JUDITH TURNER

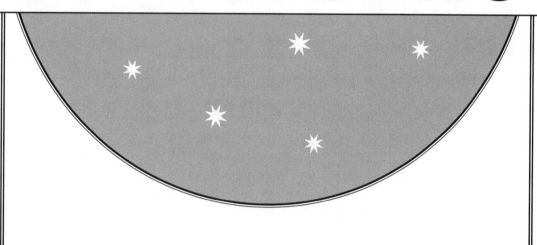

THE HIDDEN WORLD OF
BIRTHDAYS

A FIRESIDE BOOK
PUBLISHED BY SIMON & SCHUSTER

FIRESIDE
Rockefeller Center
1230 Avenue of the Americas
New York, NY 10020

The Hidden World of Birthdays copyright © 1999 by Judith Turner
The Hidden World of Relationships copyright © 2001 by Judith Turner

This Fireside Edition 2006

FIRESIDE and colophon are registered
trademarks of Simon & Schuster, Inc.

For information regarding special discounts for bulk purchases,
please contact Simon & Schuster Special Sales at
1-800-456-6798 or business@simonandschuster.com.

Designed by Eve L. Kirch and Bonnie Leon-Berman

Manufactured in the United States of America

1   3   5   7   9   10   8   6   4   2

Library of Congress Cataloging-in-Publication Data
Turner, Judith.
The hidden world of birthdays / Judith Turner.
p.   cm.
1. Birthdays.   2. Birthdays—Folklore.   I. Title.
GT2430.T87   1999
394.2—dc21   98-9699
                                                    CIP

Library of Congress Cataloging-in-Publication Data
Turner, Judith.
The hidden world of relationships / Judith Turner.
p.   cm.
1. Interpersonal relations—Psychic aspects.   I. Title.
BF1045.I58 T87   2001
131—dc21   2001033809

ISBN-13: 978-1-4165-4197-4
ISBN-10:   1-4165-4197-7

These titles were originally published individually.

MY WORDS ARE MY FEELINGS, MY FEELINGS ARE MY LIFE
MY GIFT TO YOU MY WORDS.

My parents: Judith Turner and Robert Turner. Thank you for creating such a strong foundation based on love and support and for always continuing to do so.

My siblings: Jeri Turner Sinnig, Andrew Turner, and JoAnne Connelly. For sharing not only in my joys, but trying to change my sorrows.

My children: Briane, Wojo, and Alexandria. You are my world. You are my children. You are what makes the difference in my every day.

My husband: Walter Deptuch. There could never be this fire without the "Spark."

Special People: To some who have touched my life by love and friendship along the way. Ally Walker, Eileen Breen, Susan Frusteri, Kelly Keating, Michael Toback, Robert Metzdorf, Melinda Eppy Daly, Jimmy Behrens, Daniele Gibson, Janice Holden, Miki Taylor, Marguerite Di Donato, Maryanne Colenda, Carol McCracken, Janice Meyer, Debbie Reilly, Bobby, Mike and Joey Tessel, Michele Marsh, Colleen Callaghan, Dr. Howard Adelglass and Susan Adelglass, Timmy Brown, Billy Avon, Patrick Meeuwsissen, Vicki Ullman, Christine Reilly, and Marie Kenny.

YOU HAVE ALL MADE A DIFFERENCE!

ACKNOWLEDGMENTS

Marvin Brown—for having not only an open ear, but an open mind.

Ed Stackler—for encouraging me, even though he knew he was leaving.

Paula Clark—for being kind enough to make a phone call.

Amanda Borghese—for wanting to take a chance.

Robert Metzdorf Esq.—for always believing in me.

Ally Walker—for encouragement from a friend.

Helen Horowitz "Vitamin Shoppe"—for the opportunities to ask all the questions I could.

Joe Ciccio—for the desire to help.

Gladys Callaghan—for the devotion of a friend, that all the money in the world can't buy.

Charles Fortier—"The wiz with the word." Thanks for wanting to help with anything you could.

Janice Holden Meyer—Thanks for always being there—no matter how overwhelming the work.

Pauline Black—Your support and devotion is what helped make this book. Thank you!

Leslie McHale—Your skills are amazing.

Michael Toback, Maryanne Colenda, Marguerite Di Donato "The Tuesday

Night Group"—for creating a night of sanity so I could get through this book.

Debbie Reilly—for being there, being you and always wanting to support me in all I do.

Judy Buonauito—for encouragement along the way and my introduction to astrology.

Terence Sheehan—for continuous help and support with the computer and other tasks.

Jeri Turner Sinnig—for book seeking, stapling, stuffing, collating and everything you did to contribute.

Judith Dunn Turner—for book hunting, stapling, cutting, and reading.

Cape Cod Book Hunters—Noel Keating, Carol McCracken, Judith Dunn Turner, and Jeri Turner Sinnig.

Atlantic City—Helen Schuler, Barbara Tessel, JoAnne Connelly, and Lorraine Jensen.

Miki Taylor—"The chocolate connection."

Jobes and Gertrude—for the dictionary of mythology, folklore, and symbols

Joan Hamburg—Thank you, the woman with all the answers.

Tommy Hilfiger—for your kindness when I needed it.

Pam Bernstein—for being a great agent.

Kate Ford—for wanting this book to happen for me.

Gale Hayman—When the chips were down you were supportive in picking them up.

Mark Weiss—for astrological input.

INTRODUCTION

Who is more important than you? Wouldn't it be interesting to learn important information that could enhance your life, in both large and small ways? Did you know you have a guardian angel? Has anyone explained to you there are different foods that could benefit you? Wouldn't you like to purchase a fragrance that could make others take notice of you? Some types of music should be more relaxing for you than others. You even have your own special flower based on the day you were born. Would you like to know what your lucky numbers are? Which day of the week may be best to ask for a raise? Are you seeking a mate? This book will explain the best bets in selecting a life partner for you. The tiniest things may make a difference, no matter how insignificant they may seem to you. One color may be luckier for you than another, while another color may balance your mood and enhance your environment.

You can use this book to find out all of this information about yourself. Turn to the page with *your* birthday to learn how to have a happier, more productive life. For example, my birthday is July 27. By reading that page I'd learn that I need Orange in my environment when I feel weak, I look great in Plum, and Rubies will help me overcome disappointment in love. Using this book will help you unlock the keys to your personality, needs, motivations, and dreams. You can also look up the birthdays of friends and loved ones to help you understand them better, too.

You may notice that some information repeats itself over several days. That's because there are often similarities between people born around the same time of year. But each person has qualities that are all his or her own, and each day is as special as the person born on it.

Here is a list of the information you'll find in this book:

Gems: These are jewels and precious stones that the ancients felt could be worn to bring the bearer luck, power, and encouragement. Use them carefully, as they can be powerful tools in managing your spiritual life.

Colors: Many studies have shown that the colors we surround ourselves with can change our moods, so it's vital to select the correct combinations. We each have a color that enhances our confidence and calms us when we are troubled. According to research, there are colors that will actually make you feel better, especially if your home or workplace lacks them.

Apparel Colors: There are hues and shades that are better and luckier for you to wear than others. They may give you more charm and charisma.

Astral Colors: These colors are ones you may be naturally drawn to and that may benefit you throughout your life in many subtle ways. Listed is the one that is certain to help you find your place in the universe.

Trees: Trees have the attributes of strength and power. They are full of life and offer individual meaning to each of us. You may be drawn to put a special tree in your yard or even have a memory of a certain tree when you were young. You may just look at one all the time and find that it is talking to you. See what yours might say. Once you know what tree belongs to you, you might look at and relate to your world differently.

Birds: I bet you never realized how much birds and humans really do have in common. When you read the description of birds in this book, you may find in the characterization of the birds a fascinating resemblance to yourself. You may only then recognize that without a doubt you have an attraction to a particular bird.

Health Scents: Besides finding out what to wear to smell good, you'll want to splash on what might make you feel good. There are scents that are relaxing and have better effects on particular sun signs. You may be naturally drawn to a scent because it relaxes you or you just love its smell. These scents have been selected for you for their mystical traits and ingredients.

What's Lucky: What's more fascinating than knowing what "lucky" numbers, times, days, months, and years are yours, particularly if they were picked out according to the day you were born? Do you have a lucky charm? You can now. Each lucky charm has been chosen by either its number or sign and could prove to be more than a little beneficial for you. Picking a mate isn't easy, and neither is picking a partner. Maybe this advice could help.

Spiritual Stones: These small bits of Mother Earth will guide you on your path over her. Use them in broadening your understanding of yourself or nature.

Judith's Insight: I have been a professional psychic for eighteen years and, after much meditation and thought, have developed my own insights for each day of the year. You may notice that the traits of some days are similar to those that surround them; however, each is unique. You may be able to relate to one or two items right away, but—as with the other items—each time you come back to this book you may glimpse a different part of yourself. As the person reading the book changes, the messages will alter and shift. Each insight was written to hold some meaning for you at almost any stage of your life. However, don't expect that everything will make sense right away. For example, careers that may not even interest you today could give you great satisfaction a year or two from now. The insights offer you a peek not just into who you are but who you are capable of becoming. They are crafted to give you encouragement when you may need it. All the listed information is intended to help and guide you in making the right choices for you.

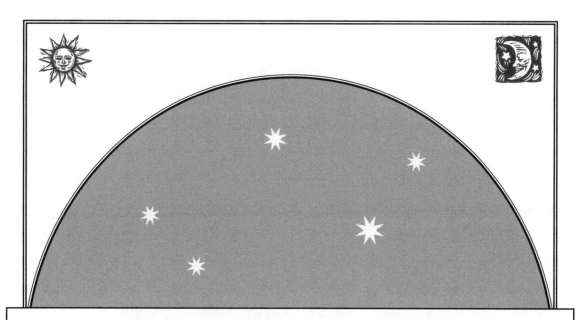

JANUARY

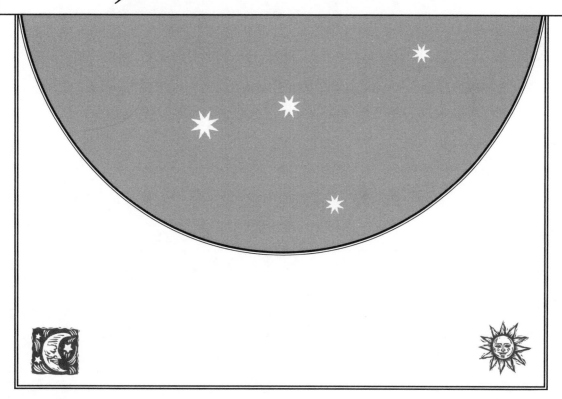

JANUARY 1 CAPRICORN • The goat of the zodiac
December 21 at 10:00 P.M. to January 21 at 3:00 A.M. • NUMEROLOGY 1

Possessions and Desires . . .

Gem: Moonstone—This gem could protect you from danger.

Flower: Oak Geranium—You are constantly open to true friendship.

Astral Color, Color Need, Apparel Color: Your Astral Color is Brown, which helps keep you grounded and stable. Blue in your environment helps you avoid becoming listless and disorganized. In your wardrobe, Green is your power color for overcoming obstacles.

Fragrance: You are stimulated by a combination of greens and flowers, such as white roses, jasmine, and greenery. They give you feelings of elegance, strength, security.

Tree: Walnut—You are unusually helpful and always looking for constant changes in your life.

Instruments: Oboe, flute, clarinet, piano, French horn, organ, piccolo

Composer: Böhm

Bird: Hummingbird—This bird is delicate and graceful. It can remain still for hours, then dart off and be as busy as a bee.

Symbol: Crown—the universal sign of dignity

Harmonious Health and Nutrition . . .

Health Scent: Strawberry—Soothing by nature, the strawberry promotes self-esteem and encourages love.

Favorable Foods: Asparagus, peaches, whole wheat, nuts, buttermilk

What's Lucky . . .

Lucky Numbers: 1, 2, 11
Best Months: March and November
Best Day of the Week: Saturday
Best Month Days: 1, 10, 19, 28
Lucky Charm: A new penny in your shoe.
Harmonious Signs for Relationships and Partnerships: Capricorn, Taurus, Virgo, and anyone born from July 27 to September 27.

Spiritual Guides . . .

Star: Vega—Those with this star can be warriors in search of victory, especially in legal situations.

Angel: Hanaeb—This angel shows us our worldly desires in order to give us strength when we are going through uncertainty.

Guardian Angel: Malachi—"Messenger of Jehovah."

Spiritual Stone: Sardonyx—This stone may cause people to be attracted to you.

✶ JUDITH'S INSIGHT ✶

A determined individual, you do not allow anything to get in your way. You're aggressive when needed, but you like to appear to be the good guy. You can back away from the demands of others; the demands you will put upon yourself are overwhelming.

Family is of key importance, and it is where your loyalty lies. Sometimes you create contradictions in your own life. You build a path on your property for others to cross, only to realize later that your property will become ruined. You are loved by all circles of people, but you need to be cautious with your language. At times your tone may be misunderstood by others.

Look for a career as a comedian, builder, lawyer, or architect. Try to keep in mind that you are creative, inventive, and strong. Look for a working environment that allows you the sense of freedom you desire. A position with growth potential is best for you. Without growth, your desire for work lessens. Be patient. It may take a while to get where you want to go, but once you do, you'll achieve the financial stability and work contentment that you so much need. When all else fails, use that great sense of humor, which is by far your second most appealing trait. Your heart is your first.

With your hands, you're a builder; emotionally, you're the foundation for others. Be cautious of what you carry on those shoulders. On your own, you can be misguided. Learn to protect yourself better. Others find you irresistibly strong.

✶ ✶ ✶

JANUARY 2   CAPRICORN • The goat of the zodiac
December 21 at 10:00 P.M. to January 21 at 3:00 A.M. • NUMEROLOGY 2

Possessions and Desires . . .

Gem: Sapphire—This gem may help you find forgiveness from those you've wronged.

Flower: Multiflora Rose—Grace covers you like a warm blanket.

Astral Color, Color Need, Apparel Color: Your Astral Color is Silver, which stimulates your imagination. Blue in your environment will prevent depression and disappointment. In your wardrobe, Green is your power color for overcoming obstacles.

Fragrance: You are stimulated by a combination of greens and flowers, such as white roses, jasmine, and greenery. They give you feelings of elegance, strength, and security.

Tree: Maple—You have great stability and flashes of intuition.

Instruments: Pipe organ, cymbal, drum

Composers: Handel, Johann Sebastian Bach

Bird: Cuckoo—A good flyer and very seldom a quitter. Some cuckoos seem more independent than they actually are and yearn for more nuturing than one would expect.

Symbol: Cross—The symbol of self-sacrifice and reconciliation.

Harmonious Health and Nutrition . . .

Health Scent: Apple—You are creative, full of joy, and nearly magical. You bring happiness.

Favorable Foods: Brussels sprouts, raspberries, rye, almonds, cottage cheese

What's Lucky . . .

Lucky Numbers: 2, 11, 20
Best Months: March and November
Best Day of the Week: Saturday
Best Month Days: 2, 11, 20, 29
Lucky Charms: Two 50-cent pieces. Give someone else one of them.
Harmonious Signs for Relationships and Partnerships: Capricorn, Taurus, Virgo, and anyone born from July 27 to September 27.

Spiritual Guides . . .

Star: Altair—Those with this star feel compelled to protect the wounded.

Angel: Hanaeb—This angel shows us our worldly desires in order to give us strength when we are going through uncertainty.

Guardian Angel: Uriel—Helps bring the light of God. "God's guidance."

Spiritual Stone: Sardonyx—This stone may cause people to be attracted to you.

✴ JUDITH'S INSIGHT ✴

You look for love in all the right places. You're a natural poet encouraged by your need for laughter. Anything and everything you try, no matter how small or large, will result in success. You're a passionate lover who is willing to work at it. Nobody likes to be without you for very long. Largely because of your capabilities, you can take on too much, too fast, never realizing the size of the burden. Have no fear, workaholics tend to survive. Stamina is your middle name. You sometimes seem to lack compassion, but those feelings are there. Keep this in mind during conflicts with loved ones and especially at work if you hold a supervisory position.

Family members will always be important to you, but check your demanding side and the demands being placed on you by others. One of these areas could pose problems for you. The outside world sees you as smart and sweet, but your loved ones pay for the constant demands you create for yourself. Family can sometimes get underfoot, especially after you've found your "significant other."

Your abilities may lead to teaching or law, but you probably have more romantic aspirations, to be something like an artist, or the head of a movie company. Try to keep your structuring abilities alive while allowing that creative soul to find its passion. Sounds like a conflict of direction, but if you start off early in a structured job, you find creativity later.

As strong as you are, you can be needy. Learn to keep your temper under wraps. The word "stubborn" doesn't begin to describe it: When you are good, you're good, but when you are bad, you're horrid.

✴ ✴ ✴

Possessions and Desires . . .

Gem: Moonstone—This gem could protect you from danger.

Flower: Cactus—You have an inner warmth like the sun to those who orbit you.

Astral Color, Color Need, Apparel Color: Your Astral Color is Black, which creates a sense of protection. Blue in your environment helps you avoid becoming listless and disorganized. In your wardrobe, many shades of Green always let you look your best.

Fragrance: You are stimulated by a combination of greens and flowers, such as white roses, jasmine, and greenery. They give you feelings of elegance, strength, and security.

Tree: Elm—You have willpower, strength, and the ability to stand alone.

Instrument: Trombone

Composers: Verdi, Mendelssohn, Schumann

Bird: Swan—Regarded as royal and sacred, this bird has the protective nature of a mother, and can become a furious fighter in the defense of its young.

Symbol: Wreath—You have been crowned with a special personality. You are strong but extremely compassionate.

Harmonious Health and Nutrition . . .

Health Scent: Rose—This scent will lead you to passionate thoughts and make you feel warm inside.

Favorable Foods: Cauliflower, peaches, whole wheat, peanuts, eggs

What's Lucky . . .

Lucky Numbers: 2, 11, 13

Best Months: March and November

Best Day of the Week: Saturday

Best Month Days: 3, 12, 21, 30

Lucky Charm: A pen that someone else has already used.

Harmonious Signs for Relationships and

Partnerships: Capricorn, Taurus, Virgo, and anyone born from July 27 to September 27.

Spiritual Guides . . .

Star: Dabih—The star of the prominent in society.

Angel: Hanaeb—This angel shows our worldly desires in order to give us strength when we are going through uncertainty.

Guardian Angel: Johiel—This angel is a protector of all those with a humble heart.

Spiritual Stone: Sardonyx—This stone may cause people to be attracted to you.

★ JUDITH'S INSIGHT ★

The more discipline and control you have, the better. Like Tom Sawyer, you have a cunning sense of power over people—they do what you want without realizing they're working so hard. Negative thinkers might call you dictatorial—you're not. A leader, even in the best of circumstances, will encounter many challenges. You have self-control, though you don't always know how to use it.

Applause and appreciation thrill you. Make sure your significant other recognizes this from the beginning. You expect your mate to intuitively know your needs. Learn to communicate better, keeping in mind it takes two to tango. All family will be important to you, especially your children. When children do enter your life, whether they're yours or not, your heart will experience a new love that will open emotional doors.

You can rise to the occasion in any career you choose. You're highly qualified for the medical field, but you thrive in any profession or career that has structure. Uniform jobs, like those of the state or federal government, will be available to you. Since you are extremely conscientious in all that you do, battling with yourself will be one of your biggest downfalls. The next will be battling with others over nothing, especially when you go through times of great frustration. Make sure you keep your mind's doors and windows open to allow the growth in your career that you greatly fear but still want badly. Don't forget to allow your childlike side out once in a while. You're a lover of travel, so stick to those activities where earth's elements are most evident: hiking, camping, boating, and so on.

★ ★ ★

JANUARY 4 CAPRICORN • The goat of the zodiac

December 21 at 10:00 P.M. to January 21 at 3:00 A.M. • NUMEROLOGY 4

Possessions and Desires . . .

Gem: Emerald—Those who carry this stone tend to be lucky in love.

Flower: Aloe—Be sure to guard against religious superstition and grieving too long.

Astral Color, Color Need, Apparel Color: Your Astral Color is Brown, which helps keep you grounded and stable. Blue in your environment helps you avoid becoming listless and disorganized. Your wardrobe should have Black to keep you confident.

Fragrance: You are stimulated by a combination of greens and flowers, such as white roses, jasmine, and greenery. They give you feelings of elegance, strength, and security.

Tree: Cherry—You will find yourself faced with constant new emotional awakenings.

Instruments: Bass, clarinet

Composers: Haydn, Wagner

Bird: Robin—The most sociable of all birds, with the ability to create quick friendships. It also can easily adapt to any home. When it wants something, it has the tendency to try and snatch it.

Symbol: Star—You are full of inner brightness and will stand out in any crowd. You will be seen as special.

Harmonious Health and Nutrition . . .

Health Scents: Vanilla—This scent will fill you with a feeling of cleanliness and stability.

Favorable Foods: String beans, cherries, rye, walnuts, cottage cheese

What's Lucky . . .

Lucky Numbers: 2, 4, 13

Best Months: March and November

Best Day of the Week: Saturday

Best Month Days: 4, 13, 22, 31

Lucky Charm: A piece of material cut from something in your home.

Harmonious Signs for Relationships and

Partnerships: Capricorn, Taurus, Virgo, and anyone born from July 27 to September 27.

Spiritual Guides . . .

Star: Gedi—The star of the best and the brightest.

Angel: Hanaeb—This angel shows us our worldly desires in order to give us strength when we are going through uncertainty.

Guardian angel: Uriel—Helps bring the light of God. "God's guidance."

Spiritual Stone: Sardonyx—This stone may cause people to be attracted to you.

✳ JUDITH'S INSIGHT ✳

You are interesting, enjoyable, and a great companion, as long as everything is going your way. Some people never reach that kind of perfection or happiness. Your tendency is to enjoy just about everything, but you need rules and regulations. You love boundaries, but you want to control. Your brains and strength give you many opportunities for relationships. It's okay to be a little cautious in love—just don't confuse caution with fear. Watch out for loneliness. Sometimes you'd rather be funny than romantic, especially when your heart is at stake.

You love your family, but you need a sense of freedom to get along. You're a little bit unconventional with your views and opinions, so you may ruffle the feathers of coworkers; just keep this in mind. You have a great business aptitude and amazing foresight for decision making. This is about the only place you may use your psychic ability and intuition. You can rebel against authority, so stick to jobs that allow you the independence to think and feel: Work in theater or film, or as a mediator, builder, or architect. You have a distinctive character and will conform when you feel safe, so learn to go with where you feel comfort and growth.

You enjoy affection—giving and getting. Try not to let your strong and protective nature get in the way of your getting it. When it comes to relationships, you have more elasticity than a rubber band. You rebound very easily from arguments. Your tendency is to conform to a loved one's needs. That is one of your greatest secrets.

✳ ✳ ✳

JANUARY 5

CAPRICORN • The goat of the zodiac

December 21 at 10:00 P.M. to January 21 at 3:00 A.M. • NUMEROLOGY 5

Possessions and Desires . . .

Gem: Moonstone—This gem could protect you from danger.

Flower: Hydrangea—Beware of being boastful or heartless.

Astral Color, Color Need, Apparel Color: Your Astral Color is Silver, which stimulates your imagination. Blue in your environment will prevent depression and disappointments. In your wardrobe, Green is your power color for overcoming obstacles.

Fragrance: You are stimulated by a combination of greens and flowers, such as white roses, jasmine, and greenery. They give you feelings of elegance, strength, and security.

Tree: Apple—You are creative, full of joy, and nearly magical. You bring happiness.

Instruments: Viola, trumpet

Composer: Liszt

Bird: Flamingo—This beautiful, gregarious bird is always careful of its enemy. It is also a caretaker of the young and tries to keep everyone happy.

Symbol: Triangle—You have the right combination of abilities.

Harmonious Health and Nutrition . . .

Health Scent: Peach—This scent may balance your good qualities so that they equal your charm.

Favorable Foods: String beans, cherries, rye, walnuts, cottage cheese

What's Lucky . . .

Lucky Numbers: 8, 5, 23

Best Months: March and November

Best Day of the Week: Saturday

Best Month Days: 5, 4, 23

Lucky Charm: A rabbit's foot or a white candle.

Harmonious Signs for Relationships and Partnerships: Capricorn, Taurus, Virgo, and anyone born from July 27 to September 27.

Spiritual Guides . . .

Star: Vega—Those with this star can be warriors in search of victory, especially in legal situations.

Angel: Hanaeb—This angel shows us our worldly desires in order to give us strength when we are going through uncertainty.

Guardian angel: Plavwell—The guardian that gives power and strength to one's presence.

Spiritual Stone: Sardonyx—This stone may cause people to be attracted to you.

✳ JUDITH'S INSIGHT ✳

You are as loyal as the day is long. You're a giver, in relationships, friendships, and business. Problems arise when you feel your efforts are not recognized. It's not so much a financial or physical reward you're hoping for, but at the very least, verbal praise for the energy you expend. If you don't feel constant growth, you tend to get bored, and then look for the nearest exit sign.

Decision making can sometimes be difficult for you. Your intuition is often correct. You don't have to be the boss, as long as you are working in an independent environment with continuous growth and new challenges. Keep this in mind when choosing your career. From actor to astronomer, you are good at just about anything. It will be finding your career and staying with it that keeps you challenged. Don't be surprised if you have multiple careers. You're the jack and the master of all trades.

You'll want proof of consistency from your mate before you commit. Doing this earlier rather than later will work better for you. When you do finally commit, you are extremely loyal, but you can be frustrated, because everyone else is aware of your extreme devotion to your mate—except your mate. You tend to keep quiet about your emotions; otherwise you will chatter until the dawn. The problem here is there isn't anyone around to listen.

★ ★ ★

JANUARY 6
CAPRICORN • The goat of the zodiac

December 21 at 10:00 P.M. to January 21 at 3:00 A.M. • NUMEROLOGY 6

Possessions and Desires . . .

Gem: Moonstone—This gem could protect you from danger.

Flower: Ice Plant—Your cold exterior hides a passionate nature.

Astral color, Color Need, Apparel Color: Your Astral Color is Brown, which helps to keep you grounded and stable. Blue in your environment helps you avoid becoming listless and disorganized. In your wardrobe, Emerald Green keeps you confident and always looking great.

Fragrance: You are stimulated by a combination of greens and flowers, such as white roses, jasmine, and greenery. They give you feelings of elegance, strength, and security.

Tree: Palm—You tend to be very healthy and creative.

Instruments: Tambourine, lyre

Composer: Schubert

Bird: Lark—Known for the beauty of its song, which is sometimes very unusual. It is also credited with extraordinary intelligence.

Symbol: Crescent—You are likely to be influenced by the phases of the moon. Your easygoing manner leads you to peaceful situations.

Harmonious Health and Nutrition . . .

Health Scent: Orange Blossom—This scent may balance your body, mind, and soul.

Favorable Foods: Lettuce, blackberries, whole wheat, almonds, buttermilk

What's Lucky . . .

Lucky Numbers: 1, 6, 15
Best Months: March and November
Best Day of the Week: Saturday
Best Month Days: 6, 15, 24
Lucky Charm: A religious token or card from any religion.
Harmonious Signs for Relationships and Partnerships: Capricorn, Taurus, Virgo, and anyone born from July 27 to September 27.

Spiritual Guides . . .

Star: Altair—Those with this star feel compelled to protect the wounded.

Angel: Hanaeb—This angel shows us our worldly desires in order to give us strength when we are going through uncertainty.

Guardian angel: Michael—"Who is like God."

Spiritual Stone: Sardonyx—This stone may cause people to become attracted to you.

✴ JUDITH'S INSIGHT ✴

With your knowledge and understanding, you epitomize common sense. There are downfalls, but as a "naturally smart" person you are quite capable of any number of things. Taking on quite a lot of responsibility at an early age may not have allowed too much room for childhood, so at some point in your life you could rebel and decide you want the childhood you never really had. The problem here is that you could be doing this at fifty.

Sometimes you seem demanding and selfish in love; at other times, you could be content with someone else who behaves that way. You will have no problem attracting a significant other. A weakness could be your lack of participation after the relationship gets underway. Challenges are what you need. If you feel you have trouble with love, then it may be time to open yourself up and stop protecting your heart. One thing you will need to learn about yourself is that balancing your head means balancing your heart. Along the way, you may encounter an unconventional relationship—at first it may be enthralling; later it could be devastating. You're good-looking, which attracts unwanted advances. Remember to keep your distance at the onset of a strong emotional relationship. Don't allow your restlessness to get you into emotionally crazy situations.

Your career can be a little sticky. One of the most beneficial careers for you is working with money: in a bank or as a merchant, accountant, or broker, or in any other job where you handle money. There are other types of careers you could pursue, but keep money in mind as a priority. Somehow money seems to find you in your lifetime.

✴ ✴ ✴

JANUARY 7   CAPRICORN • The goat of the zodiac
December 21 at 10:00 P.M. to January 21 at 3:00 A.M. • NUMEROLOGY 7

Possessions and Desires . . .

Gem: Ruby—This stone may lead you to energy, friendship, and happiness.

Flower: Japanese Rose—Beauty isn't your only attraction.

Astral Color, Color Need, Apparel Color: Your Astral Color is Black, which creates a sense of protection. Blue in your environment helps you avoid becoming listless and disorganized. Your wardrobe should have many shades of Green to keep you confident and always looking great.

Fragrance: You are stimulated by a combination of greens and flowers such as white roses, jasmine, and greenery. They give you feelings of elegance, strength, and security.

Tree: Sycamore—Yours is the ability to love, communicate honestly with others, and have lasting relationships.

Instrument: Harp

Composers: Gluck, Brahms.

Bird: Skylark—This handsome bird is beautiful when it sings. It always whistles as it works.

Symbol: Heart—You are enthusiastic, empathetic, and full of generosity and love.

Harmonious Health and Nutrition . . .

Health Scent: Jasmine—This scent may make you more easygoing when you are stressed.

Favorable Foods: Celery, strawberries, rye, nuts, cottage cheese

What's Lucky . . .

Lucky Numbers: 1, 7, 16
Best Months: March and November
Best Day of the Week: Saturday
Best Month Days: 6, 15, 24
Lucky Charm: An old key.
Harmonious Signs for Relationships and Partnerships: Capricorn, Taurus, Virgo, and anyone born from July 27 to September 27.

Spiritual Guides . . .

Star: Dabih—The star of the prominent in society.
Angel: Hanaeb—This angel shows us our worldly desires in order to give us strength when we are going through uncertainty.
Guardian angel: Raphael—The angel that attends to all of your needs when you are looking for guidance.
Spiritual Stone: Sardonyx—This stone may cause people to be attracted to you.

✷ JUDITH'S INSIGHT ✷

You are charitable in many ways, yet you are not always recognized for it. With a strong sense of intuition, you understand others without rhyme or reason. You have a magnetic personality, and others are drawn to your strength and humor. Others see abilities in you that you may not necessarily see yourself. Listen to those who give you praise.

You'll have relationships, but be cautious that you don't seem cold when it comes down to intimacy. Learn to set your body free as well as your uninhibited mind. You may be empathetic and understanding, but when it comes to loved ones, it can be hard work. Nobody gets too far without showing their sense of loyalty and devotion. Make sure your family gets to see all the warm and sensible parts of you that others do. Watch out for a tendency to behave insensitively. Love does prevail at least once. Partnerships could work quite well, even if they don't last forever.

With your style and refinement, it will be no wonder that you have strong success in your lifetime. Ready, set, go is the kind of worker you are, as long as the environment remains unstressed. Don't create your own limitations because of fear, or take too long to decide on things. Doctor, lawyer, businessperson: any career will do. You could be a world traveler or maintain a job that requires travel on a regular basis. Plain as day—you add simple pleasures in the lives you touch. Keep your own desires clear for yourself, so you can have the happiness you deserve.

✷ ✷ ✷

Possessions and Desires . . .

Gem: Moonstone—This gem could protect you from danger.

Flower: Laburnum—You tend to be pensive and known for your inner beauty.

Astral Color, Color Need, Apparel Color: Your Astral Color is Brown, which helps to keep you grounded and stable. Blue in your environment helps you avoid becoming listless and disorganized. In your wardrobe, many shades of Green keep you confident and always looking great.

Fragrance: You are stimulated by a combination of greens and flowers such as white roses, jasmine, and greenery. They give you feelings of elegance, strength, and security.

Tree: Pine—Your relationships tend to be harmonious and balanced, both emotionally and mentally.

Instrument: Cello

Composer: Mozart

Bird: Bobolink—This charming singer is equally good as a soloist or a member of an orchestra. It is a very romantic bird, useful as an insect destroyer, and elegant, with beautiful feathers and always pleasant to have around.

Symbol: Wings—You are the source of balance in your world—this will bring you contentment.

Harmonious Health and Nutrition . . .

Health Scent: Almond—This scent may revitalize you and open you to greater possibilities.

Favorable Foods: Beans, pineapple, whole wheat, walnuts, eggs

What's Lucky . . .

Lucky Numbers: 8, 17, 26
Best Months: March and November
Best Day of the Week: Saturday
Best Month Days: 8, 17, 26
Lucky Charm: A red ribbon in your wallet or over home entranceway.
Harmonious Signs for Relationships and

Partnerships: Capricorn, Taurus, Virgo, and anyone born from July 27 to September 27.

Spiritual Guides . . .

Star: Gedi—The star of the best and the brightest.
Angel: Hanaeb—This angel shows us our worldly desires in order to give us strength when we are going through uncertainty.
Guardian angel: Seraphim—An angel that brings love, light, and passion.
Spiritual Stone: Sardonyx—This stone may cause people to be attracted to you.

✶ JUDITH'S INSIGHT ✶

"Good intentions" could be your first name, and "means well" should be your last. It's a shame you don't get paid for this virtue. Those who don't recognize who you are could describe you as cunning or manipulative. With your strength and perseverance, it's no wonder you always get what you want. You don't, won't, and shouldn't let other opinions interfere with the way you handle your life. You will have the sensitivity to maintain long-lasting relationships, the sensuality to ignite great passion, and the common sense to enjoy them both. You do well when faced with life's challenges. Watch for carelessness with your body. Be careful where and while you walk. How many back, bone, muscle, and neck problems have you had? You are the helping hand for many. Friends count on your love. Just remember, when your shoulders are heavy—it's you who puts all the burdens there.

Business is a great thing; just don't delegate with such coldness. You love many and trust very few. Don't allow this skeptical side to be well known in your career. You need to communicate a bit better. Lawyer, prison warden, inventor, landscaper, or detective are all good career choices. Don't be surprised if later in life you come into a second career, or seek out a hobby that allows you the sense of growth and reward that may be lacking in your career. Strong and stable is fine, but learn to occasionally throw caution to the winds. Family matters are always a priority for you.

✶ ✶ ✶

JANUARY 9

CAPRICORN • The goat of the zodiac

December 21 at 10:00 P.M. to January 21 at 3:00 A.M. • NUMEROLOGY 9

Possessions and Desires . . .

Gem: Moonstone—This gem could protect you from danger.

Flower: Lavender—Be careful of mistrusting others too much.

Astral Color, Color Need, Apparel Color: Your Astral Color is Silver, which stimulates your imagination. Blue in your environment will prevent depression and disappointment. In your wardrobe, Maroon gives you confidence.

Fragrance: You are stimulated by a combination of greens and flowers, such as white roses, jasmine, and greenery. They give you feelings of elegance, strength, and security.

Tree: Holly—Beware that you are not carried away by your passionate nature. The only way to grow is to be open to new experiences.

Instruments: Violin, tympanum

Composer: Gluck

Bird: Mockingbird—The most proficient minstrel in the world's orchestra; graceful and enthusiastic.

Symbol: Anchor—This tranquil symbol signifies stability and strength, and stands for strong commitments in relationships.

Harmonious Health and Nutrition . . .

Health Scent: Lavender—This scent might lead others to trust you and make you patient.

Favorable Foods: Cabbage, watermelon, rye, beechnuts, buttermilk

What's Lucky . . .

Lucky Numbers: 9, 18, 27

Best Months: March and November

Best Day of the Week: Saturday

Best Month Days: 9, 18, 27

Lucky Charm: A U.S. coin or a bill of any amount from the year you were born.

Harmonious Signs for Relationships and Partnerships: Capricorn, Taurus, Virgo, and anyone born from July 27 to September 27.

Spiritual Guides . . .

Star: Vega—Those with this star can be warriors in search of victory, especially in legal situations.

Angel: Hanaeb—This angel shows us our worldly desires in order to give us strength when we are going through uncertainty.

Guardian Angel: Gabriel—"God is my strength."

Spiritual Stone: Sardonyx—This stone may cause people to be attracted to you.

✷ JUDITH'S INSIGHT ✷

Yours is the inquiring mind that always wants to know. Education is not the only way you gain knowledge. With a strong need to investigate things, you get pure enjoyment out of working. Some may say you have natural intelligence, natural intuition, and/or psychic ability.

Success always finds you. Your charm and wit help in finding a mate. Spontaneity can be very attractive, but don't allow your independence to make you seem cold and removed. Family relationships will be a bit erratic. At times, it may seem as if your relations are fine, at other times they will seem pretentious and plastic. Look inside yourself when things seem removed. You have a tendency to be guarded and distant.

In your career, you have all the makings of a born leader and may be drawn to authority. Your resourcefulness and curiosity may lead you down many different career paths. Look for a career in law or research, or with the government or utilities. You can look other places, but these areas may draw you. At some point, you may be wounded or may have a health issue due to stress at work.

Friends will use your ear for your great advice and excellent input. Sometimes, this may be a little more taxing than you think. You may be a thinker, but you're also a dreamer; that's the side that most will never know. That's not such a bad thing.

✷ ✷ ✷

JANUARY 10 CAPRICORN • The goat of the zodiac

December 21 at 10:00 P.M. to January 21 at 3:00 A.M. • NUMEROLOGY 1

Possessions and Desires . . .

Gem: Agate—This stone may promote health and lead you to a long life.
Flower: Withered Leaf—You tend to enjoy feeling blue more than is good for you.
Astral Color, Color Need, Apparel Color: Your Astral Color is Black, which creates a sense of protection. Blue in your environment helps you avoid becoming listless and disorganized. In your wardrobe, Green is your power color for overcoming obstacles.
Fragrance: You are stimulated by a combination of greens and flowers, such as white roses, jasmine, and greenery. They give you feelings of elegance, strength, and security.
Tree: Walnut—You are unusually helpful and always looking for constant changes in your life.
Instruments: Oboe, flute, clarinet, piano, French horn, organ, piccolo
Composer: Böhm
Bird: Bird of paradise—The "bird of the gods." You will shine and love extraordinary form.
Symbol: Crown—The universal sign of dignity.

Harmonious Health and Nutrition . . .

Health Scent: Strawberry—soothing by nature, the strawberry promotes self-esteem and encourages love.
Favorable Foods: Asparagus, cherries, rye, almonds, pressed cheese

What's Lucky . . .

Lucky Numbers: 2, 8, 19
Best Months: March and November
Best Day of the Week: Saturday
Best Month Days: 1, 10, 19, 28
Lucky Charm: A new penny in your shoe.
Harmonious Signs for Relationships and Partnerships: Capricorn, Taurus, Virgo, and anyone born from July 27 to September 27.

Spiritual Guides . . .

Star: Altair—Those with this star feel compelled to protect the wounded.
Angel: Hanaeb—This angel shows us our worldly desires in order to give us strength when we are going through uncertainty.
Guardian Angel: Malachi—"Messenger of Jehovah."
Spiritual Stone: Sardonyx—This stone may cause people to be attracted to you.

✴ JUDITH'S INSIGHT ✴

Precise, organized, and clearly intelligent—this is exactly who you are. Although you do balance the emotional issues very well, be careful when you feel overwhelmed with emotions. You tend to take life too seriously at times.

Devotion will be there with your mate. It takes time for you to get over disappointments from loved ones. You're so strong and easygoing, others may never recognize when you are hurting. Most of the time you will know how and when to be funny. Lucky in love, one way or another don't be surprised if you are one of those late bloomers. Family does tend to take you a little for granted, and vice versa. Just be a little better at recognizing which is which. You seem to wear uniforms—or somewhere through your life people around you could be wearing them.

There is no work ethic better than yours, when your mind is in the right place. Broker, banker, detective, or contractor—it all works for you. As long as you get to take the stage for a moment or two, you will be fine.

Creativity is there, so allow that part of you to shine when you get the courage. Yours are the purest and best intentions. You have a great instinct for cause and effect, but don't be surprised if others see you as complicated.

✴ ✴ ✴

JANUARY 11 CAPRICORN • The goat of the zodiac

December 21 at 10:00 P.M. to January 21 at 3:00 A.M. • NUMEROLOGY 2

Possessions and Desires . . .

Gem: Sapphire—This gem may help you find forgiveness from those you've wronged.

Flower: Lemon—will give you energy and passion.

Astral Color, Color Need, Apparel Color: Your Astral Color is Brown, which helps to keep you grounded and stable. Blue in your environment helps you avoid becoming listless and disorganized. In your wardrobe, many shades of Green always let you look your best.

Fragrance: You are stimulated by a combination of greens and flowers, such as white roses, jasmine, and greenery. They give you feelings of elegance, strength, and security.

Tree: Maple—You have both great stability and flashes of intuition.

Instruments: Pipe organ, cymbal, drum

Composers: Handel, Johann Sebastian Bach

Bird: Cuckoo—a good flyer and very seldom a quitter. Some cuckoos tend to think they favor lonely isolation, but what they really yearn for is a family relationship.

Symbol: Cross—The symbol of self-sacrifice and reconciliation.

Harmonious Health and Nutrition . . .

Health Scent: Apple—You are creative, full of joy, and nearly magical. You bring happiness.

Favorable Foods: Brussels sprouts, blackberries, whole wheat, peanuts, cottage cheese

What's Lucky . . .

Lucky Numbers: 2, 11, 13
Best Months: March and November
Best Day of the Week: Saturday
Best Month Days: 2, 11, 20, 29
Lucky Charms: Two 50-cent pieces. Give someone else one of them.

Harmonious Signs for Relationships and Partnerships: Capricorn, Taurus, Virgo, and anyone born from July 27 to September 27.

Spiritual Guides . . .

Star: Dabih—the star of the prominent in society.

Angel: Hanaeb—This angel shows us our worldly desires in order to give us strength when we are going through uncertainty.

Guardian angel: Uriel—"The light of God."

Spiritual Stone: Sardonyx—This stone may cause people to be attracted to you.

✷ JUDITH'S INSIGHT ✷

They may say that money is the root of all evil, but for ultradetermined you, it just creates the desire for life, and you love it. Eventually it will spell success for you. A generally enthusiastic character makes you quite a desirable catch. Fascinating and charming most of the time, you seem always to draw a bit of a crowd. Somewhere along the way you must watch out for your ego running amok.

You're usually sympathetic, but don't always show it. This can sometimes create problems with friends, family, and relationships. You will do anything for those whom you love and even those you don't. Don't spend too much time helping everyone around you and neglecting those you shouldn't. As a parent, you will be very devoted; beyond, you need to take care with your demands.

Your career can range from top trader to storekeeper to attorney to doctor. You will feel rewarded by people throughout your life, and recognition that boosts your ego may mostly come from complete strangers. You work better with a well-organized plan and can carry out even the tallest of orders. Keep others from pressuring you even half as much as you do yourself.

✷ ✷ ✷

JANUARY 12   CAPRICORN • The goat of the zodiac
December 21 at 10:00 P.M. to January 21 at 3:00 A.M. • NUMEROLOGY 3

Possessions and Desires . . .

Gem: Emerald—Those who carry this stone tend to be lucky in love.
Flower: Lemon Blossom—You are very loyal to those you care for.
Astral Color, Color Need, Apparel Color: Your Astral Color is Silver, which stimulates your imagination. Blue in your environment prevents depression and disappointments. In your wardrobe, Black keeps you confident.
Fragrance: You are stimulated by a combination of greens and flowers, such as white roses, jasmine, and greenery. They give you feelings of elegance, strength, and security.
Tree: Elm—You have willpower, strength, and the ability to stand alone.
Instrument: Trombone
Composers: Verdi, Mendelssohn, Schumann
Bird: Swan—Regarded as royal and sacred, this bird has the protective nature of a mother and can become a furious fighter in the defense of its young.
Symbol: Wreath—You have been crowned with a special personality. You are strong but extremely compassionate.

Harmonious Health and Nutrition . . .

Health Scent: Rose—This scent will lead you to passionate thoughts and make you feel warm inside.
Favorable Foods: Cauliflower, peaches, rye, peanuts, buttermilk

What's Lucky . . .

Lucky Numbers: 3, 8, 21
Best Months: March and November
Best Day of the Week: Saturday
Best Month Days: 3, 12, 21, 30
Lucky Charm: A pen that someone else has already used.
Harmonious Signs for Relationships and

Partnerships: Capricorn, Taurus, Virgo, and anyone born from July 27 to September 27.

Spiritual Guides . . .

Star: Gedi—The star of the best and the brightest.
Angel: Hanaeb—This angel shows us our worldly desires in order to give us strength when we are going through uncertainty.
Guardian angel: Johiel—This angel is a protector of all those with a humble heart.
Spiritual Stone: Sardonyx—This stone may cause people to be attracted to you.

✴ JUDITH'S INSIGHT ✴

You are distinctly ambitious and readily open to just about anything. You have the ability to get in there and make wheels spin and heads turn and bring to life what has long been dead. With a special knack for being in the right place at the right time, you see things clearly in just about any business situation. Your problems will arise in love, if you don't keep a balance of home and work.

Getting relationships will never be your problem—keeping them will take all your attention. Passion you have, and charm you'll provide. You imagine yourself as the great communicator, but in reality that is what you are here to learn. You have the habit of assuming that everybody has the same mind as you. This can cause problems. You may sometimes need to keep your opinions just a little under wraps. Friends and family always adore you.

You are often brilliant, which allows you to succeed in almost any career. You will have to be careful not to get bored, otherwise you may find yourself going from workaholic to another addiction not as attractive. You can be anything from a computer whiz to a Broadway star, a professor or a philosopher. When you finally reach the right track, there won't be any stopping you.

With character and presence as outgoing as yours, one would think you would like praise and compliments, but that is where you can be seen as shy. A final reward you will welcome. Verbally you will be shy.

✶ ✶ ✶

JANUARY 13 CAPRICORN • The goat of the zodiac
December 21 at 10:00 P.M. to January 21 at 3:00 A.M. • NUMEROLOGY 4

Possessions and Desires . . .

Gem: Emerald—Those who carry this stone tend to be lucky in love.

Flower: Imperial lily—You are in utter awe of all your life can offer you.

Astral Color, Color Need, Apparel Color: Your Astral Color is Black, which creates a sense of protection. Blue in your environment helps you avoid becoming listless and disorganized. In your wardrobe, many shades of Green always let you look your best.

Fragrance: You are stimulated by a combination of greens and flowers, such as white roses, jasmine, and greenery. They give you feelings of elegance, strength, and security.

Tree: Cherry—You will find yourself faced with constant new emotional awakenings.

Instruments: Bass, clarinet

Composers: Haydn, Wagner

Bird: Robin—The most sociable of all birds, with the ability to create quick friendships. It also can easily adapt to any home. When it wants something, it has the tendency to try and snatch it.

Symbol: Star—You are full of inner brightness and will stand out in any crowd. You will be seen as special.

Harmonious Health and Nutrition . . .

Health Scent: Vanilla—This scent will fill you with a feeling of cleanliness and stability.

Favorable Foods: Watercress, prunes, whole wheat, almonds, cottage cheese

What's Lucky . . .

Lucky Numbers: 4,13,14
Best Months: March and November
Best Day of the Week: Saturday
Best Month Days: 4, 13, 22, 31
Lucky Charm: A piece of material cut from something in your home.

Harmonious Signs for Relationships and Partnerships: Capricorn, Taurus, Virgo, and anyone born from July 27 to September 27.

Spiritual Guides . . .

Star: Vega—Those with this star can be warriors in search of victory, especially in legal situations.

Angel: Hanaeb—This angel shows us our worldly desires in order to give us strength when we are going through uncertainty.

Guardian Angel: Uriel—This angel brings the light of God's guidance.

Spiritual Stone: Sardonyx—This stone may cause people to be attracted to you.

✶ JUDITH'S INSIGHT ✶

You're inventive and creative, and have lots of initiative—you have the right mix for a perfect businessperson. You have many friends. You are easily bored by old war stories, unless they're your own. You are impeccable in your dress, even with the most casual clothes, and your physical presence is striking.

Home means a lot, and the order in which it is kept means more. You're direct with your love; sometimes a little too direct. With a flirtatious style all your own, you remain devoted to a significant other when you find one. To family, you stand as the king even if you are the queen. Understanding and kind, make sure you have time to hear others out. Generosity can be a good characteristic, so long as you hold the checkbook and write the check.

You would make a great prosecutor, debater, or even a civil rights activist. You love a fight for the underdog; you don't mind the recognition for your "wins." As much as you will be fond of sports and recreational activities, you never let fun interfere with work. You will be a hard worker, making a bit of room for Sunday relaxation. Just remember: to some fun is play, to you it may be building a house, or reorganizing the kitchen.

★ ★ ★

JANUARY 14   CAPRICORN • The goat of the zodiac

December 21 at 10:00 P.M. to January 21 at 3:00 A.M. • NUMEROLOGY 5

Possessions and Desires . . .

Gem: Moonstone—This gem could protect you from danger.

Flower: Hyssop—You like your surroundings and relationships to be neat and orderly.

Astral Color, Color Need, Apparel Color: Your Astral Color is Black, which creates a sense of protection. Blue in your environment helps you avoid becoming listless and disorganized. In your wardrobe, many shades of Green always let you look your best.

Fragrance: You are stimulated by a combination of greens and flowers, such as white roses, jasmine, and greenery. They give you feelings of elegance, strength, and security.

Tree: Apple—You are creative, full of joy, and nearly magical. You bring happiness.

Instruments: Viola, trumpet

Composer: Liszt

Bird: Flamingo—This beautiful, gregarious bird is always careful of its enemy. It is also a caretaker of the young and tries to keep everyone happy.

Symbol: Triangle—You have the right combination of abilities.

Harmonious Health and Nutrition . . .

Health Scent: Peach—This scent may balance your good qualities so that they equal your charm.

Favorable Foods: String beans, raspberries, rye, beechnuts, pressed cheese

What's Lucky . . .

Lucky Numbers: 5, 8, 23
Best Months: March and November
Best Day of the Week: Saturday
Best Month Days: 4, 5, 23
Lucky Charms: A rabbit's foot or a white candle.

Harmonious Signs for Relationships and Partnerships: Capricorn, Taurus, Virgo, and anyone born from July 27 to September 27.

Spiritual Guides . . .

Star: Altair—Those with this star feel compelled to protect the wounded.

Angel: Hanaeb—This angel shows us our worldly desires in order to give us strength when we are going through uncertainty.

Guardian angel: Plavwell—"Strength in presence."

Spiritual Stone: Sardonyx—This stone may cause people to be attracted to you.

✶ JUDITH'S INSIGHT ✶

Friendship and loyalty mean the world to you. Since you have a protective nature, it is no wonder everyone depends on you. You're strong, willing, and able. You're dependable for all that you love, and for even those that you merely like. Two wonderful traits are your sense of humor and good sense.

For some you will seem like the perfect mate. To others you will act remote and pretentiously humorous, afraid of having your heart stolen. It will be a hint you're definitely in love when you start to back up and run. Scared until caught, you're great in the beginning and great at the end; it is definitely the middle that gives you all the trouble. You love many and trust very few.

You need to have a career that will create a sense of fun and freedom. You could be the kind of person who could find fun and freedom in careers such as law or retail, whereas others may consider them too structured.

You crave excitement, even with that serious look about you. You rebound from just about anything. Just allow yourself a little room for emotional issues. You don't have to worry about others being hard on you. That you do on your own.

✶ ✶ ✶

JANUARY 15   CAPRICORN • The goat of the zodiac

December 21 at 10:00 P.M. to January 21 at 3:00 A.M. • NUMEROLOGY 6

Possessions and Desires . . .

Gem: Topaz—An excellent gift to be exchanged between very loyal friends.

Flower: Marigold—You may try hard to protect yourself from sorrow.

Astral Color, Color Need, Apparel Color: Your Astral Color is Brown, which helps to keep you grounded and stable. Blue in your environment helps you avoid becoming listless and disorganized. In your wardrobe, many shades of Green always let you look your best.

Fragrance: You are stimulated by a combination of greens and flowers, such as white roses, jasmine, and greenery. They give you feelings of elegance, strength, and security.

Tree: Palm—You tend to be very healthy and creative.

Instruments: Tambourine, lyre

Composer: Schubert

Bird: Goldfinch—These gentle creatures can be quite moody, according to the weather. Otherwise they are quite charming.

Symbol: Crescent—You are more likely to be influenced by the phases of the moon. Your easygoing manner leads you to peaceful situations.

Harmonious Health and Nutrition . . .

Health Scent: Orange Blossom—This scent may balance your body, mind, and soul.

Favorable Foods: Cauliflower, peaches, whole wheat, nuts, buttermilk

What's Lucky . . .

Lucky Numbers: 2, 15, 24
Best Months: March and November
Best Day of the Week: Saturday
Best Month Days: 6, 15, 24
Lucky Charms: A religious token or card from any religion.

Harmonious Signs for Relationships and Partnerships: Capricorn, Taurus, Virgo, and those born between July 27 and September 27.

Spiritual Guides . . .

Star: Dabih—The star of the prominent in society.
Angel: Hanaeb—This angel shows us our worldly desires in order to give us strength when we are going through uncertainty.
Guardian angel: Michael—"Who is like God."
Spiritual Stone: Sardonyx—This stone may cause people to be attracted to you.

✷ JUDITH'S INSIGHT ✷

Responsible? You're almost too responsible for your own good. You learned right from wrong much too early in life. This allowed you no freedom to be the bad child; you knew better. Somewhere along the way you could claim responsibility, but you blame everyone else, even when you're the one to blame.

You desire a little spontaneity in your love life. If your significant other recognizes this and supplies the fun and frolic, you may be able to maintain happiness. If not, you go find it for yourself. No, it doesn't mean an affair. But you can put that extra energy to work in other facets of your life by becoming consumed with sports, exercise, spas, shopping, clothes, or entertainment. Allow the freedom and allow the fun; there are fantasies in there, and it's all right to have them. Leave Mom and Dad, the church, and society behind when in the bedroom.

Legal matters will find you—just make sure you're on the right side of the law. Your determination and strength make you a good worker. Earlier in your life you'll have a serious job, then later you'll have more fun, like a lawyer who turns politician. Just stay away from being anyone's therapist until you have seen your own. Give yourself a break; leave the pressure behind as much as you can.

✷ ✷ ✷

JANUARY 16   CAPRICORN • The goat of the zodiac

December 21 at 10:00 P.M. to January 21 at 3:00 A.M. • NUMEROLOGY 7

Possessions and Desires . . .

Gem: Ruby—This stone may lead you to energy, friendship, and happiness.
Flower: Yarrow—You can usually trust in your own abilities.
Astral Color, Color Need, Apparel Color: Your Astral Color is Silver, which stimulates your imagination. Blue in your environment prevents depression and disappointments. In your wardrobe, Maroon will give you confidence.
Fragrance: You are stimulated by a combination of greens and flowers, such as white roses, jasmine, and greenery. They give you feelings of elegance, strength, and security.
Tree: Sycamore—Yours is the ability to love, communicate honestly with others, and have lasting relationships.
Instrument: Harp.
Composers: Gluck, Brahms
Bird: Warbling Parakeet—The most beautiful of all birds, known as the love bird. It does seem to have the powers of imitation.
Symbol: Heart—You are enthusiastic, empathetic, and full of generosity and love.

Harmonious Health and Nutrition . . .

Health Scent: Jasmine—This scent may make you more easygoing when you are stressed.
Favorable Foods: Cabbage, prunes, rye, peanuts, eggs

What's Lucky . . .

Lucky Numbers: 1, 6, 24
Best Months: March and November
Best Day of the Week: Saturday
Best Month Days: 6, 15, 24.
Lucky Charm: An old key.
Harmonious Signs for Relationships and Partnerships: Capricorn, Taurus, Virgo, and persons born from July 27 to September 27.

Spiritual Guides . . .

Star: Gedi—The star of the best and the brightest.
Angel: Hanaeb—This angel shows us our worldly desires in order to give us strength when we are going through uncertainty.
Guardian angel: Raphael—This angel attends to all of your needs when you are looking for guidance.
Spiritual Stone: Sardonyx—This stone may cause people to be attracted to you.

✷ JUDITH'S INSIGHT ✷

A philosopher to some, a judge to others—you will wear different hats throughout your life. You have executive ability with a spiritual charm. Trust your gut feelings—you have an uncanny ability to see through situations and people. This will give others a strong desire to reach out to you. You may find people you hardly know just pouring out their hearts to you. Your quick wit and intelligence will attract others for even more advice. Lovers, family, and friends will always seem to overwhelm you because of your distinct capabilities. This will warm your ego. At other times you will be the one complaining and feeling sorry for yourself, and there's the contradiction.

Love does prevail for you several times in your lifetime. Whether or not you live it out is up to you. Opportunity will always be there. Family members and siblings will be close, but be aware of who is doing all of the work and who is reaping all of the benefits. Aim for more balance and equality in family situations.

You could be an artist, decorator, clergy-person, or therapist. Loving at times, you possess an artistic and poetic nature. You can be charitable in your own way, but have expectations of others. You tend to be on the more cautious side when it comes to spending money, and you love a bargain. Others must win your trust and respect. Move slowly with new undertakings and learn to allow yourself room for making mistakes—even though you are perfect.

★ ★ ★

JANUARY 17　CAPRICORN • The goat of the zodiac

December 21 at 10:00 P.M. to January 21 at 3:00 A.M.　•　NUMEROLOGY 8

Possessions and Desires . . .

Gem: Chrysolite—This gem may help you clear your mind of sadness and worry.
Flower: Rosemary—You tend to have an excellent memory.
Astral Color, Color Need, Apparel Color: Your Astral Color is Brown, which helps to keep you grounded and stable. Blue in your environment helps you avoid becoming listless and disorganized. In your wardrobe, many shades of Green always let you look your best.
Fragrance: You are stimulated by a combination of greens and flowers, such as white roses, jasmine, and greenery. They give you feelings of elegance, strength, and security.
Tree: Pine—Your relationships tend to be harmonious, both emotionally and mentally.
Instrument: Cello
Composer: Mozart
Bird: Bobolink—This charming singer is equally good as a soloist or a member of an orchestra. It is a very romantic bird, useful as an insect destroyer, elegant, with beautiful feathers, and always pleasant to have around.
Symbol: Wings—You are the source of balance in your world; this will bring you contentment.

Harmonious Health and Nutrition . . .

Health Scent: Almond—This scent may revitalize you and open you to greater possibilities.
Favorable Foods: Peas, pineapple, whole wheat, almonds, cottage cheese

What's Lucky . . .

Lucky Numbers: 8, 17, 35
Best Months: March and November
Best Day of the Week: Saturday
Best Month Days: 8, 17, 26
Lucky Charm: Red ribbon in your wallet or doorway.
Harmonious Signs for Relationships and

Partnerships: Capricorn, Taurus, Virgo, and anyone born from July 27 to September 27.

Spiritual Guides . . .

Star: Vega—Those with this star can be warriors in search of victory, especially in legal situations.
Angel: Hanaeb—This angel shows us our worldly desires in order to give us strength when we are going through uncertainty.
Guardian angel: Seraphim—love, light, and passion.
Spiritual Stone: Sardonyx—This stone may cause people to be attracted to you.

✴ JUDITH'S INSIGHT ✴

Dreamer that you are, you work to hide that side of yourself. You play the protector of yourself and of others. Cautious by nature, distrusting at times, you exude love only to those you allow to get close, yet you believe you're very open. Patient, honest, and earnest—you're classic when it comes to personal ethics. Be cautious of your fears causing depression. Release yourself from times when you have a desire to be reclusive. Don't analyze so much, especially beyond the age of 35.

Tender person that you are, you will have no problem seeking a mate. Your problems will sometimes be choosing among them. Use caution and good sense when selecting. You get into relationships easily; getting out will be problematic. Sudden and strange experiences will pepper your life, but will generally be uplifting, though at a later time. Others doubt your sensitivity. Let them. In time, they come to know who you are. The strength you display confuses others.

You could do well at a number of different careers, such as banker, merchant, journalist, artist, or psychic. Trust that you'll find more than one title throughout your work life. At times you can be considered cheap, but you're really not, you're just conservative with cash. Friendly to all, cautious with most, you are somewhat dogmatic, a ready and sound reasoner with strong convictions, honest and sincere. Just watch your temper at times. Learn to relax and be happy.

✴ ✴ ✴

Possessions and Desires . . .

Gem: Moonstone—This gem could protect you from danger.

Flower: Rue—If you look too often for faults in others, you may overlook those you need to correct in yourself.

Astral Color, Color Need, Apparel Color: Your Astral Color is Brown, which helps to keep you grounded and stable. Blue in your environment helps you avoid becoming listless and disorganized. In your wardrobe, Green is your power color for overcoming obstacles.

Fragrance: You are stimulated by a combination of greens and flowers, such as white roses, jasmine, and greenery. They give you feelings of elegance, strength, and security.

Tree: Holly—Beware that you are not carried away by your passionate nature. The only way to grow is to be open to new experiences.

Instruments: Violin, tympanum

Composer: Gluck

Bird: Mockingbird—the most proficient minstrel in the world's orchestra; graceful and enthusiastic.

Symbol: Anchor—This tranquil symbol signifies stability and strength, and stands for strong commitments in relationships.

Harmonious Health and Nutrition . . .

Health Scent: Lavender—This scent might lead others to trust you and make you patient.

Favorable Foods: Beans, strawberries, rye, walnuts, buttermilk

What's Lucky . . .

Lucky Numbers: 2, 7, 9, 27

Best Months: March and November

Best Day of the Week: Saturday

Preferential Month Days: 9, 18, 27

Lucky Charm: A U.S. coin or a bill of any amount from the year you were born.

Harmonious Signs for Relationships and

Partnerships: Capricorn, Taurus, Virgo, and anyone born from July 27 to September 27.

Spiritual Guides . . .

Star: Altair—Those with this star feel compelled to protect the wounded.

Angel: Hanaeb—This angel shows us our worldly desires in order to give us strength when we are going through uncertainty.

Guardian angel: Gabriel—"God is my strength."

Spiritual Stone: Sardonyx—This stone may cause people to be attracted to you.

✷ JUDITH'S INSIGHT ✷

You have great executive ability, acute reasoning powers, and a fine intellect. You have a keen and discriminating mind and are always leaping to new heights with ideas. You are an honest person. You respect honor of any kind. You're powerful in your presentation of yourself or anything you touch. You're tough at work, but at home you are a teddy bear, kind, sweet, and affectionate.

You're fussy in love, and can be judgmental at first. Marrying you will probably be better than dating you. You're cynical in the early years, but you grow spiritual as you get older. Love will find you even when you aren't looking. Your sex appeal, the trait you don't think you have, is your magnet. Once you have that significant other, it would probably take a bomb to change this. But if that bomb hits, it will be hard to get you to change back.

You were born to lead. Success finds you whether it be in politics, law, or construction. And the list just goes on. How about president of the PTA, head of the little league or scout troop? You'll find who you are sooner or later. It will find you, if you eat when you're hungry, drink when you're thirsty, and take time to enjoy the jokes that you tell. You will be happy. You're easy and fascinating; but when things don't go your way, you become self-absorbed. Just remember, what gets absorbed becomes all dried up.

✷ ✷ ✷

JANUARY 19

CAPRICORN • The goat of the zodiac

December 21 at 10:00 P.M. to January 21 at 3:00 A.M. • NUMEROLOGY 1

Possessions and Desires . . .

Gem: Moonstone—This gem could protect you from danger.

Flower: Sage—You tend to have a great gift for things relating to the home.

Astral Color, Color Need, Apparel Color: Your Astral Color is Brown, which helps to keep you grounded and stable. Have Blue in your environment to avoid becoming listless and disorganized. In your wardrobe, Emerald Green keeps you confident and always looking great.

Fragrance: You are stimulated by a combination of greens and flowers, such as white roses, jasmine, and greenery. They give you feelings of elegance, strength, and security.

Tree: Walnut—You are unusually helpful and always looking for new beginnings.

Instruments: Oboe, flute, clarinet, piano, French horn, organ, and piccolo

Composer: Böhm

Bird: Hummingbird—This bird is delicate and graceful. It can remain still for hours, then dart off and be as busy as a bee.

Symbol: Crown—The universal sign of a dignified person.

Harmonious Health and Nutrition . . .

Health Scent: Strawberry—soothing by nature, the strawberry promotes self-esteem and encourages love.

Favorable Foods: Brussels sprouts, raspberries, whole wheat, beechnuts

What's Lucky . . .

Lucky Numbers: 1, 2, 8, 37
Best Months: March and November
Best Day of the Week: Saturday

Best Month Days: 1, 10, 19, 28
Lucky Charm: A new penny in your shoe.
Harmonious Signs for Relationships and Partnerships: Capricorn, Taurus, Virgo, and anyone born from July 27 to September 27.

Spiritual Guides . . .

Star: Dabih—the star of the prominent in society.
Angel: Hanaeb—This angel shows us our worldly desires in order to give us strength when we are going through uncertainty.
Guardian angel: Malachi—"Messenger of Jehovah."
Spiritual Stone: Sardonyx—This stone may cause people to be attracted to you.

✶ JUDITH'S INSIGHT ✶

Spontaneity isn't the only great quality about you; you have a brilliant mind, broad intuition, and a wit that keeps everyone laughing. You are the truest of friends as long as others are true to you; otherwise, a bit of the tiger appears. Listen to yourself more often.

Another strong trait is your versatility. You have little difficulty in love, family, or work. Your willingness to accommodate attracts many significant others. Your devotion to family may be your best attribute or your worst, and at times it will be hard to tell.

Actor, dressmaker, cook, and artist are good professions for you. You can do just about anything as long as it allows you creativity. If not, you will be prone to depressions and won't know why. Your desire and ability for work are outrageous.

As thoughtful as you are, you tend to get grumpy when your thoughtful gestures are not taken the way you intend them. Just remember, life is not a movie script, and if it is, sometimes others are not on the same page. Every once in a while your mood will get just enough of a twist to it to keep others guessing.

✶ ✶ ✶

JANUARY 20

CAPRICORN • The goat of the zodiac

December 21 at 10:00 P.M. to January 21 at 3:00 A.M. • NUMEROLOGY 2

Possessions and Desires . . .

Gem: Sapphire—This gem may help you find forgiveness from those you've wronged.

Flower: Snowdrop—Your life is most often filled with hopes realized.

Astral Color, Color Need, Apparel Color: Your Astral Color is Silver, which stimulates your imagination. Blue in your environment will prevent depression and disappointments. In your wardrobe, Maroon gives you confidence.

Fragrance: You are stimulated by a combination of greens and flowers, such as white roses, jasmine, and greenery. They give you feelings of elegance, strength, and security.

Tree: Maple—You have great stability and flashes of intuition.

Instruments: Pipe organ, cymbal, drum

Composers: Handel, Johann Sebastian Bach

Bird: Stork—Turkish bird, held in high esteem the world over. This bird is intelligent but may have strange tendencies.

Symbol: Cross—the symbol of self-sacrifice and reconciliation.

Harmonious Health and Nutrition . . .

Health Scent: Apple—You are creative, full of joy, and nearly magical. You bring happiness.

Favorable Foods: Watercress, peaches, rye, beechnuts, eggs

What's Lucky . . .

Lucky Numbers: 2, 8, 11
Best Months: March and November
Best Day of the Week: Saturday
Best Month Days: 2, 11, 20, 29
Lucky Charms: Two 50-cent pieces. Give someone else one of them.

Harmonious Signs for Relationships and Partnerships: Capricorn, Taurus, Virgo, and anyone born from July 27 to September 27.

Spiritual Guides . . .

Star: Gedi—the star of the best and the brightest.

Angel: Hanaeb—This angel shows us our worldly desires in order to give us strength when we are going through uncertainty.

Guardian angel: Uriel—Helps bring the light of God's guidance.

Spiritual Stone: Sardonyx—This stone may cause people to be attracted to you.

✱ JUDITH'S INSIGHT ✱

You have only the purest of hearts and a loving nature. You enjoy being the good guy. Others sometimes think you overdo it. So what, let them! They are the ones in the doctor's office trying to figure you out. The intuition you have allows you to know the right things to do at the right moment; so if you are getting it wrong, you are not paying attention to yourself.

Relationships will come and go. You do not like to be without a partner, so watch your moodiness at these times. You do tend to be a bit of a dreamer and love to fantasize. This will help when relationships aren't going well. Family, for you, will sometimes get under your skin. That's only because you want to help so much. Watch out for the monster you create; you give and demand love without limits.

Successful you are, patient you are not. Great executive ability will allow you a career as any one of the following: journalist, banker, lawyer, mediator, decorator—the list is endless. Just keep in mind that you always need and desire a sense of freedom in any job you do, along with constant growth.

Remember to allow yourself enough fun so you don't resent others for knowing how to enjoy themselves.

★ ★ ★

JANUARY 21 CAPRICORN • The goat of the zodiac

December 21 at 10:00 P.M. to January 21 at 3:00 A.M. • NUMEROLOGY 3

Possessions and Desires . . .

Gem: Sapphire—This gem may help you find forgiveness from those you've wronged.

Flower: Southernwood—You tend to enjoy bantering as a means of expressing your deepest feelings.

Astral Color, Color Need, Apparel Color: Your Astral Color is Blue, which creates calmness and brings promise. Blue in your environment helps stabilize your mood. In your wardrobe, many shades of Green always let you look your best.

Fragrance: You are stimulated by a combination of greens and flowers, such as white roses, jasmine, and greenery. They give you feelings of elegance, strength, and security.

Tree: Elm—You have willpower, strength, and the ability to stand alone.

Instrument: Trombone

Composers: Verdi, Mendelssohn, Schumann

Bird: Eagle—This bird is quick to use its powers of flight. It can see immeasurable distances in a single glance, and can sometimes appear to be indifferent.

Symbol: Wreath—You have been crowned with a special personality. You are strong but extremely compassionate.

Harmonious Health and Nutrition . . .

Health Scent: Rose—This scent will lead you to passionate thoughts and make you feel warm inside.

Favorable Foods: Celery, grapes, rye, almonds, buttermilk

What's Lucky . . .

Lucky Numbers: 3, 8, 21
Best Months: March and November
Best Day of the Week: Saturday
Best Month Days: 3, 12, 21, 30
Lucky Charm: A pen that someone else has already used.
Harmonious Signs for Relationships and

Partnerships: Capricorn, Taurus, Virgo, and anyone born from July 27 to September 27.

Spiritual Guides . . .

Star: Vega—Those with this star can be warriors in search of victory, especially in legal situations.

Angel: Hanaeb—This angel shows us our worldly desires in order to give us strength when we are going through uncertainty.

Guardian Angel: Phanuel—Protection against the negative.

Spiritual Stone: Sardonyx—This stone may cause people to be attracted to you.

✴ JUDITH'S INSIGHT ✴

You are a cute, cuddly teddy bear. Your strength will allure others; your sweet personality will keep them. Although you're generally truthful, you aren't always direct. Watch out while looking through those rose-colored glasses. Most times it will not hurt you, but sometimes it could be devastating. You will have strong bouts with low self-esteem, though your looks aren't the problem. Taking what others say too personally could hurt you. Try to eliminate this behavior.

You love strong, attractive, funny, flirtatious people. Remember, sometimes we get what we wish for. Your fickle nature won't help your love life. Learn to be comfortable with yourself first, then look for the significant other. You can be protective to a fault, so remember, we don't own our loved ones, friends, or family. They may consider you overbearing sometimes, even though others know your intentions are only positive. There is nobody more devoted than you. Rejection from loved ones is hurtful.

As a natural psychic, you should do well as a stockbroker, schoolteacher, insurance agent, artist of any kind, or in business. Decide whether you want to be liked as the boss or not. Others may see you as moody.

Promises aren't made to be broken; so don't make them unless you intend to keep them. Trust in yourself first; the rest will come easily. Allow your strengths to be used in the right places and recognize your weaknesses. These are the keys to happiness and success, which, for you, are not necessarily the same thing.

✴ ✴ ✴

JANUARY 22

AQUARIUS • The sign of the son of man

January 21 at 3:00 A.M. to February 19 at 5:00 P.M. • NUMEROLOGY 4

Possessions and Desires . . .

Gem: Sapphire—This gem may help you find forgiveness from those you've wronged.

Flower: Mullein—Your good nature may take you as far as you want to go.

Astral Color, Color Need, Apparel Color: Your Astral Color is Blue, which creates calmness and brings promise. Blue in your environment helps stabilize your mood. In your wardrobe, Rose brings you balance and harmony.

Fragrance: Put together a collection of orange blossoms and jasmine with touches of greenery. Always pick scents that are straight from nature instead of manufactured or processed when searching for a scent. This will keep you as unique as you wish to be.

Tree: Cherry—You will find yourself faced with constant new emotional awakenings.

Instrument: Bass

Composer: Haydn

Bird: Robin—the most sociable of all birds, with the ability to create quick friendships. It also can easily adapt to any home. When it wants something, it has the tendency to try and snatch it.

Symbol: Star—You are full of inner brightness and will stand out in any crowd. You will be seen as special.

Harmonious Health and Nutrition . . .

Health Scent: Vanilla—This scent will fill you with a feeling of cleanliness and stability.

Favorable Foods: Lentils, bananas, sugar, chicken, eggs

What's Lucky . . .

Lucky Numbers: 1, 4, 22

Best Months: April and August

Best Days of the Week: Wednesday, Saturday

Best Month Days: 4, 13, 22, 31

Lucky Charm: A piece of material cut from something in your home.

Harmonious Signs for Relationships and

Partnerships: Gemini, Aquarius, Libra, and anyone born from July 30 to August 31.

Spiritual Guides . . .

Star: Deneb Algiedi—This star gives strong spiritual guidance and sound judgment.

Angel: Gambiel—This angel governs health issues. He teaches us the mystery of life, both on earth and in the heavens.

Guardian Angel: Gabriel—"God is my strength."

Spiritual Stone: Sardius (Ruby)—This stone may drive you to make positive changes in your life.

✷ JUDITH'S INSIGHT ✷

Sensitive is not how most would see you, nor would they use words like shy, intimidated, or even humble. However, that side of your personality does exist. You put on a strong, capable, and independent face. You feel the need to protect yourself.

Ironically, your most wonderful attributes cause your downfalls: your family and your desire to be overly generous. But have no fear; as you mature, this will change—or perhaps you'll just hide it better. Learn to trust your intuition when choosing a mate. Attracting others will not pose a problem, but keeping them will. You send mixed signals. Love will prevail at least once for you. This doesn't always mean a formal commitment either—keep that in mind. Unique things will happen to you in your lifetime. You'll realize this when it happens, or years later when you look back on the crazy life you have led.

You are full of ideas but don't always have the energy to go with them. You have a strong sense of intuition and are a dreamer, so you need to be in a creative field. Perhaps being a computer whiz could do for a while; that would also depend on the kind of working environment and whether it allows freedom and growth. You could be boss or manager, though this may take time to manifest itself, so allow time. At the very least, you will retire successfully.

Stop having so many expectations of life. Guess what? You will be happy! Do not depend on others too much and vice versa. Just when you think it can't get any better, it does.

✷ ✷ ✷

24

JANUARY 23

AQUARIUS • The sign of the son of man

January 21 at 3:00 A.M. to February 19 at 5:00 P.M. • NUMEROLOGY 5

Possessions and Desires . . .

Gem: Sardius—this stone could give the wearer unusual insights into his or her own heart.

Flower: Nightshade—What you know is true will always stay true.

Astral Color, Color Need, Apparel Color: Your Astral Color is Blue, which creates calmness and brings promise. Blue in your environment helps stabilize your mood. In your wardrobe, many shades of Green always let you look your best.

Fragrance: Put together a collection of orange blossoms and jasmine with touches of greenery. Always pick scents that are straight from nature instead of manufactured or processed when searching for a scent. This will keep you as unique as you wish to be.

Tree: Apple—You are creative, full of joy, and nearly magical. You bring happiness.

Instrument: Viola

Composer: Liszt

Bird: Flamingo—This beautiful, gregarious bird is always careful of its enemy. It is also a caretaker of the young and tries to keep everyone happy.

Symbol: Triangle—You have the right combination of abilities.

Harmonious Health and Nutrition . . .

Health Scent: Peach—this scent may balance your good qualities so that they equal your charm.

Favorable Foods: Beets, strawberries, honey, oysters, pressed cheese

What's Lucky . . .

Lucky Numbers: 7, 14, 23

Best Months: April and August

Best Days of the Week: Wednesday, Saturday

Best Month Days: 4, 5, 23

Lucky Charms: A rabbit's foot or a white candle.

Harmonious Signs for Relationships and Partnerships: Gemini, Aquarius, Libra, and anyone born from July 30 to August 31.

Spiritual Guides

Star: Markab—Those with this star often receive more than they give.

Angel: Gambiel—This angel governs health issues. He teaches us the mystery of life, both on earth and in the heavens.

Guardian Angel: Gabriel—"God is my strength."

Spiritual Stone: Sardius (Ruby)—This stone may drive you to make positive changes in your life.

✴ JUDITH'S INSIGHT ✴

You're extremely inventive with a mathematical mind, and have the ability to do amazing things. Do not ever underestimate the power and the know-how that are yours naturally. You are distinctive, cute, and somewhat cunning. Your mind goes where others wish to. Just don't fear your capabilities; this could hinder you. You seem a little different to most who know you, strange to those who don't. You'll have an interesting life if you choose to take the high road. Otherwise, you could find yourself depressed, fighting feelings, always searching for and never really finding that inner peace.

You will have problems with those you love, but none that you will not be able to handle. Your grandest love will probably be your children, if you choose to have them. If not, it will be with things that make you feel like a child. One way or another, the relationship makes you feel young, that will mean the most to you. Make time to spend with family so you don't become overwhelmed. Enjoy the moment and stop obsessing about the next time. Allow the true reality of things to prevail, and you will feel true happiness.

You could be an architect, computer analyst, financial advisor, poet, actor, or director. Bring all the things you do well together, without pushing tomorrow onto today. Allow yourself mental growth, constant stimulation, and an occasional pat on the back.

Good things come to those who wait, and sometimes it may seem like the wait is forever. But don't worry—love, work, money, and friends do come your way. Just remember that sometimes the delivery person is not who we might expect.

✳ ✳ ✳

JANUARY 24
AQUARIUS • The sign of the son of man
January 21 at 3:00 A.M. to February 19 at 5:00 P.M. • NUMEROLOGY 6

Possessions and Desires . . .

Gem: Topaz—This is an excellent gift to be exchanged between very loyal friends.
Flower: Oak—You should always be able to rely on yourself.
Astral Color, Color Need, Apparel Color: Your Astral Color is Blue, which creates calmness and brings promise. Blue in your environment helps stabilize your mood. In your wardrobe, Rose gives you balance and harmony.
Fragrance: Put together a collection of orange blossoms and jasmine with touches of greenery. Always pick scents that are straight from nature instead of manufactured or processed when searching for a scent. This will keep you as unique as you wish to be.
Tree: Palm—You tend to be very healthy and creative.
Instrument: Tambourine
Composer: Schubert
Bird: Falcon—an expert hunter. When well-trained, it can adapt to many tasks and is usually obedient.
Symbol: Crescent—You are more likely to be influenced by the phases of the moon. Your easy-going manner leads you to peaceful situations.

Harmonious Health and Nutrition . . .

Health Scent: Orange Blossom—This scent may balance your body, mind, and soul.
Favorable Foods: Carrots, grapes, sugar, liver, buttermilk

What's Lucky . . .

Lucky Numbers: 1, 15, 24
Best Months: April and August
Best Days of the Week: Wednesday, Saturday
Best Month Days: 6, 15, 24
Lucky Charms: A religious token or card from any religion.
Harmonious Signs for Relationships and

Partnerships: Gemini, Aquarius, Libra, and anyone born from July 30 to August 31.

Spiritual Guides . . .

Star: Sa'ad Melik—This star hangs over those who are generous.
Angel: Gambiel—This angel governs health issues. He teaches us the mystery of life, both on earth and in the heavens.
Guardian Angel: Michael—"Who is like God."
Spiritual Stone: Sardius (Ruby)—This stone may drive you to make positive changes in your life.

✷ JUDITH'S INSIGHT ✷

You will make your statement. Allow yourself time to grow the way you would allow anyone else. Rome wasn't built in a day. You are a perfectionist, especially with yourself. At times you will project this onto others, so be cautious. You will be successful in more than one career. You tend to take on the grandest of responsibilities no matter what the cause, especially when it comes to family and children.

Relationships, in general, are your specialty. You could be a therapist. Seeing things clearly comes easily for you, especially when it comes to others. Be prepared to be a bit more humble. Love will bring you your greatest happiness and your greatest sadness. Family will play a big role in your life; if not in your early years, then later. You can be the one that keeps it all together.

Careers for you could get a little sticky: you want so much. You tend to idealize situations and stay in them too long. Be careful to recognize this. One minute your ego is running high, the next it is searching for your self-esteem at the pit's bottom. You do have that authority, along with a bit of creativity. At times this can be a complicated combination.

Being universally loved helps in almost every way of your life. Stay the good person that you are; all else will eventually fall right into place. Stop looking so hard for happiness; watched pots never seem to boil.

✷ ✷ ✷

JANUARY 25 AQUARIUS • The sign of the son of man

January 21 at 3:00 A.M. to February 19 at 5:00 P.M. • NUMEROLOGY 7

Possessions and Desires . . .

Gem: Garnet—This gem might show you how to find faith and emotional stability.

Flower: Motherwort—You may find to your dismay that love unexpressed is love lost.

Astral Color, Color Need, Apparel Color: Your Astral Color is Blue, which creates calmness and brings promise. Blue in your environment helps stabilize your mood. In your wardrobe, Purple reflects your giving personality and brings you luck.

Fragrance: Put together a collection of orange blossoms and jasmine with touches of greenery. Always pick scents that are straight from nature instead of manufactured or processed when searching for a scent. This will keep you as unique as you wish to be.

Tree: Sycamore—Yours is the ability to love, communicate honestly with others, and have lasting relationships.

Instrument: Harp

Composer: Gluck

Bird: Mockingbird—the most proficient minstrel in the world's orchestra; graceful and enthusiastic.

Symbol: Heart—You are enthusiastic, empathetic, and full of generosity and love.

Harmonious Health and Nutrition . . .

Health Scent: Jasmine—This scent may make you more easygoing when you are stressed.

Favorable Foods: Spinach, bananas, sugar, salmon, eggs

What's Lucky . . .

Lucky Numbers: 1, 25, 34

Best Months: April and August

Best Days of the Week: Wednesday, Saturday

Best Month Days: 7, 15, 34

Lucky Charm: An old key.

Harmonious Signs for Relationships and Partnerships: Gemini, Aquarius, Libra, and anyone born from July 30 to August 31.

Spiritual Guides . . .

Star: Sa'ad al Su'ud—The star of hope.

Angel: Gambiel—This angel governs health issues. He teaches us the mystery of life, both on earth and in the heavens

Guardian Angel: Raphael—This angel attends to all of your needs when you are looking for guidance.

Spiritual Stone: Sardius (Ruby)—This stone may drive you to make positive changes in your life.

✳ JUDITH'S INSIGHT ✳

You are intellectual but inclined to work at something in the arts. Your intelligence should lead you into a significant position. Socializing is important to you, you like to be a part of a group or in the midst of a lot of friends. You will desire a long-term relationship, and you will have one. You can put too many expectations on others, so watch that. Relationships of any kind will not be hard for you to obtain; your talk is alluring all on its own. You're a natural beauty. Communication within relationships could be your downfall—you'll always think it's the other person's fault. It isn't.

Family is important to you, but you seem to allow them freedom to pressure you. When they don't, you find ways of doing it yourself. Listen to your own intuition a bit more often. You tend to be extremely enthusiastic in the beginning of a new relationship or a new job. You can get bored easily, so make sure there is enough to keep you going.

In choosing a career, look for opportunities to wear many different hats, whether as office manager, insurance agent, broker, computer whiz, actor, or even psychic. It may take time, but you will find your niche. You sometimes have big ideas that aren't entirely realistic, but at some point at least one of those big ideas will pay off.

✳ ✳ ✳

JANUARY 26

AQUARIUS • The sign of the son of man

January 21 at 3:00 A.M. to February 19 at 5:00 P.M. • NUMEROLOGY 8

Possessions and Desires . . .

Gem: Chrysolite—This gem may help you clear your mind of sadness and worry.

Flower: Orange blossom—Your fairness equals your loveliness.

Astral Color, Color Need, Apparel Color: Your Astral Color is Blue, which creates calmness and brings promise. Blue in your environment helps stabilize your mood. In your wardrobe, Gray gives you encouragement.

Fragrance: Put together a collection of orange blossoms and jasmine with touches of greenery. Always pick scents that are straight from nature instead of manufactured or processed when searching for a scent. This will keep you as unique as you wish to be.

Tree: Pine—Your relationships tend to be harmonious, both emotionally and mentally.

Instrument: Cello

Composer: Mozart

Bird: Bobolink—This charming singer is equally good as a soloist or a member of an orchestra. It is a very romantic bird, useful as an insect destroyer, and elegant, with beautiful feathers, and always pleasant to have around.

Symbol: Wings—You are the source of balance in your world. This will bring you contentment.

Harmonious Health and Nutrition . . .

Health Scent: Almond—This scent may revitalize you and open you to greater possibilities.

Favorable Foods: Okra, apples, honey, chicken, buttermilk

What's Lucky . . .

Lucky Numbers: 7, 8, 26

Best Months: April and August

Best Days of the Week: Wednesday, Saturday

Best Month Days: 8, 17, 26

Lucky Charm: A red ribbon in your wallet or doorway.

Harmonious Signs for Relationships and Partnerships: Gemini, Aquarius, Libra, and anyone born from July 30 to August 31.

Spiritual Guides . . .

Star: Deneb Algiedi—This star gives strong spiritual guidance and sound judgment.

Angel: Gambiel—This angel governs health issues. He teaches us the mysteries of life, both on earth and in the heavens.

Guardian Angel: Seraphim—the angel that brings love, light, and passion.

Spiritual Stone: Sardius (Ruby)—This stone may drive you to make positive changes in your life.

✴ JUDITH'S INSIGHT ✴

You are conscientious and possess great reasoning abilities. You can carry out any order from beginning to end with no complications. You tend to be very ambitious, so don't listen to negativity from the outside world. Others around you can sometimes bring you down. Your greatest problem will be learning to recognize the difference between good input and bad.

Learn to deal more with gut feelings and common sense. You have it: just trust it more often. Significant others will be there. Stop anticipating disaster in love, even though you feel you've had your share. Those of you who have stability with your mate could be overwhelmed by family members and issues.

Artist, musician, healer, social worker, or teacher: any one of these positions would be great for you. You may have to clear a lot of hurdles to feel stable in your job. Once you do, you'll be fine. Money will be there. Have faith and patience.

With your great reasoning powers, you could also be a mediator. You are sensible and have a changeable disposition. You must learn patience; in time your dreams do come true. Unfortunately, some of your life's nightmares will be in there, too. You do survive. You will do much better when you don't sit around feeling sorry for yourself. Think about doing more, and you will get more.

✴ ✴ ✴

JANUARY 27   AQUARIUS • The sign of the son of man
January 21 at 3:00 A.M. to February 19 at 5:00 P.M. • NUMEROLOGY 9

Possessions and Desires . . .

Gem: Opal—Holding this stone may help you discover enough hope to go on.

Flower: Burning Nettle—You can be too quick to put others down.

Astral Color, Color Need, Apparel Color: Your Astral Color is Blue, which creates calmness and brings promise. Blue in your environment helps stabilize your mood. In your wardrobe, Rose gives you balance and harmony.

Fragrance: Put together a collection of orange blossoms and jasmine with touches of greenery. Always pick scents that are straight from nature instead of manufactured or processed when searching for a scent. This will keep you as unique as you wish to be.

Tree: Holly—Beware that you are not carried away by your passionate nature. The only way to grow is to be open to new experiences.

Instrument: Violin

Composer: Gluck

Bird: Mockingbird—The most proficient minstrel in the world's orchestra; graceful and enthusiastic.

Symbol: Anchor—This tranquil symbol signifies stability and strength, and stands for strong commitments in relationships.

Harmonious Health and Nutrition . . .

Health Scent: Lavender—This scent might lead others to trust you and make you patient.

Favorable Foods: Cucumbers, cherries, sugar, oysters, pressed cheese

What's Lucky . . .

Lucky Numbers: 2, 7, 9, 36

Best Months: April and August

Best Days of the Week: Wednesday, Saturday

Best Month Days: 9, 18, 27

Lucky Charms: A U.S. coin or a bill of any amount, from the year you were born.

Harmonious Signs for Relationships and

Partnerships: Gemini, Aquarius, Libra, and anyone born from July 30 to August 31.

Spiritual Guides . . .

Star: Markab—Those with this star often receive more than they give.

Angel: Gambiel—This angel governs health issues. He teaches us the mystery of life, both on earth and in the heavens.

Guardian Angel: Gabriel—"God is my strength."

Spiritual Stone: Sardius (Ruby)—This stone may drive you to make positive changes in your life.

✶ JUDITH'S INSIGHT ✶

You are ambitious and conscientious. Your nature is warm and loving. You have a higher sense of spirituality than most, although this may not be something everyone knows about you. Most think of you as an open book. There is indeed a much more mysterious nature about you than most people see. You have the ability to accomplish much more in life than you can ever imagine. Keep that self-esteem intact and you will be very successful. You have a calming effect on people—when people are drawn to you, remember this.

If you are a woman, you will be a devoted wife and mother. Instinctively you will find the right answers for your family. If you are a man, not only will you be devoted to your wife and children, but also there is a very special place in your heart for your mother and sisters, if you have them. Either gender will have strong psychic abilities.

You're a bit idealistic, poetic, and artistic by nature, so many career doors are open. Just be aware that you sometimes lack endurance. Nevertheless, you will have great achievements within your lifetime. Creative writing, healing, or even working in the garment or beauty industry could work for you. Allow yourself a constant creativity and freedom in anything you do. This will enhance your degree of success.

Don't take life's difficulties too personally. This can be your worst downfall. Keep away from the "poor me" syndrome when the going is rough. When things do get overwhelming, remember to put one good day in front of the other, and soon you will have had a great year.

✶ ✶ ✶

JANUARY 28 AQUARIUS • The sign of the son of man

January 21 at 3:00 A.M. to February 19 at 5:00 P.M. • NUMEROLOGY 1

Possessions and Desires . . .

Gem: Agate—This stone may promote health and lead you to a long life.

Flower: Narcissus—You must be careful not to be so focused on your life that you ignore the needs of those around you.

Astral Color, Color Need, Apparel Color: Your Astral Color is Blue, which creates calmness and brings promise. Blue in your environment helps stabilize your mood. In your wardrobe, Purple reflects your giving personality and brings you luck.

Fragrance: Put together a collection of orange blossoms and jasmine with touches of greenery. Always pick scents that are straight from nature instead of manufactured or processed when searching for a scent. This will keep you as unique as you wish to be.

Tree: Walnut—You are unusually helpful and always looking for constant changes in your life.

Instruments: Flute, clarinet

Composer: Böhm

Bird: Hummingbird—This bird is delicate and graceful. It can remain still for hours, then dart off and be as busy as a bee.

Symbol: Crown—the universal sign of dignity.

Harmonious Health and Nutrition . . .

Health Scent: Strawberry—Soothing by nature, the strawberry promotes self-esteem and encourages love.

Favorable Foods: Carrots, figs, honey, liver, eggs

What's Lucky . . .

Lucky Numbers: 1, 19, 28
Best Months: April and August
Best Days of the Week: Wednesday, Saturday
Best Month Days: 1, 10, 19, 28
Lucky Charm: New penny in your shoe.
Harmonious Signs for Relationships and

Partnerships: Gemini, Aquarius, Libra, and anyone born from July 30 to August 31.

Spiritual Guides . . .

Star: Sa'ad Melik—This star hangs over those who are generous.

Angel: Gambiel—This angel governs health issues. He teaches us the mystery of life, both on earth and in the heavens.

Guardian Angel: Malachi—"Messenger of Jehovah."

Spiritual Stone: Sardius (Ruby)—This stone may drive you to make positive changes in your life.

✦ JUDITH'S INSIGHT ✦

You are an artist by nature with a flair for all kinds of design. You're emotional, sensitive, and enthusiastic. It doesn't take a lot to make you happy or to keep you that way. When the kind of devotion you give is given back, life for you is complete. As you get older, you can become disillusioned and things are less easy, although you try to keep things going smoothly.

Allow others to be closer. Life's downfalls may be difficult for you to adapt to—not because of selfishness, but because of your tendency toward idealism. Family and friends, lovers and mates, and even your children will always make you feel a sense of guilt. Don't let them—except, of course, for the few times when they will be right.

Music may be the right career, or even just a great hobby. You will probably have a strong desire to be a caretaker of some kind. If you don't select this as a career, it will find you somewhere else in your life. Your idealism will draw you to the realm of teaching, or art director, or owner of a photography studio. Make sure structure exists in your life along with the creativity.

You're known to take the long road, but you do get there eventually. Try to listen to your intuition more. Unlike most, you have it naturally. Learn to go with it. Expect the unexpected throughout your life.

★ ★ ★

JANUARY 29 AQUARIUS • The sign of the son of man

January 21 at 3:00 A.M. to February 19 at 5:00 P.M. • NUMEROLOGY 2

Possessions and Desires . . .

Gem: Sapphire—This gem may help you find forgiveness from those you've wronged.

Flower: Liverwort—You are very confident in your ability to succeed.

Astral Color, Color Need, Apparel Color: Your Astral Color is Blue, which creates calmness and brings promise. Blue in your environment helps stabilize your mood. In your wardrobe, Green is your power color for overcoming obstacles.

Fragrance: Put together a collection of orange blossoms and jasmine with touches of greenery. Always pick scents that are straight from nature instead of manufactured or processed when searching for a scent. This will keep you as unique as you wish to be.

Tree: Maple—You have great stability and flashes of intuition.

Instrument: Pipe organ

Composer: Handel

Bird: Cuckoo—a good flyer and very seldom a quitter. Some cuckoos tend to think they favor lonely isolation, but what they really yearn for is a family relationship.

Symbol: Cross—the symbol of self-sacrifice and reconciliation.

Harmonious Health and Nutrition . . .

Health Scents: Apple—You are creative, full of joy, and nearly magical. You bring happiness.

Favorable Foods: Lima beans, cherries, sugar, salmon, buttermilk

What's Lucky . . .

Lucky Numbers: 1, 2, 29, 36
Best Months: April and August
Best Days of the Week: Wednesday, Saturday
Best Month Days: 2, 11, 20, 29
Lucky Charms: Two 50-cent pieces. Give someone else one of them.
Harmonious Signs for Relationships and

Partnerships: Gemini, Aquarius, Libra, and anyone born from July 30 to August 31.

Spiritual Guides . . .

Star: Sa'ad al Su'ud—This star is the harbinger of the outpouring of hopes.

Angel: Gambiel—This angel governs health issues. He teaches us the mystery of life, both on earth and in the heavens.

Guardian Angel: St. John—This angel simplifies that which is complicated.

Spiritual Stone: Sardius (Ruby)—This stone may drive you to make positive changes in your life.

✷ JUDITH'S INSIGHT ✷

You could be a saint if you just followed your instincts. You're sensible, warm, and witty, with a gentle disposition. You're sensitive to others' feelings, and patience is your most valuable asset. A dreamer by nature, you believe almost anything can happen, and it does! You handle most of life's pitfalls well.

Your kind, compassionate nature leads many to your door. You love to be around people. Contentment comes in the form of a longtime mate, a marriage partner or otherwise. Partnerships in business can work for you as well. You always know how to settle an argument. With your diplomacy and tact, you have no problem being humble.

You're intellectual and artistic, which can lead you to dual careers. Success in more than one career would not be surprising. Somewhere throughout your lifetime, you will be recognized for your contributions—even if it's head of the PTA or coach of the year. You may want to protect your finances by taking on a very stable position, yet you should continue to pursue a more artistic or spiritual career. Sooner or later, you do find work you love. It will come. You have high hopes; higher than you show.

It's all right to keep your favorite toys hidden. Just don't spend too much of your life protecting your heart. Let people in and allow them to help fulfill your dreams.

✷ ✷ ✷

JANUARY 30   AQUARIUS • The sign of the son of man
January 21 at 3:00 A.M. to February 19 at 5:00 P.M. • NUMEROLOGY 3

Possession and Desires . . .

Gem: Ruby—This stone may lead you to energy, friendship, and happiness.

Flower: Mignonette—Your best qualities tend to be overlooked.

Astral Color, Color Need, Apparel Color: Your Astral Color is Blue, which creates calmness and brings promise. Blue in your environment helps stabilize your mood. In your wardrobe, many shades of Green keep you confident and always looking great.

Fragrance: Put together a collection of orange blossoms and jasmine with touches of greenery. Always pick scents that are straight from nature instead of manufactured or processed when searching for a scent. This will keep you as unique as you wish to be.

Tree: Elm—You have willpower, strength, and the ability to stand alone.

Instrument: Trombone

Composer: Verdi

Bird: Swan—Regarded as royal and sacred, this bird has the protective nature of a mother, and can become a furious fighter in the defense of its young.

Symbol: Wreath—You have been crowned with a special personality. You are strong but extremely compassionate.

Harmonious Health and Nutrition . . .

Health Scent: Rose—This scent will lead you to passionate thoughts and make you feel warm inside.

Favorable Foods: String beans, gooseberries, honey, chicken, pressed cheese

What's Lucky . . .

Lucky Numbers: 7, 21, 30
Best Months: April and August
Best Days of the Week: Wednesday, Saturday
Best Month Days: 3, 12, 21, and 30
Lucky Charm: A pen that someone else has already used.
Harmonious Signs for Relationships and Partnerships: Gemini, Aquarius, Libra, and anyone born from July 30 to August 31.

Spiritual Guides . . .

Star: Deneb Algiedi—This star gives strong spiritual guidance and sound judgment.

Angel: Gambiel—This angel governs health issues. He teaches us the mystery of life, both on earth and in the heavens.

Guardian Angel: Johiel—This angel is a protector of all those with a humble heart.

Spiritual Stone: Sardius (Ruby)—This stone may tend to drive you to make positive changes in your life.

✴ JUDITH'S INSIGHT ✴

Faithful, loving, and loyal all describe you. You're not perfect, but with your traits, it sometimes seems that way. Unfortunately, you can be a little impatient, stubborn, and idealistic to the point of frustration. All in all, you always try to put your best foot forward, although your parents, teachers, and bosses may not always see it that way. In time, they know you better and become more understanding.

Relationships for you are like wine: they get better with age. You like to keep busy, and your mate must learn this from the get-go—or the relationship won't last. You may seem lazy sometimes—this is far from the truth; you have the energy to do what you want. Love doesn't come easy, so make sure when you're pushing potential partners out the door that it's what you really want. You tend to change your mind once they are gone. But love will prevail. Just have patience.

You're the perfect employee, except for your tardiness. Allow a sense of creativity in your work, or else you won't be there too long. Long-term jobs appeal to you. In fact, all your relationships benefit with time. Watch out for drops in endurance, especially when you're bored or tired. Routine tasks just aren't for you. You could be a consultant of any kind, head of a department, troubleshooter, physician, social worker, actor, or even a producer or director.

Nothing in love, family, friends, work, or money is out of your reach. Keep this in mind when you're struggling with yourself. Remember, everyone gets a turn at happiness, but only some of us recognize it.

✴ ✴ ✴

JANUARY 31   AQUARIUS • The sign of the son of man

January 21 at 3:00 A.M. to February 19 at 5:00 P.M. • NUMEROLOGY 4

Possessions and Desires . . .

Gem: Emerald—Those who carry this stone tend to be lucky in love.

Flower: Periwinkle—You tend to live your life so as to have many fond memories.

Astral Color, Color Need, Apparel Color: Your Astral Color is Blue, which creates calmness and brings promise. Blue in your environment helps stabilize your mood. In your wardrobe, Purple reflects your giving personality and brings you luck.

Fragrance: Put together a collection of orange blossoms and jasmine with touches of greenery. Always pick scents that are straight from nature instead of manufactured or processed when searching for a scent. This will keep you as unique as you wish to be.

Tree: Cherry—You will find yourself faced with constant new emotional awakenings.

Instrument: Bass

Composer: Haydn

Bird: Robin—is the most sociable of all birds, with the ability to create quick friendships. It also can easily adapt to any home. When it wants something, it has the tendency to try to snatch it.

Symbol: Star—You are full of inner brightness and will stand out in any crowd. You will be seen as special.

Harmonious Health and Nutrition . . .

Health Scent: Vanilla—This scent will fill you with a feeling of cleanliness and stability.

Favorable Foods: Lentils, cherries, sugar, salmon, eggs

What's Lucky . . .

Lucky Numbers: 1, 4, 22, 31

Best Months: April and August

Best Days of the Week: Wednesday, Saturday

Best Month Days: 4, 13, 22, 31

Lucky Charm: A piece of material cut from something in your home.

Harmonious Signs for Relationships and Partnerships: Gemini, Aquarius, Libra, and anyone born from July 30 to August 31.

Spiritual Guides . . .

Star: Markab—Those with this star often receive more than they give.

Angel: Gambiel—This angel governs health issues. He teaches us the mystery of life, both on earth and in the heavens.

Guardian Angel: St. Thomas—This angel brings affection from others and encourages you in all that you do.

Spiritual Stone: Sardius (Ruby)—This stone may drive you to make positive changes in your life.

✴ JUDITH'S INSIGHT ✴

You are practical and very intuitive; some view this as a contradiction. Actually, nothing could be better than someone with psychic inclinations who is practical about it. Your vivid imagination remains grounded. You will feel blessed or guided—others may say protected. Your gentle ways will open a lot of doors in your lifetime. Strong intuitive skills bring things that may make you feel very lucky. This could take years to recognize. Let time pass, and then look back. People are drawn to you.

Home life, although you might not know it, is very important to you, as are friends. The friendships you cultivate will serve as a second family for you. Your comfortable home life may become a haven for others—don't overdo this. Loved ones are important, but don't lose yourself in other people. When your significant others have trouble, they usually have something valid to complain about.

Work as a philosopher, teacher, preacher, healer, or even scientist may be enticing. You could have many careers. You're great at instilling confidence in others—make sure to keep your own confidence up. A long-term position helps boost your faith in yourself. Watch out for sudden changes—don't let the ship sink. Success may come in many ways: in your career, as a volunteer, or in a hobby or sport.

Be cautious about keeping secrets. Stay away from the desire for drugs or alcohol, and be aware of those around you and their dependencies. No, you are not your brother's keeper, but you are your own. Temptations will present themselves; make sure you are doubly aware of your own.

✴ ✴ ✴

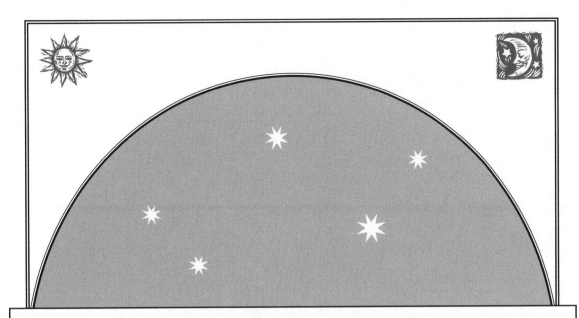

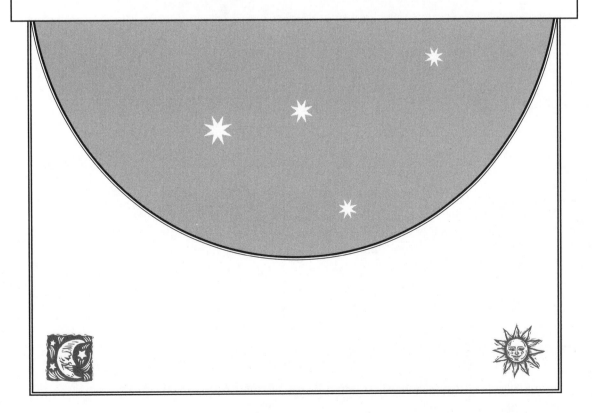

FEBRUARY

FEBRUARY 1

AQUARIUS • The sign of the son of man

January 21 at 3:00 A.M. to February 19 at 5:00 P.M. • NUMEROLOGY 1

Possessions and Desires . . .

Gem: Agate—This stone may promote health and lead you to a long life.
Flower: Sweet Pea—Delicate pleasures await you in every season.
Astral Color, Color Need, Apparel Color: Your Astral Color is Blue, which creates calmness and brings promise. Blue in your environment helps stabilize your mood. In your wardrobe, Rose gives you balance and harmony.
Fragrance: Put together a collection of orange blossoms and jasmine with touches of greenery. Always pick scents that are straight from nature instead of manufactured or processed when searching for a scent. This will keep you as unique as you wish to be.
Tree: Walnut—You are unusually helpful and always looking for constant changes in your life.
Instruments: Oboe, flute, clarinet, piano, French horn, organ, piccolo
Composer: Böhm
Bird: Hummingbird—This bird is delicate and graceful. It can remain still for hours, then dart off and be as busy as a bee.
Symbol: Crown—the universal sign of dignity.

Harmonious Health and Nutrition . . .

Health Scent: Jasmine—This scent may make you more easygoing when you are stressed.
Favorable Foods: Lima beans, bananas, honey, liver, buttermilk

What's Lucky . . .

Lucky Numbers: 1, 7, 19, 28
Best Months: April and August
Best Days of the Week: Wednesday, Saturday
Best Month Days: 1, 10, 19, 28
Lucky Charm: A new penny in your shoe.

Harmonious Signs for Relationships and Partnerships: Gemini, Aquarius, Libra, and anyone born from July 30 to August 31.

Spiritual Guides . . .

Star: Sa'ad Melik—This star hangs over those who are generous.
Angel: Gambiel—This angel governs health issues. He teaches us the mystery of life, both on earth and in the heavens.
Guardian Angel: Malachi—"Messenger of Jehovah."
Spiritual Stone: Sardius (Ruby)—This stone may drive you to make positive changes in your life.

✳ *JUDITH'S INSIGHT* ✳

You are naturally alluring, a powerful, positive presence. Your appealing personality will attract many. Others may be just drawn to you even though they may not necessarily like you. Your name appears on everybody's party list. People find you fascinating, and your sense of humor could have something to do with it. One way or another, you'll step into the limelight.

Family and friends are very important to you. Watch out with love affairs; you crave attention, the romance, the challenge. But poor judgment could lead to many heartaches. Some will just be affairs of the mind that you keep to yourself. Work with what you know; use your intuition in love; it may be hard, but it works. Eventually, you do find the one and only in your life.

Actor, politician, leader, counselor, teacher, professor, or writer: you can do one or you can do them all. And you just might. You are a jack of all trades and definitely a master of some of them. All in all, there is work to be done, and you will do more than your share in more than one career.

You just might get what you wish for. Allow time for things to manifest themselves. Happiness is at your doorstep more than once—open the door and enjoy.

✴ ✴ ✴

FEBRUARY 2 AQUARIUS • The sign of the son of man
January 21 at 3:00 A.M. to February 19 at 5:00 P.M. • NUMEROLOGY 2

Possessions and Desires . . .

Gem: Sapphire—This gem may help you find forgiveness from those you've wronged.
Flower: Yellow Rose—You usually hate any hint of falsehood.
Astral Color, Color Need, Apparel Color: Your Astral Color is Blue, which creates calmness and brings promise. Blue in your environment helps stabilize your mood. In your wardrobe, Rose gives you balance and harmony.
Fragrance: Put together a collection of orange blossoms and jasmine with touches of greenery. Always pick scents that are straight from nature instead of manufactured or processed when searching for a scent. This will keep you as unique as you wish to be.
Tree: Maple—You have great stability and flashes of intuition.
Instruments: Pipe organ, cymbal, drum
Composers: Handel, Johann Sebastian Bach
Bird: Cuckoo—A good flyer and very seldom a quitter. Some cuckoos tend to think they favor lonely isolation, but what they really yearn for is a family relationship.
Symbol: Cross—the symbol of self-sacrifice and reconciliation.

Harmonious Health and Nutrition . . .

Health Scent: Apple—You are creative, full of joy, and nearly magical. You bring happiness.
Favorable Foods: Spinach, strawberries, sugar, salmon, pressed cheese

What's Lucky . . .

Lucky Numbers: 2, 7, 11, 20
Best Months: April and August
Best Days of the Week: Wednesday, Saturday
Best Month Days: 2, 11, 20, 29
Lucky Charms: Two 50-cent pieces. Give someone else one of them.
Harmonious Signs for Relationships and

Partnerships: Gemini, Aquarius, Libra, and anyone born from July 30 to August 31.

Spiritual Guides . . .

Star: Sa'ad al Su'ud—This star is the harbinger of the outpouring of hopes.
Angel: Gambiel—This angel governs health issues. He teaches us the mystery of life, both on earth and in the heavens.
Guardian Angel: St. John—This angel simplifies that which is complicated.
Spiritual Stone: Sardius (Ruby)—This stone may drive you to make positive changes in your life.

✷ JUDITH'S INSIGHT ✷

Proud and capable, you are fascinated by just about everything in life, especially in your youth. You're open to all things and especially easy to get along with. When you start something, you never give up. Be careful of your tenacity; you could get too comfortable and not look for growth. Self-respect is important, too—as long as there are plenty of pats on the back, you won't worry too much about titles.

Should you have children, your opinions will run strong. Protect the family. You will probably find a love mate with a strong personality. You love feeling needed. When you don't, you think something is lacking. If you are neglected or abused in any way, you're out the door. Issues with women in the family may result in some egos clashing.

A career involving mysticism should intrigue you. Teacher would be all right; a decorator or nutritionist could work. You're artistic by nature, so use this ability in some unusual way. You may not be a designer, but the seamstress who does all the beautiful handiwork. Opportunities present themselves throughout your life. Learn to recognize them. Trust your knowledge and your art. Allow time for growth in the career you choose. Check your opinion, particularly with the boss—being a bit humble can come in handy.

You love to spend money, and when depressions hit, you tend to overspend. Those who say money can't buy happiness have never met you.

✷ ✷ ✷

FEBRUARY 3   AQUARIUS • The sign of the son of man

January 21 at 3:00 A.M to February 19 at 5:00 P.M. • NUMEROLOGY 3

Possessions and Desires . . .

Gem: Ruby—This stone may lead you to energy, friendship, and happiness.

Flower: Saffron—You should beware of excess emotions in the early morning.

Astral Color, Color Need, Apparel Color: Your Astral Color is Blue, which creates calmness and brings promise. Blue in your environment helps stabilize your mood. In your wardrobe, Purple reflects your giving personality and brings you luck.

Fragrance: Put together a collection of orange blossoms and jasmine with touches of greenery. Always pick scents that are straight from nature instead of manufactured or processed when searching for a scent. This will keep you as unique as you wish to be.

Tree: Elm—You have willpower, strength, and the ability to stand alone.

Instrument: Trombone

Composers: Verdi, Mendelssohn, Schumann

Bird: Swan—Regarded as royal and sacred, this bird has the protective nature of a mother, and can become a furious fighter in the defense of its young.

Symbol: Wreath—You have been crowned with a special personality. You are strong but extremely compassionate.

Harmonious Health and Nutrition . . .

Health Scent: Rose—This scent will lead you to passionate thoughts and make you feel warm inside.

Favorable Foods: Lentils, grapes, sugar, oysters, eggs

What's Lucky . . .

Lucky Numbers: 3, 7, 21
Best Months: April and August
Best Days of the Week: Wednesday, Saturday
Best Month Days: 3, 12, 21, 30
Lucky Charm: A pen that someone else has already used.

Harmonious Signs for Relationships and Partnerships: Gemini, Aquarius, Libra, and anyone born from July 30 to August 31.

Spiritual Guides . . .

Star: Deneb Algiedi—This star gives strong spiritual guidance and sound judgment.

Angel: Gambiel—This angel governs health issues. He teaches us the mystery of life, both on earth and in the heavens.

Guardian Angel: Johiel—This angel is a protector of all those with a humble heart.

Spiritual Stone: Sardius (Ruby)—This stone may drive you to make positive changes in your life.

✶ JUDITH'S INSIGHT ✶

You can be a showoff and love every minute of it. You have looks, smarts, sensuality, sensitivity, and a desire to be noticed—and you will be! Your ego can run high, and when it does, you're the best. Rejections hurt, and picking yourself up afterward can be work. You're exceptionally resilient, so you eventually bounce back. You do like to hold on to things for sentimental reasons. Friends hold on to you like you hold on to money; you're still friends with your nursery schoolmates. You'll have a million crushes—some good, some bad. Heartstrings break here and there, but you do find that devoted mate; it just takes awhile. You'll pine and pine for the "one that got away," only to thank your lucky stars later in life.

A career in which you give advice is best for you. You could be a politician, teacher, preacher, camp counselor, healer, psychic—the list is endless. You may seem quiet to some, but you need to have a place to speak out and be creative. Patience is not your strong point, but you get by. Success comes and goes because you like to start anew. Strive for balance at work—sooner or later it comes.

If all else fails, start recording some of your fantastic ideas, your daydreaming schemes. You're cunning and cute; it's a great combination. Remember that you don't have to keep both feet on the ground; one foot will help you maintain and the other sustain. Learning which is which is the trick.

✶ ✶ ✶

FEBRUARY 4

AQUARIUS • The sign of the son of man

January 21 at 3:00 A.M. to February 19 at 5:00 P.M. • NUMEROLOGY 4

Possessions and Desires . . .

Gem: Emerald—Those who carry this stone tend to be lucky in love.

Flower: Pansy—You shouldn't do anything unless you clearly think things through.

Astral Color, Color Need, Apparel Color: Your Astral Color is Blue, creating calmness and bringing promise. Keep Blue in your environment to help stabilize your mood. In your wardrobe, Rose gives you balance and harmony.

Fragrance: Put together a collection of orange blossoms and jasmine with touches of greenery. Always pick scents that are straight from nature instead of manufactured or processed when searching for a scent. This will keep you as unique as you wish to be.

Tree: Cherry—You will find yourself faced with constant new emotional awakenings.

Instruments: Bass, clarinet

Composers: Haydn, Wagner

Bird: Robin—The most sociable of all birds, with the ability to create quick friendships. It also can easily adapt to any home. When it wants something, it has the tendency to try to snatch it.

Symbol: Star—You are full of inner brightness and will stand out in any crowd. You will be seen as special.

Harmonious Health and Nutrition . . .

Health Scent: Vanilla—This scent will fill you with a feeling of cleanliness and stability.

Favorable Foods: Romaine lettuce, figs, honey, chicken, buttermilk

What's Lucky . . .

Lucky Numbers: 1, 4, 13, 22

Best Months: April and August

Best Days of the Week: Wednesday, Saturday

Best Month Days: 4, 13, 22, 31

Lucky Charm: A piece of material cut from something in your home.

Harmonious Signs for Relationships and

Partnerships: Gemini, Aquarius, Libra, and anyone born from July 30 to August 31.

Spiritual Guides . . .

Star: Markab—Those with this star often receive more than they give.

Angel: Gambiel—This angel governs health issues. He teaches us the mystery of life, both on earth and in the heavens.

Guardian Angel: St. Thomas—This angel brings affection from others and encourages you in all that you do.

Spiritual Stone: Sardius (Ruby)—This stone may drive you to make positive changes in your life.

✶ JUDITH'S INSIGHT ✶

You have an awesome sense of concentration. With focus like yours, you could master anything. Do you recognize that you see life much clearer than most? You are kind and considerate by nature, and others are fascinated by you. The fact that your looks are quite good doesn't hurt. Frequently throughout your life you'll encounter strange situations: some really good, some not. You know the difference.

You may not think it, but ask others around you: you're a flirt. Family relationships are what you make of them; at times you will need to be tolerant, but mostly it's the other way around. Love mates are usually the ones in the public eye. That's what you want, so don't feel sorry for yourself if they receive all the attention.

You will do great in just about any career having to do with people and creativity. You'd be happy as a clothing designer for the movies or theater. You will love working in an environment that will eventually lead you to glory and glamour. Fear not—you get it. Just keep in mind that opportunities that aren't here today could be here tomorrow. When your biggest dreams seem to be on hold, have patience, your day does come.

Feeling sorry for yourself never helps; it only creates more anxiety. Learn to trust your instincts more often, and temper that vivid imagination. You can have a positive impact on a lot of people's lives; make sure you are as positive for yourself.

FEBRUARY 5   AQUARIUS • The sign of the son of man

January 21 at 3:00 A.M. to February 19 at 5:00 P.M. • NUMEROLOGY 5

Possessions and Desires . . .

Gem: Sapphire—This gem may help you find forgiveness from those you've wronged.

Flower: Marsh Mallow—The course of your life will tend to surprise you.

Astral Color, Color Need, Apparel Color: Your Astral Color is Blue, which creates calmness and brings promise. Blue in your environment helps stabilize your mood. In your wardrobe, Green is your power color for overcoming obstacles.

Fragrance: Put together a collection of orange blossoms and jasmine with touches of greenery. Always pick scents that are straight from nature instead of manufactured or processed when searching for a scent. This will keep you as unique as you wish to be.

Tree: Apple—You are creative, full of joy, and nearly magical. You bring happiness.

Instruments: Viola, trumpet

Composer: Liszt

Bird: Flamingo—This beautiful and gregarious bird is always careful of its enemy. It is also a caretaker of the young and tries to keep everyone happy.

Symbol: Triangle—You have the right combination of abilities.

Harmonious Health and Nutrition . . .

Health Scent: Peach—this scent may balance your good qualities so that they equal your charm.

Favorable Foods: Carrots, cherries, honey, salmon, eggs

What's Lucky . . .

Lucky Numbers: 5, 7, 14, 23
Best Months: April and August
Best Days of the Week: Wednesday, Saturday
Best Month Days: 4, 5, 23
Lucky Charms: A rabbit's foot or a white candle.
Harmonious Signs for Relationships and

Partnerships: Gemini, Aquarius, Libra, and anyone born from July 30 to August 31.

Spiritual Guides . . .

Star: Markab—Those with this star often receive more than they give.

Angel: Gambiel—This angel governs health issues. He teaches us the mystery of life, both on earth and in the heavens.

Guardian Angel: Gabriel—"God is my strength."

Spiritual Stone: Sardius (Ruby)—This stone may drive you to make positive changes in your life.

✶ JUDITH'S INSIGHT ✶

Creativity is the main word that describes you. You present yourself as perfect; most will think of you as unique. You can seem mysterious, yet you are warm and loving with a fascination for things unknown or off-color. You can be temperamental.

All your relationships border on the unusual. You root for the underdog. At the same time, you have a strong desire to be needed, so you may find yourself the caretaker of family, friends, and any other stranger that wanders across your path. You have a sweet soul and a nurturing quality. Because of your fun-loving attitude, your children may wonder who's the parent and who's the child.

You're a caretaker by nature, and this could open career doors in such fields as medicine or education. With all your other talents, a career in the arts, film, or design is recommended. One way or another, you'll be successful. But just when you think your career is set, you'll be daydreaming. All of a sudden you'll find yourself in a new career, even if it is at age 65.

Intuitive and imaginative as you are, try to maintain some balance, even if it means keeping a journal. You see the world differently from most. It would be interesting to see how you would explain all the journeys of your life and the detours you've taken to get there. You do it with kindness, love, and laughter. Who would believe it? Time to go get the pen and write!

✶ ✶ ✶

FEBRUARY 6

AQUARIUS • The sign of the son of man

January 21 at 3:00 A.M. to February 19 at 5:00 P.M. • NUMEROLOGY 6

Possessions and Desires . . .

Gem: Topaz—This is an excellent gift to be exchanged between very loyal friends.

Flower: Mistletoe—You may need to discover that you are your best ally in surmounting difficulties.

Astral Color, Color Need, Apparel Color: Your Astral Color is Blue, which creates calmness and brings promise. Blue in your environment helps stabilize your mood. In your wardrobe, Purple reflects your giving personality and brings you luck.

Fragrance: Put together a collection of orange blossoms and jasmine with touches of greenery. Always pick scents that are straight from nature instead of manufactured or processed when searching for a scent. This will keep you as unique as you wish to be.

Tree: Palm—You tend to be very healthy and creative.

Instruments: Tambourine, lyre

Composer: Schubert

Symbol: Crescent—You are more likely to be influenced by the phases of the moon. Your easygoing manner leads you to peaceful situations.

Bird: Falcon—an expert hunter. When well-trained, it can adapt to many tasks and is usually obedient.

Harmonious Health and Nutrition . . .

Health Scent: Orange Blossom—This scent may balance your body, mind, and soul.

Favorable Foods: Beets, strawberries, sugar, oysters, pressed cheese

What's Lucky . . .

Lucky Numbers: 1, 6, 15, 24

Best Months: April and August

Best Days of the Week: Wednesday, Saturday

Best Month Days: 6, 15, 24

Lucky Charms: A religious token or card from any religion.

Harmonious Signs for Relationships and Partnerships: Gemini, Aquarius, Libra, and anyone born from July 30 to August 31.

Spiritual Guides . . .

Star: Sa'ad Melik—This star hangs over those who are generous.

Angel: Gambiel—This angel governs health issues. He teaches us the mystery of life, both on earth and in the heavens.

Guardian Angel: Michael—"Who is like God."

Spiritual Stone: Sardius (Ruby)—This stone may drive you to make positive changes in your life.

✴ JUDITH'S INSIGHT ✴

Resourceful and creative by nature, you do wonders with leftovers. You can build shelves from coffee cans or make quilts from scraps. You're thoughtful when it comes to others, not so when it comes to yourself. A lack of spare time and unrealistic expectations can drain you.

You'll want challenge in relationships, especially in love. Your warmth and sensitivity captivate people; your unusual personality can scare them. But that personality is exactly what they're attracted to in the first place. Don't underestimate your power. Passion comes in several unconventional connections in your life, especially in the beginning of relationships. Your love mate has style, and may be in the public eye.

It may take a few jobs to get you settled—not because you're fickle, but because of your diversity. Be patient. With your passion for art, you should look to that field. You could also find satisfaction as a social worker, therapist, or doctor or working with children. You can be team leader or team player. You have no problem with criticism or authority. Others may find you lazy, but it may be simple boredom. You need constant stimulation at work and, perhaps, a bit of freedom. You may be more interested in hobbies than in your job. You may find yourself in the limelight somewhere along the way. You are luckier than you think, and as you mature, you recognize this. Early years are more difficult than later ones—you think others have it better than you. Stop feeling sorry for yourself. As you grow, you learn you have it better than most.

✴ ✴ ✴

FEBRUARY 7
AQUARIUS • The sign of the son of man
January 21 at 3:00 A.M. to February 19 at 5:00 P.M. • NUMEROLOGY 7

Possessions and Desires . . .

Gem: Garnet—This gem might show you how to find faith and emotional stabilty.

Flower: Linden—You don't tend to need much help in seducing someone you care for.

Astral Color, Color Need, Apparel Color: Your Astral Color is Blue, which creates calmness and brings promise. Blue in your environment helps stabilize your mood. In your wardrobe, Purple reflects your giving personality and brings you luck.

Fragrance: Put together a collection of orange blossoms and jasmine with touches of greenery. Always pick scents that are straight from nature instead of manufactured or processed when searching for a scent. This will keep you as unique as you wish to be.

Tree: Sycamore—Yours is the ability to love, communicate honestly with others, and have lasting relationships.

Instrument: Harp

Composers: Gluck, Brahms

Bird: Mockingbird—the most proficient minstrel in the world's orchestra; graceful and enthusiastic.

Symbol: Heart—You are enthusiastic, empathetic, and full of generosity and love.

Harmonious Health and Nutrition . . .

Health Scent: Jasmine—This scent may make you more easygoing when you are stressed.

Favorable Foods: Spinach, grapes, honey, liver, buttermilk

What's Lucky . . .

Lucky Numbers: 7, 25, 43

Best Months: April and August

Best Days of the Week: Wednesday, Saturday

Best Month Days: 6, 15, 24

Lucky Charm: An old key.

Harmonious Signs for Relationships and

Partnerships: Gemini, Aquarius, Libra, and anyone born from July 30 to August 31.

Spiritual Guides . . .

Star: Sa'ad al Su'ud—The star of hope.

Angel: Gambiel—This angel governs health issues. He teaches us the mystery of life, both on earth and in the heavens.

Guardian Angel: Raphael—This angel attends to all of your needs when you are looking for guidance.

Spiritual Stone: Sardius (Ruby)—This stone may drive you to make positive changes in your life.

✶ JUDITH'S INSIGHT ✶

A collector by nature, you love to shop. You love to have fun and you enjoy parties. There simply aren't enough dances to dance for you. If you don't have a career or hobby in the arts, theater, or communication, it would be surprising.

Relationships come and go—many you will keep to yourself—until, of course, you meet that devoted, significant other. Spontaneity and style will keep you coming back for more. Your family grows to know you and appreciate your unique ways and talents. Tolerate each other. You have your own, intuitive ideas in the raising and managing of children, and most of the time you're correct.

Your friendly nature and theatrical mind attract many friends. You'd be a great artist, musician, educator, or scientist. Follow your artistic desires, but watch that possessive nature. Tension in the workplace should be avoided. You're mostly funny and original, but moods will swing. Think before you speak, especially under the age of 28. Afterward, you're less anxious.

Learn to look at the pretty colors and breathe the fresh air around you. You're a very pleasant person to have around. Others like to feel that they have your attention. Learn to enjoy the moment a little more. When you "stop and smell the roses," enjoy the colors as well as the fragrance.

✶ ✶ ✶

FEBRUARY 8   AQUARIUS • The sign of the son of man

January 21 at 3:00 A.M. to February 19 at 5:00 P.M. • NUMEROLOGY 8

Possessions and Desires . . .

Gem: Garnet—This gem might show you how to find faith and emotional stability.

Flower: Pineapple—You are considered by many to be well-mannered.

Astral Color, Color Need, Apparel Color: Your Astral Color is Blue, which creates calmness and brings promise. Blue in your environment helps stabilize your mood. In your wardrobe, Purple reflects your giving personality and brings you luck.

Fragrance: Put together a collection of orange blossoms and jasmine with touches of greenery. Always pick scents that are straight from nature instead of manufactured or processed when searching for a scent. This will keep you as unique as you wish to be.

Tree: Pine—Your relationships tend to be harmonious, both emotionally and mentally.

Instrument: Cello

Composer: Mozart

Bird: Bobolink—This charming singer is equally good as a soloist or a member of an orchestra. It is a very romantic bird, useful as an insect destroyer, and elegant, with beautiful feathers, and always pleasant to have around.

Symbol: Wings—You are the source of balance in your world; this will bring you contentment.

Harmonious Health and Nutrition . . .

Health Scent: Almond—This scent may revitalize you and open you to greater possibilities.

Favorable Foods: Lentils, gooseberries, sugar, chicken, eggs

What's Lucky . . .

Lucky Numbers: 17, 26, 44

Best Months: April and August

Best Days of the Week: Wednesday, Saturday

Best Month Days: 8, 17, 26

Lucky Charm: A red ribbon in your wallet, or doorway.

Harmonious Signs for Relationships and Partnerships: Gemini, Aquarius, Libra, and anyone born from July 30 to August 31.

Spiritual Guides . . .

Star: Deneb Algiedi—This star gives strong spiritual guidance and sound judgment.

Angel: Gambiel—This angel governs health issues. He teaches us the mystery of life, both on earth and in the heavens.

Guardian Angel: Seraphim—This angel brings love, light and passion.

Spiritual Stone: Sardius (Ruby)—This stone may drive you to make positive changes in your life.

✳ JUDITH'S INSIGHT ✳

You are unusual in many ways: the way you live, dress, and even the way you make a living. Some may see you as strange, but I will call you the unique child. One can find you in a dream state about 15 times a day. You are spiritual with or without religion. You're easily misunderstood, and can feel quite sorry for yourself if things don't go your way.

Your significant other is in the media or the limelight, hopefully for good reasons. You're drawn to the artist and the underdog, which could lead to a relationship with a person of poor character. Don't fret, you'll wind up with someone sane and look back upon your earlier relationships as funny. Family members will be patient, and in turn, you learn to be patient with them. Devotion to your friends brings you much harmony.

With your artistic nature, you may have a career so unique that a title hasn't been created for you, and you will probably be very successful at it. Watch out for becoming bored—it may hinder your rise to the top. Make sure you choose a diverse career.

Generosity is a great trait to have just as long as your pocketbook allows it. You tend to rob Peter to pay Paul. You have the ability to meditate and dream. Use this as a positive trait to learn patience. In time you do prevail.

✳ ✳ ✳

Possessions and Desires . . .

Gem: Turquoise—This stone might help you find material gain.

Flower: Leek—You should practice charity whenever possible.

Astral Color, Color Need, Apparel Color: Your Astral Color is Blue, which creates calmness and brings promise. Blue in your environment helps stabilize your mood. In your wardrobe, Purple reflects your giving personality and brings you luck.

Fragrance: Put together a collection of orange blossoms and jasmine with touches of greenery. Always pick scents that are straight from nature instead of manufactured or processed when searching for a scent. This will keep you as unique as you wish to be.

Tree: Holly—Beware that you are not carried away by your passionate nature. The only way to grow is to be open to new experiences.

Instruments: Violin, tympanum

Composer: Gluck

Bird: Mockingbird—the most proficient minstrel in the world's orchestra; graceful and enthusiastic.

Symbol: Anchor—This tranquil symbol signifyies stability and strength, and stands for strong commitments in relationships.

Harmonious Health and Nutrition . . .

Health Scent: Lavender—This scent might lead others to trust you and make you patient.

Favorable Foods: Okra, bananas, honey, liver, pressed cheese

What's Lucky . . .

Lucky Numbers: 9, 26, 36

Best Months: April and August

Best Days of the Week: Wednesday, Saturday

Best Month Days: 9, 18, 27

Lucky Charms: A U.S. coin or a bill of any amount from the year you were born.

Harmonious Sign for Relationships and Part-

nerships: Gemini, Aquarius, Libra, and anyone born from July 30 to August 31.

Spiritual Guides . . .

Star: Markab—Those with this star often receive more than they give.

Angel: Gambiel—This angel governs health issues. He teaches us the mystery of life, both on earth and in the heavens.

Guardian Angel: Gabriel—"God is my strength."

Spiritual Stone: Sardius (Ruby)—This stone may drive you to make positive changes in your life.

✳ JUDITH'S INSIGHT ✳

You have a highly evolved mind. You're a teacher by nature, but you may or may not choose that career. You're dependable and honorable and have great organizational skills. Your greatest trait of all is philanthropy—you have a heart. Good reasoning powers allow you continuity with all relationships. People are drawn to you, and you take on relationships thinking they are filling a need, later to realize they provided a need to another. This may pose problems: it's hard for you to get away from old flames; you probably want to keep them as friends. If not, they want to be friends with you. You give so much, you sometimes get restless in relationships. Beware of that complication.

Your multifaceted personality leads to your involvement in more than one career and hobby. Science would allow you freedom and growth. Educator, architect, musician, therapist, or technocrat are other possible career choices. You can raise money with the best of them, and your intuitive nature reveals psychic abilities.

With a heart as big as the ocean, you allow many people in your life. As you get older, this may become overwhelming—allow yourself a mental timeout from others. One way or another, you may find yourself in the role of messenger or teacher. Your natural intelligence and common sense will bring you success in your lifetime. Still, hard lessons are there to learn. At the time you may not believe them, but as time goes on you will. You'll make your mark, and it may be surprising just how you do.

✳ ✳ ✳

Possessions and Desires . . .

Gem: Agate—This stone may promote health and lead you to a long life.

Flower: Hawthorn—You may have an unconquerable belief in yourself.

Astral Color, Color Need, Apparel Color: Your Astral Color is Blue, which creates calmness and brings promise. Blue in your environment helps stabilize your mood. In wardrobe, Purple reflects your giving personality and brings you luck.

Fragrance: Put together a collection of orange blossoms and jasmine with touches of greenery. Always pick scents that are straight from nature instead of manufactured or processed when searching for a scent. This will keep you as unique as you wish to be.

Tree: Walnut—You are unusually helpful and always looking for constant changes in your life.

Instruments: Oboe, flute, clarinet, piano, French horn, organ, piccolo

Composer: Böhm

Bird: Bird of paradise—the "bird of the gods." You will shine and love extraordinary circumstances.

Symbol: Crown—the universal sign of dignity.

Harmonious Health and Nutrition . . .

Health Scent: Strawberry—Soothing by nature, the strawberry promotes self-esteem and encourages love.

Favorable Foods: Lima beans, cherries, sugar, salmon, buttermilk

What's Lucky . . .

Lucky Numbers: 1, 19, 37
Best Months: April and August
Best Days of the Week: Wednesday, Saturday
Best Month Days: 1, 10, 19, and 28
Lucky Charm: A new penny in your shoe.

Harmonious Signs for Relationships and Partnerships: Gemini, Aquarius, Libra, and anyone born from July 30 to August 31.

Spiritual Guides . . .

Star: Sa'ad Melik—This star hangs over those who are generous.

Angel: Gambiel—This angel governs health issues. He teaches us the mystery of life, both on earth and in the heavens.

Guardian Angel: Malachi—"Messenger of Jehovah."

Spiritual Stone: Sardius (Ruby)—This stone may drive you to make positive changes in your life.

✶ JUDITH'S INSIGHT ✶

You are affectionate, tolerant, and truthful; you're also strong-willed and obstinate. Keeping your good and bad traits in balance is the hard part. Your restlessness may create heartaches for you and others. Appearance is important to you, and your neat, though funky, style of dress shows this. To some extent you are materialistic. Your skepticism makes you unpredictable.

Stay away from moody people—they don't blend with your need for affection. At first you appear too nurturing—until others get to know you; then they love it. Be careful with ending relationships; old flames want to hang on. Family grows more important as you mature. It's easier for you to handle constant obligations when you're older.

You could be a marine architect, sculptor, lawyer, actor, or director. How about two or three of them? You may have multiple careers, hobbies, and, certainly, interests. As a collector, you find treasures in the trash. You're motivated by creativity, diversity, and cash, and success will come. Use sports to unleash all your exuberance. Constantly look to stimulate your super-abundant mental energy. Depression and laziness are the worst for you. Aim high and have great expectations, and you'll love every minute of it.

✶ ✶ ✶

FEBRUARY 11 AQUARIUS • The sign of the son of man

January 21 at 3:00 A.M. to February 19 at 5:00 P.M. • NUMEROLOGY 2

Possessions and Desires . . .

Gem: Sapphire—This gem may help you find forgiveness from those you've wronged.

Flower: Cypress Vine—You are happiest when facing new beginnings.

Astral Color, Color Need, Apparel Color: Your Astral Color is Blue, creating calm, bringing promise. Blue in your environment helps stabilize your mood. In your wardrobe, Purple reflects your giving personality and brings luck.

Fragrance: Put together a collection of orange blossoms and jasmine with touches of greenery. Always pick scents that are straight from nature instead of manufactured or processed when searching for a scent. This will keep you as unique as you wish to be.

Tree: Maple—You have both great stability and flashes of intuition.

Instruments: Pipe organ, cymbal, drum

Composers: Handel, Johann Sebastian Bach

Bird: Stork—Turkish bird, held in high esteem the world over. This bird is intelligent but may have strange tendencies.

Symbol: Cross—the symbol of self-sacrifice and reconciliation.

Harmonious Health and Nutrition . . .

Health Scent: Apple—You are creative, full of joy, and nearly magical. You bring happiness.

Favorable Foods: Beets, apples, honey, chicken, eggs

What's Lucky . . .

Lucky Numbers: 2, 7, 38
Best Months: April and August
Best Days of the Week: Wednesday, Saturday
Best Month Days: 2, 11, 20, 29
Lucky Charms: Two 50-cent pieces. Give someone else one of them.
Harmonious Signs for Relationships and Part- nerships: Gemini, Aquarius, Libra, and anyone born from July 30 to August 31.

Spiritual Guides . . .

Star: Sa'ad al Su'ud—This star is the harbinger of the outpouring of hopes.

Angel: Gambiel—This angel governs health issues. He teaches us the mystery of life, both on earth and in the heavens.

Guardian Angel: St. John—This angel simplifies that which is complicated.

Spiritual Stone: Sardius (Ruby)—This stone may drive you to make positive changes in your life.

✶ JUDITH'S INSIGHT ✶

Some may see you as strong and ambitious, others as gentle and imaginative. You have all these qualities, depending on the situation. One may be your home personality, the other your work side. In relationships, you can be fickle, or drawn to the underdog—but you know better! Depending on where you are in life, you could be the late bloomer or the early riser. Either way, mates are strong and loyal; it just may take awhile to find the right fit. Don't allow friends and family to overburden you—they will—though you place your share of burdens upon them.

Partnerships in business work well for you. You may work with your significant other or just meet that person at work. You do things better in teams than most and may have more than one career before you find the right one. Listen to the good advice of others. As a partner in a law firm, you do well. As an actor, you could have both a partnership and relationship with the producer. Think partnership!

Team leader or teammate, you'll find your way to the top in life. It infuriates you to be seen as the bad guy—you're not. You're very strong and capable, and this creates a lot of pressure. You make it your own way in life. Others may not always see it that way—they only see what you have, not what it took for you to get it. Your spiritual side will get you through.

★ ★ ★

FEBRUARY 12

AQUARIUS • The sign of the son of man

January 21 at 3:00 A.M. to February 19 at 5:00 P.M. • NUMEROLOGY 3

Possessions and Desires . . .

Gem: Ruby—This stone may lead you to energy, friendship, and happiness.

Flower: Dew Plant—You always seem to have a song in your heart.

Astral Color, Color Need, Apparel Color: Your Astral Color is Blue, which creates calmness and brings promise. Blue in your environment helps stabilize your mood. In your wardrobe, Gray gives you encouragement.

Fragrance: Put together a collection of orange blossoms and jasmine with touches of greenery. Always pick scents that are straight from nature instead of manufactured or processed when searching for a scent. This will keep you as unique as you wish to be.

Tree: Elm—You have willpower, strength, and the ability to stand alone.

Instrument: Trombone

Composers: Verdi, Mendelssohn, Schumann

Bird: Swan—Regarded as royal and sacred, this bird has the protective nature of a mother, and can become a furious fighter in the defense of its young.

Symbol: Wreath—You have been crowned with a special personality. You are strong but extremely compassionate.

Harmonious Health and Nutrition . . .

Health Scent: Rose—This scent will lead you to passionate thoughts and make you feel warm inside.

Favorable Foods: Cucumbers, figs, sugar, salmon, pressed cheese

What's Lucky . . .

Lucky Numbers: 1, 7, 12, 32
Best Months: April and August
Best Days of the Week: Wednesday, Saturday
Best Month Days: 3, 12, 21, 30

Lucky Charm: A pen that someone else has already used.

Harmonious Signs for Relationships and Partnerships: Gemini, Aquarius, Libra, and anyone born from July 30 to August 31.

Spiritual Guides . . .

Star: Deneb Algiedi—This star gives strong spiritual guidance and sound judgment.

Angel: Gambiel—This angel governs health issues. He teaches us the mystery of life, both on earth and in the heavens.

Guardian Angel: Johiel—This angel is a protector of all those with a humble heart.

Spiritual Stone: Sardius (Ruby)—This stone may drive you to make positive changes in your life.

✶ JUDITH'S INSIGHT ✶

Why do you show others your bad side? There are so many good things about you. Why do you insist on being negative, selfish, and domineering when you know you're caring and loving when it really counts? When you don't get your way, you're pesky; when you're tired, you get cranky. You're always doing everything for everybody. Well, have no fear . . . your devoted mate sees you for who you really are. With few words, your wit and charm get all the attention. Loyalty is your strong suit, no matter in what kind of relationship. As the devoted child, you pick up the slack for other family members. If they take you for granted, however, you will rebel. You can raise hell if need be.

Have you considered politics? You could be the head of something somewhere along the way, perhaps the principal of a school or a scout leader. You show great strength, devotion, and character. You will be successful—but when?

You love many but trust few, at least until they prove themselves. Since you're a hard worker, your stamina keeps you at the task longer than most. You're generous with your time and money, and you want and expect that generosity in return. Those around you learn this in order to keep you happy.

✶ ✶ ✶

FEBRUARY 13 AQUARIUS • The sign of the son of man

January 21 at 3:00 A.M. to February 19 at 5:00 P.M. • NUMEROLOGY 4

Possessions and Desires . . .

Gem: Emerald—Those who carry this stone tend to be lucky in love.

Flower: Clematis—You are more drawn to mental beauty than the physical kind.

Astral Color, Color Need, Apparel Color: Your Astral Color is Blue, which creates calmness and brings promise. Blue in your environment helps stabilize your mood. In your wardrobe, Rose gives you balance and harmony.

Fragrance: Put together a collection of orange blossoms and jasmine with touches of greenery. Always pick scents that are straight from nature instead of manufactured or processed when searching for a scent. This will keep you as unique as you wish to be.

Tree: Cherry—You will find yourself faced with constant new emotional awakenings.

Instruments: Bass, Clarinet

Composers: Haydn, Wagner

Bird: Robin—the most sociable of all birds, with the ability to create quick friendships. It also can easily adapt to any home. When it wants something, it has the tendency to try to snatch it.

Symbol: Star—You are full of inner brightness and will stand out in any crowd. You will be seen as special.

Harmonious Health and Nutrition . . .

Health Scent: Vanilla—This scent will fill you with a feeling of cleanliness and stability.

Favorable Foods: Lima beans, strawberries, sugar, salmon, eggs

What's Lucky . . .

Lucky Numbers: 1, 4, 22, 31
Best Months: April and August
Best Days of the Week: Wednesday, Saturday
Best Month Days: 4, 13, 22, 31
Lucky Charm: A piece of material cut from something in your home.
Harmonious Signs for Relationships and

Partnerships: Gemini, Aquarius, Libra, and anyone born from July 30 to August 31.

Spiritual Guides . . .

Star: Markab—Those with this star often receive more than they give.

Angel: Gambiel—This angel governs health issues. He teaches us the mystery of life, both on earth and in the heavens.

Guardian Angel: St. Thomas—This angel brings affection from others and encourages you in all that you do.

Spiritual Stone: Sardius (Ruby)—This stone may drive you to make positive changes in your life.

✳ JUDITH'S INSIGHT ✳

You see things differently from the rest of us. You may be an expert in one field or another, considered a genius by some and lucky by others, without even trying. Sudden and inexplicable things happen that will later benefit you. Your life has an "unexpected" quality about it. Because of your quick mind, you find fault in others, which could create heartache for you.

You're happy with home and family, and are affectionate to those in your life. Your strong, protective nature can be misread—keep this in mind. You will debate your position vehemently. The success of relationships actually has more to do with your mate's patience and tolerance than your own. Once you fall, there usually is no turning back, except if you are deceived in any way. Then the tables will turn, and your extreme devotion could change to extreme anger.

Your intuitive nature allows you a role as great caretaker. Many possible careers await you with your creativity. Your ability to defend an issue could lead you right into the courtroom. No matter what career you choose, there are several successful moments in it for you. You are one of those rare creatures who can succeed in more than one way and be recognized for it. Look to develop programs in the area of communications. Advertising may showcase your many talents.

You are driven in all that you do, but recognize that others lack your endurance. Give yourself a break and others, too!

✴ ✴ ✴

FEBRUARY 14 AQUARIUS • The sign of the son of man

January 21 at 3:00 A.M. to February 19 at 5:00 P.M. • NUMEROLOGY 5

Possessions and Desires . . .

Gem: Sapphires—This gem may help you find forgiveness from those you've wronged.

Flower: Carnation—Your heart's fulfillment is your only destination.

Astral Color, Color Need, Apparel Color: Your Astral Color is Blue, which creates calmness and brings promise. Blue in your environment helps stabilize your mood. In your wardrobe, Purple reflects your giving personality and brings you luck.

Fragrance: Put together a collection of orange blossoms and jasmine with touches of greenery. Always pick scents that are straight from nature instead of manufactured or processed when searching for a scent. This will keep you as unique as you wish to be.

Tree: Apple—You are creative, full of joy, and nearly magical. You bring happiness.

Instruments: Viola, Trumpet

Composer: Liszt

Bird: Flamingo—This beautiful, gregarious bird is always careful of its enemy. It is also a caretaker of the young and tries to keep everyone happy.

Symbol: Triangle—You have the right combination of abilities.

Harmonious Health and Nutrition . . .

Health Scent: Peach—This scent may balance your good qualities so that they equal your charm.

Favorable Foods: Lima beans, strawberries, sugar, salmon, eggs

What's Lucky . . .

Lucky Numbers: 5, 14, 23
Best Months: April and August
Best Days of the Week: Wednesday, Saturday
Best Month Days: 4, 5, 23
Lucky Charms: A rabbit's foot or a white candle
Harmonious Signs for Relationships and

Partnerships: Gemini, Aquarius, Libra and anyone born from July 30 to August 31.

Spiritual Guides . . .

Star: Markab—Those with this star often receive more than they give.

Angel: Gambiel—This angel governs health issues. He teaches us the mystery of life, both on earth and in the heavens.

Guardian Angel: Gabriel—"God is my strength."

Spiritual Stone: Sardius (Ruby)—This stone may drive you to make positive changes in your life.

✶ JUDITH'S INSIGHT ✶

You are a romantic soul. Full of fun and fantasy, you enjoy a good time. You're smart and hard-working, yet you love to play. Your penetrating knowledge of human nature is uncanny. You're inventive and creative and look at the world differently from the rest of us. Family and children are important, but you expect them to be closer to you than you are to them. You only let people see what you want them to see. Devotion plays a large part in all your relationships. Romance is ongoing—through reality or fantasy. Love prevails at least once in your lifetime. You make it happen.

Your energy and enthusiasm could allow you a career in the theater. Your playful ways will get you anywhere. With style and class, you can accomplish more than most in a short amount of time. Keep it interesting and make sure there's growth, otherwise you'll take off. The combination of structure and creativity in photography may interest you.

You're fun to be with (though you don't know it), but your ego can be big, especially in competition. You may love to gamble, or experiment in playlike careers: horse racing, for example. Be careful of overdoing it financially—you're a spender. Money will come and it will definitely go. Eventually the small coins you save will add up. When your ship finally comes in, it won't be a dinghy.

✶ ✶ ✶

FEBRUARY 15

AQUARIUS • The sign of the son of man

January 21 at 3:00 A.M. to February 19 at 5:00 P.M. • NUMEROLOGY 6

Possessions and Desires . . .

Gem: Sapphire—This gem may help you find forgiveness from those you've wronged.

Flower: Hemlock—The bad things in life are there to teach us the value of the good.

Astral Color, Color Need, Apparel Color: Your Astral Color is Blue, which creates calmness and brings promise. Blue in your environment helps stabilize your mood. In your wardrobe, Green is your power color for overcoming obstacles.

Fragrance: Put together a collection of orange blossoms and jasmine with touches of greenery. Always pick scents that are straight from nature instead of manufactured or processed when searching for a scent. This will keep you as unique as you wish to be.

Tree: Palm—You tend to be very healthy and creative.

Instruments: Tambourine, lyre

Composer: Schubert

Bird: Falcon—an expert hunter. When well-trained, it can adapt to many tasks and is usually obedient.

Symbol: Crescent—You are more likely to be influenced by the phases of the moon. Your easygoing manner leads you to peaceful situations.

Harmonious Health and Nutrition . . .

Health Scent: Orange Blossom—This scent may balance your body, mind, and soul.

Favorable Foods: Cucumbers, apples, honey, chicken, pressed cheese

What's Lucky . . .

Lucky Numbers: 1, 6, 15, 33
Best Months: April and August
Best Days of the Week: Wednesday, Saturday
Best Month Days: 6, 15, 24

Lucky Charms: A religious token or card from any religion.

Harmonious Signs for Relationships and Partnerships: Gemini, Aquarius, Libra, and anyone born from July 30 to August 31.

Spiritual Guides . . .

Star: Sa'ad Melik—This star hangs over those who are generous.

Angel: Gambiel—This angel governs health issues. He teaches us the mystery of life, both on earth and in the heavens.

Guardian Angel: Michael—"Who is like God."

Spiritual Stone: Sardius (Ruby)—This stone may drive you to make positive changes in your life.

✷ JUDITH'S INSIGHT ✷

You are faithful and earnest. Although you're practical by nature, you also have psychic abilities, though you may not admit it. You see beauty in everything. You're quick with your thoughts, but less so in your actions. You're highly intelligent, with a strong desire for reading and learning. Animals and kids love you.

You are often the favorite in the family and love it, but you work at it. Your self-sufficiency delays finding the perfect mate. Be patient. Watch out where your own children are concerned—it may take time to recognize problems.

Any company would be happy to have you. Your inventiveness and creativity should allow you many career possibilities. You could easily be an artist or involved in photography. The media and communications could entice you.

You're saddened by disappointments, no matter how small, but you're also hopelessly optimistic, so negative emotions don't linger for long. Find a sympathetic ear—though most of the time, you're the listener. Be thankful and try to enjoy all the wonderful things in life. You were born with the "happy gene."

✷ ✷ ✷

FEBRUARY 16 AQUARIUS • The sign of the son of man
January 21 at 3:00 A.M. to February 19 at 5:00 P.M. • NUMEROLOGY 7

Possessions and Desires . . .

Gem: Garnet—This gem might show you how to find faith and emotional stability.
Flower: Moss—You often love others with parental fervor.
Astral Color, Color Need, Apparel Color: Your Astral Color is Blue, which creates calmness and brings promise. Blue in your environment helps stabilize your mood. In your wardrobe, Green is your power color for overcoming obstacles.
Fragrance: Put together a collection of orange blossoms and jasmine with touches of greenery. Always pick scents that are straight from nature instead of manufactured or processed when searching for a scent. This will keep you as unique as you wish to be.
Tree: Sycamore—Yours is the ability to love, communicate honestly with others, and have lasting relationships.
Instrument: Harp
Composers: Gluck, Brahms
Bird: Mockingbird—the most proficient minstrel in the world's orchestra; graceful and enthusiastic.
Symbol: Heart—You are enthusiastic, empathetic, and full of generosity and love.

Harmonious Health and Nutrition . . .

Health Scent: Jasmine—This scent may make you more easygoing when you are stressed.
Favorable Foods: Spinach, figs, sugar, salmon, buttermilk

What's Lucky . . .

Lucky Numbers: 7, 25, 34
Best Months: April and August
Best Days of the Week: Wednesday, Saturday
Best Month Days: 7, 14, 21
Lucky Charm: An old key.
Harmonious Signs for Relationships and Partnerships: Gemini, Aquarius, Libra, and anyone born from July 30 to August 31.

Spiritual Guides . . .

Star: Sa'ad al Su'ud—This star is the harbinger of the outpouring of hopes.
Angel: Gambiel—This angel governs health issues. He teaches us the mystery of life, both on earth and in the heavens.
Guardian Angel: Raphael—This angel attends to all of your needs when you are looking for guidance.
Spiritual Stone: Sardius (Ruby)—This stone may drive you to make positive changes in your life.

✷ JUDITH'S INSIGHT ✷

You're curious by nature, so you need to explore anything and everything unique and different. You are often the teacher's pet or favorite child. You're faithful and loyal. A dreamer, you tend see things through rose-colored glasses. But when it comes to disappointments, you aren't too resilient. Change bothers you.

Your affectionate and tender nature leads you into relationships. You look for energy and fire in a partner. You may be with someone in the public eye, or you could wind up there yourself. You're romantic to a fault; watch out for idealizing your mate in relationships. In love, you desire fantasy and may look to a past love to get it. Don't spend too much time living in the past or acting out your fantasies.

Your imaginative gifts give you many career choices, whether it be writer, painter, teacher, musician, dancer, cartoonist, or comedian, for those of you who feel comfortable showing their humor. You lean toward low self-esteem, but you have the determination to make it to the top.

Since you're extremely sensitive to the environment and the vibrations of others, be careful with your surroundings, where you live, and the people you associate with. Your calling will come in this life. You just have to learn to open the door to opportunity when it is knocking.

✷ ✷ ✷

FEBRUARY 17

AQUARIUS • The sign of the son of man

January 21 at 3:00 A.M. to February 19 at 5:00 P.M. • NUMEROLOGY 8

Possessions and Desires . . .

Gem: Garnet—This gem might show you how to find faith and emotional stability.

Flower: Pea—You are someone who can really enjoy what life offers.

Astral Color, Color Need, Apparel Color: Your Astral Color is Blue, which creates calmness and brings promise. Blue in your environment helps stabilize your mood. In your wardrobe, Rose gives you balance and harmony.

Fragrance: Put together a collection of orange blossoms and jasmine with touches of greenery. Always pick scents that are straight from nature instead of manufactured or processed when searching for a scent. This will keep you as unique as you wish to be.

Tree: Pine—Your relationships tend to be harmonious, both emotionally and mentally.

Instrument: Cello

Composer: Mozart

Bird: Bobolink—This charming singer is equally good as a soloist or a member of an orchestra. It is a very romantic bird, most useful as an insect destroyer, and elegant, with beautiful feathers, and always pleasant to have around.

Symbol: Wings—You are the source of balance in your world; this will bring you contentment.

Harmonious Health and Nutrition . . .

Health Scent: Almond—This scent may revitalize you and open you to greater possibilities.

Favorable Foods: Cabbage, cherries, sugar, oysters, pressed cheese

What's Lucky . . .

Lucky Numbers: 8, 26, 35

Best Months: April and August

Best Days of the Week: Wednesday, Saturday

Best Month Days: 8, 17, 26

Lucky Charm: A red ribbon in your wallet or doorway.

Harmonious Signs for Relationships and

Partnerships: Gemini, Aquarius, Libra, and anyone born from July 30 to August 31.

Spiritual Guides . . .

Star: Deneb Algiedi—This star gives strong spiritual guidance and sound judgment.

Angel: Gambiel—This angel governs health issues. He teaches us the mystery of life, both on earth and in the heavens

Guardian Angel: Seraphim—Brings love, light, and passion.

Spiritual Stone: Sardius (Ruby)—This stone may drive you to make positive changes in your life.

✷ JUDITH'S INSIGHT ✷

Conscientious, intuitive, and beautiful—you are the general favorite around the house and easily loved by all. Using your well-balanced mind and strong artistic talents, you may be attracted to the sciences and nature. You have an eye for all that is beautiful. You're slow to start things, but you do learn to move steadily. You desire great things and eventually achieve them.

Your family simply adores you. At times this could be more like a burden than a blessing. Learn to balance the family scale better. With your charm and allure, relationships will appear at your feet. Even your naiveté intrigues people. Try to notice when people are good to you. Don't feel sorry for yourself when things don't go your way

Artist, psychic, schoolteacher, movie director, or editor: any one of these careers could indeed work for you. Time and patience is the key. At times you will quit too easily when things don't move fast enough. No one around you will ever do as good a job as you. You must show them how it should be done. When you finally learn to stick to it, you prevail and make it to the top. How long this takes is entirely up to you.

You have a good and sensitive soul. Make sure you learn to laugh along the way and enjoy yourself. Generosity is truly one of your greatest attributes, and many people will be drawn to your good nature. It's easy to love you. Trust your intuition. Stay optimistic, and good things will happen.

★ ★ ★

FEBRUARY 18

AQUARIUS • The sign of the son of man

January 21 at 3:00 A.M. to February 19 at 5:00 P.M. • NUMEROLOGY 9

Possessions and Desires . . .

Gem: Opal—Holding this stone may help you discover enough hope to go on.

Flower: Rye Grass—You may have a very changeable disposition.

Astral Color, Color Need, Apparel Color: Your Astral Color is Blue, which creates calmness and brings promise. Blue in your environment helps stabilize your mood. In your wardrobe, Purple reflects your giving personality and brings you luck.

Fragrance: Put together a collection of orange blossoms and jasmine with touches of greenery. Always pick scents that are straight from nature instead of manufactured or processed when searching for a scent. This will keep you as unique as you wish to be.

Tree: Holly—Beware that you are not carried away by your passionate nature. The only way to grow is to be open to new experiences.

Instruments: Violin, tympanum

Composer: Gluck

Bird: Mockingbird—the most proficient minstrel in the world's orchestra; graceful and enthusiastic.

Symbol: Anchor—This tranquil symbol signifies stability and strength, and stands for strong commitments in relationships.

Harmonious Health and Nutrition . . .

Health Scent: Lavender—This scent might lead others to trust you and make you patient.

Favorable Foods: Carrots, strawberries, honey, chicken, eggs

What's Lucky . . .

Lucky Numbers: 9, 27, 36
Best Months: April and August
Best Days of the Week: Wednesday, Saturday
Best Month Days: 9, 18, 27
Lucky Charms: A U.S. coin or a bill of any amount from the year you were born.

Harmonious Signs for Relationships and Partnerships: Gemini, Aquarius, Libra, and anyone born from July 30 to August 31.

Spiritual Guides . . .

Star: Markab—Those with this star often receive more than they give.

Angel: Gambiel—This angel governs health issues. He teaches us the mystery of life, both on earth and in the heavens.

Guardian Angel: Gabriel—"God is my strength."

Spiritual Stone: Sardius (Ruby)—This stone may drive you to make positive changes in your life.

✳ JUDITH'S INSIGHT ✳

Beautiful deserves beautiful things. You will have them—if not today, then tomorrow. Kindness brings good things, and your great intuition helps your sense of timing in life. You have your own style of doing things. Others will adjust and later respect you for it. You have strong convictions; others are drawn to you and fascinated by this, usually in a positive way.

You will be the envy of your friends and family. Lovers will be drawn and but are sometimes intimidated by your almost pure nature. Once they get to know you better they will just adore you even more. Relationships can be great or not: timing will determine that. Sometimes family can be a burden. If you don't have any, this in itself could be troublesome.

Artistic and psychic only begin to describe you. You could have any business you choose. Your inner sense of what is right lures customers. You could be a star as a computer programmer, graphic designer, architect, writer, filmmaker, or actor.

Great reasoning powers help you in your career and throughout your lifetime. You have many hidden talents and carry the mark of excellence. It's time you showed it.

★ ★ ★

FEBRUARY 19

AQUARIUS • The sign of the son of man

January 21 at 3:00 A.M. to February 19 at 5:00 P.M. • NUMEROLOGY 1

Possessions and Desires . . .

Gem: Turquoise—You may find this stone helps you gain material wealth.

Flower: Spruce—You should have many reasons to celebrate during your life.

Astral Color, Color Need, Apparel Color: Your Astral Color is Emerald Green, which gives you confidence. Violet in your environment keeps you empathetic toward others. In your wardrobe, Green is your power color for overcoming obstacles.

Fragrance: Put together a collection of orange blossoms and jasmine with touches of greenery. Always pick scents that are straight from nature instead of manufactured or processed when searching for a scent. This will keep you as unique as you wish to be.

Tree: Walnut—You are unusually helpful and always looking for constant changes in your life.

Instruments: Oboe, flute, clarinet, piano, French horn, piccolo

Composer: Böhm

Bird: Bird of paradise—the "bird of the gods." You will shine and love extraordinary circumstances.

Symbol: Crown—the universal sign of dignity.

Harmonious Health and Nutrition . . .

Health Scent: Strawberry—Soothing by nature, the strawberry promotes self-esteem and encourages love.

Favorable Foods: Beets, apples, sugar, salmon, buttermilk

What's Lucky . . .

Lucky Numbers: 1, 19, 28
Best Months: April and August
Best Days of the Week: Wednesday, Saturday
Best Month Days: 1, 10, 19, 28
Lucky Charm: A new penny in your shoe.
Harmonious Signs for Relationships and

Partnerships: Gemini, Aquarius, Libra, and anyone born from July 30 to August 31.

Spiritual Guides . . .

Star: Sa'ad Melik—This star hangs over those who are generous.

Angel: Gambiel—This angel governs health issues. He teaches us the mystery of life, both on earth and in the heavens.

Guardian Angel: Malachi—"Messenger of Jehovah."

Spiritual Stone: Sardius (Ruby)—This stone may drive you to make positive changes in your life.

✳ JUDITH'S INSIGHT ✳

Versatile and full of great ideas, you have the ambition and determination to carry out anything. Good opportunities will come out of nowhere. Others bring you luck, and your kindness and tact come through in all situations.

You want commitment, but you may run away before it happens. Eventually you will find that commitment is what makes relationships work. When you end relationships, you act unaffected. You hide your emotions, though not very well. You love your family and they you. Learn to communicate better in relationships.

With your determination and independence, you should own your own business. You have a unique style and could invent or create things never done before. You should avoid gambling or speculation when it comes to other people's money. A career as a stockbroker is not advisable. You take on responsibility early on in life, either working at a young age or caretaking of some kind.

Your share of family crises hurt you. Your youth may not necessarily be an easy one. You may take on adult responsibility at an early age. Make your own way and create the path for yourself and others. Life can be an obstacle course. You will get exhausted and often drained. Determination does win out, so keep reaching for that big brass ring. It will look great on you!

✳ ✳ ✳

FEBRUARY 20   PISCES • The fish that swim in the pure sea

February 19 at 5:00 P.M. to March 20 at 5:00 P.M. • NUMEROLOGY 2

Possessions and Desires . . .

Gem: Moonstone—This gem could protect you from danger.

Flower: Carnation—Your heart fulfillment is your only destination.

Astral Color, Color Need, Apparel Color: Your Astral Color is Pink, reflecting your compassion. Violet in your environment keeps you empathetic toward others. In your wardrobe, Maroon gives you confidence.

Fragrance: Sandalwood or other rare spices are the scents you need to have on hand. You crave attention, and your perfume or cologne should be your most powerful ally. It will enhance your irresistible charm.

Tree: Maple—You have both great stability and flashes of intuition.

Composers: Handel, Johann Sebastian Bach

Instruments: Pipe organ, cymbal, drum

Bird: Flamingo—This beautiful, gregarious bird is always careful of its enemy. It is also a caretaker of the young and tries to keep everyone happy.

Symbol: Cross—the symbol of self-sacrifice and reconciliation.

Harmonious Health and Nutrition . . .

Health Scent: Apple—You are creative, full of joy, and nearly magical. You bring happiness.

Favorable Foods: Raw beets, prunes, rice, brown sugar, egg yolks

What's Lucky . . .

Lucky Numbers: 6, 11, 20

Best Months: May and June

Best Day of the Week: Saturday

Best Month Days: 2, 4, 11

Lucky Charms: Two 50-cent pieces. Give someone else one of them.

Harmonious Signs for Relationships and Partnerships: Cancer, Scorpio, Virgo

Spiritual Guides . . .

Star: Al Phergal Muachher—Those with this star often cling too long to fond memories.

Angel: Barchiel—This angel shows us right from wrong, encourages us in good decision making, and teaches us to protect ourselves and others.

Guardian Angel: Uriel—This angel brings the light of God's guidance.

Spiritual Stone: Chrysolite—This stone might help you keep things together when you feel frayed.

✷ JUDITH'S INSIGHT ✷

You're faithful and devoted, and a loyal employee. You never shirk your duty—when you give your word, you keep it. Considerable ambition will get you where you want to go. You have a keen way of expressing yourself, and you may be mystical in some way.

Idealism and romanticism bring you some interesting relationships. Drawn to the unusual, you may have many long-term unconventional associations. You may be attracted to foreigners or desire to live in another country at some point—foreigners fit into your life somewhere along the line. Marriage or commitment is good for you, for personal growth and the self-confidence you hope for. Of course, that depends on the partners you pick. It could be just the opposite, if you are not careful

You have many talents but are inclined to develop your gift of imagination. You want to express yourself in art, literature, music, or drama. A career in fashion may be yours. You may become quite wealthy in later years. Keep this in mind if you are struggling now.

Honors could enter into your life, perhaps, also in an unconventional way. Travel is important to you. You may own property in another country. Many challenges and opportunities will come your way, and you find your way to those of influence. Success will find you. At times it won't seem possible, so keep on plugging away.

✱ ✱ ✱

FEBRUARY 21

PISCES • The fish that swim in the pure sea

February 19 at 5:00 P.M. to March 20 at 5:00 P.M. • NUMEROLOGY 3

Possessions and Desires . . .

Gem: Crystallite—You tend to be able to free yourself from unwanted passions and sadness.
Flower: Veronica—You are very loyal.
Astral Color, Color Need, Apparel Color: Your Astral Color is White, which gives you clarity. Violet in your environment keeps you empathetic toward others. In your wardrobe, Cinnamon gives you encouragement and stamina.
Fragrance: Sandalwood or other rare spices are the scents you need to have on hand. You crave attention, and your perfume or cologne should be your most powerful ally. It will enhance your irresistible charm.
Tree: Elm—You have willpower, strength, and the ability to stand alone.
Instrument: Trombone
Composers: Verdi, Mendelssohn, Schumann
Bird: Flamingo—This beautiful, gregarious bird is always careful of its enemy. It is also a caretaker of the young and tries to keep everyone happy.
Symbol: Wreath—You have been crowned with a special personality. You are strong but extremely compassionate.

Harmonious Health and Nutrition . . .

Health Scent: Rose—encourages passion and creates an inner warmth.
Favorable Foods: Sorrel, plums, barley, honey, cottage cheese

What's Lucky . . .

Lucky Numbers: 3, 12, 21
Best Months: May and June
Best Day of the Week: Saturday
Best Month Days: 3, 12, 21, 30
Lucky Charm: A pen that someone else has already used.
Harmonious Signs for Relationships and Partnerships: Cancer, Scorpio, Virgo

Spiritual Guides . . .

Star: Al Risha—Those who have this band of stars as theirs will be happiest as part of a family.
Angel: Barchiel—This angel shows us right from wrong, encourages us in good decision making, and teaches us to protect ourselves and others.
Guardian Angel: Johiel—This angel is a protector of all those with a humble heart.
Spiritual Stone: Chrysolite—This stone might help you keep things together when you feel frayed.

✳ JUDITH'S INSIGHT ✳

Although you are very self-contained, you deeply appreciate encouragement and pats on the back from those around you. You have an open mind and an ability to see things clearly. Use your independence in positive ways, otherwise you may be perceived as domineering.

You seem to attract people out of nowhere. You may not keep these relationships, but you have a knack for getting attention, and you love every minute of it. All your relationships have an element of romance. You are a social butterfly—if not in younger years, then later in life. You're on everybody's "A" list, and your generous ways put you at the center of things.

With your desire for fun and keen insight, critic might be a good career. Food critic could also work; you are so precise, you could probably spot the herbs by taste. Musician, physician, mechanic, journalist, or public relations are also good options, though it's advisable to stick to the arts. You may have more than one career or, perhaps, change careers suddenly midlife.

Remember to keep control of your own money, no matter how much you may trust your stockbroker, wife, husband, or accountant. Others will not do you justice when it comes to money—you will do much better on your own. You sometimes have serious mood swings and can learn to control this. Then again, you may not want to.

✳ ✳ ✳

FEBRUARY 22

PISCES • The fish that swim in the pure sea

February 19 at 5:00 P.M. to March 20 at 5:00 P.M. • NUMEROLOGY 4

Possessions and Desires . . .

Gem: Chrysolite—This gem may help you clear your mind of sadness and worry.

Flower: Amaryllis—You should beware of continually swinging between the extremes of arrogance and shyness.

Astral Color, Color Need, Apparel Color: Your Astral Color is Emerald, which gives you confidence. Violet in your environment keeps you empathetic toward others. In your wardrobe, Green is your power color for overcoming obstacles.

Fragrance: Sandalwood or other rare spices are the scents you need to have on hand. You crave attention, and your perfume or cologne should be your most powerful ally. It will enhance your irresistible charm.

Tree: Cherry—You will find yourself faced with constant new emotional awakenings.

Instruments: Bass, clarinet

Composers: Haydn, Wagner

Bird: Robin—the most sociable of all birds, with the ability to create quick friendships. It also can easily adapt to any home. When it wants something, it has the tendency to try to snatch it.

Symbol: Star—You are full of inner brightness and will stand out in any crowd. You will be seen as special.

Harmonious Health and Nutrition . . .

Health Scent: Vanilla—This scent will fill you with a feeling of cleanliness and stability.

Favorable Foods: Leeks, Concord grapes, bran, brown sugar, egg yolks

What's Lucky . . .

Lucky Numbers: 4, 13, 31

Best Months: May and June

Best Day of the Week: Saturday

Best Month Days: 4, 13, 22, 31

Lucky Charm: A piece of material cut from something in your home.

Harmonious Signs for Relationships and Partnerships: Cancer, Scorpio, Virgo

Spiritual Guides . . .

Star: Al Phergal Muachher—Those with this star often cling too long to fond memories.

Angel: Barchiel—This angel shows us right from wrong, encourages us in good decision making, and teaches us to protect ourselves and others.

Guardian Angel: Uriel—This angel brings the light of God's guidance.

Spiritual Stone: Chrysolite—This stone might help you keep things together when you feel frayed.

✷ JUDITH'S INSIGHT ✷

You are generally honest, sincere, and reliable, not only in your work but with friends and family. You can be a worry wart and create imaginary disasters that never happen. Slow down with your imagination, unless of course you are being paid for it. Your views can sometimes be a little unconventional. This is not a bad thing—it's what gets you noticed. Your appearance is almost perfect, and you like it that way.

You love a nice home. You may be drawn to water. Attracted to outgoing as well as quiet types, you may seek out someone very successful or perhaps someone who seems to be, someone from another country or, possibly, with an unusual career or lifestyle. Family matters to you, but be wary of those who are dependent—on you and on substances. You can easily be misread as uncaring, so make sure your signals are clear.

A plumber or doctor—sound confusing? You would be great at either. You could also be a photographer, scientist, mechanic, philanthropist, social worker, school counselor, or artist. When you find a good working environment, stick with it. It may be hard for you to find serenity, but you work circles around everyone when the atmosphere is right.

Your sweetness and adoring charm will win awards for you. To know you is to love you; those who don't could have a hard time.

✷ ✷ ✷

FEBRUARY 23

PISCES • The fish that swim in the pure sea

February 19 at 5:00 P.M. to March 20 at 5:00 P.M. • NUMEROLOGY 5

Possessions and Desires . . .

Gem: Moonstone—This gem could protect you from danger.

Flower: Pansy—You may incorrectly feel that others are declaring war against you.

Astral Color, Color Need, Apparel Color: Your Astral Color is Pink, reflecting your compassion. Violet in your environment keeps you empathetic toward others. In your wardrobe, Maroon gives you confidence.

Fragrance: Sandalwood or other rare spices are the scents you need to have on hand. You crave attention, and your perfume or cologne should be your most powerful ally. It will enhance your irresistible charm.

Tree: Apple—You are creative, full of joy, and nearly magical. You bring happiness.

Instruments: Viola, trumpet

Composer: Liszt

Bird: Flamingo—This beautiful, gregarious bird is always careful of its enemy. It is also a caretaker of the young and tries to keep everyone happy.

Symbol: Triangle—You have the right combination of abilities.

Harmonious Health and Nutrition . . .

Health Scent: Peach—This scent may balance your good qualities so that they equal your charm.

Favorable Foods: Raw beets, prunes, whole grains, honey, cottage cheese

What's Lucky . . .

Lucky Numbers: 6, 14, 23
Best Months: May and June
Best Day of the Week: Saturday
Best Month Days: 5, 4, 23
Lucky Charms: A rabbit's foot or a white candle.
Harmonious Signs for Relationships and Partnerships: Cancer, Scorpio, Virgo

Spiritual Guides . . .

Star: Al Phergal Muachher—Those with this star often cling too long to fond memories.

Angel: Barchiel—This angel shows us right from wrong, encourages us in good decision making, and teaches us to protect ourselves and others.

Guardian Angel: Plavwell—"Strength in presence."

Spiritual Stone: Chrysolite—This stone might help you keep things together when you feel frayed.

✶ JUDITH'S INSIGHT ✶

You have a sensitive but changeable disposition. You are naturally intuitive and learn how to use your intuition more and more each day. You try to understand everyone around you, but others find you difficult to know. You can accomplish many things if you put your energies in the right place at the right time. You're quite ambitious. You're a good listener and know how to help others.

The more romantic the situation, the more devoted you become. Funny as anything, you don't take criticism well. Your good nature makes you the one who takes on the responsibility of your spouse's family. You seem strong, and others don't recognize when you are hurt—they think you're moody.

Artistic, intelligent, and intuitive, you may take on one career for love and another for money. You would make a fine chemist, inventor, professor, composer, or family physician. Since you are physically fit most of your life, you should be active in sports. You would make a great sports agent.

When it comes to money, you may do better giving advice than taking it. You keep a keen eye on money, especially other people's money, that is, your wife's or husband's. The second half of your life may be better than the first: keep it in mind. You may feel the people around you are takers and want to give very little in return. Have no fear—the angels keep score, and when you're in need, they'll be there.

★ ★ ★

FEBRUARY 24

PISCES • The fish that swim in the pure sea

February 19 at 5:00 P.M. to March 20 at 5:00 P.M. • NUMEROLOGY 6

Possessions and Desires . . .

Gem: Topaz—This is an excellent gift to be exchanged between very loyal friends.

Flower: Straw—You tend to form strong unions with others.

Astral Color, Color Need, Apparel Color: Your Astral Color is Pink, reflecting your compassion. Violet in your environment keeps you empathetic toward others. In your wardrobe, Maroon gives you confidence.

Fragrance: Sandalwood or other rare spices are the scents you need to have on hand. You crave attention, and your perfume or cologne should be your most powerful ally. It will enhance your irresistible charm.

Tree: Palm—You tend to be very healthy and creative.

Instruments: Tambourine, lyre

Composer: Schubert

Bird: Goldfinch—These gentle creatures can seem moody especially in unsettled weather.

Symbol: Crescent—You are more likely to be influenced by the phases of the moon. Your easy-going manner leads you to peaceful situations.

Harmonious Health and Nutrition . . .

Health Scent: Orange Blossom—This scent may balance your body, mind, and soul.

Favorable Foods: Unhulled barley, peaches, rice, brown sugar, egg yolks

What's Lucky . . .

Lucky Numbers: 6, 17, 24
Best Months: May and June
Best Day of the Week: Saturday
Best Month Days: 6, 15, 24
Lucky Charms: A religious card or token from any religion.
Harmonious Signs for Relationships and Partnerships: Cancer, Scorpio, Virgo

Spiritual Guides . . .

Star: Al Phergal Muachher—Those with this star often cling too long to fond memories.

Angel: Barchiel—This angel shows us right from wrong, encourages us in good decision making, and teaches us to protect ourselves and others.

Guardian Angel: Michael—"Who is like God."

Spiritual Stone: Chrysolite—This stone might help you keep things together when you feel frayed.

✶ JUDITH'S INSIGHT ✶

Why are you totally misunderstood? Your overprotective personality sends out the wrong vibes. Don't make yourself an example of love and self-sacrifice. You have a strong and commanding nature with a heart of gold. You may think of yourself as unlucky, especially in love, but in time this proves untrue.

You can attract mates who are beneath your social status or inferior in some way. Several heartbreaks will plague you before you become content in a relationship. Family relationships can sometimes be a task, but you manage to keep things together. You can be the most devoted child. Take extra care with the in-laws. There may be "words" exchanged. You can be moody; so depending on when you're asked something, you may give different responses.

Disappointments come too often in your career. You will most definitely have more than one. You can become a workaholic—this will be the only way you can get where you want to go. You may make your mark in reading, writing, or arithmetic—in other words, you could be a teacher, actor, agent, artist, or professor; maybe even a therapist. Unfortunately, your lucky years come later. Your unique mind may create successful schemes or slogans.

You like nice things, and at times you can be materialistic. Making a good impression and "appearances" are important to you, so you're absolutely driven to success.

★ ★ ★

FEBRUARY 25

PISCES • The fish that swim in the pure sea

February 19 at 5:00 P.M. to March 20 at 5:00 P.M. • NUMEROLOGY 7

Possessions and Desires . . .

Gem: Moonstone—This gem could protect you from danger.

Flower: Spearmint—The spice in your life happens when you shake it up.

Astral Color, Color Need, Apparel Color: Your Astral Color is Pink, reflecting your compassion. Violet in your environment keeps you empathetic toward others. In your wardrobe, Maroon gives you confidence.

Fragrance: Sandalwood or other rare spices are the scents you need to have on hand. You crave attention, and your perfume or cologne should be your most powerful ally. It will enhance your irresistible charm.

Tree: Sycamore—Yours is the ability to love, communicate honestly with others, and have lasting relationships.

Instrument: Harp

Composers: Gluck, Brahms

Bird: Warbling Parakeet—the most beautiful of all birds, known as the love bird. It does seem to have the powers of imitation.

Symbol: Heart—You are enthusiastic, empathetic, and full of generosity and love.

Harmonious Health and Nutrition . . .

Health Scent: Jasmine—This scent may make you more easygoing when you are stressed.

Favorable Foods: Cucumbers, apples, bran, honey, cottage cheese

What's Lucky . . .

Lucky Numbers: 7, 17, 27

Best Months: May and June

Best Day of the Week: Saturday

Best Month Days: 7, 14, 21

Lucky Charm: An old key.

Harmonious Signs for Relationships and Partnerships: Cancer, Scorpio, Virgo

Spiritual Guides . . .

Star: Al Phergal Muachher—Those with this star often cling too long to fond memories.

Angel: Barchiel—This angel shows us right from wrong, encourages us in good decision making, and teaches us to protect ourselves and others.

Guardian Angel: Raphael—This angel attends to all of your needs when you are looking for guidance.

Spiritual Stone: Chrysolite—This stone might help you keep things together when you feel frayed.

✷ JUDITH'S INSIGHT ✷

Oh, cautious one: everything needs to be in its place. Be careful that this doesn't cause anxiety. You feel better keeping things to yourself. You don't like conflict; you have a vivid imagination and strong hope. Although a natural artist, you have great business abilities.

Your devotion runs deep—from friends and family to coworkers and employer. Your unusually sympathetic ear and sensitivity can cause your feelings to be hurt very easily. You may come across as needy and melodramatic. Unhappy when not in a relationship, you gravitate to romance and extravagance. Love prevails for you, including the possibility of a great long-term relationship.

You will be an author of one kind or another, whether it is in books, film, music, or education. You should have something published, even if it is your picture in the paper. Make sure you stay on the right side of the law. Motion pictures, a screen career—anything is in the cards for you. You may be born to money or earn it later in life.

Not one to run away from fear, you're more likely to investigate it. You have a gleam in your eyes when things are going well, and this enhances your good looks. But if things aren't going your way, your eyes won't lie, and the world will know of your sadness.

✷ ✷ ✷

FEBRUARY 26

PISCES • The fish that swim in the pure sea

February 19 at 5:00 P.M. to March 20 at 5:00 P.M. • NUMEROLOGY 8

Possessions and Desires . . .

Gem: Chrysolite—This gem may help you clear your mind of sadness and worry.

Flower: Lady's Delight—You have rigid ideas of what you find beautiful.

Astral Color, Color Need, Apparel Colors: Your Astral Color is Pink, reflecting your compassion. Violet in your environment keeps you empathetic toward others. In your wardrobe, Green is your power color for overcoming obstacles.

Fragrance: Sandalwood or other rare spices are the scents you need to have on hand. You crave attention, and your perfume or cologne should be your most powerful ally. It will enhance your irresistible charm.

Tree: Pine—Your relationships tend to be harmonious, both emotionally and mentally.

Instrument: Cello

Composer: Mozart

Bird: Bobolink—This charming singer is equally good as a soloist or a member of an orchestra. It is a very romantic bird, most useful as an insect destroyer, and elegant, with beautiful feathers, and always pleasant to have around.

Symbol: Wings—You are the source of balance in your world; this will bring you contentment.

Harmonious Health and Nutrition . . .

Health Scent: Almond—This scent may revitalize you and open you to greater possibilities.

Favorable Foods: Spinach, cherries, barley, brown sugar, egg yolks.

What's Lucky . . .

Lucky Numbers: 8, 17, 35

Best Months: May and June.

Best Day of the Week: Saturday.

Best Month Days: 8, 17, 26.

Lucky Charm: A red ribbon in your wallet or doorway.

Harmonious Signs for Relationships and Partnerships: Cancer, Scorpio, Virgo

Spiritual Guides . . .

Star: Al Risha—Those who have this band of stars as theirs will be happiest as part of a family.

Angel: Barchiel—This angel shows us right from wrong, encourages us in good decision making, and teaches us to protect ourselves and others.

Guardian Angel: Seraphim—Brings love, light and passion.

Spiritual Stone: Chrysolite—This stone might help you keep things together when you feel frayed.

✶ JUDITH'S INSIGHT ✶

You are a deep thinker who takes life too seriously at times. People will tend to think of you as "hard." You have a strong and commanding nature and a deep sensitivity—others don't always recognize when you are hurting. You're resourceful, and have great organizational skills that can help or hurt. You take on responsibilities. There is caution in what you wish for in your life.

Earlier in life, you may find it difficult to find the perfect mate. Later, it gets easier as your confidence grows. Marriage or a significant relationship may bring unusual circumstances to your life, both good and bad. Family may bring you sorrow in one way or another, but in time should bring you great joy. The dutiful child, you walk around guilty a lot of the time. Just remember, it's you who jumps into the pressure cooker.

You are great at so many things; the problem is your battle with ego and self-esteem. It may take time to find your niche in life, but you have many great qualities. You can be an artist, photographer, journalist, critic, media person, nutritionist, dietitian, and more. You'll strive for great accomplishment, and when you finally achieve it, you may still feel unsatisfied.

Once you recognize that you are content, a sense of freedom and a world of happiness will open. You have no enemies except yourself, that is more than you need. Take more time for self-exploration—this will bring you the greatest peace.

✶ ✶ ✶

FEBRUARY 27

PISCES • The fish that swim in the pure sea

February 19 at 5:00 P.M. to March 20 at 5:00 P.M. • NUMEROLOGY 9

Possessions and Desires . . .

Gem: Chrysolite—This gem may help you clear your mind of sadness and worry.

Flower: Bachelor's Button—Be careful not to spend too much time alone.

Astral Color, Color Need, Apparel Colors: Your Astral Color is White, which gives you clarity. Violet in your environment keeps you empathetic toward others. In your wardrobe, Maroon gives you confidence.

Fragrance: Sandalwood or other rare spices are the scents you need to have on hand. You crave attention, and your perfume or cologne should be your most powerful ally. It will enhance your irresistible charm.

Tree: Holly—Beware that you are not carried away by your passionate nature. The only way to grow is to be open to new experiences.

Instruments: Violin, tympanum

Composer: Gluck

Bird: Flamingo—This beautiful, gregarious bird is always careful of its enemy. It is also a caretaker of the young and tries to keep everyone happy.

Symbol: Wings—You are the source of balance in your world; this will bring you contentment.

Harmonious Health and Nutrition . . .

Health Scent: Lavender—This scent might lead others to trust you and make you patient.

Favorable Foods: Red cabbage, cranberry, bran, honey, cottage cheese

What's Lucky . . .

Lucky Numbers: 9, 27, 36

Best Months: May and June

Best Day of the Week: Saturday

Best Month Days: 2, 9, 18

Lucky Charms: A U.S. coin or a bill of any amount from the year you were born.

Harmonious Signs for Relationships and Partnerships: Cancer, Scorpio, Virgo

Spiritual Guides . . .

Star: Al Risha—Those who have this band of stars as theirs will be happiest as part of a family.

Angel: Barchiel—This angel shows us right from wrong, encourages us in good decision making, and teaches us to protect ourselves and others.

Guardian angel: Gabriel—"God is my strength."

Spiritual Stone: Chrysolite—This stone might help you keep things together when you feel frayed.

✶ JUDITH'S INSIGHT ✶

You should be in the limelight, and sooner or later, you will be. You're good-looking, funny, charming—a star in your own right. You're fickle in just about everything you do, except work. You are in harmony with those around you—but only if that's what you want. Watch your moody side. You are spiritual and psychic beyond your years, and it may take time for you to recognize this. You're imaginative and optimistic. You need a constant flow of mental and physical stimulation.

There isn't enough romance in the world for you. You will have many significant others and a few more insignificant others. You may find yourself alone for a portion of your life, although this is not your style. When you really, really want that special someone, you'll just go and find them. You are a good family member and are deeply devoted, though not necessarily on a daily basis.

You should be in the psychic field. If not, you should be a health care worker—hospital environments will work well for you, at least for a while. Without the public eye, you feel depressed and restless. You'll enjoy some success in your younger years, but much more as you mature. You never feel older—something to keep in mind as you approach the second half of your life. Watch for a new beginning after a dry spell. This may bring you into the limelight. One way or another, you will be a star.

You're criticized for your directness, but still win people over with your magnetic personality. Don't overlook your humanitarian qualities—they may help your dreams prevail.

✶ ✶ ✶

FEBRUARY 28

PISCES • The fish that swim in the pure sea

February 19 at 5:00 P.M. to March 20 at 5:00 P.M. • NUMEROLOGY 1

Possessions and Desires . . .

Gem: Moonstone—This gem could protect you from danger.

Flower: Calla Lily—You may be seen as a magnificent beauty if you surround yourself with these.

Astral Color, Color Need, Apparel Colors: Your Astral Color is Emerald, which gives you confidence. Violet in your environment keeps you empathetic toward others. In your wardrobe, Blue Green enhances your luck and makes you feel secure.

Fragrance: Sandalwood or other rare spices are the scents you need to have on hand. You crave attention, and your perfume or cologne should be your most powerful ally. It will enhance your irresistible charm.

Tree: Walnut—You are unusually helpful and aways looking for new beginnings.

Instruments: Oboe, flute, clarinet, piano, French horn, organ, piccolo

Composer: Böhm

Bird: Flamingo—This beautiful, gregarious bird is always careful of its enemy. It is also a caretaker of the young and tries to keep everyone happy.

Symbol: Crown—the universal sign of dignity.

Harmonious Health and Nutrition . . .

Health Scent: Strawberry—soothing by nature, the strawberry promotes self-esteem and encourages love.

Favorable Foods: Artichokes, raisins, rice, brown sugar, egg yolks

What's Lucky . . .

Lucky Numbers: 2, 6, 10
Best Months: May and June
Best Day of the Week: Saturday
Best Month Days: 1, 10, 19, 28
Lucky Charm: A new penny in your shoe.
Harmonious Signs for Relationships and Partnerships: Cancer, Scorpio, Virgo

Spiritual Guides . . .

Star: Al Phergal Muachher: Those with this star often cling too long to fond memories.

Angel: Barchiel—This angel shows us right from wrong, encourages us in good decision making, and teaches us to protect ourselves and others.

Guardian Angel: Malachi—"Messenger of Jehovah."

Spiritual Stone: Chrysolite—This stone might help you keep things together when you feel frayed.

✷ JUDITH'S INSIGHT ✷

You are the good guy/girl on the block. Warm, sensitive, and mild-mannered, you are loved by all. Adorable and giving, in time you will learn unfortunate lessons that, hopefully, allow you to grow. You take on responsibilities like a champ while limiting your ability to enjoy life. You'll gain more confidence as you mature. Use your wit more often—it helps get you by. Taking on the world way too early has forced you to think "old." Problems arise from negative and fatalistic thinking. Don't be so quick to blame others when things go wrong.

Charm and sensitivity will bring you love as long as you work to keep it. Stay clear of passive-aggressive types. Communicate with your significant other, and all will work nicely. You make a wonderful, devoted parent. Family can be overwhelming at times—so find time for yourself, but don't pull away entirely. It may take you time to realize how much family life means to you.

You may have a few careers, but you will find your way. If you find yourself on the unemployment line, remember to try to be more forthright about your career desires. You can be anything from a healer or builder to a caterer to a plumber. You could run a business. If all else fails, check out a career in the health care field or government or a unionized job.

You are a late bloomer; the second half of your life is better. You may wish to live near the water. You are a person with a heart of gold. In your later years the gold will not only be in your heart but in your pockets.

✷ ✷ ✷

FEBRUARY 29

PISCES • The fish that swim in the pure sea

February 19 at 5:00 P.M. to March 20 at 5:00 P.M. • NUMEROLOGY 2

Possessions and Desires . . .

Gem: Chrysolite—This gem may help you clear your mind of sadness and worry.

Flower: Grass—You may give in too easily.

Astral Color, Color Need, Apparel Colors: Your Astral Color is Emerald, which gives you confidence. Violet in your environment keeps you empathetic toward others. In your wardrobe, Blue Green enhances your luck and makes you feel secure.

Fragrance: Sandalwood or other rare spices are the scents you need to have on hand. You crave attention, and your perfume or cologne should be your most powerful ally. It will enhance your irresistible charm.

Tree: Maple—You have both great stability and flashes of intuition.

Instruments: Pipe organ, cymbal, drum

Composers: Handel, Johann Sebastian Bach

Bird: Cuckoo—a good flyer and very seldom a quitter. Some cuckoos tend to think they favor lonely isolation, but what they really yearn for is a family relationship.

Symbol: Cross—This is the symbol of self-sacrifice and reconciliation.

Harmonious Health and Nutrition . . .

Health Scent: Apple—You are creative, full of joy, and nearly magical. You bring happiness.

Favorable Foods: Leeks, cherries, honey, cottage cheese

What's Lucky . . .

Lucky Numbers: 2, 11, 20

Best Months: May and June

Best Day of the Week: Saturday

Best Month Days: 2, 11, 20, 29

Lucky Charms: Two 50-cent pieces. Give someone else one of them.

Harmonious Signs for Relationships and Partnerships: Cancer, Scorpio, Virgo

Spiritual Guides . . .

Star: Al Risha—Those who have this band of stars as theirs will be happiest as part of a family.

Angel: Barchiel—This angel shows us right from wrong, encourages us in good decision making, and teaches us to protect ourselves and others.

Guardian Angel: Uriel—This angel brings the light of God's guidance.

Spiritual Stone: Chrysolite—This stone might help you keep things together when you feel frayed.

✷ JUDITH'S INSIGHT ✷

Special as the day you were born—you were born for unique reasons; even if it takes a lifetime to figure it out. You have a soft, sweet, sensitive style and will be recognized for it. Strong intelligence, dry wit, and good common sense allow you to be very inventive or creative. Drawn to the unknown, somewhere along the way you make a statement. The strange and unusual can also happen to you—good and not so good.

Relationships can be easy or hard, depending on where you are in life. You are likely to have an adoring soul mate or significant other. Not everyone is lucky enough to have both in one relationship—you are. Your originality may attract some interesting mates, and you could probably write a book on unusual incidents and people. You are dedicated to family, but they could bring you heartache at times. Trust that the love and dedication are there.

You are creative and arty; look for a career as a writer, scientist or professor. Take care to stay on the right side of the law. You may even have the desire to fly a plane or head a large organization. Poet, philosopher, even astrologer would be great careers for you. You will make a mark one way or another. Sports, particularly water sports, may appeal to you, either as a hobby or career.

You're intriguing, smart, and sometimes very intense; try to enjoy life. Partnerships will flourish if you let them. You may make a strong mark on your generation, or your generation could make a strong impact on you.

✷ ✷ ✷

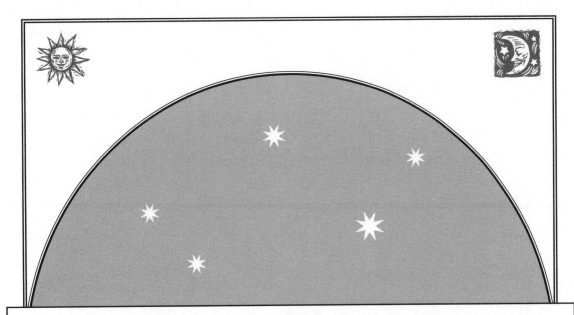

MARCH

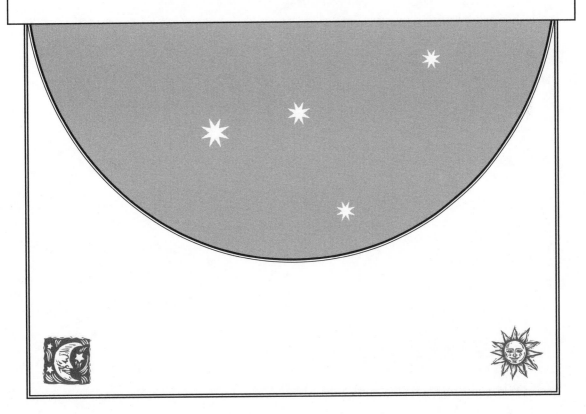

MARCH 1

PISCES • The fish that swim in the pure sea

February 19 at 5:00 P.M. to March 20 at 5:00 P.M. • NUMEROLOGY 1

Possessions and Desires . . .

Gem: Turquoise—This stone may help you find material wealth.

Flower: Heliotrope—You are faithful and devoted.

Astral Color, Color Need, Apparel Color: Your Astral Color is Pink, which reflects your compassion. Violet in your environment keeps you empathetic toward others. In your wardrobe, Cinnamon gives you encouragement and stamina.

Fragrance: Sandalwood or other rare spices are the scents you need to have on hand. You crave attention and your perfume or cologne should be your most powerful ally. It will enhance your irresistible charm.

Tree: Walnut—You are unusually helpful and always looking for new beginnings.

Instruments: Oboe, flute, clarinet, piano, French horn, organ, piccolo

Composer: Böhm

Bird: Flamingo—This beautiful, gregarious bird is always careful of its enemy. It is also a caretaker of the young and tries to keep everyone happy.

Symbol: Crown—The universal sign of a dignified person.

Harmonious Health and Nutrition . . .

Health Scent: Strawberry—Soothing by nature, the strawberry promotes self-esteem and encourages love.

Favorable Foods: Spinach, raisins, barley, honey, cottage cheese

What's Lucky . . .

Lucky Numbers: 1, 10, 37
Best Months: May and June
Best Day of the Week: Saturday
Best Month Days: 1, 10, 19, 28
Lucky Charm: A new penny in your shoe.

Harmonious Signs for Relationships and Partnerships: Cancer, Scorpio, Virgo

Spiritual Guides . . .

Star: Al Phergal Muachher—Those with this star often cling too long to fond memories.

Angel: Barchiel—This angel shows us right from wrong, encourages us in good decision making, and teaches us to protect ourselves and others.

Guardian Angel: Malachi—"Messenger of Jehovah."

Spiritual Stone: Chrysolite—This stone might help you keep things together when you feel frayed.

✳ JUDITH'S INSIGHT ✳

You have more faith and confidence in your abilities than the average person. Your application of life experience creates many positive outcomes. Your sense of concentration and focus is strong. You are true and loyal to your friends, bitter and spiteful to enemies. You work hard to obtain the better things in life.

You make new friends but do not always maintain friendships because you can be fickle, and easily dissatisfied and disillusioned with them. You have a self-protective nature, and it may take some time to connect with the right mate. In time you do, but you will go through many variable relationships first. You will find yourself frustrated by the demands of some people around you. Your intense personality makes it hard for others to always understand you. You may already be aware that you are the responsible child.

A career in nutrition, holistic medicine, or social work would work for you. You may go back and forth for a while before finally settling on one career. Your artistic abilities or creativity could also play a role either in career or extracurricular activity.

Although this may not be the first thing people notice about you, you really are good-natured. You are honest and pure, and with your determination, you will find not only success but also happiness.

✳ ✳ ✳

MARCH 2

PISCES • The fish that swim in the pure sea

February 19 at 5:00 P.M. to March 20 at 5:00 P.M. • NUMEROLOGY 2

Possessions and Desires . . .

Gem: Sapphire—This gem may help you find forgiveness from those you've wronged.

Flower: Thorn—You may be too severe in your judgements.

Astral Color, Color Need, Apparel Color: Your Astral Color is White, which gives clarity. Violet in your environment keeps you empathetic toward others. In your wardrobe, Green is your power color for overcoming obstacles.

Fragrance: Sandalwood or other rare spices are the scents you need to have on hand. You crave attention and your perfume or cologne should be your most powerful ally. It will enhance your irresistible charm.

Tree: Maple—You have both great stability and flashes of intuition.

Instruments: Pipe organ, cymbal, drum

Composers: Handel, Johann Sebastian Bach

Bird: Stork—Turkish bird, held in high esteem the world over. This bird is intelligent but may have strange tendencies.

Symbol: Cross—the symbol of self-sacrifice and reconciliation.

Harmonious Health and Nutrition . . .

Health Scent: Apple—You are creative, full of joy, and nearly magical. You bring happiness.

Favorable Foods: Spinach, raisins, barley, honey, cottage cheese

What's Lucky . . .

Lucky Numbers: 2, 11, 22
Best Months: May and June
Best Day of the Week: Saturday
Best Month Days: 2, 11, 20, 29
Lucky Charms: Two 50-cent pieces. Give someone else one of them.
Harmonious Signs for Relationships and Partnerships: Cancer, Scorpio, Virgo

Spiritual Guides . . .

Star: Al Risha—Those who have this band of stars as theirs will be happiest as part of a family.

Angel: Barchiel—This angel shows us right from wrong, encourages us in good decision making, and teaches us to protect ourselves and others.

Guardian Angel: Uriel—This angel brings the light of God's guidance.

Spiritual Stone: Chrysolite—This stone might help you keep things together when you feel frayed.

✷ JUDITH'S INSIGHT ✷

Sensitive and nurturing by nature, others may see you as weaker than you are. You have strong convictions, but you know better than to push your opinions onto others. Early in life you may have difficulty making ends meet because of your views about money and your nonmaterialistic tendencies. This changes later on. You deeply appreciate and are moved by beautiful scenery, nuances of color, and the harmony of sound. You have not only a dry sense of humor but a warm and witty way with words.

You're a devoted partner. It's not that your mate is difficult, you'll just be doing most of the bending, at least early in the relationship. Tact and style draw others to you easily. Unfortunately, you'll have your share of heartaches (even after the perfect mate is found). Your trusting nature allows others a sense of freedom. Don't become overconfident in your mate, or problems are bound to arise.

You make a sensitive and devoted parent. Through your children (if you have them), you experience the fun childhood you may have missed as a youngster. You have nicer toys now, too.

Your love of sports such as hunting or fishing could lead you into a career, but they'll more likely be a hobby. You're interested in many careers when you are young. After you finally settle on a career, you may still find yourself there twenty years later. Your work environment can't be too serious or intense. You would make a great superintendent, manager, utilities specialist, or graphics designer. You can be secretive, holding your cards close to your chest.

✷ ✷ ✷

MARCH 3

PISCES • The fish that swim in the pure sea

February 19 at 5:00 P.M. to March 20 at 5:00 P.M. • NUMEROLOGY 3

Possessions and Desires . . .

Gem: Ruby—This stone may lead you to energy, friendship and happiness.

Flower: Red Pink—You are pure with your emotions no matter what kind of relationship you're in.

Astral Color, Color Need, Apparel Color: Your Astral Color is Emerald, which gives you confidence. Violet in your environment keeps you empathetic toward others. In your wardrobe, Maroon gives you confidence.

Fragrance: Sandalwood or other rare spices are the scents you need to have on hand. You crave attention and your perfume or cologne should be your most powerful ally. It will enhance your irresistible charm.

Tree: Elm—You have willpower, strength, and the ability to stand alone.

Instrument: Trombone

Composers: Verdi, Mendelssohn, Schumann

Bird: Flamingo—This beautiful, gregarious bird is always careful of its enemy. It is also a caretaker of the young who tries to keep everyone happy.

Symbol: Wreath—You have been crowned with a special personality. You are strong but extremely compassionate.

Harmonious Health and Nutrition . . .

Health Scent: Rose—This scent will lead you to passionate thoughts and make you feel warm inside.

Favorable Foods: Artichokes, peaches, bran, honey, cottage cheese

What's Lucky . . .

Lucky Numbers: 3, 12, 30
Best Months: May and June
Best Day of the Week: Saturday
Best Month Days: 3, 12, 21, 30
Lucky Charm: A pen that someone else has already used.

Harmonious Signs for Relationships and Partnerships: Cancer, Scorpio, Virgo

Spiritual Guides . . .

Star: Al Phergal Muachher—Those with this star often cling too long to fond memories.

Angel: Barchiel—This angel shows us right from wrong, encourages us in good decision making, and teaches us to protect ourselves and others.

Guardian Angel: Johiel—This angel is a protector of all those with a humble heart.

Spiritual Stone: Chrysolite—This stone might help you keep things together when you feel frayed.

✳ JUDITH'S INSIGHT ✳

You have a strong, clear mind and great abilities to go along with it. You usually mean what you say.

If others are loyal, you're loyal back. You become outrageously angry and hold a grudge if you are humiliated. Recognize your mate's point of view, or you could end up alone. You like to be the more controlling partner, although you may never recognize that part of yourself. You have a warm heart and are usually harmless, but when you need to defend yourself, you can be ruthless. You do not make many close friends, but are reliable and worthy of the confidence that people generally have in you.

Your fondness for water could lead to an ideal career. You may have talents in music or poetry. You're also very organized. So working for the government, a large institution, or other structural company might satisfy you. The arts and theater hold a special interest for you. You will achieve success, and your accomplishments will be billboards for all the world to see.

You seem cranky and moody to some. Fearful and protective is more like it. You can jump right out of your skin when things go wrong. You are equally practical, idealistic, and altruistic. You should look forward to earning honors from the community. You have the elements to be a success in whatever you do. So do it all!

★ ★ ★

MARCH 4   PISCES • The fish that swim in the pure sea
February 19 at 5:00 P.M. to March 20 at 5:00 P.M. • NUMEROLOGY 4

Possessions and Desires . . .

Gem: Emerald—Those who carry this stone tend to be lucky in love.

Flower: Rose Geranium—You have a strong desire for life.

Astral Color, Color Need, Apparel Color: Your Astral Color is Pink, which reflects your compassion. Violet in your environment keeps you empathetic toward others. In your wardrobe, Blue-Green enhances your luck and makes you feel secure.

Fragrance: Sandalwood or other rare spices are the scents you need to have on hand. You crave attention and your perfume or cologne should be your most powerful ally. It will enhance your irresistible charm.

Tree: Cherry—You will find yourself faced with constant new emotional awakenings.

Instruments: Bass, clarinet

Composers: Haydn, Wagner

Bird: Killdeer—This bird is usually found consorting with other species, and can adapt to any environment.

Symbol: Star—You are full of inner brightness and will stand out in any crowd. You will be seen as special.

Harmonious Health and Nutrition . . .

Health Scent: Vanilla—This scent will fill you with a feeling of cleanliness and stability.

Favorable Foods: Raw beets, Concord grapes, rice, brown sugar, egg yolks

What's Lucky . . .

Lucky Numbers: 4, 22, 31
Best Months: May and June
Best Day of the Week: Saturday
Best Month Days: 4, 13, 22, 31
Lucky Charm: A piece of material cut from something in your home.
Harmonious Signs for Relationships and Partnerships: Cancer, Scorpio, Virgo

Spiritual Guides . . .

Star: Al Phergal Muachher—Those with this star often cling too long to fond memories.

Angel: Barchiel—This angel shows us right from wrong, encourages us in good decision making, and teaches us to protect ourselves and others.

Guardian Angel: Uriel—Individual archangel meaning "The Light of God."

Spiritual Stone: Chrysolite—This stone might help you keep things together when you feel frayed.

✶ JUDITH'S INSIGHT ✶

You can be unconventional. You have lots of style and love beautiful things. You maintain a neat home as well as a neat appearance. Your early years may be filled with sorrows, or you just may tend to feel sad. As you get older, life blossoms and develops into more fun and less heartache. Your independence is striking. Others may find the need to criticize because of the style in which you handle your life. Once in a while, they're right. You have a style that will leave people with their mouths open.

On occasion, you let people get to you. This may cause some bumpy relationships. You're drawn to unusual people or, perhaps, foreigners, and you like unconventional relationships. Your family life will be decent enough, but you complain about it from time to time. Love prevails, and you settle in for a while, but may become restless in the relationship.

Painting and art may be part of your career. You could also be involved in architecture, teaching, metaphysical counseling, or working for a large corporation or government. You will have visions, dreams, and keen intuition about people and things and may be drawn to mysticism and psychic research. Unusual experiences will pepper your life. You may try to express your "soul nature" in art, literature and music, but you will do well in the collecting of fine art, antiques, and so on. Some call you a bit of an eccentric.

Because your style is considered different, you sometimes create turmoil at work. You may sometimes feel others are laughing at you. In time, when you're on top, you'll laugh all the way to the bank.

✶ ✶ ✶

MARCH 5

PISCES • The fish that swim in the pure sea

February 19 at 5:00 P.M. to March 20 at 5:00 P.M. • NUMEROLOGY 5

Possessions and Desires . . .

Gem: Sardius—This stone could give the wearer unusual insights into his or her own heart.

Flower: Holly—You usually are wise when you plan ahead.

Astral Color, Color Need, Apparel Color: Your Astral Color is White, which gives you clarity. Violet in your environment keeps you empathetic toward others. In your wardrobe, Cinnamon gives you encouragement and stamina.

Fragrance: Sandalwood or other rare spices are the scents you need to have on hand. You crave attention and your perfume or cologne should be your most powerful ally. It will enhance your irresistible charm.

Tree: Apple—You are creative, full of joy, and nearly magical. You bring happiness.

Instruments: Viola, trumpet

Composer: Liszt

Bird: Flamingo—This beautiful, gregarious bird is always careful of its enemy. It is also a caretaker of the young who tries to keep everyone happy.

Symbol: Triangle—You have the right combination of abilities.

Harmonious Health and Nutrition . . .

Health Scents: Peach—this scent may balance your good qualities so that they equal your charm.

Favorable Foods: Leeks, raisins, barley, honey, cottage cheese

What's Lucky . . .

Lucky Numbers: 5, 15, 25

Best Months: May and June

Best Day of the Week: Saturday

Best Month Days: 5, 14, 23

Lucky Charms: A rabbit's foot or a white candle.

Harmonious Signs for Relationships and Partnerships: Cancer, Scorpio, Virgo

Spiritual Guides . . .

Star: Al Phergal Muachher—Those with this star often cling too long to fond memories.

Angel: Barchiel—This angel shows us right from wrong, encourages us in good decision making, and teaches us to protect ourselves and others.

Guardian Angel: Plavwell—Gives power and strength to one's presence.

Spiritual Stone: Chrysolite—This stone might help you keep things together when you feel frayed.

✳ JUDITH'S INSIGHT ✳

You have uncommon intellectual gifts, great adaptability, and can understand just about anything. Your ready wit enables you to turn difficult things around and make them easy. You can be very ingenious and inventive.

You really hate being tied down, so having a mate who allows you freedom would work. You don't like living in the same environment for long periods of time and may have to move often. Perhaps you will just change the furniture and join the "couch of the month club." Maybe you just have a need for a lot of people in your life. You create friendships easily, and this makes life eventful. You are not the kind who ends old friendships, and your network reaches far and wide.

You will have many great ideas that could lead you to a career as an inventor, designer, or journalist, or a job in the movies. You could work with computers, or as a manager, builder, or building manager. Give in to your desire for unusual career options. Be sure to take care of money matters in order to ensure financial stability later on.

You are inclined to self-indulgence of all kinds. Have a little more perseverance, and you will do well. Your life isn't one that starts easily and at times feels as if it is only getting harder. But soon you'll see your happiness grow to your satisfaction.

★ ★ ★

MARCH 6

PISCES • The fish that swim in the pure sea

February 19 at 5:00 P.M. to March 20 at 5:00 P.M. • NUMEROLOGY 6

Possessions and Desires . . .

Gem: Topaz—This is an excellent gift to be exchanged between very loyal friends.

Flower: Dogbane—You may want to guard against your tendency to let your little white lies veer into shady hues of gray.

Astral Color, Color Need, Apparel Color: Your Astral Color is Emerald, which gives you confidence. Violet in your environment keeps you empathetic toward others. In your wardrobe, Maroon gives you confidence.

Fragrance: Sandalwood or other rare spices are the scents you need to have on hand. You crave attention and your perfume or cologne should be your most powerful ally. It will enhance your irresistible charm.

Tree: Palm—You tend to be very healthy and creative.

Instruments: Tambourine, lyre

Composer: Schubert

Bird: Falcon—an expert hunter. When well-trained, it can adapt to many tasks and is usually obedient.

Symbol: Crescent—You are more likely to be influenced by the phases of the moon. Your easygoing manner leads you to peaceful situations.

Harmonious Health and Nutrition . . .

Health Scent: Orange Blossom—This scent may balance your body, mind, and soul.

Favorable Foods: Raw beets, apples, rice, brown sugar, egg yolks

What's Lucky

Lucky Numbers: 6, 16, 26
Best Months: May and June
Best Day of the Week: Saturday
Best Month Days: 6, 15, 24
Lucky Charms: A religious token or card from any religion.

Harmonious Signs for Relationships and Partnerships: Cancer, Scorpio, Virgo

Spiritual Guides . . .

Star: Al Risha—Those who have this band of stars as theirs will be happiest as part of a family.

Angel: Barchiel—This angel shows us right from wrong, encourages us in good decision making, and teaches us to protect ourselves and others.

Guardian Angel: Michael—"Who is like God."

Spiritual Stone: Chrysolite—This stone might help you keep things together when you feel frayed.

✱ JUDITH'S INSIGHT ✱

You have executive ability and a keen, active mind. You often show good, solid judgment. You demand reasons for every thought and action. Your personality is quite consistent to some, while those close to you may see you as more changeable. You're friendly to all, but you are easily hurt. Others see you as strong, but you are quite the sensitive one.

You are a devoted mate and parent. As a child you feel you take on more than your share of family responsibility. With a longtime mate you will have trials and tribulations all along the way. You do the most to maintain the relationship. Try learning to take advice, even though you're better at giving it. You love beautiful things, and the older you get, the more beautiful your surroundings. You love entertaining in your home.

Music, art, poetry, literature, and sculpture all fascinate you, but your career choice may be more structured. To start with, you could work at any level of government. You will be drawn to authority and religion. Careers in art, film, construction, music, or public service are all possibilities. It may take time for you to learn to balance your structured side with your more artistic side. All in all, you eventually find the right path and succeed at work. Your devote yourself to all you do.

Allow yourself a little more fun. When you're unhappy, you shut down your mind and mouth! Give yourself a break and allow yourself more emotional freedom.

★ ★ ★

MARCH 7

PISCES • The fish that swim in the pure sea

February 19 at 5:00 P.M. to March 20 at 5:00 P.M. • NUMEROLOGY 7

Possessions and Desires . . .

Gem: Ruby—This stone may lead you to energy, friendship, and happiness.

Flower: Hyacinth—You usually see the beauty that other people miss.

Astral Color, Color Need, Apparel Color: Your Astral Color is Pink, which reflects your compassion. Violet in your environment keeps you empathetic toward others. In your wardrobe, Blue-green enhances your luck and makes you feel secure.

Fragrance: Sandalwood or other rare spices are the scents you need to have on hand. You crave attention and your perfume or cologne should be your most powerful ally. It will enhance your irresistible charm.

Tree: Sycamore—Yours is the ability to love, communicate honestly with others, and have lasting relationships.

Instrument: Harp

Composers: Gluck, Brahms

Bird: Warbling Parakeet—the most beautiful of all birds, known as the love bird. It does seem to have the powers of imitation.

Symbol: Heart—You are enthusiastic, empathetic, and full of generosity and love.

Harmonious Health and Nutrition . . .

Health Scent: Jasmine—This scent may make you more easygoing when you are stressed.

Favorable Foods: Cucumber, raspberry, bran, honey, cottage cheese

What's Lucky . . .

Lucky Numbers: 7, 17, 34

Best Months: May and June

Best Day of the Week: Saturday

Best Month Days: 7, 16, 25

Harmonious Signs for Relationships and Partnerships: Cancer, Scorpio, Virgo

Lucky Charm: An old key.

Spiritual Guides . . .

Star: Al Risha—Those who have this band of stars as theirs will be happiest as part of a family.

Angel: Barchiel—This angel shows us right from wrong, encourages us in good decision making, and teaches us to protect ourselves and others.

Guardian Angel: Raphael—This angel attends to all of your needs when you are looking for guidance.

Spiritual Stone: Chrysolite—This stone might help you keep things together when you feel frayed.

✶ JUDITH'S INSIGHT ✶

Beauty in any form moves you. You have a taste for the good things in life. High ideals and great ambitions make you inclined to live an independent and unconventional life. You're broad minded and curious, so the mystical or psychic world intrigues you. Vivid dreams and unusual images lead you in your work.

In romantic relationships, you may start out as the weaker partner, only to prove to be stronger later on. Eventually, you take the bull by the horns and either make or break any relationship you are in. Others may see you as quiet, though this is not the case. If handled correctly, you can be the most devoted child ever to your parents. Be careful of overwhelming family dynamics. Family is important, especially your children, if you have them. They become a driving force in your life.

These may be the most natural career choices for you: beautician, fashion consultant, artist, creator, or designer. Stick to what you know instinctively, beauty and the arts. You can find a job either behind the scenes or in front of a camera. You'd also be a perfect model or spokesperson for beauty products.

You are much less complex than people seem to think. Money is important to you and you acquire great things, especially fine jewelry. So now you that know what road to take—drive!

✶ ✶ ✶

MARCH 8

PISCES • The fish that swim in the pure sea

February 19 at 5:00 P.M. to March 20 at 5:00 P.M. • NUMEROLOGY 8

Possessions and Desires . . .

Gem: Chrysolite—This gem may help you clear your mind of sadness and worry.

Flower: Olive—You tend to hope more for peace than happiness.

Astral Color, Color Need, Apparel Color: Your Astral Color is White, which gives you clarity. Violet in your environment keeps you empathetic toward others. In your wardrobe, Cinnamon gives you encouragement and stamina.

Fragrance: Sandalwood or other rare spices are the scents you need to have on hand. You crave attention and your perfume or cologne should be your most powerful ally. It will enhance your irresistible charm.

Tree: Pine—Your relationships tend to be harmonious, both emotionally and mentally.

Instrument: Cello

Composer: Mozart

Bird: Bobolink—This charming singer is equally good as a soloist or a member of an orchestra. It is a very romantic bird, useful as an insect destroyer, and elegant, with beautiful feathers, and always pleasant to have around.

Symbol: Wings—You are the source of balance in your world—this will bring you contentment.

Harmonious Health and Nutrition . . .

Health Scent: Almond—This scent may revitalize you and open you to greater possibilities.

Favorable Foods: Red cabbage, cherries, rice, brown sugar, egg yolks

What's Lucky . . .

Lucky Numbers: 8, 18, 28
Best Months: May and June
Best Day of the Week: Saturday
Best Month Days: 8, 17, 26
Lucky Charm: Red ribbon in your wallet or doorway.
Harmonious Signs for Relationships and Partnerships: Cancer, Scorpio, Virgo

Spiritual Guides . . .

Star: Al Phergal Muachher—Those with this star often cling too long to fond memories.

Angel: Barchiel—This angel shows us right from wrong, encourages us in good decision making, and teaches us to protect ourselves and others.

Guardian Angel: Seraphim—Angel that brings love light and passion.

Spiritual Stone: Chrysolite—This stone might help you keep things together when you feel frayed.

✴ JUDITH'S INSIGHT ✴

You have an active mind and a lot of determination, and that's what keeps you going. A kind nature and sensitive soul are great characteristics, but, sadly, these qualities don't always get you through the hard times. It is your tenacity and principles that ease you through.

Heavy family responsibilities dominate your life, and you take them very seriously. At times, you feel overwhelmed. Conflict about decisions causes you to question your choice of partners. Most of us go through that in our lifetime—you just may have a tougher time with it. You want freedom from time to time because you may not get out often enough. Others will not restrict you—you restrict yourself and then blame others.

Career choices for you could vary a lot. You're a natural caretaker, so health care or education are perfect. You're open to others' needs, so you'd make a great social worker or member of the clergy. Your visual sense could lead you to photography. Your desire for beauty may bring you to the cosmetics industry. You could be a plumber, nurse, or doctor. Talk about diversity! Your mind is your power, it doesn't matter what career. You will be successful, but your life will be like a roller coaster ride.

Responsibility is the key to your life, and you willingly take it on. Sure, it becomes burdensome and feels too heavy. But you are a winner and a survivor. Look forward to your future. It'll all be worth it!

✴ ✴ ✴

MARCH 9

PISCES • The fish that swim in the pure sea

February 19 at 5:00 P.M. to March 20 at 5:00 P.M. • NUMEROLOGY 9

Possessions and Desires . . .

Gem: Moonstone—This gem could protect you from danger.

Flower: Anemone—Be sure to not set your expectations too high.

Astral Color, Color Need, Apparel Color: Your Astral Color is Emerald, which gives you confidence. Violet in your environment keeps you empathetic toward others. In your wardrobe, Green is your power color for overcoming obstacles.

Fragrance: Sandalwood or other rare spices are the scents you need to have on hand. You crave attention and your perfume or cologne should be your most powerful ally. It will enhance your irresistible charm.

Tree: Holly—Beware that you are not carried away by your passionate nature. The only way to grow is to be open to new experiences.

Instruments: Violin, Tympanum

Composer: Gluck

Bird: Mockingbird—The most proficient minstrel in the world's orchestra; graceful and enthusiastic.

Symbol: Anchor—This tranquil symbol signifies stability and strength, and stands for strong commitments in relationships.

Harmonious Health and Nutrition . . .

Health Scent: Lavender—This scent might lead others to trust you and make you patient.

Favorable Foods: Sorrel, prunes, whole grains, honey, cottage cheese

What's Lucky . . .

Lucky Numbers: 9, 19, 29
Best Months: May and June
Best Day of the Week: Saturday
Best Month Days: 9, 18, 27
Lucky Charms: A U.S. coin or a bill of any amount from the year you were born.

Harmonious Signs for Relationships and Partnerships: Cancer, Scorpio, Virgo

Spiritual Guides . . .

Star: Al Phergal Muachher—Those with this star often cling too long to fond memories.

Angel: Barchiel—This angel shows us right from wrong, encourages us in good decision making, and teaches us to protect ourselves and others.

Guardian Angel: Gabriel—"God is my strength."

Spiritual Stone: Chrysolite—This stone might help you keep things together when you feel frayed.

✳ JUDITH'S INSIGHT ✳

You have zest and ambition—what desirable qualities! When you sit with things long enough, you can accomplish anything. Your great mental abilities, combined with an unstoppable energy, will earn you recognition. Curb your tendency to be impulsive. Neighbors may not always be aware of your temper.

Family can be your strongest asset or your greatest downfall. Sometime throughout your life you will feel both extremes, but with different family members. Yes, conflicts may even arise with the same person. You need time away from the family to maintain a healthy balance. At the same time, you need constant reassurance from them. You tend to waffle a bit, and although you're emotionally intelligent, it may be difficult to maintain this balance with regard to intimacy.

Look to your career to bring you into the public eye in one way or another. You do a better job of it when you're in control, because that's when you're at your happiest. Learn to use your terrific intuition—don't be such a skeptic. You could be good at several careers, including movie star, movie writer, police officer, or head of an undercover operation.

You always have the best of intentions, though you may seem selfish. Believe it or not, that is your protection. You dream the dream and then make it happen!

✳ ✳ ✳

MARCH 10

PISCES • The fish that swim in the pure sea

February 19 at 5:00 P.M. to March 20 at 5:00 P.M. • NUMEROLOGY 1

Possessions and Desires . . .

Gem: Turquoise—This stone may help you find material wealth.

Flower: Marsh Mallow—The course of your life will tend to often surprise you.

Astral Color, Color Need, Apparel Color: Your Astral Color is Pink, which emanates compassion. Violet in your environment keeps you empathetic toward others. In your wardrobe, Maroon gives you confidence.

Fragrance: Sandalwood or other rare spices are the scents you need to have on hand. You crave attention and your perfume or cologne should be your most powerful ally. It will enhance your irresistible charm.

Tree: Walnut—You are unusually helpful and always looking for new beginnings.

Instruments: Oboe, flute, clarinet, piano, French horn, organ, piccolo

Composer: Böhm

Bird: Flamingo—This beautiful, gregarious bird is always careful of its enemy. It is also a caretaker of the young who tries to keep everyone happy.

Symbol: Crown—the universal sign of dignity.

Harmonious Health and Nutrition . . .

Health Scent: Jasmine—This scent may make you more easygoing when you are stressed.

Favorable Foods: Spinach, plums, rice, brown sugar, egg yolks

What's Lucky . . .

Lucky Numbers: 10, 20, 28

Best Months: May and June

Best Day of the Week: Saturday

Best Month Days: 1, 10, 19, 28

Lucky Charm: A new penny in your shoe.

Harmonious Signs for Relationships and Partnerships: Cancer, Scorpio, Virgo

Spiritual Guides . . .

Star: Al Risha—Those who have this band of stars as theirs will be happiest as part of a family.

Angel: Barchiel—This angel shows us right from wrong, encourages us in good decision making, and teaches us to protect ourselves and others.

Guardian Angel: Malachi—"Messenger of Jehovah."

Spiritual Stone: Chrysolite—This stone might help you keep things together when you feel frayed.

✶ JUDITH'S INSIGHT ✶

You have strong convictions, a strong mind, and a strong will. You know exactly what you want. Early on in life and the hard way, you learn to be tactful. You like nice things and intend to have them. Don't worry if you don't come into this world with money—you find a way to make it. You have a style all your own and are capable of doing just about anything.

You're a sympathetic ear to some, but you won't give the time of day to others. If you like someone, you move mountains. Dedication to those you love brings you happiness along the way. People try to rattle your cage: your strength threatens them, and they want to know it's genuine. Your love life may be a rocky road, but with your sensuality and charm, romance will come knocking at your door (and more than once). Check your flippant comments and learn patience with others.

Motivated as you are, don't be surprised if you balance two careers at once. Fashion designer, beauty consultant, doctor, lawyer, writer, or movie star—you'll find your niche. As you're inclined to be impetuous and headstrong, you will be enterprising and original in all that you do.

You will encounter long journeys in your life and may be drawn to international things. Overly optimistic at times, you usually bounce back quite well after a temper tantrum. Slowly, you develop the sense of power and self-confidence that are missing in your early years. Then the world will be yours.

✶ ✶ ✶

MARCH 11

PISCES • The fish that swim in the pure sea

February 19 at 5:00 P.M. to March 20 at 5:00 P.M. • NUMEROLOGY 2

Possessions and Desires . . .

Gem: Sapphire—This gem may help you find forgiveness from those you've wronged.

Flower: Blue Violet—You are loyal and faithful in relationships.

Astral Color, Color Need, Apparel Color: Your Astral Color is Pink, which reflects your compassion. Violet in your environment keeps you empathetic toward others. In your wardrobe, Maroon gives you confidence.

Fragrance: Sandalwood or other rare spices are the scents you need to have on hand. You crave attention and your perfume or cologne should be your most powerful ally. It will enhance your irresistible charm.

Tree: Maple—You have both great stability and flashes of intuition.

Instruments: Pipe organ, cymbal, drum

Composers: Handel, Johann Sebastian Bach

Bird: Cuckoo—a good flyer and very seldom a quitter. Some cuckoos do tend to think they favor lonely isolation, but what they really yearn for is a family relationship.

Symbol: Cross—the symbol of self-sacrifice and reconciliation.

Harmonious Health and Nutrition . . .

Health Scent: Apple—You are creative, full of joy, and nearly magical. You bring happiness.

Favorable Foods: Spinach, apple, barley, honey, cottage cheese

What's Lucky . . .

Lucky Numbers: 2, 11, 22
Best Months: May and June
Best Day of the Week: Saturday
Best Month Days: 2, 11, 20, 29
Lucky Charms: Two 50-cent pieces. Give someone else one of them.
Harmonious Signs for Relationships and Partnerships: Cancer, Scorpio, Virgo

Spiritual Guides . . .

Star: Al Risha—Those who have this band of stars as theirs will be happiest as part of a family.

Angel: Barchiel—This angel shows us right from wrong, encourages us in good decision making, and teaches us to protect ourselves and others.

Guardian Angel: Uriel—This angel brings the light of God's guidance.

Spiritual Stone: Chrysolite—This stone might help you keep things together when you feel frayed.

✷ JUDITH'S INSIGHT ✷

Your ambition and enthusiasm inspire those around you. A great drive for accomplishment colors every thing you do. You have extremely good taste in the fine arts and in beauty. You keep your poetic side under wraps. Your dreamlike nature will bring you luck.

Most of the time your family doesn't quite understand you, but that could work in your favor. Early in your life you are needy, and as a youth you may have fantasized about being adopted (or maybe you were). Once you're in touch with your own style, you'll feel less the outsider. Relationships with friends and family undergo a metamorphosis, taking on a whole different dynamic.

When your relationships don't work, your imagination does. You will fill your life with fantasy and romance, and later you will live them out. Communication with your mate may be a problem. You will find people popping back into your life out of nowhere, and you welcome them with open arms.

Musician, scientist, doctor, woodworker, fashion consultant, machinist, computer whiz: you are capable of doing it all. You could also be a police officer or commissioner, screenwriter or movie star. Your career may be difficult at times, but don't worry. You get through it and take it as an opportunity to grow. Staring into space or the closest pond, you can think about nothing for hours. With your visual imagination, reading a book for you is like watching a movie.

✷ ✷ ✷

MARCH 12

PISCES • The fish that swim in the pure sea

February 19 at 5:00 P.M. to March 20 at 5:00 P.M. • NUMEROLOGY 3

Possessions and Desires . . .

Gem: Ruby—This stone may lead you to energy, friendship, and happiness.

Flower: Maple—You are very reserved emotionally.

Astral Color, Color Need, Apparel Color: Your Astral Color is White, which gives you clarity. Violet in your environment keeps you empathetic toward others. In your wardrobe, Blue-green enhances your luck and makes you feel secure.

Fragrance: Sandalwood or other rare spices are the scents you need to have on hand. You crave attention and your perfume or cologne should be your most powerful ally. It will enhance your irresistible charm.

Tree: Elm—You have willpower, strength, and the ability to stand alone.

Instrument: Trombone

Composers: Verdi, Mendelssohn, Schumann

Bird: Swan—Regarded as royal and sacred, this bird has the protective nature of a mother, and can become a furious fighter in the defense of its young.

Symbol: Wreath—You have been crowned with a special personality. You are strong but extremely compassionate.

Harmonious Health and Nutrition . . .

Health Scent: Rose—This scent will lead you to passionate thoughts and make you feel warm inside.

Favorable Foods: Artichokes, prunes, whole grains, brown sugar, egg yolks

What's Lucky . . .

Lucky Numbers: 3, 6, 12, 21
Best Months: May and June.
Best Day of the Week: Saturday
Best Month Days: 3, 12, 21, 30
Lucky Charm: A pen that someone else has already used.

Harmonious Signs for Relationships and Partnerships: Cancer, Scorpio, Virgo

Spiritual Guides . . .

Star: Al Phergal Muachher—Those with this star often cling too long to fond memories.

Angel: Barchiel—This angel shows us right from wrong, encourages us in good decision making, and teaches us to protect ourselves and others.

Guardian Angel: Johiel—This angel is a protector of all those with a humble heart.

Spiritual Stone: Chrysolite—This stone might help you keep things together when you feel frayed.

✳ JUDITH'S INSIGHT ✳

A natural caretaker, always ready to help, you always lend a hand, even when you don't have an extra. Good-natured, pure, practical, and idealistic—what a combination! Your friends are devoted to you. You love to travel, and you make a delightful travel companion. You try to understand others, but when disappointments occur, you don't bounce back so easily.

A long-term mate (or two) should be in your future. The second relationship is better. Family and friends adore you because you work at being a good person and keep their feelings in mind. You have a natural instinct for what is right. You are fond of your home but exceedingly sensitive to the emotional environment, especially when there's discord. Old treasures and toys fascinate you, and as you mature, you grow even more sentimental.

It may take you a little time to find your career because many things interest you. You could be a fisherman, hunter, nurse, doctor, or therapist. Try writing, if not early in life, perhaps later on—even if you write for a town newsletter or keep a journal. Look to your younger years to tap into those old dreams and goals. You may find you have hidden talent that you haven't been in touch with in years. Your need to communicate may draw you to a career involving the theater.

A born ham, you love to have a good time. You may like to play too much at times—some may see that as lazy. You have the makings of a good soul, and you have good karma.

✳ ✳ ✳

MARCH 13

PISCES • The fish that swim in the pure sea

February 19 at 5:00 P.M. to March 20 at 5:00 P.M. • NUMEROLOGY 4

Possessions and Desires . . .

Gem: Emerald—Those who carry this stone tend to be lucky in love.

Flower: Ivy—You are more faithful to your ideals than to other people.

Astral Color, Color Need, Apparel Color: Your Astral Color is Emerald, which gives you confidence. Violet in your environment keeps you empathetic toward others. In your wardrobe, Cinnamon gives you encouragement and stamina.

Fragrance: Sandalwood or other rare spices are the scents you need to have on hand. You crave attention and your perfume or cologne should be your most powerful ally. It will enhance your irresistible charm.

Tree: Cherry—You will find yourself faced with constant new emotional awakenings.

Instruments: Bass, clarinet

Composers: Haydn, Wagner

Bird: Robin—the most sociable of all birds, with the ability to create quick friendships. It also can easily adapt to any home. When it wants something, it has the tendency to try to snatch it.

Symbol: Star—You are full of inner brightness and will stand out in any crowd. You will be seen as special.

Harmonious Health and Nutrition . . .

Health Scent: Vanilla—This scent will fill you with a feeling of cleanliness and stability.

Favorable Foods: Leeks, cherries, bran, honey, cottage cheese

What's Lucky . . .

Lucky Numbers: 4, 13, 26

Best Months: May and June

Best Day of the Week: Saturday

Best Month Days: 4, 13, 22, 31

Lucky Charm: A piece of material cut from something in your home.

Harmonious Signs for Relationships and Partnerships: Cancer, Scorpio, Virgo

Spiritual Guides . . .

Star: Al Phergal Muachher—Those with this star often cling too long to fond memories.

Angel: Barchiel—This angel shows us right from wrong, encourages us in good decision making, and teaches us to protect ourselves and others.

Guardian Angel: Uriel—This angel brings the light of God's guidance.

Spiritual Stone: Chrysolite—This stone might help you keep things together when you feel frayed.

✶ JUDITH'S INSIGHT ✶

You love to play sports and have a good time expending that energy. Unconventional or eccentric qualities emerge after a considerable amount of sorrow. At these low times, your strong will and desire to enjoy life will pull you out of the depths. Later in life, you are drawn to the mystical or psychic.

A nice home is vital to you. When it comes to family, things may not be so easy, but your drive and determination will smooth things over. You're an eternal optimist. Love brings the greatest joy and some heartache, too. You can lean toward the selfish side until you have a family or meet the right mate. You find that special mate in the second part of your life.

You are a good egg, so a career in health care or nonprofits could work well. You may be drawn to volunteerism. Until your forties, you may dabble in many careers. After that, you'll find your love. If you are in a secure career until forty, you may wake up one morning and want something new. You would also do well as a designer, author, or editor. Research may be a profitable option.

You like things crisp and new. You must have variety, especially when it comes to fashion. Your home and furniture may change over the years, or you may decide to trade last year's car for this year's model. Maybe you just want to paint the house a different color? No, you are not fickle, but you like environmental changes. Maybe it's because you don't like emotional ones.

✶ ✶ ✶

MARCH 14

PISCES • The fish that swim in the pure sea

February 19 at 5:00 P.M. to March 20 at 5:00 P.M. • NUMEROLOGY 5

Possessions and Desires . . .

Gem: Sardius—this stone could give the wearer unusual insights into his or her own heart.

Flower: White Violet—You tend to be drawn to creative expression.

Astral Color, Color Need, Apparel Color: Your Astral Color is Pink, which reflects your compassion. Violet in your environment keeps you empathetic toward others. In your wardrobe, Green is your power color for overcoming obstacles.

Fragrance: Sandalwood or other rare spices are the scents you need to have on hand. You crave attention and your perfume or cologne should be your most powerful ally. It will enhance your irresistible charm.

Instruments: Viola, trumpet

Composer: Liszt

Tree: Apple—You are creative, full of joy, and nearly magical. You bring happiness.

Bird: Flamingo—This beautiful, gregarious bird is always careful of its enemy. It is also a caretaker of the young who tries to keep everyone happy.

Symbol: Triangle—You have the right combination of abilities.

Harmonious Health and Nutrition . . .

Health Scent: Peach—this scent may balance your good qualities so that they equal your charm.

Favorable Foods: Red cabbage, apple, barley, brown sugar, egg yolks

What's Lucky . . .

Lucky Numbers: 15, 5, 23

Best Months: May and June

Best Day of the Week: Saturday

Best Month Days: 5, 14, 23

Lucky Charms: A rabbit's foot or a white candle.

Harmonious Signs for Relationships and Partnerships: Cancer, Scorpio, Virgo

Spiritual Guides . . .

Star: Al Risha—Those who have this band of stars as theirs will be happiest as part of a family.

Angel: Barchiel—This angel shows us right from wrong, encourages us in good decision making, and teaches us to protect ourselves and others.

Guardian Angel: Phanuel—protection against the negative.

Spiritual Stone: Chrysolite—This stone might help you keep things together when you feel frayed.

✷ JUDITH'S INSIGHT ✷

You're on everyone's party list. Your presence is truly joyful, and you pick good presents, too. You are generally creative and may have many hidden talents that come about later in life. You were born with uncommon intellectual gifts and a great adaptability to any type of interesting, ingenious, inventive work.

In love, there may be some disappointments, but some day, you will definitely be lucky in love. You allow no interference in your relationships. As long as your mate understands your sense of freedom, you two will do just fine. With the right partner, children may be your greatest accomplishment. Be careful not to compete with the kids—you so love being a child yourself. As long as you are getting the attention you need, you will be in a good place.

You are a great employee and would be a better employer. You do like the occasional pat on the back. As you mature, intuition will manifest itself. See what career you start off having and which one you wind up in.

You are here to have fun and to be entertained. With that need met, you're a happy camper. If you do become depressed, it's usually because the fun has been absent from your life. You need constant mental stimulation. While your serious youth may not have been a joyful one, as an adult you want to have fun!

★ ★ ★

MARCH 15

PISCES • The fish that swim in the pure sea

February 19 at 5:00 P.M. to March 20 at 5:00 P.M. • NUMEROLOGY 6

Possessions and Desires . . .

Gem: Topaz—This is an excellent gift to be exchanged between very loyal friends.

Flower: Walnut—You tend to have a very clear mind and bright intellect.

Astral Color, Color Need, Apparel Color: Your Astral Color is White, which gives you clarity. Violet in your environment keeps you empathetic toward others. In your wardrobe, Maroon gives you confidence.

Fragrance: Sandalwood or other rare spices are the scents you need to have on hand. You crave attention and your perfume or cologne should be your most powerful ally. It will enhance your irresistible charm.

Tree: Palm—You tend to be very healthy and creative.

Instruments: Tambourine, lyre

Composer: Schubert

Bird: Lark—known for the beauty of its song, which is sometimes very unusual. It is also credited with extraordinary intelligence.

Symbol: Crescent—You are more likely to be influenced by the phases of the moon. Your easygoing manner leads you to peaceful situations.

Harmonious Health and Nutrition . . .

Health Scent: Orange Blossom—This scent may balance your body, mind, and soul.

Favorable Foods: Unhulled barley, figs, bran, honey, cottage cheese

What's Lucky . . .

Lucky Numbers: 6, 16, 24
Best Months: May and June
Best Day of the Week: Saturday
Best Month Days: 6, 15, 24
Lucky Charms: A religious token or card from any religion.

Harmonious Signs for Relationships and Partnerships: Cancer, Scorpio, Virgo

Spiritual Guides . . .

Star: Al Risha—Those who have this band of stars as theirs will be happiest as part of a family.

Angel: Barchiel—This angel shows us right from wrong, encourages us in good decision making, and teaches us to protect ourselves and others.

Guardian Angel: Michael—"Who is like God."

Spiritual Stone: Chrysolite—This stone might help you keep things together when you feel frayed.

✷ JUDITH'S INSIGHT ✷

You were born under a "lucky star" and good things will come your way. If you don't succeed careerwise, it will be your own fault. The potential to lead a fascinating life is there. Opportunities will present themselves all the time. You make many friends who will be devoted to you. You're attracted to beauty and order, and have great organizational skills.

You were born to be loved. Most are lucky if they get that once in a lifetime love; you get it twice. Your children, if you have them, will bring you great joy. Your home environment will be warm and nurturing. You check your selfish ways at the door once you find a home. At times you can be difficult to get along with, but your family and friends put up with you.

Although you will have to work hard for a living, you rise to a secure position. You could wind up in your own business as a designer, or decorator, and be very successful. You have a tendency to work too hard, but you may have to in order to achieve your goals. Science may interest you or writing as a career should intrigue you as well.

You love being on the water or maybe living there. A strong constitution will help ward off fits of overindulgence. You can be very extravagant. Save some money for retirement. Your energy wanes later in life. You are not the one who finds success: it will find you! Learn to manage it well.

✷ ✷ ✷

MARCH 16

PISCES • The fish that swim in the pure sea

February 19 at 5:00 P.M. to March 20 at 5:00 P.M. • NUMEROLOGY 7

Possessions and Desires . . .

Gem: Agate—This stone may promote health and lead you to a long life.

Flower: Valerian—You may be very easy to get along with.

Astral Color, Color Need, Apparel Color: Your Astral Color is Emerald, which gives you confidence. Violet in your environment keeps you empathetic toward others. In your wardrobe, Blue-Green enhances your luck and makes you feel secure.

Fragrance: Sandalwood or other rare spices are the scents you need to have on hand. You crave attention and your perfume or cologne should be your most powerful ally. It will enhance your irresistible charm.

Tree: Sycamore—Yours is the ability to love, communicate honestly with others, and have lasting relationships.

Instrument: Harp

Composers: Gluck, Brahms

Bird: Skylark—This handsome bird is beautiful when it sings. It always whistles as it works.

Symbol: Heart—You are enthusiastic, empathetic, and full of generosity and love.

Harmonious Health and Nutrition . . .

Health Scent: Jasmine—This scent may make you more easygoing when you are stressed.

Favorable Foods: Artichokes, cherries, rice, brown sugar, egg yolks

What's Lucky . . .

Lucky Numbers: 7, 27, 17
Best Months: May and June
Best Day of the Week: Saturday
Best Month Days: 7, 16, 25
Lucky Charm: An old key.
Harmonious Signs for Relationships and Partnerships: Cancer, Scorpio, Virgo

Spiritual Guides . . .

Star: Al Phergal Muachher—Those with this star often cling too long to fond memories.

Angel: Barchiel—This angel shows us right from wrong, encourages us in good decision making, and teaches us to protect ourselves and others.

Guardian Angel: Raphael—This angel attends to all of your needs when you are looking for guidance.

Spiritual Stone: Chrysolite—This stone might help you keep things together when you feel frayed.

✶ JUDITH'S INSIGHT ✶

You have a head for business and the determination to succeed. To some, you seem materialistic. You can be a bit impractical. Working with others is easy, provided they give you space. You are as kind and considerate as you are treated, and you adapt to almost any atmosphere. Your persistence enables you to succeed.

You're a bundle of contradictions, and can be strong and weak all at once. Watch for this in relationships. Somehow you know better, but you still encounter traps when it comes to falling in love. It should stop once you decide to get your act together. Family matters may trip you up—here, allow yourself more freedom. You're a good humanitarian most of the time, but you may tire of this. But your giving nature always returns.

You are creative, but will probably end up in a company or office. Structured environments calm you, as long as they allow you freedom. The more restrictive and controlling the environment, the more you rebel and want out. Marketing or advertising may be a good fit, and you're drawn to the beauty industry. You may surprise yourself by how "corporate" you become, either with your own company or someone else's.

Although you achieve your career goals, your vision and desire could change very easily. You make your mark on this world through altruism, even if it is by supporting your local school district or a family on your block. You can be misunderstood, but sooner or later, the smoke clears.

✶ ✶ ✶

MARCH 17

PISCES • The fish that swim in the pure sea

February 19 at 5:00 P.M. to March 20 at 5:00 P.M. • NUMEROLOGY 8

Possessions and Desires . . .

Gem: Chrysolite—This gem may help you clear your mind of sadness and worry.

Flower: Sorrel—You are very affectionate to others.

Astral Color, Color Need, Apparel Color: Your Astral Color is Pink, which reflects your compassion. Violet in your environment keeps you empathetic toward others. In your wardrobe, Cinnamon gives you encouragement and stamina.

Fragrance: Sandalwood or other rare spices are the scents you need to have on hand. You crave attention and your perfume or cologne should be your most powerful ally. It will enhance your irresistible charm.

Tree: Pine—Your relationships tend to be harmonious, both emotionally and mentally.

Instrument: Cello

Composer: Mozart

Bird: Bobolink—This charming singer is equally good as a soloist or a member of an orchestra. It is a very romantic bird, useful as an insect destroyer, and elegant, with beautiful feathers, and always pleasant to have around.

Symbol: Wings—You are the source of balance in your world—this will bring you contentment.

Harmonious Health and Nutrition . . .

Health Scent: Almond—This scent may revitalize you and open you to greater possibilities.

Favorable Foods: Beets, grapes, barley, honey, cottage cheese

What's Lucky . . .

Lucky Numbers: 8, 26, 28

Best Months: May and June

Best Day of the Week: Saturday

Best Month Days: 8, 17, 26

Lucky Charm: Red ribbon in your wallet or doorway.

Harmonious Signs for Relationships and Partnerships: Cancer, Scorpio, Virgo

Spiritual Guides . . .

Star: Al Phergal Muachher—Those with this star often cling too long to fond memories.

Angel: Barchiel—This angel shows us right from wrong, encourages us in good decision making, and teaches us to protect ourselves and others.

Guardian Angel: Seraphim—An angel that brings love, light and passion.

Spiritual Stone: Chrysolite—This stone might help you keep things together when you feel frayed.

✴ JUDITH'S INSIGHT ✴

Showing off your serious side first makes you more comfortable, especially early in life. Although you were very intelligent, you had low self-esteem as a child. You feel misunderstood most of the time, even though you mean well. You try not to show your sadness and need to learn to express your emotions better. Your confidence grows as you mature. You love it when others recognize your humor.

It seems as though your love life takes forever to take off. When it finally does, you scare easily. You relationships take forever to unfold. You could date someone for years before a commitment is mentioned. The longer you put off marriage, the better. But no matter how long you wait, you'll still have second thoughts. You love family; you use them and drive them crazy. If you weren't born with a silver spoon in your mouth, someone will put one there.

Look for a career in communications. You may end up on stage. If you do, stick with comedy: you are a great storyteller. Work is important because you love spending money. You're very inventive. If all else fails, tap into your intuition. Stop laughing and start listening.

Yours is a life far from charmed, though it may look that way to others. You can be quite selective about what you choose to reveal about yourself and what you don't. Ups and downs trouble you during your thirties and forties. Once your confidence grows and reality sets in, you may have that chance to live on Easy Street.

★ ★ ★

MARCH 18

PISCES • The fish that swim in the pure sea

February 19 at 5:00 P.M. to March 20 at 5:00 P.M. • NUMEROLOGY 9

Possessions and Desires . . .

Gem: Moonstone—This gem could protect you from danger.

Flower: Shamrock—You may find that a light heart floats over the highest troubles.

Astral Color, Color Need, Apparel Color: Your Astral Color is White, which gives you clarity. Violet in your environment keeps you empathetic toward others. In your wardrobe, Green is your power color for overcoming obstacles.

Fragrance: Sandalwood or other rare spices are the scents you need to have on hand. You crave attention and your perfume or cologne should be your most powerful ally. It will enhance your irresistible charm.

Tree: Holly—Beware that you are not carried away by your passionate nature. The only way to grow is to be open to new experiences.

Instruments: Violin, tympanum

Composer: Gluck

Bird: Mockingbird—the most proficient minstrel in the world's orchestra; graceful and enthusiastic.

Symbol: Anchor—This tranquil symbol signifies stability and strength, and stands for strong commitments in relationships.

Harmonious Health and Nutrition . . .

Health Scent: Lavender—This scent might lead others to trust you and make you patient.

Favorable Foods: Artichokes, watermelon, bran, brown sugar, egg yolks

What's Lucky . . .

Lucky Numbers: 9, 29, 19
Best Months: May and June
Best Day of the Week: Saturday
Best Month Days: 9, 18, 27
Lucky Charm: A U.S. coin or a bill of any amount from the year you were born.
Harmonious Signs for Relationships and Partnerships: Cancer, Scorpio, Virgo

Spiritual Guides . . .

Star: Al Phergal Muachher—Those with this star often cling too long to fond memories.

Angel: Barchiel—This angel shows us right from wrong, encourages us in good decision making, and teaches us to protect ourselves and others.

Guardian Angel: Gabriel—"God is my strength."

Spiritual Stone: Chrysolite—This stone might help you keep things together when you feel frayed.

✶ JUDITH'S INSIGHT ✶

You were born with power and presence. The lives you touch will be changed forever. You have the gift of gab and the smarts to go with it. You have a strong spiritual nature and are known as "one of a kind." You are gentle when need be, but your strength puts you in the right place at the right time. Others think you are blessed. Enthusiasm and playfulness keep you sane during difficult times. You can overcome depression and sadness with your perseverance and joyful personality.

Devotion and kindness bring the love of your life, and it may be someone you considered "just a friend." An independent soul, you do require a sense of freedom, and your mate understands this. Your relationships are sprinkled with fun and fantasy, and that's what helps keep them interesting. Family can be both your strength and your weakness. Be sure to keep this in mind on life's roller coaster.

You could have more than one career. Your creativity is enhanced with the passing years. Consider the role of caretaker early in life. Try something more creative later on. Success can come from anywhere, but you are recognized publicly at some point in your life. As you get older, intuitive gifts manifest themselves.

As an adult, you learn to enjoy life. Bad moments turn to good. Your mind is more highly evolved than you think, and you'll learn to recognize this as you mature. You take risks along the way that seem easy for you. The older you get, the better life gets! Ambition colors your life, so money is not likely to be much of a problem. You do enjoy good things and are happy to work for them.

✶ ✶ ✶

MARCH 19

PISCES • The fish that swim in the pure sea

February 19 at 5:00 P.M. to March 20 at 5:00 P.M. • NUMEROLOGY 1

Possessions and Desires . . .

Gem: Agate—This stone may promote health and lead you to a long life.

Flower: Cohosh—You must learn to wait for life to bestow its lessons and its gifts.

Astral Color, Color Need, Apparel Color: Your Astral Color is Pink, which reflects your compassion. Violet in your environment keeps you empathetic toward others. In your wardrobe, Blue-Green enhances your luck and makes you feel secure.

Fragrance: Sandalwood or other rare spices are the scents you need to have on hand. You crave attention and your perfume or cologne should be your most powerful ally. It will enhance your irresistible charm.

Tree: Walnut—You are unusually helpful and always looking for new beginnings.

Instruments: Viola, trumpet

Composer: Liszt

Bird: Hummingbird—This birds is delicate and graceful. It can remain still for hours, then dart off and be as busy as a bee.

Symbol: Crown—the universal sign of dignity.

Harmonious Health and Nutrition . . .

Health Scent: Strawberry—Soothing by nature, the strawberry promotes self-esteem and encourages love.

Favorable Foods: Raw beets, raisins, barley, honey, cottage cheese

What's Lucky . . .

Lucky Numbers: 1, 11, 28
Best Months: May and June
Best Day of the Week: Saturday
Best Month Days: 1, 10, 19, 28
Lucky Charm: A new penny in your shoe.

Harmonious Signs for Relationships and Partnerships: Cancer, Scorpio, Virgo

Spiritual Guides . . .

Star: Al Risha—Those who have this band of stars as theirs will be happiest as part of a family.

Angel: Barchiel—This angel shows us right from wrong, encourages us in good decision making, and teaches us to protect ourselves and others.

Guardian Angel: Malachi—"Messenger of Jehovah."

Spiritual Stone: Chrysolite—This stone might help you keep things together when you feel frayed.

✳ JUDITH'S INSIGHT ✳

You respect law and order. Knowledge flows to and from you, especially history. You love to explore and invent. Friends remain loyal, no matter how long you know them. You take on responsibility quite easily, although you're not usually inclined to take the initiative. Take extra care with self-indulgence.

You do well in marriage, partnerships, or unions. Fickle early in life, you later want a well-grounded, stable family life. You need your freedom; avoid smothering relationships. You may wander off emotionally or physically if needs and desires aren't met.

Enterprising and original, you become successful at one longstanding job. You would work well as a teacher, professor, caretaker, or in computers. Just don't limit yourself to these! Your artistic nature may draw you to the fine arts. Sooner or later you'll take on multiple titles and careers.

You mean well, but can be misunderstood. You can be impetuous and headstrong, and your actions may be misinterpreted by others. Others may not understand because you walk around with a smile, even when there is sadness in your eyes.

✳ ✳ ✳

MARCH 20

PISCES • The fish that swim in the pure sea

February 19 at 5:00 P.M. to March 20 at 5:00 P.M. • NUMEROLOGY 2

Possessions and Desires . . .

Gem: Sapphire—This gem may help you find forgiveness from those you've wronged.
Flower: Lettuce—You tend to think that love is an emotion that you can keep on leash.
Astral Color, Color Need, Apparel Color: Your Astral Color is White, which gives you clarity. Red in your environment gives you energy and stamina. In your wardrobe, Green is your power color for overcoming obstacles.
Fragrance: Sandalwood or other rare spices are the scents you need to have on hand. You crave attention and your perfume or cologne should be your most powerful ally. It will enhance your irresistible charm.
Tree: Maple—You have both great stability and flashes of intuition.
Instruments: Pipe organ, cymbal, drum
Composers: Handel, Johann Sebastian Bach
Bird: Cuckoo—a good flyer, and very seldom a quitter. Some cuckoos tend to think they favor lonely isolation, but what they really yearn for is a family relationship.
Symbol: Cross—the symbol of self-sacrifice and reconciliation.

Harmonious Health and Nutrition . . .

Health Scent: Apple—You are creative, full of joy, and nearly magical. You bring happiness.
Favorable Foods: Parsley, gooseberries, rye crisps, chocolate, buttermilk

What's Lucky . . .

Lucky Numbers: 2, 22, 29
Best Months: May and June
Best Day of the Week: Saturday
Best Month Days: 2, 11, 20, 29
Lucky Charms: Two 50-cent pieces. Give someone else one of them.
Harmonious Signs for Relationships and Partnerships: Cancer, Scorpio, Virgo

Spiritual Guides . . .

Star: Al Phergal Muachher—Those with this star often cling too long to fond memories.
Angel: Barchiel—This angel shows us right from wrong, encourages us in good decision making, and teaches us to protect ourselves and others.
Guardian Angel: Uriel—This angel brings the light of God's guidance.
Spiritual Stone: Chrysolite—This stone might help you keep things together when you feel frayed.

✶ JUDITH'S INSIGHT ✶

You can be rather judgmental, thinking others don't notice. Your affectionate nature is strong, but you are masterful, dictatorial, and sometimes impatient. Sometimes you lack common sense. You can be inconsistent with others, which makes you seem flighty. Childhood is tough, and you carry that around until your forties. You're a good humanitarian and usually good-natured.

You desire a stable home life. Some day, you get it and keep it that way. "Long-term relationship" spells S-E-C-U-R-I-T-Y to you. Your home will be difficult to let go of. Children's themes appear over and over in your lifetime. You can be the most devoted and the most difficult child. Your tendency to feel sorry for yourself is valid—you do most of the work. But learn to recognize that doesn't mean nobody else is doing anything.

Careers in law or government, education or health care could easily sustain your interest. Whatever the job, make sure there is enough of a creative outlet. You have great enthusiasm for your work, and may be very social in the workplace. Since you're a workaholic, some would think you are very materialistic—you're not. Sometimes you should treat yourself to something nice.

You are extremely talented, and at times seem to have all the confidence in the world, but low self-esteem will plague you all your life. Your view of life is romantic. As you get older your willpower gets stronger, as does your self-image. As you learn to know yourself better, so will others around you.

✶ ✶ ✶

MARCH 21

ARIES • The lamb of god

March 20 at 5:00 P.M. to April 20 at 4:00 A.M. • NUMEROLOGY 3

Possessions and Desires . . .

Gem: Amethyst—This stone could be good for meditation and concentration.

Flower: Pine—You may find that those you pity are really better off than you are.

Astral Color, Color Need, Apparel Color: Your Astral Color is Pink, which reflects your compassion. Red in your environment gives you energy and stamina. In your wardrobe, Maroon gives you confidence.

Fragrance: Use the subtlest hints of lemon or other citrus fruits to bring freshness into your surroundings. These scents will give you the energy to make things happen in your life.

Tree: Elm—You have willpower, strength, and the ability to stand alone.

Instrument: Trombone

Composers: Verdi, Mendelssohn, and Schumann

Bird: Warbling Parakeet—the most beautiful of all birds. It is known as the love bird. It does seem to have the powers of imitation.

Symbol: Wreath—You have been crowned with a special personality. You are strong but extremely compassionate.

Harmonious Health and Nutrition . . .

Health Scent: Rose—This scent will lead you to passionate thoughts and make you feel warm inside.

Favorable Foods: Endive, strawberries, caraway seeds, molasses, cottage cheese

What's Lucky . . .

Lucky Numbers: 3, 9, 30
Best Months: June and July
Best Day of the Week: Tuesday
Best Month Days: 3, 12, 21, 30

Lucky Charm: A pen that someone else has already used.

Harmonious Signs for Relationships and Partnerships: Sagittarius and Leo

Spiritual Guides . . .

Star: Al Botein—Those with this star often feel that they are under lots of pressure.

Angel: Malchidiel—This is the angel of new beginnings and innovative ideas.

Guardian Angel: Johiel—This angel is a protector of all those with a humble heart.

Spiritual Stone: Beryl—This stone is good for meditation and concentration.

✴ JUDITH'S INSIGHT ✴

Because of your wit and charm, you attract friends easily. You take life too seriously, especially in your early years. You can be practical and idealistic all at once. You have that powerful combination of endless mental energy along with great ambition. If you were paid for your thoughts, you would be a millionaire and that is at a penny a thought.

You look and talk as if you have it all together, and most of the time you do. This is key in attracting a mate—your mind pulls in people like a magnet. You are neat in your appearance, and your manners would make any mother proud. You're top banana in all social situations. Your family will rely on you for constant support. Unfortunately, you have no real communication skills when the conversation turns emotional.

You will be drawn to the sea either for career or pleasure. Athletics play a big role in your life. Look for a career in a large institution, such as a school, college, hospital, or charity. Eventually, you earn a lot.

Partnerships are equally lucky for you. Marriage or marriagelike arrangements bring you happiness and success. You have what it takes to get there. So go ahead and do it!

★ ★ ★

MARCH 22 ARIES • The lamb of god

March 20 at 5:00 P.M. to April 20 at 4:00 A.M. • NUMEROLOGY 4

Possessions and Desires . . .

Gem: Ruby—This stone may lead you to energy, friendship, and happiness.

Flower: Maidenhair—You may have an ability to create great beauty.

Astral Color, Color Need, Apparel Color: Your Astral Color is White, which gives you clarity. Red in your environment gives you energy and stamina. In your wardrobe, Raspberry gives you power and stimulation.

Fragrance: Use the subtlest hints of lemon or other citrus fruits to bring freshness into your surroundings. These scents will give you the energy to make things happen in your life.

Tree: Cherry—You will find yourself faced with constant new emotional awakenings.

Instruments: Bass, Clarinet

Composers: Haydn, Wagner

Bird: Killdeer—This bird is usually found consorting with other species, and can adapt to any environment.

Symbol: Star—You are full of inner brightness and will stand out in any crowd. You will be seen as special.

Harmonious Health and Nutrition . . .

Health Scent: Vanilla—This scent will fill you with a feeling of cleanliness and stability.

Favorable Foods: Swiss chard, prunes, rye crisps, raw sugar, eggs

What's Lucky . . .

Lucky Numbers: 2, 11, 22
Best Months: June and July
Best Day of the Week: Tuesday
Best Month Days: 4, 13, 22, 31
Lucky Charm: A piece of material cut from something in your home.

Harmonious Signs for Relationships and Partnerships: Sagittarius and Leo

Spiritual Guides . . .

Star: Al Thurauya—Woe to the enemies of those with this star!

Angel: Malchidiel—This is the angel of new beginnings and innovative ideas.

Guardian Angel: Uriel—This angel brings the light of God's guidance.

Spiritual Stone: Beryl—This stone is good for meditation and concentration.

✴ JUDITH'S INSIGHT ✴

Your determination, drive, and faithfulness inspire others around you. Since you're enthusiastic and kind, you take on projects and work and handle them with great care, right down to the tiniest detail. You may be criticized for your independence.

If you are a woman, you will have many admirers, but you will not be drawn into marriage unless the man wins your affection and desires by his own worthiness—then he becomes your king.

If you are a man, you will be apt to "shop around" before settling down. You are not a creature of impulse. You will wait to be sure your mate is loyal before commitment. For either gender: once you make a commitment, you are generous and sharing. Stability and love at home are vital.

You can be a judge, lawyer, teacher, business manager, or financier. You have great mental ability, but you may at times overdo it at work. You may have your hand in more than one business venture. You'll own quite a bit of real estate. Your mind is mathematical, peaceful, and shrewd.

You enjoy life most when your loved ones enjoy themselves—even if it is at your expense. You are quite fair when it comes to the rights of others. Just remember that success is at your feet, because you know how to use your head!

✴ ✴ ✴

MARCH 23 ARIES • The lamb of god

March 20 at 5:00 P.M. to April 20 at 4:00 A.M. • NUMEROLOGY 5

Possessions and Desires . . .

Gem: Sardius—This stone could give the wearer unusual insights into his or her own heart.

Flower: Woodbine—You may see everyone as your brothers and sisters.

Astral Color, Color Need, Apparel Color: Your Astral Color is Pink, which reflects your compassion. Red in your environment gives you energy and stamina. In your wardrobe, Copper gives you confidence and a sharp appearance.

Fragrance: Use the subtlest hints of lemon or other citrus fruits to bring freshness into your surroundings. These scents will give you the energy to make things happen in your life.

Tree: Apple—You are creative, full of joy, and nearly magical. You bring happiness.

Instruments: Viola, trumpet

Composer: Liszt

Bird: Flamingo—This beautiful, gregarious bird is always careful of its enemy. It is also a caretaker of the young who tries to keep everyone happy.

Symbol: Triangle—You have the right combination of abilities.

Harmonious Health and Nutrition . . .

Health Scent: Peach—this scent may balance your good qualities so that they equal your charm.

Favorable Foods: Eggplant, apricots, caraway seeds, maple sugar, cottage cheese

What's Lucky . . .

Lucky Numbers: 5, 23, 32

Best Months: June and July

Best Day of the Week: Tuesday

Best Month Days: 5, 23, 25

Lucky Charms: A rabbit's foot or a white candle.

Harmonious Signs for Relationships and Partnerships: Sagittarius and Leo

Spiritual Guides . . .

Star: Al Botein—Those with this star often feel that they are under lots of pressure.

Angel: Malchidiel—This is the angel of new beginnings and innovative ideas.

Guardian Angel: Plavwell—gives power and strength to one's presence.

Spiritual Stone: Beryl—This stone is good for meditation and concentration.

✴ JUDITH'S INSIGHT ✴

You're enterprising, refined, subtle, ambitious, and enthusiastic; if you're not successful, it is your own fault. Some will call you lucky. You're often in the right place at the right time. This is not to say you won't have your share of struggle or heartache—you just sail through it so well. The power of positive thinking is your philosophy.

You want commitment but will test the waters over and over until you are absolutely one hundred percent sure. Then you'll test them again. A romantic, devoted mate who understands your sense of humor is essential to you. You're a harmless flirt, but when you get caught, you tend to stay loyal. You are solid as a rock, and family members look to you for your intelligence as well as your support emotionally. Watch out for impulsiveness.

You love secrets and living on the edge. A career in law may satisfy these proclivities. You do have a flair for theater and performing, even if you don't want to act. A career that would bring you into the limelight will work just fine.

You have many talents and, along the way, you discover some of them. You may jump from one career to another, or you may just do them all. At some point you will have your hand in more than one basket—for charity, that is. As you get older, you'll tap into your spiritual side, not something you thus far feel at home with. You enjoy a party as much as the next guy, but you are usually the host.

✴ ✴ ✴

MARCH 24

ARIES • The lamb of god

March 20 at 5:00 P.M. to April 20 at 4:00 A.M. • NUMEROLOGY 6

Possessions and Desires . . .

Gem: Topaz—This is an excellent gift to be exchanged between very loyal friends.
Flower: Fern—You are fascinated with all the beauty that life offers you.
Astral Color, Color Need, Apparel Color: Your Astral Color is Pink, which reflects your compassion. Red in your environment gives you energy and stamina. In your wardrobe, Copper gives you confidence and a sharp appearance.
Fragrance: Use the subtlest hints of lemon or other citrus fruits to bring freshness into your surroundings. These scents will give you the energy to make things happen in your life.
Tree: Palm—You tend to be very healthy and creative.
Instruments: Tambourine, lyre
Composer: Schubert
Bird: Falcon—an expert hunter. When well-trained it can adapt to many tasks and is usually obedient.
Symbol: Crescent—You are more likely to be influenced by the phases of the moon. Your easygoing manner leads you to peaceful situations.

Harmonious Health and Nutrition . . .

Health Scent: Orange Blossom—This scent may balance your body, mind, and soul.
Favorable Foods: Mustard greens, pomegranates, rye crisps, molasses, eggs

What's Lucky . . .

Lucky Numbers: 6, 16, 26
Best Months: June and July
Best Day of the Week: Tuesday
Best Month Days: 6, 15, 24
Lucky Charms: A religious token or card from any religion.

Harmonious Signs for Relationships and Partnerships: Sagittarius and Leo

Spiritual Guides . . .

Star: Al Sheratan—Those with this star hide their pain from those who could help them.
Angel: Malchidiel—This is the angel of new beginnings and innovative ideas.
Guardian Angel: Michael—"Who is like God."
Spiritual Stone: Beryl—This stone is good for meditation and concentration.

✱ *JUDITH'S INSIGHT* ✱

Hosting parties is your strong suit, and you enjoy every minute of it. You have a knack of handling and juggling. You love beautiful things and will work hard to acquire them. You don't look for a handout unless you put your hand in. Generosity, kindness, and charity are themes that run through your life.

You tend to have unusual relationships, maybe even an unusual marriage. Relatives of your significant other may be a problem—maybe there are too many of them. Be careful about letting your partner's family's and friends' problems become your own; you take on responsibility so well. In love, balance takes time, and patience is not one of your virtues. Generosity is, and this may be a blessing or a downfall.

As a general rule, you are lucky with money matters and careers. If you want to own a business, you could. Likewise, if you prefer government or real estate, these might make you happy. You get a natural high from new beginnings in business. You may find a longtime career and then moonlight or own a business on the side. Or you may just retire early and do something on your own then.

One way or another you'll have money, even if it comes after age fifty. Your magnanimous personality attracts friends from all walks of life. Childhood friends stick it out. You have the ability to create great things in your life—with or without a paintbrush.

✱ ✱ ✱

MARCH 25

ARIES • The lamb of god

March 20 at 5:00 P.M. to April 20 at 4:00 A.M. • NUMEROLOGY 7

Possessions and Desires . . .

Gem: Ruby—This stone may lead you to energy, friendship, and happiness.

Flower: Allspice—You have compassion for every living thing.

Astral Color, Color Need, Apparel Color: Your Astral Color is White, which gives you clarity. Red in your environment gives you energy and stamina. In your wardrobe, Rose gives you balance and harmony.

Fragrance: Use the subtlest hints of lemon or other citrus fruits to bring freshness into your surroundings. These scents will give you the energy to make things happen in your life.

Tree: Sycamore—Yours is the ability to love, communicate honestly with others, and have lasting relationships.

Composers: Gluck, Brahms

Instrument: Harp

Bird: Warbling Parakeet—the most beautiful of all birds, known as the love bird. It does seem to have the powers of imitation.

Symbol: Heart—You are enthusiastic, empathetic, and full of generosity and love.

Harmonious Health and Nutrition . . .

Health Scent: Jasmine—This scent may make you more easygoing when you are stressed.

Favorable Foods: Spinach, apples, chocolate, buttermilk

What's Lucky . . .

Lucky Numbers: 7, 17, 27
Best Months: June and July
Best Day of the Week: Tuesday
Best Month Days: 6, 15, 24
Lucky Charm: An old key.

Harmonious Signs for Relationships and Partnerships: Sagittarius and Leo

Spiritual Guides . . .

Star: Al Botein—Those with this star often feel that they are under lots of pressure.

Angel: Malchidiel—This is the angel of new beginnings and innovative ideas.

Guardian Angel: Raphael—This angel attends to all of your needs when you are looking for guidance.

Spiritual Stone: Beryl—This stone is good for meditation and concentration.

✳ JUDITH'S INSIGHT ✳

You have a mathematical mind, high ideals, and great ambition. Because you're inclined to be extremely independent, you may lead a rather unconventional life. You are broadminded, with a very curious nature. You love to flirt, but you display a sense of purity. No one will ever know what you're thinking—you hide your secrets well.

Drawn to unusual environments and relationships, you may desire to live in an unconventional place. You may desire wooded areas instead of cleared properties. And your home is a palace, no matter where you live. In time, you will make a devoted mate.

Your career may be anything connected with government, law, state institutions, or schools, and you should advance early on. Do not rule out a more creative position either. You may aspire to paint, compose music, or write screenplays.

People will be drawn to you, especially for business advice. The most eventful, unexpected things seem to happen to you all the time. You have high ideals and great aspirations. Once you figure which one you really want, you'll go out and get it!

✳ ✳ ✳

MARCH 26
ARIES • The lamb of god
March 20 at 5:00 P.M. to April 20 at 4:00 A.M. • Numerology 8

Possessions and Desires . . .

Gem: Chrysolite—This gem may help you clear your mind of sadness and worry.

Flower: Pitch Pine—You can be very philosophical.

Astral Color, Color Need, Apparel Color: Your Astral Color is Pink, which reflects your compassion. Red in your environment gives you energy and stamina. In your wardrobe, Green is your power color for overcoming obstacles.

Fragrance: Use the subtlest hints of lemon or other citrus fruits to bring freshness into your surroundings. These scents will give you the energy to make things happen in your life.

Tree: Pine—Your relationships tend to be harmonious, both emotionally and mentally.

Instrument: Cello

Composer: Mozart

Bird: Bobolink—This charming singer is equally good as a soloist or a member of an orchestra. It is a very romantic bird, useful as an insect destroyer, elegant, with beautiful feathers, and is always pleasant to have around.

Symbol: Wings—You are the source of balance in your world—this will bring you contentment.

Harmonious Health and Nutrition . . .

Health Scent: Raspberry—This scent might bring you a feeling of harmony with the universe.

Favorable Foods: Spinach, apples, chocolate, buttermilk

What's Lucky . . .

Lucky Numbers: 8, 17, 26

Best Months: June and July

Best Day of the Week: Tuesday

Best Month Days: 8, 17, 26

Lucky Charm: Red ribbon in your wallet or doorway.

Harmonious Signs for Relationships and Partnerships: Sagittarius and Leo

Spiritual Guides . . .

Star: Al Thurauya—Woe to the enemies of those with this star!

Angel: Malchidiel—This is the angel of new beginnings and innovative ideas.

Guardian Angel: Seraphim—An angel that brings love, light, and passion

Spiritual Stone: Beryl—This stone is good for meditation and concentration.

✦ JUDITH'S INSIGHT ✦

Obstacles don't faze you. You meet life's sorrow and disappointment head on. Early on in life, heavy responsibility follows you, and this is where you develop your strength of character and sheer will. You may work early or marry early. Groups and teams cramp your style. You do better working alone.

You may desire children early in life. You can be the big kid or the mature adult, depending on the situation. Although you're usually extremely loyal, you may need to pull away sometimes. You are everyone's rock and always make the best of everything. Make sure you don't let the needs of others overshadow your own. You tend to have strong influence over friends, family, and significant others.

You have the ability to take on more than one career. A business you start will succeed. State or government jobs might appeal to you; your investigative nature lends itself to police work. The desire for a stable work environment and long-term employment is there. Your jobs tend to last forever. At one time or another, you may be involved with a family business. Longevity combined with talent make you an ideal worker.

Aim for as much fun as responsibility, or you may feel resentment along the way. Because of your strength, you can be misread and misunderstood. You may be the head of the class, and you love and desire the finer things. Don't worry; you'll have them. Slow down and smell the roses. While you're there, take time to enjoy the pretty colors.

✱ ✱ ✱

MARCH 27 ARIES • The lamb of god
March 20 at 5:00 P.M. to April 20 at 4:00 A.M. • NUMEROLOGY 9

Possessions and Desires . . .

Gem: Diamond—This stone is thought to encourage harmony in relationships and gives strength to the troubled.

Flower: Fir—You may need to take more time for yourself in order to discover who you are.

Astral Color, Color Need, Apparel Color: Your Astral Color is White, which gives you clarity. Red in your environment gives you energy and stamina. In your wardrobe, Maroon gives you confidence.

Fragrance: Use the subtlest hints of lemon or other citrus fruits to bring freshness into your surroundings. These scents will give you the energy to make things happen in your life.

Tree: Holly—Beware that you are not carried away by your passionate nature. The only way to grow is to be open to new experiences.

Instruments: Violin, tympanum

Composer: Gluck

Bird: Mockingbird—the most proficient minstral in the world's orchestra; graceful and enthusiastic.

Symbol: Anchor—This tranquil symbol signifies stability and strength, and stands for strong commitments in relationships.

Harmonious Health and Nutrition . . .

Health Scents: Almond—This scent may revitalize you and open you to greater possibilities.

Favorable Foods: Watercress, gooseberries, caraway seeds, maple sugar, pressed cheese

What's Lucky . . .

Lucky Numbers: 9, 19, 29
Best Months: June and July
Best Day of the Week: Tuesday
Best Month Days: 9, 18, 27
Lucky Charms: A U.S. coin or a bill of any amount from the year you were born.

Harmonious Signs for Relationships and Partnerships: Sagittarius and Leo

Spiritual Guides . . .

Star: Al Thurauya—Woe to the enemies of those with this star!

Angel: Malchidiel—This is the angel of new beginnings and innovative ideas.

Guardian Angel: Gabriel—"God is my strength."

Spiritual Stone: Beryl—This stone is good for meditation and concentration.

✴ JUDITH'S INSIGHT ✴

You have a great spirit and strong desire for life. Enthusiasm alone will take you places. You're easygoing and friendly no matter what the situation and people will recognize this. Your ambitious style may lead you in many different directions, not necessarily connected to your work. Sports, extracurricular activities, and even volunteer work should all satisfy you. You have many good ideas and may find yourself throwing parties at the last minute.

The ideal mate for you is out there. Family life can get overwhelming, but probably because you're making it that way. You draw your strength from nurturing relationships. Although you may be the domineering partner, you do it with class and style, so it doesn't appear that way.

You should engage in business or industry. Counseling or metaphysics may be attractive to you. You would do very well as an artist, architect, judge, or jewelry maker. You find your niche after a few emotional battles. Do not rule out all areas of professional sports. You have high energy and great endurance.

Avoid mood-altering substances as much as possible. You have a tendency to become addicted. However, when habits do form, you recognize you have the willpower to overcome anything. You will enjoy friends in high places. The odds are that you can be there yourself eventually.

✴ ✴ ✴

MARCH 28 ARIES • The lamb of god

March 20 at 5:00 P.M. to April 20 at 4:00 A.M. • NUMEROLOGY 1

Possessions and Desires . . .

Gem: Amethyst—This stone is said to give calmness and peace.

Flower: Sweetbriar—The simpler you keep things the more settled you'll be.

Astral Color, Color Need, Apparel Color: Your Astral Color is Pink, which reflects your compassion. Red in your environment gives you energy and stamina. In your wardrobe, Raspberry gives power and stimulation.

Fragrance: Use the subtlest hints of lemon or other citrus fruits to bring freshness into your surroundings. These scents will give you the energy to make things happen in your life.

Tree: Walnut—You are unusually helpful and always looking for new beginnings.

Instruments: Oboe, flute, clarinet, piano, French horn, organ, piccolo

Composer: Böhm

Bird: Bird of paradise—the "bird of the gods." You will shine and love extraordinary form.

Symbol: Crown—the universal sign of dignity.

Harmonious Health and Nutrition . . .

Health Scent: Jasmine—This scent may make you more easygoing when you are stressed.

Favorable Foods: Watercress, gooseberries, caraway seeds, maple sugar, pressed cheese

What's Lucky . . .

Lucky Numbers: 1, 10, 11
Best Months: June and July
Best Day of the Week: Tuesday
Best Month Days: 1, 10, 19, and 28
Lucky Charm: A new penny in your shoe

Harmonious Signs for Relationships and Partnerships: Sagittarius and Leo

Spiritual Guides . . .

Star: Al Sheratan—Those with this star hide their pain from those who could thelp them.

Angel: Malchidiel—This is the angel of new beginnings and innovative ideas.

Guardian Angel: Malachi—"Messenger of Jehovah."

Spiritual Stone: Beryl—This stone is good for meditation and concentration.

✴ JUDITH'S INSIGHT ✴

You have organizational skills and much executive ability. A quick study, you have an unusually long attention span. You love to live high on the hog. You will lead an eventful life. Anything can happen, with you around. You possess strength and strong will, and your independent character is well recognized and respected.

Stable home life and strong family ties dominate your life. Your bark can be worse than your bite: you can get into arguments but retain close connections. Love does prevail. Your presence and charm and sense of humor are noticed. You can flirt but are unlikely to stray unless living under extreme circumstances for a long period of time.

In your career, you're the initiator, or the boss. If not, you're unhappy. You need recognition and high rank. You will do well in whatever career you choose. You could be a car mechanic, salesperson, lawyer, detective, or even surgeon. Whatever the career, you shoot for the moon and don't settle until you get it.

You are faithful, smart, and sympathetic, surprisingly domestic, and desirous of an orderly home life. Sounds stuffy, but no! For you, every day will have a certain element of surprise.

✴ ✴ ✴

MARCH 29 ARIES • The lamb of god

March 20 at 5:00 P.M. to April 20 at 4:00 A.M. • NUMEROLOGY 2

Possessions and Desires . . .

Gem: Sapphire—This gem may help you find forgiveness from those you've wronged.

Flower: Elder—You can be overzealous when faced with what should be small problems.

Astral Color, Color Need, Apparel Color: Your Astral Color is Pink, which reflects your compassion. Red in your environment gives you energy and stamina. In your wardrobe, Maroon gives you confidence

Fragrance: Use the subtlest hints of lemon or other citrus fruits to bring freshness into your surroundings. These scents will give you the energy to make things happen in your life.

Tree: Maple—You have both great stability and flashes of intuition.

Instruments: Pipe organ, cymbal, drum

Composers: Handel, Johann Sebastian Bach

Bird: Cuckoo—a good flyer and very seldom a quitter. Some cuckoos tend to think they favor lonely isolation, but what they really yearn for is a family relationship.

Symbol: Cross—the symbol of self-sacrifice and reconciliation.

Harmonious Health and Nutrition . . .

Health Scents: Apple—You are creative, full of joy, and nearly magical. You bring happiness.

Favorable Foods: Dill, prunes, rye crisps, raw sugar, cottage cheese

What's Lucky . . .

Lucky Numbers: 2, 20, 22
Best Months: June and July
Best Day of the Week: Tuesday
Best Month Days: 2, 11, 20, 29
Lucky Charms: Two 50-cent pieces. Give someone else one of them.

Harmonious Signs for Relationships and Partnerships: Sagittarius and Leo

Spiritual Guides . . .

Star: Al Botein—Those with this star often feel that they are under lots of pressure.

Angel: Malchidiel—This is the angel of new beginnings and innovative ideas.

Guardian Angel: Uriel—This angel brings the light of God's guidance.

Spiritual Stone: Beryl—This stone is good for meditation and concentration.

✳ JUDITH'S INSIGHT ✳

You have a presence that demands attention and a smile that can change the world. You are faithful, just, sympathetic, and kind—sometimes to a fault. You grasp things very easily, and are strong and ambitious. Even when others step on your toes, you stay out of their way. You can endure just about any situation that arises.

You're loyal and devoted to family, which may not always be to your best advantage. You attract friends easily. You're a good friend, and you occasionally check that friends are as devoted as you. You make a great parent or guardian and seem to understand children better that most. Much love and devotion comes your way, especially as you get older.

You start off with one longstanding career that will keep you grounded, only later to desire a sense of freedom. This may come after retirement! You may never get the total career recognition you wish, but you do gain the respect of others in your chosen field. Whether you are a police officer, police commissioner, politician, decorator, or CEO of a large corporation, your greatest satisfaction comes when you're in love.

You have a way with words and may aspire to use it. You have many hidden talents. Your greatest attribute, however, is your joie de vive. You know how to enjoy life and bring others along for the ride.

✶ ✶ ✶

MARCH 30
ARIES • The lamb of god
March 20 at 5:00 P.M. to April 20 at 4:00 A.M. • NUMEROLOGY 3

Possessions and Desires . . .

Gem: Ruby—This stone may lead you to energy, friendship, and happiness.
Flower: Horehound—You usually see beyond the surface of things.
Astral Color, Color Need, Apparel Color: Your Astral Color is White, which gives you clarity. Red in your environment gives you energy and stamina. In your wardrobe, Raspberry gives power and stimulation.
Fragrance: Use the subtlest hints of lemon or other citrus fruits to bring freshness into your surroundings. These scents will give you the energy to make things happen in your life.
Tree: Elm—You have willpower, strength, and the ability to stand alone.
Instrument: Trombone
Composers: Verdi, Mendelssohn, Schumann
Bird: Swan—Regarded as royal and sacred, this bird has the protective nature of a mother and can become a furious fighter in the defense of its young.
Symbol: Wreath—You have been crowned with a special personality. You are strong but extremely compassionate.

Harmonious Health and Nutrition . . .

Health Scent: Rose—This scent will lead you to passionate thoughts and make you feel warm inside.
Favorable Foods: Eggplant, tomatoes, maple sugar, pressed cheese

What's Lucky . . .

Lucky Numbers: 3, 12, 30
Best Months: June and July
Best Day of the Week: Tuesday
Best Month Days: 3, 12, 21, 30
Lucky Charm: A pen that someone else has already used.

Harmonious Signs for Relationships and Partnerships: Sagittarius and Leo

Spiritual Guides . . .

Star: Al Thurauya—Woe to the enemies of those with this star!
Angel: Malchidiel—This is the angel of new beginnings and innovative ideas.
Guardian Angel: Johiel—This angel is a protector of all those with a humble heart.
Spiritual Stone: Beryl—This stone is good for meditation and concentration.

✴ JUDITH'S INSIGHT ✴

You have great ideas and you know how to put them to good use. A gentle person with a strong exterior, you are loving and nurturing with ambition and enthusiasm to boot. Hidden charms abound, and you are noticed for your high energy. People are drawn to you, even the ones who don't like you. You have great organizational abilities.

Family is your greatest love, and sometimes your greatest pain in the neck. You like a smoothly running household. Sometimes you may go a bit overboard. If mates are consistent with their affection, you will have a harmonious partnership. If not, you may feel indifferent. You have distinct needs and tendencies when it comes to a love relationship. This may be the only area of your life where you follow instead of lead.

You are the top banana in whatever you do. Any one of these careers would work well for you and bring you success and recognition: architect, building contractor, lawyer, writer, or artist.

Your wit and charm attract crowds of onlookers. You have a strong will and are far from lazy. Sometimes your opinions can be taken wrong, but you're willing to back down, especially when nobody's listening. The older you get, the less challenged you feel by your environment. Eventually, you learn to stop challenging it.

★ ★ ★

MARCH 31 ARIES • The lamb of god

March 20 at 5:00 P.M. to April 20 at 4:00 A.M. • NUMEROLOGY 4

Possessions and Desires . . .

Gem: Emerald—Those who carry this stone tend to be lucky in love.
Flower: Love-lies-bleeding—It tends to take a long time for you to fall in love.
Astral Color, Color Need, Apparel Color: Your Astral Color is Pink, which reflects your compassion. Red in your environment gives you energy and stamina. In your wardrobe, green is your power color for overcoming obstacles.
Fragrance: Use the subtlest hints of lemon or other citrus fruits to bring freshness into your surroundings. These scents will give you the energy to make things happen in your life.
Tree: Cherry—You will find yourself faced with constant new emotional awakenings.
Instruments: Bass, clarinet
Composers: Haydn, Wagner
Bird: Robin—the most sociable of all birds, with the ability to create quick friendships. It also can easily adapt to any home. When it wants something, it has the tendency to try to snatch it.
Symbol: Star—You are full of inner brightness and will stand out in any crowd. You will be seen as special.

Harmonious Health and Nutrition . . .

Health Scent: Vanilla—This scent will fill you with a feeling of cleanliness and stability.
Favorable Foods: Parsley, apples, caraway seeds, chocolate

What's Lucky . . .

Lucky Numbers: 4, 14, 24
Best Months: June and July
Best Day of the Week: Tuesday
Best Month Days: 4, 13, 22, 3
Lucky Charm: A piece of material cut from something in your home.

Harmonious Signs for Relationships and Partnerships: Sagittarius and Leo

Spiritual Guides . . .

Star: Al Thurauya—Woe to the enemies of those with this star!
Angel: Malchidiel—This is the angel of new beginnings and innovative ideas.
Guardian Angel: Uriel—This angel brings the light of God's guidance.
Spiritual Stone: Beryl—This stone is good for meditation and concentration.

✶ JUDITH'S INSIGHT ✶

You are a strong thinker and reasoner, somewhat opinionated, and you distrust everything people tell you. You enjoy a good time and the good life. When you get nervous, you get cranky. Although you aren't lazy, you can go through some unproductive stages. Strange and unusual events seem to find you.

You adapt to things quite easily and enjoy harmony at home. Your home must be neat and organized. You command respect throughout the family. Try to dwell less on things that go wrong in your love life. An unconventional marriage or relationship may alleviate this. You make a devoted parent and child.

You could own your own clothing company or be president of someone else's. You take on responsibility with ease. You may also be attracted to law or government. Be careful to stay on the right side of the law. Work around cars may be appealing, or you may be a collector. A knack with mechanical things lends itself to a hands-on career. You have great expectations and the karma to achieve even greater ones. Try to be fair with all those around you, even when your instincts tell you not to.

You may be strong in a hobby or take on outside interests. You'll accomplish many things. Some may consider you a bit eccentric, and you know what? You like it that way!

★ ★ ★

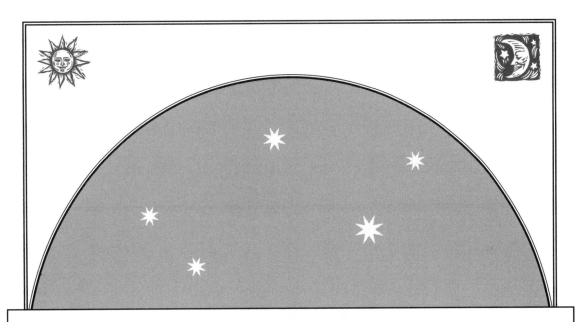

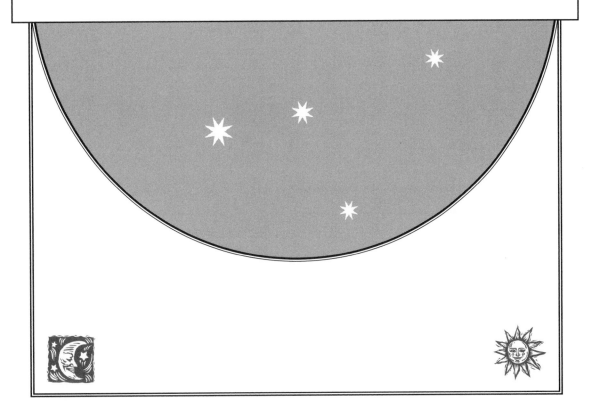

APRIL

APRIL 1 ARIES • The lamb of god

March 20 at 5:00 P.M. to April 20 at 4:00 A.M. • NUMEROLOGY I

Possessions and Desires . . .

Gem: Turquoise—This stone may help you find material wealth.

Flower: Columbine—You can be seen as foolish in some of your more passionate quests.

Astral Color, Color Need, Apparel Color: Your Astral Color is White, which gives you clarity. Red in your environment gives you energy and stamina. In your wardrobe, Maroon gives you confidence.

Fragrance: Use the subtlest hints of lemon or other citrus fruits to bring freshness into your surroundings. These scents will give you the energy to make things happen in your life.

Tree: Walnut—You are unusually helpful and always looking for new beginnings.

Instruments: Oboe, flute, piano, French horn, organ, piccolo

Composer: Böhm

Bird: Skylark—This handsome bird is beautiful when it sings. It always whistles as it works.

Symbol: Crown—the universal sign of dignity.

Harmonious Health and Nutrition . . .

Health Scent: Strawberry—soothing by nature, the strawberry promotes self-esteem and encourages love.

Favorable Foods: Dried beans, prunes, raw sugar, pressed cheese

What's Lucky . . .

Lucky Numbers: 1, 9, 18
Best Months: June and July
Best Day of the Week: Tuesday
Best Month Days: 1, 10, 19, 28
Lucky Charm: A new penny in your shoe.
Harmonious Signs for Relationships and Partnerships: Sagittarius and Leo

Spiritual Guides . . .

Star: Al Thuraya—Woe to the enemies of those with this star!

Angel: Malchidiel—This is the angel of new beginnings and innovative ideas.

Guardian Angel: Malachi—"Messenger of Jehovah."

Spiritual Stone: Beryl—This stone is good for meditation and concentration.

✳ JUDITH'S INSIGHT ✳

You have great ideas. You adapt to and grasp things easily and are generally good with details. Oddly, you're either bursting with energy or lacking it, depending on whether something sparks your fancy. Known for your philosophical mind and sympathetic nature, you can achieve great heights. You like having friends in high places. You love to learn. You can be belligerent on occasion and should keep your guard up, or your aggression could be destructive.

Home is important as long as you have chosen it for yourself. You desire order and live by the phrase "A place for everything and everything in its place." Your friends are your family. Friends are important to you; sometimes so important that they may cloud your thinking. You are faithful and loyal as long as you feel the same in return from your partner. In the early years of life, you may have a roving eye or perhaps just be flirtatious.

Careerwise, you are talented enough to do anything you desire—be it architect or psychologist. Your success may lie in building and/or designing. You're intensely independent, especially at work, and you have great organizational skills. Let no dust collect on things you get involved in, or you will get bored. You set hard goals for yourself, but you achieve them. Beware of going to extremes. Think first—you can be frank and outspoken. Most often, you throw caution to the wind and are impulsive. You are accustomed to overcoming obstacles, but you should carefully evaluate which obstacles you really want to remove. Be cautious of overzealousness in resolving problems.

✳ ✳ ✳

APRIL 2 ARIES • The lamb of god

March 20 at 5:00 P.M. to April 20 at 4:00 A.M. • NUMEROLOGY 2

Possessions and Desires . . .

Gem: Diamond—This stone is thought to encourage harmony in relationships and gives strength to the troubled.

Flower: Rush—You may be too anxious to adhere to other people's opinions of you.

Astral Color, Color Need, Apparel Color: Your Astral Color is Pink, which reflects your compassion. Red in your environment gives you energy and stamina. In your wardrobe, Gray brings out the best in your looks.

Fragrance: Use the subtlest hints of lemon or other citrus fruits to bring freshness into your surroundings. These scents will give you the energy to make things happen in your life.

Tree: Maple—You have both great stability and flashes of intuition.

Instruments: Pipe organ, cymbal, drum

Composers: Handel, Johann Sebastian Bach

Bird: Warbling Parakeet—the most beautiful of all birds, known as the love bird. It does seem to have the powers of imitation.

Symbol: Cross—the symbol of self-sacrifice and reconciliation.

Harmonious Health and Nutrition . . .

Health Scent: Apple—You are creative, full of joy, and nearly magical. You bring happiness.

Favorable Foods: Asparagus, apricots, rye crisps, maple sugar, buttermilk

What's Lucky . . .

Lucky Numbers: 1, 9, 27
Best Months: June and July
Best Day of the Week: Tuesday
Best Month Days: 2, 11, 20, 29
Lucky Charms: Two 50-cent pieces. Give someone else one of them.

Harmonious Signs for Relationships and Partnerships: Sagittarius and Leo

Spiritual Guides . . .

Star: Al Botein—Those with this star often feel that they are under lots of pressure.

Angel: Malchidiel—This is the angel of new beginnings and innovative ideas.

Guardian Angel: Uriel—This angel brings the light of God's guidance.

Spiritual Stone: Beryl—This stone is good for meditation and concentration.

✷ JUDITH'S INSIGHT ✷

You are energetic, impulsive, and sensuous, with lots of creativity, imagination, and common sense. If one were to say you were psychic, you'd probably respond that you have natural intelligence and insight. You could be an inventor, doctor, creator, or producer, combining your creativity and intelligence. You're a jack-of-all trades. You have artistic talent, and if art is not your career, pursue it as a hobby for personal fulfillment. Golf, cars, and sports all appeal to you, as do antiques.

You need attention and get it. If those around you are inattentive, you become cranky. You are sympathetic and kind, a true, faithful friend. Your aspirations and impulsiveness make you a most intriguing and alluring companion. You want a long-term mate. You often bite off more than you can chew and may have problems interacting in unfamiliar groups. You're comfortable as a social butterfly and as a caterpillar in the cocoon. Society accepts you at work or play, and you may find yourself with people in high places. When you get bored, find a good book or great movie, and you'll soon be climbing mountains with the cast, or fighting the bad guys. Such escapism is therapeutic for you. Although you may think you are escaping into the darkness, you are, in reality, finding the light.

✷ ✷ ✷

APRIL 3   ARIES • The lamb of god
March 20 at 5:00 P.M. to April 20 at 4:00 A.M. • NUMEROLOGY 3

Possessions and Desires . . .

Gem: Ruby—This stone may lead you to energy, friendship, and happiness.

Flower: Meadow Saffron—You tend to dwell too much on past experiences.

Astral Color, Color Need, Apparel Color: Your Astral Color is White, which gives you clarity. Red in your environment gives you energy and stamina. In your wardrobe, Raspberry brings you power and stimulation.

Fragrance: Use the subtlest hints of lemon or other citrus fruits to bring freshness into your surroundings. These scents will give you the energy to make things happen in your life.

Tree: Elm—You have willpower, strength, and the ability to stand alone.

Instrument: Trombone

Composers: Verdi, Mendelssohn, Schumann

Bird: Swan—Regarded as royal and sacred, this bird has the protective nature of a mother, and can become a furious fighter in the defense of its young.

Symbol: Wreath—You have been crowned with a special personality. You are strong but extremely compassionate.

Harmonious Health and Nutrition . . .

Health Scent: Raspberry—This scent might bring you a feeling of harmony with the universe.

Favorable Foods: Mustard greens, strawberries, caraway seeds, chocolate, eggs

What's Lucky . . .

Lucky Numbers: 1, 9, 19

Best Months: June and July

Best Day of the Week: Tuesday

Best Month Days: 3, 12, 21, 30

Lucky Charm: A pen that someone else has already used.

Harmonious Signs for Relationships and Partnerships: Sagittarius and Leo

Spiritual Guides . . .

Star: Al Thurauya—Woe to the enemies of those with this star!

Angel: Malchidiel—This is the angel of new beginnings and innovative ideas.

Guardian Angel: Johiel—This angel is a protector of all those with a humble heart.

Spiritual Stone: Beryl—This stone is good for meditation and concentration.

✷ JUDITH'S INSIGHT ✷

You are gifted with great mental energy, innovative schemes, and original plans for interesting things. Since you're strong and self-willed, you make things happen. There is nothing you cannot accomplish. You're candid, positive, forceful, even heroic. You're a natural leader, with many followers. Your leadership ability could enhance or injure a relationship.

Much depends on your mate. Your enterprising and venturesome ways are attractive, and your mate appreciates your spontaneity. Pure energy and ambition will carry you far, even in relationships. In all likelihood your significant other adores you year after year. If a love relationship does fail, another will appear in its place. You are the responsible one—serene yet caring—the one who picks up the pieces for the family. You gain respect from friends in social situations. Children and family mean the world to you, but be on guard—you do not own them. Distinguish between favor and obligation. You will have powerful friends but could make powerful enemies. Most definitely you will be head of the house and possibly even the Senate. Friends and family think you live a charmed life because you make things look easy. What throws others doesn't faze you. You conquer major obstacles as if you were tying your shoes.

When it comes to your life's work, your capabilities are endless and your choices inexhaustible. You could be anything from critic to editor, banker, accountant, police officer and very possibly lawyer, or judge, and you have no problem maintaining dual careers. If not, one career and many hobbies may be for you. You are at your best when your energy is up; just be careful to watch your blood pressure. Your toughness is complemented by your warmth—you are a true diamond in the rough.

APRIL 4
ARIES • The lamb of god
March 20 at 5:00 P.M. to April 20 at 4:00 A.M. • NUMEROLOGY 4

Possessions and Desires . . .

Gem: Emerald—Those who carry this stone tend to be lucky in love.

Flower: Reed—You tend to love music and may be very gifted in that art.

Astral Color, Color Need, Apparel Color: Your Astral Color is Pink, which reflects your compassion. Red in your environment gives you energy and stamina. In your wardrobe, Copper brings you confidence and a sharp appearance.

Fragrance: Use the subtlest hints of lemon or other citrus fruits to bring freshness into your surroundings. These scents will give you the energy to make things happen in your life.

Tree: Cherry—You will find yourself faced with constant new emotional awakenings.

Instruments: Bass, clarinet

Composers: Haydn, Wagner

Bird: Robin—the most sociable of all birds with the ability to create quick friendships. It also can easily adapt to any home. When it wants something, it has the tendency to try to snatch it.

Symbol: Star—You are full of inner brightness and will stand out in any crowd. You will be seen as special.

Harmonious Health and Nutrition . . .

Health Scent: Vanilla—This scent will fill you with a feeling of cleanliness and stability.

Favorable Foods: Lentils, apples, rye crisps, molasses, cottage cheese

What's Lucky . . .

Lucky Numbers: 1, 4, 9

Best Months: June and July

Best Day of the Week: Tuesday

Best Month Days: 4, 13, 22, 31

Lucky Charm: A piece of material cut from something in your home.

Harmonious Signs for Relationships and Partnerships: Sagittarius and Leo

Spiritual Guides . . .

Star: Al Thurauya—Woe to the enemies of those with this star!

Angel: Malchidiel—This is the angel of new beginnings and innovative ideas.

Guardian Angel: Uriel—This angel brings the light of God's guidance.

Spiritual Stone: Beryl—This stone is good for meditation and concentration.

✳ JUDITH'S INSIGHT ✳

Your place is at the bargaining table or in a debate. The skills you have could be fine-tuned for the White House. You are a thinker, a reasoner, and the one with imagination. To top it off, you possess an endearing sense of humor. You have the admiration of friends and family, since you not only bring home the bacon, you fry it up and present it to your neighbor so she can feed her man. Others view you as nice and kind-hearted, but you're terrible if someone double-crosses you. You lean toward unconventional relationships. You welcome responsibility but must guard against taking on more than you want to handle.

Your mate sees you as challenging and steadfast. Be careful that others don't misread you. Poor communication on your part could pose relationship problems. Sometimes you seem demanding and must soften your approach. Your relationships improve tremendously when you listen. Your charm and wit bring many to you, and your social calendar will be full. The pressures of trying to balance friends and family may feel burdensome, but you can do it.

You're inventive and creative with many ideas, and you also know how to implement them. Your efforts could mean a novel yet lucrative career for you. In this computer age, programming or analysis could work well for you. Develop those original ideas, keep your hands busy stirring more than one pot, and you can have a very good income. Lucky in financial affairs and capable of adapting quickly, you can respond favorably to sudden, unexpected changes. For such a conventional person with a conventional lifestyle, you can expect very unconventional things to happen.

✳ ✳ ✳

APRIL 5   ARIES • The lamb of god

March 20 at 5:00 P.M. to April 20 at 4:00 A.M. • NUMEROLOGY 5

Possessions and Desires . . .

Gem: Amethyst—This stone is said to give calmness and peace.

Flower: Mouse-ear Chickweed—You are usually clever enough to see that keeping life simple works best for you.

Astral Color, Color Need, Apparel Color: Your Astral Color is White, which gives you clarity. Red in your environment gives you energy and stamina. In your wardrobe, Green is your power color for overcoming obstacles.

Fragrance: Use the subtlest hints of lemon or other citrus fruits to bring freshness into your surroundings. These scents will give you the energy to make things happen in your life.

Tree: Apple—You are creative, full of joy, and nearly magical. You bring happiness.

Instruments: viola, trumpet

Composer: Liszt

Bird: Flamingo—This beautiful, gregarious bird is always careful of its enemy. It is also a caretaker of the young who tries to keep everyone happy.

Symbol: Triangle—You have the right combination of abilities.

Harmonious Health and Nutrition . . .

Health Scents: Peach—This scent may balance your good qualities so that they equal your charm.

Favorable Foods: Endive, prunes, caraway seeds, chocolate, buttermilk

What's Lucky . . .

Lucky Numbers: 1, 5, 9
Best Months: June and July
Best Day of the Week: Tuesday
Best Month Days: 4, 5, 23
Lucky Charms: A rabbit's foot or a white candle
Harmonious Signs for Relationships and Partnerships: Sagittarius and Leo

Spiritual Guides . . .

Star: Al Botein—Those with this star often feel that they are under lots of pressure.

Angel: Malchidiel—This is the angel of new beginnings and innovative ideas.

Guardian Angel: Phanuel—protection against the negative.

Spiritual Stone: Beryl—This stone is good for meditation and concentration.

✷ JUDITH'S INSIGHT ✷

Confident, courageous, convinced, impulsive, stubborn, and strong-willed are all terms that could describe you. These traits usually complement each other, but occasionally they collide. Confidence in your own judgment carries you far, but watch out whose feathers you may ruffle. Generally, to know you is to like you. But sometimes knowing you is loving you, and sometimes those who love you most have a tough time liking you. Anything you devote yourself to can be achieved. Your intuition is good and the outcome is usually always right, but you are not always satisfied with the results. Trust your intuitions more. As you age, relationships improve as more people learn that everything you do comes first from the heart. You have a roving eye, but when you get into a monogamous relationship, you are dedicated.

Your diligence at work and at play brings success. Your employer is satisfied with your performance. You, the employee, are not so satisfied. You demand much of yourself. When your turn comes, you are a terrific manager and a great boss. By not overdelegating to others, you share the workload, and everyone benefits by your teaching. Talented with things mechanical, you like to build, create, and sometimes critique. This could lead to one of many different careers for you. You must work from the bottom up, whether it be funding a foundation or building an empire. You'll be successful—it just may take time. This poses problems for you; patience is not your strongest virtue.

You love money and enjoy being the breadwinner. You could be less demanding, more easygoing. You can be all work and no play, or all play and no work at all. You must somehow learn to balance the two.

★ ★ ★

APRIL 6

ARIES • The lamb of god

March 20 at 5:00 P.M. to April 20 at 4:00 A.M. • NUMEROLOGY 6

Possessions and Desires . . .

Gem: Topaz—This is an excellent gift to be exchanged between very loyal friends.

Flower: Myrrh—You have many reasons to be glad just to be alive.

Astral Color, Color Need, Apparel Color: Your Astral Color is Pink, which reflects your compassion. Red in your environment gives you energy and stamina. In your wardrobe, Maroon gives you confidence.

Fragrance: Use the subtlest hints of lemon or other citrus fruits to bring freshness into your surroundings. These scents will give you the energy to make things happen in your life.

Tree: Palm—You tend to be very healthy and creative.

Instruments: Tambourine, lyre

Composer: Schubert

Bird: Falcon—an expert hunter. When well-trained, it can adapt to many tasks and is usually obedient.

Symbol: Crescent—You are more likely to be influenced by the phases of the moon. Your easygoing manner leads you to peaceful situations.

Harmonious Health and Nutrition . . .

Health Scent: Orange Blossom—This scent may balance your body, mind, and soul.

Favorable Foods: Asparagus, apricots, rye crisps, maple sugar, pressed cheese

What's Lucky . . .

Lucky Numbers: 1, 9, 24, 33
Best Months: June and July
Best Day of the Week: Tuesday
Best Month Days: 6, 15, 24
Lucky Charms: A religious token or card from any religion.
Harmonious Signs for Relationships and Partnerships: Sagittarius and Leo

Spiritual Guides . . .

Star: Al Sheratan—Those with this star hide their pain from those who could help them.

Angel: Malchidiel—This is the angel of new beginnings and innovative ideas.

Guardian Angel: Michael—"Who is like God."

Spiritual Stone: Beryl—This stone is good for meditation and concentration.

✶ JUDITH'S INSIGHT ✶

The key to your happiness is to stop taking life so seriously. You work hard and play hard, and take things to extremes. It's not that your expectations are too high, just that you don't always allow yourself enough time to achieve them. You will be successful, no doubt; you just need to get out of your own way and pay less attention to those who get in your way. Live more in the present and enjoy your dreams as you have them. You are harder on yourself than anyone else.

You're affectionate, demonstrative and warm-hearted. Passionate, too—you are especially attractive to the opposite sex. You are popular socially and make friends wherever you go. Make sure low self-esteem doesn't interfere with letting relationships happen. A satisfying love relationship generally comes later in life. You love to spend money and show off your home and surroundings. You insist on having nice things. Be careful, though, and curb your generosity so it doesn't impoverish you.

Success awaits in artistic circles, such as painting, music, sculpture, poetry, or literature. Your fondness of theater and opera can also result in professional possibilities. You are a caretaker by nature, so if an artistic career doesn't develop, be sure to utilize your nurturing qualities in caring for others. Because you are so emotional, you empathize with others' needs. Pursuing a profession in psychiatry, nursing, or teaching would work well for you.

In money matters, you're lucky during the early part of your life, but less so as the years pass. After forty, you will again enjoy financial success. Remember, opening the palm of your hand makes it more likely that another will place something in it, including his or her hand.

✶ ✶ ✶

APRIL 7   ARIES • The lamb of god
March 20 at 5:00 P.M. to April 20 at 4:00 A.M. • NUMEROLOGY 7

Possessions and Desires . . .

Gem: Diamond—This stone is thought to encourage harmony in relationships and gives strength to the troubled.

Flower: Hop—You tend to loathe injustice.

Astral Color, Color Need, Apparel Color: Your Astral Color is White, which gives you clarity. Red in your environment gives you energy and stamina. In your wardrobe, Raspberry gives you power and stimulation.

Fragrance: Use the subtlest hints of lemon or other citrus fruits to bring freshness into your surroundings. These scents will give you the energy to make things happen in your life.

Tree: Sycamore—Yours is the ability to love, communicate honestly with others, and have lasting relationships.

Instrument: Harp

Composers: Gluck, Brahms

Bird: Warbling Parakeet—the most beautiful of all birds, known as the love bird. It does seem to have the powers of imitation.

Symbol: Heart—You are enthusiastic, empathetic, and full of generosity and love.

Harmonious Health and Nutrition . . .

Health Scent: Jasmine—This scent may make you more easygoing when you are stressed.

Favorable Foods: Asparagus, apricots, rye crisps, maple sugar, pressed cheese

What's Lucky . . .

Lucky Numbers: 1, 7, 9

Best Months: June and July

Best Day of the Week: Tuesday

Best Month Days: 6, 15, 24

Lucky Charm: An old key.

Harmonious Signs for Relationships and Partnerships: Sagittarius and Leo

Spiritual Guides . . .

Star: Al Thurauya—Woe to the enemies of those with this star!

Angel: Malchidiel—This is the angel of new beginnings and innovative ideas.

Guardian Angel: Raphael—This angel attends to all of your needs when you are looking for guidance.

Spiritual Stone: Beryl—This stone is good for meditation and concentration.

✷ JUDITH'S INSIGHT ✷

You are cautious by nature; sometimes your prudence prevents you from doing the things you really want. You are a shining star—the only one that doesn't know the brightness of your shining is you. Others see you in a completely different light from how you see yourself. Unfortunately, your keen intuition benefits others more than yourself. Your heart is made of gold, but be careful where you spend it. You like to explore the unknown, and would make a fine detective. Develop your deep love for music and your hidden love for the theatre. Passion couples well with your original ideas. You are likely to be considered a crank or eccentric by those who don't understand you. You will always have an intense desire for travel away from your birthplace and experience a restlessness because of it. You are always looking to change your surroundings.

You will not be happy with a commonplace job. I wouldn't be surprised to find you racing cars, or inventing new parts for them. More inventive and creative than you give yourself credit for, you will feel more satisfied once you recognize your own skills. Your home is where your heart will be, and a place you create for yourself. You're inclined to live in the land of dreams and illusions regarding the opposite sex, so expect some disappointments. Fear not, though, for you will meet your soul mate and feel at last you have found someone who really understands you, even if you don't yet fully understand yourself.

★ ★ ★

APRIL 8   ARIES • The lamb of god
March 20 at 5:00 P.M. to April 20 at 4:00 A.M.   •   NUMEROLOGY 8

Possessions and Desires . . .

Gem: Diamond—This stone is thought to encourage harmony in relationships and gives strength to the troubled.

Flower: Almond Tree—You always have hope in your heart that things will get better.

Astral Color, Color Need, Apparel Color: Your Astral Color is Pink, which reflects your compassion. Red in your environment gives you energy and stamina. In your wardrobe, Gray brings out the best in your looks.

Fragrance: Use the subtlest hints of lemon or other citrus fruits to bring freshness into your surroundings. These scents will give you the energy to make things happen in your life.

Tree: Pine—Your relationships tend to be balanced, both emotionally and mentally.

Instrument: Cello

Composer: Mozart

Bird: Bobolink—This charming singer is equally good as a soloist or a member of an orchestra. It is a very romantic bird, most useful as an insect destroyer, and elegant, with beautiful feathers, and always pleasant to have around.

Symbol: Wings—You are the source of balance in your world—this will bring you contentment.

Harmonious Health and Nutrition . . .

Health Scent: Almond—This scent may revitalize you and open you to greater possibilities.

Favorable Foods: Endive, strawberries, caraway seeds, molasses, buttermilk

What's Lucky . . .

Lucky Numbers: 1, 8, 9

Best Months: June and July

Best Day of the Week: Tuesday

Best Month Days: 8, 17, 26

Lucky Charm: Red ribbon in your wallet or doorway

Harmonious Signs for Relationships and Partnerships: Sagittarius and Leo

Spiritual Guides . . .

Star: Al Sheratan—Those with this star hide their pain from those who could help them.

Angel: Malchidiel—This is the angel of new beginnings and innovative ideas.

Guardian Angel: Seraphim—An angel that brings love, light, and passion.

Spiritual Stone: Beryl—This stone is good for meditation and concentration

✶ JUDITH'S INSIGHT ✶

Suspicious, inquisitive, and skeptical by nature, you are extremely reserved and distrustful of people, but you become devoted to those who do pass your test. You are very patient and kind, and ultraconsiderate, in a relationship—once you get there. Although you will do anything for your family, there are times when family overwhelms you. You would make a good government official, detective or investigator. Your tenacity can persevere to the end. You are dedicated and productive no matter what job you take on: attorney, judge, critic, journalist, supervisor, or machinist. You will get the job done and do it well. Remarkable ideas and plans for starting new industries or developing business on any scale, large or small, start with you. They say money does not make the man or woman, but you are the man or woman that will make the money.

Your greatest difficulty will be in finding others who see eye to eye with you. With your perseverance, personal power, and determination, you are likely to carry anything through to the end. Eventually you will enjoy the financial fruit of your labor. Your life, however, brims with contradictions. You want to make your mark and will be confronted with much opposition in carrying out your plans. You can overcome the hurdles, easily or not, and achieve your goals. When it comes to hobby or work, look for things that enlarge your life. Developing or marketing perfumes or cultivating or selling flowers, plants, or trees will bring you satisfaction. If you are unable to work in these or other such fields, your creativity will be expanded through your fondness for music and the decorative arts.

✶ ✶ ✶

APRIL 9

ARIES • The lamb of god

March 20 at 5:00 P.M. to April 20 at 4:00 A.M. • NUMEROLOGY 9

Possessions and Desires . . .

Gem: Amethyst—This stone is said to give calmness and peace.

Flower: Balsam—You are a very sympathetic person.

Astral Color, Color Need, Apparel Color: Your Astral Color is White, which gives you clarity. Red in your environment gives you energy and stamina. In your wardrobe, Copper gives you confidence and a sharp appearance.

Fragrance: Use the subtlest hints of lemon or other citrus fruits to bring freshness into your surroundings. These scents will give you the energy to make things happen in your life.

Tree: Holly—Beware that you are not carried away by your passionate nature. The only way to grow is to be open to new experiences.

Instruments: Violin, tympanum

Composer: Gluck

Bird: Warbling Parakeet—the most beautiful of all birds, known as the love bird. It does seem to have the powers of imitation.

Symbol: Anchor—This tranquil symbol signifies stability and strength, and stands for strong commitments in relationships.

Harmonious Health and Nutrition . . .

Health Scent: Lavender—This scent might lead others to trust you and make you patient.

Favorable Foods: Dried beans, watermelon, rye crisps, raw sugar, pressed cheese

What's Lucky . . .

Lucky Numbers: 1, 9, 10

Best Months: June and July

Best Day of the Week: Tuesday

Best Month Days: 9, 18, 27

Lucky Charms: A U.S. coin or a bill of any amount from the year you were born.

Harmonious Signs for Relationships and Partnerships: Sagittarius and Leo

Spiritual Guides . . .

Star: Al Botein—Those with this star often feel that they are under lots of pressure.

Angel: Malchidiel—This is the angel of new beginnings and innovative ideas.

Guardian Angel: Gabriel—"God is my strength."

Spiritual Stone: Beryl—This stone is good for meditation and concentration.

✶ JUDITH'S INSIGHT ✶

You're extremely independent in thought and action, and have a strong dislike for restrictions and limitations of any kind. You are inclined to candidly express your opinions, sometimes too frankly, while disregarding the feelings of others. You are sometimes combative, and you rush into quarrels or arguments simply because of your impulsive nature. You love running risks and are fearless in the face of danger. At the same time, you can be very nurturing, and are a good volunteer, caretaker, or listener, anxious to lend a helping hand. Be careful of minor accidents: you may slip and fall on ice, crash the car, or trip down the stairs. Don't worry, there won't be any permanent damage, but you are a lawyer's dream. You will have more than your share of love affairs, even if no one in your family knows about them. You are flirtatious by nature, but in a naive way. You are blessed with endless vitality and recover quickly from illness.

You are likely to be more fortunate in money matters after midlife, but you will still be comfortable in earlier years. You'll have to work hard for your money. Your friends admire you. Remember to look for a career that allows independence and creativity, like a computer specialist or graphic artist. Do not be surprised if you find yourself searching for a new career after a few years, even if it is within the same company. You desire authority and would like that at work. Somewhere along the way, your creativity has to come in to play.

✶ ✶ ✶

APRIL 10 ARIES • The lamb of god

March 20 at 5:00 P.M. to April 20 at 4:00 A.M. • NUMEROLOGY 1

Possessions and Desires . . .

Gem: Beryl—This gem could be good for meditation and concentration.

Flower: Barberry—You can have very black moods sometimes.

Astral Color, Color Need, Apparel Color: Your Astral Color is Pink, which emanates compassion. Red in your environment gives you energy and stamina. In your wardrobe, Green is your power color for overcoming obstacles.

Fragrance: Use the subtlest hints of lemon or other citrus fruits to bring freshness into your surroundings. These scents will give you the energy to make things happen in your life.

Tree: Walnut—You are unusually helpful and always looking for new beginnings.

Instruments: Oboe, flute, clarinet, piano, French horn, organ, and piccolo

Composer: Böhm

Bird: Hummingbird—This bird is delicate and graceful. It can remain still for hours, then dart off and be as busy as a bee.

Symbol: Crown—the universal sign of dignity.

Harmonious Health and Nutrition . . .

Health Scent: Strawberry—soothing by nature, the strawberry promotes self-esteem and encourages love.

Favorable Foods: Endive, strawberries, caraway seeds, molasses, buttermilk

What's Lucky . . .

Lucky Numbers: 10, 19, 20
Best Months: June and July
Best Day of the Week: Tuesday
Best Month Days: 1, 10, 19, 28
Lucky Charm: A new penny in your shoe.
Harmonious Signs for Relationships and Partnerships: Sagittarius and Leo

Spiritual Guides . . .

Star: Al Botein—Those with this star often feel that they are under lots of pressure.

Angel: Malchidiel—This is the angel of new beginnings and innovative ideas.

Guardian Angel: Malachi—"Messenger of Jehovah."

Spiritual Stone: Beryl—This stone is good for meditation and concentration.

✳ JUDITH'S INSIGHT ✳

Energetic and courageous, for you honesty is not just the best policy . . . it's the *only* one. Life must be full of problem-solving and challenges to keep you happy. You are well spoken, especially when talking of something about which you care deeply. Sometimes you let difficulties cloud your sparkling zest for life. Don't allow others to sabotage your energy.

Your fiery and forceful nature may sometimes complicate relationships, but because of your smooth, cunning way, you win more hearts than you lose. If you actually caught the person who is your romantic ideal, you'd more than likely be miserable, for what you want and what you need are two different things. Family and friends mean everything to you even though you rarely express this aloud.

Your drive and determination are powerful propellers. The only time "vice" is mentioned in connection with you is when it's paired with "president." Careers in law, finance, or sales are best for you. Working or just dabbling in real estate could bring big rewards. A property inheritance may turn up in your lifetime.

Fun to be with, you have a terrific sense of humor, except when the joke's on you. Your gift for mixing things up makes your parties amusing and diverse. Don't be surprised if you find yourself in the public eye. You make a loyal friend as long as you receive loyalty in return. Seemingly reckless, make sure those around you realize you know exactly what you're doing.

✳ ✳ ✳

APRIL 11

ARIES • The lamb of god

March 20 at 5:00 P.M. to April 20 at 4:00 A.M. • NUMEROLOGY 2

Possessions and Desires . . .

Gem: Sapphire—This gem may help you find forgiveness from those you've wronged.

Flower: Beech Tree—You will have a life of emotional prosperity.

Astral Color, Color Need, Apparel Color: Your Astral Color is White, which gives you clarity. Red in your environment gives you energy and stamina. In your wardrobe, Maroon gives you confidence.

Fragrance: Use the subtlest hints of lemon or other citrus fruits to bring freshness into your surroundings. These scents will give you the energy to make things happen in your life.

Tree: Maple—You have both great stability and flashes of intuition.

Instruments: Pipe organ, cymbal, drum

Composers: Handel, Johann Sebastian Bach

Bird: Stork—Turkish bird, held in high esteem the world over. This bird is intelligent but may have strange tendencies.

Symbol: Cross—the symbol of self-sacrifice and reconciliation.

Harmonious Health and Nutrition . . .

Health Scent: Apple—You are creative, full of joy, and nearly magical. You bring happiness.

Favorable Foods: Parsley, prunes, caraway seeds, buttermilk

What's Lucky . . .

Lucky Numbers: 1, 2, 9

Best Months: June and July

Best Day of the Week: Tuesday

Best Month Days: 2, 11, 20, 29

Lucky Charms: Two 50-cent pieces. Give someone else one of them.

Harmonious Signs for Relationships and Partnerships: Sagittarius and Leo

Spiritual Guides . . .

Star: Al Sheratan—Those with this star hide their pain from those who could help them

Angel: Malchidiel—This is the angel of new beginnings and innovative ideas.

Guardian Angel: Uriel—This angel brings the light of God's guidance.

Spiritual Stone: Beryl—This stone is good for meditation and concentration.

✷ JUDITH'S INSIGHT ✷

You have original, unconventional ideas with an imagination beyond compare. You are a pleasure to be around, and your genuine enthusiasm even makes work pleasurable for coworkers. You not only accomplish just about everything you attempt, but you often exceed your expectations. You work well in partnerships. You may often change your occupation simply because you tire of things if you are tied down too long at one job. With enough diversity, however, you find it easier to remain in one position longer.

Your restlessness could be detrimental at home. You need someone who understands your desire for spontaneity and constant adventure. Marriage can work if it has unconventional overtones in a conventional life setting.

A wide choice of occupations awaits you—there are few things you cannot accomplish. Your inventive nature draws you to creative jobs, although you possess the ability to maintain and sustain just about any career. You may be particularly attracted to jobs that utilize your mechanical aptitude, from fixing computers to repairing airplane engines. You'd also be a dedicated teacher or police officer. You are exceptionally self-reliant and decisive and seek authority over others, even when there is no authority to be had. Watch your sarcasm and criticism. Your forcefulness will make you friends or stir up enemies.

You stick like glue to a friend who is good to you. Through thick and thin, you will always be there to offer support. You know how to keep a promise. Fond of fun and frolic, you show devotion to those devoted to you, and you go to great lengths to ensure their good time.

★ ★ ★

APRIL 12

ARIES • The lamb of god

March 20 at 5:00 P.M. to April 20 at 4:00 A.M. • NUMEROLOGY 3

Possessions and Desires . . .

Gem: Ruby—This stone may lead you to energy, friendship, and happiness.

Flower: Bindweed—You are usually too humble.

Astral Color, Color Need, Apparel Color: Your Astral Color is Pink, which reflects your compassion. Red in your environment gives you energy and stamina. In your wardrobe, Copper gives you confidence and a sharp appearance.

Fragrance: Use the subtlest hints of lemon or other citrus fruits to bring freshness into your surroundings. These scents will give you the energy to make things happen in your life.

Tree: Elm—You have willpower, strength, and the ability to stand alone.

Instrument: Trombone

Composers: Verdi, Mendelssohn, Schumann

Bird: Swan—Regarded as royal and sacred, this bird has the protective nature of a mother and can become a furious fighter in the defense of its young.

Symbol: Wreath—You have been crowned with a special personality. You are strong but extremely compassionate.

Harmonious Health and Nutrition . . .

Health Scent: Rose—This scent will lead you to passionate thoughts and make you feel warm inside.

Favorable Foods: Asparagus, strawberries, raw sugar, cottage cheese

What's Lucky . . .

Lucky Numbers: 1, 3, 6, 9

Best Months: June and July

Best Day of the Week: Tuesday

Best Month Days: 3, 12, 21, 30

Lucky Charm: A pen that someone else has already used.

Harmonious Signs for Relationships and Partnerships: Sagittarius and Leo

Spiritual Guides . . .

Star: Al Botein—Those with this star often feel that they are under lots of pressure.

Angel: Malchidiel—This is the angel of new beginnings and innovative ideas.

Guardian Angel: Johiel—This angel is a protector of all those with a humble heart.

Spiritual Stone: Beryl—This stone is good for meditation and concentration.

✷ JUDITH'S INSIGHT ✷

You are viewed as leading an enchanted life, and for the most part, you do. You're a good person and a caring friend, and are much more independent than you think. Your ambition takes you to great heights, and you appreciate the prestige and the company of high-achieving friends. You have a more philosophical mind and sympathetic nature than most get to see. Part of you is always hidden behind a door—very few get to see what you are all about. You're protective by nature and fearful of hurting yourself. Somewhere along the way, someone hurt you and never apologized. It may seem to take forever, but love does prevail. Be sure you don't sacrifice yourself for your mate. Happiness could be yours if your courage is as strong as your honor.

Your executive skills should bring you to the top, but unfortunately this does not mean overnight. Give it time. Don't be alarmed should you switch careers in midlife and delve into something you never dreamed possible. Your talents are varied and many. You would make a great psychologist, stockbroker, lawyer, or master of ceremonies. Lose the fear of committing to your own business now, and later in life you'll see that's where you should be. Prepare yourself for an entirely independent situation. You are endowed with a strong sense of responsibility and along the way will assume the obligations of others. Just remember to smile—laughter and happiness are truly your best medicine.

✶ ✶ ✶

APRIL 13
ARIES • The lamb of god
March 20 at 5:00 P.M. to April 20 at 4:00 A.M. • NUMEROLOGY 4

Possessions and Desires . . .

Gem: Emerald—Those who carry this stone tend to be lucky in love.

Flower: Cinquefoil—You tend be the advisor to friends and family.

Astral Color, Color Need, Apparel Color: Your Astral Color is White, which gives you clarity. Red in your environment gives you energy and stamina. In your wardrobe, Raspberry gives you power and stimulation.

Fragrance: Use the subtlest hints of lemon or other citrus fruits to bring freshness into your surroundings. These scents will give you the energy to make things happen in your life.

Tree: Cherry—You will find yourself faced with constant new emotional awakenings.

Instruments: Bass, clarinet

Composers: Haydn, Wagner

Bird: Skylark—This handsome bird is beautiful when it sings. It always whistles as it works.

Symbol: Star—You are full of inner brightness and will stand out in any crowd. You will be seen as special.

Harmonious Health and Nutrition . . .

Health Scent: Vanilla—This scent will fill you with a feeling of cleanliness and stability.

Favorable Foods: Lentils, apples, maple sugar, eggs

What's Lucky . . .

Lucky Numbers: 1, 4, 8, 9

Best Months: June and July

Best Day of the Week: Tuesday

Best Month Days: 4, 13, 22, 31

Lucky Charm: A piece of material cut from something in your home.

Harmonious Signs for Relationships and Partnerships: Sagittarius and Leo

Spiritual Guides . . .

Star: Al Sheratan—Those with this star hide their pain from those who could help them

Angel: Malchidiel—This is the angel of new beginnings and innovative ideas.

Guardian Angel: Uriel—This angel brings the light of God's guidance.

Spiritual Stone: Beryl—This stone is good for meditation and concentration.

✴ JUDITH'S INSIGHT ✴

Anticipate the unexpected and go with the flow in making changes in your life, career, home, and family. Feelings of restlessness will resonate through your life. A great reader with a deep love for literature, you possess intense mental energy and activity. You want to be successful and your trump card may be in writing or graphic arts. Perhaps you'll run your own company. You work easily with others but are wary of tense atmospheres. Don't let these moments rattle you. You may become a schoolteacher or work with children in another capacity. You know how to interact with young people, and you reap the rewards as they respond to you. When you look for a job, disregard monotonous positions. You could be an attorney, financier, or salesperson. You simply thrive on change and spontaneity. You are idealistic, with strong personal ethics; when it comes to devotion to a mate or a friend, there is none better than you. While you generate much power and energy, take care to prevent others from draining you. Don't expend more than you can give. Many times you stick to an undertaking long after you should. You love your home and environment but are not averse to relocating if necessary. No matter where you build your nest, it will be a true home.

★ ★ ★

APRIL 14 ARIES • The lamb of god

March 20 at 5:00 P.M. to April 20 at 4:00 A.M. • NUMEROLOGY 5

Possessions and Desires . . .

Gem: Diamond—This stone is thought to encourage harmony in relationships and gives strength to the troubled.

Flower: Birch—Your meekness disguises a vibrant fantasy life.

Astral Color, Color Need, Apparel Color: Your Astral Color is Pink, which emanates confidence. Red in your environment gives you energy and stamina. In your wardrobe, Gray brings out the best in your looks.

Fragrance: Use the subtlest hints of lemon or other citrus fruits to bring freshness into your surroundings. These scents will give you the energy to make things happen in your life.

Tree: Apple—You are creative, full of joy, and nearly magical. You bring happiness.

Instruments: Viola, trumpet

Composer: Liszt

Bird: Flamingo—this beautiful, gregarious bird is always careful of its enemy. It is also a caretaker of the young who tries to keep everyone happy.

Symbol: Triangle—You have the right combination of abilities.

Harmonious Health and Nutrition . . .

Health Scent: Peach—This scent may balance your good qualities so that they equal your charm.

Favorable Foods: Peas, apricots, caraway seeds, chocolate, pressed cheese

What's Lucky . . .

Lucky Numbers: 1, 5, 9, 10
Best Months: June and July
Best Day of the Week: Tuesday
Best Month Days: 4, 5, 23
Lucky Charms: A rabbit's foot or a white candle

Harmonious Signs for Relationships and Partnerships: Sagittarius and Leo

Spiritual Guides . . .

Star: Al Thurauya—Woe to the enemies of those with this star!

Angel: Malchidiel—This is the angel of new beginnings and innovative ideas.

Guardian Angel: Plavwell—gives power and strength to one's presence.

Spiritual Stone: Beryl—This stone is good for meditation and concentration.

✳ JUDITH'S INSIGHT ✳

You're admired by friends and family, and you welcome their company. You can make anything happen. The only person to get in your way is you. Because you're clever, intelligent, and versatile, accomplishments come easily to you. You never shun hard work. Your contagious smile endears you to others. Quick wit and good reasoning enable you to adapt to anything. Your generosity of pocket and self is far better received than your generosity with advice. You will be most comfortable with the way you handle gifts, but do withhold the advice unless you're specifically asked for it. You're a good listener. You're one of the lucky ones, who seem to find a mate that you want to stick to and wants to stick to you. To know you is to love you so keep this in mind.

Authoritative careers beckon. You feel drawn to government careers. With your intense mind, however, big business is not far behind. You have many dreams and will attempt to follow them all. Remember to allow time for things to happen. Heavy responsibilities will burden you at an early age, and you take them seriously. Resolved responsibilities will be repeatedly replaced with new ones. You would make a great detective with your inherent curiosity and investigative qualities. You are an honorable friend and devoted parent. Loyalty is your best quality.

✳ ✳ ✳

APRIL 15 ARIES • The lamb of god
March 20 at 5:00 P.M. to April 20 at 4:00 A.M. • NUMEROLOGY 6

Possessions and Desires . . .

Gem: Topaz—This is an excellent gift to be exchanged between very loyal friends.

Flower: China Aster—You like a lot of variety in your life.

Astral Color, Color Need, Apparel Color: Your Astral Color is Pink, which reflects your compassion. Red in your environment gives you energy and stamina. In your wardrobe, Maroon gives you confidence.

Fragrance: Use the subtlest hints of lemon or other citrus fruits to bring freshness into your surroundings. These scents will give you the energy to make things happen in your life.

Tree: Palm—You tend to be very healthy and creative.

Instruments: Tambourine, lyre

Composer: Schubert

Bird: Lark—known for the beauty of its song, which is sometimes very unusual. It is also credited with extraordinary intelligence.

Symbol: Crescent—You are more likely to be influenced by the phases of the moon. Your easy-going manner leads you to peaceful situations.

Harmonious Health and Nutrition . . .

Health Scent: Orange Blossom—This scent may balance your body, mind, and soul.

Favorable Foods: Spinach, prunes, rye crisps, molasses, buttermilk

What's Lucky . . .

Lucky Numbers: 1, 6, 9, 18
Best Months: June and July
Best Day of the Week: Tuesday
Best Month Days: 6, 15, 24
Lucky Charms: A religious token or card from any religion.

Harmonious Signs for Relationships and Partnerships: Sagittarius and Leo

Spiritual Guides . . .

Star: Al Botein—Those with this star often feel that they are under lots of pressure.

Angel: Malchidiel—This is the angel of new beginnings and innovative ideas.

Guardian Angel: Michael—"Who is like God,"

Spiritual Stone: Beryl—This stone is good for meditation and concentration.

✶ JUDITH'S INSIGHT ✶

A challenge here, a challenge there, you seek challenge everywhere. Develop that power of yours to resolve conflict, and you will rise to the top. Your overabundance of energy, however, must be contained and redirected. Freedom of mind, body, and soul is important to you. Your sense of freedom permeates your life, and you are denied little. Powerful within the family and much respected by friends, you love a homey atmosphere and need a settled haven. But you can stir the pot if things don't go your way. On occasion, you may be overbearing, but your good intentions prevail when a matter concerns your loved ones. These traits may both hinder and help you and your loved ones. Your task is recognizing what works for you and when. Have patience with yourself when it comes to finding a mate. It will take time.

Activity careers offer the best for you. Always include physical work for yourself, even if you are the boss. You could make a successful salesperson, as well as find satisfaction in police work or as an artist or medical assistant. You have a great scientific ability, whether you use it at work or play. You are diligent and principled and finish what you attempt. You take your responsibilities very seriously. You enjoy a battle of wits.

★ ★ ★

APRIL 16   ARIES • The lamb of god

March 20 at 5:00 P.M. to April 20 at 4:00 A.M. • NUMEROLOGY 7

Possessions and Desires . . .

Gem: Amethyst—This stone is said to give calmness and peace.
Flower: Crocus—You may spend too much time stewing over those who have innocently harmed you.
Astral Color, Color Need, Apparel Color: Your Astral Color is White, giving you clarity. Red in your environment gives you energy and stamina. In your wardrobe, Copper gives you confidence and a sharp appearance.
Fragrance: Use the subtlest hints of lemon or other citrus fruits to bring freshness into your surroundings. These scents will give you the energy to make things happen in your life.
Tree: Sycamore—Yours is the ability to love, communicate honestly with others, and have lasting relationships.
Instrument: Harp
Composers: Gluck, Brahms
Bird: Skylark—This handsome bird is beautiful when it sings. It always whistles as it works.
Symbol: Heart—You are enthusiastic, empathetic, and full of generosity and love.

Harmonious Health and Nutrition . . .

Health Scent: Jasmine—This scent may make you more easygoing when you are stressed.
Favorable Foods: Spinach, watermelon, caraway seeds, maple sugar, cottage cheese

What's Lucky . . .

Lucky Numbers: 1, 7, 9, 21
Best Months: June and July
Best Day of the Week: Tuesday
Best Month Days: 6, 15, 24
Lucky Charm: An old key.

Harmonious Signs for Relationships and Partnerships: Sagittarius and Leo

Spiritual Guides . . .

Star: Al Sheratan—Those with this star hide their pain from those who could help them.
Angel: Malchidiel—This is the angel of new beginnings and innovative ideas.
Guardian Angel: Raphael—This angel attends to all of your needs when you are looking for guidance.
Spiritual Stone: Beryl—This stone is good for meditation and concentration.

✴ JUDITH'S INSIGHT ✴

You have a great spiritual side, but you may need more maturity to recognize it. You let caution rule your life. Out of fear and sensitivity, you allow yourself more disappointments than you should. You are naturally intelligent, but you tend to hide this from others and even yourself.

You have to put family in its place at times. Family cohesion will come in time, as does balance. Friends are occasionally almost too important to you, and you place far too much stock in what others say. All others are not smarter than you. Harmony in relationships is surfacing—allow it to be seen. When you want to, you can be a delightful, insightful soul. Let yourself be inspired by positive thoughts, and don't hide behind a cranky, negative exterior. If you want more out of life, go after it. The one you lie to most is yourself. Set yourself free! Decide you want happiness and you will find it.

In your career you will need time to reach the top. You could be a painter, sculptor, or you could also be a hospital administrator, law officer, or executive secretary. You're held back by thinking you don't want to go to the top. Believe it or not, that's where you belong. When you get there, you realize this.

✴ ✴ ✴

APRIL 17 ARIES • The lamb of god
March 20 at 5:00 P.M. to April 20 at 4:00 A.M. • NUMEROLOGY 8

Possessions and Desires . . .

Gem: Amethyst—This stone is said to give calmness and peace.

Flower: Daisy—You are probably very naïve.

Astral Color, Color Need, Apparel Color: Your Astral Color is Pink, which reflects your compassion. Red in your environment gives you energy and stamina. In your wardrobe, Raspberry gives you power and stimulation.

Fragrance: Use the subtlest hints of lemon or other citrus fruits to bring freshness into your surroundings. These scents will give you the energy to make things happen in your life.

Tree: Pine—Your relationships tend to be balanced, both emotionally and mentally.

Instrument: Cello

Composer: Mozart

Bird: Skylark—This handsome bird is beautiful when it sings. It always whistles as it works.

Symbol: Wings—You are the source of balance in your world—this will bring you contentment.

Harmonious Health and Nutrition . . .

Health Scent: Almond—This scent may revitalize you and open you to greater possibilities.

Favorable Foods: Parsley, strawberries, chocolate, buttermilk

What's Lucky . . .

Lucky Numbers: 1, 8, 9, 24
Best Months: June and July
Best Day of the Week: Tuesday
Best Month Days: 8, 17, 26
Lucky Charm: Red ribbon in your wallet or doorway.

Harmonious Signs for Relationships and Partnerships: Sagittarius and Leo

Spiritual Guides . . .

Star: Al Sheratan—Those with this star hide their pain from those who could help them.

Angel: Malchidiel—This is the angel of new beginnings and innovative ideas.

Guardian angel: Seraphim—An Angel that brings love, light, and passion.

Spiritual Stone: Beryl—This stone is good for meditation and concentration.

✶ JUDITH'S INSIGHT ✶

You're very sweet, very kind—almost to a fault. You give until there is no more to give. If only others could recognize your needs. You want everyone to be happy, because you deeply feel if those around you are happy, you'll be happy, too. Responsibility rests on your shoulders; sometimes you must learn to knock it off. Family can be your greatest love and your greatest detractor. Children often get the best of you in there younger years, but later they will give their best to you.

Be more selective in relationships because you're inclined to pick critical, controlling lovers. Choose the not-so-needy, and you'll get more out of the relationship. Don't be misled by your tendency to want to settle down. What you are doing is settling to avoid having to make decisions. Since you're the one that mends everybody's heart, it is hard for you to break anyone's heart.

You could be a lawyer but one with a nurturing and caring personality. You will probably find yourself doing a lot of pro bono work. You'll be a terrific parent. You will succeed.

✶ ✶ ✶

APRIL 18   ARIES • The lamb of god

March 20 at 5:00 P.M. to April 20 at 4:00 A.M. • NUMEROLOGY 9

Possessions and Desires . . .

Gem: Ruby—This stone may lead you to energy, friendship, and happiness.

Flower: Wild Grape—You tend to be charitable to those you feel deserve your help.

Astral Color, Color Need, Apparel Color: Your Astral Color is White, which gives you clarity. Red in your environment gives you energy and stamina. In your wardrobe, Gray brings out the best in your looks.

Fragrance: Use the subtlest hints of lemon or other citrus fruits to bring freshness into your surroundings. These scents will give you the energy to make things happen in your life.

Tree: Holly—Beware that you are not carried away by your passionate nature. The only way to grow is to be open to new experiences.

Instruments: Violin, tympanum

Composer: Gluck

Bird: Mockingbird—the most proficient minstrel in the world's orchestra; graceful and enthusiastic.

Symbol: Anchor—This tranquil symbol signifies stability and strength, and stands for strong commitments in relationships.

Harmonious Health and Nutrition . . .

Health Scent: Lavender—This scent might lead others to trust you and make you patient.

Favorable Foods: Mustard greens, apples, caraway seeds, molasses, eggs

What's Lucky . . .

Lucky Numbers: 1, 9, 18, 27
Best Months: June and July
Best Day of the Week: Tuesday
Best Month Days: 9, 18, 27
Lucky Charms: A U.S. coin or bill of any amount from the year you were born.

Harmonious Signs for Relationships and Partnerships: Sagittarius and Leo

Spiritual Guides . . .

Star: Al Botein—Those with this star often feel that they are under lots of pressure.

Angel: Malchidiel—This is the angel of new beginnings and innovative ideas.

Guardian Angel: Gabriel—"God is my strength."

Spiritual Stone: Beryl—This stone is good for meditation and concentration.

✶ JUDITH'S INSIGHT ✶

Because you're determined and focused, you should get anywhere you want to go. Though you will encounter obstacles, they need not deter you, and in time you will arrive at the destination you desire. It's entirely up to you. Some may think you pushy and anxious at times, but you do get the job done. You accomplish what you set out to do. Since you can be quick-tempered, you sometimes encumber your relationships. In time you will find a tolerant mate who doesn't take you so seriously and helps you to lighten up. You enjoy taking risks, but be forewarned—you could head right into the danger zone if you are not careful. You can use this risk taking to your advantage by choosing a career in law enforcement. Should you not be so inclined, your slot will be in a government institution, perhaps the post office, or a medical office or large company.

You must learn to balance your personality as well as your checkbook. You have the ability to make money, and you will do so, but you must curb your fondness for extravagant things and the desire to spend like mad. You are drawn to the extraordinary or unconventional and may find that you are only satisfied if you are driving an exotic sports car. You see life as a game—just remember, in games you can't always win; with every win there is a loss.

APRIL 19

ARIES • The lamb of god

March 20 at 5:00 P.M. to April 20 at 4:00 A.M. • NUMEROLOGY 1

Possessions and Desires . . .

Gem: Turquoise—This stone may help you find material wealth.

Flower: Honey Flower—Your life tends to be sweet and sincere.

Astral Color, Color Need, Apparel Color: Your Astral Color is White, which gives you clarity. Red in your environment gives you energy and stamina. In your wardrobe, Gray brings out the best in your looks.

Fragrance: Use the subtlest hints of lemon or other citrus fruits to bring freshness into your surroundings. These scents will give you the energy to make things happen in your life.

Tree: Walnut—You are unusually helpful and always looking for new beginnings

Instruments: Oboe, flute, clarinet, piano, French horn, organ, piccolo

Composer: Böhm

Bird: Hummingbird—This bird is delicate and graceful. It can remain still for hours, then dart off and be as busy as a bee.

Symbol: Crown—the universal sign of dignity.

Harmonious Health and Nutrition . . .

Health Scent: Strawberry—soothing by nature, the strawberry promotes self-esteem and encourages love.

Favorable Foods: Beans, prunes, rye crisps, maple sugar, cottage cheese

What's Lucky . . .

Lucky Numbers: 1, 9, 20
Best Months: June and July
Best Day of the Week: Tuesday
Best Month Days: 1, 10, 19, 28

Lucky Charm: A new penny in your shoe.
Harmonious Signs for Relationships and Partnerships: Sagittarius and Leo

Spiritual Guides . . .

Star: Al Thurauya—Woe to the enemies of those with this star!

Angel: Malchidiel—This is the angel of new beginnings and innovative ideas.

Guardian Angel: Malachi—"Messenger of Jehovah."

Spiritual Stone: Beryl—This stone is good for meditation and concentration.

✷ JUDITH'S INSIGHT ✷

Generosity is only one of your fine traits. You are decidedly ambitious and will surpass those around you. You are likely to be the most successful and prominent member of your immediate family, eclipsing all your relations as well. Keep this in mind: you find more success with partners than without. This is where you need to develop patience. You're very creative. Your fearlessness and determination prompt success in whatever you decide to do. Lean toward careers that offer steady advancement. Take a job in the mail room at a Fortune 500 company; you will likely advance near the top even if it takes awhile. You would do well running a non-profit organization. You may end up in the public eye as a politician or actor.

You need romance as much as love. You need to be with a sentimental person who will not only adore you, but allow you freedom to have an unconventional home atmosphere. Children will definitely create and foster disputes in your life, but later on, children and family bring you harmony. Those around you require tolerance. As you learn to better communicate, you will be able to have and hold an enduring love.

✷ ✷ ✷

APRIL 20   ARIES • The lamb of god

March 20 at 5:00 P.M. to April 20 at 4:00 A.M. • NUMEROLOGY 2

Possessions and Desires . . .

Gem: Sapphire—This gem may help you find forgiveness from those you've wronged.
Flower: Withered Rose—Your love tends to last forever.
Astral Color, Color Need, Apparel Color: Your Astral Color is Pink, which reflects your compassion. Red in your environment gives you energy and stamina. In your wardrobe, Green is your power color for overcoming obstacles.
Fragrance: Use the subtlest hints of lemon or other citrus fruits to bring freshness into your surroundings. These scents will give you the energy to make things happen in your life.
Tree: Maple—You have both great stability and flashes of intuition.
Instruments: Pipe organ, cymbal, drum
Composers: Handel, Johann Sebastian Bach
Bird: Stork—Turkish bird, held in high esteem the world over. This bird is intelligent but may have strange tendencies.
Symbol: Cross—the symbol of self-sacrifice and reconciliation.

Harmonious Health and Nutrition . . .

Health Scent: Apple—You are creative, full of joy, and nearly magical. You bring happiness.
Favorable Foods: Dill, gooseberries, raw sugar, pressed cheese

What's Lucky . . .

Lucky Numbers: 1, 2, 4, 9
Best Months: June and July
Best Day of the Week: Tuesday
Best Month Days: 2, 11, 20, 29
Lucky Charms: Two 50-cent pieces. Give someone else one of them.

Harmonious Signs for Relationships and Partnerships: Sagittarius and Leo

Spiritual Guides . . .

Star: Al Botein—Those with this star often feel that they are under lots of pressure.
Angel: Malchidiel—This is the angel of new beginnings and innovative ideas.
Guardian Angel: Uriel—This angel brings the light of God's guidance.
Spiritual Stone: Beryl—This stone is good for meditation and concentration.

✶ JUDITH'S INSIGHT ✶

Tenacity is one of your most evident traits. You are also independent, ambitious, and determined. Be on guard, as your loved ones and others around you may feel neglected at times. Occupational changes may occur frequently, unless the atmosphere around you offers constant change. Although your desire for independence is strong, your desire to be with someone is even stronger. You like to be waited on hand and foot and on occasion are inclined to put your foot in your mouth. Relationships will work if you learn to better manage your emotions. Recognize that others may feel you don't want to let them in. All things considered, you have to be alert to recognize red flags' matters of love. Definitely admired by your friends and family and well-respected in the community, you will remember many fond flirtations along the way.

You will work hard for that high standing in the community, but once you get there, don't sit down. You must work at maintaining that status, for it can be fleeting. You love beautiful things and beautiful people. Working in the beauty or fashion industry would work well for you. You have plenty of talent, but you need a constant challenge.

✶ ✶ ✶

APRIL 21

TAURUS • The winged bull of the zodiac

April 20 at 4:00 A.M. to May 21 at 4:00 A.M. • NUMEROLOGY 3

Possessions and Desires . . .

Gem: Emerald—Those who carry this stone tend to be lucky in love.

Flower: Honeysuckle—You are a person filled with generous and devoted affections.

Astral Color, Color Need, Apparel Color: Your Astral Color is Red, which enhances passion, power, excitement, and strength. Yellow in your environment stimulates and exhilarates you. In your wardrobe, Blue-green enhances your luck and makes you feel secure.

Fragrance: You are devoted to the scent of roses. Choose the buds that have the strongest fragrance to create the special emotions you need.

Tree: Elm—You have willpower, strength, and the ability to stand alone.

Instrument: Trombone

Composers: Verdi, Mendelssohn, Schumann

Bird: Eagle—this bird is quick to use its powers of flight. It can see immeasurable distances in a single glance, and can sometimes appear to be indifferent.

Symbol: Wreath—You have been crowned with a special personality. You are strong but extremely compassionate.

Harmonious Health and Nutrition . . .

Health Scent: Rose—This scent will lead you to passionate thoughts and make you feel warm inside.

Favorable Foods: Kale, peaches, eggs, beef

What's Lucky . . .

Lucky Numbers: 3, 4, 5, 6

Best Months: May and July

Best Day of the Week: Friday

Best Month Days: 3, 12, 21, 30

Lucky Charm: A pen that someone else has already used.

Harmonious Signs for Relationships and Partnerships: Virgo, Capricorn, and sometimes Libra.

Spiritual Guides . . .

Star: Al Heka—Those with this star are driven to succeed.

Angel: Asmodel—This angel governs business and other transactions and aids in negotiations.

Guardian Angel: Johiel—This angel is a protector of all those with a humble heart.

Spiritual Stone: Topaz—This stone may protect the bearer from the effects of allergies.

✳ JUDITH'S INSIGHT ✳

Success awaits you in positions of authority, even if you don't think so now. Ambition gets you where you want to go. You are exceptionally capable, independent, and energized. In many areas, you lead a charmed life. Your mate is enamored with you and thrives on the spontaneity in your relationship. You are the romantic, however. Cultivate your sensibilities and let others touch your heart. You may wander through the school of hard knocks occasionally or even accept a few subliminal hard punches from time to time, but this growth can only help you become a better person.

You are best at delegating rather than undertaking matters yourself. This is true even in emotional situations, especially when it comes to family. If you have children, let them enjoy themselves even if you never had that opportunity as a child. You remain a child at heart but shield it well with your ultraresponsible nature. Strive for balance between being an adult and a child. Learn to take the best from both worlds.

Enjoying your friends is high on your list. Don't be surprised if they have relocated once or twice since you last called them. You are definitely a contradiction in every sense of the word. But that keeps them all guessing—even you.

★ ★ ★

APRIL 22 TAURUS • The winged bull of the zodiac
April 20 at 4:00 A.M. to May 21 at 4:00 A.M. • NUMEROLOGY 4

Possessions and Desires . . .

Gem: Sapphire—This gem may help you find forgiveness from those you've wronged.
Flower: Yellow Jasmine—You are most often graceful and elegant.
Astral Color, Color Need, Apparel Color: Your Astral Color is Red, which enhances passion, power, excitement, and strength. Yellow in your environment stimulates and exhilarates you. In your wardrobe, Cream gives you encouragement and style.
Fragrance: You are devoted to the scent of roses. Choose the buds that have the strongest fragrance to create the special emotions you need.
Tree: Cherry—You will find yourself faced with constant new emotional awakenings.
Instruments: Bass, clarinet
Composers: Haydn and Wagner
Bird: Robin—the most sociable of all birds, with the ability to create quick friendships. It also can easily adapt to any home. When it wants something, it has the tendency to try to snatch it.
Symbol: Star—You are full of inner brightness and will stand out in any crowd. You will be seen as special.

Harmonious Health and Nutrition . . .

Health Scents: Vanilla—This scent will fill you with a feeling of cleanliness and stability.
Favorable Foods: Cabbage, bananas, cheese, salmon

What's Lucky . . .

Lucky Numbers: 4, 6, 8, 12
Best Months: May and July
Best Day of the Week: Friday
Best Month Days: 4, 13, 22, 31
Lucky Charm: A piece of material cut from something in your home.
Harmonious Signs for Relationships and Partnerships: Virgo, Capricorn, and sometimes Libra.

Spiritual Guides . . .

Star: Al Debaran—Those with this star are born leaders.
Angel: Asmodel—This angel governs business and other transactions and aids in negotiations.
Guardian Angel: Uriel—This angel brings the light of God's guidance.
Spiritual Stone: Topaz—This stone may protect the bearer from the effects of allergies.

✴ JUDITH'S INSIGHT ✴

Strong yet sensitive describes you. Although you are fond of the arts and drawn to creative things, you feel awkward with them. You are uncomfortable with your creative nature, but that's because you haven't found your niche. You think you would be most satisfied with a structured career, but undoubtedly you'll have a career that's both creative and structured, such as entertainment lawyer, an actress-turned-agent, a doctor who writes a book, an artist who becomes a museum curator. The balance of structure and creativity will be most rewarding for you.

You do like a nice home, and you fear an empty nest—you want someone in it with you. This can be really up to you, but be sure you choose the proper mate. Friends are true, but you are truer. You have an open-door policy with friends and family alike and should not be dismayed when you become overwrought from having so many demands put on you. Learn when to say yes and no. Aware that you're less than perfect, you take great strides to create the opposite impression. This false superiority incites enemies from time to time, and you know it. You are also smart enough to recognize your enemies and deal appropriately with them.

To be imperfect is to be human. The ability to laugh at yourself will bring much satisfaction. You can be pretentious; it would be better if you could just let it all hang out. With your philosophical nature, it is safe to say that still waters run deep, and your depth runs for miles.

✴ ✴ ✴

APRIL 23   TAURUS • The winged bull of the zodiac
April 20 at 4:00 A.M. to May 21 at 4:00 A.M. • NUMEROLOGY 5

Possessions and Desires . . .

Gem: Amethyst—This stone is said to give calmness and peace.

Flower: Lady's Slipper—What you find beautiful may change as swiftly as the pages of the calendar.

Astral Color, Color Need, Apparel Color: Your Astral Color is Red, which enhances passion, power, excitement, and strength. Yellow in your environment stimulates and exhilarates you. In your wardrobe, Blue-green enhances your luck and makes you feel secure.

Fragrance: You are devoted to the scent of roses. Choose the buds that have the strongest fragrance to create the special emotions you need.

Tree: Apple—You are creative, full of joy, and nearly magical. You bring happiness.

Instruments: Viola, trumpet

Composer: Liszt

Bird: Flamingo—This beautiful, gregarious bird is always careful of its enemy. It is also a caretaker of the young who tries to keep everyone happy.

Symbol: Triangle—You have the right combination of abilities.

Harmonious Health and Nutrition . . .

Health Scent: Peach—This scent may balance your good qualities so that they equal your charm.

Favorable Foods: Romaine lettuce, grapes, buttermilk, beef

What's Lucky . . .

Lucky Numbers: 4, 5, 6, 15
Best Months: May and July
Best Day of the Week: Friday
Best Month Days: 4, 5, 23
Lucky Charms: A rabbit's foot or a white candle.
Harmonious Signs for Relationships and Partnerships: Virgo, Capricorn, and sometimes Libra.

Spiritual Guides . . .

Star: Al Debaran—Those with this star are born leaders.

Angel: Asmodel—This angel governs business and other transactions and aids in negotiations.

Guardian Angel: Plavwell—This angel gives power and strength to one's presence.

Spiritual Stone: Topaz—This stone may protect the bearer from the effects of allergies.

✳ JUDITH'S INSIGHT ✳

You are alluring, charming and witty; you attract the passionate—just like you. What a salesperson you would make with your wonderful gift of gab! It is uncanny how you can prepare a gourmet meal from leftovers and attractively decorate the house from the neighbor's discarded trash. Challenges become you, except when the challenge is in sustaining a relationship. You could use some help here. You see things through your eyes only and rarely accept the views of others. At times your imagination and uninhibited nature can run amok—and it's not necessarily a bad thing. Taking action is not your strong point, but in the midst of a traumatic situation your levelheaded understanding and warmth save the day.

You are a valued worker and an asset and fun to have around. You have a tendency to be somewhat scattered; this might be beneficial if you are pursuing an acting career. Your deep-seated yearning for success is undermined by your lack of dedication to do what it takes to achieve the goal. It may take as many as twenty jobs to find the place where you belong. Don't be discouraged; you will eventually find your vocation and avocation while you have fun along the way. Hospital administrator, public relations, or marketing are jobs that you could do well. You handle problems well, so a troubleshooter in any business would be a good career choice for you. Time and space will shower you with harmony; it's just unclear whether the harmony evolves sooner or later.

★ ★ ★

APRIL 24 TAURUS • The winged bull of the zodiac
April 20 at 4:00 A.M. to May 21 at 4:00 A.M. • NUMEROLOGY 6

Possessions and Desires . . .

Gem: Topaz—This is an excellent gift to be exchanged between very loyal friends.

Flower: Musk Plant—Knowing your weakness can be your greatest strength.

Astral Color, Color Need, Apparel Color: Your Astral Color is Red, which enhances passion, power, excitement, and strength. Yellow in your environment stimulates and exhilarates you. In your wardrobe, Rose gives you balance and harmony.

Fragrance: You are devoted to the scent of roses. Choose the buds that have the strongest fragrance to create the special emotions you need.

Tree: Palm—You tend to be very healthy and creative.

Instruments: Tambourine, lyre

Composer: Schubert

Bird: Falcon—an expert hunter. When well-trained, it can adapt to many tasks and is usually obedient.

Symbol: Crescent—You are more likely to be influenced by the phases of the moon. Your easygoing manner leads you to peaceful situations.

Harmonious Health and Nutrition . . .

Health Scent: Orange Blossom—This scent may balance your body, mind, and soul.

Favorable Foods: Kale, black figs, cheese, oysters

What's Lucky . . .

Lucky Numbers: 4, 6, 12, 24
Best Months: May and July
Best Day of the Week: Friday
Best Month Days: 6, 15, 24
Lucky Charms: A religious token or card from any religion.
Harmonious Signs for Relationships and Partnerships: Virgo, Capricorn, and sometimes Libra.

Spiritual Guides . . .

Star: Al Debaran—Those with this star are born leaders.

Angel: Asmodel—This angel governs business and other transactions and aids in negotiations.

Guardian Angel: Michael—"Who is like God."

Spiritual Stone: Topaz—This stone may protect the bearer from the effects of allergies.

✶ JUDITH'S INSIGHT ✶

You are passionate about all things in your life. Unfortunately, you tend to listen to others too much and take on their burdens. You wear your heart on your sleeve. You're vulnerable in your early years. You are not necessarily persuaded by others, but you're susceptible to their ideas. You're in love with love—the true romantic. Your fantasies make it unlikely that real life can measure up to your dreams. You swim with the tides of love and drift much more toward realism with each passing year. In fact, the scales of love and friendship do balance. In one way or another, family will cause a crisis. Many times you could be overwhelmed with family, but only if you allow it. Keep things in perspective, for you tend to be dependent on family members and blame your disappointments on them. Be aware that your expectations may sometimes be out of reach.

Look for a career in health or beauty or perhaps upholstery or tailoring. You have a knack for fixing things and may even utilize your skills as a physician or therapist. As long as you feel needed and confront different problems on a daily basis, you do very well. Many hidden talents will evolve. Eventually you will fall in love with what you do and derive much satisfaction from it. It shouldn't surprise you to find yourself doing what you always wanted to do, but you might be held back by your own inhibitions. You tend to pull away from your own psychic intuition and spiritual desires. When feeling depressed, do something! Keep yourself busy and stay focused.

✶ ✶ ✶

APRIL 25

TAURUS • The winged bull of the zodiac

April 20 at 4:00 A.M. to May 21 at 4:00 A.M. • NUMEROLOGY 7

Possessions and Desires . . .

Gem: Ruby—This stone may lead you to energy, friendship, and happiness.

Flower: Peach Blossom—You tend to want to own those you love instead of having a relationship of equality.

Astral Color, Color Need, Apparel Color: Your Astral Color is Red, which enhances passion, power, excitement, and strength. Yellow in your environment stimulates and exhilarates you. In your wardrobe, Cream gives you encouragement and style.

Fragrance: You are devoted to the scent of roses. Choose the buds that have the strongest fragrance to create the special emotions you need.

Tree: Sycamore—Yours is the ability to love, communicate honestly with others, and have lasting relationships.

Instrument: Harp

Composers: Gluck, Brahms

Bird: Warbling Parakeet—the most beautiful of all birds, known as the love bird. It does seem to have the powers of imitation.

Symbol: Heart—You are enthusiastic, empathetic, and full of generosity and love.

Harmonious Health and Nutrition . . .

Health Scents: Jasmine—This scent may make you more easygoing when you are stressed.

Favorable Foods: Carrots, lime, eggs, chicken

What's Lucky . . .

Lucky Numbers: 4, 6, 7, 21

Best Months: May and July

Best Day of the Week: Friday

Best Month Days: 6, 15, 24

Lucky Charm: An old key.

Harmonious Signs for Relationships and Partnerships: Virgo, Capricorn, and sometimes Libra.

Spiritual Guides . . .

Star: Al Heka—Those with this star are driven to succeed.

Angel: Asmodel—This angel governs business and other transactions and aids in negotiations.

Guardian Angel: Raphael—This angel attends to all of your needs when you are looking for guidance.

Spiritual Stone: Topaz—This stone may protect the bearer from the effects of allergies.

✴ JUDITH'S INSIGHT ✴

You are a caretaker of fine things, and this attribute will contribute to your financial success. Alas, it also means you often take on too much responsibility. You take life much too seriously. Learn to laugh a little more; laugh from the pit of your stomach. You will feel such relief. Try enjoying some moments without analyzing them, and go with the flow. As you lighten up the whole world lightens, too. You have a strong will. Your common sense and your intelligence put you over the top. You believe others think you are stupid; just remember, you do that to yourself. You can get defensive in a working environment, and you certainly don't like your work to be criticized. You will be rather successful, despite this negativity. You're sympathetic and kind when you want to be. Family values are important, particularly when you have your own family. You feel good if catered to, and, more important, you are ready and willing to do some catering of your own. You will be a professional one way or another. You might be a doctor, dentist, or attorney.

You love the niceties in life—the more designer labels, the better. Cut up those credit cards, though, or you could become a candidate for bankruptcy. You will experiment in varied positions before you find satisfaction and success—and dollars. You want to be a landowner and should forget some of the designer labels and work toward owning your own property.

★ ★ ★

Possessions and Desires . . .

Gem: Sardonyx—A gift of this stone might help in keeping relationships faithful.

Flower: Bridal Rose—You should be very happy in love.

Astral Color, Color Need, Apparel Color: Your Astral Color is Red, which enhances passion, power, excitement, and strength. Yellow in your environment stimulates and exhilarates you. In your wardrobe, Blue-green enhances your luck and makes you feel secure.

Fragrance: You are devoted to the scent of roses. Choose the buds that have the strongest fragrance to create the special emotions you need.

Tree: Pine—Your relationships tend to be balanced, both emotionally and mentally.

Instrument: Cello

Composer: Mozart

Bird: Bobolink—This charming singer is equally good as a soloist or a member of an orchestra. It is a very romantic bird, most useful as an insect destroyer, and elegant, with beautiful feathers and always pleasant to have around.

Symbol: Wings—You are the source of balance in your world—this will bring you contentment.

Harmonious Health and Nutrition . . .

Health Scents: Almond—This scent may revitalize you and open you to greater possibilities.

Favorable Foods: Celery, apples, buttermilk, salmon

What's Lucky . . .

Lucky Numbers: 4, 6, 8, 16

Best Months: May and July

Best Day of the Week: Friday

Best Month Days: 8, 17, 26

Lucky Charm: Red ribbon in your wallet or doorway.

Harmonious Signs for Relationships and Partnerships: Virgo, Capricorn, and sometimes Libra.

Spiritual Guides . . .

Star: Al Debaran—Those with this star are born leaders.

Angel: Asmodel—This angel governs business and other transactions and aids in negotiations.

Guardian Angel: Seraphim—An angel that brings love, light, and passion.

Spiritual Stone: Topaz—This stone may protect the bearer from the effects of allergies.

✴ JUDITH'S INSIGHT ✴

Mistakes happen; learn from them instead of dwelling on them. You are at home before large audiences. Your wit and charm are enticing. You give family matters top priority, so much so that when they move down your list, family members don't always understand. Your refreshing style and presence attract others, but your intensity and stubbornness often drive them away.

Your tendency to jump to conclusions quickly may make your companion feel overwhelmed by you. Only when a relationship is over do you begin to realize how good it was. Your mom or another motherlike figure, at some point, will be the apple of your eye who holds the key to your heart. If you are already a parent, it could be your child who holds that position in your heart. You do tend to hold onto things and not let them go. This may not work in a conflict, but when it comes to being the devoted mate that you are, it is definitely a desired trait.

You do know how to give a party and impress everyone with your decorations. Explore using these talents as your life's work. Your impeccable taste and organizational aptitude suggest success for you in designing or catering. You could also be a great showperson or entertainer. Your strong desire to see that others have a good time will ensure many a success, now and later.

✳ ✳ ✳

APRIL 27

TAURUS • The winged bull of the zodiac

April 20 at 4:00 A.M. to May 21 at 4:00 A.M. • NUMEROLOGY 9

Possessions and Desires . . .

Gem: Emerald—Those who carry this stone tend to be lucky in love.

Flower: Broken Straw—You tend to want to quickly leave unpleasant situations instead of staying to deal with them.

Astral Color, Color Need, Apparel Color: Your Astral Color is Red, which enhances passion, power, excitement, and strength. Yellow in your environment stimulates and exhilarates you. In your wardrobe, Rose gives you balance and harmony.

Fragrance: You are devoted to the scent of roses. Choose the buds that have the strongest fragrance to create the special emotions you need.

Tree: Holly—Beware that you are not carried away by your passionate nature. The only way to grow is to be open to new experiences.

Instruments: Violin, tympanum

Composer: Gluck

Bird: Mockingbird—the most proficient minstrel in the world's orchestra; graceful and enthusiastic.

Symbol: Anchor—This tranquil symbol signifies stability and strength, and stands for strong commitments in relationships.

Harmonious Health and Nutrition . . .

Health Scents: Lavender—This scent might lead others to trust you and make you patient.

Favorable Foods: Celery, apples, buttermilk, salmon

What's Lucky . . .

Lucky Numbers: 4, 6, 9, 18

Best Months: May and July.

Best Day of the Week: Friday

Best Month Days: 9, 18, 27

Lucky Charms: A U. S. coin or bill of any amount from the year you were born.

Harmonious Signs for Relationships and Partnerships: Virgo, Capricorn, and sometimes Libra.

Spiritual Guides . . .

Star: Al Debaran—Those with this star are born leaders.

Angel: Asmodel—This angel governs business and other transactions and aids in negotiations.

Guardian Angel: Gabriel—"God is my strength."

Spiritual Stone: Topaz—This stone may protect the bearer from the effects of allergies.

✶ JUDITH'S INSIGHT ✶

Generous and kind, you frequently do not hesitate to inform others of your self-sacrifices. Alternatively, you can be very secretive about your own affairs. A teacher at heart, you could take teaching to different dimensions, conventional and unconventional. You are very perceptive, and you inspire those around you. You may consider careers in psychology, or work as a writer, doctor, or counselor. You absorb knowledge from every possible source and have great recall for things you read about or see on television. You are multitalented, with the gift of gab; so working with people is for you. Beautician or makeup artist could also be occupations you'd do well. You do have a dab of drama, so acting could be a consideration. Stocks and finance also intrigue you, as long as you are not the one dotting the i's or crossing the t's. You prefer to distance yourself from paperwork.

Avoid the extremes, especially when it comes to relationships. You may be comfortable with one now, but eventually you'll be challenged by the intricacies of many different relationships. You strive to have a truly beautiful home for your family that will mean everything to you. Resist the temptation to refurbish and redecorate your home at every whim. Antiques and oddities will permeate throughout, as somehow you have identified these as feeling like nature. You are here to seek and find answers. Answers may surface for you when you reach that particular chapter in that particular book.

✶ ✶ ✶

APRIL 28 TAURUS • The winged bull of the zodiac

April 20 at 4:00 A.M. to May 21 at 4:00 A.M. • NUMEROLOGY 1

Possessions and Desires . . .

Gem: Emerald—Those who carry this stone tend to be lucky in love.

Flower: Yellow Violet—You tend to be happiest surrounded by nature.

Astral Color, Color Need, Apparel Color: Your Astral Color is Red, which enhances passion, power, excitement, and strength. Yellow in your environment stimulates and exhilarates you. In your wardrobe, Rose gives you balance and harmony.

Fragrance: You are devoted to the scent of roses. Choose the buds that have the strongest fragrance to create the special emotions you need.

Tree: Walnut—You are unusually helpful and always looking for new beginnings.

Instruments: Oboe, flute, clarinet, piano, French horn, organ, and piccolo

Composer: Böhm

Bird: Bird of paradise—the "bird of the gods." You will shine and love extraordinary circumstances.

Symbol: Crown—the universal sign of dignity.

Harmonious Health and Nutrition . . .

Health Scent: Strawberry—soothing by nature, the strawberry promotes self-esteem and encourages love.

Favorable Foods: Celery, grapes, cheese, beef

What's Lucky . . .

Lucky Numbers: 4, 6, 10, 20
Best Months: May and July
Best Day of the Week: Friday
Best Month Days: 1, 10, 19, 28
Lucky Charm: A new penny in your shoe.
Harmonious Signs for Relationships and Partnerships: Virgo, Capricorn, and sometimes Libra.

Spiritual Guides . . .

Star: Al Heka—Those with this star are driven to succeed.

Angel: Asmodel—This angel governs business and other transactions and aids in negotiations.

Guardian Angel: Malachi—"Messenger of Jehovah."

Spiritual Stone: Topaz—This stone may protect the bearer from the effects of allergies.

✦ JUDITH'S INSIGHT ✦

Enthusiastic by nature, you reach out to the people in your life. Sometimes perfectionism makes you too choosy for your own good. You are the epitome of independence and rarely feel needy. Though you are an unconventional person, you will be most content with conventional relationships. You're afraid to be bored and will become dissatisfied if your relationship doesn't bring you a certain amount of excitement. Unfortunately, you may feel lonely even while you have a partner. Remember, you must be the one to make things stimulating. Ordinarily you face and solve problems as they arise. You are forceful and, some might say, dictatorial. This is definitely a deterrent to business partnerships, and you should try to be more diplomatic. Tact will enhance all your relationships; it brings out your other good aspects. You always give 110 percent to every commitment, be it work or love. You welcome change, however, and must guard against jumping out of relationships too quickly.

Strong aggressions surface to put you at the top. Use caution at play and with entertainment. Obstacles will present themselves, but you overcome them easily. You may desire a career in government or business and could do well in both. Either way, take precautions with the legalities. No matter what you take on, you'll rise to the top. Most others recognize your wit and charm; they appreciate your sense of humor. You love to be popular, and your laughter is infectious. You do your best work before a hand-picked audience. You believe less means more when it comes to friends. You prefer having a few close friends and spending quality time with them. Your devotion to your friends will come back to you tenfold.

✷ ✷ ✷

Possessions and Desires . . .

Gem: Amethyst—This stone is said to give calmness and peace.

Flower: Wormwood—You tend to focus on what you left behind instead of where you could be going.

Astral Color, Color Need, Apparel Color: Your Astral Color is Red, which enhances passion, power, excitement, and strength. Yellow in your environment stimulates and exhilarates you. In your wardrobe, Rose gives you balance and harmony.

Fragrance: You are devoted to the scent of roses. Choose the buds that have the strongest fragrance to create the special emotions you need.

Tree: Maple—You have both great stability and flashes of intuition.

Instrument: Pipe organ, cymbal, drum

Composers: Handel, Johann Sebastian Bach

Bird: Cuckoo—a good flyer and very seldom a quitter. Some cuckoos tend to think they favor lonely isolation, but what they really yearn for is a family relationship.

Symbol: Cross—the symbol of self-sacrifice and reconciliation.

Harmonious Health and Nutrition . . .

Health Scent: Apple—You are creative, full of joy, and nearly magical. You bring happiness.

Favorable Foods: Watercress, peaches, eggs, salmon

What's Lucky . . .

Lucky Numbers: 4, 6, 11, 22
Best Months: May and July
Best Day of the Week: Friday
Best Month Days: 2, 11, 20, 29
Lucky Charms: Two 50-cent pieces. Give someone else one of them.

Harmonious Signs for Relationships and Partnerships: Virgo, Capricorn, and sometimes Libra.

Spiritual Guides . . .

Star: Al Heka—Those with this star are driven to succeed.

Angel: Asmodel—This angel governs business and other transactions and aids in negotiations.

Guardian Angel: Uriel—This angel brings the light of God's guidance.

Spiritual Stone: Topaz—This stone may protect the bearer from the effects of allergies.

✷ JUDITH'S INSIGHT ✷

Although you definitely have the ability to go it alone, the possibilities are enhanced when you join your efforts with another's. Determination and ambition will take you where you want to go in due course. Unfortunately, in this area, you're a little impatient, and it will seem at times like your life is taking you the long way around to your goals. You are beholden to family members and sometimes give too much importance to those relationships. Your frankness gets you into trouble occasionally, but you will have the respect of those around you. Witty and charming, you're welcome in everyone's circle. You flit through relationships at first, but as you mature you won't want to let go. This may pose a problem, but awareness of this tendency to stretch things out will help you make better choices. Your strong presence makes you stand out in the crowd, even when your inner self would rather hide against the wall. You're very honorable, and this attribute will bring you much contentment and happiness, although it may seem like it takes forever.

Money will come and go, but along the way the worries of finance will dissipate. A large windfall will be bestowed upon you more than once during your life. Although you insist on looking good now, as you mature your looks matter even more. Vanity will eventually play a bigger part in your life than your anticipate.

✷ ✷ ✷

APRIL 30
TAURUS • The winged bull of the zodiac
April 20 at 4:00 A.M. to May 21 at 4:00 A.M. • NUMEROLOGY 3

Possessions and Desires . . .

Gem: Ruby—this stone may lead you to energy, friendship, and happiness.

Flower: Vernal Grass—It usually doesn't take a whole lot to make you happy.

Astral Color, Color Need, Apparel Color: Your Astral Color is Red, which enhances passion, power, excitement, and strength. Yellow in your environment stimulates and exhilarates you. In your wardrobe, Rose gives you balance and harmony.

Fragrance: You are devoted to the scent of roses. Choose the buds that have the strongest fragrance to create the special emotions you need.

Tree: Elm—You have willpower, strength, and the ability to stand alone.

Instrument: Trombone

Composers: Verdi, Mendelssohn, Schumann

Bird: Eagle—This bird is quick to use its powers of flight. It can see immeasurable distances in a single glance, and can sometimes appear to be indifferent.

Symbol: Wreath—You have been crowned with a special personality. You are strong but extremely compassionate.

Harmonious Health and Nutrition . . .

Health Scent: Rose—This scent will lead you to passionate thoughts and make you feel warm inside.

Favorable Foods: Turnips, raspberries, buttermilk, beef

What's Lucky . . .

Lucky Numbers: 3, 4, 6, 9
Best Months: May and July
Best Day of the Week: Friday
Best Month Days: 3, 12, 21, 30
Lucky Charm: A pen that someone else has already used.

Harmonious Signs for Relationships and Partnerships: Virgo, Capricorn, and sometimes Libra.

Spiritual Guides . . .

Star: Al Debaran—Those with this star are born leaders.

Angel: Asmodel—This angel governs business and other transactions and aids in negotiations.

Guardian Angel: Johiel—This angel is a protector of all those with a humble heart.

Spiritual Stone: Topaz—This stone may protect the bearer from the effects of allergies.

✴ JUDITH'S INSIGHT ✴

"Strong as a bull" describes both your physical and emotional strength. You can handle just about anything. While others will view your life as charmed, that's not the case. You work hard at building on your strengths, which will always serve you and others. You enjoy overcoming obstacles, and you do this well.

Children, yours and others, are very important in your life. You shine through and around them. You may kiss some toads before you find your prince or princess. After being disillusioned a few times, you will find an appreciative mate. You are somewhat idealistic, but you will eventually balance that tendency with your materialism. You love spending money—it makes you feel good. Disregard those negative thoughts about not accomplishing enough financially; you do climb up the financial ladder.

Your appreciation of others tends to make you the caretaker in most situations, regardless of whether another is outwardly taking care of you or vice versa. Your sense of humor develops little by little. Peace of mind comes in time. Don't watch the clock.

✱ ✱ ✱

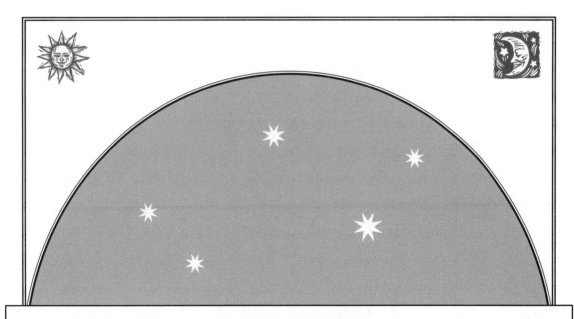

MAY

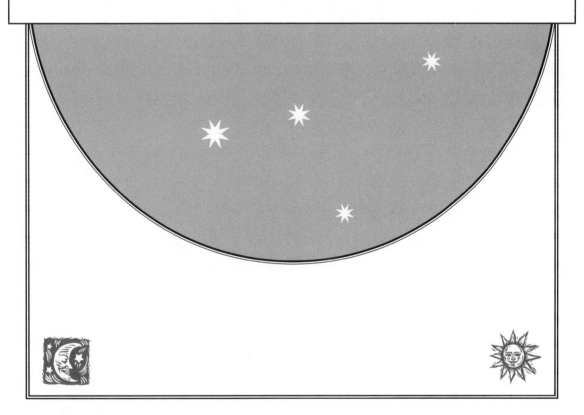

MAY 1

TAURUS • The winged bull of the zodiac

April 20 at 4:00 A.M. to May 21 at 4:00 A.M. • NUMEROLOGY I

Possessions and Desires . . .

Gem: Turquoise—This stone may help you find material wealth.

Flower: American Aster—You are always thoughtful of others.

Astral Color, Color Need, Apparel Color: Your Astral Color is Red, which enhances passion, power, excitement, and strength. Yellow in your environment stimulates and exhilarates you. In your wardrobe, Rose gives you balance and harmony.

Fragrance: You are devoted to the scent of roses. Choose the buds that have the strongest fragrance to create the special emotions you need.

Tree: Walnut—You are unusually helpful and aways looking for new beginnings.

Instruments: Oboe, flute, clarinet, piano, French horn, organ, piccolo

Composer: Böhm

Bird: Hummingbird—This birds is delicate and graceful. It can remain still for hours, then dart off and be as busy as a bee.

Symbol: Crown—the universal sign of dignity.

Harmonious Health and Nutrition . . .

Health Scent: Strawberry—Soothing by nature, the strawberry promotes self-esteem and encourages love.

Favorable Foods: Romaine lettuce, black figs, eggs, chicken

What's Lucky . . .

Lucky Numbers: 1, 2, 4, 6
Best Months: May and July
Best Day of the Week: Friday
Best Month Days: 1, 10, 19, 28
Lucky Charm: A new penny in your shoe.
Harmonious Signs for Relationships and

Partnerships: Virgo, Capricorn, and sometimes Libra.

Spiritual Guides . . .

Star: Al Debaran—Those with this star are born leaders.

Angel: Asmodel—This angel governs business and other transactions and aids in negotiations.

Guardian Angel: Malachi—"Messenger of Jehovah."

Spiritual Stone: Topaz—This stone may protect the bearer from the effects of allergies.

✳ JUDITH'S INSIGHT ✳

Creativity, originality, and self-reliance bring you an independence that carries you through just about every situation. A good head on your shoulders and a sensitive nature ensure that doors open for you. You can develop your career utilizing either or both your artistic and counseling talents. Follow your larger vision enthusiastically. Whether you crawl or leap up the ladder of success depends on your devotion to the task.

You dislike being alone and thrive on the attention of others. Eat it up while others are interested—there will be lonely spells in your life. Keep it all in perspective. Try not to see the quiet times as lonely—view them as rest and recuperation, and you won't make mistakes in your love life based on loneliness. Your friends and family know you need the occasional pat on the back, and they offer it instinctively. You attract more flies with honey than with vinegar.

Success awaits you, but you must make it happen, and it could take awhile. Fashion and beauty, or perhaps the theater, could offer the most to you. You will not only meet your own burdens in life but also help carry the burdens of others. Because of who and what you are, you probably wouldn't want it any other way. This is your forte.

✳ ✳ ✳

MAY 2 TAURUS • The winged bull of the zodiac

April 20 at 4:00 A.M. to May 21 at 4:00 A.M. • NUMEROLOGY 2

Possessions and Desires . . .

Gem: Amethyst—This stone is said to give calmness and peace.

Flower: Chickweed—You will find your way in life is a very curvy road.

Astral Color, Color Need, Apparel Color: Your Astral Color is Red, which enhances passion, power, excitement, and strength. Yellow in your environment stimulates and exhilarates you. In your wardrobe, Rose gives you balance and harmony.

Fragrance: You are devoted to the scent of roses. Choose the buds that have the strongest fragrance to create the special emotions you need.

Tree: Maple—You have both great stability and flashes of intuition.

Instruments: Pipe organ, cymbal, drum

Composers: Handel, Johann Sebastian Bach

Bird: Stork—Turkish bird, held in high esteem the world over. This bird is intelligent but may have strange tendencies.

Symbol: Cross—the symbol of self-sacrifice and reconciliation.

Harmonious Health and Nutrition . . .

Health Scents: Apple—You are creative, full of joy, and nearly magical. You bring happiness.

Favorable Foods: Turnips, cranberries, buttermilk, salmon

What's Lucky . . .

Lucky Numbers: 2, 4, 6, 11

Best Months: May and July

Best Day of the Week: Friday

Best Month Days: 2, 11, 20, 29

Lucky Charms: Two 50-cent pieces. Give someone else one of them.

Harmonious Signs for Relationships and Partnerships: Virgo, Capricorn, and sometimes Libra.

Spiritual Guides . . .

Star: Al Heka—Those with this star are driven to succeed.

Angel: Asmodel—This angel governs business and other transactions and aids in negotiations.

Guardian Angel: St. John—This angel simplifies that which is complicated.

Spiritual Stone: Topaz—This stone may protect the bearer from the effects of allergies.

✴ JUDITH'S INSIGHT ✴

A diehard romantic, you have a great capacity for love and all that goes with it. You could write compelling love stories drawn from your dreams and imagination. Fear not—your logical side keeps you rooted to earth. To no one's surprise, you may be that lucky one who experiences the love of a lifetime, but it's more likely you'll find love in many places along the way. Love brings happiness, at least once, for you. You will be able to act out some of those romantic fantasies of yours.

Your life's work should involve the arts, beauty, or spirituality, and you'd be an asset and find fulfillment in the theater. Be cognizant of keeping both feet planted on the ground. Your hobbies should also be associated with literature, art, or theater. You may find mystical studies alluring, as well. Follow your need to express yourself. Someday you may find yourself in the public eye, or the public may eventually find you.

You have other hidden talents and a certain style about you. You're put together well, and could easily be a decorator, personal dresser, or personal shopper.

You are most sympathetic to the needs of others and often lean toward helping the underdog. Be wary of your stubbornness. Catch yourself when you are tempted to complain about others—think twice about your own behavior. Let any negative stubbornness give way to a gentler, more positive diligence.

✶ ✶ ✶

MAY 3 TAURUS • The winged bull of the zodiac

April 20 at 4:00 A.M. to May 21 at 4:00 A.M. • NUMEROLOGY 3

Possessions and Desires . . .

Gem: Ruby—This stone may lead you to energy, friendship, and happiness.
Flower: May Rose—Your life will be filled with love and warmth.
Astral Color, Color Need, Apparel Color: Your Astral Color is Red, which enhances passion, power, excitement, and strength. Yellow in your environment stimulates and exhilarates you. In your wardrobe, Rose gives you balance and harmony.
Fragrance: You are devoted to the scent of roses. Choose the buds that have the strongest fragrance to create the special emotions you need.
Tree: Elm—You have willpower, strength, and the ability to stand alone.
Instrument: Trombone
Composers: Verdi, Mendelssohn, Schumann
Bird: Swan—Regarded as royal and sacred, this bird has the protective nature of a mother, and can become a furious fighter in the defense of its young.
Symbol: Wreath—You have been crowned with a special personality. You are strong but extremely compassionate.

Harmonious Health and Nutrition . . .

Health Scents: Rose—This scent will lead you to passionate thoughts and make you feel warm inside.
Favorable Foods: Tomatoes, raspberries, cheese, oysters

What's Lucky . . .

Lucky Numbers: 4, 6, 8
Best Month: May and July
Best Day of the Week: Friday
Best Month Days: 3, 12, 21, 30
Lucky Charm: A pen that someone else has already used.
Harmonious Signs for Relationships and Partnerships: Virgo, Capricorn, and sometimes Libra.

Spiritual Guides . . .

Star: Al Debaran—Those with this star are born leaders.
Angel: Asmodel—This angel governs business and other transactions and aids in negotiations.
Guardian Angel: Johiel—This angel is a protector of all those with a humble heart.
Spiritual Stone: Topaz—This stone may protect the bearer from the effects of allergies.

✷ JUDITH'S INSIGHT ✷

The best kind of contradiction shines through your personality. You are creative, talented, enthusiastic, and energetic, yet down to earth, logical, and loyal. It's a dynamic combination that you struggle with, but you will eventually fall into step. Your compassion and kindness bring you many friends. Your feisty side will work to your advantage in defense of your ideas. Quite possibly you will find yourself resolving legal issues. Once angered, however, you find it difficult to let go. Time and the persuasion of others usually alter your stance. You crave attention, particularly in your younger years. Good or bad, any attention bodes well for you. It is indifference you cannot tolerate.

Be selective when it comes to romance. You love attractive things and looking good. Sometimes we ought not judge a book by its cover, but merely gaze without being judgmental. Your looks entice others to flirt with you or get closer. But you're very loyal, and you won't find yourself in hot water too often.

Creativity will shine through everything you do. Make laughter your best medicine. Learn to appreciate those funny moments. Simply lighten up and enjoy.

Money is a high priority, and you will be preoccupied with your financial status as you mature. You can be generous as well as miserly. You should seek the middle ground, when it comes to your checkbook, to ensure financial stability.

✷ ✷ ✷

MAY 4   TAURUS • The winged bull of the zodiac

April 20 at 4:00 A.M. to May 21 at 4:00 A.M. • NUMEROLOGY 4

Possessions and Desires . . .

Gem: Emerald—Those who carry this stone tend to be lucky in love.
Flower: Myrtle—Love is yours if you pay close attention to your heartbeat.
Astral Color, Color Need, Apparel Color: Your Astral Color is Red, which enhances passion, power, excitement, and strength. Yellow in your environment stimulates and exhilarates you. In your wardrobe, Rose gives you balance and harmony.
Fragrance: You are devoted to the scent of roses. Choose the buds that have the strongest fragrance to create the special emotions you need.
Tree: Cherry—You will find yourself faced with constant new emotional awakenings.
Instruments: Bass, clarinet
Composers: Haydn, Wagner
Bird: Robin—the most sociable of all birds, with the ability to create quick friendships. It also can easily adapt to any home. When it wants something, it has the tendency to try to snatch it.
Symbol: Star—You are full of inner brightness and will stand out in any crowd. You will be seen as special.

Harmonious Health and Nutrition . . .

Health Scents: Vanilla—This scent will fill you with a feeling of cleanliness and stability.
Favorable Foods: Peaches, eggs, beef, carrots

What's Lucky . . .

Lucky Numbers: 4, 6, 8
Best Months: May and July
Best Day of the Week: Friday
Best Month Days: 4, 13, 22, 31
Lucky Charm: A piece of material cut from something in your home.
Harmonious Signs for Relationships and

Partnerships: Virgo, Capricorn, and sometimes Libra.

Spiritual Guides . . .

Star: Al Heka—Those with this star are driven to succeed.
Angel: Asmodel—This angel governs business and other transactions and aids in negotiations.
Guardian Angel: Uriel—This angel brings the light of God's guidance.
Spiritual Stone: Topaz—This stone may protect the bearer from the effects of allergies.

✴ JUDITH'S INSIGHT ✴

Versatility and flexibility ensure many successes for you. Your adaptability and independent spirit leads others to reach out for you. You remain influential all your life. Friends and family most often relate to you but occasionally back away because you project your high expectations of yourself onto them. They fear you will demand more of them and thus they back off. Nonetheless, your circle of friends will continue to grow, as does the love and understanding of your beloved ones. One minute you welcome your family's dependence on you, the next you urge them to exercise more independence. It all comes together when you take it less seriously.

Success is very much in the picture, particularly if you are self-employed. A natural leader, you can achieve much when coupled with the right partners. Be choosy and take care. Life will reward your efforts financially. Good things develop when you give it your best. You may find a comfortable slot in big business, a home business, or in the public eye—say, in politics. Your creativity ensures retail success.

In matters of the heart, learn patience. Your goodness as a person shines through, and others clamor to share that goodness. You will find stability in your mate, and your mate will support your pursuits.

✶ ✶ ✶

MAY 5   TAURUS • The winged bull of the zodiac
April 20 at 4:00 A.M. to May 21 at 4:00 A.M. • NUMEROLOGY 5

Possessions and Desires . . .

Gem: Sardius—this stone could give the wearer unusual insights into his or her own heart.

Flower: Ophrys—You usually are a delight to be with.

Astral Color, Color Need, Apparel Color: Your Astral Color is Red, which enhances passion, power, excitement, and strength. Yellow in your environment stimulates and exhilarates you. In your wardrobe, Rose gives you balance and harmony.

Fragrance: You are devoted to the scent of roses. Choose the buds that have the strongest fragrance to create the special emotions you need.

Tree: Apple—You are creative, full of joy, and nearly magical. You bring happiness.

Instruments: Viola, trumpet

Composer: Liszt

Bird: Flamingo—This beautiful, gregarious bird is always careful of its enemy. It is also a caretaker of the young who tries to keep everyone happy.

Symbol: Triangle—You have the right combination of abilities.

Harmonious Health and Nutrition . . .

Health Scent: Peach—This scent may balance your good qualities so they equal your charm.

Favorable Foods: Carrots, apples, cheese, chicken

What's Lucky . . .

Lucky Numbers: 4, 5, 6, 10
Best Months: May and July
Best Day of the Week: Friday
Best Month Days: 4, 5, 23
Lucky Charms: A rabbit's foot or a white candle
Harmonious Signs for Relationships and Partnerships: Virgo, Capricorn, and sometimes Libra.

Spiritual Guides . . .

Star: Al Debaran—Those with this star are born leaders.

Angel: Asmodel—This angel governs business and other transactions and aids in negotiations.

Guardian Angel: Plavwell—This angel gives power and strength to one's presence.

Spiritual Stone: Topaz—This stone may protect the bearer from the effects of allergies.

✴ JUDITH'S INSIGHT ✴

You are so special—unusually keen—an original in all you do. You have far-reaching reasoning powers. You are perceptive, analytical, and observant. An independent spirit, you approach situations amiably. You are a master of creativity and you enjoy everything from carpentry to counseling. You're great at anything you try, and you will aspire for more. To no one's surprise, a company of your own would definitely succeed. More than you care to admit, you desire fame. Although you are successful in what you do, you may seek other interests, perhaps a hobby with more guts and glamour. Even if you don't actively seek it, it may find you. You could get involved in golf, boating, organizational writing, or heading the PTA.

Family holds a strong connection for you. Although you're influenced by your mate in a strong way, you remain comfortably independent. Hopefully your youthful love affairs will help anchor your shifting affections. It is wiser for you to marry later rather than sooner. Your mate will understand you.

Financially, you may not win the lottery, but you will be comfortable. With the passing years, you become less spiritual and more materialistic. You appear to be a strong presence, your gentle heart will embrace a chosen few who will be lucky to have been touched by you.

✴ ✴ ✴

MAY 6   TAURUS • The winged bull of the zodiac
April 20 at 4:00 A.M. to May 21 at 4:00 A.M.   • NUMEROLOGY 6

Possessions and Desires . . .

Gem: Topaz—This is an excellent gift to be exchanged between very loyal friends.

Flower: Quince—You enjoy the excitement life has to offer.

Astral Color, Color Need, Apparel Color: Your Astral Color is Red, which enhances passion, power, excitement, and strength. Yellow in your environment stimulates and exhilarates you. In your wardrobe, Rose gives you balance and harmony.

Fragrance: You are devoted to the scent of roses. Choose the buds that have the strongest fragrance to create the special emotions you need.

Tree: Palm—You tend to be very healthy and creative.

Instruments: Tambourine, lyre

Composer: Schubert

Bird: Lark—known for the beauty of its song, which is sometimes very unusual. It is also credited with extraordinary intelligence.

Symbol: Crescent—You are more likely to be influenced by the phases of the moon. Your easygoing manner leads you to peaceful situations.

Harmonious Health and Nutrition . . .

Health Scent: Orange Blossom—This scent may balance your body, mind, and soul.

Favorable Foods: Carrots, apples, cheese, chicken

What's Lucky . . .

Lucky Numbers: 4, 6, 12, 16

Best Months: May and July

Best Day of the Week: Friday

Best Month Days: 6, 15, 24

Lucky Charms: A religious token or card from any religion.

Harmonious Signs for Relationships and Partnerships: Virgo, Capricorn, and sometimes Libra.

Spiritual Guides . . .

Star: Al Debaran—Those with this star are born leaders.

Angel: Asmodel—This angel governs business and other transactions and aids in negotiations.

Guardian Angel: Michael—"Who is like God."

Spiritual Stone: Topaz—This stone may protect the bearer from the effects of allergies.

✷ JUDITH'S INSIGHT ✷

Sharing is where your heart is—you have such an intense desire to give of yourself. The kindness of friends tends to overwhelm you. You are very decisive and do not appreciate being diverted from your chosen path. Your enthusiasm for life and your many skills open up many different careers to you.

You can be both angel and devil. Your emotional contradictions may seem unfortunate to you, but to others they're fascinating. Your random acts of kindness come from the heart with no strings attached. You may take many small steps before you arrive at your ultimate career, but you'll derive success from what you've accomplished along the way.

As you reach various plateaus in life, you will in all likelihood seek change. Each plateau represents a period of growth. Family will be your strongest foundation, and you will, despite your career, find the way to have a solid family of your own. You will expand your immediate circle and thrive on the enjoyment of not only yourself but others, particularly in social events. You're certainly equipped to be a politician, but more likely an activist for children, the infirm, or the homeless. The legal arena may have possibilities for you.

Because of your compassion, people are always around you. Although your creativity is strong, your compassion is stronger. Once your career taps into your emotional side you will be happy. Stylish, with some vanity, you'll always try to improve your appearance, and you'll retain your stylish looks as though you'd found the fountain of youth.

✶ ✶ ✶

MAY 7

TAURUS • The winged bull of the zodiac

April 20 at 4:00 A.M. to May 21 at 4:00 A.M. • NUMEROLOGY 7

Possessions and Desires . . .

Gem: Agate—This stone may promote health and lead you to a long life.

Flower: Primrose—You never lose sight of the simple pleasures of childhood.

Astral Color, Color Need, Apparel Color: Your Astral Color is Red, which enhances passion, power, excitement, and strength. Yellow in your environment stimulates and exhilarates you. In your wardrobe, Rose gives you balance and harmony.

Fragrance: You are devoted to the scent of roses. Choose the buds that have the strongest fragrance to create the special emotions you need.

Tree: Sycamore—Yours is the ability to love, communicate honestly with others, and have lasting relationships.

Instrument: Harp

Composers: Gluck, Brahms

Bird: Warbling Parakeet—the most beautiful of all birds, known as the love bird. It does seem to have the powers of imitation.

Symbol: Heart—You are enthusiastic, empathetic, and full of generosity and love.

Harmonious Health and Nutrition . . .

Health Scent: Jasmine—This scent may make you more easygoing when you are stressed.

Favorable Foods: Carrots, cherries, cheese, liver

What's Lucky . . .

Lucky Numbers: 4, 6, 7, 15
Best Months: May and July
Best Day of the Week: Friday
Best Month Days: 6, 15, 24
Lucky Charm: An old key.
Harmonious Signs for Relationships and Partnerships: Virgo, Capricorn, and sometimes Libra.

Spiritual Guides . . .

Star: Al Debaran—Those with this star are born leaders.

Angel: Asmodel—This angel governs business and other transactions and aids in negotiations.

Guardian Angel: Raphael—This angel attends to all of your needs when you are looking for guidance.

Spiritual Stone: Topaz—This stone may protect the bearer from the effects of allergies.

✳ JUDITH'S INSIGHT ✳

You are a dreamer with extraordinary curiosity about nature. With encouragement and support, you could succeed as an inventor, author, or designer, or in almost anything that you originate. Your hands will serve you well, but your heart works best. You are strong mentally which complements your intuitiveness, common sense, and natural intelligence. You search for the unknown. Natural kindness makes you generous, but not foolish. You tend to have predetermined views when it comes to managing money or giving it away. Some may think you eccentric because of your desire for the unusual. You would be likely to collect antiques, especially dolls, games, and toys. If could be you searching for buried treasure or mining for gold.

Perhaps a career as a writer, poet, painter, musician, or inventor would bring you success and happiness. Financial rewards should find you early in life, but most assuredly in your later years. You will share your money to benefit others. Friends and family appreciate your generosity, as will a favorite charity or the local hospital. Public welfare permeates your life in one way or another, whether you will be receiving help or, on a more positive note, being the one who helps others. At first any love commitment would be difficult, but once you have made some minor adjustments, the relationship will do well. You are the mule in the relationship most of the time so keep this in mind.

★ ★ ★

MAY 8   TAURUS • The winged bull of the zodiac
April 20 at 4:00 A.M. to May 21 at 4:00 A.M. • NUMEROLOGY 8

Possessions and Desires . . .

Gem: Emerald—Those who carry this stone tend to be lucky in love.

Flower: White Poppy—You may need more sleep than other people you know.

Astral Color, Color Need, Apparel Color: Your Astral Color is Red, which enhances passion, power, excitement, and strength. Yellow in your environment stimulates and exhilarates you. In your wardrobe, Rose gives you balance and harmony.

Fragrance: You are devoted to the scent of roses. Choose the buds that have the strongest fragrance to create the special emotions you need.

Tree: Pine—Your relationships tend to be harmonious, both emotionally and mentally.

Instrument: Cello

Composer: Mozart

Bird: Bobolink—This charming singer is equally good as a soloist or a member of an orchestra. It is a very romantic bird, useful as an insect destroyer, and elegant, with beautiful feathers, and is always pleasant to have around.

Symbol: Wings—You are the source of balance in your world—this will bring you contentment.

Harmonious Health and Nutrition . . .

Health Scent: Almond—This scent may revitalize you and open you to greater possibilities.

Favorable Foods: Celery, apples, buttermilk, beef

What's Lucky . . .

Lucky Numbers: 4, 6, 8
Best Months: May and July
Best Day of the Week: Friday
Best Month Days: 8, 17, 26

Lucky Charm: Red ribbon in your wallet or doorway.

Harmonious Signs for Relationships and Partnerships: Virgo, Capricorn, and sometimes Libra.

Spiritual Guides . . .

Star: Al Debaran—Those with this star are born leaders.

Angel: Asmodel—This angel governs business and other transactions and aids in negotiations.

Guardian Angel: Seraphim—This angel brings love, light, and passion.

Spiritual Stone: Topaz—this stone may protect the bearer from the effects of allergies.

✶ JUDITH'S INSIGHT ✶

In the early years, nagging loneliness makes you crave attention, sometimes more than others are prepared to give. Be not dismayed or distracted, as you eventually find yourself in a loving and nurturing relationship. Restrictive relationships smother, and you thrive on freely exploring your world. There's a natural glow about you that will brighten as you mature. Your innate sense of responsibility ensures that you'll carry out any task before you. You enthusiasm for life makes things happen around you. You will maintain a high position in such areas as the theater, the arts, decorating, or consulting in beauty.

You are a pleasure to love, and the more amenities in life for you, the better. Love mates will praise you; there will seldom be times when attention is lacking. Your attractiveness lures many, but be watchful to not become complacent about your relationships.

You will succeed financially and will be surrounded with the niceties in life: a wonderful home and family and, eventually, after all the hurdles, a good life.

✶ ✶ ✶

MAY 9
TAURUS • The winged bull of the zodiac
April 20 at 4:00 A.M. to May 21 at 4:00 A.M. • NUMEROLOGY 9

Possessions and Desires

Gem: Emerald—Those who carry this stone tend to be lucky in love.

Flower: Snowball—You tend to bounce back from times of distress.

Astral Color, Color Need, Apparel Color: Your Astral Color is Red, which enhances passion, power, excitement, and strength. Yellow in your environment stimulates and exhilarates you. In your wardrobe, Rose gives you balance and harmony.

Fragrance: You are devoted to the scent of roses. Choose the buds that have the strongest fragrance to create the special emotions you need.

Tree: Holly—Beware that you are not carried away by your passionate nature. The only way to grow is to be open to new experiences.

Instruments: Violin, tympanum

Composer: Gluck

Bird: Mockingbird—the most proficient minstrel in the world's orchestra; graceful and enthusiastic.

Symbol: Anchor—This tranquil symbol signifies stability and strength, and stands for strong commitments in relationships.

Harmonious Health and Nutrition . . .

Health Scent: Lavender—This scent might lead others to trust you and make you patient.

Favorable Foods: Turnips, raspberries, cheese, chicken

What's Lucky . . .

Lucky Numbers: 4, 6, 9, 18

Best Months: May and July

Best Day of the Week: Friday

Best Month Days: 9, 18, 27

Lucky Charms: A U.S. coin or a bill of any amount from the year you were born.

Harmonious Signs for Relationships and

Partnerships: Virgo, Capricorn, and sometimes Libra.

Spiritual Guides . . .

Star: Al Heka—Those with this star are driven to succeed.

Angel: Asmodel—This angel governs business and other transactions and aids in negotiations.

Guardian Angel: Gabriel—"God is my strength."

Spiritual Stone: Topaz—This stone may protect the bearer from the effects of allergies.

✳ JUDITH'S INSIGHT ✳

Persistence and consistency are the key to who you are, perhaps even the key to your heart. You maintain a steady course, though unexpected changes rock your boat. You are confident in your own abilities and have a strong, but not inflated, opinion of yourself. Your self-confidence attracts others.

Your abilities and talents, which are many, add to your charm. Though not surrounded by a fan club, others respect and admire you. If you choose, you will be at the head of the class or department, in whatever career you desire. You manage people well, despite your stubborn nature. Your fun-loving, playful side keeps the balance.

You have exquisite taste and love beautiful ornaments. Not only do you know how to decorate, you know how to conceal the blemishes. You accentuate what is already attractive and make good things better. These skills and experience may foster a career from construction to beauty consulting and everything in between. Any career that would utilize your style and creativity will bring contentment to you. Anything you put your handprint on is unique.

Love gives you a run for your money early in life, when you're really not ready to settle. The powerful person you are seeks powerful mates. You can escape the few tangled webs along the way. You love your mate and are a loyal soul.

✳ ✳ ✳

MAY 10 TAURUS • The winged bull of the zodiac

April 20 at 4:00 A.M. to May 21 at 4:00 A.M. • NUMEROLOGY 1

Possessions and Desires . . .

Gem: Turquoise—This stone may help you find material wealth.

Flower: Red Poppy—You usually are a source of consolation to others.

Astral Color, Color Need, Apparel Colors: Your Astral Color is Red, which enhances passion, power, excitement, and strength. Yellow in your environment stimulates and exhilarates you. In your wardrobe, Rose gives you balance and harmony.

Fragrance: You are devoted to the scent of roses. Choose the buds that have the strongest fragrance to create the special emotions you need.

Tree: Walnut—You are unusually helpful and aways looking for new beginnings.

Instruments: Oboe, flute, clarinet, piano, French horn, organ, piccolo

Composer: Böhm

Bird: Bird of Paradise—the "birds of the Gods." You will shine and love extraordinary circumstances.

Symbol: Crown—the universal sign of dignity.

Harmonious Health and Nutrition . . .

Health Scent: Strawberry—soothing by nature, the strawberry promotes self-esteem and encourages love.

Favorable Foods: Kale, peaches, eggs, salmon

What's Lucky . . .

Lucky Numbers: 2, 4, 6
Best Months: May and July
Best Day of the Week: Friday
Best Month Days: 1, 10, 19, 28
Lucky Charm: A new penny in your shoe.
Harmonious Signs for Relationships and

Partnerships: Virgo, Capricorn, and sometimes Libra.

Spiritual Guides . . .

Star: Al Debaran—Those with this star are born leaders.

Angel: Asmodel—This angel governs business and other transactions and aids in negotiations.

Guardian Angel: Malachi—"Messenger of Jehovah."

Spiritual Stone: Topaz—This stone may protect the bearer from the effects of allergies.

✶ JUDITH'S INSIGHT ✶

Faithful and loyal, you stand up for yourself and those around you. You are not to be messed with when angry. Ultraresponsible in all undertakings, you succeed at work, school, or play. When it comes to love and sex, you are generous to the nth degree. You consider no sacrifice too great for your loved one and often end a crisis with openness, honesty, and fair dealing.

You have all the makings of an excellent public servant and could attain a high government position. You may work around uniformed people one way or another. This caretaker personality of yours may lead you down another path: medicine or teaching may be your niche. A lover of animals and gardening, you could be a veterinarian or a landscaper. Lo and behold, you find one way or another to help out your fellow man! This desire is strong, and this is how your humanity shines.

Your creative nature leaves you desirous of a little fame and a bit of fortune, too. Willing to work endlessly and tirelessly, you find yourself in the limelight from time to time. Your personal integrity exposes you to many a splendid thing.

✶ ✶ ✶

MAY 11   TAURUS • The winged bull of the zodiac

April 20 at 4:00 A.M. to May 21 at 4:00 A.M.   •   NUMEROLOGY 2

Possessions and Desires . . .

Gem: Sapphire—This gem may help you find forgiveness from those you've wronged.

Flower: Sensitive Plant—You may be oversensitive to imagined slights.

Astral Color, Color Need, Apparel Color: Your Astral Color is Red, which enhances passion, power, excitement, and strength. Yellow in your environment stimulates and exhilarates you. In your wardrobe, Rose gives you balance and harmony.

Fragrance: You are devoted to the scent of roses. Choose the buds that have the strongest fragrance to create the special emotions you need.

Tree: Maple—You have both great stability and flashes of intuition.

Instruments: Pipe organ, cymbal, drum

Composers: Handel, Johann Sebastian Bach

Bird: Stork—Turkish bird, held in high esteem the world over. This bird is intelligent but may have strange tendencies.

Symbol: Cross—the symbol of self-sacrifice and reconciliation.

Harmonious Health and Nutrition . . .

Health Scent: Apple—You are creative, full of joy, and nearly magical. You bring happiness.

Favorable Foods: Radishes, watermelon, buttermilk, salmon

What's Lucky . . .

Lucky Numbers: 2, 4, 6, 11

Best Months: May and July

Best Day of the Week: Friday

Best Month Days: 2, 11, 20, 29

Lucky Charms: Two 50-cent pieces. Give someone else one of them.

Harmonious Signs for Relationships and

Partnerships: Virgo, Capricorn, and sometimes Libra.

Spiritual Guides . . .

Star: Al Heka—Those with this star are driven to succeed.

Angel: Asmodel—This angel governs business and other transactions and aids in negotiations.

Guardian Angel: St. John—This angel simplifies that which is complicated.

Spiritual Stone: Topaz—This stone may protect the bearer from the effects of allergies.

✳ JUDITH'S INSIGHT ✳

You become increasingly versatile each day. You like reading and writing and can baffle those around you with your sharp knowledge of history and science. You can be the great observer, you know how to play any kind of game. You enjoy debating, whether it's serious or just for the fun of it.

Fond of travel, you are very likely to relocate often. Should you remain in one place, you will probably vacation frequently. You would make a great florist, designer, landscaper, or developer. You simply love improving, creating, or designing. You have a knack for producing beauty and should pursue a career that showcases that talent. You will find the arts very appealing, whether as part of your life's work or your hobby. Sarcastic and unpredictable is quite a combination, but you will catch many fish with your lures and flirtations. Your undying loyalty ensures the best for you but be aware there will be times when you will be in conflict. Your word is your bond. You like to make those around you happy. Often, you deliver before the recipient is even aware of a need.

As you mature, you learn to accept criticism with more grace and see that it doesn't always have to be destructive.

✳ ✳ ✳

MAY 12

TAURUS • The winged bull of the zodiac

April 20 at 4:00 A.M. to May 21 at 4:00 A.M. • NUMEROLOGY 3

Possessions and Desires . . .

Gem: Ruby—This stone may lead you to energy, friendship, and happiness.

Flower: Star of Bethlehem—You tend not be happy when things are even a little messy.

Astral Color, Color Need, Apparel Color: Your Astral Color is Red, which enhances passion, power, excitement, and strength. Yellow in your environment stimulates and exhilarates you. In your wardrobe, Rose gives you balance and harmony.

Fragrance: You are devoted to the scent of roses. Choose the buds that have the strongest fragrance to create the special emotions you need.

Tree: Elm—You have willpower, strength, and the ability to stand alone.

Instrument: Trombone

Composers: Verdi, Mendelssohn, Schumann

Bird: Eagle—This bird is quick to use its powers of flight. It can see immeasurable distances in a single glance, and can sometimes appear to be indifferent.

Symbol: Wreath—You have been crowned with a special personality. You are strong but extremely compassionate.

Harmonious Health and Nutrition . . .

Health Scent: Rose—This scent will lead you to passionate thoughts and make you feel warm inside.

Favorable Foods: Celery, grapes, cheese, liver

What's Lucky . . .

Lucky Numbers: 3, 4, 6, 12

Best Months: May and July

Best Day of the Week: Friday

Best Month Days: 3, 12, 21, 30

Lucky Charm: A pen that someone else has already used.

Harmonious Signs for Relationships and

Partnerships: Virgo, Capricorn, and sometimes Libra.

Spiritual Guides . . .

Star: Al Debaran—Those with this star are born leaders.

Angel: Asmodel—This angel governs business and other transactions and aids in negotiations.

Guardian Angel: Johiel—This angel is a protector of all those with a humble heart.

Spiritual Stone: Topaz—This stone may protect the bearer from the effects of allergies.

✶ JUDITH'S INSIGHT ✶

You inspire those around you with your love and devotion, despite some displays of bullheadedness. Your charm and wit make it hard for people to turn away. Relationships with friends and family improve steadily through the second half of your life. You are a philosopher in your own right; someday you'll understand just how intuitive you really are. The more you're drawn to the unknown, the more mysteries you unravel and conquer.

You're very versatile and develop talents and then take them for granted. Explore and build on those everyday skills, and eventually you will use them for both pleasure and profit. A career in painting, art, music, or literature brings harmony, although somewhere along the way you may desire something in the public life such as politics or law. You have an inborn sense of justice and believe in standing up for principles.

It's very likely that you will find "the one" easily and marry early. You can also expect to have a minimum of three loves during your lifetime. You seek beauty and are most content when you are surrounded by it. You are equally impressed with natural beauty and man-made creations. Generosity is your most honorable trait. As a highly respected member of the community, you will teach and touch others. Your kindness will be felt by many along your trail of life.

✶ ✶ ✶

MAY 13 TAURUS • The winged bull of the zodiac

April 20 at 4:00 A.M. to May 21 at 4:00 A.M. • NUMEROLOGY 4

Possessions and Desires . . .

Gem: Emerald—Those who carry this stone tend to be lucky in love.

Flower: Strawberry—You may not be able to love what you don't first respect.

Astral Color, Color Need, Apparel Color: Your Astral Color is Red, which enhances passion, power, excitement, and strength. Yellow in your environment stimulates and exhilarates you. In your wardrobe, Rose gives you balance and harmony.

Fragrance: You are devoted to the scent of roses. Choose the buds that have the strongest fragrance to create the special emotions you need.

Tree: Cherry—You will find yourself faced with constant new emotional awakenings.

Instruments: Bass, clarinet

Composers: Haydn, Wagner

Bird: Swan—Regarded as royal and sacred, this bird has the protective nature of a mother, and can become a furious fighter in the defense of its young.

Symbol: Star—You are full of inner brightness and will stand out in any crowd. You will be seen as special.

Harmonious Health and Nutrition . . .

Health Scent: Vanilla—This scent will fill you with a feeling of cleanliness and stability.

Favorable Foods: Brussels sprouts, apples, eggs, chicken

What's Lucky . . .

Lucky Numbers: 4, 6, 8, 13

Best Months: May and July

Best Day of the Week: Friday

Best Month Days: 4, 13, 22, 31

Lucky Charm: A piece of material cut from something in your home.

Harmonious Signs for Relationships and Partnerships: Virgo, Capricorn, and sometimes Libra.

Spiritual Guides . . .

Star: Al Debaran—Those with this star are born leaders.

Angel: Asmodel—This angel governs business and other transactions and aids in negotiations.

Guardian Angel: Uriel—This angel brings the light of God's guidance.

Spiritual Stone: Topaz—This stone may protect the bearer from the effects of allergies.

✳ JUDITH'S INSIGHT ✳

Set boundaries for yourself; balancing the world on your shoulders will become so much easier if you were to take baby steps instead of giant steps. Your strong desires lead you to many accomplishments, along with a barrel-full of struggles. These same desires, accomplishments, and struggles provide you with a foundation to build multiple careers and/or hobbies. Your dedication to achieving the goals you set for yourself ensures success for you. You seldom fail—you are very good at overcoming obstacles and responding to emergencies of every kind. You handle stress like a champ. Your independent approach to life makes you somewhat of a loner, but you very much enjoy the company of others and generally prefer companionship.

Peculiar circumstances surround your family and loved ones. The unusual is commonplace in your life, and the unexpected is most likely to happen around you. Somewhere along the way, you will be impressed with one or two foreign-born mates who come into your life. It appears you may have unusual living situations, or it may just be that you live in unusual living quarters. You work best alone but are comfortable with teamwork. Your performance continues to improve at a steady pace.

You expect the unexpected, and you often resort to stirring the pot merely to create challenges. Writing books or short stories or poetry would suit you, but you might also be content working in a car wash or as a chef.

Very possibly you'll support yourself in one thing while you concentrate on another. You may feel like a puddle-jumper when it comes to career, but you'll find your niche and have a story to tell. Very likely, this is how you become that renowned writer or poet. Hang in there!

✳ ✳ ✳

MAY 14

TAURUS • The winged bull of the zodiac

April 20 at 4:00 A.M. to May 21 at 4:00 A.M. • NUMEROLOGY 5

Possessions and Desires . . .

Gem: Amethyst—This stone is said to give calmness and peace.

Flower: Sumac—You may need to have things perfect before you can enjoy them.

Astral Color, Color Need, Apparel Color: Your Astral Color is Red, which enhances passion, power, excitement, and strength. Yellow in your environment stimulates and exhilarates you. In your wardrobe, Rose gives you balance and harmony.

Fragrance: You are devoted to the scent of roses. Choose the buds that have the strongest fragrance to create the special emotions you need.

Tree: Apple—You are creative, full of joy, and nearly magical. You bring happiness.

Instruments: Viola, trumpet

Composer: Liszt

Bird: Flamingo—This beautiful, gregarious bird is always careful of its enemy. It is also a caretaker of the young who tries to keep everyone happy.

Symbol: Triangle—You have the right combination of abilities.

Harmonious Health and Nutrition . . .

Health Scents: Peach—This scent may balance your good qualities so they equal your charm.

Favorable Foods: Radishes, peaches, eggs, beef

What's Lucky . . .

Lucky Numbers: 4, 5, 6, 14

Best Months: May and July

Best Day of the Week: Friday

Best Month Days: 4, 5, 23

Lucky Charms: A rabbit's foot or a white candle.

Harmonious Signs for Relationships and Partnerships: Virgo, Capricorn, and sometimes Libra.

Spiritual Guides . . .

Star: Al Heka—Those with this star are driven to succeed.

Angel: Asmodel—This angel governs business and other transactions and aids in negotiations.

Guardian Angel: Plavwell—This angel gives power and strength to one's presence.

Spiritual Stone: Topaz—This stone may protect the bearer from the effects of allergies.

✶ JUDITH'S INSIGHT ✶

You have the gift of gab and are quite the talker. Others feel close to you. You somehow manage to keep your left hand from knowing what your right hand is doing. Talk about being complicated! You have a marvelous look and are so appealing to the eye, you'll have no problem in attracting a mate. You do have to be cautious of that occasional sharp tongue, as this could create havoc in any relationship. You can take a lot and are slow to anger, but when you finally lose it, the steam that has been building bursts forth. Passionate to a fault, you have a tendency to avoid too much conversational intimacy.

You should strive for more independence when it comes to your career. Your exceptionally fine brain works well for you, no matter what the demands. Your decision that you are better off working on your own is delayed because you work so well with others. You eventually recognize your capability to take charge. You expect others to pull their own weight, like you, and are intolerant of lazy people.

Working along with others is fine for you, but needing them bothers you. Whether you become the butcher, the baker, or the television producer, you will have many opportunities to use your various talents. You underestimate your own skills, and it's hard for you to realize that others aren't as skilled as you and may lack your keen eye or strong sense of originality.

Be patient with others, and you learn to tolerate yourself better.

✶ ✶ ✶

MAY 15

TAURUS • The winged bull of the zodiac

April 20 at 4:00 A.M. to May 21 at 4:00 A.M. • NUMEROLOGY 6

Possessions and Desires . . .

Gem: Topaz—This is an excellent gift to be exchanged between very loyal friends.

Flower: Sweet William—You love gallantry above all other virtues.

Astral Color, Color Need, Apparel Color: Your Astral Color is Red, which enhances passion, power, excitement, and strength. Yellow in your environment stimulates and exhilarates you. In your wardrobe, Rose gives you balance and harmony.

Fragrance: You are devoted to the scent of roses. Choose the buds that have the strongest fragrance to create the special emotions you need.

Tree: Palm—You tend to be very healthy and creative.

Instruments: Tambourine, lyre

Composer: Schubert

Bird: Lark—known for the beauty of its song, which is sometimes very unusual. It is also credited with extraordinary intelligence.

Symbol: Crescent—You are more likely to be influenced by the phases of the moon. Your easygoing manner leads you to peaceful situations.

Harmonious Health and Nutrition . . .

Health Scent: Orange Blossom—This scent may balance your body, mind, and soul.

Favorable Foods: Turnips, lime, cheese, oysters

What's Lucky . . .

Lucky Numbers: 4, 6, 12, 15

Best Months: May and July

Best Day of the Week: Friday

Best Month Days: 6, 15, 24

Lucky Charms: A religious token or card from any religion.

Harmonious Signs for Relationships and

Partnerships: Virgo, Capricorn, and sometimes Libra.

Spiritual Guides . . .

Star: Al Debaran—Those with this star are born leaders.

Angel: Asmodel—This angel governs business and other transactions and aids in negotiations.

Guardian Angel: Michael—"Who is like God."

Spiritual Stone: Topaz—This stone may protect the bearer from the effects of allergies.

✳ JUDITH'S INSIGHT ✳

You love entertaining friends and family, especially the children. Often considered intense and meticulous, you appreciate a grand home and a designer office. You're always willing to go all out to make things happen, not only for yourself but also for others.

You must be cautious when it comes to finding the right partner. Your ability to idealize relationships also puts strain on them. Your romantic desires sometimes can be more important than simply maintaining a good relationship or keeping harmony within it. You can be both angel or devil with trident in hand, depending on the situation. Most often the angel is readily apparent, but look out when that devil surfaces!

You should seek to work with beauty one way or another. Some options you should consider: architect, landscaper, builder, designer, or florist. The possibilities are endless. You may find your most fulfilling role as a physician, perhaps a plastic surgeon. Beauty is everywhere!

You have a weak spot for animals or the underdogs in life. Keep these emotions and this enthusiasm burning in your heart and devote yourself to a good cause. Try volunteering your time and services or become a caretaker in some other way. Your good nature will inevitably ensure that your kindness will be noticed by others, even if you don't know it at the time.

✳ ✳ ✳

MAY 16

TAURUS • The winged bull of the zodiac

April 20 at 4:00 A.M. to May 21 at 4:00 A.M. • NUMEROLOGY 7

Possessions and Desires . . .

Gem: Agate—This stone may promote health and lead you to a long life.

Flower: Lilac—You may have a phenomenal memory.

Astral Color, Color Need, Apparel Color: Your Astral Color is Red, which enhances passion, power, excitement, and strength. Yellow in your environment stimulates and exhilarates you. In your wardrobe, Rose gives you balance and harmony.

Fragrance: You are devoted to the scent of roses. Choose the buds that have the strongest fragrance to create the special emotions you need.

Tree: Sycamore—Yours is the ability to love, communicate honestly with others, and have lasting relationships.

Instrument: Harp

Composers: Gluck, Brahms

Bird: Skylark—This handsome bird is beautiful when it sings. It always whistles as it works.

Symbol: Heart—You are enthusiastic, empathetic, and full of generosity and love.

Harmonious Health and Nutrition . . .

Health Scent: Jasmine—This scent may make you more easygoing when you are stressed.

Favorable Foods: Spinach, strawberries, liver, eggs

What's Lucky . . .

Lucky Numbers: 4, 6, 7, 16
Best Months: May and July
Best Day of the Week: Friday
Best Month Days: 6, 15, 24
Lucky Charm: An old key.
Harmonious Signs for Relationships and Partnerships: Virgo, Capricorn, and sometimes Libra.

Spiritual Guides . . .

Star: Al Heka—Those with this star are driven to succeed.

Angel: Asmodel—This angel governs business and other transactions and aids in negotiations.

Guardian Angel: Raphael—This angel attends to all of your needs when you are looking for guidance.

Spiritual Stone: Topaz—This stone may protect the bearer from the effects of allergies.

✶ JUDITH'S INSIGHT ✶

Your very presence gives encouragement to others. Friends and family are loyal throughout your life. They know your devotion to them. You are good-natured, kind, and honorable. You are a giver by nature. This benevolence may be detrimental to you, because you give of yourself and your pocketbook to the utmost. You are self-indulgent at times, especially as you pursue the quality things. A nonconformist, you may appear eccentric, and others may view you as peculiar.

Monetary rewards manifest themselves one way or another during your lifetime. You may be successful in the legal issues of your life; maybe an inheritance ensures your fortune. You are better at expressing your feelings through writing rather than speaking. There are many opportunities in which to invest your skills. You may have a career as a nurse or teacher. You will also find much satisfaction as a devoted guardian or parent. Family members residing with you will benefit from your caring ways. This leads to other acts of good will, such as being responsible for getting a new wing on the local hospital, or devoting your time as a volunteer to local charities. Your humanitarian efforts will go far.

Listen to yourself and learn to follow your dreams. Unusual events in life help you and guide you. Let your dreams give you the answers you seek. You count on that guardian angel looking out for you, and in turn you provide great protection to many others.

✶ ✶ ✶

MAY 17

TAURUS • The winged bull of the zodiac

April 20 at 4:00 A.M. to May 21 at 4:00 A.M. • NUMEROLOGY 8

Possessions and Desires . . .

Gem: Sapphire—This gem may help you find forgiveness from those you've wronged.

Flower: Thistle—You tend to feel that to avoid excess is the way to success.

Astral Color, Color Need, Apparel Color: Your Astral Color is Red, which enhances passion, power, excitement, and strength. Yellow in your environment stimulates and exhilarates you. In your wardrobe, Rose gives you balance and harmony.

Fragrance: You are devoted to the scent of roses. Choose the buds that have the strongest fragrance to create the special emotions you need.

Tree: Pine—Your relationships tend to be harmonious, both emotionally and mentally.

Instrument: Cello

Composer: Mozart

Bird: Bobolink—This charming singer is equally good as a soloist or a member of an orchestra. It is a very romantic bird, most useful as an insect destroyer, and elegant, with beautiful feathers, and always pleasant to have around.

Symbol: Wings—You are the source of balance in your world—this will bring you contentment.

Harmonious Health and Nutrition . . .

Health Scent: Almond—This scent may revitalize you and open you to greater possibilities.

Favorable Foods: Spinach, raspberries, cheese, salmon

What's Lucky . . .

Lucky Numbers: 4, 6, 8, 17

Best Months: May and July

Best Day of the Week: Friday

Best Month Days: 8, 17, 26

Lucky Charm: Red ribbon in your wallet or doorway.

Harmonious Signs for Relationships and

Partnerships: Virgo, Capricorn, and sometimes Libra.

Spiritual Guides . . .

Star: Al Heka—Those with this star are driven to succeed.

Angel: Asmodel—This angel governs business and other transactions and aids in negotiations.

Guardian Angel: Seraphim—An angel that brings love, light, and passion.

Spiritual Stone: Topaz—This stone may protect the bearer from the effects of allergies.

✶ JUDITH'S INSIGHT ✶

Craving love and affection the way you do could take you down the wrong paths. So keep this in mind; be cautious about taking unnecessary chances or letting yourself be careless in these matters. You are called the child of fate. This stems from the numerous changes in your surroundings from the time of your birth. Being strong-willed makes it difficult for you to express your emotions. Throughout your life, this will be a challenge all its own. You sacrifice yourself often for others, especially family members, but all the while you are seeking their approval.

The search is on when it comes to love matters—it will indeed take time and patience, yet the outcome is ultimately worth waiting for. Watch out for feelings of loneliness, even when you are in a good, loving relationship. Friendships, however, may be your greatest source of support and contentment, although you tend to underestimate the power of your friends.

Your financial gains come not only from hard work but also through careful investments in solid, grounded companies. You would be good at developing land or landscape architecture. Your talent for innovative ideas is best put to use there, or in the arts, as long as it's in a hands-on situation. Most others must follow their hearts. You, however, must follow your gut. You have great intuition and great instincts. These attributes will enable you to succeed in business.

✶ ✶ ✶

MAY 18   TAURUS • The winged bull of the zodiac
April 20 at 4:00 A.M. to May 21 at 4:00 A.M. • NUMEROLOGY 9

Possessions and Desires . . .

Gem: Emerald—Those who carry this stone tend to be lucky in love.
Flower: Vervain—You usually seem extremely charming to those around you.
Astral Color, Color Need, Apparel Color: Your Astral Color is Red, which enhances passion, power, excitement, and strength. Yellow in your environment stimulates and exhilarates you. In your wardrobe, Rose gives you balance and harmony.
Fragrance: You are devoted to the scent of roses. Choose the buds that have the strongest fragrance to create the special emotions you need.
Tree: Holly—Beware that you are not carried away by your passionate nature. The only way to grow is to be open to new experiences.
Instruments: Violin, tympanum
Composer: Gluck
Bird: Mockingbird—the most proficient minstrel in the world's orchestra; graceful and enthusiastic.
Symbol: Anchor—This tranquil symbol signifies stability and strength, and stands for strong commitments in relationships.

Harmonious Health and Nutrition . . .

Health Scent: Lavender—This scent might lead others to trust you and make you patient.
Favorable Foods: Watercress, bananas, eggs, chicken

What's Lucky . . .

Lucky Numbers: 4, 6, 9, 18
Best Months: May and July
Best Day of the Week: Friday
Best Month Days: 9, 18, 27
Lucky Charms: A U.S. coin or a bill of any amount from the year you were born.
Harmonious Signs for Relationships and

Partnerships: Virgo, Capricorn, and sometimes Libra.

Spiritual Guides . . .

Star: Al Debaran—Those with this star are born leaders.
Angel: Asmodel—This angel governs business and other transactions and aids in negotiations.
Guardian Angel: Gabriel—"God is my strength."
Spiritual Stone: Topaz—This stone may protect the bearer from the effects of allergies.

✶ JUDITH'S INSIGHT ✶

Organization? Nobody does it better than you. You enjoy working and are capable of producing almost anything. In time, and with your natural talents, you will be quite successful. Unfortunately, you get in your own way. Learn to step around yourself, and don't hold back. Competitive by nature, you can debate most topics. A challenge whets your appetite and will be what drives you to get the job done. Just remember, be careful of what you wish for; in time and after skirting many obstacles, you get the golden ring.

The emotional part isn't as easy for you. Your strong will and impatience can sometimes ruin relationships because of your inability to allow them time to work. People can get to you and ruffle your feathers with their indecisiveness. You tend to have more successes in business than you do with love, but inevitably you do find mates who understand and appreciate you.

Your practicality will take you far. It would not be surprising if you sought structure in your career, perhaps with the military or the police force or in a position in government or politics. You may be in charge. You yearn for intrigue and some action, and it is likely you will have dual careers and/or hobbies.

Family members play a big role in your life. You do, however, pull away from time to time because of the pressures on you. Self-confidence will bring you to the door of success and provide the key to open it.

✶ ✶ ✶

MAY 19
TAURUS • The winged bull of the zodiac
April 20 at 4:00 A.M. to May 21 at 4:00 A.M. • NUMEROLOGY 1

Possessions and Desires . . .

Gem: Turquoise—This stone may help you find material wealth.

Flower: Trillium—You are usually very modest about your many gifts.

Astral Color, Color Need, Apparel Color: Your Astral Color is Red, which enhances passion, power, excitement, and strength. Yellow in your environment stimulates and exhilarates you. In your wardrobe, Rose gives you balance and harmony.

Fragrance: You are devoted to the scent of roses. Choose the buds that have the strongest fragrance to create the special emotions you need.

Tree: Walnut—You are unusually helpful and always looking for new beginnings.

Instruments: Oboe, flute, clarinet, piano, French horn, organ, piccolo

Composer: Böhm

Bird: Bird of Paradise—the "bird of the Gods." You will shine and love extraordinary circumstances.

Symbol: Crown—the universal sign of dignity.

Harmonious Health and Nutrition . . .

Health Scent: Strawberry—Soothing by nature, the strawberry promotes self-esteem and encourages love.

Favorable Foods: Watercress, bananas, eggs, chicken

What's Lucky . . .

Lucky Numbers: 1, 4, 6, 10
Best Months: May and July
Best Day of the Week: Friday
Best Month Days: 1, 10, 19, 28
Lucky Charm: A new penny in your shoe.
Harmonious Signs for Relationships and

Partnerships: Virgo, Capricorn, and sometimes Libra.

Spiritual Guides . . .

Star: Al Heka—Those with this star are driven to succeed.

Angel: Asmodel—This angel governs business and other transactions and aids in negotiations.

Guardian Angel: Malachi—"Messenger of Jehovah."

Spiritual Stone: Topaz—This stone may protect the bearer from the effects of allergies.

✷ JUDITH'S INSIGHT ✷

Self-reliance and creativity are your foundation, and you also have a compassionate and nurturing nature. You recoil from criticism, but do not discount everything; some criticism is constructive. Your kindness may be misunderstood by those not as nice as you. You could work well in a hospital either volunteering your services or pursuing a career. Your keen eye and delightful bedside manner would be most appreciated. You stand tall in such a setting. You are happiest with a specific goal, but do not narrow your options when fixing goals. You are likely to aspire to many, and accomplish much.

How you view yourself is far more important than how others see you. You can be your own worst enemy, especially when it comes to love. An adoring mate doesn't ruffle your feathers easily, but that independent companion puts you through many a hurdle. Your tolerance here pays off when your independent companion becomes your adoring mate.

Give yourself a break. It's okay not to extend your helping hand every time. Learn to sit back, enjoy the music, and watch the show, even if you are worrying about your neighbor's needs. The kindness you provide comes back to you.

✷ ✷ ✷

MAY 20

TAURUS • The winged bull of the zodiac

April 20 at 4:00 A.M. to May 21 at 4:00 A.M. • NUMEROLOGY 2

Possessions and Desires . . .

Gem: Sapphire—This gem may help you find forgiveness from those you've wronged.
Flower: Wallflower—You usually have the strength to get through any adversity.
Astral Color, Color Need, Apparel Color: Your Astral Color is Red, which enhances passion, power, excitement, and strength. Yellow in your environment stimulates and exhilarates you. In your wardrobe, Rose gives you balance and harmony.
Fragrance: You are devoted to the scent of roses. Choose the buds that have the strongest fragrance to create the special emotions you need.
Tree: Maple—You have both great stability and flashes of intuition.
Instruments: Pipe organ, cymbal, drum
Composers: Handel, Johann Sebastian Bach
Bird: Stork—Turkish bird, held in high esteem the world over. This bird is intelligent but may have strange tendencies.
Symbol: Cross—the symbol of self-sacrifice and reconciliation.

Harmonious Health and Nutrition . . .

Health Scent: Apple—You are creative, full of joy, and nearly magical. You bring happiness.
Favorable Foods: Turnips, grapes, buttermilk, oysters

What's Lucky . . .

Lucky Numbers: 2, 4, 6
Best Months: May and July
Best Day of the Week: Friday
Best Month Days: 2, 11, 20, 29
Lucky Charms: Two 50-cent pieces. Give someone else one of them.
Harmonious Signs for Relationships and

Partnerships: Virgo, Capricorn, and sometimes Libra.

Spiritual Guides . . .

Star: Al Heka—Those with this star are driven to succeed.
Angel: Asmodel—This angel governs business and other transactions and aids in negotiations.
Guardian Angel: St. John—This angel simplifies that which is complicated.
Spiritual Stone: Topaz—This stone may protect the bearer from the effects of allergies.

✶ JUDITH'S INSIGHT ✶

Community-minded and sociable, you simply love to entertain. You seek that perfect appearance at all times. Your well-balanced mind brings much peace. You can be rather shrewd, but you keep that hidden. Your inquisitive, inventive nature, coupled with your wit, ensures a good future as a counselor, teacher, police detective, or even an incredibly successful politician. You are a leader; you can do anything from being the president of the PTA to being the president of the United States. You'll probably be in government. Somewhere along the way, the law enters your lifestyle. With your questioning mind, you may find yourself taking on some great attorneys or defending renowned criminals.

Early in life your vanity contributes to your condescending attitude toward your love mate. Maturity brings balance and after some emotional bumps and bruises, you become comfortable with close relationships and are very much better at working on those alliances.

Entertainment simply intrigues you; don't be surprised if you occasionally seek a bit of excess. Your fondness for fine art and music may enhance a career or provide a satisfying hobby that consumes all your spare time.

✶ ✶ ✶

MAY 21 TAURUS • The winged bull of the zodiac

April 20 at 4:00 A.M. to May 21 at 4:00 A.M. • NUMEROLOGY 3

Possessions and Desires . . .

Gem: Ruby—This stone may lead you to energy, friendship, and happiness.

Flower: Weeping Willow—You may spend too much time focusing on what you've lost instead of what you have to gain.

Astral Color, Color Need, Apparel Color: Your Astral Color is Red, which enhances passion, power, excitement, and strength. Yellow in your environment stimulates and exhilarates you. In your wardrobe, Rose gives you balance and harmony.

Fragrance: You are devoted to the scent of roses. Choose the buds that have the strongest fragrance to create the special emotions you need.

Tree: Elm—You have willpower, strength, and the ability to stand alone.

Instrument: Trombone

Composers: Verdi, Mendelssohn, Schumann

Bird: Swan—Regarded as royal and sacred, this bird has the protective nature of a mother, and can become a furious fighter in the defense of its young.

Symbol: Wreath—You have been crowned with a special personality. You are strong but extremely compassionate.

Harmonious Health and Nutrition . . .

Health Scent: Rose—This scent will lead you to passionate thoughts and make you feel warm inside.

Favorable Foods: Tomatoes, black figs, eggs, beef

What's Lucky . . .

Lucky Numbers: 3, 4, 6
Best Months: May and July
Best Day of the Week: Friday
Best Month Days: 3, 12, 21, 30
Lucky Charm: A pen that someone else has already used.
Harmonious Signs for Relationships and Partnerships: Virgo, Capricorn, and sometimes Libra.

Spiritual Guides . . .

Star: Al Debaran—Those with this star are born leaders.

Angel: Asmodel—This angel governs business and other transactions and aids in negotiations.

Guardian Angel: Johiel—This angel is a protector of all those with a humble heart.

Spiritual Stone: Topaz—This stone may protect the bearer from the effects of allergies.

✳ JUDITH'S INSIGHT ✳

Your sense of freedom dictates your actions and reactions. It is not surprising if you follow through with those unexpected urges to change your lifestyle by redoing your house or relocating out of state. You are meticulous about your appearance to friends, relatives, and strangers alike. You seek the social environment and everything it has to offer. You rebel against injustice in any form and tend to fight for the underdog. Your artistic nature draws you to the arts one way or another, whether through music, poetry, or the ballet, or merely as a frequent patron of the theater. Staying up late watching movies, you project yourself into nearly every scene.

That strong, devoted love of friends and family makes you more than willing to take on the responsibilities of others, be it giving of yourself or slipping some dollars into pockets. Don't permit your inherent love of home to blind you to the manipulations of some undeserving characters. Although fiercely loyal to your family, you can be fickle with your friends. You enjoy having children around you, and you play a strong role in children's lives. This could be as a loving parent, but more than likely you will be a Dutch uncle, the godmother/godfather, or just the neighbor willing to listen.

You love receiving invitations, whether or not you go where you're invited. You are anxious to be more of a socialite than you are. As time passes, you get to that desired place in society. You can seem eccentric. You like unusual decorations in your home or office. It's possible you will deal in antiques. Whatever path you take, your career takes off, and in time, success means money.

✳ ✳ ✳

MAY 22
GEMINI • The twins of the zodiac
May 21 at 4:00 A.M. to June 21 at 12:00 P.M. • NUMEROLOGY 4

Possessions and Desires . . .

Gem: Topaz—This is an excellent gift to be exchanged between very loyal friends.

Flower: Willow—You love to be free so much that any boundary feels like a prison.

Astral Color, Color Need, Apparel Color: Your Astral Color is Red, which enhances passion, power, excitement, and strength. Violet in your environment will keep you empathetic toward others. In your wardrobe, Green is your power color for overcoming obstacles.

Fragrance: You should flood your living space with the scent of distilled floral bouquet or freshly cut wood. This will give your ever-curious mind a rest from its constant search for new experiences.

Tree: Cherry—You will find yourself faced with constant new emotional awakenings.

Instrument: Bass, clarinet

Composers: Haydn, Wagner

Bird: Robin—the most sociable of all birds, with the ability to create quick friendships. It also can easily adapt to any home. When it wants something, it has the tendency to try to snatch it.

Symbol: Star—You are full of inner brightness and will stand out in any crowd. You will be seen as special.

Harmonious Health and Nutrition . . .

Health Scent: Vanilla—This scent will fill you with a feeling of cleanliness and stability.

Favorable Foods: Kale, grapes, whole-wheat breads, molasses, goat's milk

What's Lucky . . .

Lucky Numbers: 4, 5, 8, 9
Best Months: April and August
Best Day of the Week: Wednesday
Best Month Days: 4, 13, 22, 31
Lucky Charm: A piece of material cut from something in your home.

Harmonious Signs for Relationships and Partnerships: Aquarius and Libra

Spiritual Guides . . .

Star: Al Divah—Those with this star could feel that they are mistreated by relatives.

Angel: Ambriel—This angel governs travel and transportation, particularly over water, and helps to create love and good communication.

Guardian Angel: Uriel—This angel brings the light of God's guidance.

Spiritual Stone: Chrysoprasus—This stone aids in relaxation.

✴ JUDITH'S INSIGHT ✴

You are magnetic. Others are drawn to you and they don't know why. You can hypnotize with your charm. You are loved by all. Your innate desire to be conscientious attracts people. You have a style of your own; you enjoy music and science. It's possible that at a young age you were either dissecting worms or mentally testing social issues in political situations. You can write well and may find yourself in some type of media position, perhaps as a journalist or photographer. Although art is a real pull for you, the camera would be more your style as it captures your analytical ability. You very well could develop your talents and handle both sides of the camera well: behind it, directing motion pictures, or in front, acting in a film.

Fear and doubt inhibit you at times, but you can rise above these things. You like to help those in need. Independent, yet gentle and kind, you are drawn to the security of a stable relationship. Would-be mates are attracted by your magnetism, but you often discount possibilities because of some underlying fear. Remain open-minded.

You set high standards, not only for yourself, but also for others. In rising to meet these top standards, there will be falls, yet you find you easily pick yourself up and dust yourself off. Not having sufficient patience and understanding of your mate raises much more conflict, but when you learn to do so, the rewards are great.

★ ★ ★

MAY 23 GEMINI • The twins of the zodiac

May 21 at 4:00 A.M. to June 21 at 12:00 P.M. • NUMEROLOGY 5

Possessions and Desires . . .

Gem: Topaz—This is an excellent gift to be exchanged between very loyal friends.

Flower: Water Lily—Your motives are always for the best.

Astral Color, Color Need, Apparel Color: Your Astral Color is Red, which enhances passion, power, excitement, and strength. Violet in your environment keeps you empathetic towards others. In your wardrobe, Coral brings you a brilliant and sharp appearance.

Fragrance: You should flood your living space with the scent of distilled floral bouquet or freshly cut wood. This will give your ever-curious mind a rest from its constant search for new experiences.

Tree: Apple—You are creative, full of joy, and nearly magical. You bring happiness.

Instruments: Viola, trumpet

Composer: Liszt

Bird: Flamingo—This beautiful, gregarious bird is always careful of its enemy. It is also a caretaker of the young who tries to keep everyone happy.

Symbol: Triangle—You have the right combination of abilities.

Harmonious Health and Nutrition . . .

Health Scent: Peach—This scent may balance your good qualities so that they equal your charm.

Favorable Foods: Parsnips, oranges, whole-wheat bread, molasses, eggs

What's Lucky . . .

Lucky Numbers: 5, 9, 10, 23

Best Months: April and August

Best Day of the Week: Wednesday

Best Month Days: 5, 4, 23

Lucky Charms: A rabbit's foot or a white candle.

Harmonious Signs for Relationships and Partnerships: Aquarius and Libra

Spiritual Guides . . .

Star: Al Divah—Those with this star could feel that they are mistreated by relatives.

Angel: Ambriel—This angel governs travel and transportation, particularly over water, and helps to create love and good communication.

Guardian Angel: Plavwell—This angel gives power and strength to one's presence.

Spiritual Stone: Chrysoprasus—This stone aids in relaxation.

✷ JUDITH'S INSIGHT ✷

You like to play the role of hero/heroine, whether it is on the screen or in real life. Perhaps you most enjoy writing about heroic people. Analytical by nature, you could become overcritical unless, of course, you are that well-paid, published critic. Versatility abounds when it comes to your career—you can do anything from editing or writing the books to performing on stage or screen. You will be involved with literature or publishing or heading a media company. As long as you have pen and paper, you will be successful.

You find mates perhaps too early in life. You're independent in almost every aspect of your life—except your emotional ties. Love affairs are frequent, and you can be moody when it comes to showing affection. Once you have loved people in your life, your loyalty and devotion make it difficult for your significant other to sever the ties.

Family members play you like a fine violin, but you allow it. Having children involved in your life, in one way or another, is of great importance to you. The fun and spontaneity in your relationships enable you to maintain them easily. When it comes to real intimacy, these relationships require more work, as you tend to shy away. Lucky when it comes to earning money, you will have opportunities to do so in many different capacities throughout your life. You particularly desire beautiful things—even if you don't realize it. This may be expressed in a well-manicured lawn or the fine suits you wear. Eventually you feel more balanced, and harmony finds you in later years.

✷ ✷ ✷

MAY 24 GEMINI • The twins of the zodiac

May 21 at 4:00 A.M. to June 21 at 12:00 P.M. • NUMEROLOGY 6

Possessions and Desires . . .

Gem: Topaz—This is an excellent gift to be exchanged between very loyal friends.

Flower: Aconite—You need to work on liking people more.

Astral Color, Color Need, Apparel Color: Your Astral Color is Red, which enhances passion, excitement, and strength. Violet in your environment keeps you empathetic toward others. In your wardrobe, Green is your power color for overcoming obstacles.

Fragrance: You should flood your living space with the scent of distilled floral bouquet or freshly cut wood. This will give your ever-curious mind a rest from its constant search for new experiences.

Tree: Palm—You tend to be very healthy and creative.

Instruments: Tambourine, lyre

Composer: Schubert

Bird: Goldfinch—there are forty-four different species of finches which vary greatly. This can sometimes be the most charming of birds. These gentle creatures can be very moody in unsettled weather.

Symbol: Crescent—You are more likely to be influenced by the phases of the moon. Your easygoing manner leads you to peaceful situations.

Harmonious Health and Nutrition . . .

Health Scent: Orange Blossom—This scent may balance your body, mind, and soul.

Favorable Foods: Cabbage, huckleberries, whole-wheat bread, buttermilk

What's Lucky . . .

Lucky Numbers: 5, 6, 9, 12
Best Months: April and August
Best Day of the Week: Wednesday
Best Month Days: 6, 15, 24
Lucky Charms: A religious token or card from any religion.
Harmonious Signs for Relationships and Partnerships: Aquarius and Libra

Spiritual Guides . . .

Star: Al Henah—Those born under this star are easily wounded.

Angel: Ambriel—This angel governs travel and transportation, particularly over water, and helps to create love and good communication.

Guardian Angel: Michael—"Who is like God."

Spiritual Stone: Chrysoprasus—This stone aids in relaxation.

✴ JUDITH'S INSIGHT ✴

You enjoy writing, especially about issues of a mysterious nature. You love music, art, and the sciences. You could find yourself drawn to a career in science. Generally, you have a lot of enthusiasm about which direction you take in life, but occasionally you are stifled when your environment is no longer stimulating and comfortable. Small annoyances from people bother you more than you think, but the atmosphere at the moment has much to do with it. Watch out for those who drink too much around you.

Lighthearted and sympathetic, you yearn for love, and when you find it, you appreciate how much being loved means to you. You reap what you sow and cultivate great relationships with current friends, while maintaining friendships from childhood. Relationships continue to emerge as you get older. Family occupies a large role in your life, especially your father or another male—be aware that this could be a vulnerable situation for you. Your enthusiasm can make you appear intense in relationships. All in all, you will have an understanding mate and will learn to keep the balance.

As for your career, make sure you gravitate toward putting your thoughts on paper. If you are a caretaker, for example, a nurse, doctor, therapist, or psychologist, keep that pen handy and maintain a journal. This will not only assist you in ousting emotions so that they have no place to hide, but give you a basis for perhaps a literary piece. It may not seem creative, but becoming a detective or investigator could bring out things in you that you don't realize are there. You can be shrewd when needed, and this, too, supports your aspirations. You prefer working alone, but you recognize that team work can be more advantageous. You circulate with people in high positions and sometimes are intrigued by them. As time passes, you'll be at the top.

MAY 25 GEMINI • The twins of the zodiac

May 21 at 4:00 A.M. to June 21 at 12:00 P.M. • NUMEROLOGY 7

Possessions and Desires . . .

Gem: Ruby—This stone may lead you to energy, friendship, and happiness.

Flower: Rhubarb—You may love to give advice, but you are not apt to take it.

Astral Color, Color Needs, Apparel Color: Your Astral Color is Red, which enhances passion, excitement, and strength. Violet in your environment keeps you empathetic toward others. In your wardrobe, Wine gives you energy.

Fragrance: You should flood your living space with the scent of distilled floral bouquet or freshly cut wood. This will give your ever-curious mind a rest from its constant search for new experiences.

Tree: Sycamore—Yours is the ability to love, communicate honestly with others, and have lasting relationships.

Instrument: Harp

Composers: Gluck, Brahms

Bird: Skylark—This handsome bird is beautiful when it sings. It always whistles as it works.

Symbol: Heart—You are enthusiastic, empathetic, and full of generosity and love.

Harmonious Health and Nutrition . . .

Health Scent: Jasmine—This scent may make you more easygoing when you are stressed.

Favorable Foods: Prunes, whole-wheat bread, molasses, goat's milk

What's Lucky . . .

Lucky Numbers: 5, 7, 9, 14

Best Months: April and August

Best Day of the Week: Wednesday

Best Month Days: 6, 15, 24

Lucky Charm: An old key.

Harmonious Signs for Relationships and Partnerships: Aquarius and Libra

Spiritual Guides . . .

Star: Al Divah—Those with this star could feel that they are mistreated by relatives.

Angel: Ambriel—This angel governs travel and transportation, particularly over water, and helps to create love and good communication.

Guardian Angel: Raphael—This angel attends to all of your needs when you are looking for guidance.

Spiritual Stone: Chrysoprasus—This stone aids in relaxation.

✳ JUDITH'S INSIGHT ✳

You are at times impractical; your fondness for pleasure attracts you to sports, entertainment, and amusements. One of these areas may be a great place to work: in the movies, entertaining people on stage, or on the athletic field. You do anything to entertain others and enjoy yourself. You switch easily from having a good time to being more serious. You also long for knowledge and may have many years of education or take classes in different fields for your own enjoyment. Be cautious about getting sidetracked and leaving things undone. Even if you don't attend classes, you will make the effort to learn by observing others.

You are basically content and free from anxieties. Sympathetic at times, you can also be demanding. You enjoy being generous, but you fear being taken advantage of. When you feel comfortable and believe you are receiving, you give more freely. Your skepticism of others' generosity fades with the years. With family members, you swing back and forth from closeness and security to feeling insecure, which, at times, creates distance.

Despite your intuition and good sense, you allow people into your life too quickly and may give too much credence to what they say. Trust your instincts—your first impression is most often right. You are critical at times, and your analytical side could foster a career in computers, working from your home or office. You may find that two careers surface simultaneously. You're capable of doing both, but one will most likely become a hobby. You feel complete with a partner in harmonious situations, be it marriage, partnership, or friendship. Stay active—loneliness may bring about depression. Not to say there isn't harmony in being alone. You just prefer to hold hands through life.

✳ ✳ ✳

MAY 26 GEMINI • The twins of the zodiac

May 21 at 4:00 A.M. to June 21 at 12:00 P.M. • NUMEROLOGY 8

Possessions and Desires . . .

Gem: Topaz—This is an excellent gift to be exchanged between very loyal friends.

Flower: Phlox—You may go along with the crowd more than could be good for you.

Astral Color, Color Need, Apparel Color: Your Astral Color is Red, which enhances passion, excitement, and strength. Violet in your environment keeps you empathetic toward others. In your wardrobe, Coral brings you a brilliant and sharp appearance.

Fragrance: You should flood your living space with the scent of distilled floral bouquet or freshly cut wood. This will give your ever-curious mind a rest from its constant search for new experiences.

Tree: Pine—Your relationships tend to be balanced, both emotionally and mentally.

Instrument: Cello

Composer: Mozart

Bird: Bobolink—This charming singer is equally good as a soloist or a member of an orchestra. It is a very romantic bird, useful as an insect destroyer, and elegant, with beautiful feathers, and always pleasant to have around.

Symbol: Wings—You are the source of balance in your world—this will bring you contentment.

Harmonious Health and Nutrition . . .

Health Scent: Almond—This scent may revitalize you and open you to greater possibilities.

Favorable Foods: Kale, grapes, whole-wheat bread, eggs

What's Lucky . . .

Lucky Numbers: 5, 8, 9, 16

Best Months: April and August

Best Day of the Week: Wednesday

Best Month Days: 8, 17, 26

Lucky Charm: Red ribbon in your wallet or doorway.

Harmonious Signs for Relationships and Partnerships: Aquarius and Libra

Spiritual Guides . . .

Star: Al Henah—Those born under this star are easily wounded.

Angel: Ambriel—This angel governs travel and transportation, particularly over water, and helps to create love and good communication

Guardian Angel: Seraphim—An angel that brings love, light, and passion.

Spiritual Stone: Chrysoprasus—This stone aids in relaxation.

✴ JUDITH'S INSIGHT ✴

You appreciate the finer things in life. You like Paris, the carnival, and springtime. You have extreme likes and dislikes. Strong and confident as you leave the house, you are easily discouraged and arrive home depressed and unmotivated. You could live two different lives, and no one would know it. You always wish you were someplace else. Easily distracted, you switch from project to project. If channeled properly, your drive could further a successful life's work. You will probably seek multiple educational degrees or vocational skills. Just about any job in education would be a number one choice.

Keep a journal, and you'll see progress. You will be pleasantly surprised how good a writer you are. Keep track, too, of your dreams—you feel comfortably connected to them. Your fear of publicity curbs your need to be known and heard. One way or another you seek to contribute to others; if not on stage, perhaps, through your writing. With your distinctive voice, you may have the opportunity to write song lyrics, and record the songs as well! If singing is not a career, you should join your local choir or other choral group.

Balancing the scales is learning about yourself while including family and loved ones. Childhood friends support you. You may have many careers before you find a balance in your mid-forties, but the trip along the way is more than satisfactory. You know how to have a good time by leaving your mind at home. When things become overwhelming, you recognize you must turn off your mind for a while.

✴ ✴ ✴

MAY 27   GEMINI • The twins of the zodiac

May 21 at 4:00 A.M. to June 21 at 12:00 P.M. • NUMEROLOGY 9

Possessions and Desires . . .

Gem: Topaz—This is an excellent gift to be exchanged between very loyal friends.

Flower: Meadowsweet—You should guard against thinking that there is no purpose to whatever challenge the universe gives you.

Astral Color, Color Need, Apparel Color: Your Astral Color is Red, which enhances passion, excitement, and strength. Violet in your environment keeps you empathetic toward others. In your wardrobe, Coral brings you a brilliant and sharp appearance.

Fragrance: You should flood your living space with the scent of distilled floral bouquet or freshly cut wood. This will give your ever-curious mind a rest from its constant search for new experiences.

Tree: Holly—Beware that you are not carried away by your passionate nature. The only way to grow is to be open to new experiences..

Instruments: Violin, tympanum

Composer: Gluck

Bird: Mockingbird—the most proficient minstrel in the world's orchestra; graceful and enthusiastic.

Symbol: Anchor—This tranquil symbol signifies stability and strength, and stands for strong commitments in relationships.

Harmonious Health and Nutrition . . .

Health Scent: Lavender—This scent might lead others to trust you and make you patient.

Favorable Foods: Cucumbers, oranges, whole-wheat bread, cottage cheese

What's Lucky . . .

Lucky Numbers: 5, 9, 18, 27

Best Months: April and August

Best Day of the Week: Wednesday

Best Month Days: 9, 18, 27

Lucky Charms: A U.S. coin or a bill of any amount from the year you were born.

Harmonious Signs for Relationships and Partnerships: Aquarius and Libra

Spiritual Guides . . .

Star: Al Divah—Those with this star could feel that they are mistreated by relatives.

Angel: Ambriel—This angel governs travel and transportation, particularly over water, and helps to create love and good communication.

Guardian Angel: Gabriel—"God is my strength."

Spiritual Stone: Chrysoprasus—This stone aids in relaxation.

✳ JUDITH'S INSIGHT ✳

Your intuition and active mind form a strong desire for the mystical and the unknown. Your niche may be in psychic work or another spiritual field. Your practical side, however, creates contradiction, unless you write about it. You have talent for organization, and you desire conquest on a large scale. The ability to acquire wealth and power is yours, but watch out for unnecessary spending. You find power exciting and thrive on conflict. You'd do well on a debating team or in the political arena. Legal contests will present themselves. Be careful that you're not on the losing side. Be on guard for feeling out of control and overreacting.

In love, you lean toward obsessiveness or possessiveness. Demonstrate the affection you want others to. Think less and act more. You have more of a romantic mind than a romantic heart. In younger years, you are flirtatious. Luck in love comes in your thirties. If you marry earlier, you may fear you've chosen the wrong person or have years of dispute, but all gets resolved if that's what you want.

There is no undertaking too large for you, but your overzealous style may cause career downfalls. Fear not, most things work out. As for family, you assume enough responsibility to feel consumed. You may move away—not necessarily to create distance from the emotional drain—circumstances may simply bring this about. Don't fight it. You may choose a strong mate, and then find that strength and vitality are too much for you. In time, there will be balance and harmony. Financially, you do reasonably well. You accumulate many possessions to reassure yourself of your wealth and stability, but you must learn to share and to develop your generosity.

✳ ✳ ✳

MAY 28   GEMINI • The twins of the zodiac

May 21 at 4:00 A.M. to June 21 at 12:00 P.M. • NUMEROLOGY 1

Possessions and Desires . . .

Gem: Turquoise—This stone may help you find material wealth.

Flower: Oleander—You tend to hope more for peace than happiness.

Astral Color, Color Need, Apparel Color: Your Astral Color is Red, which enhances passion, excitement, and strength. Violet in your environment keeps you empathetic toward others. In your wardrobe, Wine gives you energy.

Fragrance: You should flood your living space with the scent of distilled floral bouquet or freshly cut wood. This will give your ever-curious mind a rest from its constant search for new experiences.

Tree: Walnut—You are unusually helpful and always looking for constant changes in your life.

Instruments: Oboe, flute, clarinet, piano, French horn, organ, piccolo

Composer: Böhm

Bird: Hummingbird—This bird is delicate and graceful. It can remain still for hours, then suddenly dart off and be as busy as a bee.

Symbol: Crown—the universal sign of dignity.

Harmonious Health and Nutrition . . .

Health Scent: Strawberry—Soothing by nature, the strawberry promotes self-esteem and encourages love.

Favorable Foods: Beets, cherries, whole-wheat bread, goat's milk

What's Lucky . . .

Lucky Numbers: 1, 5, 9, 10
Best Months: April and August
Best Day of the Week: Wednesday
Best Month Days: 1, 10, 19, 28
Lucky Charm: A new penny in your shoe.
Harmonious Signs for Relationships and Partnerships: Aquarius and Libra

Spiritual Guides . . .

Star: Al Henah—Those born under this star are easily wounded.

Angel: Ambriel—This angel governs travel and transportation, particularly over water, and helps to create love and good communication.

Guardian Angel: Malachi—"Messenger of Jehovah."

Spiritual Stone: Chrysoprasus—This stone aids in relaxation.

✶ JUDITH'S INSIGHT ✶

Creative, original and self-reliant, you are also impractical at times. You love your independence, but sometimes have to recognize your need for others. You should learn to develop your sensitivities and let people in. Build on your artistic capabilities in a career, be it photographer, artist, decorator, architect, or builder. You should follow your inclination toward the larger visions in life. When you do, you achieve. Although you seem strong and ambitious, self-esteem is sometimes low, which is the source of most of your problems. You dislike being alone and possess a driving need to always be with that special someone.

You have little patience for slow career advancement. You much prefer to simply be placed at the top. This is an immature outlook and could leave you perched at the top with little to offer. You crave recognition from friends and family. The more they stroke, the more you respond. Likewise, people get in with you with honey, not vinegar. Success awaits you, but you must make it happen. Whether your spot is in theater, fashion or beauty, you have a style all your own. The fashion industry really beckons, and you could do well. You are drawn to creative pursuits, but sometimes cannot draw on your own creativity. Be patient here until you get to a powerful situation.

Recognize that you alone don't always have to bear all the burdens. Extend your hand, take from others, and share the weight. In time, as you cultivate your sense of partnership, be it a love relationship, work, or play, you achieve harmony.

✶ ✶ ✶

MAY 29 GEMINI • The twins of the zodiac
May 21 at 4:00 A.M. to June 21 at 12:00 P.M. • NUMEROLOGY 2

Possessions and Desires . . .

Gem: Sapphire—This gem may help you find forgiveness from those you've wronged.
Flower: French Marigold—You may need to learn to trust those you love and get over being so jealous.
Astral Color, Color Need, Apparel Color: Your Astral Color is Red, which enhances passion, excitement, and strength. Violet in your environment keeps you empathetic toward others. In your wardrobe, Green is your power color for overcoming obstacles.
Fragrance: You should flood your living space with the scent of distilled floral bouquet or freshly cut wood. This will give your ever-curious mind a rest from its constant search for new experiences.
Tree: Maple—You have great stability and flashes of intuition.
Instruments: Pipe organ, cymbal, drum
Composers: Handel, Johann Sebastian Bach
Bird: Cuckoo—a good flyer and very seldom a quitter. Some cuckoos tend to think they favor lonely isolation, but what they really yearn for is a family relationship.
Symbol: Cross—the symbol of self-sacrifice and reconciliation.

Harmonious Health and Nutrition . . .

Health Scent: Apple—You are creative, full of joy, and nearly magical. You bring happiness.
Favorable Foods: Cabbage, huckleberries, whole-wheat bread, margarine

What's Lucky . . .

Lucky Numbers: 1, 5, 9, 11
Best Months: April and August
Best Day of the Week: Wednesday
Best Month Days: 2, 11, 20, 29
Lucky Charms: Two 50-cent pieces. Give someone else one of them.
Harmonious Signs for Relationships and Partnerships: Aquarius and Libra

Spiritual Guides . . .

Star: Al Henah—Those born under this star are easily wounded.
Angel: Ambriel—This angel governs travel and transportation, particularly over water, and helps to create love and good communication.
Guardian angel: St. John—The guardian that brings simplicity to all that is complicated.
Spiritual Stone: Chrysoprasus—This stone aids in relaxation.

✶ JUDITH'S INSIGHT ✶

It is easier for you to stick to something than to make changes in your life. You may dwell on your purpose in life, yet your lack of adventurousness keeps you where you are. Determined and dedicated, you prefer being on one ladder until you reach the top. It may feel like you're taking the long road. Family members are too important to you; you're often overly responsible for family and sometimes feel underappreciated. Others may see you as a drifting rebel rather than the solid rock that you are. You seem to deal with conflict on one level or another, on a daily basis. Learn to recognize you are not here to solve everyone's difficulties. Your frankness gets you in trouble, particularly with those who don't know you well. You are witty and charming. Consider writing about what goes on around you.

Relationships appear to be slow to develop at first; you tend to rush things. Be patient—you do better in time as you and your mate grow together and overcome the trouble spots. You push away those you love when angry. When you do devote yourself to someone, you give 110 percent. As long as your partner accepts your romanticism, your relationship has no limits. Stubbornness can be your greatest flaw. When you find yourself complaining, stop and listen. Others may complain about the same things about you. Your sympathetic side allows you to commiserate with others and may lead to a public, humanitarian career, as in a state hospital, school or medical institution, or perhaps making laws to improve life for the unfortunate. Creating boundaries for yourself, as well as others, will be very, very important. Once you learn to do this, you no longer need to go overboard in your emotional, physical, or professional life; the balance will contribute much to your happiness.

✶ ✶ ✶

MAY 30 GEMINI • The twins of the zodiac

May 21 at 4:00 A.M. to June 21 at 12:00 P.M. • NUMEROLOGY 3

Possessions and Desires . . .

Gem: Topaz—This is an excellent gift to be exchanged between very loyal friends.

Flower: Carolina Rose—You could fear losing yourself in love.

Astral Color, Color Need, Apparel Color: Your Astral Color is Red, which enhances passion, excitement, and strength. Violet in your environment keeps you empathetic toward others. In your wardrobe, Green is your power color for overcoming obstacles.

Fragrance: You should flood your living space with the scent of distilled floral bouquet or freshly cut wood. This will give your ever-curious mind a rest from its constant search for new experiences.

Tree: Elm—You have willpower, strength, and the ability to stand alone.

Instrument: Trombone

Composers: Verdi, Mendelssohn, Schumann

Bird: Swan—Regarded as royal and sacred, this bird has the protective nature of a mother, and can become a furious fighter in the defense of its young.

Symbol: Wreath—You have been crowned with a special personality. You are strong but extremely compassionate.

Harmonious Health and Nutrition . . .

Health Scent: Rose—This scent will lead you to passionate thoughts and make you feel warm inside.

Favorable Foods: Celery, peaches, whole-wheat bread, cottage cheese

What's Lucky . . .

Lucky Numbers: 3, 5, 6, 9
Best Months: April and August
Best Day of the Week: Wednesday
Best Month Days: 3, 12, 21, 30
Lucky Charm: A pen that someone else has already used.

Harmonious Signs for Relationships and Partnerships: Aquarius and Libra

Spiritual Guides . . .

Star: Al Henah—Those born under this star are easily wounded.

Angel: Ambriel—This angel governs travel and transportation, particularly over water, and helps to create love and good communication.

Guardian Angel: Johiel—This angel is a protector of all those with a humble heart.

Spiritual Stone: Chrysoprasus—This stone aids in relaxation.

✷ JUDITH'S INSIGHT ✷

You are enthusiastic, energetic, and ambitious. You can adapt to nearly any work scenario and efficiently accomplish it. There are no holds barred when it comes to your work. Contradiction may exist in your personality—you can be best friend or worst enemy to another. Compassionate and kind, you attract love mates easily. Be wary that you don't make commitments before you are ready. Once you commit, you are generally loyal, but you love to flirt. If you reassure your partner that the flirting is harmless, you'll fare better in the relationship. You are consistent and tolerant; it is difficult for you to let go. You can be the best child or the worst, the best parent or the worst, all in the same day. You're a bundle of contradictions, but your unfailing loyalty outweighs the conflict. Full of pride, you value beautiful things, and you're willing to work for them. A well-rounded environment makes you happiest. Since you're always looking for a new challenge, more than one career beckons. Accept this as you will grow in strength with each accomplishment. Reporter, critic, reviewer, musician, and artist are all good careers for you. Since you have such a talent with dress and style, you may even find a career in designing clothing.

You thrive among people who are warm and witty, and friendships come easily to you. You like leaving your door ajar, but be careful of unworthy persons who may walk in seeking to take advantage.

✷ ✷ ✷

MAY 31 GEMINI • The twins of the zodiac

May 21 at 4:00 A.M. to June 21 at 12:00 P.M. • NUMEROLOGY 4

Possessions and Desires . . .

Gem: Emerald—Those who carry this stone tend to be lucky in love.
Flower: Pink—Your boldness may take you far.
Astral Color, Color Need, Apparel Color: Your Astral Color is Red, which enhances passion, excitement, and strength. Violet in your environment keeps you empathetic toward others. In your wardrobe, Coral brings you a brilliant and sharp appearance.
Fragrance: You should flood your living space with the scent of distilled floral bouquet or freshly cut wood. This will give your ever-curious mind a rest from its constant search for new experiences.
Tree: Cherry—You will find yourself faced with constant new emotional awakenings.
Instruments: Bass, clarinet
Composers: Haydn, Wagner
Bird: Killdeer—This bird is usually found consorting with other species, and can adapt to any environment.
Symbol: Star—You are full of inner brightness and will stand out in any crowd. You will be seen as special.

Harmonious Health and Nutrition . . .

Health Scent: Vanilla—This scent will fill you with a feeling of cleanliness and stability.
Favorable Foods: Celery, mulberry, whole-wheat bread, buttermilk

What's Lucky . . .

Lucky Numbers: 4, 5, 8, 9
Best Months: April and August
Best Day of the Week: Wednesday
Best Month Days: 4, 13, 22, and 31
Lucky Charm: A piece of material cut from something in your home.
Harmonious Signs for Relationships and Partnerships: Aquarius and Libra

Spiritual Guides . . .

Star: Al Divah—Those with this star could feel that they are mistreated by relatives.
Angel: Ambriel—This angel governs travel and transportation, particularly over water, and helps to create love and good communication.
Guardian Angel: St. John—This angel simplifies that which is complicated.
Spiritual Stone: Chrysoprasus—This stone aids in relaxation.

✴ JUDITH'S INSIGHT ✴

You must develop tact. When you master being more diplomatic, you will have it made. You can sometimes be overly frank, despite veiling your frankness in a subtle way. Learning finesse will be your number one hurdle. Mostly satisfied with yourself, you can be critical of others, although most often with good reason. Others may view you as conceited; you do have a high regard for yourself. If you have low self-esteem, the last thing you would do is let anybody else know.

Fond of your family and friends and eager to spend time with them, you put on a party in a matter of minutes. You work at enhancing your charm and augmenting your natural beauty, but this is done subtly. With regard to spending and investing your money, you are quite cautious, although willing to spend on yourself and family members. You respect others' boundaries and create your own. You could be a great reporter, critic, reviewer, publisher, writer, musician, or artist. As well as you work on your own, you also do well with others—except in situations where others get the credit.

Owning your own home and property is definitely important—you will have both. You tend to allow your mate freedom without letting it be known just how closely you're watching. As you mature, you relax more and are less intense; as a result, you enjoy life much more than ever before, and likewise, others enjoy you more.

✴ ✴ ✴

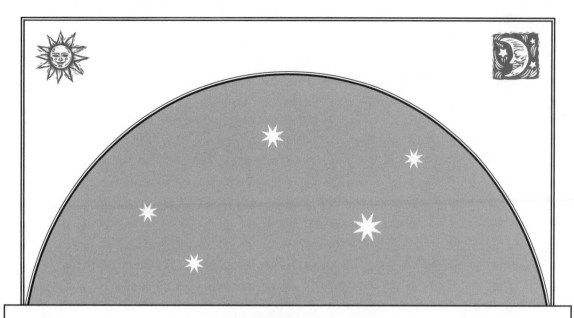

JUNE

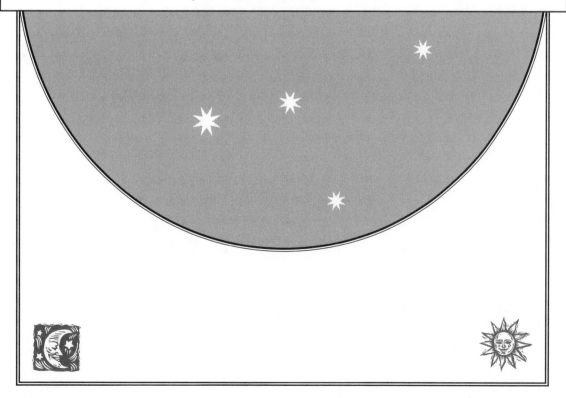

JUNE 1 GEMINI • The twins of the zodiac

May 21 at 4:00 A.M. to June 21 at 12:00 P.M. • NUMEROLOGY 1

Possessions and Desires . . .

Gem: Turquoise—This stone may help you find material wealth.

Flower: Marjoram—You tend to blush easily.

Astral Color, Color Need, Apparel Color: Your Astral Color is Red, which enhances passion, excitement, and strength. Violet in your environment keeps you empathetic toward others. In your wardrobe, Wine gives you energy.

Fragrance: You should flood your living space with the scent of distilled floral bouquet or freshly cut wood. This will give your ever-curious mind a rest from its constant search for new experiences.

Tree: Walnut—You are unusually helpful and always looking for constant changes in your life.

Instruments: Oboe, flute, clarinet, piano, French horn, organ, piccolo

Composer: Böhm

Bird: Bird of paradise—the "bird of the gods." You will shine and love extraordinary circumstances.

Symbol: Crown—the universal sign of dignity.

Harmonious Health and Nutrition . . .

Health Scent: Strawberry—Soothing by nature, the strawberry promotes self-esteem and encourages love.

Favorable Foods: Beets, apricots, whole-wheat bread, margarine

What's Lucky . . .

Lucky Numbers: 5, 9, 11
Best Months: April and August
Best Day of the Week: Wednesday
Best Month Days: 1, 10, 19, 28
Lucky Charm: A new penny in your shoe.

Harmonious Signs for Relationships and Partnerships: Aquarius and Libra

Spiritual Guides . . .

Star: Al Henah—Those born under this star are easily wounded.

Angel: Ambriel—This angel governs travel and transportation, particularly over water, and helps to create love and good communication.

Guardian Angel: Malachi—"Messenger of Jehovah."

Spiritual Stone: Chrysoprasus—This stone aids in relaxation.

✶ JUDITH'S INSIGHT ✶

"Fascinating" is a good word to describe you. You are also exceptionally kindhearted, hopeful, insightful, and full of enthusiasm. Your loving instinct allows you to nurture those around you, causing them to admire you. Your desire to please others will make you an adoring partner in love. You tend to hide your flirtatious side, allowing only a chosen few in.

You'll have more than one career in creative fields—perhaps art or writing. Expect to work with books, paper, and pencil: reading, writing, or possibly drawing. With your ability, you are capable of handling more than one job at a time. You can be torn between different directions in your life and at times may feel frustrated. When you put your efforts into a project, the results should be positive.

Some think of you as brilliant. Don't be discouraged when you hit those pitfalls that seem to come out of nowhere. You tend to spring right back with no problem.

✶ ✶ ✶

JUNE 2

GEMINI • The twins of the zodiac

May 21 at 4:00 A.M. to June 21 at 12:00 P.M. • NUMEROLOGY 2

Possessions and Desires . . .

Gem: Sapphire—This gem may help you find forgiveness from those you've wronged.

Flower: Double Red Pink—Your life will be full of love and affection.

Astral Color, Color Need, Apparel Color: Your Astral Color is Red, which enhances passion, excitement, and strength. Violet in your environment keeps you empathetic toward others. In your wardrobe, Green gives you confidence.

Fragrance: You should flood your living space with the scent of distilled floral bouquet or freshly cut wood. This will give your ever-curious mind a rest from its constant search for new experiences.

Tree: Maple—You have great stability and flashes of intuition.

Instruments: Pipe organ, cymbal, drum

Composers: Handel, Johann Sebastian Bach

Bird: Stork—Turkish bird, held in high esteem the world over. This bird is intelligent but may have strange tendencies.

Symbol: Cross—the symbol of self-sacrifice and reconciliation.

Harmonious Health and Nutrition . . .

Health Scent: Apple—You are creative, full of joy, and nearly magical. You bring happiness.

Favorable Foods: Peas, grapes, whole-wheat bread, eggs

What's Lucky . . .

Lucky Numbers: 9, 5, 11
Best Months: April and August
Best Day of the Week: Wednesday
Best Month Days: 2, 11, 20, 29

Lucky Charms: Two 50-cent pieces. Give someone else one of them.

Harmonious Signs for Relationships and Partnerships: Aquarius and Libra

Spiritual Guides . . .

Star: Al Divah—Those with this star could feel that they are mistreated by relatives.

Angel: Ambriel—This angel governs travel and transportation, particularly over water, and helps to create love and good communication.

Guardian Angel: St. John—This angel simplifies that which is complicated.

Spiritual Stone: Chrysoprasus—This stone aids in relaxation.

✴ JUDITH'S INSIGHT ✴

Your inventive ways can bring you a lot of new beginnings in your life. You are the one who gets there first. You love literature, history, and books. Somewhere along the way, you search to make history yourself. You have a sharp mind and an overwhelming intelligence, which will make you work hard to get to the top.

When it comes to love, be wary of your fickle side. Finding that special someone may take some time. You are warmhearted and receptive, which is beneficial to all relationships and partnerships. Look for the one with whom you feel harmony.

When it comes to understanding all sides of an issue, you outdo yourself. You would make a great debater. Professor, historian, inventor, or publisher—none of these careers is out of your reach. It wouldn't be surprising if you found a career in computers; you could be a leader in either hardware or software.

Remember the word *choices*, because you will have a life full of them.

✴ ✴ ✴

JUNE 3

GEMINI • The twins of the zodiac

May 21 at 4:00 A.M. to June 21 at 12:00 P.M. • NUMEROLOGY 3

Possessions and Desires . . .

Gem: Ruby—This stone may lead you to energy, friendship, and happiness.

Flower: Yellow Pink—Be careful what you refuse isn't what you will desire above all at a later time.

Astral Color, Color Need, Apparel Color: Your Astral Color is Red, which enhances passion, excitement, and strength. Violet in your environment keeps you empathetic toward others. In your wardrobe, Coral brings you a brilliant and sharp appearance.

Fragrance: You should flood your living space with the scent of distilled floral bouquet or freshly cut wood. This will give your ever-curious mind a rest from its constant search for new experiences.

Tree: Elm—You have willpower, strength, and the ability to stand alone.

Instrument: Trombone

Composers: Verdi, Mendelssohn, Schumann

Bird: Swan—Regarded as royal and sacred, this bird has the protective nature of a mother, and can become a furious fighter in the defense of its young.

Symbol: Wreath—You have been crowned with a special personality. You are strong but extremely compassionate.

Harmonious Health and Nutrition . . .

Health Scent: Rose—This scent will lead you to passionate thoughts and make you feel warm inside.

Favorable Foods: Beets, prunes, whole-wheat bread, molasses, cottage cheese

What's Lucky . . .

Lucky Numbers: 3, 5, 9

Best Months: April and August

Best Day of the Week: Wednesday

Best Month Days: 3, 12, 21, 30

Lucky Charm: A pen that someone else has already used.

Harmonious Signs for Relationships and Partnerships: Aquarius and Libra

Spiritual Guides . . .

Star: Al Henah—Those born under this star are easily wounded.

Angel: Ambriel—This angel governs travel and transportation, particularly over water, and helps to create love and good communication.

Guardian Angel: Johiel—This angel is a protector of all those with a humble heart.

Spiritual Stone: Chrysoprasus—This stone aids in relaxation.

✳ JUDITH'S INSIGHT ✳

You are cunning and smooth. These aspects of your personality, along with your charm and wit, will help bring you just about everything in life you could want. You know how to use these gifts to your advantage.

Fortunate in love, it may take someone hopelessly devoted to put up with you and your mood swings. Keeping you satisfied will be your partner's biggest challenge. As long as you can enjoy your freedom, friends, and many social contacts, you will be fine. The more invitations the better.

Ambition is one of your strongest qualities, and you use it well. You will work hard to get to the top, while experiencing your share of downfalls. Lower your standards a bit. In the end, you are likely to have multiple successes. You do well either owning your own company or, on a larger scale, being the head of an organization or president of a company. Any skill you care to develop will only improve with time. You may fancy a position in government, whether it be a municipal, state, or federal job.

You make friends easily enough, but you try to dominate the crowd. Force yourself to hold back; one way or another you become the leader.

★ ★ ★

JUNE 4   GEMINI • The twins of the zodiac
May 21 at 4:00 A.M. to June 21 at 12:00 P.M. • NUMEROLOGY 4

Possessions and Desires . . .

Gem: Emerald—Those who carry this stone tend to be lucky in love.
Flower: Daily Rose—Many people will wish they were as happy as you.
Astral Color, Color Need, Apparel Color: Your Astral Color is Red, which enhances passion, excitement, and strength. Violet in your environment keeps you empathetic toward others. In your wardrobe, Wine gives you energy.
Fragrance: You should flood your living space with the scent of distilled floral bouquet or freshly cut wood. This will give your ever-curious mind a rest from its constant search for new experiences.
Tree: Cherry—You will find yourself faced with constant new emotional awakenings.
Instruments: Bass, clarinet
Composers: Haydn, Wagner
Bird: Robin—the most sociable of all birds, with the ability to create quick friendships. It also can easily adapt to any home. When it wants something, it has the tendency to try to snatch it.
Symbol: Star—You are full of inner brightness and will stand out in any crowd. You will be seen as special.

Harmonious Health and Nutrition . . .

Health Scent: Vanilla—this scent will fill you with a feeling of cleanliness and stability.
Favorable Foods: Celery, whole-wheat bread, molasses, eggs

What's Lucky . . .

Lucky Numbers: 5, 9, 22
Best Months: April and August
Best Day of the Week: Wednesday
Best Month Days: 4, 13, 22, 31
Lucky Charm: A piece of material cut from something in your home.

Harmonious Signs for Relationships and Partnerships: Aquarius and Libra

Spiritual Guides . . .

Star: Al Henah—Those born under this star are easily wounded.
Angel: Ambriel—This angel governs travel and transportation, particularly over water, and helps to create love and good communication.
Guardian Angel: Uriel—This angel brings the light of God's guidance.
Spiritual Stone: Chrysoprasus—This stone aids in relaxation.

✳ JUDITH'S INSIGHT ✳

You think you're smart, and you are, but your strong intuition is your major gift. You have an investigative nature and present a challenge to others around you. The unknown fascinates you; those around you find *you* fascinating.

You are likely to have unusual relationships or to be drawn to unusual individuals. Making commitments will be the great challenge for you. Family may think of you as a rebel; others might say the black sheep. You simply march to the beat of a different drummer and love it when others notice.

Without question, you would succeed at undercover work. You love the exotic, thrills, and adventure. It would not be surprising if you had all of them. Many different careers present possibilities to you, as long as you are using your creativity. Somewhere along the way, try picking up a pen and paper—whether it is working on designing contracts or signing them. The greater the challenge, the better. Any kind of investigative or police work should appeal to you as well.

Friends think of you often, but your flamboyant style may sometimes make them uneasy. Still, your kind ways and warm heart keep people in your life. Be careful that your erratic tendencies don't discourage them. Stop beating yourself up when things don't move quickly enough—you'll just end up with a lot of bruises.

★ ★ ★

JUNE 5
GEMINI • The twins of the zodiac
May 21 at 4:00 A.M. to June 21 at 12:00 P.M. • NUMEROLOGY 5

Possessions and Desires . . .

Gem: Sardius—this stone could give the wearer unusual insights into his or her own heart.
Flower: Lancaster Rose—Many people may be envious of your cheerful nature.
Astral Color, Color Need, Apparel Color: Your Astral Color is Red, which enhances passion, excitement, and strength. Violet in your environment keeps you empathetic toward others. In your wardrobe, Green gives you confidence.
Fragrance: You should flood your living space with the scent of distilled floral bouquet or freshly cut wood. This will give your ever-curious mind a rest from its constant search for new experiences.
Tree: Apple—You are creative, full of joy, and nearly magical. You bring happiness.
Instruments: Viola, trumpet
Composer: Liszt
Bird: Flamingo—This beautiful, gregarious bird is always careful of its enemy. It is also a caretaker of the young who tries to keep everyone happy.
Symbol: Triangle—You have the right combination of abilities.

Harmonious Health and Nutrition . . .

Health Scent: Peach—This scent may balance your good qualities so that they equal your charm.
Favorable Foods: Parsnips, prunes, whole-wheat bread, molasses, margarine

What's Lucky . . .

Lucky Numbers: 5, 9, 23
Best Months: April and August
Best Day of the Week: Wednesday
Best Month Days: 4, 5, 23
Lucky Charms: A rabbit's foot or a white candle.
Harmonious Signs for Relationships and Partnerships: Aquarius and Libra

Spiritual Guides . . .

Star: Al Divah—Those with this star could feel that they are mistreated by relatives.
Angel: Ambriel—This angel governs travel and transportation, particularly over water, and helps to create love and good communication.
Guardian Angel: Plavwell—This angel gives power and strength to one's presence.
Spiritual Stone: Chrysoprasus—This stone aids in relaxation.

✳ JUDITH'S INSIGHT ✳

Your keen intelligence and resourcefulness make you very much a live one. You are energetic and enthusiastic; everything around you fascinates and intrigues you. Your love of travel should lead you to visit a lot of exotic places or, at the very least, to create an exotic environment. Your suitcase is always packed.

Falling in love and keeping it will be your greatest challenge. You waffle and brood and keep yourself from being totally devoted. When it comes to love, try to get out of your own way. It's easier to blame others than to take responsibility for your own actions. In due time you find balance, once you're in a relationship for a considerable amount of time. Have no fear, you eventually find someone who is patient with you.

In any working environment, you have the talent to make yourself shine. Consider a career in entertainment, writing, publishing, or computer graphics. You might own a resort hotel or hold a job in that industry. Talented as you are, you may find yourself hunting and hunting. Before you know it, you may find yourself on stage. Have faith—not only will you find yourself at some time connected to the theater or arts, but you may be the one doing the writing. Or you could be involved in astronomy, astrology, or art. Make sure your career brings you many challenges.

You are a risk taker and won't be happy unless there are challenges. From jumping out of an airplane to climbing the tallest mountain—you always take the risk.

★ ★ ★

JUNE 6   GEMINI • The twins of the zodiac

May 21 at 4:00 A.M. to June 21 at 12:00 P.M.   •   NUMEROLOGY 6

Possessions and Desires . . .

Gem: Topaz—This is an excellent gift to be exchanged between very loyal friends.

Flower: Thorn Apple—You may not be above fibbing to win the heart of the one you want.

Astral Color, Color Need, Apparel Color: Your Astral Color is Red, which enhances passion, excitement, and strength. Violet in your environment keeps you empathetic toward others. In your wardrobe, Coral brings you a brilliant and sharp appearance.

Fragrance: You should flood your living space with the scent of distilled floral bouquet or freshly cut wood. This will give your ever-curious mind a rest from its constant search for new experiences.

Tree: Palm—You tend to be very healthy and creative.

Instruments: Tambourine, lyre

Composer: Schubert

Bird: Falcon—an expert hunter. When well-trained, it can adapt to many tasks and is usually obedient.

Symbol: Crescent—You are more likely to be influenced by the phases of the moon. Your easygoing manner leads you to peaceful situations.

Harmonious Health and Nutrition . . .

Health Scent: Orange Blossom—This scent may balance your body, mind, and soul.

Favorable Foods: Red raspberries, whole-wheat bread, molasses, cottage cheese

What's Lucky . . .

Lucky Numbers: 5, 9, 24
Best Months: April and August
Best Day of the Week: Wednesday
Best Month Days: 6, 15, 24

Lucky Charms: A religious token or card from any religion.

Harmonious Signs for Relationships and Partnerships: Aquarius and Libra

Spiritual Guides . . .

Star: Al Henah—Those born under this star are easily wounded.

Angel: Ambriel—This angel governs travel and transportation, particularly over water, and helps to create love and good communication.

Guardian Angel: Michael—"Who is like God."

Spiritual Stone: Chrysoprasus—This stone aids in relaxation.

✷ JUDITH'S INSIGHT ✷

You have a strong, magnetic personality and a hand to bring you whatever you wish for. Others may see you as lucky. Your charm and wit enhance your career, especially if you choose politics. You are more devoted and loyal than most people think. When it comes to romance, your style is subtle. This is most attractive, particularly to your mate, who must be a powerhouse. At times, you might lack flexibility in your relationship. Look before you leap. Otherwise, in love, you could experience some heartache. Keep both feet on the ground. As a lover, you are deep and emotional in all your thoughts. The problem here is that you are afraid to let others know who you really are. If a mate takes the time to know you in a relationship and removes those bricks one by one, eventually you will find happiness.

It will seem as if money just falls into your lap, and at some point or another it does. But consider the possibility that you could invent, create, or design architecture that will bring you fame. As a salesperson, you'll be the one who lands the largest contract in company history. No matter what career you choose you'll eventually be wealthy.

✷ ✷ ✷

JUNE 7 GEMINI • The twins of the zodiac

May 21 at 4:00 A.M. to June 21 at 12:00 P.M. • NUMEROLOGY 7

Possessions and Desires . . .

Gem: Ruby—This stone may lead you to energy, friendship, and happiness.

Flower: Red Tulip—You will hear many open declarations of love in your life.

Astral Color, Color Need, Apparel Color: Your Astral Color is Red, which enhances passion, excitement, and strength. Violet in your environment keeps you empathetic toward others. In your wardrobe, Green gives you confidence.

Fragrance: You should flood your living space with the scent of distilled floral bouquet or freshly cut wood. This will give your ever-curious mind a rest from its constant search for new experiences.

Tree: Sycamore—Yours is the ability to love, communicate honestly with others, and have lasting relationships.

Instrument: Harp

Composers: Gluck, Brahms

Bird: Goldfinch—there are forty-four different species of finches which vary greatly. This can sometimes be the most charming of birds. These gentle creatures can be very moody in unsettled weather.

Symbol: Heart—You are enthusiastic, empathetic, and full of generosity and love.

Harmonious Health and Nutrition . . .

Health Scent: Jasmine—This scent may make you more easygoing when you are stressed.

Favorable Foods: Lettuce, apricots, whole-wheat bread, molasses, buttermilk

What's Lucky . . .

Lucky Numbers: 5, 7, 9
Best Months: April and August
Best Day of the Week: Wednesday
Best Month Days: 6, 15, 24

Lucky Charm: An old key.
Harmonious Signs for Relationships and Partnerships: Aquarius and Libra

Spiritual Guides . . .

Star: Al Henah—Those born under this star are easily wounded.

Angel: Ambriel—This angel governs travel and transportation, particularly over water, and helps to create love and good communication.

Guardian Angel: Raphael—This angel attends to all of your needs when you are looking for guidance.

Spiritual Stone: Chrysoprasus—This stone aids in relaxation.

✶ JUDITH'S INSIGHT ✶

You are profound in your thinking—dwelling on things that occupy your mind. If only you could just turn it off. This constant thinking could be great for work and bad for love or emotional circumstances. Your mind never shutting down often leads you on an emotional roller coaster ride. People seem to overwhelm you, though it just may be your mood. Work on calming techniques. Keep yourself from getting overwrought and burned out because you don't like to say No.

Extremely loyal on the one hand, you do have a tendency to flirt. In fact at times you may even want to do more than flirt. You adore your family, but you will create situations in life that give you distance. You provide a sense of power to others around you and may be the comfort zone for your friends and family.

You will go back and forth with your career. A career in writing would be comfortable for you. Although it may take years for you to recognize your talent, your imagination could transform any boring story. You may find yourself in multiple careers or taking on multiple jobs—one for structure, the other for love.

Order pleases you both at home and in your relationships. Write about it in a play or script. With your talent, you may just be published.

★ ★ ★

JUNE 8 GEMINI • The twins of the zodiac

May 21 at 4:00 A.M. to June 21 at 12:00 P.M. • NUMEROLOGY 8

Possessions and Desires . . .

Gem: Chrysolite—This gem may help you clear your mind of sadness and worry.

Flower: Variegated Tulip—You usually see the beauty in things that others miss.

Astral Color, Color Need, Apparel Color: Your Astral Color is Red, which enhances passion, excitement, and strength. Violet in your environment keeps you empathetic toward others. In your wardrobe, Wine gives you energy.

Fragrance: You should flood your living space with the scent of distilled floral bouquet or freshly cut wood. This will give your ever-curious mind a rest from its constant search for new experiences.

Tree: Pine—Your relationships tend to be balanced, both emotionally and mentally.

Instrument: Cello

Composer: Mozart

Bird: Lark—known for the beauty of its song, which is sometimes very unusual. It is also credited with extraordinary intelligence.

Symbol: Wings—You are the source of balance in your world—this will bring you contentment.

Harmonious Health and Nutrition . . .

Health Scent: Almond—This scent may revitalize you and open you to greater possibilities.

Favorable Foods: Peas, prunes, whole-wheat bread, molasses, eggs

What's Lucky . . .

Lucky Numbers: 5, 8, 9

Best Months: April and August

Best Day of the Week: Wednesday

Best Month Days: 8, 17, 26

Lucky Charm: Red ribbon in your wallet or doorway.

Harmonious Signs for Relationships and Partnerships: Aquarius and Libra

Spiritual Guides . . .

Star: Al Henah—Those born under this star are easily wounded.

Angel: Ambriel—This angel governs travel and transportation, particularly over water, and helps to create love and good communication.

Guardian Angel: Seraphim—An angel that brings love, light, and passion.

Spiritual Stone: Chrysoprasus—This stone aids in relaxation.

✴ JUDITH'S INSIGHT ✴

Quite the observer, you take in just about everything that is humanly possible—all at once. You are deep, thoughtful, and charming. Life for you may not be easy because you take on too much at one time. Give yourself a break. You reject restrictions of any kind and thrive on your independence.

Since you've been misunderstood for most of your life, you may eventually find a relationship with a soul mate who understands you. Hopefully you will be single at the time. Be patient—finding the right mate takes some time. Be cautious because you could have trouble with your neighbors. Others may seem as if they are tracking you and following what you are doing.

Your philosophical nature will probably put you in serious literary work, science, or mathematics. Somewhere along the way you may even have a desire for architecture. Your strong spiritual sense may draw you to learn more about mysticism. A teacher or counselor by nature, be selective about who and what you listen to. Be especially careful about taking things too seriously.

You are a dear friend with a select few close companions with whom you find balance and harmony and total security. Eventually you do seem to find that harmony in friendships and relationships gets easier, and you tend not to be so scattered with your emotions.

★ ★ ★

JUNE 9

GEMINI • The twins of the zodiac

May 21 at 4:00 A.M. to June 21 at 12:00 P.M. • NUMEROLOGY 9

Possessions and Desires . . .

Gem: Topaz—This is an excellent gift to be exchanged between very loyal friends.

Flower: Thyme—You tend not to be happy unless you are very active.

Astral Color, Color Need, Apparel Color: Your Astral Color is Red, which enhances passion, excitement, and strength. Violet in your environment keeps you empathetic toward others. In your wardrobe, Coral brings you a brilliant and sharp appearance.

Fragrance: You should flood your living space with the scent of distilled floral bouquet or freshly cut wood. This will give your ever-curious mind a rest from its constant search for new experiences.

Tree: Holly—Beware that you are not carried away by your passionate nature. The only way to grow is to be open to new experiences.

Instruments: Violin, tympanum

Composer: Gluck

Bird: Mockingbird—the most proficient minstrel in the world's orchestra; graceful and enthusiastic.

Symbol: Anchor—This tranquil symbol signifies stability and strength, and stands for strong commitments in relationships.

Harmonious Health and Nutrition . . .

Health Scent: Lavender—This scent might lead others to trust you and make you patient.

Favorable Foods: Cabbage, bananas, wholewheat bread, molasses, cottage cheese

What's Lucky . . .

Lucky Numbers: 5, 9, 36
Best Months: April and August
Best Day of the Week: Wednesday
Best Month Days: 9, 18, 27

Lucky Charms: A U.S. coin or a bill of any amount from the year you were born.

Harmonious Signs for Relationships and Partnerships: Aquarius and Libra

Spiritual Guides . . .

Star: Al Henah—Those born under this star are easily wounded.

Angel: Ambriel—This angel governs travel and transportation, particularly over water, and helps to create love and good communication.

Guardian Angel: Gabriel—"God is my strength."

Spiritual Stone: Chrysoprasus—This stone aids in relaxation.

✶ JUDITH'S INSIGHT ✶

Your combination of intelligence, wit, charm, shrewdness, and attractiveness are a handful, and so are you. With your high energy, any career is possible. You will accomplish much in your lifetime because you're good at everything you try.

More flirtatious than loyal? Not really. You're more loyal and devoted, though others may beg to differ. You want a secure relationship but love to be recognized. Many opportunities for love affairs present themselves. It is likely you'll turn away more than you take on, at least in your later years. Otherwise, you may create unnecessary headaches for yourself.

Success will knock at your door rather often. From head of the class to head of the corporation, you are a born leader, and life will take you places. You clear obstacles and hurdles like a professional athlete. Be sure to exercise caution when it comes to legal issues, unless, of course, you choose to be an attorney and spend your life in the courtroom. One way or the other, legal issues appear throughout your life.

Your love of words and gift with them makes you a terrific conversationalist. This could actually be your greatest asset.

✶ ✶ ✶

JUNE 10   GEMINI • The twins of the zodiac
May 21 at 4:00 A.M. to June 21 at 12:00 P.M. • NUMEROLOGY 1

Possessions and Desires . . .

Gem: Agate—This stone may promote health and lead you to a long life.

Flower: Pomegranate—You may find that a little foolishness can be a lot of fun.

Astral Color, Color Need, Apparel Color: Your Astral Color is Red, which enhances passion, excitement, and strength. Violet in your environment keeps you empathetic toward others. In your wardrobe, Green gives you confidence.

Fragrance: You should flood your living space with the scent of distilled floral bouquet or freshly cut wood. This will give your ever-curious mind a rest from its constant search for new experiences.

Tree: Walnut—You are unusually helpful and always looking for constant changes in your life.

Instruments: Oboe, flute, clarinet, piano, French horn, organ, piccolo

Composer: Böhm

Bird: Bird of paradise—the "bird of the gods." You will shine and love extraordinary circumstances.

Symbol: Crown—the universal sign of dignity.

Harmonious Health and Nutrition . . .

Health Scent: Strawberry—Soothing by nature, the strawberry promotes self-esteem and encourages love.

Favorable Foods: Radishes, grapes, whole-wheat bread, molasses, goat's milk

What's Lucky . . .

Lucky Numbers: 5, 9, 10
Best Months: April and August
Best Day of the Week: Wednesday
Best Month Days: 1, 10, 19, 28
Lucky Charm: A new penny in your shoe.
Harmonious Signs for Relationships and Partnerships: Aquarius and Libra

Spiritual Guides . . .

Star: Al Henah—Those born under this star are easily wounded.

Angel: Ambriel—This angel governs travel and transportation, particularly over water, and helps to create love and good communication.

Guardian Angel: Malachi—"Messenger of Jehovah."

Spiritual Stone: Chrysoprasus—This stone aids in relaxation.

✶ JUDITH'S INSIGHT ✶

"Fascinating" could describe you. You have a good heart, and you lend a helping hand whenever you can. Did you know you have psychic abilities? It's no surprise that you may back away from that. A strong sense of independence and enthusiasm and a positive attitude will bring others to you. You love to be loved, and you become the nurturer whether you want to or not.

You do tend to have luck with friends because your natural instinct is to give a lot. Your loving instincts do allow you to have harmony in your family. At times, siblings could cause conflict, but you do tend to have decent relationships with them at one time or another.

Expect the unexpected when it comes to work. Multiple careers await you. You have the ability to do more than one career and may choose to do so. Expect to work with paper, whether it is writing, reading, or arithmetic. But no matter what the job, you always put your all into it. There may be jobs that tend to bring out your brilliance: professor, head of the college, or top sales rep, it doesn't matter; you will find that you will get to the top.

Don't get discouraged when you hit the puddles in a rainstorm and get splashed, because you will be able to overcome just about any and every obstacle that lands in your path. It takes time for things to happen. You do tend to find love and laughter as you get older.

✶ ✶ ✶

JUNE 11 GEMINI • The twins of the zodiac

May 21 at 4:00 A.M. to June 21 at 12:00 P.M. • NUMEROLOGY 2

Possessions and Desires . . .

Gem: Sapphire—This gem may help you find forgiveness from those you've wronged.
Flower: Black Poplar—You are courageous in the face of strife.
Astral Color, Color Need, Apparel Color: Your Astral Color is Red, which enhances passion, excitement, and strength. Violet in your environment keeps you empathetic toward others. In your wardrobe, Wine gives you energy.
Fragrance: You should flood your living space with the scent of distilled floral bouquet or freshly cut wood. This will give your ever-curious mind a rest from its constant search for new experiences.
Tree: Maple—You have great stability and flashes of intuition.
Instruments: Pipe organ, cymbal, drum
Composers: Handel, Johann Sebastian Bach
Bird: Stork—Turkish bird, held in high esteem the world over. This bird is intelligent but may have strange tendencies.
Symbol: Cross—the symbol of self-sacrifice and reconciliation.

Harmonious Health and Nutrition . . .

Health Scent: Apple—You are creative, full of joy, and nearly magical. You bring happiness.
Favorable Foods: Brussels sprouts, blackberries, whole wheat, peanuts, cottage cheese

What's Lucky . . .

Lucky Numbers: 2, 5, 9
Best Months: April and August
Best Day of the Week: Wednesday
Best Month Days: 2, 11, 20, 29
Lucky Charms: Two 50-cent pieces. Give someone else one of them.

Harmonious Signs for Relationships and Partnerships: Aquarius and Libra

Spiritual Guides . . .

Star: Al Divah—Those with this star could feel that they are mistreated by relatives.
Angel: Ambriel—This angel governs travel and transportation, particularly over water, and helps to create love and good communication.
Guardian Angel: St. John—This angel simplifies that which is complicated.
Spiritual Stone: Chrysoprasus—This stone aids in relaxation.

✳ JUDITH'S INSIGHT ✳

You have a keen understanding and tend to look closely at people. Where can you usually be found? At the center of attention! You are intrigued with literature, history, and books. Somewhere along the way you may even make a little history yourself. Quite the inventor, you create a lot of new beginnings, whether you father or you bear a lot of children. New beginnings will be important in your life.

You're an inspiration to everyone around you. When it comes to love, you go through some stages of indecisiveness or whimsy. You're generally better with a mate, but make sure you don't settle for the wrong one just for companionship. Be patient. Your kindness and gentleness are enhanced when in a relationship.

Your sharp mind and deep intelligence would make you a great attorney, county leader, political leader, or publisher. Your great communication skills could help you do wonders with computers or media jobs.

Remember, you will experience a lot of quick changes and detours. Expect the unexpected. You may have a strong desire to travel and could be interested in somebody who is from another country; you may have an opportunity to move out of the country somewhere along the way.

★ ★ ★

JUNE 12 GEMINI • The twins of the zodiac

May 21 at 4:00 A.M. to June 21 at 12:00 P.M. • NUMEROLOGY 3

Possessions and Desires . . .

Gem: Ruby—This stone may lead you to energy, friendship, and happiness.

Flower: Prickly Pear—You are sometimes too quick to make fun of the shortcomings of others.

Astral Color, Color Need, Apparel Color: Your Astral Color is Red, which enhances passion, excitement, and strength. Violet in your environment keeps you empathetic toward others. In your wardrobe, Coral brings you a brilliant and sharp appearance.

Fragrance: You should flood your living space with the scent of distilled floral bouquet or freshly cut wood. This will give your ever-curious mind a rest from its constant search for new experiences.

Tree: Elm—You have willpower, strength, and the ability to stand alone.

Instrument: Trombone

Composers: Verdi, Mendelssohn, Schumann

Bird: Swan—Regarded as royal and sacred, this bird has the protective nature of a mother, and can become a furious fighter in the defense of its young.

Symbol: Wreath—You have been crowned with a special personality. You are strong but extremely compassionate.

Harmonious Health and Nutrition . . .

Health Scent: Rose—This scent will lead you to passionate thoughts and make you feel warm inside.

Favorable Foods: Cauliflower, peaches, rye, peanuts, buttermilk

What's Lucky . . .

Lucky Numbers: 3, 5, 9
Best Months: April and August
Best Day of the Week: Wednesday
Best Month Days: 3, 12, 21, 30
Lucky Charm: A pen that someone else has already used.

Harmonious Signs for Relationships and Partnerships: Aquarius and Libra

Spiritual Guides . . .

Star: Al Henah—Those born under this star are easily wounded.

Angel: Ambriel—This angel governs travel and transportation, particularly over water, and helps to create love and good communication.

Guardian Angel: Johiel—This angel is a protector of all those with a humble heart.

Spiritual Stone: Chrysoprasus—This stone aids in relaxation.

✶ JUDITH'S INSIGHT ✶

You know how to get what you want. Some call you a smooth operator, but because you are genuinely kindhearted and warm, people are willing to do what you want. You make new friends easily and keep old friends for decades. It's not that you're dominating, but people simply allow you to take control. One way or another, you become the leader of the pack.

You are mostly lucky in love; if a relationship does fail, another is forming right around the corner. You definitely can be more secure at work than with love. At times you can be moody and try to blame it on your partner. Keep in mind that the hardest task for you is recognizing your multidimensional personality.

You're more likely to succeed than not. You will do well in whatever job you choose, whether you work in or with an organization or large company. Your skills, whether they be mechanical or mental, operate on a grand scale. A position in government wouldn't be surprising.

You love a good party and respond to any social invitation—the more social, the better. Whether it be fishing, hunting, playing racquetball or tennis—it is not so much the sport, but the desire for the interaction with other people that attracts you.

You can be demanding, and sooner or later you get what you want. Have no fear, somewhere along the way you learn to give more than you get.

✶ ✶ ✶

JUNE 13   GEMINI • The twins of the zodiac

May 21 at 4:00 A.M. to June 21 at 12:00 P.M. • NUMEROLOGY 4

Possessions and Desires . . .

Gem: Emerald—Those who carry this stone tend to be lucky in love.

Flower: Potato Blossom—You should discover that what you give to others is really a gift to yourself.

Astral Color, Color Need, Apparel Color: Your Astral Color is Red, which enhances passion, excitement, and strength. Violet in your environment keeps you empathetic toward others. In your wardrobe, Green gives you confidence.

Fragrance: You should flood your living space with the scent of distilled floral bouquet or freshly cut wood. This will give your ever-curious mind a rest from its constant search for new experiences.

Tree: Cherry—You will find yourself faced with constant new emotional awakenings.

Instruments: Bass, clarinet

Composers: Haydn, Wagner

Bird: Lark—These birds are known for the beauty of their song which is sometimes very unusual. It is also credited with having extraordinary intelligence.

Symbol: Star—You are full of inner brightness and will stand out in any crowd. You will be seen as special.

Harmonious Health and Nutrition . . .

Health Scent: Vanilla—this scent will fill you with a feeling of cleanliness and stability.

Favorable Foods: Watercress, prunes, whole wheat, almonds, cottage cheese

What's Lucky . . .

Lucky Numbers: 4, 5, 13

Best Months: April and August

Best Day of the Week: Wednesday

Best Month Days: 4, 13, 22, 31

Lucky Charm: A piece of material cut from something in your home.

Harmonious Signs for Relationships and Partnerships: Aquarius and Libra

Spiritual Guides . . .

Star: Al Henah—Those born under this star are easily wounded.

Angel: Ambriel—This angel governs travel and transportation, particularly over water, and helps to create love and good communication.

Guardian Angel: St. John—This angel simplifies that which is complicated.

Spiritual Stone: Chrysoprasus—This stone aids in relaxation.

✶ JUDITH'S INSIGHT ✶

You are a born adventurer; if it isn't exotic, thrilling, or challenging, you don't want to go. You are extremely strong and intuitive, and you have a keen intellect and a strong, unusual mind. Likewise, relationships with unique people attract and draw you in. Commitments themselves will be a great challenge for you. You tend to keep close to your family, but maybe you're seen as the rebel every so often. You're a bit eccentric, and your living environment may be considered different or out of the realm of the ordinary.

Because of your investigative nature, you may find yourself digging through the dirt at a young age. Career possibilities may include being a rocket scientist, creating a television story, writing a script, or starring in the most popular film. Whether or not you write or direct doesn't matter; you will tend to have two or three jobs.

You like a challenge and, at the same time, you present a challenge. Fascinated with yourself, you create scenarios in which you even compete with yourself! But your impatience can pose problems. You are willful, determined, shrewd, and penetrating, and so you can be read as harsh at times. But your depth and kind and loving nature will eventually allow others to see you as you are—warm and sensitive.

✶ ✶ ✶

JUNE 14

GEMINI • The twins of the zodiac

May 21 at 4:00 A.M. to June 21 at 12:00 P.M. • NUMEROLOGY 5

Possessions and Desires . . .

Gem: Sardius—this stone could give the wearer unusual insights into his or her own heart.

Flower: Mountain Peak—Your aspirations tend to carry you where you wish to go.

Fragrance: You should flood your living space with the scent of distilled floral bouquet or freshly cut wood. This will give your ever-curious mind a rest from its constant search for new experiences.

Astral Color, Color Need, Apparel Color: Your Astral Color is Red, which enhances passion, excitement, and strength. Violet in your environment keeps you empathetic toward others. In your wardrobe, Wine gives you energy.

Tree: Apple—You are creative, full of joy, and nearly magical. You bring happiness.

Instruments: Viola, trumpet

Composer: Liszt

Bird: Flamingo—This beautiful, gregarious bird is always careful of its enemy. It is also a caretaker of the young who tries to keep everyone happy.

Symbol: Triangle—You have the right combination of abilities.

Harmonious Health and Nutrition . . .

Health Scent: Peach—This scent may balance your good qualities so that they equal your charm.

Favorable Foods: String beans, raspberries, rye, beechnuts, pressed cheese

What's Lucky . . .

Lucky Numbers: 5, 9, 14
Best Months: April and August
Best Day of the Week: Wednesday
Best Month Days: 4, 5, 23
Lucky Charms: A rabbit's foot or a white candle.
Harmonious Signs for Relationships and Partnerships: Aquarius and Libra

Spiritual Guides . . .

Star: Al Henah—Those born under this star are easily wounded.

Angel: Ambriel—This angel governs travel and transportation, particularly over water, and helps to create love and good communication.

Guardian Angel: Plavwell—This angel gives power and strength to one's presence.

Spiritual Stone: Chrysoprasus—This stone aids in relaxation.

✶ JUDITH'S INSIGHT ✶

You can be very tight with money, then suddenly show extreme generosity, especially when it comes to a gift for a friend. You're a good, loyal friend, and can be trusted with a secret. Energetic, enthusiastic, and very much alive, you are intrigued by others as much as they are by you.

When there is a crisis, you can be more warm-hearted than usual. You are loving, kind, and imaginative. However, your need for independence could isolate you. While in a relationship, learn to demonstrate how much you need closeness. You tend to behave as if it's not that important. This could be your greatest downfall. Allow your emotional side to be as directed as your working one, and you will find much more harmony in your life.

You are hard-working, intelligent, and resourceful; your career goals could range from computer graphics to writing or publishing. Somewhere along the way, you may make multiple career changes in the space of a year. Keep looking for the right fit. Inevitably, you lean toward using your creativity. You have a flare for the dramatic, in addition to a keen attraction to research, science, or mathematics. You could succeed in astronomy, astrology, or designing of any kind. Many chances to change your job and your residence present themselves along the way. You are a risk taker and could be the one air ballooning, power shooting or, perhaps, running for public office.

★ ★ ★

JUNE 15   GEMINI • The twins of the zodiac
May 21 at 4:00 A.M. to June 21 at 12:00 P.M. • NUMEROLOGY 6

Possessions and Desires . . .

Gem: Topaz—This is an excellent gift to be exchanged between very loyal friends.

Flower: Wild Plum—You tend to love with the heat of a forest fire.

Fragrance: You should flood your living space with the scent of distilled floral bouquet or freshly cut wood. This will give your ever-curious mind a rest from its constant search for new experiences.

Astral Color, Color Need, Apparel Color: Your Astral Color is Red, which enhances passion, excitement, and strength. Violet in your environment keeps you empathetic toward others. In your wardrobe, Coral brings you a brilliant and sharp appearance.

Tree: Palm—You tend to be very healthy and creative.

Instruments: Tambourine, lyre

Composer: Schubert

Bird: Lark—known for the beauty of its song, which is sometimes very unusual. It is also credited with extraordinary intelligence.

Symbol: Crescent—You are more likely to be influenced by the phases of the moon. Your easygoing manner leads you to peaceful situations.

Harmonious Health and Nutrition . . .

Health Scent: Orange Blossom—This scent may balance your body, mind, and soul.

Favorable Foods: Cauliflower, peaches, whole wheat, nuts, buttermilk

What's Lucky . . .

Lucky Numbers: 5, 6, 9
Best Months: April and August
Best Day of the Week: Wednesday
Best Month Days: 6, 15, 24
Lucky Charms: A religious token or card from any religion.

Harmonious Signs for Relationships and Partnerships: Aquarius and Libra

Spiritual Guides . . .

Star: Al Divah—Those with this star could feel that they are mistreated by relatives.

Angel: Ambriel—This angel governs travel and transportation, particularly over water, and helps to create love and good communication.

Guardian Angel: Michael—"Who is like God."

Spiritual Stone: Chrysoprasus—This stone aids in relaxation.

✶ JUDITH'S INSIGHT ✶

You have a strong magnetic personality that brings you what you wish for in this lifetime. Your charm and good sense of humor get you through many a tight spot. No matter what anybody else says about you, you're faithful and loyal, and you consider doing whatever it takes to make others happy.

Your subtle style is most attractive, and you make a devoted mate. When it comes to romance, you like challenge and require a little spontaneity. Be more open in relationships, and try not to put up so many roadblocks. Your flirtatious ways are alluring, and you need and will choose a mate who takes the time to understand you.

Remember to keep both feet on the ground when it comes to work, because you may do three jobs at once. Although you may be one to rock the boat at work, you're dependable and seen as a hard worker. You catch on to things quickly and have no problem doing many things at once. Many hidden talents come out when you are older, especially in sports or creative talents. You may start off as an attorney who then becomes a golf pro, or perhaps a football player who turns into a sportscaster. You should have several careers, but you like diversification.

Eventually you could come across windfalls in your life, or maybe you'll invent or create something that generates a lot of money for you. Financially, you take what you have and do very well with it.

✶ ✶ ✶

JUNE 16 GEMINI • The twins of the zodiac

May 21 at 4:00 A.M. to June 21 at 12:00 P.M. • NUMEROLOGY 7

Possessions and Desires . . .

Gem: Agate—This stone may promote health and lead you to a long life.

Flower: Fly Orchis—You tend not to have a problem admitting when you have made a mistake.

Fragrance: You should flood your living space with the scent of distilled floral bouquet or freshly cut wood. This will give your ever-curious mind a rest from its constant search for new experiences.

Astral Color, Color Need, Apparel Color: Your Astral Color is Red, which enhances passion, excitement, and strength. Violet in your environment keeps you empathetic toward others. In your wardrobe, Green gives you confidence.

Tree: Sycamore—Yours is the ability to love, communicate honestly with others, and have lasting relationships.

Instrument: Harp

Composers: Gluck, Brahms

Bird: Skylark—This handsome bird is beautiful when it sings. It always whistles as it works.

Symbol: Heart—You are enthusiastic, empathetic, and full of generosity and love.

Harmonious Health and Nutrition . . .

Health Scent: Jasmine—This scent may make you more easygoing when you are stressed.

Favorable Foods: Cabbage, prunes, rye, peanuts, eggs

What's Lucky . . .

Lucky Numbers: 5, 7, 9
Best Months: April and August
Best Day of the Week: Wednesday
Best Month Days: 6, 15, 2
Lucky Charm: An old key.
Harmonious Signs for Relationships and Partnerships: Aquarius and Libra

Spiritual Guides . . .

Star: Al Henah—Those born under this star are easily wounded.

Angel: Ambriel—This angel governs travel and transportation, particularly over water, and helps to create love and good communication.

Guardian Angel: Raphael—This angel attends to all of your needs when you are looking for guidance.

Spiritual Stone: Chrysoprasus—This stone aids in relaxation.

✶ JUDITH'S INSIGHT ✶

You are profound in your thinking and would make an excellent writer. Unfortunately, your mind doesn't turn off easily, so you dwell on things entirely too much. You see life through rose-colored glasses, yet you analyze things to death. Overwhelming hurdles will present themselves, and you handle them with remarkable ease. Learn to check your criticism of others; this could trip you up. At the same time, try being a little less self-doubting and hard on yourself.

You learn the value of friendship early on, and as you mature, this feeling deepens. You are quite loyal. Someone you're attracted to may consider you a friend. Don't feel cast aside. This is a great compliment. Inevitably you find harmony in love.

At times you pull away from the family, either emotionally or physically. You provide a strong sense of power to those around you and will be a comfort zone for friends and family. Expect a tidy home—you value order! You enjoy the luxuries of life, and you find a way to make your home quite comfortable.

It may take time to recognize your true talents. Your wonderfully creative nature makes you impractical in business. You have the capabilities for a career as a musician or poet. Bookkeeper, cashier, accountant, literary agent, editor, confidential clerk, or psychologist would make a nice fit.

Foreign things intrigue you and inspire you to travel. Living in a foreign country or with a family of another culture awakens a strong connection to another time.

✶ ✶ ✶

JUNE 17   GEMINI • The twins of the zodiac

May 21 at 4:00 A.M. to June 21 at 12:00 P.M. • NUMEROLOGY 8

Possessions and Desires . . .

Gem: Chrysolite—This gem may help you clear your mind of sadness and worry.

Flower: Palm—You may know much success in life.

Fragrance: You should flood your living space with the scent of distilled floral bouquet or freshly cut wood. This will give your ever-curious mind a rest from its constant search for new experiences.

Astral Color, Color Need, Apparel Color: Your Astral Color is Red, which enhances passion, excitement, and strength. Violet in your environment keeps you empathetic toward others. In your wardrobe, Wine gives you energy.

Tree: Pine—Your relationships tend to be balanced, both emotionally and mentally.

Instrument: Cello

Composer: Mozart

Bird: Lark—known for the beauty of their song, which is sometimes very unusual. It is also credited with extraordinary intelligence.

Symbol: Wings—You are the source of balance in your world—this will bring you contentment.

Harmonious Health and Nutrition . . .

Health Scent: Almond—This scent may revitalize you and open you to greater possibilities.

Favorable Foods: Peas, pineapple, whole wheat, almonds, cottage cheese

What's Lucky . . .

Lucky Numbers: 5, 7, 8

Best Months: April and August

Best Day of the Week: Wednesday

Best Month Days: 8, 17, 26

Lucky Charm: Red ribbon in your wallet or doorway.

Harmonious Signs for Relationships and Partnerships: Aquarius and Libra

Spiritual Guides . . .

Star: Al Henah—Those born under this star are easily wounded.

Angel: Ambriel—This angel governs travel and transportation, particularly over water, and helps to create love and good communication.

Guardian Angel: Seraphim—An angel that brings love, light, and passion.

Spiritual Stone: Chrysoprasus—This stone aids in relaxation.

✴ JUDITH'S INSIGHT ✴

You have a nurturing, sympathetic, and generous nature. You take in everything. You're often in deep thought, and you tend to analyze everything. Your surroundings are quite important, and you like them comfortable and homey. You appreciate nice things, but that's not what makes you tick. It is more important for you to give than take for yourself, although this may not be the case in your early years.

The worst thing that could happen is having restrictions placed on you. This could be a problem when cultivating a relationship. The mate who provides you with a sense of freedom and trust could be the perfect match. Although you're a dear friend to those close to you, intimate friendships are few and far between. You probably only have a handful of dear friends throughout life, and usually you've known them since childhood.

Your signature personality trait is your willingness to take on responsibility. Life will be easier once you learn to resist the urge to take on the responsibilities of others. You have a philosophical nature and could wind up with a literary career—or with something in science or mathematics. In this technological age, you might also find yourself the head of a computer or New Age environmental company. The unknown and mystical intrigues you. You can sometimes be misunderstood and don't like to explain yourself to others.

The older you get, the less pressure you put on yourself, and your life tends to forge ahead with less stress.

✴ ✴ ✴

JUNE 18 GEMINI • The twins of the zodiac

May 21 at 4:00 A.M. to June 21 at 12:00 P.M. • NUMEROLOGY 9

Possessions and Desires . . .

Gem: Topaz—This is an excellent gift to be exchanged between very loyal friends.
Flower: Mustard—No one is fooled when you try to act indifferent.
Astral Color, Color Need, Apparel Color: Your Astral Color is Red, which enhances passion, excitement, and strength. Violet is your environment, keeps you empathetic toward others. In your wardrobe, Coral brings you a brilliant and sharp appearance.
Fragrance: You should flood your living space with the scent of distilled floral bouquet or freshly cut wood. This will give your ever-curious mind a rest from its constant search for new experiences.
Tree: Holly—Beware that you are not carried away by your passionate nature. The only way to grow is to be open to new experiences.
Instruments: Violin, tympanum
Composer: Gluck
Bird: Mockingbird—the most proficient minstrel in the world's orchestra; graceful and enthusiastic.
Symbol: Anchor—This tranquil symbol signifies stability and strength, and stands for strong commitments in relationships.

Harmonious Health and Nutrition . . .

Health Scent: Lavender—This scent might lead others to trust you and make you patient.
Favorable Foods: Beans, strawberries, rye, walnuts, buttermilk

What's Lucky . . .

Lucky Numbers: 5, 9, 18
Best Months: April and August
Best Day of the Week: Wednesday
Best Month Days: 9, 18, 27
Lucky Charms: A U.S. coin or a bill of any amount from the year you were born.

Harmonious Signs for Relationships and Partnerships: Aquarius and Libra

Spiritual Guides . . .

Star: Al Henah—Those born under this star are easily wounded.
Angel: Ambriel—This angel governs travel and transportation, particularly over water, and helps to create love and good communication.
Guardian Angel: Gabriel—"God is my strength."
Spiritual Stone: Chrysoprasus—This stone aids in relaxation.

✶ JUDITH'S INSIGHT ✶

Because you're charming, attractive, and alluring, you have no problem finding a mate. You are highly energetic and a willing participant in just about any sport. Inspired by challenge, you're one of those rare people who can do just about anything. Watch out for intense relationships—they can zap your energy. You need to allow yourself more patience for things to come to fruition, in their own time frame.

Keeping the balance with family will be much easier for you than keeping the balance in a love relationship. Family members understand you better and, therefore, have more patience. You tend toward extremes: you can give one hundred percent or be cold and completely isolate yourself from others. This may pose problems when it comes to maintaining long-term relationships. A lot of your emotional conflict will be fear-based—fear of what you really want, and fear of not getting it.

Be cautious that your interaction with the law finds you on the right side. You have to watch out for times where you will have problems with the IRS or just incur a lot of legal problems or situations. Unless, of course, you find yourself working for them. You may have a career, with reading, writing, or arithmetic, but not necessarily as a teacher. You will be surrounded by books or magazines at one time or another.

✶ ✶ ✶

JUNE 19 GEMINI • The twins of the zodiac

May 21 at 4:00 A.M. to June 21 at 12:00 P.M. • NUMEROLOGY 1

Possessions and Desires . . .

Gem: Agate—This stone may promote health and lead you to a long life.

Flower: Mulberry Tree—You may be considered very wise by your peers.

Astral Color, Color Need, Apparel Color: Your Astral Color is Red, enhancing passion, excitement, and strength. Violet in your environment keeps you empathetic toward others. In your wardrobe, Green gives you confidence.

Fragrance: You should flood your living space with the scent of distilled floral bouquet or freshly cut wood. This will give your ever-curious mind a rest from its constant search for new experiences.

Tree: Walnut—You are unusually helpful and always looking for constant changes in your life.

Instruments: Oboe, flute, clarinet, piano, French horn, organ, piccolo

Composer: Böhm

Bird: Bird of Paradise—the "birds of the Gods." You will shine and love extraordinary circumstances.

Symbol: Crown—the universal sign of dignity.

Harmonious Health and Nutrition . . .

Health Scent: Strawberry—Soothing by nature, the strawberry promotes self-esteem and encourages love.

Favorable Foods: Brussels sprouts, raspberries, whole wheat, beechnuts, pressed cheese

What's Lucky . . .

Lucky Numbers: 5, 9, 10
Best Months: April and August
Best Day of the Week: Wednesday
Best Month Days: 1, 10, 19, 28
Lucky Charm: A new penny in your shoe.
Harmonious Signs for Relationships and Partnerships: Aquarius and Libra

Spiritual Guides . . .

Star: Al Henah—Those born under this star are easily wounded.

Angel: Ambriel—This angel governs travel and transportation, particularly over water, and helps to create love and good communication.

Guardian Angel: Malachi—"Messenger of Jehovah."

Spiritual Stone: Chrysoprasus—This stone aids in relaxation.

✴ JUDITH'S INSIGHT ✴

You are exceptional, kindhearted, hopeful, insightful, and full of enthusiasm. But you tend to waver when a decision is warranted, whether it be in your career or in your relationships. Feeling as if you're at a crossroads is a frequent theme throughout your life. Being torn in many different directions can be frustrating, but when you put your efforts into something and have direction, there is nothing that can stop you.

Your loving instincts provide nurturing beyond compare. You are a devoted friend and one of the most responsible family members; people respect you for your stamina and ability to carry things out. Because people depend on you, you tend to take on too much responsibility—whether you want to or not. Avoid feeling trapped by friends and family by saying No once in a while. It's healthy to go through stages of seclusion, but you dwell on things entirely too much and too long.

At some point in your life, your work will involve pen and paper, whether it be writing, sketching, or creating contracts. You might be a teacher or even a salesperson for a paper company.

Your mind is brilliant and your strong suit. Don't get discouraged when you encounter pitfalls—you are probably going to have to run an obstacle course here and there. Have no fear, not only do you get back on the horse, you learn to ride in the right direction.

✴ ✴ ✴

JUNE 20 GEMINI • The twins of the zodiac

May 21 at 4:00 A.M. to June 21 at 12:00 P.M. • NUMEROLOGY 2

Possessions and Desires . . .

Gem: Sapphire—This gem may help you find forgiveness from those you've wronged.
Flower: Black Mulberry—You will hold onto all of your childhood friends.
Astral Color, Color Need, Apparel Color: Your Astral Color is Red, which enhances passion, excitement, and strength. Violet in your environment keeps you empathetic toward others. In your wardrobe, Wine gives you energy.
Fragrance: You should flood your living space with the scent of distilled floral bouquet or freshly cut wood. This will give your ever-curious mind a rest from its constant search for new experiences.
Tree: Maple—You have great stability and flashes of intuition.
Instruments: Pipe organ, cymbal, drum
Composers: Handel, Johann Sebastian Bach
Bird: Cuckoo—a good flyer and very seldom a quitter. Some cuckoos tend to think they favor lonely isolation, but what they really yearn for is a family relationship.
Symbol: Cross—the symbol of self-sacrifice and reconciliation.

Harmonious Health and Nutrition . . .

Health Scent: Apple—You are creative, full of joy, and nearly magical. You bring happiness.
Favorable Foods: Watercress, peaches, rye, beechnuts, eggs

What's Lucky . . .

Lucky Numbers: 2, 5, 9
Best Months: April and August
Best Day of the Week: Wednesday
Best Month Days: 2, 11, 20, 29
Lucky Charms: Two 50-cent pieces. Give someone else one of them.

Harmonious Signs for Relationships and Partnerships: Aquarius and Libra

Spiritual Guides . . .

Star: Al Divah—Those with this star could feel that they are mistreated by relatives.
Angel: Ambriel—This angel governs travel and transportation, particularly over water, and helps to create love and good communication.
Guardian Angel: St. John—This angel simplifies that which is complicated.
Spiritual Stone: Chrysoprasus—This stone aids in relaxation.

✳ JUDITH'S INSIGHT ✳

You are loving and generous to a fault. You educate others on the art of giving. Kindness will allow you more happiness than you might otherwise believe. Remember the word *choices* because you will have plenty—especially in love. You can be quite fickle in love. Inevitably and later in life, you find peace and a long-lasting relationship and will do anything to make it work. Astute and receptive to the outside world, you don't seem to be as highly evolved when it comes to your own emotions. You are, unfortunately, drawn to someone who doesn't understand you.

Your healthy imagination may actually help your career choices. Whether you are putting things together for your children or working in the media or advertising, somewhere along the way your creativity will enhance your job. You may be on stage, but you're more likely to take a role in the writing process. You are sharp and intelligent, and education or preparing educational materials seem to play a role in your life. You may also have an interest in history, science, or research. If you don't, you could be rallying the community and fighting for the rights of neighbors and friends, the underdog and yourself. Learn to recognize and appreciate your humanitarianism.

Financially, you need to keep the balance until the time money and your generosity go hand in hand. Ultimately you will be financially secure.

✳ ✳ ✳

JUNE 21   GEMINI • The twins of the zodiac

May 21 at 4:00 A.M. to June 21 at 12:00 P.M.   •   NUMEROLOGY 3

Possessions and Desires . . .

Gem: Ruby—This stone may lead you to energy, friendship, and happiness.
Flower: Peony—You may find yourself being too forgiving when others hurt you.
Astral Color, Color Need, Apparel Color: Your Astral Color is Green, which gives you confidence. Green in your environment enhances your luck, because you will feel secure. In your wardrobe, Brown gives you confidence and a sharp look.
Fragrance: You should flood your living space with the scent of distilled floral bouquet or freshly cut wood. This will give your ever-curious mind a rest from its constant search for new experiences.
Tree: Elm—You have willpower, strength, and the ability to stand alone.
Instrument: Trombone
Composers: Verdi, Mendelssohn, Schumann
Bird: Swan—Regarded as royal and sacred, this bird has the protective nature of a mother, and can become a furious fighter in the defense of its young.
Symbol: Wreath—You have been crowned with a special personality. You are strong but extremely compassionate.

Harmonious Health and Nutrition . . .

Health Scent: Rose—This scent will lead you to passionate thoughts and make you feel warm inside.
Favorable Foods: Celery, grapes, rye, almonds, buttermilk

What's Lucky . . .

Lucky Numbers: 3, 5, 9
Best Months: April and August
Best Day of the Week: Wednesday
Best Month Days: 3, 12, 21, and 30
Lucky Charm: A pen that someone else has already used.

Harmonious Signs for Relationships and Partnerships: Aquarius and Libra

Spiritual Guides . . .

Star: Al Henah—Those born under this star are easily wounded.
Angel: Ambriel—This angel governs travel and transportation, particularly over water, and helps to create love and good communication.
Guardian Angel: Johiel—This angel is a protector of all those with a humble heart.
Spiritual Stone: Chrysoprasus—This stone aids in relaxation.

✶ JUDITH'S INSIGHT ✶

You are cunning and smooth, charming and funny; your sense of humor can get you through any tough situation. You may endure battles in relationships before you find harmony. It has a lot to do with you. As you get older, you change remarkably and have more patience and consideration for your partner. But keeping yourself satisfied will be a bit of a task when it comes to love. You need a lot of freedom, social invitations, and friends to keep you satisfied. You will be called selfish at times because you demand a lot, want a lot, and get a lot. Have no fear, for your turn will come to give back, and this is where you learn one of life's greatest lessons. An epiphany of sorts will be your teacher, and from then on, you undergo considerable change and give more than you receive.

You do well in your own business or working for a larger company—the bigger the better. With your organizational skills, there aren't many jobs you can't handle. It wouldn't be surprising for you to end up in a government position. At some point in your life, you may take a position where a uniform is required. You may have a job where frequent travel is involved. All in all, you do have a successful career.

You make friends quite easily and try to dominate the crowd. When you're not vying for control, the power is usually handed right over to you. One way or another you are placed in a powerful position.

✶ ✶ ✶

JUNE 22

CANCER • The waves of the moon of the zodiac

June 21 at 12:00 P.M. to July 22 at 11:00 P.M. • NUMEROLOGY 4

Possessions and Desires . . .

Gem: Sapphire—This gem may help you find forgiveness from those you've wronged.

Flower: Passionflower—Religion tends to be a very important factor in your life.

Astral Color, Color Need, Apparel Color: Your Astral Color is Green, which gives you confidence. Green in your environment enhances your luck, because you will feel secure. In your wardrobe, Silver is very stimulating for you.

Fragrance: You will be calmed by the scent of fresh linen dried in the breeze or wild orchids.

Tree: Cherry—You will find yourself faced with constant new emotional awakenings.

Instruments: Bass, clarinet

Composers: Haydn, Wagner

Bird: Killdeer—This bird is usually found consorting with other species, and can adapt to any environment.

Symbol: Star—You are full of inner brightness and will stand out in any crowd. You will be seen as special.

Harmonious Health and Nutrition . . .

Health Scent: Vanilla—This scent will fill you with a feeling of cleanliness and stability.

Favorable Foods: Lentils, bananas, sugar, chicken, eggs

What's Lucky . . .

Lucky Numbers: 3, 4, 7

Best Months: February and September

Best Day of the Week: Monday

Best Month Days: 4, 13, 22, 31

Lucky Charm: A piece of material cut from something in your home.

Harmonious Signs for Relationships and Partnerships: Pisces, Scorpio, and Taurus

Spiritual Guides . . .

Star: Al Nethra—Those with this star are treasured as friends.

Angel: Muriel—This angel aids us during times of emotional stress.

Guardian Angel: St. John—This angel simplifies that which is complicated.

Spiritual Stone: Chrysoprasus—This stone aids in relaxation.

✷ JUDITH'S INSIGHT ✷

You are a challenge to others and quite fascinating even to yourself. Bouts with self-doubt and low self-esteem could possibly be your greatest downfall. Because of your strong personality, people don't always realize how sensitive you are and can actually expect too much of you. Watch that this doesn't pull you down at times. You tend to stand secure even though your personality can be overwhelming.

You are likely to have unusual relationships or be drawn to a unique person. You may also desire to live in unusual situations or maybe choose a mate who is foreign born. Family may see you as a rebel or the black sheep. You are quite eccentric, and you love every minute of it. The more conversation pieces you have around you, the better. As you get older you tend to become more family oriented, and you make take a 180-degree turn to the more conservative. Later, a more structured family environment will appeal to you.

You will undertake many challenges and love the exotic, the thrilling, and the adventurous. Tap into your strong intuition more often. You could be a psychic, an astrologer, investigator, or detective. With your love of work, you can have a very successful career; you just need patience to get there.

✷ ✷ ✷

JUNE 23 CANCER • The waves of the moon of the zodiac
June 21 at 12:00 P.M. to July 22 at 11:00 P.M. • NUMEROLOGY 5

Possessions and Desires . . .

Gem: Sardius—This stone could give the wearer unusual insights into his or her own heart.

Flower: Pasqueflower—You tend to not ask other people to give you what you need.

Astral Color, Color Need, Apparel Color: Your Astral Color is Green, which gives you confidence. Green in your environment enhances your luck, because you will feel secure. In your wardrobe, Brown gives you confidence and a sharp appearance.

Fragrance: You will be calmed by the scent of fresh linen dried in the breeze or wild orchids.

Tree: Apple—You are creative, full of joy, and nearly magical. You bring happiness.

Instruments: Viola, trumpet

Composer: Liszt

Bird: Cuckoo—a good flyer and very seldom a quitter. Some cuckoos tend to think they favor lonely isolation, but what they really yearn for is a family relationship.

Symbol: Triangle—You have the right combination of abilities.

Harmonious Health and Nutrition . . .

Health Scent: Peach—This scent may balance your good qualities so that they equal your charm.

Favorable Foods: Beets, strawberries, honey, oysters, pressed cheese

What's Lucky . . .

Lucky Numbers: 3, 5, 7
Best Months: February and September
Best Day of the Week: Monday
Best Month Days: 4, 5, 23
Lucky Charms: A rabbit's foot or a white candle
Harmonious Signs for Relationships and Partnerships: Pisces, Scorpio, and Taurus

Spiritual Guides . . .

Star: Al Nethra—Those with this star are treasured as friends.

Angel: Muriel—This angel aids us during times of emotional stress.

Guardian Angel: Plavwell—This angel gives power and strength to one's presence.

Spiritual Stone: Jacinth—Holding this stone could aid in memory retention.

✳ JUDITH'S INSIGHT ✳

Some may call you a showoff, and you display yourself and your home like museum pieces. Things of beauty and taste appeal to you. Your energy and enthusiasm are addictive, so your name appears first on the invitation list. You have many hidden talents, and you might be in your mid-thirties before you figure out what you really want to do.

One big downfall is your impatience with those not as quick as you. When it comes to love, you are totally devoted to one mate, even if it lasts only a week or two. You find it easier to blame others than to take responsibility for problems. After forty, though, you tend to balance that.

It is most likely that you will have more than one job. A career in entertaining, writing, publishing, or computer graphics could please you. With your restlessness, it wouldn't be surprising if you were in a job with many changes or more than one title.

You have a strong desire to travel on a constant basis. Your suitcase should always be ready and packed. Or, since you are a risk taker, you could parachute out of planes. You are intrigued by the unusual and unknown, like astrology or psychology. You may come up with some of your own theories on life. Consider psychology as a possibility. You take on life and use every minute of your time to enjoy it. But, watch out for less active times—this could send you into a depression. So when you're feeling low, all you have to do is get your engine started again.

✳ ✳ ✳

JUNE 24   CANCER • The waves of the moon of the zodiac

June 21 at 12:00 P.M. to July 22 at 11:00 P.M. • NUMEROLOGY 6

Possessions and Desires . . .

Gem: Topaz—This is an excellent gift to be exchanged between very loyal friends.

Flower: Hemp—You may need to just accept that the universe will always have its own way.

Astral Color, Color Need, Apparel Color: Your Astral Color is Green, which gives you confidence. Green in your environment enhances your luck, because you will feel secure. In your wardrobe, Silver is very stimulating for you.

Fragrance: You will be calmed by the scent of fresh linen dried in the breeze or wild orchids.

Tree: Palm—You tend to be very healthy and creative.

Instruments: Tambourine, lyre

Composer: Schubert

Bird: Goldfinch—There are forty-four different species of finches which vary greatly. This can sometimes be the most charming bird. These gentle creatures can be very moody in unsettled weather.

Symbol: Crescent—You are more likely to be influenced by the phases of the moon. Your easygoing manner leads you to peaceful situations.

Harmonious Health and Nutrition . . .

Health Scent: Orange Blossom—This scent may balance your body, mind, and soul.

Favorable Foods: Carrots, grapes, sugar, liver, buttermilk

What's Lucky . . .

Lucky Numbers: 3, 6, 7

Best Months: February and September

Best Day of the Week: Monday

Best Month Days: 6, 15, 24

Lucky Charms: A religious token or card from any religion.

Harmonious Signs for Relationships and Partnerships: Pisces, Scorpio, and Taurus

Spiritual Guides . . .

Star: Al Terpha—The people born under this star are often delivered from trouble by luck.

Angel: Muriel—This angel aids us during times of emotional stress.

Guardian Angel: Michael—"Who is like God."

Spiritual Stone: Jacinth—Holding this stone could aid in memory retention.

✶ JUDITH'S INSIGHT ✶

There isn't anything you can't do. You are a great talker and avid reader. Seldom do you go into a deep conversation you can't handle. You seem pretty certain about how to get over the obstacles that inevitably come in your way. Eventually you learn to accept criticism, although at first you can be quite defensive.

When it comes to finding a mate, look before you leap. You have a tendency to jump in without really knowing the other person. Your worst heartaches come from not thinking before you speak. As a lover, you are deep and emotional. The problem is very few people ever get to see that. Too bad you're afraid to let others in, especially since you crave intimacy most. Your subtle style is most attractive, but your mate must be a powerhouse when it comes to romance. If that person doesn't appreciate spontaneity, they may never put a smile on your face. Don't worry, you fare quite well in your love life and other relationships. Work to send out more receptive signals. Harmony and happiness tend to come when you decide you're ready.

Although you like a challenge, from time to time you could just stop something in the middle and decide you want something else. It will seem as if money just falls into your lap. It is also very possible that you will create something and bring yourself to significant wealth.

✶ ✶ ✶

JUNE 25 CANCER • The waves of the moon of the zodiac
June 21 at 12:00 P.M. to July 22 at 11:00 A.M. • NUMEROLOGY 7

Possessions and Desires . . .

Gem: Ruby—This stone may lead you to energy, friendship, and happiness.
Flower: Hollyhock—You don't mind working for the security you want from life.
Astral Color, Color Need, Apparel Color: Your Astral Color is Green, which gives confidence. Green in your environment enhances your luck, because you will feel secure. In your wardrobe, Brown gives confidence and a sharp look.
Fragrance: You will be calmed by the scent of fresh linen dried in the breeze or wild orchids.
Tree: Sycamore—Yours is the ability to love, communicate honestly with others, and have lasting relationships.
Instrument: Harp
Composers: Gluck, Brahms
Bird: Skylark—This handsome bird is beautiful when it sings. It always whistles as it works.
Symbol: Heart—You are enthusiastic, empathetic, and full of generosity and love.

Harmonious Health and Nutrition . . .

Health Scent: Jasmine—This scent may make you more easygoing when you are stressed.
Favorable Foods: Spinach, bananas, sugar, salmon, eggs

What's Lucky . . .

Lucky Numbers: 3, 7, 25
Best Months: February and September
Best Day of the Week: Monday
Best Month Days: 6, 15, 24
Lucky Charm: An old key.

Harmonious Signs for Relationships and Partnerships: Pisces, Scorpio, and Taurus

Spiritual Guides . . .

Star: Al Nethra—Those with this star are treasured as friends.
Angel: Muriel—This angel aids us during times of emotional stress.
Guardian Angel: Ralphael—This angel attends to all of your needs when you are looking for guidance.
Spiritual Stone: Jacinth—Holding this stone could aid in memory retention.

✴ JUDITH'S INSIGHT ✴

You are kind, gentle, sweet, and nurturing. You love your home to look neat and tidy. Highly sensitive, you can be quick on the defense as well as on the offense. When people are nice to you, you are at your best; and the nicer they are, the nicer you are in return. You can be secretive, and sometimes a bit flirtatious and even promiscuous. Try to relax that mind: you dwell on things far too long. That is okay for work, but unhealthy emotionally. Your tendency is to be extremely loyal.

You are a comfort zone for your friends and family, but you don't know how to say No. Keep yourself from getting worked up when it comes to love. Use your sense of humor as much as you want, and then use it some more.

You are profound in your thinking; a career in writing would be a nice fit for you. Although it may take you years to recognize all your talents, your number one talent is your imagination. Family members remind you from time to time how inventive you were as a child. You may go back and forth with careers until your thirties; then you will, without a doubt, find the right path and follow it to the end of the rainbow.

✱ ✱ ✱

JUNE 26 CANCER • The waves of the moon of the zodiac

June 21 at 12:00 P.M. to July 22 at 11:00 P.M. • NUMEROLOGY 8

Possessions and Desires . . .

Gem: Chrysolite—This gem may help you clear your mind of sadness and worry.

Flower: Sweet Scabiosa—That which you love tends to be what you see as genuine.

Astral Color, Color Need, Apparel Color: Your Astral Color is Green, which gives you confidence. Green in your environment enhances your luck, because you will feel secure. In your wardrobe, Brown gives you confidence and a sharp appearance.

Fragrance: You will be calmed by the scent of fresh linen dried in the breeze or wild orchids.

Tree: Pine—Your relationships tend to be balanced, both emotionally and mentally.

Instrument: Cello

Composer: Mozart

Bird: Bobolink—This charming singer is equally good as a soloist or a member of an orchestra. It is a very romantic bird, most useful as an insect destroyer, and elegant, with beautiful feathers, and always pleasant to have around.

Symbol: Wings—You are the source of balance in your world—this will bring you contentment.

Harmonious Health and Nutrition . . .

Health Scent: Almond—This scent may revitalize you and open you to greater possibilities.

Favorable Foods: Okra, apples, honey, chicken, buttermilk

What's Lucky . . .

Lucky Numbers: 3, 7, 8

Best Months: February and September

Best Day of the Week: Monday

Best Month Days: 8, 17, 26

Lucky Charm: Red ribbon in your wallet or doorway.

Harmonious Signs for Relationships and Partnerships: Pisces, Scorpio, and Taurus

Spiritual Guides . . .

Star: Al Nethra—Those with this star are treasured as friends.

Angel: Muriel—This angel aids us during times of emotional stress.

Guardian Angel: Seraphim—An angel that brings love, light, and passion.

Spiritual Stone: Jacinth—Holding this stone could aid in memory retention.

✦ JUDITH'S INSIGHT ✦

Although you're charming and giving, you can be too serious. You don't miss much: you take it in, store it, and review it like a movie. You can be misunderstood and considered intense. Few people really get to know that mind of yours. You rarely speak without something concrete to say. Every once in a while you have a tendency to go overboard either with spending or partying. Your small circle of friends from childhood will stick with your almost forever.

It may take work for a mate to please you. Your serious soul locks others out. You may find life uneasy at times, and others may see you as a lonely heart looking for a place to connect. Certain special people bring out your terrific sense of humor. And you're better with a partner than alone.

For you there aren't enough hours in a day. Remember not to bite off more than you can chew. This is yet another way you overdo it. When it comes to family ties, you keep them. Family for you could also be close, dear friends or even former lovers. You're a free bird who needs a secure nest where you can always come in for a landing and feel safe. So although you may have one appearance, you really are someone else.

You love to teach and instruct and are a wealth of information, not only from books but your own philosophies of life. You would make a great teacher, professor, or instructor. You can even do well with emotional counseling, guidance counseling, or nurturing of any kind. Not to say that you are not smart enough to be the head of the company—that side of you exists as well. Of course, you would be the boss with a heart.

★ ★ ★

JUNE 27   CANCER • The waves of the moon of the zodiac
June 21 at 12:00 P.M. to July 22 at 11:00 P.M. • NUMEROLOGY 9

Possessions and Desires . . .

Gem: Sapphire—This gem may help you find forgiveness from those you've wronged.

Flower: Schinus—You may find much peace in actively practicing your chosen religion.

Astral Color, Color Need, Apparel Color: Your Astral Color is Green, which gives you confidence. Green in your environment enhances your luck, because you will feel secure. In your wardrobe, Silver is very stimulating for you.

Fragrance: You will be calmed by the scent of fresh linen dried in the breeze or wild orchids.

Tree: Holly—Beware that you are not carried away by your passionate nature. The only way to grow is to be open to new experiences.

Instruments: Violin, tympanum

Composer: Gluck

Bird: Mockingbird—the most proficient minstrel in the world's orchestra; graceful and enthusiastic.

Symbol: Anchor—This tranquil symbol signifies stability and strength, and stands for strong commitments in relationships.

Harmonious Health and Nutrition . . .

Health Scents: Lavender—This scent might lead others to trust you and make you patient.

Favorable Foods: Cucumbers, cherries, sugar, oysters, pressed cheese

What's Lucky . . .

Lucky Numbers: 3, 7, 9

Best Month: February and September

Best Day of the Week: Monday

Best Month Days: 9, 18, 27

Lucky Charm: A U.S. coin or a bill of any amount from the year you were born.

Harmonious Signs for Relationships and Partnerships: Pisces, Scorpio, and Taurus

Spiritual Guides . . .

Star: Al Terpha—The people born under this star are often delivered from trouble by luck.

Angel: Muriel—This angel aids us during times of emotional stress.

Guardian Angel: Gabriel—"God is my strength."

Spiritual Stone: Jacinth—Holding this stone could aid in memory retention.

✶ JUDITH'S INSIGHT ✶

You are the truest and most loyal of friends. A combination of intelligence and wit makes you charming, shrewd, and attractive. You really are a great conversationalist, though others may see you as quiet. Your gift with words may be your greatest asset, although your kind advice and good heart are the cornerstones of your makeup.

Your search for love may not be complete until you are a little older. And be careful when you find it—that's when the challenges really begin. A nurturing soul, you really do love your domestic side. Somewhere along the way, you learn to recognize this.

You do tend to be more creative than you think, and, as you get older, you may put that creativity to work—painting, writing, or building sand castles. You may find work as caregiver in a hospital. A career in publishing, as an editor or a writer, may present itself to you. Success will knock at your door often, and you will have chances to move. Make sure that you are not in a stagnant situation. In time you could be head of a corporation or wind up in your own business or assisting your mate in his or hers.

A few legal issues may arise, or you may just work for attorneys. You encounter an obstacle or two, but you hurdle them like a master athlete. The older you get, the better you become. As you get older when it comes to work, your tendency is to stay in one place for the security it provides.

✶ ✶ ✶

Possessions and Desires . . .

Gem: Emerald—Those who carry this stone tend to be lucky in love.

Flower: Snapdragon—Be careful to get the facts before assuming you know another's intentions.

Astral Color, Color Need, Apparel Color: Your Astral Color is Green, which gives you confidence. Green in your environment enhances your luck, because you will feel secure. In your wardrobe, Brown gives you confidence and a sharp look.

Fragrance: You will be calmed by the scent of fresh linen dried in the breeze or wild orchids.

Tree: Walnut—You are unusually helpful and always looking for new beginnings.

Instruments: Oboe, flute, clarinet, piano, French horn, organ, piccolo

Composer: Böhm

Bird: Bird of Paradise—the "bird of the Gods." You will shine and love extraordinary form.

Symbol: Crown—the universal sign of dignity.

Harmonious Health and Nutrition . . .

Health Scent: Strawberry—Soothing by nature, the strawberry promotes self-esteem and encourages love.

Favorable Foods: Carrots, figs, honey, liver, eggs

What's Lucky . . .

Lucky Numbers: 3, 7, 10

Best Months: February and September

Best Day of the Week: Monday

Best Month Days: 1, 10, 19, 28

Lucky Charm: A new penny in your shoe.

Harmonious Signs for Relationships and Partnerships: Pisces, Scorpio, and Taurus

Spiritual Guides . . .

Star: Al Nethra—Those with this star are treasured as friends.

Angel: Muriel—This angel aids us during times of emotional stress.

Guardian Angel: Malachi—"Messenger of Jehovah."

Spiritual Stone: Jacinth—Holding this stone could aid in memory retention.

✴ JUDITH'S INSIGHT ✴

You're essentially kindhearted and nice to others. You're definitely one who is interested in material things. You will have a lot of things, from a beautiful home to a nice car to attractive clothes. You are sympathetic and kind in spite of your changeable mood. When it comes to friendship, you are true and loyal. You consider gossip an art and may be intrigued by what others have to say. In financial matters you can be rather intractable, not outwardly generous with others, because a lot of the time you spend your money on yourself.

In love, allow doors and windows to open. You tend to be too closed-minded. Give yourself a chance to find the right mate, otherwise you may be doing double duty and amid a lot of conflict. A triangle of some sort is quite possible. Family matters do have an important role in your life.

It would be very surprising if you weren't intrigued by the art of poetry and love. If you are male, you may find that these things play a valuable role in your life. You are quite artistic or will be attracted to the arts and to beauty. You can be anything from an upholsterer to a decorator or a sculptor. Your nurturing side may lead you to medicine and helping others.

Don't be discouraged when you hit curves in the road, because you will have many. As time goes on, you get used to them and master them like a professional race car driver. If you have a car, it may be a valuable asset to you and something you treat like a child.

✶ ✶ ✶

JUNE 29 CANCER • The waves of the moon of the zodiac

June 21 at 12:00 P.M. to July 22 at 11:00 P.M. • NUMEROLOGY 2

Possessions and Desires . . .

Gem: Sapphire—This gem may help you find forgiveness from those you've wronged.
Flower: Saint Johnswort—Be careful not to let superstitions rule your life.
Astral Color, Color Need, Apparel Color: Your Astral Color is Green, which gives you confidence. Green in your environment enhances your luck, because you will feel secure. In your wardrobe, Silver is stimulating for you.
Fragrance: You will be calmed by the scent of fresh linen dried in the breeze or wild orchids.
Tree: Maple—You have both great stability and flashes of intuition.
Instruments: Pipe organ, cymbal, drum
Composers: Handel, Johann Sebastian Bach
Bird: Cuckoo—a good flyer and very seldom a quitter. Some cuckoos tend to think they favor lonely isolation, but what they really yearn for is a family relationship.
Symbol: Cross—the symbol of self-sacrifice and reconciliation.

Harmonious Health and Nutrition . . .

Health Scent: Apple—You are creative, full of joy, and nearly magical. You bring happiness.
Favorable Foods: Lima beans, cherries, sugar, salmon, buttermilk

What's Lucky . . .

Lucky Numbers: 3, 7, 11
Best Months: February and September
Best Day of the Week: Monday
Best Month Days: 2, 11, 20, 29
Lucky Charms: Two 50-cent pieces. Give someone else one of them.

Harmonious Signs for Relationships and Partnerships: Pisces, Scorpio, and Taurus

Spiritual Guides . . .

Star: Al Nethra—Those with this star are treasured as friends.
Angel: Muriel—This angel aids us during times of emotional stress.
Guardian Angel: Uriel—This angel brings the light of God's guidance.
Spiritual Stone: Jacinth—Holding this stone could aid in memory retention.

✷ JUDITH'S INSIGHT ✷

Beginnings are important to you, and you will thrive on change. You welcome new things—new love, a new house, new clothes, new furniture. When it comes to love, you weave a tangled web. Expect the unexpected, especially in your twenties. As you get older you become less erratic, and your chances of finding a mate improve. When you do, look for some security. Warmhearted and kind, you do put up barricades when it comes to relationships. Sometimes you listen with only one ear. Your life will be full of choices over and over again.

As far as career is concerned, it is doubtful that you will pick one early in life and stick with it. If you do, however, somewhere along the way you will either hold a second career or take up a hobby that will consume most of your time. Your love of literature, history, and books will present itself; you may even make a little history yourself. You do have a sharp mind and an overwhelming intelligence that may lead you to become a professor, historian, writer, inventor, or publisher. The way the world is going today, you may be a leader in hardware or software in computers.

✷ ✷ ✷

JUNE 30   CANCER • The waves of the moon of the zodiac

June 21 at 12:00 P.M. to July 22 at 11:00 P.M. • NUMEROLOGY 3

Possessions and Desires . . .

Gem: Sapphire—This gem may help you find forgiveness from those you've wronged.
Flower: Sunflower—You should be adored by the one that you love.
Astral Color, Color Need, Apparel Color: Your Astral Color is Green, which gives you confidence. Green in your environment enhances your luck, because you will feel secure. In your wardrobe, Brown gives you confidence and a sharp appearance.
Fragrance: You will be calmed by the scent of fresh linen dried in the breeze or wild orchids.
Tree: Elm—You have willpower, strength, and the ability to stand alone.
Instrument: Trombone
Composers: Verdi, Mendelssohn, Schumann
Bird: Swan—Regarded as royal and sacred, this bird has the protective nature of a mother, and can become a furious fighter in the defense of its young.
Symbol: Wreath—You have been crowned with a special personality. You are strong but extremely compassionate.

Harmonious Health and Nutrition . . .

Health Scent: Rose—This scent will lead you to passionate thoughts and make you feel warm inside.
Favorable Foods: String beans, gooseberries, honey, chicken, pressed cheese

What's Lucky . . .

Lucky Numbers: 3, 7, 30
Best Months: February and September
Best Day of the Week: Monday
Best Month Days: 3, 12, 21, 30
Lucky Charm: A pen that someone else has already used.

Harmonious Signs for Relationships and Partnerships: Pisces, Scorpio, and Taurus

Spiritual Guides . . .

Star: Al Nethra—Those with this star are treasured as friends.
Angel: Muriel—This angel aids us during times of emotional stress.
Guardian Angel: Johiel—This angel is a protector of all those with a humble heart.
Spiritual Stone: Jacinth—Holding this stone could aid in memory retention.

✷ JUDITH'S INSIGHT ✷

Your personality will bring you just about anything you want in life. You have wit, charm, and a sense of humor. Cunning and smooth, you have loads of self-reliance and love to rule. You make friends easily but dominate the crowd. You are a social butterfly and need a lot of friends. The more social invitations, the better.

You emerge as a leader early on. You are fortunate in love, and relationships fall at your feet. Unfortunately, being with the wrong person will cause you to get into many a rut. Take your time in choosing the right partner. In order for someone to keep you satisfied, they have to know you well enough to provide the freedom you require. Trust is vital in your relationship.

You would do well owning your own company, but if you work for a large company, the larger it is, the better. Your excellent organizational skills are superb in any office situation. It wouldn't be surprising if you decide on a career working in government—municipal or otherwise. You are quite a handy person and do have a knack for mechanical things. Fast things (like cars) intrigue you, and you seek out all kinds of challenges.

You can be considered a handful because you demand a lot. You are here to live life to the fullest.

✱ ✱ ✱

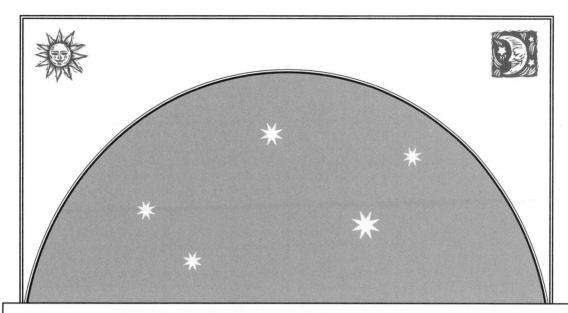

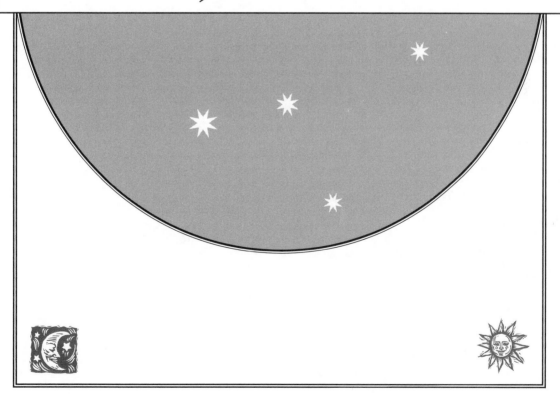

JULY

JULY 1 CANCER • The waves of the moon of the zodiac
June 21 at 12:00 P.M. to July 22 at 11:00 P.M. • NUMEROLOGY 1

Possessions and Desires . . .

Gem: Emerald—Those who carry this stone tend to be lucky in love.

Flower: Sycamore—You may have a strong curiosity about everything around you.

Astral Color, Color Need, Apparel Color: Your Astral Color is Green, which gives you confidence. Green in your environment enhances your luck, because you will feel secure. In your wardrobe, Silver is a stimulating color for you.

Fragrance: You will be calmed by the scent of fresh linen dried in the breeze or wild orchids.

Tree: Walnut—You are unusually helpful and always looking for constant changes in your life.

Instruments: Oboe, flute, clarinet, piano, French horn, organ, piccolo

Composer: Böhm

Bird: Cuckoo—A good flyer and very seldom a quitter. Many seem more independent than they actually are. Yearn for more nurturing than one would expect.

Symbol: Crown—the universal sign of dignity.

Harmonious Health and Nutrition . . .

Health Scent: Strawberry—Soothing by nature, the strawberry promotes self-esteem and encourages love.

Favorable Foods: Parsley, honey, oysters, buttermilk

What's Lucky . . .

Lucky Numbers: 3, 7, 11
Best Months: February and September.
Best Day of the Week: Monday
Best Month Days: 1, 10, 19, 28

Lucky Charm: A new penny in your shoe.
Harmonious Signs for Relationships and Partnerships: Pisces, Scorpio, and Taurus

Spiritual Guides . . .

Star: Al Nethra—Those with this star are treasured as friends.

Angel: Muriel—This angel aids us during times of emotional stress.

Guardian Angel: Malachi—"Messenger of Jehovah."

Spiritual Stone: Jacinth—Holding this stone could aid in memory retention.

✦ JUDITH'S INSIGHT ✦

You are kind, loving, loyal, and true. You are a great humanitarian and giving will be very important to you. It will be more important for you to give than receive. You are so attached to your home and family sometimes it will seem hard for you to make decisions without considering everybody's happiness. It is more likely than not that you will find harmony in loving relationships. Children and marriage could play a large role in your life at one time or another.

Your nurturing side will probably lead you into a profession as a doctor, nurse, or medical assistant. It wouldn't be surprising if, somewhere along the way, you were brought to the public eye with whatever career you choose. You are independent and can adapt to changes very easily. You are fond of theater and drama, and you may have a career in that field. There is a good chance you will attain wealth.

You have a great love for the unknown and are intrigued by mysterious environments. Strange things happen to you. You may even be a bit psychic. Your life will probably be quite unpredictable.

✶ ✶ ✶

JULY 2   CANCER • The waves of the moon of the zodiac
June 21 at 12:00 P.M. to July 22 at 11:00 P.M. • NUMEROLOGY 2

Possessions and Desires . . .

Gem: Sapphire—This gem may help you find forgiveness from those you've wronged.

Flower: Xanthium—You sometimes are rude without meaning to be.

Astral Color, Color Need, Apparel Color: Your Astral Color is Green, which gives you confidence. Green in your environment enhances your luck, because you will feel secure. In your wardrobe, Brown gives you confidence and a sharp look.

Fragrance: You will be calmed by the scent of fresh linen dried in the breeze or wild orchids.

Tree: Maple—You have both great stability and flashes of intuition.

Instruments: Pipe organ, cymbal, drum

Composers: Handel, Johann Sebastian Bach

Bird: Stork—Turkish bird, held in high esteem the world over. This bird is intelligent but may have strange tendencies.

Symbol: Cross—the symbol of self-sacrifice and reconciliation.

Harmonious Health and Nutrition . . .

Health Scent: Apple—You are creative, full of joy, and nearly magical. You bring happiness.

Favorable Foods: Cabbage, grapefruit, whole oats, molasses, cottage cheese

What's Lucky . . .

Lucky Numbers: 2, 3, 7

Best Months: February and September

Best Day of the Week: Monday

Best Month Days: 2, 11, 20, 29

Lucky Charms: Two 50-cent pieces. Give someone else one of them.

Harmonious Signs for Relationships and Partnerships: Pisces, Scorpio, and Taurus

Spiritual Guides . . .

Star: Al Nethra—Those with this star are treasured as friends.

Angel: Muriel—This angel aids us during times of emotional stress.

Guardian Angel: Uriel—This angel brings the light of God's guidance.

Spiritual Stone: Jacinth—Holding this stone could aid in memory retention.

✵ JUDITH'S INSIGHT ✵

You show much persistence and consistency through your life. You are as stable as the day is long. You always show good judgment in whatever you do. You conscience is very strong. You can be moody, neat as a pin, strong as an ox, and cranky as a crab. You can be bothered by things in your environment because of your sensitive nature.

Your tendency is to do better with relationships than not. Your home is important, even if it is the garage. You have a strong determination. Not only do you create a successful career for yourself, you look to enhance the success of other people, especially those with whom you have a friendship or relationship. Your career could be in a counseling or homemaking environment. You could also be anything from a carpenter to chiropractor. Whatever you do, you will nurture and serve those around you.

You like to create drama in life. Travel will be important to you, but you'll be luckier on sea or surrounded by water. You are inspired by anything you do around water. If you want to write, do it near a lake. Your more romantic and sentimental times will be better when you are surrounded by water. If you are feeling low and need to stimulate yourself, walk along the beach, and look for answers in the waves.

✳ ✳ ✳

JULY 3   CANCER • The waves of the moon of the zodiac
June 21 at 12:00 P.M. to July 22 at 11:00 P.M. • NUMEROLOGY 3

Possessions and Desires . . .

Gem: Emerald—Those who carry this stone tend to be lucky in love.
Flower: Wood Sorrel—You may mother those you care for.
Astral Color, Color Need, Apparel Color: Your Astral Color is Green, which gives you confidence. Green in your environment enhances your luck, because you will feel secure. In your wardrobe, Silver is a stimulating color for you.
Fragrance: You will be calmed by the scent of fresh linen dried in the breeze or wild orchids.
Tree: Elm—You have willpower, strength, and the ability to stand alone.
Instrument: Trombone
Composers: Verdi, Mendelssohn, Schumann
Bird: Stork—Turkish bird, held in high esteem the world over. This bird is intelligent but may have strange tendencies.
Symbol: Wreath—You have been crowned with a special personality. You are strong but extremely compassionate.

Harmonious Health and Nutrition . . .

Health Scent: Rose—This scent will lead you to passionate thoughts and make you feel warm inside.
Favorable Foods: Cauliflower, peaches, caraway, honey, salmon, eggs

What's Lucky . . .

Lucky Numbers: 3, 7, 21
Best Months: February and September
Best Day of the Week: Monday
Best Month Days: 3, 12, 21, 30
Lucky Charm: A pen that someone else has already used.

Harmonious Signs for Relationships and Partnerships: Pisces, Scorpio, and Taurus

Spiritual Guides . . .

Star: Al Nethra—Those with this star are treasured as friends.
Angel: Muriel—This angel aids us during times of emotional stress.
Guardian Angel: Johiel—This angel is a protector of all those with a humble heart.
Spiritual Stone: Jacinth—Holding this stone could aid in memory retention.

✳ JUDITH'S INSIGHT ✳

You are intelligent and intuitive and sometimes too logical for your own good. You do tend to have strong opinions. Yet, usually you speak only when you really have something to say. Others in your life may think you are serious by nature, but you are just shy. You may not truly realize your independent nature.

You want a happy home and do what you must to make it happen. The challenge for you is keeping from doing too much for others; whether it be furniture that has to be moved or a neighbor in need of a helping hand, you are always there to help.

You may desire a career in the health field, which means that you could eventually be the head of a facility or perhaps the owner. You would be a successful entrepeneur. You do lean toward a public life at one time or another. It won't be surprising if your name is in print at some point. Though it does take some time for you to find your niche, you will be quite successful in whatever you choose.

Your home is most important to you, especially living with a long term mate. Just don't make this decision hastily. You will be the one who does it all to keep your relationship going, friends or lovers. When others don't return the same energies, you will take all you can, but eventually leave. If affections and devotion are returned, you can live happily ever after.

✳ ✳ ✳

JULY 4   CANCER • The waves of the moon of the zodiac
June 21 at 12:00 P.M. to July 22 at 11:00 P.M. • NUMEROLOGY 4

Possessions and Desires . . .

Gem: Sapphire—This gem may help you find forgiveness from those you've wronged.
Flower: Water willow: Patience is hard for you, but you will learn it along the way.
Astral Color, Color Need, Apparel Color: Your Astral Color is Green, which gives you confidence. Green in your environment enhances your luck, because you will feel secure. In your wardrobe, Brown gives you confidence and a sharp look.
Fragrance: You will be calmed by the scent of fresh linen dried in the breeze or wild orchids.
Tree: Cherry—You will find yourself faced with constant new emotional awakenings.
Instruments: Bass, clarinet
Composers: Haydn, Wagner
Bird: Stork—Turkish bird, held in high esteem the world over. This bird is intelligent but may have strange tendencies.
Symbol: Star—You are full of inner brightness and will stand out in any crowd. You will be seen as special.

Harmonious Health and Nutrition . . .

Health Scent: Vanilla—This scent will fill you with a feeling of cleanliness and stability.
Favorable Foods: Celery, black figs, whole oats, molasses, oysters, cream

What's Lucky . . .

Lucky Numbers: 3, 4, 7
Best Months: February and September
Best Day of the Week: Monday
Best Month Days: 4, 13, 22, 31
Lucky Charm: A piece of material cut from something in your home.

Harmonious Signs for Relationships and Partnerships: Pisces, Scorpio, and Taurus

Spiritual Guides . . .

Star: Al Nethra—Those with this star are treasured friends.
Angel: Muriel—This angel aids us during times of emotional stress.
Guardian Angel: Uriel—This angel brings the light of God's guidance.
Spiritual Stone: Jacinth—Holding this stone could aid in memory retention

✳ JUDITH'S INSIGHT ✳

You are exceptionally sensitive and have a warm heart that could heat the world. You surround yourself with loads of people, yet you seem lonely. Many strange, unusual things occur throughout your life. Believe it or not, these experiences will enhance your life, though at the time they may seem devastating. Later on, you will have learned from them.

It is extremely easy for you to make friends, although you allow relationships to drift away. You blame others for not being there when it is you who pushes them away. What you feel is not necessarily what you show, and this could create problems.

You could be a great doctor, lawyer, or teacher. You could be successful working in film or theater. No matter what career you eventually become active in, with time you will rise almost to the top—it would be quite surprising if you didn't.

You tend to stand apart from the crowd. You have a strong sense of loyalty, not only to your family, but to your country. You tend to be the one that lends the helping hand.

★ ★ ★

JULY 5

CANCER • The waves of the moon of the zodiac

June 21 at 12:00 P.M. to July 22 at 11:00 P.M. • NUMEROLOGY 5

Possessions and Desires . . .

Gem: Emerald—Those who carry this stone tend to be lucky in love.

Flower: Crown of Roses—You will be recognized as a very moral person.

Astral Color, Color Need, Apparel Color: Your Astral Color is Green, which gives you confidence. Green in your environment enhances your luck, because you will feel secure. In your wardrobe, Silver is a stimulating color for you.

Fragrance: You will be calmed by the scent of fresh linen dried in the breeze or wild orchids.

Tree: Apple—You are creative, full of joy, and nearly magical. You bring happiness.

Instruments: Viola, trumpet

Composer: Liszt

Bird: Cuckoo—a good flyer and very seldom a quitter. Some cuckoos tend to think they favor lonely isolation, but what they really yearn for is a family relationship.

Symbol: Triangle—You have the right combination of abilities.

Harmonious Health and Nutrition . . .

Health Scent: Peach—This scent may balance your good qualities so that they equal your charm.

Favorable Foods: Beets, watermelon, caraway, salmon, buttermilk

What's Lucky . . .

Lucky Numbers: 3, 5, 7

Best Months: February and September

Best Day of the Week: Monday

Best Month Days: 4, 5, 23

Lucky Charms: A rabbit's foot or a white candle.

Harmonious Signs for Relationships and Partnerships: Pisces, Scorpio, and Taurus

Spiritual Guides . . .

Star: Al Nethra—Those with this star are treasured as friends.

Angel: Muriel—This angel aids us during times of emotional stress.

Guardian Angel: Plavwell—The guardian that gives power and strength to one's presence.

Spiritual Stone: Jacinth—Holding this stone could aid in memory retention.

✳ JUDITH'S INSIGHT ✳

Don't judge your whole life by your childhood. You may feel as if you will never be happy, but you will. Stop fulfilling your own negative prophecies and start thinking more positively. Your sound mind and sharp intellect will lead you down a path of strong learning and teaching. Your confidence does waver, however, and you may have trouble with your self-esteem. But when your kind heart and deep soul become evident, life is bound to be better for you. Others may take advantage of you because of your kind and sympathetic nature. Yes, you are warm and sensitive, but when things don't go your way you can be cold and removed.

As kind and giving as you are, your communication skills need some work. Friends never realize what they mean to you unless you tell them. Relationships will bring you the most happiness and your greatest sadness, not necessarily from the same people. It may seem as if it takes forever to find the perfect love, but you must remain patient—in time there is balance. Security is almost more important to you than romance, so pay attention to your choices. Learn to not force issues. You don't always need to be right.

Charming personality that you have, you would work well with people. Your nuturing attitude makes it easy for you to do anything from homemaker to caretaker. You would do well working with children. But you would do well as a counselor, whether it is a guidance counselor or psychiatrist.

✳ ✳ ✳

JULY 6 CANCER • The waves of the moon of the zodiac
June 21 at 12:00 P.M. to July 22 at 11:00 P.M. • NUMEROLOGY 6

Possessions and Desires . . .

Gem: Sapphire—This gem may help you find forgiveness from those you've wronged.
Flower: White Rosebud—The lessons you learned in your early youth never cease to be of use.
Astral Color, Color Need, Apparel Color: Your Astral Color is Green, which gives you confidence. Green in your environment enhances your luck, because you will feel secure. In your wardrobe, Brown gives you confidence and a sharp look.
Fragrance: You will be calmed by the scent of fresh linen dried in the breeze or wild orchids.
Tree: Palm—You tend to be very healthy and creative.
Instruments: Tambourine, lyre
Composer: Schubert
Bird: Goldfinch—These gentle creatures can seem moody, especially in unsettled weather.
Symbol: Crescent—You are more likely to be influenced by the phases of the moon. Your easygoing manner leads you to peaceful situations.

Harmonious Health and Nutrition . . .

Health Scent: Orange Blossom—This scent may balance your body, mind, and soul.
Favorable Foods: Cauliflower, oranges, honey, oysters, eggs

What's Lucky . . .

Lucky Numbers: 3, 6, 7
Best Months: February and September
Best Day of the Week: Monday
Best Month Days: 6, 15, 24
Lucky Charms: A religious token or card from any religion.

Harmonious Signs for Relationships and Partnerships: Pisces, Scorpio, and Taurus

Spiritual Guides . . .

Star: Al Nethra—Those with this star are treasured as friends.
Angel: Muriel—This angel aids us during times of emotional stress.
Guardian Angel: Michael—"Who is like God."
Spiritual Stone: Jacinth—Holding this stone could aid in memory retention.

✷ JUDITH'S INSIGHT ✷

Your kind heart will lead you down the right path and help you find everything you want. You sometimes view things through rose-colored glasses. Your magnetic personality will take you anywhere you want to go. With your magical charisma, life appears to be quite easy. You are a quality-of-life person with honorable charm. Be careful to keep that cranky, crab side under control.

You tend to protect yourself when it comes to intimacy. Your strong love and devotion for your family will bring harmony and happiness. You do get intense without realizing it, and it may be hard for others to make that clear to you.

You have a great determination. With your powerful ambition you will go far, but it does take you many tries to get there. You tend to advance in careers such as teaching, counseling, law, building, government, and politics.

You tend to carry the problems of the world on your shoulders. Just remember to shrug them off every once in a while and let unwanted pressures fade.

✷ ✷ ✷

JULY 7 CANCER • The waves of the moon of the zodiac
June 21 at 12:00 P.M. to July 22 at 11:00 P.M. • NUMEROLOGY 7

Possessions and Desires . . .

Gem: Sapphire—This gem may help you find forgiveness from those you've wronged.
Flower: Red Rosebud—Love brings only little disappointments.
Astral Color, Color Need, Apparel Color: Your Astral Color is Green, which gives you confidence. Green in your environment enhances your luck, because you will feel secure. In your wardrobe, Silver is a stimulating color for you.
Fragrance: You will be calmed by the scent of fresh linen dried in the breeze or wild orchids.
Tree: Sycamore—Yours is the ability to love, communicate honestly with others, and have lasting relationships.
Instrument: Harp
Composers: Gluck, Brahms
Bird: Warbling Parakeet—the most beautiful of all birds, known as the love bird. It does seem to have the powers of imitation.
Symbol: Heart—You are enthusiastic, empathetic, and full of generosity and love.

Harmonious Health and Nutrition . . .

Health Scent: Jasmine—This scent may make you more easygoing when you are stressed.
Favorable Foods: Turnips, caraway, molasses, salmon, cottage cheese

What's Lucky . . .

Lucky Numbers: 3, 7, 25
Best Months: February and September
Best Day of the Week: Monday
Best Month Days: 6, 15, 24
Lucky Charm: An old key.

Harmonious Signs for Relationships and Partnerships: Pisces, Scorpio, and Taurus

Spiritual Guides . . .

Star: Al Nethra—Those with this star are treasured as friends.
Angel: Muriel—This angel aids us during times of emotional stress.
Guardian Angel: Raphael—This angel attends to all of your needs when you are looking for guidance.
Spiritual Stone: Jacinth—Holding this stone could aid in memory retention.

✶ JUDITH'S INSIGHT ✶

You have a great sense of humor, along with strong loyalties and devotion. You are just and fair in your regard and feeling for others. You have only the best intentions, even if others aren't receptive to your advice when you offer it. You are capable of overcoming just about any condition.

You give your all, and gladly, especially when it comes to your family. In turn, they will do anything for you. You hit many obstacles and emotional hurdles, which makes you and your immediate family draw close. Love is a challenge at times, but you are the devoted mate who really does try to make your partner happy. Even though you may be settled in a relationship, you may look for another mate, only to realize that you could not find anyone better.

You are much more creative than you give yourself credit for. You accomplish more than you think. No matter what job you take, responsibility is no challenge. You are a delightful, well-organized, and faithful employee. When it comes to hard work, devotion, and loyalty, you win hands down.

You may have a bout with the legal system or with the law. It wouldn't be too serious an issue.

✶ ✶ ✶

JULY 8 CANCER • The waves of the moon of the zodiac

June 21 at 12:00 P.M. to July 22 at 11:00 P.M. • NUMEROLOGY 8

Possessions and Desires . . .

Gem: Emerald—Those who carry this stone tend to be lucky in love.

Flower: White Rose—The lessons you learned in your early youth never cease to be of use.

Astral Color, Color Need, Apparel Color: Your Astral Color is Green, which gives you confidence. Green in your environment enhances your luck, because you will feel secure. In your wardrobe, Brown gives you confidence and a sharp look.

Fragrance: You will be calmed by the scent of fresh linen dried in the breeze or wild orchids.

Tree: Pine—Your relationships tend to be balanced, both emotionally and mentally.

Instrument: Cello

Composer: Mozart

Bird: Bobolink—This charming singer is equally good as a soloist or a member of an orchestra. It is a very romantic bird, most useful as an insect destroyer, and elegant, with beautiful feathers, and always pleasant to have around.

Symbol: Wings—You are the source of balance in your world. This will bring you contentment.

Harmonious Health and Nutrition . . .

Health Scent: Almond—This scent may revitalize you and open you to greater possibilities.

Favorable Foods: Cabbage, whole oats, honey, oysters, cream

What's Lucky . . .

Lucky Numbers: 3, 7, 8

Best Months: February and September

Best Day of the Week: Monday

Best Month Days: 8, 17, 26

Lucky Charm: Red ribbon in your wallet or doorway.

Harmonious Signs for Relationships and Partnerships: Pisces, Scorpio, and Taurus

Spiritual Guides . . .

Star: Al Nethra—Those with this star are treasured as friends.

Angel: Muriel—This angel aids us during times of emotional stress.

Guardian Angel: Seraphim—An angel that brings love, light and passion.

Spiritual Stone: Jacinth—Holding this stone could aid in memory retention.

✴ JUDITH'S INSIGHT ✴

You are very sensitive and try to be stronger than you are. You take life a bit too seriously. You can be ego-driven and strong-minded, and your aims may be high. As you mature, you learn to be quite charitable and generous. Believe it or not, after your forties, life gets easier for you.

You want love and security in your family. In time, you will find the perfect mate. Unfortunately, you have to have patience and faith in order for things to become more harmonious. You go out of your way for friends and family and sometimes feel like nobody understands. A beautiful home and a structured family are nevertheless important to you. If you settle down by the beach or the sea, you may feel more relaxed and happy.

A perfectionist at work, you would make a great builder, designer, artist, writer, teacher, or poet. Whatever you create, you devote time and talent to it. Allow your knowledge to grow and, in time, good things only tend to get greater.

Financially, you have to watch out and expect the unexpected, although at times you may have a few windfalls, which just tend to accumulate. Just remember, not everyone around you is a psychic, and it would be better for you to communicate than think that life is written as a script. Take the time to not only be kind but to have an open mind.

★ ★ ★

JULY 9 CANCER • The waves of the moon of the zodiac
June 21 at 12:00 P.M. to July 22 at 11:00 P.M. • NUMEROLOGY 9

Possessions and Desires . . .

Gem: Sapphire—This gem may help you find forgiveness from those you've wronged.
Flower: Wild Rose—You tend to love with the heat of a forest fire.
Astral Color, Color Need, Apparel Color: Your Astral Color is Green, which gives you confidence. Green in your environment enhances your luck, because you will feel secure. In your wardrobe, Silver is a stimulating color for you.
Fragrance: You will be calmed by the scent of fresh linen dried in the breeze or wild orchids.
Tree: Holly—Beware that you are not carried away by your passionate nature. The only way to grow is to be open to new experiences.
Instruments: Violin, tympanum
Composer: Gluck
Bird: Mockingbird—the most proficient minstrel in the world's orchestra; graceful and enthusiastic.
Symbol: Anchor—This tranquil symbol signifies stability and strength, and stands for strong commitments in relationships.

Harmonious Health and Nutrition . . .

Health Scent: Lavender—This scent might lead others to trust you and make you patient.
Favorable Foods: Cauliflower, dates, caraway, salmon, eggs

What's Lucky . . .

Lucky Numbers: 3, 7, 9
Best Months: February and September
Best Day of the Week: Monday
Best Month Days: 9, 18, 27
Lucky Charms: A U.S. coin or a bill of any amount from the year you were born.
Harmonious Signs for Relationships and Partnerships: Pisces, Scorpio, and Taurus

Spiritual Guides . . .

Star: Al Nethra—Those with this star are treasured as friends.
Angel: Muriel—This angel aids us during times of emotional stress.
Guardian Angel: Gabriel—"God is my strength."
Spiritual Stone: Jacinth—Holding this stone could aid in memory retention.

✶ JUDITH'S INSIGHT ✶

A true original, you're daring and fearless in just about everything you do. You have a legal mind—inventive, imaginative, and not very easily discouraged. You aim high, and you certainly are able to reach those heights. You have much more control of yourself than you recognize. You are capable of much self-sacrifice in your life, and you are more a giver than a taker. You pass through much mental suffering with few complaints. You may find yourself in unique and unfortunate situations, but you tend to get through these challenges unscathed.

You are a good friend to many because you are conscientious about what and how others feel. Your intuitive nature allows you inner knowledge. Listen to yourself more. Love is overwhelming around you—your family members adore you. But it takes time to find the right mate, even though you may think you have found someone special early in life. Challenges exist not only in work but in your love life.

You do many things in the blink of an eye. You will find success in any career you choose, whether it's lawyer, psychic, counselor, actor, writer, or restaurateur.

You walk away from things when you feel nobody is listening. You will travel on many streets and paths and down many highways. You will definitely leave your mark, no matter what the situation, and you never really understand just how much you affect other people.

✶ ✶ ✶

JULY 10 CANCER • The waves of the moon of the zodiac
June 21 at 12:00 P.M. to July 22 at 11:00 P.M. • NUMEROLOGY 1

Possessions and Desires . . .

Gem: Emerald—Those who carry this stone tend to be lucky in love.
Flower: Fig Tree—Whatever you do you tend to do a lot.
Astral Color, Color Need, Apparel Color: Your Astral Color is Green, which gives you confidence. Green in your environment enhances your luck, because you will feel secure. In your wardrobe, Brown gives you confidence and a sharp look.
Fragrance: You will be calmed by the scent of fresh linen dried in the breeze or wild orchids.
Tree: Walnut—You are unusually helpful and always looking for new beginnings.
Instruments: Oboe, flute, clarinet, piano, French horn, organ, piccolo
Composer: Böhm
Bird: Hummingbird—This bird is delicate and graceful. It can remain still for hours, then dart off and be as busy as a bee.
Symbol: Crown—the universal sign of dignity.

Harmonious Health and Nutrition . . .

Health Scent: Strawberry—Soothing by nature, the strawberry promotes self-esteem and encourages love.
Favorable Foods: Asparagus, lemons, whole oats, molasses, oysters, buttermilk

What's Lucky . . .

Lucky Numbers: 3, 7, 10
Best Months: February and September
Best Day of the Week: Monday
Best Month Days: 1, 10, 19, 28
Lucky Charm: A new penny in your shoe.

Harmonious Signs for Relationships and Partnerships: Pisces, Scorpio, and Taurus

Spiritual Guides . . .

Star: Al Nethra—Those with this star are treasured as friends.
Angel: Muriel—This angel aids us during times of emotional stress.
Guardian Angel: Malachi—"Messenger of Jehovah."
Spiritual Stone: Jacinth—Holding this stone could aid in memory retention.

✳ JUDITH'S INSIGHT ✳

At times, you wear your heart on your sleeve, but other times you hide it. You may go through a lot of changes; expect the unexpected. You tend to be somewhat fearful, in spite of the fact that you appear very secure and always seem like you know what you're doing. A great humanitarian, you will always try to imagine what you can do for other people.

At heart, you have very strong values, and family means a lot to you. Your kind and loyal nature brings you closer to your home and family. Although you are independent, you shy away from too much change.

You have a great love for the unknown and for mysterious environments. It also wouldn't be surprising for you to be involved in the arts, theater, or drama. You may succeed as a lawyer or doctor. You can sell all right—as long as the buyer comes to you.

You have a good chance of gaining wealth and may not want to live in ways that let other people know about it. Your dress will be modest and simple, and your home will be decorated with fine furniture and antiques.

✳ ✳ ✳

JULY 11 CANCER • The waves of the moon of the zodiac
June 21 at 12:00 P.M. to July 22 at 11:00 P.M. • NUMEROLOGY 2

Possessions and Desires . . .

Gem: Sapphire—This gem may help you find forgiveness from those you've wronged.
Flower: Angelica—You will be an inspiration for those you allow to know you.
Astral Color, Color Need, Apparel Color: Your Astral Color is Green, which gives you confidence. Green in your environment enhances your luck, because you will feel secure. In your wardrobe, Silver is a stimulating color for you.
Fragrance: You will be calmed by the scent of fresh linen dried in the breeze or wild orchids.
Tree: Maple—You have both great stability and flashes of intuition.
Instruments: Pipe organ, cymbal, drum
Composers: Handel, Johann Sebastian Bach
Bird: Cuckoo—a good flyer and very seldom a quitter. Some cuckoos tend to think they favor lonely isolation, but what they really yearn for is a family relationship.
Symbol: Cross—the symbol of self-sacrifice and reconciliation.

Harmonious Health and Nutrition . . .

Health Scent: Apple—You are creative, full of joy, and nearly magical. You bring happiness.
Favorable Foods: Kale, watermelon, caraway, salmon, cream

What's Lucky . . .

Lucky Numbers: 2, 3, 7
Best Months: February and September
Best Day of the Week: Monday
Best Month Days: 2, 11, 20, 29
Lucky Charms: Two 50-cent pieces. Give someone else one of them.
Harmonious Signs for Relationships and Partnerships: Pisces, Scorpio, and Taurus

Spiritual Guides . . .

Star: Al Nethra—Those with this star are treasured as friends.
Angel: Muriel—This angel aids us during times of emotional stress.
Guardian Angel: St. John—This angel simplifies that which is complicated.
Spiritual Stone: Jacinth—Holding this stone could aid in memory retention.

✴ JUDITH'S INSIGHT ✴

You are gentle, sympathetic, thoughtful, determined, and interested in other human beings. Most may view you as moody. You show much persistence and consistency throughout your life and exercise good judgment. You are as stable as the day is long. You always have good intentions, almost to a fault. Others may misunderstand or take offense at that. You have a lot of success with relationships, partners, and your own social environment. Once you get a friend, you never seem to have to let go. You have some strong ties to home life.

You could have a successful career as a doctor, counselor, chiropractor, even carpenter. No matter what you do, you lean toward nurturing others. You have a conscientious side and a good bedside manner. Because of your sensitivity and strong intuitive qualities, you tend to be very aware of the atmosphere and surroundings. Of course, your tendency is to always want to do better than yesterday, and you could be overly ambitious. At times you create drama.

You look for inspiration in everything. Travel will be important . . . more so as you age. You need to be around water, whether it is living, working, or playing. It would be very surprising if water sports would not appeal to you. When you are feeling low and need to stimulate yourself, take yourself for a walk along the beach or a swim in the pool, and if all else fails, drink some water.

★ ★ ★

JULY 12

CANCER • The waves of the moon of the zodiac

June 21 at 12:00 P.M. to July 22 at 11:00 P.M. • NUMEROLOGY 3

Possessions and Desires . . .

Gem: Sapphire—This gem may help you find forgiveness from those you've wronged.

Flower: Basil—Be careful that the things you hate don't distract you from living a full life.

Astral Color, Color Need, Apparel Color: Your Astral Color is Green, which gives you confidence. Green in your environment enhances your luck, because you will feel secure. In your wardrobe, Brown gives you confidence and a sharp look.

Fragrance: You will be calmed by the scent of fresh linen dried in the breeze or wild orchids.

Tree: Elm—You have willpower, strength, and the ability to stand alone.

Instrument: Trombone

Composers: Verdi, Mendelssohn, Schumann

Bird: Swan—Regarded as royal and sacred, this bird has the protective nature of a mother, and can become a furious fighter in the defense of its young.

Symbol: Wreath—You have been crowned with a special personality. You are strong but extremely compassionate.

Harmonious Health and Nutrition . . .

Health Scent: Rose—This scent will lead you to passionate thoughts and make you feel warm inside.

Favorable Foods: Onions, oranges, whole oats, honey, cottage cheese

What's Lucky . . .

Lucky Numbers: 3, 4, 7
Best Months: February and September
Best Day of the Week: Monday
Best Month Days: 3, 12, 21, 30
Lucky Charm: A pen that someone else has already used.
Harmonious Signs for Relationships and Partnerships: Pisces, Scorpio, and Taurus

Spiritual Guides . . .

Star: Al Nethra—Those with this star are treasured as friends.

Angel: Muriel—This angel aids us during times of emotional stress.

Guardian Angel: Johiel—This angel is a protector of all those with a humble heart.

Spiritual Stone: Jacinth—Holding this stone could aid in memory retention.

✳ JUDITH'S INSIGHT ✳

You are a quiet person and a deep thinker. As a general rule, you tend to have a bit of a hot temper and act on impulse. You are somewhat critical by nature and can get yourself involved in big, crucial problems. Your judgments aren't always the best, even though you have a good heart and act with good intentions. You can be the great humanitarian and want to offer a helping hand. However, you don't always know how to show this side of yourself. You tend to live in a world of your own and like it that way. Although you dislike being needy, you do tend to rely on other people a great deal. You're intelligent and intuitive but somewhat illogical at times. You have to learn to think before you speak and wait until you really have something to say.

You love your home and try to make it beautiful and harmonious, but you tend to weave many tangled webs. You aim high and are quite capable; however, as responsible as you are, you're always the last one out of bed. You accomplish much more in your later life than you do in earlier years, and you do veer off the track at times. Once you get out of your own way, you will become quite successful.

You may jump around in careers and look for something that offers adventure and spontaneity. Unfortunately, you need to be around something with more security. Watch out for bouts with the law or legal issues that may arise around you. It may be that you choose a legal career: attorney, judge, or police officer. You tend to lead an erratic life, and one way or another you will be in the public eye and in the newspaper. The publicity will, hopefully, be good. Eventually you find harmony and stop creating obstacles for yourself.

✳ ✳ ✳

JULY 13   CANCER • The waves of the moon of the zodiac

June 21 at 12:00 P.M. to July 22 at 11:00 P.M. • NUMEROLOGY 4

Possessions and Desires . . .

Gem: Emerald—Those who carry this stone tend to be lucky in love.
Flower: Daffodil—You may need to strengthen your self-regard.
Astral Color, Color Need, Apparel Color: Your Astral Color is Green, which gives you confidence. Green in your environment enhances your luck, because you will feel secure. In your wardrobe, Silver is a stimulating color for you.
Fragrance: You will be calmed by the scent of fresh linen dried in the breeze or wild orchids.
Tree: Cherry—You will find yourself faced with constant new emotional awakenings.
Instruments: Bass, clarinet
Composers: Haydn, Wagner
Bird: Killdeer—This bird is usually found consorting with other species, and can adapt to any environment.
Symbol: Star—You are full of inner brightness and will stand out in any crowd. You will be seen as special.

Harmonious Health and Nutrition . . .

Health Scent: Vanilla—This scent will fill you with a feeling of cleanliness and stability.
Favorable Foods: Celery, peaches, caraway, salmon, buttermilk

What's Lucky . . .

Lucky Numbers: 3, 7, 13
Best Months: February and September
Best Day of the Week: Monday
Best Month Days: 4, 13, 22, 31
Lucky Charm: A piece of material cut from something in your home.

Harmonious Signs for Relationships and Partnerships: Pisces, Scorpio, and Taurus

Spiritual Guides . . .

Star: Al Nethra—Those with this star are treasured as friends.
Angel: Muriel—This angel aids us during times of emotional stress.
Guardian Angel: Uriel—This angel brings the light of God's guidance.
Spiritual Stone: Jacinth—Holding this stone could aid in memory retention.

✷ JUDITH'S INSIGHT ✷

You are exceptionally sensitive, have a warm heart, and, if you had the chance, would do a lot for the world. You dwell too long on things. You have hidden talents and experience many strange circumstances. But believe it or not, these experiences eventually enhance your life.

It is extremely easy for you to make friends, although you push people away. What you want and what you say are two different things. This can be your downfall. You tend to blame others when things don't go your way, but you are a loyal and always helpful friend and would do anything for those you care about. Family can be overwhelming and overzealous and at times create conflict for you.

With your energy, there is no reason why you cannot accomplish many things in your lifetime. Unfortunately what you really want out of life takes time. The second part of your life will bring you closer to what you want. Watch that you don't make the wrong choices just because the choices are there. You would be a great doctor, lawyer, or teacher, but your aim eventually may be more in theater or film. No matter what career you eventually choose, somewhere along the way that actor in you comes out. You need to stand out in a crowd and, in due time, you will.

★ ✷ ★

JULY 14

CANCER • The waves of the moon of the zodiac

June 21 at 12:00 P.M. to July 22 at 11:00 P.M. • NUMEROLOGY 5

Possessions and Desires . . .

Gem: Sapphire—This gem may help you find forgiveness from those you've wronged.
Flower: Bay—You are serene even when those about you are awash in chaos.
Astral Color, Color Need, Apparel Color: Your Astral Color is Green, which gives you confidence. Green in your environment enhances your luck, because you will feel secure. In your wardrobe, Brown gives you confidence and a sharp look.
Fragrance: You will be calmed by the scent of fresh linen dried in the breeze or wild orchids.
Tree: Apple—You are creative, full of joy, and nearly magical. You bring happiness.
Instruments: Viola, trumpet
Composer: Liszt
Bird: Flamingo—This beautiful, gregarious bird is always cautious of its enemy. It is also a caretaker of the young who tries to keep everyone happy.
Symbol: Triangle—You have the right combination of abilities.

Harmonious Health and Nutrition . . .

Health Scent: Peach—This scent may balance your good qualities so they equal your charm.
Favorable Foods: Cauliflower, blackberries, whole oats, honey, cottage cheese

What's Lucky . . .

Lucky Numbers: 3, 5, 7
Best Months: February and September
Best Day of the Week: Monday
Best Month Days: 4, 5, 23
Lucky Charms: A rabbit's foot or a white candle.
Harmonious Signs for Relationships and Partnerships: Pisces, Scorpio, and Taurus

Spiritual Guides . . .

Star: Al Nethra—Those with this star are treasured as friends.
Angel: Muriel—This angel aids us during times of emotional stress.
Guardian Angel: Plavwell—The guardian that gives power and strength to one's presence.
Spiritual Stone: Jacinth—Holding this stone could aid in memory retention.

✶ JUDITH'S INSIGHT ✶

You can be taken advantage of because of your sensitivity, kindness, and sympathetic nature. Friends really never do know what they mean to you, because as kind and as giving as you are, you lack the communication skills to be that intimate. Your confidence does waver from time to time, and you go through periods of low self-esteem. But, it seems to others as if you have a very strong ego.

Your domestic, loving, and sympathetic nature may lead you to think that no matter what you do, you would make a perfect mother, father, or nanny. You seem to have great discipline. Don't judge your entire life by your early years, which may contain many unhappy moments. The relationships that bring you the most happiness also tend to bring you the most pain. Whether it is your mother or father, you tend to go through many challenges with parents. As a parent, if you become one, you go through your own challenges with your children. You do tend to have an open-door policy with your home, but unfortunately that never leaves you quiet time, and you need that to keep your balance.

You do best in careers where you are allowed freedom and are nurtured. You would do very well as a doctor, lawyer, clerk, inventor, promoter, or publicity agent. But with your kindness and your sweetness, you may want to work with children. Money does seem to roll in and roll out. You like to live well.

✶ ✶ ✶

JULY 15
CANCER • The waves of the moon of the zodiac
June 21 at 12:00 P.M. to July 22 at 11:00 P.M. • NUMEROLOGY 6

Possessions and Desires ...

Gem: Sapphire—This gem may help you find forgiveness from those you've wronged.
Flower: Belladonna—You may find you treasure the times you spend in silence.
Astral Color, Color Need, Apparel Color: Your Astral Color is Green, which gives you confidence. Green in your environment enhances your luck, because you will feel secure. In your wardrobe, Silver is a stimulating color for you.
Fragrance: You will be calmed by the scent of fresh linen dried in the breeze or wild orchids.
Tree: Palm—You tend to be very healthy and creative.
Instruments: Tambourine, lyre
Composer: Schubert
Bird: Falcon—an expert hunter. When well-trained, it can adapt to many tasks and is usually obedient.
Symbol: Crescent—You are more likely to be influenced by the phases of the moon. Your easygoing manner leads you to peaceful situations.

Harmonious Health and Nutrition ...

Health Scent: Orange Blossom—This scent may balance your body, mind, and soul.
Favorable Foods: Asparagus, cranberries, molasses, eggs

What's Lucky ...

Lucky Numbers: 3, 7, 15
Best Months: February and September
Best Day of the Week: Monday
Best Month Days: 6, 15, 24
Lucky Charms: A religious token or card from any religion.
Harmonious Signs for Relationships and Partnerships: Pisces, Scorpio, and Taurus

Spiritual Guides ...

Star: Al Nethra—Those with this star are treasured as friends.
Angel: Muriel—This angel aids us during times of emotional stress.
Guardian Angel: Michael—"Who is like God."
Spiritual Stone: Jacinth—Holding this stone could aid in memory retention.

✴ JUDITH'S INSIGHT ✴

You have a magical charisma and a sense of devotion to those around you that tends to make anyone you know always feel at home. You wear your heart on your sleeve. You never seem to let anybody else down; you never seem to turn a deaf ear; you always seem to have an open mind. You are respected and honored by those who know you. Your magnetic personality will bring you right down the path of life and get you where you want to go.

You protect yourself when it comes to intimacy with others, and you won't allow too many people to get close. Your domestic nature may afford you a perfect manicured lawn, an impeccable home, or a hand-designed kitchen that you made yourself. You can go through a hard time when it comes to finding a mate. Potential mates may see you as a more cranky person than you really are. Not to say that you are always unhappy, but the crab does seem to rear its head.

With your powerful ambitions, you tend to go far in any job. You would make a great trader, salesperson, lawyer, or professional of any kind. Your great devotion and determination help advance you in your career. You have no problem with taking on the responsibilities of others and may find yourself doing other people's work to make their lives easier. Remember to not bite off more than you can chew. You may become depressed in your middle years if you don't relax and have a little more fun.

✴ ✴ ✴

JULY 16 CANCER • The waves of the moon of the zodiac

June 21 at 12:00 P.M. to July 22 at 11:00 P.M. • NUMEROLOGY 7

Possessions and Desires . . .

Gem: Emerald—Those who carry this stone tend to be lucky in love.

Flower: Harebell—If you give into feeling sad you may forget what happiness is like.

Astral Color, Color Need, Apparel Color: Your Astral Color is Green, which gives you confidence. Green in your environment enhances your luck, because you will feel secure. In your wardrobe, Brown gives you confidence and a sharp look.

Fragrance: You will be calmed by the scent of fresh linen dried in the breeze or wild orchids.

Tree: Sycamore—Yours is the ability to love, communicate honestly with others, and have lasting relationships.

Instrument: Harp

Composers: Gluck, Brahms

Bird: Skylark—This handsome bird is beautiful when it sings. It always whistles as it works.

Symbol: Heart—You are enthusiastic, empathetic, and full of generosity and love.

Harmonious Health and Nutrition . . .

Health Scent: Jasmine—This scent may make you more easygoing when you are stressed.

Favorable Foods: Watercress, black figs, honey, oysters, cream

What's Lucky . . .

Lucky Numbers: 3, 7, 16

Best Months: February and September.

Best Day of the Week: Monday

Best Month Days: 6, 15, 24

Lucky Charm: An old key.

Harmonious Signs for Relationships and Partnerships: Pisces, Scorpio, and Taurus

Spiritual Guides . . .

Star: Al Nethra—Those with this star are treasured as friends.

Angel: Muriel—This angel aids us during times of emotional stress.

Guardian Angel: Raphael—This angel attends to all of your needs when you are looking for guidance.

Spiritual Stone: Jacinth—Holding this stone could aid in memory retention.

✳ JUDITH'S INSIGHT ✳

You are commanding, self-willed, and capable of great poise. You attract people very easily. Others may rely on your advice because you tend to see things quite clearly. You are a loyal soul and you like to help others. You can be defensive and argumentative, if need be. You can either love very strongly or hate very strongly, depending on the situation. You would make a great debater because you do see both sides of an issue clearly.

You are devoted to family members and their needs. You will do just about anything to help others overcome obstacles. Love at times tends to be a bit of a challenge, but you do bring a devoted mate into your life. Just remember, not all things come in the same package. It may take time for your mate to commit or even for you to commit. You may have a relationship that goes back and forth for years. Inevitably you may have the romance of your dreams, and this is what will really make you happy.

No job is too big or too small. You tend to handle responsibility as if it is no challenge at all. The more responsibility you're given, the more diligent and organized you become. Even as a employee, you're the one everyone looks to talk to. You start off all right financially, but there are times when money, or lack of it, can become stressful. Eventually you do get the balance, and you will be given a helping hand. Say thank you and give back when things do get better.

✶ ✶ ✶

JULY 17 CANCER • The waves of the moon of the zodiac
June 21 at 12:00 P.M. to July 22 at 11:00 P.M. • NUMEROLOGY 8

Possessions and Desires . . .

Gem: Sapphire—This gem may help you find forgiveness from those you've wronged.
Flower: Bilberry—You are generous to a fault.
Astral Color, Color Need, Apparel Color: Your Astral Color is Green, which gives you confidence. Green in your environment enhances your luck, because you will feel secure. In your wardrobe, Silver is a stimulating color for you.
Fragrance: You will be calmed by the scent of fresh linen dried in the breeze or wild orchids.
Tree: Pine—Your relationships tend to be balanced, both emotionally and mentally.
Instrument: Cello
Composer: Mozart
Bird: Bobolink—This charming singer is equally good as a soloist or a member of an orchestra. It is a very romantic bird, most useful as an insect destroyer, and elegant, with beautiful feathers, and always pleasant to have around.
Symbol: Wings—You are the source of balance in your world—this will bring you contentment.

Harmonious Health and Nutrition . . .

Health Scent: Almond—This scent may revitalize you and open you to greater possibilities.
Favorable Foods: Onions, watermelon, whole oats, cottage cheese

What's Lucky . . .

Lucky Numbers: 3, 7, 8
Best Months: February and September
Best Day of the Week: Monday
Best Month Days: 8, 17, 26
Lucky Charm: Red ribbon in your wallet or doorway.

Harmonious Signs for Relationships and Partnerships: Pisces, Scorpio, and Taurus

Spiritual Guides . . .

Star: Al Nethra—Those with this star are treasured as friends.
Angel: Muriel—This angel aids us during times of emotional stress.
Guardian Angel: Seraphim—An angel that brings love, light, and passion.
Spiritual Stone: Jacinth—Holding this stone could aid in memory retention.

✳ JUDITH'S INSIGHT ✳

You are quite sensitive and you have a desire to make the world a better place. You are fully aware of what it takes to make change, and you have no problem with working hard. You like things your own way, and if your efforts benefit others or yourself, that's all that matters. You hate the sin, and you love the sinner. You can be considered indifferent and cold when it comes to relationships, because you tend to be a bit fearful. Your sensitivity can go a long way. You may find that friends come and go in life, but never really that far. There may be more than one mate in your life. Depending on what kind of life you lead, this could be good or bad.

You could be a bit of a perfectionist when it comes to work and may be frustrated when it comes to working with other people. Be careful about your frustration. You could be a great counselor or advisor because of your kind soul, but you require a lot of physical activity for a career to be best for you. You would do well in any physical activity, whether it be sports or a job that requires mechanical or physical ability. You have a lot of energy. The more it is used up, the better.

JULY 18 CANCER • The waves of the moon of the zodiac
June 21 at 12:00 P.M. to July 22 at 11:00 P.M. • NUMEROLOGY 9

Possessions and Desires . . .

Gem: Emerald—Those who carry this stone tend to be lucky in love.

Flower: Bittersweet—You only wish to hear or tell the absolute truth.

Astral Color, Color Need, Apparel Color: Your Astral Color is Green, which gives you confidence. Green in your environment enhances your luck, because you will feel secure. In your wardrobe, Brown gives you confidence and a sharp look.

Fragrance: You will be calmed by the scent of fresh linen dried in the breeze or wild orchids.

Tree: Holly—Beware that you are not carried away by your passionate nature. The only way to grow is to be open to new experiences.

Instruments: Violin, tympanum

Composer: Gluck

Bird: Mockingbird—the most proficient minstrel in the world's orchestra; graceful and enthusiastic.

Symbol: Anchor—This tranquil symbol signifies stability and strength, and stands for strong commitments in relationships.

Harmonious Health and Nutrition . . .

Health Scent: Lavender—This scent might lead others to trust you and make you patient.

Favorable Foods: Cabbage, lemons, molasses, salmon, eggs

What's Lucky . . .

Lucky Numbers: 3, 7, 9
Best Months: February and September
Best Day of the Week: Monday
Best Month Days: 9, 18, 27
Lucky Charms: A U.S. coin or a bill of any amount from the year you were born.

Harmonious Signs for Relationships and Partnerships: Pisces, Scorpio, and Taurus

Spiritual Guides . . .

Star: Al Nethra—Those with this star are treasured as friends.

Angel: Muriel—This angel aids us during times of emotional stress.

Guardian Angel: Gabriel—"God is my strength."

Spiritual Stone: Jacinth—Holding this stone could aid in memory retention.

✷ JUDITH'S INSIGHT ✷

You love the good times—to just enjoy. Whether you know it or not, you have a burning desire to sacrifice yourself and help other people. You may have to overcome your share of obstacles. You pass through much mental suffering quietly and with few complaints. Your intuitive nature allows you a great deal of time to listen to yourself. You go through periods of sadness, but you are a survivor and get through them all.

You make a great parent. You have a loving home and kind heart and are very sensible and sensitive. You are original and daring and fearless in just about anything you do. You are creative and not easily discouraged. Your aims in life are high and you certainly possess the capabilities to achieve them. You eat challenges for breakfast, and it wouldn't be surprising if you had more than one career. There will be opportunities early, but be patient and don't choose the wrong one. You accomplish a lot because you set a lot of goals. You could be a psychologist, lawyer, owner of a restaurant, or laborer. It takes more time for you to find the right love, and if you exercise patience, you will have great success.

You will walk down many roadways and meet many people. Every road you travel on you will travel on twice. Remember that.

✦ ✦ ✦

JULY 19   CANCER • The waves of the moon of the zodiac
June 21 at 12:00 P.M. to July 22 at 11:00 P.M. • NUMEROLOGY 1

Possessions and Desires . . .

Gem: Sapphire—This gem may help you find forgiveness from those you've wronged.
Flower: Blackberry—You have as much energy as the sun.
Astral Color, Color Need, Apparel Color: Your Astral Color is Green, which gives you confidence. Green in your environmental enhances your luck, because you will feel secure. In your wardrobe, Silver is a stimulating color for you.
Fragrance: You will be calmed by the scent of fresh linen dried in the breeze or wild orchids.
Tree: Walnut—You are unusually helpful and always looking for new beginnings.
Instruments: Oboe, flute, clarinet, piano, French horn, organ, and piccolo
Composer: Böhm
Bird: Bird of Paradise—the "bird of the Gods." You will shine and love extraordinary circumstances.
Symbol: Crown—the universal sign of dignity.

Harmonious Health and Nutrition . . .

Health Scent: Strawberry—Soothing by nature, the strawberry promotes self-esteem and encourages love.
Favorable Foods: Parsley, dates, honey, oysters, cream

What's Lucky . . .

Lucky Numbers: 3, 7, 19
Best Months: February and September
Best Day of the Week: Monday
Best Month Days: 1, 10, 19, 28
Lucky Charm: A new penny in your shoe.
Harmonious Signs for Relationships and Partnerships: Pisces, Scorpio, and Taurus

Spiritual Guides . . .

Star: Al Nethra—Those with this star are treasured as friends.
Angel: Muriel—This angel aids us during times of emotional stress.
Guardian Angel: Malachi—"Messenger of Jehovah."
Spiritual Stone: Jacinth—Holding this stone could aid in memory retention.

✳ JUDITH'S INSIGHT ✳

You are kind and levelheaded. It will be a challenge to keep your dependency and independence in balance. You do tend to go through many strange circumstances in your lifetime and may even have a psychic encounter. You are a bit unpredictable, and you like it that way. You love to have a good time; the more invitations, the better.

You are attached to home and family and will work hard to keep your relationships stable. You can be a little self-sacrificing and may give up a little to keep harmony at home. Your nurturing side will inevitably bring you a family. Whether you have children of your own, adopt, or marry someone with children, it would be very surprising if children were not in your life.

You have strong values and morals. They may be threatened at times. Being the humanitarian that you are, it would not be surprising if you either worked as a volunteer or in a caretaking environment. You have a great love for the unknown and the mysterious. It may be that you'll become a detective or work in the theater or on a TV drama.

There is a good chance that you will have great wealth, either by lucrative investments or by inheriting money. You may live a little more simply than your bank account allows.

✳ ✳ ✳

JULY 20 CANCER • The waves of the moon of the zodiac
June 21 at 12:00 P.M. to July 22 at 11:00 P.M. • NUMEROLOGY 2

Possessions and Desires . . .

Gem: Emerald—Those who carry this stone tend to be lucky in love.
Flower: Bulrush—Be discreet in your dealing with others.
Astral Color, Color Need, Apparel Color: Your Astral Color is Green, which gives you confidence. Green in your environment enhances your luck, because you will feel secure. In your wardrobe, Brown gives you confidence and a sharp look.
Fragrance: You will be calmed by the scent of fresh linen dried in the breeze or wild orchids.
Tree: Maple—You have both great stability and flashes of intuition.
Instruments: Pipe organ, cymbal, drum
Composers: Handel, Johann Sebastian Bach
Bird: Cuckoo—a good flyer and very seldom a quitter. Some cuckoos tend to think they favor lonely isolation, but what they really yearn for is a family relationship.
Symbol: Cross—the symbol of self-sacrifice and reconciliation.

Harmonious Health and Nutrition . . .

Health Scent: Apple—You are creative, full of joy, and nearly magical. You bring happiness.
Favorable Foods: Beets, oranges, whole oats, salmon, eggs

What's Lucky . . .

Lucky Numbers: 3, 7, 20
Best Months: February and September
Best Day of the Week: Monday
Best Month Days: 2, 11, 20, 29
Lucky Charms: Two 50-cent pieces. Give someone else one of them.
Harmonious Signs for Relationships and Partnerships: Pisces, Scorpio, and Taurus

Spiritual Guides . . .

Star: Al Nethra—Those with this star are treasured as friends.
Angel: Muriel—This angel aids us during times of emotional stress.
Guardian Angel: St. Thomas—This angel brings affection from others and encourages you in all that you do.
Spiritual Stone: Jacinth—Holding this stone could aid in memory retention.

✴ JUDITH'S INSIGHT ✴

You can be quite inquisitive. You're also secretive and don't like to let anybody know what you're up to. Most people won't recognize this because of your open appearance and consistently caring nature. You have a kind heart and are considerate, yet you can be very moody. You tend to do better with relationships than not and work hard to keep them happy. You want to maintain friendships throughout your life. You do like stability, and it would be surprising for you not to live in the same home for a long time. You can be very neat and yet very disorganized at the same time. Your home is important, whether it's a garage, basement, palace, or attic.

Careerwise, you may have your hands in more than one pot. You could be a counselor, chiropractor, or carpenter. You have a bit of a creative mind and may desire to invent something. If you would like to be a creator or writer, you will probably find that you are more inspired when you are looking at the water. You are determined to be successful. No matter what the job is, you tend to rise to the top quickly, get bored, and then make a change.

Most of the romantic and sentimental times throughout your life will probably just coincidentally happen near the beach. When you are feeling low and look for a little stimulation or energy, find a beach and take a walk, or drink a pitcher of water. Travel will become important to you later in life. Choose places near water.

✴ ✴ ✴

JULY 21   CANCER • The waves of the moon of the zodiac
June 21 at 12:00 P.M. to July 22 at 11:00 P.M. • NUMEROLOGY 3

Possessions and Desires . . .

Gem: Sapphire—This gem may help you find forgiveness from those you've wronged.
Flower: Canterbury Bell—You tend to constantly seek approval from those around you.
Astral Color, Color Need, Apparel Color: Your Astral Color is Green, which gives you confidence. Green in your environment enhances your luck, because you will feel secure. In your wardrobe, Silver is a stimulating color for you.
Fragrance: You will be calmed by the scent of fresh linen dried in the breeze or wild orchids.
Tree: Elm—You have willpower, strength, and the ability to stand alone.
Instrument: Trombone
Composers: Verdi, Mendelssohn, Schumann
Bird: Cuckoo—a good flyer and very seldom a quitter. Some cuckoos tend to think they favor lonely isolation, but what they really yearn for is a family relationship.
Symbol: Wreath—You have been crowned with a special personality. You are strong but extremely compassionate.

Harmonious Health and Nutrition . . .

Health Scent: Rose—This scent will lead you to passionate thoughts and make you feel warm inside.
Favorable Foods: Turnips, huckleberry, caraway, oysters, buttermilk

What's Lucky . . .

Lucky Numbers: 3, 7, 21
Best Months: February and September
Best Day of the Week: Monday
Best Month Days: 3, 12, 21, 30
Lucky Charm: A pen that someone else has already used.
Harmonious Signs for Relationships and Partnerships: Pisces, Scorpio, and Taurus

Spiritual Guides . . .

Star: Al Nethra—Those with this star are treasured as friends.
Angel: Muriel—This angel aids us during times of emotional stress.
Guardian Angel: Johiel—This angel is a protector of all those with a humble heart.
Spiritual Stone: Jacinth—Holding this stone could aid in memory retention.

✳ JUDITH'S INSIGHT ✳

You live in a world of your own, and other people don't necessarily know this about you. You seem more outgoing than you are, and your nature is fearless and courageous. You like your quiet time, and are quite sentimental about any gifts or anything that you do in life. You are a bit of a daydreamer. You create your own story in your own mind on a day-to-day basis. You are naturally intelligent, intuitive, and quite logical. You speak with an impeccable vocabulary and usually have something very intelligent to say.

You want a happy home, and eventually you find it. The challenge for you will be to find harmony with your mate. Eventually you do. Watch out for relationship choices because you can be fickle at times. You can be overwhelmed by friends and family and by the tasks you tend to take on. Simply put, you do too much for others.

You want to lend a helping hand, but sometimes you go overboard. You will be quite successful in whatever you choose, but should put yourself in an energetic environment. You would do very well as an entrepreneur or in business—although, your creativity won't necessarily be used there. The best thing for you would be to create something and go into business on your own. You lean toward the public or publicity at one time or another—hopefully for the good and not the bad. A born politician, you can be charming and witty, and you can win people over to your side. People will be drawn to you one way or another and will want to do what you ask.

✳ ✳ ✳

JULY 22   CANCER • The waves of the moon of the zodiac

June 21 at 12:00 P.M. to July 22 at 11:00 P.M. • NUMEROLOGY 4

Possessions and Desires . . .

Gem: Emerald—Those who carry this stone tend to be lucky in love.

Flower: Celandine—Your happiness tends to occur later in life.

Astral Color, Color Need, Apparel Color: Your Astral Color is Green, which gives you confidence. Green in your environment enhances your luck, because you will feel secure. In your wardrobe, Brown gives you confidence and a sharp look.

Fragrance: You will be calmed by the scent of fresh linen dried in the breeze or wild orchids.

Tree: Cherry—You will find yourself faced with constant new emotional awakenings.

Instruments: Bass, clarinet

Composers: Haydn, Wagner

Bird: Stork—Turkish bird, held in high esteem the world over. This bird is intelligent but may have strange tendencies.

Symbol: Star—You are full of inner brightness and will stand out in any crowd. You will be seen as special.

Harmonious Health and Nutrition . . .

Health Scent: Vanilla—This scent will fill you with a feeling of cleanliness and stability.

Favorable Foods: Cauliflower, dates, molasses, salmon, cottage cheese

What's Lucky . . .

Lucky Numbers: 3, 4, 7

Best Months: February and September

Best Day of the Week: Monday

Best Month Days: 4, 13, 22, 31

Lucky Charm: A piece of material cut from something in your home.

Harmonious Signs for Relationships and Partnerships: Pisces, Scorpio, and Taurus

Spiritual Guides . . .

Star: Al Nethra—Those with this star are treasured as friends.

Angel: Muriel—This angel aids us during times of emotional stress.

Guardian Angel: Uriel—This angel brings the light of God's guidance.

Spiritual Stone: Jacinth—Holding this stone could aid in memory retention.

✳ JUDITH'S INSIGHT ✳

You fit into almost any situation with ease. You are full of life and activity, and your energy levels are boundless. Failures do not suit you—you have no time for negativity. You tend to procrastinate, but inevitably you rise to the occasion. You are exceptionally sensitive and have a warm heart. You do tend to be lonely sometimes and others may see you as a lost puppy.

It is extremely easy for you to make friends, but you must watch out for losing old friends. This, undoubtedly, is your worst shortcoming. You will share anything you have with your friends and family and do have many true and loving friends when you put a lot of energy into it. You can waver with love and find yourself chasing someone only to find it is not necessarily what you want.

You are not really fickle, but others may see you this way. Sometimes you look for the stage, screen, or limelight. Whether you become president of the PTA, run for town council, or appear in the local newspaper, somewhere or other notoriety will find you. You could be a great doctor, lawyer, teacher, even actor. You do have many wonderful talents, although you tend to be a bit scattered in the early part of your life. As you get older, you get more centered, and instead of feeling disillusioned by life, you follow your chosen path and get where you want to go.

✳ ✳ ✳

JULY 23 LEO • The heart of the zodiac

July 22 at 11:00 P.M. to August 23 at 6:00 A.M. • NUMEROLOGY 5

Possessions and Desires . . .

Gem: Diamond—This stone is thought to encourage harmony in relationships and gives strength to the troubled.

Flower: Indian Plum—You may find that the process of going without is more fun than the having.

Astral Color, Color Need, Apparel Color: Your Astral Color is Red, which enhances passion, power, excitement, and strength. Orange in your environment gives you confidence. In your wardrobe, Green is your power color for overcoming obstacles.

Fragrance: Surround yourself with the most romantic flowers you can find such as roses, lilies, and violets. The lavish scents will give an added boost to your natural enthusiasm.

Tree: Apple—You are creative, full of joy, and nearly magical. You bring happiness.

Instruments: Viola, trumpet

Composer: Liszt

Bird: Skylark—This handsome bird is beautiful when it sings. It always whistles as it works.

Symbol: Triangle—You have the right combination of abilities.

Harmonious Health and Nutrition . . .

Health Scent: Peach—This scent may balance your good qualities so that they equal your charm.

Favorable Foods: Watercress, raspberries, barley, red meat

What's Lucky . . .

Lucky Numbers: 5, 14, 23
Best Months: January and October
Best Day of the Week: Sunday
Best Month Days: 4, 5, 23
Lucky Charms: A rabbit's foot or a white candle.
Harmonious Signs for Relationships and Partnerships: Sagittarius and Aries

Spiritual Guides . . .

Star: Al Zubra—Those with this star fear punishment they don't deserve.

Angel: Verchiel—This angel enhances our ability to enjoy what life offers and gives much luck in legal dealings.

Guardian Angel: Plavwell—The guardian that gives power and strength to one's presence.

Spiritual Stone: Amethyst—This stone is thought to be a mood stabilizer and balances the emotions.

✷ JUDITH'S INSIGHT ✷

Your heart alone can set the world on fire. You love with ease, and your character is naturally sensational. You always look for something new and for the good in everything. You demand absolute honesty and faithfulness in others, and you give nothing less. Generous to a fault, you don't judge people, and you don't like being judged. You tend to be warm and sensitive, but you can be selfish and hung up on what is important to you. There aren't many obstacles you cannot overcome. You have a strong mind, an especially strong body, and an ego to match. Your self-esteem, however, wavers when things do go wrong in your life. Have no fear, the train will derail, but eventually you get back on track.

You go through a lot of emotional situations as a child; but fear not, your future is better. Friends really never truly realize what they have until you are gone. Relationships give you happiness, but you bring more happiness to others than they to you. It may seem life is taking forever to bring you harmony in love. Be patient—the more romance, the better you respond. Someone you trust and honor who can feed your ego is your perfect mate, and once you find that person, you'll stay.

You would do well in any career. A born leader, you can be head designer or head of the company. You are a teacher in your own right. You can start in the mailroom and work your way right up to the top of a company. There aren't many things you won't be good at.

✷ ✷ ✷

JULY 24 LEO • The heart of the zodiac

July 22 at 11:00 P.M. to August 23 at 6:00 A.M. • NUMEROLOGY 6

Possessions and Desires . . .

Gem: Agate—This stone may promote health and lead you to a long life.

Flower: White Lilac—You may keep the wisdom of childhood all your life.

Astral Color, Color Need, Apparel Color: Your Astral Color is Red, which enhances passion, power, excitement, and strength. Orange in your environment gives you confidence. In your wardrobe, Plum brings out the best in your looks.

Fragrance: Surround yourself with the most romantic flowers you can find such as roses, lilies, and violets. The lavish scents will give an added boost to your natural enthusiasm.

Tree: Palm—You tend to be very healthy and creative.

Instruments: Tambourine, lyre

Composer: Schubert

Bird: Lark—known for the beauty of its song, which is sometimes very unusual. It is also credited with extraordinary intelligence.

Symbol: Crescent—You are more likely to be influenced by the phases of the moon. Your easygoing manner leads you to peaceful situations.

Harmonious Health and Nutrition . . .

Health Scent: Orange Blossom—Balances the mind, body, and soul.

Favorable Foods: Radishes, lemons, whole oats, buttermilk

What's Lucky . . .

Lucky Numbers: 8, 15, 42

Best Months: January and October

Best Day of the Week: Sunday

Best Month Days: 6, 15, 24

Lucky Charms: A religious token or card from any religion.

Harmonious Signs for Relationships and Partnerships: Sagittarius and Aries

Spiritual Guides . . .

Star: Al Serpha—Those with this star know how special life can be.

Angel: Verchiel—This angel enhances our ability to enjoy what life offers and gives much luck in legal dealings.

Guardian Angel: Michael—"Who is like God."

Spiritual Stone: Amethyst—This stone is thought to be a mood stabilizer and balances the emotions.

✶ JUDITH'S INSIGHT ✶

No matter how you come into this life, you will soar to the top. You may enter the up elevator, but at times you will reach obstacles, like the doors getting jammed. You may find yourself back on the first floor only to begin your rise all over again. You could bear the world's problems; just make sure you have a place for your own. Pride is important to you, and you may hold on to things longer than you should. You have a great gift of turning your life around. Cranky when you're younger, as you get older you tend to be a little more sentimental and bring out your caring heart.

You love and heat intensely. Your accurate memory is long-lasting. You will stick by a friend and never forget a favor. Through thick or thin, you give and give and always put your best foot forward. You have a strong presence and a powerful mind. Ambition will take you where you want to go. Opportunities will present themselves, and you can go from one extreme to another. Friendships will be deep and may even help you advance in your careers. You tend to get what you give, as most people don't.

You are a powerful figure, and at times you may intimidate others. Your random acts of kindness will put you ahead in life, so keep doing the right thing, and when you are at the top, you don't have to worry about falling back down.

When you're in a long term relationship, you're looking for the exit door or searching avidly for the perfect mate.

Careers you would excel in are: dress designer and personal shopper. If you're interested in film, you could find yourself in the wardrobe department. School plays a role whether you are a perpetual student or professor.

JULY 25   LEO • The heart of the zodiac

July 22 at 11:00 P.M. to August 23 at 6:00 A.M.   •   NUMEROLOGY 7

Possessions and Desires . . .

Gem: Ruby—This stone may lead you to energy, friendship, and happiness.

Flower: Lilac—You tend to let your own horn become a very rusty instrument; a loud toot now and again couldn't hurt.

Astral Color, Color Need, Apparel Color: Your Astral Color is Red, which enhances passion, power, excitement, and strength. Orange in your environment gives you confidence. In your wardrobe, Purple reflects your giving personality and brings you luck.

Fragrance: Surround yourself with the most romantic flowers you can find such as roses, lilies, and violets. The lavish scents will give an added boost to your natural enthusiasm.

Tree: Sycamore—Yours is the ability to love, communicate honestly with others, and have lasting relationships.

Instrument: Harp

Composers: Gluck, Brahms

Bird: Skylark—This handsome bird is beautiful when it sings. It always whistles as it works.

Symbol: Heart—You are enthusiastic, empathetic, and full of generosity and love.

Harmonious Health and Nutrition . . .

Health Scent: Jasmine—This scent may make you more easygoing when you are stressed.

Favorable Foods: Cabbage, grapefruit, caraway seeds, red meat

What's Lucky . . .

Lucky Numbers: 7, 14, 34
Best Months: January and October
Best Day of the Week: Sunday
Best Month Days: 6, 15, 24
Lucky Charm: An old key.
Harmonious Signs for Relationships and Partnerships: Sagittarius and Aries

Spiritual Guides . . .

Star: Al Gieba—The lucky born with this star are treated like royalty.

Angel: Verchiel—This angel enhances our ability to enjoy what life offers and gives much luck in legal dealings.

Guardian Angel: Raphael—This angel attends to all of your needs when you are looking for guidance.

Spiritual Stone: Amethyst—This stone is thought to be a mood stabilizer and balances the emotions.

✷ JUDITH'S INSIGHT ✷

You are sympathetic and kind and have an intensely loving nature. Your smile can bring great warmth to others. Honorable, strong and loyal, you have only the best intentions with regard to other people's feelings and would do anything for them. Other people see you better than you see yourself. You are a responsible soul, and no challenge is too great as long as you are doing for others.

You are capable of overcoming just about any condition, especially when it comes to family. You give your all and gladly. Family will do anything for you because of your devotion to them. You will overcome obstacles and emotional hurdles and create happiness and harmony for yourself. At times love is a challenge; you tend to choose powerful mates, and at times there could be intense struggles.

You are much more creative than you think. You can be well-organized when it comes to work, and you would make a loyal employee. If you are the employer, you tend to be open to the emotional needs of others. Financially, you endure peaks and valleys, and at times you feel like you'll never make it. Eventually, there is a balance, and later on in life you will be in fine financial shape.

You are a good humanitarian, and you lend a helping hand to whomever needs it. You are as good as the other guy, and you just need to have as much faith in yourself as you do in others.

Leadership qualities could make you a supervisor in any career. Human resources, computer programming, and clinical psychology may be some of the careers that you excel at; not to mention a schoolteacher or television producer.

✷ ✷ ✷

JULY 26 LEO • The heart of the zodiac

July 22 at 11:00 P.M. to August 23 at 6:00 A.M. • NUMEROLOGY 8

Possessions and Desires . . .

Gem: Diamond—This stone is thought to encourage harmony in relationships and gives strength to the troubled.

Flower: Magnolia—You have a great love of nature.

Astral Color, Color Need, Apparel Color: Your Astral Color is Red, which enhances passion, power, excitement, and strength. Orange in your environment gives you confidence. In your wardrobe, Green is your power color for overcoming obstacles.

Fragrance: Surround yourself with the most romantic flowers you can find such as roses, lilies, and violets. The lavish scents will give an added boost to your natural enthusiasm.

Tree: Pine—Your relationships tend to be harmonious, both emotionally and mentally.

Instrument: Cello

Composer: Mozart

Bird: Bobolink—This charming singer is equally good as a soloist or a member of an orchestra. It is a very romantic bird, most useful as an insect destroyer, and elegant, with beautiful feathers, and always pleasant to have around.

Symbol: Wings—You are the source of balance in your world—this will bring you contentment.

Harmonious Health and Nutrition . . .

Health Scent: Almond—This scent may revitalize you and open you to greater possibilities.

Favorable Foods: Green lima beans, sour plums, rice bran, buttermilk

What's Lucky . . .

Lucky Numbers: 8, 17, 26
Best Months: January and October
Best Day of the Week: Sunday
Best Month Days: 8, 17, 26
Lucky Charm: Red ribbon in your wallet or doorway.
Harmonious Signs for Relationships and Partnerships: Sagittarius and Aries

Spiritual Guides . . .

Star: Al Zubra—Those with this star fear punishment they don't deserve.

Angel: Verchiel—This angel enhances our ability to enjoy what life offers and gives much luck in legal dealings.

Guardian Angel: Seraphim—An angel that brings love, light and passion.

Spiritual Stone: Amethyst—This stone is thought to be a mood stabilizer and balances the emotions.

✷ JUDITH'S INSIGHT ✷

You are a loving, sensitive, and giving person, inclined to be poetic and musical. Because of your sensitivity, you must try to be stronger. Keeping emotional balance will be your great challenge. Your aim is high, and you wish the best for others. When it comes to love, you want nothing more than to settle down. Unfortunately, there are times when commitments will require work. Be patient. With a lot of love, timing, and perseverance, your home will eventually be just the way you want it.

You seem to amaze people with your ability to juggle many things. You can be a perfectionist, not only when it comes to your home and family, but when it comes to how you look in public. You're quite vain, and you may even look to alter your appearance. It would be very surprising if you didn't have a desire to create or invent something. You know how to do everything, and you love bargains. You can be anything from artist to writer, teacher to poet. Besides your career, a hobby may take a lot of your time. Your keen sense of knowledge allows you to do any job with ease. Responsibility does not scare you. You can be motivated by a new job.

You will be great with money and generous with your friends. You like the act of giving and expect others to recognize you for it. You also like the occasional pat on the back. Your communication skills could use polishing—your bark is worse than your bite. Somewhat impractical, you can get into battles over principles and might be considered stubborn. You are indeed a good person—don't take life so seriously.

JULY 27

LEO • The heart of the zodiac

July 22 at 11:00 P.M. to August 23 at 6:00 A.M. • NUMEROLOGY 9

Possessions and Desires . . .

Gem: Ruby—This stone may lead you to energy, friendship, and happiness.
Flower: Saxifrage—You may need too much affection from others because you don't care enough for yourself.
Astral Color, Color Need, Apparel Color: Your Astral Color is Red, which enhances passion, power, excitement, and strength. Orange in your environment gives you confidence. In your wardrobe, Plum brings out the best in your looks.
Fragrance: Surround yourself with the most romantic flowers you can find such as roses, lilies, and violets. The lavish scents will give an added boost to your natural enthusiasm.
Tree: Holly—Beware that you are not carried away by your passionate nature. The only way to grow is to be open to new experiences.
Instruments: Violin, tympanum
Composer: Gluck
Bird: Mockingbird—the most proficient minstrel in the world's orchestra; graceful and enthusiastic.
Symbol: Anchor—This tranquil symbol signifies stability and strength, and stands for strong commitments in relationships.

Harmonious Health and Nutrition . . .

Health Scent: Lavender—This scent might lead others to trust you and make you patient.
Favorable Foods: Cucumbers, limes, barley, red meat

What's Lucky . . .

Lucky Numbers: 7, 17, 27
Best Months: January and October
Best Day of the Week: Sunday
Best Month Days: 9, 18, 27
Lucky Charms: A U.S. coin or a bill of any amount from the year you were born.

Harmonious Signs for Relationships and Partnerships: Sagittarius and Aries

Spiritual Guides . . .

Star: Al Gieba—The lucky born with this star are treated like royalty.
Angel: Verchiel—This angel enhances our ability to enjoy what life offers and gives much luck in legal dealings.
Guardian Angel: Gabriel—"God is my strength."
Spiritual Stone: Amethyst—This stone is thought to be a mood stabilizer and balances the emotions.

✷ JUDITH'S INSIGHT ✷

You are an original. Daring in thought, fearless, and determined in just about anything you do, you have lofty goals. You are capable of accomplishing just about anything you set out to. Born independent, you only become more so as you get older. You are enjoyable, bright, cheerful, and sensitive. In later years, your more altruistic qualities will present themselves. You have a grand mind and intellect. Some unique and unfortunate things will happen in your life, but you survive them. You pass through mental suffering quietly and without complaints. Your intuitive nature makes you aware of others, and you know how to put yourself in their shoes. Because of this sensitivity, you are a good friend.

It will take time for you to find the right love, but you will. You may push the right one away a couple of times before realizing who you have. There will be many challenges, and you can conquer not just one but maybe all. Challenges exist in your love life and also in your work and career. Your past always pops up in your future. You can be a counselor, psychologist, psychic, writer, or restaurant owner.

You have an inner knowledge that will take you far beyond the ordinary places. You accomplish a lot because you set out to do a lot.

✷ ✷ ✷

JULY 28 LEO • The heart of the zodiac

July 22 at 11:00 P.M. to August 23 at 6:00 A.M. • NUMEROLOGY 1

Possessions and Desires . . .

Gem: Ruby—This stone may lead you to energy, friendship, and happiness.
Flower: Money Plant—You are sometimes too honest.
Astral Color, Color Need, Apparel Color: Your Astral Color is Red, which enhances passion, power, excitement, and strength. Orange in your environment gives you confidence. In your wardrobe, Purple reflects your giving personality and brings you luck.
Fragrance: Surround yourself with the most romantic flowers you can find such as roses, lilies, and violets. The lavish scents will give an added boost to your natural enthusiasm.
Tree: Walnut—You are unusually helpful and always looking for constant changes in your life.
Instruments: Oboe, flute, clarinet, piano, French horn, organ, piccolo
Composer: Böhm
Bird: Bird of Paradise—the "bird of the Gods." You will shine and love extraordinary form.
Symbol: Crown—the universal sign of dignity.

Harmonious Health and Nutrition . . .

Health Scent: Strawberry—Soothing by nature, the strawberry promotes self-esteem and encourages love.
Favorable Foods: Brussels sprouts, sour cherries, caraway seeds, buttermilk

What's Lucky . . .

Lucky Numbers: 2, 8, 10
Best Months: January and October
Best Day of the Week: Sunday
Best Month Days: 1, 10, 19, 28

Lucky Charm: A new penny in your shoe.
Harmonious Signs for Relationships and Partnerships: Sagittarius and Aries

Spiritual Guides . . .

Star: Al Zubra—Those with this star fear punishment they don't deserve.
Angel: Verchiel—This angel enhances our ability to enjoy what life offers and gives much luck in legal dealings.
Guardian Angel: Malachi—"Messenger of Jehovah."
Spiritual Stone: Amethyst—This stone is thought to be a mood stabilizer and balances the emotions.

✷ JUDITH'S INSIGHT ✷

You will become a good humanitarian. You may have a bit of psychic ability. You have a great love for the unknown and will thrive on mysterious environments.

Your kind, loving, and loyal nature will allow you happiness at home with family and friends. You are so attached to home and family that sometimes it will be difficult for you to make decisions without considering everybody else's happiness and well-being while leaving your own behind. Children and marriage play a large part in your life and may be a place where decisions are made with your heart.

You have a love of the arts: theater, drama, and music. This may lead you to a career, but your nurturing side will probably lead you to a profession in health care. Somewhere along the way you may be in the public eye or have a bit of notoriety.

You will do very well with financial investments. You may not always want others to recognize the money you have.

✷ ✷ ✷

JULY 29   LEO • The heart of the zodiac

July 22 at 11:00 P.M. to August 23 at 6:00 A.M. • NUMEROLOGY 2

Possessions and Desires . . .

Gem: Agate—This stone may promote health and lead you to a long life.
Flower: Verbena—You may feel that your life is in some way enchanted.
Astral Color, Color Need, Apparel Color: Your Astral Color is Red, which enhances passion, power, excitement, and strength. Orange in your environment gives you confidence. In your wardrobe, Green is your power color for overcoming obstacles.
Fragrance: Surround yourself with the most romantic flowers you can find such as roses, lilies, and violets. The lavish scents will give an added boost to your natural enthusiasm.
Tree: Holly—Beware that you are not carried away by your passionate nature. The only way to grow is to be open to new experiences.
Instruments: Violin, tympanum
Composer: Gluck
Bird: Goldfinch—These gentle creatures can seem moody, especially in unsettled weather.
Symbol: Anchor—This tranquil symbol signifies stability and strength, and stands for strong commitments in relationships.

Harmonious Health and Nutrition . . .

Health Scent: Lavender—This scent might lead others to trust you and make you patient.
Favorable Foods: Radishes, pomegranates, barley, red meat

What's Lucky . . .

Lucky Numbers: 2, 11, 22
Best Months: January and October
Best Day of the Week: Sunday
Best Month Days: 9, 18, 27
Lucky Charms: A U.S. coin or a bill of any amount from the year you were born.
Harmonious Signs for Relationships and Partnerships: Sagittarius and Aries

Spiritual Guides . . .

Star: Al Zubra—Those with this star fear punishment they don't deserve.
Angel: Verchiel—This angel enhances our ability to enjoy what life offers and gives much luck in legal dealings.
Guardian Angel: Gabriel—"God is my strength."
Spiritual Stone: Amethyst—This stone is thought to be a mood stabilizer and balances the emotions.

✳ JUDITH'S INSIGHT ✳

You are capable of attaining anything you set your mind to. You're almost too enthusiastic and energetic for some people, and they may misinterpret this behavior and view you as showy. You could do very well in sports and may be recognized at some point in your life for your athletic abilities. You have an idealistic, curious mind.

You're giving and loving, and you have a strong sense of responsibility when it comes to the family. Whether you are the oldest, the youngest, or in the middle, you're the one everybody turns to. Family is very important to you, and it would be unusual if you didn't have your own. Whether you do or not, children and family values have heavy influence over you, and you lend your heart out a whole lot.

Travel is important to you, and at some point in your life you may be inspired by someone or something foreign or the desire to live abroad. If you write, you may even choose an exotic atmosphere for stimulation. You are fond of singing, and you look for an occupation or occasion where you can do so. You will always have a strong desire to be successful, although for years you may not know exactly what you'll be successful at. Keep believing, because you will do very well and bring yourself into the public eye (even if it is on a municipal board or the PTA).

The vitality you possess is there for a reason. In your earlier years, you may seem like the rebel and the one who fights for the underdog. You do better financially after your forties.

✳ ✳ ✳

JULY 30   LEO • The heart of the zodiac

July 22 at 11:00 P.M. to August 23 at 6:00 A.M. • NUMEROLOGY 3

Possessions and Desires . . .

Gem: Ruby—This stone may lead you to energy, friendship, and happiness.

Flower: Patagonian (mint)—You may have very strong scruples.

Astral Color, Color Need, Apparel Color: Your Astral Color is Red, which enhances passion, power, excitement, and strength. Orange in your environment gives you confidence. In your wardrobe, Purple reflects your giving personality and brings you luck.

Fragrance: Surround yourself with the most romantic flowers you can find such as roses, lilies, and violets. The lavish scents will give an added boost to your natural enthusiasm.

Tree: Holly—Beware that you are not carried away by your passionate nature. The only way to grow is to be open to new experiences.

Instruments: Violin, tympanum

Composer: Gluck

Bird: Stork—Turkish bird, held in high esteem the world over. This bird is intelligent but may have strange tendencies.

Symbol: Wreath—You have been crowned with a special personality. You are strong but extremely compassionate.

Harmonious Health and Nutrition . . .

Health Scent: Lavender—This scent might lead others to trust you and make you patient.

Favorable Foods: Cabbage, grapefruit, caraway seeds, buttermilk

What's Lucky . . .

Lucky Numbers: 3, 12, 21

Best Months: January and October

Best Day of the Week: Sunday

Best Month Days: 9, 18, 27

Lucky Charms: A U.S. coin or a bill of any amount from the year you were born.

Harmonious Signs for Relationships and Partnerships: Sagittarius and Aries

Spiritual Guides . . .

Star: Al Gieba—The lucky born with this star are treated like royalty.

Angel: Verchiel—This angel enhances our ability to enjoy what life offers and gives much luck in legal dealings.

Guardian Angel: Gabriel—"God is my strength."

Spiritual Stone: Amethyst—This stone is thought to be a mood stabilizer and balances the emotions.

✳ JUDITH'S INSIGHT ✳

You tend to lend a helping hand to others around you, only they may not necessarily take it so readily. Sometimes you can be misunderstood because you can be such a giver. Material things could be important to you. You have a style all your own and enjoy life in the comfort zone.

A late bloomer when it comes to love, you can be overwhelmed by family and friends because you put yourself out for everyone else. Be sure to save time for yourself and a partner, otherwise you may become resentful.

Careerwise, you can fit into just about any situation. If you cook, you will shine. If you are on stage, you will be the star. If you are a lawyer, you win cases. No matter what you do, you will rise to the top. In the beginning your aims may be low, but as you grow, aim higher. Your ambition will be there, but sometimes it could use a jolt. Your enthusiasm could be knocked down by negativity from others around you. Remember to turn a deaf ear to anything negative. You would do well as an entrepreneur. That does not mean that your caretaking personality won't lead to the health field. You might become a successful doctor or an administrator of a hospital.

You do tend to lean towards the public or publicity, so at some point or another you may find your name in the news.

✳ ✳ ✳

JULY 31　LEO • The heart of the zodiac

July 22 at 11:00 P.M. to August 23 at 6:00 A.M. • NUMEROLOGY 4

Possessions and Desires . . .

Gem: Agate—This stone may promote health and lead you to a long life.

Flower: Osier—You tend to be very frank in your opinions.

Astral Color, Color Need, Apparel Color: Your Astral Color is Red, which enhances passion, power, excitement, and strength. Orange in your environment gives you confidence. In your wardrobe, Plum brings out the best in your looks.

Fragrance: Surround yourself with the most romantic flowers you can find such as roses, lilies, and violets. The lavish scents will give an added boost to your natural enthusiasm.

Tree: Cherry—You will find yourself faced with constant new emotional awakenings.

Instruments: Bass, clarinet

Composers: Haydn, Wagner

Bird: Skylark—This handsome bird is beautiful when it sings. It always whistles as it works.

Symbol: Star—You are full of inner brightness and will stand out in any crowd. You will be seen as special.

Harmonious Health and Nutrition . . .

Health Scent: Vanilla—This scent will fill you with a feeling of cleanliness and stability.

Favorable Foods: Cabbage, grapefruit, caraway seeds, buttermilk

What's Lucky . . .

Lucky Numbers: 4, 13, 24

Best Months: January and October

Best Day of the Week: Sunday

Best Month Days: 4, 13, 22, 31

Lucky Charm: A piece of material cut from something in your home.

Harmonious Signs for Relationships and Partnerships: Sagittarius and Aries

Spiritual Guides . . .

Star: Al Gieba—The lucky born with this star are treated like royalty.

Angel: Verchiel—This angel enhances our ability to enjoy what life offers and gives much luck in legal dealings.

Guardian Angel: Uriel—This angel brings the light of God's guidance.

Spiritual Stone: Amethyst—This stone is thought to be a mood stabilizer and balances the emotions.

✴ JUDITH'S INSIGHT ✴

You are exceptionally sensitive and have quite a heart. You tend to have too much pride for your own good. You are as loyal as the day is long, and you are an honorable friend. You want to stop bad things from happening, not only to yourself; you sometimes stand in the way so bad things don't happen to other people. You do have unusual experiences throughout your life, but you eventually handle them and recognize that they did enhance your life. You could take a tragedy and turn it into a major motion picture. You need a sense of independence in what you are doing and to not allow yourself to get bored.

Your energies will dwindle if you are not emotionally fed. You go through a lot of entanglements, and you tend to blame others when things go wrong. Just remember, don't stand in your own way, and don't stand in others' way of helping you.

It is extremely easy for you to make friends, although you do have to watch out for falling into periods of feeling sorry for yourself. You can be your own worst enemy. You can also allow relationships to drift apart because you are waiting to see who calls first and can't bring yourself to pick up the phone.

You could be a great doctor, lawyer, teacher; just about anything you want, you can do. You have extraordinary power, energy, and perseverance.

✴ ✴ ✴

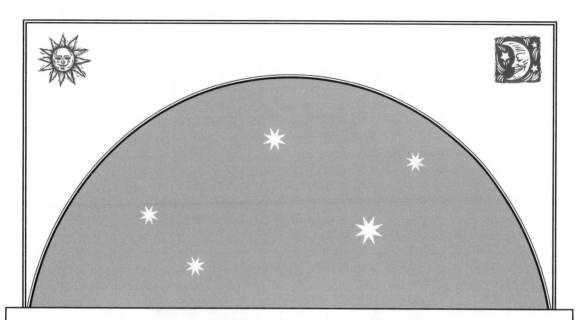

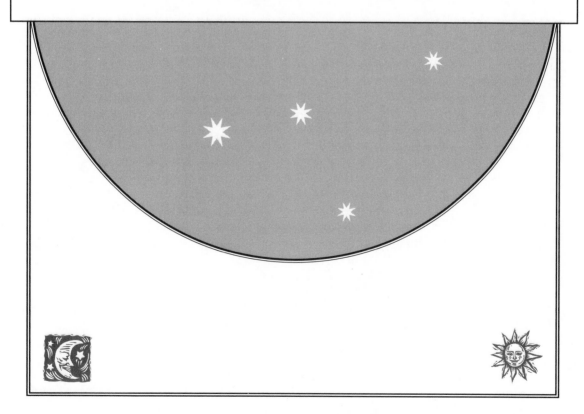

AUGUST

AUGUST 1

LEO • The heart of the zodiac

July 22 at 11:00 P.M. to August 23 at 6:00 A.M. • NUMEROLOGY 1

Possessions and Desires . . .

Gem: Ruby—This stone may lead you to energy, friendship, and happiness.

Flower: Burgundy Rose—You often don't realize just how much love you carry inside.

Astral Color, Color Need, Apparel Color: Your Astral Color is Red, which enhances passion, power, excitement, and strength. Orange in your environment gives you confidence. In your wardrobe, Purple reflects your giving personality and brings you luck.

Fragrance: Surround yourself with the most romantic flowers you can find such as roses, lilies, and violets. The lavish scents will give an added boost to your natural enthusiasm.

Tree: Walnut—You are unusually helpful and aways looking for new beginnings.

Instruments: Oboe, flute, clarinet, piano, French horn, organ, piccolo

Composer: Böhm

Bird: Cuckoo—A good flyer and very seldom a quitter. Many seem more independent than they actually are; yearn for more nurturing than one would expect.

Symbol: Crown—the universal sign of dignity.

Harmonious Health and Nutrition . . .

Health Scent: Strawberry—Soothing by nature, the strawberry promotes self-esteem and encourages love.

Favorable Foods: Spinach, apples, whole oats, red meat

What's Lucky . . .

Lucky Numbers: 1, 2, 17
Best Months: January and October
Best Day of the Week: Sunday
Best Month Days: 1, 10, 19, 28
Lucky Charm: A new penny in your shoe.

Harmonious Signs for Relationships and Partnerships: Sagittarius and Aries

Spiritual Guides . . .

Star: Al Gieba—The lucky born with this star are treated like royalty.

Angel: Verchiel—This angel enhances our ability to enjoy what life offers and gives much luck in legal dealings.

Guardian Angel: Malachi—"Messenger of Jehovah."

Spiritual Stone: Amethyst—This stone is thought to be a mood stabilizer and balances the emotions.

✳ JUDITH'S INSIGHT ✳

Because you're energetic and enthusiastic, everyone always wants to be around you. You are exceptionally loyal to family and friends. Your desire for love will bring it right to you; just be sure to keep your eyes open. It may take some time to meet the right person. Your mate should understand your need for romance and spontaneity, otherwise a struggle could arise.

Your strong business instincts may result in many opportunities coming your way. There aren't too many jobs you can't tackle. One way or the other, you will take on the role of caretaker, whether with your own children, your parents, or work. Several careers, from nursing to music to performing, are all possibilities for you. You may have more than one career, and it may take time to find out exactly what you want to do.

You like a neat and tidy home and enjoy changes around your environment. New things, whether it be furniture, clothing or housing, delight you. Because of your curious nature, you cannot resist the temptation to see what everyone else is up to. Don't be surprised if you take on too much at times. You may have a tendency to burn out. Regardless of career, it is highly likely that you will take on a hobby or two. Find something that suits you, and remember to enjoy the fun things in life.

✳ ✳ ✳

AUGUST 2

LEO • The heart of the zodiac

July 22 at 11:00 P.M. to August 23 at 6:00 A.M. • NUMEROLOGY 2

Possessions and Desires . . .

Gem: Ruby—This stone may lead you to energy, friendship, and happiness.

Flower: Damask Rose—You seem to have an inner glow that warms other people's hearts.

Astral Color, Color Need, Apparel Color: Your Astral Color is Red, which enhances passion, power, excitement, and strength. Orange in your environment gives you confidence. In your wardrobe, Green is your power color for overcoming obstacles.

Fragrance: Surround yourself with the most romantic flowers you can find such as roses, lilies, and violets. The lavish scents will give an added boost to your natural enthusiasm.

Tree: Maple—You have both great stability and flashes of intuition.

Instruments: Pipe organ, cymbal, drum

Composers: Handel, Johann Sebastian Bach

Bird: Skylark—This handsome bird is beautiful when it sings. It always whistles as it works.

Symbol: Cross—the symbol of self-sacrifice and reconciliation.

Harmonious Health and Nutrition . . .

Health Scent: Apple—You are creative, full of joy, and nearly magical. You bring happiness.

Favorable Foods: Cabbage, limes, barley, red meat, buttermilk

What's Lucky . . .

Lucky Numbers: 2, 8, 28

Best Months: January and October

Best Day of the Week: Sunday

Best Month Days: 2, 11, 20, 29

Lucky Charms: Two 50-cent pieces. Give someone else one of them.

Harmonious Signs for Relationships and Partnerships: Sagittarius and Aries

Spiritual Guides . . .

Star: Al Zubra—Those with this star fear punishment they don't deserve.

Angel: Verchiel—This angel enhances our ability to enjoy what life offers and gives much luck in legal dealings.

Guardian Angel: Uriel—This angel brings the light of God's guidance.

Spiritual Stone: Amethyst—This stone is thought to be a mood stabilizer and balances the emotions.

✷ JUDITH'S INSIGHT ✷

Original, daring, and fearless in all your actions, you uplift those around you mentally and socially. People trust in you and have confidence in you. Your personality alone will bring you advancement in life one way or the other. Opportunities present themselves seemingly out of nowhere.

With a flair for the dramatic, you are likely to be drawn to the arts, literature, music, theater, and film. Your natural talent in these areas can enhance any career choice. Your gift of gab and your skill with words and communicating could make you a good preacher, teacher, writer, poet, publisher, or editor.

You have good intuition and a great memory. With your style, you will have no trouble attracting a mate. In love, you may find yourself with too many rather than too few choices. Pick the right mate for the right reasons. You are magnanimous and broad-minded, and very few people don't like you. Steer clear of entanglements when it comes to friendship.

Work comes easily, but you may actually have to "work" at play! Without the proper time to enjoy yourself, you have a tendency to get cranky and even depressed. Take as much time for yourself as you do for others. Watch out for family matters that drain your energy.

★ ★ ★

AUGUST 3 LEO • The heart of the zodiac

July 22 at 11:00 P.M. to August 23 at 6:00 A.M. • NUMEROLOGY 3

Possessions and Desires . . .

Gem: Agate—This stone may promote health and lead you to a long life.

Flower: Moss Rose—You tend to let those you love know how you feel.

Astral Color, Color Need, Apparel Color: Your Astral Color is Red, which enhances passion, power, excitement, and strength. Orange in your environment gives you confidence. In your wardrobe, Purple reflects your giving personality and brings you luck.

Fragrance: Surround yourself with the most romantic flowers you can find such as roses, lilies, and violets. The lavish scents will give an added boost to your natural enthusiasm.

Tree: Elm—You have willpower, strength, and the ability to stand alone.

Instrument: Trombone

Composers: Verdi, Mendelssohn, Schumann

Bird: Warbling Parakeet—the most beautiful of all birds, known as the love bird. It does seem to have the powers of imitation.

Symbol: Wreath—You have been crowned with a special personality. You are strong but extremely compassionate.

Harmonious Health and Nutrition . . .

Health Scent: Rose—This scent will lead you to passionate thoughts and make you feel warm inside.

Favorable Foods: Turnips, limes, rice bran, red meat, buttermilk

What's Lucky . . .

Lucky Numbers: 5, 23, 32

Best Months: January and October

Best Day of the Week: Sunday

Best Month Days: 3, 12, 21, 30

Lucky Charm: A pen that someone has already used.

Harmonious Signs for Relationships and Partnerships: Sagittarius and Aries

Spiritual Guides . . .

Star: Al Serpha—Those with this star know how special life can be.

Angel: Verchiel—This angel enhances our ability to enjoy what life offers and gives much luck in legal dealings.

Guardian Angel: Johiel—This angel is a protector of all those with a humble heart.

Spiritual Stone: Amethyst—This stone is thought to be a mood stabilizer and balances the emotions.

✳ JUDITH'S INSIGHT ✳

Ultraresponsible, you always know how to carry out every task you want to accomplish. At times you may lack enthusiasm, and this could pose problems for you. Be careful of feeling sorry for yourself and putting yourself into positions that you know perfectly well will make you unhappy. Take time with big decisions—you could rush into things at times.

Your intense mind will lead you into careers involving reading or writing, but your passion for design may lead you to the arts or some other creative endeavor. Look for hobbies that fully utilize your physical power. A career such as physical therapy, construction, or even waiting on tables could also work for you. Your nurturing side may lead to a career in counseling. Just learn to recognize when it's you that needs the counseling.

Legal matters of one kind or another will be important. It may be that you choose law enforcement or advocacy as your life's work. Make sure you stay on the right side of the law.

A good and loyal friend, you know how to keep a secret (particularly your own). Family plays a large role in your life. You may grow up adoring someone and, as you mature, recognize that this someone should instead adore you.

Your life's lesson is accepting balance. You love the fun and romance in a relationship, but when things get too serious, you want to run. Once you begin to practice balance in your life, you should be able to make better choices. Your work is cut out for you.

✳ ✳ ✳

AUGUST 4 LEO • The heart of the zodiac
July 22 at 11:00 P.M. to August 23 at 6:00 A.M. • NUMEROLOGY 4

Possessions and Desires . . .

Gem: Diamond—This stone is thought to encourage harmony in relationships and gives strength to the troubled.

Flower: Morning Glory—You have honest and open intentions.

Astral Color, Color Need, Apparel Color: Your Astral Color is Red, which enhances passion, power, excitement, and strength. Orange in your environment gives you confidence. In your wardrobe, Plum brings out the best in your looks.

Fragrance: Surround yourself with the most romantic flowers you can find such as roses, lilies, and violets. The lavish scents will give an added boost to your natural enthusiasm.

Tree: Cherry—You will find yourself faced with constant new emotional awakenings.

Instruments: Bass, clarinet

Composers: Haydn, Wagner

Bird: Skylark—This handsome bird is beautiful when it sings. It always whistles as it works.

Symbol: Star—You are full of inner brightness and will stand out in any crowd. You will be seen as special.

Harmonious Health and Nutrition . . .

Health Scent: Vanilla—This scent will fill you with a feeling of cleanliness and stability.

Favorable Foods: Savory, raspberries, rice bran, red meat, buttermilk

What's Lucky . . .

Lucky Numbers: 4, 8, 44

Best Months: January and October

Best Day of the Week: Sunday

Best Month Days: 4, 13, 22, 31

Lucky Charm: A piece of material cut from something in your home.

Harmonious Signs for Relationships and Partnerships: Sagittarius and Aries

Spiritual Guides . . .

Star: Al Gieba—The lucky born with this star are treated like royalty.

Angel: Verchiel—This angel enhances our ability to enjoy what life offers and gives much luck in legal dealings.

Guardian Angel: St. Thomas—This angel brings affection from others and encourages you in all that you do.

Spiritual Stone: Amethyst—This stone is thought to be a mood stabilizer and balances the emotions.

✴ JUDITH'S INSIGHT ✴

You have a desire to be heard one way or another, whether it be through music, art, or writing, and eventually, you will. Nothing less than all is enough for you. You give more than you take. The more glitz and light in your life, the better you like it. You can turn a small event into an ongoing affair. The unconventional and unique appeals to your sense of creativity. Some may see you as eccentric or strange.

Learn to be patient, especially in love relationships. In time, you will learn balance. It is much simpler to blame others than take responsibility for things running amok in a relationship. You give and give to a fault—it is by far your best attribute. But sometimes your partner may feel overwhelmed by your generosity.

Steer clear of addictions of any kind. You have a tendency to act compulsively when you try to ride both sides of the seesaw. As long as your work is rewarding, you will get the most out of life. If people are nice to you, you are at your best.

Watch closely those extremes! You can stand on the stage and be afraid no one sees you.

Some possible careers are: movie star, singer, director, writer, restaurateur, deli manager, chef, and magazine editor.

✷ ✷ ✷

AUGUST 5 LEO • The heart of the zodiac

July 22 at 11:00 P.M. to August 23 at 6:00 A.M. • NUMEROLOGY 5

Possessions and Desires . . .

Gem: Ruby—This stone may lead you to energy, friendship, and happiness.

Flower: Hundred-leaved Rose—You will have many reasons to be proud of yourself.

Astral Color, Color Need, Apparel Color: Your Astral Color is Red, which enhances passion, power, excitement, and strength. Orange in your environment gives you confidence. In your wardrobe, Green is your power color for overcoming obstacles.

Fragrance: Surround yourself with the most romantic flowers you can find such as roses, lilies, and violets. The lavish scents will give an added boost to your natural enthusiasm.

Tree: Apple—You are creative, full of joy, and nearly magical. You bring happiness.

Instruments: Viola, trumpet

Composer: Liszt

Bird: Skylark—This handsome bird is beautiful when it sings. It always whistles as it works.

Symbol: Triangle—You have the right combination of abilities.

Harmonious Health and Nutrition . . .

Health Scent: Peach—Balances your good qualities so that they equal your charm.

Favorable Foods: Watercress, oranges, caraway seeds, red meat, buttermilk

What's Lucky . . .

Lucky Numbers: 8, 9, 23
Best Months: January and October
Best Day of the Week: Sunday
Best Month Days: 4, 5, 23
Lucky Charms: A rabbit's foot or a white candle.
Harmonious Signs for Relationships and Partnerships: Sagittarius and Aries

Spiritual Guides . . .

Star: Al Zubra—Those with this star fear punishment they don't deserve.

Angel: Verchiel—This angel enhances our ability to enjoy what life offers and gives much luck in legal dealings.

Guardian Angel: Plavwell—The guardian that gives power and strength to one's presence.

Spiritual Stone: Amethyst—This stone is thought to be a mood stabilizer and balances the emotions.

✷ JUDITH'S INSIGHT ✷

Talented in many ways, you love to be entertained and have the energy to do it. Good times and parties are when you are at your best.

You love the law and may look for a career in it. Your energy is contagious, and even two jobs may not be enough. In all likelihood you'll take up a time-consuming hobby in addition to your life's work. Keep a close eye on the higher-ups on the job and work to make them happy. Be careful of your directness, particularly with family and friends. Some may ask you to back off, even when all you're trying to do is help.

Your flair for fashion leaves others breathless, so impeccable is your manner of dress. Perhaps a career in retail would satisfy you. Aspirations and goals are high, and you have the skill to achieve all of them. You may experience a pitfall or two, maybe as early as age twenty, but your resiliency is one of your finest qualities.

In love, you allow yourself just enough freedom to hang yourself. You crave attention too much and are a nonstop flirt. Flattery will get them everywhere, but you do see right through the phonies in life.

You'll need to keep one eye on the purse strings and one eye on those fingers that love to spend. More than once in your life, you will have to tighten up the budget. While you are certainly capable of living on a budget, if you didn't spend money, you probably wouldn't enjoy working so hard for it.

✷ ✷ ✷

AUGUST 6   LEO   •   The heart of the zodiac

July 22 at 11:00 P.M. to August 23 at 6:00 A.M.   •   NUMEROLOGY 6

Possessions and Desires . . .

Gem: Diamond—This stone is thought to encourage harmony in relationships and gives strength to the troubled.

Flower: Sardony—You tend to feel the universe has an ironic sense of humor.

Astral Color, Color Need, Apparel Color: Your Astral Color is Red, which enhances passion, power, excitement, and strength. Orange in your environment gives you confidence. In your wardrobe, Purple reflects your giving personality and brings you luck.

Fragrance: Surround yourself with the most romantic flowers you can find such as roses, lilies, and violets. The lavish scents will give an added boost to your natural enthusiasm.

Tree: Palm—You tend to be very healthy and creative.

Instruments: Tambourine, lyre

Composer: Schubert

Bird: Cuckoo—A good flyer and very seldom a quitter. Many seem more independent than they actually are; yearn for more nurturing than one would expect.

Symbol: Crescent—You are more likely to be influenced by the phases of the moon. Your easygoing manner leads you to peaceful situations.

Harmonious Health and Nutrition . . .

Health Scent: Orange Blossom—This scent may balance your body, mind, and soul.

Favorable Foods: Radishes, sour cherries, barley, red meat, buttermilk

What's Lucky . . .

Lucky Numbers: 8, 9, 42
Best Months: January and October
Best Day of the Week: Sunday
Best Month Days: 6, 15, 24
Lucky Charms: A religious token or card from any religion.

Harmonious Signs for Relationships and Partnerships: Sagittarius and Aries

Spiritual Guides . . .

Star: Al Serpha—This star makes special things happen in one's life.

Angel: Verchiel—This angel enhances our ability to enjoy what life offers and gives much luck in legal dealings.

Guardian Angel: Michael—"Who is like God."

Spiritual Stone: Amethyst—This stone is thought to be a mood stabilizer and balances the emotions.

✶ JUDITH'S INSIGHT ✶

Good things come to those who wait or to those who have the stamina to stand in line as long as you do. Sometimes it may seem your life is going nowhere or even moving backwards. Be patient; you'll get what you want.

As a young person, your judgment could get you into your share of trouble for things you don't do. As you mature, so do your choices. You love to party, and that could be a problem. Learn to exercise some balance. You do take life seriously sometimes, and perhaps your need to socialize somehow compensates for this. Mostly, others take pride in knowing you.

A pleasant surprise of money, an inheritance, or some other windfall comes into your life. Perhaps you invent a product that brings you a large sum of money.

It make take a lifetime (or seem that way) to find the perfect mate. You should work harder to keep things together and take a less aloof attitude when it comes to love. Many relationship opportunities will present themselves along the way, but you may have trouble choosing the right one. Take your time; even your loyalty has its limits.

Careers for you could be in politics, law, or firefighting. You are mechanically inclined and definitely have a flair for entertainment. Perhaps you may find yourself behind the curtain or cameras as a photographer, lighting technician, or stage hand. Somewhere along the way, the spotlight is there.

✶ ✶ ✶

AUGUST 7
LEO • The heart of the zodiac
July 22 at 11:00 P.M. to August 23 at 6:00 A.M. • NUMEROLOGY 7

Possessions and Desires . . .

Gem: Ruby—This stone may lead you to energy, friendship, and happiness.

Flower: Saint foil—Your emotions tend to be easily understood.

Astral Color, Color Need, Apparel Color: Your Astral Color is Red, which enhances passion, power, excitement, and strength. Orange in your environment gives you confidence. In your wardrobe, Plum brings out the best in your looks.

Fragrance: Surround yourself with the most romantic flowers you can find such as roses, lilies, and violets. The lavish scents will give an added boost to your natural enthusiasm.

Tree: Sycamore—Yours is the ability to love, communicate honestly with others, and have lasting relationships.

Instrument: Harp

Composers: Gluck, Brahms

Bird: Warbling Parakeet—The most beautiful of all birds, known as the love bird. It does seem to have the powers of imitation.

Symbol: Heart—You are enthusiastic, empathetic, and full of generosity and love.

Harmonious Health and Nutrition . . .

Health Scent: Jasmine—This scent may make you more easygoing when you are stressed.

Favorable Foods: Lima beans, lemons, whole oats, red meat, buttermilk

What's Lucky . . .

Lucky Numbers: 8, 9, 34
Best Months: January and October
Best Day of the Week: Sunday
Best Month Days: 6, 15, 24
Lucky Charm: An old key.

Harmonious Signs for Relationships and Partnerships: Sagittarius and Aries

Spiritual Guides . . .

Star: Al Serpha—This star makes special things happen in one's life.

Angel: Verchiel—This angel enhances our ability to enjoy what life offers and gives much luck in legal dealings.

Guardian Angel: Raphael—This angel attends to all of your needs when you are looking for guidance.

Spiritual Stone: Amethyst—This stone is thought to be a mood stabilizer and balances the emotions.

✱ JUDITH'S INSIGHT ✱

Boy, what a handful . . . that's how others describe you, and you love each and every minute of it. You are generous, energetic, and funny. No wonder everyone invites you to the party. You not only know how to have a good time, but you put on a good time for family and friends. Party planning or catering may be good career choices for you. The great organizer, you could also be head of an organization, nonprofit or otherwise. Business is the way to go for you, and you may have something to do with the health care industry.

Your love mate may enjoy your energy but wish you to slow down at times. Find a way to uncomplicate things for your own sake as well as your partner's. Keep your eyes focused on the road, because at times you feel like your life is changing so fast you can't hold on.

You are known to create havoc. Challenges in whatever you do will keep you awake at night. Dignified and stylish, you can be the envy of relatives and neighbors and even your devoted mate. Watch out for a tendency to demand too much from others. Very few possess the energy you have.

✱ ✱ ✱

AUGUST 8 LEO • The heart of the zodiac

July 22 at 11:00 P.M. to August 23 at 6:00 A.M. • NUMEROLOGY 8

Possessions and Desires . . .

Gem: Ruby—This stone may lead you to energy, friendship, and happiness.

Flower: Scabiosa—You will find that even the untidiest love affairs are important lessons on the way to a suitable one.

Astral Color, Color Need, Apparel Color: Your Astral Color is Red, which enhances passion, power, excitement, and strength. Orange in your environment gives you confidence. In your wardrobe, Purple reflects your giving personality and brings you luck.

Fragrance: Surround yourself with the most romantic flowers you can find such as roses, lilies, and violets. The lavish scents will give an added boost to your enthusiasm.

Tree: Pine—Your relationships tend to be harmonious, both emotionally and mentally.

Instrument: Cello

Composer: Mozart

Bird: Skylark—This handsome bird is beautiful when it sings. It always whistles as it works.

Symbol: Wings—You are the source of balance in your world—this will bring you contentment.

Harmonious Health and Nutrition . . .

Health Scents: Almond—This scent may revitalize you and open you to greater possibilities.

Favorable Foods: Cucumbers, limes, rice bran, red meat, buttermilk

What's Lucky . . .

Lucky Numbers: 8, 17, 26
Best Months: January and October
Best Day of the Week: Sunday
Best Month Days: 8, 17, 26
Lucky Charm: Red ribbon in your wallet or doorway

Harmonious Signs for Relationships and Partnerships: Sagittarius and Aries

Spiritual Guides . . .

Star: Al Serpha—This star makes special things happen in one's life.

Angel: Verchiel—This angel enhances our ability to enjoy what life offers and gives much luck in legal dealings.

Guardian Angel: Seraphim—An angel that brings love, light, and passion.

Spiritual Stone: Amethyst—This stone is thought to be a mood stabilizer and balances the emotions.

✷ JUDITH'S INSIGHT ✷

You may spend half your life trying to convince others of your way of thinking. Your persistence, consistency, and energy are unbeaten! You can be a contradiction at times, and you want to have a piece of everything. You'd be wise to learn to practice some balance in your life. As you mature and your self-esteem increases, you'll be better equipped to equalize things.

Your career is more important to you than you let on. As a youth, you have great expectations, and if everything goes along as planned, you'll be fine. If not, you could backslide and feel indifferent and drained of energy. Work in the public eye seems to be very lucky for you. Any profession that brings you into the limelight is where you belong. Around the age of forty, you may choose a completely different career track and be on the road to success.

Some people see you as unusual because of your attraction to the exotic. You like being noticed and wearing different things. Your love life may experience a lot of emotional peaks and valleys. Your family or friends may run you ragged emotionally as well. Recognize your need for a pat on the back every now and then for all the hard work you do. Without it, you lose enthusiasm and energy.

★ ★ ★

AUGUST 9   LEO • The heart of the zodiac

July 22 at 11:00 P.M. to August 23 at 6:00 A.M. • NUMEROLOGY 9

Possessions and Desires . . .

Gem: Agate—This stone may promote health and lead you to a long life.
Flower: Witch Hazel—Be careful that you don't allow other people's troubles to overwhelm you.
Astral Color, Color Need, Apparel Color: Your Astral Color is Red, which enhances passion, power, excitement, and strength. Orange in your environment gives you confidence. In your wardrobe, Green is your power color for overcoming obstacles.
Fragrance: Surround yourself with the most romantic flowers you can find such as roses, lilies, and violets. The lavish scents will give an added boost to your enthusiasm.
Tree: Holly—Beware that you are not carried away by your passionate nature. The only way to grow is to be open to new experiences.
Instruments: Violin, tympanum
Composer: Gluck
Bird: Warbling Parakeet—The most beautiful of all birds, known as the love bird. It does seem to have the powers of imitation.
Symbol: Anchor—This tranquil symbol signifies stability and strength, and stands for strong commitments in relationships.

Harmonious Health and Nutrition . . .

Health Scent: Lavender—This scent might lead others to trust you and make you patient.
Favorable Foods: Turnips, sour cherries, barley, red meat, buttermilk

What's Lucky . . .

Lucky Numbers: 8, 9, 45
Best Months: January and October
Best Day of the Week: Sunday

Best Month Days: 9, 18, 27
Lucky Charms: A U.S. coin or a bill of any amount from the year you were born.
Harmonious Signs for Relationships and Partnerships: Sagittarius and Aries

Spiritual Guides . . .

Star: Al Zubra—Those with this star fear punishment they don't deserve.
Angel: Verchiel—This angel enhances our ability to enjoy what life offers and gives much luck in legal dealings.
Guardian Angel: Gabriel—"God is my strength."
Spiritual Stone: Amethyst—This stone is thought to be a mood stabilizer and balances the emotions.

✶ JUDITH'S INSIGHT ✶

You have determination, enthusiasm, and extravagance—you like to do things in a big way. You have great style, charm, and a terrific sense of humor. You love travel, music, and entertainment of any kind. You can be emotional, and with your sheer strength, that may confuse others. Inclined to have unusual relationships, you are lucky with friends and seem to hang onto them forever. Sometimes you might try turning off that mind of yours to give yourself a much-needed rest.

You have hidden talents that would let you thrive in a business setting, publishing, entertainment, or medicine. Watch your tendency to behave erratically—that energy can go both ways!

In love relationships, be cautious of feeling trapped once committed. Your ambition is strong and can dominate the other person, especially in the beginning. If they last more than three or four months, you tend to temper that better. Make sure your partner has the stamina to keep up with you.

Your impeccable taste and style may lead you to either a career or hobby in fine art.

✶ ✶ ✶

AUGUST 10   LEO • The heart of the zodiac

July 22 at 11:00 P.M. to August 23 at 6:00 A.M. • NUMEROLOGY 1

Possessions and Desires . . .

Gem: Ruby—This stone may lead you to energy, friendship, and happiness.

Flower: Whortleberry—You sometimes betray yourself without meaning to.

Astral Color, Color Need, Apparel Color: Your Astral color is Red, which enhances passion, power, excitement, and strength. Orange in your environment gives you confidence. In your wardrobe, Plum brings out the best in your looks.

Fragrance: Surround yourself with the most romantic flowers you can find such as roses, lilies, and violets. The lavish scents will give an added boost to your enthusiasm.

Tree: Walnut—You are unusually helpful and aways looking for new beginnings.

Instruments: Oboe, flute, clarinet, piano, French horn, organ, piccolo

Composer: Böhm

Bird: Cuckoo—A good flyer and very seldom a quitter. Many seem more independent than they actually are. They yearn for more nurturing than one would expect.

Symbol: Crown—the universal sign of dignity.

Harmonious Health and Nutrition . . .

Health Scent: Strawberry—soothing by nature, the strawberry promotes self-esteem and encourages love.

Favorable Foods: Spinach, grapefruit, whole oats, red meat, buttermilk

What's Lucky . . .

Lucky Numbers: 8, 9, 37
Best Months: January and October
Best Day of the Week: Sunday
Best Month Days: 1, 10, 19, 28

Lucky Charm: A new penny in your shoe.
Harmonious Signs for Relationships and Partnerships: Sagittarius and Aries

Spiritual Guides . . .

Star: Al Gieba—The lucky born with this star are treated like royalty.

Angel: Verchiel—This angel enhances our ability to enjoy what life offers and gives much luck in legal dealings.

Guardian Angel: Malachi—"Messenger of Jehovah."

Spiritual Stone: Amethyst—This stone is thought to be a mood stabilizer and balances the emotions.

✷ JUDITH'S INSIGHT ✷

Exceptionally loyal to friends and family, you have an overwhelming amount of energy. You love to be loved, and anything that will bring the attention around to you makes you happy. As long as your partner is able to bring romance and spontaneity to you, no one is a more loyal mate. If you wait until you're a little older before making that commitment, odds are you will find love that lasts and only gets better.

Somewhere along the way, you may have a desire to entertain. You could succeed in any line of work from theater business manager to car salesperson to lawyer. Remember these are all connected to performing! Stay in touch with your nurturing side as well. Teaching or nursing are both good job choices.

Whether cleaning out the garage, picking up your room, or rearranging the office, your intense energy always makes you eager to do something new. Be careful to measure that verve . . . others may be overwhelmed by it. You, too, may give in to depression simply because you think life lacks a constant stream of stimulation. New projects and beginnings help corral that awesome drive of yours.

★ ★ ✷

AUGUST 11
LEO • The heart of the zodiac
July 22 at 11:00 P.M. to August 23 at 6:00 A.M.. • NUMEROLOGY 2

Possessions and Desires . . .

Gem: Ruby—This stone may lead you to energy, friendship, and happiness.

Flower: Fireweed—You have an inner solidity that holds up those who rely on you.

Astral Color, Color Need, Apparel Color: Your Astral Color is Red, which enhances passion, power, excitement, and strength. Orange in your environment gives you confidence. In your wardrobe, Purple reflects your giving personality and brings you luck.

Fragrance: Surround yourself with the most romantic flowers you can find such as roses, lilies, and violets. The lavish scents will give an added boost to your enthusiasm.

Tree: Maple—You have both great stability and flashes of intuition.

Instruments: Pipe organ, cymbal, drum

Composers: Handel, Johann Sabastian Bach

Bird: Skylark—This handsome bird is beautiful when it sings. It always whistles as it works.

Symbol: Cross—the symbol of self-sacrifice and reconciliation.

Harmonious Health and Nutrition . . .

Health Scent: Apple—You are creative, full of joy, and nearly magical. You bring happiness.

Favorable Foods: Lima beans, raspberries, caraway seeds, red meat

What's Lucky . . .

Lucky Numbers: 8, 9, 22

Best Months: January and October

Best Day of the Week: Sunday

Best Month Days: 2, 11, 20, 29

Lucky Charms: Two 50-cent pieces. Give someone else one of them.

Harmonious Signs for Relationships and Partnerships: Sagittarius and Aries

Spiritual Guides . . .

Star: Al Gieba—The lucky born with this star are treated like royalty.

Angel: Verchiel—This angel enhances our ability to enjoy what life offers and gives much luck in legal dealings.

Guardian Angel: St. John—This angel simplifies that which is complicated.

Spiritual Stone: Amethyst—This stone is thought to be a mood stabilizer and balances the emotions.

✳ JUDITH'S INSIGHT ✳

Daring, fearless . . . sound familiar? You have the necessary confidence and personality to bring advancement into your life and into others'. People enjoy you and your natural way of communicating. Music, the dramatic arts, or writing: somewhere along the way, you words will be taken seriously. You are here to teach and learn. Your good intuition and memory make lots of choices available to you.

In love, you must be cautious when connecting with a mate. You tend to be overzealous when it comes to commitment. Happiness will come to you, especially in the area of family, where you gain most of your strength. As a youth, you may not be as aware of this.

As magnanimous as you are, you have a few enemies, particularly in the workplace. With friends and in social situations, however, you look for harmony as much as possible. Jobs will come easy to you because you are able to do so many different things. Titles don't mean much to you, although along the way, you do have the opportunity to take your place at the top. It's not necessary for you to go out of your way to make your presence known.

Financially, you'll do fine, and as you mature, you'll become more charitable with your money. Your charitable nature may make you seek an opportunity to raise money for nonprofit organizations. With your inventiveness, you may end up in careers such as computer programming, product development, or arts and crafts.

★ ★ ★

AUGUST 12 LEO • The heart of the zodiac
July 22 at 11:00 P.M. to August 23 at 6:00 A.M. • NUMEROLOGY 3

Possessions and Desires . . .

Gem: Agate—This stone may promote health and lead you to a long life.

Flower: Vine—You will have happiness and laughter in your life.

Astral Color, Color Need, Apparel Color: Your Astral Color is Red, which enhances passion, power, excitement, and strength. Orange in your environment gives you confidence. In your wardrobe, Green is your power color for overcoming obstacles.

Fragrance: Surround yourself with the most romantic flowers you can find such as roses, lilies, and violets. The lavish scents will given an added boost to your enthusiasm.

Tree: Elm—You have willpower, strength, and the ability to stand alone.

Instrument: Trombone

Composers: Verdi, Mendelssohn, Schumann

Bird: Warbling Parakeet—the most beautiful of all birds, known as the love bird. It does seem to have the powers of imitation.

Symbol: Wreath—You have been crowned with a special personality. You are strong but extremely compassionate.

Harmonious Health and Nutrition . . .

Health Scent: Rose—This scent will lead you to passionate thoughts and make you feel warm inside.

Favorable Foods: Cucumbers, lemons, rice bran, red meat, buttermilk

What's Lucky . . .

Lucky Number: 3, 12, 21
Best Months: January and October
Best Day of the Week: Sunday
Best Month Days: 3, 12, 21, 30

Lucky Charm: A pen that someone else has already used.

Harmonious Signs for Relationships and Partnerships: Sagittarius and Aries

Spiritual Guides . . .

Star: Al Zubra—Those with this star fear punishment they don't deserve.

Angel: Verchiel—This angel enhances our ability to enjoy what life offers and gives much luck in legal dealings.

Guardian Angel: Johiel—This angel is a protector of all those with a humble heart.

Spiritual Stone: Amethyst—This stone is thought to be a mood stabilizer and balances the emotions.

✷ JUDITH'S INSIGHT ✷

Capable is your middle name. There isn't much that you don't like, and with your enthusiasm and energy, you go out of your way for others. If you did have a weakness, it would be your tendency to dwell on things too long. Don't think so much.

You are strong and able and can do anything from designing cabinets to building them. Try putting your verve into something physical, whether it be a sport (or a career in sports), physical therapy, or sports medicine. Around your mid-thirties, you begin a life-long self-improvement journey. You could be a great counselor largely because you make such a good friend.

Law and authority are lucky for you, but you may have a lawsuit or two to contend with. Family plays a huge role in your life, but when it comes to relationships, you may have disagreements and feel misunderstood. You let others in only so far. Try being more patient.

As far as giving goes, you have a big heart. Watch our for the urge to give more than you have.

✷ ✷ ✷

AUGUST 13   LEO • The heart of the zodiac

July 22 at 11:00 P.M. to August 23 at 6:00 A.M. • NUMEROLOGY 4

Possessions and Desires . . .

Gem: Diamond—This stone is thought to encourage harmony in relationships and gives strength to the troubled.

Flower: Vetch—You may be a great person to have as a friend.

Astral Color, Color Need, Apparel Color: Your Astral Color is Red, which enhances passion, power, excitement, and strength. Orange in your environment gives you confidence. In your wardrobe, Plum brings out the best in your looks.

Fragrance: Surround yourself with the most romantic flowers you can find such as roses, lilies, and violets. The lavish scents will give an added boost to you enthusiasm.

Tree: Cherry—You will find yourself faced with constant new emotional awakenings.

Instruments: Bass, clarinet

Composers: Haydn, Wagner

Bird: Skylark—This handsome bird is beautiful when it sings. It always whistles as it works.

Symbol: Star—You are full of inner brightness and will stand out in any crowd. You will be seen as special.

Harmonious Health and Nutrition . . .

Health Scent: Vanilla—This scent will fill you with a feeling of cleanliness and stability.

Favorable Foods: Spinach, sour cherries, barley, red meat, buttermilk

What's Lucky . . .

Lucky Numbers: 4, 13, 31

Best Months: January and October

Best Day of the Week: Sunday

Best Month Days: 4, 13, 22, 31

Lucky Charm: A piece of material cut from something in your home.

Harmonious Signs for Relationships and Partnerships: Sagittarius and Aries

Spiritual Guides . . .

Star: Al Zubra—Those with this star fear punishment they don't deserve.

Angel: Verchiel—This angel enhances our ability to enjoy what life offers and gives much luck in legal dealings.

Guardian Angel: St. Thomas—This angel brings affection from others and encourages you in all that you do.

Spiritual Stone: Amethyst—This stone is thought to be a mood stabilizer and balances the emotions.

✷ JUDITH'S INSIGHT ✷

You always want what you can't have, and eventually you get it anyway. Drawn to music, acting, and writing, somewhere along the way, these will play a great role in your life. You give more than you take because it's easier to you that way. Some may see you as strange or eccentric, spiritual, or drawn to the underdog.

Patience is your life's lesson, particularly when it comes to love and family. This could be a setback. You're better with friends and social life than with intimate relationships, however much you desire to have one. Unfortunately, you want your partner to do all the work. You like to watch and see how much others are willing to put into a relationship first.

Watch out for addictions. You can be extreme at times . . . both at work and play. Try to listen more to your terrific intuition and less to what others may be saying. That's what intuition is for! When things get too out of balance, you can be depressed. It's not that you feel sorry for yourself, but you may throw a little pity party now and then. Try not to overdo things. Your tendency is to make things come to life with your positive attitude.

You need to find more than one career in your lifetime. You could do anything from building houses to decorating them. You have more leadership qualities than you think.

✦ ✦ ✦

AUGUST 14   LEO • The heart of the zodiac

July 22 at 11:00 P.M. to August 23 at 6:00 A.M. • NUMEROLOGY 5

Possessions and Desires . . .

Gem: Ruby—This stone may lead you to energy, friendship, and happiness.

Flower: Thrift—You usually have a very sympathetic nature.

Astral Color, Color Need, Apparel Color: Your Astral Color is Red, which enhances passion, power, excitement, and strength. Orange in your environment gives you confidence. In your wardrobe, Purple reflects your giving personality and brings you luck.

Fragrance: Surround yourself with the most romantic flowers you can find such as roses, lilies, and violets. The lavish scents will give an added boost to your enthusiasm.

Tree: Apple—You are creative, full of joy, and nearly magical. You bring happiness.

Instruments: Viola, trumpet

Composer: Liszt

Bird: Skylark—This handsome bird is beautiful when it sings. It always whistles as it works.

Symbol: Triangle—You have the right combination of abilities.

Harmonious Health and Nutrition . . .

Health Scent: Peach—Balances your good qualities so they equal your charm.

Favorable Foods: Turnips, oranges, caraway seeds, red meat, buttermilk

What's Lucky . . .

Lucky Numbers: 5, 15, 32

Best Months: January and October

Best Day of the Week: Sunday

Best Month Days: 4, 5, 23

Lucky Charms: A rabbit's foot or a white candle.

Harmonious Signs for Relationships and Partnerships: Sagittarius and Aries

Spiritual Guides . . .

Star: Al Serpha—This star makes special things happen in one's life.

Angel: Verchiel—This angel enhances our ability to enjoy what life offers and gives much luck in legal dealings.

Guardian angel: Plavwell—The guardian that gives power and strength to one's presence.

Spiritual Stone: Amethyst—This stone is thought to be a mood stabilizer and balances the emotions.

✷ JUDITH'S INSIGHT ✷

You are talented in many ways, and your energy can outlast all those around you. Entertainment, sports, or any kind of physical job would work wonderfully for you. You crave entertainment somewhere along the way; you love fun and games, no matter how daring, adventurous, or exciting.

Your love of justice may lead you to a career in law. You are interested in the unknown, and people thrive on your energy and inclination toward the exotic. Socially, you can be quite popular. Travel and outdoor sports should appeal to you.

Watch out for your fiery temper; people sometimes let you down, especially in love relationships. When you feel secure, you can pour on the affection. Otherwise, you might be shy and pessimistic.

Aim high—you're assertive enough to accomplish a lot. There may be two or three jobs over the course of your life, or you just may wear so many hats that it seems that way. Good executive abilities and communication skills may guide you to a job in the media.

Lots of your energy goes into keeping things neat, and this could drive others (especially those living with you) a bit crazy. This may completely reverse itself at some time, and the clutter may build for years!

★ ★ ★

AUGUST 15   LEO • The heart of the zodiac

July 22 at 11:00 P.M. to August 23 at 6:00 A.M. • NUMEROLOGY 6

Possessions and Desires . . .

Gem: Diamond—This stone is thought to encourage harmony in relationships and gives strength to the troubled.

Flower: Throatwort—Your best gifts are often neglected.

Astral Color, Color Need, Apparel Color: Your Astral Color is Red, which enhances passion, power, excitement, and strength. Orange in your environment gives you confidence. In your wardrobe, Green is your power color for overcoming obstacles.

Fragrance: Surround yourself with the most romantic flowers you can find such as roses, lilies, and violets. The lavish scents will give an added boost to your enthusiasm.

Tree: Palm—You tend to be very healthy and creative.

Instruments: Tambourine, lyre

Composer: Schubert

Bird: Skylark—This handsome bird is beautiful when it sings. It always whistles as it works.

Symbol: Crescent—You are more likely to be influenced by the phases of the moon. Your easygoing manner leads you to peaceful situations.

Harmonious Health and Nutrition . . .

Health Scent: Orange Blossom—This scent may balance your body, mind, and soul.

Favorable Foods: Radishes, figs, whole oats, red meat, buttermilk

What's Lucky . . .

Lucky Numbers: 6, 9, 32
Best Months: January and October
Best Day of the Week: Sunday
Best Month Days: 6, 15, 24
Lucky Charms: A religious token or card from any religion.
Harmonious Signs for Relationships and Partnerships: Sagittarius and Aries

Spiritual Guides . . .

Star: Al Serpha—This star makes special things happen in one's life.

Angel: Verchiel—This angel enhances our ability to enjoy what life offers and gives much luck in legal dealings.

Guardian Angel: Michael—"Who is like God."

Spiritual Stone: Amethyst—This stone is thought to be a mood stabilizer and balances the emotions.

✳ JUDITH'S INSIGHT ✳

You are an inspiration to all your friends. Most of the time you can melt ice with your love and tenderness, but watch out for that fiery temper that surfaces from time to time. You have no problem demonstrating devotion to your family and friends. You must learn to be patient.

You can be either energetic or downright lazy, depending on the situation. When things are going your way, your stamina runs high. If you get knocked down a bit, however, you could lean toward depression, and you keep this to yourself. A party person at heart, you need to exercise some moderation with food, drink, and spending. Most of the time, you're aware of what makes you and those around you happy. Your family will be high priority either early in life or later on. Because of your ability to inspire others, people feel that need and want you around.

As smart as you are and as strong as your ego is, you do experience bouts of low self-esteem every once in awhile. Watch out for being misguided in love relationships—you may choose the wrong kind of person in your hurry to settle down. Take your time in looking for the right someone. You tend to want a high-maintenance individual (like yourself!).

As far as career goes, you are naturally mechanically inclined and have a flair for computers, drawing, graphics, and camera work. If you don't go into photography as your life's work, take it up as a hobby. You will come into money, whether you win the lottery or inherit a significant sum.

Keep your head high and watch your emotional gauge. Balance for you is key.

✳ ✳ ✳

AUGUST 16 LEO • The heart of the zodiac

July 22 at 11:00 P.M. to August 23 at 6:00 A.M. • NUMEROLOGY 7

Possessions and Desires . . .

Gem: Ruby—This stone may lead you to energy, friendship, and happiness.

Flower: Butterfly Orchid—You tend to be a very happy person.

Astral Color, Color Need, Apparel Color: Your Astral Color is Red, which enhances passion, power, excitement, and strength. Orange in your environment gives you confidence. In your wardrobe, Plum brings out the best in your looks.

Fragrance: Surround yourself with the most romantic flowers you can find such as roses, lilies, and violets. The lavish scents will give an added boost to your enthusiasm.

Tree: Sycamore—Yours is the ability to love, communicate honestly with others, and have lasting relationships.

Instrument: Harp

Composer: Brahms

Bird: Skylark—This handsome bird is beautiful when it sings. It always whistles as it works.

Symbol: Heart—You are enthusiastic, empathetic, and full of generosity and love.

Harmonious Health and Nutrition . . .

Health Scent: Jasmine—This scent may make you more easygoing when you are stressed.

Favorable Foods: Radishes, figs, whole oats, red meat, buttermilk

What's Lucky . . .

Lucky Numbers: 8, 9, 61

Best Months: January and October

Best Day of the Week: Sunday

Best Month Days: 6, 15, 24

Lucky Charm: An old key.

Harmonious Signs for Relationships and Partnerships: Sagittarius and Aries

Spiritual Guides . . .

Star: Al Zubra—Those with this star fear punishment they don't deserve.

Angel: Verchiel—This angel enhances our ability to enjoy what life offers and gives much luck in legal dealings.

Guardian Angel: Raphael—This angel attends to all of your needs when you are looking for guidance.

Spiritual Stone: Amethyst—This stone is thought to be a mood stabilizer and balances the emotions.

✷ JUDITH'S INSIGHT ✷

Others may see you as a handful, but you are actually very kind, funny, and generous. Born with the gift to entertain, you make a great host, party planner, or caterer. You may even go into the entertainment business. But if you choose a more "serious" profession, such as law, you will give impassioned speeches and presentations. Regardless of what career you choose, there will have to be some thrill or notoriety involved.

You tend to want a "good time" and don't always understand when things go wrong in love relationships. This could be problematic, and a lot of the time, you're the source of the complications. It upsets you when your mate changes moods. When your partner is easygoing, you enjoy that; but if things get tough, you head for the hills. Try and keep yourself centered. Put yourself in your mate's shoes; you may be a bit more understanding.

Not everyone is born with such high intellect as you. Your instincts and intuition are natural, and you should try to follow them. More often than not, they're right on the money. Smart as you are, you will need to find a career that provides enough challenge to interest you. Your life's lesson: practice patience.

✷ ✷ ✷

AUGUST 17 LEO • The heart of the zodiac
July 22 at 11:00 P.M. to August 23 at 6:00 A.M. • NUMEROLOGY 8

Possessions and Desires ...

Gem: Ruby—This stone may lead you to energy, friendship, and happiness.

Flower: Pear—You may express your affections too frequently.

Astral Color, Color Need, Apparel Color: Your Astral Color is Red, which enhances passion, power, excitement, and strength. Orange in your environment gives you confidence. In your wardrobe, Purple reflects your giving personality and brings you luck.

Fragrance: Surround yourself with the most romantic flowers you can find such as roses, lilies, and violets. The lavish scents will give an added boost to your enthusiasm.

Tree: Pine—Your relationships tend to be harmonious, both emotionally and mentally.

Instrument: Cello

Composer: Mozart

Bird: Skylark—This handsome bird is beautiful when it sings. It always whistles as it works.

Symbol: Wings—You are the source of balance in your world—this will bring you contentment.

Harmonious Health and Nutrition ...

Health Scent: Almond—This scent may revitalize you and open you to greater possibilities.

Favorable Foods: Cabbage, sour plums, barley, red meat, buttermilk

What's Lucky ...

Lucky Numbers: 8, 17, 22

Best Months: January and October

Best Day of the Week: Sunday

Best Month Days: 8, 17, 26

Lucky Charm: Red ribbon in your wallet or doorway

Harmonious Signs for Relationships and Partnerships: Sagittarius and Aries

Spiritual Guides ...

Star: Al Gieba—The lucky born with this star are treated like royalty.

Angel: Verchiel—This angel enhances our ability to enjoy what life offers and gives much luck in legal dealings.

Guardian Angel: Seraphim—An angel that brings love, light, and passion.

Spiritual Stone: Amethyst—This stone is thought to be a mood stabilizer and balances the emotions.

✷ JUDITH'S INSIGHT ✷

Consistent and persistent ... you could win awards! You have a strong mind and strong views and spend a great deal of time trying to convince others of your way of thinking. You are impulsive, intuitive, and (at times) authoritative; should you give up on school, your natural intelligence more than makes up for it. You're highly energetic, but look for ways to corral that verve. You're better off when you're in control.

When it comes to love, because you're so giving, people could take advantage of you. Often they see your strength, but you may hide how much you really take on. You are loyal in every way, and your family, friends, and lovers all tend to lean on you. Be careful of emotional obstacles that could cause you heartache.

Career is more important to you than you think, and you may wind up later in life at a job you only dreamed of as a youth. You may take on a hobby and, later on, make it your career. Someone you know may help you land a job. People like you, and things seem like they're handed to you. .Be sure to get the recognition you deserve for the work you do.

From clergyperson to salesperson, business manager to teacher, no matter what job you do, it must have a creative or artistic outlet of some kind.

✷ ✷ ✷

AUGUST 18   LEO • The heart of the zodiac

July 22 at 11:00 P.M to August 23 at 6:00 A.M. • NUMEROLOGY 9

Possessions and Desires . . .

Gem: Ruby—This stone may lead you to energy, friendship, and happiness.

Flower: Blue Periwinkle—You are in harmony with nature.

Astral Color, Color Need, Apparel Color: Your Astral Color is Red, which enhances passion, power, excitement, and strength. Orange in your environment gives you confidence. In your wardrobe, Green is your power color for overcoming obstacles.

Fragrance: Surround yourself with the most romantic flowers you can find such as roses, lilies, and violets. The lavish scents will give an added boost to your enthusiasm.

Tree: Holly—Beware that you are not carried away by your passionate nature. The only way to grow is to be open to new experiences.

Instruments: Violin, tympanum

Composer: Gluck

Bird: Skylark—This handsome bird is beautiful when it sings. It always whistles as it works.

Symbol: Heart—You are enthusiastic, empathetic, and full of generosity and love.

Harmonious Health and Nutrition . . .

Health Scent: Lavender—This scent might lead others to trust you and make you patient.

Favorable Foods: Watercress, apples, rice bran, red meat, buttermilk

What's Lucky . . .

Lucky Numbers: 8, 9, 99

Best Months: January and October

Best Day of the Week: Sunday

Best Month Days: 9, 18, 27

Lucky Charm: A U.S. coin or a bill of any amount from the year you were born.

Harmonious Signs for Relationships and Partnerships: Sagittarius and Aries

Spiritual Guides . . .

Star: Al Gieba—The lucky born with this star are treated like royalty.

Angel: Verchiel—This angel enhances our ability to enjoy what life offers and gives much luck in legal dealings.

Guardian Angel: Gabriel—"God is my strength."

Spiritual Stone: Amethyst—This stone is thought to be a mood stabilizer and balances the emotions.

✷ JUDITH'S INSIGHT ✷

You have style, charm, and a great sense of humor. You tend to look for the unusual and may be drawn to exotic things or perhaps live in another country. You may simply create an atmosphere that stands out as different from everybody else's. Get used to extravagance! You love it and grow into it as you mature.

Some see you as eccentric and strange, though this is not the case. You like unusual things around you; you dare to be different. You're one of those gifted people who succeed at almost everything they try. Watch your energy levels—they could be erratic and drive people crazy. In love, you go through many flirtations and affairs of the heart because you tend to fall in love with your friends. Avoid feelings of entrapment in relationships by waiting until later to settle down. Your ambition makes you a controller, and this can get in the way, especially during intimacy.

Fine things in life appeal to you. You love the theater, arts, and travel. High-quality taste may bring high-quality desires. Somewhere along the way, you do take your chances with others around the world by traveling.

The perfect career would be in the theater, but that may not come to you.

✷ ✷ ✷

AUGUST 19 LEO • The heart of the zodiac

July 22 at 11:00 P.M. to August 23 at 6:00 A.M. • NUMEROLOGY 1

Possessions and Desires . . .

Gem: Agate—This stone may promote health and lead you to a long life.

Flower: Pimpernel—You usually like a life of constant change.

Astral Color, Color Need, Apparel Color: Your Astral Color is Red, which enhances passion, power, excitement, and strength. Orange in your environment gives you confidence. In your wardrobe, Plum brings out the best in your looks.

Fragrance: Surround yourself with the most romantic flowers you can find such as roses, lilies, and violets. The lavish scents will give an added boost to your enthusiasm.

Tree: Walnut—You are unusually helpful and aways looking for new beginnings.

Instruments: Oboe, flute, clarinet, piano, French horn, organ, piccolo

Composer: Böhm

Bird: Warbling Parakeet—the most beautiful of all birds, known as the love bird. It does seem to have the powers of imitation.

Symbol: Crown—the universal sign of dignity.

Harmonious Health and Nutrition . . .

Health Scent: Strawberry—Soothing by nature, the strawberry promotes self-esteem and encourages love.

Favorable Foods: Spinach, grapefruit, whole oats, red meat, buttermilk

What's Lucky . . .

Lucky Numbers: 8, 9, 91
Best Months: January and October
Best Day of the Week: Sunday
Best Month Days: 1, 10, 19, 28
Lucky Charm: A new penny in your shoe.

Harmonious Signs for Relationships and Partnerships: Sagittarius and Aries

Spiritual Guides . . .

Star: Al Gieba—The lucky born with this star are treated like royalty.

Angel: Verchiel—This angel enhances our ability to enjoy what life offers and gives much luck in legal dealings.

Guardian Angel: Malachi—"Messenger of Jehovah."

Spiritual Stone: Amethyst—This stone is thought to be a mood stabilizer and balances the emotions.

✸ JUDITH'S INSIGHT ✸

Versatility is your middle name. Few tasks exist that you cannot tackle and master. You always look for symmetry in your life, and organization to you spells H-A-R-M-O-N-Y. Your life is neatly arranged. Your passions run to the extreme, and you push yourself to your physical limits. Watch out for exhaustion causing health problems.

You are capable of seeing the talent in others, and sports or coaching should interest you. You are likely to be a workaholic, but then "extreme" is a theme throughout your life. Be careful of overindulging in any area. Quite the shopper, you look for oddities and unusual things. Your job may satisfy your appetite for the unconventional.

Your desire for love brings out the best in you, though it may take time to find that special someone. You may have to kiss a few toads, but when you least expect it and stop trying, you'll turn around one day and notice the perfect partner who was there all along. Romance and spontaneity must be important to your spouse.

Your life's lesson: take time to stop and smell the roses. Living near the water may inspire you.

✸ ✸ ✸

AUGUST 20   LEO • The heart of the zodiac

July 22 at 11:00 P.M. to August 23 at 6:00 A.M. • NUMEROLOGY 2

Possessions and Desires . . .

Gem: Ruby—This stone may lead you to energy, friendship, and happiness.

Flower: Crowfoot—You may want to try to be more grateful to others for their generosity.

Astral Color, Color Need, Apparel Color: Your Astral Color is Red, which enhances passion, power, excitement, and strength. Orange in your environment gives you confidence. In your wardrobe, Purple reflects your giving personality and brings you luck.

Fragrance: Surround yourself with the most romantic flowers you can find such as roses, lilies, and violets. The lavish scents will give an added boost to your enthusiasm.

Tree: Maple—You have both great stability and flashes of intuition.

Instruments: Pipe organ, cymbal, drum

Composers: Handel, Johann Sebastian Bach

Bird: Skylark—This handsome bird is beautiful when it sings. It always whistles as it works.

Symbol: Cross—the symbol of self-sacrifice and reconciliation.

Harmonious Health and Nutrition . . .

Health Scent: Apple—You are creative, full of joy, and nearly magical. You bring happiness.

Favorable Foods: Lima beans, pomegranates, rice bran, red meat, buttermilk

What's Lucky . . .

Lucky Numbers: 2, 8, 9
Best Months: January and October
Best Day of the Week: Sunday
Best Month Days: 2, 11, 20, 29

Lucky Charms: Two 50-cent pieces. Give someone else one of them.
Harmonious Signs for Relationships and Partnerships: Sagittarius and Aries

Spiritual Guides . . .

Star: Al Serpha—This star makes special things happen in one's life.

Angel: Verchiel—This angel enhances our ability to enjoy what life offers and gives much luck in legal dealings.

Guardian Angel: St. John—This angel simplifies that which is complicated.

Spiritual Stone: Amethyst—This stone is thought to be a mood stabilizer and balances the emotions.

✳ *JUDITH'S INSIGHT* ✳

Brilliant and capable, you could do anything you set your mind to. A bit extreme at times, check your tendencies to spend too much, give too much, eat too much . . . get the picture? Socially, others find you inspiring, and somewhere along the way, opportunities will present themselves through your many friends.

Drawn to art, music, literature, or drama, you love the theater and movies. A terrific communicator, you may find in yourself a desire to write a book, a play, or perhaps a newspaper article. Learn to trust your intuition more—yours is exceptional. Your personality is magnanimous, attracting others to you. Be careful who you let into your life. When it comes to relationships, people expect you to have few faults. Surprise—you are not perfect, and you know it. However, this may be difficult for others to accept. In love and in business, you work better with a partner. Take your time choosing the right ones.

✳ ✳ ✳

AUGUST 21

LEO • The heart of the zodiac

July 22 at 11:00 P.M. to August 23 at 6:00 A.M. • NUMEROLOGY 3

Possessions and Desires . . .

Gem: Ruby—This stone may lead you to energy, friendship, and happiness.

Flower: Cuckooflower—Your passions run as hot as a candle flame and are just as easily extinguished.

Astral Color, Color Need, Apparel Color: Your Astral Color is Red, which enhances passion, power, excitement, and strength. Orange in your environment gives you confidence. In your wardrobe, Green is your power color for overcoming obstacles.

Fragrance: Surround yourself with the most romantic flowers you can find such as roses, lilies, and violets. The lavish scents will give an added boost to your enthusiasm.

Tree: Elm—You have willpower, strength, and the ability to stand alone.

Instrument: Trombone

Composers: Verdi, Mendelssohn, Schumann

Bird: Skylark—This handsome bird is beautiful when it sings. It always whistles as it works.

Symbol: Wreath—You have been crowned with a special personality. You are strong but extremely compassionate.

Harmonious Health and Nutrition . . .

Health Scent: Rose—This scent will lead you to passionate thoughts and make you feel warm inside.

Favorable Foods: Sprouts, black figs, barley, red meat, buttermilk

What's Lucky . . .

Lucky Numbers: 8, 9, 12
Best Months: January and October
Best Day of the Week: Sunday

Best Month Days: 3, 12, 21, 30
Lucky Charm: A pen that someone else has already used.
Harmonious Signs for Relationships and Partnerships: Sagittarius and Aries

Spiritual Guides . . .

Star: Al Zubra—Those with this star fear punishment they don't deserve.

Angel: Verchiel—This angel enhances our ability to enjoy what life offers and gives much luck in legal dealings.

Guardian Angel: St. Thomas—This angel brings affection from others and encourages you in all that you do.

Spiritual Stone: Amethyst—This stone is thought to be a mood stabilizer and balances the emotions.

✴ JUDITH'S INSIGHT ✴

Whether you're the boss or not, you should be. You are a highly responsive person who can take on tons of responsibility. People recognize this, so they tend to heap it on. Fortunately, you can take it, but taking on too much at one time will drain your enthusiasm. Watch out for feeling sorry for yourself. You may be pushed into a corner, feel trapped, and then complain about it. Whether it's in love, at work, or with your family, learn to ease up on yourself and listen to your inner voice. Saying No is not the end of the world.

You are a great friend and could enjoy a counseling career, such as law or therapy. Because you accomplish everything you try, you may have more than one career in your lifetime. Anything to do with investigating or research finds you breathless with excitement. Look for careers that exploit this inclination.

Family plays a large role in your life. There, too, you must watch out for extremes.

✳ ✳ ✳

AUGUST 22 LEO • The heart of the zodiac

July 22 at 11:00 P.M. to August 23 at 6:00 A.M. • NUMEROLOGY 4

Possessions and Desires . . .

Gem: Agate—This stone may promote health and lead you to a long life.

Flower: Currant—You should guard against spending too much time feeling depressed.

Astral Color, Color Need, Apparel Color: Your Astral Color is Red, which enhances passion, power, excitement, and strength. Orange in your environment gives you confidence. In your wardrobe, Plum brings out the best in your looks.

Fragrance: Surround yourself with the most romantic flowers you can find such as roses, lilies, and violets. The lavish scents will give an added boost to your enthusiasm.

Tree: Cherry—You will find yourself faced with constant new emotional awakenings.

Instruments: Bass, clarinet

Composers: Haydn, Wagner

Bird: Skylark—This handsome bird is beautiful when it sings. It always whistles as it works.

Symbol: Star—You are full of inner brightness and will stand out in any crowd. You will be seen as special.

Harmonious Health and Nutrition . . .

Health Scent: Vanilla—This scent will fill you with a feeling of cleanliness and stability.

Favorable Foods: Cabbage, raspberries, barley, red meat, buttermilk

What's Lucky . . .

Lucky Numbers: 8, 9, 32
Best Months: January and October
Best Day of the Week: Sunday

Best Month Days: 4, 13, 22, 31
Lucky Charm: A piece of material cut from something in your home.
Harmonious Signs for Relationships and Partnerships: Sagittarius and Aries

Spiritual Guides . . .

Star: Al Serpha—This star makes special things happen in one's life.

Angel: Verchiel—This angel enhances our ability to enjoy what life offers and gives much luck in legal dealings.

Guardian Angel: Uriel—This angel brings the light of God's guidance.

Spiritual Stone: Amethyst—This stone is thought to be a mood stabilizer and balances the emotions.

✴ JUDITH'S INSIGHT ✴

You live by the seat of your pants and love it. Everything you try is a breeze. You accept help only when you are able to give too. Love means everything to you, and you're willing to work at your relationship. Your mate must champion you and your undertakings, and a sense of humor is mandatory. As long as your partner understands you, your love life will flourish.

Reading and writing don't seem to interest you as much as an uncanny knack for details. Sometimes coworkers misinterpret your giving acts. Even friends can misunderstand you—they don't always appreciate your sunny, selfless disposition.

Material possessions are important to you, and you surround yourself with things. Make sure you don't clutter yourself right out of your room.

✴ ✴ ✴

AUGUST 23 LEO • The heart of the zodiac

August 23 at 6:00 A.M. to September 23 at 3:00 A.M. • NUMEROLOGY 5

Possessions and Desires . . .

Gem: Ruby—This stone may lead you to energy, friendship, and happiness.

Flower: Daffodil—You may need to strengthen your self-regard.

Astral Color, Color Need, Apparel Color: Your Astral Color is Red, which enhances passion, power, excitement, and strength. Orange in your environment gives you confidence. In your wardrobe, Purple reflects your giving personality and brings you luck.

Fragrance: Surround yourself with the most romantic flowers you can find such as roses, lilies, and violets. The lavish scents will give an added boost to your enthusiasm.

Tree: Apple—You are creative, full of joy, and nearly magical. You bring happiness.

Instruments: Viola, trumpet

Composer: Liszt

Bird: Warbling Parakeet—the most beautiful of all birds, know as the love bird. It does seem to have the powers of imitation.

Symbol: Triangle—You have the right combination of abilities.

Harmonious Health and Nutrition . . .

Health Scent: Peach—This scent may balance your good qualities so that they equal your charm.

Favorable Foods: Cucumbers, limes, whole oats, red meat, buttermilk

What's Lucky . . .

Lucky Numbers: 8, 9, 32
Best Months: January and October
Best Day of the Week: Sunday
Best Month Days: 5, 4, 23
Lucky Charms: A rabbit's foot or a white candle.
Harmonious Signs for Relationships and Partnerships: Sagittarius and Aries

Spiritual Guides . . .

Star: Al Serpha—This star makes special things happen in one's life.

Angel: Verchiel—This angel enhances our ability to enjoy what life offers and gives much luck in legal dealings.

Guardian Angel: St. Thomas—This angel brings affection from others and encourages you in all that you do.

Spiritual Stone: Amethyst—This stone is thought to be a mood stabilizer and balances the emotions.

✦ JUDITH'S INSIGHT ✦

Get out of your own way. You have talent and energy enough for two. You love to entertain and be entertained. So long as you're the center of attention, things are just fine by you. This may take you a lifetime to recognize. You have a strong devotion toward family, though they may misunderstand your actions at times.

You dress impeccably and have a flair for fashion. Look for a career in retail or the beauty industry. Even if you don't work in the beauty business, you always look like you do. High aims and aspirations lead you into great responsibility.

When it comes to love, allow yourself just enough freedom. You bring on attention and flattery, but you spot the phonies a mile away. You may have a volatile relationship, but you are mostly devoted to your spouse or partner, and you would do anything to keep things from coming apart. You make a great friend as well.

Be sure to keep an eye on finances—sometimes you give away more than you should. For some reason, you may be secretive about money, always hiding something away for a rainy day. Life's hurdles will present themselves, but you take them on and clear them like a trained athlete.

✶ ✶ ✶

AUGUST 24

VIRGO • The festivities and celebrations of the zodiac

August 23 at 6:00 A.M. to September 23 at 3:00 A.M. • NUMEROLOGY 6

Possessions and Desires . . .

Gem: Jasper—This stone could grant the bearer protection from sadness.

Flower: Dahlia—You may crave stability in all situations.

Astral Color, Color Need, Apparel Color: Your Astral Color is Navy Blue—the color of style and refinement. Violet in your environment keeps you empathetic toward others. In your wardrobe, Green is your power color for overcoming obstacles.

Fragrance: Try never to mix scents. Purchase your products all from the same company so your environment will be clean and harmonious.

Tree: Palm—You tend to be very healthy and creative.

Instruments: Tambourine, lyre

Composer: Schubert

Bird: Stork—Turkish bird, held in high esteem the world over. This bird is intelligent but may have strange tendencies.

Symbol: Crescent—You are more likely to be influenced by the phases of the moon. Your easygoing manner leads you to peaceful situations.

Harmonious Health and Nutrition . . .

Health Scent: Orange Blossom—This scent may balance your body, mind, and soul.

Favorable Foods: Asparagus, strawberries, molasses, beef, cottage cheese

What's Lucky . . .

Lucky Numbers: 3, 5, 42

Best Months: February and November

Best Day of the Week: Wednesday

Best Month Days: 6, 15, 24

Lucky Charms: A religious token or card from any religion.

Harmonious Signs for Relationships and Partnerships: Capricorn and Taurus

Spiritual Guides . . .

Star: Al Awa—Those with this star are often objects of others' desire.

Angel: Hamaliel—This angel governs logic and shows us what is real. His lessons in personal ethics always improve our karma.

Guardian Angel: Michael—"Who is like God."

Spiritual Stone: Jasper—This stone may soothe bruised emotions.

✴ JUDITH'S INSIGHT ✴

If you would just learn patience, everything will come to your door. Be sure to recognize when someone is knocking. One step at a time, especially in love, is the best approach for you. People are devoted to you, and half the time you don't even know it. Try to take the time to enjoy yourself more; otherwise your negativity can get the best of you.

Your very good mind makes you hungry for knowledge. An avid reader and traveler, you should think less about trying things and just try them. Sometimes you think yourself right out of an idea. You are a great worker; it takes a lot to tire you out. You'd make a good writer or communicator of some kind. Politics and, yes, firefighting may tempt you. Again, you may spend too much time thinking about career and not enough time doing what you really want.

Your sweet soul makes you an understanding parent and good partner. Sometimes you play too hard in love and don't always reveal your inner thoughts. Try using those terrific communication skills in your relationship. Your partner will appreciate it.

✴ ✴ ✴

Possessions and Desires . . .

Gem: Hyacinth—This stone might aid the memory.

Flower: Sweet Flag—If you don't follow your own sense of honor don't expect to ever be honored.

Astral Color, Color Need, Apparel Color: Your Astral Color is Navy Blue—the color of style and refinement. Violet in your environment keeps you empathetic toward others. In your wardrobe, Light Blue gives you strength and determination.

Fragrance: Try never to mix scents. Purchase your products all from the same company so your environment will be clean and harmonious.

Tree: Sycamore—Yours is the ability to love, communicate honestly with others, and have lasting relationships.

Instrument: Harp

Composers: Gluck, Brahms

Bird: Killdeer—This bird is usually found consorting with other species, and can adapt to any environment.

Symbol: Heart—You are enthusiastic, empathetic, and full of generosity and love.

Harmonious Health and Nutrition . . .

Health Scent: Jasmine—This scent may make you more easygoing when you are stressed.

Favorable Foods: Peas, huckleberries, chocolate, oysters, eggs

What's Lucky . . .

Lucky Numbers: 3, 5, 26
Best Months: February and November
Best Day of the Week: Wednesday
Best Month Days: 6, 15, 24

Lucky Charm: An old key.
Harmonious Signs for Relationships and Partnerships: Capricorn and Taurus

Spiritual Guides . . .

Star: Sumak al Azel—Those with this star are called upon to serve.

Angel: Hamaliel—This angel governs logic and shows us what is real. His lessons in personal ethics always improve our karma.

Guardian Angel: Raphael—This angel attends to all of your needs when you are looking for guidance.

Spiritual Stone: Jasper—This stone may soothe bruised emotions.

✴ JUDITH'S INSIGHT ✴

Anyone who is as generous, funny, and energetic as you is bound to be a handful at times. You know how to party and have a good time. With that, there's this shy side, though most people see you as the comedian. You may want to attempt a career in entertainment, if not on stage, then on the business end. You may attempt writing a screenplay.

Your instincts seem good, and although your heart may say one thing, your levelheaded reason keeps you from making mistakes. It may take time for find that special someone. When you recognize love, your heart is open and you let it in. That is not to say you won't have your share of headaches. The friends and family who give you the most devotion are the ones you give back to. You need only a few close friends around you, and that seems to work fine.

Life's ups and downs don't seem to dampen your stylish approach to things. A class act, really, you will have your share of opportunities, but it may take a long time before you recognize what they are.

✴ ✴ ✴

Possessions and Desires . . .

Gem: Jasper—This stone could grant the bearer protection from sadness.

Flower: Everlasting—What you love you tend to love forever.

Astral Color, Color Need, Apparel Color: Your Astral Color is Navy Blue—the color of style and refinement. Violet in your environment keeps you empathetic toward others. In your wardrobe, Green is your power color for overcoming obstacles.

Fragrance: Look for those classic scents that give you the feeling of freshness and sparkling clean, scents containing jasmine, ylang ylang, and roses.

Tree: Pine—Your relationships tend to be harmonious, both emotionally and mentally.

Instrument: Cello

Composer: Mozart

Bird: Cuckoo—A good flyer and very seldom a quitter. Many seem more independent than they actually are; yearn for more nurturing than one would expect.

Symbol: Wings—You are the source of balance in your world—this will bring you contentment.

Harmonious Health and Nutrition . . .

Health Scent: Almond—This scent may revitalize you and open you to greater possibilities.

Favorable Foods: Peas, huckleberries, chocolate, oysters, eggs

What's Lucky . . .

Lucky Numbers: 3, 5, 62

Best Months: February and November

Best Day of the Week: Wednesday

Best Month Days: 8, 17, 26

Lucky Charm: Red ribbon in your wallet or doorway.

Harmonious Signs for Relationships and Partnerships: Capricorn and Taurus

Spiritual Guides . . .

Star: Al Awa—Those with this star are often objects of others' desire.

Angel: Hamaliel—This angel governs logic and shows us what is real. His lessons in personal ethics always improve our karma.

Guardian Angel: Seraphim—An angel that brings love, light, and passion.

Spiritual Stone: Jasper—This stone may soothe bruised emotions.

✦ JUDITH'S INSIGHT ✦

You are never at a loss for words; it would be surprising were you not to do something with language. Conscientious to a fault, you get irritated with opinionated, controlling people. Somehow you put people at ease, make a good friend, and certainly know how to keep a secret.

You're far-sighted and intuitive, even psychic, and would do well with anything involving books, publishing, editing, or writing. No matter what the job, business will be good to you. Your flair for detail may lead you to designing, whether it be flower arrangements or landscapes. Science is another possibility. Searching for answers and mystery fascinate you. Computers may interest you.

Sometimes you can be too fussy with people and should learn to give out those necessary pats on the back. You don't necessarily need the spotlight, but you could be the one in charge of directing it.

✦ ✦ ✦

Possessions and Desires . . .

Gem: Jasper—This stone could grant the bearer protection from sadness.

Flower: Filbert—You may constantly find yourself reconnecting with those you care about.

Astral Color, Color Need, Apparel Color: Your Astral Color is Navy Blue—the color of style and refinement. Violet in your environment keeps you empathetic toward others. In your wardrobe, Light Blue gives you strength and determination.

Fragrance: Look for those classic scents that give you the feeling of freshness and sparkling clean scents containing jasmine, ylang ylang, and roses.

Tree: Holly—Beware that you are not carried away by your passionate nature. The only way to grow is to be open to new experiences.

Instruments: Violin, tympanum

Composer: Gluck

Bird: Goldfinch—These gentle creatures can seem moody, especially in unsettled weather.

Symbol: Anchor—This tranquil symbol signifies stability and strength, and stands for strong commitments in relationships.

Harmonious Health and Nutrition . . .

Health Scent: Strawberry—Soothing by nature, the strawberry promotes self-esteem and encourages love.

Favorable Foods: Mushrooms, pineapple, raw sugar, liver, buttermilk

What's Lucky . . .

Lucky Numbers: 3, 5, 28

Best Months: February and November

Best Day of the Week: Wednesday

Best Month Days: 9, 18, 27

Lucky Charms: A U.S. coin or a bill of any amount from the year you were born.

Harmonious Signs for Relationships and Partnerships: Capricorn and Taurus

Spiritual Guides . . .

Star: Al Awa—Those with this star are often objects of others' desire.

Angel: Hamaliel—This angel governs logic and shows us what is real. His lessons in personal ethics always improve our karma.

Guardian Angel: Gabriel—"God is my strength."

Spiritual Stone: Jasper—This stone may soothe bruised emotions.

✳ JUDITH'S INSIGHT ✳

Fond of travel, a lover of music, you are a fine judge of paintings and recognize good work. You could be an art critic. Determination and extravagance seem to polarize you. You're extremely emotional, but others see you as strong. You're drawn to unusual relationships, so a long-distance love affair may work for you. Maintaining friendships comes easily to you—you seem to hang on to them forever. In love relationships, however, once you've made that commitment, you have a tendency to feel trapped. Your ambitious nature requires a good deal of freedom. Unless your mate knows this and respects it, problems could arise.

You're a classy, sharp dresser and look rich in the way you present yourself (even if you're not). Sometimes you get anxious because you think too much and overstep your mark, but this is all self-inflicted and can be worked on.

✳ ✳ ✳

AUGUST 28

VIRGO • The festivities and celebrations of the zodiac

August 23 at 6:00 A.M. to September 23 at 3:00 A.M. • **NUMEROLOGY 1**

Possessions and Desires . . .

Gem: Jasper—This stone could grant the bearer protection from sadness.

Flower: Flax—You are comfortable letting the universe guide you where it wants you to go.

Astral Color, Color Need, Apparel Color: Your Astral Color is Navy Blue—the color of style and refinement. Violet in your environment keeps you empathetic toward others. In your wardrobe, Green is your power color for overcoming obstacles.

Fragrance: Look for those classic scents that give you the feeling of freshness and sparkling clean scents containing jasmine, ylang ylang, and roses.

Tree: Walnut—You are unusually helpful and always looking for constant changes in your life.

Instruments: Oboe, flute, clarinet, piano, French horn, organ, piccolo

Composer: Böhm

Bird: Robin—the most sociable of all birds, with the ability to create quick friendships. It also can easily adapt to any home. When it wants something, it has the tendency to try to snatch it.

Symbol: Crown—the universal sign of dignity.

Harmonious Health and Nutrition . . .

Health Scent: Strawberry—Soothing by nature, the strawberry promotes self-esteem and encourages love.

Favorable Foods: Turnips, cranberries, molasses, beef, goat's milk

What's Lucky . . .

Lucky Numbers: 3, 5, 10
Best Months: February and November
Best Day of the Week: Wednesday
Best Month Days: 1, 10, 19, 28

Lucky Charm: A new penny in your shoe.
Harmonious Signs for Relationships and Partnerships: Capricorn and Taurus

Spiritual Guides . . .

Star: Sumak al Azel—Those with this star are called upon to serve.

Angel: Hamaliel—This angel governs logic and shows us what is real. His lessons in personal ethics always improve our karma.

Guardian Angel: Malachi—"Messenger of Jehovah."

Spiritual Stone: Jasper—This stone may soothe bruised emotions.

✦ JUDITH'S INSIGHT ✦

Your versatility makes you desirable. A lover of music and art, you have a lot of energy and a terrific mind, even if you may not have the degree to back it up. Striving for the more materialistic things in life or dealing with the sadder issues of life will drain you of all of your energies. You can go from compassion and advocacy for the downtrodden to cocktail parties with the rich and famous with equal contentment. Your energy and enthusiasm will take you places. A more loyal friend or family loved one is difficult to find.

Your deep desire for love will bring it right to you. Sometimes, however, your choices are made with blinders on. The need for romance is strong, and you require lots of spontaneity.

You are a classic workaholic; a nine to five job is fine, but you may devote yourself to other endeavors three times more. Journalism and publishing as well as music and theater all appeal to your creative nature. There will be very few jobs you take on that you don't master, if any.

Your energy levels and drive toward perfection usually take you in a positive direction.

✱ ✱ ✱

AUGUST 29 VIRGO • The festivities and celebrations of the zodiac

August 23 at 6:00 A.M. to September 23 at 3:00 A.M. • NUMEROLOGY 2

Possessions and Desires . . .

Gem: Hyacinth—This stone might aid the memory.

Flower: Flower-of-an-hour—You usually see the beauty in the smallest things that others tend to overlook.

Astral Color, Color Need, Apparel Color: Your Astral Color is Navy Blue—the color of style and refinement. Violet in your environment keeps you empathetic toward others. In your wardrobe, Light Blue gives you strength and determination.

Fragrance: Look for those classic scents that give you the feeling of freshness and sparkling clean scents containing jasmine, ylang ylang, and roses.

Tree: Maple—You have both great stability and flashes of intuition.

Instruments: Pipe organ, cymbal, drum

Composers: Handel, Johann Sebastian Bach

Bird: Stork—Turkish bird, held in high esteem the world over. This bird is intelligent but may have strange tendencies.

Symbol: Cross—the symbol of self-sacrifice and reconciliation.

Harmonious Health and Nutrition . . .

Health Scents: Apple—You are creative, full of joy, and nearly magical. You bring happiness.

Favorable Foods: Celery, strawberry, chocolate, chicken, cottage cheese

What's Lucky . . .

Lucky Numbers: 3, 5, 11

Best Months: February and November

Best Day of the Week: Wednesday

Best Month Days: 2, 11, 20, 29

Lucky Charms: Two 50-cent pieces. Give someone else one of them.

Harmonious Signs for Relationships and Partnerships: Capricorn and Taurus

Spiritual Guides . . .

Star: Al Awa—Those with this star are often objects of others' desire.

Angel: Hamaliel—This angel governs logic and shows us what is real. His lessons in personal ethics always improve our karma.

Guardian Angel: St. Thomas—This angel brings affection from others and encourages you in all that you do.

Spiritual Stone: Jasper—This stone may soothe bruised emotions.

✴ JUDITH'S INSIGHT ✴

Others see you as living in your own world—that's how original you are. Daring and fearless, adventure colors all your actions. Your personality alone will bring advancement into your life. Others are inspired just being around you. Career opportunities will fall at your feet.

Attention from prospective lovers comes easily. Your appearance is neat and distinguished. It takes you time to warm up to someone in order for you to feel comfortable. You demonstrate affection only when others show theirs for you.

You are drawn to a meticulous environment, whether it be work, school, or home life. A career as a builder or in an artistic field should appeal to you, so fond are you of the arts. Don't rule out a career that has something to do with water. Writing and journalism are both possibilities for you. Jobs always seem to come your way.

As unselfish and broad-minded as you are, almost everyone likes you. Your family is more proud of you than you believe. The biggest success comes with family and friends, with a business a close second.

✴ ✴ ✴

AUGUST 30

VIRGO • The festivities and celebrations of the zodiac

August 23 at 6:00 A.M. to September 23 at 3:00 A.M. • NUMEROLOGY 3

Possessions and Desires . . .

Gem: Jasper—This stone could grant the bearer protection from sadness.

Flower: Flowering Reed—You allow the universe to be your guide when it comes to finding happiness.

Astral Color, Color Need, Apparel Color: Your Astral Color is Navy Blue—the color of style and refinement. Violet in your environment keeps you empathetic toward others. In your wardrobe, Green is your power color for overcoming obstacles.

Fragrance: Look for those classic scents that give you the feeling of freshness and sparkling clean, scents containing Jasmine, ylang ylang, and roses.

Tree: Elm—You have willpower, strength, and the ability to stand alone.

Instrument: Trombone

Composers: Verdi, Mendelssohn, Schumann

Bird: Stork—Turkish bird, held in high esteem the world over. This bird is intelligent but may have strange tendencies.

Symbol: Wreath—You have been crowned with a special personality. You are strong but extremely compassionate.

Harmonious Health and Nutrition . . .

Health Scent: Rose—This scent will lead you to passionate thoughts and make you feel warm inside.

Favorable Foods: Sorrel, raspberries, raw sugar, fish, eggs

What's Lucky . . .

Lucky Numbers: 3, 5, 30
Best Months: February and November
Best Day of the Week: Wednesday

Best Month Days: 3, 12, 21, 30
Lucky Charm: A pen that someone else has already used.
Harmonious Signs for Relationships and Partnerships: Capricorn and Taurus

Spiritual Guides . . .

Star: Sumak al Azel—Those with this star are called upon to serve.

Angel: Hamaliel—This angel governs logic and shows us what is real. His lessons in personal ethics always improve our karma.

Guardian Angel: Johiel—This angel is a protector of all those with a humble heart.

Spiritual Stone: Jasper—This stone may soothe bruised emotions.

✷ JUDITH'S INSIGHT ✷

As responsible as you are, be careful of others taking advantage of you. You get more jobs than you know what to do with because everyone sees you as so capable. It may take time for your career to evolve. An intensely strong mind may lead you to research or writing or working with small, fine things. You have the physical presence to be an athlete or a physical therapist or both.

Overindulgence will be a problem for you. You will be tempted to do things you know are wrong for you. Try to resist those impulses.

A dear friend, you know how to keep a secret. You may enjoy practicing law or a career in law enforcement because of this tight-lipped quality. A bout or two with the law could shake things up. Make sure you are on the right side.

Family and romances are all fulfilling to you. Just try to be patient and don't rush into things. Everything can't happen overnight.

✷ ✷ ✷

AUGUST 31

VIRGO • The festivities and celebrations of the zodiac

August 23 at 6:00 A.M. to September 23 at 3:00 A.M. • NUMEROLOGY 4

Possessions and Desires . . .

Gem: Emerald—Those who carry this stone tend to be lucky in love.

Flower: Foxglove—You may need to learn that sincerity will get you farther than empty flattery.

Astral Color, Color Need, Apparel Color: Your Astral Color is Navy Blue—the color of style and refinement. Violet in your environment keeps you empathetic toward others. In your wardrobe, Light Blue gives you strength and determination.

Fragrance: Try never to mix scents. Purchase your products all from the same company so your environment will be clean and harmonious.

Tree: Cherry—You will find yourself faced with constant new emotional awakenings.

Instruments: Bass, clarinet

Composers: Haydn, Wagner

Bird: Killdeer—This bird is usually found consorting with other species, and can adapt to any environment.

Symbol: Star—You are full of inner brightness and will stand out in any crowd. You will be seen as special.

Harmonious Health and Nutrition . . .

Health Scent: Vanilla—This scent will fill you with a feeling of cleanliness and stability.

Favorable Foods: Brussels sprouts, prunes, molasses, liver, buttermilk

What's Lucky . . .

Lucky Numbers: 3, 4, 5

Best Months: February and November

Best Day of the Week: Wednesday

Best Month Days: 4, 13, 22, 31

Lucky Charm: A piece of material cut from something in your home.

Harmonious Signs for Relationships and Partnerships: Capricorn and Taurus

Spiritual Guides . . .

Star: Al Awa—Those with this star are often objects of others' desire.

Angel: Hamaliel—This angel governs logic and shows us what is real. His lessons in personal ethics always improve our karma.

Guardian Angel: Uriel—This angel brings the light of God's guidance.

Spiritual Stone: Jasper—This stone may soothe bruised emotions.

✴ JUDITH'S INSIGHT ✴

You want to be seen and heard, and you just might have your way. Most likely, it will be through writing of some kind or, possibly, music. You give your all, no matter what—you don't know any other way. Drawn to unusual places and people, you may travel a bit or even live abroad at one point in your life.

Patience and patience . . . that's the key in love. Sometimes you doubt another's affection simply because they have their mind on other things. You want and need a secure relationship, and someday you realize it's you who needs to feel secure in yourself. Giving too much or too little can overwhelm you and your partner. Shyness may be a problem for you at the beginning of a relationship.

Be careful to check your tendencies to overdo it, whether it be work or play. You are known to go to extremes, both good and bad. You may have to clear a few hurdles in your work life before you can relax and really perform, which you eventually do and do well. Later in your life is better—the second half of your life really takes off once you learn to stop taking things so personally.

✴ ✴ ✴

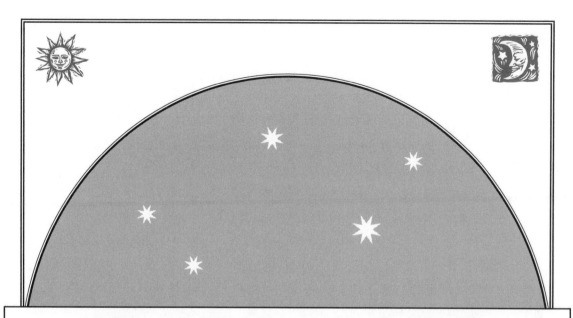

SEPTEMBER

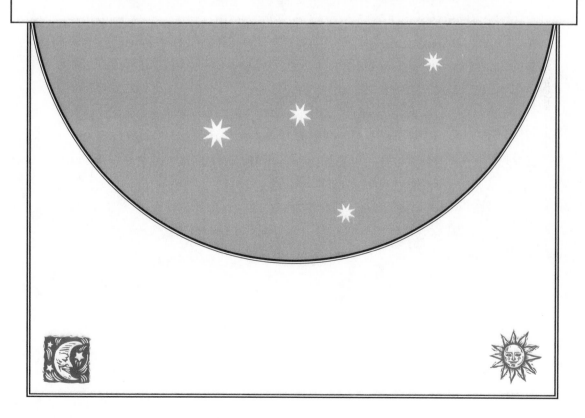

SEPTEMBER 1
VIRGO • The festivities and celebrations of the zodiac

August 23 at 6:00 A.M. to September 23 at 3:00 A.M. • NUMEROLOGY 1

Possessions and Desires . . .

Gem: Jasper—This stone could grant the bearer protection from sadness.

Flower: Fumitory—You may spend too much time complaining about what can't be altered.

Astral Color, Color Need, Apparel Color: Your Astral Color is Navy Blue—the color of style and refinement. Violet in your environment keeps you empathetic toward others. In your wardrobe, Green is your power color for overcoming obstacles.

Fragrance: Look for those classic scents that give you the feeling of fresh and sparkling clean, scents containing jasmine, ylang ylang, and roses.

Tree: Cherry—You will find yourself faced with constant new emotional awakenings.

Instruments: Bass, clarinet

Composers: Haydn, Wagner

Bird: Stork—Turkish bird, held in high esteem the world over. This bird is intelligent but may have strange tendencies.

Symbol: Star—You are full of inner brightness and will stand out in any crowd. You will be seen as special.

Harmonious Health and Nutrition . . .

Health Scent: Strawberry—Soothing by nature, the strawberry promotes self-esteem and encourages love.

Favorable Foods: Watercress, raspberries, raw sugar, chicken, goat's milk

What's Lucky . . .

Lucky Numbers: 1, 3, 5
Best Months: February and November
Best Day of the Week: Wednesday
Best Month Days: 4, 13, 22, 31
Lucky Charm: A new penny in your shoe.

Harmonious Signs for Relationships and Partnerships: Capricorn and Taurus

Spiritual Guides . . .

Star: Al Awa—Those with this star are often objects of others' desire.

Angel: Hamaliel—This angel governs logic and shows us what is real. His lessons in personal ethics always improve our karma.

Guardian Angel: Malachi—"Messenger of Jehovah."

Spiritual Stone: Jasper—This stone may soothe bruised emotions.

✶ JUDITH'S INSIGHT ✶

You have unbelievable concentration as well as a well-balanced mind. You are mechanically inclined. You might be annoying to those around you because you constantly need everything in perfect order. You make friends easily, but some will pull away due to your frankness and impatience. It is possible to be *too* honest. You are loyal, comforting, and always there for your friends in their time of need.

You would do well in government jobs related to accounting. Maybe you could work for the IRS. If the word *audit* gives you chills, consider a career as a chef or restaurateur. Your impeccable organizational skills could be put to good use in acting, writing, directing, and, definitely, editing. You love to sing, though you may not be very good at it.

As you get older, losing your looks would be something you take very seriously. You are capital *V* Vain. When you're in love, you can be cloying because you look to your relationships to provide you with self-esteem—you need *constant* reassurance. You are loyal and faithful to your mate but overthink the union to the point your spouse will wonder if you have nothing but doubts. Realize your brain is way too active, and relax!

Financially, you do well and enjoy great success.

✶ ✶ ✶

SEPTEMBER 2 VIRGO • The festivities and celebrations of the zodiac
August 23 at 6:00 A.M. to September 23 at 3:00 A.M. • NUMEROLOGY 2

Possessions and Desires . . .

Gem: Jasper—This stone could grant the bearer protection from sadness.
Flower: Helenium—You may need to learn that letting tears go washes away the hurt more quickly than holding them in.
Astral Color, Color Need, Apparel Color: Your Astral Color is Navy Blue—the color of style and refinement. Violet in your environment keeps you empathetic toward others. In your wardrobe, Light Blue gives you strength and determination.
Fragrance: Look for those classic scents that give you the feeling of fresh and sparkling clean, scents containing jasmine, ylang ylang, and roses.
Tree: Maple—You have both great stability and flashes of intuition.
Instruments: Pipe organ, cymbal, drum
Composers: Handel, Johann Sebastian Bach
Bird: Goldfinch—These gentle creatures can seem moody, especially in unsettled weather.
Symbol: Cross—the symbol of self-sacrifice and reconciliation.

Harmonious Health and Nutrition . . .

Health Scent: Apple—A vivacious scent encouraging energy. Will help you to be more creative, intuitive, and positive.
Favorable Foods: Turnips, cherries, chocolate, beef, cottage cheese

What's Lucky . . .

Lucky Numbers: 3, 5, 11
Best Months: February and November
Best Day of the Week: Wednesday
Best Month Days: 2, 11, 20, 29
Lucky Charms: Two 50-cent pieces. Give someone else one of them.
Harmonious Signs for Relationships and Partnerships: Capricorn and Taurus

Spiritual Guides . . .

Star: Al Awa—Those with this star are often objects of others' desire.
Angel: Hamaliel—This angel governs logic and shows us what is real. His lessons in personal ethics always improve our karma.
Guardian Angel: St. John—This angel simplifies that which is complicated.
Spiritual Stone: Jasper—This stone may soothe bruised emotions.

✶ JUDITH'S INSIGHT ✶

You are trustworthy and conscientious in whatever you do, be it work, home life, or play. It's likely that you will work in a job that utilizes your mind, but you could be a professional athlete. The best of both worlds would be employment where you can sweat while you think and still be paid for it. You have a lifelong insatiable love of learning. It's too bad library cards don't accumulate frequent flyer miles! You soak knowledge up like a sponge. A strong desire for travel only enhances your thirst for knowledge. You are so curious you catch yourself eavesdropping on conversations in restaurants, on the bus, or at parties.

Temperamentally suited to work with nature, you'd make a very happy flower arranger, designer, gardener, or landscaper. Otherwise you may find yourself working with waterways, the ocean, or even—believe it or not—vitamins! (You're talented in science and chemistry.) Your sharp mind may lead you to consider journalism, editing, proofreading, or anchoring the evening news.

Your frankness could threaten many friendships. Aim at being less judgmental and feeling superior to others. Learn to notice how words affect people and measure your meaning against their interpretation. You can control this if you recognize it, for you are as loyal as they come. You enjoy fast responses to your romantic overtures, but when it comes to you and love, slower is better. If you're impatient, you had better formulate a quick escape route.

The person you believe in most should be you. Listen to your insights more often.

SEPTEMBER 3 VIRGO • The festivities and celebrations of the zodiac
August 23 at 6:00 A.M. to September 23 at 3:00 A.M. • NUMEROLOGY 3

Possessions and Desires . . .

Gem: Jasper—This stone could grant the bearer protection from sadness.

Flower: Hepatica—You tend to have enough self-confidence to fight your way through what you get yourself into.

Astral Color, Color Need, Apparel Color: Your Astral Color is Navy Blue—the color of style and refinement. Violet in your environment keeps you empathetic toward others. In your wardrobe, Green is your power color for overcoming obstacles.

Fragrance: Look for those classic scents that give you the feeling of fresh and sparkling clean, scents containing jasmine, ylang ylang, and roses.

Tree: Elm—You have willpower, strength, and the ability to stand alone.

Instrument: Trombone

Composers: Verdi, Mendelssohn, Schumann

Bird: Killdeer—This bird is usually found consorting with other species, and can adapt to any environment.

Symbol: Star—You are full of inner brightness and will stand out in any crowd. You will be seen as special.

Harmonious Health and Nutrition . . .

Health Scent: Rose—This scent will lead you to passionate thoughts and make you feel warm inside.

Favorable Foods: Peas, strawberry, molasses, liver, eggs

What's Lucky . . .

Lucky Numbers: 3, 5, 21
Best Months: February and November
Best Day of the Week: Wednesday
Best Month Days: 3, 12, 21, 30
Lucky Charm: A pen that someone else has already used.

Harmonious Signs for Relationships and Partnerships: Capricorn and Taurus

Spiritual Guides . . .

Star: Al Awa—Those with this star are often objects of others' desire.

Angel: Hamaliel—This angel governs logic and shows us what is real. His lessons in personal ethics always improve our karma.

Guardian Angel: Johiel—This angel is a protector of all those with a humble heart.

Spiritual Stone: Jasper—This stone may soothe bruised emotions.

✷ JUDITH'S INSIGHT ✷

You are excellent with details and designs. Though you may not have much interest in it, you could be a great decorator. Anything related to architecture, movie set design, engineering, or computer programming should appeal to you. It is imperative that you find a job that will send you home mentally exhausted, or your home life could be chaos.

You love constant change not only with your furniture but your body. New glasses, different hairstyle—the list is endless. Romance is another area where you always want something new. You may have at least one very important relationship that you choose to leave, later regret leaving, and then can never get back. You want stability, but you run from it like the wind.

As long as things are stimulating, you won't be bored. You know you have the ability to do just about anything. The reason every one calls you pushy and impatient is because, well, you are. You just don't suffer fools well. When you need to be, you can be kind, open-minded, and nurturing. If you take time to notice that other people have lives too, your heart goes out to them.

With very little effort but a lot of focus you can control any situation and effect change in your world. You can make things happen.

★ ★ ★

SEPTEMBER 4 VIRGO • The festivities and celebrations of the zodiac

August 23 at 6:00 A.M. to September 23 at 3:00 A.M. • NUMEROLOGY 4

Possessions and Desires . . .

Gem: Jasper—This stone could grant the bearer protection from sadness.

Flower: Hoya—You may carve your place in the world through your sharp wits and hard work.

Astral Color, Color Need, Apparel Color: Your Astral Color is Navy Blue—the color of style and refinement. Violet in your environment keeps you empathetic towards others. In your wardrobe, Light Blue, gives you strength and determination.

Fragrance: Look for those classic scents that give you the feeling of fresh and sparkling clean, scents containing jasmine, ylang ylang, and roses.

Tree: Cherry—You will find yourself faced with constant new emotional awakenings.

Instruments: Bass, clarinet

Composers: Haydn, Wagner

Bird: Cuckoo—A good flyer and very seldom a quitter. Many seem more independent than they actually are; yearn for more nurturing than one would expect.

Symbol: Star—You are full of inner brightness and will stand out in any crowd. You will be seen as special.

Harmonious Health and Nutrition . . .

Health Scent: Vanilla—This scent will fill you with a feeling of cleanliness and stability.

Favorable Foods: Parsnips, peaches, raw sugar, fish, goat's milk

What's Lucky . . .

Lucky Numbers: 3, 5, 22
Best Months: February and November
Best Day of the Week: Wednesday
Best Month Days: 4, 13, 22, 31
Lucky Charm: A piece of material cut from something in your home.
Harmonious Signs for Relationships and Partnerships: Capricorn and Taurus

Spiritual Guides . . .

Star: Al Awa—Those with this star are often objects of others' desire.

Angel: Hamaliel—This angel governs logic and shows us what is real. His lessons in personal ethics always improve our karma.

Guardian Angel: St. Thomas—This angel brings affection from others and encourages you in all that you do.

Spiritual Stone: Jasper—This stone may soothe bruised emotions.

✶ JUDITH'S INSIGHT ✶

No matter how large the crowd, you stand out. Solid, sensible and headstrong, under many layers of ego, you have a golden vein of kindness and always wear your heart on your sleeve. Your intentions may be good, but you must be cautious in selecting your methods. Sometimes your actions will be grossly misunderstood.

You may be so fascinated by all the opportunities for employment that you can't find anything to do. Multiple talents and determination are usually gifts, not curses. There are very few jobs you can't do; your skills and abilities make you well suited to be a builder, clockmaker, artist, engineer, or teacher. Your love of finding fault can also lead you into a career as a theater critic or even government troubleshooter. You could also be a counselor, mediator, or designer.

You'll make an excellent parent once you're completely past the "me" stage in your life. There is no doubt that you can be selfish to an extreme. You can't become a well-rounded human being if you think the world revolves around you. You enjoy helping others with their problems, but are limited when it comes to keeping promises. Give others time to forgive you. Your style is *yours;* nobody understands it or would be caught dead doing it, but they all admire your moves anyway. You like unusual things and may be drawn to out-of-the ordinary people, those like no one else on the planet. Among the wildly different you manage to fit in.

✶ ✶ ✶

Possessions and Desires . . .

Gem: Jasper—This stone could grant the bearer protection from sadness.

Flower: Mimosa—You may be too sensitive to criticism.

Astral Color, Color Need, Apparel Color: Your Astral Color is Navy Blue—the color of style and refinement. Violet in your environment keeps you empathetic toward others. In your wardrobe, Green is your power color for overcoming obstacles.

Fragrance: Look for those classic scents that give you the feeling of fresh and sparkling clean, scents containing jasmine, ylang ylang, and roses.

Tree: Apple—You are creative, full of joy, and nearly magical. You bring happiness.

Instruments: Viola, trumpet

Composer: Liszt

Bird: Robin—the most sociable of all birds, with the ability to create quick friendships. It also can easily adapt to any home. When it wants something, it has the tendency to try to snatch it.

Symbol: Triangle—You have the right combination of abilities.

Harmonious Health and Nutrition . . .

Health Scent: Peach—This scent may balance your good qualities so that they equal your charm.

Favorable Foods: Parsley, prunes, molasses, chicken, buttermilk

What's Lucky . . .

Lucky Numbers: 3, 5, 23

Best Months: February and November

Best Day of the Week: Wednesday

Best Month Days: 4, 5, 23

Lucky Charms: A rabbit's foot or a white candle.

Harmonious Signs for Relationships and Partnerships: Capricorn and Taurus

Spiritual Guides . . .

Star: Al Awa—Those with this star are often objects of others' desire.

Angel: Hamaliel—This angel governs logic and shows us what is real. His lessons in personal ethics always improve our karma.

Guardian Angel: Plavwell—The guardian that gives power and strength to one's presence.

Spiritual Stone: Jasper—This stone may soothe bruised emotions.

✳ JUDITH'S INSIGHT ✳

Versatility is your greatest asset. Happiest doing many things at once, you're busy holding down the fort and propping up the sky. This creates a very interesting problem. Others feel free to burden you because you appear to be so capable. You are often disappointed, wishing others would rise to your high standards. The person who fails you the most is you because you expect altogether too much of yourself.

You have a kind heart but can be hotheaded and complaining at times. The complaining part can trip you up. You love changes and may need to make many of them in your life: new clothes, new cars; you trade things in easily.

The yellow caution flag is waving when it comes to relationships. Romantic ties remain difficult for you. Committing to one for you may be more objectionable than having your teeth pulled. Getting you to decide to get married, live together, or even go on a second date will make your prospects crazy. After taking the dreaded plunge, you happily bond to your family with bands of steel. Once you're in, you give yourself totally to your spouse and children.

Loyal and dependable, you're the one that family and friends call when they need advice or help. A great listener, your wide-open ear even takes in strangers. Friends of friends you haven't even met call you because they've heard how understanding you can be. Unfortunately, because you can resent this, you're prone to mood swings and can easily snap at people with the least provocation.

In your career you will be the great communicator as a writer, director, telephone operator, computer analyst, and film critic.

✳ ✳ ✳

SEPTEMBER 6 VIRGO • The festivities and celebrations of the zodiac
August 23 at 6:00 A.M. to September 23 at 3:00 A.M. • NUMEROLOGY 6

Possessions and Desires . . .

Gem: Jasper—This stone could grant the bearer protection from sadness.

Flower: Iris—You are the one with an open ear for your friends.

Astral Color, Color Need, Apparel Color: Your Astral Color is Navy Blue—the color of style and refinement. Violet in your environment keeps you empathetic toward others. In your wardrobe, Light Blue gives you strength and determination.

Fragrance: Look for those classic scents that give you the feeling of fresh and sparkling clean, scents containing jasmine, ylang ylang, and roses.

Tree: Palm—You tend to be very healthy and creative.

Instruments: Tambourine, lyre

Composer: Schubert

Bird: Killdeer—This bird is usually found consorting with other species, and can adapt to any environment.

Symbol: Star—You are full of inner brightness and will stand out in any crowd. You will be seen as special.

Harmonious Health and Nutrition . . .

Health Scent: Orange Blossom—This scent may balance your mind, body, and soul.

Favorable Foods: Swiss chard, black figs, chocolate, beef, cottage cheese

What's Lucky . . .

Lucky Numbers: 3, 5, 42
Best Months: February and November
Best Day of the Week: Wednesday
Best Month Days: 6, 15, 24
Lucky Charms: A religious token or card from any religion.
Harmonious Signs for Relationships and Partnerships: Capricorn and Taurus

Spiritual Guides . . .

Star: Sumak al Azel—Those with this star are called upon to serve.

Angel: Hamaliel—This angel governs logic and shows us what is real. His lessons in personal ethics always improve our karma.

Guardian Angel: Michael—"Who is like God."

Spiritual Stone: Jasper—This stone may soothe bruised emotions.

✴ *JUDITH'S INSIGHT* ✴

You have a good head on your shoulders and learned to be very responsible at an early age. You have limitless sympathy for your fellow human beings. You enjoy helping others even though you complain that people take advantage of you. Sometimes you feel like a fish out of water, and because of drastic living changes, you never really settle in at the new place. It may be a different state or country, or perhaps the neighborhood has completely altered. You yearn for travel to exotic places but never seem to get around to it. Life seems boring without frequent challenges.

When it comes to relationships, you always secretly wish your mate was more romantic. At the same time, you'd die if anyone found out how mushy you are. You love freedom and adventure, so keep this in mind. You may experience a whirlwind courtship followed by a hasty marriage. Not too much later you may regret not giving the matter more thought and time.

Work for you must be stable and provide enough room to explore your creative side. This flair for innovation should translate into a career at a museum, theater, apparel design firm, or fragrance manufacturer. If you feel your urge to nurture is stronger, you may desire employment as a doctor, teacher, or day care provider. You are more likely to do many things because of your strong ambition and determination. Your lesson in life is learning patience. If it feels like your whole life is spent standing in line waiting for your share, you're correct. But look at it this way: you're in the right line for success. Just after you turn fifty you shoot to the top of your field—farther than you ever expected.

★ ★ ★

SEPTEMBER 7 VIRGO • The festivities and celebrations of the zodiac
August 23 at 6:00 A.M. to September 23 at 3:00 A.M. • NUMEROLOGY 7

Possessions and Desires . . .

Gem: Hyacinth—This stone might aid the memory.

Flower: Madder—You have a lot of attention being paid to you.

Astral Color, Color Need, Apparel Color: Your Astral Color is Navy Blue—the color of style and refinement. Violet in your environment keeps you empathetic toward others. In your wardrobe, Green is your power color for overcoming obstacles.

Fragrance: Look for those classic scents that give you the feeling of fresh and sparkling clean, scents containing jasmine, ylang ylang, and roses.

Tree: Pine—Your relationships tend to be harmonious, both emotionally and mentally.

Instrument: Cello

Composer: Mozart

Bird: Stork—Turkish bird, held in high esteem the world over. This bird is intelligent but may have strange tendencies.

Symbol: Wings—You are the source of balance in your world—this will bring you contentment.

Harmonious Health and Nutrition . . .

Health Scent: Almond—This scent may revitalize you and open you to greater possibilities.

Favorable Foods: Radishes, raspberries, chocolate, oysters, buttermilk

What's Lucky . . .

Lucky Numbers: 3, 5, 44

Best Months: February and November

Best Day of the Week: Wednesday

Best Month Days: 8, 17, 26

Lucky Charm: An old key.

Harmonious Signs for Relationships and Partnerships: Capricorn and Taurus

Spiritual Guides . . .

Star: Al Awa—Those with this star are often objects of others' desire.

Angel: Hamaliel—This angel governs logic and shows us what is real. His lessons in personal ethics always improve our karma.

Guardian Angel: Seraphim—An angel that brings love, light, and passion.

Spiritual Stone: Jasper—This stone may soothe bruised emotions.

✴ JUDITH'S INSIGHT ✴

Optimistic, steady, determined, and both mentally and physically capable, you can expect many accomplishments in life because you allow nothing to stand in your way. You may have years that seem excruciating to live through, but later on you will remember them as not so bad. Although you like to think of yourself as liberal, you have a strong conservative streak that refuses to be buried.

Make sure your surroundings are in order. You go ballistic when you put something on the table and later find it's disappeared. Many things that you see as a reflection of you, like clothes, house, garage, attic, or car, must be in perfect condition, even if they're twenty years old. You like a stable home and family, but you have to be the one that keeps it that way.

Love will be what you make it; luckily you're the one in control. If you ever lose what you see as your due authority, you become very upset. Your family can always rely on you in spite of how much heartache they sometimes give in return. Don't be blinded to your pushy and possessive nature.

When you decide to do things, you tend to overdo them. You have great organizational skills, but may have trouble balancing everyday demands made on you. Try not to overreact to daily pressures. A physical job that makes use of your strength may appeal to you. You are nurturing and probably attracted to careers in medicine; you would make an excellent emergency room nurse or plastic surgeon.

★ ★ ★

SEPTEMBER 8 VIRGO • The festivities and celebrations of the zodiac
August 23 at 6:00 A.M. to September 23 at 3:00 A.M. • NUMEROLOGY 8

Possessions and Desires . . .

Gem: Emerald—Those who carry this stone tend to be lucky in love.
Flower: Monkshood—You may wish you lived in times of great chivalry.
Astral Color, Color Need, Apparel Color: Your Astral Color is Navy Blue—the color of style and refinement. Violet in your environment keeps you empathetic toward others. In your wardrobe, Light Blue gives you strength and determination.
Fragrance: Look for those classic scents that give you the feeling of fresh and sparkling clean, scents containing jasmine, ylang ylang, and roses.
Tree: Holly—Beware that you are not carried away by your passionate nature. The only way to grow is to be open to new experiences.
Instruments: Violin, tympanum
Composer: Gluck
Bird: Goldfinch—These gentle creatures can seem moody, especially in unsettled weather.
Symbol: Star—You are full of inner brightness and will stand out in any crowd. You will be seen as special.

Harmonious Health and Nutrition . . .

Health Scent: Lavender—This scent might lead others to trust you and make you patient.
Favorable Foods: Sorrel, huckleberries, raw sugar, chicken, cottage cheese

What's Lucky . . .

Lucky Numbers: 3, 5, 36
Best Months: February and November
Best Day of the Week: Wednesday
Best Month Days: 9, 18, 27
Lucky Charm: Red ribbon in your wallet or doorway
Harmonious Signs for Relationships and Partnerships: Capricorn and Taurus

Spiritual Guides . . .

Star: Al Awa—Those with this star are often objects of others' desire.
Angel: Hamaliel—This angel governs logic and shows us what is real. His lessons in personal ethics always improve our karma.
Guardian Angel: Gabriel—"God is my strength."
Spiritual Stone: Jasper—This stone may soothe bruised emotions.

✶ JUDITH'S INSIGHT ✶

You're a terrific person! Given your many abilities, you're on the express elevator right up to the top. You are intelligent and know how to make the most of your challenging personality. You are wise beyond your years; people are drawn to your way of thinking. Please remember that energy is a flow that you have to keep in motion. When it comes to your work, home, or play, don't ever impede your own momentum.

Some say you're nosy—you see it as a healthy curiosity and thirst for knowledge. You may want to get paid for this quality. Work as an investigator, research scientist, paralegal, or creative director may find you. You are a dependable employer; your crew soon learns how to keep you happy. When your employees disappoint you, though, sometimes you may be so grouchy that you frighten yourself.

You desire constant change and attention in romance. Find a mate who takes life as seriously as you, or you'll be very frustrated much of the time. You have a dry wit and great sense of humor, but use them sparingly. Your family may subject you to lots of pressure, and you tend to "adopt" your friends. Remember to create reasonable boundaries, or other people will press you beneath the weight of their need.

Give yourself some slack every now and then. You are a stylish perfectionist who is seldom satisfied. Lighten up! Leave the dishes in the sink or let the grass grow if it means getting more enjoyment out of today.

✶ ✶ ✶

SEPTEMBER 9 VIRGO • The festivities and celebrations of the zodiac
August 23 at 6:00 A.M. to September 23 at 3:00 A.M. • NUMEROLOGY 9

Possessions and Desires . . .

Gem: Jasper—This stone could grant the bearer protection from sadness.

Flower: Monkshood—You may wish you lived in times of great chivalry.

Astral Color, Color Need, Apparel Color: Your Astral Color is Navy Blue—the color of style and refinement. Violet in your environment keeps you empathetic toward others. In your wardrobe, Green is your power color for overcoming obstacles.

Fragrance: Look for those classic scents that give you the feeling of fresh and sparkling clean, scents containing jasmine, ylang ylang, and roses.

Tree: Holly—Beware that you are not carried away by your passionate nature. The only way to grow is to be open to new experiences.

Instruments: Violin, tympanum

Composer: Gluck

Bird: Robin—the most sociable of all birds, with the ability to create quick friendships. It also can easily adapt to any home. When it wants something, it has the tendency to try to snatch it.

Symbol: Anchor—This tranquil symbol signifies stability and strength, and stands for strong commitments in relationships.

Harmonious Health and Nutrition . . .

Health Scent: Lavender—This scent might lead others to trust you and make you patient.

Favorable Foods: Parsnips, cherries, molasses, brains, eggs

What's Lucky . . .

Lucky Numbers: 3, 5, 81

Best Months: February and November

Best Day of the Week: Wednesday

Best Month Days: 9, 18, 27

Lucky Charms: A U.S. coin or a bill of any amount from the year you were born.

Harmonious Signs for Relationships and Partnerships: Capricorn and Taurus

Spiritual Guides . . .

Star: Al Awa—Those with this star are often objects of others' desire.

Angel: Hamaliel—This angel governs logic and shows us what is real. His lessons in personal ethics always improve our karma.

Guardian Angel: Gabriel—"God is my strength."

Spiritual Stone: Jasper—This stone may soothe bruised emotions.

✳ JUDITH'S INSIGHT ✳

If you could muster enough belief in yourself, you would be the perfect athlete. People stare at you for one reason or another. It goes beyond your well-groomed outer appearance. Was that you on the cover of that fashion or news magazine? You would love it if you could find a job where they paid you for ideas. You'd be a millionaire ten times over! However, the next time you go to work you know you'll be doing something physical. For example, you could be a personal trainer.

Romance for you takes energy. You can be loyal to the right someone, but until then, you're a shameless flirt who dashes in and out of relationships. Use your own insights to write or create a book like this. Your intuition is one of your strongest assets. Right now this may be a dream, but a great work waits inside. One day you will let it out.

You are passionate when you speak or write, molding feelings into strong sentences. People around you know you understand their meaning. You would make an excellent counselor. Listen closely for opportunity to tap you out a coded message concerning a second or third career. You could be someone who has "postal worker" on the bottom of your résumé and "best-selling author" at the top.

Okay, some see you as a know-it-all; so what if it's true? Learn to give others only what they can handle of your wisdom. This is particularly good advice when dealing with your spouse or the constant stream of *I told you so's* could be the grounds for your divorce. Surprisingly, you may be happier if you jump into things without thinking them through completely.

✳ ✳ ✳

SEPTEMBER 10
VIRGO • The festivities and celebrations of the zodiac
August 23 at 6:00 A.M. to September 23 at 3:00 A.M. • NUMEROLOGY 1

Possessions and Desires . . .

Gem: Jasper—This stone could grant the bearer protection from sadness.

Flower: Tear Drop—You are happier when you are patient.

Astral Color, Color Need, Apparel Color: Your Astral Color is Navy Blue—the color of style and refinement. Violet in your environment keeps you empathetic toward others. In your wardrobe, Light Blue gives you strength and determination.

Fragrance: Look for those classic scents that give you the feeling of fresh and sparkling clean, scents containing jasmine, ylang ylang, and roses.

Tree: Walnut—You are unusually helpful and always looking for constant changes in your life.

Instruments: Oboe, flute, clarinet, piano, French horn, organ, piccolo

Composer: Böhm

Bird: Cuckoo—A good flyer and very seldom a quitter. Many seem more independent than they actually are; yearn for more nurturing than one would expect.

Symbol: Crown—the universal sign of dignity.

Harmonious Health and Nutrition . . .

Health Scent: Strawberry—Soothing by nature, the strawberry promotes self-esteem and encourages love.

Favorable Foods: Turnips, black figs, raw sugar, barley, buttermilk

What's Lucky . . .

Lucky Numbers: 3, 5, 28
Best Months: February and November
Best Day of the Week: Wednesday
Best Month Days: 1, 10, 19, 28
Lucky Charm: A new penny in your shoe
Harmonious Signs for Relationships and Partnerships: Capricorn and Taurus

Spiritual Guides . . .

Star: Al Awa—Those with this star are often objects of others' desire.

Angel: Hamaliel—This angel governs logic and shows us what is real. His lessons in personal ethics always improve our karma.

Guardian Angel: Malachi—"Messenger of Jehovah."

Spiritual Stone: Jasper—This stone may soothe bruised emotions.

✳ *JUDITH'S INSIGHT* ✳

You have mind like a laser light. There is nothing your executive abilities can't handle. You have a well-balanced intellect and a well-rounded personality. If you don't earn your living by thinking, you're likely to work at jobs that require mechanical or technical skills. You only need to put your hands on a failing device to get it to work better than the designer intended.

Kind and giving, you readily make friends. Acquaintances, however, may blanch at your cutting and hurtful remarks. When your friends need you, you are loyal and comforting in the beginning, but you lack patience if they don't recover as quickly as you would.

Government or accounting positions look good. Your taste and organizational skills may be better suited for the fashion industry. Sing out your love for music, but limit it to the shower. You may be better off as the person who comes up with the lyrics.

When the first gray hairs and facial lines appear, you overreact. Spending money you may not have won't impress people for long or bring back your youth. Use that well-developed sense of humor to help you relax and accept normal changes.

Relationships come easily to you. However, once you enter into one, the thrill usually leaves. Small things about your mate irritate you. Make sure you really get to know your partner before you marry. The more adjusting you do before the bond, the less friction there will be after. Choose a partner for other reasons than how cute you two look together in photos.

★ ★ ★

SEPTEMBER 11 VIRGO • The festivities and celebrations of the zodiac
August 23 at 6:00 A.M. to September 23 at 3:00 A.M. • NUMEROLOGY 2

Possessions and Desires . . .

Gem: Jasper—This stone could grant the bearer protection from sadness.

Flower: Cranberry—You may need to learn the only cure for heartache is to accept the bitter with the sweet.

Astral Color, Color Need, Apparel Color: Your Astral Color is Navy Blue—the color of style and refinement. Violet in your environment keeps you empathetic toward others. In your wardrobe, Green is your power color for overcoming obstacles.

Fragrance: Look for those classic scents that give you the feeling of fresh and sparkling clean, scents containing jasmine, ylang ylang, and roses.

Tree: Maple—You have both great stability and flashes of intuition.

Instruments: Pipe organ, cymbal, drum

Composers: Handel, Johann Sebastian Bach

Bird: Killdeer—This bird is usually found consorting with other species, and can adapt to any environment.

Symbol: Cross—the symbol of self-sacrifice and reconciliation.

Harmonious Health and Nutrition . . .

Health Scent: Apple—A vivacious scent encouraging energy. Will help you to be more creative, intuitive and positive.

Favorable Foods: Mushrooms, cranberries, chocolate, liver, cottage cheese

What's Lucky . . .

Lucky Numbers: 2, 3, 5
Best Months: February and November
Best Day of the Week: Wednesday
Best Month Days: 2, 11, 20, 29
Lucky Charms: Two 50-cent pieces. Give someone else one of them.

Harmonious Signs for Relationships and Partnerships: Capricorn and Taurus

Spiritual Guides . . .

Star: Al Awa—Those with this star are often objects of others' desire.

Angel: Hamaliel—This angel governs logic and shows us what is real. His lessons in personal ethics always improve our karma.

Guardian Angel: St. John—This angel simplifies that which is complicated.

Spiritual Stone: Jasper—This stone may soothe bruised emotions.

✶ JUDITH'S INSIGHT ✶

You are a faithful and ardent mate, and your scrupulous and principled approach to life is award-winning. Once committed to a task, you dedicate yourself to it. Your biggest hindrance is your overactive mind. A high achiever, you sometimes go overboard in setting impossible goals.

As you mature, you learn to drink up knowledge. You're most comfortable in a natural setting, and would choose to relax sitting by a pond or picnicking in the woods, roasting marshmallows over a campfire. These opportunities are rare, but with proper planning you fit them into your busy lifestyle.

You may work for the government in the sciences, perhaps chemistry, but you may supplement your income through journalism, editing, or proofreading. Your unrehearsed and outspoken responses get you into trouble at times, and you could lose a friend by speaking harshly. Put more energy into the rewarding relationships, and let the unworkable ones go. Beware of quick responses and look before you leap.

LIsten to your inner self. It's time to believe in yourself more than you do. There's nothing to be feared from your own insight. You are a genuinely good person and a caring soul. It will take time for you to recognize this. Other people already do.

✷ ✷ ✷

SEPTEMBER 12 VIRGO • The festivities and celebrations of the zodiac
August 23 at 6:00 A.M. to September 23 at 3:00 A.M. • NUMEROLOGY 3

Possessions and Desires . . .

Gem: Jasper—This stone could grant the bearer protection from sadness.

Flower: Jonquil—Your affections tend to be readily returned.

Astral Color, Color Need, Apparel Color: Your Astral Color is Navy Blue—the color of style and refinement. Violet in your environment keeps you empathetic toward others. In your wardrobe, Light Blue gives you strength and determination.

Fragrance: Look for those classic scents that give you the feeling of fresh and sparkling clean, scents containing jasmine, ylang ylang, and roses.

Tree: Elm—You have willpower, strength, and the ability to stand alone.

Instrument: Trombone

Composers: Verdi, Mendelssohn, Schumann

Bird: Cuckoo—A good flyer and very seldom a quitter. Many seem more independent than they actually are; yearn for more nurturing than one would expect.

Symbol: Wreath—You have been crowned with a special personality. You are strong but extremely compassionate.

Harmonious Health and Nutrition . . .

Health Scent: Rose—This scent will lead you to passionate thoughts and make you feel warm inside.

Favorable Foods: Brussels sprouts, pineapple, chocolate, chicken, buttermilk

What's Lucky . . .

Lucky Numbers: 3, 5, 66
Best Months: February and November
Best Day of the Week: Wednesday
Best Month Days: 3, 12, 21, 30
Lucky Charm: A pen that someone else has already used.
Harmonious Signs for Relationships and Partnerships: Capricorn and Taurus

Spiritual Guides . . .

Star: Al Awa—Those with this star are often objects of others' desire.

Angel: Hamaliel—This angel governs logic and shows us what is real. His lessons in personal ethics always improve our karma.

Guardian Angel: Johiel—This angel is a protector of all those with a humble heart.

Spiritual Stone: Jasper—This stone may soothe bruised emotions.

✶ JUDITH'S INSIGHT ✶

Your splendid mind is just one of your great qualities. When a situation calls for good judgment, smart advice, or clever decisions, you're *the* person to ask. Much of the time, you're right. You can be expected to resolve disputes honestly, firmly, clearly, and without prejudice. You remember thousands of details and are skilled at planning. Good jobs for you are computer programmer, architect, set designer, or engineer. You should also explore law or a related career. Change excites you in your earlier years.

You won't find it difficult making friends. People struggle to get closer to you because of your attractive personality and good looks. Getting stuck in one place frightens you, but a more stable life offers a peace you've never known. You're a sweetheart when things are going your way: affectionate and caring to those around you. When misunderstandings occur, however, your stubborn temperament emerges.

Determined and assertive, you set clear goals. Huge obstacles seem to suddenly drop out of the sky, usually landing on your head. For a while you're dazed, but when the dust settles, you get right back on track. Others can count on you for comfort. Why are you surprised when your abruptness is met with disaster?

There are so many jobs you can see yourself doing that choosing the best is daunting. Eventually you discover the secret to your own happiness is to have more than one. You may work nine to five for someone else and turn a favorite hobby into a moneymaking sideline.

You have no trouble finding mates. Staying happy with them may be a problem. You have a habit of being too critical, but you will grow out of that. When you do, love tends to turn into a fairytale of love.

SEPTEMBER 13 VIRGO • The festivities and celebrations of the zodiac
August 23 at 6:00 A.M. to September 23 at 3:00 A.M. • NUMEROLOGY 4

Possessions and Desires . . .

Gem: Hyacinth—This stone might aid the memory.

Flower: Love-in-a-mist—Your emotions usually are an unknown land you need to explore.

Astral Color, Color Need, Apparel Color: Your Astral Color is Navy Blue—the color of style and refinement. Violet in your environment keeps you empathetic toward others. In your wardrobe, Green is your power color for overcoming obstacles.

Fragrance: Look for those classic scents that give you the feeling of fresh and sparkling clean, scents containing jasmine, ylang ylang, and roses.

Tree: Cherry—You will find yourself faced with constant new emotional awakenings.

Instruments: Bass, clarinet

Composers: Haydn, Wagner

Bird: Stork—Turkish bird, held in high esteem the world over. This bird is intelligent but may have strange tendencies.

Symbol: Star—You are full of inner brightness and will stand out in any crowd. You will be seen as special.

Harmonious Health and Nutrition . . .

Health Scent: Vanilla—This scent will fill you with a feeling of cleanliness and stability.

Favorable Foods: Celery, cranberries, raw sugar, liver, cottage cheese

What's Lucky . . .

Lucky Numbers: 3, 5, 67

Best Months: February and November

Best Day of the Week: Wednesday

Best Month Days: 4, 13, 22, 31

Lucky Charm: A piece of material cut from something in your home.

Harmonious Signs for Relationships and Partnerships: Capricorn and Taurus

Spiritual Guides . . .

Star: Al Awa—Those with this star are often objects of others' desire.

Angel: Hamaliel—This angel governs logic and shows us what is real. His lessons in personal ethics always improve our karma.

Guardian Angel: Uriel—This angel brings the light of God's guidance.

Spiritual Stone: Jasper—This stone may soothe bruised emotions.

✶ JUDITH'S INSIGHT ✶

You have a powerful body that you keep in great shape. Stop worrying that people are out to get you. If you wait until you get older to find courage, you may miss out on much. Try not to wince when people want to get close to you. You have an impressive mind and good judgment. You're honest and usually correct. You are unique and most likely a star athlete.

What you end up doing will shock some. Your secret desires are marketable skills. Some examples of work you'd be good at include building trades, clock-making, law, journalism, writing, inventing, or the merchant marine.

You make a excellent parent once you get over your self-absorbed phase. Unresolved childhood fears need sorting out. Getting older means growing up. You are amiable enough and lucky in love. You may have to choose between two or more wonderful partners who have an equal hold on your affections.

For you, a promise made is a promise kept. With your unusual style that yields surprising results, you enjoy exotic art. As you learn more of life's lessons, you work to help those who are less fortunate. Many different types of people are drawn to you. Your eclectic group of friends all regard you highly.

★ ★ ★

SEPTEMBER 14 VIRGO • The festivities and celebrations of the zodiac
August 23 at 6:00 A.M. to September 23 at 3:00 A.M. • NUMEROLOGY 5

Possessions and Desires . . .

Gem: Emerald—Those who carry this stone tend to be lucky in love.

Flower: Acacia—You will have more than your share of close friends in your life.

Astral Color, Color Need, Apparel Color: Your Astral Color is Navy Blue—the color of style and refinement. Violet in your environment keeps you empathetic toward others. In your wardrobe, Light Blue gives you strength and determination.

Fragrance: Look for those classic scents that give you the feeling of fresh and sparkling clean, scents containing jasmine, ylang ylang, and roses.

Tree: Apple—You are creative, full of joy, and nearly magical. You bring happiness.

Instruments: Viola, trumpet

Composer: Liszt

Bird: Goldfinch—These gentle creatures can seem moody, especially in unsettled weather.

Symbol: Triangle—You have the right combination of abilities.

Harmonious Health and Nutrition . . .

Health Scent: Peach—This scent may balance your good qualities so that they equal your charm.

Favorable Foods: Endive, black figs, chocolate, beef, goat's milk

What's Lucky . . .

Lucky Numbers: 3, 5, 14
Best Months: February and November
Best Day of the Week: Wednesday
Best Month Days: 4, 5, 23
Lucky Charms: A rabbit's foot or a white candle.
Harmonious Signs for Relationships and Partnerships: Capricorn and Taurus

Spiritual Guides . . .

Star: Al Awa—Those with this star are often objects of others' desire.

Angel: Hamaliel—This angel governs logic and shows us what is real. His lessons in personal ethics always improve our karma.

Guardian Angel: Plavwell—The guardian that gives power and strength to one's presence.

Spiritual Stone: Jasper—This stone may soothe bruised emotions

✷ JUDITH'S INSIGHT ✷

You are kindhearted and hotheaded. Once the bills are paid, you can be generous. You may live in two places, probably owning a vacation home or living in the suburbs with an apartment in the city. If you aren't moving every year, you are always getting different furniture. Even when you're new in town, your address book is packed. You need constant variety in cars, clothes, and friends.

There's a flashing yellow warning light when it comes to you and relationships. Those who have dated you can only wonder what they did to make you so completely avoid them afterward. They didn't know you were fussy, finicky, and fickle. You make some commitments along the way, but they usually don't last. If you do manage to find a partner who is as comfortable with change as you, you can be a faithful spouse. It will seem like you are both married to different people every month.

Employers love you; you're trustworthy, capable, and reliable. You are witty and fun to be with. Your soul desires a deep connection with religion or a spiritual movement. Beware of losing yourself in a cult. You can be a legal clerk, freelance magazine writer, telemarketer, scientist, or research assistant. No matter what type of company issues the checks, they tend to be big ones. Cash seems to fall out of the sky and into your pockets. Expect to be very secure by middle age.

✷ ✷ ✷

SEPTEMBER 15 VIRGO • The festivities and celebrations of the zodiac

August 23 at 6:00 A.M. to September 23 at 3:00 A.M. • NUMEROLOGY 6

Possessions and Desires . . .

Gem: Jasper—This stone could grant the bearer protection from sadness.

Flower: Rose Acacia—You tend to want to surround yourself with elegant things.

Astral Color, Color Need, Apparel Color: Your Astral Color is Navy Blue—the color of style and refinement. Violet in your environment keeps you empathetic toward others. In your wardrobe, Green is your power color for overcoming obstacles.

Fragrance: Look for those classic scents that give you the feeling of fresh and sparkling clean, scents containing jasmine, ylang ylang, and roses.

Tree: Palm—You tend to be very healthy and creative.

Instruments: Tambourine, lyre

Composer: Schubert

Bird: Cuckoo—A good flyer and very seldom a quitter. Many seem more independent than they actually are; yearn for more nurturing than one would expect.

Symbol: Crescent—You are more likely to be influenced by the phases of the moon. Your easygoing manner leads you to peaceful situations.

Harmonious Health and Nutrition . . .

Health Scent: Orange Blossom—This scent may balance your body, mind, and soul.

Favorable Foods: Watercress, cranberries, molasses, liver, eggs

What's Lucky . . .

Lucky Numbers: 3, 5, 6
Best Months: February and November
Best Day of the Week: Wednesday
Best Month Days: 6, 15, 24
Lucky Charms: A religious token or card from any religion.
Harmonious Signs for Relationships and Partnerships: Capricorn and Taurus

Spiritual Guides . . .

Star: Al Awa—Those with this star are often objects of others' desire.

Angel: Hamaliel—This angel governs logic and shows us what is real. His lessons in personal ethics always improve our karma.

Guardian Angel: Michael—"Who is like God."

Spiritual Stone: Jasper—This stone may soothe bruised emotions.

✷ JUDITH'S INSIGHT ✷

The world dumped itself on your shoulders at a very young age. Through it all, you learned to keep your head held high. You're never without three or four strays who look to you for assistance. They could be either animals or people. Your hobby could be helping people; you have time for little else. You are a ball of energy and as funny as a comic. You have talents that can be used in business; maybe you should start your own.

You seem to like doing things the hard way. You are lonely and wish with all your heart to have someone special. You attract needy people with your cloying personality. You usually find a solid commitment with a kindred spirit who loves you without making you feel drained.

You think too much and should seek a career that will keep your mind occupied. You would do very well as a law professor, court clerk, gossip columnist, or host of a radio call-in show.

You are always involved in volunteer activities. Everyone else on the PTA knows who to ask to bake eight dozen cookies at the last minute and chaperone the fifth-grade dance. Later in life you may make time for sports. You might pick golf because the space around you feels immense.

Most people enjoy when life is easy. You only have gears for uphill and are uncomfortable on downward slopes. Heaven forbid you should coast: something would snap. You are selflessly kind, which is rare, and you are one of the universe's gifts to the world.

✷ ✷ ✷

SEPTEMBER 16 VIRGO • The festivities and celebrations of the zodiac
August 23 at 6:00 A.M. to September 23 at 3:00 A.M. • NUMEROLOGY 7

Possessions and Desires . . .

Gem: Emerald—Those who carry this stone tend to be lucky in love.

Flower: Adonis Flos—You spend too much time dwelling on past hurts.

Astral Color, Color Need, Apparel Color: Your Astral Color is Navy Blue—the color of style and refinement. Violet in your environment keeps you empathetic toward others. In your wardrobe, Light Blue gives you strength and determination.

Fragrance: Look for those classic scents that give you the feeling of fresh and sparkling clean, scents containing jasmine, ylang ylang, and roses.

Tree: Sycamore—Yours is the ability to love, communicate honestly with others, and have lasting relationships.

Instrument: Harp

Composers: Gluck, Brahms

Bird: Killdeer—This bird is usually found consorting with other species, and can adapt to any environment.

Symbol: Heart—You are enthusiastic, empathetic, and full of generosity and love.

Harmonious Health and Nutrition . . .

Health Scent: Jasmine—This scent may make you more easygoing when you are stressed.

Favorable Foods: Parsnips, raspberries, raw sugar, oysters, cottage cheese

What's Lucky . . .

Lucky Numbers: 3, 5, 7
Best Months: February and November
Best Day of the Week: Wednesday
Best Month Days: 6, 15, 24
Lucky Charm: An old key.
Harmonious Signs for Relationships and Partnerships: Capricorn and Taurus

Spiritual Guides . . .

Star: Sumak al Azel—Those with this star are called upon to serve.

Angel: Hamaliel—This angel governs logic and shows us what is real. His lessons in personal ethics always improve our karma.

Guardian Angel: Raphael—This angel attends to all of your needs when you are looking for guidance.

Spiritual Stone: Jasper—This stone may soothe bruised emotions.

✶ JUDITH'S INSIGHT ✶

You are physically and mentally powerful; life is going to be an endless stream of accomplishments. You want to champion liberal causes, but your conservative friends make so much sense you guiltily agree with them. You like to have a place for everything and everything in its place. Others may see you as obsessively tidy, both on the job and in your appearance. Your hair always looks perfect. You put your outfits together with great flair.

Known for creating harmony out of chaos, you should consider a career in movies behind the scenes: as art director, set decorator, costume designer, or wardrobe person. If you're not ready for the big time, you may want to volunteer for a community theatrical company.

Pushy and possessive by nature, you can't stand to see things done in a half-baked manner. Keeping the balance in everyday life is sometimes difficult for you because you are very meticulous. Things simply must be a certain way, which you see as the right or only way.

You may raise the levels of stress for yourself and those around you. The warning whistle blows on the pressure-cooker when you try to enter into relationships. You are so set in your ways that you may experience difficulty finding a person who can understand you. You probably won't deviate much from the mental picture you have in your head of the proper mate. Eventually you will find your other half, but it may take longer than you hoped. This extended search will teach you your most-needed life lesson: patience. As usual, everything comes together for you.

✶ ✶ ✶

Possessions and Desires . . .

Gem: Jasper—This stone could grant the bearer protection from sadness.

Flower: Box (tree)—You have a very dry sense of humor and are not very outgoing.

Astral Color, Color Need, Apparel Color: Your Astral Color is Navy Blue—the color of style and refinement. Violet in your environment keeps you empathetic toward others. In your wardrobe, Green is your power color for overcoming obstacles.

Fragrance: Look for those classic scents that gives you the feeling of fresh and sparkling clean, scents containing jasmine, ylang ylang, and roses.

Tree: Pine—Your relationships tend to be harmonious, both emotionally and mentally.

Instrument: Cello

Composer: Mozart

Bird: Goldfinch—These gentle creatures can seem moody, especially in unsettled weather.

Symbol: Wings—You are the source of balance in your world—this will bring you contentment.

Harmonious Health and Nutrition . . .

Health Scent: Almond—This scent may revitalize you and open you to greater possibilities.

Favorable Foods: Asparagus, cranberries, chocolate, chicken, goat's milk

What's Lucky . . .

Lucky Numbers: 3, 5, 8

Best Months: February and November

Best Day of the Week: Wednesday

Best Month Days: 8, 17, 26

Lucky Charm: Red ribbon in your wallet or doorway

Harmonious Signs for Relationships and Partnerships: Capricorn and Taurus

Spiritual Guides . . .

Star: Caphir—People born under this star catch what they chase.

Angel: Hamaliel—This angel governs logic and shows us what is real. His lessons in personal ethics always improve our karma.

Guardian Angel: Seraphim—An angel that brings love, light, and passion.

Spiritual Stone: Jasper—This stone may soothe bruised emotions.

✴ JUDITH'S INSIGHT ✴

Intelligent and charismatic, you are always willing to lend a helping hand. You always want to learn new things. Your career choices reflect this, as you are inclined to work as a researcher, investigator, scientist, paralegal, or attorney.

You are a most dependable employee if the workplace is one that you enjoy. Your intuitive tendencies can be thrown off if your environment is not right. You are wise beyond your years. A very serious person, you should seek a mate who won't expect you to be too frivolous. Not to say you can't have a good time, but you need to ponder situations and are very calm emotionally. Any spouse of yours has to understand all sides of you.

Even if you know you're right most of the time, don't offer advice too often to family and friends. Sometimes they should learn lessons on their own, and they may become dependent on your telling them what to do. Hard feelings may arise. You like things to be perfect; you tastefully create your own world. Learn that nothing is perfect, and even perfect chaos sometimes can be a higher order.

You insist on harmony in all things: career, love, friends, your home, and family. Financially, it may take time for you to feel secure. You will learn that security is sometimes not what you have accumulated monetarily but what you have gained emotionally.

✴ ✴ ✴

SEPTEMBER 18 VIRGO • The festivities and celebrations of the zodiac

August 23 at 6:00 A.M. to September 23 at 3:00 A.M. • NUMEROLOGY 9

Possessions and Desires . . .

Gem: Jasper—This stone could grant the bearer protection from sadness.

Flower: Buttercup—You have more than the angels protecting you.

Astral Color, Color Need, Apparel Color: Your Astral Color is Navy Blue—the color of style and refinement. Violet in your environment keeps you empathetic toward others. In your wardrobe, Light Blue gives you strength and determination.

Fragrance: Look for those classic scents that give you the feeling of fresh and sparkling clean, scents containing jasmine, ylang ylang, and roses.

Tree: Holly—Beware that you are not carried away by your passionate nature. The only way to grow is to be open to new experiences.

Instruments: Violin, tympanum

Composer: Gluck

Bird: Robin—the most sociable of all birds, with the ability to create quick friendships. It also can easily adapt to any home. When it wants something, it has the tendency to try to snatch it.

Symbol: Anchor—This tranquil symbol signifies stability and strength, and stands for strong commitments in relationships.

Harmonious Health and Nutrition . . .

Health Scent: Lavender—This scent might lead others to trust you and make you patient.

Favorable Foods: Endive, strawberries, raw sugar, liver, eggs

What's Lucky . . .

Lucky Numbers: 3, 5, 81

Best Months: February and November

Best Day of the Week: Wednesday

Best Month Days: 9, 18, 27

Lucky Charms: A U.S. coin or a bill of any amount from the year you were born.

Harmonious Signs for Relationships and Partnerships: Capricorn and Taurus

Spiritual Guides . . .

Star: Al Awa—Those with this star are often objects of others' desire.

Angel: Hamaliel—This angel governs logic and shows us what is real. His lessons in personal ethics always improve our karma.

Guardian Angel: Gabriel—"God is my strength."

Spiritual Stone: Jasper—This stone may soothe bruised emotions.

✶ *JUDITH'S INSIGHT* ✶

A natural athlete, you are so energetic, you can't find enough ways to release it. You would be good at anything that requires a physically fit body. You have the knack for doing things quite well, and others think everything comes very easily to you.

You probably prefer to work at a job where you can use your mind. Your outward appearance may lead you into a career such as modeling, acting, or consulting in the beauty and glamour trade. You do have a good head on your shoulders, but you may have more success in life by showing off those shoulders.

Your passionate nature leads to large, mostly good, changes in your life. It may take you time to recognize this asset. You are a very wise person, and other people could benefit from what you know naturally. Your philosophy of life has the potential to open doors for others by giving them powerful insights and by teaching them kindness and understanding. If you have no desire to write or give speeches, you should at least keep a journal of your dreams, thoughts, and feelings. This emotional diary could be the basis of a completely different career from the one you are currently in. You may be considered a know-it-all because you're right most of the time. You must learn that some people don't always recognize wisdom, especially when it comes in such a good-looking package.

Playfully affectionate at times, you make a loyal mate in a committed relationship. Recognize the pressures you sometimes put on people because of your obsession with order. Relax your standards to a level that makes those around you comfortable.

★ ★ ★

SEPTEMBER 19 VIRGO • The festivities and celebrations of the zodiac
August 23 at 6:00 A.M. to September 23 at 3:00 A.M. • NUMEROLOGY 1

Possessions and Desires . . .

Gem: Jasper—This stone could grant the bearer protection from sadness.

Flower: Cabbage—You tend to focus too much on what's in it for you.

Astral Color, Color Need, Apparel Color: Your Astral Color is Navy Blue—the color of style and refinement. Violet in your environment keeps you empathetic toward others. In your wardrobe, Green is your power color for overcoming obstacles.

Fragrance: Look for those classic scents that give you the feeling of fresh and sparkling clean, scents containing jasmine, ylang ylang, and roses.

Tree: Walnut—You are unusually helpful and always looking for constant changes in your life.

Instruments: Oboe, flute, clarinet, piano, French horn, organ, piccolo

Composer: Böhm

Bird: Killdeer—This bird is usually found consorting with other species, and can adapt to any environment.

Symbol: Crown—the universal sign of dignity.

Harmonious Health and Nutrition . . .

Health Scent: Strawberry—Soothing by nature, the strawberry promotes self-esteem and encourages love.

Favorable Foods: Parsley, black figs, molasses, chicken, goat's milk

What's Lucky . . .

Lucky Numbers: 3, 5, 19
Best Months: February and November
Best Day of the Week: Wednesday
Best Month Days: 10, 19, 28
Lucky Charm: A new penny in your shoe.
Harmonious Signs for Relationships and Partnerships: Capricorn and Taurus

Spiritual Guides . . .

Star: Sumak al Azel—Those with this star are called upon to serve.

Angel: Hamaliel—This angel governs logic and shows us what is real. His lessons in personal ethics always improve our karma.

Guardian Angel: Malachi—"Messenger of Jehovah."

Spiritual Stone: Jasper—This stone may soothe bruised emotions.

✸ JUDITH'S INSIGHT ✸

You are truthful and conscientious, almost pure, by nature. Others fail to see the real you and think of you as prudish. They mistake your intensity for coldness. Cautious when it comes to getting close to people, you constantly evaluate and reevaluate situations before you act. You can be a pain in the neck because you do everything by the book.

You make friends easily, but some take offense at your honesty and directness. Most people can't face the whole truth. A loyal and comforting friend, nobody is more dependable than you. You will succeed if you decide to work in jobs involving money such as a government clerk, banker, accountant, or cashier.

An avid reader, you feel that it's impossible to study too much. You never stop taking classes and will make a great scholar. Be sure to save some time to have fun. Your love of music may lead to a career there. You might not be able to sing but would make a fine songwriter.

The older you get, the more important your appearance will become. Vanity could be your weakness. You may have a strong desire to travel. You were the kid sitting over a microscope or taking apart a computer. Your attraction to nature may lead you into hobbies like flower arranging, gardening, and environmental activism.

When it comes to relationships, strong emotions make you uncomfortable and guarded. The more affection you receive, the happier you are. You wait for others to approach you. Be cautious about pushing others away. You must follow your intuition.

✸ ✸ ✸

SEPTEMBER 20
VIRGO • The festivities and celebrations of the zodiac
August 23 at 6:00 A.M. to September 23 at 3:00 A.M. • NUMEROLOGY 2

Possessions and Desires . . .

Gem: Hyacinth—This stone might aid the memory.

Flower: China Pink—It takes time, but your wishes do come true.

Astral Color, Color Need, Apparel Colors: Your Astral Color is Navy Blue—the color of style and refinement. Violet in your environment keeps you empathetic toward others. In your wardrobe, Light Blue gives you strength and determination.

Fragrance: Look for those classic scents that give you the feeling of fresh and sparkling clean, scents containing jasmine, ylang ylang, and roses.

Tree: Maple—You have both great stability and flashes of intuition.

Instruments: Pipe organ, cymbal, drum

Composers: Handel, Johann Sebastian Bach

Bird: Cuckoo—A good flyer and very seldom a quitter. Many seem more independent than they actually are; yearn for more nurturing than one would expect.

Symbol: Cross—the symbol of self-sacrifice and reconciliation.

Harmonious Health and Nutrition . . .

Health Scent: Apple—A vivacious scent encouraging energy. Will help you to be more creative, intuitive and positive.

Favorable Foods: Celery, huckleberries, molasses, beef, buttermilk

What's Lucky . . .

Lucky Numbers: 3, 5, 20

Best Months: February and November

Best Day of the Week: Wednesday

Best Month Days: 2, 11, 20, 29

Lucky Charms: Two 50-cent pieces. Give someone else one of them.

Harmonious Signs for Relationships and Partnerships: Capricorn and Taurus

Spiritual Guides . . .

Star: Al Awa—Those with this star are often objects of others' desire.

Angel: Hamaliel—This angel governs logic and shows us what is real. His lessons in personal ethics always improve our karma.

Guardian Angel: Uriel—This angel brings the light of God's guidance.

Spiritual Stone: Jasper—This stone may soothe bruised emotions.

✴ JUDITH'S INSIGHT ✴

Many may see you as shy, but you love being noticed. In love, you long for stability and security. You go out of your way to understand others, and you should look for a partner who could understand you. Take time selecting that special someone. Later in life you learn that love is not always neat and orderly the way you would like it.

You have an eye for fine things and are drawn to excitement of any kind. The older you get, the more confident and determined you seem. You seek adventure in your own way. Your love of nature and the unusual should make you a great camper, and you may have the desire to climb mountains or sail around the world.

Plan a career in journalism, research, or law. You would make an excellent paralegal. Because of your love of travel and nature, anthropology fascinates you. Stay out of other people's way, and at the same time, be careful not to trip over your own feet.

As much as you explore the world and all it has to offer, it will be your home that is your palace.

✴ ✴ ✴

SEPTEMBER 21 VIRGO • The festivities and celebrations of the zodiac

August 23 at 6:00 A.M. to September 23 at 3:00 A.M. • NUMEROLOGY 3

Possessions and Desires . . .

Gem: Jasper—This stone could grant the bearer protection from sadness.

Flower: Cornflower—You have an abundance of inner riches.

Astral Color, Color Need, Apparel Color: Your Astral Color is Navy Blue—the color of style and refinement. Violet in your environment keeps you empathetic toward others. In your wardrobe, Green is your power color for overcoming obstacles.

Fragrance: Look for those classic scents that give you the feeling of fresh and sparkling clean, scents containing jasmine, ylang ylang, and roses.

Tree: Elm—You have willpower, strength, and the ability to stand alone.

Instrument: Trombone

Composers: Verdi, Mendelssohn, Schumann

Bird: Killdeer—This bird is usually found consorting with other species, and can adapt to any environment.

Symbol: Wreath—You have been crowned with a special personality. You are strong but extremely compassionate.

Harmonious Health and Nutrition . . .

Health Scent: Rose—This scent will lead you to passionate thoughts and make you feel warm inside.

Favorable Foods: Swiss chard, pineapple, raw sugar, liver, buttermilk

What's Lucky . . .

Lucky Numbers: 3, 5, 12
Best Months: February and November
Best Day of the Week: Wednesday
Best Month Days: 3, 12, 21, 30

Lucky Charm: A pen that someone else has already used.

Harmonious Signs for Relationships and Partnerships: Capricorn and Taurus

Spiritual Guides . . .

Star: Caphir—People born under this star catch what they chase.

Angel: Hamaliel—This angel governs logic and shows us what is real. His lessons in personal ethics always improve our karma.

Guardian Angel: Johiel—This angel is a protector of all those with a humble heart.

Spiritual Stone: Jasper—This stone may soothe bruised emotions.

✳ JUDITH'S INSIGHT ✳

Intrigued with any knowledge you can drink up, you make the perfect student, even if you never expand your formal education. You have more hidden talent than you know. You may seem egotistical and have bouts of low self-esteem.

Your polite charm attracts others to you. Unfortunately, you should avoid some of them. You always look great and are really a very tender soul. Avoid falling victim to your moods and appearing cranky.

Your ability to have all your ducks in a row at times makes it easy for you to adapt to most working environments, especially those in accounting, law, journalism, or business. Even if it's counting change, you have a knack with numbers. As a general rule, you love money, and it wouldn't be surprising for your career to be centered on it.

Impeccable taste in style and fashion, you love being dressed in a sharp suit or outfit. A born critic, you take on that role even when no one asks. Lucky in love, you have a certain sweetness and charm that attracts prospective partners to you. Your lesson in life: learn when to walk and when to run.

✳ ✳ ✳

SEPTEMBER 22 VIRGO • The festivities and celebrations of the zodiac
August 23 at 6:00 A.M. to September 23 at 3:00 A.M. • NUMEROLOGY 4

Possessions and Desires . . .

Gem: Emerald—Those who carry this stone tend to be lucky in love.

Flower: Primrose—You will never lose sight of the simple pleasures of childhood.

Astral Color, Color Need, Apparel Color: Your Astral Color is Navy Blue—the color of style and refinement. Violet in your environment keeps you empathetic toward others. In your wardrobe, Light Blue gives you strength and determination.

Fragrance: Look for those classic scents that give you the feeling of fresh and sparkling clean, scents containing jasmine, ylang ylang, and roses.

Tree: Cherry—You will find yourself faced with constant new emotional awakenings.

Instruments: Bass, clarinet

Composers: Haydn, Wagner

Bird: Goldfinch—These gentle creatures can seem moody, especially in unsettled weather.

Symbol: Star—You are full of inner brightness and will stand out in any crowd. You will be seen as special.

Harmonious Health and Nutrition . . .

Health Scent: Vanilla—This scent will fill you with a feeling of cleanliness and stability.

Favorable Foods: Endive, raspberries, chocolate, chicken, cottage cheese

What's Lucky . . .

Lucky Numbers: 3, 5, 44

Best Months: February and November

Best Day of the Week: Wednesday

Best Month Days: 4, 13, 22, 31

Lucky Charm: A piece of material cut from something in your home.

Harmonious Signs for Relationships and Partnerships: Capricorn and Taurus

Spiritual Guides . . .

Star: Al Awa—Those with this star are often objects of others' desire.

Angel: Hamaliel—This angel governs logic and shows us what is real. His lessons in personal ethics always improve our karma.

Guardian Angel: St. Thomas—This angel brings affection from others and encourages you in all that you do.

Spiritual Stone: Jasper—This stone may soothe bruised emotions.

✷ JUDITH'S INSIGHT ✷

You stand out in a crowd. Strong, sensible, and a bit headstrong, you must be cautious about how people are perceiving you. Sometimes it may not be enough to mean well. You have many talents, and your determination takes you places. The possibilities are endless.

You are creative to some degree and may do very well in theater, engineering, teaching, or government. You make an excellent parent because you're so good to your own. Learn to conquer the urge toward self-centeredness. There is no doubt you'll have stages in your life when your own needs will blind you to the needs of others.

In relationships of any kind, you will be the more eager to please and easygoing. You need things to have rules and follow an established order. You should always agree to find a balance acceptable for everyone involved. Your word is law. You are just as good at making promises as following them through.

Known for your different style in doing things, you like unique art and insist on a very well-organized home. Your living arrangements, relationships, and family are very important to you. You can take things very seriously. You are a sensitive soul and subject yourself to way more stress than you should. When you begin to feel overwhelmed, step back and free your thoughts before you lose perspective.

✷ ✷ ✷

SEPTEMBER 23 VIRGO • The festivities and celebrations of the zodiac
August 23 at 6:00 A.M. to September 23 at 3:00 A.M. • NUMEROLOGY 5

Possessions and Desires . . .

Gem: Jasper—This stone could grant the bearer protection from sadness.

Flower: Ivy Spig—You may spend so much time trying to please others that you forget to take care of you.

Astral Color, Color Need, Apparel Color: Your Astral Color is Crimson, which reflects your ability to nurture. Yellow in your environment stimulates and exhilarates you. In your wardrobe, Brown brings you stability.

Fragrance: Look for those classic scents that give you the feeling of fresh and sparkling clean, scents containing jasmine, ylang ylang, and roses.

Tree: Apple—You are creative, full of joy, and nearly magical. You bring happiness.

Instruments: Viola, trumpet

Composer: Liszt

Bird: Stork—Turkish bird, held in high esteem the world over. This bird is intelligent but may have strange tendencies.

Symbol: Triangle—You have the right combination of abilities.

Harmonious Health and Nutrition . . .

Health Scent: Peach—This scent may balance your good qualities so that they equal your charm.

Favorable Foods: Watercress, raspberries, molasses, beef, cottage cheese

What's Lucky . . .

Lucky Numbers: 3, 5, 32

Best Months: February and November

Best Day of the Week: Wednesday

Best Month Days: 4, 5, 23

Lucky Charms: A rabbit's foot or a white candle.

Harmonious Signs for Relationships and Partnerships: Capricorn and Taurus

Spiritual Guides . . .

Star: Al Awa—Those with this star are often objects of others' desire.

Angel: Hamaliel—This angel governs logic and shows us what is real. His lessons in personal ethics always improve our karma.

Guardian Angel: Plavwell—The guardian that gives power and strength to one's presence.

Spiritual Stone: Jasper—This stone may soothe bruised emotions.

✶ JUDITH'S INSIGHT ✶

You have a kind heart and a warm soul combined with a hair-trigger temper. A quality person who has a strong desire for success, you love frequent changes, especially in your home. You can never get your furniture quite the way you want, and you rearrange rooms on a regular basis. A frequent shopper, you express who you are through your manner of dress. Every day you have a completely different style of clothing. Versatility is a recurring theme throughout your life.

Extremely flexible, you're capable of handling just about any predicament and command respect from others. You would do well in the legal profession. Your methodical and organized mind lends itself to research. You do tend to overanalyze at times, which results in your taking things too seriously. Balance and harmony are key. Usually, you get what you want, but not without expending a lot of effort.

Listen to that little voice inside your head more often. You were blessed with fine instincts for a reason.

No challenge is too great for you, and you'll have many to meet. You could be offered many career opportunities because of the quality of your work. At some time, you may want to write a book that could be published. Some of your work may make you famous. While you are struggling so to get ahead and keep up with the neighbors, be sure to take time to love and laugh. You are a person who thrives on work but still needs to fit in some enjoyment. Otherwise, what's the point of working so hard?

You put a lot of energy into everything you do including romance and love relationships. But you are one who needs a lot of attention. Keep this in mind when picking a mate.

✶ ✶ ✶

SEPTEMBER 24 LIBRA • The scales of justice

September 23 at 3:00 A.M. to October 23 at 12:00 P.M. • NUMEROLOGY 6

Possessions and Desires . . .

Gem: Diamond—This stone is thought to encourage harmony in relationships and gives strength to the troubled.

Flower: Cress—You like to be in control of your world.

Astral Color, Color Need, Apparel Color: Your Astral color is Crimson, which reflects your ability to nurture. Yellow in your environment stimulates and exhilarates you. In your wardrobe, Brown brings you stability.

Fragrance: Pick scents that are soft and not overwhelming, like eclectic mixtures of wildflowers.

Tree: Palm—You tend to be very healthy and creative.

Instruments: Tambourine, lyre

Composer: Schubert

Bird: Goldfinch—there are no less than forty-four species of the finch, from the dull and inviting, to the extraordinarily active and exquisite. This can sometimes be the most charming bird. These gentle creatures can be very shy in unsettled weather.

Symbol: Crescent—You are more likely to be influenced by the phases of the moon. Your easygoing manner leads you to peaceful situations.

Harmonious Health and Nutrition . . .

Health Scent: Orange Blossom—This scent may balance your body, mind, and soul.

Favorable Foods: Radishes, watermelon, wholewheat bread, walnuts

What's Lucky . . .

Lucky Numbers: 6, 9

Best Months: August and December

Best Day of the Week: Friday

Best Month Days: 6, 15, 24

Lucky Charms: A religious token or card from any religion.

Harmonious Signs for Relationships and Partnerships: Aquarius and Gemini

Spiritual Guides . . .

Star: Al Icliel—This is the star for those who easily submit to authority.

Angel: Zuriel—This angel lends us the power to find balance when we desperately need it.

Guardian Angel: Michael—"Who is like God."

Spiritual Stone: Sapphire—The stone of serenity and prosperity.

✶ JUDITH'S INSIGHT ✶

You have a great head on your shoulders, but you take responsibility too seriously. Why must you worry about everyone else's problems? Your family and friends are extremely important to you. But you often focus your intense concentration on problems for so long, you may miss the big picture.

You love drama in relationships. Stability and loyalty are equally important. Sometimes you like to stir the emotional pot and keep your partner on his or her toes. Usually you give love only after having received it. You yearn for freedom and adventure, but must have the security of knowing someone waits at home for you. Keep all this in mind when you choose a mate; you might forget and pick an unsuitable, inflexible partner.

No matter what career you choose, you'll earn a good living. Your early years will be steady and calm, but age loosens your thirst for freedom and spontaneity after a mild midlife crisis. You may work for one place faithfully for twenty years and then suddenly quit.

You have a creative way of nurturing and will do well as a teacher, day care provider, or doctor. Your love of art and fashion may lead you to a museum, an apparel or fragrance manufacturer, or the theater. It is most likely that you will have more than one career in your lifetime.

A good friend, you must check your temper at times. You are genuine, well-organized, and well-prepared in all your dealings. The more stable you can make your environment, the more settled you find your emotions.

✶ ✶ ✶

SEPTEMBER 25
LIBRA • The scales of justice

September 23 at 3:00 A.M. to October 23 at 12:00 P.M. • NUMEROLOGY 7

Possessions and Desires . . .

Gem: Agate—This stone may promote health and lead you to a long life.
Flower: Crocus—You love it when your home is in harmony.
Astral Color, Color Need, Apparel Color: Your Astral color is Crimson, which reflects your ability to nurture. Yellow in your environment stimulates and exhilarates you. In your wardrobe, Rose gives you balance and harmony.
Fragrance: Pick scents that are soft and not overwhelming, like eclectic mixtures of wildflowers.
Tree: Sycamore—The ability to have love, communicate with others, and have lasting relationships.
Instrument: Cello
Composers: Gluck, Brahms
Bird: Skylark—This handsome bird is beautiful when it sings. It always whistles while it works.
Symbol: Heart—You are enthusiastic, empathetic, and full of generosity and love.

Harmonious Health and Nutrition . . .

Health Scent: Jasmine—This scent may make you more easygoing when you are stressed.
Favorable Foods: Asparagus, prunes, wholewheat bread, Brazil nuts

What's Lucky . . .

Lucky Numbers: 6, 9
Best Months: August and December
Best Day of the Week: Friday
Best Month Days: 6, 15, 24
Lucky Charm: An old key.
Harmonious Signs for Relationships and Partnerships: Aquarius and Gemini

Spiritual Guides . . .

Star: Al Zubena—Those with this star often seek and find redemption.
Angel: Zuriel—This angel lends us the power to find balance when we desperately need it.
Guardian Angel: Raphael—This angel attends to all of your needs when you are looking for guidance.
Spiritual Stone: Sapphire—the stone of serenity and prosperity.

✴ JUDITH'S INSIGHT ✴

Positive, strong, and determined—both physically and mentally—you will accomplish much in life. Family and friends rely on you. Some expect you to meet all their needs. Make sure you don't take on more than you should. Relationships will be difficult because you want predictability at all times, as if you were following a script. It's impossible to live life with no surprises, and you'd be better off accepting the unexpected.

You have a pushy nature and need to be in control of your own life. Try to balance this by choosing your challenges, or everyday life will be very strenuous for you. You are too organized and prone to losing the big picture in an ocean of detail.

You are a snappy dresser and love it when people comment—which they often do—on your impeccable taste. There are several careers that you should find appealing. You would make a great nurse, computer analyst, actor, builder, or artist. What a range! There are so many different and competing sides to your personality, you do best if you use your abundant energy to further your ambitions. This is the key to unlocking your potential.

You are considerate, smart, and sweet. You are liberal minded, and there will be times in life you'll have so much freedom you'll feel uncomfortable. Stability and boundaries are needed much more than you realize.

✶ ✶ ✶

SEPTEMBER 26 LIBRA • The scales of justice

September 23 at 3:00 A.M. to October 23 at 12:00 P.M. • NUMEROLOGY 8

Possessions and Desires . . .

Gem: Chrysolite—This gem may help you clear your mind of sadness and worry.

Flower: Dock—You tend to be a very patient person.

Astral Color, Color Need, Apparel Color: Your Astral Color is Crimson, which reflects your ability to nurture. Yellow in your environment stimulates and exhilarates you. In your wardrobe, Brown brings you stability.

Fragrance: Pick scents that are soft and not overwhelming, like eclectic mixtures of wildflowers.

Tree: Pine—Your relationships tend to be harmonious, both emotionally and mentally.

Instrument: Cello

Composer: Mozart

Bird: Bobolink—This charming singer is equally good as a soloist or a member of an orchestra. It is a very romantic bird, most useful as an insect destroyer, and elegant, with beautiful feathers, and always pleasant to have around.

Symbol: Wings—You are the source of balance in your world—this will bring you contentment.

Harmonious Health and Nutrition . . .

Health Scent: Almond—This scent may revitalize you and open you to greater possibilities.

Favorable Foods: Carrots, bananas, whole-wheat bread, walnuts

What's Lucky . . .

Lucky Numbers: 6, 9

Best Months: August and December

Best Day of the Week: Friday

Best Month Days: 8, 17, 26

Lucky Charm: Red ribbon in your wallet or doorway.

Harmonious signs for Relationships and Partnerships: Aquarius and Gemini

Spiritual Guides . . .

Star: Al Zubena—Those with this star often seek and find redemption.

Angel: Zuriel—This angel lends us the power to find balance when we desperately need it.

Guardian Angel: Seraphim—An angel that brings love, light, and passion.

Spiritual Stone: Sapphire—the stone of serenity and prosperity.

✶ JUDITH'S INSIGHT ✶

An excellent student with fantastic grades, you are on a lifelong hunt for knowledge. You'd be a terrific investigator, researcher, scientist, and participant in any way in the legal profession. Try to put your other, creative side to good use even in jobs that require rigid adherence to set rules. Unless you have something to say, you don't speak. People like the sound of your voice.

You are a responsible employee, but may want to be as independent as possible. It wouldn't be surprising if you were gifted musically or if music played an important role in your life. You could be a creative director for a recording company or write music at some point in your life. You are a super executive and have no problem solving many puzzling business problems.

Your desire for constant change may help you at work, but it doesn't in relationships. Remember that energy is a flow that works best in a circuit; pick a mate who will send back what you give him or her. You're very affectionate and need that special someone to give you hugs, kisses, and sweet smiles every single day. Your family and friends will feel that they need to give you constant advice and may turn surly if you don't follow their suggestions. Don't feel pressured away from living your own life. You can be too much the perfectionist. Try to relax and leave the vacuuming and the gardening until tomorrow when you're more rested. Take time today to enjoy life more. You deserve it.

SEPTEMBER 27 LIBRA • The scales of justice

September 23 at 3:00 A.M. to October 23 at 12:00 P.M. • NUMEROLOGY 9

Possessions and Desires . . .

Gem: Beryl—This gem could be good for meditation and concentration.

Flower: Dandelion—You can be very in tune with the universe and have a strong intuition.

Astral Color, Color Need, Apparel Color: Your Astral Color is Crimson, which reflects your ability to nurture. Yellow in your environment stimulates and exhilarates you. In your wardrobe, Rose gives you balance and harmony.

Fragrance: Pick scents that are soft and not overwhelming, like eclectic mixtures of wildflowers.

Tree: Holly—Beware that you are not carried away by your passionate nature. The only way to grow is to be open to new experiences.

Instruments: Violin, tympanum

Composer: Gluck

Bird: Mockingbird—the most proficient minstrel in the world's orchestra; graceful and enthusiastic.

Symbol: Anchor—This tranquil symbol signifies stability and strength, and stands for strong commitments in relationships.

Harmonious Health and Nutrition . . .

Health Scent: Lavender—This scent might lead others to trust you and make you patient.

Favorable Foods: Celery, plums, whole-wheat bread, peanuts

What's Lucky . . .

Lucky Numbers: 6, 9

Best Months: August and December

Best Day of the Week: Friday

Best Month Days: 9, 18, 27

Lucky Charms: A U.S. coin or a bill of any amount from the year you were born.

Harmonious Signs for Relationships and Partnerships: Aquarius and Gemini

Spiritual Guides . . .

Star: Al Icliel—This is the star of those who easily submit to authority.

Angel: Zuriel—This angel lends us the power to find balance when we desperately need it.

Guardian Angel: Gabriel—"God is my strength."

Spiritual Stone: Sapphire—the stone of serenity and prosperity.

✳ JUDITH'S INSIGHT ✳

You want to be known for your mind, but a beauty like you stands out from the crowd like an ink spot on white carpeting. Learn to deal with admiration and attention—it will follow you all your life. Just don't let it go to your head that others are always fawning over you.

You could be a writer or philosopher because of your words of wisdom. In the game of life, this is your strong suit. You have a passionate personality that speaks volumes, and if you wanted to, you could have a career in professional sports.

People really enjoy your company and fall for your charm with the force of gravity. You may have a reputation of being conceited about how much you know. Though you offer many good opinions, those around may prefer you to keep your words of wisdom to yourself. Even if you're usually right, coming from you it's unwelcome.

Don't close any doors to possible careers because you don't really know what direction you want your life to take later on. Family and friends adore you for your amiable demeanor, and you have no problem keeping active friendships. Look for the best in everybody, and don't be forced to choose between groups of bickering friends.

✳ ✳ ✳

SEPTEMBER 28
LIBRA • The scales of justice

September 23 at 3:00 A.M. to October 23 at 12:00 P.M. • NUMEROLOGY 1

Possessions and Desires . . .

Gem: Diamond—This stone is thought to encourage harmony in relationships and gives strength to the troubled.

Flower: Gooseberry—You may spend so much time waiting for something better to happen that you miss what is good about your life.

Astral Color, Color Need, Apparel Color: Your Astral color is Crimson, which reflects your ability to nurture. Yellow in your environment stimulates and exhilarates you. In your wardrobe, Brown brings you stability.

Fragrance: Pick scents that are soft and not overwhelming, like eclectic mixtures of wildflowers.

Tree: Walnut—You are unusually helpful and always looking for constant changes in your life.

Instrument: Clarinet

Composer: Böhm

Bird: Hummingbird—This bird is delicate and graceful. It can remain still for hours, then dart off and be as busy as a bee.

Symbol: Crown—the universal sign of dignity.

Harmonious Health and Nutrition . . .

Health Scent: Strawberry—Soothing by nature, the strawberry promotes self-esteem and encourages love.

Favorable Foods: Corn, raspberries, whole-wheat bread, walnuts

What's Lucky . . .

Lucky Numbers: 6, 9

Best Months: August and December

Best Day of the Week: Friday

Best Month Days: 1, 10, 19

Lucky Charm: A new penny in your shoe.

Harmonious Signs for Relationships and Partnerships: Aquarius and Gemini

Spiritual Guides . . .

Star: Al Zubena—Those with this star often seek and find redemption.

Angel: Zuriel—This angel lends us the power to find balance when we desperately need it.

Guardian Angel: Malachi—"Messenger of Jehovah."

Spiritual Stone: Sapphire—the stone of serenity and prosperity.

✳ *JUDITH'S INSIGHT* ✳

Your mind is your greatest asset. With great focus and a well-rounded mind, you are equally good at cooking and changing the oil or tuning up the car. You would find success in employment in national or local government. Tax accounting would be a perfect career for you. Since you are such a great cook, you would make an excellent chef or restaurateur. Your refined taste and organizational skills are marketable. You won't have difficulty initiating and completing projects. Your love of work and long hours pay off down the road. Watch out for jealous coworkers. Your seemingly perfect ways can annoy others.

Making new friends is useful because you may lose some along the way with your bluntness. You need to learn patience and tact with others, particularly when they are in need of consolation. Should you decide to be a physician or nurse, you'll need to work on your bedside manner.

You're fond of music and may enjoy singing. Someone close to you could be heavily involved in music. As you get older you may develop an understanding that life isn't as serious as you previously believed. For you, looser is better.

You are romantically guarded; whoever wants to storm the castle you built around your heart had better be very patient. This is not necessarily a bad thing, it's just that relationships take time for you. You may meet many different types before you discover your perfect soul mate in a surprising situation. You are loyal and faithful when you finally make a commitment.

✳ ✳ ✳

SEPTEMBER 29   LIBRA • The scales of justice

September 23 at 3:00 A.M. to October 23 at 12:00 P.M. • NUMEROLOGY 2

Possessions and Desires . . .

Gem: Chrysolite—This gem may help you clear your mind of sadness and worry.

Flower: Guelderrose—You open up when you feel emotional warmth.

Astral Color, Color Need, Apparel Color: Your Astral Color is Crimson, which reflects your ability to nurture. Yellow in your environment stimulates and exhilarates you. In your wardrobe, Rose gives you balance and harmony.

Fragrance: Pick scents that are soft and not overwhelming, like eclectic mixtures of wildflowers.

Tree: Maple—You have great stability and flashes of intuition.

Instrument: Pipe organ

Composers: Handel, Johann Sebastian Bach

Bird: Stork—Storks have a strange type of intelligence that is easily misunderstood. The stork is known to have a pleasing nature.

Symbol: Cross—the symbol of self-sacrifice and reconciliation.

Harmonious Health and Nutrition . . .

Health Scent: Apple—You are creative and full of joy, and nearly magical. You bring happiness.

Favorable Foods: Peas, prunes, whole-wheat bread, almonds

What's Lucky . . .

Lucky Numbers: 6, 9

Best Months: August and December

Best Day of the Week: Friday

Best Month Days: 2, 11, 20

Lucky Charms: Two 50-cent pieces. Give someone else one of them.

Harmonious Signs for Relationships and Partnerships: Aquarius and Gemini

Spiritual Guides . . .

Star: Al Icliel—This is the star of those who easily submit to authority.

Angel: Zuriel—This angel lends us the power to find balance when we desperately need it.

Guardian Angel: St. John—This angel simplifies that which is complicated.

Spiritual Stone: Sapphire—the stone of serenity and prosperity.

✶ JUDITH'S INSIGHT ✶

You do whatever needs to be done in the exact manner it should be done. You are pleasant to deal with and happy just to be alive. Sports will play a role in your life, if only as a hobby. You are intrigued by how things work and what people who have come before have felt and thought. One of your most cherished goals is to extensively travel the country or the world.

You will probably be a bit headstrong at times. A career connected with nature is perfect—you so love the outdoors. Gardening, flower arranging, and being near rivers and other waterways also appeal to your senses. You might live on or near the sea and love it. Follow your interest in science and chemistry. You may have ambitions of becoming a doctor.

Your frank and judgmental nature could cost you a friend or two when you are younger. Fortunately, the years teach you to be a little more balanced in what you say. You may seem cold to some people, but that's only because you're so shy. To know you is to love you, and there aren't many as loyal as you. Relationships take time for you, and you don't feel settled unless you're part of a couple. Friendships, relationships, or partners always add something vital and necessary to your life. You will learn to listen to yourself more because your self-esteem grows as you get older.

You can be your own worst enemy and need to relax and enjoy life. You have psychic abilities and really do know the right direction to take. Listen to your heart: all the answers you need are deep in your soul.

✳ ✳ ✳

SEPTEMBER 30   LIBRA • The scales of justice

September 23 at 3:00 A.M. to October 23 at 12:00 P.M. • NUMEROLOGY 3

Possessions and Desires . . .

Gem: Ruby—This stone may lead you to energy, friendship, and happiness.
Flower: Bluebell—You are steadfast and constant in your emotions.
Astral Color, Color Need, Apparel Color: Your Astral Color is Crimson, which reflects your ability to nurture. Yellow in your environment stimulates and exhilarates you. In your wardrobe, Brown brings you stability.
Fragrance: Pick scents that are soft and not overwhelming, like eclectic mixtures of wildflowers.
Tree: Elm—You have willpower, strength, and the ability to stand alone.
Instrument: Trombone
Composers: Verdi, Mendelssohn, Schumann
Bird: Swan—Regarded as royal and sacred, this bird has the protective nature of a mother, and can become a furious fighter in the defense of its young.
Symbol: Wreath—You have been crowned with a special personality. You are strong but extremely compassionate.

Harmonious Health and Nutrition . . .

Health Scent: Rose—This scent will lead you to passionate thoughts and make you feel warm inside.
Favorable Foods: Spinach, cherries, whole-wheat bread, peanuts

What's Lucky . . .

Lucky Numbers: 6, 9
Best Months: August and December
Best Day of the Week: Friday
Best Month Days: 3, 12, 21
Lucky Charm: A pen that someone else has already used.
Harmonious Signs for Relationships and Partnerships: Aquarius and Gemini

Spiritual Guides . . .

Star: Al Icliel—This is the star of those who easily submit to authority.
Angel: Zuriel—This angel lends us the power to find balance when we desperately need it.
Guardian Angel: Johiel—This angel is a protector of all those with a humble heart.
Spiritual Stone: Sapphire—the stone of serenity and prosperity.

✶ JUDITH'S INSIGHT ✶

You welcome change and love to rearrange things. Your home is your place of security. Very good at juggling thousands of small details and talented in design, you would be a good architect, set designer, engineer, project manager, or computer programmer.

You are fascinated with the process of learning, and nothing escapes your interest. Extremely good at math, you may find job satisfaction working with accounting or numbers. You have a strong physical presence that others feed off. You accomplish more in one hour than most can in a day. You make things happen.

Watch out for your arrogance. People need patience from you most. Kind and open-minded with those close to you, you can also be compassionate and caring to strangers. You may become famous through your humanitarian efforts.

When it comes to romance, you know right away who you want but can never have him or her right away. Things take time, especially a relationship to last a lifetime. Your life's lesson is to wait with grace and balance.

Order and neatness are a must, but you don't want to be the one who keeps it that way. You are a good person who would do well to understand that others don't think or rush into situations as quickly as you. Use your intuition. You know the right answers are inside you, but they usually seem too good to be true. You can be a success at work if you choose to make the effort and are patient. Remember to always be flexible, and you will get where you want to go.

✶ ✶ ✶

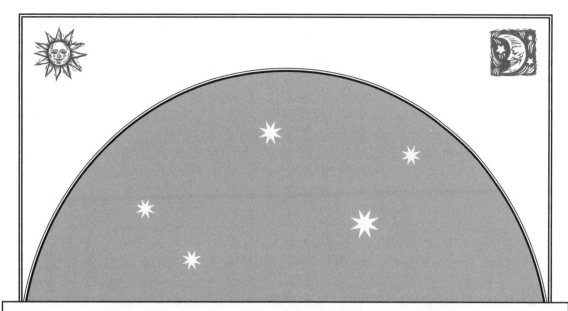

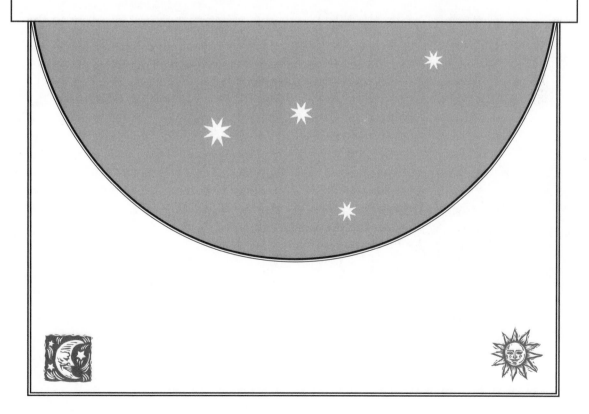

OCTOBER

OCTOBER 1

LIBRA • The scales of justice

September 23 at 3:00 A.M. to October 23 at 12:00 P.M. • NUMEROLOGY 1

Possessions and Desires . . .

Gem: Turquoise—This stone might help you find material gain.

Flower: Horse Chestnut—You may thirst for the good things in life.

Astral Color, Color Need, Apparel Color: Your Astral Color is Crimson, which reflects your ability to nurture. Yellow in your environment stimulates and exhilarates you. In your wardrobe, Rose gives you balance and harmony.

Fragrance: Pick scents that are soft and not overwhelming, like eclectic mixtures of wildflowers.

Tree: Walnut—You are unusually helpful and always looking for constant changes in your life.

Instrument: Organ

Composer: Böhm

Bird: Dove—the bird of hope during strife. It coos its song even in the dark of night.

Symbol: Crown—the universal sign of dignity.

Harmonious Health and Nutrition . . .

Health Scent: Strawberry—Soothing by nature, the strawberry promote self-esteem and encourages love

Favorable Foods: Asparagus, bananas, wholewheat bread, almonds

What's Lucky . . .

Lucky Numbers: 6, 9

Best Months: August and December

Best Day of the Week: Friday

Best Month Days: 1, 10, 19

Lucky Charm: A new penny in your shoe.

Harmonious Signs for Relationships and Partnerships: Aquarius and Gemini

Spiritual Guides . . .

Star: Al Icliel—This is the star of those who easily submit to authority.

Angel: Zuriel—This angel lends us the power to find balance when we desperately need it.

Guardian Angel: Malachi—"Messenger of Jehovah."

Spiritual Stone: Sapphire—the stone of serenity and prosperity.

✴ JUDITH'S INSIGHT ✴

You never fear showing what you feel. You are a very emotional person. Your home is your kingdom, and you are most comfortable when in your own space. Your sunny disposition makes it easy for others to like you.

You would make a wonderful teacher or professor, but your options aren't limited to education. You have talent for mathematics, bookkeeping, and sales. You may lean toward a career using your creative ability or, perhaps, one in the legal profession. You could be a skilled craftsperson or mechanic. You have a way with words and the ability to make the complex seem clear to other people. You would be a great theater or book critic.

You can be quickly knocked off balance when emotionally overwhelmed. Your intensity may be more than you or others close to you can handle. You're giving and kindhearted, so others easily attach themselves to you. Be careful to temper your generosity, or you may become exhausted. Ninety percent of the time you're a sweetie, but when things don't go your way, you can be a bitter pill.

Protecting yourself by recognizing your limitations and needs will help you avoid many heartaches in your life. Although at times undoubtedly complicated, you are happiest in a long term relationship. You find comfort in being in a partnership.

✴ ✴ ✴

OCTOBER 2 LIBRA • The scales of justice

September 23 at 3:00 A.M. to October 23 at 12:00 P.M. • NUMEROLOGY 2

Possessions and Desires . . .

Gem: Sapphire—This gem may help you find forgiveness from those you've wronged.
Flower: Juniper—You may spend too much time guarding yourself from imagined dangers.
Astral Color, Color Need, Apparel Color: Your Astral Color is Crimson, which reflects your ability to nurture. Yellow in your environment stimulates and exhilarates you. In your wardrobe, Brown brings you stability.
Fragrance: Pick scents that are soft and not overwhelming, like eclectic mixtures of wildflowers.
Tree: Maple—You have great stability and flashes of intuition.
Instrument: Cymbal
Composers: Handel, Johann Sebastian Bach
Bird: Cuckoo—a good flyer, and very seldom a quitter. Some cuckoos tend to think they favor lonely isolation, but what they really yearn for is a family relationship.
Symbol: Cross—the symbol of self-sacrifice and reconciliation.

Harmonious Health and Nutrition . . .

Health Scent: Apple—A vivacious scent encouraging energy. Will help you to be more creative, intuitive and positive.
Favorable Foods: Radishes, blackberries, wholewheat bread, Brazil nuts

What's Lucky . . .

Lucky Numbers: 6, 9
Best Months: August and December
Best Day of the Week: Friday
Best Month Days: 2, 11, 20
Lucky Charms: Two 50-cent pieces. Give someone else one of them.
Harmonious Signs for Relationships and Partnerships: Aquarius and Gemini

Spiritual Guides . . .

Star: Al Zubena—Those with this star often seek and find redemption.
Angel: Zuriel—This angel lends us the power to find balance when we desperately need it.
Guardian Angel: St. John—This angel simplifies that which is complicated.
Spiritual Stone: Sapphire—the stone of serenity and prosperity.

✶ _JUDITH'S INSIGHT_ ✶

Sincerity is your strongest characteristic. They say that nice guys finish last, and you prove them wrong. Your kindness and genuineness will bring you many good things throughout your life. Sometime around middle age or just after, you and one other person may decide to start a business. This person won't exactly be your equal, but they will still be vital to your success.

You need to be with someone in a close relationship to feel settled. You are cautious when it comes to finding love, as you should be. Finding a devoted mate may take years. Remember, don't sacrifice yourself just to have a partner. You may find that behavior brings you momentary happiness but in the long run yields only distress.

You would do well in jobs in government, engineering, or any highly structured industry. There's a side of you that yearns to be theatrical, even if it's in customer service, using humor to soothe people with complaints. You are a born communicator and will send the world a message whether as an artist or innovator. It is very important for you to find peace in the places you live and work. If the atmosphere around you is not conducive to your inner serenity, you will not succeed. You do better later in life when you don't feel the need to be so serious all the time. Most people get more fearful as they get older, but you're the reverse. Just remember to relax and laugh especially during low times. Just because balance is a difficult struggle for you doesn't mean that you can't eventually find it.

✶ ✶ ✶

OCTOBER 3

LIBRA • The scales of justice

September 23 at 3:00 A.M. to October 23 at 12:00 P.M. • NUMEROLOGY 3

Possessions and Desires . . .

Gem: Ruby—This stone may lead you to energy, friendship, and happiness.

Flower: Wheat—You could end up very wealthy.

Astral Color, Color Need, Apparel Color: Your Astral Color is Crimson, which reflects your ability to nurture. Yellow in your environment stimulates and exhilarates you. In your wardrobe, Rose gives you balance and harmony.

Fragrance: Pick scents that are soft and not overwhelming, like eclectic mixtures of wildflowers.

Tree: Elm—You have willpower, strength, and the ability to stand alone.

Instrument: Trombone

Composers: Verdi, Mendelssohn, Schumann

Bird: Eagle—This bird is quick to use its powers of flight. It can see immeasurable distances in a single glance, and can sometimes appear to be indifferent.

Symbol: Wreath—You have been crowned with a special personality. You are strong but extremely compassionate.

Harmonious Health and Nutrition . . .

Health Scent: Rose—This scent will lead you to passionate thoughts and make you warm.

Favorable Foods: Spinach, peaches, whole-wheat bread, walnuts

What's Lucky . . .

Lucky Numbers: 6, 9

Best Months: August and December

Best Day of the Week: Friday

Best Month Days: 3, 12, 21

Lucky Charm: A pen that someone else has already used.

Harmonious Signs for Relationships and Partnerships: Aquarius and Gemini

Spiritual Guides . . .

Star: Al Zubena—Those with this star often seek and find redemption.

Angel: Zuriel—This angel lends us the power to find balance when we desperately need it.

Guardian Angel: Johiel—This angel is a protector of all those with a humble heart.

Spiritual Stone: Sapphire—the stone of serenity and prosperity.

★ JUDITH'S INSIGHT ★

You love justice, so don't be surprised to find yourself in a courthouse often during your life. If you don't choose to enter the legal profession, you may have many dealings with it, usually having to do with important documents like contracts, financial reports, or stocks and bonds. It's up to you whether you're a champion of the underdog or the underdog yourself. You would also make a great mediator, psychologist, or philosopher. You understand the secrets that lie beneath what others see. You will understand life more clearly than most people could ever hope to imagine.

You have good friends because you know relationships take work, and you're a willing, devoted friend. You find mates quite easily, and this could be beneficial if you go about it properly. Others will strive to bring you happiness, not only emotionally, but financially. You have an alluring charm and wit.

You will be successful; your career will be very important to you after you turn thirty. In your late forties, after a brief midlife crisis, you may change jobs and work in a completely different, perhaps artistic field. The real you always rises to the top.

You are great with children, either your own or those close to you. Anything you do around young people brings luck. You will make a huge difference in a lot of lives, but you may not always understand just how much your efforts mean.

★ ★ ★

OCTOBER 4   LIBRA • The scales of justice

September 23 at 3:00 A.M. to October 23 at 12:00 P.M. • NUMEROLOGY 4

Possessions and Desires . . .

Gem: Emerald—Those who carry this stone tend to be lucky in love.
Flower: Venus's Looking Glass—You are more comfortable using flattery than frankness.
Astral Color, Color Need, Apparel Color: Your Astral Color is Crimson, which reflects your ability to nurture. Yellow in your environment stimulates and exhilarates you. In your wardrobe, Brown brings you stability.
Fragrance: Pick scents that are soft and not overwhelming, like eclectic mixtures of wildflowers.
Tree: Cherry—You will find yourself faced with constant new emotional awakenings.
Instrument: Bass
Composers: Haydn, Wagner
Bird: Robin—the most sociable of all birds, with the ability to create quick friendships. It also can easily adapt to any home. When it wants something, it has the tendency to try to snatch it.
Symbol: Star—You are full of inner brightness and will stand out in any crowd. You will be seen as special.

Harmonious Health and Nutrition . . .

Health Scent: Vanilla—This scent will fill you with a feeling of cleanliness and stability.
Favorable Foods: Carrots, prunes, whole-wheat bread, peanuts

What's Lucky . . .

Lucky Numbers: 6, 9
Best Months: August and December
Best Day of the Week: Friday
Best Month Days: 4, 13, 22
Lucky Charm: A piece of material cut from something in your home.

Harmonious Signs for Relationships and Partnerships: Aquarius and Gemini

Spiritual Guides . . .

Star: Al Icliel—This is the star of those who easily submit to authority.
Angel: Zuriel—This angel lends us the power to find balance when we desperately need it.
Guardian Angel: Uriel—This angel brings the light of God's guidance.
Spiritual Stone: Sapphire—the stone of serenity and prosperity.

✳ JUDITH'S INSIGHT ✳

Here today, gone tomorrow is how you operate. It would be surprising to find you settled for more than a minute. You are a little erratic and drawn to unusual surroundings and people. The only thing you'll be patient about is working toward a lasting relationship. You are self-sacrificing or feel you are. In love matches, you tend to be a jellyfish that does what your mate dictates. Deep down you want a lot from a mate and need even more.

You can be contrary and change your mind way too often. Very close friends and family are important to you, but you push people away, which creates tension at work or social gatherings. Unfortunately, you only need to show up to have others drawn to you. You would prefer to be a professional athlete more than the work you wind up doing. Watch out for silly injuries, as you may be accident prone.

You can do any job you choose. Since you are drawn to the peculiar, you may be employed in a career that is a strange smattering of many fields. If you don't work at multiple jobs, you wear several hats at once. You would be successful doing scientific, legal, or other research.

You will be well-known for your cultural, religious, or political contributions.

✳ ✳ ✳

OCTOBER 5   LIBRA • The scales of justice

September 23 at 3:00 A.M. to October 23 at 12:00 P.M. • NUMEROLOGY 5

Possessions and Desires . . .

Gem: Sardius—This stone could give the wearer unusual insights into his or her own heart.
Flower: Turnip—You tend to greatly enjoy helping others.
Astral Color, Color Need, Apparel Color: Your Astral Color is Crimson, which reflects your ability to nurture. Yellow in your environment stimulates and exhilarates you. In your wardrobe, Rose gives you balance and harmony.
Fragrance: Pick scents that are soft and not overwhelming, like eclectic mixtures of wildflowers.
Tree: Apple—You are creative, full of joy, and nearly magical. You bring happiness.
Instrument: Trumpet
Composer: Liszt
Bird: Flamingo—This beautiful, gregarious bird is always careful of its enemy. It is also a caretaker of the young and tries to keep everyone happy.
Symbol: Triangle—You have the right combination of abilities.

Harmonious Health and Nutrition . . .

Health Scent: Peach—This scent may balance your good qualities so that they equal your charm.
Favorable Foods: Tomatoes, watermelon, wholewheat bread, almonds

What's Lucky . . .

Lucky Numbers: 6, 9
Best Months: August and December
Best Day of the Week: Friday
Best Month Days: 4, 5, 23
Lucky Charms: A rabbit's foot or a white candle.
Harmonious Signs for Relationships and Partnerships: Aquarius and Gemini

Spiritual Guides . . .

Star: Al Zubena—Those with this star often seek and find redemption.
Angel: Zuriel—This angel lends us the power to find balance when we desperately need it.
Guardian Angel: Plavwell—The guardian that gives power and strength to one's presence.
Spiritual Stone: Sapphire—the stone of serenity and prosperity.

✳ JUDITH'S INSIGHT ✳

You are highly compassionate and have no problem showing it. You love to have a good time and will do anything to smile on another's face. You have refined taste, a sharp mind, and a love of intellectual pursuits. Mentally graced with a little something extra, whether it be a high IQ, psychic abilities, extreme common sense, or all three, you are very special. Because you get so much done every day, you will accomplish much during your life. Combined with your other gifts, your patience and kindness allow you many fine opportunities to succeed. Only you can select your goals—no one else has the vision to see that far. You should make history in one way or another.

You go out of your way for everybody, even if it means sacrificing yourself. However, you are prone to be overly practical and levelheaded when it comes to romance and close relationships. You need to turn off the clattering of your computerlike mind for a moment so you can hear the symphony that your heart is playing. Choosing a mate to spend your life with isn't like buying a car or house. For one thing, there is *never* a resale value.

You always give and sacrifice without asking for your needs to be met. You may have more heartache than anyone should be forced to bear. You can adapt to almost any situation. You don't just go with the flow, you enhance it.

✳ ✳ ✳

OCTOBER 6   LIBRA • The scales of justice

September 23 at 3:00 A.M. to October 23 at 12:00 P.M. • NUMEROLOGY 6

Possessions and Desires . . .

Gem: Topaz—This is an excellent gift to be exchanged between very loyal friends.

Flower: Tuberose—You might find that you can't enjoy yourself unless there is a dash of danger.

Astral Color, Color Need, Apparel Color: Your Astral Color is Crimson, which reflects your ability to nurture. Yellow in your environment stimulates and exhilarates you. In your wardrobe, Brown brings you stability.

Fragrance: Pick scents that are soft and not overwhelming, like eclectic mixtures of wildflowers.

Tree: Palm—You tend to be very healthy and creative.

Instrument: Lyre

Composer: Schubert

Bird: Falcon—An expert hunter. When well-trained, it can adapt to many tasks and is usually obedient.

Symbol: Crescent—You are more likely to be influenced by the phases of the moon. Your easygoing manner leads you to peaceful situations.

Harmonious Health and Nutrition . . .

Health Scent: Orange Blossom—This scent may balance your body, mind, and soul.

Favorable Foods: Lettuce, prunes, whole-wheat bread, walnuts

What's Lucky . . .

Lucky Numbers: 6, 9

Best Months: August and December

Best Day of the Week: Friday

Best Month Days: 6, 15, 24

Lucky Charms: A religious token or card from any religion.

Harmonious Signs for Relationships and Partnerships: Aquarius and Gemini

Spiritual Guides . . .

Star: Al Icliel—This is the star of those who easily submit to authority.

Angel: Zuriel—This angel lends us the power to find balance when we desperately need it.

Guardian Angel: Michael—"Who is like God."

Spiritual Stone: Sapphire—the stone of serenity and prosperity.

✱ JUDITH'S INSIGHT ✱

You appreciate the art world, and maybe one day it will appreciate you. You see the world with an artist's eye. Creativity may be one of your strongest traits. You are very self-reliant except when it comes to love, where you find yourself adrift in a leaky emotional rowboat surrounded by a sea of need. Intimate relationships will mean everything to you, and you will do just about anything to find a secure partner. You don't have to be so anxious; your magnetic personality will attract a soul mate to you, but it will be difficult at first for the two of you to figure out how to adjust your powerful energies.

You have survived many disappointments; it sometimes seems that you avoid life's pitfalls just to wind up in the pits. You seem to thrive on adversity and laugh off even the greatest sorrow with style. Entertainment is important to you. You will be passionately fond of some form of the performing arts. You will be either a movie buff, music collector, or actor in a local play. You also love to celebrate living the good life by hosting frequent parties. You will be in the public eye in one way or another, whether you are the head of the PTA or the ringleader of your friends.

Your friends stay friends for life. You only lose friends when they leave this earth. But even then, they will be by your side as guardian angels. As you get older, you'll recognize everybody you meet changes you in some significant way. You are very persuasive, and others may consider you stubborn. This could be a positive thing for the most part but an obstacle in relationships. You are loyal to everyone, even if trusts are betrayed. Some see you as a rebel without a cause. Later in your life you just may find your cause.

★ ★ ★

OCTOBER 7 LIBRA • The scales of justice

September 23 at 3:00 A.M. to October 23 at 12:00 P.M. • NUMEROLOGY 7

Possessions and Desires . . .

Gem: Sapphire—This stone may help you find forgiveness from those you wronged.
Flower: Traveler's Joy—You usually can't be happy unless you first feel safe.
Astral Color, Color Need, Apparel Color: Your Astral Color is Crimson, which reflects your ability to nurture. Yellow in your environment stimulates and exhilarates you. In your wardrobe, Rose gives you balance and harmony.
Fragrance: Pick scents that are soft and not overwhelming, like eclectic mixtures of wildflowers.
Tree: Sycamore—Yours is the ability to love, communicate honestly with others, and have lasting relationships.
Instrument: Harp
Composers: Gluck, Brahms.
Bird: Warbling Parakeet—the most beautiful of all birds, known as the love bird. It does seem to have the powers of imitation.
Symbol: Heart—You are enthusiastic, empathetic, and full of generosity and love.

Harmonious Health and Nutrition . . .

Health Scent: Jasmine—This scent may make you more easygoing when you are stressed.
Favorable Foods: Tomatoes, prunes, whole-wheat bread, almonds

What's Lucky . . .

Lucky Numbers: 6, 9
Best Months: August and December
Best Day of the Week: Friday
Best Month Days: 6, 15, 24
Lucky Charm: An old key.
Harmonious Signs for Relationships and Partnerships: Aquarius and Gemini

Spiritual Guides . . .

Star: Al Zubena—Those with this star often seek and find redemption.
Angel: Zuriel—This angel lends us the power to find balance when we desperately need it.
Guardian Angel: Raphael—This angel attends to all of your needs when you are looking for guidance.
Spiritual Stone: Sapphire—the stone of serenity and prosperity.

✷ JUDITH'S INSIGHT ✷

You are ready, willing, and able to help others whenever they need you. You always like to be the good guy. You're ambitious and energetic and can be successful in out-of-the-ordinary professions. You have a tendency to dominate in all situations, usually because everyone recognizes you're the person who deserves to be in charge. You can easily see the way out of any predicament.

In every job you do, you will be the troubleshooter. If something doesn't work, gets stuck, or becomes lost or hopelessly tangled, you are the one everyone expects to solve the problem. You will develop a fondness for the fine arts and are energized by being with groups of people.

Your family and close friends give you a heaping portion of heartaches and heartburn. After tempers cool, you are the one who patches up the holes and makes everything all better.

You will have a strongly intense love relationship at least once in your life. Love and being attached are the most important things to you. Just remember to stop thinking and start doing—it's the only way to get to where you want. Never allow your fears to choke off your ability to be happy. Allow yourself the time it takes for everything to come into your life. You have patience for others; you just need patience when it comes to you.

Some careers that you may excel at: lawyer, investigator, a president or vice president of a large corporation, real estate, philosopher, writer, and doctor.

✷ ✷ ✷

OCTOBER 8 LIBRA • The scales of justice

September 23 at 3:00 A.M. to October 23 at 12:00 P.M. • NUMEROLOGY 8

Possessions and Desires . . .

Gem: Chrysolite—This gem may help you clear your mind of sadness and worry.

Flower: Tamarisk—You may get a secret thrill from tales of outlaws.

Astral Color, Color Need, Apparel Color: Your Astral Color is Crimson, which reflects your ability to nurture. Yellow in your environment stimulates and exhilarates you. In your wardrobe, Brown brings you stability.

Fragrance: Pick scents that are soft and not overwhelming, like eclectic mixtures of wildflowers.

Tree: Pine—Your relationships tend to be harmonious, both emotionally and mentally.

Instrument: Cello

Composer: Mozart

Bird: Bobolink—This charming singer is equally good as a soloist or a member of an orchestra. It is a very romantic bird, most useful as an insect destroyer, and elegant, with beautiful feathers, and is always pleasant to have around.

Symbol: Wings—You are the source of balance in your world—this will bring you contentment.

Harmonious Health and Nutrition . . .

Health Scent: Almond—This scent may revitalize you and open you to greater possibilities.

Favorable Foods: Lettuce, blackberries, whole-wheat bread, Brazil nuts

What's Lucky . . .

Lucky Numbers: 6, 9

Best Months: August and December

Best Day of the Week: Friday

Best Month Days: 8, 17, 26

Lucky Charm: Red ribbon in your wallet or doorway.

Harmonious Signs for Relationships and Partnerships: Aquarius and Gemini

Spiritual Guides . . .

Star: Al Zubena—Those with this star often seek and find redemption.

Angel: Zuriel—This angel lends us the power to find balance when we desperately need it.

Guardian Angel: Seraphim—An angel that brings love, light, and passion.

Spiritual Stone: Sapphire—the stone of serenity and prosperity.

✶ JUDITH'S INSIGHT ✶

You can take life much too seriously, especially when young. You are prone to feeling far more pressure than the situation warrants. Other people aren't the ones who are causing you to feel so much stress; the guilty party is wearing your sneakers.

You're charming and understanding; this wins you attention every time. You tend to bore easily, especially when looking for that special someone to love. It'll be much easier for you to find a job than a spouse. You are very gifted when it comes to the qualities employers look for. You may aspire to become a musician, artist, teacher, lawyer, or designer. You are original and can be considered an innovative person. Somehow great ideas always find you right when you need them. You will work well with others because you enjoy their company.

Your family is a source of grief for you. They seem to leap from one crisis to another. You and your spouse may often feel like the only sane people trapped in an asylum because of the crazy life the two of you lead. You have the nasty habit of creating difficulties for yourself without meaning to.

You should be very wealthy for at least part of your life. Opportunities don't just knock, they blow your door off the hinges. Just remember that it never hurts to save money when you have it for possible times of hardship.

You'll find that the more you try to focus on what's best in others, the more you'll like yourself.

✶ ✶ ✶

OCTOBER 9

LIBRA • The scales of justice

September 23 at 3:00 A.M. to October 23 at 12:00 P.M. • NUMEROLOGY 9

Possessions and Desires . . .

Gem: Beryl—This gem could be good for meditation and concentration.
Flower: Celandine—Your happiness tends to occur later in life.
Astral Color, Color Need, Apparel Color: Your Astral Color is Crimson, which reflects your ability to nurture. Yellow in your environment stimulates and exhilarates you. In your wardrobe, Rose gives you balance and harmony.
Fragrance: Pick scents that are soft and not overwhelming, like eclectic mixtures of wildflowers.
Tree: Holly—Beware that you are not carried away by your passionate nature. The only way to grow is to be open to new experiences.
Instruments: Violin, tympanum
Composer: Gluck
Bird: Mockingbird—the most proficient minstrel in the world's orchestra; graceful and enthusiastic.
Symbol: Anchor—This tranquil symbol signifies stability and strength, and stands for strong commitments in relationships.

Harmonious Health and Nutrition . . .

Health Scent: Lavender—This scent might lead others to trust you and make you patient.
Favorable Foods: Carrots, peaches, whole-wheat bread, walnuts

What's Lucky . . .

Lucky Numbers: 6, 9, 18
Best Months: August and December
Best Day of the Week: Friday
Best Month Days: 9, 18, 27
Lucky Charms: A U.S. coin or a bill of any amount from the year you were born.

Harmonious Signs for Relationships and Partnerships: Aquarius and Gemini

Spiritual Guides . . .

Star: Al Icliel—This is the star of those who easily submit to authority.
Angel: Zuriel—This angel lends us the power to find balance when we desperately need it.
Guardian Angel: Gabriel—"God is my strength."
Spiritual Stone: Sapphire—the stone of serenity and prosperity.

✷ JUDITH'S INSIGHT ✷

For you there is no middle ground. You are equally ready to either smile or punch your way out of any situation. Honor is very important to you. You are a natural lawyer, debater, or critic. You would also make a much-sought-after surgeon. You are easily amused; with a comfy chair and a good book, you can be quite happy. You love learning new things. You are a born leader who will earn and deserve a position of authority.

Finding a mate should be a piece of cake. You must be careful not to hold on to all you catch, as some will cause you nothing but the worst kind of trouble. You have to keep your eyes, ears, and mind very open. You may have a large number of relationships.

You have a style that's all your own, and you tend to be very independent. Others see you as a loner, but you see yourself as a member of a fun group you have yet to find. It will be your life's work to fully integrate your personality. You are kindhearted, but your head is running the show. A warm soul like yours is filled with compassion, but you believe that others should learn to take care of themselves. Your good habits multiply to drive out the bad as you get older, and you become a much happier person.

Put yourself in the middle of your own life; wallflowers don't get to grow.

✷ ✷ ✷

OCTOBER 10 LIBRA • The scales of justice

September 23 at 3:00 A.M. to October 23 at 12:00 P.M. • NUMEROLOGY 1

Possessions and Desires . . .

Gem: Opal—Holding this stone may help you discover enough hope to go on.
Flower: Stock—You tend to love what you love all your life.
Astral Color, Color Need, Apparel Color: Your Astral Color is Crimson, which reflects your ability to nurture. Yellow in your environment stimulates and exhilarates you. In your wardrobe, Brown brings you stability.
Fragrance: Pick scents that are soft and not overwhelming, like eclectic mixtures of wildflowers.
Tree: Walnut—You are unusually helpful and always looking for constant changes in your life.
Instruments: French horn, organ, violin
Composer: Böhm
Bird: Bird of Paradise—the "birds of the Gods." You will shine and love extraordinary circumstances.
Symbol: Crown—the universal sign of dignity.

Harmonious Health and Nutrition . . .

Health Scent: Strawberry—Soothing by nature, the strawberry promotes self-esteem and encourages love.
Favorable Foods: Corn, prunes, whole-wheat bread, almonds

What's Lucky . . .

Lucky Numbers: 6, 9
Best Months: August and December
Best Day of the Week: Friday
Best Month Days: 1, 10, 19
Lucky Charm: A new penny in your shoe.
Harmonious Signs for Relationships and Partnerships: Aquarius and Gemini

Spiritual Guides . . .

Star: Al Zubena—Those with this star often seek and find redemption.
Angel: Zuriel—This angel lends us the power to find balance when we desperately need it.
Guardian Angel: Malachi—"Messenger of Jehovah."
Spiritual Stone: Sapphire—the stone of serenity and prosperity.

✴ JUDITH'S INSIGHT ✴

They say that the love of money is the root of all evil, but it's not that for you. Money to you is just a way to keep score; it doesn't mean much more than that. It seems that it's always flowing in a steady stream headed your way. This is good because you love to win. You're happiest at home and never really comfortable anywhere else. If anything disturbs the security you feel there, you will become dangerously restless. Your natural optimism makes it easy for you to cultivate both friends and lovers.

You'd make a wonderful grade school teacher but are more likely to work in a tightly structured environment because you crave financial security. Government, law, publishing, or other communications-related careers will probably suit you. You may wish to be employed as a skilled craftsperson or work with machines.

You are prone to losing yourself in your relationships and not always for the better. You need to maintain your balance when dealing with those you love. You overanalyze and magnify a small fight into a disaster and then at the end of the day forget that anything happened. When you learn to be less self-centered and opinionated, you will enjoy social interactions more. You are open to the point of bluntness. This works in business but can be a problem when it comes to love.

★ ★ ★

OCTOBER 11

LIBRA • The scales of justice

September 23 at 3:00 A.M. to October 23 at 12:00 P.M. • **NUMEROLOGY 2**

Possessions and Desires . . .

Gem: Opal—Holding this stone may help you discover enough hope to go on.

Flower: Black-eyed Susan—You never stop struggling to overcome your troubles.

Astral Color, Color Need, Apparel Color: Your Astral Color is Crimson, which reflects your ability to nurture. Yellow in your environment stimulates and exhilarates you. In your wardrobe, Rose gives you balance and harmony.

Fragrance: Pick scents that are soft and not overwhelming, like eclectic mixtures of wildflowers.

Tree: Maple—You have great stability and flashes of intuition.

Instrument: Drum

Composers: Handel, Johann Sebastian Bach

Bird: Stork—Turkish bird, held in high esteem the world over. This bird is intelligent but may have strange tendencies.

Symbol: Cross—the symbol of self-sacrifice and reconciliation.

Harmonious Health and Nutrition . . .

Health Scent: Apple—A vivacious scent encouraging energy. Will help you to be more creative, intuitive, and positive.

Favorable Foods: Radishes, watermelon, wholewheat bread, peanuts

What's Lucky . . .

Lucky Numbers: 6, 9

Best Months: August and December

Best Day of the Week: Friday

Best Month Days: 2, 11, 20

Lucky Charms: Two 50-cent pieces. Give someone else one of them.

Harmonious Signs for Relationships and Partnerships: Aquarius and Gemini

Spiritual Guides . . .

Star: Al Zubena—Those with this star often seek and find redemption.

Angel: Zuriel—This angel lends us the power to find balance when we desperately need it.

Guardian Angel: St. John—This angel simplifies that which is complicated.

Spiritual Stone: Sapphire—the stone of serenity and prosperity.

✶ JUDITH'S INSIGHT ✶

Kindness and sincerity are your greatest attributes. They say nice guys finish last, but you disprove them by finishing first and way ahead of the pack. When you help others, you bring out the best both in yourself and in everyone involved. Some say you make too many sacrifices, but you get more out of giving than the effort you expend.

You are happier in a partnership or relationship than on your own. You fear going through life alone without the love you need. You may commit to several unusual, hard-to-explain relationships during your lifetime. You are independent and dependent at the same time. You find enjoyment and security doing things as a part of a group.

You could be a musician, artist, teacher, or lawyer. You will never work in a job that lacks a clearly defined structure. Chaos makes you anxious. Even something as simple as an open window in the winter or unpainted ceilings can make you restless and moody. The more you feel connected to your working space, the better your productivity.

You are thorough in anything you do, true and loyal to friends, and quite conscientious. You fight to the end for your beliefs. You have your whole life mapped out, especially when it comes to career. You are like an artist who scraps things many times before making them perfectly. Everything you do will have a finished, well-thought-out quality to it.

✶ ✶ ✶

OCTOBER 12 LIBRA • The scales of justice

September 23 at 3:00 A.M. to October 23 at 12:00 P.M. • NUMEROLOGY 3

Possessions and Desires . . .

Gem: Ruby—This stone may lead you to energy, friendship, and happiness.

Flower: Mundi Rose—If variety is the spice of life, yours is never mild.

Astral Color, Color Need, Apparel Color: Your Astral Color is Crimson, which reflects your ability to nurture. Yellow in your environment stimulates and exhilarates you. In your wardrobe, Brown brings you stability.

Fragrance: Pick scents that are soft and not overwhelming, like eclectic mixtures of wildflowers.

Tree: Elm—You have willpower, strength, and the ability to stand alone.

Instrument: Trombone

Composers: Verdi, Mendelssohn, Schumann

Bird: Eagle—This bird is quick to use its powers of flight. It can see immeasurable distances in a single glance, and can sometimes appear to be indifferent.

Symbol: Wreath—You have been crowned with a special personality. You are strong but extremely compassionate.

Harmonious Health and Nutrition . . .

Health Scent: Rose—This scent will lead you to passionate thoughts and make you feel warm inside.

Favorable Foods: Lentils, black figs, whole-wheat bread, almonds

What's Lucky . . .

Lucky Numbers: 6, 9

Best Months: August and December

Best Day of the Week: Friday

Best Month Days: 3, 12, 21

Lucky Charm: A pen that someone else has already used.

Harmonious Signs for Relationships and Partnerships: Aquarius and Gemini

Spiritual Guides . . .

Star: Al Zubena—Those with this star often seek and find redemption.

Angel: Zuriel—This angel lends us the power to find balance when we desperately need it.

Guardian Angel: Johiel—This angel is a protector of all those with a humble heart.

Spiritual Stone: Sapphire—the stone of serenity and prosperity.

★ JUDITH'S INSIGHT ★

Everything you love, you love deeply. Even the simplest things interest you. The smallest gestures are extremely important to you. You can be sentimental at heart, but you balance out the mush with a very clear and bright mind. You always understand the larger ramifications and would make an excellent author, counselor, or teacher. Your desire to learn what no one else knows may make you a scientist or surgeon. You have good friends because you work hard at maintaining connections. Nothing really comes easy to you in life, but you stubbornly keep practicing.

You have been blessed with charm, wit, and a devoted nature. You are more a giver than a taker. You have at least one great success you will remember and be well-known, respected, and admired for. You crave order and rules, both in your personal life and on the job.

Certain contracts or legal papers will be very important to you. There is every indication that you will do very well in the legal profession. More often than not you will come out on top when involved in trials. You're a winner, and your luck rubs off on others. You are generous with money. Just remember that you are here to make a difference—in large ways and small.

You like having a partner and you are usually in one relationship or another. Not every relationship will be what you want it to be, but you find yourself being more secure in having a mate than not.

★ ★ ★

OCTOBER 13 LIBRA • The scales of justice

September 23 at 3:00 A.M. to October 23 at 12:00 P.M. • NUMEROLOGY 4

Possessions and Desires . . .

Gem: Emerald—Those who carry this stone tend to be lucky in love.

Flower: Red Rose—love shouldn't disappoint you for any length of time.

Astral Color, Color Need, Apparel Color: Your Astral Color is Crimson, which reflects your ability to nurture. Yellow in your environment stimulates and exhilarates you. In your wardrobe, Rose gives you balance and harmony.

Fragrance: Pick scents that are soft and not overwhelming, like eclectic mixtures of wildflowers.

Tree: Cherry—You will find yourself faced with constant new emotional awakenings.

Instruments: Clarinet, French Horn, piano

Composers: Haydn, Wagner

Bird: Killdeer—This bird is usually found consorting with other species, and can adapt to any environment.

Symbol: Star—You are full of inner brightness and will stand out in any crowd. You will be seen as special.

Harmonious Health and Nutrition . . .

Health Scent: Vanilla—This scent will fill you with a feeling of cleanliness and stability.

Favorable Foods: Asparagus, raspberries, wholewheat bread, almonds

What's Lucky . . .

Lucky Numbers: 6, 9

Best Months: August and December

Best Day of the Week: Friday

Best Month Days: 4, 13, 22

Lucky Charm: A piece of material cut from something in your home.

Harmonious Signs for Relationships and Partnerships: Aquarius and Gemini

Spiritual Guides . . .

Star: Al Zubena—Those with this star often seek and find redemption.

Angel: Zuriel—This angel lends us the power to find balance when we desperately need it.

Guardian Angel: Uriel—This angel brings the light of God's guidance.

Spiritual Stone: Sapphire—the stone of serenity and prosperity.

✳ JUDITH'S INSIGHT ✳

You have mechanical abilities and can easily fix broken things. You are very original and will leave your mark on the world. You don't always have the time and energy you need in order to accomplish all your dreams. You know this but still won't give up the battle.

Home is extremely important, especially how it looks to others. You are overly giving in order to have a relationship that lasts. Your partner will expect you to sacrifice for him or her and then resent you for it. You will usually pick a difficult mate who has a more powerful personality. It's always your time, patience, and efforts that keep the marriage steady. At some point your partner may realize what you mean to him or her, allowing you to feel more satisfaction in love.

You learn early that acquiring things does not necessarily guarantee happiness. Family and friends are important to you. You keep people at arm's length, which leads to tension. It's easier to be distant than admit you have feelings that might hurt someone you care about.

You may love dangerous sports but tend to be a little accident prone. You should be all right if you are smart enough to be cautious. Good at everything, you would make a great salesperson, computer programmer, musician, or teacher. You have a dramatic flair, and your work belongs on stage, whether you are the actor or playwright. Your confidence takes you far. You are patient to a point but become frustrated once you reach your limits. Learn to stay grounded and continue waiting for what you need, and all will come to you.

✳ ✳ ✳

OCTOBER 14   LIBRA • The scales of justice

September 23 at 3:00 A.M. to October 23 at 12:00 P.M. • NUMEROLOGY 5

Possessions and Desires . . .

Gem: Sardius—This stone could give the wearer unusual insights into his or her own heart.

Flower: China Rose—You could fall into the trap of thinking that something new is necessarily more beautiful than what you have.

Astral Color, Color Need, Apparel Color: Your Astral Color is Crimson, which reflects your ability to nurture. Yellow in your environment stimulates and exhilarates you. In your wardrobe, Brown brings you stability.

Fragrance: Pick scents that are soft and not overwhelming, like eclectic mixtures of wildflowers.

Tree: Apple—You are creative, full of joy, and nearly magical. You bring happiness.

Instrument: Viola

Composer: Liszt

Bird: Flamingo—This beautiful, gregarious bird is always careful of its enemy. It is also a caretaker of the young, and tries to keep everyone happy.

Symbol; Triangle—You have the right combination of abilities.

Harmonious Health and Nutrition . . .

Health Scent: Peach—This scent may balance your good qualities so that they equal your charm.

Favorable Foods: Spinach, cherries, whole-wheat bread, Brazil nuts

What's Lucky . . .

Lucky Numbers: 6, 9
Best Months: August and December
Best Day of the Week: Friday
Best Month Days: 4, 5, 23
Lucky Charms: A rabbit's foot or a white candle.
Harmonious Signs for Relationships and Partnerships: Aquarius and Gemini

Spiritual Guides . . .

Star: Al Zubena—Those with this star often seek and find redemption.

Angel: Zuriel—This angel lends us the power to find balance when we desperately need it.

Guardian Angel: Plavwell—The guardian that gives power and strength to ones presence.

Spiritual Stone: Sapphire—the stone of serenity and prosperity.

✳ *JUDITH'S INSIGHT* ✳

Family is very important to you. You need complete freedom, yet crave a stable, committed home and family life. This could be a bit of a contradiction, but at times in your life you will feel like you are receiving the best of both worlds.

Work is tremendously difficult, but somehow you manage. There will be endless delays and pressures before you eventually get where you want. You love nature and need to be around flowers, trees, and running brooks for inspiration. You would do very well as an environmental lawyer or someone fighting for the rights of animals or children.

With your patience, kindness, and intelligence, you will contribute much at work. Strong compassion, a love of life, and a unique vision will make you very successful and maybe even famous. Others are very surprised when you become moody and cranky. Work to manage your levels of frustration, understimulation, and insecurity.

Romance and intimate relationships are extremely important to you. Be sure to choose someone who is openly, physically affectionate. You need to touch and be touched frequently. You connect with your soul mate only after sacrificing logic on Cupid's altar. Who you marry isn't anyone you would have chosen using your head.

You love to travel, entertain, and be entertained; you may throw large parties, rub elbows with performers, or direct a local theatrical production.

✱ ✱ ✱

OCTOBER 15
LIBRA • The scales of justice
September 23 at 3:00 A.M. to October 23 at 12:00 P.M. • NUMEROLOGY 6

Possessions and Desires . . .

Gem: Diamond—This stone is thought to encourage harmony in relationships and gives strength to the troubled.

Flower: Raspberry—You will find you are here for a multiple purpose.

Astral Color, Color Need, Apparel Color: Your Astral Color is Crimson, which reflects your ability to nurture. Yellow in your environment stimulates and exhilarates you. In your wardrobe, Rose gives you balance and harmony.

Fragrance: Pick scents that are soft and not overwhelming, like eclectic mixtures of wildflowers.

Tree: Palm—You tend to be very healthy and creative.

Instrument: Tambourine

Composer: Schubert

Bird: Lark—known for the beauty of its song, which is sometimes very unusual. It is also credited with extraordinary intelligence.

Symbol: Crescent—You are more likely to be influenced by the phases of the moon. Your easygoing manner leads you to peaceful situations

Harmonious Health and Nutrition . . .

Health Scent: Orange Blossom—This scent may balance your body, mind, and soul.

Favorable Foods: Kale, peaches, whole-wheat bread, walnuts

What's Lucky . . .

Lucky Numbers: 6, 9
Best Months: August and December
Best Day of the Week: Friday
Best Month Days: 6, 15, 24
Lucky Charms: A religious token or card from any religion.
Harmonious Signs for Relationships and Partnerships: Aquarius and Gemini

Spiritual Guides . . .

Star: Al Icliel—This is the star of those who easily submit to authority.

Angel: Zuriel—This angel lends us the power to find balance when we desperately need it.

Guardian Angel: Michael—"Who is like God."

Spiritual Stone: Sapphire—the stone of serenity and prosperity.

✶ JUDITH'S INSIGHT ✶

Your fine art appreciation may lead you to some sort of recognition for your contributions. Your refined taste draws you to the stage, concert hall, or movie studio.

Your seem so independent, people don't realize how needy you are. You have to get very close to someone before you can bring yourself to reveal your insecurities. Relationships with friends, lovers, and family mean everything to you. You have a strong magnetic personality and may find your mate at work. As much as you like challenges on the job, you loathe them in love. You want spontaneity, desire, fun, and romance—love at first sight, butterflies. You believe that true love won't ever be work. You're very lucky because love usually finds you this way.

It may be through your work or hobbies, but you should become famous. You will do well when employed as an attorney, scientist, teacher, author, or coach. You keep in contact with childhood friends; no one that you care for leaves your life for very long. You are so giving that many people see you as guardian angel.

You encounter lots of disappointments. They tend to hit unexpectedly. Fortunately, you recover quickly. Just as surprising, you may come into a sizable windfall. You might have to endure with your usual grace a number of small or chronic medical problems. You refuse to close the door on whatever life offers, and this will bring you many pleasant changes.

★ ★ ★

OCTOBER 16 LIBRA • The scales of justice

September 23 at 3:00 A.M. to October 23 at 12:00 P.M. • NUMEROLOGY 7

Possessions and Desires . . .

Gem: Agate—This stone may promote health and lead you to a long life.

Flower: Split Reed—If something feels wrong to you it usually is.

Astral Color, Color Need, Apparel Color: Your Astral Color is Crimson, which reflects your ability to nurture. Yellow in your environment stimulates and exhilarates you. In your wardrobe, Brown brings you stability.

Fragrance: Pick scents that are soft and not overwhelming, like eclectic mixtures of wildflowers.

Tree: Sycamore—Yours is the ability to love, communicate honestly with others, and have lasting relationships.

Instruments: Harp, violin, cello

Composers: Gluck, Brahms

Bird: Skylark—This handsome bird is beautiful when it sings. It always whistles as it works.

Symbol: Heart—You are enthusiastic, empathetic, and full of generosity and love.

Harmonious Health and Nutrition . . .

Health Scent: Jasmine—This scent may make you more easygoing when you are stressed.

Favorable Foods: Swiss chard, prunes, wholewheat bread, peanuts

What's Lucky . . .

Lucky Numbers: 6, 9
Best Months: August and December
Best Day of the Week: Friday
Best Month Days: 6, 15, 24
Lucky Charm: An old key
Harmonious Signs for Relationships and Partnerships: Aquarius and Gemini

Spiritual Guides . . .

Star: Al Zubena—Those with this star often seek and find redemption.

Angel: Zuriel—This angel lends us the power to find balance when we desperately need it.

Guardian Angel: Raphael—This angel attends to all of your needs when you are looking for guidance.

Spiritual Stone: Sapphire—the stone of serenity and prosperity.

✶ JUDITH'S INSIGHT ✶

You are always eager to assist, and often underappreciated; those you help may not even take the time to say thank you. You're ambitious and energetic as long as you believe in yourself. You can be successful in very odd ways. You are criticized for being domineering, but it's usually because someone hands you the reins, then complains that you have them. You have great intentions, but don't always see the big picture. You have a giving heart, but need to watch around you for what the outcome may be.

You should find employment as a troubleshooter. You were born to solve problems, large and small. You are a people person who gains energy just from being with others.

Unfortunately, love for you means heartache. After a long, dusty trail your tattered heart will find a soul mate who adores you and gives you the world. It make take you a while to accept their love because you fear your own happiness. You can complicate some situations to the point where you're unable to come to a decision. Sometimes it's impossible to please everyone.

Work on bringing some order to your scattered thoughts and get on the road to where you want to be.

★ ★ ★

OCTOBER 17 LIBRA • The scales of justice

September 23 at 3:00 A.M. to October 23 at 12:00 P.M. • NUMEROLOGY 8

Possessions and Desires . . .

Gem: Chrysolite—This gem may help you clear your mind of sadness and worry.

Flower: Single Reed—You usually have a natural sense of rhythm.

Astral Color, Color Need, Apparel Color: Your Astral Color is Crimson, which reflects your ability to nurture. Yellow in your environment stimulates and exhilarates you. In your wardrobe, Rose gives you balance and harmony.

Fragrance: Pick scents that are soft and not overwhelming, like eclectic mixtures of wildflowers.

Tree: Pine—Your relationships tend to be harmonious, both emotionally and mentally.

Instrument: Cello

Composer: Mozart

Bird: Bobolink—This charming singer is equally good as a soloist or a member of an orchestra. It is a very romantic bird, most useful as an insect destroyer, and elegant, with beautiful feathers, and always pleasant to have around.

Symbol: Wings—You are the source of balance in your world—this will bring you contentment.

Harmonious Health and Nutrition . . .

Health Scent: Almond—This scent may revitalize you and open you to greater possibilities.

Favorable Foods: Peas, raspberries, whole-wheat bread, almonds

What's Lucky . . .

Lucky Numbers: 6, 9

Best Months: August and December

Best Day of the Week: Friday

Best Month Days: 8, 17, 26

Lucky Charm: Red ribbon in your wallet or doorway.

Harmonious Signs for Relationships and Partnerships: Aquarius and Gemini

Spiritual Guides . . .

Star: Al Zubena—Those with this star often seek and find redemption.

Angel: Zuriel—This angel lends us the power to find balance when we desperately need it.

Guardian Angel: Seraphim—An angel that brings love, light, and passion.

Spiritual Stone: Sapphire—the stone of serenity and prosperity.

✳ JUDITH'S INSIGHT ✳

You are very unbalanced and tend to live your life in a rut in order to give yourself a semblance of security. You hate to choose sides because you don't like to surrender any possibilities. You blame everyone else for the enormous stress you place on yourself. You will be quite wealthy not through work but by money falling in your lap. You could be lucky with the lottery, pick the right stock, or win at gambling.

Family and friends are likely to call on you for every crisis, and you are always there for them. At some point you will find this too overwhelming and may suddenly move far away to escape. You hold the wild cards of charm and understanding in your hand; when you play them, they win for you the attention and love that you need and deserve. You get bored easily, so it may take you some time to settle on a mate who can hold your attention. You like a clean, warm environment and a harmonious home. You always give in, but you never give up on love.

It won't be hard for you to find a career, but staying in just one may prove quite difficult. You aspire to be a renowned musician, artist, or acting teacher, but are more likely to be a manager or agent. You're an excellent idea person with entrepreneurial capabilities. You define yourself through your work, so it's difficult for you to be satisfied unless you have a career you think has sufficient status. Your energy, individuality, and ability to work with others outweigh your lack of focus.

✳ ✳ ✳

OCTOBER 18　LIBRA • The scales of justice

September 23 at 3:00 A.M. to October 23 at 12:00 P.M. • NUMEROLOGY 9

Possessions and Desires . . .

Gem: Beryl—This gem could be good for meditation and concentration.
Flower: Rhododendron—You have the ability to be a winner, at just about everything.
Astral Color, Color Need, Apparel Color: Your Astral Color is Crimson, which reflects your ability to nurture. Yellow in your environment stimulates and exhilarates you. In your wardrobe, Brown brings you stability.
Fragrance: Pick scents that are soft and not overwhelming, like eclectic mixtures of wildflowers.
Tree: Holly—Beware that you are not carried away by your passionate nature. The only way to grow is to be open to new experiences.
Instruments: Violin, tympnum
Composer: Gluck
Bird: Mockingbird—the most proficient minstrel in the world's orchestra; graceful and enthusiastic.
Symbol: Anchor—This tranquil symbol signifies stability and strength, and stands for strong commitments in relationships.

Harmonious Health and Nutrition . . .

Health Scent: Lavender—This scent might lead others to trust you and make you patient.
Favorable Foods: Tomatoes, strawberries, whole-wheat bread, Brazil nuts

What's Lucky . . .

Lucky Numbers: 6, 9
Best Months: August and December
Best Day of the Week: Friday
Best Month Days: 9, 18, 27
Lucky Charm: A U.S. coin or a bill of any amount from the year you were born.

Harmonious Signs for Relationships and Partnerships: Aquarius and Gemini

Spiritual Guides . . .

Star: Al Icliel—This is the star of those who easily submit to authority.
Angel: Zuriel—This angel lends us the power to find balance when we desperately need it.
Guardian Angel: Gabriel—"God is my strength."
Spiritual Stone: Sapphire—the stone of serenity and prosperity.

✶ JUDITH'S INSIGHT ✶

You are a born leader and always will be in charge. No matter what the situation, you excel; you are the most ardent lover and vicious fighter. Your kind heart and warmth will convince others to defend you. You highly value honor and will struggle tooth-and-nail for not only yours but for others'. You are completely loyal to all that love you.

You would make a great debater because you can clearly see both sides of any issue. It will be difficult for you to narrow your choices when picking a career, as so much interests you. You would make a wonderful surgeon. No matter what career you choose, eventually you'll hold a position of responsibility and authority. You may even be publicly recognized and become very famous.

Looking for a mate may require some time and patience, though you seem to attract all the wrong ones quite easily. Be sure you understand exactly what you need from a love relationship, because mistakes in this area could be costly. The appearance of your home is very important to you. Not to say that you're too materialistic, but you do have a powerful desire to be surrounded by the finer things in life.

You will be well known for your unique style, especially as you get older.

✶ ✶ ✶

OCTOBER 19　LIBRA • THE LIONS

September 23 at 3:00 A.M. to October 23 at 12:00 P.M. • NUMEROLOGY 1

Possessions and Desires . . .

Gem: Agate—This stone may promote health and lead you to a long life.

Flower: Austrian Rose—You are artistic and drawn to beauty.

Astral Color, Color Need, Apparel Color: Your Astral Color is Crimson, which reflects your ability to nurture. Yellow in your environment stimulates and exhilarates you. In your wardrobe, Rose gives you balance and harmony.

Fragrance: Pick scents that are soft and not overwhelming, like eclectic mixtures of wildflowers.

Tree: Walnut—You are unusually helpful and always looking for constant changes in your life.

Instruments: Piccolo, violin, flute

Composer: Böhm

Bird: Hummingbird—This bird is delicate and graceful. It can remain still for hours, then be as busy as a bee.

Symbol: Crown—the universal sign of dignity.

Harmonious Health and Nutrition . . .

Health Scent: Strawberry—soothing by nature, the strawberry promotes self-esteem and encourages love.

Favorable Foods: Kale, cherries, whole-wheat bread, peanuts

What's Lucky . . .

Lucky Numbers: 6, 9
Best Months: August and December
Best Day of the Week: Friday
Best Month Days: 1, 10, 19
Lucky Charm: A new penny in your shoe
Harmonious Signs for Relationships and Partnerships: Aquarius and Gemini

Spiritual Guides . . .

Star: Al Zubena—Those with this star often seek and find redemption.

Angel: Zuriel—This angel lends us the power to find balance when we desperately need it.

Guardian Angel: Malachi—"Messenger of Jehovah."

Spiritual Stone: Sapphire—the stone of serenity and prosperity.

✷ JUDITH'S INSIGHT ✷

You are the type who suffers in silence for a long time before eventually coming into your own. Everyone has disappointments, but you feel yours more keenly than most. Because you never feel secure, you struggle to create a safe environment for everybody around you. Your home is very, very important to you. You're at your best there. If you have the opportunity to work from home, it will suit you splendidly.

You tend to make relationships last a long time, and those who leave your life usually return to it down the road. You would make a wonderful teacher, professor, scientist, chemist, or researcher. You have great skill with operating and repairing all types of machines—from cars to computers.

You get overwhelmed by other's emotions, so love can be hard for you. Intimacy quickly tosses you out of balance. Very few people will be able to tell what you are feeling. It would be preferable for you to marry a mind-reader or a very empathic mate, because you lack basic communication skills. Your kindhearted nature will bring many people into your life, but only a very few will be truly close to you. You are prone to pushing people away because your fear-driven coldness leads them to think you are incapable of caring. You are like the sun with planets in orbit around you. The lighthearted, laughing side of you lures people in while your anxieties keep them forever at arm's length.

✷ ✷ ✷

OCTOBER 20 LIBRA • The scales of justice
September 23 at 3:00 A.M. to October 23 at 12:00 P.M. • NUMEROLOGY 2

Possessions and Desires . . .

Gem: Sapphire—This gem may help you find forgiveness from those you've wronged.

Flower: Rose Campion—You tend to think that real love needs to be earned.

Astral Color, Color Need, Apparel Color: Your Astral Color is Crimson, which reflects your ability to nurture. Yellow in your environment stimulates and exhilarates you. In your wardrobe, Rose gives you balance and harmony.

Fragrance: Pick scents that are soft and not overwhelming, like eclectic mixtures of wildflowers.

Tree: Maple—You have great stability and flashes of intuition.

Instrument: Pipe organ, guitar

Composers: Handel, Johann Sebastian Bach

Bird: Cuckoo—a good flyer, and very seldom a quitter. Some cuckoos tend to think they favor lonely isolation, but what they really yearn for is a family relationship.

Symbol: Cross—the symbol of self-sacrifice and reconciliation.

Harmonious Health and Nutrition . . .

Health Scent: Apple—A vivacious scent encouraging energy. Will help you to be more creative, intuitive and positive.

Favorable Foods: Asparagus, peaches, whole-wheat bread, walnuts

What's Lucky . . .

Lucky Numbers: 6, 9
Best Months: August and December
Best Day of the Week: Friday
Best Month Days: 2, 11, 20
Lucky Charms: Two 50-cent pieces. Give someone else one of them.
Harmonious Signs for Relationships and Partnerships: Aquarius and Gemini

Spiritual Guides . . .

Star: Al Zubena—Those with this star often seek and find redemption.

Angel: Zuriel—This angel lends us the power to find balance when we desperately need it.

Guardian Angel: St. John—This angel simplifies that which is complicated.

Spiritual Stone: Sapphire—the stone of serenity and prosperity.

✴ JUDITH'S INSIGHT ✴

How you look to others means everything to you; even the crease in your pants must be absolutely perfect. You are more comfortable in relationships and partnerships than on your own. You need a sounding board and support to succeed. You could still run your own business or find yourself in positions of control, but it's much easier if you have help than if you have to do everything yourself.

You have great organizational skills and will do very well with money and finance. You can make a dollar go a long, long way. It's crucial for you to find peace and order in the environment in which you live. Even your garage is in perfect shape.

You're emotionally cool when younger. The distance becomes a problem for you as you get older. You struggle to allow laughter and love into your heart. You spend your life trying to protect yourself, only to recognize that you are your own worst enemy. You need people more than you know. Your family is extremely important. No sacrifice is too great to keep them all together. Accomplishing this may sometimes be a struggle.

You would make a great teacher, artist, designer, preacher, or counselor. You listen well and don't respond unless you really have something worthwhile to say.

✴ ✴ ✴

OCTOBER 21   LIBRA • The scales of justice

September 23 at 3:00 A.M. to October 23 at 12:00 P.M. • NUMEROLOGY 3

Possessions and Desires . . .

Gem: Ruby—This stone may lead you to energy, friendship, and happiness.

Flower: Buttercup—You become more and more graceful with age.

Astral Color, Color Need, Apparel Color: Your Astral Color is Crimson, which reflects your ability to nurture. Yellow in your environment stimulates and exhilarates you. In your wardrobe, Brown brings you stability.

Fragrance: Pick scents that are soft and not overwhelming, like eclectic mixtures of wildflowers.

Tree: Elm—You have willpower, strength, and the ability to stand alone.

Instrument: Trombone

Composers: Verdi, Mendelssohn, Schumann

Bird: Swan—Regarded as royal and sacred, this bird has the protective nature of a mother, and can become a furious fighter in the defense of its young.

Symbol: Wreath—You have been crowned with a special personality. You are strong but extremely compassionate.

Harmonious Health and Nutrition . . .

Health Scent: Rose—This scent will lead you to passionate thoughts and make you feel warm inside.

Favorable Foods: Carrots, bananas, whole-wheat bread, almonds

What's Lucky . . .

Lucky Numbers: 6, 9
Best Months: August and December
Best Day of the Week: Friday
Best Month Days: 3, 12, 21
Lucky Charm: A pen that someone else has already used.
Harmonious Signs for Relationships and Partnerships: Aquarius and Gemini

Spiritual Guides . . .

Star: Al Icliel—This is the star of those who easily submit to authority.

Angel: Zuriel—This angel lends us the power to find balance when we desperately need it.

Guardian Angel: Johiel—This angel is a protector of all those with a humble heart.

Spiritual Stone: Sapphire—the stone of serenity and prosperity.

✳ JUDITH'S INSIGHT ✳

You feel responsible for the whole world and think every burden rests on your shoulders. You know you need others, but always feel that you must struggle alone. You don't understand that reaching out for a partner's hand doesn't make you weak. Later in life you learn that accepting aid from people doesn't mean that you have to agree with everything they do. To need is to be human.

You have many good friends because you work hard to keep them. Your uncertainty makes you appear secretive. Often you will forget the many nice things you've done for others. You have a fantastic sense of humor, but at times are afraid to laugh. Letting go will be one of the great challenges of your life.

You will be successful in more ways than one; your ambition will never let you quit short of your goals. Because you're so loyal, people go out of their way for you. You love law and order; it would be very surprising if both weren't important factors in your life. You or someone close to you—maybe a spouse, child, or parent—are heavily involved with legal papers in some way.

You do tend to have luck with a buck and may have the opportunity to turn that single into a huge pile. You are naturally giving and, thankfully, as you get older you become more caring and sharing.

Some careers for you: parent, child care provider, therapist. writer, C.E.O. of a company, critic, chef, or hotel manager.

✳ ✳ ✳

OCTOBER 22

LIBRA • The scales of justice

September 23 at 3:00 A.M. to October 23 at 12:00 P.M. • NUMEROLOGY 4

Possessions and Desires . . .

Gem: Emerald—Those who carry this stone tend to be lucky in love.

Flower: Red Primrose—Your best gifts are often overlooked even by you.

Astral Color, Color Need, Apparel Color: Your Astral Color is Crimson, which reflects your ability to nurture. Yellow in your environment stimulates and exhilarates you. In your wardrobe, Rose gives you balance and harmony.

Fragrance: Pick scents that are soft and not overwhelming, like eclectic mixtures of wildflowers.

Tree: Cherry—You will find yourself faced with constant new emotional awakenings.

Instruments: Bass, clarinet

Composers: Haydn, Wagner

Bird: Robin—the most sociable of all birds, with the ability to create quick friendships. It also can easily adapt to any home. When it wants something, it has the tendency to try to snatch it.

Symbol: Star—You are full of inner brightness and will stand out in any crowd. You will be seen as special.

Harmonious Health and Nutrition . . .

Health Scent: Vanilla—This scent will fill you with a feeling of cleanliness and stability.

Favorable Foods: Spinach, peaches, wholewheat bread, peanuts

What's Lucky . . .

Lucky Numbers: 6, 9
Best Months: August and December
Best Day of the Week: Friday
Best Month Days: 4, 13, 22
Lucky Charm: A piece of material cut from something in your home.
Harmonious Signs for Relationships and Partnerships: Aquarius and Gemini

Spiritual Guides . . .

Star: Al Zubena—Those with this star often seek and find redemption.

Angel: Zuriel—This angel lends us the power to find balance when we desperately need it.

Guardian Angel: Uriel—This angel brings the light of God's guidance.

Spiritual Stone: Sapphire—the stone of serenity and prosperity.

✶ JUDITH'S INSIGHT ✶

You have an attractive personality that draws everything you wish to you with the force of gravity. Stand still and watch your career, money, and spouse come rushing your way. You are a little eccentric and are partial to unusual people, situations, and surroundings.

Just because you can pull in what you need doesn't mean you can keep it without expending any energy. This is particularly true when it comes to a lasting relationship. Love will not be easy for you until you get older because your fears loom larger than your desires. As you get older, you will experience a love that will force you to give of yourself in order to keep it. It's very difficult for you to give emotionally, so you compensate with material gifts. Friends and families are important to you, but you push them away. You run away from the slightest unpleasantness instead of seeking to solve the situation.

You will do very well in sports or any activity where you work up a sweat. If you're not a professional athlete, you will be a passionate amateur. You can do just about any job available, so long as it's something you favor. When your energy is flowing you, can make the most difficult task seem like a cakewalk.

You tend to be well known and respected for your contributions.

Some careers for you: lawyer, guidance counselor, nutritionist, doctor, paralegal, or chemist.

★ ★ ★

OCTOBER 23 SCORPIO • The resourceful one of the zodiac

October 23 at 12:00 P.M. to November 22 at 5:00 A.M. • NUMEROLOGY 5

Possessions and Desires . . .

Gems: Sardius—This stone could give the wearer unusual insights into his or her own heart.

Flower: Polyanthus—You may need to learn that everything you are proud to have earned was only what the universe chose to give you.

Astral Color, Color Need, Apparel Color: Your Astral Color is Crimson, which reflects your ability to nurture. Yellow in your environment stimulates and exhilarates you. In your wardrobe, Brown brings you stability.

Fragrance: Buy pots of cinnabar or other scents from the sunny mediterranean or Orient. You are the most passionate sign of the zodiac, and your fragrance must be as unpredictable as you are.

Tree: Apple—You are creative, full of joy, and nearly magical. You bring happiness.

Instrument: Trumpet

Composer: Liszt

Bird: Flamingo—This beautiful, gregarious bird is always careful of its enemy. It is also a caretaker of the young and tries to keep everyone happy.

Symbol: Triangle—You have the right combination of abilities.

Harmonious Health and Nutrition . . .

Health Scent: Peach—This scent may balance your good qualities so that they equal your charm.

Favorable Foods: Asparagus, raspberries, whole-wheat bread, Brazil nuts

What's Lucky . . .

Lucky Numbers: 6, 9

Best Months: August and December

Best Day of the Week: Friday

Best Month Days: 4, 5, 23

Lucky Charm: A pen that someone else has already used.

Harmonious Signs for Relationships and Partnerships: Aquarius and Gemini

Spiritual Guides . . .

Star: Al Icliel—This is the star of those who easily submit to authority.

Angel: Zuriel—This angel lends us the power to find balance when we desperately need it.

Guardian Angel: Plavwell—The guardian that gives power and strength to one's presence.

Spiritual Stone: Sapphire—the stone of serenity and prosperity

✳ JUDITH'S INSIGHT ✳

You are very compassionate and have no problem showing it, though you sometimes lose interest unless you feel committed to a cause. You love adventure, even vicariously through a book or a movie. You crave constant stimulation and expect to live an exciting adventure every day.

Relationships can be contentious if your partner doesn't share or understand your need for thrill-seeking. An imprudent union with a quiet partner will lead to severe problems that will definitely end with two broken hearts. It's like pulling teeth to get you either into or out of a relationship. You have a rich emotional life but sometimes forget to be sensible.

Your patience, kindness, and intelligence will present you many opportunities to succeed. Your love of challenging, new experiences will often distract you from your goals. You make history in one way or another. You would like to be more practical and level-headed than you are. You love to learn and are equally fascinated by science fiction and history. Something that happened in the distant past will play a very big role in your life, though you may not notice how right away. When in doubt, follow your heart rather than your head.

Some careers for you could be: philosopher, chef, investigator, graphic artist, or troubleshooter.

★ ★ ★

OCTOBER 24

SCORPIO • The resourceful one of the zodiac

October 23 at 12:00 P.M. to November 22 at 5:00 A.M. • NUMEROLOGY 6

Possessions and Desires . . .

Gems: Topaz—This is an excellent gift to be exchanged between very loyal friends.
Flower: Plane—People think you're very bright.
Astral Color, Color Need, Apparel Color: Your Astral Color is Crimson, which reflects your ability to nurture. Yellow in your environment stimulates and exhilarates you. In your wardrobe, Rose gives you balance and harmony.
Fragrance: Buy pots of cinnabar or other scents from the sunny Mediterranean or Orient. You are the most passionate sign of the zodiac, and your fragrance must be as unpredictable as you are.
Trees: Palm—You tend to be very healthy and creative.
Instruments: Tambourine, lyre
Composer: Schubert
Bird: Goldfinch—There are no less than forty-four species of the finch, from the dull and inviting, the extraordinarily active and exquisite. These gentle creatures can be very shy in unsettled weather.
Symbol: Triangle—You have the right combination of abilities.

Harmonious Health and Nutrition . . .

Health Scent: Orange Blossom—This scent may balance your body, mind, and soul.
Favorable Foods: Cabbage, strawberries, barley, beef, pressed cheese

What's Lucky . . .

Lucky Numbers: 2, 4
Best Months: January and July
Best Day of the Week: Tuesday
Best Month Days: 4, 5, 23
Lucky Charms: A religious token or card from any religion.
Harmonious Signs for Relationships and Partnerships: Cancer and Pisces

Spiritual Guides . . .

Star: Al Kalb—Those with this star are often delightful.
Angel: Ambriel—This angel governs travel and transportation, particularly over water, and helps to create love and good communication.
Guardian Angel: Michael—"Who is like God."
Spiritual Stone: Chalcedony—This stone might help when taking long trips, especially by car.

✳ JUDITH'S INSIGHT ✳

Your suspicious nature should lead you into law enforcement, auditing, or insurance investigation, although your artistic talents may put you on stage or into a gallery. You go through more emotions in an hour than most people experience in a lifetime. Your independent nature fools others into believing you aren't as needy as you are. You aren't usually a taker, but rarely are you a giver. You remain very cynical and skeptical. Disappointments come and go, and you dwell on them far too long. Learn to enjoy the moment and not take life so seriously.

While walking life's tightrope you try to balance your heavy insecurities with your massive ego. When you fall off, it's usually into a deep, self-centered depression. You frequently fail to notice all the possibilities available to you. You are a very good friend, but one who's waiting for the other shoe to drop. People must prove themselves to you over and over again, and still you expect disappointment. You have to learn that trust doesn't just sprout spontaneously; it has to be grown from seed. You think the world owes you something and are never satisfied with what you have. You never allow yourself to forget, forgive, or get over the wounds of childhood.

You are lucky with money, which is good, because you like to gamble and fail to remember the lessons of losing. As you get older you finally surmount your ingrained cynicism and learn that you are a very caring person.

✳ ✳ ✳

OCTOBER 25 SCORPIO • The resourceful one of the zodiac

October 23 at 12:00 P.M. to November 22 at 5:00 A.M. • NUMEROLOGY 7

Possessions and Desires . . .

Gem: Agate—This stone may promote health and lead you to a long life.
Flower: Indian Pink—The things you dislike greatly in your youth could be the passions of your later years.
Astral Color, Color Need, Apparel Color: Your Astral Color is Black, the color of protection, birth, and beginnings. Red in your environment gives you energy and stamina. In your wardrobe, Green is your power color for overcoming obstacles.
Fragrance: Buy pots of cinnabar or other scents from the sunny Mediterranean or Orient. You are the most passionate sign of the zodiac, and your fragrance must be as unpredictable as you are.
Tree: Sycamore—Yours is the ability to love, communicate honestly with others, and have lasting relationships.
Instruments: Viola, trumpet
Composer: Liszt
Bird: Skylark—This handsome bird is beautiful when it sings. It always whistles while it works.
Symbol: Heart—You are enthusiastic, empathetic, and full of generosity and love.

Harmonious Health and Nutrition . . .

Health Scent: Jasmine—This scent may make you more easygoing when you are stressed.
Favorable Foods: Celery, blackberries, oats, chicken, eggs

What's Lucky . . .

Lucky Numbers: 2, 4
Best Months: January and July
Best Day of the Week: Tuesday
Best Month Days: 6, 15, 24
Lucky Charm: An old key.
Harmonious Signs for Relationships and Partnerships: Cancer and Pisces

Spiritual Guides . . .

Star: Al Kalb—Those with this star are often delightful.
Angel: Ambriel—This angel governs travel and transportation, particularly over water, and helps to create love and good communication.
Guardian Angel: Raphael—This angel attends to all of your needs when you are looking for guidance.
Spiritual Stone: Chalcedon—This stone might help when taking long trips, especially by car.

✳ *JUDITH'S INSIGHT* ✳

You don't get as much from life as you should because you tend to live in your head. You are given to extremes. You need to use your imagination as it was intended—find creative ways in which to support yourself. You talk the talk, but you lack the energy to walk the walk. You can be successful in extraordinary ways.

You have a passive-aggressive personality and try to dominate in all circumstances. You won't hold the steering wheel, but you can't seem to let the driver go where he or she will. You want to get to the top, but would rather whine than work to get there. You are a fine problem-solver with excellent ideas, opinions, and advice that could be useful to any field that employs you. You just have a huge blind spot when you look in the mirror.

You make a good parent or would do very well with children, even as a teacher. Later in life you may find yourself back in school learning a different career, or else the profession you choose requires many years of study. You would be successful as a lecturer, military commander, or highly specialized physician.

You have many heartaches and disappointments early in life, and these form obstacles to mature relationships. You tend surround yourself with those you know will disappoint you because it's all you expect. Stop thinking so much and resolve to do something. Once you find your direction, you'll finally arrive at your desired destination.

✷ ✷ ✷

OCTOBER 26   SCORPIO • The resourceful one of the zodiac

October 23 at 12:00 P.M. to November 22 at 5:00 A.M.   •   NUMEROLOGY 8

Possessions and Desires . . .

Gem: Chrysolite—This gem may help you clear your mind of sadness and worry.
Flower: Larch—You may find your audacity can lead you to folly.
Astral Color, Color Need, Apparel Color: Your Astral Color is Black, the color of protection, birth, and beginnings. Red in your environment gives you energy and stamina. In your wardrobe, Wine gives you energy.
Fragrance: Buy pots of cinnabar or other scents from the sunny Mediterranean or Orient. You are the most passionate sign of the zodiac, and your fragrance must be as unpredictable as you are.
Tree: Pine—Your relationships tend to be harmonious, both emotionally and mentally.
Instruments: Viola, trumpet
Composer: Beethoven
Bird: Bobolink—This charming singer is equally good as a soloist or a member of an orchestra. It is a very romantic bird, most useful as an insect destroyer, and elegant, with beautiful feathers, and always pleasant to have around.
Symbol: Wings—You are the source of balance in your world—this will bring you contentment.

Harmonious Health and Nutrition . . .

Health Scent: Almond—This scent may revitalize you and open you to greater possibilities.
Favorable Foods: Carrots, cranberries, rye crisp, fresh oysters, buttermilk

What's Lucky . . .

Lucky Numbers: 2, 4
Best Months: January and July
Best Day of the Week: Tuesday
Best Month Days: 4, 5, 23
Lucky Charm: Red ribbon in your wallet or doorway.

Harmonious Signs for Relationships and Partnerships: Cancer and Pisces

Spiritual Guides . . .

Star: Al Shaula—People who are born with this star are careful to avoid being cruel.
Angel: Ambriel—This angel governs travel and transportation, particularly over water, and helps to create love and good communication.
Guardian Angel: Seraphim—An angel that brings love, light, and passion.
Spiritual Stone: Chalcedon—This stone might help when taking long trips, especially by car.

✴ JUDITH'S INSIGHT ✴

You tend to take on more burdens than you can carry and are far too serious while hauling them. You are overconscientious without knowing it. You doubt your own capabilities and lack self-esteem. Your off-center wit and charm are often misconstrued as egotism. You're very understanding of others but fail miserably to gauge the bone-crushing amount of pressure you place on yourself.

You think romance is boring and so may delay looking for the right mate until all the good ones are taken. Somewhere along the way, you will surprise yourself by becoming a leader, or maybe you will suddenly realize that everyone has been following you all along. You have a caring heart shivering in the shadows cast by your ever-pondering mind. You are much more intelligent than you let on. When you're older, you'll be more comfortable showing off your mental talents.

You very much need to be a part of a family. If you don't get this feeling from those who are blood relations, you seek it from very close friends. You should become quite wealthy in this lifetime, if for no other reason than that you hold your coins so tightly the presidents scream.

Some careers for you: executive chef, hotel manager, head of securities. You have excellent mechanical and physical capabilities. You are unbelievably meticulous in nature.

✴ ✴ ✴

OCTOBER 27 SCORPIO • The resourceful one of the zodiac

October 23 at 12:00 P.M. to November 22 at 5:00 A.M. • NUMEROLOGY 9

Possessions and Desires . . .

Gem: Beryl—This gem could be good for meditation and concentration.

Flower: Peppermint—Others should flock to you for warmth.

Astral Color, Color Need, Apparel Color: Your Astral Color is Black, the color of protection, birth, and beginnings. Red in your environment gives you energy and stamina. In your wardrobe, Tan gives you balance and harmony.

Fragrance: Buy pots of cinnabar or other scents from the sunny Mediterranean or Orient. You are the most passionate sign of the zodiac, and your fragrance must be as unpredictable as you are.

Tree: Holly—Beware that you are not carried away by your passionate nature. The only way to grow is to be open to new experiences.

Instruments: Viola, trumpet

Composer: Liszt

Bird: Mockingbird—the most proficient minstrel in all the world's orchestra; graceful and enthusiastic.

Symbol: Anchor—This tranquil symbol signifies stability and strength, and stands for strong commitments in relationships.

Harmonious Health and Nutrition . . .

Health Scent: Lavender—This scent might lead others to trust you and make you patient.

Favorable Foods: Spinach, watermelon, oats, beef, pressed cheese

What's Lucky . . .

Lucky Numbers: 2, 4
Best Months: January and July
Best Day of the Week: Tuesday
Best Month Days: 9, 18, 27

Lucky Charm: A U.S. coin or a bill of any amount from the year you were born.

Harmonious Signs for Relationships and Partnerships: Cancer and Pisces

Spiritual Guides . . .

Star: Al Kalb—Those with this star are often delightful.

Angel: Ambriel—This angel governs travel and transportation, particularly over water, and helps to create love and good communication.

Guardian Angel: Gabriel—"God is my strength."

Spiritual Stone: Chalcedon—This stone might help when taking long trips, especially by car.

✷ JUDITH'S INSIGHT ✷

Your secretive nature may keep others from ever really knowing the real you. You like to protect yourself unnecessarily. You are the perfect "fun" date: adventurous, energetic, and totally entertaining. Your gifts of eloquence, humor, style and charm are so alluring that attracting a mate is easy as pie, but keeping relationships may be tough for you.

The natural careers for you would be lawyer, surgeon, chemist, or clergyperson. You are witty, well-spoken, affable, clever, and curious, all of which ensure that you're rarely bored. It is very important for you to be considered successful—you need to be noticed. You seek recognition in more than one career and in your hobbies. You are authoritative and likely to gain respect and responsibility. Local, state, and national politics interest you. Very often, you volunteer to lead the PTA or local charity organization.

You can be fearful that others will discover how spiritual you are. What you feel the most strongly you conceal the most completely. Family and friends are important to you for the affection that they can give you. Most of the time, you're surrounded by many people and are a devoted friend, child, parent, spouse, or sibling.

✷ ✷ ✷

OCTOBER 28

SCORPIO • The resourceful one of the zodiac

October 23 at 12:00 P.M. to November 22 at 5:00 A.M. • NUMEROLOGY 1

Possessions and Desires . . .

Gem: Agate—This stone may promote health and lead you to a long life.

Flower: Osmunda—You tend to be a happy dreamer.

Astral Color, Color Need, Apparel Color: Your Astral Color is Black, the color of protection, birth and beginnings. Red in your environment gives you energy and stamina. In your wardrobe, Green is your power color for overcoming obstacles.

Fragrance: Buy pots of cinnabar or other scents from the sunny Mediterranean or Orient. You are the most passionate sign of the zodiac, and your fragrance must be as unpredictable as you are.

Tree: Walnut—You are unusually helpful and always looking for constant changes in your life.

Instruments: Oboe, flute, clarinet, piano, French horn, organ, piccolo

Composer: Böhm

Bird: Bird of Paradise—the "bird of the Gods." You will shine and love extraordinary circumstances.

Symbol: Crown—the universal sign of dignity.

Harmonious Health and Nutrition . . .

Health Scent: Strawberry—Soothing by nature, the strawberry promotes self-esteem and encourages love.

Favorable Foods: Cabbage, apple, barley, salmon, eggs

What's Lucky . . .

Lucky Numbers: 2, 4

Best Months: January and July

Best Day of the Week: Tuesday

Best Month Days: 4, 5, 23

Lucky Charm: A new penny in your shoe.

Harmonious Signs for Relationships and Partnerships: Cancer and Pisces

Spiritual Guides . . .

Star: Al Kalb—Those with this star are often delightful.

Angel: Ambriel—This angel governs travel and transportation, particularly over water, and helps to create love and good communication.

Guardian Angel: Plavwell—The guardian that gives power and strength to one's presence.

Spiritual Stone: Chalcedon—This stone might help when taking long trips, especially by car.

✳ *JUDITH'S INSIGHT* ✳

You have the need to dig deeply into everything. Getting to the bottom of things is your specialty, and you pursue it in careers such as scientist, chemist, astronomer, astrologer, paralegal, or inventor. For you, solving problems is as important and natural as breathing. You love to read history and are likely to make it.

You have no problem catching the hearts of others—deciding the next step in relationships, however, will always seem crippling. You simultaneously fear and yearn for a solid commitment. You are far too difficult for even you to figure out. You tend to look for problems even when none exist, but you refuse to be honest about your concerns. You tend to run from conflict. You need calm and peace so much that you force others to keep silent when open discussion would be more healing.

You change your mind on major issues three times a day. Your home is your castle, and you will always feel more secure when there. Your optimism makes it easy for others to believe that things will get better in time. You are too intense and easily overwhelmed by sentiment. Your kindhearted generosity will complicate your life in ways you can't imagine. You readily agree to help, but often don't follow through. Eventually, you will be a huge success in more than one area. You may accomplish more in one lifetime than most do in several.

✳ ✳ ✳

OCTOBER 29

SCORPIO • The resourceful one of the zodiac

October 23 at 12:00 P.M. to November 22 at 5:00 A.M. • NUMEROLOGY 2

Possessions and Desires . . .

Gem: Sapphire—This gem may help you find forgiveness from those you've wronged.

Flower: Oxeye—You usually are extremely patient.

Astral Color, Color Need, Apparel Color: Your Astral Color is Black, the color of protection, birth, and beginnings. Red in your environment gives you energy and stamina. In your wardrobe, Wine gives you energy.

Fragrance: Buy pots of cinnabar or other scents from the sunny Mediterranean or Orient. You are the most passionate sign of the zodiac, and your fragrance must be as unpredictable as you are.

Tree: Maple—You have great stability and flashes of intuition.

Instruments: Viola, trumpet

Composer: Beethoven

Bird: Stork—Turkish bird, held in high esteem the world over. This bird is intelligent but may have strange tendencies.

Symbol: Cross—the symbol of self-sacrifice and reconciliation.

Harmonious Health and Nutrition . . .

Health Scent: Apple—A vivacious scent encouraging energy. Will help you to be more creative, intuitive and positive.

Favorable Foods: Celery, raspberry, oats, beef, buttermilk

What's Lucky . . .

Lucky Numbers: 2, 4

Best Months: January and July

Best Day of the Week: Tuesday

Best Month Days: 2, 11, 20

Lucky Charms: Two 50-cent pieces. Give someone else one of them.

Harmonious Signs for Relationships and Partnerships: Cancer and Pisces

Spiritual Guides . . .

Star: Al Shaula—People who are born with this star are careful to avoid being cruel.

Angel: Ambriel—This angel governs travel and transportation, particularly over water, and helps to create love and good communication.

Guardian Angel: St. John—This angel simplifies that which is complicated.

Spiritual Stone: Chalcedon—This stone might help when taking long trips, especially by car.

✳ JUDITH'S INSIGHT ✳

Being caring, considerate, and compassionate will get you in the kind of trouble most people pray for. You will be overwhelmed by offers and opportunities in work, friendships, and relationships. People will go well out of their way just to be near your sensitivity and charm. "Popular" doesn't begin to describe it.

You do better at work where you have partners. Remember to select the right ones. You may want be on your own, thinking you should be more independent, but you will be lonely. You need someone you feel close enough to share with—whether it be an assistant, mentor, or office best buddy. Others think money is more important to you than it really is. If you become wealthy, as you should, they will finally understand you value it only as a tool to help others.

If you sacrifice too much for love, you'll only end up miserable. You are a slavishly devoted mate whose efforts are largely ignored. You have many troubles from those you love, but time will send you the perfect match. You are always searching for romance, though sometimes in horribly wrong places.

Your best careers are in government, engineering, acting, or communications. You may come up with an innovation or two that make you rich. It is very important for you to feel peace in your surroundings. Where you work and live will be the deciding factor in your success. As you get older the chains of seriousness fall away, so you can run with laughter and love to your special destiny.

✳ ✳ ✳

OCTOBER 30

SCORPIO • The resourceful one of the zodiac

October 23 at 12:00 P.M. to November 22 at 5:00 A.M. • NUMEROLOGY 3

Possessions and Desires . . .

Gem: Ruby—This stone may lead you to energy, friendship, and happiness.

Flower: Parsley—You tend to see life as one long, continuous party.

Astral Color, Color Need, Apparel Color: Your Astral Color is Black, the color of protection, birth, and beginnings. Red in your environment gives you energy and stamina. In your wardrobe, Tan gives you balance and harmony.

Fragrance: Buy pots of cinnabar or other scents from the sunny Mediterranean or Orient. You are the most passionate sign of the zodiac, and your fragrance must be as unpredictable as you are.

Tree: Elm—You have willpower, strength, and the ability to stand alone.

Instruments: Viola, trumpet

Composer: Liszt

Bird: Eagle—This bird is quick to use its powers of flight. It can see immeasurable distances in a single glance, and can sometimes appear to be indifferent.

Symbol: Wreath—You have been crowned with a special personality. You are strong but extremely compassionate.

Harmonious Health and Nutrition . . .

Health Scent: Rose—This scent will lead you to passionate thoughts and make you feel warm inside.

Favorable Foods: Mushrooms, black figs, barley, fresh oysters, pressed cheese

What's Lucky . . .

Lucky Numbers: 2, 4
Best Months: January and July
Best Day of the Week: Tuesday
Best Month Days: 4, 5, 23
Lucky Charm: A pen that someone else has already used.

Harmonious Signs for Relationships and Partnerships: Cancer and Pisces

Spiritual Guides . . .

Star: Al Kalb—Those with this star are often delightful.

Angel: Ambriel—This angel governs travel and transportation, particularly over water, and helps to create love and good communication.

Guardian Angel: Johiel—This angel is a protector of all those with a humble heart.

Spiritual Stone: Chalcedon—This stone might help when taking long trips, especially by car.

✶ *JUDITH'S INSIGHT* ✶

You love justice and fight hard for a principle you believe in. You would make a great mediator, psychologist, or advocate. You clearly understand both sides of complex issues and strive to comprehend even the opinions you don't agree with. You keep your friends for life. You find happiness in close relationships. Although you receive much heartache and disappointment from romance, you accept what life offers. You always work diligently at making things better. You're charming, devoted, and easy to love. You probably have difficulties with your siblings if you have them. It may seem that your family has neglected you in some way.

You will be successful because of your powerful vision and unstoppable attitude. If you are an entrepreneur, you may have two or three businesses fail before you succeed. In any career, years will go by before you're recognized for your talents. Don't worry if it seems like you're going downhill; you are just picking up speed. You will learn something important from every job you take.

You could do well in stocks, bonds, or anything to do with paper money. You remain optimistic because you know that eventually most things go your way. If you fully trust your intuition, you'll make better choices in life. You add balance to your environment with great organizational, intellectual, and creative skill. You possess the willingness to work very hard for what you want.

✶ ✶ ✶

OCTOBER 31 SCORPIO • The resourceful one of the zodiac

October 23 at 12:00 P.M. to November 22 at 5:00 A.M. • NUMEROLOGY 4

Possessions and Desires . . .

Gem: Emerald—Those who carry this stone tend to be lucky in love.

Flower: Common Nettle—You tend to work well with others.

Astral Color, Color Need, Apparel Color: Your Astral Color is Black, the color of protection, birth, and beginnings. Red in your environment gives you energy and stamina. In your wardrobe, green is your power color for overcoming obstacles.

Fragrance: Buy pots of cinnabar or other scents from the sunny Mediterranean or Orient. You are the most passionate sign of the zodiac, and your fragrance must be as unpredictable as you are.

Tree: Cherry—You will find yourself faced with constant new emotional awakenings..

Instruments: Bass, clarinet

Composers: Haydn, Wagner

Bird: Robin—the most sociable of all birds, with the ability to create quick friendships. It also can be easily adapt to any home. When it wants something, it has the tendency to try to snatch it.

Symbol: Star—You are full of inner brightness and will stand out in any crowd. You will be seen as special.

Harmonious Health and Nutrition . . .

Health Scent: Vanilla—This scent will fill you with a feeling of cleanliness and stability.

Favorable Foods: Tomatoes, pineapple, rye crisps, salmon, buttermilk

What's Lucky . . .

Lucky Numbers: 2, 4
Best Months: January and July
Best Day of the Week: Tuesday
Best Month Days: 4, 5, 23
Lucky Charm: A piece of material cut from something in your home.

Harmonious Signs for Relationships and Partnerships: Cancer and Pisces

Spiritual Guides . . .

Star: Al Shaula—People who are born with this star are careful to avoid being cruel.

Angel: Ambriel—This angel governs travel and transportation, particularly over water, and helps to create love and good communication.

Guardian Angel: Uriel—This angel brings the light of God's guidance.

Spiritual Stone: Chalcedon—This stone might help when taking long trips, especially by car.

✦ *JUDITH'S INSIGHT* ✦

Everybody around you will feel nurtured by you in one way or another. Your low self-esteem worsens as you get older, so you should decide to conquer it now. You see education as a tool to help yourself and others. You may not get all that you learn from books; instead, you may graduate with honors from the school of hard knocks.

You're lucky in love and have secure relationships. Love whoever you want, but be yourself. You start life being very dependent on others and only later discover your own inner strength. That's why so many others depend on you. However, someone as loyal and devoted as you usually isn't such a good flirt.

You may become more involved in strenuous physical activities such as long-distance running as you get older. Don't overdo it, or you'll be plagued by injuries. Seek jobs in which you can continually grow in knowledge and responsibility. You would do well as a nurse, researcher, teacher, or child care provider. You may even want to write or work on either side of a camera at one point. You might pursue law if you thought you could champion the rights of the downtrodden.

Some type of fame finds you in this lifetime; your name will be printed in books, though maybe in small print.

✶ ✶ ✶

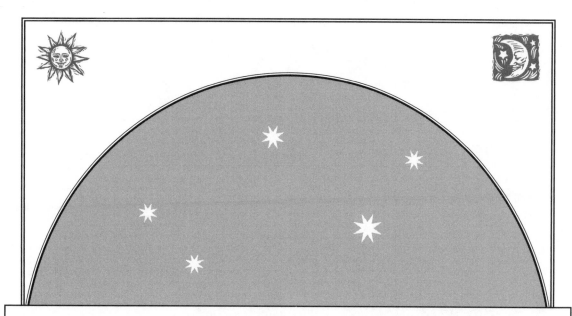

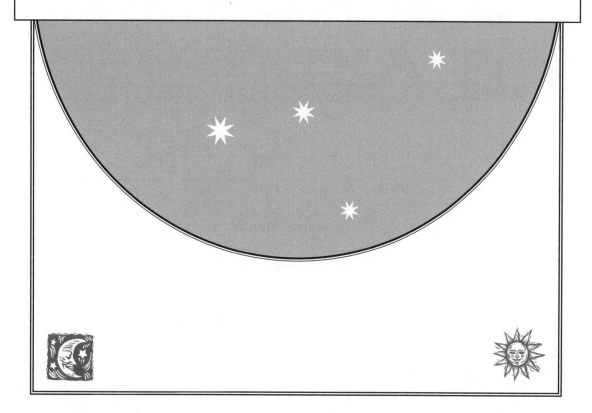

NOVEMBER

NOVEMBER 1

SCORPIO • The resourceful one of the zodiac

October 23 at 12:00 P.M. to November 22 at 5:00 A.M. • NUMEROLOGY 1

Possessions and Desires . . .

Gem: Turquoise—This stone might help you find material wealth.
Flower: Nasturtium—You have a strong love of your country.
Astral Color, Color Need, Apparel Color: Your Astral Color is Black, the color of protection, birth, and beginnings. Red in your environment gives you energy and stamina. In your wardrobe, Wine gives you energy.
Fragrance: Buy pots of cinnabar or other scents from the sunny Mediterranean or Orient. You are the most passionate sign of the zodiac, and your fragrance must be as unpredictable as you are.
Tree: Walnut—You are unusually helpful and always looking for constant changes in your life.
Instruments: Oboe, flute, clarinet, piano, French horn, organ, piccolo
Composer: Böhm
Bird: Bird of paradise—"the bird of the gods." You will shine and love extraordinary circumstances.
Symbol: Crown—the universal sign of dignity.

Harmonious Health and Nutrition . . .

Health Scent: Strawberry—Soothing by nature, the strawberry promotes self-esteem and encourages love.
Favorable Foods: Carrots, black figs, barley, beef, buttermilk

What's Lucky . . .

Lucky Numbers: 2, 4
Best Months: January and July
Best Day of the Week: Tuesday
Best Month Days: 4, 5, 23
Lucky Charm: A new penny in your shoe.

Harmonious Signs for Relationships and Partnerships: Cancer and Pisces

Spiritual Guides . . .

Star: Al Kalb—Those with this star are often delightful.
Angel: Ambriel—This angel governs travel and transportation, particularly over water, and helps to create love and good communication.
Guardian Angel: Plavwell—The guardian that gives power and strength to one's presence.
Spiritual Stone: Chalcedon—This stone might help when taking long trips, especially by car.

✶ JUDITH'S INSIGHT ✶

With your boundless energy and exceptionally powerful presence, others around you sense your zest for life. You are creative in every sense of the word, and your good ideas and imagination bring success. You are observant by nature and would make a great critic. There will definitely be success in a government job; your opinions would be extremely well received. You have many strong feelings, and when you express them, people listen.

Your keen wit and sense of humor naturally attract people. If you feel neglected in your love life, you may become sarcastic. Although you're bighearted and forgiving, you can be moody at times. You dwell on things too long when angered and need to be more resilient. On the whole, you will do well in life because you work hard at being a good person. Watch out for disillusionment. It could be difficult for you to make a comeback after experiencing disappointments.

You tend to find love, but just remember, for you it's "the more you give, the more you get." You are too practical at times and need to be more emotionally involved in what is going on around you.

✶ ✶ ✶

NOVEMBER 2

SCORPIO • The resourceful one of the zodiac

October 23 at 12:00 P.M. to November 22 at 5:00 A.M. • NUMEROLOGY 2

Possessions and Desires . . .

Gem: Sapphire—This gem may help you find forgiveness from those you've wronged.
Flower: Mountain ash—You tend to be very prudent in your business.
Astral Color, Color Need, Apparel Color: Your Astral Color is Black, the color of protection, birth, and beginnings. Red in your environment gives you energy and stamina. In your wardrobe, Tan gives you balance and harmony.
Fragrance: Buy pots of cinnabar or other scents from the sunny Mediterranean or Orient. You are the most passionate sign of the zodiac, and your fragrance must be as unpredictable as you are.
Tree: Maple—You have great stability and flashes of intuition.
Instruments: Pipe organ, cymbal, drum
Composers: Handel, Johann Sebastian Bach
Bird: Cuckoo—a good flyer, and very seldom a quitter. Some cuckoos tend to think they favor lonely isolation, but what they really yearn for is a family relationship.
Symbol: Cross—the symbol of self-sacrifice and reconciliation.

Harmonious Health and Nutrition . . .

Health Scent: Apple—A vivacious scent encouraging energy. Will help you to be more creative, intuitive and positive.
Favorable Foods: Mushrooms, cranberries, barley, fresh oysters, buttermilk

What's Lucky . . .

Lucky Numbers: 2, 4
Best Months: January and July
Best Day of the Week: Tuesday
Best Month Days: 2, 11, 20
Lucky Charms: Two 50-cent pieces. Give someone else one of them.
Harmonious Signs for Relationships and Partnerships: Cancer and Pisces

Spiritual Guides . . .

Star: Al Shaula—People born with this star are careful to avoid being cruel.
Angel: Ambriel—This angel governs travel and transportation, particularly over water, and helps to create love and good communication.
Guardian Angel: St. Thomas—This angel brings affection from others and encourages you in all that you do.
Spiritual Stone: Chalcedon—This stone might help when taking long trips, especially by car.

✶ JUDITH'S INSIGHT ✶

You can be the most frustrating human being on the planet. It may take a rocket scientist to figure you out simply because it's too scary for you to let others know who you really are. If you can keep your emotions from getting in the way, your abundant talent, energy, and imagination will help you succeed in your chosen career. You prefer to be your own boss and don't function well when others tell you what to do.

Your fearless and meticulous nature combined with your interest in the sciences would make you a great surgeon. Strong principles and a defense-oriented personality will lead you into a courtroom, either as a judge or as a lawyer fighting the good fight, usually championing the underdog. You have a strong physical and mental presence. You love challenging occupations, but you can coast on your luck as a stockbroker or market analyst. You are charged and raring to go, and never, ever need new batteries.

Relationships are more difficult for you because you choose the unusual and desire the unconventional. What can you expect from a person who finds the pursuit of material possessions so darn intriguing? You have the key to your own happiness when it comes to finding a mate. You make things as complicated or as simple as you decide.

You will get what you give in life; maybe this is the lesson you're here to learn.

✶ ✶ ✶

NOVEMBER 3

SCORPIO • The resourceful one of the zodiac

October 23 at 12:00 P.M. to November 22 at 5:00 A.M. • NUMEROLOGY 3

Possessions and Desires . . .

Gem: Ruby—This stone may lead you to energy, friendship, and happiness.

Flower: Mugwort—Happiness will be waiting for you to realize you already have it.

Astral Color, Color Need, Apparel Color: Your Astral Color is Black, the color of protection, birth, and beginnings. Red in your environment gives you energy and stamina. In your wardrobe, Green is your power color for overcoming obstacles.

Fragrance: Buy pots of cinnabar or other scents from the sunny Mediterranean or Orient. You are the most passionate sign of the zodiac, and your fragrance must be as unpredictable as you are.

Tree: Elm—You have willpower, strength, and the ability to stand alone.

Instrument: Trombone

Composers: Verdi, Mendelssohn, Schumann

Bird: Swan—Regarded as royal and sacred, this bird has the protective nature of a mother, and can become a furious fighter in the defense of its own.

Symbol: Wreath—You have been crowned with a special personality. You are strong but extremely compassionate.

Harmonious Health and Nutrition . . .

Health Scent: Rose—This scent will lead you to passionate thoughts and make you feel warm inside.

Favorable Foods: Okra, lemon, barley, salmon, eggs

What's Lucky . . .

Lucky Numbers: 2, 4
Best Months: January and July
Best Day of the Week: Tuesday
Best Month Days: 4, 5, 23
Lucky Charm: A pen that someone else has already used.

Harmonious Signs for Relationships and Partnerships: Cancer and Pisces

Spiritual Guides . . .

Star: Al Kalb—Those with this star are often delightful.

Angel: Ambriel—This angel governs travel and transportation, particularly over water, and helps to create love and good communication.

Guardian Angel: St. Thomas—This angel brings affection from others and encourages you in all that you do.

Spiritual Stone: Chalcedon—This stone might help when taking long trips, especially by car.

✷ JUDITH'S INSIGHT ✷

You're quite the challenging person and love being that way. You can't wait to travel the entire wide world and soak up all the knowledge, experiences, and excitement every corner has to offer. You would make a great journalist, photographer, or researcher. After you've traveled, seek work in government, business or other endeavors that require someone dependable. You have original ideas and are creative, but you tend to rely more on your organizational and administrative skills.

Romance depends on you. When you finally decide to be happy, you'll work at it until you make it happen. Before you're ready, prospective suitors find you a messy battlefield. Unfortunately, the person who must bear the real brunt of your combative nature is you.

You tend to be generous when you have money in your pocket. When cash is low, you give freely of your time and energy. You're very sympathetic and charitable to those people you favor, but if you feel disrespect or disloyalty, you can become overly defensive and arrogant.

Remember, you're the traveler: whether you do it early or late in life, you're sure to find a way to cram in as much as you can from the universe around you.

✶ ✶ ✶

NOVEMBER 4 SCORPIO • The resourceful one of the zodiac

October 23 at 12:00 P.M. to November 22 at 5:00 A.M. • NUMEROLOGY 4

Possessions and Desires . . .

Gem: Emerald—Those who carry this stone tend to be lucky in love.
Flower: Mushroom—You may need to learn to trust more those who care for you.
Astral Color, Color Need, Apparel Color: Your Astral Color is Black, the color of protection, birth, and beginnings. Red in your environment gives you energy and stamina. In your wardrobe, Wine gives you energy.
Fragrance: Buy pots of cinnabar or other scents from the sunny Mediterranean or Orient. You are the most passionate sign of the zodiac, and your fragrance must be as unpredictable as you are.
Tree: Cherry—You will find yourself faced with constant new emotional awakenings.
Instruments: Bass, clarinet
Composers: Haydn, Wagner
Bird: Kildeer—This common bird is usually found consorting with other species, and can adapt to any environment.
Symbol: Star—You are full of inner brightness and will stand out in any crowd. You will be seen as special.

Harmonious Health and Nutrition . . .

Health Scent: Vanilla—This scent will fill you with a feeling of cleanliness and stability.
Favorable Foods: Cabbage, blackberries, oats, fresh oysters, buttermilk

What's Lucky . . .

Lucky Numbers: 2, 4
Best Months: January and July
Best Day of the Week: Tuesday
Best Month Days: 4, 13, 22
Lucky Charm: A piece of material cut from something in your home.
Harmonious Signs for Relationships and Partnerships: Cancer and Pisces

Spiritual Guides . . .

Star: Al Kalb—Those with this star are often delightful.
Angel: Ambriel—This angel governs travel and transportation, particularly over water, and helps to create love and good communication.
Guardian Angel: Uriel—This angel brings the light of God's guidance.
Spiritual Stone: Chalcedon—This stone might help when taking long trips, especially by car.

★ JUDITH'S INSIGHT ★

Why do you feel like the underdog? Without enthusiasm for achieving your goals and finding new resolve, disappointments usually take awhile to pass. Having taken on adult responsibilities at an early age makes you feel old. Your self-esteem wavers during your younger years, but as you grow older and connect with your mate, harmony and happiness blossom. You don't realize how special you are. A kind heart, an active mind, strong values, and a vibrant imagination contribute to your uniqueness. Every day you face numerous contradictions in how you see yourself, and while you sort things out, life keeps presenting you bigger challenges. You are the dutiful child, spouse, student, parent, or worker—no matter what your role in life, you take it seriously.

Focus less on the contents of your wallet or bank account as the measure of your success. You're well-rounded and have so many different talents, you could have difficulty choosing one career. You could have a career in politics or music or you could even be a brain surgeon. You will develop a great desire to accomplish many things and may achieve them as you get older. Your strong need for justice makes you want to help underdogs, either as a public defender or an advocate for children.

You have so many uncommon gifts that finding the best way to use them takes time. Your first lesson: be patient with yourself.

★ ★ ★

NOVEMBER 5 SCORPIO • The resourceful one of the zodiac

October 23 at 12:00 P.M. to November 22 at 5:00 A.M. • NUMEROLOGY 5

Possessions and Desires . . .

Gem: Sardius—This stone could give the wearer unusual insights into his or her own heart.
Flower: Mimosa—You may be too sensitive to criticism.
Astral Color, Color Need, Apparel Color: Your Astral Color is Black, the color of protection, birth, and beginnings. Red in your environment gives you energy and stamina. In your wardrobe, Tan gives you balance and harmony.
Fragrance: Buy pots of cinnabar or other scents from the sunny Mediterranean or Orient. You are the most passionate sign of the zodiac, and your fragrance must be as unpredictable as you are.
Tree: Apple—You are creative, full of joy, and nearly magical. You bring happiness.
Instruments: Viola, trumpet
Composer: Liszt
Bird: Flamingo—This beautiful, gregarious bird is always careful of its enemy. It is also a caretaker of the young and tries to keep everyone happy.
Symbol: Triangle—You have the right combination of abilities.

Harmonious Health and Nutrition . . .

Health Scent: Peach—This scent may balance your good qualities so that they equal your charm.
Favorable Foods: Asparagus, cranberries, barley, beef, pressed cheese

What's Lucky . . .

Lucky Numbers: 2, 4
Best Months: January and July
Best Day of the Week: Tuesday
Best Month Days: 4, 5, 23
Lucky Charms: A rabbit's foot or a white candle
Harmonious Signs for Relationships and Partnerships: Cancer and Pisces

Spiritual Guides . . .

Star: Al Shaula—People born with this star are careful to avoid being cruel.
Angel: Ambriel—This angel governs travel and transportation, particularly over water, and helps to create love and good communication.
Guardian Angel: Plavwell—The guardian that gives power and strength to one's presence.
Spiritual Stone: Chalcedon—This stone might help when taking long trips, especially by car.

✳ JUDITH'S INSIGHT ✳

Organization is your strong suit, but you're talented in many other ways. You have a deep love and understanding of acting and nature. Your energy keeps you from knowing whether you're coming or going. Hint: Usually you're doing both.

Look for careers relating to art or beauty. Tell prospective employers you can be trained to do just about anything—you won't be lying. You have strong imagination and unflagging stamina. You are gifted, especially in situations that require intelligence. Expect to be frustrated when faced with stagnation. You need to be constantly learning.

Cupid could prove a challenging adversary in this lifetime. Many times through the years, your love life will suddenly swing from happy to bleak and back again. Understand that you become bored easily with your mate—although you're always or continuously loyal. Selecting a mate too early in life may trap you in a union that will bring you grief, though you cannot leave. The later you get married, the better your chances at happiness. There are lessons you must first learn when it comes to love, relationships, and family. Beware of the times when any or all of these overwhelm you.

You need your friends, and connections remain close for many years. Try not to second-guess yourself. If you learn patience and stability while focusing on what you're really looking for, you won't be so anxious all the time.

✳ ✳ ✳

NOVEMBER 6 SCORPIO • The resourceful one of the zodiac

October 23 at 12:00 P.M. to November 22 at 5:00 A.M. • NUMEROLOGY 6

Possessions and Desires . . .

Gem: Topaz—This is an excellent gift to be exchanged between very loyal friends.
Flower: Mandrake—You may tend to let your fears hold you back from enjoying life.
Astral Color, Color Need, Apparel Color: Your Astral Color is Black, the color of protection, birth, and beginnings. Red in your environment gives you energy and stamina. In your wardrobe, Green is your power color for overcoming obstacles.
Fragrance: Buy pots of cinnabar or other scents from the sunny Mediterranean or Orient. You are the most passionate sign of the zodiac, and your fragrance must be as unpredictable as you are.
Tree: Palm—You tend to be very healthy and creative.
Instruments: Tambourine, lyre
Composer: Schubert
Bird: Falcon—an expert hunter. When well-trained, it can adapt to many tasks and is usually obedient.
Symbol: Crescent—You are more likely to be influenced by the phases of the moon. Your easygoing manner leads you to peaceful situations.

Harmonious Health and Nutrition . . .

Health Scent: Orange Blossom—This scent may balance your body, mind, and soul.
Favorable Foods: Corn, watermelon, barley, fresh oysters, eggs

What's Lucky . . .

Lucky Numbers: 2, 4
Best Months: January and July
Best Day of the Week: Tuesday
Best Month Days: 6, 14, 24
Lucky Charms: A religious token or card from any religion.
Harmonious Signs for Relationships and Partnerships: Cancer and Pisces

Spiritual Guides . . .

Star: Al Shaula—People born with this star are careful to avoid being cruel.
Angel: Ambriel—This angel governs travel and transportation, particularly over water, and helps to create love and good communication.
Guardian Angel: Michael—"Who is like God."
Spiritual Stone: Chalcedon—This stone might help when taking long trips, especially by car.

✶ JUDITH'S INSIGHT ✶

You are lovable by nature, but a nuclear physicist couldn't explain yourself to you or others. Besides your extreme moods, you feel the need to keep your feelings secret until you've sorted them out. Why don't you think of asking for help? The added trouble is, on the surface, you don't seem all that complex. You can be a cheerful social butterfly or icy cold and distant, as the whim strikes you. Calling you a challenge is an understatement.

Do you want to be a philosopher, writer, electrician, government agent, lawyer, nurse, or doctor? Any of these suit you. You have a strong mind, resolute heart, and powerful energies. The right opportunities may take time to find, but when you're not looking, you discover yourself standing in the middle of exactly the right job.

Be kind to the person who eventually captures your heart. You offer them a formidable task. Maintaining a relationship with you takes a lot of energy. Keep the desire fresh, or you run the risk of taking it for granted and unwittingly tearing down all that has been built. Even though you're very kind, loving, and altogether affectionate, you require extra attention because you're so unsure of yourself and what makes you happy.

Look forward to the time when you finally discover your missing balance; the passing of time teaches you respect for yourself.

★ ★ ★

NOVEMBER 7

SCORPIO • The resourceful one of the zodiac

October 23 at 12:00 P.M. to November 22 at 5:00 A.M. • NUMEROLOGY 7

Possessions and Desires . . .

Gem: Emerald—This gem is thought to aid in soothing the connection between the desires of the soul with those of the body

Flower: Marvel-of-Peru—You tend to think that the brave are foolish.

Astral Color, Color Need, Apparel Color: Your Astral Color is Black, the color of protection, birth, and beginnings. Red in your environment gives you energy and stamina. In your wardrobe, Wine gives you energy.

Fragrance: Buy pots of cinnabar or other scents from the sunny Mediterranean or Orient. You are the most passionate sign of the zodiac, and your fragrance must be as unpredictable as you are.

Tree: Sycamore—Yours is the ability to love, communicate honestly with others, and have lasting relationships.

Instrument: Harp

Composers: Gluck, Brahms

Bird: Warbling Parakeet—the most beautiful of all birds, it is known as the love bird. It does seem to have the powers of imitation.

Symbol: Heart—You are enthusiastic, empathetic, and full of generosity and love.

Harmonious Health and Nutrition . . .

Health Scent: Jasmine—This scent may make you more easygoing when you are stressed.

Favorable Foods: Cauliflower, cranberries, barley, salmon, buttermilk

What's Lucky . . .

Lucky Numbers: 2, 4

Best Months: January and July

Best Day of the Week: Tuesday

Best Month Days: 4, 5, 23

Lucky Charm: An old key.

Harmonious Signs for Relationships and Partnerships: Cancer and Pisces

Spiritual Guides . . .

Star: Al Kalb—Those with this star are often delightful.

Angel: Ambriel—This angel governs travel and transportation, particularly over water, and helps to create love and good communication.

Guardian Angel: Raphael—This angel attends to all of your needs when you are looking for guidance.

Spiritual Stone: Chalcedon—This stone might help when taking long trips, especially by car.

✳ JUDITH'S INSIGHT ✳

If persistence and consistency count in this world, you will have all the success and happiness you'll ever need. A natural intelligence enables you to write and follow a personal book of rules you'll rely on all your life. Your sensitivity may help or hinder or both. You don't seem as passionate as you are. Family and other attachments might trip you up. It will sometimes take hard work just to keep your emotional car on the road. Try to develop relationships based on harmony.

You will do well if you decide to become a scientist, chemist, critic, philosopher, or jurist. You are quite the thinker; while that's a good thing sometimes, you don't know how to shut off your mind when necessary. You are a hard worker who is prone to overanalyzing. Unfortunately, you add way too much imagination to your rumination. This is good if you were writing a book, but not necessarily when trying to maintain a family or a relationship. At times you harm yourself by mixing in your insecurities and fear with your confidence. On a good day, spilled milk gets cleaned up. On a bad one, it could be destructive.

Keep your emotions in balance, and all you desire can be yours. It sounds like a fortune cookie, but really it's your life.

✳ ✳ ✳

NOVEMBER 8 SCORPIO • The resourceful one of the zodiac
October 23 at 12:00 P.M. to November 22 at 5:00 A.M. • NUMEROLOGY 8

Possessions and Desires . . .

Gem: Chrysolite—This gem may help you clear your mind of sadness and worry.
Flower: Lupine—You usually are very imaginative.
Astral Color, Color Need, Apparel Color: Your Astral Color is Black, the color of protection, birth, and beginnings. Red in your environment gives you energy and stamina. In your wardrobe, Tan gives you balance and harmony.
Fragrance: Buy pots of cinnabar or other scents from the sunny Mediterranean or Orient. You are the most passionate sign of the zodiac, and your fragrance must be as unpredictable as you are.
Tree: Pine—Your relationships tend to be harmonious, both emotionally and mentally.
Instrument: Cello
Composer: Mozart
Bird: Bobolink—This charming singer is equally good as a soloist or a member of an orchestra. It is a very romantic bird, useful as an insect destroyer, and elegant, with beautiful feathers, and always pleasant to have around.
Symbol: Wings—You are the source of balance in your world—this will bring you contentment.

Harmonious Health and Nutrition . . .

Health Scent: Almond—This scent may revitalize you and open you to greater possibilities.
Favorable Foods: Asparagus, strawberries, rye crisp, chicken, eggs

What's Lucky . . .

Lucky Numbers: 2, 4
Best Months: January and July
Best Day of the Week: Tuesday
Best Month Days: 4, 5, 23
Lucky Charm: Red ribbon in your wallet or doorway.
Harmonious Signs for Relationships and Partnerships: Cancer and Pisces

Spiritual Guides . . .

Star: Al Kalb—Those with this star are often delightful.
Angel: Ambriel—This angel governs travel and transportation, particularly over water, and helps to create love and good communication.
Guardian Angel: Seraphim—An angel that brings love, light, and passion.
Spiritual Stone: Chalcedon—This stone might help you keep things together when you feel frayed.

✳ JUDITH'S INSIGHT ✳

You are wonderful at planning and scheming. With your gift for organization, it's a snap for you to put together parties, events, even businesses. Impeccably stylish, you do things your own way. Your love of learning makes you a great student. With just a pen you can turn a piece of paper into a flower to fool a butterfly. Your gift for understanding others is balanced by your cluelessness when it comes to yourself. Those who don't know you see harmony and patience; however, your close friends and family experience how difficult you can be. In relationships, you love a good challenge, so why would your lover expect smooth sailing? All you're trying to do is balance your natural cynicism toward relationships with a lifelong quest for perfect love. As you get older, curbing that skepticism gets easier, so your head lets your heart discover its intended home. If you choose a mate too early in life, expect a lot of bickering before you learn to smooth out the bumpy patches on the road to serenity.

As with romance, success on the job finds you later rather than sooner. You may move from career to career, but all are likely to center around some kind of design or creation. Theater and entertainment may spark your interest, particularly in comedy. As long as you find a job that provides constant applause, your ego is satisfied. Constantly seeking growth, you crave approval and acknowledgment of your many talents. Yours is a life of new beginnings always brimming with fire, energy, and enthusiasm.

★ ★ ★

NOVEMBER 9 SCORPIO • The resourceful one of the zodiac

October 23 at 12:00 P.M. to November 22 at 5:00 A.M. • NUMEROLOGY 9

Possessions and Desires . . .

Gem: Beryl—This gem could be good for meditation and concentration.

Flower: Lotus—Be careful you don't raise barriers between yourself and what you truly love.

Astral Color, Color Need, Apparel Color: Your Astral Color is Black, the color of protection, birth, and beginnings. Red in your environment gives you energy and stamina. In your wardrobe, Green is your power color for overcoming obstacles.

Fragrance: Buy pots of cinnabar or other scents from the sunny Mediterranean or Orient. You are the most passionate sign of the zodiac, and your fragrance must be as unpredictable as you are.

Tree: Holly—Beware that you are not carried away by your passionate nature. The only way to grow is to be open to new experiences.

Instruments: Violin, tympanum

Composer: Gluck

Bird: Mockingbird—the most proficient minstrel in the world's orchestra; graceful and enthusiastic.

Symbol: Anchor—This tranquil symbol signifies stability and strength, and stands for strong commitments in relationships.

Harmonious Health and Nutrition . . .

Health Scent: Lavender—This scent might lead others to trust you and make you patient.

Favorable Foods: Cabbage, black figs, oats, salmon, pressed cheese

What's Lucky . . .

Lucky Numbers: 2, 4

Best Months: January and July

Best Day of the Week: Tuesday

Best Month Days: 9, 18, 27

Lucky Charm: A U. S. coin or a bill of any amount from the year you were born.

Harmonious Signs for Relationships and Partnerships: Cancer and Pisces

Spiritual Guides . . .

Star: Al Shaula—People born with this star are careful to avoid being cruel.

Angel: Ambriel—This angel governs travel and transportation, particularly over water, and helps to create love and good communication.

Guardian Angel: Gabriel—"God is my strength."

Spiritual Stone: Chalcedon—This stone might help when taking long trips, especially by car.

✳ JUDITH'S INSIGHT ✳

You have a very adept mind for music or art. Be cautious when it comes to extremes in the area of self-confidence. Your ego may seem inflated to others because you lack self-esteem. This may trip you up and keep you from obtaining higher rewards in life, both with money and advancement.

Naturally secretive, you don't like showing off your accomplishments, but you do well with careers in the public eye. You tend to gravitate toward those who make you feel secure, which could be a problem. Other people may find you snobbish or gossipy and not trust you. Watch for signs of being misunderstood, especially if you want to be successful. Continuing to be defensive creates enemies out of nowhere.

When it comes to love, you're a more devoted mate than most, even in light of your flirtatious manner. Again, your charm and wit draws in that special person. Give more than you take by allowing others access to that heart of yours. Fight the urge to flee when asked your feelings. At the very least, admit your fear. Tell those you care about how much they mean to you. If you can accept the challenge, you can be happy.

Relax and enjoy being the sparkling, enchanting individual that everyone loves being around.

Some careers you may excel at are: psychologist, with your analytical side; lawyer; paralegal; realtor; musician; or entertainer.

✳ ✳ ✳

NOVEMBER 10

SCORPIO • The resourceful one of the zodiac

October 23 at 12:00 P.M. to November 22 at 5:00 A.M. • NUMEROLOGY 1

Possessions and Desires . . .

Gem: Agate—This stone may promote health and lead you to a long life.

Flower: Lotus—You have very little difficulty expressing your thoughts and feelings.

Astral Color, Color Need, Apparel Color: Your Astral Color is Black, the color of protection, birth, and beginnings. Red in your environment gives you energy and stamina. In your wardrobe, Wine gives you energy.

Fragrance: Buy pots of cinnabar or other scents from the sunny Mediterranean or Orient. You are the most passionate sign of the zodiac, and your fragrance must be as unpredictable as you are.

Tree: Walnut—You are unusually helpful and always looking for constant changes in your life.

Instruments: Oboe, flute, clarinet, piano, French horn, organ, piccolo

Composer: Böhm

Bird: Bird of paradise—the "bird of the gods." You will shine and love extraordinary circumstances.

Symbol: Crown—the universal sign of dignity.

Harmonious Health and Nutrition . . .

Health Scent: Strawberry—Soothing by nature, the strawberry promotes self-esteem and encourages love.

Favorable Foods: Celery, blackberries, barley, beef, eggs

What's Lucky . . .

Lucky Numbers: 2, 4
Best Months: January and July
Best Day of the Week: Tuesday
Best Month Days: 4, 5, 23
Lucky Charm: A new penny in your shoe

Harmonious Signs for Relationships and Partnerships: Cancer and Pisces

Spiritual Guides . . .

Star: Al Shaula—people born with this star are careful to avoid being cruel.

Angel: Ambriel—This angel governs travel and transportation, particularly over water, and helps to create love and good communication.

Guardian Angel: Malachi—"Messenger of Jehovah."

Spiritual Stone: Chalcedon—This stone might help when taking long trips, especially by car.

✴ JUDITH'S INSIGHT ✴

You make things happen, not only in your life, but in the lives of those around you. Challenges are important to you, though you may not realize how much. You are blessed with creativity and love to initiate new beginnings. Control your enthusiasm and exercise caution until you have all the facts. Your naiveté may allow you to be misled or cheated. Your moods swing dramatically from sunny optimism to bleak pessimism.

You need to be with a partner more than you care to admit. Choosy in love, you force the other to prove his or her emotions first. Watch out for too much of this or you may lose one or two people who really mean a lot. Overall, you'll be lucky with partnerships and have many good friends.

You may know some people in high places who will aid you in your career, though with your determined nature, you don't really need help. You may desire multiple jobs. Areas that would be good for you are music, philosophy, law, or design. Later on, you develop an interest in humanitarian or volunteer work.

Your life is a fight for your beliefs, and you have the sensitivity and energy to battle for causes of others, too.

✶ ✶ ✶

NOVEMBER 11

SCORPIO • The resourceful one of the zodiac

October 23 at 12:00 P.M. to November 22 at 5:00 A.M. • NUMEROLOGY 2

Possessions and Desires . . .

Gem: Sapphire—This gem may help you find forgiveness from those you've wronged.

Flower: Lotus Tree—You may have the blessing of effortless agreement between yourself and your friends.

Astral Color, Color Need, Apparel Color: Your Astral Color is Black, the color of protection, birth, and beginnings. Red in your environment gives you energy and stamina. In your wardrobe, Tan gives you balance and harmony.

Fragrance: Buy pots of cinnabar or other scents from the sunny Mediterranean or Orient. You are the most passionate sign of the zodiac, and your fragrance must be as unpredictable as you are.

Tree: Maple—You have great stability and flashes of intuition.

Instruments: Pipe organ, cymbal, drum

Composers: Handel, Johann Sebastian Bach

Bird: Stork—Storks have a strange type of intelligence that is easily misunderstood. The stork is known to have a pleasing nature.

Symbol: Cross—the symbol of self-sacrifice and reconciliation.

Harmonious Health and Nutrition . . .

Health Scent: Raspberry—This scent might bring you a feeling of harmony with the universe.

Favorable Foods: Dandelion, cranberries, barley, chicken, buttermilk

What's Lucky . . .

Lucky Numbers: 2, 4
Best Months: January and July
Best Day of the Week: Tuesday
Best Month Days: 4, 5, 23
Lucky Charms: Two 50-cent pieces. Give someone else one of them.
Harmonious Signs for Relationships and Partnerships: Cancer and Pisces

Spiritual Guides . . .

Star: Al Kalb—Those with this star are often delightful.

Angel: Ambriel—This angel governs travel and transportation, particularly over water, and helps to create love and good communication.

Guardian Angel: St. John—This angel simplifies that which is complicated.

Spiritual Stone: Chalcedon—This stone might help when taking long trips, especially by car.

✴ JUDITH'S INSIGHT ✴

You are talented, energetic, and bighearted, with a strong and sensible mind. Your imagination will allow you success if you can wait for your unconventional methods to work. When you're younger, try to resist your nasty habit of making all the wrong choices. You are too busy looking to ever find anything. Others may become frustrated with you as you seem to take the longest path possible.

You need to be in control, and work is best when you're the boss. You're meticulous and organized, so consider a career in medicine, as either a surgeon or researcher. You would also do well in the legal profession.

With your strong physical power, if you don't choose a career in professional sports, you should make them a hobby—at which you'll excel. You wake up charged every day and remain energized, as long as you get your way. Obstacles drain and depress you—you take everything too personally.

You're difficult to work with, and you can be a nightmare to love. Relationships will be the most complicated part of your life, and it's usually your fault. You clutch the key to your heart and often refuse to give it out. Eventually, you'll realize that the spiritual is more important than the material and discover all the joys a relationship can offer.

Keep your head up high and that abundant energy flowing; your life's lesson is to learn to work with others as you reach your destiny.

✴ ✴ ✴

NOVEMBER 12

SCORPIO • The resourceful one of the zodiac

October 23 at 12:00 P.M. to November 22 at 5:00 A.M. • NUMEROLOGY 3

Possessions and Desires . . .

Gem: Ruby—This stone may lead you to energy, friendship, and happiness.

Flower: Lichen—You tend to love being by yourself.

Astral Color, Color Need, Apparel Color: Your Astral Color is Black, the color of protection, birth, and beginnings. Red in your environment gives you energy and stamina. In your wardrobe, Green is your power color for overcoming obstacles.

Fragrance: Buy pots of cinnabar or other scents from the sunny Mediterranean or Orient. You are the most passionate sign of the zodiac, and your fragrance must be as unpredictable as you are.

Tree: Elm—You have willpower, strength, and the ability to stand alone.

Instrument: Trombone

Composers: Verdi, Mendelssohn, Schumann

Bird: Eagle—This bird is quick to use its powers of flight. It can see immeasurable distances in a single glance, and can sometimes appear to be indifferent.

Harmonious Health and Nutrition . . .

Health Scent: Rose—This scent will lead you to passionate thoughts and make you feel warm inside.

Favorable Foods: Asparagus, watermelon, oats, salmon, pressed cheese

What's Lucky . . .

Lucky Numbers: 2, 4
Best Months: January and July
Best Day of the Week: Tuesday
Best Month Days: 3, 12, 21
Lucky Charm: A pen that someone else has already used.

Harmonious Signs for Relationships and Partnerships: Cancer and Pisces

Spiritual Guides . . .

Star: Al Kalb—Those with this star are often delightful.

Angel: Ambriel—This angel governs travel and transportation, particularly over water, and helps to create love and good communication.

Guardian Angel: Johiel—This angel is a protector of all those with a humble heart.

Spiritual Stone: Chalcedon—This stone might help when taking long trips, especially by car.

✴ JUDITH'S INSIGHT ✴

You make things happen, get the ball rolling, and keep it in motion. You are born to be famous or at least well known. Your efforts with children will be acknowledged. You're destined to make a difference in the lives of those around you, and the experience will change you forever.

Your determination and passion allow you your pick of careers, though it may take you a long time to feel successful. Think about becoming a pediatrician, as it suits your caring nature and kind heart. You need not work with children, however, to leave an impression on them. They look up to you no matter what. Charm takes you far—all the way to the bank and maybe even the Senate.

Home environment and family mean everything to you. This feeling grows deeper as you mature. You cheerfully pull everybody onto the bandwagon and enlist their help in the work you do for others.

Your ambition enables you to travel the world and experience many different cultures. Always exploring the universe, you will discover it inside yourself.

You can be hard to get a commitment from when it comes to love, until you really become ready.

✶ ✶ ✶

NOVEMBER 13 SCORPIO • The resourceful one of the zodiac

October 23 at 12:00 P.M. to November 22 at 5:00 A.M. • NUMEROLOGY 4

Possessions and Desires . . .

Gem: Emerald—Those who carry this stone tend to be lucky in love.

Flower: Field Lily—You have great humility when greatness finds you.

Astral Color, Color Need, Apparel Color: Your Astral Color is Black, the color of protection, birth, and beginnings. Red in your environment gives you energy and stamina. In your wardrobe, Wine gives you energy.

Fragrance: Buy pots of cinnabar or other scents from the sunny Mediterranean or Orient. You are the most passionate sign of the zodiac, and your fragrance must be as unpredictable as you are.

Tree: Cherry—You will find yourself faced with constant new emotional awakenings.

Instruments: Bass, clarinet

Composers: Haydn, Wagner

Bird: Robin—the most sociable of all birds, with the ability to create quick friendships. It also can easily adapt to any home. When it wants something, it has the tendency to try to snatch it.

Symbol: Star—You are full of inner brightness and will stand out in any crowd. You will be seen as special.

Harmonious Health and Nutrition . . .

Health Scent: Vanilla—This scent will fill you with a feeling of cleanliness and stability.

Favorable Foods: Spinach, strawberries, rye crisps, fresh oysters, buttermilk

What's Lucky . . .

Lucky Numbers: 2, 4

Best Months: January and July

Best Day of the Week: Tuesday

Best Month Days: 4, 13, 22

Lucky Charm: A piece of material cut from something in your home.

Harmonious Signs for Relationships and Partnerships: Cancer and Pisces

Spiritual Guides . . .

Star: Al Shaula—People born with this star are careful to avoid being cruel.

Angel: Ambriel—This angel governs travel and transportation, particularly over water, and helps to create love and good communication.

Guardian Angel: Uriel—This angel brings the light of God's guidance.

Spiritual Stone: Chalcedon—This stone might help when taking long trips, especially by car.

✳ JUDITH'S INSIGHT ✳

You draw people in without their knowing why. Your appealing manner can persuade others to do whatever you want. Your great sense of humor can disappear if the joke is on you. You have a tendency toward selfishness but really do anything for anyone you can.

You crave challenge and desire the opportunity to travel and know all the world can offer. When you're searching for a mate, remember that you dislike feeling tied down. Make it clear from the start that you need freedom and independence, or the partnership will never work. The more confined you feel, the more you struggle to be free.

Keep this in mind as well when choosing a career. Look for one that offers freedom and constant stimulation. Being a free bird doesn't necessarily mean you don't depend on others. Oddly, you do well in jobs with clearly defined structure, like those in government. You may even find yourself working for a uniform company or wearing a uniform, say as a firefighter, cop, or member of the armed forces. No matter what career you choose, your good work ethic and strong intellect bring you success.

Follow your need to travel, if not in your physical world, then with your mind and your soul.

✳ ✳ ✳

NOVEMBER 14

SCORPIO • The resourceful one of the zodiac

October 23 at 12:00 P.M. to November 22 at 5:00 A.M. • NUMEROLOGY 5

Possessions and Desires . . .

Gem: Sardius—This stone could give the wearer unusual insights into his or her own heart.
Flower: Yellow Lily—You usually hate any hint of falsehood.
Astral Color, Color Need, Apparel Color: Your Astral Color is Black, the color of protection, births, and beginnings. Red in your environment gives you energy and stamina. In your wardrobe, Tan gives you balance and harmony.
Fragrance: Buy pots of cinnabar or other scents from the sunny Mediterranean or Orient. You are the most passionate sign of the zodiac, and your fragrance must be as unpredictable as you are.
Tree: Apple—You are creative, full of joy, and nearly magical. You bring happiness.
Instruments: Viola, trumpet
Composer: Liszt
Bird: Flamingo—This beautiful, gregarious bird is always careful of its enemy. It is also a caretaker of the young and tries to keep everyone happy.
Symbol: Triangle—You have the right combination of abilities.

Harmonious Health and Nutrition . . .

Health Scent: Peach—This scent may balance your good qualities so that they equal your charm.
Favorable Foods: Cauliflower, cranberries, barley, chicken, eggs

What's Lucky . . .

Lucky Numbers: 2, 4
Best Months: January and July
Best Day of the Week: Tuesday
Best Month Days: 4, 5, 23
Lucky Charm: A rabbit's foot or a white candle.
Harmonious Signs for Relationships and Partnerships: Cancer and Pisces

Spiritual Guides . . .

Star: Al Kalb—Those with this star are often delightful.
Angel: Ambriel—This angel governs travel and transportation, particularly over water, and helps to create love and good communication.
Guardian Angel: Plavwell—The guardian that gives power and strength to one's presence.
Spiritual Stone: Chalcedon—This stone might help when taking long trips, especially by car.

✳ *JUDITH'S INSIGHT* ✳

Your deep love for the arts and natural instincts should guide you to a career that takes advantage of your imagination. Your fine investigative abilities enable you to get to the truth. Some may see you as skeptical. Personality and the gift of gab take you far at work. You'd make an excellent salesperson or worker in the beauty industry. Highly charged and very good at combining different ideas to create an entirely new product, you could be equally comfortable working in marketing or boutiques or producing a show.

Romance is a source of frustration for you. You want fresh new beginnings and challenges. Marrying later in life proves better as you will have exhausted your emotional wanderlust. You make a better friend than lover. When you put yourself in a love relationship, you lose focus. As a friend, when you feel freedom from restrictions, you're wonderfully loyal.

Expect to find yourself flying off to one country after another. You were born to visit exotic places. A wild practical joker, you can be difficult to get along with. However, you usually host the parties and comfort others with encouragement and security. Keep your home neat . . . it is vital. If you don't decide to become a professional chef, your friends and family will benefit from your culinary skill.

✳ ✳ ✳

NOVEMBER 15 SCORPIO • The resourceful one of the zodiac

October 23 at 12:00 P.M. to November 22 at 5:00 A.M. • NUMEROLOGY 6

Possessions and Desires . . .

Gem: Topaz—This is an excellent gift to be exchanged between very loyal friends.

Flower: Laurestine—If you neglect your own needs you may end up very bitter.

Astral Color, Color Need, Apparel Color: Your Astral Color is Black, the color of protection, birth, and beginnings. Red in your environment gives you energy and stamina. In your wardrobe, Green is your power color for overcoming obstacles.

Fragrance: Buy pots of cinnabar or other scents from the sunny Mediterranean or Orient. You are the most passionate sign of the zodiac, and your frangrance must be as unpredictable as you are.

Tree: Palm—You tend to be very healthy and creative.

Instruments: Tambourine, lyre

Composer: Schubert

Bird: Lark—known for the beauty of its song, which is sometimes very unusual. It is also credited with extraordinary intelligence.

Symbol: Crescent—You are more likely to be influenced by the phases of the moon. Your easygoing manner leads you to peaceful situations

Harmonious Health and Nutrition . . .

Health Scent: Orange Blossom—This scent may balance your body, mind, and soul.

Favorable Foods: Cabbage, blackberries, oats, salmon, pressed cheese

What's Lucky . . .

Lucky Numbers: 2, 4
Best Months: January and July
Best Day of the Week: Tuesday
Best Month Days: 6, 15, 14
Lucky Charm: A religious token or card from any religion.
Harmonious Signs for Relationships and Partnerships: Cancer and Pisces

Spiritual Guides . . .

Star: Al Shaula—People born with this star are careful to avoid being cruel.

Angel: Ambriel—This angel governs travel and transportation, particularly over water, and helps to create love and good communication.

Guardian Angel: Michael—"Who is like God."

Spiritual Stone: Chalcedon—This stone might help when taking long trips, especially by car.

✴ JUDITH'S INSIGHT ✴

Strong tendencies toward the sciences may entice you to consider a career studying nature. You love time spent near bodies of water and recognize this as a source of calm and contentment. If ever you're flagging in courage or depressed, a quick aquatic visit will perk you right up. You should live near the sea, a river, a lake, or at the very least, a reservoir.

You make many friends and could keep them due to your generally truthful and trustworthy nature. But remember, a person who is too truthful and frank is hard for people to accept, so curb your need to be overly direct. You are a proud person with well-developed character; people respect you.

You are completely devoted in love, and as long as each romantic interlude lasts, you feel as if it's forever. The reasons for breakups will vary as much as the unconventional relationships you choose. You may carry on multiple relationships all at once.

You are versatile and capable of doing anything well; your strong mind and energetic body govern a giving soul. The right employment may take time to discover. Stop looking for it, and it will find you. For you, job satisfaction lies beyond a journey through some disappointment. Console yourself along the way. Inevitably, you'll find the career in which you'll be a success.

Some careers that you may excel at: musician, lawyer, chemist, doctor, or scientist.

✴ ✴ ✴

NOVEMBER 16
SCORPIO • The resourceful one of the zodiac
October 23 at 12:00 P.M. to November 22 at 5:00 A.M. • NUMEROLOGY 7

Possessions and Desires . . .

Gem: Agate—This stone may promote health and lead you to a long life.

Flower: Mountain Laurel—You will always have great ambitions concerning your life.

Astral Color, Color Need, Apparel Color: Your Astral Color is Black, the color of protection, birth, and beginnings. Red in your environment gives you energy and stamina. In your wardrobe, Wine gives you energy.

Fragrance: Buy pots of cinnabar or other scents from the sunny Mediterranean or Orient. You are the most passionate sign of the zodiac, and your fragrance must be as unpredictable as you are.

Tree: Sycamore—Yours is the ability to love, communicate honestly with others, and have lasting relationships.

Instrument: Harp

Composers: Gluck, Brahms

Bird: Skylark—This handsome bird is beautiful when it sings. It always whistles as it works.

Harmonious Health and Nutrition . . .

Health Scent: Jasmine—This scent may make you more easygoing when you are stressed.

Favorable Foods: Celery, black figs, rye crisps, beef, buttermilk

What's Lucky . . .

Lucky Numbers: 2, 4

Best Months: January and July

Best Day of the Week: Tuesday

Best Month Days: 4, 5, 23

Lucky Charm: An old key.

Harmonious Signs for Relationships and Partnerships: Cancer and Pisces

Spiritual Guides . . .

Star: Al Kalb—Those with this star are often delightful.

Angel: Ambriel—This angel governs travel and transportation, particularly over water, and helps to create love and good communication.

Guardian Angel: Raphael—This angel attends to all of your needs when you are looking for guidance.

Spiritual Stone: Chalcedon—This stone might help when taking long trips, especially by car.

✶ JUDITH'S INSIGHT ✶

If you can't succeed, nobody can. Loaded with determination and perseverance, you have all the basic tools needed to conquer the world. People want to help you because of your vibrant enthusiasm. They'll be anxious to take part in your many victories. You were born to lead, and your followers are aware of your strength and appreciate your sensitivity. Somewhere along the way, you may discover certain personality traits that need work. But as you do with all other difficult obstacles, given enough time, you find a way to overcome them.

Relationships can be a struggle. It may seem you'd be better off without one or that true love will never find you. Your perfect mate understands you and is capable of sticking it out.

You are here to accomplish much and probably won't rest until you do. Besides being a born leader, you are a teacher of life. A natural philosopher, you give great advice. You would make an excellent preacher, counselor, or motivational speaker. Your charm, wit, and energy will not quit. All you need is time to reach the forefront both in your chosen field and in life.

✶ ✶ ✶

NOVEMBER 17 SCORPIO • The resourceful one of the zodiac

October 23 at 12:00 P.M. to November 22 at 5:00 A.M. • NUMEROLOGY 8

Possessions and Desires . . .

Gem: Chrysolite—This gem may help you clear your mind of sadness and worry.

Flower: Laurel—You tend to find victory even in defeat.

Astral Color, Color Need, Apparel Color: Your Astral Color is Black, the color of protection, birth, and beginnings. Red in your environment gives you energy and stamina. In your wardrobe, Tan gives you balance and harmony.

Tree: Pine—Your relationships tend to be harmonious, both emotionally and mentally.

Instrument: Cello

Composer: Mozart

Bird: Bobolink—This charming singer is equally good as a soloist or a member of an orchestra. It is a very romantic bird, most useful as an insect destroyer, and elegant, with beautiful feathers, and always pleasant to have around.

Symbol: Wings—You are the source of balance in your world—This will bring you contentment.

Harmonious Health and Nutrition . . .

Health Scent: Almond—This scent may revitalize you and open you to greater possibilities.

Favorable Foods: Dandelion, blackberries, barley, salmon, eggs

What's Lucky . . .

Lucky Numbers: 2, 4

Best Months: January and July

Best Day of the Week: Tuesday

Best Month Days: 8, 17, 26

Lucky Charm: Red ribbon in your wallet or doorway.

Harmonious Signs for Relationships and Partnerships: Cancer and Pisces

Spiritual Guides . . .

Star: Al Kalb—Those with this star are often delightful.

Angel: Ambriel—This angel governs travel and transportation, particularly over water, and helps to create love and good communication.

Guardian Angel: Seraphim—An angel that brings love, light, and passion.

Spiritual Stone: Chalcedon—This stone might help when taking long trips, especially by car.

✴ JUDITH'S INSIGHT ✴

You have skill at organization, usually pulling things together by sheer force. Consider a career as a troubleshooter—your knack for handling difficult issues lends itself to problem solving. You do things your own way and cannot tolerate interference. While you can be a great student of life, many things don't seem to interest you. You are naturally artistic and yearn for a job that utilizes your creative side.

Your love of travel deepens as you mature. You feel safe and secure around large bodies of water. While you seek serenity, you are quick-minded and sometimes even quicker tempered. Your lesson in life: learn to deal with losses and difficulties.

Better as part of a family or fellowship than on your own, you sometimes rely on luck in making choices about the people in your life. Stability in matters of the heart may take time, but you stick it out until you find a mate who understands you. The life you build together will be worth the struggle.

When you least expect it, success will fall right into your lap. The taste of victory only increases your appetite for more challenge. You should pursue many differing fields. Who else has the skills to be a great designer, artist, or teacher, and could do equally well in the stock market, gambling, or even the theater?

Understand that you have an ego that needs to be fed. Be careful not to overdo it.

✴ ✴ ✴

NOVEMBER 18

SCORPIO • The resourceful one of the zodiac

October 23 at 12:00 P.M. to November 22 at 5:00 A.M. • NUMEROLOGY 9

Possessions and Desires . . .

Gem: Beryl—This gem could be good for meditation and concentration.

Flower: Houstonia—You are content with what the universe gives you.

Astral Color, Color Need, Apparel Color: Your Astral Color is Black, the color of protection, birth, and beginnings. Red in your environment gives you energy and stamina. In your wardrobe, Green is your power color for overcoming obstacles.

Fragrance: Buy pots of cinnabar or other scents from the sunny Mediterranean or Orient. You are the most passionate sign of the zodiac, and your fragrance must be as unpredictable as you are.

Tree: Holly—Beware that you are not carried away by your passionate nature. The only way to grow is to be open to new experiences.

Instruments: Violin, tympanum

Composer: Gluck

Bird: Mockingbird—the most proficient minstrel in the world's orchestra; graceful and enthusiastic.

Symbol: Anchor—This tranquil symbol signifies stability and strength, and stands for strong commitments in relationships.

Harmonious Health and Nutrition . . .

Health Scent: Lavender—This scent might lead others to trust you and make you patient.

Favorable Foods: Asparagus, cranberries, oats, fresh oysters, buttermilk

What's Lucky . . .

Lucky Numbers: 2, 4
Best Months: January and July
Best Day of the Week: Tuesday
Best Month Days: 4, 5, 23
Lucky Charm: A U.S. coin or a bill of any amount from the year you were born.

Harmonious Signs for Relationships and Partnerships: Cancer and Pisces

Spiritual Guides . . .

Star: Al Shaula—People born with this star are careful to avoid being cruel.

Angel: Ambriel—This angel governs travel and transportation, particularly over water, and helps to create love and good communication.

Guardian Angel: Gabriel—"God is my strength."

Spiritual Stone: Chalcedon—This stone might help when taking long trips, especially by car.

✷ JUDITH'S INSIGHT ✷

No matter what career you choose, the opportunity to work in the limelight will present itself. What begins as a bit part in your grade school play may lead to you starring in a major motion picture. Be aware of your emotional extremes—your self-confidence can ride high or drop down low. Your pocketbook is either completely empty or stuffed full.

You are naturally secretive, and this makes the search for a close relationship difficult. Others may see you as untruthful because you tend to keep your feelings to yourself.

You will excel in the field of public affairs or in a public company. Consider a career in government. You don't have to be a politician, but by no means should you consider it out of your reach. By being kinder to others you'll like yourself more and fare better in life. Try being as generous as you can. The older you get, the more giving you become. If you get lucky financially, try sharing the wealth.

Usually deep in thought, you don't always let others know what you're thinking. You are strongly intuitive and need to learn to trust your inner voice. If you don't, you'll eventually wish you had. You have great executive abilities and uncanny organizational skills.

Learn to go with what you know is true, and success will find you.

✷ ✷ ✷

NOVEMBER 19 SCORPIO • The resourceful one of the zodiac

October 23 at 12:00 P.M. to November 22 at 5:00 A.M. • NUMEROLOGY 1

Possessions and Desires . . .

Gem: Turquoise—This stone might help you find material wealth.

Flower: Hornbeam—You may place more emphasis on how things look than how they really are.

Astral Color, Color Need, Apparel Color: Your Astral Color is Black, the color of protection, birth, and beginnings. Red in your environment gives you energy and stamina. In your wardrobe, Wine gives you energy.

Fragrance: Buy pots of cinnabar or other scents from the sunny Mediterranean or Orient. You are the most passionate sign of the zodiac, and your fragrance must be as unpredictable as you are.

Tree: Walnut—You are unusually helpful and always looking for constant changes in your life.

Instruments: Oboe, flute, clarinet, piano, French horn, organ, piccolo

Composer: Böhm

Bird: Bird of paradise—the "bird of the gods." You will shine and love extraordinary circumstances.

Symbol: Crown—the universal sign of dignity.

Harmonious Health and Nutrition . . .

Health Scent: Strawberry—soothing by nature, the strawberry promotes self-esteem and encourages love.

Favorable Foods: Cabbage, black figs, barley, salmon, eggs

What's Lucky . . .

Lucky Numbers: 2, 4
Best Months: January and July
Best Day of the Week: Tuesday
Best Month Days: 1, 10, 19
Lucky Charm: A new penny in your shoe.
Harmonious Signs for Relationships and Partnerships: Cancer and Pisces

Spiritual Guides . . .

Star: Al Shaula—People born with this star are careful to avoid being cruel.

Angel: Ambriel—This angel governs travel and transportation, particularly over water, and helps to create love and good communication.

Guardian Angel: Malachi—"Messenger of Jehovah."

Spiritual Stone: Chalcedon—This stone might help when taking long trips, especially by car.

✷ JUDITH'S INSIGHT ✷

Your exceptional power and energy just never quit. You glow like a long-lasting, superbright incandescent bulb. You are creative in every sense of the word; your ideas are usually the good ones. You are astute and observant by nature and would make an extraordinary critic. Although you may see it as common sense or natural intelligence, you rely heavily on intuition.

There is a job for you in government if you want it. Your opinions are well received, and you always win in debate. When you speak people really do listen. With your sense of humor and wit, everyone wants to stay part of the huge crowd that surrounds you.

You will have many friends, acquaintances, and lovers, and this is your choice. Watch out for a tendency for sarcasm—others may see you as moody. So long as the party is going your way and in your control, everything is fine by you. You can pout if you don't get your way. Try to find a better method to release that building before it gets the best of you. Try to swiftly deal with depression during difficult times in your life. You have a tendency to wallow for too long instead of going forward.

Depending on which road you take, you can accomplish as much or as little as you please.

✷ ✷ ✷

NOVEMBER 20

SCORPIO • The resourceful one of the zodiac

October 23 at 12:00 P.M. to November 22 at 5:00 A.M. • NUMEROLOGY 2

Possessions and Desires . . .

Gem: Sapphire—This gem may help you find forgiveness from those you've wronged.

Flower: Honeysuckle—You are generous and devoted.

Astral Color, Color Need, Apparel Color: Your Astral Color is Black, the color of protection, birth, and beginnings. Red in your environment gives you energy and stamina. In your wardrobe, Tan gives you balance and harmony.

Fragrance: Buy pots of cinnabar or other scents from the sunny Mediterranean or Orient. You are the most passionate sign of the zodiac, and your fragrance must be as unpredictable as you are.

Tree: Maple—You have great stability and flashes of intuition.

Instruments: Pipe organ, cymbal, drum

Composers: Handel, Johann Sebastian Bach

Bird: Stork—Turkish bird, held in high esteem the world over. This bird is intelligent but may have strange tendencies.

Symbol: Cross—The symbol of self-sacrifice and reconciliation.

Harmonious Health and Nutrition . . .

Health Scent: Raspberry—This scent might bring you a feeling of harmony with the universe.

Favorable Foods: Cauliflower, watermelon, oats, fresh oysters, pressed cheese

What's Lucky . . .

Lucky Numbers: 2, 4
Best Months: January and July
Best Day of the Week: Tuesday
Best Month Days: 2, 11, 20
Lucky Charms: Two 50-cent pieces. Give someone else one of them.

Harmonious Signs for Relationships and Partnerships: Cancer and Pisces

Spiritual Guides . . .

Star: Al Shaula—People born with this star are careful to avoid being cruel.

Angel: Ambriel—This angel governs travel and transportation, particularly over water, and helps to create love and good communication.

Guardian Angel: St. John—This angel simplifies that which is complicated.

Spiritual Stone: Chalcedon—This stone might help when taking long trips, especially by car.

✳ JUDITH'S INSIGHT ✳

You are talented and energetic with a vivid imagination. This alone could pave the way to success. Try to keep your emotional side from getting in the way. You'll do best as the boss—not only of yourself, but of your surroundings. Entertainment at home is important to you, as is an extremely tidy house. You need to feel secure at home. When things are unsettled with friends and family, you'll experience a great deal of pain. You prefer harmony around you, but you won't back away from standing up to a surly neighbor.

You may do well as an athlete and probably enjoy some physical activity every single day. You are interested in learning and will drink up knowledge whatever the source: movies, traveling, or books. You would do well as a stockbroker, analyst, or paralegal or in any career in which there is constant research.

Relationships can pose problems for you because you hang onto your heart. It is hard for you to let go once you fall in love. People must prove themselves to you before you can relax. Learn to let go. You're not holding on; you're holding yourself back.

Yes, life can be messy and complicated—jump in and get dirty.

✳ ✳ ✳

NOVEMBER 21 SCORPIO • The resourceful one of the zodiac

October 23 at 12:00 P.M. to November 22 at 5:00 A.M. • NUMEROLOGY 3

Possessions and Desires . . .

Gem: Ruby—This stone may lead you to energy, friendship, and happiness.

Flower: Hawkweed—You grasp the significance of events more quickly that those around you.

Astral Color, Color Need, Apparel Color: Your Astral Color is Black, the color of protection, birth, and beginnings. Red in your environment gives you energy and stamina. In your wardrobe, Green is your power color for overcoming obstacles.

Fragrance: Buy pots of cinnabar or other scents from the sunny Mediterranean or Orient. You are the most passionate sign of the zodiac, and your fragrance must be as unpredictable as you are.

Tree: Elm—You have willpower, strength, and the ability to stand alone.

Instrument: Trombone

Composers: Verdi, Mendelssohn, Schumann

Bird: Swan—Regarded as royal and sacred, this bird has the protective nature of a mother, and can become a furious fighter in the defense of its young.

Symbol: Wreath—This symbol is like the crown in having a special personality, but those with your mark also show lots of compassion for others.

Harmonious Health and Nutrition . . .

Health Scent: Rose—This scent will lead you to passionate thoughts and make you feel warm inside.

Favorable Foods: Cauliflower, watermelon, oats, fresh oysters, pressed cheese

What's Lucky . . .

Lucky Numbers: 2, 4

Best Months: January and July

Best Day of the Week: Tuesday

Best Month Days: 3, 12, 21

Lucky Charm: A pen that someone else has already used.

Harmonious Signs for Relationships and Partnerships: Cancer and Pisces

Spiritual Guides . . .

Star: Al Kalb—Those with this star are often delightful.

Angel: Ambriel—This angel governs travel and transportation, particularly over water, and helps to create love and good communication.

Guardian Angel: Johiel—This angel is a protector of all those with a humble heart.

Spiritual Stone: Chalcedon—This stone might help when taking long trips, especially by car.

✴ JUDITH'S INSIGHT ✴

World travel should appeal to you because of your perfect ease in any situation. You have a sort of sweetness about you, love to soak up knowledge, and do it very well. You experience exciting things nearly every day because it's in your nature to seek them out. Even if you don't actually move from place to place in ships and planes, some amount of your life will be spent seeking knowledge about other religions, foods, people, and cultures.

Your love life is up to you. First, decide you want to be happy. Your mind actually rules your heart. Try to understand that with most people, it's the other way around. A more combative or sensitive person would be difficult to find. Most of your fighting takes place within yourself. The trouble with this is you always lose.

You would do well employed in government or in jobs where you travel to new locations or environments constantly. For instance, transportation and travel industries should attract you. You act more independent than is really the case. As you mature, you learn to recognize how important friends and family are to you. Be as generous with money as you can afford to be. Your genuine love of people makes you sympathetic and charitable, even when finances are tight.

It is a diverse world, and it's all yours.

✴ ✴ ✴

NOVEMBER 22 SAGITTARIUS • The adventurous one of the zodiac

October 23 at 12:00 A.M. to November 22 at 5:00 P.M. • NUMEROLOGY 4

Possessions and Desires . . .

Gem: Emerald—Those who carry this stone tend to be lucky in love.

Flower: Gourd—You tend not to be happy unless you have an overabundance of what you want.

Astral Color, Color Need, Apparel Color: Your Astral Color is Red, the color of passion, power, excitement, and strength. Violet in your environment keeps you empathetic toward others. In your wardrobe, Purple reflects your giving personality and brings you luck.

Fragrance: You need to be bathed in exotic scents that will give your imagination room to roam. Experiment with imported incense and tinctures to show the world what a spirited individual you are.

Tree: Cherry—You will find yourself faced with constant new emotional awakenings.

Instruments: Bass, clarinet

Composers: Haydn, Wagner

Bird: Robin—The most sociable of all birds, with the ability to create quick friendships. It also can easily adapt to any home. When it wants something, it has the tendency to try to snatch it.

Symbol: Star—You are full of inner brightness and will stand out in any crowd. You will be seen as special.

Harmonious Health and Nutrition . . .

Health Scent: Vanilla—This scent will fill you with a feeling of cleanliness and stability.

Favorable Foods: Asparagus, cranberries, oats, salmon, buttermilk

What's Lucky . . .

Lucky Numbers: 5, 7
Best Months: February and June
Best Day of the Week: Thursday
Best Month Days: 4, 13, 22
Lucky Charm: A piece of material cut from something in your home.

Harmonious Signs for Relationships and Partnerships: Aries, Leo, Sagittarius

Spiritual Guides . . .

Star: Al Naim—Those with this star are often delightful.

Angel: Aduachiel—This angel governs the balance of elements—water, earth, fire, and air—and helps maintain a calm disposition.

Guardian Angel: Uriel—This angel brings the light of God's guidance.

Spiritual Stone: Emerald—This gem is thought to aid in smoothing the connection between the desires of the soul and those of the body.

✷ JUDITH'S INSIGHT ✷

You often feel older than you are because of your well-developed sense of responsibility. An appealing inner charm steadily draws others to you. When you aks why people like you so much, they won't always be able to supply a reason. There's just that special something you possess.

You may feel misunderstood until you grow up and start recognizing how out of the ordinary you are. You are unique, with a kind heart and overactive mind, and you have strong values no matter what environment you grow up in.

You can lack tact, and your sense of humor can waver, especially if the joke is on you. Life is not going to be always easy. Luckily you have the strength to meet the challenges you'll face. It's very important for you to do what you consider is your duty. In every relationship, you'll fulfill what the other person expects, even to your own detriment.

Well-rounded and with many different talents, you don't fully recognize all your gifts until you're older. You may be strongly interested in electricity, music, or politics. Your firm convictions fuel the need to accomplish much in this life. You would do very well as a social worker or in another job as a force for true justice. You have the ability to communicate your ideas clearly, and your words often find their way into the heads and hearts of many.

✷ ✷ ✷

Possessions and Desires . . .

Gem: Sardius—This stone could give the wearer unusual insights into his or her own heart.

Flower: Fuchsia—You tend to have good taste in what you wear and your surroundings.

Astral Color, Color Need, Apparel Color: Your Astral Color is Red, the color of passion, power, excitement, and strength. Violet in your environment will keep you empathetic toward others. In your wardrobe, Green is your power color for overcoming obstacles.

Fragrance: You need to be bathed in exotic scents that will give your imagination room to roam. Experiment with imported incense and tinctures to show the world what a spirited individual you are.

Tree: Apple—You are creative, full of joy, and nearly magical. You bring happiness.

Instruments: Viola, trumpet

Composer: Liszt

Bird: Flamingo—This beautiful, gregarious bird is always careful of its enemy. It is also a caretaker of the young and tries to keep everyone happy.

Symbol: Triangle—You have the right combination of abilities.

Harmonious Health and Nutrition . . .

Health Scent: Peach—This scent may balance your good qualities so that they equal your charm.

Favorable Foods: Cabbage, oranges, rice, pecans, chicken

What's Lucky . . .

Lucky Numbers: 5 & 7

Best Months: February and June

Best Day of the Week: Thursday

Best Month Days: 4, 5, 23

Lucky Charm: A rabbit's foot or a white candle.

Harmonious Signs for Relationships and Partnerships: Aries, Leo, Sagittarius

Spiritual Guides . . .

Star: Al Beldah—those with this star are sometimes the victims of hasty judgments.

Angel: Aduachiel—this angel governs the balance of elements—water, earth, fire, and air—and helps maintain a calm disposition.

Guardian Angel: Plavwell—The guardian that gives power and strength to one's presence.

Spiritual Stone: Emerald—This gem is thought to aid in smoothing the connection between the desires of the soul and those of the body.

✶ JUDITH'S INSIGHT ✶

Positive, fearless, and masterful, it's not enough for you to achieve success at work; you need recognition for your spectacular accomplishments with your family and hobbies. These strong traits can lead you to a public or political career. Even if this is not your way, you should someday find yourself in the public eye.

You'd make a great consultant or counselor. Unlike most, you can be your own best advocate and usually know what's best for you. Law and order appeal to you, and you might consider a career in that profession. You would excel as a soldier, teacher, or surgeon. Your desire for drama may lead you to some form of acting. A natural poet, you often create songs and, if you have the voice, sing them yourself.

Those you love may not always understand what you see as your purely good intentions. You want a relationship with a firm commitment, but one that allows a strong sense of freedom. Discipline yourself with your spouse and children, if you have them. You may become suspicious and jealous with your mate. Beware of acting overly demanding and rigid with those living around you. Remember, a heavy hand may lead to a heavy heart.

Your biggest challenge in life is to put to effective use the many skills and gifts you were born with. Hang onto the reins tightly because it is likely to be an eventful ride. Incorporate your love of travel into a life where you'll frequently visit very different places.

✶ ✶ ✶

NOVEMBER 24 SAGITTARIUS • The adventurous one of the zodiac

November 22 at 5:00 A.M. to December 21 at 10:00 P.M. • NUMEROLOGY 6

Possessions and Desires . . .

Gem: Topaz—This is an excellent gift to be exchanged between very loyal friends.
Flower: Dark Geranium—Allow yourself more freedom, when you yearn for it.
Astral Color, Color Need, Apparel Color: Your Astral Color is Red, the color of passion, power, excitement, and strength. Violet in your environment keeps you empathetic toward others. In your wardrobe, Green is your power color for overcoming obstacles.
Fragrance: You need to be bathed in exotic scents that will give your imagination room to roam. Experiment with imported incense and tinctures to show the world what a spirited individual you are.
Tree: Palm—You tend to be very healthy and creative.
Instruments: Tambourine, lyre
Composer: Schubert
Bird: Goldfinch—There are forty-four different species of finches which vary greatly. These gentle creatures can be very shy in unsettled weather.
Symbol: Crescent—You are more likely to be influenced by the phases of the moon. Your easygoing manner leads you to peaceful situations.

Harmonious Health and Nutrition . . .

Health Scent: Orange Blossom—This scent may balance your body, mind, and soul
Favorable Foods: Savory, apples, caraway seed, almond, chicken

What's Lucky . . .

Lucky Numbers: 5, 7
Best Months: February and June
Best Day of the Week: Thursday
Best Month Days: 6, 15, 24

Lucky Charm: A religious token or card from any religion.
Harmonious Signs for Relationships and Partnerships: Aries, Leo, Sagittarius

Spiritual Guides . . .

Star: Al Beldah—Those with this star are sometimes the victims of hasty judgments.
Angel: Aduachiel—This angel governs the balance of elements —water, earth, fire, and air—and helps maintain a calm disposition.
Guardian Angel: Michael—"Who is like God."
Spiritual Stone: Emerald—This gem is thought to aid in smoothing the connection between the desires of the soul and those of the body.

✴ JUDITH'S INSIGHT ✴

You are lovable by nature, and that quality softens your often demanding personality. Others may find you moody and complex. Although you can be quite the party animal at times, another side of you may be viewed as cold and aloof.

Because you want to do so many things, it may take you a while to get settled into a steady career. You'll plug away and chug along for years before a sudden opportunity arises leading to wealth or possibly fame.

You would do well in philosophy, writing, teaching, medicine, or law. These differing careers have one thing in common: they require strong persons who can control themselves and others. You accomplish the task with both charm and wit.

Romance is more than difficult for you. It would take a miracle for you to find somebody that wants to put up with your ever-changing desires. The other person can never be affectionate, kind, or loving enough to suit you. What's more, if your mate acts as thoughtlessly as you do sometimes, you're out the door. It doesn't have to be this way, but the only one who can change your destiny is you. If you want love in your life (and you do), you'll have to put your whole heart into it. It may take years for you to recognize this.

✴ ✴ ✴

NOVEMBER 25 SAGITTARIUS • The adventurous one of the zodiac
November 22 at 5:00 A.M. to December 21 at 10:00 P.M. • NUMEROLOGY 7

Possessions and Desires . . .

Gem: Ruby—This stone may lead you to energy, friendship, and happiness.

Flower: Nutmeg Geranium—What you let yourself expect will tend to be what you receive.

Astral Color, Color Need, Apparel Color: Your Astral Color is Red, the color of passion, power, excitement, and strength. Violet in your environment keeps you empathetic toward others. In your wardrobe, Purple reflects your giving personality and brings you luck.

Fragrance: You need to be bathed in exotic scents that will give your imagination room to roam. Experiment with imported incense and tinctures to show the world what a spirited individual you are.

Tree: Sycamore—Yours is the ability to love, communicate honestly with others, and have lasting relationships.

Instrument: Harp

Composers: Gluck, Brahms

Bird: Skylark—This handsome bird is beautiful when it sings. It always whistles as it works.

Symbol: Heart—You are enthusiastic, empathetic, and full of generosity and love

Harmonious Health and Nutrition . . .

Health Scent: Jasmine—This scent may make you more easygoing when you are stressed.

Favorable Foods: Greens, peaches, cereals, pecans, chicken

What's Lucky . . .

Lucky Numbers: 5, 7
Best Months: February and June
Best Day of the Week: Thursday
Best Month Days: 6, 15, 24
Lucky Charm: An old key.
Harmonious Signs for Relationships and Partnerships: Aries, Leo, Sagittarius

Spiritual Guides . . .

Star: Al Beldah—Those with this star are sometimes the victims of hasty judgments.

Angel: Aduachiel—This angel governs the balance of elements—water, earth, fire, and air—and helps maintain a calm disposition.

Guardian Angel: Raphael—This angel attends to all of your needs when you are looking for guidance.

Spiritual Stone: Emerald—This gem is thought to aid in smoothing the connection between the desires of the soul and those of the body.

✶ JUDITH'S INSIGHT ✶

You have more than enough power and passion for life to get all you want out of it. Give in. A career goal may include fun and frolic, but you need a challenge, too. You will work hard to be successful but are likely to be hindered or helped most by your environment. Try to keep where you are separate from who you are in your own mind. Don't let the excitement or boredom of the place control your emotions.

Your romantic soul makes you high maintenance when it comes to love and relationships. Of course, you're extremely kind, warm, and sensitive. Love for you is a forest fire whose flame seldom dies. Give your partner credit just for keeping up with you.

You can do just about anything you put your mind to except when it comes to making a quick decision. You analyze things to death, which will always interfere with your getting things done. Watch out for your mood swings hurting your cause. Many days, you may find all you'll do is argue with yourself.

You love to travel and may have the desire to visit exotic places. Your love of entertainment may lead you to a career in party planning, performing, or writing or as a critic. You're a person who clearly knows the difference between right and wrong, and there won't be a time in your life when you don't seek justice. You like helping the underdog, and it should be a comfort that you get out of life only as much as you put in.

✶ ✶ ✶

NOVEMBER 26 SAGITTARIUS • The adventurous one of the zodiac

November 22 at 5:00 A.M. to December 21 at 10:00 P.M. • NUMEROLOGY 8

Possessions and Desires . . .

Gem: Chrysolite—This gem may help you clear your mind of sadness and worry.

Flower: Silver Leaf Geranium—You seem to remember all the tiny details.

Astral Color, Color Need, Apparel Color: Your Astral Color is Red, the color of passion, power, excitement, and strength. Violet in your environment will keep you empathetic toward others. In your wardrobe, Green is your power color for overcoming obstacles.

Fragrance: You need to be bathed in exotic scents that will give your imagination room to roam. Experiment with imported incense and tinctures to show the world what a spirited individual you are.

Tree: Pine—Your relationships tend to be harmonious, both emotionally and mentally.

Instrument: Cello

Composer: Mozart

Bird: Bobolink—This charming singer is equally good as a soloist or a member of an orchestra. It is a very romantic bird, useful as an insect destroyer, and elegant, with beautiful feathers, and always pleasant to have around.

Symbol: Wings—You are the source of balance in your world—this will bring you contentment.

Harmonious Health and Nutrition . . .

Health Scent: Almond—This scent may revitalize you and open you to greater possibilities.

Favorable Foods: Horseradish, grapes, rice, pecans, fish

What's Lucky . . .

Lucky Numbers: 5, 7

Best Months: February and June

Best Day of the Week: Thursday

Best Month Days: 8, 17, 26

Lucky Charm: Red ribbon in your wallet or doorway.

Harmonious Signs for Relationships and Partnerships: Aries, Leo, Sagittarius

Spiritual Guides . . .

Star: Al Naim—Those with this star are often delightful.

Angel: Aduachiel—this angel governs the balance of elements—water, earth, fire, and air—and helps maintain a calm disposition.

Guardian Angel: Seraphim—An angel that brings love, light, and passion.

Spiritual Stone: Emerald—This gem is thought to aid in smoothing the connection between the desires of the soul and those of the body.

✶ JUDITH'S INSIGHT ✶

Provided the subject is of interest, you make a great student. Your energy will bring you success, if you can manage to find a way to channel it. You are quick-minded and, unfortunately, sometimes quick-tempered. Though very serious while younger, as you get older you become the life of many parties.

Retail, particularly sales, may bring you success. You can talk anyone into buying anything. Your conversations are bright and interesting, and you have no fear of showing or receiving affection. Others feel close to you because of your naturally cheerful disposition. Consider making the most use of your gifts by opening your own business.

Relationships will be just a matter of finding the right method of convincing that special person you're the one. It's easy for you to meet people, so you should have many choices. Explore your love of travel—you are brimming with desire to delve into nature both close to you and far away.

You will feel secure around water and are invigorated by heights. You have a talent for innovation. The only restriction you'll ever feel is time. You're so busy that even if you live to be a hundred, there will be things you haven't gotten around to.

★ ★ ★

NOVEMBER 27 SAGITTARIUS • The adventurous one of the zodiac

November 22 at 5:00 A.M. to December 21 at 10:00 P.M. • NUMEROLOGY 9

Possessions and Desires . . .

Gem: Beryl—This gem could be good for meditation and concentration.

Flower: Gentian—You are likely to live a blameless life.

Astral Color, Color Need, Apparel Color: Your Astral Color is Red, the color of passion, power, excitement, and strength. Violet in your environment will keep you empathetic toward others. In your wardrobe, Purple reflects your giving personality and brings you luck.

Fragrance: You need to be bathed in exotic scents that will give your imagination room to roam. Experiment with imported incense and tinctures to show the world what a spirited individual you are.

Tree: Holly—Beware that you are not carried away by your passionate nature. The only way to grow is to be open to new experiences.

Instruments: Violin, tympanum

Composer: Gluck

Bird: Mockingbird—the most proficient minstrel in the world's orchestra; graceful and enthusiastic.

Symbol: Anchor—This tranquil symbol signifies stability and strength, and stands for strong commitments in relationships.

Harmonious Health and Nutrition . . .

Health Scent: Lavender—This scent might lead others to trust you and make you patient.

Favorable Foods: Savory, prunes, bran, pecans, chicken

What's Lucky . . .

Lucky Numbers: 5, 7
Best Months: February and June
Best Day of the Week: Thursday
Best Month Days: 9, 18, 27
Lucky Charm: A U.S. coin or bill of any amount from the year you were born.

Harmonious Signs for Relationships and Partnerships: Aries, Leo, Sagittarius

Spiritual Guides . . .

Star: Al Beldah—Those with this star are sometimes the victims of hasty judgments.

Angel: Aduachiel—This angel governs the balance of elements—water, earth, fire, and air—and helps maintain a calm disposition.

Guardian Angel: Gabriel—"God is my strength."

Spiritual Stone: Emerald—This gem is thought to aid in smoothing the connection between the desires of the soul and those of the body.

✶ JUDITH'S INSIGHT ✶

You need plenty of excitement every day. The more pressure life gives you, the more you can get accomplished. While it's natural for you to feel stressed, you don't handle obstacles or interference very well. It's very important to you that your energies are directed in ways you consider proper. You have executive abilities and are highly skilled in organization.

Your family is a source of comfort and strength. Your inherited gifts might be either material things or your family's optimistic disposition. You love the finer things in life. Usually stylishly dressed, you are often noticed for your exquisite taste.

Not one to wear your emotions on your sleeve, you are naturally a bit secretive. Give all you can to relationships while in them. You adore making and receiving romantic gestures.

As long as you work with people, you'll do very well. You can be generous, and the more you do for others, the happier you are. Sometimes, however, you think too much. You may be troubled by regret, refusing to follow through on strong premonitions. You are well regarded by family and friends; somehow public recognition will follow you.

You have great counseling technique. Public relations, the media, any job in telecommunication or computers would suit you well.

✶ ✶ ✶

NOVEMBER 28 SAGITTARIUS • The adventurous one of the zodiac

November 22 at 5:00 A.M. to December 21 at 10:00 P.M. • NUMEROLOGY 1

Possessions and Desires . . .

Gem: Agate—This stone may promote health and lead you to a long life.

Flower: Gorse—You generally get along with everyone.

Astral Color, Color Need, Apparel Color: Your Astral Color is Red, the color of passion, power, excitement, and strength. Violet in your environment keeps you empathetic toward others. In your wardrobe, Green is your power color for overcoming obstacles.

Fragrance: You need to be bathed in exotic scents that will give your imagination room to roam. Experiment with imported incense and tinctures to show the world what a spirited individual you are.

Tree: Walnut—You are unusually helpful and always looking for constant changes in your life.

Instruments: Oboe, flute, clarinet, piano, French horn, organ, piccolo

Composer: Böhm

Bird: Bird of Paradise—the "bird of the Gods." You will shine and love extraordinary circumstances.

Symbol: Crown—the universal sign of dignity.

Harmonious Health and Nutrition . . .

Health Scent: Strawberry—Soothing by nature, the strawberry promotes self-esteem and encourages love.

Favorable Foods: Cabbage, apples, rice, almonds, fish

What's Lucky . . .

Lucky Numbers: 5, 7
Best Months: February and June
Best Day of the Week: Thursday
Best Month Days: 1, 10, 19

Lucky Charm: A new penny in your shoe.
Harmonious Signs for Relationships and Partnerships: Aries, Leo, Sagittarius

Spiritual Guides . . .

Star: Al Naim—Those with this star are often delightful.

Angel: Aduachiel—This angel governs the balance of elements—water, earth, fire, and air—and helps maintain a calm disposition.

Guardian Angel: Malachi—"Messenger of Jehovah."

Spiritual Stone: Emerald—This gem is thought to aid in smoothing the connection between the desires of the soul and those of the body.

✳ JUDITH'S INSIGHT ✳

You are fiery, determined, and generally quick in your actions. You're charming and physically fit and should have no problem cultivating relationships of any kind. You love to learn.

Your open-door policy to all possibilities only enhances your life. Be aware that your power and passion can intimidate other people. You will have intense enemies and deeply devoted friends. An iron will helps you on the job, though it's difficult admitting your mistakes. You can laugh at obstacles before and after you overcome them. A career either in acting, athletics, law, or state government could work for you.

You like to control those you love. This will cause problems with your partner and other family members. You may often be the cause of friction at home. Family is the primary focus of your life. If you choose to have them, your children and you will be very important to each other.

You do well at games of chance and may experience an occasional lucky streak. Keeping your wits about you can further the benefits of luck. Make sure you remain aware of what's going on around you.

✱ ✱ ✱

NOVEMBER 29 SAGITTARIUS • The adventurous one of the zodiac

November 22 at 5:00 A.M. to December 21 at 10:00 P.M. • NUMEROLOGY 2

Possessions and Desires . . .

Gem: Sapphire—This gem may help you find forgiveness from those you've wronged.

Flower: Goldilocks—You tend to always act like a young person.

Astral Color, Color Need, Apparel Color: Your Astral Color is Red, the color of passion, power, excitement, and strength. Violet in your environment will keep you empathetic toward others. In your wardrobe, Purple reflects your giving personality and brings you luck.

Fragrance: You need to be bathed in exotic scents that will give your imagination room to roam. Experiment with imported incense and tinctures to show the world what a spirited individual you are.

Tree: Maple—You have great stability and flashes of intuition.

Instruments: Pipe organ, cymbal, drum

Composers: Handel, Johann Sebastian Bach

Bird: Stork—Turkish bird, held in high esteem the world over. This bird is intelligent but may have strange tendencies.

Symbol: Cross—the symbol of self-sacrifice and reconciliation.

Harmonious Health and Nutrition . . .

Health Scent: Apple—A vivacious scent encouraging energy. Will help you to be more creative, intuitive and positive.

Favorable Foods: Horseradish, apricots, rice, pecans, chicken

What's Lucky . . .

Lucky Numbers: 5, 7

Best Months: February and June

Best Day of the Week: Thursday

Lucky Charms: Two 50-cent pieces. Give someone else one of them.

Harmonious Signs for Relationships and Partnerships: Aries, Leo, Sagittarius

Spiritual Guides . . .

Star: Al Beldah—Those with this star are sometimes the victims of hasty judgments.

Angel: Aduachiel—This angel governs the balance of elements—water, earth, fire, and air—and helps maintain a calm disposition.

Guardian Angel: St. John—This angel simplifies that which is complicated.

Spiritual Stone: Emerald—This gem is thought to aid in smoothing the connection between the desires of the soul and those of the body.

✳ JUDITH'S INSIGHT ✳

You love a good time. Quite the talker, you may do well in careers where you use your voice and mouth. Your vivid imagination and powerful energy sometimes frustrate other people. With the ability to turn disadvantage into success, you can make the best of just about any situation. It's better when you can be your own boss; any interference from others makes you cranky.

You do most things well but are easily flustered if sidetracked by problems. You are at your best in a party atmosphere. Your strong convictions may find you frequently defending others. You love to dig into things physically and mentally and so would be happy in employment involving research.

Your dominant concern is for those you love. Romance brings you great satisfaction and the most happiness. You're more giver than taker. Generous to a fault, you sacrifice anything and have energy to spare when working to make your family comfortable. It may take awhile to get over a disappointing love relationship.

Your passion to seek out the unusual, unknown, or international could find you seeking a career in the airline or travel industry. Wherever your particular road leads, you always want peace in the environment.

✳ ✳ ✳

NOVEMBER 30 SAGITTARIUS • The adventurous one of the zodiac

November 22 at 5:00 A.M. to December 21 at 10:00 P.M. • NUMEROLOGY 3

Possessions and Desires . . .

Gem: Ruby—This stone may lead you to energy, friendship, and happiness.

Flower: Goldenrod—You may spend so much time preparing for troubles you lose the joy of living.

Astral Color, Color Need, Apparel Color: Your Astral Color is Red, the color of passion, power, excitement, and strength. Violet in your environment keeps you empathetic toward others. In your wardrobe, Green is your power color for overcoming obstacles.

Fragrance: You need to be bathed in exotic scents that will give your imagination room to roam. Experiment with imported incense and tinctures to show the world what a spirited individual you are.

Tree: Elm—You have willpower, strength, and the ability to stand alone.

Instrument: Trombone

Composers: Verdi, Mendelssohn, Schumann

Bird: Eagle—This bird is quick to use its powers of flight. It can see immeasurable distances in a single glance, and can sometimes appear to be indifferent.

Symbol: Wreath—You have been crowned with a special personality. You are strong but extremely compassionate.

Harmonious Health and Nutrition . . .

Health Scent: Rose—This scent will lead you to passionate thoughts and make you feel warm inside.

Favorable Foods: Greens, prunes, cereals, pecans, fish

What's Lucky . . .

Lucky Numbers: 5, 7
Best Months: February and June
Best Day of the Week: Thursday
Best Month Days: 3, 12, 21

Lucky Charm: A pen that someone else has already used.

Harmonious Signs for Relationships and Partnerships: Aries, Leo, Sagittarius

Spiritual Guides . . .

Star: Al Beldah—Those with this star are sometimes the victims of hasty judgments.

Angel: Aduachiel—This angel governs the balance of elements—water, earth, fire, and air—and helps maintain a calm disposition.

Guardian Angel: Johiel—This angel is a protector of all those with a humble heart.

Spiritual Stone: Emerald—This gem is thought to aid in smoothing the connection between the desires of the soul and those of the body.

✷ JUDITH'S INSIGHT ✷

You always win and, therefore, have the most toys. You're playful and spontaneous, and you love to turn any situation into a party. You give of yourself, your time, your talent, and your money. Others depend on you for amusement, and you seldom let them down. People admire you for your worldview. Your presence is a gift all on its own.

You have no problem entering into relationships. Understand that you have so much energy that you may frighten some people. Once that special person gets to know you, they'll be ready for the commitment you so crave. Sleepyheads are not for you, and you avoid lazy types.

You waste no time and live life to its fullest. You're fun to be with, and you love to laugh. Be careful of your tendency to overdo things, both at work and play. Expect to succeed in careers that center around entertainment, hospitality, writing, reading, or children.

It may be likely that you'll have more than one career throughout your lifetime. You may have to take a job that pays the bills for awhile before landing your dream gig. You easily create bonds that become and remain true friendships forever.

✷ ✷ ✷

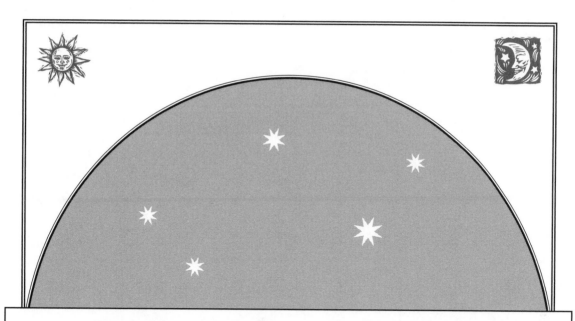

DECEMBER

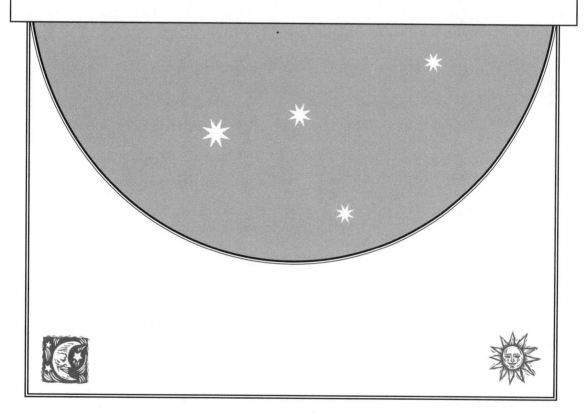

DECEMBER 1 SAGITTARIUS • The adventurous one of the zodiac

November 22 at 5:00 A.M. to December 21 at 10:00 P.M. • NUMEROLOGY 1

Possessions and Desires . . .

Gem: Turquoise—This stone might help you find material wealth.

Flower: Scarlet Geranium—You are always generous with what you have to give.

Astral Color, Color Need, Apparel Color: Your Astral Color is Red, the color of passion, power, excitement, and strength. Violet in your environment keeps you empathetic toward others. In your wardrobe, Purple reflects your giving personality and brings you luck.

Fragrance: You need to be bathed in exotic scents that will give your imagination room to roam. Experiment with imported incense and tinctures to show the world what a spirited individual you are.

Tree: Walnut—You are unusually helpful and always looking for constant changes in your life.

Instruments: Oboe, flute, clarinet, piano, French horn, organ, piccolo

Composer: Böhm

Bird: Hummingbird—This bird is delicate and graceful. It can remain still for hours, then dart off and be as busy as a bee.

Symbol: Crown—the universal sign of dignity.

Harmonious Health and Nutrition . . .

Health Scent: Strawberry—Soothing by nature, the strawberry promotes self-esteem and encourages love.

Favorable Foods: Greens, black figs, unrefined cereals, almonds, chicken

What's Lucky . . .

Lucky Numbers: 5, 7

Best Months: February and June

Best Day of the Week: Thursday

Best Month Days: 1, 10, 19

Lucky Charm: A new penny in your shoe.

Harmonious Signs for Relationships and Partnerships: Aries, Leo, Sagittarius

Spiritual Guides . . .

Star: Al Naim—Those with this star are often delightful.

Angel: Aduachiel—this angel governs the balance of elements—water, earth, fire, and air—and helps maintain a calm disposition.

Guardian Angel: Malachi—"Messenger of Jehovah."

Spiritual Stone: Emerald—This gem is thought to aid in smoothing the connection between the desires of the soul and those of the body.

✳ JUDITH'S INSIGHT ✳

Energetic, enthusiastic, and determined, you would make the perfect athlete. Just about any sport should interest you. You can adapt yourself easily to different circumstances. Your name may even appear in the paper at one time or another, probably for being absolutely brilliant at something. You have plenty of self-confidence and should find your way no matter what obstacles you encounter.

A high-quality employee or employer, you create pleasant working conditions for your coworkers. You would do well as a musician, actor, athlete, or salesman. With your flair for design, you could do something in the fashion industry. A desire for travel may lead you to pursue flying. You are a natural when it comes to business and may be inclined to have your own eventually.

Love for you is a battle zone. You desperately want a commitment and will take more grief than you should to keep things together. Do not take your own advice when it comes to love. You need more romance than your selected mate can give. You love a fiery and passionate relationship and need constant spontaneity to keep your attention engaged. In return you offer fun and a kindhearted personality. Beware of getting exactly what you wish for; you could later regret who you end up with.

★ ★ ★

DECEMBER 2 SAGITTARIUS • The adventurous one of the zodiac

November 22 at 5:00 A.M. to December 21 at 10:00 P.M. • NUMEROLOGY 2

Possessions and Desires . . .

Gem: Sapphire—This gem may help you find forgiveness from those you've wronged.

Flower: Teasel—You may not like spending much time in crowds.

Astral Color, Color Need, Apparel Color: Your Astral Color is Red, the color of passion, power, excitement, and strength. Violet in your environment keeps you empathetic toward others. In your wardrobe, Green is your power color for overcoming obstacles.

Fragrance: You need to be bathed in exotic scents that will give your imagination room to roam. Experiment with imported incense and tinctures to show the world what a spirited individual you are.

Tree: Maple—You have great stability and flashes of intuition.

Instruments: Pipe organ, cymbal, drum

Composers: Handel, Johann Sebastian Bach

Bird: Cuckoo—A good flyer and very seldom a quitter. Many seem more independent than they actually are; yearn for more nurturing than one would expect.

Symbol: Cross—the symbol of self-sacrifice and reconciliation.

Harmonious Health and Nutrition . . .

Health Scent: Apple—You are creative, full of joy, and nearly magical. You bring happiness.

Favorable Foods: Cabbage, apples, rice, pecans, fish

What's Lucky . . .

Lucky Numbers: 5 7
Best Months: February and June
Best Day of the Week: Thursday
Best Month Days: 2, 11, 20
Lucky Charms: Two 50-cent pieces. Give someone else one of them.
Harmonious Signs for Relationships and Partnerships: Aries, Leo, Sagittarius

Spiritual Guides . . .

Star: Al Naim—Those with this star are often delightful.

Angel: Aduachiel—This angel governs the balance of elements—water, earth, fire, and air—and helps maintain a calm disposition.

Guardian Angel: St. Thomas—This angel brings affection from others and encourages you in all that you do.

Spiritual Stone: Emerald—This gem is thought to aid in smoothing the connection between the desires of the soul and those of the body.

✶ JUDITH'S INSIGHT ✶

Consistent, compassionate, persistent, and brave, you are not likely to turn off course because of any obstacles that occur. You are smart but can lack self-confidence. You live life more inside your head than others ever realize. You are always heard, even when silent.

Entertainment will play a strong role in your life, as will your love of fun. You aspire to a life of art or music. At the very least you'll become an avid moviegoer or collector of CDs. You love to travel and have the desire to circle the earth one way or another.

Family and children will be very important to you, and others will have to understand that your home relationships take priority over just about anything in your life. You don't tend to leave things too quickly, and you give your spouse all your attention. So long as you work to have all the ingredients going in, your relationships turn out wonderfully well.

You want very much to be successful, and while you are looking for it, it just might find you. Remember, square pegs don't fit into round holes. Your organizational skills may lead you down many paths in search of the perfect career. You would do well in government, law, travel, or entertainment. Medical matters take on strong meaning in your life, either as an employment or as volunteer work in a hospice.

✶ ✶ ✶

DECEMBER 3 SAGITTARIUS • The adventurous one of the zodiac

November 22 at 5:00 A.M. to December 21 at 10:00 P.M. • NUMEROLOGY 3

Possessions and Desires . . .

Gem: Ruby—This stone may lead you to energy, friendship, and happiness.

Flower: French Willow—You can be a person of simple tastes and have enough courage to seek out what is truly important.

Astral Color, Color Need, Apparel Color: Your Astral Color is Red, the color of passion, power, excitement, and strength. Violet in your environment keeps you empathetic toward others. In your wardrobe, Purple reflects your giving personality and brings you luck.

Fragrance: You need to be bathed in exotic scents that will give your imagination room to roam. Experiment with imported incense and tinctures to show the world what a spirited individual you are.

Tree: Elm—You have willpower, strength, and the ability to stand alone.

Instrument: Trombone

Composers: Verdi, Mendelssohn, Schumann

Bird: Swan—Regarded as royal and sacred, this bird has the protective nature of a mother, and can become a furious fighter in the defense of its own.

Symbol: Wreath—You have been crowned with a special personality. You are strong but extremely compassionate.

Harmonious Health and Nutrition . . .

Health Scent: Rose—This scent will lead you to passionate thoughts and make you feel warm inside.

Favorable Foods: Savory, peaches, bran, almonds, chicken

What's Lucky . . .

Lucky Numbers: 5, 7
Best Months: February and June
Best Day of the Week: Thursday
Best Month Days: 3, 12, 21, 30

Lucky Charm: A pen that someone else has already used.

Harmonious Signs for Relationships and Partnerships: Aries, Leo, Sagittarius

Spiritual Guides . . .

Star: Al Naim—Those with this star are often delightful.

Angel: Aduachiel—This angel governs the balance of elements—water, earth, fire, and air—and helps maintain a calm disposition.

Guardian Angel: Johiel—This angel is a protector of all those with a humble heart.

Spiritual Stone: Emerald—This gem is thought to aid in smoothing the connection between the desires of the soul and those of the body.

✴ JUDITH'S INSIGHT ✴

You are one charming pain in the neck. It would benefit you to learn that you can get more accomplished by keeping quiet. You can be kind and hard working, but you need to find your special niche in life before you achieve happiness.

Love will be tricky for you, as you're likely to be attracted to one very difficult person after another. The only way you'll be able to make a relationship work is by constantly feeding it loads of positive energy. Family is important to you, but you need to have an agreed-on amount of space or you'll end up feeling claustrophobic.

If you lead, you succeed. You're great at administration, but when people don't listen you get easily frustrated. Not only are you a good talker, you're a good listener. You would do well in politics and government, and you follow the letter of the law. You could also do well as a law or code enforcement officer.

You would also make an excellent builder, contractor, or designer. And if you haven't reached all your goals yet, pick up a paper and pen and spell out how you'll eventually succeed. Sometimes you have trouble getting started, but you should write, even if it's the local newspaper gossip column.

Life will be a constant learning experience for you. It may take time for you to find yourself, but it'll be worth the wait.

DECEMBER 4 SAGITTARIUS • The adventurous one of the zodiac

November 22 at 5:00 A.M. to December 21 at 10:00 P.M. • NUMEROLOGY 4

Possessions and Desires . . .

Gem: Emerald—Those who carry this stone tend to be lucky in love.

Flower: Fleur-de-lis—You may have a quick temper but are just as swift to show your affections.

Astral Color, Color Need, Apparel Color: Your Astral Color is Red, the color of passion, power, excitement, and strength. Violet in your environment will keep you empathetic toward others. In your wardrobe, Green is your power color for overcoming obstacles.

Fragrance: You need to be bathed in exotic scents that will give your imagination room to roam. Experiment with imported incense and tinctures to show the world what a spirited individual you are.

Tree: Cherry—You will find yourself faced with constant new emotional awakenings.

Instruments: Bass, clarinet

Composers: Haydn, Wagner

Bird: Killdeer—This bird is usually found consorting with other species, and can adapt to any environment.

Symbol: Star—You are full of inner brightness and will stand out in any crowd. You will be seen as special.

Harmonious Health and Nutrition . . .

Health Scent: Vanilla—This scent will fill you with a feeling of cleanliness and stability.

Favorable Foods: Dandelion, oranges, caraway seed, pecans, fish

What's Lucky . . .

Lucky Numbers: 5, 7

Best Months: February and June

Best Day of the Week: Thursday

Best Month Days: 4, 13, 22

Lucky Charm: A piece of material cut from something in your home.

Harmonious Signs for Relationships and Partnerships: Aries, Leo, Sagittarius

Spiritual Guides . . .

Star: Al Naim—Those with this star are often delightful.

Angel: Aduachiel—This angel governs the balance of elements—water, earth, fire, and air—and helps maintain a calm disposition.

Guardian Angel: Uriel—This angel brings the light of God's guidance.

Spiritual Stone: Emerald—This gem is thought to aid in smoothing the connection between the desires of the soul and those of the body.

✴ *JUDITH'S INSIGHT* ✴

You are very intelligent, highly motivated, spontaneous, and enthusiastic. You have a great imagination and are remarkable at handling people. Who could ask for more? You will probably live a very unconventional life. Drawn to the unique and unusual, you love to entertain and to be entertained.

Animals make you calm and happy. You may consider a career that involves animals. At one time or another, you may have a lot of pets. Just as rewarding for you is a career in jewelry, retail, manufacturing, or music. You have great physical qualities, high energy levels, and much skill when it comes to sports.

You have no problem maintaining friends because of your sincerity. Intimate relationships can be a little more difficult, and you may suffer through a few losers before you meet your true soul mate. Forget looking for fire; instead, look for someone who understands you.

You can be cautious and reserved when you don't feel comfortable and may try to pretend you're an altogether different person. Nothing bothers you more than disrespect and ingratitude. You are rigid when you want to be. Discipline can be very important to you. Be cautious when others try to corner you and keep you there.

You need to keep both feet on the ground because you have a tendency to make yourself restless or anxious.

★ ★ ★

DECEMBER 5 SAGITTARIUS • The adventurous one of the zodiac

November 22 at 5:00 A.M. to December 21 at 10:00 P.M. • NUMEROLOGY 5

Possessions and Desires . . .

Gem: Sardius—This stone could give the wearer unusual insights into his or her own heart.
Flower: Fennel—You tend to be as strong as you need to be.
Astral Color, Color Need, Apparel Color: Your Astral Color is Red, the color of passion, power, excitement, and strength. Violet in your environment keeps you empathetic toward others. In your wardrobe, Purple reflects your giving personality and brings you luck.
Fragrance: You need to be bathed in exotic scents that will give your imagination room to roam. Experiment with imported incense and tinctures to show the world what a spirited individual you are.
Tree: Apple—You are creative, full of joy, and nearly magical. You bring happiness.
Instruments: Viola, trumpet
Composer: Liszt
Bird: Flamingo—This beautiful, gregarious bird is always careful of its enemy. It is also a caretaker of the young and tries to keep everyone happy.
Symbol: Triangle—You have the right combination of abilities.

Harmonious Health and Nutrition . . .

Health Scent: Peach—This scent may balance your good qualities so that they equal your charm.
Favorable Foods: Savory, grapes, bran, almonds, chicken

What's Lucky . . .

Lucky Numbers: 5, 7
Best Months: February and June
Best Day of the Week: Thursday
Best Month Days: 5, 4, 23
Lucky Charms: A rabbit's foot or a white candle.

Harmonious Signs for Relationships and Partnerships: Aries, Leo, Sagittarius

Spiritual Guides . . .

Star: Al Naim—Those with this star are often delightful.
Angel: Aduachiel—This angel governs the balance of elements—water, earth, fire, and air—and helps maintain a calm disposition.
Guardian Angel: Plavwell—The guardian that gives power and strength to one's presence.
Spiritual Stone: Sardonyx—This stone may cause people to be attracted to you.

✳ JUDITH'S INSIGHT ✳

You are interested in just about everything life has to offer. You're happiest creating a commotion or throwing a wild party. You know how to talk and get your point across. You are so filled with ideas that you could be an entrepreneur who starts up more than one business. You do well working with people and may be drawn to advertising, public relations, or even horse racing.

You have a style all your own. Direct your creative abilities toward fixing up your home and toward your career. Financially, you will reap rewards in unusual ways, and you won't necessarily have to work for all the money you receive.

Charm will bring relationships right to your door; your natural kindness will keep them there. You are always generous, not just with gifts but also affection. You are a pleasure to be around. There's a demanding side there, too, but in your case, the good outweighs the bad. Relationships do put you through a hoop or two, but you have enough stamina to end up where you want to be.

Follow your intuition once you recognize the voice inside.

✳ ✳ ✳

DECEMBER 6 SAGITTARIUS • The adventurous one of the zodiac

November 22 at 5:00 A.M. to December 21 at 10:00 P.M. • NUMEROLOGY 6

Possessions and Desires . . .

Gem: Topaz—This is an excellent gift to be exchanged between very loyal friends.

Flower: Dragon Plant—You are the strength for all of those around you.

Astral Color, Color Need, Apparel Color: Your Astral Color is Red, the color of passion, power, excitement, and strength. Violet in your environment will keep you empathetic toward others. In your wardrobe, Green is your power color for overcoming obstacles.

Fragrance: You need to be bathed in exotic scents that will give your imagination room to roam. Experiment with imported incense and tinctures to show the world what a spirited individual you are.

Tree: Palm—You tend to be very healthy and creative.

Instruments: Tambourine, lyre

Composer: Schubert

Bird: Falcon—an expert hunter. When well-trained, it can adapt to many tasks and is usually obedient.

Symbol: Crescent—You are more likely to be influenced by the phases of the moon. Your easygoing manner leads you to peaceful situations.

Harmonious Health and Nutrition . . .

Health Scent: Orange Blossom—This scent may balance your body, mind, and soul.

Favorable Foods: Horseradish, apples, rice, pecans, fish

What's Lucky . . .

Lucky Numbers: 5, 7
Best Months: February and June
Best Day of the Week: Thursday
Best Month Days: 6, 15, 24
Lucky Charm: A religious token or card from any religion.

Harmonious Signs for Relationships and Partnerships: Aries, Leo, Sagittarius

Spiritual Guides . . .

Star: Al Naim—Those with this star are often delightful.

Angel: Aduachiel—This angel governs the balance of elements—water, earth, fire, and air—and helps maintain a calm disposition.

Guardian Angel: Michael—"Who is like God."

Spiritual Stone: Emerald—This gem is thought to aid in smoothing the connection between the desires of the soul and those of the body.

✶ JUDITH'S INSIGHT ✶

You love to entertain and make the perfect host or hostess. You'd be clever to make a career out of this. Your friendly disposition makes it easy for you to meet and greet, and you very rarely feel out of place. In one form or another, you achieve success in the entertainment business, either as an owner or worker in a restaurant or club or as a choreographer or writer.

Your love of the outdoors and nature may lead to a career with horses. You love to gamble and must be careful this doesn't get you into some kind of trouble. Somewhere along the way, a dual income presents itself. You have two of everything; it seems as if doubles keep entering your life from a couple of directions.

There isn't a mean bone in your body, and you're a pleasure to be around. When it comes to love, you are attractive, strong, and energetic. Your positive energy and enthusiasm for life make others want to be around you, although at times you can have moments of stubbornness and mood swings.

Financial success comes to you through relationships as well as through your business. You can be very restless or very committed, depending on your partner. Somewhere along the way, finances begin to improve enough so you feel secure. Your generosity helps money come to you.

✶ ✶ ✶

DECEMBER 7 SAGITTARIUS • The adventurous one of the zodiac

November 22 at 5:00 A.M. to December 21 at 10:00 P.M. • NUMEROLOGY 7

Possessions and Desires . . .

Gem: Agate—This stone may promote health and lead you to a long life.

Flower: Diomosa—You can be very shy around those you care for deeply.

Astral Color, Color Need, Apparel Color: Your Astral Color is Red, the color of passion, power, excitement, and strength. Violet in your environment keeps you empathetic toward others. In your wardrobe, Purple reflects your giving personality and brings you luck.

Fragrance: You need to be bathed in exotic scents that will give your imagination room to roam. Experiment with imported incense and tinctures to show the world what a spirited individual you are.

Tree: Sycamore—Yours is the ability to love, communicate honestly with others, and have lasting relationships.

Instrument: Harp

Composers: Gluck, Brahms

Bird: Warbling Parakeet—the most beautiful of all birds, known as the love bird. It does seem to have the powers of imitation.

Harmonious Health and Nutrition . . .

Health Scent: Jasmine—This scent may make you more easygoing when you are stressed.

Favorable Foods: Celery, grapes, caraway seed, pecans, chicken

What's Lucky . . .

Lucky Numbers: 5, 7
Best Months: February and June
Best Day of the Week: Thursday
Best Month Days: 6, 15, 24

Lucky Charm: An old key
Harmonious Signs for Relationships and Partnerships: Aries, Leo, Sagittarius

Spiritual Guides . . .

Star: Al Beldah—those with this star are sometimes the victims of hasty judgments.

Angel: Aduachiel—This angel governs the balance of elements—water, earth, fire, and air—and helps maintain a calm disposition.

Guardian Angel: Uriel—An individual archangel meaning: "the light of God."

Spiritual Stone: Emerald—This gem is thought to aid in smoothing the connection between the desires of the soul and those of the body

✴ JUDITH'S INSIGHT ✴

Dedicated to people in one way or another, you tend to be gentle, kind, outgoing, and always available. You are charming but don't necessarily lead a charmed life. Your share of heartaches will find you, but your stiff upper lip helps you maintain a good life.

You're fascinated with your surroundings and with light and would make an incredible painter and artist. So long as you don't lose yourself, you should spend some amount of time in your own world of imagination. You have a strong, determined mind when it comes to business and could do very well in accounting, finance, or the stock market. Here, too, your dreams will connect you to where you want to be.

When it comes to relationships, you are the ultimate romantic. Just make sure to take the chance and let your ideas flow. You can rise to any occasion and effect change to your environment with the best of them. No matter what you are doing, you know how to enjoy the moment. You are generous enough to give and smart enough to save. Your warm heart enables you to keep many close relationships.

✴ ✴ ✴

DECEMBER 8 SAGITTARIUS • The adventurous one of the zodiac

November 22 at 5:00 A.M. to December 21 at 10:00 P.M. • NUMEROLOGY 8

Possessions and Desires . . .

Gem: Chrysolite—This gem may help you clear your mind of sadness and worry.

Flower: Hollyhock—You can be very persuasive when you wish to be.

Astral Color, Color Need, Apparel Color: Your Astral Color is Red, the color of passion, power, excitement, and strength. Violet in your environment keeps you empathetic toward others. In your wardrobe, Green is your power color for overcoming obstacles.

Fragrance: You need to be bathed in exotic scents that will give your imagination room to roam. Experiment with imported incense and tinctures to show the world what a spirited individual you are.

Tree: Pine—Your relationships tend to be harmonious, both emotionally and mentally.

Instrument: Cello

Composer: Mozart

Bird: Bobolink—This charming singer is equally good as a soloist or a member of an orchestra. It is a very romantic bird, useful as an insect destroyer, and elegant, with beautiful feathers, and always pleasant to have around.

Symbol: Wings—You are the source of balance in your world—this will bring you contentment.

Harmonious Health and Nutrition . . .

Health Scent: Strawberry—Soothing by nature, the strawberry promotes self-esteem and encourages love.

Favorable Foods: Cabbage, peaches, unrefined cereals, pecans, fish

What's Lucky . . .

Lucky Numbers: 5, 7
Best Months: February and June
Best Day of the Week: Thursday
Best Month Days: 8, 17, 26

Lucky Charm: Red ribbon in your wallet or doorway.

Harmonious Signs for Relationships and Partnerships: Aries, Leo, and Sagittarius

Spiritual Guides . . .

Star: Al Naim—Those with this star are often delightful.

Angel: Aduachiel—this angel governs the balance of elements—water, earth, fire, and air—and helps maintain a calm disposition.

Guardian Angel: Seraphim—An angel that brings love, light, and passion.

Spiritual Stone: Emerald—This gem is thought to aid in smoothing the connection between the desires of the soul and those of the body.

✶ JUDITH'S INSIGHT ✶

You'd make the best judge, lawyer, businessperson, or clergyperson. You have a genuine personality and can keep secrets and maintain loyalties. Your unflagging endurance would make you an excellent athlete. You love to learn and will soak up knowledge of any kind.

Your adult life will go more smoothly than your childhood because you need time to become at ease with yourself. You mature into a better person who enjoys life only after gaining wisdom. Remember periodically you need to clean the cobwebs of skepticism and the snakes of negativity out of your mind. You do find love because you give it so freely. You don't like to be criticized and crave attention; when choosing your life's partner, keep these traits in mind. You get what you receive in love and would be a terrific spouse for anyone except those who make you feel on edge.

If you handled rejection a little better, you could make a fantastic entertainer. You may experience some hard years of self-sacrifice, but you have many hidden talents and will do better as you mature. Guard your self-confidence through the tough times, expecting not just the good but the great ones to come.

✶ ✶ ✶

Possessions and Desires . . .

Gem: Beryl—This gem could be good for meditation and concentration.

Flower: Creeper—You may keep far too many things to yourself.

Astral Color, Color Need, Apparel Color: Your Astral Color is Red, the color of passion, power, excitement, and strength. Violet in your environment keeps you empathetic toward others. In your wardrobe, Purple reflects your giving personality and brings you luck.

Fragrance: You need to be bathed in exotic scents that will give your imagination room to roam. Experiment with imported incense and tinctures to show the world what a spirited individual you are.

Tree: Holly—Beware that you are not carried away by your passionate nature. The only way to grow is to be open to new experiences.

Instruments: Violin, tympanum

Composer: Gluck

Bird: Mockingbird—the most proficient minstrel in the world's orchestra; graceful and enthusiastic.

Symbol: Anchor—This tranquil symbol signifies stability and strength, and stands for strong commitments in relationships.

Harmonious Health and Nutrition . . .

Health Scent: Lavender—This scent might lead others to trust you and make you patient.

Favorable Foods: Horseradish, oranges, rice, almonds, chicken

What's Lucky . . .

Lucky Numbers: 5, 7

Best Months: February and June

Best Day of the Week: Thursday

Best Month Days: 9, 18, 27

Lucky Charms: A U.S. coin or bill of any amount from the year you were born.

Harmonious Signs for Relationships and Partnerships: Aries, Leo, Sagittarius

Spiritual Guides . . .

Star: Al Naim—Those with this star are often delightful.

Angel: Aduachiel—This angel governs the balance of elements—water, earth, fire, and air—and helps maintain a calm disposition.

Guardian Angel: Gabriel—"God is my strength."

Spiritual Stone: Emerald—This gem is thought to aid in smoothing the connection between the desires of the soul and those of the body.

✳ *JUDITH'S INSIGHT* ✳

Others see you as dependable, reliable, respectful, and capable of doing just about anything. You possess the drive to accomplish exactly what you want. You have great opinions on any number of topics. Yours is a matchless intellect.

Consider sports as a career. With your energy and enthusiasm you could be a success at any one you choose. You have the potential to really excel at the game of golf if not as a pro than as the most enthusiastic duffer on your local links. You're a born leader—everyone's pick to be head of the PTA.

You can be very generous to those you think are deserving. Otherwise, you tend to keep your money deep in your pockets. You will do well in relationships because of the effort you put into them. Seek out someone who understands you, because you don't always understand yourself. It takes time for you to figure out who you are; you'll know yourself better when you get older.

The outdoors encourages and motivates you. When you are feeling low, depressed, or achy, go outside, take a deep breath, and fill your lungs with fresh air. You get inspiration from your environment, so keep it clean and bright.

✳ ✳ ✳

DECEMBER 10

SAGITTARIUS • The adventurous one of the zodiac

November 22 at 5:00 A.M. to December 21 at 10:00 P.M. • NUMEROLOGY 1

Possessions and Desires . . .

Gem: Agate—This stone may promote health and lead you to a long life.

Flower: Coronilla—You will be successful if you can learn what you should truly wish for.

Astral Color, Color Need, Apparel Color: Your Astral Color is Red, the color of passion, power, excitement, and strength. Violet in your environment will keep you empathetic toward others. In your wardrobe, Green is your power color for overcoming obstacles.

Fragrance: You need to be bathed in exotic scents that will give your imagination room to roam. Experiment with imported incense and tinctures to show the world what a spirited individual you are.

Tree: Walnut—You are unusually helpful and always looking for constant changes in your life.

Instruments: Oboe, flute, clarinet, piano, French horn, organ, piccolo

Composer: Böhm

Bird: Bird of Paradise—the "bird of the Gods." You will shine and love extraordinary circumstances.

Symbol: Crown—the universal sign of dignity.

Harmonious Health and Nutrition . . .

Health Scent: Strawberry—Soothing by nature, the strawberry promotes self-esteem and encourages love.

Favorable Foods: Greens, apricots, rice, almonds, chicken

What's Lucky . . .

Lucky Numbers: 5, 7
Best Months: February and June
Best Day of the Week: Thursday
Best Month Days: 1, 10, 19
Lucky Charm: A new penny in your shoe.
Harmonious Signs for Relationships and Partnerships: Aries, Leo, Sagittarius

Spiritual Guides . . .

Star: Al Naim—Those with this star are often delightful.

Angel: Aduachiel—This angel governs the balance of elements—water, earth, fire, and air—and helps maintain a calm disposition.

Guardian Angel: Malachi—"Messenger of Jehovah."

Spiritual Stone: Emerald—This gem is thought to aid in smoothing the connection between the desires of the soul and those of the body.

✷ JUDITH'S INSIGHT ✷

Wise beyond your years, you have a natural intelligence that will take you anywhere you want to go. You are energetic and enthusiastic and get excited over the smallest things. You make a perfect athlete because you have strong will, steely desire, and great determination.

You should make a super parent. Even if you don't have children, people will want you to "adopt" theirs because you're so sympathetic and understanding. Family means everything to you.

You have plenty of self-confidence, but might not make use of it until you're older. You are not just a quality worker but at times a brilliant one. You will become recognized during your life for creativity and innovation. Expect something to be named for you. You know business naturally and have no qualms about hard work.

You're prone to loving drama more than your partner in relationships. Hopefully you can work off the energy on stage. You are a born comic or actor, though you fear it if you do recognize the talent. Your love life can be a battle because your biggest enemy is yourself. Making a commitment will be hard for you, but you stay almost indefinitely once it's made. Only years of misery will force you to make changes when things aren't working out. You don't believe in half measures and easily show your feelings.

Somewhere along the way you will pursue frequent travel, in either a career or ownership of property outside the borders of your state or country.

✷ ✷ ✷

Possessions and Desires . . .

Gem: Sapphire—This gem may help you find forgiveness from those you've wronged.

Flower: Cockle—You love to show your affection.

Astral Color, Color Need, Apparel Color: Your Astral Color is Red, the color of passion, power, excitement, and strength. Violet in your environment will keep you empathetic toward others. In your wardrobe, Purple reflects your giving personality and brings you luck.

Fragrance: You need to be bathed in exotic scents that will give your imagination room to roam. Experiment with imported incense and tinctures to show the world what a spirited individual you are.

Tree: Maple—You have great stability and flashes of intuition.

Instruments: Pipe organ, cymbal, drum

Composers: Handel, Johann Sebastian Bach

Bird: Stork—Turkish bird, held in high esteem the world over. This bird is intelligent but may have strange tendencies.

Symbol: Cross—the symbol of self-sacrifice and reconciliation.

Harmonious Health and Nutrition . . .

Health Scent: Apple—You are creative, full of joy, and nearly magical. You bring happiness.

Favorable Foods: Cabbage, oranges, caraway seed, pecans, fish

What's Lucky . . .

Lucky Numbers: 5, 7

Best Months: February and June

Best Day of the Week: Thursday

Best Month Days: 2, 11, 20

Lucky Charms: Two 50-cent pieces. Give someone else one of them.

Harmonious Signs for Relationships and Partnerships: Aries, Leo, Sagittarius

Spiritual Guides . . .

Star: Al Beldah—Those with this star are sometimes the victims of hasty judgments.

Angel: Aduachiel—This angel governs the balance of elements—water, earth, fire, and air—and helps maintain a calm disposition.

Guardian Angel: St. Thomas—This angel brings affection from others and encourages you in all that you do.

Spiritual Stone: Emerald—This gem is thought to aid in smoothing the connection between the desires of the soul and those of the body.

✶ JUDITH'S INSIGHT ✶

You want to take on the world and often do just that. You must be cautious of attempting too much all at once. You don't mind working hard as long as you're having fun. Once the play is gone from a situation, you will look for a change. This could be problematic when it comes to relationships. You'd never abandon your mate, but once the spark fades you could become cold and depressed.

Whether or not you recognize it, your heart is set on a life of merriment. Your aspirations lie in the arts. You may have to look for a more structured job to pay the bills. If this is the case, you'll get your entertainment from hobbies.

You have persistence and consistency and courage. Things don't usually stay stuck in the middle around you. Your environment is very important to you. You must live, work, and play in comfortable surroundings.

Your self-confidence will be challenged throughout your life. While you know where your heart lies and where your head is, keeping both organized may be a trial. You'd do well in careers having to do with government, travel, and entertainment. Whether in your day-to-day job or volunteer work, the medical field could also be very important to you.

You work hard at keeping things together and rarely lose friends because you take every relationship very seriously.

✶ ✶ ✶

DECEMBER 12 SAGITTARIUS • The adventurous one of the zodiac

November 22 at 5::00 A.M. to December 21 at 10:00 P.M. • NUMEROLOGY 3

Possessions and Desires . . .

Gem: Ruby—This stone may lead you to energy, friendship, and happiness.

Flower: Coriander—You often don't realize how special your talents are.

Astral Color, Color Need, Apparel Color: Your Astral Color is Red, the color of passion, power, excitement, and strength. Violet in your environment keeps you empathetic toward others. In your wardrobe, Green is your power color for overcoming obstacles.

Fragrance: You need to be bathed in exotic scents that will give your imagination room to roam. Experiment with imported incense and tinctures to show the world what a spirited individual you are.

Tree: Elm—You have willpower, strength, and the ability to stand alone.

Instrument: Trombone

Composers: Verdi, Mendelssohn, Schumann

Bird: Eagle—This bird is quick to use its powers of flight. It can see immeasurable distances in a single glance, and can sometimes appear to be indifferent.

Symbol: Wreath—You have been crowned with a special personality. You are strong but extremely compassionate.

Harmonious Health and Nutrition . . .

Health Scent: Rose—This scent will lead you to passionate thoughts and make you feel warm inside.

Favorable Foods: Leafy greens, apples, bran, almonds, chicken

What's Lucky . . .

Lucky Numbers: 5, 7
Best Months: February and June
Best Day of the Week: Thursday
Best Month Days: 3, 12, 21
Lucky Charm: A pen that someone else has already used.

Harmonious Signs for Relationships and Partnerships: Aries, Leo, Sagittarius

Spiritual guides . . .

Star: Al Naim—Those with this star are often delightful.

Angel: Aduachiel—This angel governs the balance of elements—water, earth, fire, and air—and helps maintain a calm disposition.

Guardian Angel: Johiel—This angel is a protector of all those with a humble heart.

Spiritual Stone: Emerald—This gem is thought to aid in smoothing the connection between the desires of the soul and those of the body.

✳ JUDITH'S INSIGHT ✳

Love will be one of your greatest challenges. You know you want it, but you live in complete fear of it. Once committed, you remain loyal, but until you cross the mental line into partnership, you fight it tooth and nail simply because the hope of happiness scares the pants off you. You are charming, yet people will not understand why you act the way you do.

It is important to you to be considered a success, and you are a born leader. You have great organizational skills and the gift of gab. You will do well in politics and government, construction, or outside sales—in short, jobs in which you can spend most of your time interacting with different kinds of people.

You follow the letter of the law and expect your neighbors to do the same. This tendency might stick you with a career as a petty bureaucrat. You would also make an excellent builder or designer in your work or hobbies. The desire to build things—whether it be model airplanes or birthday cakes—screams to come out.

You subject yourself to many emotional pitfalls. You can brood when things don't go your way. You are very good at giving advice but not so hot at taking it. You make a better talker than listener until you gain the wisdom necessary to balance the two.

✳ ✳ ✳

Possessions and Desires . . .

Gem: Emerald—Those who carry this stone tend to be lucky in love.

Flower: Citron—Be careful that your many gifts don't make you difficult to be around.

Astral Color, Color Need, Apparel Color: Your Astral Color is Red, the color of passion, power, excitement, and strength. Violet in your environment keeps you empathetic toward others. In your wardrobe, Purple reflects your giving personality and brings you luck.

Fragrance: You need to be bathed in exotic scents that will give your imagination room to roam. Experiment with imported incense and tinctures to show the world what a spirited individual you are.

Tree: Cherry—You will find yourself faced with constant new emotional awakenings.

Instruments: Bass, clarinet

Composers: Haydn, Wagner

Bird: Robin—The most sociable of all birds, with the ability to create quick friendships. It also can easily adapt to any home. When it wants something, it has the tendency to try to snatch it.

Symbol: Star—You are full of inner brightness and will stand out in any crowd. You will be seen as special.

Harmonious Health and Nutrition . . .

Health Scent: Vanilla—This scent will fill you with a feeling of cleanliness and stability.

Favorable Foods: Dandelion, oranges, rice, pecans, fish

What's Lucky . . .

Lucky Numbers: 5, 7

Best Months: February and June

Best Day of the Week: Thursday

Best Month Days: 4, 13, 22

Lucky Charm: A piece of material cut from something in your home.

Harmonious Signs for Relationships and Partnerships: Aries, Leo, Sagittarius

Spiritual Guides . . .

Star: Al Beldah—Those with this star are sometimes the victims of hasty judgments.

Angel: Aduachiel—This angel governs the balance of elements—water, earth, fire, and air—and helps maintain a calm disposition.

Guardian Angel: Uriel—This angel brings the light of God's guidance.

Spiritual Stone: Emerald—This gem is thought to aid in smoothing the connection between the desires of the soul and those of the body.

✷ JUDITH'S INSIGHT ✷

You must carefully avoid falling into ruts. A stale environment is the worst for you. You love to be challenged and always want more than you have. You have a way with people and words, and you can do a lot because you have a vivid imagination and don't recognize any obstacles until you've passed them. You're continually drawn to unique and unusual people and places and tend to lead an unconventional life.

You're creative in uncommon ways. Creativity isn't just writing or painting; it's a different way to recognize what's around you. You have brilliant ideas and can probably whip up a gourmet dinner with leftovers or make a go-cart out of junk from the back of the garage. You are highly intelligent and resourceful.

Making and maintaining friendships comes easily to you. Relationships can be trickier. You seem to think true love has to be a challenge. And you're very fussy, which doesn't help. Sooner or later you learn what's important.

You must be cautious, as you have a tendency to become overburdened to the point of explosion. Usually you have an even temperament, but every once in awhile you find the villain role attractive. You were born to help and, whether you realize it or not, to teach.

Keep yourself from being too anxious. Remember, the more stable your emotions, the easier your life becomes.

Some appealing careers: lecturer, historian, or professor. You might own a retail establishment or maybe even a restaurant.

✷ ✷ ✷

Possessions and Desires . . .

Gem: Sardius—This stone could give the wearer unusual insights into his or her own heart.

Flower: Coxcomb—Your complex personality can often bring you into conflict with others.

Astral Color, Color Need, Apparel Color: Your Astral Color is Red, the color of passion, power, excitement, and strength. Violet in your environment keeps you empathetic toward others. In your wardrobe, Green is your power color for overcoming obstacles.

Fragrance: You need to be bathed in exotic scents that will give your imagination room to roam. Experiment with imported incense and tinctures to show the world what a spirited individual you are.

Tree: Apple—You are creative, full of joy, and nearly magical. You bring happiness.

Instruments: Viola, trumpet

Composer: Liszt

Bird: Flamingo—This beautiful, gregarious bird is always careful of its enemy. It is also a caretaker of the young and tries to keep everyone happy.

Symbol: Triangle—You have the right combination of abilities.

Harmonious Health and Nutrition . . .

Health Scent: Peach—This scent may balance your good qualities so that they equal your charm.

Favorable Foods: Savory, grapes, bran, almonds, chicken

What's Lucky . . .

Lucky Numbers: 5, 7

Best Months: February and June

Best Day of the Week: Thursday

Best Month Days: 4, 5, 23

Lucky Charms: A rabbit's foot or a white candle.

Harmonious Signs for Relationships and Partnerships: Aries, Leo, Sagittarius

Spiritual Guides . . .

Star: Al Naim—Those with this star are often delightful.

Angel: Aduachiel—This angel governs the balance of elements—water, earth, fire, and air—and helps maintain a calm disposition.

Guardian Angel: Plavwell—The guardian that gives power and strength to one's presence.

Spiritual Stone: Emerald—This gem is thought to aid in smoothing the connection between the desires of the soul and those of the body.

✴ *JUDITH'S INSIGHT* ✴

You spend most of your life looking for the hurdles to jump over. The love and desire for challenge leads you to seek what most people fear. You're a gambler by nature, though not always with money. You are a collector of entertainment memorabilia, and this would be a great industry for you to work in. You would make a fine entrepreneur or toy maker.

Your high energies will lead you into becoming your own boss at one point or another. Sheer determination brings you success. You are shrewd and sharp in handling business situations. If you work for somebody else, you're sure to wind up being a leader, never a follower. You're filled with ideas and need a job with constant stimulation. You'd do well in anything in the media, public relations, or communications.

Your charm will bring relationships to your doorstep. Your natural kindness will keep people in your life for a very long time, and you always have a date. You're generous not only with gifts but also with your emotions.

Your good side should always outweigh your bad, though you can have a hot temper. Relationships will put you through a hoop here and there, but you have remarkable stamina. Financially you will reap rewards because of your knack for creativity. Follow your intuition whenever it leads you.

✶ ✶ ✶

DECEMBER 15 SAGITTARIUS • The adventurous one of the zodiac

November 22 at 5:00 A.M. to December 21 at 10:00 P.M. • NUMEROLOGY 6

Possessions and Desires . . .

Gem: Topaz—This is an excellent gift to be exchanged between very loyal friends

Flower: Coreopsis—You are nearly always very cheerful.

Astral Color, Color Need, Apparel Color: Your Astral Color is Red, the color of passion, power, excitement, and strength. Violet in your environment keeps you empathetic toward others. In your wardrobe, Purple reflects your giving personality and brings you luck.

Fragrance: You need to be bathed in exotic scents that will give your imagination room to roam. Experiment with imported incense and tinctures to show the world what a spirited individual you are.

Tree: Palm—You tend to be very healthy and creative.

Instruments: Tambourine, lyre

Composer: Schubert

Bird: Lark—known for the beauty of its song, which is sometimes very unusual. It is also credited with extraordinary intelligence.

Symbol: Crescent—You are more likely to be influenced by the phases of the moon. Your easygoing manner leads you to peaceful situations.

Harmonious Health and Nutrition . . .

Health Scent: Orange Blossom—This scent may balance your body, mind, and soul.

Favorable Foods: Celery, prunes, unrefined cereals, pecans, fish

What's Lucky . . .

Lucky Numbers: 5, 7

Best Months: February and June

Best Day of the Week: Thursday

Best Month Days: 6, 15, 24

Lucky Charm: A religious token or card from any religion.

Harmonious Signs for Relationships and Partnerships: Aries, Leo, Sagittarius

Spiritual Guides . . .

Star: Al Naim—Those with this star are often delightful.

Angel: Aduachiel—This angel governs the balance of elements—water, earth, fire, and air—and helps maintain a calm disposition.

Guardian Angel: Michael—"Who is like God."

Spiritual Stone: Emerald—This gem is thought to aid in smoothing the connection between the desires of the soul and those of the body.

✳ JUDITH'S INSIGHT ✳

Your friendly disposition makes it easy for you to enter into relationships. Friends and family are usually devoted to you because you treat them better than you treat yourself. Low self-esteem in childhood and adolescence could have a negative impact on your adulthood. If this is the case, you may want to take steps to understand the root causes. See someone who can give you good advice.

You make the perfect host or hostess and will gravitate to careers relating to entertainment, communications, or public relations. You are a people person and probably feel depressed if you are not constantly surrounded by activity and interaction with others. Your love of outdoors and nature leads you to enjoy hobbies that concern animals, children, and environmental causes.

Dual incomes pop up in your life at some point. It may not be until you are on social security, but you can confidently expect that it will happen. You may have to be very careful with money, but in your later years finances will improve.

There isn't a mean bone in your body. When it comes to love you're attracted to energetic people with strong personalities. Be very clear with prospective mates that they shouldn't try to dominate you. Life will present you with more than your share of obstacles, but you have the necessary strength to endure. Your ideas and abilities are all very good; you just have to learn to believe in yourself more.

✳ ✳ ✳

DECEMBER 16 SAGITTARIUS • The adventurous one of the zodiac

November 22 at 5:00 A.M. to December 21 at 10:00 P.M. • NUMEROLOGY 7

Possessions and Desires . . .

Gem: Ruby—This stone may lead you to energy, friendship, and happiness.

Flower: Rock Rose—Your love is usually very powerful.

Astral Color, Color Need, Apparel Color: Your Astral Color is Red, the color of passion, power, excitement, and strength. Violet in your environment keeps you empathetic toward others. In your wardrobe, Green is your power color for overcoming obstacles.

Fragrance: You need to be bathed in exotic scents that will give your imagination room to roam. Experiment with imported incense and tinctures to show the world what a spirited individual you are.

Tree: Sycamore—Yours is the ability to love, communicate honestly with others, and have lasting relationships.

Instrument: Harp

Composers: Gluck, Brahms

Bird: Skylark—This handsome bird is beautiful when it sings. It always whistles as it works.

Symbol: Heart—You are enthusiastic, empathetic, and full of generosity and love.

Harmonious Health and Nutrition . . .

Health Scent: Jasmine—This scent may make you more easygoing when you are stressed.

Favorable Foods: Horseradish, black figs, rice, almonds, chicken

What's Lucky . . .

Lucky Numbers: 5, 7
Best Months: February and June
Best Day of the Week: Thursday
Best Month Days: 6, 15, 24
Lucky Charm: An old key.
Harmonious Signs for Relationships and Partnerships: Aries, Leo, Sagittarius

Spiritual Guides . . .

Star: Al Beldah—Those with this star are sometimes the victims of hasty judgments.

Angel: Aduachiel—This angel governs the balance of elements—water, earth, fire, and air—and helps maintain a calm disposition.

Guardian Angel: Raphael—This angel attends to all of your needs when you are looking for guidance.

Spiritual Stone: Emerald—This gem is thought to aid in smoothing the connection between the desires of the soul and those of the body.

✶ JUDITH'S INSIGHT ✶

You are always charming but not always lucky. Life seems to constantly throw up roadblocks. Your profound imagination is your greatest blessing and worst curse; it's a powerful tool but one with two edges. Your intense inner focus often forces you to ignore those around you. You are determined to succeed at all costs, even if you lose a friendship or two on the way. You have a very clear opinion as to how your life should be. Your attitude is that if the real world sometimes doesn't always match your inner movie, why should you care; you don't spend much time there anyway.

You're kind and warmhearted and find delight in giving pleasure to those you care for. You can, however, appear cold to those whose gestures of affection make you uncomfortable. Because people find you intriguing, this could happen to you quite often. You have an idealized view of romance, so your relationships border on extreme passion. When you have to face the truth, you're prone to more than the usual number of heartaches. And you can't be alone for any length of time.

When things don't go your way, you pout. You are easily sucked into ditches and can never really overcome depression by yourself. Your energy supply comes from your environment or other people. You know how to enjoy life and are generous when you have resources to spare.

You would make an unbelievable casting agent or commercial photographer, so long as there was exotic travel. Antiques may be a hobby or career whether dealing with furniture or jewelry.

✶ ✶ ✶

DECEMBER 17 SAGITTARIUS • The adventurous one of the zodiac

November 22 at 5:00 A.M. to December 21 at 10:00 P.M. • NUMEROLOGY 8

Possessions and Desires . . .

Gem: Chrysolite—This gem may help you clear your mind of sadness and worry.

Flower: Chamomile—You don't spend enough time relaxing.

Astral Color, Color Need, Apparel Color: Your Astral Color is Red, the color of passion, power, excitement, and strength. Violet in your environment keeps you empathetic toward others. In your wardrobe, Purple reflects your giving personality and brings you luck.

Fragrance: You need to be bathed in exotic scents that will give your imagination room to roam. Experiment with imported incense and tinctures to show the world what a spirited individual you are.

Tree: Pine—Your relationships tend to be harmonious, both emotionally and mentally.

Instrument: Cello

Composer: Mozart

Bird: Bobolink—This charming singer is equally good as a soloist or a member of an orchestra. It is a very romantic bird, useful as an insect destroyer, and elegant, with beautiful feathers, and always pleasant to have around.

Symbol: Wings—You are the source of balance in your world—this will bring you contentment.

Harmonious Health and Nutrition . . .

Health Scent: Almond—This scent may revitalize you and open you to greater possibilities.

Favorable Foods: Greens, peaches, caraway seed, pecans, fish

What's Lucky . . .

Lucky Numbers: 5, 7

Best Months: February and June

Best Day of the Week: Thursday

Best Month Days: 8, 17, 26

Lucky Charm: Red ribbon in your wallet or doorway.

Harmonious Signs for Relationships and Partnerships: Aries, Leo, Sagittarius

Spiritual Guides . . .

Star: Al Naim—Those with this star are often delightful.

Angel: Aduachiel—This angel governs the balance of elements—water, earth, fire, and air—and helps maintain a calm disposition.

Guardian Angel: Seraphim—An angel that brings love, light, and passion.

Spiritual Stone: Emerald—This gem is thought to aid in smoothing the connection between the desires of the soul and those of the body.

✴ JUDITH'S INSIGHT ✴

Think of the world as a willing genie eagerly awaiting your wish. You approach life and learning with enthusiasm. Your childhood probably wasn't all it should have been. Don't worry: your adult years will more than make up for it. You want it all so much that your desire makes the very air around you sizzle.

Marriage is your natural state, but you need to be with someone who's willing to work with you on maintaining it. If by the third date you don't feel your prospective mate is capable of spontaneity, you know they probably aren't for you. Be sure to pick someone who doesn't get easily jealous, as you're a terrible flirt.

Along with a brighter personal life, your finances improve as you get older. You like to share that firsthand knowledge of life's pitfalls with others. You give unstintingly of your time and energy to worthwhile causes, usually through organized volunteer work.

The jobs you select early on will determine your success, so choose wisely. You'd like to become an entertainer of some kind, but shun the rejection that goes along with it. This is one area where your indomitable will may meet an immovable barrier.

Explore your natural gifts: understanding will come with time, but not without some soul-searching. Some people love justice and become judges. Others love kindness and become counselors. You, loving both, can take your pick.

✴ ✴ ✴

DECEMBER 18 SAGITTARIUS • The adventurous one of the zodiac

November 22 at 5:00 A.M. to December 21 at 10:00 P.M. • NUMEROLOGY 9

Possessions and Desires . . .

Gem: Beryl—This gem could be good for meditation and concentration.

Flower: Cedar of Lebanon—You are a truly honest person.

Astral Color, Color Need, Apparel Color: Your Astral Color is Red, the color of passion, power, excitement, and strength. Violet in your environment keeps you empathetic toward others. In your wardrobe, Green is your power color for overcoming obstacles.

Fragrance: You need to be bathed in exotic scents that will give your imagination room to roam. Experiment with imported incense and tinctures to show the world what a spirited individual you are.

Tree: Holly—Beware that you are not carried away by your passionate nature. The only way to grow is to be open to new experiences.

Instruments: Violin, tympanum

Composer: Gluck

Bird: Mockingbird—the most proficient minstrel in the world's orchestra; graceful and enthusiastic.

Symbol: Anchor—This tranquil symbol signifies stability and strength, and stands for strong commitments in relationships.

Harmonious Health and Nutrition . . .

Health Scent: Lavender—This scent might lead others to trust you and make you patient.

Favorable Foods: Savory, apricots, rice, almonds, chicken

What's Lucky . . .

Lucky Numbers: 5, 7
Best Months: February and June
Best Day of the Week: Thursday
Best Month Days: 9, 18, 27

Lucky Charms: A U.S. coin or bill of any amount from the year you were born.
Harmonious Signs for Relationships and Partnerships: Aries, Leo, Sagittarius

Spiritual Guides . . . .

Star: Al Naim—Those with this star are often delightful.

Angel: Aduachiel—This angel governs the balance of elements—water, earth, fire, and air—and helps maintain a calm disposition.

Guardian Angel: Gabriel—"God is my strength."

Spiritual Stone: Emerald—this gem is thought to aid in smoothing the connection between the desires of the soul and those of the body.

✶ JUDITH'S INSIGHT ✶

You seem to think the world exists just to wrestle with. There is no reason for you to believe otherwise, since you so often pin it to the mat. You were born to work hard, and you have more energy after accomplishing a difficult task than when you started. Reliable, responsible, and capable, you have the drive necessary to become an independent contractor or entrepreneur.

You adore adventure—the riskier the better. Sports or any activity where you could work up a good sweat should be attractive to you. You get a thrill out of fast cars in the fast lane, and even more so if the road is slick and the sky is dark. You are generous with those who truly need it, but scornful toward those who don't.

You're a good person in a relationship because you're so loyal and dependable. With the right person, you not only give what you get, you give more. Though more likely to have long, substantial relationships, you may be married more than once.

It takes time for you to figure out who you are. Expect to become more secure with yourself as you get older. You are likely to retire early and start your own business. Often the tiniest things give you the help you need when faced with difficulty. You crush obstacles that never should have existed in the first place.

✶ ✶ ✶

DECEMBER 19 SAGITTARIUS • The adventurous one of the zodiac

November 22 at 5:00 A.M. to December 21 at 10:00 P.M. • NUMEROLOGY 1

Possessions and Desires . . .

Gem: Turquoise—This stone may help you find material wealth.

Flower: Carnation—You can be too quick to refuse love or kindness.

Astral Color, Color Need, Apparel Color: Your Astral Color is Red, the color of passion, power, excitement, and strength. Violet in your environment keeps you empathetic toward others. In your wardrobe, Purple reflects your giving personality and brings you luck.

Fragrance: You need to be bathed in exotic scents that will give your imagination room to roam. Experiment with imported incense and tinctures to show the world what a spirited individual you are.

Tree: Walnut—You are unusually helpful and always looking for constant changes in your life.

Instruments: Oboe, flute, clarinet, piano, French horn, organ, piccolo

Composer: Böhm

Bird: Hummingbird—This bird is delicate and graceful. It can remain still for hours, then dart off and be as busy as a bee.

Symbol: Crown—the universal sign of dignity.

Harmonious Health and Nutrition . . .

Health Scent: Strawberry—Soothing by nature, the strawberry promotes self-esteem and encourages love.

Favorable Foods: Cabbage, apples, bran, pecans, fish

What's Lucky . . .

Lucky Numbers: 5, 7
Best Months: February and June
Best Day of the Week: Thursday
Best Month Days: 1, 10, 19
Lucky Charm: A new penny in your shoe.
Harmonious Signs for Relationships and Partnerships: Aries, Leo, Sagittarius

Spiritual Guides

Star: Al Naim—Those with this star are often delightful.

Angel: Aduachiel—This angel governs the balance of elements—water, earth, fire, and air—and helps maintain a calm disposition.

Guardian Angel: Malachi—"Messenger of Jehovah."

Spiritual Stone: Emerald—This gem is thought to aid in smoothing the connection between the desires of the soul and those of the body.

✶ JUDITH'S INSIGHT ✶

People know you're brilliant and won't be surprised when you accomplish something truly amazing and out of the ordinary. You are self-confident, enthusiastic, and generally trustworthy. A highly regarded employee, you never complain even when working conditions are terrible. You feel you're there to do the job, not to whine about it.

Expect to find enjoyment in being an actor, musician, salesperson, or any other career that offers the opportunity to make people smile. You have a strong desire to travel and may have many close relationships with people from all over the world. In business you care less about making money than contributing to the future of something you believe in.

Intimate relationships may be torture because you are too stubborn to give up on the unhealthy ones. Commitment and loyalty mean so much to you that quitting is never an option, so you are prone to experiencing real agony. It is crucial you really know everything you can about your mate before you tie the knot. You hear advice when it's given to you, but seldom take it until years later when your mind suddenly changes. You don't feel it's your place to give others your opinions.

A good soul with a kind heart and caring mind, your worst fault is that you might be violently emotional. Learning to control yourself is your key to being happy.

✶ ✶ ✶

DECEMBER 20 SAGITTARIUS • The adventurous one of the zodiac

November 22 at 5:00 A.M. to December 21 at 10:00 P.M. • NUMEROLOGY 2

Possessions and Desires . . .

Gem: Sapphire—This gem may help you find forgiveness from those you've wronged.

Flower: Cardinal Flower—You stand out from those who surround you.

Astral Color, Color Need, Apparel Color: Your Astral Color is Red, the color of passion, power, excitement, and strength. Violet in your environment keeps you empathetic toward others. In your wardrobe, Green is your power color for overcoming obstacles.

Fragrance: You need to be bathed in exotic scents that will give your imagination room to roam. Experiment with imported incense and tinctures to show the world what a spirited individual you are.

Tree: Maple—You have great stability and flashes of intuition.

Instruments: Pipe organ, cymbal, drum

Composers: Handel, Johann Sebastian Bach

Bird: Stork—Turkish bird, held in high esteem the world over. This bird is intelligent but may have strange tendencies.

Symbol: Cross—the symbol of self-sacrifice and reconciliation.

Harmonious Health and Nutrition . . .

Health Scent: Apple—You are creative, full of joy, and nearly magical. You bring happiness.

Favorable Foods: Celery, grapes, unrefined cereals, almonds, chicken

What's Lucky . . .

Lucky Numbers: 5, 7

Best Months: February and June

Best Day of the Week: Thursday

Best Month Days: 2, 11, 20

Lucky Charms: Two 50-cent pieces. Give someone else one of them.

Harmonious Signs for Relationships and Partnerships: Aries, Leo, Sagittarius

Spiritual Guides

Star: Al Beldah—Those with this star are sometimes the victims of hasty judgments.

Angel: Aduachiel—This angel governs the balance of elements—water, earth, fire, and air—and helps maintain a calm disposition.

Guardian Angel: St. Thomas—This angel brings affection from others and encourages you in all that you do.

Spiritual Stone: Emerald—This gem is thought to aid in smoothing the connection between the desires of the soul and those of the body.

✶ JUDITH'S INSIGHT ✶

You would make an incredible politician. You love to please people and crave attention. Athletics should feed your energy. Travel will work its way into your life somewhere along the way. Willing to travel on charter packages alone, you are likely to be found on a guided tour around the world.

You can be temperamental on occasion, but your personality is consistent, at least on the outside. When it comes to more intimate relationships, you will fight an uphill battle until you realize you really don't want to be alone. It may also take time for you to fall in love with being in love. It can be the biggest challenge of your life.

You love a bargain and shopping. You'd make a great personal shopper, purchasing agent, casting agent, or talent scout. A born hunter, you like to conquer with all your might, and when it comes to love, you will do it all. Money comes to those who wait, and wait and wait.

You have many tastes and even more hidden talents. Be as confident as you act. All will be fine.

✶ ✶ ✶

DECEMBER 21 SAGITTARIUS • The adventurous one of the zodiac

November 22 at 5:00 A.M. to December 21 at 10:00 P.M. • NUMEROLOGY 3

Possessions and Desires . . .

Gem: Ruby—This stone may lead you to energy, friendship, and happiness.

Flower: Japonica—You may realize that only you can free yourself of your emotional blocks.

Astral Color, Color Need, Apparel Color: Your Astral Color is Red, the color of passion, power, excitement, and strength. Violet in your environment keeps you empathetic toward others. In your wardrobe, Purple reflects your giving personality and brings you luck.

Fragrance: You need to be bathed in exotic scents that will give your imagination room to roam. Experiment with imported incense and tinctures to show the world what a spirited individual you are.

Tree: Maple—You have great stability and flashes of intuition.

Instrument: Trombone

Composers: Verdi, Mendelssohn, Schumann

Bird: Swan—Regarded as royal and sacred, this bird has the protective nature of a mother, and can become a furious fighters in the defense of its young.

Symbol: Wreath—You have been crowned with a special personality. You are strong but extremely compassionate.

Harmonious Health and Nutrition . . .

Health Scent: Rose—This scent will lead you to passionate thoughts and make you feel warm inside.

Favorable Foods: Leafy greens, black figs, rice, pecans, fish

What's Lucky . . .

Lucky Numbers: 5, 7

Best Months: February and June

Best Day of the Week: Thursday

Best Month Days: 3, 12, 21

Lucky Charm: A pen that someone else has already used.

Harmonious Signs for Relationships and Partnerships: Aries, Leo, Sagittarius

Spiritual Guides . . .

Star: Al Naim—Those with this star are often delightful.

Angel: Aduachiel—This angel governs the balance of elements—water, earth, fire, and air—and helps maintain a calm disposition.

Guardian Angel: Johiel—This angel is a protector of all those with a humble heart.

Spiritual Stone: Chalcedon—This stone might help when taking long trips, especially by car

✶ JUDITH'S INSIGHT ✶

You are in every way an original soul. Follow your heart and believe that the inner path created just for you will lead where you need to go. It often seems that everyone you know relies on you for strength. You're the one who calls to catch up first. You are eager to help others, but sometimes this trait will allow the unscrupulous to take advantage of you.

You need stability in your love life, although you prefer matters relating to bedroom activities to be a bit exotic. Moving makes you apprehensive, but on the other hand, you love to travel. You spend too much of your free time fixing up your house only to leave it behind! Stability is actually one of your prime goals. The places you live become your roots; pulling them up hurts.

Though home and relationships have to be settled and predictable, you seek work that can be downright dangerous. You take on risky projects and are more than capable of carrying them through. Taking on more than you can handle doesn't concern you because you still haven't found your limits. You are reliable, loyal, and dependable. Your positive attitude makes you a great employee, though you seem to be the only boss who could stand the strain of so daring a subordinate. Look at careers in manufacturing, art, fashion, decorating, entertainment, or communications. One or more of these could be hobbies.

You tend to bring the world to your neighborhood; you are pretty much a whole world all by yourself.

✶ ✶ ✶

DECEMBER 22

CAPRICORN • The goat of the zodiac

December 21 at 10:00 P.M. to January 21 at 3:00 A.M. • NUMEROLOGY 4

Possessions and Desires . . .

Gem: Moonstone—This gem could protect you from danger.

Flower: Petunia—You tend to be the last to realize your desires.

Astral Color, Color Need, Apparel Color: Your Astral Color is Brown, which helps keep you grounded and stable. Blue in your environment helps you avoid becoming listless and disorganized. In your wardrobe, Blue-Green enhances your luck, because you will feel secure.

Fragrance: You are stimulated by a combination of greens and flowers, such as white roses, jasmine, and greenery. They give you feelings of strength and security.

Tree: Cherry—You will find yourself faced with constant new emotional awakenings.

Instruments: Bass, clarinet

Composers: Haydn, Wagner

Bird: Hummingbird—This bird is delicate and graceful. It can remain still for hours, then dart off and be as busy as a bee.

Symbol: Star—You are full of inner brightness and will stand out in any crowd. You will be seen as special.

Harmonious Health and Nutrition . . .

Health Scent: Vanilla—This scent will fill you with a feeling of cleanliness and stability.

Favorable Foods: Cauliflower, prunes, whole wheat, walnuts, cottage cheese

What's Lucky . . .

Lucky Numbers: 1, 2, 8
Best Months: March and November
Best Day of the Week: Saturday
Best Month Days: 4, 13, 22, 31
Lucky Charm: A piece of material cut from something in your home.

Harmonious Signs for Relationships and Partnerships: Capricorn, Taurus, Virgo, and anyone born from July 27 to September 27.

Spiritual Guides . . .

Star: Vega—Those with this star can be warriors in search of victory, especially in legal situations.

Angel: Hanaeb—This angel shows us our worldly desires in order to give us strength when we are going through uncertainty.

Guardian Angel: Uriel—This angel brings the light of God's guidance.

Spiritual Stone: Sardonyx—This stone may cause people to be attracted to you.

✴ JUDITH'S INSIGHT ✴

You will be drawn to animals, and working with them brings you a happiness you never find in people or machines. You love horses in particular: their grace, power, freedom, and speed all speak to your soul with inexplicable eloquence. You might become either a veterinarian, trainer, or livestock farmer. At the very least you should own many pets. If this is the case, look for a career in businesses where you can be creative, like jewelry design, manufacturing, or music. In addition, you possess the strength and energy for athletic competition.

You have no problem maintaining lifelong friendships because you're sincere and steadfast. Expect to spend a long time searching for that special someone. This suits your cautious and reserved demeanor. You may take too long seeking perfection before you feel comfortable enough to commit to a love relationship. As long as you trust your partner, you are a loyal mate.

Nothing bothers you more than disrespect and lack of gratitude. You are rigid when you need to be. Self-discipline is extremely important to you. Avoid the tendency to get overanxious. You will shine at public functions because of your charismatic personality. People are attracted to you and don't always know why.

✴ ✴ ✴

DECEMBER 23

CAPRICORN • The goat of the zodiac

December 21 at 10:00 P.M. to January 21 at 3:00 A.M. • NUMEROLOGY 5

Possessions and Desires . . .

Gem: Moonstone—This gem could protect you from danger.

Flower: Bear's-breech—You will have luck with financial matters.

Astral Color, Color Need, Apparel Color: Your Astral Color is Brown helping to keep you grounded and stable. Have Blue in your environment to avoid becoming listless and disorganized. Your wardrobe should have Maroon, giving you confidence.

Fragrance: You are stimulated by a combination of greens and flowers, such as white roses, jasmine, and greenery. They give you feelings of elegance, strength and security.

Tree: Apple—You are creative, full of joy, and nearly magical. You bring happiness.

Instruments: Oboe, flute, clarinet, piano, French horn, organ, piccolo

Composer: Liszt

Bird: Hummingbird—This bird is delicate and graceful. It can remain still for hours, then dart off and be as busy as a bee.

Symbol: Triangle—You have the right combination of abilities.

Harmonious Health and Nutrition . . .

Health Scent: Peach—This scent may balance your good qualities so that they equal your charm.

Favorable Foods: Brussels sprouts, raspberries, rye, almonds, pressed cheese

What's Lucky . . .

Lucky Numbers: 1, 2, 8
Best Months: March and November
Best Day of the Week: Saturday
Best Month Days: 4, 5, 23
Lucky Charms: A rabbit's foot or a white candle.
Harmonious Signs for Relationships and Partnerships: Capricorn, Taurus, Virgo, and anyone born from July 27 to September 27.

Spiritual Guides . . .

Star: Vega—Those with this star can be warriors in search of victory, especially in legal situations.

Angel: Hanaeb—This angel shows us our worldly desires in order to give us strength when we are going through uncertainty.

Guardian Angel: Plavwell—The guardian that gives power and strength to one's presence.

Spiritual Stone: Sardonyx—This stone may cause people to be attracted to you.

✷ JUDITH'S INSIGHT ✷

You love to learn. You can understand the underlying circumstances of any situation easily. You see all the possible outcomes as clearly as if they had already happened and wisely choose among them. With a finely tuned mind, you know how to balance between the uncertainty of fire and steadfastness of earth. You are eager to seek out spontaneity and excitement as long as you have stability to return to at home.

There aren't many subjects that won't interest you. You could do especially well in law. An original worldview makes you a natural leader. Your warm wit and a broad sense of humor could take you into the limelight at one point or another. A job may await you in the field of communications. Your work life is so exciting that it seems like an endless stream of news bulletins. Your name belongs in flashing lights.

Charming and warm, you will have no problem finding and connecting with the right mate, although you don't see marriage as a source of excitement. You may neglect your family until later in life, and this causes friction. Because you spend so little time at home, your mate might consider the relationship dead. You will either end up changing your priorities or your address.

You do become a financial success in this lifetime. Expect your name to be remembered long after you leave this world behind.

✳ ✳ ✳

DECEMBER 24

CAPRICORN • The goat of the zodiac

December 21 at 10:00 P.M. to January 21 at 3:00 A.M. • NUMEROLOGY 6

Possessions and Desires . . .

Gem: Moonstone—This gem could protect you from danger.
Flower: Chrysanthemum—You are drawn to what you know to be true.
Astral Color, Color Need, Apparel Color: Your Astral Color is Brown, which helps keep you grounded and stable. Blue in your environment helps you avoid becoming listless and disorganized. In your wardrobe, Maroon gives you confidence.
Fragrance: You are stimulated by a combination of greens and flowers, such as white roses, jasmine, and greenery. They give you feelings of elegance, strength, and security.
Tree: Palm—You tend to be healthy and creative.
Instruments: Tambourine, lyre
Composer: Schubert
Bird: Bird of Paradise—the "bird of the Gods." You will shine and love extraordinary circumstances.
Symbol: Anchor—This tranquil symbol signifies stability and strength, and stands for strong commitments in relationships.

Harmonious Health and Nutrition . . .

Health Scent: Orange Blossom—This scent may balance your body, mind, and soul.
Favorable Foods: Watercress, blackberries, whole wheat, beechnuts, eggs

What's Lucky . . .

Lucky Numbers: 1, 2, 8
Best Months: March and November
Best Day of the Week: Saturday
Best Month Days: 6, 15, 24
Lucky Charms: A religious token or card from any religion.
Harmonious Signs for Relationships and Partnerships: Capricorn, Taurus, Virgo, and anyone born from July 27 to September 27.

Spiritual Guides . . .

Star: Vega—Those with this star can be warriors in search of victory, especially in legal situations.
Angel: Hanaeb—This angel shows us our worldly desires in order to give us strength.
Guardian Angel: Michael—"Who is like God."
Spiritual Stone: Sardonyx—This stone may cause people to be attracted to you.

✴ JUDITH'S INSIGHT ✴

Everyone recognizes your charisma but you. Old-fashioned and conventional, you think boys will be boys, and girls are supposed to be young ladies. But that doesn't mean you stay that way your whole life. If you are a man you will lend yourself to your masculine pride. If you are a woman you will love a man who opens a door to a car, but never one that closes one on you in business.

You are so charming that you usually have several possible relationships running concurrently. Keeping your partners straight is your biggest romantic challenge. Unfortunately, when you find your perfect mate, he or she will hold this against you. It's just your luck to become smitten by the one person who stays away. You will come into your own; however, it takes you some time. Family and children are important to you. You desire passion, fun, and fantasy in the early years and comfortable stability as you get older.

You are your own worst enemy. Trying to control and dictate to others does not win and keep friends. You love to give advice and relish careers in counseling. You are independent and determined enough to be a great entrepreneur. You may find other possible employment opportunities in communications, bookkeeping, or teaching music.

Good things come to those who wait; sadly enough, you have yet to learn how.

✴ ✴ ✴

DECEMBER 25

CAPRICORN • The goat of the zodiac

December 21 at 10:00 P.M. to January 21 at 3:00 A.M. • NUMEROLOGY 7

Possessions and Desires . . .

Gem: Moonstone—This gem could protect you from danger.

Flower: Christmas Rose—You may need to find a natural way to tranquilize your anxiety.

Astral Color, Color Need, Apparel Color: Your Astral Color is Brown, which helps to keep you grounded and stable. Blue in your environment helps you avoid becoming listless and disorganized. In your wardrobe, Blue-Green enhances your luck and makes you feel secure.

Fragrance: You are stimulated by a combination of greens and flowers, such as white roses, jasmine and greenery. They give you feelings of elegance, strength, and security.

Tree: Sycamore—Yours is the ability to love, communicate honestly with others, and have lasting relationships.

Instrument: Harp

Composers: Gluck, Brahms

Bird: Hummingbird—This bird is delicate and graceful. It can remain still for hours, then dart off and be as busy as a bee.

Symbol: Heart—You are enthusiastic, empathetic, and full of generosity and love.

Harmonious Health and Nutrition . . .

Health Scent: Jasmine—This scent may make you more easygoing when you are stressed.

Favorable Foods: String beans, peaches, rye, peanuts, cottage cheese

What's Lucky . . .

Lucky Numbers: 1, 2, 8

Best Months: March and November

Best Day of the Week: Saturday

Best Month Days: 6, 15, 24

Lucky Charm: An old key.

Harmonious Signs for Relationships and Partnerships: Capricorn, Taurus, Virgo, and anyone born from July 27 to September 27.

Spiritual Guides . . .

Star: Vega—Those with this star can be warriors in search of victory, especially in legal situations.

Angel: Hanaeb—This angel shows us our worldly desires in order to give us strength when we are going through uncertainty.

Guardian Angel: Raphael—This angel attends to all of your needs when you are looking for guidance.

Spiritual Stone: Sardonyx—This stone may cause people to be attracted to you.

✷ JUDITH'S INSIGHT ✷

You are strong in your mind, body, and spirit, but at times weak when it comes to matters of the heart. Your tendency to meet obstacles head-on should be tempered with knowing how to avoid them. You are enthusiastic and generally a happy person. Full of energy, you can accomplish much in this life.

Only after you have experienced the worst kind of heartache will you find love. Learning to stand up for yourself in a relationship is a lesson you should master, the sooner the better. Eventually you find luck with a love match, and your mate will be very devoted. After all you go through to win that special person, be sure you take the time to maintain the relationship, or you might find yourself alone again.

You will do well in business and could create one from scratch. Two jobs may present themselves at the same time. You're prone to overwork, so be sure to take time to enjoy the life you've built for yourself.

You are better to others than you are to yourself. Low self-esteem early in life could cripple you emotionally unless you face and overcome it. You might consider seeking a professional to help you with this problem. Your sunny disposition makes it easy to form friendships. Always the perfect host or hostess, you would do very well in careers relating to entertainment or communications. You are a people person. Social interaction energizes you.

✷ ✷ ✷

DECEMBER 26

CAPRICORN • The goat of the zodiac

December 21 at 10:00 P.M. to January 21 at 3:00 A.M. • NUMEROLOGY 1

Possessions and Desires . . .

Gem: Moonstone—This gem could protect you from danger.

Flower: Balm of Gilead—You can be a cure for other people's depressions.

Astral Color, Color Need, Apparel Color: Your Astral Color is Brown, which helps to keep you grounded and stable. Blue in your environment helps you avoid becoming listless and disorganized. In your wardrobe, Maroon brings you confidence.

Fragrance: You are stimulated by a combination of greens and flowers such as white roses, jasmine, and greenery. They give you feelings of elegance, strength, and security.

Tree: Walnut—You are unusually helpful and aways looking for constant changes in your life.

Instruments: Oboe, flute, clarinet, piano, French horn, organ, piccolo

Composer: Böhm

Bird: Bird of paradise—the "birds of the gods." You will shine and love extraordinary circumstances.

Symbol: Crown—the universal sign of dignity.

Harmonious Health and Nutrition . . .

Health Scent: Strawberry—Soothing by nature, the strawberry promotes self-esteem and encourages love.

Favorable Foods: Asparagus, pineapples, whole wheat, beechnuts, buttermilk

What's Lucky . . .

Lucky Numbers: 1, 2, 8
Best Months: March and November
Best Day of the Week: Saturday
Best Month Days: 1, 10, 19, 28
Lucky Charm: A new penny in your shoe
Harmonious Signs for Relationships and Partnerships: Capricorn, Taurus, Virgo, and anyone born from July 27 to September 27.

Spiritual Guides . . .

Star: Vega—Those with this star can be warriors in search of victory, especially in legal situations.

Angel: Hanaeb—This angel shows us our worldly desires in order to give us strength when we are going through uncertainty.

Guardian Angel: Malachi—"Messenger of Jehovah."

Spiritual Stone: Sardonyx—This stone may cause people to be attracted to you.

✳ JUDITH'S INSIGHT ✳

The question you frequently hear is, How could someone so nice be so unlucky all the time? Your energy and drive surround you like a force field. You have a kind and gentle nature, although sometimes when nervous you treat people coldly.

You are fascinated with the world around you, and you can do anything once you decide what's best. It would be more satisfying for you to work outdoors. No matter what job you find yourself in, you realize that you are a born builder; whether the construction materials are stock portfolios, businesses, or the traditional bricks, mortar, and wood. And you always create something solid.

You fantasize more than you indulge in the romance life could offer you. If you can ever get what you feel out of your head and into practice, you will find a rapt audience of one in that special person. You are the most loyal and devoted mate that anybody could have. Where you live is ultra-important. You may not pay enough attention to your family until later in life. After a major life lesson, you become devoted to your home life.

You can handle what comes your way with aplomb and safely direct your own energies. At work you are a devoted servant, even if you're the boss. You are generous to those who are generous to you.

★ ★ ★

DECEMBER 27

CAPRICORN • The goat of the zodiac

December 21 at 10:00 P.M. to January 21 at 3:00 A.M. • NUMEROLOGY 9

Possessions and Desires . . .

Gem: Moonstone—This gem could protect you from danger.

Flower: Ash Tree—The grandeur of the natural world fills you with awe and joy.

Astral Color, Color Need, Apparel Color: Your Astral Color is Brown, which helps to keep you grounded and stable. Blue in your environment helps you avoid becoming listless and disorganized. In your wardrobe, Maroon gives you confidence.

Fragrance: You are stimulated by a combination of greens and flowers, such as white roses, jasmine, and greenery. They give feelings of elegance, strength, and security.

Tree: Walnut—You are unusually helpful and always looking for constant changes in your life.

Instruments: Clarinet, piano, organ

Composer: Gluck

Bird: Hummingbird—This bird is delicate and graceful. It can remain still for hours, then dart off and be as busy as a bee.

Symbol: Anchor—This tranquil symbol signifies stability and strength, and stands for strong commitments in relationships.

Harmonious Health and Nutrition . . .

Health Scent: Lavender—This scent might lead others to trust you and make you patient.

Favorable Foods: Cauliflower, blackberries, rye, peanuts, cottage cheese

What's Lucky . . .

Lucky Numbers: 1, 2, 8
Best Months: March and November
Best Day of the Week: Saturday
Best Month Days: 9, 18, 27
Lucky Charms: A U.S. coin or a bill of any amount from the year you were born.

Harmonious Signs for Relationships and Partnerships: Capricorn, Taurus, Virgo, and anyone born from July 27 to September 27.

Spiritual Guides . . .

Star: Vega—Those with this star can be warriors in search of victory, expecially in legal situations.

Angel: Hanaeb—This angel shows us our worldly desires in order to give us strength when we are going through uncertainty.

Guardian Angel: Gabriel—"God is my strength."

Spiritual Stone: Sardonyx—This stone may cause people to be attracted to you.

✷ JUDITH'S INSIGHT ✷

You are capable, restless, and headstrong. When it comes to work, you're all business. Your fear that others may see you as weak causes you to be overly aggressive and abrupt. However, you aren't fooling anyone for long: everyone recognizes the soft, cuddly teddy bear that you really are. You would make a fine athlete, as you possess the energy, enthusiasm, and physical strength to endure. You may enjoy having several differing jobs at once.

You are more likely to find your spouse where you work and will probably have to kiss a lot of toads before discovering the one you overlooked was meant for you all along. Your wit and charm make you a very attractive catch, so luring others into your life won't be a problem. You are the most devoted person when it comes to home and family issues.

Learn to discover that you have many friends who prey on your good nature. They take full advantage of your unflagging loyalty. You put up with it because you are too stubborn to protect yourself. Even acquaintances find you to be generous and giving. After matters are settled, you still find yourself endlessly rethinking them. Your own success will surprise you.

You might become a businessperson of some kind or an entrepreneur. You would also make a good travel agent and travel coordinator.

✷ ✷ ✷

DECEMBER 28

CAPRICORN • The goat of the zodiac

December 21 at 10:00 P.M. to January 21 at 3:00 A.M. • NUMEROLOGY 1

Possessions and Desires . . .

Gem: Moonstone—This gem could protect you from danger.

Flower: Arbor Vitae—This is the flower of unchanging frendship.

Astral Color, Color Need, Apparel Color: Your Astral Color is Brown, which helps to keep you grounded and stable. Blue in your environment helps you avoid becoming listless and disorganized. In your wardrobe, Blue-Green enhances your luck and makes you feel secure.

Fragrance: You are stimulated by a combination of greens and flowers, such as white roses, jasmine, and greenery. They give you feelings of elegance, strength, and security.

Tree: Walnut—You are unusually helpful and always looking for constant changes in your life.

Instruments: Oboe, flute, clarinet, piano, French horn, organ, piccolo

Composer: Böhm

Bird: Hummingbird—This bird is delicate and graceful. It can remain still for hours, then dart off and be as busy as a bee.

Symbol: Crown—the universal sign of dignity.

Harmonious Health and Nutrition . . .

Health Scent: Strawberry—Soothing by nature, the strawberry promotes self-esteem and encourages love.

Favorable Foods: Lettuce, raspberries, whole wheat, walnuts, pressed cheese

What's Lucky . . .

Lucky Numbers: 1, 2, 8
Best Months: March and November
Best Day of the Week: Saturday
Best Month Days: 1, 10, 19, 28
Lucky Charm: A new penny in your shoe.
Harmonious Signs for Relationships and Partnerships: Capricorn, Taurus, Virgo, and anyone born from July 27 to September 27.

Spiritual Guides . . .

Star: Vega—Those with this star can be warriors in search of victory, especially in legal situations.

Angel: Hanaeb—This angel shows us our worldly desires in order to give us strength when we are going through uncertainty.

Guardian Angel: Malachi—"Messenger of Jehovah."

Spiritual Stone: Sardonyx—This stone may cause people to be attracted to you.

✷ JUDITH'S INSIGHT ✷

You can be really brilliant given the proper task. It is very likely that at some point in your life you will become well known. Your self-confidence will take you all the way to the bank and farther. Your work is always of the highest quality, and you rarely complain about tasks or working conditions. You are just as likely to end up digging ditches as holding a critical office position.

At some point in your life, you will happily find yourself on stage. The guitar may amuse your friends and lead to a career in music. People are drawn to you, and you do well working in jobs dealing with the public, such as customer service. You have a knack for art and could be a fine designer. Your love of travel may lead you to a career as an agent. A natural in business, you have no problem owning and operating your own or managing someone else's.

Your love life of peaks and valleys stabilizes once you decide you want a harmonious mate. Getting out of bad relationships can be nightmarish as a horror movie. You take advice well and are more than sensitive when other people are hurting.

You need to sharpen your communication skills. Amazing personal growth comes in your forties. Earlier on in life, you grab what you can. As you mature, however, you become just the opposite, giving beyond your means. People gravitate to you for your energy and enthusiasm.

✷ ✷ ✷

DECEMBER 29

CAPRICORN • The goat of the zodiac

December 21 at 10:00 P.M. to January 21 at 3:00 A.M. • NUMEROLOGY 2

Possessions and Desires . . .

Gem: Moonstone—This gem could protect you from danger.

Flower: Amaranth—You should have a very long life.

Astral Color, Color Need, Apparel Color: Your Astral Color is Brown, which helps to keep you grounded and stable. Blue in your environment helps you avoid becoming listless and disorganized. In your wardrobe, Maroon gives you confidence.

Fragrance: You are stimulated by a combination of greens and flowers, such as white roses, jasmine, and greenery. They give you feelings of elegance, strength, and security.

Tree: Maple—You have both great stability and flashes of intuition.

Instruments: Pipe organ, cymbal, drum

Composers: Handel, Johann Sebastian Bach

Bird: Hummingbird—This bird is delicate and graceful. It can remain still for hours, then dart off and be as busy as a bee.

Symbol: Crown—the universal sign of dignity.

Harmonious Health and Nutrition . . .

Health Scent: Strawberry—Soothing by nature, the strawberry promotes self-esteem and encourages love.

Favorable Foods: String beans, peaches, rye, almonds, cottage cheese

What's Lucky . . .

Lucky Numbers: 1, 2, 8
Best Months: March and November
Best Day of the Week: Saturday
Best Month Days: 2, 11, 20, 29
Lucky Charms: Two 50-cent pieces. Give someone else one of them.
Harmonious Signs for Relationships and Partnerships: Capricorn, Taurus, Virgo, and anyone born from July 27 to September 27.

Spiritual Guides . . .

Star: Vega—Those with this star can be warriors in search of victory, especially in legal situations.

Angel: Hanaeb—This angel shows us our worldly desires in order to give us strength when we are going through uncertainty.

Guardian Angel: Malachi—"Messenger of Jehovah."

Spiritual Stone: Sardonyx—This stone may cause people to be attracted to you.

✷ JUDITH'S INSIGHT ✷

You are persistent, consistent, brave, and not likely to turn off your chosen course because of obstacles. You endure *anything* to keep a commitment. When faced with unfamiliar circumstances, you become quiet and shy. You enjoy your version of entertainment when you make the time for it. Sadly, you tend to be a workaholic.

Though you'd like to work in the arts or music industries, it's highly likely that you find yourself in a cubicle working for a large company. You would do well as an attorney, as a teacher, or in business. You are thoughtful and have no problem showing emotion. You're convincing, smooth, and graceful in speech, which means you'd do nicely in politics or communications.

Some will consider you a worthy role model. You are loyal and possess a wicked sense of humor. Close companions always feel safe around you because you're fearless. Your spouse may even choose you for this particular quality. You are spirited and have a strong zest for life. You are capable of being somewhat reckless or headstrong. All in all, you are an extremely devoted friend and family member.

✷ ✷ ✷

Possessions and Desires . . .

Gem: Moonstone—This gem could protect you from danger.

Flower: Ambrosia—Your love will tend to be returned.

Astral Color, Color Need, Apparel Color: Your Astral Color is Brown, helping to keep you grounded and stable. Have Blue in your environment to avoid becoming listless and disorganized. Your wardrobe should have Blue-Green, enhancing your luck, because you will feel secure.

Fragrance: You are stimulated by a combination of greens and flowers, such as white roses, jasmine, and greenery. They give you feelings of elegance, strength, and security.

Tree: Elm—You have willpower, strength, and the ability to stand alone.

Instrument: Trombone

Composers: Verdi, Mendelssohn, Schumann

Bird: Hummingbird—This bird is delicate and graceful. It can remain still for hours, then dart off and be as busy as a bee.

Symbol: Wreath—You have been crowned with a special personality. You are strong but extremely compassionate.

Harmonious Health and Nutrition . . .

Health Scent: Rose—This scent will lead you to passionate thoughts and make you feel warm inside.

Favorable Foods: Watercress, prunes, whole wheat, peanuts, pressed cheese

What's Lucky . . .

Lucky Numbers: 1, 2, 8

Best Months: March and November

Best Day of the Week: Saturday

Best Month Days: 3, 12, 21, 30

Lucky Charm: A pen that someone else has already used.

Harmonious Signs for Relationships and Partnerships: Capricorn, Taurus, Virgo, and anyone born from July 27 to September 27.

Spiritual Guides . . .

Star: Vega—Those with this star can be warriors in search of victory, especially in legal situations.

Angel: Hanaeb—This angel shows us our worldly desires in order to give us strength when we are going through uncertainty.

Guardian Angel: Johiel—This angel is a protector of all those who with a humble heart.

Spiritual Stone: Sardonyx—This stone may cause people to be attracted to you.

✷ JUDITH'S INSIGHT ✷

You're always thoughtful, and will do anything to improve someone else's day. Your charm and wit serve you well. As you get older, your love of challenge only increases. You may work for others while maintaining a business of your own on the side. You are more creative than you realize, and nothing delights you more than your own accomplishments.

You are mechanically inclined and should seek opportunities to work with your hands. A career in politics, government, or law enforcement should also mesh nicely with your skills. You could be a bit more flexible. You tend to rigidly follow the letter of the law without permitting exceptions.

A stable home life is so important that without it you wither emotionally. You have a clear sense of your personal values. Allow your intuition to be a sure and steady guide to success. It will take you there. Relationships are always easy because you make them so. You and your mate are devoted to each other—it would take a crane to pry you from each other's sides.

You have difficulty relaxing. As you get older, you feel more secure and let more of your personality develop in charming ways.

You will accomplish much if you can stop chasing down dead-end streets.

✷ ✷ ✷

DECEMBER 31 CAPRICORN • The goat of the zodiac

December 21 at 10:00 P.M. to January 21 at 3:00 A.M. • NUMEROLOGY 4

Possessions and Desires . . .

Gem: Moonstone—This gem might make you safer when you're nervous.

Flower: Apple Blossom—You will be famous even if it's just in your neighborhood.

Astral Color, Color Need, Apparel Color: Your Astral Color is Brown, which helps to keep you grounded and stable. Blue in your environment helps you avoid becoming listless and disorganized. In your wardrobe, Blue-Green enhances your luck and makes you feel secure.

Fragrance: You are stimulated by a combination of greens and flowers, such as white roses, jasmine, and greenery. They give you feelings of elegance, strength, and security.

Tree: Cherry—You will find yourself faced with constant new emotional awakenings.

Instruments: Bass, clarinet

Composers: Haydn, Wagner

Bird: Bird of paradise—the "bird of the gods." You will shine and love extraordinary circumstances.

Symbol: Star—You are full of inner brightness and will stand out in any crowd. You will be seen as special.

Harmonious Health and Nutrition . . .

Health Scent: Vanilla—This scent will fill you with a feeling of cleanliness and stability.

Favorable Foods: Asparagus, cherries, rye, beechnuts, eggs

What's Lucky . . .

Lucky Numbers: 1, 2, 8

Best Months: March and November

Best Day of the Week: Saturday

Best Month Days: 4, 13, 22, 31

Lucky Charm: A piece of material cut from something in your home.

Harmonious Signs for Relationships and Partnerships: Capricorn, Taurus, Virgo, and anyone born from July 27 to September 27.

Spiritual Guides . . .

Star: Vega—Those with this star can be warriors in search of victory, especially in legal situations.

Angel: Hanaeb—This angel shows us our worldly desires in order to give us strength when we are going through uncertainty.

Guardian Angel: Uriel—This angel brings the light of God's guidance.

Spiritual Stone: Sardonyx—This stone may cause people to be attracted to you.

✳ JUDITH'S INSIGHT ✳

You have executive abilities and are a born leader. You're highly intelligent and remarkable at handling people and events. Your vivid imagination may tempt you into an artistic career. Your executive ability, however, will surely land you in a business situation. You are drawn to unique, unusual, and exotic people and places. You love entertaining as much as being entertained. Anything that makes up the natural world interests you.

You may only be able to relax while outdoors, say, camping or fishing. Some may see you as a little narrow-minded and stubborn, but your thoughtfulness always redeems you. You will do well employed as a jeweler or retail manufacturer. You are a great athlete because of your high energy levels. Look for opportunity in this area.

Your sincerity makes you a popular friend. People don't just like you, they love you. On the other hand, romantically, plan on getting through many truly difficult years. Each failed relationship seems the same horrible event with a new unspeakable twist. The up side is that your experience ultimately makes you a devoted mate. You can be cautious and reserved and, when you choose to be, shy and introspective. Respect from you is earned, and ungrateful behavior deeply offends you.

You can be very disciplined and expect the same of those around you. You should fight the urge to be overanxious and keep both feet on the ground. You're too quick to lose your temper. Find a way to expend that extra energy in a positive way. In addition to your life's work, take on more than one hobby so that you always have something to do.

✳ ✳ ✳

If you would like to share any stories about how the information in this book has touched your life, please send correspondence to the following address:

Judith Turner
1064 River Road
Edgewater, NJ 07020

RESOURCES

Our Fate and the Zodiac, Margaret Mayo. Brentano's, 1990.

Violets, Tennyson, D. Wolfe. Fiske & Co., Boston, 1898.

The Influence of the Stars, Rosa Baughan. Kegan, Paul Trench, Trubner & Co. Ltd., 1904

The Vibrations of Numbers, Mrs. L. Dow. Ballutti, Atlantic City, New Jersey, 1913.

Discourses from the Spirit World, Stephen Olin. Partridge and Butler, New York, 1853.

The Guide to Astrology, Raphael. W. Foulsham & Co., London, 1898.

A Practical Treatise of Astral Medicine and Therapeutics, Dr. M. Duz. W. Foulsham & Co., Paris, 1912.

The Philosophy of Numbers, Mrs. L. Dow. Ballutti, 1908.

The Astrologers Guide, Guido Bonatus. Jerom Cardan, Wm. C. Eldon Serjeant, London, 1886.

The Hindu Book of Astrology. The New York Magazine of Mysteries, 1908.

Astrology for All, Alan Leo, London, 1910.

A Manual of Astrology or the Book of the Stars. Thomas Tigg & Son, 1837.

Metaphysical Astrology, John Hazelrigg. Hermetric Publishing Company, 1917.

Asteophysic Principles, John Hazelrigg. Hermetric Publishing Company, 1917.

The Key of Destiny, F. Homer Curtis. E.P. Dutton, 1919.

The Occult Sciences, Arthur Edward Waite. Kegan, Paul Trench, Trubner & Co. Ltd., 1891.

The Book of Knowledge Children's Encyclopedia. The Grolier Society, 1918.

Sacred and Legendary Art, Mrs. Jameson. Longmans, Green & Co., London, 1870.

Sealed Book of Daniel Opened, William C. Thurman, 1867.

Number and Litten or Thirty-Two Paths of Wisdom, E.C.B. Peeke, 1908.

Ptolemy's Tetrabiblos, J.M. Ashmand, 1917.

The Guardian Angel, Oliver Wendell Holmes, 1895.

Mastery of Fate, C.D. Larson, The Progress Co., 1908.

Red-Letter Days, Gail Hamilton. Ticknor and Field, Boston, 1866.

Heliocentric Astrology and Solar Mentality, Yarmo Vedra. Holmes W. Morton, 1899.

The Birds Calendar, H. E. Parkhurst. Charles Scribner, 1894.

The Special Basis of Astrology, Joseph G. Dalton. McCoy Publishing, 1893.

The Book of Days, W & R Chambers. J.B. Lippincott & Co., 1864.

Practical Astrology, Comte C. de Saint-Germain. Laird & Lee Publishers, Chicago.

Astrology, M. M. MacGregor. The Penn Publishing Company, 1904.

Flower and Fruit, Jane H. Newell. Ginn & Company, 1896.

Stars of Destiny, Katherine Taylor Craig. E. P. Dutton & Company, New York, 1916.

Starlight, C. W. Leadbeater. Theosophical Publishing House, Adyar, Madras, India, 1917.

The Influence of the Stars, Rosa Baughan. George Redway, London, 1889.

Moon Lore, Rev. Timothy Harley, London, 1885.

The Influence of the Zodiac Upon Human Life, Eleanor Kirk, 1894.

The Viking Age, Paul B. Du Chaillu. Charles Scribner's Sons, 1889.

Flower Fables, Louisa May Alcott. Henry Altemus Company, Philadelphia, 1898.

The Living World, J. W. Buel. H. S. Smith, 1889.

Past, Present, and Future, J. White, Herald Publishing Association, Washington, D.C., 1909.

THE HIDDEN WORLD OF
RELATIONSHIPS

Judith Turner

A Fireside Book
Published by Simon & Schuster
New York London Toronto Sydney Singapore

In honor and memory
of
my daddy,

Robert Frederick Turner

Every day I hear your voice,
Every day I wait for your call,
Every day I learn what you taught me,
Every day I find another memory,
Every day I say a prayer,
Every day your words are spoken,
Every day you make a dream come true,
Every day you guide me from up there,
Every day your wisdom lives,
Every day I hear what you would be saying,
Every day I thank God you were my dad,
Every day I am proud of you,
Every day I hope you are proud of me,
Every day you live on inside of me,
Every day I become more like you,
Every day I do what you would have done,
Every day I wonder are you still having fun,
Every day I know you've become my Guardian Angel,
Every day I know I shouldn't worry,
Every day I feel the strength you're giving me,
Every day I learn something new about you,
Every day I find your words coming out of my mouth,
Every day I know how much you love me,
Every day I look for you,
Every day I won't let go by, that I don't allow you to take part,
Every day you are in my heart,
Every day is not the same without you.

I love you, Daddy.

ACKNOWLEDGMENTS

Caroline Sutton—Editor at Simon & Schuster; I would like to thank you for believing in my book.

Pam Bernstein—My agent; I would like to thank you for your advice and expertise.

Joan Hamburg—I would like to thank you for your support and friendship, and of course your knowledge and know-how to do everything and anything.

Kellyann Nielsen—I would like to thank you for your incredible writing and editing skills, along with your encouragement and desire to help. You should be proud of yourself and the work that you have done. I am sure this is only the beginning of a long life of writing. "Hats off to Kelly for a job well done."

Janice Meyer—Who is luckier than I to have come across not only one of the "best friends" in the whole world, she happens to know the computer and type, too. I just want to thank you again for getting me through this project.

Robert Metzdorf—Thank you for always standing next to me in all that I drag you into, for encouraging me, and for loving me. You make it easy to have dreams and desires, and never hesitate to have a good word; you are one in a "billion"—not only as an attorney but also as a friend.

Deborah Reilly—You have been through it all and you are better than an Eveready battery: you just keep going. I thank you for being you and lending me your heart as well as your hand.

Judith "Clare" Turner—You gave me life, you gave me your name, and you give me all that I need every day of my life. Thank you for your help and for the entire book hunting, among all the other things you do.

Terence A. Sheehan—Thank you for all your help, your errands, and your love. Your many talents have been used in this project, which still wouldn't be done without you. Believe in yourself; I believe in you.

Jeri Turner Sinnig—You are truly a blessing in my life. Your support allows me to do what I do with ease. I thank you for being the great person that you are and for your continuous help. "I love you."

Susie Hilfiger—I would like to thank you for lending me your "Birthday Books." Your support, encouragement, and friendship are gifts I will always cherish. You're a great lady! I can't forget the Tiffany pen.

Joanne Connelly—I would like to thank you for your love, for your support, and for your son Terence.

Andrew Turner—To think, it all started in Disney, Flea Market, and You!

Bert Morgan—I would like to thank you, not only for help, support, and friendship, but for all the diet Pepsi I could drink.

The Spa at Norwich Inn—For having an incredible view and place for me to write, so I could get this book done, as well as for the encouraging staff.

"Tuesday Night"—I could never do all this work without having a place to blow off steam . . . Marguerite Di Donato, Dr. Maryanne Colenda, Michael Toback, and Debbie Reilly.

Mary Dall—Thank you for all your help, love, and of course your cannolis.

Trisha Squires—Thank you for jumping in and helping when I was desperate.

Eileen Breen—Thank you for your help, your desire to help, and your friendship. You are my friend and my family all in one; how lucky am I.

Miki Taylor—Thank you; we are still eating the Easter candy.

Jim & Susan Frustieri—Thank you for your computer expertise . . . I'd still be working on it.

Melinda Daley—"The Pen" that made me start to write this book. Your friendship and your love do make a difference.

Katie Boyle-Monaghan—All your hard work has not been forgotten.

Gladys Callaghan—Your support, your desire, and your friendship—without book number one, there would not be number two.

Bertilotti's Bros. (John, Albert, and Ronnie, and we can't forget Judy Joseph)—Thank you for all the birthday cakes.

Astrological Consultants—Judy Bonauito, Betsy Wayman, and Claudia Trevellis.

Operation Judi—It was more than a gift of a lifetime! Thank you to Joanne Connelly, Jeri Turner, Judith Clare Turner, Barbara Tessel, Debbie Reilly, and Eileen Breen.

To my family—Without your support a job like this would be impossible. To my husband, "Sparky," I couldn't do all of this without you. P.S.: I love you. Thank you for your patience, your love, and your kindness, and your never-ending desire to help and understand, Sparky, Wojo, Briane, and Alexandria.

More family—Mommy, Andrew, Joanne, Jeri, Debora, Haley, Rickey and Rickey, Terence, Dave, Jennifer and Kelsey, Samantha, Kellyann, Melissa, and Suzanne.

Tommy and Susan Hilfiger—A special thank-you to you both for all of your love, support, and help in launching this book. To all the others who "help" from this point on . . . Thank you!

To all others who "help" from this point on . . . Thank you!

INTRODUCTION

RELATIONSHIPS. DID YOU EVER SIT AND WONDER HOW MANY DIFFERENT RELATION-SHIPS we have, and how many roles we play in other people's lives? One person can act the part of a *child,* a *parent,* a *boss,* a *best friend,* a *sister* or *brother,* and so on all in the same day. Even when we are not looking for a relationship we find ourselves creating new ones every day. They could be the people we work with, our in-laws, our neighbors, or our best friends. Here is a book with a little inside information about what makes a person tick. There is only one thing as important as you are and that is how you relate to those people in your life.

Love has a tendency to have a mind of its own. When we think of the word *Love* we have an inclination to only think about our romantically significant others, or the people we would like to have play that role in our lives. But wouldn't it be interesting to learn more about all the people we love and the relationships we enter? What about the relationships in our lives that we don't have the option of selecting? These are our *parents, siblings, teachers, bosses, co-workers,* and *employees,* and let's not forget our in-laws. In this book you will gain insight on everything from how to approach your boss to what the perfect gift is for your mother-in-law. You may already know that your sister has a defensive attitude. By reading her birthday, you can also learn that her defensiveness may grow out of her own fear. That realization could dramatically change how you look at her. Then there is the other side of the coin, the special people we may have selected to be in our lives. These are Our Friends, Lovers, Soul Mates, Business Partners, and of course, Our Husbands and Wives.

When it comes to the people we love, we never have enough **"Insider Information."** Here you may begin to get the answers to so many of your questions. Have you wondered what the perfect gift would be for that special someone? What are the best nights of the week to take him or her out on the town? Where would the best location be for your dream wedding? What about making up after a fight—wouldn't you like to have a secret glimpse into what will make things better? And if you feel as though you are looking for love in all the wrong places, you can put your best foot forward with the best possible advice. You can look for the best attributes in others along with what might help you find a lasting love.

Just as my first book, *The Hidden World of Birthdays,* was designed to help you learn about yourself according to the day you were born, this book will help you learn about how you relate to the other people in your life. At the same time, it will give you information about how those people relate to you as well. You will learn exactly what makes your partner tick, along with how to get around him or her when he or she is mad at you. Or maybe you want to know just how to capture a person's attention when his or her mind seems to be elsewhere. This book will provide the key to unlocking not only your own personality and needs, but also those of every person in your life.

Decans: There is a question that I have received from many people who have read my first book. Is there relevance to reading the day before or the day after your birthday? My answer is yes. When you are reading about your birthday, you may see a reflection of yourself throughout the days listed on the top of your page. Without getting too astrologically technical, everyone born on the same day cannot be exactly alike in every category. In astrology, "decans" break up an astrological sign into three different "subsigns." So under each date there is a decan you can refer to. I used these dates to give you some flexibility. For instance, if you have already given the gift listed on the page with the person's birthday, you could try the gifts listed on the dates given at the top of the page.

Soul Mates: What is a Soul Mate? Do we each have a Soul Mate? A Soul Mate is someone with whom you have an uncanny connection. Your Soul Mate does not have to be your life mate, but certainly can be. You can find Soul Mates not just in the romantic sector of your life, but in any type of partnering around you. We have to look at our best friends, our housekeepers, the nannies for our children, and our business partners. Do Capricorns get along with fellow Capricorns? What kind of relationship would there be between a Leo and a Virgo? These are the main types of astrological questions asked everywhere. You will never see them answered quite like this. I've put together a unique, quick reference at the beginning of every birthday; it can give you the answers to these questions even before they are asked. Maybe a Capricorn is too stubborn for you, but someone else may like that in a partner. A Leo could bring out the fire in a sluggish Pisces. If you partner up with a Virgo, he or she may be too rigid in business, but maybe that Aquarius will allow you the creative freedom to get that other job you are looking for. We may not marry someone we think is our Soul Mate, but maybe they are the catalysts in our lives that lead us down destiny's path. We do not meet people by accident. Their presence has a time and a place. The section "Soul Mates" may teach you how to recognize some of yours.

Most Charming Characteristics: Just in case you haven't figured them out for yourself! Whether you're looking at your own birthday or someone else's, it's great to know the finer qualities of a person. When you know this information you are ready, for the best is yet to come.

Gifts: What is the perfect gift? Everyone has been in this situation. A Holiday or Birthday comes up and you have to buy a gift for your boss or that special someone. Here, in black and white, will be the secret to the perfect gift for every day of the year. It's the best way to say that that person means a lot to you.

Sensual Foods: *Sensual* means different things to different people, but the title here tells all. Picking the right dish will not only entice your love's appetite but his or her heart as well.

Romantic Flowers: Everybody loves to get flowers. You receive attention not only from the one sending them, but also from anyone else who notices them. When you are sent flowers others know someone thinks that you are special. How great is that! It doesn't matter if you are sending flowers as a thank-you gift or if you have them in hand when you arrive for your first date. You want them to make a lasting impression. Here you will find out the perfect flowers to show your affection.

Best Date Nights: Do you go out on Tuesday for the first date or wait until Thursday? Imagine the benefit of knowing what night of the week your date will be in the best frame of mind before scheduling that important outing. This is also handy when scheduling business meetings. From the best day of the week to the best days of the month, timing is essential. If you are already married, looking up this day will help to rekindle the romance.

Colors of Passion: Looking to get noticed or just tantalize your date to no end? Wear the color that works best for you. This color is your "Passion Enhancer." Would that red dress work? How about that new blue tie? Many studies have shown that the colors we surround ourselves with can change our moods. These colors have been selected to enhance our desire for love and romance.

The Perfect Wedding: Here is the answer everybody is looking for without spending time and money on a party planner. If you are planning your special day or a special event, you can use these ideas to make it wonderful. You can take the process a step further and look up both birthdays to combine the results for the perfect event for both of you. After all, the setting and theme of a wedding are what make it special. There is nothing more memorable than a wedding day that truly reflects your personality and interests. Romance will radiate from a day designed in your own image.

Wise Words: What is love without romance? What is romance without poetry? In Antiquarian Birthday Books, a poem was assigned to each day of the year. These words of wisdom gave meaning to that day as well as to the people born on that day, as I've seen in the ancient birthday books I've collected over the years. Here I have hand-selected Poems, Quotes, and Phrases with care and matched them with the birthdays for which they hold meaning. This should end anyone's fear of being lost for words.

Hints of Love: This section is a secret glimpse into the heart of your partner—or the person you wish would become your partner. Knowing this information will let you see how this person feels about you before he or she has a chance to tell you. It can take the guesswork out of getting to know how a person communicates feelings.

After the Argument: The hardest thing in the world to say can be "I am sorry." There are many ways of getting this across. Sometimes even the words themselves don't have much meaning. These are times when you must put your words into action, when you need to appeal to a person's heart and mind. This section will teach you how to let the dust settle after a disagreement.

Romantic Places: Romance, like beauty, is in the eye of the beholder. Romance can be created anywhere or anytime. When you're looking for a special, unique, or intriguing setting, you will find the answer here. Ever wonder where to go and what to do once that special someone agrees to a date? Using this section, you can go someplace that will appeal to your partner's nature and romance will abound.

Lucky Love Star: In astrology, there are planets and stars for all of the signs. I found this list of stars in an ancient book. Each star correlates with a sign and enhances different emotions.

Imagine knowing that you have a special star out of the billions of stars in the sky. When it comes to making that wish upon a star, you can be ahead of the game and know just where to direct your heart's desire.

Beautiful Thought: What constitutes a beautiful thought may vary for everybody. Some people would like a line that will make them laugh. Others need it to make them think. Either way, a beautiful thought always helps to brighten even the gloomiest moment.

Sharing Secrets: I call this section "Insider Trading." It gives you the answers to all of the questions you have, but can't ask, about getting into the heart of the person you have your eye on. You may also find out how to show this person the way to your own heart. This information will come in handy in other types of relationships as well.

Judith's Insights

This is my interpretation of the person born on this day. These insights combine a little astrology with a little numerology, but always have a lot of my own experience and insight mixed in. This section gives you information on how someone might respond to your advances and why someone may act a certain way. You will learn exactly how to approach them. This section will tell you if they like quiet and refined or loud and down-to-earth. "Judith's Insights" cover topics from how to ask for a raise to how to get a date. Each insight is broken down into two headings: "About the Man" and "About the Woman."

JANUARY

Soul Mates: You should have no problem having a relationship with your own sign, Capricorn. Two peas in one pod can work well together. Taurus and Virgo would probably be two of the easiest signs for you to get along with, in or out of love. You will be a natural magnet for a Cancer, but anticipate complications at times. With Aries and Libra, the passion may draw you in. Even if it is only friendship, it can be a passionate one. Leos would be a hard relationship, but it could work if you can stand to be on the bottom occasionally. Pisces, the ingenious wit, will get you together. The great disposition of most Pisces could keep you there. Just make sure they don't get bored. Aquarius and Sagittarius could work well, but be cautious of flirtatious Gemini and Scorpio. They will drive you crazy and could test your sense when it comes to loyalty.

Most Charming Characteristics: Ambitious, studious, original.

Gifts: *For her:* hummingbird feeder. *For him:* day of golf.

Sensual Foods: Strawberries and cream; meat loaf.

Romantic Flowers: Iris is your flower if you are the gal sending subtle messages. If you are the man, you will look for clematis. This flower's mental beauty creates emotional stimulation for you.

Best Date Nights: Saturday; 1st and 19th of each month.

Colors of Passion: *For her:* green, brown, violet. *For him:* dark gray, brown.

The Perfect Wedding: Earthy goat girls feel most secure on the old terra firma, but climb, climb you must. The top of a mountain in Colorado or the top of a monument in Washington, D.C., all these locations lend themselves to your powerful persona. Inspired by tradition, you are happiest in a pleasant, conventional location. Ideal setting: Moscow; the Grand Canyon.

Wise Words: Robert Browning: "Let me be cared about, keep out of harm, and schemed for, safe in love as with a charm."

Hints of Love: They only use the three magic words when they know they mean it, and they already know it is going to be said back to them.

After the Argument: *For him:* Pay him extra attention. Send him something at work so everybody notices. Make him feel important. *For her:* Go overboard in a big way. Don't just send flowers at work, but to her home and to her mother's when she is there for Sunday dinner.

Romantic Places: Places of beauty bring romance: the rain forest; a garden; the Grand Canyon.

Lucky Love Star: Capriel—you never like the feeling of loneliness.

Beautiful Thought: It takes both ends of the shoelace to tie the shoe.

Sharing Secrets: Let them admire something about you first. Show them you have a sense of humor. *For the guys:* The way to his heart is definitely through his stomach. *For the gals:* Hold their hand and then take them to the next step.

Judith's Insights

About the Man: If you know how to read minds, this person can make a great mate. Communication is not his strong suit, so it had better be yours. Otherwise, you will turn into the "whiney one" asking questions that he will assume you know. Make sure to pay great attention to him, especially on his special days. No, don't expect the same in return. To know this partner is to truly love him. If this is a boss, getting the coffee would be a good thing. Most of us are looking for a loyal, down-to-earth mate. This guy could be it if you are on an even keel.

About the Woman: No matter what your sign is, if you are having any kind of relationship with this person expect that she is looking for security. You will learn a lot from her, if you are open to it. Most of the time you will have more than loyalty here. Remember, this woman needs to have financial security at all times. When someone is messing with her pocketbook, there could be hell to pay. If something is wrong in the bedroom, you can be sure that something is going on in the boardroom to cause it. She has a keen sense of humor as long as the joke is not on her.

Soul Mates: Capricorn and Capricorn could work as well as anything out there. You can help Aquarius and Pisces remember the little joys in life so you can find joy in each other for a lifetime. Cancer and Aries could be too rigid for your taste. A solid plan can take a partnership with Taurus and Virgo to new heights. If you like things fast and exciting, you could have loads of fun with Scorpio and Gemini. The passion can be there with Libra as long as someone is feeding the flame. Establish with Leo who the boss is and things can progress from there. You could feel your heart skip a beat with Sagittarius.

Most Charming Characteristics: Love of family; greatest charm, devotion.

Gifts: *For her:* home security system. *For him:* trip to a museum.

Sensual Foods: Cherry-apple pie; beef Stroganoff.

Romantic Flowers: A rose of any color for the lady. Roses stand for love regardless of the color. Send them with orchids and you will be saying "I love you." For the gentleman, let him know you think of him by sending pansies—and forget-me-nots for true love.

Best Date Nights: Saturday; 2nd and 29th of each month.

Colors of Passion: *For her:* green, brown, violet. *For him:* dark gray, brown.

The Perfect Wedding: Earthy goat girls feel most secure on the old terra firma, but climb, climb you must. The top of a mountain in Colorado or the top of a monument in Washington, D.C., all these locations lend themselves to your powerful persona. Inspired by tradition, you are happiest in a pleasant, conventional location. Ideal setting: Moscow; the Grand Canyon.

Wise Words: Henry Wadsworth Longfellow: "Onward its course the present keeps, / Onward the constant current sweeps / Till life is done."

Hints of Love: Don't overdo it (dress, attention) too soon or this one will run. Wait until you have them hooked before you become outrageous.

After the Argument: *For him:* Pay him extra attention. Send him something at work so everybody notices. Make him feel important. *For her:* Go overboard in a big way. Don't just send flowers at work, but to her home and to her mother's when she is there for Sunday dinner.

Romantic Places: Places of power bring romance: Russia; a courthouse; Washington, D.C.

Lucky Love Star: Capriel—you never like the feeling of loneliness.

Beautiful Thought: Expressions are the flowers in the garden of life.

Sharing Secrets: Give them the opportunity to notice you first. *For the gals:* They love to be adored; love at first sight. *For the guys:* Remember to always let them believe it was their idea.

Judith's Insights

About the Man: If you are looking for a "loyal subject," you will find it here. No matter what relationship you are having, you can't find a better partner. The challenge is going to be communication and patience. These are not his best qualities. He loves it when you go overboard, so full steam ahead. He'll need to work on his bedside manner. If you are looking for the typical burly guy, here he is. He is a man's man if there ever was one. He has wit, humor, and strength. You won't find another man who is more willing to work on what is wrong than him.

About the Woman: Her strength can mislead you right down the wrong path. No matter what size she is, she carries tremendous personal strength, along with the ability for you to feel this girl can do it all alone. Don't get easily discouraged. She loves having others with her. You just may need to be patient for when to put in your two cents. Give her plenty of compliments. She will be eating out of your hand in no time. When there is a weak link in her chain, her self-esteem may be about to falter. As long as things are going well you will have the perfect mate.

Soul Mates: You will get along with anyone just like you. That is why you would do well with another Capricorn. If Pisces and Aquarius are on the train, don't let it leave without you. They can give you a true feeling of wellness you never had before. Cancer's and Aries's unyielding nature will have you running in the other direction. Taurus and Virgo know how to turn on that irresistible charm, which you just love. It would be advisable to fasten your seat belt. You might be thrown about with Scorpio and Gemini. New and interesting things must be ever present for a relationship with Libra to work. If you can let Leo be in charge, or even think that they are, then you will get along fine. Keep open to all things new and exciting and you can fly to new heights with Sagittarius.

Most Charming Characteristics: Friendly, enjoys meeting new people, strong personality.

Gifts: *For her:* tickets to the theater. *For him:* home improvement books.

Sensual Foods: Hot fudge sundae with all the trimmings; shepherd's pie.

Romantic Flowers: These ladies like everyone to know how faithful they are, so send them violets. To surprise them, send tulips. Men like their flowers the same as their relationships, unpretending. Send them camellias with white roses to show your affection.

Best Date Nights: Saturday; 12th and 30th of each month.

Colors of Passion: *For her:* green, brown, violet. *For him:* dark gray, brown.

The Perfect Wedding: Earthy goat girls feel most secure on the old terra firma, but climb, climb you must. The top of a mountain in Colorado or the top of a monument in Washington, D.C., all these locations lend themselves to your powerful persona. Inspired by tradition, you are happiest in a pleasant, conventional location. Ideal setting: Moscow; the Grand Canyon.

Wise Words: Charles Dickens; "It's vain to recall the past, unless it works some influence upon the present."

Hints of Love: Make sure you go on more than one date before you jump to conclusions on liking and disliking.

After the Argument: *For him:* Pay him extra attention. Send him something at work so everybody notices. Make him feel important. *For her:* Go overboard in a big way. Don't just send flowers at work, but to her home and to her mother's when she is there for Sunday dinner.

Romantic Places: Places of beauty bring romance: Africa; a hot-air balloon; Yosemite, California.

Lucky Love Star: Capriel—you never like the feeling of loneliness.

Beautiful Thought: Success is a dream you have to have before you make it happen.

Sharing Secrets: This one loves a challenge. *For the gals:* Be consistently inconsistent until you have them hooked. *For the guys:* This one loves to play catch. You may feel like a yo-yo, but as long as he is calling that's all that matters.

Judith's Insights

About the Man: There is more hope than you think. You must first stand back and learn to read between the lines. Once you get that down you will be heading down the road to any kind of relationship. This one is capable of only deep feelings, so bringing them to the surface may take some time. If you're waiting for "Thank you," you may hear that, but "I love you" or "I'm glad you're here," or other complimentary words can take a while. He will drive you crazy just because he can. His stubborn side will make you want to run while his wit will make you want to stay.

About the Woman: Sensible she is, sensible she needs to be, so you must bring the unpredictable to the table. Financially, she may be quite the secret keeper. She holds the bankbooks as her most sacred possession. She can be the truest, kindest friend. She will still be around in fifty years. Make sure that you keep enhancing your intellect to keep her around. She needs mental stimulation and great conversations. She can be jealous when she feels insecure. Take her jealousy as both a compliment and a plea for attention and reinforcement.

Soul Mates: Another Capricorn could be exactly what you are looking for. With Aquarius and Pisces, you will both have a passion for life that you never experienced before. Cancer's and Aries's instinct to control all around them will leave you dreaming of greener pastures. There is not much that can shake the stable foundation you can make with Taurus and Virgo. Scorpio and Gemini will be too much energy focused in every direction for you to take lying down. Libra will fill every minute with a passion for life that can't help but rub off on you. Getting along with the dominating Leo could prove to be a difficult task for you. You and Sagittarius can make a tight partnership.

Most Charming Characteristics: Energetic, good business ability, shrewd.

Gifts: *For her:* antique furniture. *For him:* gold watch.

Sensual Foods: Whipped cream, strawberries, brown sugar, and heavy cream.

Romantic Flowers: These ladies like men with taste. Show them you love style by sending fuchsia flowers—even brightly colored wildflowers will do. To confuse this man, send him lilies along with bright daisies to show him your innocence. Keep him guessing.

Best Date Nights: Saturday; 13th and 22nd of each month.

Colors of Passion: *For her:* green, brown, violet. *For him:* dark gray, brown.

The Perfect Wedding: Earthy goat girls feel most secure on the old terra firma, but climb, climb you must. The top of a mountain in Colorado or the top of a monument in Washington, D.C., all these locations lend themselves to your powerful persona. Inspired by tradition, you are happiest in a pleasant, conventional location. Ideal setting: Moscow; the Grand Canyon.

Wise Words: Benjamin Franklin: "A false friend and a shadow attend only while the sun shines."

Hints of Love: Don't act too needy too soon. It may push this relationship away.

After the Argument: *For him:* Pay him extra attention. Send him something at work so everybody notices. Make him feel important. *For her:* Go overboard in a big way. Don't just send flowers at work, but to her home and to her mother's when she is there for Sunday dinner.

Romantic Places: Places of power bring romance: India; a marina; New York City.

Lucky Love Star: Capriel—you never like the feeling of loneliness.

Beautiful Thought: A leaf fallen from the tree is not so different from the candle that blows in the wind.

Sharing Secrets: This is a family person at heart, so your presence is most important. *For the gals:* Make sure you go to Sunday dinner with her family when you are invited. *For the guys:* If you don't like his mom, you might have a hard time catching this one.

Judith's Insights

About the Man: You may think he is cheap at first, but he really needs for others to prove themselves before he is willing to dig in his pockets. He sees no need to make any investment until he is sure that it will pay out in the end. If you hang around long enough, you may get to see the generous side. Any relationship will start as cold, almost removed. As time moves on, he becomes more demonstrative and affectionate. Time could be on your side. If you are looking for love, you may just be in the right place. This guy has wit and charm and is mostly dependable.

About the Woman: You may feel she likes no one and at times that may ring true, but it's not likely. She will like it better when others take the first step. If you are working together, invite her to lunch more than once. You'll see it takes time for her to warm up. Most of the struggles in a relationship with this one will be in her mind. Snakes, I call them, and she has plenty of them in that pretty head of hers. You may lose her to a crowd at a party. She is an entertainer at heart. The good news is that she likes to be in a secure relationship and won't wander unless the attention has been lacking.

Soul Mates: You will undoubtedly be attracted to someone of your own sign, Capricorn. You will make it a good relationship when you accept everything about yourself, for you will see it constantly in your partner. Virgo and Taurus will be great partners for you because you will each have equal responsibility and reward. Cancer will draw you in but may drive you nuts once you are there. Libra and Aries are brimming with passion. They will give you a new view of the world around you. Leo needs to be in control most of the time. Can you give up as much as they expect? Pisces's charm will prove to be irresistible for you. Keep them occupied and they will do the same for you. Aquarius and Sagittarius can be the perfect combination of yin and yang energy. You will bring out the best in each other at every turn. Gemini and Scorpio are just too much for you to take. Their flirting will leave you boiling.

Most Charming Characteristics: Honest, kind-hearted, loving, fond of children.

Gifts: *For her:* jasmine body wash. *For him:* new book.

Sensual Foods: Puddings and pastry of all kinds.

Romantic Flowers: You are the lady of distinction and only carnations will do. Any mix of colors with sprays of mignonette. Sweet peas or red carnations will appeal to this man's heart.

Best Date Nights: Saturday; 5th and 23rd of each month.

Colors of Passion: *For her:* green, brown, violet. *For him:* dark gray, brown.

The Perfect Wedding: Earthy goat girls feel most secure on the old terra firma, but climb, climb you must. The top of a mountain in Colorado or the top of a monument in Washington, D.C., all these locations lend themselves to your powerful persona. Inspired by tradition, you are happiest in a pleasant, conventional location. Ideal setting: Moscow; the Grand Canyon.

Wise Words: Webber: "What love is to man, music is to the arts and to mankind. Music is love itself. It is the purest most ethereal language of passion."

Hints of Love: Keep it fun. Look for new and exciting things to do, especially if you are in a long-term relationship.

After the Argument: *For him:* Pay him extra attention. Send him something at work so everybody notices. Make him feel important. *For her:* Go overboard in a big way. Don't just send flowers at work, but to her home and to her mother's when she is there for Sunday dinner.

Romantic Places: Places of beauty bring romance: China; an aquarium; Redwoods, California.

Lucky Love Star: Capriel—you never like the feeling of loneliness.

Beautiful Thought: A drooping rose can still have beautiful petals.

Sharing Secrets: Everything in its good time. This one works slowly, but when it is time to pick up speed, watch out. *For the gals:* Don't go by the obvious. Read between the lines. As long as the invitation is being offered, go full speed ahead. *For the guys:* Just when you thought you should walk away, he'll say, "I love you." Talk about confusing.

Judith's Insights

About the Man: You're dealing with a manly man. He lives in a practical-joke center. Seems like a bit of a contradiction, but not really. This one is the epitome of "the bigger they are the harder they fall." He wants to fall in love but does not want to give up his free nights and fun. If you want a commitment out of this guy you have to let him know that you will let him hang with his friends and not put a ball and chain around his leg. He loves attention, so listen to his war stories, even if you've heard them repeatedly. Not a bad boss if you can get him.

About the Woman: She'll fight with herself, and almost never write you. When she's angry, communication will be harder than ever. If the paychecks are down, she may become irritable or a workaholic. Things going downhill at work will affect her entire life. If you begin having a problem with her personally, ask her how work is going to get to the bottom of things. She wants security most of all. You have to be consistent in your affection and attention. I hope that patience is your strong suit. You will certainly need it.

Soul Mates: A pairing with another Capricorn could be anything but difficult. Achievement of great things is possible when you have Aquarius and Pisces in your corner. Cancer and Aries can wear you a little thin. You don't mind all of your ducks in a row, but having them nailed to the floor would drive you crazy. There is wonderful potential for big things when you combine your charm with that of Taurus and Virgo. Scorpio and Gemini will run you ragged with their teasing tendencies. Things with Leo must be up front right away before Leo decides who is running the show. Libra needs constant stimulation to keep going. You might want to take your vitamins for this one. Sagittarius can be the partner you have always been looking for.

Most Charming Characteristics: Impulsive, thinks and acts quickly, good intentions.

Gifts: *For her:* day of golf. *For him:* membership in exclusive club.

Sensual Foods: Champagne with strawberries; fillet of sole.

Romantic Flowers: You love it when you get tulips, declaring love. When you receive a variety, it shows how hopelessly in love your partner is. He will just love a single rose. This shows him you understand his pleasures.

Best Date Nights: Saturday; 6th and 15th of each month.

Colors of Passion: *For her:* green, brown, violet. *For him:* dark gray, brown.

The Perfect Wedding: Earthy goat girls feel most secure on the old terra firma, but climb, climb you must. The top of a mountain in Colorado or the top of a monument in Washington, D.C., all these locations lend themselves to your powerful persona. Inspired by tradition, you are happiest in a pleasant, conventional location. Ideal setting: Moscow; the Grand Canyon.

Wise Words: Charles Dickens: "Every traveller has a home of his own, and he learns to appreciate it the more from his wanderings."

Hints of Love: This one is a cautious soul. You may have to find a way to go around to the back door.

After the Argument: *For him:* Pay him extra attention. Send him something at work so everybody notices. Make him feel important. *For her:* Go overboard in a big way. Don't just send flowers at work, but to her home and to her mother's when she is there for Sunday dinner.

Romantic Places: Places of power bring romance: Rome; a yacht; the Lincoln Memorial.

Lucky Love Star: Capriel—you never like the feeling of loneliness.

Beautiful Thought: Just because something ends doesn't mean it has failed.

Sharing Secrets: This one is a charmer, perhaps even fickle. *For the gals:* If you are patient enough to stick around, this one is worth the wait. *For the guys:* If there is enough time on the clock, stick around past three months. Then maybe he will have noticed you are there.

Judith's Insights

About the Man: If you want a loving, loyal person in your life, make sure you are able to prove yourself first. This one watches the pot very closely. He has the nickel he got for his second birthday and wants to keep it. He is not cheap, but frugal. He can be extravagant at times, even as a boss. Did you ever hear that old saying "Good things come to those who wait"? Well, great things come to those who wait longer. Hang in there, the bonus is time off with pay, only once you have proved yourself. He is well worth the wait when he finally gives you all of himself.

About the Woman: Looking for a very best friend? Here she is! She may seem standoffish at first until you have a problem. She will be the first to call and she will be the first to come. A friend is someone who comes to your side when she can't, and that is exactly what this girl does for the ones she cares for. As a boss, expect to prove yourself first before reaping any extra rewards. After you prove your loyalty, the royal treatment isn't far behind. She may seem quite pushy for your taste, but in time you realize that she is just a very up-front type of person.

Soul Mates: How can you not get along with someone as much like you as a fellow Capricorn? Pisces and Aquarius will fill your life with never-ending passion and inspiration. Cancer and Aries may try to fence you in. You can't live like that, so make sure they never get the chance. Taurus and Virgo will give you all you need to fulfill even your craziest dreams. Scorpio and Gemini will have you turning green when they turn their flirtatious charm elsewhere. Libras will shine their warm light on you as long as you keep them interested. That feeling is well worth any work that must be done. Leo has to think that they run the show if they are to remain happy anywhere. A partnership with Sagittarius, whether love or not, can be strong and long-lived.

Most Charming Characteristics: Stimulating to others, gives good advice.

Gifts: *For her:* fine bottle of wine. *For him:* royal collectible.

Sensual Foods: Chocolates; poached salmon; anything flambé; filet mignon; potatoes.

Romantic Flowers: Send this girl sunflowers if you want her to know you adore her. You may even add some poppies for a splash of extravagance. His desire for sport and play will be understood when you send him hyacinth and geranium.

Best Date Nights: Saturday; 15th and 24th of each month.

Colors of Passion: *For her:* green, brown, violet. *For him:* dark gray, brown.

The Perfect Wedding: Earthy goat girls feel most secure on the old terra firma, but climb, climb you must. The top of a mountain in Colorado or the top of a monument in Washington, D.C., all these locations lend themselves to your powerful persona. Inspired by tradition, you are happiest in a pleasant, conventional location. Ideal setting: Moscow; the Grand Canyon.

Wise Words: Robert Browning: "My own hope is a sun will pierce the thickest cloud earth ever stretched."

Hints of Love: Passion must be in the picture at all times or you could lose this one's attention quickly.

After the Argument: *For him:* Pay him extra attention. Send him something at work so everybody notices. Make him feel important. *For her:* Go overboard in a big way. Don't just send flowers at work, but to her home and to her mother's when she is there for Sunday dinner.

Romantic Places: Places of beauty bring romance: Africa; a state capital; Miami, Florida.

Lucky Love Star: Capriel—you never like the feeling of loneliness.

Beautiful Thought: Knowing there's a tomorrow allows us to get through today.

Sharing Secrets: If you are looking for love, then you have found the right mate. *For the gals:* This one could be stubborn. It may take forever to get a relationship started, but it is as solid as they come. *For the guys:* Even when he is ready, he might not be willing and able. He will put you through more obstacles than any course. Be patient.

Judith's Insights

About the Man: Very easily misunderstood, and it's no wonder. They really aren't great at communicating what they want. Even being this guy's friend takes work. To know him is to love him, so if he's your boss, be patient. It could get better. I think he doesn't like people to know just how vulnerable he is. The nicer you are, the nicer he'll be. Time can bring out the best of him in every capacity. He will reveal new layers of his personality the more comfortable he feels with you. He is charming, loyal, and loving, but getting to the core may be hard. He is worth it.

About the Woman: Yes, she can be a moody nightmare if you are on the opposite side of her. But this gal makes a great teammate. Her ambition will make you feel like you can never keep up. After time, you may learn you don't have to. Charm lies in her and will only be brought out when she really feels safe. You can easily get around this one with jokes and wit. Watching from afar, you may wonder why everyone jumps when she needs something. In time you will see her charisma along with her loyalty, and it may be you doing the jumping.

Soul Mates: You cannot help but get along with a Capricorn like yourself. Virgo and Taurus will support you and inspire you in everything you undertake. A relationship with Cancer will start strong but will weaken as time passes. Aries and Libra will open your eyes to dreams and goals you never thought about for yourself. Leo needs someone to lord it over and control. You would be wise to walk away if you don't like giving up control. Pisces will put you under a spell you don't want to wear off. Sagittarius and Aquarius will make you become the perfect person you always dreamed you could be. Gemini and Scorpio are too much for you to handle.

Most Charming Characteristics: Self-reliant, dependable, shrewd.

Gifts: *For her:* gold jewelry. *For him:* antique furniture.

Sensual Foods: Caviar; beef tenderloin; potatoes au gratin.

Romantic Flowers: Rhododendron will let her be on the lookout for trouble. Throw in some chrysanthemum and she'll know it is you she will be looking out for. Cactus will show him warmth. Yellow daffodil is a token of a good time had by all. Chivalry is not dead.

Best Date Nights: Saturday; 8th and 17th of each month.

Colors of Passion: *For her:* green, brown, violet. *For him:* dark gray, brown.

The Perfect Wedding: Earthy goat girls feel most secure on the old terra firma, but climb, climb you must. The top of a mountain in Colorado or the top of a monument in Washington, D.C., all these locations lend themselves to your powerful persona. Inspired by tradition, you are happiest in a pleasant, conventional location. Ideal setting: Moscow, the Grand Canyon.

Wise Words: Robert Browning: " 'Twas something our two souls should mix as mists do; each is sucked into each now."

Hints of Love: A random act of kindness will go a long way with this one. What can you do for them today?

After the Argument: *For him:* Pay him extra attention. Send him something at work so everybody notices. Make him feel important. *For her:* Go overboard in a big way. Don't just send flowers at work, but to her home and to her mother's when she is there for Sunday dinner.

Romantic Places: Places of power bring romance: Athens; a stadium; Los Angeles, California.

Lucky Love Star: Capriel—you never like the feeling of loneliness.

Beautiful Thought: Enjoy the company of the one sitting next to you.

Sharing Secrets: If you can hang around and give constant stimulation, this could be your mate. *For the gals:* She is always looking for the Exit sign. Don't show her where it is or she will be gone. *For the guys:* Fast cars, fast food; he likes everything that goes fast. Put on your running shoes. If you can keep up, then he is yours.

Judith's Insights

About the Man: Are you looking for trouble or just a lot of work? It may seem like too much work, especially if you are working together. One minute he is a perfectionist, the next a procrastinator. This can be a tough combination. Just remember he sometimes wants what he wants, and he wants it *yesterday*. He can seem like a control freak. That part of his nature will lessen in time as you create a balance in your relationship. Although he can be bossy, he would love to turn the reins over to you and relax for once.

About the Woman: She makes a great co-worker, a tough boss, and a wonderful friend. She expects a lot, so be ready to give all you have to give, and I don't mean materialistically. I mean of you. Her temper can sometimes get in the way. But if you are smart, you'll learn that after the storm the weather is usually wonderful, and so is she. As much as she desires passion, she yearns for balance even more. All she wants is a person who will make sure she knows what she means to them. Appreciate her and all she does and you will have a happy girl indeed.

Soul Mates: You and a fellow Capricorn are bound to become close and get along for a lifetime. Aquarius and Pisces will have you flying in no time. Things are not so easy for you and Cancer or Aries. Control is the name of the game when it comes to a Leo. They love to have it. When you need a solid base to build your dreams, look no further than a Taurus or Virgo. Gemini and Scorpio will leave you cold with their fiery and flirty nature. Libra will have you spinning and laughing at the feeling. You and Sagittarius are natural allies.

Most Charming Characteristics: Energetic, successful, reliable.

Gifts: *For her:* vanilla-scented candles. *For him:* chess set.

Sensual Foods: Passion fruit; fillet of sole almondine.

Romantic Flowers: The magnolias you send her will let her know you will be around for a while to come. Petunia is to say never despair. Holly will let him know what he is getting into. Pansy will keep you in his thoughts.

Best Date Nights: Saturday; 9th and 27th of each month.

Colors of Passion: *For her:* green, brown, violet. *For him:* dark gray, brown.

The Perfect Wedding: Earthy goat girls feel most secure on the old terra firma, but climb, climb you must. The top of a mountain in Colorado or the top of a monument in Washington, D.C., all these locations lend themselves to your powerful persona. Inspired by tradition, you are happiest in a pleasant, conventional location. Ideal setting: Moscow; the Grand Canyon.

Wise Words: Ralph Waldo Emerson: "Begin at the beginning, proceed in order, step by step."

Hints of Love: Family and friends are important to this one. Don't try to alienate them or it will definitely backfire on you.

After the Argument: *For him:* Pay him extra attention. Send him something at work so everybody notices. Make him feel important. *For her:* Go overboard in a big way. Don't just send flowers at work, but to her home and to her mother's when she is there for Sunday dinner.

Romantic Places: Places of beauty bring romance: Jamaica; a beach; Key West, Florida.

Lucky Love Star: Capriel—you never like the feeling of loneliness.

Beautiful Thought: Rain makes the flowers grow and gives nature a bath.

Sharing Secrets: This one may seem like a lot of work. They just need the basics: love, loyalty, and respect. *For the gals:* If you can show her your best side right from the beginning it may work. Be careful of fluff, because she will see right through it. *For the guys:* He loves to be loved. Give him plenty of attention, even if you think you don't stand a chance. Perseverance will win here.

Judith's Insights

About the Man: What a guy! Everybody loves him. It's his charisma. You may even envy the attention he gets, and why not? He's the one who seems to have the world right where he wants it. He has style, class, and is a hard act to follow. Never doubt, however, how he feels once he has told you. It will rarely change. That is why it takes so long for him to let it out. He wanted to make sure that it was really how he felt and that you feel the same way. He loves to be treated like royalty. Bring him breakfast in bed and you might stay in bed for the rest of the day!

About the Woman: She could probably build a house all by herself. If she doesn't decide to conquer that task in this life, it will be something of that nature. This gal is going places. She can frustrate the best of us. That's why it takes people who really understand what she is all about. Keep in mind that her way of showing her feelings is through actions instead of words. There is no such thing as doing too much to let her know how you feel. She will definitely notice if you do too little. She loves to be adored no matter what type of relationship she is in. Compliments go a long way with her.

Soul Mates: You should have no problem having a relationship with your own sign, Capricorn. Two peas in one pod can work well together. Taurus and Virgo would probably be two of the easiest signs for you to get along with, in or out of love. You will be a natural magnet for a Cancer, but anticipate complications at times. With Aries and Libra, the passion may draw you in. Even if it is only friendship, it can be a passionate one. Leos would be a hard relationship, but it could work if you can stand to be on the bottom occasionally. Pisces, the ingenious wit, will get you together. The great disposition of most Pisces could keep you there. Just make sure they don't get bored. Aquarius and Sagittarius could work well, but be cautious of flirtatious Gemini and Scorpio. They will drive you crazy and could test your sense when it comes to loyalty.

Most Charming Characteristics: Leader, good quick thinker, true and loyal.

Gifts: *For her:* hummingbird feeder. *For him:* day of golf.

Sensual Foods: Peaches; mousse; shrimp.

Romantic Flowers: Iris is your flower if you are the gal sending subtle messages. If you are the man, you will look for clematis. This flower's mental beauty creates emotional stimulation for you.

Best Date Nights: Saturday; 10th and 19th of each month.

Colors of Passion: *For her:* green, brown, violet. *For him:* dark gray, brown.

The Perfect Wedding: Earthy goat girls feel most secure on the old terra firma, but climb, climb you must. The top of a mountain in Colorado or the top of a monument in Washington, D.C., all these locations lend themselves to your powerful persona. Inspired by tradition, you are happiest in a pleasant, conventional location. Ideal setting: Moscow; the Grand Canyon.

Wise Words: Ralph Waldo Emerson: "Next to the originator of a good sentence is the first quoter of it. Many will read the book before one thinks of quoting a passage."

Hints of Love: Show others how much you adore him or her. Your partner will revel in how others notice.

After the Argument: *For him:* Pay him extra attention. Send him something at work so everybody notices. Make him feel important. *For her:* Go overboard in a big way. Don't just send flowers at work, but to her home and to her mother's when she is there for Sunday dinner.

Romantic Places: Places of beauty bring romance: the rain forest; a garden; the Grand Canyon.

Lucky Love Star: Capriel—you never like the feeling of loneliness.

Beautiful Thought: If the wind didn't blow, you wouldn't hear the different sounds nature makes.

Sharing Secrets: Looking for love, but that is just their little secret. *For the gals:* Why shouldn't they want to be loved? Of course they do, but they want you to do all of the work. *For the guys:* You must prove yourself repeatedly. Don't expect too much until he knows you are under his thumb.

Judith's Insights

About the Man: So, he is a little opinionated sometimes. His bark is worse than his bite. If you are working for this guy, and you run into a problem, he can be the kindest and the sweetest ever. Oops, he just let out his best-kept secret, his charm. His exterior can definitely camouflage his interior. If you love a challenge, then this is the guy for you. He loves to be conquered and wants you to work hard to do so. This way he can know what you are made of before any bad times arrive. They will arrive; it is all in how the two of you handle them together.

About the Woman: You can love many and trust few, but you are in soft hands with this one. She wants everyone to like her, even if she doesn't show it. Her patience may fly out of the window now and again. We are all human. She loves a good time, so keep the environment light. Her joy is so far down in her heart that you may need a forklift to get it out. She defines love by loyalty, so make sure you keep that in mind every day. As a boss, she will constantly challenge you to do your best. That is not necessarily a bad thing.

Soul Mates: Capricorn and Capricorn can work as well as anything out there. You can help Aquarius and Pisces remember the little joys in life so you can find joy in each other for a lifetime. Cancer and Aries could be too rigid for your taste. A solid plan can take a partnership with Taurus and Virgo to new heights. If you like things fast and exciting, you could have loads of fun with Scorpio and Gemini. The passion can be there with Libra as long as someone is feeding the flame. Establish with Leo who the boss is and things can progress from there. You could feel your heart skip a beat with Sagittarius.

Most Charming Characteristics: Kind, loyal, winsome.

Gifts: *For her:* home security system. *For him:* trip to a museum.

Sensual Foods: Kiwis; cantaloupes; strawberries.

Romantic Flowers: Any rose of any color for the lady. Roses stand for love regardless of the color. Send them with orchids and you will be saying, "I love you." If you want a gentleman to know you think of him, send pansies, and forget-me-nots for true love.

Best Date Nights: Saturday; 2nd and 29th of each month.

Colors of Passion: *For her:* green, brown, violet. *For him:* dark gray, blue.

The Perfect Wedding: Earthy goat girls feel most secure on the old terra firma, but climb, climb you must. The top of a mountain in Colorado or the top of a monument in Washington, D.C., all these locations lend themselves to your powerful persona. Inspired by tradition, you are happiest in a pleasant, conventional location. Ideal setting: Moscow, the Grand Canyon.

Wise Words: Robert Browning: "I use heart, head and hands / All day, I build, scheme, study and make friends."

Hints of Love: Don't overdo it (dress, attention)

too soon or this one will run. Wait until you have them hooked before you become outrageous.

After the Argument: *For him:* Pay him extra attention. Send him something at work so everybody notices. Make him feel important. *For her:* Go overboard in a big way. Don't just send flowers at work, but to her home and to her mother's when she is there for Sunday dinner.

Romantic Places: Places of power bring romance: Russia; a courthouse; Washington, D.C.

Lucky Love Star: Capriel—you never like the feeling of loneliness.

Beautiful Thought: Birds sing so we know nature is alive.

Sharing Secrets: You had better be ready to pull out your romantic side if you want this to work. *For the gals:* Fireplaces, walks on the beach, or even winning a bear at the local carnival. *For the guys:* When you are out shopping bring him something home. Even if it is silly, he will love the thought.

Judith's Insights

About the Man: He is a manly man and enjoys every minute of it. He stands at the sideline only until he is ready to get involved. Some may look at him as a loner. In truth, he is just a boy waiting in the wings. He waits until he is certain that it is time to make his move. Once he does make his move, there is no going back for him. Does the word *powerhouse* mean anything to you? He is capable in just about every way except communicating. Not to say he can't read or write. You just may have to read his mind here and there.

About the Woman: She may come on a little strong, especially as a friend. That is certainly never her intention. She just has a lot of answers and is ready to help everybody and anybody. She won't get involved in anyone else's business unless she truly believes that she can help. If she has nothing to offer she will keep her mouth closed. Having a lot of patience will come in handy when dealing with her. Always remember that her intentions are pure. She would never try to tell you what to do if she did not care for you.

Soul Mates: You will get along with anyone just like you. That is why you would do well with another Capricorn. If Pisces and Aquarius are on the train, don't let it leave without you. They can give you a true feeling of wellness you never had before. Cancer's and Aries's unyielding nature will have you running in the other direction. Taurus and Virgo know how to turn on that irresistible charm, which you just love. It would be advisable to fasten your seat belt. You might be thrown about with Scorpio and Gemini. New and interesting things must be ever present for a relationship with Libra to work. If you can let Leo be in charge, or even think he or she is, then you will get along fine. Keep open to all things new and exciting and you can fly to new heights with Sagittarius.

Most Charming Characteristics: Original, strong, robust.

Gifts: *For her:* tickets to the theater. *For him:* home improvement books.

Sensual Foods: Caramel and chocolate syrup on anything.

Romantic Flowers: These ladies like everyone to know how faithful they are, so send them violets. To surprise them send tulips. Men like their flowers the same as their relationships, unpretending. Send them camellias with white roses to show your affection.

Best Date Nights: Saturday; 3rd and 21st of each month.

Colors of Passion: *For her:* green, brown, violet. *For him:* dark gray, blue.

The Perfect Wedding: Earthy goat girls feel most secure on the old terra firma, but climb, climb you must. The top of a mountain in Colorado or the top of a monument in Washington, D.C., all these locations lend themselves to your powerful persona. Inspired by tradition, you are happiest in a pleasant, conventional location. Ideal setting: Moscow; the Grand Canyon.

Wise Words: Ralph Waldo Emerson: "The human body is the magazine of inventions, the patent office where are the models from which every hint was taken."

Hints of Love: When those born on this day decide to sit on the fence don't try to push them off before they are ready. Let them do the jumping themselves.

After the Argument: *For him:* Pay him extra attention. Send him something at work so everybody notices. Make him feel important. *For her:* Go overboard in a big way. Don't just send flowers at work, but to her home and to her mother's when she is there for Sunday dinner.

Romantic Places: Places of beauty bring romance: Africa; a hot-air balloon; Yosemite, California.

Lucky Love Star: Capriel—you never like the feeling of loneliness.

Beautiful Thought: Our lives imitate the living waters.

Sharing Secrets: It may seem like they are not interested, but ask them out anyway. *For the gals:* Until they absolutely know you are interested, you will never find out that they are. *For the guys:* Ask him out if he doesn't ask you. He may be shy or not. Either way, he may be interested.

Judith's Insights

About the Man: His life has been very complicated, and you will be paying some part of that bill. Pamper him if he is your boss. You will have a much easier work environment. As a friend, when he whines, just give him room. To know him is to have more patience. He is much better with strangers. It isn't easy being green—or walking in this guy's shoes, either, for that matter. He is always being tugged in twenty different directions. He can feel sorry for himself every so often. When he is feeling fine he is doing everything for everyone else.

About the Woman: She loves to live in the past, how far depends only on her age. You know she can get ugly when she is under too much stress. Try to de-stress any situation for her. You can count on the fact that she will create her own obstacles, especially when she is fearful. Keep the big picture in mind. Don't pull too hard on this girl's coattails. She is constantly going somewhere to help someone. Whether or not they wanted help in the first place is a completely other matter. She can't help taking care of the people she cares for the most.

Soul Mates: Another Capricorn could be exactly what you are looking for. With Aquarius and Pisces, you will both have a passion for life that you never experienced before. Cancer's and Aries's instinct to control all around them will leave you dreaming of greener pastures. There is not much that can shake the stable foundation you can make with Taurus and Virgo. Scorpio and Gemini will be too much energy focused in every direction for you to take lying down. Libra will fill every minute with a passion for life that can't help but rub off on you. Getting along with the dominating Leo could prove to be a difficult task for you. You and Sagittarius can make a tight partnership.

Most Charming Characteristics: Energetic, ambitious, independent.

Gifts: *For her:* antique furniture. *For him:* gold watch.

Sensual Foods: Waffles with whipped cream; chocolate soufflé; French wine.

Romantic Flowers: These ladies like men with taste. Show them you love style by sending fuchsia flowers, or even brightly colored wildflowers will do. To confuse this man, send him lilies along with bright daisies to show him your innocence. Keep him guessing.

Best Date Nights: Saturday; 4th and 22nd of each month.

Colors of Passion: *For her:* green, brown, violet. *For him:* dark gray, blue.

The Perfect Wedding: Earthy goat girls feel most secure on the old terra firma, but climb, climb you must. The top of a mountain in Colorado or the top of a monument in Washington, D.C., all these locations lend themselves to your powerful persona. Inspired by tradition, you are happiest in a pleasant, conventional location. Ideal setting: Moscow; the Grand Canyon.

Wise Words: Benjamin Franklin: "A little home well filled, a little field well tilled, a little wife well willed, are great riches."

Hints of Love: Make sure you learn to compromise, but never with your principles.

After the Argument: *For him:* Pay him extra attention. Send him something at work so everybody notices. Make him feel important. *For her:* Go overboard in a big way. Don't just send flowers at work, but to her home and to her mother's when she is there for Sunday dinner.

Romantic Places: Places of power bring romance: India; a marina; New York City.

Lucky Love Star: Capriel—you never like the feeling of loneliness.

Beautiful Thought: When your shoulders carry too much of a burden, shrug them, so something falls off.

Sharing Secrets: Don't be surprised if the first date is with their family. *For the gals:* Make sure you invite her to your family functions. It will be a red flag to her if you don't. *For the guys:* He may seem like a family man, but isn't that what you were looking for?

Judith's Insights

About the Man: He can overcome any obstacle as long as he feels supported. He will regress in any situation where he feels that loyalty wavers. He may become more and more important as he gets older. You will see even more moodiness with insecurity. Early in life, he will create the balance he needs to keep his self-esteem high. Later on in life he needs it created for him. Don't forget this guy's birthday or Valentine's gift. He needs to feel as if his partner has her eyes only on him. Constant reassurance will combat his jealousy.

About the Woman: You may feel that she is very competitive, because she can be. She either brings out the very best in others or the very worst. Sometimes she can even bring out both. She can be a challenge in any relationship she enters. She is the kind of person who deserves more than most. Most of the time she get it. She loves flirting, so don't be insulted when she gleams at the opportunity of it. You should know that this girl is oh so loyal. Make sure that you are able to give her all of the respect and freedom that she gives you.

Soul Mates: You will undoubtedly be attracted to someone of your own sign, Capricorn. You will make it a good relationship when you accept everything about yourself, for you will see it constantly in your partner. Virgo and Taurus will be great partners for you because you will each have equal responsibility and reward. Cancer will draw you in but may drive you nuts once you are there. Libra and Aries are brimming with passion. They will give you a new view of the world around you. Leo needs to be in control most of the time. Can you give up as much as they expect? Pisces's charm will prove to be irresistible for you to resist. Keep them occupied and they will do the same for you. Aquarius and Sagittarius can be the perfect combination of yin and yang energy. You will bring out the best in each other at every turn. Gemini and Scorpio are just too much for you to take. Their flirting will leave you boiling.

Most Charming Characteristics: Confident, sympathetic, understanding.

Gifts: *For her:* jasmine body wash. *For him:* a new book.

Sensual Foods: Oysters; mussels; spicy foods.

Romantic Flowers: You are the lady of distinction, and only carnations will do. Any mix of colors with sprays of mignonette. Sweet peas or red carnations will appeal to this man's heart.

Best Date Nights: Saturday; 5th and 23rd of each month.

Colors of Passion: *For her:* green, brown, violet. *For him:* dark gray, blue.

The Perfect Wedding: Earthy goat girls feel most secure on the old terra firma, but climb, climb you must. The top of a mountain in Colorado or the top of a monument in Washington, D.C., all these locations lend themselves to your powerful persona. Inspired by tradition, you are happiest in a pleasant, conventional location. Ideal setting: Moscow; the Grand Canyon.

Wise Words: Robert Schumann: "Music is the outflow of a beautiful mind."

Hints of Love: If you try to take a step back, it will be noticed. It could create the domino effect, and everything will start to fall.

After the Argument: *For him:* Pay him extra attention. Send him something at work so everybody notices. Make him feel important. *For her:* Go overboard in a big way. Don't just send flowers at work, but to her home and to her mother's when she is there for Sunday dinner.

Romantic Places: Places of beauty bring romance: China; an aquarium; Redwoods, California.

Lucky Love Star: Capriel—you never like the feeling of loneliness.

Beautiful Thought: Look around. Is there someone else you would really like to be?

Sharing Secrets: "Take me as I am" could be the anthem for this one. *For the gals:* They will have strong views on just about everything. If you can hang with them, then nothing will be as important as you. *For the guys:* The thing you fall in love with may end up becoming the thing you hate. After a commitment, this one sticks around.

Judith's Insights

About the Man: He is not the most spontaneous or adventurous, so you may have to bring your unique ideas around the back door. Just dress them up to be a bit more conservative. He can be cynical, but he could feel he is just playing devil's advocate. He has great logic and intellect. So, listen to him from time to time. He really does know what he is talking about, and he only wants to help you see that. He will never mind doing the dirty work in any kind of situation. He expects reward, respect, and benefits in return for a job well done.

About the Woman: She will drive you crazy if you let her. Her ability to do fifty things at once may be a challenge to her. It may also create havoc for others to watch. Your wants and needs may not come first. At times, you may have to glue her to a seat and fill her in on your needs. You may feel like she is turning you a deaf ear, and then she hears you. No matter who is in the driver's seat, this gal is doing the steering. Just when you think that you have been calling the shots, you will look over and she will be the captain of the team as she has been all along.

Soul Mates: A pairing with another Capricorn could be anything but difficult. Achievement of great things is possible when you have Aquarius and Pisces in your corner. Cancer and Aries can wear you a little thin. You don't mind all of your ducks in a row, but having them nailed to the floor would drive you crazy. There is wonderful potential for big things when you combine your charm with that of Taurus and Virgo. Scorpio and Gemini will run you ragged with their teasing tendencies. Things with Leo must be up front right away before they decide who is running the show. Libra needs constant stimulation to keep going. You might want to take your vitamins for this one. Sagittarius can be the partner you have always been looking for.

Most Charming Characteristics: Original, good leader, shrewd.

Gifts: *For her:* day of golf. *For him:* membership in exclusive club.

Sensual Foods: Lobster; watermelon.

Romantic Flowers: You love it when you get tulips, declaring love. When you receive a variety, it shows how hopelessly in love your partner is. He will just love a single rose. This shows him you understand his pleasures.

Best Date Nights: Saturday; 15th and 24th of each month.

Colors of Passion: *For her:* green, brown, violet. *For him:* dark gray, blue.

The Perfect Wedding: Earthy goat girls feel most secure on the old terra firma, but climb, climb you must. The top of a mountain in Colorado or the top of a monument in Washington, D.C., all these locations lend themselves to your powerful persona. Inspired by tradition, you are happiest in a pleasant, conventional location. Ideal setting: Moscow; the Grand Canyon.

Wise Words: Marcus Aurelius: "Put yourself in harmony with the things among which your lot is cast; love those with whom you have your portion, with a true love."

Hints of Love: Consistence and persistence will get this prize every time. They will value the effort.

After the Argument: *For him:* Pay him extra attention. Send him something at work so everybody notices. Make him feel important. *For her:* Go overboard in a big way. Don't just send flowers at work, but to her home and to her mother's when she is there for Sunday dinner.

Romantic Places: Places of power bring romance: Rome; a yacht; the Lincoln Memorial.

Lucky Love Star: Capriel—you never like the feeling of loneliness.

Beautiful Thought: Thinking positive thoughts is a fine way to train yourself to be positive.

Sharing Secrets: Seem moody until you get to know them. *For the gals:* You may not know whether to say hello or drop dead. As relations progress you will learn not to leave her dangling and her moods will become more consistent. *For the guys:* To know him is to love him. His bark is much worse than his bite. He just wants someone to love him without criticism.

Judith's Insights

About the Man: This guy likes to be consumed with something—anything. For the most part, it may be work, but it may become diet and exercise. He puts his family first, and don't challenge that part of his life. He can become on the depressed side if there isn't enough stimulation. In the grand scheme of things, he can make a good partner in every way. In the small picture, he may drive you crazy and could be a workaholic. Getting him to relax and open up will be a job in itself. If you can get him talking about his feelings you will have a pleasant reward for your efforts.

About the Woman: She is constantly running on the tracks, running for office, or running to work. You will certainly always find her running. Don't let this one have too much time to think. It could bring things to a dead halt, including her energy. She can frustrate you or stimulate you, but there is seldom a gray area. She has a need for control and harmony. She likes to be the chief. If you don't mind being a regular Indian with her in charge, you can have a good partnership. Just remember that even chiefs started low on the totem pole.

Soul Mates: How can you not get along with someone as much like you as a fellow Capricorn? Pisces and Aquarius will fill your life with never-ending passion and inspiration. Cancer and Aries may try to fence you in. You can't live like that, so make sure they never get the chance. Taurus and Virgo will give you all you need to fulfill even your craziest dreams. Scorpio and Gemini will have you turning green when they turn their flirtatious charm elsewhere. Libras will shine their warm light on you as long as you keep them interested. That feeling is well worth any work that must be done. Leo has to think that they run the show if they are to remain happy anywhere. A partnership with Sagittarius, whether love or not, can be strong and long-lived.

Most Charming Characteristics: Courageous, ambitious, sincere.

Gifts: *For her:* fine bottle of wine. *For him:* royal collectible.

Sensual Foods: Strawberries; truffles; shish kebab.

Romantic Flowers: Send this girl sunflowers if you want her to know you adore her. You may even add some poppies for a splash of extravagance. His desire for sport and play will be understood when you send him hyacinth and geranium.

Best Date Nights: Saturday; 6th and 24th of each month.

Colors of Passion: *For her:* green, brown, violet. *For him:* dark gray, blue.

The Perfect Wedding: Earthy goat girls feel most secure on the old terra firma, but climb, climb you must. The top of a mountain in Colorado or the top of a monument in Washington, D.C., all these locations lend themselves to your powerful persona. Inspired by tradition, you are happiest in a pleasant, conventional location. Ideal setting: Moscow, the Grand Canyon.

Wise Words: Robert Browning: "Someone shall somehow run amuck / With this old world, for want of strife / Sound asleep."

Hints of Love: Be funny. Laughter will be what keeps this one coming back again and again.

After the Argument: *For him:* Pay him extra attention. Send him something at work so everybody notices. Make him feel important. *For her:* Go overboard in a big way. Don't just send flowers at work, but to her home and to her mother's when she is there for Sunday dinner.

Romantic Places: Places of beauty bring romance: Africa; state capital; Miami, Florida.

Lucky Love Star: Capriel—you never like the feeling of loneliness.

Beautiful Thought: Letting go is allowing life to flow.

Sharing Secrets: You had better be able to put your money where your mouth is. *For the gals:* It doesn't need to be lavish, but she does love the loot. The more the better. *For the guys:* He doesn't mind spending his hard-earned cash, but he loves to see you contribute to please him.

Judith's Insights

About the Man: You'll find him stubborn at first; as time goes on, he tends to lighten up. He may keep up a brick wall, as an employer or an employee. He does better with friends than with family when communicating. His home does become his castle. Make sure he has his own space. This is a jack of all trades, and he never has a problem letting everyone know it. He loves it even more when he has an admirer. Just make sure that you applaud for him whether he does a great job at it or not. He needs support as much as attention.

About the Woman: She adores being adored. She hates cat fights but always seems to be in the mix of one, whether it's with a friend or family. Controversy may come up in handling business affairs. Then she takes the attitude at work less intensely. When she is arguing, keep the door open. This one will be coming back. At first you may think that she wants to be the boss at all times. At other times, you will find that she really wants to be taken care of. She is a never-ending challenge, but the path is littered with many rewards for all of your hard work.

Soul Mates: You cannot help but get along with a Capricorn like yourself. Virgo and Taurus will support you and inspire you in everything you undertake. A relationship with Cancer will start strong but will weaken as time passes. Aries and Libra will open your eyes to dreams and goals you never thought about for yourself. Leo needs someone to lord it over and control. You would be wise to walk away if you don't like giving up control. Pisces will put you under a spell you don't want to wear off. Sagittarius and Aquarius will make you become the perfect person you always dreamed you could be all along. Gemini and Scorpio are too much for you to handle.

Most Charming Characteristics: Fair-minded, affectionate, just.

Gifts: *For her:* gold jewelry. *For him:* antique furniture.

Sensual Foods: Grapes; fine cheeses and crackers; taffy.

Romantic Flowers: Rhododendron will let her be on the lookout for trouble. Throw in some chrysanthemum and she'll know it is you she will be looking out for. Cactus will show him warmth. Yellow daffodil is a token of a good time had by all. Chivalry is not dead.

Best Date Nights: Saturday; 8th and 26th of each month.

Colors of Passion: *For her:* green, brown, violet. *For him:* dark gray, blue.

The Perfect Wedding: Earthy goat girls feel most secure on the old terra firma, but climb, climb you must. The top of a mountain in Colorado or the top of a monument in Washington, D.C., all these locations lend themselves to your powerful persona. Inspired by tradition, you are happiest in a pleasant, conventional location. Ideal setting: Moscow; the Grand Canyon.

Wise Words: Robert Browning: "If joy delays, / Be happy that no worth befell."

Hints of Love: Treat this one like royalty or precious cargo. They will love being valued in this way.

After the Argument: *For him:* Pay him extra attention. Send him something at work so everybody notices. Make him feel important. *For her:* Go overboard in a big way. Don't just send flowers at work, but to her home and to her mother's when she is there for Sunday dinner.

Romantic Places: Places of power bring romance: Athens; a stadium; Los Angeles, California.

Lucky Love Star: Capriel—you never like the feeling of loneliness.

Beautiful Thought: Seasons prepare us for the changes in our lives and ourselves.

Sharing Secrets: Nobody likes a weak link, especially not this one. *For the gals:* Make sure you treat her like a lady and act like a man. *For the guys:* Put your best foot forward. Dress your best and keep your manners in check. This man notices.

Judith's Insights

About the Man: Rome wasn't built in a day, and neither will a quick comfort zone with this guy. He has built-in defenses that have been perfected over the years. The only way past them is to learn them in and out and then figure out a way around them. He makes a better employee than an employer, but with his intellect, sooner, before later, he'll be on the top. He needs to be kept busy. Social life is of definite importance. Be creative, inventive, and open minded to hang with this one. He can be confusing, yes, but he will keep you on your toes.

About the Woman: Did you see the Do Not Disturb sign? Sometimes it will be hard to notice. This one can shut down all communication when in overload. You are more likely to be the caller than this lady. She loves to sit back and just let the moment happen. Work means everything, and when it is all done, she'll start over again, especially with decorating. Keep your favorite items. You may find they vanish when you are not paying attention. She makes a great mate when her partner makes her feel important and loved.

Soul Mates: You and a fellow Capricorn are bound to become close and get along for a lifetime. Aquarius and Pisces will have you flying in no time. Things are not so easy for you and Cancer or Aries. Control is the name of the game when it comes to a Leo. They love to have it. When you need a solid base to build your dreams, look no further than a Taurus or Virgo. Gemini and Scorpio will leave you cold with their fiery and flirty nature. Libra will have you spinning and laughing at the feeling. You and Sagittarius are natural allies.

Most Charming Characteristics: Energetic, cautious, strong.

Gifts: *For her:* vanilla-scented candles. *For him:* chess set.

Sensual Foods: Champagne; grapes; mangoes; filet mignon.

Romantic Flowers: The magnolias you send her will let her know you will be around for a while to come. Petunia is to say never despair. Holly will let him know what he is getting into. Pansy will keep you in his thoughts.

Best Date Nights: Saturday; 9th and 18th of each month.

Colors of Passion: *For her:* green, yellow, violet. *For him:* dark gray, blue.

The Perfect Wedding: Earthy goat girls feel most secure on the old terra firma, but climb, climb you must. The top of a mountain in Colorado or the top of a monument in Washington, D.C., all these locations lend themselves to your powerful persona. Inspired by tradition, you are happiest in a pleasant, conventional location. Ideal setting: Moscow; the Grand Canyon.

Wise Words: Robert Browning: "Look at the end of work, contrast / The petty Done, the Undone vast."

Hints of Love: Affection is important, but only if it comes naturally. Otherwise, the sirens will go off.

After the Argument: *For him:* Pay him extra attention. Send him something at work so everybody notices. Make him feel important. *For her:* Go overboard in a big way. Don't just send flowers at work, but to her home and to her mother's when she is there for Sunday dinner.

Romantic Places: Places of beauty bring romance: Jamaica; a beach; Key West, Florida.

Lucky Love Star: Capriel—you never like the feeling of loneliness.

Beautiful Thought: The answers are in every heartbeat; listen to the pulse.

Sharing Secrets: Attention, attention, attention. *For the gals:* Do it any way you can. Presents, phone calls, cards, or flowers. Whatever works for you will work for her. *For the guys:* He would love nostalgic gifts or T-shirts. He also likes phone calls, as long as they don't interrupt his favorite pastimes.

Judith's Insights

About the Man: There is help on the way with this one! You may feel like you need the advice of anybody and everybody. It's not so much that he is difficult, but it certainly can be looked at that way. Don't intrude on his days to himself or on his days off. He won't be very happy. His mom plays a bigger role than you may think. Make sure that you are ready to take life or work more seriously to be involved with this one. You may have to jump through a few hoops to prove yourself, but if you make it through the first round you usually make the team.

About the Woman: Everybody needs a "run for their money." That may include working for it in an environment that seems tough because it is. This gal can bring stress or break it in an instant. She may want others to do the emotional work. You may have to watch this one. She can absolutely have tunnel vision. During an argument you have to be the one to keep an open mind and try to hear what she is saying. She will be consumed with the fact that she is right and might not get the whole picture.

Soul Mates: You should have no problem having a relationship with your own sign, Capricorn. Two peas in one pod can work well together. Taurus and Virgo would probably be two of the easiest signs for you to get along with, in or out of love. You will be a natural magnet for a Cancer, but anticipate complications at times. With Aries and Libra, the passion may draw you in. Even if it is only friendship, it can be a passionate one. Leos would be a hard relationship, but it could work if you can stand to be on the bottom occasionally. Pisces, the ingenious wit, will get you together. The great disposition of most Pisces could keep you there. Just make sure they don't get bored. Aquarius and Sagittarius could work well, but be cautious of flirtatious Gemini and Scorpio. They will drive you crazy and could test your sense when it comes to loyalty.

Most Charming Characteristics: Kind, considerate, diplomatic.

Gifts: *For her:* hummingbird feeder. *For him:* day of golf.

Sensual Foods: Châteaubriand; crème brûlée.

Romantic Flowers: Iris is your flower if you are the gal sending subtle messages. If you are the man, you will look for clematis. This flower's mental beauty creates emotional stimulation for you.

Best Date Nights: Saturday; 1st and 10th of each month.

Colors of Passion: *For her:* green, yellow, violet. *For him:* dark gray, blue.

The Perfect Wedding: Earthy goat girls feel most secure on the old terra firma, but climb, climb you must. The top of a mountain in Colorado or the top of a monument in Washington, D.C., all these locations lend themselves to your powerful persona. Inspired by tradition, you are happiest in a pleasant, conventional location. Ideal setting: Moscow; the Grand Canyon.

Wise Words: Nikolay Berdyayev: "Humility is both the source of spiritual peace and also a means of union with powers higher than our own."

Hints of Love: This one likes others to make his or her dreams come true. Be the "fantasy" fulfiller.

After the Argument: *For him:* Pay him extra attention. Send him something at work so everybody notices. Make him feel important. *For her:* Go overboard in a big way. Don't just send flowers at work, but to her home and to her mother's when she is there for Sunday dinner.

Romantic Places: Places of beauty bring romance: the rain forest; a garden; the Grand Canyon.

Lucky Love Star: Capriel—you never like the feeling of loneliness.

Beautiful Thought: It's easier to change the question than the answer.

Sharing Secrets: Make sure you are not the killjoy. *For the gals:* When she has an idea, try it before you decide you don't like it. She needs to be pleased. *For the guys:* Do the things he loves to do and he will make the things you love ten times more fun.

Judith's Insights

About the Man: He wants what he wants, and he usually wants it yesterday. He is a bit impatient and sometimes impractical. When you first meet him, he shows you the more practical and conservative side. As a friend, he is only as loyal as you are. You will have to let him down more than once before he walks away, but he is certainly capable of it. You might not find his ticklish spot too quickly but you can push his sensitive buttons without even knowing it. His most tricky button is his jealousy button. Watch out for the green-eyed monster to take over his brain.

About the Woman: If you are too pushy, you may just lose your job or your next invitation to dinner. Good things come to those who tread lightly. Let her think or feel that she has some say in her destiny. It will certainly make things go easier. She has the great talent of having a temper tantrum without the kicking and screaming. This is especially true in a work environment. She is known to pout when things are not going her way. She is proud of her accomplishments and wants to be recognized for them. Her work is like a well-oiled machine.

Soul Mates: Capricorn and Capricorn can work as well as anything out there. You can help Aquarius and Pisces remember the little joys in life so you can find joy in each other for a lifetime. Cancer and Aries could be too rigid for your taste. A solid plan can take a partnership with Taurus and Virgo to new heights. If you like things fast and exciting, you could have loads of fun with Scorpio and Gemini. The passion can be there with Libra as long as someone is feeding the flame. Establish with Leo who the boss is and things can progress from there. You could feel your heart skip a beat with Sagittarius.

Most Charming Characteristics: Self-reliant, diligent, honest.

Gifts: *For her:* home security system. *For him:* trip to a museum.

Sensual Foods: Shrimp; sinful chocolate cake.

Romantic Flowers: Any rose of any color for the lady. Roses stand for love regardless of the color. Send them with orchids and you will be saying, "I love you." If you want a gentleman to know you think of him, send pansies, and forget-me-nots for true love.

Best Date Nights: Saturday; 2nd and 29th of each month.

Colors of Passion: *For her:* green, pale yellow, violet. *For him:* dark gray, blue.

The Perfect Wedding: Earthy goat girls feel most secure on the old terra firma, but climb, climb you must. The top of a mountain in Colorado or the top of a monument in Washington, D.C., all these locations lend themselves to your powerful persona. Inspired by tradition, you are happiest in a pleasant, conventional location. Ideal setting: Moscow; the Grand Canyon.

Wise Words: Charles Dickens: "There are some sweet daydreams, so they are, they put the visions of the night to shame."

Hints of Love: Stop worrying about next week's date today or there will not be one tomorrow.

After the Argument: *For him:* Pay him extra attention. Send him something at work so everybody notices. Make him feel important. *For her:* Go overboard in a big way. Don't just send flowers at work, but to her home and to her mother's when she is there for Sunday dinner.

Romantic Places: Places of power bring romance: Russia; a courthouse; Washington, D.C.

Lucky Love Star: Capriel—you never like the feeling of loneliness.

Beautiful Thought: Breathe to the rhythm of your heart with your eyes closed.

Sharing Secrets: You had better be ready to have a relationship. *For the gals:* No lies, no games, and no mistakes. She wants what she wants with as little work as possible. *For the guys:* If you have games on your mind, then move on. This one likes fun any way he can get it, but no emotional roller coasters.

Judith's Insights

About the Man: This guy will never take anything for granted. He can even go so far as to doubt that the sky is blue just because you told him it was. He is always expecting the next shoe to drop. Sometimes you'll feel like he has too much self-control. What a talker! He can impress you with knowledge he doesn't even have. He will let pride get in his way. His practical side can drive you crazy, especially when it comes to making decisions. It will surprise you when he finally does make a choice, but it is always the right one for him because of all the thought he put into it.

About the Woman: This is a lady with a lot of versatility. When she sets her mind to it, she can be successful with ten things at once. She can be rather suspicious. If you are working for her, expect that she will be checking the time clock. She will certainly have style no matter how much cash she has in the bank. It only takes a moment to fall in love with her warmth and open heart. She can be the boss of all bosses as long as you have proven that you are deserving of her respect. She wants to know that everyone around her can do their part to make things move ahead.

Soul Mates: You will get along with anyone just like you. That is why you would do well with another Capricorn. If Pisces and Aquarius are on the train, don't let it leave without you. They can give you a true feeling of wellness you never had before. Cancer's and Aries's unyielding nature will have you running in the other direction. Taurus and Virgo know how to turn on that irresistible charm, which you just love. It would be advisable to fasten your seat belt. You might be thrown about with Scorpio and Gemini. New and interesting things must be ever present for a relationship with Libra to work. If you can let Leo be in charge, or even think that they are, then you will get along fine. Keep open to all things new and exciting and you can fly to new heights with Sagittarius.

Most Charming Characteristics: Adaptable, kind, self-reliant.

Gifts: *For her:* tickets to the theater. *For him:* home improvement books.

Sensual Foods: Toasted marshmallows; chocolates.

Romantic Flowers: These ladies like everyone to know how faithful they are, so send them violets. To surprise them send tulips. Men like their flowers the same as their relationships, unpretending. Send them camellias with white roses to show your affection.

Best Date Nights: Saturday; 3rd and 21st of each month.

Colors of Passion: *For her:* indigo blue, yellow, violet. *For him:* dark gray, blue.

The Perfect Wedding: Earthy goat girls feel most secure on the old terra firma, but climb, climb you must. The top of a mountain in Colorado or the top of a monument in Washington, D.C., all these locations lend themselves to your powerful persona. Inspired by tradition, you are happiest in a pleasant, conventional location. Ideal setting: Moscow; the Grand Canyon.

Wise Words: Charles Dickens: "Painters always make ladies out prettier than they are, or they wouldn't get any custom."

Hints of Love: Keep the romance in the picture. Don't forget the long walks on the beach and camping out in front of the fireplace.

After the Argument: *For him:* Pay him extra attention. Send him something at work so everybody notices. Make him feel important. *For her:* Go overboard in a big way. Don't just send flowers at work, but to her home and to her mother's when she is there for Sunday dinner.

Romantic Places: Places of beauty bring romance: Africa; a hot-air balloon; Yosemite, California.

Lucky Love Star: Capriel—you never like the feeling of loneliness.

Beautiful Thought: Children make tomorrow easier, even if you don't think that today.

Sharing Secrets: You may have to give this one more than one chance. *For the gals:* Intriguing as she is, expect a handful. She lightens up as time goes on. *For the guys:* His quirks may make you have second thoughts, but that is what separates the men from the boys.

Judith's Insights

About the Man: He is a bit more stubborn than the usual guy. He makes a great boss, because he doesn't have to maintain a certain role form. He likes informalities, so long as you show him great respect. He likes to be more "help profile" than you might think. Get out of his way if he's having a bad day. He loves to keep his life full, even if his calendar is empty. Invite him out to a play or a unique dinner party. He may seem a bit more dull than he would like. If this guy is your boss, the office will be much happier if you invite him to be part of the gang.

About the Woman: This gal knows how to have a good time. If anything gets in her way, it will certainly bring out her worst side. Some may think of her as selfish, and at times she may be that way. But most of the time she knows what she wants and just goes and gets it. Her kindness allows doors to open for her. She can say all of the right things, but her actions can contradict her words. She likes for people to look at her and wonder. She does have a selfish and almost rude side, especially if you have wronged her. She can talk her way out of anything.

Soul Mates: You love yourself so much you could do well with any Aquarius. Both Pisces and Aries will know how to charm you into their reaches. Libra and Sagittarius will intrigue you. They can make the best partner, no matter what kind you have in mind. Capricorn will bring you right down to earth and keep you safe. You love it no matter how much you say that you don't. Leo will be your greatest challenge, depending on the mood you are in and how much both of you have grown. This could be the most fun you have had in a long time. Taurus and Scorpio will test your patience and could drive you right off the deep end if you let them. You must be willing to accept Gemini for who they are for this to work. With Cancer and Virgo, you would do better just to run, but the temptation is there. Just remember, where there is smoke there is usually fire.

Most Charming Characteristics: Self-reliant, diplomatic, affectionate.

Gifts: *For her:* onyx necklace. *For him:* telescope.

Sensual Foods: Chocolate-covered strawberries; New York steak; scallops.

Romantic Flowers: These ladies like men with taste. Show them you love style by sending fuchsia flowers, or even brightly colored wildflowers will do. To confuse this man, send him lilies along with bright daisies to show him your innocence. Keep him guessing.

Best Date Nights: Saturday; 4th and 13th of each month.

Colors of Passion: *For her:* sky blue, pale yellow. *For him:* indigo blue, bright blue.

The Perfect Wedding: Outlandish scenery—say, the view from an airplane, a Native American reservation, a national park—could enhance the sealing of your vows and make your day unique. You are moved by spectacular landscapes, and fresh air is a must. These, combined with your sweet sense of whimsy, will make your wedding day magical and filled with dreamy possibilities. Ideal setting: Arizona.

Wise Words: Percy Bysshe Shelley: "And the spirit arose on the garden fair / Like the spirit of Love felt everywhere."

Hints of Love: The mystery is important, but being evasive will create disaster. Make sure you know the difference.

After the Argument: *For him:* He can be stubborn. You might have to cook his favorite meal and buy those tickets to the concert he wanted. In other words, make sure he knows you're going out of your way. *For her:* If she was wrong, you won't have to do too much at all. If you were wrong, expect it to cost you! Grovel, grovel, and then grovel some more. Expect to go see the movies she wants and eat in the restaurant she wants to for a while. Time will be the currency for payment on this one.

Romantic Places: Places of distinction bring romance: Switzerland; a bed-and-breakfast; Hyde Park, New York.

Lucky Love Star: Aquariel—you will never lack devotion.

Beautiful Thought: Any transition is only a bridge to help you get to where you're going.

Sharing Secrets: Talk about high maintenance. *For the gals:* Once she sees that you go out of your way for her then she will for you. *For the guys:* The bark is definitely much worse than the bite. He comes on stronger and more obstinate then he actually is.

Judith's Insights

About the Man: This guy can have wonderful possibilities, if he gets out of his own way. He either has a million people around him or he has none. He would much rather the million. He hates to feel alone. Yes, he can be moody, and that makes others pull away. His diplomatic side will make it easy for others to talk to him. He can whine with the best of them, but can sometimes lack patience and compassion if others whine too much. He is drawn to the unusual and unique. You can be certain to impress him by taking him to see something he has never seen before.

About the Woman: This lady can dress to the nines and get noticed by everyone. She's got class and style and loves to show it. She can get too trapped in what others think. Her relationship with family could drive her and you crazy. This one loves to go out to the theater, art, shopping. She likes to feel a part of the action. She is extremely inventive and can do some amazing things with the smallest start. One step at a time is the best plan when approaching this girl. No one can force her to do something she isn't ready for, and those who try just get burned.

Soul Mates: When looking for a compatible sign, look no further than your own, Aquarius. Taurus's and Scorpio's terrible temper and tendency to erupt in a fury will be simply irrational to you. The match of wits with Cancer and Virgo happens fast. It will be strained just as fast if you don't really get to know each other. You will be fascinated with Pisces and Aries charisma. A union with Libra and Sagittarius could be picture-perfect. Leo is a truly worthy adversary. This could be a lot of fun. A Capricorn can keep your feet on the ground while you still have the ability to fly as high as you need to. Don't go in with the intent of changing Gemini. Learn to value them for who they are:

Most Charming Characteristics: Determined, ambitious, respectable.

Gifts: *For her:* meditation tapes. *For him:* science set or microscope.

Sensual Foods: Vanilla and strawberry mousse; tiramisù; espresso.

Romantic Flowers: You are the lady of distinction, and only carnations will do. Any mix of colors with sprays of mignonette. Sweet peas or red carnations will appeal to this man's heart.

Best Date Nights: Saturday; 5th and 23rd of each month.

Colors of Passion: *For her:* sky blue, pale yellow. *For him:* green, bright blue.

The Perfect Wedding: Outlandish scenery—say, the view from an airplane, a Native American reservation, a national park—could enhance the sealing of your vows and make your day unique. You are moved by spectacular landscapes, and fresh air is a must. These, combined with your sweet sense of whimsy, will make your wedding day magical and filled with dreamy possibilities. Ideal setting: Arizona.

Wise Words: Robert Browning: "We find great things are made of little things, and little things go lessening till at last comes God behind them."

Hints of Love: If you learn to back up when things are moving too fast, you won't have to bow out so often.

After the Argument: *For him:* He can be stubborn. You might have to cook his favorite meal and buy those tickets to the concert he wanted. In other words, make sure he knows you're going out of your way. *For her:* If she was wrong, you won't have to do too much at all. If you were wrong, expect it to cost you! Grovel, grovel, and then grovel some more. Expect to go see the movies she wants and eat in the restaurant she wants to for a while. Time will be the currency for payment on this one.

Romantic Places: Places of innovation bring romance: Japan; a science museum; Disney World.

Lucky Love Star: Aquariel—you will never lack devotion.

Beautiful Thought: Peace of mind brings peace in time.

Sharing Secrets: Make sure you have at least five dates before you make up your mind. *For the gals:* She can be cynical, so it could be a few dates before she loosens up. *For the guys:* He still has yesterday on his mind. He needs a reason to forget his past relationship. Make a new history for him.

Judith's Insight

About the Man: He is stubborn like a mule, maybe even more so. His job and all of his relationships better allow him a lot of freedom, because he will need it. He may seem different or odd to others. He does that so others keep their distance until he is sure about the select few that have been chosen to join his inner circle. He doesn't like to be disappointed in people. When he does enter any kind of relationship, even family, he makes it for life. Make him laugh and he will be instantly focused on you. It may have been a while since he has laughed.

About the Woman: This girl is one great boss lady. She allows the fun and follies while also having the ability to be a workaholic. She works hard, plays hard and sometimes harder. All that she asks from the people around her is what she is able to give herself. She understands and gives loyalty to those who give her loyalty. If you have a friend in her, you have made one for life. She has an open-minded personality that makes people want to bring her ideas and see what she thinks of them. Smile and hold her hand while she tries to help the world.

Soul Mates: With so much in common with another Aquarius, you can't go wrong. Taurus and Scorpio are powerful and stubborn. If you are attracted to each other enough, they will stick with you through thick and thin. You might be enthralled by Cancer's and Virgo's powerful imagination, but things for you guys in the real world will be much stickier. Take delight in the spell Pisces and Aries will cast upon you. Things with Libra and Sagittarius are a perfect example of what can go right. Leo is like a bet. It can be risky, but it could also end in a win-win situation. You and Capricorn will balance each other perfectly. If you don't expect Gemini to change just to suit you, the partnership will work out fine. If you are willing to accept each other for what you truly are, then by all means go for it.

Most Charming Characteristics: Truthful, affectionate, good-natured.

Gifts: *For her:* dinner at an unusual restaurant. *For him:* tickets to the circus.

Sensual Foods: Raspberries; pound cake; caviar.

Romantic Flowers: You love it when you get tulips, declaring love. When you receive a variety, it shows how hopelessly in love your partner is. He will just love a single rose. This shows him you understand his pleasures.

Best Date Nights: Wednesday; 6th and 15th of each month.

Colors of Passion: *For her:* sky blue, pale yellow. *For him:* indigo blue, bright blue.

The Perfect Wedding: Outlandish scenery—say, the view from an airplane, a Native American reservation, a national park—could enhance the sealing of your vows and make your day unique. You are moved by spectacular landscapes, and fresh air is a must. These, combined with your sweet sense of whimsy, will make your wedding day magical and filled with dreamy possibilities. Ideal setting: Arizona.

Wise Words: Robert Browning: "I say that man was made to grow, not stop."

Hints of Love: Expecting too much too soon can only build up hopes that will fall down too easily.

After the Argument: *For him:* He can be stubborn. You might have to cook his favorite meal and buy those tickets to the concert he wanted. In other words, make sure he knows you're going out of your way. *For her:* If she was wrong, you won't have to do too much at all. If you were wrong, expect it to cost you! Grovel, grovel, and then grovel some more. Expect to go see the movies she wants and eat in the restaurant she wants to for a while. Time will be the currency for payment on this one.

Romantic Places: Places of distinction bring romance: Britain; a sushi bar; Houston, Texas.

Lucky Love Star: Aquariel—you will never lack devotion.

Beautiful Thought: Ingredients make the fragrance.

Sharing Secrets: Don't be in a hurry, or it will be over before it begins. *For the gals:* Like fine wine and amazing food. Savor it a moment until an hour is created. *For the guys:* To do too much too fast will prove risky. Try to give a push and he will just jump ship.

Judith's Insights

About the Man: He can bring joy to the party or suck the life right out of it. If he is in a bad mood, he simply doesn't know how to disguise it. This one can be a bit complicated. You don't have to be psychic to figure this one out. If he is happy, everything is great. If he isn't, you should run the other way while you still can. A relationship with him may start out challenging and end up being the best comfort zone you have ever had. He can be overwhelming with his advice and ideas on how to improve your life together. He only has your, and his, best interests at heart.

About the Woman: You can call her catty but she won't like it. You can call her determined, but she probably won't like that, either. Call her beautiful and acknowledge her success and she will be eating out of your hand. She loves a compliment, attention, and for you to be loyal to her. She never can feel she is being criticized. Learn to deal with negative issues in a positive way. It is all about the spin you can put on the issue at hand. She will find ways to say I'm sorry without having to say those words. She thinks that she is simple but she is simply complicated.

Soul Mates: Looking at a fellow Aquarius is like looking at a reflection of yourself. If you don't like what you see, you have to look inside yourself before you look inside them. Taurus and Scorpio might be troubled by your judgment-free nature. Ease it up a bit. You might not learn not to go near the fire of Cancer and Virgo until you have been burned by it. Pisces's and Aries's magnetism will pull you right to them. Libra and Sagittarius are the personification of whatever image you have of a great relationship. Sharpen your edges; the ride with Leo will be a great one. When you get in over your head, Capricorn is there to help you swim to shore. Gemini must be appreciated for what they are instead of molded into your vision of what they should be.

Most Charming Characteristics: Leader, friendly, perceptive.

Gifts: *For her:* tickets to a performance art show. *For him:* astrological chart.

Sensual Foods: Flambé; lobster; oysters.

Romantic Flowers: Send this girl sunflowers if you want her to know you adore her. You may even add some poppies for a splash of extravagance. His desire for sport and play will be understood when you send him hyacinth and geranium.

Best Date Nights: Wednesday; 7th and 15th of each month.

Colors of Passion: *For her:* sky blue, pale yellow. *For him:* indigo blue, bright blue.

The Perfect Wedding: Outlandish scenery—say, the view from an airplane, a Native American reservation, a national park—could enhance the sealing of your vows and make your day unique. You are moved by spectacular landscapes, and fresh air is a must. These, combined with your sweet sense of whimsy, will make your wedding day magical and filled with dreamy possibilities. Ideal setting: Arizona.

Wise Words: William Wordsworth: "The flower of the sweetest smell is shy and lowly."

Hints of Love: Make sure all the ingredients are present before putting the cake in the oven.

After the Argument: *For him:* He can be stubborn.

You might have to cook his favorite meal and buy those tickets to the concert he wanted. In other words, make sure he knows you're going out of your way. *For her:* If she was wrong, you won't have to do too much at all. If you were wrong, expect it to cost you! Grovel, grovel, and then grovel some more. Expect to go see the movies she wants and eat in the restaurant she wants to for a while. Time will be the currency for payment on this one.

Romantic Places: Places of innovation bring romance: New York City; an air show; Silicon Valley.

Lucky Love Star: Aquariel—you will never lack devotion.

Beautiful Thought: Breathe in fresh air when you're looking for a fresh moment.

Sharing Secrets: They need to look before they leap, but only in love. *For the gals:* She needs creative and exciting dates to keep her interest. Don't take her for granted too soon. *For the guys:* You may think he gives signs of moving this relationship quickly but make sure you slow it down before he does.

Judith's Insights

About the Man: I guess the one with the most friends wins, and that is this guy. His magnetic personality brings them in by the truckload. He loves to be around people, and certainly needs his alone time or he will become very cranky. He will have his hands in everybody else's job, besides doing his own. He just loves being needed, as long as he is very appreciated. Keep the romance going or he will look some place else for what is lacking. Not to say he would cheat. Once he has made a commitment he keeps to it. He will, however, break it off if he finds someone willing to give him the attention he wants.

About the Woman: She is a leader, and nature has, in fact, created that for her. Whether she is low man on the totem pole or president, she is looked up to. But she looks to be noticed. She works at each relationship she has, and never wants to be looked at as the bad gal. She certainly works hard enough at being good. Does it really matter who wears the pants in the relationship? This is a new century. You can both wear the pants and still make it work. She hates being taken for granted, so make sure you let her know that you appreciate what she does for you.

Soul Mates: Fix your eyes on a fellow Aquarius and it will be as if you are looking at yourself. You may have to fight to be with Taurus and Scorpio, but you may be all the richer for the struggle. No matter how much you believe you can get around the blaze of Cancer and Virgo, it will be better to take another course entirely. Imagine the fun to be ensnared by such delightful captors as Pisces and Aries. Talk about perfect. You can't go wrong with Libra and Sagittarius. A relationship with Leo will test your creativity. You need to learn to settle down while your Capricorn needs to learn to play around. A pairing with Gemini can work only if you learn to accept them for who they are.

Most Charming Characteristics: Loyal, true, magnetic personality.

Gifts: *For her:* dance class. *For him:* leather journal.

Sensual Foods: Crème brûlée; poached salmon.

Romantic Flowers: Rhododendron will let her be on the lookout for trouble. Throw in some chrysanthemum and she'll know it is you she will be looking out for. Cactus will show him warmth. Yellow daffodil is a token of a good time had by all. Chivalry is not dead.

Best Date Nights: Wednesday; 8th and 26th of each month.

Colors of Passion: *For her:* sky blue, pale yellow. *For him:* indigo blue, bright blue.

The Perfect Wedding: Outlandish scenery—say, the view from an airplane, a Native American reservation, a national park—could enhance the sealing of your vows and make your day unique. You are moved by spectacular landscapes, and fresh air is a must. These, combined with your sweet sense of whimsy, will make your wedding day magical and filled with dreamy possibilities. Ideal setting: Arizona.

Wise Words: Robert Browning: "Years must teem with change untried, / With chance not easily defied / With an end somewhere undescried."

Hints of Love: Simple often turns into complicated with this one. When you overcomplicate the moment, try to step back for a breather.

After the Argument: *For him:* He can be stubborn. You might have to cook his favorite meal and buy those tickets to the concert he wanted. In other words, make sure he knows you're going out of your way. *For her:* If she was wrong, you won't have to do too much at all. If you were wrong, expect it to cost you! Grovel, grovel, and then grovel some more. Expect to go see the movies she wants and eat in the restaurant she wants to for a while. Time will be the currency for payment on this one.

Romantic Places: Places of distinction bring romance: Russia; an art museum; Savannah, Georgia.

Lucky Love Star: Aquariel—you will never lack devotion.

Beautiful Thought: Stars are the heavens winking at us.

Sharing Secrets: The possibilities are endless, if you can pay the price. *For the gals:* She is hoping chivalry is not dead, and you must be willing to be the man at all costs. *For the guys:* He can be demanding and somewhat controlling. He just needs to be trained.

Judith's Insights

About the Man: Yes, his ego can get in the way. Not to say yours doesn't. His passionate way of entertaining life will both stimulate you and drive you to the edge. He may just bring out the competitiveness in any relationship. There is that desire to always ignite the passion or fire in things. This guy is the initiator of everything. It doesn't matter if it is a party or a relationship; everyone is welcome to come and show what they have. He tends to have a calming effect on others while being hyper himself.

About the Woman: She can be your best friend and worst enemy, and sometimes both in the same day. She has a kind and giving nature, but can cut you off on a dime. She gets easily fed up with "same old, same old." She is encouraging as a pal, but more critical as a boss. She may even be a manager without the title. This is not always by her choice, but by the choice of others. The attraction is her energy and her uncanny desire for life. She can become frustrating when she is stubborn and self-absorbed. Patience will get you through any tough spot with her.

Soul Mates: How can you not be hooked on someone made from the same mold you were? Aquarius and Aquarius is exactly that. If you can get Taurus and Scorpio to open up to the world, they will be much easier for you to handle. A match with Cancer and Virgo would require a magical imagination to ever get off the ground. Pisces and Aries know exactly how to capture your attention. You will love to be around such good-natured and generous people as Libra and Sagittarius. Leo has laid the gauntlet down. Are you ready for the game? Capricorn makes sure your exuberance doesn't get you in trouble. Gemini must be accepted for the fiery and flirty people they are.

Most Charming Characteristics: Ambitious, loyal, true.

Gifts: *For her:* natural-scented body wash. *For him:* photography class.

Sensual Foods: Chocolate soufflé; filet mignon.

Romantic Flowers: The magnolias you send her will let her know you will be around for a while to come. Petunia is to say never despair. Holly will let him know what he is getting into. Pansy will keep you in his thoughts.

Best Date Nights: Wednesday; 9th and 18th of each month.

Colors of Passion: *For her:* sky blue, pale yellow. *For him:* indigo blue, bright blue.

The Perfect Wedding: Outlandish scenery—say, the view from an airplane, a Native American reservation, a national park—could enhance the sealing of your vows and make your day unique. You are moved by spectacular landscapes, and fresh air is a must. These, combined with your sweet sense of whimsy, will make your wedding day magical and filled with dreamy possibilities. Ideal setting: Arizona.

Wise Words: John Locke: "Gentleness is far more successful in all its enterprises than violence; indeed, violence generally frustrates its own purpose while gentleness scarcely ever fails."

Hints of Love: Allow them to know what is in your heart as well as what is in your head.

After the Argument: *For him:* He can be stubborn.

You might have to cook his favorite meal and buy those tickets to the concert he wanted. In other words, make sure he knows you're going out of your way. *For her:* If she was wrong, you won't have to do too much at all. If you were wrong, expect it to cost you! Grovel, grovel, and then grovel some more. Expect to go see the movies she wants and eat in the restaurant she wants to for a while. Time will be the currency for payment on this one.

Romantic Places: Places of innovation bring romance: London; a university; Los Angeles, California.

Lucky Love Star: Aquariel—you will never lack devotion.

Beautiful Thought: When the train whistle blows in the middle of the night, it can put you on the right track.

Sharing Secrets: Tomorrow is another day, but why wait? You can do it all today. *For the gals:* Have your date filled from dusk to dawn, and then some. *For the guys:* You may find he needs a nap here and there, but he can last all day and all night if he has a reason.

Judith's Insights

About the Man: Hang on to your hat. This could be a bumpy ride. You must learn to understand him if you want to stick around. He is anything but false. He can be as true as they come. Sometimes he can be a bit too truthful. He feels that if he can't give it to you straight you don't need to be there. It takes time to understand him. Once you do, the ride will get much easier. He will infuse any situation with passion and life like you have never seen. He has a no-holds-barred philosophy toward life. He is here to live it to the fullest.

About the Woman: First impressions may not be accurate for this gal. She may seem hard and fast. Her nature is to have many desires and accomplishments and do what she has to meet them. This is one lady who will never have a problem working on a problem in the relationship until there is harmony. She can be a people watcher, and doesn't usually jump without checking out every square inch of what she is getting into. Get her noticed and she will love every minute of it. She may have a sharp tongue but is still known for being approachable.

Soul Mates: How can you not be hooked on someone made from the same mold you were? Aquarius and Aquarius is exactly that. If you can get Taurus and Scorpio to open up to the world, they will be much easier for you to handle. A match with Cancer and Virgo would require a magical imagination to ever get off the ground. Pisces and Aries know exactly how to capture your attention. You will love to be around such good-natured and generous people as Libra and Sagittarius. Leo has laid the gauntlet down. Are you ready for the game? Capricorn makes sure your exuberance doesn't get you in trouble. Gemini must be accepted for the fiery and flirty people they are.

Most Charming Characteristics: Loyal, talented, sincere.

Gifts: *For her:* angel collectibles. *For him:* unusual food for dinner.

Sensual Foods: Steak au poivre; cheesecake.

Romantic Flowers: Iris is your flower if you are the gal sending subtle messages. If you are the man, you will look for clematis. This flower's mental beauty creates emotional stimulation for you.

Best Date Nights: Wednesday; 1st and 28th of each month.

Colors of Passion: *For her:* sky blue, pale yellow. *For him:* indigo blue, bright blue.

The Perfect Wedding: Outlandish scenery—say, the view from an airplane, a Native American reservation, a national park—could enhance the sealing of your vows and make your day unique. You are moved by spectacular landscapes, and fresh air is a must. These, combined with your sweet sense of whimsy, will make your wedding day magical and filled with dreamy possibilities. Ideal setting: Arizona.

Wise Words: Robert Louis Stevenson: "An aim in life is the only fortune worth finding, and it is not to be found in foreign lands but in the heart itself."

Hints of Love: Keep both feet on the ground the first time you think you want to jump. This way you won't jump too high too soon.

After the Argument: *For him:* He can be stubborn. You might have to cook his favorite meal and buy those tickets to the concert he wanted. In other words, make sure he knows you're going out of your way. *For her:* If she was wrong, you won't have to do too much at all. If you were wrong, expect it to cost you! Grovel, grovel, and then grovel some more. Expect to go see the movies she wants and eat in the restaurant she wants to for a while. Time will be the currency for payment on this one.

Romantic Places: Places of distinction bring romance: Belgium; a five-star restaurant; Nashville, Tennessee.

Lucky Love Star: Aquariel—you will never lack devotion.

Beautiful Thought: Listening to the crickets, hear what the nighttime has to say.

Sharing Secrets: It may need to start with friendship. This isn't the consolation prize; it's the grand prize. *For the gals:* Go slow and allow it to grow one seed at a time. You won't need to push; it will all come in time. *For the guys:* A step here and a step there. Before he knows it, that friendship will be love.

Judith's Insights

About the Man: His ego can be a bit fragile, and he has a big one. If you want any kind of relationship with him, be cautious with criticism. You will never know how sensitive he is until you hurt his feelings by accident. If he works for you, you will get the best out of him by skimming through the negative and accenting the positive. You have heard of testing the water. Well, this guy likes to test the entire river before he goes in. He is cautious to a fault and may let good things pass him by because of his fear of being hurt. Give him time to jump in before you give up on him.

About the Woman: All of her ducks need to be in a row. Not just her house and home, but her emotions. You don't get more genuine than this girl. Yes, she is capable of heavy mood swings. She can have a habit of looking through rose-colored glasses. Don't take them away. Just suggest other alternatives. When she falls, she falls hard. You may find that she begins to resemble glue stuck to your shoe. She will be everywhere you go and listen to everything you say with utter concentration. Don't abuse this power you have over her if you want to make anything of it.

Soul Mates: You and a fellow Aquarius are carbon copies of each other. This will help you know what the other is thinking. The road ahead with Taurus and Scorpio will be difficult, but it will be fantastically rewarding in the end. Cancer's and Virgo's confusion between emotional hunger and love may cause major problems in the relationship. Expect to be wrapped up in Pisces's and Aries's magical dreams. Libra and Sagittarius will ignore any shortcomings you might have to make the relationship work. Don't let the bumps in the road with Leo throw you off course. With Capricorn, you will feel a great sense of security that will help you reach any goals you set. Gemini is full of energy and excitement. Instead of trying to change it you should accept it and enjoy it.

Most Charming Characteristics: Ambitious, loving, talented.

Gifts: *For her:* astrological chart. *For him:* meditation tapes.

Sensual Foods: Strawberry shortcake; pineapple; ham.

Romantic Flowers: Any rose of any color for the lady. Roses stand for love regardless of the color. Send them with orchids and you will be saying, "I love you." If you want a gentleman to know you think of him, send pansies, and forget-me-nots for true love.

Best Date Nights: Wednesday; 11th and 20th of each month.

Colors of Passion: *For her:* sky blue, pale yellow. *For him:* indigo blue, bright blue.

The Perfect Wedding: Outlandish scenery—say, the view from an airplane, a Native American reservation, a national park—could enhance the sealing of your vows and make your day unique. You are moved by spectacular landscapes, and fresh air is a must. These, combined with your sweet sense of whimsy, will make your wedding day magical and filled with dreamy possibilities. Ideal setting: Arizona.

Wise Words: William Gladstone: "Men have no business to talk of disenchantment; ideals are never realized—that is no reason why men should not persist, and toil, and hope."

Hints of Love: Laughter alleviates the tension, but so can understanding where another is sitting.

After the Argument: *For him:* He can be stubborn. You might have to cook his favorite meal and buy those tickets to the concert he wanted. In other words, make sure he knows you're going out of your way. *For her:* If she was wrong, you won't have to do too much at all. If you were wrong, expect it to cost you! Grovel, grovel, and then grovel some more. Expect to go see the movies she wants and eat in the restaurant she wants to for a while. Time will be the currency for payment on this one.

Romantic Places: Places of innovation bring romance: Hong Kong; virtual reality arcade; Chicago.

Lucky Love Star: Aquariel—you will never lack devotion.

Beautiful Thought: Cobwebs let you know you're never alone.

Sharing Secrets: This one needs to be the one and only, even if it is only the first date. *For the gals:* Don't talk about your past relationships. Do all you can to make her feel cherished from the first moment. *For the guys:* Play up your innocence. Let him take charge, even in paying the bill. He needs to wear the pants.

Judith's Insights

About the Man: You can't find a more loyal subject for your army, or even for a friend. He doesn't like things to get too intense. Handle this one with care. If you are in a mood, then stay away. It could create war that will take you both nowhere fast. He does have his rebellious side. He can love many, trust few, and always insist on paddling his own canoe. He can be in and out of a relationship at the same time. He won't jump in completely until he knows that you can be trusted with his heart. Once he does jump in, he will make quite a splash.

About the Woman: Don't corner this gal. Like a cornered rat, she could snap at you. She is idealistic and will create the best in any situation. She is more sensitive then one may think, and she does bleed when cut. Look at her strength as an asset instead of a liability. She loves to have plenty of people around her. If the one with the most friends wins, then consider her the winner. Sincerity at flirting may seem limited in the beginning. She has to move gradually into things before she will put all of her feelings into them. She can become a true and deep love if given the time.

Soul Mates: A union with another Aquarius will definitely appeal to your sense of self. Don't let your logic overshadow Taurus's and Scorpio's love for the dramatic. If you are willing to take on the challenge of Cancer and Virgo, you had better be ready for a difficult run. Pisces and Aries will stir your inner strengths to reach higher goals than you had ever imagined before. A partnership with Libra and Sagittarius is a dream made real and even better than the dream to begin with. The rise and fall of the Leo roller coaster is what makes it so much fun to ride. Any time you need a reality check, Capricorn will be there to provide it gently and honestly. Things are exactly what they seem with Gemini. Make sure you can accept what your eyes are telling you.

Most Charming Characteristics: Influential, passionate, kind.

Gifts: *For her:* intricately carved glass vase. *For him:* night out dancing.

Sensual Foods: Steak fondue; cheese fondue and French bread.

Romantic Flowers: These ladies like everyone to know how faithful they are, so send them violets. To surprise them send tulips. Men like their flowers the same as their relationships, unpretending. Send them camellias with white roses to show your affection.

Best Date Nights: Wednesday; 12th and 30th of each month.

Colors of Passion: *For her:* sky blue, pale yellow. *For him:* indigo blue, bright blue.

The Perfect Wedding: Outlandish scenery—say, the view from an airplane, a Native American reservation, a national park—could enhance the sealing of your vows and make your day unique. You are moved by spectacular landscapes, and fresh air is a must. These, combined with your sweet sense of whimsy, will make your wedding day magical and filled with dreamy possibilities. Ideal setting: Arizona.

Wise Words: W. S. Landor: "Those who are quite satisfied sit still and do nothing; those who are not quite satisfied are the sole benefactors of the world."

Hints of Love: Communication is important here.

A script isn't provided for you. You must write it for yourself.

After the Argument: *For him:* He can be stubborn. You might have to cook his favorite meal and buy those tickets to the concert he wanted. In other words, make sure he knows you're going out of your way. *For her:* If she was wrong, you won't have to do too much at all. If you were wrong, expect it to cost you! Grovel, grovel, and then grovel some more. Expect to go see the movies she wants and eat in the restaurant she wants to for a while. Time will be the currency for payment on this one.

Romantic Places: Places of distinction bring romance: Germany; ornate theater; New Orleans, Louisiana.

Lucky Love Star: Aquariel—you will never lack devotion.

Beautiful Thought: Windows are doors without handles.

Sharing Secrets: You need to remember never to forget. *For the gals:* Her birthday, holidays, and your anniversary. Even down to each dinner date. *For the guys:* His birthday, his laundry, his mother's birthday, and of course, him any other day of the year.

Judith's Insights

About the Man: Red rover, red rover, this life is boring. Please send me a new one, over. He likes the new and exciting. He loves a rowboat, a fast car, and a trip to anywhere with anyone. Keep it going. If this guys works for you, change his job or give him a title change occasionally. It will keep him loyal. He has a tremendous amount of hope and desire for the future. He will look for love all over the place and never find it because he won't let go of his emotions. Teach him to share his feelings with you if you have any hope of being this guy's partner.

About the Woman: She can be Little Miss Competitive. That is how and why she stimulates all of those around her. If she isn't calling, it's okay. To do the calling, she wants to be prodded. She has values and uses them. A bit on the intense side, but she is always loving. You have hit the jackpot. Not only does she have it all, she is willing to share it all with the right person. Before she does, you have to prove that you can be trusted with it. She is excellent at understanding the unusual happenings in one's life. She just may drive you crazy with her search for perfection.

Soul Mates: You love yourself so much you could do well with any Aquarius. Both Pisces and Aries will know how to charm you into their reaches. Libra and Sagittarius will intrigue you. They can make the best partner, no matter what kind you have in mind. Capricorn will bring you right down to earth and keep you safe. Gemini will love you for who you are as long as you are willing to do the same for them. You love it no matter how much you say that you don't. Leo will be your greatest challenge, depending on the mood you are in and how much both of you have grown. This could be the most fun you have had in a long time Taurus and Scorpio will test your patience and could drive you right off the deep end if you let them. With Cancer and Virgo, you would do better just to run, but the temptation is there. Just remember, where there is smoke there is usually fire.

Most Charming Characteristics: Ambitious, kind, generous.

Gifts: *For her:* onyx necklace. *For him:* telescope.

Sensual Foods: Baked Alaska; seafood.

Romantic Flowers: These ladies like men with taste. Show them you love style by sending fuchsia flowers, or even brightly colored wildflowers will do. To confuse this man, send him lilies along with bright daisies to show your innocence. Keep him guessing.

Best Date Nights: Wednesday; 4th and 22nd of each month.

Colors of Passion: *For her:* sky blue, pale yellow. *For him:* indigo blue, bright blue.

The Perfect Wedding: Outlandish scenery—say, the view from an airplane, a Native American reservation, a national park—could enhance the sealing of your vows and make your day unique. You are moved by spectacular landscapes, and fresh air is a must. These, combined with your sweet sense of whimsy, will make your wedding day magical and filled with dreamy possibilities. Ideal setting: Arizona.

Wise Words: Charles Dickens: "We are not all arrayed in two opposite ranks, the offensive and defensive. Some few there are who can walk between; who help the needy as they go; and take no part with either side."

Hints of Love: Don't dissect every minute of every day. Learn to appreciate each minute as it comes.

After the Argument: *For him:* He can be stubborn. You might have to cook his favorite meal and buy those tickets to the concert he wanted. In other words, make sure he knows you're going out of your way. *For her:* If she was wrong, you won't have to do too much at all. If you were wrong, expect it to cost you! Grovel, grovel, and then grovel some more. Expect to go see the movies she wants and eat in the restaurant she wants to for a while. Time will be the currency for payment on this one.

Romantic Places: Places of distinction bring romance: Switzerland; a bed-and-breakfast; Hyde Park, New York.

Lucky Love Star: Aquariel—you will never lack devotion.

Beautiful Thought: If you never spent time looking at a clock, think of how many more minutes you'd have.

Sharing Secrets: My house should be your house, especially if you don't have one of your own *For the gals:* All for one and one for all. Yours and mine must become ours. *For the guys:* If he needs to stand on ceremony, even for the first five minutes, it will be a definite turnoff for this one.

Judith's Insights

About the Man: Pay a lot of attention to him. If he works for you, answer his questions right away. He is confident and confusing. He can come off so secure you might think he needs nothing from you. What he really needs, though, is everything. He can have a heavy heart that comes from too many missed opportunities. He needs to be taught how to risk things to get what he dreams of. Without risk there is no joy in the prize. He can be more serious than he wants others to realize. Help him relax and enjoy what he has, and he will want to reach for more.

About the Woman: Just because she is smart and is a good "one-man show," don't make the mistake of not offering your help. She will take that as abandonment. She can bring home the bacon and fry it up, but never take her for granted or she will be gone. "Thank you" is something you must be able to say to her, but not only in words. She needs cuddling as if she were a teddy bear. She can put too much on her shoulders and then wonder how it got there in the first place. Don't tell her it is there. Just lift it off gently without her knowing.

FEBRUARY

Soul Mates: You and a fellow Aquarius will revel in all of your shared characteristics. Taurus and Scorpio will help you share all of the feelings you are uncomfortable with. Cancer and Virgo will retreat into themselves at the first sign of trouble, leaving you bewildered and ready to move on. Pisces and Aries make sure that your feet stay on the ground while you are enjoying the wonderful spell you are under. Libra's and Sagittarius's honesty and respect will leave you feeling very secure in the relationship. Things between you and Leo will be interesting indeed. Capricorn will give you a realistic view of all of your greatest dreams. Gemini can't be changed into something different. You will just have to accept this or move on.

Most Charming Characteristics: Artistic, staunch friend, loyal.

Gifts: *For her:* meditation tapes. *For him:* science set or microscope.

Sensual Foods: Strawberries and cream; meat loaf.

Romantic Flowers: Iris is your flower if you are the gal sending subtle messages. If you are the man, you will look for clematis. This flower's mental beauty creates emotional stimulation for you.

Best Date Nights: Wednesday; 10th and 28th of each month.

Colors of Passion: *For her:* sky blue, pale yellow. *For him:* indigo blue, bright blue.

The Perfect Wedding: Outlandish scenery—say, the view from an airplane, a Native American reservation, a national park—could enhance the sealing of your vows and make your day unique. You are moved by spectacular landscapes, and fresh air is a must. These, combined with your sweet sense of whimsy, will make your wedding day magical and filled with dreamy possibilities. Ideal setting: Arizona.

Wise Words: Haweis: "Love is a many-sided sacrifice; it means thoughtfulness for others; it means putting their good before self-gratification. Love is impulse, no doubt, but true love is impulse wisely directed."

Hints of Love: They only use the three magic words when they know they mean it, and they already know it is going to be said back to them.

After the Argument: *For him:* He can be stubborn. You might have to cook his favorite meal and buy those tickets to the concert he wanted. In other words, make sure he knows you're going out of your way. *For her:* If she was wrong, you won't have to do too much at all. If you were wrong, expect it to cost you! Grovel, grovel, and then grovel some more. Expect to go see the movies she wants and eat in the restaurant she wants to for a while. Time will be the currency for payment on this one.

Romantic Places: Places of innovation bring romance: Japan; a science museum; Disney World.

Lucky Love Star: Aquariel—you will never lack devotion.

Beautiful Thought: The grass is always greener on the other side, so look at your yard from across the street.

Sharing Secrets: Let them admire something about you first. Show them you have a sense of humor. *For the gals:* Hold her hand and then take her to the next step. *For the guys:* The way to his heart is definitely through his stomach.

Judith's Insights

About the Man: You might not think he is as thoughtful as he really can be. He most certainly has the wandering mind. When you look into his eyes, you will find his mind is not into space. His thoughts are firmly affixed to one subject or another. He means well, but you must get to know him to understand him. Kindness brings the best out of him. Today you will think he is a flake and tomorrow you will think he is a genius. His fascination with life itself can lead him to so many interesting subjects that he can get lost in thought for hours.

About the Woman: She may lack concentration, although she has great intellect. Her emotions run high, especially when put under any kind of stress. She can love you in the morning, hate you in the afternoon, and then love you again in the evening. You need patience to be this one's friend. When you don't take her actions so personally, things tend to work better. She is imaginative and is always looking for an adventure, especially in love. Don't allow this girl to get bored or you will find her wandering toward other loves.

Soul Mates: You and a fellow Aquarius are carbon copies of each other. This will help you know what the other is thinking. The road ahead with Taurus and Scorpio will be difficult, but it will be fantastically rewarding in the end. Cancer's and Virgo's confusion between emotional hunger and love may cause major problems in the relationship. Expect to be wrapped up in Pisces's and Aries's magical dreams. Libra and Sagittarius will ignore any shortcomings you might have to make the relationship work. Don't let the bumps in the road with Leo throw you off course. With Capricorn, you will feel a great sense of security that will help you reach any goals you set. Gemini is full of energy and excitement. Instead of trying to change it you should accept it and enjoy it.

Most Charming Characteristics: Charming, dreamer, conversationalist.

Gifts: *For her:* dinner at an unusual restaurant. *For him:* tickets to the circus.

Sensual Foods: Cherry-apple pie; beef Stroganoff.

Romantic Flowers: Any rose of any color for the lady. Roses stand for love regardless of the color. Send them with orchids and you will be saying, "I love you." If you want a gentleman to know you think of him, send pansies, and forget-me-nots for true love.

Best Date Nights: Wednesday; 2nd and 20th of each month.

Colors of Passion: *For her:* sky blue, pale yellow. *For him:* indigo blue, bright blue.

The Perfect Wedding: Outlandish scenery—say, the view from an airplane, a Native American reservation, a national park—could enhance the sealing of your vows and make your day unique. You are moved by spectacular landscapes, and fresh air is a must. These, combined with your sweet sense of whimsy, will make your wedding day magical and filled with dreamy possibilities. Ideal setting: Arizona.

Wise Words: Charles Dickens: "Natural affections and instincts . . . are the most beautiful of the Almighty's works, but like other beautiful works of His, they must be reared and fostered."

Hints of Love: Remember to keep the dating fun. Don't act like you are married before your time.

After the Argument: *For him:* He can be stubborn. You might have to cook his favorite meal and buy those tickets to the concert he wanted. In other words, make sure he knows you're going out of your way. *For her:* If she was wrong, you won't have to do too much at all. If you were wrong, expect it to cost you! Grovel, grovel, and then grovel some more. Expect to go see the movies she wants and eat in the restaurant she wants to for a while. Time will be the currency for payment on this one.

Romantic Places: Places of distinction bring romance: Britain; a sushi bar; Houston, Texas.

Lucky Love Star: Aquariel—you will never lack devotion.

Beautiful Thought: Style is made by fashion; class is made by actions.

Sharing Secrets: Give them the opportunity to notice you first. *For the gals:* They love to be adored; love at first sight. *For the guys:* Remember to always let them believe it was their idea.

Judith's Insights

About the Man: He does better when you let him believe he is the one in charge. He doesn't necessarily have to be the one actually in charge. He just has to believe he is. He is a good instigator but may lose interest after a while. Let him get things started, and then you take over. You may have to teach him style, even though he thinks he has it already. He is practical, but responsibility can waver depending on the company he is keeping. He loves feeling needed, so ask him for his help whenever you can.

About the Woman: This one loves money and anything it can purchase. She is capable of making those almighty dollars and spending them twice as fast. She can be generous, but can go through her cheap moods. She is drawn to the unique and unusual, especially when it comes to the company she keeps. Expect to be hanging outdoors with this gal. When she falls in love it should last forever. Even when the relationship doesn't last forever the love will. She loves to be cuddled and cherished. Her emotions may run high but she is low maintenance.

Soul Mates: A union with another Aquarius will definitely appeal to your sense of self. Don't let your logic overshadow Taurus's and Scorpio's love for the dramatic. If you are willing to take on the challenge of Cancer and Virgo, you had better be ready for a difficult run. Pisces and Aries will stir your inner strengths to reach higher goals than you had ever imagined before. A partnership with Libra or Sagittarius is a dream made real and even better than the dream to begin with. The rise and fall of the Leo roller coaster is what makes it so much fun to ride. Any time you need a reality check, Capricorn will be there to provide it gently and honestly. Things are exactly what they seem with Gemini. Make sure you can accept what your eyes are telling you.

Most Charming Characteristics: Generous, good-natured, self-restraint.

Gifts: *For her:* tickets to a performance art show. *For him:* astrological chart.

Sensual Foods: Hot fudge sundae with all the trimmings; shepherd's pie.

Romantic Flowers: These ladies like everyone to know how faithful they are, so send them violets. To surprise them send tulips. Men like their flowers the same as their relationships, unpretending. Send them camellias with white roses to show your affection.

Best Date Nights: Wednesday; 12th and 21st of each month.

Colors of Passion: *For her:* sky blue, pale yellow. *For him:* indigo blue, bright blue.

The Perfect Wedding: Outlandish scenery—say, the view from an airplane, a Native American reservation, a national park—could enhance the sealing of your vows and make your day unique. You are moved by spectacular landscapes, and fresh air is a must. These, combined with your sweet sense of whimsy, will make your wedding day magical and filled with dreamy possibilities. Ideal setting: Arizona.

Wise Words: Anonymous: "Where true love bestows its sweetness, where true friendship lays its hand, dwells all greatness, all completeness, all the wealth of every land."

Hints of Love: Make sure you go on more than one date before you jump to conclusions on liking and disliking.

After the Argument: *For him:* He can be stubborn. You might have to cook his favorite meal and buy those tickets to the concert he wanted. In other words, make sure he knows you're going out of your way. *For her:* If she was wrong, you won't have to do too much at all. If you were wrong, expect it to cost you! Grovel, grovel, and then grovel some more. Expect to go see the movies she wants and eat in the restaurant she wants to for a while. Time will be the currency for payment on this one.

Romantic Places: Places of innovation bring romance: New York City; an air show; Silicon Valley.

Lucky Love Star: Aquariel—you will never lack devotion.

Beautiful Thought: A true friend is the one you never think is there for you but always is.

Sharing Secrets: This one loves a challenge. *For the gals:* Be consistently inconsistent until you have them hooked. *For the guys:* This one loves to play catch. You may feel like a yo-yo, but as long as he is calling that's all that matters.

Judith's Insights

About the Man: Who is better than he is? Not too many men you will meet. He seems to have it all, although he doesn't. Just don't tell him that he doesn't. He feels as if he has what any man wants and is very happy about it. There are no flies on him. He won't allow others to get in his way. You can definitely expect him to get in your way, though. He complains about his family if given the chance. Not to say they don't give a reason to complain, but he doesn't need a reason to do so in the first place.

About the Woman: What she doesn't know won't hurt her. This definitely rings true with this one. If it isn't positive, then she does not want to hear it. Positive input only, please. She has a strong heart and an even stronger mind. She doesn't appreciate a catlike environment. Don't bring up petty arguments. This girl can walk and chew gum at the same time, just for starters. She has many hidden talents but won't mind revealing them to the right person. She wants a partner who is willing to do what it takes to keep things moving. If you do your work, then she will do hers.

Soul Mates: You love yourself so much you could do well with any Aquarius. Both Pisces and Aries will know how to charm you into their reaches. Libra and Sagittarius will intrigue you. They can make the best partner, no matter what kind you have in mind. Capricorn will bring you right down to earth and keep you safe. You love it no matter how much you say that you don't. Hooking up with Gemini will work only if you don't try to mold them into something they aren't. Leo will be your greatest challenge, depending on the mood you are in and how much both of you have grown. This could be the most fun you have had in a long time. Taurus and Scorpio will test your patience and could drive you right off the deep end if you let them. With Cancer and Virgo, you would do better just to run, but the temptation is there. Just remember, where there is smoke there is usually fire.

Most Charming Characteristics: Honest, shrewd, strong personality.

Gifts: *For her:* dance class. *For him:* leather journal.

Sensual Foods: Whipped cream, strawberries, brown sugar, and heavy cream.

Romantic Flowers: These ladies like men with taste. Show them you love style by sending fuchsia flowers, or even brightly colored wildflowers will do. To confuse this man, send him lilies along with bright daisies to show your innocence. Keep him guessing.

Best Date Nights: Wednesday; 4th and 31 of each month.

Colors of Passion: *For her:* sky blue, pale yellow. *For him:* indigo blue, bright blue.

The Perfect Wedding: Outlandish scenery—say, the view from an airplane, a Native American reservation, a national park—could enhance the sealing of your vows and make your day unique. You are moved by spectacular landscapes, and fresh air is a must. These, combined with your sweet sense of whimsy, will make your wedding day magical and filled with dreamy possibilities. Ideal setting: Arizona.

Wise Words: Gail Hamilton: "Wisdom dwells in blue skies and broad sunshine and the wide hills and the indefinite waters, in peace of mind, freedom, ownership of the earth."

Hints of Love: Don't act too needy too soon. It may push this relationship away.

After the Argument: *For him:* He can be stubborn. You might have to cook his favorite meal and buy those tickets to the concert he wanted. In other words, make sure he knows you're going out of your way. *For her:* If she was wrong, you won't have to do too much at all. If you were wrong, expect it to cost you! Grovel, grovel, and then grovel some more. Expect to go see the movies she wants and eat in the restaurant she wants to for a while. Time will be the currency for payment on this one.

Romantic Places: Places of distinction bring romance: Russia; an art museum; Savannah, Georgia.

Lucky Love Star: Aquariel—you will never lack devotion.

Beautiful Thought: Looking through rose-colored glasses is fine, but even they may need Windex.

Sharing Secrets: This is a family person at heart; your presence is most important. *For the gals:* Make sure you go to Sunday dinner with her family when you are invited. *For the guys:* If you don't like his mom, you might have a hard time catching this one.

Judith's Insights

About the Man: His hobby is his work. His entertainment is his work. Work is everything to him. You have to make it interesting or he will not stray from it. He is a challenge, even to his mother, although he adores her. If you are working for this guy, you must prove yourself. Only then will you receive pats on the back. He has the looks, smarts, and sensitivity to stand out in a crowd, and he does. He will put as much effort into playing as he does working as long as the game is exciting and competitive. Challenge him to do his best and he will do even better than that.

About the Woman: It may take her some time to get where she wants to go. Rest assured, however, this gal knows just what she wants. She is not in a hurry to settle into anything too quickly. There is still much to be seen in this world and she wants to see it all. Her friends are from kindergarten. Once you have reached her inner circle, odds are you will be there for life. You wouldn't be there if she did not think you had what it takes. She is not exactly cheap, but she would rather spend your money than hers. Maybe that is why she always has money.

Soul Mates: When looking for a compatible sign, look no further than your own, Aquarius. Taurus's and Scorpio's terrible temper and tendency to erupt in a fury will be simply irrational to you. The match of wits with Cancer and Virgo happens fast. It will be strained just as fast if you don't really get to know each other. You will be fascinated with Pisces and Aries charisma. A union with Libra and Sagittarius could be picture-perfect. Leo is a truly worthy adversary. This could be a lot of fun. A Capricorn can keep your feet on the ground while you still have the ability to fly as high as you need to. Don't go in with the intent of changing Gemini. Learn to value them for who they are.

Most Charming Characteristics: Dreamer, generous, kind.

Gifts: *For her:* natural-scented body wash. *For him:* unusual food for dinner.

Sensual Foods: Puddings and pastry of all kinds.

Romantic Flowers: You are the lady of distinction and only carnations will do. Any mix of colors with sprays of mignonette. Sweet peas or red carnations will appeal to this man's heart.

Best Date Nights: Wednesday; 4th and 5th of each month.

Colors of Passion: *For her:* sky blue, pale yellow. *For him:* indigo blue, bright blue.

The Perfect Wedding: Outlandish scenery—say, the view from an airplane, a Native American reservation, a national park—could enhance the sealing of your vows and make your day unique. You are moved by spectacular landscapes, and fresh air is a must. These, combined with your sweet sense of whimsy, will make your wedding day magical and filled with dreamy possibilities. Ideal setting: Arizona.

Wise Words: Blaise Pascal: "All our dignity comes from thought. We are ennobled by this and not by space or duration which we cannot fill. Let us endeavor then to think rightly."

Hints of Love: Keep it fun. Look for new and exciting things to do, especially if you are in a long-term relationship.

After the Argument: *For him:* He can be stubborn. You might have to cook his favorite meal and buy those tickets to the concert he wanted. In other words, make sure he knows you're going out of your way. *For her:* If she was wrong, you won't have to do too much at all. If you were wrong, expect it to cost you! Grovel, grovel, and then grovel some more. Expect to go see the movies she wants and eat in the restaurant she wants to for a while. Time will be the currency for payment on this one.

Romantic Places: Places of innovation bring romance: London; a university; Los Angeles, California.

Lucky Love Star: Aquariel—you will never lack devotion.

Beautiful Thought: Relationships really start to work when you realize there are many kinds.

Sharing Secrets: Everything in its good time. This one works slowly, but when it is time to pick up speed, watch out. *For the gals:* Don't go by the obvious. Read between the lines. As long as the invitation is being offered, go full speed ahead. *For the guys:* Just when you thought you should walk away, he'll say, "I love you." Talk about confusing.

Judith's Insights

About the Man: He will have fun at a party only if he is hosting it. Maybe this is because he feels better when he is in charge. Even if he isn't throwing the party he will mingle with everyone just like a true host. He can have fun in his own way, but other times he will feel like he is stuck in neutral. There is no middle when it comes to his energy. He can either run a marathon or can't get off the couch. You may find he whines a little when he doesn't get his own way. Step away and let him wallow. When he is done with the self-pity he will bounce right back to his old self.

About the Woman: She stands up for everyone else and then sits down for herself. Words will come easily only when she is writing or saying them on someone else's behalf. You can make her cry very easily. She can change with the company she keeps. She thinks of herself as independent. I think she is more impressionable. Show her how to be her own person while still having fun with you. She loves romance. There is almost an ache in her heart for it. She will expect no more from others than they are capable of giving. She lives by the Golden Rule.

Soul Mates: With so much in common with another Aquarius, you can't go wrong. Taurus and Scorpio are powerful and stubborn. If you are attracted to each other enough, they will stick with you through thick and thin. You might be enthralled by Cancer's and Virgo's powerful imagination, but things for you guys in the real world will be much stickier. Take delight in the spell Pisces and Aries will cast upon you. Things with Libra and Sagittarius are a perfect example of what can go right. Leo is like a bet. It can be risky, but it could also end in a win-win situation. You and Capricorn will balance each other perfectly. Gemini needs to be loved for who they are. Accept their quirks and your life will be richer. If you are willing to accept each other for what you truly are, then by all means go for it.

Most Charming Characteristics: Witty, prudent, adaptable.

Gifts: *For her:* astrological chart. *For him:* meditation tapes.

Sensual Foods: Champagne with strawberries; fillet of sole.

Romantic Flowers: You love it when you get tulips, declaring love. When you receive a variety, it shows how hopelessly in love your partner is. He will just love a single rose. This shows him you understand his pleasures.

Best Date Nights: Wednesday; 6th and 15th of each month.

Colors of Passion: *For her:* sky blue, pale yellow. *For him:* indigo blue, bright blue.

The Perfect Wedding: Outlandish scenery—say, the view from an airplane, a Native American reservation, a national park—could enhance the sealing of your vows and make your day unique. You are moved by spectacular landscapes, and fresh air is a must. These, combined with your sweet sense of whimsy, will make your wedding day magical and filled with dreamy possibilities. Ideal setting: Arizona.

Wise Words: Edmund Burke: "Love for one's fellows, and a brave heart, are the most useful gifts to go through life with."

Hints of Love: This one is a cautious soul. You may have to find a way to go around to the back door.

After the Argument: *For him:* He can be stubborn. You might have to cook his favorite meal and buy those tickets to the concert he wanted. In other words, make sure he knows you're going out of your way. *For her:* If she was wrong, you won't have to do too much at all. If you were wrong, expect it to cost you! Grovel, grovel, and then grovel some more. Expect to go see the movies she wants and eat in the restaurant she wants to for a while. Time will be the currency for payment on this one.

Romantic Places: Places of distinction bring romance: Belgium; a five-star restaurant; Nashville, Tennessee.

Lucky Love Star: Aquariel—you will never lack devotion.

Beautiful Thought: The strength of emotions between two people is the marriage.

Sharing Secrets: This one is a charmer, perhaps even fickle. *For the gals:* If you are patient enough to stick around, this one is worth the wait. *For the guys:* If there is enough time on the clock, stick around past three months. Then maybe he will have noticed you are there.

Judith's Insights

About the Man: He knows what is on your mind. This one has a lot of intuition but does not like to admit it. He likes to keep his hand a secret until all bets have been put in the pot. He can be challenging, even as a friend. People who work with him see a better-adjusted personality. Once things get to the personal level, he will become oddly irresponsible. Time and patience on your part will level him out. His energy is matched only by his sensitivity. Getting him to settle down and live a "normal" life will not work for this guy. Commitment is fine without the ball and chain.

About the Woman: She can take on any work or job responsibilities, but not those that are related to emotions. She not only runs from them, she hides from them. You may have to trap her at times and make her communicate. She can make a case for anyone else more convincing than saying the sky is blue. Her words just won't come when they are about herself. She is incredibly well rounded, but needs constant stimulation. Find ways of making her laugh at herself. Once she is more comfortable with her insecurities she will be more accepting of yours.

Soul Mates: Looking at a fellow Aquarius is like looking at a reflection of yourself. If you don't like what you see, you have to look inside yourself before you look inside your partner. Taurus and Scorpio might be troubled by your judgment-free nature. Ease it up a bit. You might not learn not to go near the fire of Cancer and Virgo until you have been scalded by it. Pisces's and Aries's magnetism will pull you right to them. Libra and Sagittarius are the personification of whatever image you have of a great relationship. Sharpen your edges; the ride with Leo will be a great one. When you get in over your head, Capricorn is there to help you swim to shore. Gemini must be appreciated for what they are instead of molded into your vision of what they should be.

Most Charming Characteristics: Witty, loving, perceptive.

Gifts: *For her:* angel collectibles. *For him:* photography class.

Sensual Foods: Chocolates; poached salmon; flambé; filet mignon; potatoes.

Romantic Flowers: Send this girl sunflowers if you want her to know you adore her. You may even add some poppies for a splash of extravagance. His desire for sport and play will be understood when you send him hyacinth and geranium.

Best Date Nights: Wednesday; 15th and 24th of each month.

Colors of Passion: *For her:* sky blue, pale yellow. *For him:* indigo blue, bright blue.

The Perfect Wedding: Outlandish scenery—say, the view from an airplane, a Native American reservation, a national park—could enhance the sealing of your vows and make your day unique. You are moved by spectacular landscapes, and fresh air is a must. These, combined with your sweet sense of whimsy, will make your wedding day magical and filled with dreamy possibilities. Ideal setting: Arizona.

Wise Words: Charles Dickens: "What joy and cheerfulness it wakes up within us to see all nature beaming in brightness and sunshine!"

Hints of Love: Passion must be in the picture at all times or you could lose this one's attention quick.

After the Argument: *For him:* He can be stubborn. You might have to cook his favorite meal and buy those tickets to the concert he wanted. In other words, make sure he knows you're going out of your way. *For her:* If she was wrong, you won't have to do too much at all. If you were wrong, expect it to cost you! Grovel, grovel, and then grovel some more. Expect to go see the movies she wants and eat in the restaurant she wants to for a while. Time will be the currency for payment on this one.

Romantic Places: Places of innovation bring romance: Hong Kong; virtual reality arcade; Chicago.

Lucky Love Star: Aquariel—you will never lack devotion.

Beautiful Thought: Birds sing, bells ring, a baby cries—the simple sounds of life.

Sharing Secrets: If you are looking for love, then you have found the right mate. *For the gals:* This one could be stubborn. It may take forever to get a relationship started, but it is as solid as they come. *For the guys:* Even when he is ready, he might not be willing and able. He will put you through more obstacles than any course. Be patient.

Judith's Insights

About the Man: If you can't find him, he is probably out rescuing someone or something. *Activist* is not the word to describe him. *World savior* is a better term. He has the character to be a nurturer or a caretaker. He goes overboard when he is interested in a person. He is sensitive to a fault, and is known to wear his heart on his sleeve. Be careful of how you tell him bad news—or anything, for that matter. He is always on the run, trying to do everything on his to-do list and visiting his friends. Help him sit down and relax and he will look at you in a new way.

About the Woman: What a great humanitarian this girl is. She will seldom leave room for anyone or anything else. Stand close and lend a helping hand to her cause and you will be noticed. You can put anything before her needs in the beginning. Once she has committed, however, she will want more attention. Ask her for ten minutes and she will give you twenty. Demand ten and she will give you five. You will get much further with her if you use a nice approach. She will never expect love to work out. Maybe that is why she works so hard at it.

Soul Mates: Fix your eyes on a fellow Aquarius and it will be as if you are looking at yourself. You may have to fight to be with Taurus and Scorpio, but you may be all the richer for the struggle. No matter how much you believe you can get around the blaze of Cancer and Virgo, you will be wiser to take another course entirely. Imagine the fun to be ensnared by such delightful captors as Pisces and Aries. Talk about perfect. You can't go wrong with Libra and Sagittarius. A relationship with Leo will test your creativity. You need to learn to settle down while your Capricorn needs to learn to play around. A pairing with Gemini can work only if you learn to accept them for who they are.

Most Charming Characteristics: Loving, economical, loyal.

Gifts: *For her:* intricately carved glass vase. *For him:* night out dancing.

Sensual Foods: Caviar; beef tenderloin; potatoes au gratin.

Romantic Flowers: Rhododendron will let her be on the lookout for trouble. Throw in some chrysanthemum and she'll know it is you she will be looking out for. Cactus will show him warmth. Yellow daffodil is a token of a good time had by all. Chivalry is not dead.

Best Date Nights: Wednesday; 8th and 17th of each month.

Colors of Passion: *For her:* sky blue, pale yellow. *For him:* indigo blue, bright blue.

The Perfect Wedding: Outlandish scenery—say, the view from an airplane, a Native American reservation, a national park—could enhance the sealing of your vows and make your day unique. You are moved by spectacular landscapes, and fresh air is a must. These, combined with your sweet sense of whimsy, will make your wedding day magical and filled with dreamy possibilities. Ideal setting: Arizona.

Wise Words: Robert Browning: "Man must pass from old to new, / From vain to real, from mistake to fact, / From what once seemed good to what now proves best."

Hints of Love: A random act of kindness will go a long way with this one. What can you do for them today?

After the Argument: *For him:* He can be stubborn. You might have to cook his favorite meal and buy those tickets to the concert he wanted. In other words, make sure he knows you're going out of your way. *For her:* If she was wrong, you won't have to do too much at all. If you were wrong, expect it to cost you! Grovel, grovel, and then grovel some more. Expect to go see the movies she wants and eat in the restaurant she wants to for a while. Time will be the currency for payment on this one.

Romantic Places: Places of distinction bring romance: Germany; ornate theater; New Orleans, Louisiana.

Lucky Love Star: Aquariel—you will never lack devotion.

Beautiful Thought: Fantasies are dreams that we fear will never happen.

Sharing Secrets: If you can hang around and give constant stimulation, this could be your mate. *For the gals:* She is always looking for the Exit sign. Don't show her where it is or she will be gone. *For the guys:* Fast cars, fast food; he likes everything that goes fast. Put on your running shoes. If you can keep up, then he is yours.

Judith's Insights

About the Man: You will find that he has friends from all walks of life. He can make being popular a career. You will find them on every guest list. This one could be having a beer with his enemy. He will never know what lonely is. You will very seldom see him alone. If at first you don't succeed, try, try again. All of a sudden he may notice you or even be ready to give you a chance. He can be his own worst enemy, but he will always make the best of friends. There is nothing he would not do for someone he cares for, and he expects the same in return.

About the Woman: This is a lady with an agenda. When she sets her mind to something, no person can change it. Her anger only lasts five minutes, but then so can everything else in her life. You will find her needing constant change. If you get her angry, don't expect her to call until you have apologized more than once. This footloose and fancy-free girl takes disappointment more seriously than you may think. She can be only as good as her mate. If she is with someone who is congenial and loving, she will be also. What you have in yourself is what you will find in her.

Soul Mates: How can you not be hooked on someone made from the same mold you were? Aquarius and Aquarius are exactly that. If you can get Taurus and Scorpio to open up to the world, they will be much easier for you to handle. A match with Cancer and Virgo would require a magical imagination to ever get off the ground. Pisces and Aries know exactly how to capture your attention. You will love to be around such good-natured and generous people as Libra and Sagittarius. Leo has laid the gauntlet down. Are you ready for the game? Capricorn makes sure your exuberance doesn't get you in trouble. Gemini must be accepted for the fiery and flirty people they are.

Most Charming Characteristics: Loyal, energetic, generous.

Gifts: *For her:* onyx necklace. *For him:* telescope.

Sensual Foods: Passionfruit; fillet of sole almondine.

Romantic Flowers: The magnolias you send her will let her know you will be around for a while to come. Petunia is to say never despair. Holly will let him know what he is getting into. Pansy will keep you in his thoughts.

Best Date Nights: Wednesday; 9th and 27th of each month.

Colors of Passion: *For her:* sky blue, pale yellow. *For him:* indigo blue, bright blue.

The Perfect Wedding: Outlandish scenery—say, the view from an airplane, a Native American reservation, a national park—could enhance the sealing of your vows and make your day unique. You are moved by spectacular landscapes, and fresh air is a must. These, combined with your sweet sense of whimsy, will make your wedding day magical and filled with dreamy possibilities. Ideal setting: Arizona.

Wise Words: Robert Browning: "Pause here upon this strip of time / Allotted you out of eternity."

Hints of Love: Family and friends are important to this one. Don't try to alienate them or it will definitely backfire on you.

After the Argument: *For him:* He can be stubborn. You might have to cook his favorite meal and buy those tickets to the concert he wanted. In other words, make sure he knows you're going out of your way. *For her:* If she was wrong, you won't have to do too much at all. If you were wrong, expect it to cost you! Grovel, grovel, and then grovel some more. Expect to go see the movies she wants and eat in the restaurant she wants to for a while. Time will be the currency for payment on this one.

Romantic Places: Places of distinction bring romance: Switzerland; a bed-and-breakfast; Hyde Park, New York.

Lucky Love Star: Aquariel—you will never lack devotion.

Beautiful Thought: The one who makes you laugh will be the one you'll always remember.

Sharing Secrets: This one may seem like a lot of work. They just need the basics: love, loyalty, and respect. *For the gals:* If you can show her your best side right from the beginning, it may work. Be careful of fluff, because she will see right through it. *For the guys:* He loves to be loved. Give him plenty of attention, even if you think you don't stand a chance. Perseverance will win here.

Judith's Insights

About the Man: You will think he is a big bully at times. At other times, he will be a pussycat who just wants to curl up on your lap. He isn't necessarily moody but can change with his environment. Depending on the situation, he will bring out the best or the worst in himself. There is certainly both in there. Approach him with kindness and you can accomplish anything. Try to force him to give you something he is not ready to give and he will turn on you. The best way to his heart is to give him time to get used to the idea of being part of a team.

About the Woman: Where there is smoke there is fire. She can also be a fun-loving individual. You just can't cross her and get away with it. Even during conflict, if you treat her with respect that is exactly what you will get in return. Don't take her kindness for weakness. She will give to you until it hurts before you start to expect it. Once you start getting used to it she will step back and wait to see if you will give to her. She will have joy in her heart as long as you are respectful. If you treat her like a lady she can be a breath of fresh air in any environment.

Soul Mates: You and a fellow Aquarius will revel in all of your shared characteristics. Taurus and Scorpio will help you share all of the feelings you are uncomfortable with. Cancer and Virgo will retreat into themselves at the first sign of trouble, leaving you bewildered and ready to move on. Pisces and Aries make sure that your feet stay on the ground while you are enjoying the wonderful spell you are under. Libra's and Sagittarius's honesty and respect will leave you feeling very secure in the relationship. Things between you and Leo will be interesting indeed. Capricorn will give you a realistic view of all of your greatest dreams. Gemini can't be changed into something different. You will just have to accept this or move on.

Most Charming Characteristics: Energetic, kind, affectionate.

Gifts: *For her:* meditation tapes. *For him:* science set or microscope.

Sensual Foods: Peaches; mousse; shrimp.

Romantic Flowers: Iris is your flower if you are the gal sending subtle messages. If you are the man, you will look for clematis. This flower's mental beauty creates emotional stimulation for you.

Best Date Nights: Wednesday; 10th and 28th of each month.

Colors of Passion: *For her:* sky blue, pale yellow. *For him:* indigo blue, bright blue.

The Perfect Wedding: Outlandish scenery—say, the view from an airplane, a Native American reservation, a national park—could enhance the sealing of your vows and make your day unique. You are moved by spectacular landscapes, and fresh air is a must. These, combined with your sweet sense of whimsy, will make your wedding day magical and filled with dreamy possibilities. Ideal setting: Arizona.

Wise Words: Charles Dickens: "Old Time, that greatest o'er us although we refuse it, nature thro' dust clouds we fling her."

Hints of Love: Show others how much you adore this partner. They will revel in how others notice.

After the Argument: *For him:* He can be stubborn. You might have to cook his favorite meal and buy those tickets to the concert he wanted. In other words, make sure he knows you're going out of your way. *For her:* If she was wrong, you won't have to do too much at all. If you were wrong, expect it to cost you! Grovel, grovel, and then grovel some more. Expect to go see the movies she wants and eat in the restaurant she wants to for a while. Time will be the currency for payment on this one.

Romantic Places: Places of innovation bring romance: Japan; a science museum; Disney World.

Lucky Love Star: Aquariel—you will never lack devotion.

Beautiful Thought: Candles are our own little heavenly lights.

Sharing Secrets: They're looking for love, but that is just their little secret. *For the gals:* Why shouldn't they want to be loved? Of course they do, but they want you to do all of the work. *For the guys:* You must prove yourself repeatedly. Don't expect too much until he knows you are under his thumb.

Judith's Insights

About the Man: He never looks before he leaps. He will usually find himself paying for it the hard way. So does everyone around him. He can have a selfish side that can become obvious in a work environment. He likes to look out for number one. If he likes you, he usually loves you. If he doesn't, it will take a lot to change his mind. This guy will have trouble keeping his good and bad traits in balance. Competition is something that makes him thrive, but it can also get out of control. Just ask his siblings! Letting him win in small situations may help when he loses in the big ones.

About the Woman: Learn to take the sting out of the bell. In other words, once you find out what works and what doesn't, use it to maintain a relationship with this gal. She allows others in only when she feels safe. You could work with her for a year and never know her. Then she will suddenly feel like your best friend. She can be loyal to her mate for longer than the average person. Even when someone walks all over her she will take it until she finally explodes. Once this girl walks away she will be extremely hard to turn around. You will get exactly what you give here.

Soul Mates: You and a fellow Aquarius are carbon copies of each other. This will help you know what the other is thinking. The road ahead with Taurus and Scorpio will be difficult, but it will be fantastically rewarding in the end. Cancer's and Virgo's confusion between emotional hunger and love may cause major problems in the relationship. Expect to be wrapped up in Pisces's and Aries's magical dreams. Libra and Sagittarius will ignore any shortcomings you might have to make the relationship work. Don't let the bumps in the road with Leo throw you off course. With Capricorn, you will feel a great sense of security that will help you reach any goals you set. Gemini is full of energy and excitement. Instead of trying to change this, you should accept it and enjoy it.

Most Charming Characteristics: Talented, passionate, exciting.

Gifts: *For her:* dinner at an unusual restaurant. *For him:* tickets to the circus.

Sensual Foods: Kiwis; cantaloupes; strawberries.

Romantic Flowers: Any rose of any color for the lady. Roses stand for love regardless of the color. Send them with orchids and you will be saying, "I love you." If you want a gentleman to know you think of him, send pansies, and forget-me-nots for true love.

Best Date Nights: Wednesday; 2nd and 11th of each month.

Colors of Passion: *For her:* sky blue, pale yellow. *For him:* indigo blue, bright blue.

The Perfect Wedding: Outlandish scenery—say, the view from an airplane, a Native American reservation, a national park—could enhance the sealing of your vows and make your day unique. You are moved by spectacular landscapes, and fresh air is a must. These, combined with your sweet sense of whimsy, will make your wedding day magical and filled with dreamy possibilities. Ideal setting: Arizona.

Wise Words: Robert Browning: "But let the sun shine! wherefore repine? / With thee to lead me, oh day of mine."

Hints of Love: Don't overdo it (dress, attention) too soon or this one will run. Wait until you have them hooked before you become outrageous.

After the Argument: *For him:* He can be stubborn. You might have to cook his favorite meal and buy those tickets to the concert he wanted. In other words, make sure he knows you're going out of your way. *For her:* If she was wrong, you won't have to do too much at all. If you were wrong, expect it to cost you! Grovel, grovel, and then grovel some more. Expect to go see the movies she wants and eat in the restaurant she wants to for a while. Time will be the currency for payment on this one.

Romantic Places: Places of distinction bring romance: Britain; a sushi bar; Houston, Texas.

Lucky Love Star: Aquariel—you will never lack devotion.

Beautiful Thought: Next time a raindrop falls, try to catch it before it catches you.

Sharing Secrets: You had better be ready to pull out your romantic side if you want this to work. *For the gals:* Fireplaces, walks on the beach, or even winning a bear at the local carnival. *For the guys:* When you are out shopping, bring him something home. Even if it is silly, he will love the thought.

Judith's Insights

About the Man: Don't overcomplicate the picture. Be precise and talk about the issues. Otherwise, you will lose this guy. He loves attention and he will find it any way he can. You will find that he becomes a best friend with a stranger in a minute. He is likable and open-minded. That brings a lot to his door. It will take time for him to shuffle through what comes his way to find the good parts. Prove yourself worthy by how you treat others around you. You will capture the attention of this humanitarian by simply being the best version of yourself.

About the Woman: She is quiet and demure, but that does not mean that you can mess with her. She makes new friends while keeping the old. She can be strong when she needs to be. It is likely that she will be the boss someday. If her quirkiness brings laughter to lunch, others tend to be drawn to her. She loves attention. Any type of attention will do, but she especially enjoys compliments. Pamper this girl and you will have her wrapped around your finger. She makes it easy to be kind to her because she is always kind to those who love and care for her.

Soul Mates: A union with another Aquarius will definitely appeal to your sense of self. Don't let your logic overshadow Taurus's and Scorpio's love for the dramatic. If you are willing to take on the challenge of Cancer and Virgo, you had better be ready for a difficult run. Pisces and Aries will stir your inner strengths to reach higher goals than you had ever imagined before. A partnership with Libra and Sagittarius is a dream made real and even better than the dream to begin with. The rise and fall of the Leo roller coaster is what makes it so much fun to ride. Any time you need a reality check, Capricorn will be there to provide it gently and honestly. Things are exactly what they seem with Gemini. Make sure you can accept what your eyes are telling you.

Most Charming Characteristics: Charming, clear thinker, artistic.

Gifts: *For her:* tickets to a performance art show. *For him:* astrological chart.

Sensual Foods: Caramel and chocolate syrup on anything.

Romantic Flowers: These ladies like everyone to know how faithful they are, so send them violets. To surprise them send tulips. Men like their flowers the same as their relationships, unpretending. Send them camellias with white roses to show your affection.

Best Date Nights: Wednesday; 3rd and 21st of each month.

Colors of Passion: *For her:* sky blue, pale yellow. *For him:* indigo blue, bright blue.

The Perfect Wedding: Outlandish scenery—say, the view from an airplane, a Native American reservation, a national park—could enhance the sealing of your vows and make your day unique. You are moved by spectacular landscapes, and fresh air is a must. These, combined with your sweet sense of whimsy, will make your wedding day magical and filled with dreamy possibilities. Ideal setting: Arizona.

Wise Words: Benjamin Franklin: "Fear not death, for the sooner we die the longer we shall be immortal."

Hints of Love: When this one decides to sit on the fence don't try to push them off before they are ready. Let them do the jumping themselves.

After the Argument: *For him:* He can be stubborn. You might have to cook his favorite meal and buy those tickets to the concert he wanted. In other words, make sure he knows you're going out of your way. *For her:* If she was wrong, you won't have to do too much at all. If you were wrong, expect it to cost you! Grovel, grovel, and then grovel some more. Expect to go see the movies she wants and eat in the restaurant she wants to for a while. Time will be the currency for payment on this one.

Romantic Places: Places of innovation bring romance: New York City; an air show; Silicon Valley.

Lucky Love Star: Aquariel—you will never lack devotion.

Beautiful Thought: Nothing is better than a favor you would never ask for.

Sharing Secrets: They may seem like they are not interested, but ask them out anyway. *For the gals:* Until they absolutely know you are interested, you will never find out that they are. *For the guys:* Ask him out if he doesn't ask you. He may be shy or not. Either way he may be interested.

Judith's Insights

About the Man: He won't let you in until you prove yourself over and over again. He loves to be mysterious. Cautious is his way in the world of employment. He is the best bluff player at the card table and will never let you know what is in his hand until all of the betting is done. You can know this guy for years and never really have a handle on him. Then all at once he will pour his soul out to you. He can only do so if he is truly comfortable. His sensitive side may be camouflaged but it's there indeed. Bring your ideas to this open-minded guy for some real advice.

About the Woman: She is the achiever of hope. She really would love to give it a chance, but she tends to be more skeptical of people. She can have an outrageous wardrobe or a very understated one, depending on the stage of her life. She looks for people who are down-to-earth and open to unusual happenstance, just like her. She will rule the road by being quiet. This girl won't have to say a word to have the whole room listening. People naturally look to her for advice and counsel. She can have a talent for getting away with murder if you don't watch it.

61

Soul Mates: You love yourself so much you could do well with any Aquarius. Both Pisces and Aries will know how to charm you into their reaches. Libra and Sagittarius will intrigue you. They can make the best partner, no matter what kind you have in mind. Capricorn will bring you right down to earth and keep you safe. You love it no matter how much you say that you don't. Gemini will not change just to please you. You have to accept everything they bring to the table. Leo will be your greatest challenge, depending on the mood you are in and how much both of you have grown. This could be the most fun you have had in a long time. Taurus and Scorpio will test your patience and could drive you right off the deep end if you let them. With Cancer and Virgo, you would do better just to run, but the temptation is there. Just remember, where there is smoke there is usually fire.

Most Charming Characteristics: Considerate, refined, charming.

Gifts: *For her:* dance class. *For him:* leather journal.

Sensual Foods: Waffles with whipped cream; chocolate soufflé; French wine.

Romantic Flowers: These ladies like men with taste. Show them you love style by sending fuchsia flowers, or even brightly colored wildflowers will do. To confuse this man, send him lilies along with bright daisies to show your innocence. Keep him guessing.

Best Date Nights: Wednesday; 4th and 13th of each month.

Colors of Passion: *For her:* sky blue, pale yellow. *For him:* indigo blue, bright blue.

The Perfect Wedding: Outlandish scenery—say, the view from an airplane, a Native American reservation, a national park—could enhance the sealing of your vows and make your day unique. You are moved by spectacular landscapes, and fresh air is a must. These, combined with your sweet sense of whimsy, will make your wedding day magical and filled with dreamy possibilities. Ideal setting: Arizona.

Wise Words: Benjamin Franklin: "Nothing in human affairs and schemes is perfect, and perhaps that is the case of our opinions."

Hints of Love: Make sure you learn to compromise, but never with your principles.

After the Argument: *For him:* He can be stubborn. You might have to cook his favorite meal and buy those tickets to the concert he wanted. In other words, make sure he knows you're going out of your way. *For her:* If she was wrong, you won't have to do too much at all. If you were wrong, expect it to cost you! Grovel, grovel, and then grovel some more. Expect to go see the movies she wants and eat in the restaurant she wants to for a while. Time will be the currency for payment on this one.

Romantic Places: Places of distinction bring romance: Russia; an art museum; Savannah, Georgia.

Lucky Love Star: Aquariel—you will never lack devotion.

Beautiful Thought: Enjoy your moments out in space; it's okay to leave for a moment with no trace.

Sharing Secrets: Don't be surprised if the first date is with their family. *For the gals:* Make sure you invite her to your family functions. It will be a red flag to her if you don't. *For the guys:* He may seem like a family man, but isn't that what you were looking for?

Judith's Insights

About the Man: This one is a unique blend like a fine wine or coffee. Mix compassion and intellect with inspiration and insight and you get a powerful result. He gives life to every project he touches. It is the same with any relationship he is in. Whether you are friends or co-workers with this guy, your life will never be the same once linked with his. He can be a true friend. His emotions will remain secret until he feels that you have proven yourself reliable to be told about them. Time is the only way to prove that you are a safe investment for his heart.

About the Woman: Here is a needle in a haystack. She is as good as it gets, even when you push her too far. She can be patient and understanding, almost to a fault. She can tend to become indignant at times. Eventually, though, she brings herself right back up to par. Relying on her is easy. Getting her to rely on you is a different story. You had better be ready to put your best foot forward. Nothing but your best effort will do at all for her. It does not matter if you work or play with her. She wants to be the best friend you have and won't settle for anything less.

Soul Mates: When looking for a compatible sign, look no further than your own, Aquarius. Taurus's and Scorpio's terrible temper and tendency to erupt in a fury will be simply irrational to you. The match of wits with Cancer and Virgo happens fast. It will be strained just as fast if you don't really get to know each other. You will be fascinated with Pisces and Aries charisma. A union with Libra and Sagittarius could be picture-perfect. Leo is a truly worthy adversary. This could be a lot of fun. A Capricorn can keep your feet on the ground while you still have the ability to fly as high as you need to. Don't go in with the intent of changing Gemini. Learn to value them for who they are.

Most Charming Characteristics: Independent, masterful, talented.

Gifts: *For her:* natural-scented body wash. *For him:* unusual food for dinner.

Sensual Foods: Oysters; mussels; spicy foods.

Romantic Flowers: You are the lady of distinction, and only carnations will do. Any mix of colors with sprays of mignonette. Sweet peas or red carnations will appeal to this man's heart.

Best Date Nights: Wednesday; 5th and 23rd of each month.

Colors of Passion: *For her:* sky blue, pale yellow. *For him:* indigo blue, bright blue.

The Perfect Wedding: Outlandish scenery—say, the view from an airplane, a Native American reservation, a national park—could enhance the sealing of your vows and make your day unique. You are moved by spectacular landscapes, and fresh air is a must. These, combined with your sweet sense of whimsy, will make your wedding day magical and filled with dreamy possibilities. Ideal setting: Arizona.

Wise Words: Robert Burns: "Yon rose-buds in the morning dew, / How pure among the leaves sae green."

Hints of Love: If you try to take a step back, it will be noticed. It could create the domino effect, and everything will start to fall.

After the Argument: *For him:* He can be stubborn. You might have to cook his favorite meal and buy those tickets to the concert he wanted. In other words, make sure he knows you're going out of your way. *For her:* If she was wrong, you won't have to do too much at all. If you were wrong, expect it to cost you! Grovel, grovel, and then grovel some more. Expect to go see the movies she wants and eat in the restaurant she wants to for a while. Time will be the currency for payment on this one.

Romantic Places: Places of innovation bring romance: London; a university; Los Angeles, California.

Lucky Love Star: Aquariel—you will never lack devotion.

Beautiful Thought: The wind will whisper your angel's words.

Sharing Secrets: Take me as I am could be the anthem for this one. *For the gals:* They will have strong views on just about everything. If you can hang with them, then nothing will be as important as you. *For the guys:* The thing you fall in love with may end up becoming the thing you hate. After a commitment, this one sticks around.

Judith's Insights

About the Man: He loves to be liked and fears any type of criticism. He handles people very well and has a constant positive attitude. He can be so nice that he won't let you know when you have crossed the line. He will let his feelings stay inside and cook until they spill out whether he wants them to or not. Expect this guy to cook you dinner and clean up the dishes afterward. He wants the people he loves to love him unconditionally because that is how he loves them. If he is the boss, he will have lunch in the cafeteria with everyone else.

About the Woman: She is friends with her pals from kindergarten and doesn't like to wander when it comes to forming friendships. She keeps her mind focused. She can sometimes be formal, but doesn't mean to be standoffish. She is a friend who stands with you until she falls over. This girl is a lover, not a fighter, although she can be temperamental. When things are going well she will exude happiness from every pore. She tries to keep her best foot forward at all times. When people step on her emotions she can be amazingly sensitive.

Soul Mates: With so much in common with another Aquarius, you can't go wrong. Taurus and Scorpio are powerful and stubborn. If you are attracted to each other enough, they will stick with you through thick and thin. You might be enthralled by Cancer's and Virgo's powerful imagination, but things for you guys in the real world will be much stickier. Take delight in the spell Pisces and Aries will cast upon you. Things with Libra and Sagittarius are a perfect example of what can go right. Leo is like a bet. It can be risky, but it could also end in a win-win situation. You and Capricorn will balance each other perfectly. Partnering with Gemini can be good only if you can love them for all that they are today instead of molding them into what they could be. If you are willing to accept each other for what you truly are, then by all means go for it.

Most Charming Characteristics: Talented, independent, conscientious.

Gifts: *For her:* astrological chart. *For him:* meditation tapes.

Sensual Foods: Lobster; watermelon.

Romantic Flowers: You love it when you get tulips, declaring love. When you receive a variety, it shows how hopelessly in love your partner is. He will just love a single rose. This shows him you understand his pleasures.

Best Date Nights: Wednesday; 6th and 15th of each month.

Colors of Passion: *For her:* sky blue, pale yellow. *For him:* indigo blue, bright blue.

The Perfect Wedding: Outlandish scenery—say, the view from an airplane, a Native American reservation, a national park—could enhance the sealing of your vows and make your day unique. You are moved by spectacular landscapes, and fresh air is a must. These, combined with your sweet sense of whimsy, will make your wedding day magical and filled with dreamy possibilities. Ideal setting: Arizona.

Wise Words: Benjamin Franklin: "Virtue alone is sufficient to make a man great, glorious and happy."

Hints of Love: Consistence and persistence will get this prize every time. They will value the effort.

After the Argument: *For him:* He can be stubborn.

You might have to cook his favorite meal and buy those tickets to the concert he wanted. In other words, make sure he knows you're going out of your way. *For her:* If she was wrong, you won't have to do too much at all. If you were wrong, expect it to cost you! Grovel, grovel, and then grovel some more. Expect to go see the movies she wants and eat in the restaurant she wants to for a while. Time will be the currency for payment on this one.

Romantic Places: Places of distinction bring romance: Belgium; a five-star restaurant; Nashville, Tennessee.

Lucky Love Star: Aquariel—you will never lack devotion.

Beautiful Thought: Just think, the sun never wakes up or goes to sleep alone.

Sharing Secrets: They seem moody until you get to know them. *For the gals:* You may not know whether to say hello or drop dead. As relations progress you will learn not to leave her dangling, and her moods will become more consistent. *For the guys:* To know him is to love him. His bark is much worse than his bite. He just wants someone to love him without criticism.

Judith's Insights

About the Man: He can love many, but only a select few will ever get to know him fully. He can have a wall surrounding him, and he will allow you to take it down only one brick at a time. He can be guarded with his emotions, even with his family members. Earning his trust will be a test that you are not allowed to fail. There is no second chance with this guy if you have betrayed him. He is saddened by disappointments no matter how small. You have to be careful about what he can misunderstand about your intentions. Honor is your best tool to pry open his door.

About the Woman: Everybody wants to hear her advice. She is very inclined to give all of the answers. Her bedside manner is the best around. No matter how much you pester her, she will stick around. If she is an employee of yours, she would rather take the day off than come in and do a job halfway. Her work will be done right or not at all. She looks for love in all of the wrong places until she meets her match. She can be the epitome of a wanderer, changing her mood and ways of doing things in an instant. She wants a demonstrative mate who goes over the top for her.

Soul Mates: Looking at a fellow Aquarius is like looking at a reflection of yourself. If you don't like what you see, you have to look inside yourself before you look inside your partner. Taurus and Scorpio might be troubled by your judgment-free nature. Ease it up a bit. You might not learn not to go near the fire of Cancer and Virgo until you have been scalded by it. Pisces's and Aries's magnetism will pull you right to them. Libra and Sagittarius are the personification of whatever image you have of a great relationship. Sharpen your edges; the ride with Leo will be a great one. When you get in over your head, Capricorn is there to help you swim to shore. Gemini must be appreciated for what they are instead of molded into your vision of what they should be.

Most Charming Characteristics: Conscientious, honorable, considerate.

Gifts: *For her:* angel collectibles. *For him:* photography class.

Sensual Foods: Strawberries; truffles; shish kebab.

Romantic Flowers: Send this girl sunflowers if you want her to know you adore her. You may even add some poppies for a splash of extravagance. His desire for sport and play will be understood when you send him hyacinth and geranium.

Best Date Nights: Wednesday; 7th and 21st of each month.

Colors of Passion: *For her:* sky blue, pale yellow. *For him:* indigo blue, bright blue.

The Perfect Wedding: Outlandish scenery—say, the view from an airplane, a Native American reservation, a national park—could enhance the sealing of your vows and make your day unique. You are moved by spectacular landscapes, and fresh air is a must. These, combined with your sweet sense of whimsy, will make your wedding day magical and filled with dreamy possibilities. Ideal setting: Arizona.

Wise Words: Benjamin Franklin: "If men are so wicked with religion, what would they have been without it?"

Hints of Love: Be funny. Laughter will keep this one coming back again and again.

After the Argument: *For him:* He can be stubborn. You might have to cook his favorite meal and buy those tickets to the concert he wanted. In other words, make sure he knows you're going out of your way. *For her:* If she was wrong, you won't have to do too much at all. If you were wrong, expect it to cost you! Grovel, grovel, and then grovel some more. Expect to go see the movies she wants and eat in the restaurant she wants to for a while. Time will be the currency for payment on this one.

Romantic Places: Places of innovation bring romance: Hong Kong; virtual reality arcade; Chicago.

Lucky Love Star: Aquariel—you will never lack devotion.

Beautiful Thought: Life is full of perfect imperfections.

Sharing Secrets: You had better be able to put your money where your mouth is. *For the gals:* It doesn't need to be lavish, but she does love the loot. The more the better. *For the guys:* He doesn't mind spending his hard-earned cash, but he loves to see you contribute to please him.

Judith's Insights

About the Man: He likes his home, his garden, and his car. The way he does things will change with the blink of an eye. He is always on the lookout for the newest idea on how to make his life better. He cherishes gifts from friends. The best gift for this guy is your time and thought put into making him happy. He has a strong sentimental side. If you can make a gift or take him to a place from his childhood, it will capture more than his attention; also his heart. His wildness will fall by the wayside when he finds his passion in his career.

About the Woman: She is here today and gone tomorrow. You need to wear roller skates to keep up with her. She can intimidate her co-workers with a dive-in, accomplished, and fast-paced manner. One minute she is two weeks behind in her work, the next minute she is two weeks ahead. She will keep you on your toes. She can be rather wishy-washy when entering a new relationship. She is just feeling things out before she gets too much invested. She has the gift to gab, and gab, and gab some more. Where this girl goes there are sure to be many following.

Soul Mates: Fix your eyes on a fellow Aquarius and it will be as if you are looking at yourself. You may have to fight to be with Taurus and Scorpio, but you may be all the richer for the struggle. No matter how much you believe you can get around the blaze of Cancer and Virgo, you will be wiser to take another course entirely. Imagine the fun to be ensnared by such delightful captors as Pisces and Aries. Talk about perfect. You can't go wrong with Libra and Sagittarius. A relationship with Leo will test your creativity. You need to learn to settle down while your Capricorn needs to learn to play around. A pairing with Gemini can work only if you learn to accept them for who they are.

Most Charming Characteristics: Talented, independent, charming.

Gifts: *For her:* intricately carved glass vase. *For him:* night out dancing.

Sensual Foods: Grapes; fine cheeses and crackers; taffy.

Romantic Flowers: Rhododendron will let her be on the lookout for trouble. Throw in some chrysanthemum and she'll know it is you she will be looking out for. Cactus will show him warmth. Yellow daffodil is a token of a good time had by all. Chivalry is not dead.

Best Date Nights: Wednesday; 8th and 17th of each month.

Colors of Passion: *For her:* sky blue, light green. *For him:* indigo blue, bright blue.

The Perfect Wedding: Outlandish scenery—say, the view from an airplane, a Native American reservation, a national park—could enhance the sealing of your vows and make your day unique. You are moved by spectacular landscapes, and fresh air is a must. These, combined with your sweet sense of whimsy, will make your wedding day magical and filled with dreamy possibilities. Ideal setting: Arizona.

Wise Words: Ralph Waldo Emerson: "Earth laughs in flowers."

Hints of Love: Treat this one like royalty or precious cargo. They will love being valued in this way.

After the Argument: *For him:* He can be stubborn. You might have to cook his favorite meal and buy those tickets to the concert he wanted. In other words, make sure he knows you're going out of your way. *For her:* If she was wrong, you won't have to do too much at all. If you were wrong, expect it to cost you! Grovel, grovel, and then grovel some more. Expect to go see the movies she wants and eat in the restaurant she wants to for a while. Time will be the currency for payment on this one.

Romantic Places: Places of distinction bring romance: Germany; ornate theater; New Orleans, Louisiana.

Lucky Love Star: Aquariel—you will never lack devotion.

Beautiful Thought: What's more seducing, the raging waves or the calming of the waters?

Sharing Secrets: Nobody likes a weak link, especially not this one. *For the gals:* Make sure you treat her like a lady and act like a man. *For the guys:* Put your best foot forward. Dress your best and keep your manners in check. This man notices.

Judith's Insights

About the Man: He is a butterfly who starts in a cocoon but is soon flying here, and there, and everywhere. Have car; will travel. That is this guy's way of life. He always keeps his eye on the Exit sign when entering a room—or a relationship. When all else fails to make things work, he will be able to make a clean getaway. He can be the worst or best employee. His work effort can be erratic if he does not have passion for what he is doing. He can be a better employer. People will look to him for advice and inspiration, and he will never hesitate to give either.

About the Woman: She can feel challenged by the smallest thing. She constantly rides an emotional roller coaster and is somewhat defensive in a calm and quiet way. She loves people to notice her moods. That is probably why she has them in the first place. Make sure you help her pick up the pieces when they fall. She can be a real do-gooder if she gets the opportunity. The best way to her heart is not to try so hard. She needs to feel a sense of control that can come only if she thinks she is the one who noticed you first.

Soul Mates: How can you not be hooked on someone made from the same mold you were? Aquarius and Aquarius are exactly that. If you can get Taurus and Scorpio to open up to the world, they will be much easier for you to handle. A match with Cancer and Virgo would require a magical imagination to ever get off the ground. Pisces and Aries know exactly how to capture your attention. You will love to be around such good-natured and generous people as Libra and Sagittarius. Leo has laid the gauntlet down. Are you ready for the game? Capricorn makes sure your exuberance doesn't get you in trouble. Gemini must be accepted for the fiery and flirty people they are.

Most Charming Characteristics: Determined, reliable, honest.

Gifts: *For her:* onyx necklace. *For him:* telescope.

Sensual Foods: Champagne; grapes; mangoes; filet mignon.

Romantic Flowers: The magnolias you send her will let her know you will be around for a while to come. Petunia is to say never despair. Holly will let him know what he is getting into. Pansy will keep you in his thoughts.

Best Date Nights: Wednesday; 9th and 18th of each month.

Colors of Passion: *For her:* sky blue, light green. *For him:* indigo blue, bright blue.

The Perfect Wedding: Outlandish scenery—say, the view from an airplane, a Native American reservation, a national park—could enhance the sealing of your vows and make your day unique. You are moved by spectacular landscapes, and fresh air is a must. These, combined with your sweet sense of whimsy, will make your wedding day magical and filled with dreamy possibilities. Ideal setting: Arizona.

Wise Words: Benjamin Franklin: "Useful attainments in your minority will procure riches in maturity, of which writing and accounts are not the meanest."

Hints of Love: Affection is important, but only if it comes naturally. Otherwise, the sirens will go off.

After the Argument: *For him:* He can be stubborn.

You might have to cook his favorite meal and buy those tickets to the concert he wanted. In other words, make sure he knows you're going out of your way. *For her:* If she was wrong, you won't have to do too much at all. If you were wrong, expect it to cost you! Grovel, grovel, and then grovel some more. Expect to go see the movies she wants and eat in the restaurant she wants to for a while. Time will be the currency for payment on this one.

Romantic Places: Places of distinction bring romance: Switzerland; a bed and breakfast; Hyde Park, New York.

Lucky Love Star: Aquariel—you will never lack devotion.

Beautiful Thought: A tree changes many times in its lifetime.

Sharing Secrets: Attention, attention, attention. *For the gals:* Do it any way you can. Presents, phone calls, cards, or flowers. Whatever works for you will work for her. *For the guys:* He would love nostalgic gifts or T-shirts. He also likes phone calls, as long as they don't interrupt his favorite pastimes.

Judith's Insights

About the Man: If you can't find him he's probably lost in space, right in the next room. He lives in a world of his own. It's safer, although it is sometimes unrealistic. When others challenge him, he will exit stage left and find no need to return. Once he is gone it will be nearly impossible to get him back, so make sure you keep his feelings in mind in all that you do. He won't show it right away when things bother him. Instead, he will let it simmer until the top pops off and he boils over. The more love and understanding you give him, the more he will be able to return them to you.

About the Woman: She thinks with her heart at every given moment. She is naturally smart but others don't always see that. She can hold a conversation with the best of them, but she certainly needs a reason to do so. You won't find this girl wasting her time with a person who won't get her to where she wants to be. Where she wants to be is in a partnership that grows stronger each day. She has seen too many relationships that start strong and steadily lose their power. She'll create her own barriers, if need be. To take them down will be your test.

Soul Mates: You and a fellow Aquarius will revel in all of your shared characteristics. Taurus and Scorpio will help you share all of the feelings you are uncomfortable with. Cancer and Virgo will retreat into themselves at the first sign of trouble, leaving you bewildered and ready to move on. Pisces and Aries make sure that your feet stay on the ground while you are enjoying the wonderful spell you are under. Libra's and Sagittarius's honesty and respect will leave you feeling very secure in the relationship. Things between you and Leo will be interesting indeed. Capricorn will give you a realistic view of all of your greatest dreams. Gemini can't be changed into something different. You will just have to accept this or move on.

Most Charming Characteristics: Honest, loving, adventurous.

Gifts: *For her:* meditation tapes. *For him:* science set or microscope.

Sensual Foods: Châteaubriand; crème brûlée.

Romantic Flowers: Iris is your flower if you are the gal sending subtle messages. If you are the man, you will look for clematis. This flower's mental beauty creates emotional stimulation for you.

Best Date Nights: Wednesday; 1st and 28th of each month.

Colors of Passion: *For her:* turquoise, light green. *For him:* indigo blue, bright blue.

The Perfect Wedding: Outlandish scenery—say, the view from an airplane, a Native American reservation, a national park—could enhance the sealing of your vows and make your day unique. You are moved by spectacular landscapes, and fresh air is a must. These, combined with your sweet sense of whimsy, will make your wedding day magical and filled with dreamy possibilities. Ideal setting: Arizona.

Wise Words: Princess Helena: "If I fall, It shall be like myself; Setting sun should leave a track of glory in the skies."

Hints of Love: This one likes others to make his or her dreams come true. Be the "fantasy" fulfiller.

After the Argument: *For him:* He can be stubborn. You might have to cook his favorite meal and buy those tickets to the concert he wanted. In other words, make sure he knows you're going out of your way. *For her:* If she was wrong, you won't have to do too much at all. If you were wrong, expect it to cost you! Grovel, grovel, and then grovel some more. Expect to go see the movies she wants and eat in the restaurant she wants to for a while. Time will be the currency for payment on this one.

Romantic Places: Places of innovation bring romance: Japan; a science museum; Disney World.

Lucky Love Star: Aquariel—you will never lack devotion.

Beautiful Thought: We are all on loan to each other, some of us just have more interest than others.

Sharing Secrets: Make sure you are not the killjoy. *For the gals:* When she has an idea, try it before you decide you don't like it. She needs to be pleased. *For the guys:* Do the things he loves to do and he will make the things you love ten times more fun.

Judith's Insights

About the Man: He is definitely indecisive. This guy can change his mind more often than his clothes. He can give any type of relationship a run for its money. He wants a lot, and the older he gets, the more he wants of it. Make sure that you let him know what you are ready to give right up front. If you don't, he will expect it all. He won't ever expect more than he is willing to give, however. But if he begins to see that the relationship is unbalanced he will harbor ill feelings that will grow like a cancer and kill the relationship.

About the Woman: It's a real good thing it is a woman's prerogative to change her mind. That often is top on her list. If she is your employer she'll drive you up a wall and back down again. Even her friendships can be wishy-washy at times. You'll never really feel totally stable when you are in a relationship with her. She tries to get the most out of every situation. Just stand by and watch how easy she makes it all seem. She never even realizes what a smooth operator she is. In her head are all of the emotions she fights through to get to her goal and never lets anyone see.

Soul Mates: Pisces and Pisces: you two fish have your own language. Aries's and Taurus's need for self-preservation may bring out your insecurities. There is loads of water here with Cancer and Scorpio. Try not to drown in it. Gemini and Sagittarius will urge you to reach out and expand. Virgo's perfectionism can get out of control. This can pull the rug out from under you. Extremes are rampant with Libra and Leo. Make sure to balance self-confidence with humility. Capricorn and Aquarius can be the stabilizing force you need so much.

Most Charming Characteristics: Passionate, leader, emotional.

Gifts: *For her:* dinner at an unusual restaurant. *For him:* tickets to the circus.

Sensual Foods: Shrimp; sinful chocolate cake.

Romantic Flowers: Any rose of any color for the lady. Roses stand for love regardless of the color. Send them with orchids and you will be saying, "I love you." If you want a gentleman to know you think of him, send pansies, and forget-me-nots for true love.

Best Date Nights: Saturday; 2nd and 4th of each month.

Colors of Passion: *For her:* light green, violet. *For him:* blue-green, turquoise.

The Perfect Wedding: Choose a relaxed, romantic atmosphere, most likely inspired by a body of water. An inlet or a lagoon at either dawn or dusk . . . or, perhaps, a winter wedding in a cozy room with a picturesque, snowy view. You might choose a grand room with roaring, blazing fireplaces. Ideal setting: Mediterranean island; Greece.

Wise Words: Charles Dickens: "It is pleasant to find real merit appreciated, whatever its particular walk in life may be."

Hints of Love: Stop worrying about next week's date today or there will not be one tomorrow.

After the Argument: *For him:* Promise him anything, but give him yourself and your time. If you can make him smile, you're on your way. A little attention goes a long way, but this is one whose ego you don't want to inflate or he could milk it for a while. *For her:* You had better be ready to be on your best behavior for a long time. This one could be tough even if she is the one who was wrong.

Romantic Places: Places of fantasy bring romance: Ireland; Renaissance fair; Hollywood, California.

Lucky Love Star: Pisciel—you will never lack magnetism.

Beautiful Thought: Love is like the glow of the radiant sun on a clear day.

Sharing Secrets: You had better be ready to have a relationship. *For the gals:* No lies, no games, and no mistakes. She wants what she wants with as little amount of work as possible. *For the guys:* If you have games on your mind, then move on. This one likes fun any way he can get it, but no emotional roller coasters.

Judith's Insights

About the Man: This guy is highly emotional, and for good reasons—at least, that's what he believes. He can feel sorry for himself and he isn't so good at feeling sorry for others. He can be the diplomat when he wants to be. His words will always come so much easier when they are on someone else's behalf. That's how he tends to gain affection from others around him. When it comes to facing or vocalizing his own emotions, he will get stuck in a corner he can't find his way out of. Lend him a hand and guide him slowly into the light without pulling him too fast.

About the Woman: You may find her moody or just swimming in both directions at the same time. You think you're confused—that's how you find her most of her life, unless the right situation grounds her. Otherwise, she's like a fish out of water. When the light is on that usually means someone is home. Then it is okay to proceed. Keep putting out the bait. As long as she is moving forward it is safe to inch your way toward her. The minute she has stopped taking the bait the interest has died. It will take more than fancy footwork to get her back on track.

Soul Mates: No one can know you like a copy of yourself, Pisces. That is why a relationship with another Pisces will be solid. Aries and Taurus may be the solid ground you seek. You might have to fight for the territory, though. Water signs need to give and receive feelings. If you pair with Cancer and Scorpio, make sure you each have that opportunity. Your receptivity will slow Gemini's and Sagittarius's impatient desire to move way too fast. Your insecurities are on trial constantly with Virgo. Walk away while you can. Beware of dependency coming from just plain enjoying each other's company when you deal with Leo and Libra. You help Capricorn and Aquarius become less rigid while they help you build structure. A perfect balance.

Most Charming Characteristics: Studious, passionate, generous.

Gifts: *For her:* tickets to a performance art show. *For him:* astrological chart.

Sensual Foods: Toasted marshmallows; chocolates.

Romantic Flowers: These ladies like everyone to know how faithful they are, so send them violets. To surprise them send tulips. Men like their flowers the same as their relationships, unpretending. Send them camellias with white roses to show your affection.

Best Date Nights: Saturday; 3rd and 12th of each month.

Colors of Passion: *For her:* light green, violet. *For him:* blue, light green, turquoise.

The Perfect Wedding: Choose a relaxed, romantic atmosphere, most likely inspired by a body of water. An inlet or a lagoon at either dawn or dusk . . . or, perhaps, a winter wedding in a cozy room with a picturesque, snowy view. You might choose a grand room with roaring, blazing fireplaces. Ideal setting: Mediterranean island; Greece.

Wise Words: Charles Dickens: "Ride on over all obstacles and win the race."

Hints of Love: Keep the romance in the picture. Don't forget the long walks on the beach and camping out in front of the fireplace.

After the Argument: *For him:* Promise him anything, but give him yourself and your time. If you can make him smile, you're on your way. A little attention goes a long way, but this is one whose ego you don't want to inflate or he could milk it for a while. *For her:* You had better be ready to be on your best behavior for a long time. This one could be tough even if she is the one who was wrong.

Romantic Places: Places of spirituality bring romance: Rome; yoga class; the mountains of Colorado.

Lucky Love Star: Pisciel—you will never lack magnetism.

Beautiful Thought: Close your eyes on a rainy day, take a breath of the cool mist; it's one of life's finest comforts.

Sharing Secrets: You may have to give this one more than one chance. *For the gals:* Intriguing as she is, expect a handful. She lightens up as time goes on. *For the guys:* His quirks may make you have second thoughts, but that is what separates the men from the boys.

Judith's Insights

About the Man: He can be a friend, but you may not even know it. He won't call or write unless it is in response to your advance. Then one day he'll do something wonderful for you. He demands nothing but will accept everything you have to give. He is not ignoring you on purpose. Things crowd his mind more than most people, and he has only so much attention span. If his focus is on his emotions, then the only way you can get through to him is identifying with those emotions. He will be hard to read unless you know what to look for. Time is the only way you will know the signs.

About the Woman: She was looking in all the wrong places, until the right one found her. You could be standing on your head in the middle of the road and she may not notice you. If she writes your paycheck make sure she knows not only your name, but your number also. Holding her attention will be a test in itself. She enjoys the cheap thrills. A picnic in the park, private practical jokes, and sentimental gifts are all keys that will work in the lock around her heart. This girl is wise beyond her years, so lying will only get you in trouble. Sincerity and honesty are the best ways to get noticed.

Soul Mates: What is better than finding someone as faithful and devoted as you? That is exactly what you can find in a fellow Pisces. Aries's and Taurus's unfolding energy can make a relationship with them into an interesting ride. Cancer's and Scorpio's strong desire to love and be loved can result in an overflow of emotions. Gemini and Sagittarius push you to connect with others instead of standing back and waiting for them to come to you. Virgo's analytical nature will leave you feeling powerless. Leo and Libra may have trouble making decisions because they are worried about being fair. Your receptiveness will calm the rebellion in Capricorn's and Aquarius's energy.

Most Charming Characteristics: Generous, passionate, loyal.

Gifts: *For her:* dinner cruise. *For him:* fishing trip with the guys.

Sensual Foods: Chocolate-covered strawberries; New York steak; scallops.

Romantic Flowers: These ladies like men with taste. Show them you love style by sending fuchsia flowers, or even brightly colored wildflowers will do. To confuse this man, send him lilies along with bright daisies to show your innocence. Keep him guessing.

Best Date Nights: Saturday; 13th and 22nd of each month.

Colors of Passion: *For her:* light green, violet. *For him:* blue-green, turquoise.

The Perfect Wedding: Choose a relaxed, romantic atmosphere, most likely inspired by a body of water. An inlet or a lagoon at either dawn or dusk . . . or, perhaps, a winter wedding in a cozy room with a picturesque, snowy view. You might choose a grand room with roaring, blazing fireplaces. Ideal setting: Mediterranean island; Greece.

Wise Words: Charles Dickens: "In very many cases of friendship, or what passes for it, the old axiom is reversed, and like clings to unlike more than to like."

Hints of Love: The mystery is important, but being evasive will create disaster. Make sure you know the difference.

After the Argument: *For him:* Promise him anything, but give him yourself and your time. If you can make him smile, you're on your way. A little attention goes a long way, but this is one whose ego you don't want to inflate or he could milk it for a while. *For her:* You had better be ready to be on your best behavior for a long time. This one could be tough even if she is the one who was wrong.

Romantic Places: Places of fantasy bring romance: China; a carnival; Mardi Gras.

Lucky Love Star: Pisciel—you will never lack magnetism.

Beautiful Thought: It takes both sun and rain to make a rainbow.

Sharing Secrets: Talk about high maintenance . . . *For the gals:* Once she sees that you go out of your way for her, then she will for you. *For the guys:* The bark is definitely much worse than the bite. He comes on stronger and more obstinate then he actually is.

Judith's Insights

About the Man: If it weren't for his lack of patience, he would be pretty perfect. I wouldn't go and tell him that. His ego has a tendency to run on high to begin with. His sensitivity to everyone is what makes him on the top of everyone's list, however. Having a friend in him is like having an angel watching over you. He will always listen to new ideas, and he loves to visit new places. The look on his face when you take him on an unusual date will be worth any amount of work it may have taken to pull it off. Once you please him you will want to do it again and again.

About the Woman: She's not so bad. In fact, she's one of the best. You'll find she does better with men than women. Her nose gets out of joint on occasion. Others may find that her attitude is carried in the air. All in all, the worst you can say is that she's too good to those she cares for. They can get away with murder if they try. Just beware of the explosion that eventually happens when her feelings of being taken advantage of finally get to be too much for her to take. That explosion could ruin anything in her path.

Soul Mates: Pisces can always lean on another stable Pisces. Balance with Aries and Taurus comes through adding gentleness to their need for independence. Cancer and Scorpio may try to go too far within or too far outside. Gemini and Sagittarius bring into your life a very active and extroverted energy. Until Virgo realizes that imperfection is okay, your ego will not be safe in their arms. Make sure that a relationship with Leo and Libra maintains your sense of self as well as part of the whole. When you help Capricorn and Aquarius remember the little joys in life, you will find joy in each other for a lifetime.

Most Charming Characteristics: Determined, loving, just.

Gifts: *For her:* diamond earrings. *For him:* romantic cruise.

Sensual Foods: Vanilla and strawberry mousse; tiramisù; espresso.

Romantic Flowers: You are the lady of distinction, and only carnations will do. Any mix of colors with sprays of mignonette. Sweet peas or red carnations will appeal to this man's heart.

Best Date Nights: Saturday; 5th and 23rd of each month.

Colors of Passion: *For her:* light green, violet. *For him:* bright blue-green, turquoise.

The Perfect Wedding: Choose a relaxed, romantic atmosphere, most likely inspired by a body of water. An inlet or a lagoon at either dawn or dusk . . . or, perhaps, a winter wedding in a cozy room with a picturesque, snowy view. You might choose a grand room with roaring, blazing fireplaces. Ideal setting: Mediterranean island; Greece.

Wise Words: Charles Dickens: "When duty calls we must obey."

Hints of Love: If you learn to back up when things are moving too fast, you won't have to bow out so often.

After the Argument: *For him:* Promise him anything, but give him yourself and your time. If you can make him smile, you're on your way. A little attention goes a long way, but this is one whose ego you don't want to inflate or he could milk it for a while. *For her:* You had better be ready to be on your best behavior for a long time. This one could be tough even if she is the one who was wrong.

Romantic Places: Places of spirituality bring romance: India; a cathedral or temple; the Grand Canyon.

Lucky Love Star: Pisciel—you will never lack magnetism.

Beautiful Thought: Know you made the difference in someone else's life today.

Sharing Secrets: Make sure you have at least five dates before you make up your mind. *For the gals:* They can be cynical, so it could be a few dates before she loosens up. *For the guys:* He still has yesterday on his mind. He needs a reason to forget his past relationship. Make a new history for him.

Judith's Insights

About the Man: He needs a constant flow of attention, and he really doesn't care how he gets it. Compliment, encourage, console, and you will form a bond beyond bonds. This guy is looking for fireworks when it comes to love. He wants overwhelming passion to last a lifetime without fading. If you are in a relationship with him you can't let the love get dull. His interest is easily swayed to bigger and better things if he is not completely focused on you. Excitement is not only a great way to get his attention, it is also a great way to keep it.

About the Woman: She loves her pals. Whether it's coffee klatching with the girls or having a drink with the guys after work, any socializing will do. So, don't expect this one to sit around for more than five minutes. She needs to be constantly moving and having fun. Fancy dinners whet this girl's palate. Traveling will appeal to her desire for new experiences. A carnival will appeal to her sense of adventure. In younger years, she loves crashing parties and investigating the neighborhood. New beginnings of any kind will do to keep her blood flowing.

Soul Mates: As long as you understand each other's need to be independent at times, a relationship with another Pisces will work nicely. Aries's and Taurus's assertiveness may become too willful. This is when you must take full advantage of your receptivity. Try to build gates in the walls Cancer and Scorpio put up around themselves. Gemini and Sagittarius bring to the table communication and interaction to merge with your compassion. Virgo's tendency to try too hard will leave your head spinning. Keep the picture of your true self inside you at all times when getting together with Leo and Libra. You will need that picture when things get too dependent. Capricorn and Aquarius will give you the best combination of yin and yang energy. You will bring out the best in each other at every turn.

Most Charming Characteristics: Kind, acquiescent, good-natured.

Gifts: *For her:* seafood and champagne dinner at sunset. *For him:* custom aquarium.

Sensual Foods: Raspberries; pound cake; caviar.

Romantic Flowers: You love it when you get tulips, declaring love. When you receive a variety, it shows how hopelessly in love your partner is. He will just love a single rose. This shows him you understand his pleasures.

Best Date Nights: Saturday; 6th and 15th of each month.

Colors of Passion: *For her:* light green, white. *For him:* blue-green, light blue.

The Perfect Wedding: Choose a relaxed, romantic atmosphere, most likely inspired by a body of water. An inlet or a lagoon at either dawn or dusk . . . or, perhaps, a winter wedding in a cozy room with a picturesque, snowy view. You might choose a grand room with roaring, blazing fireplaces. Ideal setting: Mediterranean island; Greece.

Wise Words: Charles Dickens: "As I have observed that Time confuses facts occasionally, I hardly know what weight to give to its authority."

Hints of Love: Expecting too much too soon can only build up hopes that will fall down too easily.

After the Argument: *For him:* Promise him anything, but give him yourself and your time. If you can make him smile, you're on your way. A little attention goes a long way, but this is one whose ego you don't want to inflate or he could milk it for a while. *For her:* You had better be ready to be on your best behavior for a long time. This one could be tough even if she is the one who was wrong.

Romantic Places: Places of fantasy bring romance: Russia; the theater; New York City.

Lucky Love Star: Pisciel—you will never lack magnetism.

Beautiful Thought: A phone call can be the hug you were looking for:

Sharing Secrets: Don't be in a hurry, or it will be over before it begins. *For the gals:* Like fine wine and amazing food. Savor a moment until an hour is created. *For the guys:* To do too much too fast will prove risky. Try to give a push and he will just jump ship.

Judith's Insights

About the Man: You have to win his approval at first and always. It's seldom that he will say yes right away. My bet is he likes to procrastinate, just in case a better offer comes along. If you pat him on the back from time to time, he may stay around forever. Without acknowledgment of his accomplishment he will fade out of your life. He can be completely misunderstood by those who do not take the time to truly get to know him. His intentions will almost always be misrepresented by his actions. Give him time to help you understand what he was trying to do before you get angry with him.

About the Woman: Some will see the spoiled brat in her nature. This one put the silver spoon in her own mouth. She is a great boss, as long as you keep up your end of the deal. If you do your job, it will be a piece of cake. If you are being lazy, you will see the dark side of her personality. Don't step on her toes. Make sure that you give her plenty of room to breathe if you want her to stay with you for any long period of time. She can be impatient from time to time but never on a regular basis. She loves it when people pay attention, so let her know that you noticed her.

Soul Mates: A pairing with another Pisces could be just what you need. The two of you can take turns leaning on each other in your insecure times that only another Pisces could understand. Be prepared to step back and understand exactly where Aries and Taurus are coming from. Their independence may be about something else. Cancer and Scorpio are oh so very sensitive, just like you. Gemini and Sagittarius will urge you to reach out and communicate your feelings more aptly. A confident Pisces is no match for a nagging and picky Virgo. Don't become completely reliant on a partnership with Leo and Libra. You might find yourself wrapped up in everything but what is important to you. Capricorn and Aquarius, like you, have the ability and willingness to adapt to each other. This will carry you through anything you need to face together.

Most Charming Characteristics: Perceptive, entertaining, considerate.

Gifts: *For her:* book of poetry and quotes. *For him:* tickets to a film festival.

Sensual Foods: Flambé; lobster; oysters.

Romantic Flowers: Send this girl sunflowers if you want her to know you adore her. You may even add some poppies for a splash of extravagance. His desire for sport and play will be understood when you send him hyacinth and geranium.

Best Date Nights: Saturday; 14th and 21st of each month.

Colors of Passion: *For her:* light green, violet. *For him:* blue-green, white.

The Perfect Wedding: Choose a relaxed, romantic atmosphere, most likely inspired by a body of water. An inlet or a lagoon at either dawn or dusk . . . or, perhaps, a winter wedding in a cozy room with a picturesque, snowy view. You might choose a grand room with roaring, blazing fireplaces. Ideal setting: Mediterranean island; Greece.

Wise Words: Charles Dickens: "There are dark shadows on the earth, but its lights are stronger in contrast."

Hints of Love: Make sure all the ingredients are present before putting the cake in the oven.

After the Argument: *For him:* Promise him anything, but give him yourself and your time. If you can make him smile, you're on your way. A little attention goes a long way, but this is one whose ego you don't want to inflate or he could milk it for a while. *For her:* You had better be ready to be on your best behavior for a long time. This one could be tough even if she is the one who was wrong.

Romantic Places: Places of spirituality bring romance: Nepal; mountain trail; Waikiki, Hawaii.

Lucky Love Star: Pisciel—you will never lack magnetism.

Beautiful Thought: The sentimental feeling of receiving flowers.

Sharing Secrets: They need to look before they leap, but only in love. *For the gals:* She needs creative and exciting dates to keep her interested. Don't take her for granted too soon. *For the guys:* You may think he gives signs of moving this relationship quickly, but make sure you slow it down before he does.

Judith's Insights

About the Man: He can have his hands in a little bit of everything. He is on everyone's invitation list. This guy knows how to work the room, including the boardroom and the lunchroom. Watching this one could make everyone dizzy. You could also learn a lot from him if you let yourself admit that he knows more than you do. A smile across the room can make this guy's day. He loves to know that people have noticed what he does and how he does it. Imitation is the ultimate compliment to him. Doing things his way is just what you need to make him happy.

About the Woman: She's got it all, and knows just how to use it to her advantage. Yes, she can flaunt it, too. This one dresses to be noticed, even when going to the grocery store. She will make sure she knows any and all the gossip. She can sit and talk to you and never actually hear what you are saying. She has to be really interested to hang on a person's every word. If you find her quoting you to her friends you can be sure that she likes you more than just a little. She cherishes every gift she gets but loves the expensive ones even more.

Soul Mates: Use that Pisces support for another Pisces. You will both need it for tough times in your life. Aries and Taurus love their freedom just as much as they love having you there to listen to their adventures. When Cancer and Scorpio get together with you there could be a flood of emotions no one can control. Change is important. Gemini and Sagittarius won't hesitate to initiate it. Virgo's tendency to critique your every move will break even your compassionate energy. Your receptive nature may become too susceptible to suggestion when in the hands of Leo and Libra. You will love to bask in the warm smiles of Capricorn and Aquarius for a long time to come.

Most Charming Characteristics: Affectionate, entertaining, intellectual.

Gifts: *For her:* romantic evening at home. *For him:* fishing rod and reel.

Sensual Foods: Crème brûleé; poached salmon.

Romantic Flowers: Rhododendron will let her be on the lookout for trouble. Throw in some chrysanthemum and she'll know it is you she will be looking out for. Cactus will show him warmth. Yellow daffodil is a token of a good time had by all. Chivalry is not dead.

Best Date Nights: Saturday; 8th and 17th of each month.

Colors of Passion: *For her:* light green, violet. *For him:* blue-green, white.

The Perfect Wedding: Choose a relaxed, romantic atmosphere, most likely inspired by a body of water. An inlet or a lagoon at either dawn or dusk . . . or, perhaps, a winter wedding in a cozy room with a picturesque, snowy view. You might choose a grand room with roaring, blazing fireplaces. Ideal setting: Mediterranean island; Greece.

Wise Words: Charles Dickens: "It is a poor heart that never rejoices, and our hearts are not poor! No!"

Hints of Love: Simple often turns into complicated with this one. When you overcomplicate the moment, try to step back for a breather.

After the Argument: *For him:* Promise him anything, but give him yourself and your time. If you can make him smile, you're on your way. A little attention goes a long way, but this is one whose ego you don't want to inflate or he could milk it for a while. *For her:* You had better be ready to be on your best behavior for a long time. This one could be tough even if she is the one who was wrong.

Romantic Places: Places of fantasy bring romance: Saint Petersburg, Russia; a movie set; Las Vegas, Nevada.

Lucky Love Star: Pisciel—you will never lack magnetism.

Beautiful Thought: Our hearts create the moment; listen to the beat.

Sharing Secrets: The possibilities are endless, if you can pay the price. *For the gals:* She is hoping chivalry is not dead, and you must be willing to be the man at all costs. *For the guys:* He can be demanding and somewhat controlling. He just needs to be trained.

Judith's Insights

About the Man: What does yesterday have to do with today? Nothing! He can change his mind in an instant. He can have a strong conviction today, yet a few days later he will have already moved on. He will never look at that as moody. He just wants what he wants until he doesn't want it anymore. Compliments are a sure way to get his attention. Pat him on the back for his accomplishments and he will be looking at you in a whole new way. It may take a few times to get him to agree to meet you. Once he does you can be sure that he is interested.

About the Woman: *Temperamental* is a great word to describe this girl. It is not a good thing to cross her, even at work. She'll cut you out with her mental pair of scissors. If you want something from her, prepare in advance. Do her two or three favors before you ask for yours. Does anyone ever really know her? She is an expert at hiding behind herself for protection. She has ways of getting what she wants without having to ask. When you make her angry you had better be ready to pay for it for a while. It takes the best effort to bring out her good side.

Soul Mates: A fellow Pisces will be just as compassionate and nurturing as you are. Keep in mind how much you love their willfulness when Aries and Taurus get a bit full of themselves. Water signs are more introverted. When you are with Cancer and Scorpio, someone has to bring out your independent side. Quiet contemplation can heighten Gemini's and Sagittarius's intuition and temper their fire. Run away from Virgo's nitpicking behavior. Severe swings in the feel of the relationship with Leo and Libra are sure to come. Achievements of great things are possible when you have Capricorn and Aquarius in your corner.

Most Charming Characteristics: Perceptive, intellectual, entertaining.

Gifts: *For her:* tickets to the local Renaissance fair. *For him:* a beach weekend.

Sensual Foods: Chocolate soufflé; filet mignon.

Romantic Flowers: The magnolias you send her will let her know you will be around for a while to come. Petunia is to say never despair. Holly will let him know what he is getting into. Pansy will keep you in his thoughts.

Best Date Nights: Saturday; 2nd and 18th of each month.

Colors of Passion: *For her:* light green, violet. *For him:* blue-green, white.

The Perfect Wedding: Choose a relaxed, romantic atmosphere, most likely inspired by a body of water. An inlet or a lagoon at either dawn or dusk . . . or, perhaps, a winter wedding in a cozy room with a picturesque, snowy view. You might choose a grand room with roaring, blazing fireplaces. Ideal setting: Mediterranean island; Greece.

Wise Words: Charles Dickens: "Cheerfulness and content are great beautifiers, and are famous preservers of youthful looks, depend upon it."

Hints of Love: Allow them to know what is in your heart as well as what is in your head.

After the Argument: *For him:* Promise him anything, but give him yourself and your time. If you can make him smile, you're on your way. A little attention goes a long way, but this is one whose ego you don't want to inflate or he could milk it for a while. *For her:* You had better be ready to be on your best behavior for a long time. This one could be tough even if she is the one who was wrong.

Romantic Places: Places of spirituality bring romance: Israel; a Japanese garden; the Grand Canyon.

Lucky Love Star: Pisciel—you will never lack magnetism.

Beautiful Thought: When you are about to fall apart, someone builds you up.

Sharing Secrets: Tomorrow is another day, but why wait? You can do it all today. *For the gals:* Have your date filled from dusk to dawn, and then some. *For the guys:* You may find he needs a nap here and there, but he can last all day and all night if he has a reason.

Judith's Insights

About the Man: This one can be a son of a gun when he wants to. Don't cross him if you think you'll ever need a favor from him. His memory is awfully good, and he will repay any injustice as well as any good deed done in the past. He can exhaust you or energize you. Don't take him too literally. He can be a taker. He means well. Somehow his intentions are always lost in actions. He will do something for someone and get confused when that person gets angry. He was only trying to help. Letting him know that you noticed the things he has done right will give him hope after all.

About the Woman: She does better with men friends than with the ladies. Men are just easier for her to work or play with. She can be one of the boys. Maybe it's her power or maybe her passion. Either way, it still is who she is. She needs to feel in total control even when she is doing something completely out of control. It is very hard for this girl to relax. She does know how to have fun, however. Enjoy her company when you have it. If she takes the time to be with you at all she is already enjoying yours.

Soul Mates: Pisces understand each other, so this can be a great start. Aries and Taurus will attract you with their strength, but watch out for power struggles here and there. Otherwise, it is a go. Cancer and Scorpio tend to go with the flow, as do you. Sometimes, too much water gets in the room and it all gets washed up, though. Capricorn and Aquarius are a great basis for any relationship. Passion and true friendship are something you don't see every day. Gemini and Sagittarius are feisty, flirty, and furious. *Critical* is written all over Virgo. Leo and Libra will bring out the best or worst in you. Sometimes it can be a little bit of both.

Most Charming Characteristics: Loving, sincere, adventurous.

Gifts: *For her:* sailing adventures. *For him:* write him a poem from your heart.

Sensual Foods: Steak au poìvre; cheesecake.

Romantic Flowers: Iris is your flower if you are the gal sending subtle messages. If you are the man, you will look for clematis. This flower's mental beauty creates emotional stimulation for you.

Best Date Nights: Saturday; 10th and 19th of each month.

Colors of Passion: *For her:* light green, violet. *For him:* blue-green, white.

The Perfect Wedding: Choose a relaxed, romantic atmosphere, most likely inspired by a body of water. An inlet or a lagoon at either dawn or dusk . . . or, perhaps, a winter wedding in a cozy room with a picturesque, snowy view. You might choose a grand room with roaring, blazing fireplaces. Ideal setting: Mediterranean island; Greece.

Wise Words: Charles Dickens: "Most men live in a world of their own, and in that limited circle alone are they ambitious for distinction and applause."

Hints of Love: Keep both feet on the ground the first time you think you want to jump. This way you won't jump too high too soon.

After the Argument: *For him:* Promise him anything, but give him yourself and your time. If you can make him smile, you're on your way. A little attention goes a long way, but this is one whose ego you don't want to inflate or he could milk it for a while. *For her:* You had better be ready to be on your best behavior for a long time. This one could be tough even if she is the one who was wrong.

Romantic Places: Places of fantasy bring romance: Russia; the theater; New York City.

Lucky Love Star: Pisciel—you will never lack magnetism.

Beautiful Thought: Remembering the gifts of yesterday, never knowing they would be important tomorrow.

Sharing Secrets: This may need to start with friendship. That isn't the consolation prize; it's the grand prize. *For the gals:* Go slow and allow it to grow one seed at a time. You won't need to push; it will all come in time. *For the guys:* A step here and a step there. Before he knows it, that friendship will be love.

Judith's Insights

About the Man: He stands for loyal and loving. He can sometimes feel like he is lost at sea or maybe he just relates better to nature than people. It may seem that way sometimes. He is very approachable and likable. He is warm and sensitive and can be loved by many people. The only way he can bring love into his life is to work at it. Once he knows that things won't run smoothly without regular maintenance, he will make a much better partner. He will live life on his own terms and won't let anyone tell him he should do it differently.

About the Woman: Frankly, she doesn't give a damn what anyone thinks. You can see she beats to the rhythm of her own drum. If you are lucky enough to win this one over, she will become a better friend/mate/employee every day in every way. This is someone to give a chance to. It may take time and patience, but it is certainly worth the effort. Don't listen to what she says but notice the way she acts. That is where the real truth lies. Talk about looking for love in all of the right places. Here it is with her. All you have to do is give it time to bloom.

Soul Mates: Pisces and Pisces: you two fish have your own language. Aries's and Taurus's need for self-preservation may bring out your insecurities. There is loads of water here with Cancer and Scorpio. Try not to drown in it. Gemini and Sagittarius will urge you to reach out and expand. Virgo's perfectionism can get out of control. This can pull the rug out from under you. Extremes are rampant with Libra and Leo. Make sure to balance self-confidence with humility. Capricorn and Aquarius can be the stabilizing force you need so much.

Most Charming Characteristics: Gentle, sympathetic, true.

Gifts: *For her:* fantasy novel. *For him:* dinner next to the water.

Sensual Foods: Strawberry shortcake; pineapple; ham.

Romantic Flowers: Any rose of any color for the lady. Roses stand for love regardless of the color. Send them with orchids and you will be saying, "I love you." If you want a gentleman to know you think of him, send pansies, and forget-me-nots for true love.

Best Date Nights: Saturday; 11th and 20th of each month.

Colors of Passion: *For her:* light green, violet. *For him:* blue-green, white.

The Perfect Wedding: Choose a relaxed, romantic atmosphere, most likely inspired by a body of water. An inlet or a lagoon at either dawn or dusk . . . or, perhaps, a winter wedding in a cozy room with a picturesque, snowy view. You might choose a grand room with roaring, blazing fireplaces. Ideal setting: Mediterranean island; Greece.

Wise Words: Charles Dickens: "Things cannot be expected to turn up of themselves. We must, in a measure, assist to turn them up."

Hints of Love: Laughter alleviates the tension, but so can understanding where another is sitting.

After the Argument: *For him:* Promise him anything, but give him yourself and your time. If you can make him smile, you're on your way. A little attention goes a long way, but this is one whose ego you don't want to inflate or he could milk it for a while. *For her:* You had better be ready to be on your best behavior for a long time. This one could be tough even if she is the one who was wrong.

Romantic Places: Places of fantasy bring romance: Ireland; Renaissance fair; Hollywood, California.

Lucky Love Star: Pisciel—you will never lack magnetism.

Beautiful Thought: Everything needs a beginning, a middle, and an end.

Sharing Secrets: This one needs to be the one and only, even if it is only the first date. *For the gals:* Don't talk about your past relationships. Do all you can to make her feel cherished from the first moment. *For the guys:* Play up your innocence. Let him take charge, even in paying the bill. He needs to wear the pants.

Judith's Insights

About the Man: His life is unique and unusual, and that's how he likes it. His work environment needs to be harmonious or he will be miserable to work with. He enjoys a night out on the town. Bring him to some swanky party of a premiere and he will be in heaven. He loves to stand by and watch others before he dives in. Let him have time to study his surroundings before you pull him on to that dance floor. Once he has the lay of the land he will join you with a great big smile on his face.

About the Woman: She can dance in more ways than one. Sure, she dances at the nightclub, but she's better at dancing around the truth and emotions. She hates to be nailed down, unless she is doing the nailing. This girl never seems to be on an even keel. Just when she has all of her ducks in a row she will kick one out and start over. Is she looking for trouble or excitement? Perhaps to her they are one and the same. Allow her freedom to start a fire and she will want to tie the knot down the road.

MARCH

Soul Mates: Pisces understand each other, so this can be a great start. Aries and Taurus will attract you with their strength, but watch out for power struggles here and there. Otherwise, it is a go. Cancer and Scorpio tend to go with the flow, as do you. Sometimes, too much water gets in the room and it all gets washed up, though. Capricorn and Aquarius are a great basis for any relationship. Passion and true friendship are something you don't see every day. Gemini and Sagittarius are feisty, flirty, and furious. Critical is written all over Virgo. Leo and Libra will bring out the best or worst in you. Sometimes it can be a little bit of both.

Most Charming Characteristics: Artistic, honest, good-natured.

Gifts: *For her:* movie night at home. *For him:* sailboat.

Sensual Foods: Strawberries and cream; meat loaf.

Romantic Flowers: Iris is your flower if you are the gal sending subtle messages. If you are the man, you will look for clematis. This flower's mental beauty creates emotional stimulation for you.

Best Date Nights: Saturday; 1st and 10th of each month.

Colors of Passion: *For her:* light green, violet. *For him:* blue-green, turquoise.

The Perfect Wedding: Choose a relaxed, romantic atmosphere, most likely inspired by a body of water. An inlet or a lagoon at either dawn or dusk . . . or, perhaps, a winter wedding in a cozy room with a picturesque, snowy view. You might choose a grand room with roaring, blazing fireplaces. Ideal setting: Mediterranean island; Greece.

Wise Words: Charles Dickens: "Think and speak and act like an accountable creature."

Hints of Love: They only use the three magic words when they know they mean it, and they already know it is going to be said back to them.

After the Argument: *For him:* Promise him anything, but give him yourself and your time. If you can make him smile, you're on your way. A little attention goes a long way, but this is one whose ego you don't want to inflate or he could milk it for a while. *For her:* You had better be ready to be on your best behavior for a long time. This one could be tough even if she is the one who was wrong.

Romantic Places: Places of spirituality bring romance: Rome; yoga class; the mountains of Colorado.

Lucky Love Star: Pisciel—you will never lack magnetism.

Beautiful Thought: Any bonus is cause for celebration.

Sharing Secrets: Let them admire something about you first. Show them you have a sense of humor. *For the gals:* Hold their hand and then take them to the next step. *For the guys:* The way to his heart is definitely through his stomach.

Judith's Insights

About the Man: Don't let him get to the point where you can't tell the difference between an obligation and a favor. He can be Mr. Nice Guy, and will certainly feel drained if too much is put on his shoulders. He is childlike in many ways and will make people of all ages attracted to him, including dogs. His ability to make you smile no matter what the day has brought you will make you want to hang around him as often as possible. Getting into a relationship with this guy may take longer than you think. He needs to make sure that the ice is thick enough to walk on.

About the Woman: I wish I had a nickel for every time she changes her mind. We could all retire on it. You may have to wear roller skates to keep up with this gal. She loves her dance card to be full, and if the phone isn't ringing, then she will start to dial it. If the romance is not there she will not hesitate to seek it out elsewhere. If you can't take the heat you have to have enough common sense to stay out of the kitchen. This girl has a very passionate heart and can often live in her own head. Make sure you give her plenty of attention without losing yourself in the meantime.

Soul Mates: Pisces and Pisces: you two fish have your own language. Aries's and Taurus's need for self-preservation may bring out your insecurities. There is loads of water here with Cancer and Scorpio. Try not to drown in it. Gemini and Sagittarius will urge you to reach out and expand. Virgo's perfectionism can get out of control. This can pull the rug out from under you. Extremes are rampant with Libra and Leo. Make sure to balance self-confidence with humility. Capricorn and Aquarius can be the stabilizing force you need so much.

Most Charming Characteristics: Intuitive, affectionate, good-natured.

Gifts: *For her:* dinner cruise. *For him:* fishing trip with the guys.

Sensual Foods: Cherry-apple pie; beef Stroganoff.

Romantic Flowers: Any rose of any color for the lady. Roses stand for love regardless of the color. Send them with orchids and you will be saying, "I love you." If you want a gentleman to know you think of him, send pansies, and forget-me-nots for true love.

Best Date Nights: Saturday; 11th and 20th of each month.

Colors of Passion: *For her:* light green, violet. *For him:* blue-green, turquoise.

The Perfect Wedding: Choose a relaxed, romantic atmosphere, most likely inspired by a body of water. An inlet or a lagoon at either dawn or dusk . . . or, perhaps, a winter wedding in a cozy room with a picturesque, snowy view. You might choose a grand room with roaring, blazing fireplaces. Ideal setting: Mediterranean island; Greece.

Wise Words: Charles Dickens: "We must meet reverses boldly, and not suffer them to frighten us."

Hints of Love: Remember to keep the dating fun. Don't act like you are married before your time.

After the Argument: *For him:* Promise him anything, but give him yourself and your time. If you can make him smile, you're on your way. A little attention goes a long way, but this is one whose ego you don't want to inflate or he could milk it for a while. *For her:* You had better be ready to be on your best behavior for a long time. This one could be tough even if she is the one who was wrong.

Romantic Places: Places of fantasy bring romance: China; a carnival; Mardi Gras.

Lucky Love Star: Pisciel—you will never lack magnetism.

Beautiful Thought: Swimming upstream and getting there.

Sharing Secrets: Give them the opportunity to notice you first. *For the gals:* They love to be adored; love at first sight. *For the guys:* Remember to always let them believe it was their idea.

Judith's Insights

About the Man: He is looking out for number one, and he is number two. You can count on the fact that this guy will put you before himself. This is the kind of boss everybody dreams of and seldom gets. Yes, he is a bit of a dreamer, but he dreams with his eyes open and his mouth shut. He can certainly make you laugh, and you know what that means. You will want to stick around for more of his loving ways. He is sensitive and nurturing by nature. People who do not know any better may think him weak. His convictions and passion will show you otherwise.

About the Woman: Her words will stick in your mind long after she is out of your life. This one has a lasting impression on any relationship she is in, good or bad. Even the passersby she meets on the street will feel her pull. She has a unique attractiveness in everything she does. Her kindness lures you in, and her kindness is what makes you want to stay. She has many fantasies and will find many ways of living them out. This gal is not only a dreamer but a doer as well. Oh, the things she could teach you! She believes that the spirit of life is to make things happen.

Soul Mates: No one can know you like a copy of yourself, Pisces. That is why a relationship with another Pisces will be solid. Aries and Taurus may be the solid ground you seek. You might have to fight for the territory, though. Water signs need to give and receive feelings. If you pair with Cancer and Scorpio, make sure you each have that opportunity. Your receptivity will slow Gemini's and Sagittarius's impatient desire to move way too fast. Your insecurities are on trial constantly with Virgo. Walk away while you can. Beware of dependency coming from just plain enjoying each other's company when you deal with Leo and Libra. You help Capricorn and Aquarius become less rigid while they help you build structure. A perfect balance.

Most Charming Characteristics: Magnetic personality, passionate, faithful.

Gifts: *For her:* diamond earrings. *For him:* romantic cruise.

Sensual Foods: Hot-fudge sundae with all the trimmings; shepherd's pie.

Romantic Flowers: These ladies like everyone to know how faithful they are, so send them violets. To surprise them send tulips. Men like their flowers the same as their relationships, unpretending. Send them camellias with white roses to show your affection.

Best Date Nights: Saturday; 12th and 21st of each month.

Colors of Passion: *For her:* light green, violet. *For him:* blue-green, turquoise.

The Perfect Wedding: Choose a relaxed, romantic atmosphere, most likely inspired by a body of water. An inlet or a lagoon at either dawn or dusk . . . or, perhaps, a winter wedding in a cozy room with a picturesque, snowy view. You might choose a grand room with roaring, blazing fireplaces. Ideal setting: Mediterranean island; Greece.

Wise Words: Charles Dickens: "I don't care; nothing puts me out; I am resolved to be happy."

Hints of Love: Make sure you go on more than one date before you jump to conclusions on liking and disliking.

After the Argument: *For him:* Promise him anything, but give him yourself and your time. If you can make him smile, you're on your way. A little attention goes a long way, but this is one whose ego you don't want to inflate or he could milk it for a while. *For her:* You had better be ready to be on your best behavior for a long time. This one could be tough even if she is the one who was wrong.

Romantic Places: Places of spirituality bring romance: India; a cathedral or temple; the Grand Canyon.

Lucky Love Star: Pisciel–you will never lack magnetism.

Beautiful Thought: A fallen leaf starts a new life when someone picks it up from the ground.

Sharing Secrets: This one loves a challenge. *For the gals:* Be consistently inconsistent until you have them hooked. *For the guys:* This one loves to play catch. You may feel like a yo-yo, but as long as he is calling that's all that matters.

Judith's Insights

About the Man: He can be the life of the party or the one who is letting the air out of the tires in the parking lot. I guess it depends on your idea of fun. He is up for anything and everything, especially if it is impetuous. He has a class and a style all his own. To know him is to love him. Getting to know his true self may prove to be harder than you can imagine. It is not that he does not want to let you in. His appearance is so different from his true self that you may have a hard time believing that he is so sensitive and kind inside.

About the Woman: She knows exactly what she wants, but she doesn't always like stepping on others to get what she wants. If you show her loyalty, you will have a friend for life and then some. Others feel competitive with her just because of the appearance that she does everything with ease. It isn't as easy as she makes it look. She simply has no problem with putting in the work necessary for attaining her dreams. Her good nature and disposition make her approachable, but this one has a soft heart and may bleed easily. Be careful how you approach sensitive subjects.

Soul Mates: What is better than finding someone as faithful and devoted as you? That is exactly what you can find in a fellow Pisces. Aries's and Taurus's unfolding energy can make a relationship with them into an interesting ride. Cancer's and Scorpio's strong desire to love and be loved can result in an overflow of emotions. Gemini and Sagittarius push you to connect with others instead of standing back and waiting for them to come to you. Virgo's analytical nature will leave you feeling powerless. Leo and Libra may have trouble making decisions because they are worried about being fair. Your receptiveness will calm the rebellion in Capricorn's and Aquarius's energy.

Most Charming Characteristics: Shrewd, gracious, passionate.

Gifts: *For her:* seafood and champagne dinner at sunset. *For him:* custom aquarium.

Sensual Foods: Whipped cream, strawberries, brown sugar, and heavy cream.

Romantic Flowers: These ladies like men with taste. Show them you love style by sending fuchsia flowers, or even brightly colored wildflowers will do. To confuse this man, send him lilies, along with bright daisies to show your innocence. Keep him guessing.

Best Date Nights: Saturday; 13th and 22nd of each month.

Colors of Passion: *For her:* light green, violet. *For him:* blue-green, turquoise.

The Perfect Wedding: Choose a relaxed, romantic atmosphere, most likely inspired by a body of water. An inlet or a lagoon at either dawn or dusk . . . or, perhaps, a winter wedding in a cozy room with a picturesque, snowy view. You might choose a grand room with roaring, blazing fireplaces. Ideal setting: Mediterranean island; Greece.

Wise Words: Charles Dickens: "Constancy in love is a good thing; but it means nothing and is nothing, without constancy in every kind of effort."

Hints of Love: Don't act too needy too soon. It may push this relationship away.

After the Argument: *For him:* Promise him anything, but give him yourself and your time. If you can make him smile, you're on your way. A little attention goes a long way, but this is one whose ego you don't want to inflate or he could milk it for a while. *For her:* You had better be ready to be on your best behavior for a long time. This one could be tough even if she is the one who was wrong.

Romantic Places: Places of fantasy bring romance: Russia; the theater; New York City.

Lucky Love Star: Pisciel—you will never lack magnetism.

Beautiful Thought: Even a small pebble can make many ripples in the water.

Sharing Secrets: This is a family person at heart; your presence is most important. *For the gals:* Make sure you go to Sunday dinner with her family when you are invited. *For the guys:* If you don't like his mom, you might have a hard time catching this one.

Judith's Insights

About the Man: Here is a guy who will open the door for you, even when he might not see you coming. He can wear his heart on his sleeve or keep it in his back pocket. It depends on what time of the day it is. Yes, he can be a little moody. He has an open ear but doesn't necessarily take input too easily. This one has boundaries, and others need to know exactly what they are before proceeding. Be cautious, especially if it is time to ask for a raise. This guy needs a little reassurance and someone to give him a hug. You would be surprised at how sensitive he can be.

About the Woman: All she wants is to be happy and for others in her life to help her do that. If for a moment she is looking through rose-colored glasses, let her do so. Don't try to take them away or she will push you away. She is a good friend and needs encouragement. If you tend to disapprove of what she is doing she will shut the door. Didn't your mother ever teach you that if you don't have something nice to say you shouldn't say anything? This rule is especially important when approaching this girl. She doesn't want to hear the bad news. She wants to focus on the good.

Soul Mates: Pisces can always lean on another stable Pisces. Balance with Aries and Taurus comes through adding gentleness to their need for independence. Cancer and Scorpio may try to go too far within or too far outside. Gemini and Sagittarius bring into your life a very active and extroverted energy. Until Virgo realizes that imperfection is okay, your ego will not be safe in their arms. Make sure that a relationship with Leo and Libra maintains your sense of self as well as part of the whole. When you help Capricorn and Aquarius remember the little joys in life, you will find joy in each other for a lifetime.

Most Charming Characteristics: True, ardent lover; perceptive.

Gifts: *For her:* book of poetry and quotes. *For him:* tickets to a film festival.

Sensual Foods: Puddings and pastry of all kinds.

Romantic Flowers: You are the lady of distinction, and only carnations will do. Any mix of colors with sprays of mignonette. Sweet peas or red carnations will appeal to this man's heart.

Best Date Nights: Saturday; 14th and 23rd of each month.

Colors of Passion: *For her:* light green, violet. *For him:* blue-green, turquoise.

The Perfect Wedding: Choose a relaxed, romantic atmosphere, most likely inspired by a body of water. An inlet or a lagoon at either dawn or dusk . . . or, perhaps, a winter wedding in a cozy room with a picturesque, snowy view. You might choose a grand room with roaring, blazing fireplaces. Ideal setting: Mediterranean island; Greece.

Wise Words: Charles Dickens: "The ceaseless work of time had been performed, in storm and sunshine. Through a whole year the tides of human chance and change had set in their allotted courses."

Hints of Love: Keep it fun. Look for new and exciting things to do, especially if you are in a long-term relationship.

After the Argument: *For him:* Promise him any-thing, but give him yourself and your time. If you can make him smile, you're on your way. A little attention goes a long way, but this is one whose ego you don't want to inflate or he could milk it for a while. *For her:* You had better be ready to be on your best behavior for a long time. This one could be tough even if she is the one who was wrong.

Romantic Places: Places of spirituality bring romance: Nepal; mountain trail; Waikiki, Hawaii.

Lucky Love Star: Pisciel—you will never lack magnetism.

Beautiful Thought: Thinking you threw away today, then catching it tomorrow.

Sharing Secrets: Everything in its good time. This one works slowly, but when it is time to pick up speed, watch out. *For the gals:* Don't go by the obvious. Read between the lines. As long as the invitation is being offered, go full speed ahead. *For the guys:* Just when you thought you should walk away, he'll say, "I love you." Talk about confusing.

Judith's Insights

About the Man: There isn't much difference here between the men and the boys when it comes to this fella. They just both want to have fun. He has an open heart and an open mind, and most of the time an open-door policy. But be cautious about stepping over boundaries. He put them up with such small curves it is hard to notice where they are. He needs to feel as if he is cherished by the one he loves. He cherishes her more than you could realize. There is nothing he would not do to attain a goal he has set for himself. He believes that all things are possible.

About the Woman: You didn't remember her birthday and you are expecting a raise? I wouldn't leave this one out of any party or she will take it personally, especially if there should have been one for her. She has more emotional needs than most people notice. She may not be the life of the party, but she can be, depending on what situation she is in. If you establish a standard of overwhelming demonstrations of your feelings early on in the relationship, you have to be able to sustain that level for the entire life of the relationship. She will expect nothing less.

Soul Mates: As long as you understand each other's need to be independent at times, a relationship with another Pisces will work nicely. Aries's and Taurus's assertiveness may become too willful. This is when you must take full advantage of your receptivity. Try to build gates in the walls Cancer and Scorpio put up around them. Gemini and Sagittarius bring to the table communication and interaction to merge with your compassion. Virgo's tendency to try too hard will leave your head spinning. Keep the picture of your true self inside of you at all times when getting together with Leo and Libra. You will need that picture when things get too dependent. Capricorn and Aquarius will give you the best combination of yin and yang energy. You will bring out the best in each other at every turn.

Most Charming Characteristics: Diligent, adventurous, loyal.

Gifts: *For her:* romantic evening at home. *For him:* fishing rod and reel.

Sensual Foods: Champagne with strawberries; fillet of sole.

Romantic Flowers: You love it when you get tulips, declaring love. When you receive a variety, it shows how hopelessly in love your partner is. He will just love a single rose. This shows him you understand his pleasures.

Best Date Nights: Saturday; 6th and 15th of each month.

Colors of Passion: *For her:* light green, violet. *For him:* blue-green, turquoise.

The Perfect Wedding: Choose a relaxed, romantic atmosphere, most likely inspired by a body of water. An inlet or a lagoon at either dawn or dusk . . . or, perhaps, a winter wedding in a cozy room with a picturesque, snowy view. You might choose a grand room with roaring, blazing fireplaces. Ideal setting: Mediterranean island; Greece.

Wise Words: Charles Dickens: "Time and tide will wait for no man, saith the adage, but all men have to wait for time and tide."

Hints of Love: This one is a cautious soul. You may have to find a way to go around to the back door.

After the Argument: *For him:* Promise him anything, but give him yourself and your time. If you can make him smile, you're on your way. A little attention goes a long way, but this is one whose ego you don't want to inflate or he could milk it for a while. *For her:* You had better be ready to be on your best behavior for a long time. This one could be tough even if she is the one who was wrong.

Romantic Places: Places of fantasy bring romance: Saint Petersburg; Russia; a movie set; Las Vegas, Nevada.

Lucky Love Star: Pisciel—you will never lack magnetism.

Beautiful Thought: Looking into someone's eyes and hearing all that person has to say.

Sharing Secrets: This one is a charmer, perhaps even fickle. *For the gals:* If you are patient enough to stick around, this one is worth the wait. *For the guys:* If there is enough time on the clock, stick around past three months. Then maybe he will have noticed you are there.

Judith's Insights

About the Man: He is so simple. If you are nice, he is nicer. If you are kind, he is kinder. If you are giving, he will give more. You just have to watch that you keep an even balance in any type of relationship you have with this guy. He can attain any goal or dream he has because he does not mind putting in the time to attain it. When others don't put as much effort in he won't understand why. This one can be moody, especially in a work environment. He can allow himself to be taken advantage of, but then pushes away from everybody around him.

About the Woman: She has a mouth but doesn't push to use it. She would prefer an even-tempered environment and for every situation to be cool, calm, and collected. You can push her only so far before she changes the rules. Allow her space and keep the door open; she will walk in almost every time. Others misjudge her because of her strength. She is loyal to a fault, and when it backfires she may blame it on you. It is not her fault that she was born so kind. You have to be cautious not to underestimate this girl. You will find that she is in the driver's seat and you will lose.

Soul Mates: A pairing with another Pisces could be just what you need. The two of you can take turns leaning on each other in your insecure times that only another Pisces could understand. Be prepared to step back and understand exactly where Aries and Taurus are coming from. Their independence may be about something else. Cancer and Scorpio are oh so very sensitive, just like you. Gemini and Sagittarius will urge you to reach out and communicate your feelings more aptly. A confident Pisces is no match for a nagging and picky Virgo. Don't become completely reliant on a partnership with Leo and Libra. You might find yourself wrapped up in everything but what is important to you. Capricorn and Aquarius, like you, have the ability and willingness to adapt to each other. This will carry you through anything you need to face together.

Most Charming Characteristics: Generous, tenderhearted, honest.

Gifts: *For her:* tickets to the local Renaissance fair. *For him:* a beach weekend.

Sensual Foods: Chocolates; poached salmon; flambé; filet mignon; potatoes.

Romantic Flowers: Send this girl sunflowers if you want her to know you adore her. You may even add some poppies for a splash of extravagance. His desire for sport and play will be understood when you send him hyacinth and geranium.

Best Date Nights: Saturday; 16th and 25th of each month.

Colors of Passion: *For her:* light green, violet. *For him:* blue-green, turquoise.

The Perfect Wedding: Choose a relaxed, romantic atmosphere, most likely inspired by a body of water. An inlet or a lagoon at either dawn or dusk . . . or, perhaps, a winter wedding in a cozy room with a picturesque, snowy view. You might choose a grand room with roaring, blazing fireplaces. Ideal setting: Mediterranean island; Greece.

Wise Words: Oliver Wendell Holmes: "You can laugh over that as much as you like—in private."

Hints of Love: Passion must be in the picture at all times or you could lose this one's attention quickly.

After the Argument: *For him:* Promise him anything, but give him yourself and your time. If you can make him smile, you're on your way. A little attention goes a long way, but this is one whose ego you don't want to inflate or he could milk it for a while. *For her:* You had better be ready to be on your best behavior for a long time. This one could be tough even if she is the one who was wrong.

Romantic Places: Places of spirituality bring romance: Israel; a Japanese garden; the Grand Canyon.

Lucky Love Star: Pisciel—you will never lack magnetism.

Beautiful Thought: A quiet sound can create the loudest noise.

Sharing Secrets: If you are looking for love, then you have found the right mate. *For the gals:* This one could be stubborn. It may take forever to get a relationship started, but it is as solid as they come. *For the guys:* Even when he is ready, he might not be willing and able. He will put you through more obstacles than any course. Be patient.

Judith's Insights

About the Man: He seems to lead a charmed life. In his head he can, but in his heart it is a bit more complicated than that. He can second-guess any type of relationship he has: family, friends, co-workers, and lovers. Things could get too overwhelming for him, and then he will have doubts and questions in his mind. He is a good worker but may seem defensive with others around him. You must prove yourself to him and then he will follow. He can be nurturing to all around him. At times, he can be so devoted to everyone else that he forgets to take care of himself.

About the Woman: She will never feel she is on board with you 100 percent. She will hold back in any endeavor until she feels others recognize her worth. It is her nature to question laziness in her relationships. Maybe it is because she puts so much of her heart into them. If she is there, her heart is there. Once she believes that you are at her side, she will move forward without so much anguish. You may have an obstacle between you and her heart but this could also be part of the fun. The prize on the other side is more than worth the effort to get there.

Soul Mates: Use that Pisces support for another Pisces. You will both need it for tough times in your life. Aries and Taurus love their freedom just as much as they love having you there to listen to their adventures. When Cancer and Scorpio get together with you there could be a flood of emotions no one can control. Change is important. Gemini and Sagittarius won't hesitate to initiate it. Virgo's tendency to critique your every move will break even your compassionate energy. Your receptive nature may become too susceptible to suggestion when in the hands of Leo and Libra. You will love to bask in the warm smiles of Capricorn and Aquarius for a long time to come.

Most Charming Characteristics: Scrupulously honest, sincere, generous.

Gifts: *For her:* sailing adventures. *For him:* write him a poem from your heart.

Sensual Foods: Caviar; beef tenderloin; potatoes au gratin.

Romantic Flowers: Rhododendron will let her be on the lookout for trouble. Throw in some chrysanthemum and she'll know it is you she will be looking out for. Cactus will show him warmth. Yellow daffodil is a token of a good time had by all. Chivalry is not dead.

Best Date Nights: Saturday; 8th and 17th of each month.

Colors of Passion: *For her:* light green, violet. *For him:* blue-green, turquoise.

The Perfect Wedding: Choose a relaxed, romantic atmosphere, most likely inspired by a body of water. An inlet or a lagoon at either dawn or dusk . . . or, perhaps, a winter wedding in a cozy room with a picturesque, snowy view. You might choose a grand room with roaring, blazing fireplaces. Ideal setting: Mediterranean island; Greece.

Wise Words: Oliver Wendell Holmes: "Take care that the phrase or sentence you commend is not warmth but is in quotation marks."

Hints of Love: A random act of kindness will go a long way with this one. What can you do for them today?

After the Argument: *For him:* Promise him anything, but give him yourself and your time. If you can make him smile, you're on your way. A little attention goes a long way, but this is one whose ego you don't want to inflate or he could milk it for a while. *For her:* You had better be ready to be on your best behavior for a long time. This one could be tough even if she is the one who was wrong.

Romantic Places: Places of fantasy bring romance: Russia; the theater; New York City.

Lucky Love Star: Pisciel—you will never lack magnetism.

Beautiful Thought: Breathe in, breathe deep; this will allow for a peaceful sleep.

Sharing Secrets: If you can hang around and give constant stimulation, this could be your mate. *For the gals:* She is always looking for the Exit sign. Don't show her where it is or she will be gone. *For the guys:* Fast car, fast food; he likes everything that goes fast. Put on your running shoes. If you can keep up, then he is yours.

Judith's Insights

About the Man: Powerful emotions may make him seem moody. He tries to keep his calendar full. He hates feeling as if his life is empty, so you may find that he fills it with busy work. This work is never frivolous, however. There is always a dream or goal that he is striving for. When he attains that goal he will simply set another to work toward. To him, life is all about the fun you have living it and the things you can achieve on the way. He certainly is approachable, but it may take him time to notice you. Have a lot of patience if you are interested in this one.

About the Woman: She is one of those who would rather stay home and wash her hair than fill her schedule with people she doesn't really like. So, if you happen to be hanging out with this gal, she certainly already enjoys your company. Having just a coffee break with this gal means she is not interested in wasting her time, and if she is having dinner with you, she is really in love. Sometimes she can have a hard time getting out of her own way, especially when it comes to love. She seems more free-spirited than she really is. She will always be looking ahead.

Soul Mates: A fellow Pisces will be just as compassionate and nurturing as you. Keep in mind how much you love their willfulness when Aries and Taurus get a bit full of themselves. Water signs are more introverted. When you are with Cancer and Scorpio, someone has to bring out your independent side. Quiet contemplation can heighten Gemini's and Sagittarius's intuition and temper their fire. Run away from Virgo's nit-picking behavior. Severe swings in the feel of the relationship with Leo and Libra are sure to come. Achievements of great things are possible when you have Capricorn and Aquarius in your corner.

Most Charming Characteristics: Gracious, perceptive, understanding.

Gifts: *For her:* fantasy novel. *For him:* dinner next to the water.

Sensual Foods: Passion fruit; fillet of sole almondine.

Romantic Flowers: The magnolias you send her will let her know you will be around for a while to come. Petunia is to say never despair. Holly will let him know what he is getting into. Pansy will keep you in his thoughts.

Best Date Nights: Saturday; 9th and 18th of each month.

Colors of Passion: *For her:* light green, violet. *For him:* blue-green, turquoise.

The Perfect Wedding: Choose a relaxed, romantic atmosphere, most likely inspired by a body of water. An inlet or a lagoon at either dawn or dusk . . . or, perhaps, a winter wedding in a cozy room with a picturesque, snowy view. You might choose a grand room with roaring, blazing fireplaces. Ideal setting: Mediterranean island; Greece.

Wise Words: Oliver Wendell Holmes: "Because a man does not say much, it does not follow that he may not have an exalted intense inner life."

Hints of Love: Family and friends are important to this one. Don't try to alienate them or it will definitely backfire on you.

After the Argument: *For him:* Promise him anything, but give him yourself and your time. If you can make him smile, you're on your way. A little attention goes a long way, but this is one whose ego you don't want to inflate or he could milk it for a while. *For her:* You had better be ready to be on your best behavior for a long time. This one could be tough even if she is the one who was wrong.

Romantic Places: Places of spirituality bring romance: Rome; yoga class; the mountains of Colorado.

Lucky Love Star: Pisciel—you will never lack magnetism.

Beautiful Thought: A question you ask today could answer itself tomorrow.

Sharing Secrets: This one may seem like a lot of work. They just need the basics: love, loyalty, and respect. *For the gals:* If you can show her your best side right from the beginning it may work. Be careful of fluff, because she will see right through it. *For the guys:* He loves to be loved. Give him plenty of attention, even if you think you don't stand a chance. Perseverance will win here.

Judith's Insights

About the Man: Everybody loves him, including his mom. If you can break that chain, that would be surprising. He loves the rat pack. You will find him traveling in groups of people—the Men's Club, the Boy's Club, and the Yacht Club. He needs to be one of the boys, and, yes, he is the one with the most toys, so appeal to that. He has a reason for surrounding himself with everyone he does hang with. You won't find this guy in the company of someone he does not like. To him, that is just a waste of time. If he is asking you out, there is already strong interest there.

About the Woman: She lives in a world of her own and is able to shut out the world. People think they know her and then realize one day that they don't. Sometimes the closer you get, the farther apart you feel. Time is one of the things that will allow you to feel close. They are constantly building walls, and you are constantly taking them down. Expect a little work. She likes to believe that she is in charge of her own life and emotions. As long as you let her continue to believe that, she will allow you to get close to her. Show her that your heart and hands are open to get even closer.

Soul Mates: Pisces understand each other, so this can be a great start. Aries and Taurus will attract you with their strength but watch out for power struggles here and there. Otherwise, it is a go. Cancer and Scorpio tend to go with the flow, as do you. Sometimes, too much water gets in the room and it all gets washed up, though. Capricorn and Aquarius are a great basis for any relationship. Passion and true friendship are something you don't see every day. Gemini and Sagittarius are feisty, flirty, and furious. Critical is written all over Virgo. Leo and Libra will bring out the best or worst in you. Sometimes it can be a little bit of both.

Most Charming Characteristics: Engaging personality, intuitive, impulsive.

Gifts: *For her:* movie night at home. *For him:* sailboat.

Sensual Foods: Peaches; mousse; shrimp.

Romantic Flowers: Iris is your flower if you are the gal sending subtle messages. If you are the man, you will look for clematis. This flower's mental beauty creates emotional stimulation for you.

Best Date Nights: Saturday; 1st and 10th of each month.

Colors of Passion: *For her:* light green, violet. *For him:* blue-green, turquoise.

The Perfect Wedding: Choose a relaxed, romantic atmosphere, most likely inspired by a body of water. An inlet or a lagoon at either dawn or dusk . . . or, perhaps, a winter wedding in a cozy room with a picturesque, snowy view. You might choose a grand room with roaring, blazing fireplaces. Ideal setting: Mediterranean island; Greece.

Wise Words: John Keats: "Here are sweet peas, on tiptoe for a flight; With wings of gentle flush o'er delicate white. / And taper fingers catching all things, To bind them all about with tiny rings."

Hints of Love: Show others how much you adore him or her. They will revel in how others notice.

After the Argument: *For him:* Promise him anything, but give him yourself and your time. If you can make him smile, you're on your way. A little attention goes a long way, but this is one whose ego you don't want to inflate or he could milk it for a while. *For her:* You had better be ready to be on your best behavior for a long time. This one could be tough even if she is the one who was wrong.

Romantic Places: Places of fantasy bring romance: China; a carnival; Mardi Gras.

Lucky Love Star: Pisciel—you will never lack magnetism.

Beautiful Thought: Sometimes you just need time to pass in order for things to happen.

Sharing Secrets: They're looking for love, but that is just their little secret. *For the gals:* Why shouldn't they want to be loved? Of course they do, but they want you to do all of the work. *For the guys:* You must prove yourself repeatedly. Don't expect too much until he knows you are under his thumb.

Judith's Insights

About the Man: It would be easier to send a message in a bottle across the ocean than to pry things from this guy's heart that he might not be ready to let you know. He hates confrontation. Allow him to think he is in total control and then take baby steps, tiny baby steps. If this is your boss, don't overstep your boundaries. Too much pressure on this one will make him run. Don't come to any conclusions about how he may be feeling before you give him time to figure that out for himself. He needs to weigh all sides of the issue at hand before making a statement.

About the Woman: She has her own way of challenging every situation. Her intention could be as good as gold and still she will have a tendency to drive you crazy somehow. Don't take her too personally. You are better off letting time tell things more clearly, especially when you are dealing with business. She needs to be sure of things before she jumps in. She needs to hesitate at times to look back and make sure that the road was as smooth as it seemed at the time. Her careful way about her will make her more approachable, but her hesitations will make you feel as if you have to pull back.

Soul Mates: Pisces and Pisces: you two fish have your own language. Aries's and Taurus's need for self-preservation may bring out your insecurities. There is loads of water here with Cancer and Scorpio. Try not to drown in it. Gemini and Sagittarius will urge you to reach out and expand. Virgo's perfectionism can get out of control. This can pull the rug out from under you. Extremes are rampant with Libra and Leo. Make sure to balance self-confidence with humility. Capricorn and Aquarius can be the stabilizing forces you need so much.

Most Charming Characteristics: Conscientious, congenial, appreciative.

Gifts: *For her:* dinner cruise. *For him:* fishing trip with the guys.

Sensual Foods: Kiwis; cantaloupes; strawberries.

Romantic Flowers: Any rose of any color for the lady. Roses stand for love regardless of the color. Send them with orchids and you will be saying, "I love you." If you want a gentleman to know you think of him, send pansies, and forget-me-nots for true love.

Best Date Nights: Saturday; 11th and 20th of each month.

Colors of Passion: *For her:* light green, violet. *For him:* blue-green, turquoise.

The Perfect Wedding: Choose a relaxed, romantic atmosphere, most likely inspired by a body of water. An inlet or a lagoon at either dawn or dusk . . . or, perhaps, a winter wedding in a cozy room with a picturesque, snowy view. You might choose a grand room with roaring, blazing fireplaces. Ideal setting: Mediterranean island; Greece.

Wise Words: Oliver Wendell Holmes: "Why, the truths a man carries about with him are his tools."

Hints of Love: Don't overdo it (dress, attention) too soon or this one will run. Wait until you have them hooked before you become outrageous.

After the Argument: *For him:* Promise him anything, but give him yourself and your time. If you can make him smile, you're on your way. A little attention goes a long way, but this is one whose ego you don't want to inflate or he could milk it for a while. *For her:* You had better be ready to be on your best behavior for a long time. This one could be tough even if she is the one who was wrong.

Romantic Places: Places of spirituality bring romance: India; a cathedral or temple; the Grand Canyon.

Lucky Love Star: Pisciel—you will never lack magnetism.

Beautiful Thought: All you need is time, and time will show you the place.

Sharing Secrets: You had better be ready to pull out your romantic side if you want this to work. *For the gals:* Fireplaces, walks on the beach, or even winning a bear at the local carnival. *For the guys:* When you are out shopping, bring him something home. Even if it is silly, he will love the thought.

Judith's Insights

About the Man: Some like it hot. Do you think he does? He loves a little bit of controversy to keep things interesting, but he can't stand outright confrontations. Yes, he thinks he has it all, and maybe he does. Certainly a little bit of wit can go a long way. When it comes down to love, his attitude can become bitter if things don't work out the way he has planned. He will never understand why someone would not work as hard as possible to reach a dream. If you can't work toward the dream of a happy life with this guy, he won't waste his time trying for you.

About the Woman: She has a need to feel important. Don't we all? But this one is constantly searching it out. She needs to make a difference. With this one, if you get past the tollbooth, it's not over. There are many more tolls along the road, as well as a few potholes you have to look out for. She wants you to put your emotions where your mouth is and create a steady hand of loyalty. She will give you nothing less. She can be a keeper and has a true ability to not overcomplicate the situation. She may need a little constant intrigue. Even when she has made a commitment she is not dead.

Soul Mates: No one can know you like a copy of yourself, Pisces. That is why a relationship with another Pisces will be solid. Aries and Taurus may be the solid ground you seek. You might have to fight for the territory, though. Water signs need to give and receive feelings. If you pair with Cancer and Scorpio, make sure you each have that opportunity. Your receptivity will slow Gemini's and Sagittarius's impatient desire to move way too fast. Your insecurities are on trial constantly with Virgo. Walk away while you can. Beware of dependency coming from just plain enjoying each other's company when you deal with Leo and Libra. You help Capricorn and Aquarius become less rigid while they help you build structure. A perfect balance.

Most Charming Characteristics: Engaging personality, impulsive, honest.

Gifts: *For her:* diamond earrings. *For him:* romantic cruise.

Sensual Foods: Caramel and chocolate syrup on anything.

Romantic Flowers: These ladies like everyone to know how faithful they are, so send them violets. To surprise them send tulips. Men like their flowers the same as their relationships, unpretending. Send them camellias with white roses to show your affection.

Best Date Nights: Saturday; 3rd and 12th of each month.

Colors of Passion: *For her:* light green, violet. *For him:* blue-green, turquoise.

The Perfect Wedding: Choose a relaxed, romantic atmosphere, most likely inspired by a body of water. An inlet or a lagoon at either dawn or dusk . . . or, perhaps, a winter wedding in a cozy room with a picturesque, snowy view. You might choose a grand room with roaring, blazing fireplaces. Ideal setting: Mediterranean island; Greece.

Wise Words: Thomas Hardy: "But with a disposition to be happy, it is neither this place nor the other that can render us the reverse. In short, each man's happiness depends upon himself, and his ability for doing with little."

Hints of Love: When these folks decide to sit on the fence don't try to push them off before they are ready. Let them do the jumping themselves.

After the Argument: *For him:* Promise him anything, but give him yourself and your time. If you can make him smile, you're on your way. A little attention goes a long way, but this is one whose ego you don't want to inflate or he could milk it for a while. *For her:* You had better be ready to be on your best behavior for a long time. This one could be tough even if she is the one who was wrong.

Romantic Places: Places of fantasy bring romance: Russia; the theater; New York City.

Lucky Love Star: Pisciel—you will never lack magnetism.

Beautiful Thought: Learn what you need to balance yourself, then everything else will even out.

Sharing Secrets: It may seem like they are not interested, but ask them out anyway. *For the gals:* Until they absolutely know you are interested, you will never find out that they are. *For the guys:* Ask him out if he doesn't ask you. He may be shy or not. Either way, he may be interested.

Judith's Insights

About the Man: You may think this one is Mr. Know It All, and since he is so diverse it may get to you that he just could be. He is a little too cocky from time to time, but full of vim and vigor. He continuously adds a little spice to the situation, and that is why people rarely get bored when in his company. Tension excites him while confrontation turns him off. He is not here to fight for the sake of fighting. Instead, he craves a good solid debate from time to time. Don't agree with everything he says. Just make sure that you can back up your opinions with solid arguments.

About the Woman: She can play follow the leader for only so long. She decides what she likes and doesn't like in someone and is sure to look at the person's best quality and try to enhance it. This one not only tries to bring the best out of herself but of other people. She is easily approachable, easily obtainable, and easily enjoyable. She might even come off as unusual. She is ready, willing, and able to learn from others. All she wants is for you to be as open. She starts off in any relationship in a cocoon. Before you realize what has happened, the butterfly she truly is will come out.

Soul Mates: What is better than finding someone as faithful and devoted as you? That is exactly what you can find in a fellow Pisces. Aries's and Taurus's unfolding energy can make a relationship with them into an interesting ride. Cancer's and Scorpio's strong desire to love and be loved can result in an overflow of emotions. Gemini and Sagittarius push you to connect with others instead of standing back and waiting for them to come to you. Virgo's analytical nature will leave you feeling powerless. Leo and Libra may have trouble making decisions because they are worried about being fair. Your receptiveness will calm the rebellion in Capricorn's and Aquarius's energy.

Most Charming Characteristics: Ambitious, faithful, understanding.

Gifts: *For her:* seafood and champagne dinner at sunset. *For him:* custom aquarium.

Sensual Foods: Waffles with whipped cream; chocolate soufflé; French wine.

Romantic Flowers: These ladies like men with taste. Show them you love style by sending fuchsia flowers, or even brightly colored wildflowers will do. To confuse this man, send him lilies along with bright daisies to show your innocence. Keep him guessing.

Best Date Nights: Saturday; 4th and 13th of each month.

Colors of Passion: *For her:* light green, violet. *For him:* blue-green, turquoise.

The Perfect Wedding: Choose a relaxed, romantic atmosphere, most likely inspired by a body of water. An inlet or a lagoon at either dawn or dusk . . . or, perhaps, a winter wedding in a cozy room with a picturesque, snowy view. You might choose a grand room with roaring, blazing fireplaces. Ideal setting: Mediterranean island; Greece.

Wise Words: Thomas Moore: "Words, once my stock, are wanting, to commend so great a poet, and so good a friend."

Hints of Love: Make sure you learn to compromise, but never with your principles.

After the Argument: *For him:* Promise him anything, but give him yourself and your time. If you can make him smile, you're on your way. A little attention goes a long way, but this is one whose ego you don't want to inflate or he could milk it for a while. *For her:* You had better be ready to be on your best behavior for a long time. This one could be tough even if she is the one who was wrong.

Romantic Places: Places of spirituality bring romance: Nepal; mountain trail; Waikiki, Hawaii.

Lucky Love Star: Pisciel—you will never lack magnetism.

Beautiful Thought: Understand that everything cannot happen in a single day.

Sharing Secrets: Don't be surprised if the first date is with the family. *For the gals:* Make sure you invite her to your family functions. It will be a red flag to her if you don't. *For the guys:* He may seem like a family man, but isn't that what you were looking for?

Judith's Insights

About the Man: He is capable of being very charismatic, but you will only see him put his best foot forward when he is interested. He is extremely guarded, so get to know him before making harsh judgments. It will be easier to ask him for things when he knows where you are coming from. Explain your reasons clearly and he will be much likelier to give you what you need. He loves giving so much that he has had to train himself to be cautious about what and to whom. He just wants to know that there is someone who will be willing to give to him in return.

About the Woman: There isn't much you can do to rattle this one's cage. She loves very few people and for just no reason. She consistently tests the hands of fate and questions life at every hand's turn, a skeptic living an emotional dream. She has an interesting way of going about life, but her spiritual side takes her through. She will come off as more flirtatious than she really is. She wants to cultivate a secure relationship more than anything. All she needs is a little action in the picture to make things perfect. A bit of spice is just the thing to cheer her up if she seems bored or withdrawn.

Soul Mates: Pisces can always lean on another stable Pisces. Balance with Aries and Taurus comes through, adding gentleness to their need for independence. Cancer and Scorpio may try to go too far within or too far outside. Gemini and Sagittarius bring into your life a very active and extroverted energy. Until Virgo realizes that imperfection is okay, your ego will not be safe in their arms. Make sure that a relationship with Leo and Libra maintains your sense of self as well as part of the whole. When you help Capricorn and Aquarius remember the little joys in life, you will find joy in each other for a lifetime.

Most Charming Characteristics: Conversationalist, energetic, ambitious.

Gifts: *For her:* book of poetry and quotes. *For him:* tickets to a film festival.

Sensual Foods: Oysters; mussels; spicy foods.

Romantic Flowers: You are the lady of distinction, and only carnations will do. Any mix of colors with sprays of mignonette. Sweet peas or red carnations will appeal to this man's heart.

Best Date Nights: Saturday; 5th and 23rd of each month.

Colors of Passion: *For her:* light green, violet. *For him:* blue-green, turquoise.

The Perfect Wedding: Choose a relaxed, romantic atmosphere, most likely inspired by a body of water. An inlet or a lagoon at either dawn or dusk . . . or, perhaps, a winter wedding in a cozy room with a picturesque, snowy view. You might choose a grand room with roaring, blazing fireplaces. Ideal setting: Mediterranean island; Greece.

Wise Words: Thomas Campbell: "Who shall say that Fortune grieves him, While the star of hope she leaves him?"

Hints of Love: If you try to take a step back, it will be noticed. It could create the domino effect, and everything will start to fall.

After the Argument: *For him:* Promise him anything, but give him yourself and your time. If you can make him smile, you're on your way. A little

attention goes a long way, but this is one whose ego you don't want to inflate or he could milk it for a while. *For her:* You had better be ready to be on your best behavior for a long time. This one could be tough even if she is the one who was wrong.

Romantic Places: Places of fantasy bring romance: Saint Petersburg, Russia; a movie set; Las Vegas, Nevada.

Lucky Love Star: Piscel—you will never lack magnetism.

Beautiful Thought: Speaking the word of today, having it heard tomorrow.

Sharing Secrets: Take me as I am could be the anthem for this one. *For the gals:* They will have strong views on just about everything. If you can hang with them, then nothing will be as important as you. *For the guys:* The thing you fall in love with may end up becoming the thing you hate. After a commitment, this one sticks around.

Judith's Insights

About the Man: Always ready to make a new friend, this guy is open to just about anything. He loves his wardrobe and his words to be diversified. He is easy to please. This is a guy who just wants to have fun and doesn't give in to gossip or controversy. He is usually the person in a crowd everyone tries to be next to. It is no wonder people are attracted to him. He will give all of himself to the right person and will never ask for anything that he can't give himself. You will find no one who is more loving than this guy when he feels cherished by his partner.

About the Woman: Don't ask too many questions; she will feel picked on. Her life is like being the cat's meow but constantly chased by dogs. She is strong and likes it when others around her understand her strength. She can come on too strong at times, but she is certainly a little kitten when she is petted the right way. You need no fancy approach to get into her heart; just be real. If you can be straightforward and honest, she will be sure to be intrigued. She is more than able to sustain a long and loving relationship as long as she feels that she is getting the same in return.

Soul Mates: As long as you understand each other's need to be independent at times, a relationship with another Pisces will work nicely. Aries's and Taurus's assertiveness may become too willful. This is when you must take full advantage of your receptivity. Try to build gates in the walls Cancer and Scorpio put up around them. Gemini and Sagittarius bring to the table communication and interaction to merge with your compassion. Virgo's tendency to try too hard will leave your head spinning. Keep the picture of your true self inside you at all times when getting together with Leo and Libra. You will need that picture when things get too dependent. Capricorn and Aquarius will give you the best combination of yin and yang energy. You will bring out the best in each other at every turn.

Most Charming Characteristics: Modest, unassuming, wholehearted, sincere.

Gifts: *For her:* romantic evening at home. *For him:* fishing rod and reel.

Sensual Foods: Lobster; watermelon.

Romantic Flowers: You love it when you get tulips, declaring love. When you receive a variety, it shows how hopelessly in love your partner is. He will just love a single rose. This shows him you understand his pleasures.

Best Date Nights: Saturday; 6th and 15th of each month.

Colors of Passion: *For her:* light green, violet. *For him:* blue-green, turquoise.

The Perfect Wedding: Choose a relaxed, romantic atmosphere, most likely inspired by a body of water. An inlet or a lagoon at either dawn or dusk . . . or, perhaps, a winter wedding in a cozy room with a picturesque, snowy view. You might choose a grand room with roaring, blazing fireplaces. Ideal setting: Mediterranean island; Greece.

Wise Words: John Locke: "He is the freeman whom the truth makes free, and all are slaves beside."

Hints of Love: Consistence and persistence will get this prize every time. They will value the effort.

After the Argument: *For him:* Promise him anything, but give him yourself and your time. If you can make him smile, you're on your way. A little attention goes a long way, but this is one whose ego you don't want to inflate or he could milk it for a while. *For her:* You had better be ready to be on your best behavior for a long time. This one could be tough even if she is the one who was wrong.

Romantic Places: Places of spirituality bring romance: Israel; a Japanese garden; the Grand Canyon.

Lucky Love Star: Pisciel—you will never lack magnetism.

Beautiful Thought: A good laugh tonight will give you the need for less sleep tomorrow.

Sharing Secrets: They seem moody until you get to know them. *For the gals:* You may not know whether to say hello or drop dead. As relations progress, you will learn not to leave her dangling, and her moods will become more consistent. *For the guys:* To know him is to love him. His bark is much worse than his bite. He just wants someone to love him without criticism.

Judith's Insights

About the Man: He has a passion for power and the people in it. He is drawn to social excitement of all kinds. You can usually find him where the movers and shakers are. He is the politician in many situations, even if he is not interested in being one. If you have the opportunity, invite him out to a political event or to an opening of some kind. Make him feel important. That will get his attention. Keeping his attention is as easy as you make it. The relationship must be balanced to keep him interested. A little give and take never hurt anyone. A lack of it will hurt him.

About the Woman: She knows everybody and everybody knows her, and by her first name. She is a peaceful person. People envy her just because she exists. She makes things look so easy while she has worked her buns off for everything she has. She lives life and gets the best out of it. She is easy to please and eager for others to be in her life. Make her feel important and she will be linked to you for a long time. She would rather the people in her life be easy and simple. The constant soap opera will never be concentrated around her, and she is all the happier for it.

Soul Mates: A pairing with another Pisces could be just what you need. The two of you can take turns leaning on each other in your insecure times that only another Pisces could understand. Be prepared to step back and understand exactly where Aries and Taurus are coming from. Their independence may be about something else. Cancer and Scorpio are oh so very sensitive, just like you. Gemini and Sagittarius will urge you to reach out and communicate your feelings more aptly. A confident Pisces is no match for a nagging and picky Virgo. Don't become completely reliant on a partnership with Leo and Libra. You might find yourself wrapped up in everything but what is important to you. Capricorn and Aquarius, like you, have the ability and willingness to adapt to each other. This will carry you through anything you need to face together.

Most Charming Characteristics: Confident, sincere, ambitious.

Gifts: *For her:* tickets to the local Renaissance fair. *For him:* a beach weekend.

Sensual Foods: Strawberries; truffles; shish kebab.

Romantic Flowers: Send this girl sunflowers if you want her to know you adore her. You may even add some poppies for a splash of extravagance. His desire for sport and play will be understood when you send him hyacinth and geranium.

Best Date Nights: Saturday; 7th and 16th of each month.

Colors of Passion: *For her:* light green, violet. *For him:* blue-green, turquoise.

The Perfect Wedding: Choose a relaxed, romantic atmosphere, most likely inspired by a body of water. An inlet or a lagoon at either dawn or dusk . . . or, perhaps, a winter wedding in a cozy room with a picturesque, snowy view. You might choose a grand room with roaring, blazing fireplaces. Ideal setting: Mediterranean island; Greece.

Wise Words: M. M. Kass Jr.: "It is a sad day for a young man when he first arouses himself to believe that there is an easier way of making a dollar than by honest work."

Hints of Love: Be funny. Laughter will be what keeps this one coming back again and again.

After the Argument: *For him:* Promise him anything, but give him yourself and your time. If you can make him smile, you're on your way. A little attention goes a long way, but this is one whose ego you don't want to inflate or he could milk it for a while. *For her:* You had better be ready to be on your best behavior for a long time. This one could be tough even if she is the one who was wrong.

Romantic Places: Places of fantasy bring romance: Russia; the theater; New York City.

Lucky Love Star: Pisciel—you will never lack magnetism.

Beautiful Thought: Fantasies and dreams carry us through, for now it's hope that will do.

Sharing Secrets: You had better be able to put your money where your mouth is. *For the gals:* It doesn't need to be lavish, but she does love the loot. The more the better. *For the guys:* He doesn't mind spending his hard-earned cash, but he loves to see you contribute to please him.

Judith's Insights

About the Man: The importance of what others think of him will subside as he gets older. It will also make him more approachable in many ways. The older he gets, the kinder he gets. That is saying a lot for a person who will give you anything you need if you only give a reason. This man likes others to appreciate him and know who he is. He is like a fine wine that gets better with age. He has a head for business and a drive to succeed at anything that is before him. Once he has achieved a certain level of success he will turn and look for something else to accomplish.

About the Woman: This gal knows what she wants and doesn't let much get in her way of getting it. If she likes you she will let you know, and if she doesn't, she will let you know that. If she is asking you to hang with her, that is a clear sign that she does like you. She won't waste her time with a person she doesn't like. Let's put it this way: it may be subtle, but she will get her point across in very specific ways. Don't get in the way of any of her goals and don't challenge her to come up with answers she hasn't had time to think of.

Soul Mates: Use that Pisces support for another Pisces. You will both need it for tough times in your life. Aries and Taurus love their freedom just as much as they love having you there to listen to their adventures. When Cancer and Scorpio get together with you there could be a flood of emotions no one can control. Change is important. Gemini and Sagittarius won't hesitate to initiate it. Virgo's tendency to critique your every move will break even your compassionate energy. Your receptive nature may become too susceptible to suggestion when in the hands of Leo and Libra. You will love to bask in the warm smiles of Capricorn and Aquarius for a long time to come.

Most Charming Characteristics: Philosophical, thoughtful, congenial.

Gifts: *For her:* sailing adventures. *For him:* write him a poem from your heart.

Sensual Foods: Grapes; fine cheeses and crackers; taffy.

Romantic Flowers: Rhododendron will let her be on the lookout for trouble. Throw in some chrysanthemum and she'll know it is you she will be looking out for. Cactus will show him warmth. Yellow daffodil is a token of a good time had by all. Chivalry is not dead.

Best Date Nights: Saturday; 8th and 26th of each month.

Colors of Passion: *For her:* light green, violet. *For him:* blue-green, turquoise.

The Perfect Wedding: Choose a relaxed, romantic atmosphere, most likely inspired by a body of water. An inlet or a lagoon at either dawn or dusk . . . or, perhaps, a winter wedding in a cozy room with a picturesque, snowy view. You might choose a grand room with roaring, blazing fireplaces. Ideal setting: Mediterranean island; Greece.

Wise Words: Charles Dickens: "All good ends can be worked out by good means. Those that cannot are bad; and may be counted so at once, and left alone."

Hints of Love: Treat this one like royalty or precious cargo. They will love being valued in this way.

After the Argument: *For him:* Promise him anything, but give him yourself and your time. If you can make him smile, you're on your way. A little attention goes a long way, but this is one whose ego you don't want to inflate or he could milk it for a while. *For her:* You had better be ready to be on your best behavior for a long time. This one could be tough even if she is the one who was wrong.

Romantic Places: Places of spirituality bring romance: Rome; yoga class; the mountains of Colorado.

Lucky Love Star: Pisciel—you will never lack magnetism.

Beautiful Thought: If we could only catch a glimpse of our yesterday, bottle it, and preserve it for tomorrow.

Sharing Secrets: Nobody likes a weak link, especially not this one. *For the gals:* Make sure you treat her like a lady and act like a man. *For the guys:* Put your best foot forward. Dress your best and keep your manners in check. This man notices.

Judith's Insights

About the Man: After he learns to get out of his own way, he may find his way into yours. It is not so much that he is full of himself, but he is the type of person who can do it all on his own, and it takes him a while to figure out why he may decide to have anybody he needs fit in his life. He may come across as cocky, but it is just that he never wants to feel too needy. This guy is in no way an impossible person to love. He is actually quite easy to love once you have seen what his soul is made of. To get there all you have to be is the loving and giving person you are.

About the Woman: Since she can be a little full of herself, she sets her goals and accomplishes them. Her attitude surprises everybody because one minute she is grounded and the next she is set free. Expect a lot of frequent flyer miles with this gal. Her experiences are many, and she will have plenty to write about. Handling her will be a hard task because she spends most of her life trying to figure out what makes her tick. Save her the trouble by showing her how much she has done for the people in her life without even realizing it. Imagine what she could do if she actually tried.

Soul Mates: A fellow Pisces will be just as compassionate and nurturing as you. Keep in mind how much you love their willfulness when Aries and Taurus get a bit full of themselves. Water signs are more introverted. When you are with Cancer and Scorpio, someone has to bring out your independent side. Quiet contemplation can heighten Gemini's and Sagittarius's intuition and temper their fire. Run away from Virgo's nit-picking behavior. Severe swings in the feel of the relationship with Leo and Libra are sure to come. Achievements of great things are possible when you have Capricorn and Aquarius in your corner.

Most Charming Characteristics: Quick-witted, confident, loyal.

Gifts: *For her:* fantasy novel. *For him:* dinner next to the water.

Sensual Foods: Champagne; grapes; mangoes; filet mignon.

Romantic Flowers: The magnolias you send her will let her know you will be around for a while to come. Petunia is to say never despair. Holly will let him know what he is getting into. Pansy will keep you in his thoughts.

Best Date Nights: Saturday; 9th and 18th of each month.

Colors of Passion: *For her:* light green, violet. *For him:* blue-green, turquoise.

The Perfect Wedding: Choose a relaxed, romantic atmosphere, most likely inspired by a body of water. An inlet or a lagoon at either dawn or dusk . . . or, perhaps, a winter wedding in a cozy room with a picturesque, snowy view. You might choose a grand room with roaring, blazing fireplaces. Ideal setting: Mediterranean island, Greece.

Wise Words: Charles Dickens: "How much wiser to take action at once than to trust to uncertain time."

Hints of Love: Affection is important, but only if it comes naturally. Otherwise, the sirens will go off.

After the Argument: *For him:* Promise him anything, but give him yourself and your time. If you can make him smile, you're on your way. A little attention goes a long way, but this is one whose ego you don't want to inflate or he could milk it for a while. *For her:* You had better be ready to be on your best behavior for a long time. This one could be tough even if she is the one who was wrong.

Romantic Places: Places of fantasy bring romance: China; a carnival; Mardi Gras.

Lucky Love Star: Pisciel—you will never lack magnetism.

Beautiful Thought: There are not enough good surprises.

Sharing Secrets: Attention, attention, attention. *For the gals:* Do it any way you can. Presents, phone calls, cards, or flowers. Whatever works for you will work for her. *For the guys:* He would love nostalgic gifts or T-shirts. He also likes phone calls, as long as they don't interrupt his favorite pastimes.

Judith's Insights

About the Man: What about him makes him so appealing to all around him? It is his simple and giving nature that creates a following that he will never understand. He will never know why his family and friends admire him so much. He has to know when, where, what, and how all the time. He doesn't like to be left in the lurch. He has more than a sensitive side and guards that side so others don't notice. When he feels exposed he may withdraw like a turtle. Keep him informed at all times and he will be more manageable.

About the Woman: She is a gal and knows how to use it. You would like to think that with all of the chattering she does, she is an open book. Well, guess again. As you get to know her, you should take note; this one is a puzzle and not easily put together. Just when you think you have it together you will realize that you are missing many pieces. She may seem as if she is giving you orders when that is not what she is trying to do. She is a natural leader, and you can learn a lot from her as soon as she learns how to give you advice without telling you what to do.

Soul Mates: Pisces understand each other, so this can be a great start. Aries and Taurus will attract you with their strength but watch out for power struggles here and there. Otherwise, it is a go. Cancer and Scorpio tend to go with the flow, as do you. Sometimes, too much water gets in the room and it all gets washed up, though. Capricorn and Aquarius are a great basis for any relationship. Passion and true friendship are something you don't see every day. Gemini and Sagittarius are feisty, flirty, and furious. Critical is written all over Virgo. Leo and Libra will bring out the best or worst in you. Sometimes it can be a little bit of both.

Most Charming Characteristics: Generous, affectionate, thoughtful.

Gifts: *For her:* movie night at home. *For him:* sailboat.

Sensual Foods: Châteaubriand; crème brûlée.

Romantic Flowers: Iris is your flower if you are the gal sending subtle messages. If you are the man, you will look for clematis. This flower's mental beauty creates emotional stimulation for you.

Best Date Nights: Saturday; 10th and 19th of each month.

Colors of Passion: *For her:* dark red, violet. *For him:* blue-green, turquoise.

The Perfect Wedding: Choose a relaxed, romantic atmosphere, most likely inspired by a body of water. An inlet or a lagoon at either dawn or dusk . . . or, perhaps, a winter wedding in a cozy room with a picturesque, snowy view. You might choose a grand room with roaring, blazing fireplaces. Ideal setting: Mediterranean island; Greece.

Wise Words: Charles Dickens; "Every man of true genius has his peculiarity."

Hints of Love: They like others to make their dreams come true. Be the "fantasy" fulfiller.

After the Argument: *For him:* Promise him anything, but give him yourself and your time. If you can make him smile, you're on your way. A little at-tention goes a long way, but this is one whose ego you don't want to inflate or he could milk it for a while. *For her:* You had better be ready to be on your best behavior for a long time. This one could be tough even if she is the one who was wrong.

Romantic Places: Places of spirituality bring romance: India; a cathedral or temple; the Grand Canyon.

Lucky Love Star: Pisciel—you will never lack magnetism.

Beautiful Thought: Appreciation is the greatest reward.

Sharing Secrets: Make sure you are not the killjoy. *For the gals:* When she has an idea, try it before you decide you don't like it. She needs to be pleased. *For the guys:* Do the things he loves to do and he will make the things you love ten times more fun.

Judith's Insights

About the Man: Nostalgia is his life's blood. Maybe that's why he is always reminiscing about the past. Even when he has a new job, you will wonder why he ever left the last one. Keep an open mind and an open schedule, because he doesn't like to be that organized. He may spring a get-together at the last minute. He loves to flirt, and he may not seem as loyal as he really is. This is a guy who will go to the ends of the earth for the one he loves. Once he makes a commitment, he will make sure that there is nothing in the way. Until he finds the right person, however, he will have a great time with the wrong ones.

About the Woman: Don't ever let her think you are being too bossy, even if you are her boss. She knows exactly how to get the job done. That is why she is there. She can be so much fun with her warm and witty side intact. She does get mood swings, so watch out. They can swing right open and hit you in the face if you are not careful about where you are walking. If you can get to know these swings, you will be prepared to run when they kick in. She can bruise easily. She may seem strong, but you really have to be careful how you say things. Her sensitive side goes hand in hand with her nurturing side.

Soul Mates: Pisces and Pisces: you two fish have your own language. Aries's and Taurus's need for self-preservation may bring out your insecurities. There is loads of water here with Cancer and Scorpio. Try not to drown in it. Gemini and Sagittarius will urge you to reach out and expand. Virgo's perfectionism can get out of control. This can pull the rug out from under you. Extremes are rampant with Libra and Leo. Make sure to balance self-confidence with humility. Capricorn and Aquarius can be the stabilizing force you need so much.

Most Charming Characteristics: Logical, diligent, philosophical.

Gifts: *For her:* dinner cruise. *For him:* fishing trip with the guys.

Sensual Foods: Shrimp; sinful chocolate cake.

Romantic Flowers: Any rose of any color for the lady. Roses stand for love regardless of the color. Send them with orchids and you will be saying, "I love you." If you want a gentleman to know you think of him, send pansies, and forget-me-nots for true love.

Best Date Nights: Saturday; 2nd and 11th of each month.

Colors of Passion: *For her:* light green, violet. *For him:* blue-green, turquoise.

The Perfect Wedding: Choose a relaxed, romantic atmosphere, most likely inspired by a body of water. An inlet or a lagoon at either dawn or dusk . . . or, perhaps, a winter wedding in a cozy room with a picturesque, snowy view. You might choose a grand room with roaring, blazing fireplaces. Ideal setting: Mediterranean island; Greece.

Wise Words: Charles Dickens: "What is the odds so long as the fire of souls is kindled at the taper of conviviality and the wing of friendship never moults a feather."

Hints of Love: Stop worrying about next week's date today, or there will not be one tomorrow.

After the Argument: *For him:* Promise him anything, but give him yourself and your time. If you can make him smile, you're on your way. A little at-tention goes a long way, but this is one whose ego you don't want to inflate or he could milk it for a while. *For her:* You had better be ready to be on your best behavior for a long time. This one could be tough even if she is the one who was wrong.

Romantic Places: Places of fantasy bring romance: Saint Petersburg; Russia; a movie set; Las Vegas, Nevada.

Lucky Love Star: Pisciel—you will never lack magnetism.

Beautiful Thought: It's always great to run into an old lover when you look great, or are not caring if you don't.

Sharing Secrets: You had better be ready to have a relationship. *For the gals:* No lies, no games, and no mistakes. She wants what she wants with as little amount of work possible. *For the guys:* If you have games on your mind, then move on. This one likes fun any way he can get it, but no emotional roller coasters.

Judith's Insights

About the Man: Now, here is a guy who knows what he wants. When he sets a goal there is no telling how far he will soar. Yes, nine times out of ten he gets exactly what he wants. Competitive is his middle name, maybe even his first. He is passionate about so many things that he may seem fickle. His attention can be on more than one thing as long as they all excite him. There is much fun to be had with a man like this. This guy can put the fire in the fireplace with no match. Just watch out that being too close too fast doesn't burn you.

About the Woman: Everyone thinks she is stronger than she is. She has a heart of gold and gets it broken way too often. She is a breath of fresh air to everyone she gets close to, although they may be few and far between. It is not that she puts up walls, but she is very hard for others to read. She likes what she likes how she likes it. She won't differ from that mind-set very often. This is a straight shooter right from the hip. Watch out, she can get her nose out of joint if you try to push her before she has had time to settle on the idea of commitment.

Soul Mates: Aries, Leo, and Sagittarius dish out just as much energy as you do. Let Aquarius and Pisces into your life and you definitely won't regret it. Virgo and Scorpio will have you twisted in knots trying to keep up with their mood swings. Don't lead Taurus and Gemini on. Let them know if you are not in for the long haul. Teach Libra the joy of independence you so love and they will be a joy to be around. Cancer's and Capricorn's unyielding nature will have you running in the other direction.

Most Charming Characteristics: Impetuous, persistent, incredibly kindhearted.

Gifts: *For her:* expensive perfume. *For him:* fine cologne.

Sensual Foods: Toasted marshmallows; chocolates.

Romantic Flowers: These ladies like everyone to know how faithful they are, so send them violets. To surprise them send tulips. Men like their flowers the same as their relationships, unpretending. Send them camellias with white roses to show your affection.

Best Date Nights: Tuesday; 3rd and 21st of each month.

Colors of Passion: *For her:* dark red, crimson. *For him:* reddish brown, black.

The Perfect Wedding: Flamboyant and dynamic . . . ring a bell? A wonderfully romantic, resplendent theme wedding is most suited to your personality. Don't laugh—you may want to consider a Disneyland setting (if not, maybe honeymoon?) that is steeped in fantasy and mystery. You love unusual dining places, and good entertainment for your guests is a must. It is essential that a splendid time is had by all, not just you and your love. Ideal setting: Florence.

Wise Words: Charles Dickens: "We must be hopeful, and we must at least try to be, if not generous, just."

Hints of Love: Keep the romance in the picture. Don't forget the long walks on the beach and camping out in front of the fireplace.

After the Argument: *For him:* Start kissing up. Inflate that ego until it pops. You usually will have two fights before the resolution of the first one. If he is wrong, don't expect the "I'm sorry." The fight will just end quickly. If you're wrong, start washing the car or shining his shoes. Then give him a night out with his friends. *For her:* Make sure she is good and calm, then say you're sorry for what you did, even if the fight wasn't your fault. If you want to make up, just start saying you're sorry for something. You will have her eating out of your hand in no time.

Romantic Places: Places of excitement bring romance: New Orleans; an amusement park; Times Square.

Lucky Love Star: Ariel—you will never lack affection.

Beautiful Thought: Simple says more.

Sharing Secrets: You may have to give this one more than one chance. *For the gals:* Intriguing as she is, expect a handful. She lightens up as time goes on. *For him:* His quirks may make you have second thoughts, but that is what separates the men from the boys.

Judith's Insights

About the Man: This guy is much, much more emotional than he allows the world to see. He can be a bit covert and shy, and he tends to let those he really knows into his heart as well as his head. He can be a bit of a tyrant when it comes to work, but certainly always gets the job done. Whether you work with him or live with him, you have to be able to do your part to get things done. Otherwise, he will grow to resent you. If he feels vulnerable, he will become even more hard-nosed than he already is. Be sensitive to his sensitive nature.

About the Woman: Only love can break her heart, and it has done a good job. Loyalty and security are the two things that can change her life. Many enter her life, but there are few who have stayed. She allows limited engagements only. It takes a special individual to get close to this one. The search is on. She knows just how to enjoy passion. If you struggle for her attention she may be testing to see what you are made of before she lets you in. If she is spending time with you at all it is a good sign that she cares for you. Be straightforward and honest and things will go well.

Soul Mates: Does the phrase "life of the party" mean anything to you? With Aries, Leo, and Sagittarius you will certainly be exactly that. Let yourself open up to all of the joy Aquarius and Pisces can bring to you. Nothing is what it seems to be with Virgo and Scorpio. Trying to uncover the truth can be exhausting. Taurus and Gemini are all about connecting. Are you willing to be permanently connected? Libra may become too dependent on the partnership and you may feel strangled. You have no patience for the overbearing nature of Cancer and Capricorn.

Most Charming Characteristics: Friendly, sincere, thoughtful.

Gifts: *For her:* horseback riding. *For him:* tickets to the races.

Sensual Foods: Chocolate-covered strawberries; New York steak; scallops.

Romantic Flowers: These ladies like men with taste. Show them you love style by sending fuchsia flowers, or even brightly colored wildflowers will do. To confuse this man, send him lilies along with bright daisies to show your innocence. Keep him guessing.

Best Date Nights: Tuesday; 13th and 22nd of each month.

Colors of Passion: *For her:* dark red, crimson. *For him:* violet, black.

The Perfect Wedding: Flamboyant and dynamic . . . ring a bell? A wonderfully romantic, resplendent theme wedding is most suited to your personality. Don't laugh—you may want to consider a Disneyland setting (if not, maybe honeymoon?) that is steeped in fantasy and mystery. You love unusual dining places, and good entertainment for your guests is a must. It is essential that a splendid time is had by all, not just you and your love. Ideal setting: Florence.

Wise Words: Charles Dickens: "There is little doubt that troubles are exceedingly gregarious in their nature, and flying in flocks are apt to perch capriciously."

Hints of Love: The mystery is important, but being evasive will create disaster. Make sure you know the difference.

After the Argument: *For him:* Start kissing up. Inflate that ego until it pops. You usually will have two fights before the resolution of the first one. If he is wrong, don't expect the "I'm sorry." The fight will just end quickly. If you're wrong, start washing the car or shining his shoes. Then give him a night out with his friends. *For her:* Make sure she is good and calm, then say you're sorry for what you did, even if the fight wasn't your fault. If you want to make up, just start saying you're sorry for something. You will have her eating out of your hand in no time.

Romantic Places: Places of enthusiasm bring romance: Rio de Janeiro; an air show; Disney World.

Lucky Love Star: Ariel—you will never lack affection.

Beautiful Thought: Giving someone something they have always wanted.

Sharing Secrets: Talk about high maintenance. *For the gals:* Once she sees that you go out of your way for her, then she will for you. *For the guys:* The bark is definitely much worse than the bite. He comes on stronger and more obstinate than he actually is.

Judith's Insights

About the Man: If he could only take that almighty chip off his shoulder, it would certainly make him more approachable. It is not that he doesn't know it exists, he just uses it for protection. A big heart he does have, and most people, when they get to know him, say he is a really good guy. But you must get past that almighty chip. He will use it as an excuse not to get close. Walk right around that excuse to let him know that you can take anything he throws your way. Proving that you can take his bad side will let him show you his good side.

About the Woman: She can be hard to reach. She likes to keep everything pulled together, exterior and interior. At times, it seems as if there is not an emotional bone in her body. Then all of a sudden the simplest thing can start her emotional waters running. It may have a lot to do with the company she is keeping and the environment that makes her feel safe. She is much more sensitive than you would ever guess. Her heart is way too big to be anything else. She may have just learned how to weed out those who will waste her time, leaving those who will bring her happiness.

Soul Mates: When you have Aries, Leo, and Sagittarius in your life, the journey will be thrilling. Only when you are receptive to inspiration can you enjoy a partnership with Aquarius and Pisces. Virgo and Scorpio will aggravate you with their emotional roller coaster. Are you ready for your seeds to take root? If so, Taurus and Gemini are the perfect soil for them to grow in. Allow Libra to value things outside of the relationship and you will enjoy it much more. Cancer's and Capricorn's mood swings will have your head spinning.

Most Charming Characteristics: Meticulous, sincere, intellectual.

Gifts: *For her:* sparkling bracelet. *For him:* personalized briefcase.

Sensual Foods: Vanilla and strawberry mousse; tiramisù; espresso.

Romantic Flowers: You are the lady of distinction, and only carnations will do. Any mix of colors with sprays of mignonette. Sweet peas or red carnations will appeal to this man's heart.

Best Date Nights: Tuesday; 5th and 25th of each month.

Colors of Passion: *For her:* dark red, crimson. *For him:* reddish brown, black.

The Perfect Wedding: Flamboyant and dynamic . . . ring a bell? A wonderfully romantic, resplendent theme wedding is most suited to your personality. Don't laugh—you may want to consider a Disneyland setting (if not, maybe honeymoon?) that is steeped in fantasy and mystery. You love unusual dining places, and good entertainment for your guests is a must. It is essential that a splendid time is had by all, not just you and your love. Ideal setting: Florence.

Wise Words: Charles Dickens: "The freedom of the subject and the liberty of the individual are among the first and proudest boasts of the true-hearted Englishman."

Hints of Love: If you learn to back up when things are moving too fast, you won't have to bow out so often.

After the Argument: *For him:* Start kissing up. Inflate that ego until it pops. You usually will have two fights before the resolution of the first one. If he is wrong, don't expect the "I'm sorry." The fight will just end quickly. If you're wrong, start washing the car or shining his shoes. Then give him a night out with his friends. *For her:* Make sure she is good and calm, then say you're sorry for what you did, even if the fight wasn't your fault. If you want to make up, just start saying you're sorry for something. You will have her eating out of your hand in no time.

Romantic Places: Places of excitement bring romance: Spain; a nightclub; Hollywood, California.

Lucky Love Star: Ariel—you will never lack affection.

Beautiful Thought: Random acts of kindness, for someone who needs them.

Sharing Secrets: Make sure you have at least five dates before you make up your mind. *For the gals:* They can be cynical, so it could be a few dates before she loosens up. *For the guys:* He still has yesterday on his mind. He needs a reason to forget his past relationship. Make a new history for him.

Judith's Insights

About the Man: Do you really need to walk before you can run? If you don't, then tell this guy. He just thinks at his own pace, and others may look at it as if he does it ass-backward. He is a kind guy, absolutely easy to hang with, but you may need a little more than patience. Those walls are there for his protection. You can get through those walls by showing that you are all that you seem to be and there are no hidden dangers. His family and friends look to him for inspiration. He can be so creative that it is enough for more than one person.

About the Woman: You will find yourself playing follow the leader no matter what kind of relationship you have. You will wind up following her. Yes, even if she works for you, or perhaps you are her boss, it will be you who takes the lead from her. She just has a way about her and tends to have everything under control. She has a style all her own, and others tend to follow her. There are times when she has almost too many options and too many relationships. This girl is not good at handling emotional crises. Keep things nonconfrontational to keep her comfortable.

Soul Mates: You can finally find someone to keep up with you in Aries, Leo, and Sagittarius. Aquarius and Pisces are a blessing you must be willing to receive. Virgo and Scorpio are too easily offended for your liking. Be ready to give Taurus and Gemini the consistency they deserve or move on to other things. Libra is a real team player and will fight for you all the way. Just make sure they don't forget to fight for themselves also. Cancer and Capricorn are too focused on the order of things for your impulsive nature. This is not recommended.

Most Charming Characteristics: Affectionate, intuitive, quick-witted.

Gifts: *For her:* new clothes from her fave designer. *For him:* newest trend in ties.

Sensual Foods: Raspberries; pound cake; caviar.

Romantic Flowers: You love it when you get tulips, declaring love. When you receive a variety, it shows how hopelessly in love your partner is. He will just love a single rose. This shows him you understand his pleasures.

Best Date Nights: Tuesday; 6th and 15th of each month.

Colors of Passion: *For her:* dark red, crimson. *For him:* reddish brown, black.

The Perfect Wedding: Flamboyant and dynamic . . . ring a bell? A wonderfully romantic, resplendent theme wedding is most suited to your personality. Don't laugh—you may want to consider a Disneyland setting (if not, maybe honeymoon?) that is steeped in fantasy and mystery. You love unusual dining places, and good entertainment for your guests is a must. It is essential that a splendid time is had by all, not just you and your love. Ideal setting: Florence.

Wise Words: Charles Dickens: "Man wants but little here below, nor wants that little long—how true that is!—after dinner."

Hints of Love: Expecting too much too soon can only build up hopes that will fall down too easily.

After the Argument: *For him:* Start kissing up. Inflate that ego until it pops. You usually will have two fights before the resolution of the first one. If he is wrong, don't expect the "I'm sorry." The fight will just end quickly. If you're wrong, start washing the car or shining his shoes. Then give him a night out with his friends. *For her:* Make sure she is good and calm, then say you're sorry for what you did, even if the fight wasn't your fault. If you want to make up, just start saying you're sorry for something. You will have her eating out of your hand in no time.

Romantic Places: Places of enthusiasm bring romance: Buenos Aires; a comedy club; Nashville, Tennessee.

Lucky Love Star: Ariel—you will never lack affection.

Beautiful Thought: It's a great feeling to do a favor you didn't want to do, then have it work out for your benefit, for one reason or another.

Sharing Secrets: Don't be in a hurry or it will be over before it begins. *For the gals:* Like fine wine and amazing food. Savor a moment until an hour is created. *For the guys:* To do too much too fast will prove risky. Try to give a push and he will just jump ship.

Judith's Insights

About the Man: He can be generous with everything he has. Don't mistake that for his liking you. He also has a passion for everything he does. He doesn't put his foot in the dirt unless he is happy to be where he is walking. He can be easily misread, so proceed with an open mind and open loyalty. He will test the waters again and again before he is ready to take a dip. He wants to make sure that things are stable before he gets too far to change his mind. He loves hosting parties. To capture his attention, you can ask him to help you throw a bash at your place.

About the Woman: The spotlight is on her, and people either love her or hate her. You will seldom see people in the middle. You will have to be subtle to approach this one, especially if you are going for a raise. Don't let her know you are coming. She might give you the wrong impression at first. She is everybody's life of the party, especially when it is her party. At times she will have too much to do and not enough time to do it. It may be exhausting to go through life with her dance card full, but that is the way she likes it. Even when she has many people around she may feel lonely.

Soul Mates: There is electricity in the air when you hook up with Aries, Leo, and Sagittarius. Aquarius and Pisces will delight you when you are open-hearted. Virgo's and Scorpio's tendency to worry will drive you up a wall. When you want to firmly establish yourself, turn no further than Taurus and Gemini. When you and Libra strike a happy medium between independence and dependence, things will flow smoothly. Dependency is a big turnoff for you. Cancer and Capricorn build walls around themselves so fast that you might even get stuck in them.

Most Charming Characteristics: Openhearted, positive, analytical.

Gifts: *For her:* a reason to dress up. *For him:* rare bottle of wine.

Sensual Foods: Flambé; lobster; oysters.

Romantic Flowers: Send this girl sunflowers if you want her to know you adore her. You may even add some poppies for a splash of extravagance. His desire for sport and play will be understood when you send him hyacinth and geranium.

Best Date Nights: Tuesday; 6th and 15th of each month.

Colors of Passion: *For her:* dark red, crimson. *For him:* reddish brown, black.

The Perfect Wedding: Flamboyant and dynamic . . . ring a bell? A wonderfully romantic, resplendent theme wedding is most suited to your personality. Don't laugh—you may want to consider a Disneyland setting (if not, maybe honeymoon?) that is steeped in fantasy and mystery. You love unusual dining places, and good entertainment for your guests is a must. It is essential that a splendid time is had by all, not just you and your love. Ideal setting: Florence.

Wise Words: Charles Dickens: "Men's courses will foreshadow certain ends, to which, if persevered in, they must lead. But if the courses be departed from the ends will change."

Hints of Love: Make sure all the ingredients are present before putting the cake in the oven.

After the Argument: *For him:* Start kissing up. Inflate that ego until it pops. You usually will have two fights before the resolution of the first one. If he is wrong, don't expect the "I'm sorry." The fight will just end quickly. If you're wrong, start washing the car or shining his shoes. Then give him a night out with his friends. *For her:* Make sure she is good and calm, then say you're sorry for what you did, even if the fight wasn't your fault. If you want to make up, just start saying you're sorry for something. You will have her eating out of your hand in no time.

Romantic Places: Places of excitement bring romance: Mexico; a sports event; Las Vegas, Nevada.

Lucky Love Star: Ariel—you will never lack affection.

Beautiful Thought: It's more satisfying when someone actually comes back and tips you for the help you gave him or her.

Sharing Secrets: They need to look before they leap, but only in love. *For the gals:* She needs creative and exciting dates to keep her interested. Don't take her for granted too soon. *For the guys:* You may think he gives signs of moving this relationship quickly; make sure you slow it down before he does.

Judith's Insights

About the Man: His friends mean everything to him, and he could still be hanging with the guys from kindergarten. The only thing you will get from trying to break this bond is out of his life. He needs to be kept busy and have more work than hours in the day. You just may have to find a way to fit in there on the fine line, if you want to get noticed. He is drawn to the unusual. This may be reflected in where he lives or even how he dresses. Stand out from the crowd of people that are clamoring for his attention and you will have a better chance of winning his heart.

About the Woman: She loves a party and a peaceful walk in the park. She is not moody but diversified. She makes her own language and is clear in speaking and hearing. She can most certainly make you feel like she is always waiting for a better offer to come along, although she would never admit that. She loves to live life by the seat of her pants. She yearns for excitement and is ready for anything new. Bring some ideas to the table when asking to spend time with her. She will be impressed by the thought you put into it before you even asked.

Soul Mates: Spontaneity is the name of the game when it is played with Aries, Leo, and Sagittarius. Don't let the gift of joy Aquarius and Pisces are willing to give you go unclaimed. Virgo and Scorpio need constant affirmation. This could leave you exhausted. Reliability is the expectation of Taurus and Gemini. You must decide if you want to be the one to be relied on before you enter anything. You must come to an understanding with Libra about where this relationship is sailing before it sinks. The tendency for Cancer and Capricorn to cling to you is a definite push for you to move on.

Most Charming Characteristics: Generous, original, resourceful.

Gifts: *For her:* long back rub. *For him:* sports tickets.

Sensual Foods: Crème brûlée; poached salmon.

Romantic Flowers: Rhododendron will let her be on the lookout for trouble. Throw in some chrysanthemum and she'll know it is you she will be looking out for. Cactus will show him warmth. Yellow daffodil is a token of a good time had by all. Chivalry is not dead.

Best Date Nights: Tuesday; 8th and 26th of each month.

Colors of Passion: *For her:* dark red, crimson. *For him:* reddish brown, black.

The Perfect Wedding: Flamboyant and dynamic . . . ring a bell? A wonderfully romantic, resplendent theme wedding is most suited to your personality. Don't laugh—you may want to consider a Disneyland setting (if not, maybe honeymoon?) that is steeped in fantasy and mystery. You love unusual dining places, and good entertainment for your guests is a must. It is essential that a splendid time is had by all, not just you and your love. Ideal setting: Florence.

Wise Words: Oliver Wendell Holmes: "The 'amen' of nature is always a flower."

Hints in Love: Simple often turns into complicated with this one. When you overcomplicate the moment, try to step back for a breather.

After the Argument: *For him:* Start kissing up. Inflate that ego until it pops. You usually will have two fights before the resolution of the first one. If he is wrong, don't expect the "I'm sorry." The fight will just end quickly. If you're wrong, start washing the car or shining his shoes. Then give him a night out with his friends. *For her:* Make sure she is good and calm, then say you're sorry for what you did, even if the fight wasn't your fault. If you want to make up, just start saying you're sorry for something. You will have her eating out of your hand in no time.

Romantic Places: Places of enthusiasm bring romance: London; carnival; Cape Canaveral, Florida.

Lucky Love Star: Ariel—you will never lack affection.

Beautiful Thought: Kindness is a virtue.

Sharing Secrets: The possibilities are endless, if you can pay the price. *For the gals:* She is hoping chivalry is not dead, and you must be willing to be the man at all costs. *For the guys:* He can be demanding and somewhat controlling. He just needs to be trained.

Judith's Insights

About the Man: He always wants to be the good guy. He likes to be loved. I guess that is what he is searching for. He does better communicating with his buddies and peers at work than with his loved ones at home. He may be much more approachable when he is given many options instead of only one. Be clear and put your emotions on the table. He will test you over and over to make sure that his heart is safe in your hands. Just because you pass the test, it doesn't mean that he will jump right into a commitment. Things have to be taken one at a time when it comes to this guy's emotions.

About the Woman: Her loyalty may waver until relationships get committed. She is simply trying to keep her options open. You need to step up to the plate with this one and wear your honor on your sleeve. Expect the unexpected and try to keep the environment light. She excels in every way when laughter is in the air. Keep humor in the mix and things will go smoothly. All this girl needs is constant and unquestioning love. She is a pussycat when she is happy. The lion inside her will rear its head if you make her doubt your intentions.

Soul Mates: Say good-bye to the mundane and hello to fiery passion when you meet Aries, Leo, and Sagittarius. No person is an island. Open the channels to Aquarius and Pisces. They have much to bring. Overly sensitive signs like Virgo and Scorpio are too much for you to bear. Taurus and Gemini need a completely devoted partner. If that is not you, let them know as soon as you can. Things with Libra are up to you and your willingness to compromise. Cancer and Capricorn won't deviate from the predetermined plan that you never agreed to in the first place.

Most Charming Characteristics: Original, generous, affectionate.

Gifts: *For her:* newest book from her fave chef. *For him:* book about success.

Sensual Foods: Chocolate soufflé; filet mignon.

Romantic Flowers: The magnolias you send her will let her know you will be around for a while to come. Petunia is to say never despair. Holly will let him know what he is getting into. Pansy will keep you in his thoughts.

Best Date Nights: Tuesday; 18th and 27th of each month.

Colors of Passion: *For her:* dark red, crimson. *For him:* reddish brown, black.

The Perfect Wedding: Flamboyant and dynamic . . . ring a bell? A wonderfully romantic, resplendent theme wedding is most suited to your personality. Don't laugh—you may want to consider a Disneyland setting (if not, maybe honeymoon?) that is steeped in fantasy and mystery. You love unusual dining places, and good entertainment for your guests is a must. It is essential that a splendid time is had by all, not just you and your love. Ideal setting: Florence.

Wise Words: William Cullen Bryant: "The struggling tides of life that seem in wayward endless course to tend are eddies of a mighty stream that rolls to its appointed end."

Hints of Love: Allow them to know what is in your heart as well as what is in your head.

After the Argument: *For him:* Start kissing up. Inflate that ego until it pops. You usually will have two fights before the resolution of the first one. If he is wrong, don't expect the "I'm sorry." The fight will just end quickly. If you're wrong, start washing the car or shining his shoes. Then give him a night out with his friends. *For her:* Make sure she is good and calm, then say you're sorry for what you did, even if the fight wasn't your fault. If you want to make up, just start saying you're sorry for something. You will have her eating out of your hand in no time.

Romantic Places: Places of excitement bring romance: Brazil; an amusement park; New Orleans.

Lucky Love Star: Ariel—you will never lack affection.

Beautiful Thought: Listening is only half, hearing makes it whole.

Sharing Secrets: Tomorrow is another day, but why wait? You can do it all today. *For the gals:* Have your date filled from dusk to dawn, and then some. *For the guys:* You may find he needs a nap here and there, but he can last all day and all night if he has a reason.

Judith's Insights

About the Man: He just wants to have a little bit of fun. Life to him should be a buffet full of his favorite foods. As long as there is a lot to choose from he will be happy. It can take a lot to nail him down to do anything. When he enters the room, the first thing he searches out is the Exit sign. Don't be too pushy, but be steady instead. He likes consistency. The walls will come down in no time if you are consistent. There will be no one more loyal than this guy once he has made his choice of who he wants to spend his life with. Until then there are no rules.

About the Woman: She needs to know who you are before she can enter into any type of relationship. Even as a friend, she can be somewhat cynical. Socializing is everything and everybody knows her name. Don't be overbearing in any kind of relationship or you will push her away. She will let you in on the secret if you prove yourself first. She likes to keep her options open until she is sure of a single plan of action. You may find that she has several love interests waiting for her to choose one.

Soul Mates: Aries, Leo, and Sagittarius bring so much adventure and passion into your life it would be hard to bore even you. Taurus and Gemini are a go as long as you can make a complete commitment. Otherwise, they can bring out the worst in everyone. Aquarius and Pisces would bring constant stimulation and enjoyment, if you would only let them. Cancer and Capricorn could wear you a little thin. Libra could go either way. You complement each other, but if compromise is not in the picture, then neither are you. Virgo and Scorpio will give you a run for your money, then want to go spend it all.

Most Charming Characteristics: Humorous, positive, thoughtful.

Gifts: *For her:* getaway to a spa. *For him:* intimate dinner for two.

Sensual Foods: Steak au poivre; cheesecake.

Romantic Flowers: Iris is your flower if you are the gal sending subtle messages. If you are the man, you will look for clematis. This flower's mental beauty creates emotional stimulation for you.

Best Date Nights: Tuesday; 1st and 19th of each month.

Colors of Passion: *For her:* dark red, crimson. *For him:* reddish brown, black.

The Perfect Wedding: Flamboyant and dynamic . . . ring a bell? A wonderfully romantic, resplendent theme wedding is most suited to your personality. Don't laugh—you may want to consider a Disneyland setting (if not, maybe honeymoon?) that is steeped in fantasy and mystery. You love unusual dining places, and good entertainment for your guests is a must. It is essential that a splendid time is had by all, not just you and your love. Ideal setting: Florence.

Wise Words: Johann Wolfgang von Goethe: "I can tell you, honest friend, what to believe: Believe life; it teaches better than book and orator."

Hints of Love: Keep both feet on the ground the first time you think you want to jump. This way you won't jump too high too soon.

After the Argument: *For him:* Start kissing up. Inflate that ego until it pops. You usually will have two fights before the resolution of the first one. If he is wrong, don't expect the "I'm sorry." The fight will just end quickly. If you're wrong, start washing the car or shining his shoes. Then give him a night out with his friends. *For her:* Make sure she is good and calm, then say you're sorry for what you did, even if the fight wasn't your fault. If you want to make up, just start saying you're sorry for something. You will have her eating out of your hand in no time.

Romantic Places: Places of enthusiasm bring romance: French Riviera; an outdoor festival; Hollywood, California.

Lucky Love Star: Ariel—you will never lack affection.

Beautiful Thought: It's a blast when someone you never expected to remembers your birthday.

Sharing Secrets: It may need to start with friendship. This isn't the consolation prize; it's the grand prize. *For the gals:* Go slow and allow it to grow one seed at a time. You won't need to push; it will all come in time. *For the guys:* A step here and a step there. Before he knows it, that friendship will be love.

Judith's Insights

About the Man: He needs to be in charge, even if he does it in a not-so-obvious way. He can be a handful if you don't find a way to where his buttons are. If he is your co-worker or boss, payday is the best day to ask him for anything. Favors will be honored if you keep your end of the bargain at all times. If he starts to feel that your relationship is not based on give-and-take, he will move on to bigger and better things. There are many waiting in the wings for his attention. The only way for you to keep it on you is to give him space to roam.

About the Woman: She can shut you out with a snap of her fingers if you cross her, but that is only if you haven't touched her heart first. She can create obstacles that don't exist. It takes patience and time to get close to this one. The walls are there for her protection. Keep that in mind and you won't take it personally. She can love many but trust few. She will always be looking for the newest thing in town. She is not fickle to hurt your feelings; she just likes to know what is around in case she needs to move on to something new.

Soul Mates: Look out when you get together with an Aries, Leo, or Sagittarius, you guys will be on fire! Loosen up; Aquarius and Pisces just might inspire you. Just when you think you know Virgo and Scorpio, more layers will appear out of nowhere. Taurus and Gemini crave stability. If you are not ready to settle down, move on. Libra doesn't feel complete without a partner. Are you willing to be the other half? Cancer and Capricorn are way too rigid for your taste.

Most Charming Characteristics: Affectionate, sincere, a good sport.

Gifts: *For her:* day at the horse races. *For him:* tickets to the big game.

Sensual Foods: Strawberry shortcake; pineapple; ham.

Romantic Flowers: Any rose of any color for the lady. Roses stand for love regardless of the color. Send them with orchids and you will be saying, "I love you." If you want a gentleman to know you think of him, send pansies, and forget-me-nots for true love.

Best Date Nights: Tuesday; 11th and 29th of each month.

Colors of Passion: *For her:* dark red, crimson. *For him:* reddish brown, black.

The Perfect Wedding: Flamboyant and dynamic . . . ring a bell? A wonderfully romantic, resplendent theme wedding is most suited to your personality. Don't laugh—you may want to consider a Disneyland setting (if not, maybe honeymoon?) that is steeped in fantasy and mystery. You love unusual dining places, and good entertainment for your guests is a must. It is essential that a splendid time is had by all, not just you and your love. Ideal setting: Florence.

Wise Words: Bertrand Russell: "A happy life must be to a great extent a quiet life, where it is only in an atmosphere of quiet that true joy can live."

Hints of Love: Laughter alleviates the tension, but so can understanding where another is sitting.

After the Argument: *For him:* Start kissing up. Inflate that ego until it pops. You usually will have two fights before the resolution of the first one. If he is wrong, don't expect the "I'm sorry." The fight will just end quickly. If you're wrong, start washing the car or shining his shoes. Then give him a night out with his friends. *For her:* Make sure she is good and calm, then say you're sorry for what you did, even if the fight wasn't your fault. If you want to make up, just start saying you're sorry for something. You will have her eating out of your hand in no time.

Romantic Places: Places of excitement bring romance: Cannes, France; a carnival; New York City.

Lucky Love Star: Ariel—you will never lack affection.

Beautiful Thought: Being present can be the present.

Sharing Secrets: This one needs to be the one and only, even if it is only the first date. *For the gals:* Don't talk about your past relationships. Do all you can to make her feel cherished from the first moment. *For the guys:* Play up your innocence. Let him take charge, even in paying the bill. He needs to wear the pants.

Judith's Insights

About the Man: He is looking for a thrill, and not a cheap one. He is ready to spend the cash to have a good time as long as you are ready to match it. It is practically burning a hole in his pocket. He will bring into your life not only a spark but the flame of passion as well. Anyone around him needs to at least have a desire to enjoy life. If they don't, he won't bother with them at all. He will be looking for the unusual things that many people miss in their lives. Dates are not the classic dinner and movie for this guy. Inviting him out means doing something off the beaten track.

About the Woman: She can be a piece of cake or a royal pain. She loves to be the center of attention. The best way to get to her is to create that image for her. Give her center stage and don't forget to applaud afterward. She will be eating out of your hand in no time. She loves to be in a relationship for the simple comfort of having a companion. This is not a game player. Instead, she will shoot straight from the hip. She is constantly surrounded by friends and is always looking for a good time. It is easy to get the first date, but the second will take a good impression.

Soul Mates: Aries, Leo, and Sagittarius dish out just as much energy as you do. Let Aquarius and Pisces into your life and you definitely won't regret it. Virgo and Scorpio will have you twisted in knots trying to keep up with their mood swings. Don't lead Taurus and Gemini on. Let them know if you are not in for the long haul. Teach Libra the joy of independence you so love and they will be a joy to be around. Cancer's and Capricorn's unyielding nature will have you running in the other direction.

Most Charming Characteristics: Affectionate, generous, analytical.

Gifts: *For her:* expensive perfume. *For him:* fine cologne.

Sensual Foods: Steak fondue; cheese fondue and French bread.

Romantic Flowers: These ladies like everyone to know how faithful they are, so send them violets. To surprise them send tulips. Men like their flowers the same as their relationships, unpretending. Send them camellias with white roses to show your affection.

Best Date Nights: Tuesday; 3rd and 30th of each month.

Colors of Passion: *For her:* dark red, crimson. *For him:* reddish brown, black.

The Perfect Wedding: Flamboyant and dynamic . . . ring a bell? A wonderfully romantic, resplendent theme wedding is most suited to your personality. Don't laugh—you may want to consider a Disneyland setting (if not, maybe honeymoon?) that is steeped in fantasy and mystery. You love unusual dining places, and good entertainment for your guests is a must. It is essential that a splendid time is had by all, not just you and your love. Ideal setting: Florence.

Wise Words: W. Barbellion: "To be selfish is to imprison in a tiny cage the glorious ego capable of penetrations to the farthest confines of the universe."

Hints of Love: Communication is important here. A script isn't provided for you. You must write it for yourself.

After the Argument: *For him:* Start kissing up. Inflate that ego until it pops. You usually will have two fights before the resolution of the first one. If he is wrong, don't expect the "I'm sorry." The fight will just end quickly. If you're wrong, start washing the car or shining his shoes. Then give him a night out with his friends. *For her:* Make sure she is good and calm, then say you're sorry for what you did, even if the fight wasn't your fault. If you want to make up, just start saying you're sorry for something. You will have her eating out of your hand in no time.

Romantic Places: Places of excitement bring romance: New Orleans; an amusement park; Times Square.

Lucky Love Star: Ariel—you will never lack affection.

Beautiful Thought: It's not as bad as you thought; in fact, it's not bad at all.

Sharing Secrets: You need to remember never to forget. *For the gals:* Her birthday, holidays, and your anniversary. Even down to each dinner date. *For the guys:* His birthday, his laundry, his mother's birthday, and, of course, him any other day of the year.

Judith's Insights

About the Man: He can talk a lot about nothing yet always have plenty to say. He never seems to run out of friends or something to do. He doesn't like feeling lonely or even being alone. You can be sure that there will be plenty of friends coming and going at his place. He is a very easy one to approach because he is so open. If he has room on his dance card, you can be sure that he is searching for someone to fill it. The only way to get on his dance card is to show your ability to keep up with him. It may sound easier than it really is.

About the Woman: She is not moody, but you may get the impression she is at times. She feels like you are her best friend at times, other times like you don't know her at all. This may mean she is not feeling comfortable in her own environment. Make a stronger effort to make her feel secure and you may feel her open up more. She will get attention from everyone she meets. Even strangers walking in the street will stop and check out this girl radiating this energy. Her approachable and uncomplicated ways make it easy for her to get along with a wide range of people.

Soul Mates: Does the phrase "life of the party" mean anything to you? With Aries, Leo, and Sagittarius you will certainly be exactly that. Let yourself open up to all of the joy Aquarius and Pisces can bring to you. Nothing is what it seems to be with Virgo and Scorpio. Trying to uncover the truth can be exhausting. Taurus and Gemini are all about connecting. Are you willing to be permanently connected? Libra may become too dependent on the partnership and you may feel strangled. You have no patience for the overbearing nature of Cancer and Capricorn.

Most Charming Characteristics: Devoted, open-minded, congenial.

Gifts: *For her:* horseback riding. *For him:* tickets to the races.

Sensual Foods: baked Alaska; seafood.

Romantic Flowers: These ladies like men with taste. Show them you love style by sending fuchsia flowers, or even brightly colored wildflowers will do. To confuse this man, send him lilies along with bright daisies to show your innocence. Keep him guessing.

Best Date Nights: Tuesday; 4th and 22nd of each month.

Colors of Passion: *For her:* dark red, crimson. *For him:* reddish brown, black.

The Perfect Wedding: Flamboyant and dynamic . . . ring a bell? A wonderfully romantic, resplendent theme wedding is most suited to your personality. Don't laugh—you may want to consider a Disneyland setting (if not, maybe honeymoon?) that is steeped in fantasy and mystery. You love unusual dining places, and good entertainment for your guests is a must. It is essential that a splendid time is had by all, not just you and your love. Ideal setting: Florence.

Wise Words: Seneca: "True friends are the whole world to one another; and he that is a friend to himself, is also a friend to mankind."

Hints of Love: Don't dissect every minute of every day. Learn to appreciate each minute as it comes.

After the Argument: *For him:* Start kissing up. Inflate that ego until it pops. You usually will have two fights before the resolution of the first one. If he is wrong, don't expect the "I'm sorry." The fight will just end quickly. If you're wrong, start washing the car or shining his shoes. Then give him a night out with his friends. *For her:* Make sure she is good and calm, then say you're sorry for what you did, even if the fight wasn't your fault. If you want to make up, just start saying you're sorry for something. You will have her eating out of your hand in no time.

Romantic Places: Places of enthusiasm bring romance: Rio de Janeiro; an air show; Disney World.

Lucky Love Star: Ariel—you will never lack affection.

Beautiful Thought: The sun shines on your day.

Sharing Secrets: My house should be your house, especially if you don't have one of your own. *For the gals:* All for one and one for all. Yours and mine must become ours. *For the guys:* If he needs to stand on ceremony, even for the first five minutes, it will be a definite turnoff for this one.

Judith's Insights

About the Man: He does have a heart, and it is very easily found. He just doesn't want to be tied down. He likes to be the king and have all of his subjects surrounding him. Grounding this one could be a difficult task. If you hang in there it might happen by accident. Otherwise, it will take much work. Even if he does make a commitment he will need a certain amount of freedom if he is to stay for very long. Try to fence him in and he will learn how to jump. Let him roam around when he feels the need and he will be coming back before you know it.

About the Woman: Other girls will take her as competitive. Do not think that she is not. She is just fueled by competition. She is open-minded, openhearted, and vacillates on what she truly wants and what will make her happy. She can be quiet and then funny and friendly. It is not that she is fickle, but sometimes people can bring out the best in her or the worst, depending on the situation. Everyone seems to follow this girl. She is the person everyone assumes has a date and then Friday night she is calling her friends to come over so she doesn't have to be alone.

APRIL

Soul Mates: Aries, Leo, and Sagittarius bring so much adventure and passion into your life it would be hard to bore even you. Taurus and Gemini are a go as long as you can make a complete commitment. Otherwise, they can bring out the worst in everyone. Aquarius and Pisces would bring constant stimulation and enjoyment, if you would only let them. Cancer and Capricorn could wear you a little thin. Libra could go either way. You complement each other, but if compromise is not in the picture, then neither are you. Virgo and Scorpio will give you a run for your money, then want to go spend it all.

Most Charming Characteristics: Good sport, aggressive, original.

Gifts: *For her:* sparkling bracelet. *For him:* personalized briefcase.

Sensual Foods: Strawberries and cream; meat loaf.

Romantic Flowers: Iris is your flower if you are the gal sending subtle messages. If you are the man, you will look for clematis. This flower's mental beauty creates emotional stimulation for you.

Best Date Nights: Tuesday; 1st and 28th of each month.

Colors of Passion: *For her:* dark red, crimson. *For him:* reddish brown, black.

The Perfect Wedding: Flamboyant and dynamic . . . ring a bell? A wonderfully romantic, resplendent theme wedding is most suited to your personality. Don't laugh—you may want to consider a Disneyland setting (if not, maybe honeymoon?) that is steeped in fantasy and mystery. You love unusual dining places, and good entertainment for your guests is a must. It is essential that a splendid time is had by all, not just you and your love. Ideal setting: Florence.

Wise Words: James Russell Lowell: "Love's nobility is shown in this, that it strengthens us to make sacrifices for others, and not for the object of our love alone."

Hints of Love: They use the three magic words only when they know they mean it, and they already know it is going to be said back to them.

After the Argument: *For him:* Start kissing up. Inflate that ego until it pops. You usually will have two fights before the resolution of the first one. If he is wrong, don't expect the "I'm sorry." The fight will just end quickly. If you're wrong, start washing the car or shining his shoes. Then give him a night out with his friends. *For her:* Make sure she is good and calm, then say you're sorry for what you did, even if the fight wasn't your fault. If you want to make up, just start saying you're sorry for something. You will have her eating out of your hand in no time.

Romantic Places: Places of excitement bring romance: Spain; a nightclub; Hollywood.

Lucky Love Star: Ariel—you will never lack affection.

Beautiful Thought: Your neighbor gives you a helping hand.

Sharing Secrets: Let them admire something about you first. Show them you have a sense of humor. *For the gals:* Hold their hand and then take them to the next step. *For the guys:* The way to his heart is definitely through his stomach.

Judith's Insights

About the Man: What fortitude he has, including all his hobbies, work, and relationships. He can be a juggler with all of his time. You have to be tolerant to hang out with this guy; even as a best friend he can become exhausting. Just when you think that he has no time for you anymore, he will surprise you. He can be critically cautious about what he gets himself into. Then he will surprise you and throw caution to the wind and act impulsively. He is a walking contradiction who will bring you a lot of joy while you try to figure him out.

About the Woman: You need to be able to walk on a balance beam; the only problem is that she is the only one who knows where it starts and ends. Her emotions are erratic, so it may be a job having any sort of relationship, including being a sister. When her attention is upon you it will feel as if you are in the sun's rays. When she turns her attention elsewhere you will be hit with the cold loneliness that comes after you have known someone so warm. Everybody may play the fool but not this girl. You would have a hard time trying to put something over on her.

Soul Mates: Look out when you get together with an Aries, Leo, or Sagittarius, you guys will be on fire! Loosen up; Aquarius and Pisces just might inspire you. Just when you think you know Virgo and Scorpio, more layers will appear out of nowhere. Taurus and Gemini crave stability. If you are not ready to settle down, move on. Libra doesn't feel complete without a partner. Are you willing to be the other half? Cancer and Capricorn are way too rigid for your taste.

Most Charming Characteristics: Extremely generous, sociable, strong.

Gifts: *For her:* new clothes from her fave designer. *For him:* newest trend in ties.

Sensual Foods: Cherry-apple pie; beef Stroganoff.

Romantic Flowers: Any rose of any color for the lady. Roses stand for love regardless of the color. Send them with orchids and you will be saying, "I love you." If you want a gentleman to know you think of him, send pansies, and forget-me-nots for true love.

Best Date Nights: Tuesday; 11th and 20th of each month.

Colors of Passion: *For her:* dark red, crimson. *For him:* reddish brown, black.

The Perfect Wedding: Flamboyant and dynamic . . . ring a bell? A wonderfully romantic, resplendent theme wedding is most suited to your personality. Don't laugh—you may want to consider a Disneyland setting (if not, maybe honeymoon?) that is steeped in fantasy and mystery. You love unusual dining places, and good entertainment for your guests is a must. It is essential that a splendid time is had by all, not just you and your love. Ideal setting: Florence.

Wise Words: Charles Dickens: "Good training is always desirable."

Hints of Love: Remember to keep the dating fun. Don't act like you are married before your time.

After the Argument: *For him:* Start kissing up. Inflate that ego until it pops. You usually will have two fights before the resolution of the first one. If he is wrong, don't expect the "I'm sorry." The fight will just end quickly. If you're wrong, start washing the car or shining his shoes. Then give him a night out with his friends. *For her:* Make sure she is good and calm, then say you're sorry for what you did, even if the fight wasn't your fault. If you want to make up, just start saying you're sorry for something. You will have her eating out of your hand in no time.

Romantic Places: Places of enthusiasm bring romance: Buenos Aires; a comedy club; Nashville, Tennessee.

Lucky Love Star: Ariel—you will never lack affection.

Beautiful Thought: You realize your mate had good intentions.

Sharing Secrets: Give them the opportunity to notice you first. *For the gals:* They love to be adored; love at first sight. *For the guys:* Remember to always let them believe it was their idea.

Judith's Insights

About the Man: He is filled with wisdom like an old man. The only problem with that is he can get old before his time. Certainly he demands, and commands, the best. He believes he deserves it. Anger and laughter are only a thin line away from each other. Try stepping away if you feel him leaning toward the anger side. What this guy craves is to be cherished. This is what he wants and this is what he needs. Anything less and he will be roaming off before you know it. He knows that someone is out there who will give him what he needs.

About the Woman: She is the Energizer bunny, and if you are lucky, you can catch up with her. Then maybe she can be yours. She has a goal of where, when, and what she wants to be, and allows nobody to get in her way. She needs to always have something to do and—more important—something to look forward to. She never settles for second best. The first date with her had better be a fine restaurant, even if she is the one paying. She has class and she loves to display it. Make sure that you are up to par before you even attempt to get close to her.

Soul Mates: Aries, Leo, and Sagittarius dish out just as much energy as you do. Let Aquarius and Pisces into your life and you definitely won't regret it. Virgo and Scorpio will have you twisted in knots trying to keep up with their mood swings. Don't lead Taurus and Gemini on. Let them know if you are not in for the long haul. Teach Libra the joy of independence you so love and they will be a joy to be around. Cancer's and Capricorn's unyielding nature will have you running in the other direction.

Most Charming Characteristics: Precise, interesting, entertaining.

Gifts: *For her:* a reason to dress up. *For him:* rare bottle of wine.

Sensual Foods: Hot fudge sundae with all the trimmings; shepherd's pie.

Romantic Flowers: These ladies like everyone to know how faithful they are, so send them violets. To surprise them send tulips. Men like their flowers the same as their relationships, unpretending. Send them camellias with white roses to show your affection.

Best Date Nights: Tuesday; 3rd and 12th of each month.

Colors of Passion: *For her:* dark red, crimson. *For him:* reddish brown, black.

The Perfect Wedding: Flamboyant and dynamic . . . ring a bell? A wonderfully romantic, resplendent theme wedding is most suited to your personality. Don't laugh—you may want to consider a Disneyland setting (if not, maybe honeymoon?) that is steeped in fantasy and mystery. You love unusual dining places, and good entertainment for your guests is a must. It is essential that a splendid time is had by all, not just you and your love. Ideal setting: Florence.

Wise Words: Charles Dickens: "Nothing is too bad to be retrieved."

Hints of Love: Make sure you go on more than one date before you jump to conclusions on liking and disliking.

After the Argument: *For him:* Start kissing up. Inflate that ego until it pops. You usually will have two fights before the resolution of the first one. If he is wrong, don't expect the "I'm sorry." The fight will just end quickly. If you're wrong, start washing the car or shining his shoes. Then give him a night out with his friends. *For her:* Make sure she is good and calm, then say you're sorry for what you did, even if the fight wasn't your fault. If you want to make up, just start saying you're sorry for something. You will have her eating out of your hand in no time.

Romantic Places: Places of excitement bring romance: Mexico; a sports event; Las Vegas, Nevada.

Lucky Love Star: Ariel—you will never lack affection.

Beautiful Thought: Someone offers you a job, so you can quit the one you hate.

Sharing Secrets: This one loves a challenge. *For the gals:* Be consistently inconsistent until you have them hooked. *For the guys:* This one loves to play catch. You may feel like a yo-yo, but as long as he is calling that's all that matters.

Judith's Insights

About the Man: He may seem a little bit passive-aggressive. Everything is okay one minute, until it is not. He has a vision of what he wants things to be and how they should happen, and he has a hard time diverting from it. Working with him could just about drive you crazy; living with him could make you want to move. Loving him could do both. He will notice when you flirt with others but never when he does. He can be as jealous as they come. Allay his fears by smiling and holding his hand. The only way to let him know you are his is by showing him.

About the Woman: She is more sensitive than anyone could ever imagine. She takes life more seriously, especially with family. If you want her attention, you will have to feed her emotional needs. To get this one's door open you will have to play nice, very nice. If you can do that, you will be golden. She will act like she knows exactly what she wants but she is much more fickle than she would ever care to admit. She is also more needy than she would ever admit to, even to her mother. The ability to read minds would come in handy in this relationship.

Soul Mates: Does the phrase "life of the party" mean anything to you? With Aries, Leo, and Sagittarius, you will certainly be exactly that. Let yourself open up to all of the joy Aquarius and Pisces can bring to you. Nothing is what it seems to be with Virgo and Scorpio. Trying to uncover the truth can be exhausting. Taurus and Gemini are all about connecting. Are you willing to be permanently connected? Libra may become too dependent on the partnership and you may feel strangled. You have no patience for the overbearing nature of Cancer and Capricorn.

Most Charming Characteristics: Ambitious, resourceful, humorous.

Gifts: *For her:* long back rub. *For him:* sports tickets.

Sensual Foods: Whipped cream, strawberries, brown sugar, and heavy cream.

Romantic Flowers: These ladies like men with taste. Show them you love style by sending fuchsia flowers, or even brightly colored wildflowers will do. To confuse this man, send him lilies along with bright daisies to show your innocence. Keep him guessing.

Best Date Nights: Tuesday; 4th and 22nd of each month.

Colors of Passion: *For her:* dark red, crimson. *For him:* reddish brown, black.

The Perfect Wedding: Flamboyant and dynamic . . . ring a bell? A wonderfully romantic, resplendent theme wedding is most suited to your personality. Don't laugh—you may want to consider a Disneyland setting (if not, maybe honeymoon?) that is steeped in fantasy and mystery. You love unusual dining places, and good entertainment for your guests is a must. It is essential that a splendid time is had by all, not just you and your love. Ideal setting: Florence.

Wise Words: Benjamin Franklin: "It is generally agreed to be folly to hazard the loss of a friend rather than to lose a just."

Hints of Love: Don't act too needy too soon. It may push this relationship away.

After the Argument: *For him:* Start kissing up. Inflate that ego until it pops. You usually will have two fights before the resolution of the first one. If he is wrong, don't expect the "I'm sorry." The fight will just end quickly. If you're wrong, start washing the car or shining his shoes. Then give him a night out with his friends. *For her:* Make sure she is good and calm, then say you're sorry for what you did, even if the fight wasn't your fault. If you want to make up, just start saying you're sorry for something. You will have her eating out of your hand in no time.

Romantic Places: Places of enthusiasm bring romance: London; a carnival; Cape Canaveral, Florida.

Lucky Love Star: Ariel—you will never lack affection.

Beautiful Thought: Someone was watching over you today; you realize they've been watching over you all along.

Sharing Secrets: This is a family person at heart; your presence is most important. *For the gals:* Make sure you go to Sunday dinner with her family when you are invited. *For the guys:* If you don't like his mom, you might have a hard time catching this one.

Judith's Insights

About the Man: If you could bottle his energy you could make millions. His work ethic is beyond belief. His bedside manner is better with strangers than with most of his loved ones. He has a million and one friends. It is hard to know where anything else could fit in. You may feel abandoned when his energy takes him elsewhere. He wants to be king of the castle and everyone else to be his subjects. He will likely pass on the crown when he feels safe and not intruded upon. Things must always be balanced in this relationship for him to be happy.

About the Woman: She is pushy and gets what she wants all the time. Her kind heart makes it easy to give to her. She is a friend to everyone. Approaching her can be difficult if you feel like you are not in her inner circle. Once you are in her inner circle, you may feel as if you are the only person in the world. She will give you the shirt off her back as long as you are willing and able to do the same. She firmly believes in give-and-take and might even have a mental scorecard when it comes to her friends and lovers. Make sure the numbers are all equal.

Soul Mates: When you have Aries, Leo, and Sagittarius in your life, the journey will be thrilling. Only when you are receptive to inspiration can you enjoy a partnership with Aquarius and Pisces. Virgo and Scorpio will aggravate you with their emotional roller coaster. Are you ready for your seeds to take root? If so, Taurus and Gemini are the perfect soil for them to grow in. Show Libra how to value things outside of the relationship and you will enjoy it much more. Cancer's and Capricorn's mood swings will have your head spinning.

Most Charming Characteristics: Magnetic, generous, a leader.

Gifts: *For her:* newest book from her fave chef. *For him:* book about success.

Sensual Foods: Puddings and pastry of all kinds.

Romantic Flowers: You are the lady of distinction, and only carnations will do. Any mix of colors with sprays of mignonette. Sweet peas or red carnations will appeal to this man's heart.

Best Date Nights: Tuesday; 5th and 23rd of each month.

Colors of Passion: *For her:* dark red, crimson. *For him:* reddish brown, black.

The Perfect Wedding: Flamboyant and dynamic . . . ring a bell? A wonderfully romantic, resplendent theme wedding is most suited to your personality. Don't laugh—you may want to consider a Disneyland setting (if not, maybe honeymoon?) that is steeped in fantasy and mystery. You love unusual dining places, and good entertainment for your guests is a must. It is essential that a splendid time is had by all, not just you and your love. Ideal setting: Florence.

Wise Words: Confucius: "However great the ills man may have to bear, he but adds to them when he allows himself to give way to despair."

Hints of Love: Keep it fun. Look for new and exciting things to do, especially if you are in a long-term relationship.

After the Argument: *For him:* Start kissing up. Inflate that ego until it pops. You usually will have two fights before the resolution of the first one. If he is wrong, don't expect the "I'm sorry." The fight will just end quickly. If you're wrong, start washing the car or shining his shoes. Then give him a night out with his friends. *For her:* Make sure she is good and calm, then say you're sorry for what you did, even if the fight wasn't your fault. If you want to make up, just start saying you're sorry for something. You will have her eating out of your hand in no time.

Romantic Places: Places of excitement bring romance: Brazil; an amusement park; New Orleans.

Lucky Love Star: Ariel—you will never lack affection.

Beautiful Thought: Someone really goes out of his or her way for you on the day you need it the most.

Sharing Secrets: Everything in its good time. This one works slowly, but when it is time to pick up speed, watch out. *For the gals:* Don't go by the obvious. Read between the lines. As long as the invitation is being offered go full speed ahead. *For the guys:* Just when you thought you should walk away, he'll say, "I love you." Talk about confusing.

Judith's Insights

About the Man: He wants joy, and fun, and life out in the sun. He doesn't like feeling cooped up, especially when it comes to a relationship. Don't smother this one, even if you are his best friend. If he is allowed his space to roam he will be much happier, as will your relationship with him. If you don't want to go to the party, expect that he will go alone. It does not mean he is being disloyal. He needs the stimulation of others. Believe me, he will come home much happier than if he was made to stay away from the good time.

About the Woman: She has six best friends; then there are always more. She is a people person. I think she just likes having something to do and people to do it with. But I can't say she is just about quantity. She certainly finds the best of the best and has quality along with quantity. Double standard is written all over this girl. When you go out, the first thing she may do is leave you to mingle. If the role was reversed she might consider it abandonment. She just feels like she needs the extra attention only a roomful of people can give her.

Soul Mates: You can finally find someone to keep up with you in Aries, Leo, and Sagittarius. Aquarius and Pisces are a blessing you must be willing to receive. Virgo and Scorpio are too easily offended for your liking. Be ready to give Taurus and Gemini the consistency they deserve or move on to other things. Libra is a real team player and will fight for you all the way. Just make sure that they don't forget to fight for themselves also. Cancer and Capricorn are too focused on the order of things for your impulsive nature. This is not recommended.

Most Charming Characteristics: Artistic, humorous, incredibly loyal.

Gifts: *For her:* day at the horse races. *For him:* tickets to the big game.

Sensual Foods: Champagne with strawberries; fillet of sole.

Romantic Flowers: You love it when you get tulips, declaring love. When you receive a variety, it shows how hopelessly in love your partner is. He will just love a single rose. This shows him you understand his pleasures.

Best Date Nights: Tuesday; 6th and 24th of each month.

Colors of Passion: *For her:* dark red, crimson. *For him:* reddish brown, black.

The Perfect Wedding: Flamboyant and dynamic . . . ring a bell? A wonderfully romantic, resplendent theme wedding is most suited to your personality. Don't laugh—you may want to consider a Disneyland setting (if not, maybe honeymoon?) that is steeped in fantasy and mystery. You love unusual dining places, and good entertainment for your guests is a must. It is essential that a splendid time is had by all, not just you and your love. Ideal setting: Florence.

Wise Words: Charles Dickens: "The smile, the cheerful, happy smile was made for home and fireside. Peace and happiness."

Hints of Love: This one is a cautious soul. You may have to find a way to go around to the back door.

After the Argument: *For him:* Start kissing up. Inflate that ego until it pops. You usually will have two fights before the resolution of the first one. If he is wrong, don't expect the "I'm sorry." The fight will just end quickly. If you're wrong, start washing the car or shining his shoes. Then give him a night out with his friends. *For her:* Make sure she is good and calm, then say you're sorry for what you did, even if the fight wasn't your fault. If you want to make up, just start saying you're sorry for something. You will have her eating out of your hand in no time.

Romantic Places: Places of enthusiasm bring romance: French Riviera; an outdoor festival; Hollywood.

Lucky Love Star: Ariel—you will never lack affection.

Beautiful Thought: The tree that falls is the one you were going to have to pay to have cut down.

Sharing Secrets: This one is a charmer, perhaps even fickle. *For the gals:* If you are patient enough to stick around, this one is worth the wait. *For the guys:* If there is enough time on the clock, stick around past three months. Then maybe he will have noticed you are there.

Judith's Insights

About the Man: He knows better but likes to live life on the edge. His approach needs work, although he sees himself as suave. His temper can use a little work also, but he is really a pussycat in a bear's body. If you can get past his burly and tempestuous exterior, you will be pleasantly surprised. He is guaranteed to be looking for love in all of the wrong places early in life. It may take him forever to figure this out. He will spend half of his life fighting to find love and the second half of it wondering why it is so important to him. Time is all this guy needs to put his head right.

About the Woman: She is the wanderer of life. She is searching aimlessly through life to figure out where she actually belongs. She is easy to be a friend to, but hard to nail down. She never sees what she demands, but always feels what others command. Treat her like a lady. It works every time. She tends to overcomplicate the picture by putting too many things in it. Teach her that less is more. Don't get insulted if she doesn't get that concept right away. She can be the work of art that she creates after the lesson has had time to sink in.

Soul Mates: There is electricity in the air when you hook up with Aries, Leo, and Sagittarius. Aquarius and Pisces will delight you when you are open-hearted. Virgo's and Scorpio's tendency to worry will drive you up a wall. When you want to firmly establish yourself, turn no further than Taurus and Gemini. When you and Libra strike a happy medium between independence and dependence things will flow smoothly. Dependency is a big turnoff for you. Cancer and Capricorn build walls around themselves so fast that you might even get stuck in them.

Most Charming Characteristics: Sincere, quick-witted, passionate.

Gifts: *For her:* expensive perfume. *For him:* fine cologne.

Sensual Foods: Chocolates; poached salmon; flambé; filet mignon; potatoes.

Romantic Flowers: Send this girl sunflowers if you want her to know you adore her. You may even add some poppies for a splash of extravagance. His desire for sport and play will be understood when you send him hyacinth and geranium.

Best Date Nights: Tuesday; 6th and 15th of each month.

Colors of Passion: *For her:* dark red, crimson. *For him:* reddish brown, black.

The Perfect Wedding: Flamboyant and dynamic . . . ring a bell? A wonderfully romantic, resplendent theme wedding is most suited to your personality. Don't laugh—you may want to consider a Disneyland setting (if not, maybe honeymoon?) that is steeped in fantasy and mystery. You love unusual dining places, and good entertainment for your guests is a must. It is essential that a splendid time is had by all, not just you and your love. Ideal setting: Florence.

Wise Words: Charles Dickens: "Personal considerations sink into nothing afore a common cause."

Hints of Love: Passion must be in the picture at all times or you could lose this one's attention quickly.

After the Argument: *For him:* Start kissing up. Inflate that ego until it pops. You usually will have two fights before the resolution of the first one. If he is wrong, don't expect the "I'm sorry." The fight will just end quickly. If you're wrong, start washing the car or shining his shoes. Then give him a night out with his friends. *For her:* Make sure she is good and calm, then say you're sorry for what you did, even if the fight wasn't your fault. If you want to make up, just start saying you're sorry for something. You will have her eating out of your hand in no time.

Romantic Places: Places of excitement bring romance: Cannes, France; a carnival; New York City.

Lucky Love Star: Ariel—you will never lack affection.

Beautiful Thought: You learn how to relax and enjoy a massage.

Sharing Secrets: If you are looking for love, then you have found the right mate. *For the gals:* This one could be stubborn. It may take forever to get a relationship started, but it is as solid as they come. *For the guys:* Even when he is ready, he might not be willing and able. He will put you through more obstacles than any course. Be patient.

Judith's Insights

About the Man: His style may be on the harsh side, but his strength is both intriguing and alluring. You may be sucked into it before you even know it. If you work together, you may be doing all of his work for him and never even noticing. Once you have been pulled in, it will be tough to pull away. He will never see the way things really are. He will only see how he wants them to be. His restless soul can make him so impatient that he talks himself out of going on the first date before he even gets a chance to enjoy it. Show him how to slow down and enjoy the moment.

About the Woman: She needs constant attention and reassurance. If you work together you may think she is being competitive when she isn't. She is just searching for security. She is not selfish but may seem that way because she has so many needs. Once the relationship has progressed to the point where she feels comfortable she will realize all that you have endured by being with her. This is when her sense of balance will kick in and she will do all that she can to make it up to you. The next few months will be absolute heaven. Just don't get too used to doing nothing.

Soul Mates: Spontaneity is the name of the game when it is played with Aries, Leo, and Sagittarius. Don't let the gift of joy Aquarius and Pisces are willing to give you go unclaimed. Virgo and Scorpio need constant affirmation. This could leave you exhausted. Reliability is the expectation of Taurus and Gemini. You must decide if you want to be the one to be relied on before you enter anything. You must come to an understanding with Libra where this relationship is sailing before it sinks. The tendency of Cancer and Capricorn to cling to you is a definite push for you to move on.

Most Charming Characteristics: Considerate, vivacious, ambitious.

Gifts: *For her:* horseback riding. *For him:* tickets to the races.

Sensual Foods: Caviar; beef tenderloin; potatoes au gratin.

Romantic Flowers: Rhododendron will let her be on the lookout for trouble. Throw in some chrysanthemum and she'll know it is you she will be looking out for. Cactus will show him warmth. Yellow daffodil is a token of a good time had by all. Chivalry is not dead.

Best Date Nights: Tuesday; 8th and 26th of each month.

Colors of Passion: *For her:* dark red, crimson. *For him:* reddish brown, black.

The Perfect Wedding: Flamboyant and dynamic . . . ring a bell? A wonderfully romantic, resplendent theme wedding is most suited to your personality. Don't laugh—you may want to consider a Disneyland setting (if not, maybe honeymoon?) that is steeped in fantasy and mystery. You love unusual dining places, and good entertainment for your guests is a must. It is essential that a splendid time is had by all, not just you and your love. Ideal setting: Florence.

Wise Words: Charles Dickens: "Although a skilful flatterer is a most delightful companion if you can keep him all to yourself his taste becomes very doubtful when he takes to complimenting other people."

Hints of Love: A random act of kindness will go a long way with this one. What can you do for them today?

After the Argument: *For him:* Start kissing up. Inflate that ego until it pops. You usually will have two fights before the resolution of the first one. If he is wrong, don't expect the "I'm sorry." The fight will just end quickly. If you're wrong, start washing the car or shining his shoes. Then give him a night out with his friends. *For her:* Make sure she is good and calm, then say you're sorry for what you did, even if the fight wasn't your fault. If you want to make up, just start saying you're sorry for something. You will have her eating out of your hand in no time.

Romantic Places: Places of excitement bring romance: New Orleans; an amusement park; Times Square.

Lucky Love Star: Ariel—you will never lack affection.

Beautiful Thought: You might find a boss who really appreciates you.

Sharing Secrets: If you can hang around and give constant stimulation, this could be your mate. *For the gals:* She is always looking for the Exit sign. Don't show her where it is or she will be gone. *For the guys:* Fast car, fast food; he likes everything that goes fast. Put on your running shoes. If you can keep up, then he is yours.

Judith's Insights

About the Man: This guy isn't too fond of laziness, whether with an employee or with a friendship. His lack of patience with people flares up when he doesn't feel the effort. The good news is he is bursting with energy and open to just about anything. If you can hold up your end of the bargain he will love you for it. If you are looking for romance this guy will give you a run for your money. Just don't try to hinder his independence. If he feels as if he can't go out on the town with his friends without you he may decide to drop you altogether.

About the Woman: This one could be your dream or your complete nightmare. She doesn't like anyone to know how vulnerable she is, so don't expect too much of her too fast. Once she places herself in a relationship, she looks at it as if she will be there forever. You must be able to hold up your end of the deal to get anywhere with her. Keep the reins loose and tighten them only when you know that it isn't going to create a noose. If she feels crowded in any way she may lash out at you. Give her enough space to be the same girl you fell for in the beginning.

Soul Mates: Say good-bye to the mundane and hello to fiery passion when you meet Aries, Leo, and Sagittarius. No person is an island. Open the channels to Aquarius and Pisces. They have much to bring. Overly sensitive signs like Virgo and Scorpio are too much for you to bear. Taurus and Gemini need a completely devoted partner. If that is not you, let them know as soon as you can. Things with Libra are up to you and your willingness to compromise. Cancer and Capricorn won't deviate from the predetermined plan that you never agreed to in the first place.

Most Charming Characteristics: Artistic, considerate, magnetic.

Gifts: *For her:* sparkling bracelet. *For him:* personalized briefcase.

Sensual Foods: Passion fruit; fillet of sole almondine.

Romantic Flowers: The magnolias you send her will let her know you will be around for a while to come. Petunia is to say never despair. Holly will let him know what he is getting into. Pansy will keep you in his thoughts.

Best Date Nights: Tuesday; 9th and 18th of each month.

Colors of Passion: *For her:* dark red, crimson. *For him:* reddish brown, black.

The Perfect Wedding: Flamboyant and dynamic . . . ring a bell? A wonderfully romantic, resplendent theme wedding is most suited to your personality. Don't laugh—you may want to consider a Disneyland setting (if not, maybe honeymoon?) that is steeped in fantasy and mystery. You love unusual dining places, and good entertainment for your guests is a must. It is essential that a splendid time is had by all, not just you and your love. Ideal setting: Florence.

Wise Words: Charles Dickens: "A person is never known till a person is proved."

Hints of Love: Family and friends are important to this one. Don't try to alienate them or it will definitely backfire on you.

After the Argument: *For him:* Start kissing up. Inflate that ego until it pops. You usually will have two fights before the resolution of the first one. If he is wrong, don't expect the "I'm sorry." The fight will just end quickly. If you're wrong, start washing the car or shining his shoes. Then give him a night out with his friends. *For her:* Make sure she is good and calm, then say you're sorry for what you did, even if the fight wasn't your fault. If you want to make up, just start saying you're sorry for something. You will have her eating out of your hand in no time.

Romantic Places: Places of enthusiasm bring romance: Rio de Janeiro; an air show; Disney World.

Lucky Love Star: Ariel—you will never lack affection.

Beautiful Thought: Finding a fortune is finding a friend.

Sharing Secrets: This one may seem like a lot of work. They just need the basics: love, loyalty, and respect. *For the gals:* If you can show her your best side right from the beginning it may work. Be careful of fluff, because she will see right through it. *For the guys:* He loves to be loved. Give him plenty of attention, even if you think you don't stand a chance. Perseverance will win here.

Judith's Insights

About the Man: He is the fire you can't try to smother or you will find yourself surrounded by smoke. You need to keep him fed without allowing him to get out of control. He can be blunt and even raw at times. Don't try to go up against him if he is your boss. He will usually win, and even if you win, you will really lose. Try to go around him. You won't have to second-guess if this guy is interested in you. You will be able to spot that gleam in his eye from across the room. If things get too hot he might go out for some air, but don't worry, he'll be back in a second.

About the Woman: You need to enter from the heart and appeal to her needs. If she is your boss or co-worker, lend her a helping hand without her asking. She can push people away with a blink of an eye. If you hang in there no matter how much she tries to push you away, you will be the winner. She only tries to do that when she is scared. It is actually a good sign. If she is scared enough to push you away, then she has some pretty strong feelings for you that need to be explored. Hanging around no matter what she throws your way is the only way that will happen.

Soul Mates: Aries, Leo, and Sagittarius bring so much adventure and passion into your life it would be hard to bore even you. Taurus and Gemini are a go as long as you can make a complete commitment. Otherwise, they can bring out the worst in everyone. Aquarius and Pisces would bring constant stimulation and enjoyment, if you would only let them. Cancer and Capricorn could wear you a little thin. Libra could go either way. You complement each other, but if compromise is not in the picture, then neither are you. Virgo and Scorpio will give you a run for your money, then want to go spend it all.

Most Charming Characteristics: Adaptable, determined, considerate.

Gifts: *For her:* new clothes from her fave designer. *For him:* newest trend in ties.

Sensual Foods: Peaches; mousse; shrimp.

Romantic Flowers: Iris is your flower if you are the gal sending subtle messages. If you are the man, you will look for clematis. This flower's mental beauty creates emotional stimulation for you.

Best Date Nights: Tuesday; 10th and 19th of each month.

Colors of Passion: *For her:* dark red, crimson. *For him:* reddish brown, black.

The Perfect Wedding: Flamboyant and dynamic . . . ring a bell? A wonderfully romantic, resplendent theme wedding is most suited to your personality. Don't laugh—you may want to consider a Disneyland setting (if not, maybe honeymoon?) that is steeped in fantasy and mystery. You love unusual dining places, and good entertainment for your guests is a must. It is essential that a splendid time is had by all, not just you and your love. Ideal setting: Florence.

Wise Words: William Shakespeare: "Let me not to the marriage of two minds admit impediments. Love is not love which alters when alteration finds or bends with the remover to remove."

Hints of Love: Show others how much you adore him or her. They will revel in how others notice.

After the Argument: *For him:* Start kissing up. Inflate that ego until it pops. You usually will have two fights before the resolution of the first one. If he is wrong, don't expect the "I'm sorry." The fight will just end quickly. If you're wrong, start washing the car or shining his shoes. Then give him a night out with his friends. *For her:* Make sure she is good and calm, then say you're sorry for what you did, even if the fight wasn't your fault. If you want to make up, just start saying you're sorry for something. You will have her eating out of your hand in no time.

Romantic Places: Places of excitement bring romance: Spain; a nightclub; Hollywood, California.

Lucky Love Star: Ariel—you will never lack affection.

Beautiful Thought: Your very best friend thinks you are his or her best friend, too.

Sharing Secrets: They are looking for love, but that is just their little secret. *For the gals:* Why shouldn't they want to be loved? Of course they do, but they want you to do all of the work. *For the guys:* You must prove yourself repeatedly. Don't expect too much until he knows you are under his thumb.

Judith's Insights

About the Man: He likes it when he is feeling like he has an entourage following behind him. He is not very picky; he just likes constant devotion and praise. Think of devotion and praise as oil and gasoline that feed him, as if he were a car. Getting to know his particular brand will help your cause immensely. Capturing his attention is the easy part. A compliment here and a sly glance there and he will know. Keeping his attention is the hard part. He has a tendency to look around at the rest of the room when things are slow. You have to be ready to give your all.

About the Woman: She wants to feel as proud as a peacock, even if she is only having dinner with you. She demands a lot from anybody in her life. This can be one of her faults if she lets it get out of control. If you can meet her demands, things can work well. If it starts feeling like it is work meeting all of these demands you have to let her know. She might not even realize what she is asking. There is nothing that she expects from you that she is not willing to give herself. If you feel a lack of effort on her part it may be a simple oversight.

Soul Mates: Look out when you get together with an Aries, Leo, or Sagittarius, you guys will be on fire! Loosen up; Aquarius and Pisces just might inspire you. Just when you think you know Virgo and Scorpio, more layers will appear out of nowhere. Taurus and Gemini crave stability. If you are not ready to settle down, move on. Libra doesn't feel complete without a partner. Are you willing to be the other half? Cancer and Capricorn are way too rigid for your taste.

Most Charming Characteristics: Faithful, respectful, sincere.

Gifts: *For her:* a reason to dress up. *For him:* rare bottle of wine.

Sensual Foods: Kiwis; cantaloupes; strawberries.

Romantic Flowers: Any rose of any color for the lady. Roses stand for love regardless of the color. Send them with orchids and you will be saying, "I love you." If you want a gentleman to know you think of him, send pansies, and forget-me-nots for true love.

Best Date Nights: Tuesday; 2nd and 29th of each month.

Colors of Passion: *For her:* dark red, crimson. *For him:* reddish brown, black.

The Perfect Wedding: Flamboyant and dynamic . . . ring a bell? A wonderfully romantic, resplendent theme wedding is most suited to your personality. Don't laugh—you may want to consider a Disneyland setting (if not, maybe honeymoon?) that is steeped in fantasy and mystery. You love unusual dining places, and good entertainment for your guests is a must. It is essential that a splendid time is had by all, not just you and your love. Ideal setting: Florence.

Wise Words: Alfred, Lord Tennyson: "He that shuts Love out, in turn shall be shut out from Love."

Hints of Love: Don't overdo it (dress, attention) too soon or this one will run. Wait until you have them hooked before you become outrageous.

After the Argument: *For him:* Start kissing up. Inflate that ego until it pops. You usually will have two fights before the resolution of the first one. If he is wrong, don't expect the "I'm sorry." The fight will just end quickly. If you're wrong, start washing the car or shining his shoes. Then give him a night out with his friends. *For her:* Make sure she is good and calm, then say you're sorry for what you did, even if the fight wasn't your fault. If you want to make up, just start saying you're sorry for something. You will have her eating out of your hand in no time.

Romantic Places: Places of enthusiasm bring romance: Buenos Aires; a comedy club; Nashville, Tennessee.

Lucky Love Star: Ariel—you will never lack affection.

Beautiful Thought: Your mate read your mind, so you don't have to talk.

Sharing Secrets: You had better be ready to pull out your romantic side if you want this to work. *For the gals:* Fireplaces, walks on the beach, or even winning a bear at the local carnival. *For the guys:* When you are out shopping bring him something home. Even if it is silly, he will love the thought.

Judith's Insights

About the Man: You have to keep him guessing. Don't give this guy all you have got right up front. If he is your boss or your buddy, hold back. As time goes by, let him know more about you and give more to him. Never let him take you for granted. Otherwise, he will be running around assuming that you will always be waiting there in the end. Give him enough rope and he will never feel the need to leave your side. If that rope is too thin, he will chew his way free just for the principle. Give him his freedom and he will always have a place to come back to.

About the Woman: Don't think you can play her for a fool. She is too smart for any of that nonsense. She is so smart she will not let her left hand be aware of what her right hand is doing. There is a fine line she draws between being mysterious and secretive. It is for you to figure out how not to cross it. She has an uncanny ability to read people but will most likely keep the information to herself. She doesn't want to reveal what she has in her hand until all bets are in. It is her way of controlling the game. Cherish her and she will be your best, and most fun, opponent.

Soul Mates: Aries, Leo, and Sagittarius dish out just as much energy as you do. Let Aquarius and Pisces into your life and you definitely won't regret it. Virgo and Scorpio will have you twisted in knots trying to keep up with their mood swings. Don't lead Taurus and Gemini on. Let them know if you are not in for the long haul. Teach Libra the joy of independence you so love and they will be a joy to be around. Cancer's and Capricorn's unyielding nature will have you running in the other direction.

Most Charming Characteristics: Pleasant, perceptive, social.

Gifts: *For her:* long back rub. *For him:* sports tickets.

Sensual Foods: Caramel and chocolate syrup on anything.

Romantic Flowers: These ladies like everyone to know how faithful they are, so send them violets. To surprise them send tulips. Men like their flowers the same as their relationships, unpretending. Send them camellias with white roses to show your affection.

Best Date Nights: Tuesday; 3rd and 12th of each month.

Colors of Passion: *For her:* dark red, crimson. *For him:* reddish brown, black.

The Perfect Wedding: Flamboyant and dynamic . . . ring a bell? A wonderfully romantic, resplendent theme wedding is most suited to your personality. Don't laugh—you may want to consider a Disneyland setting (if not, maybe honeymoon?) that is steeped in fantasy and mystery. You love unusual dining places, and good entertainment for your guests is a must. It is essential that a splendid time is had by all, not just you and your love. Ideal setting: Florence.

Wise Words: James Anthony Froude: "The essence of true nobility is neglect of self. Let the thought of self pass on, and the beauty of a great action is gone like the bloom from a soiled flower."

Hints of Love: When these folks decide to sit on the fence don't try to push them off before they are ready. Let them do the jumping themselves.

After the Argument: *For him:* Start kissing up. Inflate that ego until it pops. You usually will have two fights before the resolution of the first one. If he is wrong, don't expect the "I'm sorry." The fight will just end quickly. If you're wrong, start washing the car or shining his shoes. Then give him a night out with his friends. *For her:* Make sure she is good and calm, then say you're sorry for what you did, even if the fight wasn't your fault. If you want to make up, just start saying you're sorry for something. You will have her eating out of your hand in no time.

Romantic Places: Places of excitement bring romance: Mexico; a sports event; Las Vegas, Nevada.

Lucky Love Star: Ariel—you will never lack affection.

Beautiful Thought: Remember the first time you held someone's hand when you really needed it.

Sharing Secrets: It may seem like they are not interested, but ask them out anyway. *For the gals:* Until they absolutely know you are interested, you will never find out that they are. *For the guys:* Ask him out if he doesn't ask you. He may be shy or not. Either way, he may be interested.

Judith's Insights

About the Man: You may never know just how to approach him, which is frustrating to most who meet him. His response can be slow. He lives in his head more than his heart. He takes emotional responsibility seriously. I guess that is why he always has so much apprehension about whether to give in to it. It is as simple as it gets to be involved with this guy. Love him and he will love you back. Be good to him and he will be good to you in return. The more you invest in a relationship with this guy the more you will see invested in you.

About the Woman: She's quieter than usual, and it takes time to assess everything in her head. She doesn't like to make a move without feeling as if she has had a chance to see the whole picture. She just wants to keep it simple. It could be good to go slowly and would be better if you play no games. You will always get your money's worth with this one. Cross her and she will hang around long enough for you to think she never noticed. Then one day she will be gone. She can put up with anything but the unforgivable. Figuring out what the unforgivable is will be left to you.

Soul Mates: Does the phrase "life of the party" mean anything to you? With Aries, Leo, and Sagittarius you will certainly be exactly that. Let yourself open up to all of the joy Aquarius and Pisces can bring to you. Nothing is what it seems to be with Virgo and Scorpio. Trying to uncover the truth can be exhausting. Taurus and Gemini are all about connecting. Are you willing to be permanently connected? Libra may become too dependent on the partnership and you may feel strangled. You have no patience for the overbearing nature of Cancer and Capricorn.

Most Charming Characteristics: Energetic, strong, sincere.

Gifts: *For her:* newest book from her fave chef. *For him:* book about success.

Sensual Foods: Waffles with whipped cream; chocolate soufflé; French wine.

Romantic Flowers: These ladies like men with taste. Show them you love style by sending fuchsia flowers, or even brightly colored wildflowers will do. To confuse this man, send him lilies along with bright daisies to show your innocence. Keep him guessing.

Best Date Nights: Tuesday; 22nd and 31st of each month.

Colors of Passion: *For her:* dark red, crimson. *For him:* reddish brown, black.

The Perfect Wedding: Flamboyant and dynamic . . . ring a bell? A wonderfully romantic, resplendent theme wedding is most suited to your personality. Don't laugh—you may want to consider a Disneyland setting (if not, maybe honeymoon?) that is steeped in fantasy and mystery. You love unusual dining places, and good entertainment for your guests is a must. It is essential that a splendid time is had by all, not just you and your love. Ideal setting: Florence.

Wise Words: Ralph Waldo Emerson: "Every thought which genius and piety throw into the world alters the world."

Hints of Love: Make sure you learn to compromise, but never with your principle.

After the Argument: *For him:* Start kissing up. Inflate that ego until it pops. You usually will have two fights before the resolution of the first one. If he is wrong, don't expect the "I'm sorry." The fight will just end quickly. If you're wrong, start washing the car or shining his shoes. Then give him a night out with his friends. *For her:* Make sure she is good and calm, then say you're sorry for what you did, even if the fight wasn't your fault. If you want to make up, just start saying you're sorry for something. You will have her eating out of your hand in no time.

Romantic Places: Places of enthusiasm bring romance: London; a carnival; Cape Canaveral, Florida.

Lucky Love Star: Ariel—you will never lack affection.

Beautiful Thought: Someone who once wouldn't give you the time of day now gives you the time of your life.

Sharing Secrets: Don't be surprised if the first date is with their family. *For the gals:* Make sure you invite her to your family functions. It will be a red flag to her if you don't. *For the guys:* He may seem like a family man, but isn't that what you were looking for?

Judith's Insights

About the Man: He demands what he gives and doesn't understand anything in between. He would take your siding with someone else as being disloyal. You will feel him cold as ice and then he will very slowly leave without your noticing. Treat him as you would want to be treated to keep him around. He can be the strength in the relationship yet let his sensitive side show more and more each day. He will never let his pride get in the way of loving those around him, especially his mate. The better he is treated the better he will treat you.

About the Woman: She has an uncanny nurturing side. Others may feel that this is disguised. She can be strong and sweet at the same time. Never question her loyalty or you will lose her. Don't ever take her kindness for weakness, especially if she signs your paycheck. Repay all of her good deeds with one of your own. Balance in the work done in any relationship is extremely important to her. Allow her to love you the best that she knows how to. That is simply to give all that she receives.

Soul Mates: When you have Aries, Leo, and Sagittarius in your life, the journey will be thrilling. Only when you are receptive to inspiration can you enjoy a partnership with Aquarius and Pisces. Virgo and Scorpio will aggravate you with their emotional roller coaster. Are you ready for your seeds to take root? If so, Taurus and Gemini are the perfect soil for them to grow in. Show Libra how to value things outside of the relationship and you will enjoy it much more. Cancer's and Capricorn's mood swings will have your head spinning.

Most Charming Characteristics: Kind, extravagant, humorous.

Gifts: *For her:* day at the horse races. *For him:* tickets to the big game.

Sensual Foods: Oysters; mussels; spicy foods.

Romantic Flowers: You are the lady of distinction, and only carnations will do. Any mix of colors with sprays of mignonette. Sweet peas or red carnations will appeal to this man's heart.

Best Date Nights: Tuesday; 4th and 5th of each month.

Colors of Passion: *For her:* dark red, crimson. *For him:* reddish brown, black.

The Perfect Wedding: Flamboyant and dynamic . . . ring a bell? A wonderfully romantic, resplendent theme wedding is most suited to your personality. Don't laugh—you may want to consider a Disneyland setting (if not, maybe honeymoon?) that is steeped in fantasy and mystery. You love unusual dining places, and good entertainment for your guests is a must. It is essential that a splendid time is had by all, not just you and your love. Ideal setting: Florence.

Wise Words: Henry Wadsworth Longfellow: "No action, whether foul or fair, is ever done, but it leaves somewhere a record."

Hints of Love: If you try to take a step back, it will be noticed. It could create the domino effect, and everything will start to fall.

After the Argument: *For him:* Start kissing up. Inflate that ego until it pops. You usually will have two fights before the resolution of the first one. If he is wrong, don't expect the "I'm sorry." The fight will just end quickly. If you're wrong, start washing the car or shining his shoes. Then give him a night out with his friends. *For her:* Make sure she is good and calm, then say you're sorry for what you did, even if the fight wasn't your fault. If you want to make up, just start saying you're sorry for something. You will have her eating out of your hand in no time.

Romantic Places: Places of excitement bring romance: Brazil; an amusement park; New Orleans.

Lucky Love Star: Ariel—you will never lack affection.

Beautiful Thought: You fall and someone is there to catch you, only you don't know you have been caught at the time.

Sharing Secrets: Take me as I am could be the anthem for this one. *For the gals:* They will have strong views on just about everything. If you can hang with them, then nothing will be as important as you. *For the guys:* The thing you fall in love with may end up becoming the thing you hate. After a commitment, this one sticks around.

Judith's Insights

About the Man: He has many acquaintances but only few loyal friends. He will give you the shirt off his back but you had better be willing to give yours. All things must be equal when dealing with this guy. He never understands conflict and strives for harmony in every situation in his life. He is admired by his friends and is never far away from company. People tend to hang on his every word and he can't figure out why. He has a demonstrative way of showing his love that leaves you with a hug that lasts forever.

About the Woman: All she needs is love, appreciation, and plenty of attention. If she works with you, compliment her before you give her the bad news. You may bring out her defensive side if you don't tread carefully. You don't have to proceed with caution, but with honor. She needs to know that you are giving as much effort as she is. She can brighten the entire room just with her smile and she knows it. The minute she walks in there will be several people making their way toward her to join her conversation. Don't worry, there will be plenty to talk about with this gal.

Soul Mates: You can finally find someone to keep up with you in Aries, Leo, and Sagittarius. Aquarius and Pisces are a blessing you must be willing to receive. Virgo and Scorpio are too easily offended for your liking. Be ready to give Taurus and Gemini the consistency they deserve or move on to other things. Libra is a real team player and will fight for you all the way. Just make sure that they don't forget to fight for themselves also. Cancer and Capricorn are too focused on the order of things for your impulsive nature. This is not recommended.

Most Charming Characteristics: Energetic, versatile, generous.

Gifts: *For her:* expensive perfume. *For him:* fine cologne.

Sensual Foods: Lobster; watermelon.

Romantic Flowers: You love it when you get tulips, declaring love. When you receive a variety, it shows how hopelessly in love your partner is. He will just love a single rose. This shows him you understand his pleasures.

Best Date Nights: Tuesday; 15th and 24th of each month.

Colors of Passion: *For her:* dark red, crimson. *For him:* reddish brown, black.

The Perfect Wedding: Flamboyant and dynamic . . . ring a bell? A wonderfully romantic, resplendent theme wedding is most suited to your personality. Don't laugh—you may want to consider a Disneyland setting (if not, maybe honeymoon?) that is steeped in fantasy and mystery. You love unusual dining places, and good entertainment for your guests is a must. It is essential that a splendid time is had by all, not just you and your love. Ideal setting: Florence.

Wise Words: Henry Wadsworth Longfellow: "Tell me not in mournful numbers, / Life is but an empty dream! / For the soul is dead that slumbers, / And things are not what they seem."

Hints of Love: Consistence and persistence will get this prize every time. They will value the effort.

After the Argument: *For him:* Start kissing up. Inflate that ego until it pops. You usually will have two fights before the resolution of the first one. If he is wrong, don't expect the "I'm sorry." The fight will just end quickly. If you're wrong, start washing the car or shining his shoes. Then give him a night out with his friends. *For her:* Make sure she is good and calm, then say you're sorry for what you did, even if the fight wasn't your fault. If you want to make up, just start saying you're sorry for something. You will have her eating out of your hand in no time.

Romantic Places: Places of enthusiasm bring romance: French Riviera; an outdoor festival; Hollywood, California.

Lucky Love Star: Ariel—you will never lack affection.

Beautiful Thought: Believing in Santa Claus, the Easter Bunny, the Tooth Fairy, and tomorrow.

Sharing Secrets: They seem moody until you get to know them. *For the gals:* You may not know whether to say hello or drop dead. As relations progress you will learn not to leave her dangling, and her moods will become more consistent. *For the guys:* To know him is to love him. His bark is much worse than his bite. He just wants someone to love him without criticism.

Judith's Insights

About the Man: He makes a splash in any water. He treads and never does it lightly, and why should he? If you want to be a part of his team, you will just have to do a little swimming until you capture his attention. Even if you are the boss, let him think it is his idea. Let him think he is in control, even if you are asking for a raise. You may feel as if you have to make a lifelong commitment just to get the first date. There is something incredibly investigative about his nature. He wants to know what you are made of before he gives you a chance.

About the Woman: Love is important to her, but she won't be wearing that on her sleeve. You may have to do a little dance to get her attention, and throw a big party to keep it. Perseverance is needed in any relationship with this gal. She is full of enthusiasm and yet you may get to know her cynical side out of the blue. A date with her will be great or a disaster. You have to be on the same page to make it great. You can bring out the best in her by showing the best in yourself.

Soul Mates: There is electricity in the air when you hook up with Aries, Leo, and Sagittarius. Aquarius and Pisces will delight you when you are open-hearted. Virgo's and Scorpio's tendency to worry will drive you up a wall. When you want to firmly establish yourself, turn no further than Taurus and Gemini. When you and Libra strike a happy medium between independence and dependence things will flow smoothly. Dependency is a big turnoff for you. Cancer and Capricorn build walls around themselves so fast that you might even get stuck in them.

Most Charming Characteristics: Extravagant, courageous, considerate.

Gifts: *For her:* horseback riding. *For him:* tickets to the races.

Sensual Foods: Strawberries; truffles; shish kebab.

Romantic Flowers: Send this girl sunflowers if you want her to know you adore her. You may even add some poppies for a splash of extravagance. His desire for sport and play will be understood when you send him hyacinth and geranium.

Best Date Nights: Tuesday; 6th and 24th of each month.

Colors of Passion: *For her:* dark red, crimson. *For him:* reddish brown, black.

The Perfect Wedding: Flamboyant and dynamic . . . ring a bell? A wonderfully romantic, resplendent theme wedding is most suited to your personality. Don't laugh—you may want to consider a Disneyland setting (if not, maybe honeymoon?) that is steeped in fantasy and mystery. You love unusual dining places, and good entertainment for your guests is a must. It is essential that a splendid time is had by all, not just you and your love. Ideal setting: Florence.

Wise Words: Henry Wadsworth Longfellow: "For the structure that we raise; / Time is with materials filled; / Our to-days and yesterdays / Are the blocks with which we build."

Hints of Love: Be funny. Laughter will be what keeps this one coming back again and again.

After the Argument: *For him:* Start kissing up. Inflate that ego until it pops. You usually will have two fights before the resolution of the first one. If he is wrong, don't expect the "I'm sorry." The fight will just end quickly. If you're wrong, start washing the car or shining his shoes. Then give him a night out with his friends. *For her:* Make sure she is good and calm, then say you're sorry for what you did, even if the fight wasn't your fault. If you want to make up, just start saying you're sorry for something. You will have her eating out of your hand in no time.

Romantic Places: Places of excitement bring romance: Cannes, France; a carnival; New York City.

Lucky Love Star: Ariel—you will never lack affection.

Beautiful Thought: You can have a bad day without anyone realizing it.

Sharing Secrets: You had better be able to put your money where your mouth is. *For the gals:* It doesn't need to be lavish, but she does love the loot. The more the better. *For the guys:* He doesn't mind spending his hard-earned cash, but he loves to see you contribute to please him.

Judith's Insights

About the Man: This guy will be right up front. He will put his desires right on the table. He is certainly candid as a boss and an employee. Others may feel he is overconfident and too fearless for his own good. For the most part he is, except when it comes to his emotions. They are scattered to all four corners of the world. His emotional side can get the best of him if he is not careful to think things out before he opens his mouth. It is no wonder. He handles everything else in his life with ease. His emotions have a mind of their own.

About the Woman: She creates her own opportunity. She waits for nobody, except for when she is in love. She may be assertive, but that can take a back seat if her intuition feels a ripple in the water. She needs complete alliance. Show her that you will be there through thick and thin by each action. Consistency is the key. She puts herself on a roller coaster of love and then she will decide to take herself off when nobody else can. The only person she will lie to is herself. She is an expert at hiding her emotions until they decide to come out whether she likes it or not.

Soul Mates: Spontaneity is the name of the game when it is played with Aries, Leo, and Sagittarius. Don't let the gift of joy Aquarius and Pisces are willing to give you go unclaimed. Virgo and Scorpio need constant affirmation. This could leave you exhausted. Reliability is the expectation of Taurus and Gemini. You must decide if you want to be the one to be relied on before you enter anything. You must come to an understanding with Libra about where this relationship is sailing before it sinks. The tendency of Cancer and Capricorn to cling to you is a definite push for you to move on.

Most Charming Characteristics: Intelligent, affectionate, reliable.

Gifts: *For her:* sparkling bracelet. *For him:* personalized briefcase.

Sensual Foods: Grapes; fine cheeses and crackers; taffy.

Romantic Flowers: Rhododendron will let her be on the lookout for trouble. Throw in some chrysanthemum and she'll know it is you she will be looking out for. Cactus will show him warmth. Yellow daffodil is a token of a good time had by all. Chivalry is not dead.

Best Date Nights: Tuesday; 8th and 17th of each month.

Colors of Passion: *For her:* dark red, crimson. *For him:* reddish brown, black.

The Perfect Wedding: Flamboyant and dynamic . . . ring a bell? A wonderfully romantic, resplendent theme wedding is most suited to your personality. Don't laugh—you may want to consider a Disneyland setting (if not, maybe honeymoon?) that is steeped in fantasy and mystery. You love unusual dining places, and good entertainment for your guests is a must. It is essential that a splendid time is had by all, not just you and your love. Ideal setting: Florence.

Wise Words: Henry Wadsworth Longfellow: "Thus, at the flaming forge of life / Our fortunes must be wrought; thus, on it sounding anvil shaped / Each burning deed and thought!"

Hints of Love: Treat this one like royalty or precious cargo. They will love being valued in this way.

After the Argument: *For him:* Start kissing up. Inflate that ego until it pops. You usually will have two fights before the resolution of the first one. If he is wrong, don't expect the "I'm sorry." The fight will just end quickly. If you're wrong, start washing the car or shining his shoes. Then give him a night out with his friends. *For her:* Make sure she is good and calm, then say you're sorry for what you did, even if the fight wasn't your fault. If you want to make up, just start saying you're sorry for something. You will have her eating out of your hand in no time.

Romantic Places: Places of excitement bring romance: New Orleans; an amusement park; Times Square.

Lucky Love Star: Ariel—you will never lack affection.

Beautiful Thought: Your significant other apologizes when he or she was right and you were wrong.

Sharing Secrets: Nobody likes a weak link, especially not this one. *For the gals:* Make sure you treat her like a lady and act like a man. *For the guys:* Put your best foot forward. Dress your best and keep your manners in check. This man notices.

Judith's Insights

About the Man: He is a guy with a lot of class and wants to be treated as such. He can be reckless at times. He only stands in his own way, never in anyone else's. If you can prove yourself to him, then a true friendship awaits you. Make sure you are honest and straightforward at all times. Spend a buck or two on him. He is worth every dollar, and it will be returned to you in the most surprising ways. For every dollar you spend on this guy he will spend two on you. It is not about the denomination but the effort with this guy.

About the Woman: She can be way too shy at the first encounter. She comes around, though, as soon as she warms up. All that she is looking for is someone to be next to her with no complications. She is willing to do all the work, as long as she gets time to play. Playing is only fun for her if she has someone to do it with. She wants to be loved just like everyone else in this world. You may get more than you pay for with her. She rewards efforts to make her feel special by giving back more than received.

Soul Mates: Say good-bye to the mundane and hello to fiery passion when you meet Aries, Leo, and Sagittarius. No person is an island. Open the channels to Aquarius and Pisces. They have much to bring. Overly sensitive signs like Virgo and Scorpio are too much for you to bear. Taurus and Gemini need a completely devoted partner. If that is not you, let them know as soon as you can. Things with Libra are up to you and your willingness to compromise. Cancer and Capricorn won't deviate from the predetermined plan that you never agreed to in the first place.

Most Charming Characteristics: Ambitious, clever, artistic.

Gifts: *For her:* new clothes from her fave designer. *For him:* newest trend in ties.

Sensual Foods: Champagne; grapes; mangoes; filet mignon.

Romantic Flowers: The magnolias you send her will let her know you will be around for a while to come. Petunia is to say never despair. Holly will let him know what he is getting into. Pansy will keep you in his thoughts.

Best Date Nights: Tuesday; 9th and 27th of each month.

Colors of Passion: *For her:* dark red, crimson. *For him:* reddish brown, black.

The Perfect Wedding: Flamboyant and dynamic . . . ring a bell? A wonderfully romantic, resplendent theme wedding is most suited to your personality. Don't laugh—you may want to consider a Disneyland setting (if not, maybe honeymoon?) that is steeped in fantasy and mystery. You love unusual dining places, and good entertainment for your guests is a must. It is essential that a splendid time is had by all, not just you and your love. Ideal setting: Florence.

Wise Words: Henry Wadsworth Longfellow: "All your strength is in your union, / All your danger is in discord; therefore be at peace henceforward, / And as brothers live together."

Hints of Love: Affection is important, but only if it comes naturally. Otherwise, the sirens will go off.

After the Argument: *For him:* Start kissing up. Inflate that ego until it pops. You usually will have two fights before the resolution of the first one. If he is wrong, don't expect the "I'm sorry." The fight will just end quickly. If you're wrong, start washing the car or shining his shoes. Then give him a night out with his friends. *For her:* Make sure she is good and calm, then say you're sorry for what you did, even if the fight wasn't your fault. If you want to make up, just start saying you're sorry for something. You will have her eating out of your hand in no time.

Romantic Places: Places of enthusiasm bring romance: Rio de Janeiro; an air show; Disney World.

Lucky Love Star: Ariel—you will never lack affection.

Beautiful Thought: Sometimes life is like dropping your wallet with your paycheck in it but then getting it back with all your money in it.

Sharing Secrets: Attention, attention, attention. *For the gals:* Do it any way you can. Presents, phone calls, cards, or flowers. Whatever works for you will work for her. *For the guys:* He would love nostalgic gifts or T-shirts. He also like phone calls, as long as they don't interrupt his favorite pastimes.

Judith's Insights

About the Man: A red light may still mean go with this guy. His actions can, and will, contradict his words. His emotions are a different story. He will try his hardest to keep them hidden deep inside until they come out all at once. He has a way about him that can easily attract crowds. This may baffle you at times if you know him better than most. You may feel intimidated by his life and become an onlooker. Just let him enjoy his time in the sun and he will return the favor. Before you know it you will be the center of his world for life.

About the Woman: Don't let her do all of the work or you will lose her for sure. She can't stand it when she sees others get lazy. This is especially true in relationships, even with her family. If she is your boss or co-worker, you had better be holding up your end of the stick. Otherwise, you will hear it from her instantly. She rewards those who work hard to keep harmony in her world. Her energy allows her to do what would regularly exhaust others. Don't take the wind out of her sails. Instead, take some vitamins and work on keeping up with her.

Soul Mates: Aries, Leo, and Sagittarius bring so much adventure and passion into your life it would be hard to bore even you. Taurus and Gemini are a go as long as you can make a complete commitment. Otherwise, they can bring out the worst in everyone. Aquarius and Pisces would bring constant stimulation and enjoyment, if you would only let them. Cancer and Capricorn could wear you a little thin. Libra could go either way. You complement each other, but if compromise is not in the picture, then neither are you. Virgo and Scorpio will give you a run for your money, then want to go spend it all.

Most Charming Characteristics: Artistic, intellectual, sincere.

Gifts: *For her:* a reason to dress up. *For him:* rare bottle of wine.

Sensual Foods: Châteaubriand, crème brûlée.

Romantic Flowers: Iris is your flower if you are the gal sending subtle messages. If you are the man, you will look for clematis. This flower's mental beauty creates emotional stimulation for you.

Best Date Nights: Tuesday; 1st and 10th of each month.

Colors of Passion: *For her:* dark red, crimson. *For him:* reddish brown, green.

The Perfect Wedding: Flamboyant and dynamic . . . ring a bell? A wonderfully romantic, resplendent theme wedding is most suited to your personality. Don't laugh—you may want to consider a Disneyland setting (if not, maybe honeymoon?) that is steeped in fantasy and mystery. You love unusual dining places, and good entertainment for your guests is a must. It is essential that a splendid time is had by all, not just you and your love. Ideal setting: Florence.

Wise Words: Henry Wadsworth Longfellow: "Man-like is it to fall into sin, / Fiendlike is to dwell therein, / Christ-like is it for sin to grieve, / God-like is it all sin to leave."

Hints of Love: This one likes others to make his or her dreams come true. Be the "fantasy" fulfiller.

After the Argument: *For him:* Start kissing up. Inflate that ego until it pops. You usually will have two fights before the resolution of the first one. If he is wrong, don't expect the "I'm sorry." The fight will just end quickly. If you're wrong, start washing the car or shining his shoes. Then give him a night out with his friends. *For her:* Make sure she is good and calm, then say you're sorry for what you did, even if the fight wasn't your fault. If you want to make up, just start saying you're sorry for something. You will have her eating out of your hand in no time.

Romantic Places: Places of excitement bring romance: Spain; a nightclub; Hollywood, California.

Lucky Love Star: Ariel—you will never lack affection.

Beautiful Thought: When you're feeling desperate, someone steps in to take away your sadness.

Sharing Secrets: Make sure you are not the killjoy. *For the gals:* When she has an idea, try it before you decide you don't like it. She needs to be pleased. *For the guys:* Do the things he loves to do and he will make the things you love ten times more fun.

Judith's Insights

About the Man: He is stubborn, and he gets even more stubborn the closer you get to him. His tough exterior becomes armor when his emotions come into play. Underneath that rough toughness is a real softy. All is well that ends well. If you can get under his armor there will be no one better to get along with than this guy. It is very easy for him to overcome any obstacles that enter his path. His simply being in your life will instantly influence you and how you approach things. He can teach you just as much as you can teach him.

About the Woman: Some may think that she is tough as nails. She can certainly seem that way at times. She lets very little emotion flow to the surface. She likes to be in total control, and no one can tell her that you can't control everything. If she is your boss you may think that you can do nothing right. She does notice the good job you do but may not be able to let you know it. If and when you fall for her you will fall hard. There is something about her that knocks people right off their feet. Make sure you wear your protective gear until she is ready to join you on the floor.

Soul Mates: Look out when you get together with an Aries, Leo, or Sagittarius, you guys will be on fire! Loosen up; Aquarius and Pisces just might inspire you. Just when you think you know Virgo and Scorpio, more layers will appear out of nowhere. Taurus and Gemini crave stability. If you are not ready to settle down, move on. Libra doesn't feel complete without a partner. Are you willing to be the other half? Cancer and Capricorn are way too rigid for your taste.

Most Charming Characteristics: Intellectual, kindhearted, ambitious.

Gifts: *For her:* long back rub. *For him:* sports tickets.

Sensual Foods: Shrimp; sinful chocolate cake.

Romantic Flowers: Any rose of any color for the lady. Roses stand for love regardless of the color. Send them with orchids and you will be saying, "I love you." If you want a gentleman to know you think of him, send pansies, and forget-me-nots for true love.

Best Date Nights: Tuesday; 20th and 29th of each month.

Colors of Passion: *For her:* dark red, crimson. *For him:* reddish brown, black.

The Perfect Wedding: Flamboyant and dynamic . . . ring a bell? A wonderfully romantic, resplendent theme wedding is most suited to your personality. Don't laugh—you may want to consider a Disneyland setting (if not, maybe honeymoon?) that is steeped in fantasy and mystery. You love unusual dining places, and good entertainment for your guests is a must. It is essential that a splendid time is had by all, not just you and your love. Ideal setting: Florence.

Wise Words: Henry Wadsworth Longfellow: "From the earth's loosened mould the sapling draws its sustenance, and thrives; though stricken to the heart with winter's cold, The drooping tree revives."

Hints of Love: Stop worrying about next week's date today or there will not be one tomorrow.

After the Argument: *For him:* Start kissing up. Inflate that ego until it pops. You usually will have two fights before the resolution of the first one. If

he is wrong, don't expect the "I'm sorry." The fight will just end quickly. If you're wrong, start washing the car or shining his shoes. Then give him a night out with his friends. *For her:* Make sure she is good and calm, then say you're sorry for what you did, even if the fight wasn't your fault. If you want to make up, just start saying you're sorry for something. You will have her eating out of your hand in no time.

Romantic Places: Places of enthusiasm bring romance: Buenos Aries; a comedy club; Nashville, Tennessee.

Lucky Love Star: Ariel—you will never lack affection.

Beautiful Thought: Just when you feel like asking for a loan, you might receive a check that was due you a long time ago.

Sharing Secrets: You had better be ready to have a relationship. *For the gals:* No lies, no games, and no mistakes. She wants what she wants with as little amount of work possible. *For the guys:* If you have games on your mind, then move on. This one likes fun any way he can get it, but no emotional roller coasters.

Judith's Insights

About the Man: First things must be first here. You must learn to appreciate and praise this guy first. This will certainly make for a much more open response. He can tend to become a bit dominating in every relationship he has. If this gets overwhelming, you can let him know as long it is accompanied by positive feedback as well. He can be very hard to handle if you do not take the time to get to know him well before handing over your heart. When you do you will see that his idea of romance might be different but his intentions are the same.

About the Woman: She can appear too strong and seem to have no emotions. It is actually because she has such strong emotions that she also has such strong convictions. She runs a tight ship at all times. Keep that in mind if she is your boss. She makes it look effortless, but there is a lot of work behind it. Don't let her independent attitude make you think that she is not interested in a relationship. That happens to be exactly what she is looking for. She might not want to let on until she is certain that it is all clear and safe to come out and tell you.

Soul Mates: Try to integrate some flexible material into the tightly woven foundation you build with Taurus, Capricorn, and Virgo. Let Sagittarius and Libra expand your boundaries and stop fighting it. The combo of you and Pisces or Aries can be quite scintillating. You and Aquarius are wildly different and stubborn about those differences. Both you and Gemini must take each other at face value to enjoy life together. Cancer delights in the world just like you do. You just want something to come home to. Concentrate on your similarities and the differences between you and Leo and Scorpio won't seem as big.

Most Charming Characteristics: Generous, ambitious, artistic.

Gifts: *For her:* puppy or kitten. *For him:* tree to help grow.

Sensual Foods: Toasted marshmallows; chocolates.

Romantic Flowers: These ladies like everyone to know how faithful they are, so send them violets. To surprise them send tulips. Men like their flowers the same as their relationships, unpretending. Send them camellias with white roses to show your affection.

Best Date Nights: Friday; 3rd and 21st of each month.

Colors of Passion: *For her:* white, dark red. *For him:* green.

The Perfect Wedding: Serene and natural, sensual and glamorous—that's you all over. You enjoy savoring the moment and are continually impressed and inspired by beauty and classic taste. A brilliant outdoor wedding dripping in greens and fresh florals most appeals to you. Choose lots of fresh-cut, fragrant flowers to decorate an elegant, traditional wedding. Ideal setting: Ireland.

Wise Words: Henry Wadsworth Longfellow: "Whene'er a noble deed is wrought, / Whene'er is spoken a noble thought, / Our hearts, in glad surprise, / To higher levels rise."

Hints of Love: Keep the romance in the picture. Don't forget the long walks on the beach and camping out in front of the fireplace.

After the Argument: *For him:* Once the fight is over don't ever bring it up again. You can make a fight go in a minute if you change the subject and move on. If you need to get that last word in, this fight will never seem to end. Making up then will take a lot of stroking. *For her:* She is stubborn, but easily bought off, especially if she is in love. They say diamonds are a girl's best friends. Well, just about any real jewels will do, and only the best will do for this one.

Romantic Places: Places of luxury bring romance: Japan; a spa; Florence, Italy.

Lucky Love Star: Tawnel—you will never lack passion.

Beautiful Thought: You must have an open mind to fill your heart.

Sharing Secrets: You may have to give this one more than one chance. *For the gals:* Intriguing as she is, expect a handful. She lightens up as time goes on. *For the guys:* His quirks may make you have second thoughts, but that is what separates the men from the boys.

Judith's Insights

About the Man: They have an uncanny influence over others, sometimes even over strangers. The arts and culture of all kinds stimulate them. Appeal to his likes and at the very least you will capture his attention. The rest depends on whether you can keep a hold on it. The only way to keep him at all interested is to work as hard as he does at keeping things going. If he suspects that he is left holding the bag he will walk away before you even notice. He doesn't ask for much from those he loves. All he wants is someone who feels that the relationship is as important as he does.

About the Woman: She is a great judge of character as long as it does not involve her emotions. When the emotions are entered into the mix, there is no telling where her mind is. Her executive ability can turn any dinner party into a debate. She keeps like and love separate as well as her work and pleasure. Don't try to put up boundaries too early in a relationship with her or you will lose her interest quickly. She likes to have a sense of freedom while being attached. If you become defensive she will only assume that you are hiding something. Honesty is the best policy here.

Soul Mates: Try to integrate some flexible material into the tightly woven foundation you build with Taurus, Capricorn, and Virgo. Let Sagittarius and Libra expand your boundaries and stop fighting it. The combo of you and Pisces or Aries can be quite scintillating. You and Aquarius are wildly different and stubborn about those differences. Both you and Gemini must take each other at face value to enjoy life together. Cancer delights in the world just like you do. You just want something to come home to. Concentrate on your similarities and the differences between you and Leo and Scorpio won't seem as big.

Most Charming Characteristics: Talented, positive, keen foresight.

Gifts: *For her:* soft sweater. *For him:* antique clock.

Sensual Foods: Chocolate-covered strawberries; New York steak; scallops.

Romantic Flowers: These ladies like men with taste. Show them you love style by sending fuchsia flowers, or even brightly colored wildflowers will do. To confuse this man, send him lilies along with bright daisies to show your innocence. Keep him guessing.

Best Date Nights: Friday; 4th and 13th of each month.

Colors of Passion: *For her:* crimson, silver. *For him:* black.

The Perfect Wedding: Serene and natural, sensual and glamorous—that's you all over. You enjoy savoring the moment and are continually impressed and inspired by beauty and classic taste. A brilliant outdoor wedding dripping in greens and fresh florals most appeals to you. Choose lots of fresh-cut, fragrant flowers to decorate an elegant, traditional wedding. Ideal setting: Ireland.

Wise Words: Charles Dickens: "How true it is in all art, that what seems the easiest done, is often the most difficult to do."

Hints of Love: The mystery is important, but being evasive will create disaster. Make sure you know the difference.

After the Argument: *For him:* Once the fight is over, don't ever bring it up again. You can make a fight go in a minute if you change the subject and move on. If you need to get that last word in, this fight will never seem to end. Making up then will take a lot of stroking. *For her:* She is stubborn, but easily bought off, especially if she is in love. They say diamonds are a girl's best friends. Well, just about any real jewels will do, and only the best will do for this one.

Romantic Places: Places of vastness bring romance: Africa; a farm; the Grand Canyon.

Lucky Love Star: Tawnel—you will never lack passion.

Beautiful Thought: The bus stops, without your chasing it, when you are running late.

Sharing Secrets: Talk about high maintenance. *For the gals:* Once she sees that you go out of your way for her then she will for you. *For the guys:* The bark is definitely much worse than the bite. He comes on stronger and more obstinate than he actually is.

Judith's Insights

About the Man: If you want to get his attention, you can get it through music. He loves the arts. Even if you do not win him over, you will most certainly get his attention. You need stamina to keep up with this guy. Being able to prove you do will also capture his attention. Once you have it, it will be up to you to keep it. Life with this guy can be as simple as you make it. He would prefer to be in charge but he will never demand to be. Recognizing that he is much more at ease when he has input on how things are done will make your job of making him happy that much easier.

About the Woman: There is no such thing as trying too hard with her. She will love the attention you lavish upon her. She has incredible self-control. You might have to go overboard before she gives in. When she does give in you will also have to work hard at keeping her interested. Take your vitamins. You will need the extra nutrition to keep up with this gal. She is not fickle. She just has many passions and enjoys exploring them. She loves getting her own way. Let her win the debate over where you will eat on the first date and go from there.

Soul Mates: Being stable and quiet as you are, Capricorn, Virgo, and Taurus will need urging to open up. The foundation for a lasting pairing is there. You must be patient with the impulsive nature of Sagittarius and Libra. Your rare blowups may leave you with one less prized possession in Pisces and Aries. Be careful what comes out and what simmers to a boil. A match with an Aquarius can be a recipe for disaster or endless fascination. Gemini will look to you for direction on how to reach their goals. Generosity will deepen your relationship with Cancer and keep life sweet. Find a way to become flexible so you can make a relationship with Leo and Scorpio a nurturing one.

Most Charming Characteristics: Passionate, confident, successful.

Gifts: *For her:* Broadway show. *For him:* day at a zoo or aquarium.

Sensual Foods: Vanilla and strawberry mousse; tiramisù; espresso.

Romantic Flowers: You are the lady of distinction, and only carnations will do. Any mix of colors with sprays of mignonette. Sweet peas or red carnations will appeal to this man's heart.

Best Date Nights: Friday; 5th and 23rd of each month.

Colors of Passion: *For her:* white, silver. *For him:* green.

The Perfect Wedding: Serene and natural, sensual and glamorous—that's you all over. You enjoy savoring the moment and are continually impressed and inspired by beauty and classic taste. A brilliant outdoor wedding dripping in greens and fresh florals most appeals to you. Choose lots of fresh-cut, fragrant flowers to decorate an elegant, traditional wedding. Ideal setting: Ireland.

Wise Words: Charles Dickens: "Some men are disappointed in life somehow or other, and influenced by their disappointment."

Hints of Love: If you learn to back up when things are moving too fast, you won't have to bow out so often.

After the Argument: *For him:* Once the fight is over, don't ever bring it up again. You can make a fight go in a minute if you change the subject and move on. If you need to get that last word in, this fight will never seem to end. Making up then will take a lot of stroking. *For her:* She is stubborn, but easily bought off, especially if she is in love. They say diamonds are a girl's best friends. Well, just about any real jewels will do, and only the best will do for this one.

Romantic Places: Places of luxury bring romance: Britain; a mountain resort; Beverly Hills, California.

Lucky Love Star: Tawnel—you will never lack passion.

Beautiful Thought: Apple pie and hot cider on a Sunday afternoon are very cozy.

Sharing Secrets: Make sure you have at least five dates before you make up your mind. *For the gals:* They can be cynical, so it could be a few dates before she loosens up. *For the guys:* He still has yesterday on his mind. He needs a reason to forget his past relationship. Make a new history for him.

Judith's Insights

About the Man: He can have the patience of a saint. He loves to be around people but does not let them cramp his style. He will give you all of the room you need, because he would like you to do the same. If you work for him, just do your job right and you will have nothing to worry about. It is that simple. The one thing he will demand from you is honesty. He can be honest to the point of being brutal. He is not trying to cause you pain. He just feels that it would be an injustice to lay it out any other way. He wants things to be as uncomplicated as possible.

About the Woman: Don't ever dare to make her look like a fool. This is true of any type of relationship. If you want something, you must approach her before you tell anyone else. She likes to get her information firsthand. This one will never settle for sloppy seconds. Always give her first shot to say yes or no. If you are honorable, then life with her will be a piece of cake. If you can't be as upfront as she is, or you can't take her way of telling you the truth, you might want to look elsewhere for a mate. She wants to be as simple and honest as she can possibly be.

Soul Mates: No architect can draw plans for a building that can be stronger than the bond you can have with Taurus, Capricorn, and Virgo. Approach the match with Sagittarius and Libra with a playful attitude and you will get along famously. With two such generous spirits as Pisces and Aries, fine-tuning the relationship will be a joy. Aquarius's regard for logic as the only reason for being will make you blow your stack. Gemini will do almost anything in the name of fun. Don't take anything too personally. Don't let Cancer's moodiness push your patience to the limits. Just step back and breathe for a minute. A match with Leo and Scorpio can work magnificently when you both recognize your differences.

Most Charming Characteristics: Knowledgeable, sociable, entertaining.

Gifts: *For her:* topaz necklace. *For him:* sports tickets.

Sensual Foods: Raspberries; pound cake; caviar.

Romantic Flowers: You love it when you get tulips, declaring love. When you receive a variety, it shows how hopelessly in love your partner is. He will just love a single rose. This shows him you understand his pleasures.

Best Date Nights: Friday; 6th and 24th of each month.

Colors of Passion: *For her:* white, silver. *For him:* green.

The Perfect Wedding: Serene and natural, sensual and glamorous—that's you all over. You enjoy savoring the moment and are continually impressed and inspired by beauty and classic taste. A brilliant outdoor wedding dripping in greens and fresh florals most appeals to you. Choose lots of fresh-cut, fragrant flowers to decorate an elegant, traditional wedding. Ideal setting: Ireland.

Wise Words: Charles Dickens: "No man who was not a true gentleman at heart, ever was, since the world began, a true gentleman in manner."

Hints of Love: Expecting too much too soon can only build up hopes that will fall down too easily.

After the Argument: *For him:* Once the fight is over, don't ever bring it up again. You can make a fight go in a minute if you change the subject and move on. If you need to get that last word in, this fight will never seem to end. Making up then will take a lot of stroking. *For her:* She is stubborn, but easily bought off, especially if she is in love. They say diamonds are a girl's best friends. Well, just about any real jewels will do, and only the best will do for this one.

Romantic Places: Places of vastness bring romance: Israel; a state park; the Colorado mountains.

Lucky Love Star: Tawnel—you will never lack passion.

Beautiful Thought: Your life is like reading the whole newspaper without any interruptions.

Sharing Secrets: Don't be in a hurry, or it will be over before it begins. *For the gals:* Like fine wine and amazing food. Savor it a moment until an hour is created. *For the guys:* To do too much too fast will prove risky. Try to give a push and he will just jump ship.

Judith's Insights

About the Man: He wants to keep things for tomorrow. He is much more likely to do three things in three days than three things all in one day. This guy lives for today, but he always has tomorrow in mind. You may think that he is a procrastinator. He just simply wants to have things to look forward to later. He will find his own unique way of putting his emotions across. This may cause problems for him because people just don't know what to make of what he is telling them. Romance to this guy is walking the dog or taking your mom to the store instead of moonlight and roses.

About the Woman: She needs the visual effects along with the emotional ones. The party is always at her house and company is always on its way over. She can create hurdle after hurdle for you, so expect to do some jumping. Keep her interested with constant stimulation of her friends and family. You will have to think twice to figure out if she is really sending you signals. It is almost as if she is speaking another language and trying to figure out why people can't understand her. She writes the fairy tale in her own style. You might have to look closer to see the glass slipper.

Soul Mates: It will be a perfect recipe for a tasty relationship when the ingredients include Taurus, Capricorn, or Virgo. A romance with Sagittarius and Libra can be a hands-on, happy one if you loosen your grip on the reins. There will be a decadent streak in a pairing with Pisces and Aries, no matter how practical you are. A common goal with Aquarius can change this to a wonderful life instead of a horrifying ride. When Gemini's juggling act careens into your life, you can forget about relaxing for a while. Flexibility is the key to life with Cancer. Don't let it get too bad before you realize this. The initial allure of being from a different world than Leo and Scorpio may prove hard to swallow quite quickly.

Most Charming Characteristics: Clever, skillful, irresistible.

Gifts: *For her:* soft, comfy blanket. *For him:* savings bond.

Sensual Foods: Flambé; lobster; oysters.

Romantic Flowers: Send this girl sunflowers if you want her to know you adore her. You may even add some poppies for a splash of extravagance. His desire for sport and play will be understood when you send him hyacinth and geranium.

Best Date Nights: Friday; 6th and 15th of each month.

Colors of Passion: *For her:* white, silver. *For him:* green.

The Perfect Wedding: Serene and natural, sensual and glamorous—that's you all over. You enjoy savoring the moment and are continually impressed and inspired by beauty and classic taste. A brilliant outdoor wedding dripping in greens and fresh florals most appeals to you. Choose lots of fresh-cut, fragrant flowers to decorate an elegant, traditional wedding. Ideal setting: Ireland.

Wise Words: Henry Wadsworth Longfellow: "The softly-warbled song / Comes from the pleasant woods, and colored wings. / Glance quick in the bright sun, that moves along / The forest openings."

Hints of Love: Make sure all the ingredients are present before putting the cake in the oven.

After the Argument: *For him:* Once the fight is over, don't ever bring it up again. You can make a fight go in a minute if you change the subject and move on. If you need to get that last word in, this fight will never seem to end. Making up then will take a lot of stroking. *For her:* She is stubborn, but easily bought off, especially if she is in love. They say diamonds are a girl's best friends. Well, just about any real jewels will do, and only the best will do for this one.

Romantic Places: Places of luxury bring romance: Italy; a five-star hotel; Savannah, Georgia.

Lucky Love Star: Tawnel—you will never lack passion.

Beautiful Thought: A leaf has fallen in the snow.

Sharing Secrets: They need to look before they leap, but only in love. *For the gals:* She needs creative and exciting dates to keep her interested. Don't take her for granted too soon. *For the guys:* You may think he gives signs of moving this relationship quickly; make sure you slow it down before he does.

Judith's Insights

About the Man: He is sentimental inside, although he may never seem to be on the outside. He walks through life as if he is a bull when all he really is, is a cute, housebroken puppy. He is just looking for people to be nice to him. Feed him, pet him, and love him. This guy can be so easy if you know how to treat him well. When do you know that he is interested? He will show up at your side and just never leave. This is the only way he knows that he won't be misunderstood. It is the best way for him to show you he means business.

About the Woman: Everybody reads her wrong. They think that she is much tougher than she really is. If you take the time to know her, you will find that no one else has a heart of gold quite like hers. But she will never tell you that herself. You have to get past the rough exterior to find it. Get mushy? Not this gal! Everyone at work thinks of her as a coffee klatcher. While everyone is working hard she will be sitting back at her desk, chatting. That is because this girl's work is all done. She makes it seem so easy.

Soul Mates: Taurus, Capricorn, and Virgo are signs you can relate to on many important and comforting levels. Freedom is not negotiable for Sagittarius and Libra. Don't try to take it away, because you'll be in for a fight. You will be frequently dazzled by admiration for Pisces and Aries. Being constantly asked for advice by Aquarius will drive you crazy. This is especially true when they don't take the advice you give. You and Gemini share a strong optimism and will love pleasing each other. Don't let routine stunt the growth of your partnership with Cancer. Open the window for some fresh air. A match with Leo and Scorpio can work only when you recognize your differences and accept them.

Most Charming Characteristics: Ambitious, confident, family minded, loyal.

Gifts: *For her:* scented body products. *For him:* back rub with scented oils.

Sensual Foods: Crème brûleé; poached salmon.

Romantic Flowers: Rhododendron will let her be on the lookout for trouble. Throw in some chrysanthemum and she'll know it is you she will be looking out for. Cactus will show him warmth. Yellow daffodil is a token of a good time had by all. Chivalry is not dead.

Best Date Nights: Friday; 8th and 17th of each month.

Colors of Passion: *For her:* white, silver. *For him:* green.

The Perfect Wedding: Serene and natural, sensual and glamorous—that's you all over. You enjoy savoring the moment and are continually impressed and inspired by beauty and classic taste. A brilliant outdoor wedding dripping in greens and fresh florals most appeals to you. Choose lots of fresh-cut, fragrant flowers to decorate an elegant, traditional wedding. Ideal setting: Ireland.

Wise Words: Benjamin Franklin: "People will pay as freely to gratify one passion as another, —their resentment as their pride."

Hints of Love: Simple often turns into complicated with this one. When you overcomplicate the moment, try to step back for a breather.

After the Argument: *For him:* Once the fight is over, don't ever bring it up again. You can make a fight go in a minute if you change the subject and move on. If you need to get that last word in, this fight will never seem to end. Making up then will take a lot of stroking. *For her:* She is stubborn, but easily bought off, especially if she is in love. They say diamonds are a girl's best friends. Well, just about any real jewels will do, and only the best will do for this one.

Romantic Places: Places of vastness bring romance: Brazil; a national forest; the Great Lakes.

Lucky Love Star: Tawnel—you will never lack passion.

Beautiful Thought: The baby smiles at you, and your smile has tears.

Sharing Secrets: The possibilities are endless, if you can pay the price. *For the gals:* She is hoping chivalry is not dead, and you must be willing to be the man at all costs. *For the guys:* He can be demanding and somewhat controlling. He just needs to be trained.

Judith's Insights

About the Man: He can be full of contradictions. That will make him hard to get to know. Sometimes you might not know whether you are coming or going with this guy. He thinks that he communicates well, but you know better. The good news is that he has great fortitude and sticks to who and what he likes. He loves being on the go and having something to look forward to tomorrow. He will be constantly planning his next vacation or project at work. This is a guy who also knows how to enjoy today. He is a walking contradiction that actually works.

About the Woman: She will respond to things that excite her. Invite her to a show or a hot social party. Front-row tickets will work wonders. If you appeal to her love of style, class, and the finer things in life, she will be hooked on you in seconds. She will appreciate it even if she can't find the words to say so. She will never hesitate to take time out of her busy schedule for a special occasion. It could be a friend's birthday bash or that romantic evening in front of the fire. She wants to be tantalized. For every date, give her something to remember.

Soul Mates: Taurus, Capricorn, and Virgo understand your need to step back and take things for themselves because they need to do the same. Sagittarius and Libra are a nightmare waiting to happen. You will love the excitement of Aries's and Pisces's nature. Aquarius's need to constantly try new things may interfere with your need to kick back and relax. Be flexible with how things are done and Gemini will have fun changing things around. There will be a long life of peace and stability when you and Cancer get together. Once the arguments begin with Leo and Scorpio they will go on forever.

Most Charming Characteristics: Sincere, affectionate, sympathetic.

Gifts: *For her:* romantic dinner all alone. *For him:* home-made dessert.

Sensual Foods: Chocolate soufflé; filet mignon.

Romantic Flowers: The magnolias you send her will let her know you will be around for a while to come. Petunia is to say never despair. Holly will let him know what he is getting into. Pansy will keep you in his thoughts.

Best Date Nights: Friday; 18th and 27th of each month.

Colors of Passion: *For her:* white, silver. *For him:* green.

The Perfect Wedding: Serene and natural, sensual and glamorous—that's you all over. You enjoy savoring the moment and are continually impressed and inspired by beauty and classic taste. A brilliant outdoor wedding dripping in greens and fresh florals most appeals to you. Choose lots of fresh-cut, fragrant flowers to decorate an elegant, traditional wedding. Ideal setting: Ireland.

Wise Words: Charles Dickens: "If our inclinations are but good and open-hearted, let us gratify them boldly, though they bring upon us loss instead of profit."

Hints of Love: Allow them to know what is in your heart as well as what is in your head.

After the Argument: *For him:* Once the fight is over, don't ever bring it up again. You can make a fight go in a minute if you change the subject and move on. If you need to get that last word in, this fight will never seem to end. Making up then will take a lot of stroking. *For her:* She is stubborn, but easily bought off, especially if she is in love. They say diamonds are a girl's best friends. Well, just about any real jewels will do, and only the best will do for this one.

Romantic Places: Places of luxury bring romance: Bermuda; a cruise; New York City.

Lucky Love Star: Tawnel—you will never lack passion.

Beautiful Thought: When you're driving down the highway, look and see your rainbow in the distance.

Sharing Secrets: Tomorrow is another day, but why wait? You can do it all today. *For the gals:* Have your date filled from dusk to dawn, and then some. *For the guys:* You may find he needs a nap here and there, but he can last all day and all night if he has a reason.

Judith's Insights

About the Man: At first, you might think that there is not a serious bone in his body. When you get to know him, you will realize he is all about doing right and being real. He does like to have a good time. He always keeps his emotional responsibility as a priority. You will never have to worry about him messing with your head. All that he asks is that you don't mess with his. He will never put your needs in front of his, but he will place them right next to his on the priority list. Keeping things balanced and harmonious is his key to happiness.

About the Woman: You can always notice her walking down a crowded street, and she loves that. They are interested in how things look, feel, and taste. Keep the senses in mind at all times when trying to impress her. You need no special approach. Just being up front and honest will work every time. She is looking to be loved the old-fashioned way. To know that you adore her and that you are not looking anywhere else is all the peace of mind that this girl needs. If you are not ready to make her your one and only, let her know up front.

Soul Mates: Taurus, Capricorn, and Virgo will know how to turn on that irresistible charm, which you just love. Leo and Scorpio will create an attraction, but this is one that is harder to maintain. Sagittarius and Libra will be your dream only in a nightmare. With Pisces and Aries you will find a quick harmony, but remember that it is you who likes the finer things. Aquarius could bore you with being so needy. This is only suggested if you are in the mood for being the nurturer. Things with Gemini will be fun as long as you are the only person they are flirting with. When you are totally ready for that commitment, there is no reason you can't curl right up to that Cancer.

Most Charming Characteristics: Determined, thoughtful, considerate.

Gifts: *For her:* day at museum. *For him:* hike in the woods.

Sensual Foods: Steak au poivre; cheesecake.

Romantic Flowers: Iris is your flower if you are the gal sending subtle messages. If you are the man, you will look for clematis. This flower's mental beauty creates emotional stimulation for you.

Best Date Nights: Friday; 10th and 28th of each month.

Colors of Passion: *For her:* white, silver. *For him:* green.

The Perfect Wedding: Serene and natural, sensual and glamorous—that's you all over. You enjoy savoring the moment and are continually impressed and inspired by beauty and classic taste. A brilliant outdoor wedding dripping in greens and fresh florals most appeals to you. Choose lots of fresh-cut, fragrant flowers to decorate an elegant, traditional wedding. Ideal setting: Ireland.

Wise Words: Charles Dickens: "If we all had hearts like those which beat so lightly in the bosoms of the young and beautiful, what a Heaven this earth would be."

Hints of Love: Keep both feet on the ground the first time you think you want to jump. This way you won't jump too high too soon.

After the Argument: *For him:* Once the fight is over, don't ever bring it up again. You can make a fight go in a minute if you change the subject and move on. If you need to get that last word in, this fight will never seem to end. Making up then will take a lot of stroking. *For her:* She is stubborn, but easily bought off, especially if she is in love. They say diamonds are a girl's best friends. Well, just about any real jewels will do, and only the best will do for this one.

Romantic Places: Places of vastness bring romance: the Swiss Alps; the ocean; Redwoods, California.

Lucky Love Star: Tawnel—you will never lack passion.

Beautiful Thought: Clouds are pillows for angels.

Sharing Secrets: It may need to start with friendship. This isn't the consolation prize; it's the grand prize. *For the gals:* Go slow and allow it to grow one seed at a time. You won't need to push; it will all come in time. *For the guys:* A step here and a step there. Before he knows it, that friendship will be love.

Judith's Insights

About the Man: He has style and knows exactly how to flaunt it. He loves people to notice him. He may look like a good-time Charlie, but he does have his defensive side. Let the dust settle after an argument or disappointment if you want to ask him something. Once he is calm again he will be his old self. He can make the best mate because he never minds having someone on his arm. In fact, that is just what he is searching for. He won't settle for anything less than what he wants. What he wants is a person who cares enough to do the work to make him happy.

About the Woman: This gal is quieter than one would anticipate. The way she handles her work and her life gives the opposite impression. She may be something you never expect. She can spend her money frivolously. Never question her motives or methods or the claws will come out. Just let her do things her way and she will be happy. She mixes well with her loves as well as her friends. Her tendency to elaborate and be generous to a fault will put her in her own way more times than not. She wants the ones she loves to be happy and to want to make her happy.

Soul Mates: You will want to count on the bond you have with Taurus, Capricorn, and Virgo for a long time. If you let your insecurities get the best of you, it will drive you mad. Try to enjoy Sagittarius's and Libra's excitement among people. When you meet Pisces and Aries, the right attitude about the relationship will keep you together. Unless you enjoy taking care of the world, you would be advised to move away from Aquarius. Gemini's quick changes may baffle you at first, but they can become exhilarating. Cancers make great friends, but any commitment would mean one of you would have to forgo natural leadership to keep the peace. Be on guard with Leo and Scorpio. They are anything but soft and naïve.

Most Charming Characteristics: Positive, intuitive, devoted.

Gifts: *For her:* CD of her favorite singer. *For him:* dinner at his favorite bistro.

Sensual Foods: Strawberry shortcake; pineapple; ham.

Romantic Flowers: Any rose of any color for the lady. Roses stand for love regardless of the color. Send them with orchids and you will be saying, "I love you." If you want a gentleman to know you think of him, send pansies, and forget-me-nots for true love.

Best Date Nights: Friday; 11th and 20th of each month.

Colors of Passion: *For her:* white, silver. *For him:* green.

The Perfect Wedding: Serene and natural, sensual and glamorous—that's you all over. You enjoy savoring the moment and are continually impressed and inspired by beauty and classic taste. A brilliant outdoor wedding dripping in greens and fresh florals most appeals to you. Choose lots of fresh-cut, fragrant flowers to decorate an elegant, traditional wedding. Ideal setting: Ireland.

Wise Words: Charles Dickens: "Reflect upon your present blessings—of which every man has many—not on your past misfortunes, of which all men have some."

Hints of Love: Laughter alleviates the tension, but so can understanding where another is sitting.

After the Argument: *For him:* Once the fight is over, don't ever bring it up again. You can make a fight go in a minute if you change the subject and move on. If you need to get that last word in, this fight will never seem to end. Making up then will take a lot of stroking. *For her:* She is stubborn, but easily bought off, especially if she is in love. They say diamonds are a girl's best friends. Well, just about any real jewels will do, and only the best will do for this one.

Romantic Places: Places of luxury bring romance: India; a horse-drawn carriage; Hilton Head, South Carolina.

Lucky Love Star: Tawnel—you will never lack passion.

Beautiful Thought: Thinking you made the wrong decision, then suddenly realizing it was right all along.

Sharing Secrets: This one needs to be the one and only, even if it is only the first date. *For the gals:* Don't talk about your past relationships. Do all you can to make her feel cherished from the first moment. *For the guys:* Play up your innocence. Let him take charge, even in paying the bill. He needs to wear the pants.

Judith's Insights

About the Man: He loves his friends and the camaraderie that comes with that type of relationship. He really does not like going it alone. As soon as a relationship ends, he has a new one ready to begin. If you can be friends with him, he will do all he can to keep you that way as long as you are putting in the work as well. If you are in love with him, the only way to prove that is to do all that you can to make him feel safe and able to roam. He won't ask for more than he is able to give. The hard truth is written on the wall and it is written quite legibly.

About the Woman: She may seem like the commander and chief of everything. It is only because the job has been left on her shoulders. If she doesn't get it done no one else will. You might think she is unapproachable but she is just a kitten. Just keep in mind that even the sweetest kitten can scratch you, even if it doesn't mean to. She is up-front and honest to the point of it being painful. She despises games of any kind when they are aimed at her heart. She will be able to put up with anything as long as you are honest about the how and why.

Soul Mates: There is no telling where a match with Taurus, Capricorn, and Virgo can take you. Just make sure there is a bit of play to go along with your hard work. While you treasure the fine things in life, Sagittarius and Libra treasure their freedom. If you can live with that, then you can live with them. Pisces and Aries can give you much to feed and grow on. When you meet the Zodiac's equivalent of a shock jock in Aquarius, the attraction will be instant or not at all. Teach Gemini to slow down and enjoy the finer things around them like you love to do. You and Cancer are both concerned with safety. You can wrap each other in a cozy safety net. You can't help but be drawn to the powerful Leo and Scorpio, but you might feel overwhelmed once you are there.

Most Charming Characteristics: Faithful, dependable, conscientious.

Gifts: *For her:* puppy or kitten. *For him:* tree to help grow.

Sensual Foods: Steak fondue; cheese fondue and French bread.

Romantic Flowers: These ladies like everyone to know how faithful they are, so send them violets. To surprise them send tulips. Men like their flowers the same as their relationships, unpretending. Send them camellias with white roses to show your affection.

Best Date Nights: Friday; 3rd and 12th of each month.

Colors of Passion: *For her:* white, silver. *For him:* green.

The Perfect Wedding: Serene and natural, sensual and glamorous—that's you all over. You enjoy savoring the moment and are continually impressed and inspired by beauty and classic taste. A brilliant outdoor wedding dripping in greens and fresh florals most appeals to you. Choose lots of fresh-cut, fragrant flowers to decorate an elegant, traditional wedding. Ideal setting: Ireland.

Wise Words: Charles Dickens: "How much great minds have suffered for the truth in every age and time."

Hints of Love: Communication is important here. A script isn't provided for you. You must write it for yourself.

After the Argument: *For him:* Once the fight is over, don't ever bring it up again. You can make a fight go in a minute if you change the subject and move on. If you need to get that last word in, this fight will never seem to end. Making up then will take a lot of stroking. *For her:* She is stubborn, but easily bought off, especially if she is in love. They say diamonds are a girl's best friends. Well, just about any real jewels will do, and only the best will do for this one.

Romantic Places: Places of luxury bring romance: Japan; a spa; Florence, Italy.

Lucky Love Star: Tawnel—you will never lack passion.

Beautiful Thought: A compliment from your children is high praise for you.

Sharing Secrets: You need to remember never to forget. *For the gals:* Her birthday, holidays, and your anniversary. Even down to each dinner date. *For the guys:* His birthday, his laundry, his mother's birthday, and, of course, him any other day of the year.

Judith's Insights

About the Man: Where there is music and art, you will find him. He likes culture and all things that go with it. He can certainly give you a run for your money when it comes to his social calendar. He will always have a lot on his plate but will never mind making room for the right project or person. Just remember that he will always leave room for dessert. He knows what he wants—and even better, he knows how to get it. He can teach you a lot about giving it your all no matter what is at stake. The only important thing at stake for him is the principle.

About the Woman: She knows just how to use her gifts. Her looks, her words, and her style are always coming in handy. She has it all figured out except when it comes to her deep and hidden pain. Don't try to dig into her closets or you will be shut out pretty fast. If you give her time, she will share with you when she is ready. This is especially true when it comes to matters of the heart. You will only hear about how her heart has been broken in the past when she is sure that you won't repeat the pain. Don't point out things you have noticed that she might not be ready for you to know.

MAY

Soul Mates: Taurus, Capricorn, and Virgo will know how to turn on that irresistible charm, which you just love. Leo and Scorpio will create an attraction, but this is one that is harder to maintain. Sagittarius and Libra will be your dream only in a nightmare. With Pisces and Aries you will find a quick harmony, but remember that it is you who likes the finer things. Aquarius could bore you with being so needy. This is only suggested if you are in the mood for being the nurturer. Things with Gemini will be fun as long as you are the only person they are flirting with. When you are totally ready for that commitment, there is no reason you can't curl right up to that Cancer.

Most Charming Characteristics: Vivid personality, energetic.

Gifts: *For her:* Broadway show. *For him:* day at zoo or aquarium.

Sensual Foods: Strawberries and cream; meat loaf.

Romantic Flowers: Iris is your flower if you are the gal sending subtle messages. If you are the man, you will look for clematis. This flower's mental beauty creates emotional stimulation for you.

Best Date Nights: Friday; 1st and 10th of each month.

Colors of Passion: *For her:* white, silver. *For him:* green.

The Perfect Wedding: Serene and natural, sensual and glamorous—that's you all over. You enjoy savoring the moment and are continually impressed and inspired by beauty and classic taste. A brilliant outdoor wedding dripping in greens and fresh florals most appeals to you. Choose lots of fresh-cut, fragrant flowers to decorate an elegant, traditional wedding. Ideal setting: Ireland.

Wise Words: Charles Dickens: "There are some truths—cold, bitter, taunting truths—wherein your worldly scholars are very apt and punctual, which bind men down to earth with leaden chains."

Hints of Love: They only use the three magic words when they know they mean it, and they already know it is going to be said back to them.

After the Argument: *For him:* Once the fight is over, don't ever bring it up again. You can make a fight go in a minute if you change the subject and move on. If you need to get that last word in, this fight will never seem to end. Making up then will take a lot of stroking. *For her:* She is stubborn, but easily bought off, especially if she is in love. They say diamonds are a girl's best friends. Well, just about any real jewels will do, and only the best will do for this one.

Romantic Places: Places of vastness bring romance: Africa; a farm; the Grand Canyon.

Lucky Love Star: Tawnel—you will never lack passion.

Beautiful Thought: Your parents want to be you.

Sharing Secrets: Let them admire something about you first. Show them you have a sense of humor. *For the gals:* Hold their hand and then take them to the next step. *For the guys:* The way to his heart is definitely through his stomach.

Judith's Insights

About the Man: He gets carried away with anything and everything. He tends to be generous to a fault. People may take advantage of that. He loves to be loved and wants others to notice him and his efforts. He can be very easy to talk to as long as you stay away from politics. If you go there, he will have you arguing till the day is done. His intentions are easily misunderstood. He loves to date and wants to be treated like royalty when he is involved with someone. His charm might reel you in but his temper could have you running for cover. The best thing to do when his temper flares is to give him time to calm down before finishing the conversation.

About the Woman: There is no beating around the bush with this gal. She likes everything to be up-front and things told to her straight. Her sense of humor can vary with her mood. Make sure you feel her out before asking for any favors. If you can get to know her moods, then you can really get somewhere with her. She can be much more important to her friends than she realizes. People around her value her advice and love but forget to let her know. Don't let her good deeds go unnoticed. Let her know exactly how much she means to you. If you can ride out the storms of this girl's emotions she will notice immediately.

Soul Mates: You will want to count on the bond you have with Taurus, Capricorn, and Virgo for a long time. If you let your insecurities get the best of you, it will drive you mad. Try to enjoy Sagittarius's and Libra's excitement among people. When you meet Pisces and Aries, the right attitude about the relationship will keep you together. Unless you enjoy taking care of the world, you would be advised to move away from Aquarius. Gemini's quick changes may baffle you at first, but they can become exhilarating. Cancers make great friends, but any commitment would mean one of you would have to forgo natural leadership to keep the peace. Be on guard with Leo and Scorpio. They are anything but soft and naïve.

Most Charming Characteristics: Patient, kind, understanding.

Gifts: *For her:* topaz necklace. *For him:* sports tickets.

Sensual Foods: Cherry-apple pie; beef Stroganoff.

Romantic Flowers: Any rose of any color for the lady. Roses stand for love regardless of the color. Send them with orchids and you will be saying, "I love you." If you want a gentleman to know you think of him, send pansies, and forget-me-nots for true love.

Best Date Nights: Friday; 11th and 20th of each month.

Colors of Passion: *For her:* white, silver. *For him:* green.

The Perfect Wedding: Serene and natural, sensual and glamorous—that's you all over. You enjoy savoring the moment and are continually impressed and inspired by beauty and classic taste. A brilliant outdoor wedding dripping in greens and fresh florals most appeals to you. Choose lots of fresh-cut, fragrant flowers to decorate an elegant, traditional wedding. Ideal setting: Ireland.

Wise Words: Charles Dickens: "Love, though said to be afflicted with blindness, is a vigilant watchman."

Hints of Love: Remember to keep the dating fun. Don't act like you are married before your time.

After the Argument: *For him:* Once the fight is over, don't ever bring it up again. You can make a fight go in a minute if you change the subject and move on. If you need to get that last word in, this fight will never seem to end. Making up then will take a lot of stroking. *For her:* She is stubborn, but easily bought off, especially if she is in love. They say diamonds are a girl's best friends. Well, just about any real jewels will do, and only the best will do for this one.

Romantic Places: Places of luxury bring romance: Britain; a mountain resort; Beverly Hills, California.

Lucky Love Star: Tawnel—you will never lack passion.

Beautiful Thought: Your parents think you are doing an excellent job raising your children.

Sharing Secrets: Give them the opportunity to notice you first. *For the gals:* They love to be adored; love at first sight. *For the guys:* Remember to always let them believe it was their idea.

Judith's Insights

About the Man: Despite his talent for words, you can get him tongue-tied when it comes to his emotions. He will try to talk around them but never about them if he can help it. He may come on as a know-it-all if you don't already know him. He can tend to be on the serious side, even when he is trying not to be. Although it may not seem like it at a distance, he needs a person around to keep him balanced. Love is the glue that keeps this guy from falling apart. Without it he will tend to be much too serious for his own good. Lighten up his life by simply giving him your company and support when he feels life tearing him apart.

About the Woman: She always looks fresh from a beauty parlor. Presentation is everything to her. She takes all relationships very seriously. Sometimes she can be too serious. There is nothing casual about this gal. Not even her emotions. They could not be casual even if she wanted them that way. If you have patience and intellect she might just give you the opportunity to show her what you are made of. She is a diehard romantic and has a great capacity for love and all of the fluff that goes with it. Wine and dine her and you would only be scratching the surface with this gal.

Soul Mates: There is no telling where a match with Taurus, Capricorn, and Virgo can take you. Just make sure there is a bit of play to go along with your hard work. While you treasure the fine things in life, Sagittarius and Libra treasure their freedom. If you can live with that, then you can live with them. Pisces and Aries can give you much to feed and grow on. When you meet the Zodiac's equivalent of a shock jock in Aquarius, the attraction will be instant or not at all. Teach Gemini to slow down and enjoy the finer things around them like you love to do. You and Cancer are both concerned with safety. You can wrap each other in a cozy safety net. You can't help but be drawn to the powerful Leo and Scorpio, but you might feel overwhelmed once you are there.

Most Charming Characteristics: Devoted, witty, charming.

Gifts: *For her:* soft, comfy blanket. *For him:* savings bond.

Sensual Foods: Hot fudge sundae with all the trimmings; shepherd's pie.

Romantic Flowers: These ladies like everyone to know how faithful they are, so send them violets. To surprise them send tulips. Men like their flowers the same as their relationships, unpretending. Send them camellias with white roses to show your affection.

Best Date Nights: Friday; 3rd and 12th of each month.

Colors of Passion: *For her:* white, silver. *For him:* green.

The Perfect Wedding: Serene and natural, sensual and glamorous—that's you all over. You enjoy savoring the moment and are continually impressed and inspired by beauty and classic taste. A brilliant outdoor wedding dripping in greens and fresh florals most appeals to you. Choose lots of fresh-cut, fragrant flowers to decorate an elegant, traditional wedding. Ideal setting: Ireland.

Wise Words: Arthur Schopenhauer: "A man will love or hate solitude, that is his own society, according as he, himself, worthy or worthless."

Hints of Love: Make sure you go on more than one date before you jump to conclusions on liking and disliking.

After the Argument: *For him:* Once the fight is over, don't ever bring it up again. You can make a fight go in a minute if you change the subject and move on. If you need to get that last word in, this fight will never seem to end. Making up then will take a lot of stroking. *For her:* She is stubborn, but easily bought off, especially if she is in love. They say diamonds are a girl's best friends. Well, just about any real jewels will do, and only the best will do for this one.

Romantic Places: Places of vastness bring romance: Israel; a state park; the Colorado Mountains.

Lucky Love Star: Tawnel—you will never lack passion.

Beautiful Thought: Making a child smile, knowing you're doing something right.

Sharing Secrets: This one loves a challenge. *For the gals:* Be consistently inconsistent until you have them hooked. *For the guys:* This one loves to play catch. You may feel like a yo-yo, but as long as he is calling that's all that matters.

Judith's Insights

About the Man: If things are going his way, he can be the happiest person in the world. If they are not, then you should be advised to stay clear of him until he has time to simmer down. Give him a call in a month or two. He does much better when he is in his own environment. If you stay close to his home he will be much more receptive. He can tend to be dramatic. This is probably because he craves being a movie star deep down. He craves attention, especially in his early years. Compliments are a great way of opening the door. True love is the only way to stay there.

About the Woman: If you go just by appearances, you would think that having her for a friend would be a piece of cake. Most of the time that could be true, as long as you don't make her angry. If you do make her angry, start trying to make it up to her right away. Even if she doesn't realize she is angry, start making it up to her anyway. She will realize it quickly. Make an impact even before your first date. Don't just arrive with flowers but send them, along with chocolates, the day before. Just make sure that you can sustain the same level of romance that was displayed in the beginning.

Soul Mates: Try to integrate some flexible material into the tightly woven foundation you build with Taurus, Capricorn, and Virgo. Let Sagittarius and Libra expand your boundaries and stop fighting it. The combo of you and Pisces or Aries can be quite scintillating. You and Aquarius are wildly different and stubborn about those differences. Both you and Gemini must take each other at face value to enjoy life together. Cancer delights in the world just like you do. You just want something to come home to. Concentrate on your similarities and the differences between you and Leo and Scorpio won't seem as big.

Most Charming Characteristics: Witty, intelligent, faithful.

Gifts: *For her:* scented body products. *For him:* back rub with scented oils.

Sensual Foods: Whipped cream, strawberries, brown sugar, and heavy cream.

Romantic Flowers: These ladies like men with taste. Show them you love style by sending fuchsia flowers, or even brightly colored wildflowers will do. To confuse this man, send him lilies along with bright daisies to show your innocence. Keep him guessing.

Best Date Nights: Friday; 4th and 13th of each month.

Colors of Passion: *For her:* white, silver. *For him:* green.

The Perfect Wedding: Serene and natural, sensual and glamorous—that's you all over. You enjoy savoring the moment and are continually impressed and inspired by beauty and classic taste. A brilliant outdoor wedding dripping in greens and fresh florals most appeals to you. Choose lots of fresh-cut, fragrant flowers to decorate an elegant, traditional wedding. Ideal setting: Ireland.

Wise Words: Charles Dickens: "You mustn't laugh at life; you have got a game to play; a very serious game indeed! Everybody's playing against you, you know, and you are playing against them."

Hints of Love: Don't act too needy too soon. It may push this relationship away.

After the Argument: *For him:* Once the fight is over, don't ever bring it up again. You can make a fight go in a minute if you change the subject and move on. If you need to get that last word in, this fight will never seem to end. Making up then will take a lot of stroking. *For her:* She is stubborn, but easily bought off, especially if she is in love. They say diamonds are a girl's best friends. Well, just about any real jewels will do, and only the best will do for this one.

Romantic Places: Places of luxury bring romance: Italy; a five-star hotel; Savannah, Georgia.

Lucky Love Star: Tawnel—you will never lack passion.

Beautiful Thought: Go with the desire to make someone else happy; you will love every minute of it.

Sharing Secrets: This is a family person at heart; your presence is most important. *For the gals:* Make sure you go to Sunday dinner with her family when you are invited. *For the guys:* If you don't like his mom, you might have a hard time catching this one.

Judith's Insights

About the Man: Just give him three chances. Sometimes it takes that long for him to relax. He makes a great boss. He is buddies with his employees or co-workers. You will find him in the cafeteria with everyone else. He wants to be one of the guys. If you treat him like one he will definitely notice. Give him attention with a great night out on the town. Stir in great music and you will have this guy eating out of your hand. Take him to a place where all of the attention will be focused on him. You might feel as if you are on the outside, but he will never forget it.

About the Woman: She can do anything she puts her mind to. At the same time she can get anyone she sets her heart on also. This lady is a trendsetter. There is nothing she loves more than being an example for others. She loves all of the attention she receives, and she is worth all of that attention. Romance is in her blood, and she is just waiting for the person she can treat the way she wants to be treated. If you see her sending cards it is your clue to start sending flowers and asking her out for a true romantic evening.

Soul Mates: Being stable and quiet as you are, Capricorn, Virgo, and Taurus will need urging to open up. The foundation for a lasting pairing is there. You must be patient with the impulsive nature of Sagittarius and Libra. Your rare blowups may leave you with one less prized possession in Pisces and Aries. Be careful what comes out and what simmers to a boil. A match with an Aquarius can be a recipe for disaster or endless fascination. Gemini will look to you for direction on how to reach their goals. Generosity will deepen your relationship with Cancer and keep life sweet. Find a way to become flexible so you can make a relationship with Leo and Scorpio a nurturing one.

Most Charming Characteristics: Pleasant, responsible, humble.

Gifts: *For her:* romantic dinner all alone. *For him:* homemade dessert.

Sensual Foods: Puddings and pastry of all kinds.

Romantic Flowers: You are the lady of distinction, and only carnations will do. Any mix of colors with sprays of mignonette. Sweet peas or red carnations will appeal to this man's heart.

Best Date Nights: Friday; 5th and 23rd of each month.

Colors of Passion: *For her:* white, silver. *For him:* green.

The Perfect Wedding: Serene and natural, sensual and glamorous—that's you all over. You enjoy savoring the moment and are continually impressed and inspired by beauty and classic taste. A brilliant outdoor wedding dripping in greens and fresh florals most appeals to you. Choose lots of fresh-cut, fragrant flowers to decorate an elegant, traditional wedding. Ideal setting: Ireland.

Wise Words: Maurice Maeterlinck: "An obstacle is not a discouragement. It may become one, but only with our own consent. So long as we refuse to be discouraged, we cannot be discouraged."

Hints of Love: Keep it fun. Look for new and exciting things to do, especially if you are in a long-term relationship

After the Argument: *For him:* Once the fight is over, don't ever bring it up again. You can make a fight go in a minute if you change the subject and move on. If you need to get that last word in, this fight will never seem to end. Making up then will take a lot of stroking. *For her:* She is stubborn, but easily bought off, especially if she is in love. They say diamonds are a girl's best friends. Well, just about any real jewels will do, and only the best will do for this one.

Romantic Places: Places of vastness bring romance: Brazil; a national forest; the Great Lakes.

Lucky Love Star: Tawnel—you will never lack passion.

Beautiful Thought: Enjoy giving a gift more than receiving one?

Sharing Secrets: Everything in its good time. This one works slowly, but when it is time to pick up speed, watch out. *For the gals:* Don't go by the obvious. Read between the lines. As long as the invitation is being offered go full speed ahead. *For the guys:* Just when you thought you should walk away, he'll say, "I love you." Talk about confusing.

Judith's Insights

About the Man: He may not wear his heart on his sleeve, but he certainly has one there. He has a deep connection to his friends like no one else. Don't try to break up his night out with the boys. If you do, it will be you who loses. He makes a better employer than an employee. That way he can do things his way. You may think that he does not have a romantic bone in his body until you have a chance to reflect on the past. He will never say "I love you" until he is certain he means it. By the same token, he does not want you to say it until you are certain you mean it as well.

About the Woman: She wants to be wanted. She will try to take everyone up on their offers, as long as they intrigue her. She can be a tough boss. She follows the straight and narrow. If you can figure out her preferences on how things get done and follow them, you will be on her good side. If you cross her, you are out of here. Success surrounds her. This is not only true in business but in love affairs as well. You may feel as if she would not have time on her dance card for you, but ask anyway. She may be busy but she will always make time for the right person.

Soul Mates: No architect can draw plans for a building that can be stronger than the bond you can have with Taurus, Capricorn, and Virgo. Approach the match with Sagittarius and Libra with a playful attitude and you will get along famously. With two such generous spirits as Pisces and Aries, fine-tuning the relationship will be a joy. Aquarius's regard for logic as the only reason for being will make you blow your stack. Gemini will do almost anything in the name of fun. Don't take anything too personally. Don't let Cancer's moodiness push your patience to the limits. Just step back and breathe for a minute. A match with Leo and Scorpio can work magnificently when you both recognize your differences.

Most Charming Characteristics: Proud, persevering, conscientious.

Gifts: *For her:* day at museum. *For him:* hike in the woods.

Sensual Foods: Champagne with strawberries; fillet of sole.

Romantic Flowers: You love it when you get tulips, declaring love. When you receive a variety, it shows how hopelessly in love your partner is. He will just love a single rose. This shows him you understand his pleasures.

Best Date Nights: Friday; 6th and 15th of each month.

Colors of Passion: *For her:* white, silver. *For him:* green.

The Perfect Wedding: Serene and natural, sensual and glamorous—that's you all over. You enjoy savoring the moment and are continually impressed and inspired by beauty and classic taste. A brilliant outdoor wedding dripping in greens and fresh florals most appeals to you. Choose lots of fresh-cut, fragrant flowers to decorate an elegant, traditional wedding. Ideal setting: Ireland.

Wise Words: Henry Wadsworth Longfellow: "Be merciful, be patient, and ere long, Thou shalt have more."

Hints of Love: This one is a cautious soul. You may have to find a way to go around to the back door.

After the Argument: *For him:* Once the fight is over, don't ever bring it up again. You can make a fight go in a minute if you change the subject and move on. If you need to get that last word in, this fight will never seem to end. Making up then will take a lot of stroking. *For her:* She is stubborn, but easily bought off, especially if she is in love. They say diamonds are a girl's best friends. Well, just about any real jewels will do, and only the best will do for this one.

Romantic Places: Places of luxury bring romance: Bermuda; a cruise; New York City.

Lucky Love Star: Tawnel—you will never lack passion.

Beautiful Thought: Making someone who barely smiles laugh.

Sharing Secrets: This one is a charmer, perhaps even fickle. *For the gals:* If you are patient enough to stick around, this one is worth the wait. *For the guys:* If there is enough time on the clock, stick around past three months. Then maybe he will have noticed you are there.

Judith's Insights

About the Man: He can have a bit of a temper tantrum occasionally. Keep in mind that it works. He always gets his way one way or another. Even at work, everyone gets instantly motivated when they hear that sharp tone in his voice. It will be his charm that will make you look in the first place. He has impeccable style. His mother taught him great manners, and he uses them daily. The quickest way to make him lose interest is to act crude and rude. The quickest way into his heart is to treat all around you well, even when he is not looking. Family and friends are important to him. Make friends with them to ensure your place in his heart.

About the Woman: You had better expect to put your hands in your pocket. If she works for you, she will command a mighty buck. If you date her, she will want the finer things in life. If she is your friend, she won't hesitate to spend those hard-earned bucks on you and her circle of friends. If she is not interested in you, don't bother wasting your time or your money. She can push you away even if she is interested in you. She may not be ready for love yet. Take a step back. Let her know that you will never be far away. When she is ready she will come knocking on your door.

Soul Mates: It will be a perfect recipe for a tasty relationship when the ingredients include Taurus, Capricorn, or Virgo. A romance with Sagittarius and Libra can be a hands-on, happy one if you loosen your grip on the reins. There will be a decadent streak in a pairing with Pisces and Aries, no matter how practical you are. A common goal with Aquarius can change this to a wonderful life instead of a horrifying ride. When Gemini's juggling act careens into your life, you can forget about relaxing for a while. Flexibility is the key to life with Cancer. Don't let it get too bad before you realize this. The initial allure of being from a different world than Leo and Scorpio may prove hard to swallow quite quickly.

Most Charming Characteristics: Clear-sighted, ambitious, pleasant.

Gifts: *For her:* CD of her favorite singer. *For him:* dinner at his favorite bistro.

Sensual Foods: Chocolates; poached salmon; flambé; filet mignon; potatoes.

Romantic Flowers: Send this girl sunflowers if you want her to know you adore her. You may even add some poppies for a splash of extravagance. His desire for sport and play will be understood when you send him hyacinth and geranium.

Best Date Nights: Friday; 15th and 24th of each month.

Colors of Passion: *For her:* white, silver. *For him:* green.

The Perfect Wedding: Serene and natural, sensual and glamorous—that's you all over. You enjoy savoring the moment and are continually impressed and inspired by beauty and classic taste. A brilliant outdoor wedding dripping in greens and fresh florals most appeals to you. Choose lots of fresh-cut, fragrant flowers to decorate an elegant, traditional wedding. Ideal setting: Ireland.

Wise Words: Henry Wadsworth Longfellow: "Come back! Ye friends, whose lives are ended! come back, with all light attended, / Which seemed to darken and decay / When that ye arose and went away!"

Hints of Love: Passion must be in the picture at all times or you could lose this one's attention quickly.

After the Argument: *For him:* Once the fight is over, don't ever bring it up again. You can make a fight go in a minute if you change the subject and move on. If you need to get that last word in, this fight will never seem to end. Making up then will take a lot of stroking. *For her:* She is stubborn, but easily bought off, especially if she is in love. They say diamonds are a girl's best friends. Well, just about any real jewels will do, and only the best will do for this one.

Romantic Places: Places of vastness bring romance: the Swiss Alps; the ocean; Redwoods, California.

Lucky Love Star: Tawnel—you will never lack passion.

Beautiful Thought: Surround yourself with bright colors and bright people to brighten up your life.

Sharing Secrets: If you are looking for love, then you have found the right mate. *For the gals:* This one could be stubborn. It may take forever to get a relationship started, but it is as solid as they come. *For the guys:* Even when he is ready, he might not be willing and able. He will put you through more obstacles than any course. Be patient.

Judith's Insights

About the Man: He likes to be in good company. He has a burning desire to win over the crowd. You can win him over by showing him who you are and that you play no games. He knows how to have fun. He certainly has a sensitive side. If you let him show it and don't offend it, his sensitivity will be to your advantage. He can be a real gem or a sharp rock. It is all up to how you treat him and how you approach him. He is willing to do all that he can to make the relationship run smoothly. All that he asks is that you are willing to do the same.

About the Woman: Expect to be ready to put your best foot forward at all times. She never likes to play games with her emotions—or anyone else's, for that matter. This includes any games at work. If she is your employer, make sure you do the work or you will lose your job. There is no middle ground here. She is a true romantic and will love treating you well. If she goes overboard for you and sees that you have not made an effort, she will turn hard and cold. If you don't watch your step she might just throw you over the bow.

Soul Mates: Taurus, Capricorn, and Virgo are signs you can relate to on many important and comforting levels. Freedom is not negotiable for Sagittarius and Libra. Don't try to take it away, because you'll be in for a fight. You will be frequently dazzled by admiration for Pisces and Aries. Being constantly asked for advice by Aquarius will drive you crazy. This is especially true when they don't take the advice you give. You and Gemini share a strong optimism and will love pleasing each other. Don't let routine stunt the growth of your partnership with Cancer. Open the window for some fresh air. A match with Leo and Scorpio can work only when you recognize your differences and accept them.

Most Charming Characteristics: Sunny disposition, entertaining, imaginative.

Gifts: *For her:* puppy or kitten. *For him:* tree to help grow.

Sensual Foods: Caviar; beef tenderloin; potatoes au gratin.

Romantic Flowers: Rhododendron will let her be on the lookout for trouble. Throw in some chrysanthemum and she'll know it is you she will be looking out for. Cactus will show him warmth. Yellow daffodil is a token of a good time had by all. Chivalry is not dead.

Best Date Nights: Friday; 8th and 17th of each month.

Colors of Passion: *For her:* white, silver. *For him:* green.

The Perfect Wedding: Serene and natural, sensual and glamorous—that's you all over. You enjoy savoring the moment and are continually impressed and inspired by beauty and classic taste. A brilliant outdoor wedding dripping in greens and fresh florals most appeals to you. Choose lots of fresh-cut, fragrant flowers to decorate an elegant, traditional wedding. Ideal setting: Ireland.

Wise Words: Henry Wadsworth Longfellow: "A lovely morning; the warm sun shining through a soft haze. / The hoar frost, the haze, the genial sun. All are beautiful."

Hints of Love: A random act of kindness will go a long way with this one. What can you do for them today?

After the Argument: *For him:* Once the fight is over, don't ever bring it up again. You can make a fight go in a minute if you change the subject and move on. If you need to get that last word in, this fight will never seem to end. Making up then will take a lot of stroking. *For her:* She is stubborn, but easily bought off, especially if she is in love. They say diamonds are a girl's best friends. Well, just about any real jewels will do, and only the best will do for this one.

Romantic Places: Places of luxury bring romance: India; a horse-drawn carriage; Hilton Head, South Carolina.

Lucky Love Star: Tawnel—you will never lack passion.

Beautiful Thought: On a clear day, look up to the sky and imagine you can see heaven.

Sharing Secrets: If you can hang around and give constant stimulation, this could be your mate. *For the gals:* She is always looking for the Exit sign. Don't show her where it is or she will be gone. *For the guys:* Fast car, fast food; he likes everything that goes fast. Put on your running shoes. If you can keep up, then he is yours.

Judith's Insights

About the Man: He can have the patience of a saint when it comes to what others want. When it comes to what he is looking for, he can lose that patience pretty fast. You may have to defend yourself and your intentions right up front if you want to get your foot in the door. Be straightforward, because he does not like to play games. He can make a great mate for long-term commitments. His goal in life is to maintain a lifetime relationship. The work entailed to make this work is no problem for him. He is willing to do all that he can to keep the relationship harmonious as long as you are willing to do the same.

About the Woman: She wants, and needs, to be noticed. Hers is the voice that is usually picked up in a crowd. You can be casual with her at work because she is very down-to-earth. If she is your boss, you will get along like buddies. She loves demonstrative attention. Don't forget to hug her and hold her hand. She takes pride in all that she does. You will often hear about her accomplishments and good deeds. Pat her on the back and she will toot her own horn a little less. She wants to be recognized for who she is and what she does.

Soul Mates: Taurus, Capricorn, and Virgo understand your need to step back and take things for themselves because they need to do the same. Sagittarius and Libra are a nightmare waiting to happen. You will love the excitement of Aries's and Pisces's nature. Aquarius's need to constantly try new things may interfere with your need to kick back and relax. Be flexible with how things are done and Gemini will have fun changing things around. There will be a long life of peace and stability when you and Cancer get together. Once the arguments begin with Leo and Scorpio they will go on forever.

Most Charming Characteristics: Creative, level-headed, good sport.

Gifts: *For her:* soft sweater. *For him:* antique clock.

Sensual Foods: Passion fruit; fillet of sole almondine.

Romantic Flowers: The magnolias you send her will let her know you will be around for a while to come. Petunia is to say never despair. Holly will let him know what he is getting into. Pansy will keep you in his thoughts.

Best Date Nights: Friday; 18th and 27th of each month.

Colors of Passion: *For her:* white, silver. *For him:* green.

The Perfect Wedding: Serene and natural, sensual and glamorous—that's you all over. You enjoy savoring the moment and are continually impressed and inspired by beauty and classic taste. A brilliant outdoor wedding dripping in greens and fresh florals most appeals to you. Choose lots of fresh-cut, fragrant flowers to decorate an elegant, traditional wedding. Ideal setting: Ireland.

Wise Words: Henry Wadsworth Longfellow: "Life is real, life is earnest, and the grave is not its goal, dust thou are to dust returneth, was not spoken of the soul."

Hints of Love: Family and friends are important to this one. Don't try to alienate them or it will definitely backfire on you.

After the Argument: *For him:* Once the fight is over, don't ever bring it up again. You can make a fight go in a minute if you change the subject and move on. If you need to get that last word in, this fight will never seem to end. Making up then will take a lot of stroking. *For her:* She is stubborn, but easily bought off, especially if she is in love. They say diamonds are a girl's best friends. Well, just about any real jewels will do, and only the best will do for this one.

Romantic Places: Places of luxury bring romance: Japan; a spa; Florence, Italy.

Lucky Love Star: Tawnel—you will never lack passion.

Beautiful Thought: Your first hunch is usually the right one.

Sharing Secrets: This one may seem like a lot of work. They just need the basics: love, loyalty, and respect. *For the gals:* If you can show her your best side right from the beginning it may work. Be careful of fluff, because she will see right through it. *For the guys:* He loves to be loved. Give him plenty of attention, even if you think you don't stand a chance. Perseverance will win here.

Judith's Insights

About the Man: He has many people in his life. You could feel intimidated, even if you are his best friend. If he is your boss, you will want to get noticed. This may be hard in the sea of people vying for his attention. Make sure you go far out of your way. Find out how he likes things done and then do them his way. He loves to be in love. While some people are born with a silver spoon in their mouth, this guy was born with a Cupid's arrow planted firmly in his heart. Romance is this guy's lifeblood. Cater to this by going out of your way for him. He is sure to notice.

About the Woman: This gal is no wallflower. If you aren't paying her enough attention she will find someone who will. She hates to take a backseat to anything or anyone. Put her first or you will be the last she calls. This is especially true at work. If you want that perfect assignment, you have to pay her special attention. Her family and friends may feel as if she is difficult to live with when she does not have someone to love. She wants a person to make memories with. Her intention is to find the love of her life, and she may kiss a few frogs on the way.

Soul Mates: Taurus, Capricorn, and Virgo will know how to turn on that irresistible charm, which you just love. Leo and Scorpio will create an attraction, but this is one that is harder to maintain. Sagittarius and Libra will be your dream only in a nightmare. With Pisces and Aries you will find a quick harmony, but remember that it is you who likes the finer things. Aquarius could bore you with being so needy. This is only suggested if you are in the mood for being the nurturer. Things with Gemini will be fun as long as you are the only person they are flirting with. When you are totally ready for that commitment, there is no reason you can't curl right up to that Cancer.

Most Charming Characteristics: Charming, persistent, creative.

Gifts: *For her:* Broadway show. *For him:* day at zoo or aquarium.

Sensual Foods: Peaches; mousse; shrimp.

Romantic Flowers: Iris is your flower if you are the gal sending subtle messages. If you are the man, you will look for clematis. This flower's mental beauty creates emotional stimulation for you.

Best Date Nights: Friday; 1st and 10th of each month.

Colors of Passion: *For her:* white, silver. *For him:* green.

The Perfect Wedding: Serene and natural, sensual and glamorous—that's you all over. You enjoy savoring the moment and are continually impressed and inspired by beauty and classic taste. A brilliant outdoor wedding dripping in greens and fresh florals most appeals to you. Choose lots of fresh-cut, fragrant flowers to decorate an elegant, traditional wedding. Ideal setting: Ireland.

Wise Words: Henry Wadsworth Longfellow: "Beautiful after a week of rain, a day full of sunshine blossoms and song of birds and of tender memories."

Hints of Love: Show others how much you adore him or her. They will revel in how others notice.

After the Argument: *For him:* Once the fight is over, don't ever bring it up again. You can make a fight go in a minute if you change the subject and move on. If you need to get that last word in, this fight will never seem to end. Making up then will take a lot of stroking. *For her:* She is stubborn, but easily bought off, especially if she is in love. They say diamonds are a girl's best friends. Well, just about any real jewels will do, and only the best will do for this one.

Romantic Places: Places of vastness bring romance: Africa; a farm; the Grand Canyon.

Lucky Love Star: Tawnel—you will never lack passion.

Beautiful Thought: After the pop of the cork, the glistening pouring of the champagne, the smiles while raising the glass, the toast is for you.

Sharing Secrets: They're looking for love, but that is just their little secret. *For the gals:* Why shouldn't they want to be loved? Of course they do, but they want you to do all of the work. *For the guys:* You must prove yourself repeatedly. Don't expect too much until he knows you are under his thumb.

Judith's Insights

About the Man: He can make or break the moment by how he is handling it. Be subtle, because he does not like anyone to know his business. He can take or leave any surface relationships. It all depends on the offers he is getting. Be genuine and you will stand out from the other offers. He can sweep you right off your feet, even if it is you who is the sweeping kind. He has a quiet control about him. You may think that you have everything under control when it suddenly dawns on you that it has been him all along. You may find that is just the way you like it.

About the Woman: Some may think she is catty. There is nothing catty about this lady. She is blunt to the point of pain. If you snub her once, you will not have to worry about doing it twice. You can be whatever you want with her. It does not matter if you are casual or serious, as long as you are up-front at all times. Be all that you can be and she will be happy to be there with you. She is open and loving with those she cares for. You will find her not only standing up for herself but for those around her as well. All she asks for is honesty and love, and she will give you the same.

Soul Mates: You will want to count on the bond you have with Taurus, Capricorn, and Virgo for a long time. If you let your insecurities get the best of you, it will drive you mad. Try to enjoy Sagittarius's and Libra's excitement among people. When you meet Pisces and Aries, the right attitude about the relationship will keep you together. Unless you enjoy taking care of the world, you would be advised to move away from Aquarius. Gemini's quick changes may baffle you at first, but they can become exhilarating. Cancers make great friends, but any commitment would mean one of you would have to forgo natural leadership to keep the peace. Be on guard with Leo and Scorpio. They are anything but soft and naïve.

Most Charming Characteristics: Levelheaded, amusing, charming.

Gifts: *For her:* topaz necklace. *For him:* sports tickets.

Sensual Foods: Kiwis; cantaloupes; strawberries.

Romantic Flowers: Any rose of any color for the lady. Roses stand for love regardless of the color. Send them with orchids and you will be saying, "I love you." If you want a gentleman to know you think of him, send pansies, and forget-me-nots for true love.

Best Date Nights: Friday; 2nd and 29th of each month.

Colors of Passion: *For her:* white, silver. *For him:* green.

The Perfect Wedding: Serene and natural, sensual and glamorous—that's you all over. You enjoy savoring the moment and are continually impressed and inspired by beauty and classic taste. A brilliant outdoor wedding dripping in greens and fresh florals most appeals to you. Choose lots of fresh-cut, fragrant flowers to decorate an elegant, traditional wedding. Ideal setting: Ireland.

Wise Words: Benjamin Franklin: "Traveling is one way of lengthening life—at least in appearance."

Hints of Love: Don't overdo it (dress, attention) too soon or this one will run. Wait until you have them hooked before you become outrageous.

After the Argument: *For him:* Once the fight is over, don't ever bring it up again. You can make a fight go in a minute if you change the subject and move on. If you need to get that last word in, this fight will never seem to end. Making up then will take a lot of stroking. *For her:* She is stubborn, but easily bought off, especially if she is in love. They say diamonds are a girl's best friends. Well, just about any real jewels will do, and only the best will do for this one.

Romantic Places: Places of luxury bring romance: Britain; a mountain resort; Beverly Hills, California.

Lucky Love Star: Tawnel—you will never lack passion.

Beautiful Thought: The date may be fate, but the future is destiny.

Sharing Secrets: You had better be ready to pull out your romantic side if you want this to work. *For the gals:* Fireplaces, walks on the beach, or even winning a bear at the local carnival. *For the guys:* When you are out shopping bring him something home. Even if it is silly, he will love the thought.

Judith's Insights

About the Man: He likes to hang on to what he has. It would take a lot to break this guy from his favorite chair. He finds his way into your heart by the way he helps you. He can walk into your life in business and it could turn into a pleasure. This is a man you could be friends with for life. Sometimes you may feel as if he starts a fight just so you can kiss and make up. There is no harm here as long as you truly do make up. Make sure there are no underlying issues left over. He will resolve conflicts openly and honestly to make sure things are okay afterward.

About the Woman: This one is one hundred percent pure-hearted. That doesn't mean she can't lose her head. Don't push her when you know that she is already giving all that she has got. Doing that will only make her leave you behind while she regroups and plans her next stop. She loves a lot of passion and can be a great tease. Jokes and fun are a large part of her vocabulary. Her sense of humor can get lost a lot easier when the joke is on her. Never act underhanded when dealing with this gal. Direct and up front is the only way to get anywhere with her.

Soul Mates: There is no telling where a match with Taurus, Capricorn, and Virgo can take you. Just make sure there is a bit of play to go along with your hard work. While you treasure the fine things in life, Sagittarius and Libra treasure their freedom. If you can live with that, then you can live with them. Pisces and Aries can give you much to feed and grow on. When you meet the Zodiac's equivalent of a shock jock in Aquarius, the attraction will be instant or not at all. Teach Gemini to slow down and enjoy the finer things around them like you love to do. You and Cancer are both concerned with safety. You can wrap each other in a cozy safety net. You can't help but be drawn to the powerful Leo and Scorpio, but you might feel overwhelmed once you are there.

Most Charming Characteristics: Loyal, entertaining, generous.

Gifts: *For her:* soft, comfy blanket. *For him:* savings bond.

Sensual Foods: Caramel and chocolate syrup on anything.

Romantic Flowers: These ladies like everyone to know how faithful they are, so send them violets. To surprise them send tulips. Men like their flowers the same as their relationships, unpretending. Send them camellias with white roses to show your affection.

Best Date Nights: Friday; 12th and 21st of each month.

Colors of Passion: *For her:* white, silver. *For him:* green.

The Perfect Wedding: Serene and natural, sensual and glamorous—that's you all over. You enjoy savoring the moment and are continually impressed and inspired by beauty and classic taste. A brilliant outdoor wedding dripping in greens and fresh florals most appeals to you. Choose lots of fresh-cut, fragrant flowers to decorate an elegant, traditional wedding. Ideal setting: Ireland.

Wise Words: Benjamin Franklin: "Good sense is a thing all need, few have, and none think they want."

Hints of Love: When these folks decide to sit on the fence, don't try to push them off before they are ready. Let them do the jumping themselves.

After the Argument: *For him:* Once the fight is over, don't ever bring it up again. You can make a fight go in a minute if you change the subject and move on. If you need to get that last word in, this fight will never seem to end. Making up then will take a lot of stroking. *For her:* She is stubborn, but easily bought off, especially if she is in love. They say diamonds are a girl's best friends. Well, just about any real jewels will do, and only the best will do for this one.

Romantic Places: Places of vastness bring romance: Israel; a state park; the Colorado mountains.

Lucky Love Star: Tawnel—you will never lack passion.

Beautiful Thought: Your life is like finding forgotten jars of peanut butter and jelly just when you have forgotten to go food shopping.

Sharing Secrets: It may seem like they are not interested, but ask them out anyway. *For the gals:* Until they absolutely know you are interested, you will never find out that they are. *For the guys:* Ask him out if he doesn't ask you. He may be shy or not. Either way, he may be interested.

Judith's Insights

About the Man: Where there is smoke, you can usually find fire. You may find this guy helping even if he is not really a fireman or it isn't his field of expertise. You will always find him in the center of a lot of things. He is a social guy. He loves to be on the way to somewhere with someone. You may not even know where to begin with this guy. Always begin at the beginning. Don't try to go too fast unless you are sure that he is ready to go with you. He is searching for that special someone to spend his life with. He does not want to waste time with people who won't fit the bill.

About the Woman: Everyone admires the way she dresses, works, and lives. She does it all with style. You need to capture her attention before anything happens. Do it with the best style you know how, and you just might get the chance. Just keep in mind that you will get only one chance, so use it well. Allow her to be partially in charge, but you never have to let her know it. Take advantage of every chance to impress her. I am not talking diamonds and rubies here, although she does love those fine things. Use your ability to help others to strike a chord with her.

Soul Mates: Try to integrate some flexible material into the tightly woven foundation you build with Taurus, Capricorn, and Virgo. Let Sagittarius and Libra expand your boundaries and stop fighting it. The combo of you and Pisces or Aries can be quite scintillating. You and Aquarius are wildly different and stubborn about those differences. Both you and Gemini must take each other at face value to enjoy life together. Cancer delights in the world just like you do. You just want something to come home to. Concentrate on your similarities and the differences between you and Leo and Scorpio won't seem as big.

Most Charming Characteristics: Sincere, honest, intelligent.

Gifts: *For her:* scented body products. *For him:* back rub with scented oils.

Sensual Foods: Waffles with whipped cream; chocolate soufflé; French wine.

Romantic Flowers: These ladies like men with taste. Show them you love style by sending fuchsia flowers, or even brightly colored wildflowers will do. To confuse this man, send him lilies along with bright daisies to show your innocence. Keep him guessing.

Best Date Nights: Friday; 4th and 31st of each month.

Colors of Passion: *For her:* white, silver. *For him:* green.

The Perfect Wedding: Serene and natural, sensual and glamorous—that's you all over. You enjoy savoring the moment and are continually impressed and inspired by beauty and classic taste. A brilliant outdoor wedding dripping in greens and fresh florals most appeals to you. Choose lots of fresh-cut, fragrant flowers to decorate an elegant, traditional wedding. Ideal setting: Ireland.

Wise Words: Charles Dickens: "Real love and truth are stronger in the end than any evil or misfortune in the world."

Hints of Love: Make sure you learn to compromise, but never with your principles.

After the Argument: *For him:* Once the fight is over, don't ever bring it up again. You can make a fight go in a minute if you change the subject and move on. If you need to get that last word in, this fight will never seem to end. Making up then will take a lot of stroking. *For her:* She is stubborn, but easily bought off, especially if she is in love. They say diamonds are a girl's best friends. Well, just about any real jewels will do, and only the best will do for this one.

Romantic Places: Places of luxury bring romance: Italy; a five-star hotel; Savannah, Georgia.

Lucky Love Star: Tawnel—you will never lack passion.

Beautiful Thought: Anybody can show up; it takes a special person to be there.

Sharing Secrets: Don't be surprised if the first date is with their family. *For the gals:* Make sure you invite her to your family functions. It will be a red flag to her if you don't. *For the guys:* He may seem like a family man, but isn't that what you were looking for?

Judith's Insights

About the Man: Keep your eyes, and his, on the goal and all answers will be available to you. He does not like to play games and does not like to be left wondering. Make sure he has all information ready for him. Allow him his space while giving him respect. Approach him with a steady pace. He does not like surprises. He is the guy standing there with a large Welcome sign on his chest. If he is searching for love he will leave no stone unturned and no call unanswered. Beware of this guy's temper. All he needs is time to cool down before he can approach the problem, ready to fix it.

About the Woman: She can light up a room like magic. Her congenial attitude makes it easy to pay her attention. If you are wearing your Sunday best, then you can be sure she will notice you. She loves the finer things in life. She is ready to be impressed, so the rest is up to you and your imagination. She will analyze every person and every date to make sure that things are the way she feels that they should be. If you make it past the three-month mark you might be the lucky winner with this gal. If she didn't see potential she wouldn't have stuck around so long.

Soul Mates: Being stable and quiet as you are, Capricorn, Virgo, and Taurus will need urging to open up. The foundation for a lasting pairing is there. You must be patient with the impulsive nature of Sagittarius and Libra. Your rare blowups may leave you with one less prized possession in Pisces and Aries. Be careful what comes out and what simmers to a boil. A match with an Aquarius can be a recipe for disaster or endless fascination. Gemini will look to you for direction on how to reach their goals. Generosity will deepen your relationship with Cancer and keep life sweet. Find a way to become flexible so you can make a relationship with Leo and Scorpio a nurturing one.

Most Charming Characteristics: Determined, intelligent, creative, loyal.

Gifts: *For her:* romantic dinner all alone. *For him:* home-made dessert.

Sensual Foods: Oysters; mussels; spicy foods.

Romantic Flowers: You are the lady of distinction, and only carnations will do. Any mix of colors with sprays of mignonette. Sweet peas or red carnations will appeal to this man's heart.

Best Date Nights: Friday; 4th and 23rd of each month.

Colors of Passion: *For her:* white, silver. *For him:* green.

The Perfect Wedding: Serene and natural, sensual and glamorous—that's you all over. You enjoy savoring the moment and are continually impressed and inspired by beauty and classic taste. A brilliant outdoor wedding dripping in greens and fresh florals most appeals to you. Choose lots of fresh-cut, fragrant flowers to decorate an elegant, traditional wedding. Ideal setting: Ireland.

Wise Words: Charles Dickens: "There can be no disparity in marriage like unsuitability of mind and purpose."

Hints of Love: If you try to take a step back, it will be noticed. It could create the domino effect, and everything will start to fall.

After the Argument: *For him:* Once the fight is over, don't ever bring it up again. You can make a fight go in a minute if you change the subject and move on. If you need to get that last word in, this fight will never seem to end. Making up then will take a lot of stroking. *For her:* She is stubborn, but easily bought off, especially if she is in love. They say diamonds are a girl's best friends. Well, just about any real jewels will do, and only the best will do for this one.

Romantic Places: Places of vastness bring romance: Brazil; a national forest; the Great Lakes.

Lucky Love Star: Tawnel—you will never lack passion.

Beautiful Thought: Close your eyes and finish the beautiful dream you had yesterday.

Sharing Secrets: Take me as I am could be the anthem for this one. *For the gals:* They will have strong views on just about everything. If you can hang with them, then nothing will be as important as you. *For the guys:* The thing you fall in love with may end up becoming the thing you hate. After a commitment, this one sticks around.

Judith's Insights

About the Man: Instead of spending money taking you out to fancy places, he is more likely to stop by and bring you groceries. He is a down-to-earth guy whose romantic skills must be appreciated for their intentions. He would love it if you took him to fancy places. It has nothing to do with his expense account, but more with his natural practicality. Just play it straight and call a spade a spade. That is exactly what this guy needs to keep interested. He is never ready for games of the heart. He simply wants someone to share his life and dreams with, nothing less.

About the Woman: She might not sit around waiting for your phone call. If you pick up the phone, and it is her at the other end, you are in. She can sometimes put the cart before the horse. She just needs to slow down and think. If she is your boss, keep in mind that she needs people to be on time at all times. Don't leave her hanging if you ever want to ask her out on a second date. Never play the "I'll call later" game with this gal. Call when you say you will. If you can't, just be honest about why. That is all she asks for.

Soul Mates: No architect can draw plans for a building that can be stronger than the bond you can have with Taurus, Capricorn, and Virgo. Approach the match with Sagittarius and Libra with a playful attitude and you will get along famously. With two such generous spirits as Pisces and Aries, fine-tuning the relationship will be a joy. Aquarius's regard for logic as the only reason for being will make you blow your stack. Gemini will do almost anything in the name of fun. Don't take anything too personally. Don't let Cancer's moodiness push your patience to the limits. Just step back and breathe for a minute. A match with Leo and Scorpio can work magnificently when you both recognize your differences.

Most Charming Characteristics: Smart, sensitive, strong.

Gifts: *For her:* day at a museum. *For him:* hike in the woods.

Sensual Foods: Lobster; watermelon.

Romantic Flowers: You love it when you get tulips, declaring love. When you receive a variety, it shows how hopelessly in love your partner is. He will just love a single rose. This shows him you understand his pleasures.

Best Date Nights: Friday; 6th and 15th of each month.

Colors of Passion: *For her:* white, silver. *For him:* green.

The Perfect Wedding: Serene and natural, sensual and glamorous—that's you all over. You enjoy savoring the moment and are continually impressed and inspired by beauty and classic taste. A brilliant outdoor wedding dripping in greens and fresh florals most appeals to you. Choose lots of fresh-cut, fragrant flowers to decorate an elegant, traditional wedding. Ideal setting: Ireland.

Wise Words: Charles Dickens: "All good things perverted to evil purposes are worse than those which are naturally bad. A thoroughly wicked woman is wicked indeed."

Hints of Love: Consistence and persistence will get this prize every time. They will value the effort.

After the Argument: *For him:* Once the fight is over, don't ever bring it up again. You can make a fight go in a minute if you change the subject and move on. If you need to get that last word in, this fight will never seem to end. Making up then will take a lot of stroking. *For her:* She is stubborn, but easily bought off, especially if she is in love. They say diamonds are a girl's best friends. Well, just about any real jewels will do, and only the best will do for this one.

Romantic Places: Places of luxury bring romance: Bermuda; a cruise; New York City.

Lucky Love Star: Tawnel—you will never lack passion.

Beautiful Thought: You always find one light bulb that still works.

Sharing Secrets: They seem moody until you get to know them. *For the gals:* You may not know whether to say hello or drop dead. As relations progress you will learn not to leave her dangling, and her moods will become more consistent. *For the guys:* To know him is to love him. His bark is much worse than his bite. He just wants someone to love him without criticism.

Judith's Insights

About the Man: Give him the great outdoors and here you could have a very happy man. Take him for a drive in the country or fishing or camping. He does know how to put on a suit jacket, but only when he is forced. He can be flexible but that does not take away from what he likes. Give him what he wants and he will cooperate when it comes to what you want. Depending on his mood, he can be offensive or defensive. All he really wants is to be treated as if someone cares about him. Showing you care can be as lavish as a romantic dinner or as simple as picking up the fish food he needed.

About the Woman: You can be candid with her, but never attempt to change her. No matter how independent you think she is, she wants to be nurtured. The more luxuriously you treat her, the better. If she is given the silver spoon treatment, she will be expecting it forever. She will also love the person who gave it to her. If you go on a trip without her, make sure that you bring home a gift for her. It doesn't matter if it is jewels or a simple trinket. She just wants to know that you thought of her while you were gone.

Soul Mates: It will be a perfect recipe for a tasty relationship when the ingredients include Taurus, Capricorn, or Virgo. A romance with Sagittarius and Libra can be a hands-on, happy one if you loosen your grip on the reins. There will be a decadent streak in a pairing with Pisces and Aries, no matter how practical you are. A common goal with Aquarius can change this to a wonderful life instead of a horrifying ride. When Gemini's juggling act careens into your life, you can forget about relaxing for a while. Flexibility is the key to life with Cancer. Don't let it get too bad before you realize this. The initial allure of being from a different world than Leo and Scorpio may prove hard to swallow quite quickly.

Most Charming Characteristics: Humorous, determined, honest.

Gifts: *For her:* CD of her favorite singer. *For him:* dinner at his favorite bistro.

Sensual Foods: Strawberries; truffles; shish kebab.

Romantic Flowers: Send this girl sunflowers if you want her to know you adore her. You may even add some poppies for a splash of extravagance. His desire for sport and play will be understood when you send him hyacinth and geranium.

Best Date Nights: Friday; 6th and 24th of each month.

Colors of Passion: *For her:* white, silver. *For him:* green.

The Perfect Wedding: Serene and natural, sensual and glamorous—that's you all over. You enjoy savoring the moment and are continually impressed and inspired by beauty and classic taste. A brilliant outdoor wedding dripping in greens and fresh florals most appeals to you. Choose lots of fresh-cut, fragrant flowers to decorate an elegant, traditional wedding. Ideal setting: Ireland.

Wise Words: Charles Dickens: "Have the courage to be ignorant of a great number of things, in order that you may avoid the calamity of being ignorant of everything."

Hints of Love: Be funny. Laughter will be what keeps this one coming back again and again.

After the Argument: *For him:* Once the fight is over, don't ever bring it up again. You can make a fight go in a minute if you change the subject and move on. If you need to get that last word in, this fight will never seem to end. Making up then will take a lot of stroking. *For her:* She is stubborn, but easily bought off, especially if she is in love. They say diamonds are a girl's best friends. Well, just about any real jewels will do, and only the best will do for this one.

Romantic Places: Places of vastness bring romance: the Swiss Alps; the ocean; Redwoods, California.

Lucky Love Star: Tawnel—you will never lack passion.

Beautiful Thought: You know you respect someone when you start using his or her words.

Sharing Secrets: You had better be able to put your money where your mouth is. *For the gals:* It doesn't need to be lavish, but she does love the loot. The more the better. *For the guys:* He doesn't mind spending his hard-earned cash, but he loves to see you contribute to please him.

Judith's Insights

About the Man: Keep your eyes only on him. He will hate it if he thinks that he is not the priority. He will do just about anything for anybody. He has an unusually good relationship with all of his co-workers. You may see a secretive side to him, especially when it comes to money. Information about his finances will only come out when he is sure you will be around for quite some time. You can be cut off at the snap of a finger if you cross him. To him, what he wants is simple and down-to-earth. Some think he is even boring at times.

About the Woman: She is stubborn but never mean. She likes what she likes and that is all there is to it. She needs to have everything in order, including her house, her business, and any relationships. She can be your best friend one minute and an enemy the next if you cross her. Never push her too hard if you want to be close. She just wants someone to treat her like royalty, not with expensive items but with luxurious treatment. Sounds idealistic, but it's not. She just wants the basic "Be good to me and I'll be better to you."

Soul Mates: Taurus, Capricorn, and Virgo are signs you can relate to on many important and comforting levels. Freedom is not negotiable for Sagittarius and Libra. Don't try to take it away, because you'll be in for a fight. You will be frequently dazzled by admiration for Pisces and Aries. Being constantly asked for advice by Aquarius will drive you crazy. This is especially true when they don't take the advice you give. You and Gemini share a strong optimism and will love pleasing each other. Don't let routine stunt the growth of your partnership with Cancer. Open the window for some fresh air. A match with Leo and Scorpio can work only when you recognize your differences and accept them.

Most Charming Characteristics: Levelheaded, smart, generous.

Gifts: *For her:* puppy or kitten. *For him:* tree to help grow.

Sensual Foods: Grapes; fine cheeses and crackers; taffy.

Romantic Flowers: Rhododendron will let her be on the lookout for trouble. Throw in some chrysanthemum and she'll know it is you she will be looking out for. Cactus will show him warmth. Yellow daffodil is a token of a good time had by all. Chivalry is not dead.

Best Date Nights: Friday; 8th and 26th of each month.

Colors of Passion: *For her:* white, silver. *For him:* green.

The Perfect Wedding: Serene and natural, sensual and glamorous—that's you all over. You enjoy savoring the moment and are continually impressed and inspired by beauty and classic taste. A brilliant outdoor wedding dripping in greens and fresh florals most appeals to you. Choose lots of fresh-cut, fragrant flowers to decorate an elegant, traditional wedding. Ideal setting: Ireland.

Wise Words: Charles Dickens: "There is a passion for hunting something deeply implanted in the human breast."

Hints of Love: Treat this one like royalty or precious cargo. They will love being valued in this way.

After the Argument: *For him:* Once the fight is over, don't ever bring it up again. You can make a fight go in a minute if you change the subject and move on. If you need to get that last word in, this fight will never seem to end. Making up then will take a lot of stroking. *For her:* She is stubborn, but easily bought off, especially if she is in love. They say diamonds are a girl's best friends. Well, just about any real jewels will do, and only the best will do for this one.

Romantic Places: Places of luxury bring romance: India; a horse-drawn carriage; Hilton Head, South Carolina.

Lucky Love Star: Tawnel—you will never lack passion.

Beautiful Thought: Encouragement is the key to enthusiasm.

Sharing Secrets: Nobody likes a weak link, especially not this one. *For the gals:* Make sure you treat her like a lady and act like a man. *For the guys:* Put your best foot forward. Dress your best and keep your manners in check. This man notices.

Judith's Insights

About the Man: When you first get to know him, it may seem as if he doesn't have a heart. He spends so much time protecting himself. He seldom lets people in. As a co-worker, he can have a lot to say, but keeps to himself. If you befriend him, he will respond. He needs to feel as if he is in control. Even if he isn't you can ask for his input to make him feel as if he is. His friends are extremely important to him. Never ask him to choose between you and them. You won't like his choice, even if you have been together for a long time. Instead, make friends with his friends.

About the Woman: Just when you think she isn't interested, she will call. She isn't moody, just choosy. She won't waste time with someone who has no potential of becoming that lifelong love she is searching for. If you want her attention, appeal to her desires. She loves social situations, even fundraising political events. She likes to be a part of the society page if she can. If she does not get enough attention she may become cranky but never admit what is wrong. She might even know why she feels lonely.

Soul Mates: Taurus, Capricorn, and Virgo understand your need to step back and take things for themselves because they need to do the same. Sagittarius and Libra are a nightmare waiting to happen. You will love the excitement of Aries's and Pisces's nature. Aquarius's need to constantly try new things may interfere with your need to kick back and relax. Be flexible with how things are done and Gemini will have fun changing things around. There will be a long life of peace and stability when you and Cancer get together. Once the arguments begin with Leo and Scorpio they will go on forever.

Most Charming Characteristics: Domestic, cultured, congenial.

Gifts: *For her:* soft sweater. *For him:* antique clock.

Sensual Foods: Champagne; grapes; mangoes; filet mignon.

Romantic Flowers: The magnolias you send her will let her know you will be around for a while to come. Petunia is to say never despair. Holly will let him know what he is getting into. Pansy will keep you in his thoughts.

Best Date Nights: Friday; 18th and 27th of each month.

Colors of Passion: *For her:* white, silver. *For him:* green.

The Perfect Wedding: Serene and natural, sensual and glamorous—that's you all over. You enjoy savoring the moment and are continually impressed and inspired by beauty and classic taste. A brilliant outdoor wedding dripping in greens and fresh florals most appeals to you. Choose lots of fresh-cut, fragrant flowers to decorate an elegant, traditional wedding. Ideal setting: Ireland.

Wise Words: Charles Dickens: "No hand can make the clock for me which will strike again for me the hours that are gone."

Hints of Love: Affection is important, but only if it comes naturally. Otherwise, the sirens will go off.

After the Argument: *For him:* Once the fight is over, don't ever bring it up again. You can make a fight go in a minute if you change the subject and move on. If you need to get that last word in, this fight will never seem to end. Making up then will take a lot of stroking. *For her:* She is stubborn, but easily bought off, especially if she is in love. They say diamonds are a girl's best friends. Well, just about any real jewels will do, and only the best will do for this one.

Romantic Places: Places of luxury bring romance: Japan; a spa; Florence, Italy.

Lucky Love Star: Tawnel—you will never lack passion.

Beautiful Thought: You do have a second chance to make a first impression.

Sharing Secrets: Attention, attention, attention. *For the gals:* Do it any way you can. Presents, phone calls, cards, or flowers. Whatever works for you will work for her. *For the guys:* He would love nostalgic gifts or T-shirts. He also likes phone calls, as long as they don't interrupt his favorite pastimes.

Judith's Insights

About the Man: This is a guy who will like the silk boxers you got him for his birthday. He loves the finer things in life yet loves the everyday joys just as much. Just give him the basics and he'll look at it as if you gave him the world. He treasures his friends and his family. Make friends with them and you will have a friend in him. If you ask this guy for something, consider it yours. He will do anything and everything for someone he loves. He does not know how to put limits on what he would give you, so try to put limits on what you ask for.

About the Woman: Her emotions could be flowing like Niagara Falls, but she will keep them in check when it comes to business. Personally, she'll find ways of letting you know, but it may take some time to let you in. Just remember that if you ask you will eventually get what you need from her. She can be a people pleaser, and it drains her more often than not. She loves having company at her house. That way she can receive the attention she craves without having to leave her safety net. When she feels safe there is no telling how happy she will be.

Soul Mates: Taurus, Capricorn, and Virgo will know how to turn on that irresistible charm, which you just love. Leo and Scorpio will create an attraction, but this is one that is harder to maintain. Sagittarius and Libra will be your dream only in a nightmare. With Pisces and Aries you will find a quick harmony, but remember that it is you who likes the finer things. Aquarius could bore you with being so needy. This is only suggested if you are in the mood for being the nurturer. Things with Gemini will be fun as long as you are the only person they are flirting with. When you are totally ready for that commitment, there is no reason you can't curl right up to that Cancer.

Most Charming Characteristics: Energetic, fun-loving, affectionate.

Gifts: *For her:* Broadway show. *For him:* day at zoo or aquarium.

Sensual Foods: Châteaubriand; crème brûlée.

Romantic Flowers: Iris is your flower if you are the gal sending subtle messages. If you are the man, you will look for clematis. This flower's mental beauty creates emotional stimulation for you.

Best Date Nights: Friday; 1st and 19th of each month.

Colors of Passion: *For her:* pink, silver. *For him:* green.

The Perfect Wedding: Serene and natural, sensual and glamorous—that's you all over. You enjoy savoring the moment and are continually impressed and inspired by beauty and classic taste. A brilliant outdoor wedding dripping in greens and fresh florals most appeals to you. Choose lots of fresh-cut, fragrant flowers to decorate an elegant, traditional wedding. Ideal setting: Ireland.

Wise Words: Charles Dickens: "In journeys, as in life, it is a great deal easier to go downhill than up."

Hints of Love: This one likes others to make his or her dreams come true. Be the "fantasy" fulfiller.

After the Argument: *For him:* Once the fight is over, don't ever bring it up again. You can make a fight go in a minute if you change the subject and move on. If you need to get that last word in, this fight will never seem to end. Making up then will take a lot of stroking. *For her:* She is stubborn, but easily bought off, especially if she is in love. They say diamonds are a girl's best friends. Well, just about any real jewels will do, and only the best will do for this one.

Romantic Places: Places of vastness bring romance: Africa; a farm; the Grand Canyon.

Lucky Love Star: Tawnel—you will never lack passion.

Beautiful Thought: Perfect is different for everybody; everybody is perfectly different.

Sharing Secrets: Make sure you are not the killjoy. *For the gals:* When she has an idea, try it before you decide you don't like it. She needs to be pleased. *For the guys:* Do the things he loves to do and he will make the things you love ten times more fun.

Judith's Insights

About the Man: He wants what he wants, and he usually wants it yesterday. But he won't allow you to know that side. Until you are very close to each other, he will be good at keeping his emotions in check. Time will tell if he lets you in to that part of his life. Until then, try to figure out what he wants and give it to him before he has a chance to ask for it. As long as you can justify your actions this guy can get over anything. He can become jealous but would never be able to admit to it. Most of the time he doesn't know that is why he gets so grumpy.

About the Woman: Appeal to her tender side if you want to capture this gal's heart. Ever loyal as a friend, she's important enough to go out of your way for. Find ways to flatter her without seeming as if you are trying to butter her up for the kill. Games are not her strong suit, so make sure that it comes from your heart. She wants your complete devotion. If she feels that you have swayed from that you will lose her quickly. Treat her like no one has ever treated her by making her the center of your attention. Call her at work just to say you were thinking of her.

Soul Mates: You will want to count on the bond you have with Taurus, Capricorn, and Virgo for a long time. If you let your insecurities get the best of you, it will drive you mad. Try to enjoy Sagittarius's and Libra's excitement among people. When you meet Pisces and Aries, the right attitude about the relationship will keep you together. Unless you enjoy taking care of the world, you would be advised to move away from Aquarius. Gemini's quick changes may baffle you at first, but they can become exhilarating. Cancers make great friends, but any commitment would mean one of you would have to forgo natural leadership to keep the peace. Be on guard with Leo and Scorpio. They are anything but soft and naïve.

Most Charming Characteristics: Serious, intense, fun-loving.

Gifts: *For her:* topaz necklace. *For him:* sports tickets.

Sensual Foods: Shrimp; sinful chocolate cake.

Romantic Flowers: Any rose of any color for the lady. Roses stand for love regardless of the color. Send them with orchids and you will be saying, "I love you." If you want a gentleman to know you think of him, send pansies, and forget-me-nots for true love.

Best Date Nights: Friday; 2nd and 11th of each month.

Colors of Passion: *For her:* white, lavender. *For him:* green, red.

The Perfect Wedding: Serene and natural, sensual and glamorous—that's you all over. You enjoy savoring the moment and are continually impressed and inspired by beauty and classic taste. A brilliant outdoor wedding dripping in greens and fresh florals most appeals to you. Choose lots of fresh-cut, fragrant flowers to decorate an elegant, traditional wedding. Ideal setting: Ireland.

Wise Words: Charles Dickens: "It is so pleasant to find real merit appreciated, whatever its particular walk in life may be."

Hints of Love: Stop worrying about next week's date today or there will not be one tomorrow.

After the Argument: *For him:* Once the fight is over, don't ever bring it up again. You can make a fight go in a minute if you change the subject and move on. If you need to get that last word in, this fight will never seem to end. Making up then will take a lot of stroking. *For her:* She is stubborn, but easily bought off, especially if she is in love. They say diamonds are a girl's best friends. Well, just about any real jewels will do, and only the best will do for this one.

Romantic Places: Places of luxury bring romance: Britain; a mountain resort; Beverly Hills, California.

Lucky Love Star: Tawnel—you will never lack passion.

Beautiful Thought: Bad news just became good.

Sharing Secrets: You had better be ready to have a relationship. *For the gals:* No lies, no games, and no mistakes. She wants what she wants with as little amount of work possible. *For the guys:* If you have games on your mind, then move on. This one likes fun any way he can get it, but no emotional roller coasters.

Judith's Insights

About the Man: He will do anything to get your attention! It is what he thrives on. If he is interested, you probably won't have to do much at all. He has a way of letting people know exactly what he thinks without using words. You will be able to read his body language like a morning newspaper. Even if this guy is simply your friend he will be an incredible asset to you. He does everything in an honorable way and gives the people he cares for anything they need, even at the expense of himself and his happiness.

About the Woman: Nobody has more compassion than this gal, but don't overdo it. If you lie to her, she will lose all faith in you. She can be your lightest angel or your darkest nightmare if you don't stay on the up-and-up. It is all up to you and your ability to play it straight. If you are honest and sincere, she will be your friend for life. Never push for a commitment until long after this girl proves that she is ready for it. Otherwise, just when you think that everything is wonderful she will pull back and offer no explanation. The best bet is to take it slow.

Soul Mates: There is no telling where a match with Taurus, Capricorn, and Virgo can take you. Just make sure there is a bit of play to go along with your hard work. While you treasure the fine things in life, Sagittarius and Libra treasure their freedom. If you can live with that, then you can live with them. Pisces and Aries can give you much to feed and grow on. When you meet the Zodiac's equivalent of a shock jock in Aquarius, the attraction will be instant or not at all. Teach Gemini to slow down and enjoy the finer things around them like you love to do. You and Cancer are both concerned with safety. You can wrap each other in a cozy safety net. You can't help but be drawn to the powerful Leo and Scorpio, but you might feel overwhelmed once you are there.

Most Charming Characteristics: Confident, original, serious.

Gifts: *For her:* soft, comfy blanket. *For him:* savings bond.

Sensual Foods: Toasted marshmallows; chocolates.

Romantic Flowers: These ladies like everyone to know how faithful they are, so send them violets. To surprise them send tulips. Men like their flowers the same as their relationships, unpretending. Send them camellias with white roses to show your affection.

Best Date Nights: Friday; 3rd and 21st of each month.

Colors of Passion: *For her:* white, silver. *For him:* green, white.

The Perfect Wedding: Serene and natural, sensual and glamorous—that's you all over. You enjoy savoring the moment and are continually impressed and inspired by beauty and classic taste. A brilliant outdoor wedding dripping in greens and fresh florals most appeals to you. Choose lots of fresh-cut, fragrant flowers to decorate an elegant, traditional wedding. Ideal setting: Ireland.

Wise Words: Robert Browning: "Truth is within ourselves, it takes no lies. From outward things whatever you may believe, there is an inmost center in us all where truth abides in fullness."

Hints of Love: Keep the romance in the picture. Don't forget the long walks on the beach and camping out in front of the fireplace.

After the Argument: *For him:* Once the fight is over, don't ever bring it up again. You can make a fight go in a minute if you change the subject and move on. If you need to get that last word in, this fight will never seem to end. Making up then will take a lot of stroking. *For her:* She is stubborn, but easily bought off, especially if she is in love. They say diamonds are a girl's best friends. Well, just about any real jewels will do, and only the best will do for this one.

Romantic Places: Places of vastness bring romance: Israel; a state park; the Colorado mountains.

Lucky Love Star: Tawnel—you will never lack passion.

Beautiful Thought: Make someone else's day and that will make yours.

Sharing Secrets: You may have to give this one more than one chance. *For the gals:* Intriguing as she is, expect a handful. She lightens up as time goes on. *For him:* His quirks may make you have second thoughts, but that is what separates the men from the boys.

Judith's Insights

About the Man: This guy is no fighter, and may be too much of a loner. He gets along with everyone, but sometimes it will seem like he only has surface relationships. He can be a difficult guy to know and a more difficult one to get a commitment from. Once you are in the mix, though, there is no getting out. He will never understand why people think of him as fickle. It is his love of all things new that makes him seem as if he is jumping from flower to flower without really smelling one. Keep things interesting to keep him interested.

About the Woman: Don't ask her what she wants! She changes her mind every other minute. If you ask her out today and she says no, then wait a week or two. Don't be surprised if things flip-flop and she's the one chasing you. She can be a great friend if you give her space to be a little fickle. She loves to meet new people and try new things. To sustain a relationship with this gal you have to keep the rejuvenation going at all times. If she can feel as if there is stability and variety with you at the same time, she will stick with you for life.

Soul Mates: When looking for a compatible sign look no further than your own, Gemini. Make sure you don't change a thing for the benefit of Aquarius and Cancer. They will just have to accept you at face value. Your tendency to play fast and loose with the truth may have Aries and Taurus seeing red. Be careful of what comes out in haste. Libra and Leo will let you revel in your true and best self. If you truly get to know Virgo and Pisces it may work, but it may take a lot of elbow grease. Try to use the bad times with Sagittarius to appreciate the good times. You may come out bruised when you get together with Scorpio and Capricorn.

Most Charming Characteristics: Gentle, kind, sincere.

Gifts: *For her:* tickets to the ballet. *For him:* tickets to a dramatic play.

Sensual Foods: Chocolate-covered strawberries; New York steak; scallops.

Romantic Flowers: These ladies like men with taste. Show them you love style by sending fuchsia flowers, or even brightly colored wildflowers will do. To confuse this man, send him lilies along with bright daisies to show your innocence. Keep him guessing.

Best Date Nights: Wednesday; 4th and 13th of each month.

Colors of Passion: *For her:* pink, white. *For him:* green, red.

The Perfect Wedding: Vivacious and sophisticated, lively and diverse—these qualities apply to you and the day you plan. A garden cocktail party or huge banquet hall would work. A five-star hotel with plenty of amenities will ensure your guests have lots to do. Ideal setting: New York.

Wise Words: Henry Wadsworth Longfellow: "To give me the meanest flower that blows can give thoughts that often lie too deep for tears."

Hints of Love: The mystery is important, but being evasive will create disaster. Make sure you know the difference.

After the Argument: *For him:* You know he is moody, so you first must find out how mad he is.

The best thing for this one is to let him sit and stew for a while. Then when it comes to making up make sure he thinks it is his idea. There is a need for a lot of game playing with this one. He likes to feel he's the suave one. Let him believe he is. *For her:* This one is a little tricky. You have to have several plans; sometimes flowers will work, other times it will be love letters. Yet another time it may be a night out or even a romantic night in, with a romantic movie. This one can take a ton of work or none at all.

Romantic Places: Places of knowledge bring romance: Oxford University; a museum; Rome, Italy.

Lucky Love Star: Geminiel—you will never lack commitment.

Beautiful Thought: Remembering before it's too late.

Sharing Secrets: Talk about high maintenance. *For the gals:* Once she sees that you go out of your way for her, then she will for you. *For the guys:* The bark is definitely much worse than the bite. He comes on stronger and more obstinate then he actually is.

Judith's Insights

About the Man: He takes pride in anything he does, including who and how he loves. He gets great satisfaction from both friends and lovers. He loves to be in the middle of things. He is like a child who loves to dance with the falling leaves around him. Give him space to play and he will be coming back for more before you know it. Don't confuse his generosity with love. They can be one and the same when it comes to this guy's showing his feelings, but he doesn't have to have both in the equation. Being friends with this guy is being loved by him as well.

About the Woman: She craves for her environment to be peaceful. She wants no games, and would rather step away from anyone who tries to create them. She wants an uncomplicated friendship or nothing. It is that simple. If you can be that simple, then you will have a friend for a long time with this gal. She enjoys the company she keeps and that company is often full of new people. When entering into a commitment, she needs for her partner to understand her flirtatious nature. Jealousy will do you no good because of her friendly side.

Soul Mates: The many faces of you and another Gemini will prove to be a fun-filled adventure. Aquarius and Cancer can only change what you let them change. Try to get them to accept who and what you are instead. Aries and Taurus will be the perfect places to turn when you need direction. Libra and Leo bring to light all of the goodness that was there all along but you couldn't see. When the day with Virgo and Pisces is over you may be too tired to continue. One minute Sagittarius has you in the clouds, the next minute you will feel stuck to the floor. Scorpio and Cancer may leave you a bit bruised and broken when all is said and done.

Most Charming Characteristics: Enthusiastic, confident, cultured.

Gifts: *For her:* language tapes. *For him:* magic set.

Sensual Foods: Vanilla and strawberry mousse; tiramisù; espresso.

Romantic Flowers: You are the lady of distinction, and only carnations will do. Any mix of colors with sprays of mignonette. Sweet peas or red carnations will appeal to this man's heart.

Best Date Nights: Wednesday; 5th and 23rd of each month.

Colors of Passion: *For her:* pink, lavender. *For him:* white, green.

The Perfect Wedding: Vivacious and sophisticated, lively and diverse—these qualities apply to you and the day you plan. A garden cocktail party or huge banquet hall would work. A five-star hotel with plenty of amenities will ensure your guests have lots to do. Ideal setting: New York.

Wise Words: Alfred, Lord Tennyson: "A man is not as God, but then most God-like being most a man."

Hints of Love: If you learn to back up when things are moving too fast, you won't have to bow out so often.

After the Argument: *For him:* You know he is moody, so you first must find out how mad he is. The best thing for this one is to let him sit and stew for a while. Then when it comes to making up make sure he thinks it is his idea. There is a need for a lot of game playing with this one. He likes to feel he's the suave one. Let him believe he is. *For her:* This one is a little tricky. You have to have several plans; sometimes flowers will work, other times it will be love letters. Yet another time it may be a night out or even a romantic night in, with a romantic movie. This one can take a ton of work or none at all.

Romantic Places: Places of history bring romance: Denmark; an Indian reservation; Fort Worth, Texas.

Lucky Love Star: Geminiel—you will never lack commitment.

Beautiful Thought: Keeping all your promises.

Sharing Secrets: Make sure you have at least five dates before you make up your mind. *For the gals:* She can be cynical, so it could be a few dates before she loosens up. *For the guys:* He still has yesterday on his mind. He needs a reason to forget his past relationship. Make a new history for him.

Judith's Insights

About the Man: This one is self-confident and self-assured at every turn. No wonder he is the envy of all his friends and relatives. He makes it look easy because that is how he would like to keep it. Be clear and be ready at all times. If he feels you can keep up he will let you tag along. He makes a great lover. Don't take your emotions too seriously until you know that he wants more than a casual relationship. Falling for him can be hard on the heart if he is not ready to be linked to someone. He will someday. Waiting is the hard part.

About the Woman: Her cavalier attitude makes it hard for anyone to understand her. Her feet are never on the ground long enough to catch her. If you want this gal in your life, expect it to take some time to win her over. Running shoes would come in handy if you plan to try to keep up with her. She does casual very well but has a hard time if she feels as if she is getting nailed down. Don't get in over your head when it comes to falling for this girl, as if you could help it. Just keep a safe distance if you want to have your heart stay in one piece.

Soul Mates: No one can understand your varied personality quite like a fellow Gemini. If Aquarius and Cancer love you for who you are, you will do the same for them. If love doesn't work out for you and Aries or Taurus, then friendship is a definite possibility. Libra and Leo will help you reach new heights faster than you ever thought possible. A pairing with Virgo and Pisces is not advised for those with weak constitutions. It will take a lot out of you. A relationship with Sagittarius is one of wild extremes. You will get along famously or not at all. Scorpio and Cancer are an accident waiting to happen.

Most Charming Characteristics: Sincere, trustworthy, devoted.

Gifts: *For her:* spur-of-the-moment getaway. *For him:* night out with the guys.

Sensual Foods: Raspberries; pound cake; caviar.

Romantic Flowers: You love it when you get tulips, declaring love. When you receive a variety, it shows how hopelessly in love your partner is. He will just love a single rose. This shows him you understand his pleasures.

Best Date Nights: Wednesday; 6th and 24th of each month.

Colors of Passion: *For her:* pink, lavender. *For him:* white, red.

The Perfect Wedding: Vivacious and sophisticated, lively and diverse—these qualities apply to you and the day you plan. A garden cocktail party or huge banquet hall would work. A five-star hotel with plenty of amenities will ensure your guests have lots to do. Ideal setting: New York.

Wise Words: Benjamin Franklin: "Great pride and great meanness are merely allied. Avoid them both. Great modesty often hides great merit."

Hints of Love: Expecting too much too soon can only build up hopes that will fall down too easily.

After the Argument: *For him:* You know he is moody, so you first must find out how mad he is.

The best thing for this one is to let him sit and stew for a while. Then when it comes to making up make sure he thinks it is his idea. There is a need for a lot of game playing with this one. He likes to feel he's the suave one. Let him believe he is. *For her:* This one is a little tricky. You have to have several plans; sometimes flowers will work, other times it will be love letters. Yet another time it may be a night out or even a romantic night in, with a romantic movie. This one can take a ton of work or none at all.

Romantic Places: Places of knowledge bring romance: Egypt; a poetry-and-quotes reading; Washington, D.C.

Lucky Love Star: Geminiel—you will never lack commitment.

Beautiful Thought: When you can be truly happy for others; you will find yourself to be happier.

Sharing Secrets: Don't be in a hurry or it will be over before it begins. *For the gals:* Like fine wine and amazing food. Savor a moment until an hour is created. *For the guys:* To do too much too fast will prove risky. Try to give a push and he will just jump ship.

Judith's Insights

About the Man: He is so easy to spot. He's the guy in high school everyone loved because everyone thinks he loved him or her. He likes it that way. He is flirty, funny, and has a large audience. This guy's hot; proceed with caution or you will get burned. Keep a level head at all times and you will do fine.

About the Woman: To say she is a challenge is an understatement. This challenge can be obtained. This gal never says what she wants, at least early on in the relationship. She makes a great boss and co-worker because she gets along with everyone and anyone. Just don't take anything she says or does personally. It is all in good fun. She will call you after months of absence and expect to pick up where you left off last time. If you have dated her, expect that she will be stopping by again. Things may change but she is usually the same.

Soul Mates: Another Gemini can be the picture-perfect partner for you. Aquarius and Cancer will only be a good idea if they are willing to love you for you and not try to change you. You might have doubts about Aries and Taurus at first. Just make sure you get to know them before any decisions are made. Everything you wished but never wanted to admit to will suddenly seem possible with Libra and Leo standing by your side. You may find yourself feeling like a limp dish towel after a day with Virgo and Pisces. Like a valley, a pairing with Sagittarius will have its ups and downs. The road with Scorpio and Capricorn is not without its bumps.

Most Charming Characteristics: Loving, tenacious, trustworthy.

Gifts: *For her:* fine writing paper. *For him:* a travel journal.

Sensual Foods: Flambé; lobster; oysters.

Romantic Flowers: Send this girl sunflowers if you want her to know you adore her. You may even add some poppies for a splash of extravagance. His desire for sport and play will be understood when you send him hyacinth and geranium.

Best Date Nights: Wednesday; 6th and 15th of each month.

Colors of Passion: *For her:* pink, lavender. *For him:* white, red.

The Perfect Wedding: Vivacious and sophisticated, lively and diverse—these qualities apply to you and the day you plan. A garden cocktail party or huge banquet hall would work. A five-star hotel with plenty of amenities will ensure your guests have lots to do. Ideal setting: New York.

Wise Words: Elizabeth Barrett Browning: "There are nettles everywhere, but the smooth, green grasses are more common still, / The blue of Heaven is larger than the cloud."

Hints of Love: Make sure all the ingredients are present before putting the cake in the oven.

After the Argument: *For him:* You know he is moody, so you first must find out how mad he is. The best thing for this one is to let him sit and stew for a while. Then when it comes to making up make sure he thinks it is his idea. There is a need

for a lot of game playing with this one. He likes to feel he's the suave one. Let him believe he is. *For her:* This one is a little tricky. You have to have several plans; sometimes flowers will work, other times it will be love letters. Yet another time it may be a night out or even a romantic night in, with a romantic movie. This one can take a ton of work or none at all.

Romantic Places: Places of history bring romance: the Taj Mahal; a national monument; Gettysburg, Pennsylvania.

Lucky Love Star: Geminiel—you will never lack commitment.

Beautiful Thought: Someone takes the time to make you feel special.

Sharing Secrets: They need to look before they leap, but only in love. *For the gals:* She needs creative and exciting dates to keep her interested. Don't take her for granted too soon. *For the guys:* You may think he gives signs of moving this relationship quickly; make sure you slow it down before he does.

Judith's Insights

About the Man: He can like many but love only one. It may take time to nail this guy down to anything. This includes when you might be getting that raise. Don't be pushy or bossy. Try to find other ways to nail him down, like with little gifts or favors to win him over. Once you get him to decide, he won't change his mind. He wants someone to be demonstrative with her affections toward him. He never wants to feel as if he is the one chasing love. He wants to be the one being chased. That is why it may take a few tries before he takes you up on an invitation.

About the Woman: She will keep a list of her wins and losses like a check-and-balance sheet next to her heart. She likes a lot to be going on around her. That is why she thrives in a profession that has her deal with many people. She can sometimes create havoc on purpose just to feel fulfilled. Try not to be caught in the stream of people. Don't go dangling emotional carrots in front of her to get her moving unless you are prepared to go through with giving her the reward. Games are fine with her if they have a good emotional outcome.

Soul Mates: All signs point to a great partnership with another Gemini. Make Aquarius and Cancer aware of your need to be loved for who you are and things will work out from there. Give Aries and Taurus time. You never know if the planets are in the right place. Libra and Leo will help you recognize how wonderful you have been all along. Daily living with Virgo and Pisces would prove to be difficult. You must decide if it is worth the work. It is either feast or famine with Sagittarius. There is no such thing as middle ground. Scorpio and Capricorn may leave you all shook up.

Most Charming Characteristics: Exuberant, fun-loving, friendly.

Gifts: *For her:* surprise party. *For him:* night out bowling.

Sensual Foods: Creme brûlée; poached salmon.

Romantic Flowers: Rhododendron will let her be on the lookout for trouble. Throw in some chrysanthemum and she'll know it is you she will be looking out for. Cactus will show him warmth. Yellow daffodil is a token of a good time had by all. Chivalry is not dead.

Best Date Nights: Wednesday; 17th and 26th of each month.

Colors of Passion: *For her:* pink, lavender. *For him:* white, red.

The Perfect Wedding: Vivacious and sophisticated, lively and diverse—these qualities apply to you and the day you plan. A garden cocktail party or huge banquet hall would work. A five-star hotel with plenty of amenities will ensure your guests have lots to do. Ideal setting: New York.

Wise Words: Rudolph Steiner: "Keep watch over each of your actions and each of your words, in order that you may not hinder the free will of any human being."

Hints of Love: Simple often turns into complicated with this one. When you overcomplicate the moment, try to step back for a breather.

After the Argument: *For him:* You know he is moody, so you first must find out how mad he is. The best thing for this one is to let him sit and stew

for a while. Then when it comes to making up make sure he thinks it is his idea. There is a need for a lot of game playing with this one. He likes to feel he's the suave one. Let him believe he is. *For her:* This one is a little tricky. You have to have several plans; sometimes flowers will work, other times it will be love letters. Yet another time it may be a night out or even a romantic night in, with a romantic movie. This one can take a ton of work or none at all.

Romantic Places: Places of knowledge bring romance: Israel; a planetarium; Baltimore, Maryland.

Lucky Love Star: Geminiel—you will never lack commitment.

Beautiful Thought: Givers are more likely to get.

Sharing Secrets: The possibilities are endless, if you can pay the price. *For the gals:* She is hoping chivalry is not dead, and you must be willing to be the man at all costs. *For the guys:* He can be demanding and somewhat controlling. He just needs to be trained.

Judith's Insights

About the Man: This guy is looking for love in all of the right places. At the same time, he can have the worst timing in the world. As a boss, he may drive you crazy with his constantly changing mind. What he needs by when will constantly change at a moment's notice. If you can keep up he will be sure to notice. Restlessness and love are the continual activities and the outstanding traits of this guy's character. You may feel as if you are a human yo-yo until a relationship with him gets off the ground. Just step back and wait for his active nature to settle a bit.

About the Woman: This gal makes an incredible friend. If she is your enemy, she is downright lethal. You will adore her until you have your first fight. The side of her that you see then will not only bring a dose of reality into the relationship, but it might leave you questioning it at the same time. She can lead two different lives and no one would notice. She may seem bold and confident on the outside, but she is easily discouraged and can come home defeated and drained. Until she can learn to balance her emotions she will be a hard one to keep track of.

Soul Mates: With a fellow Gemini, you will have all of the variety you have ever wanted. Aquarius and Cancer must be told that you are not willing to change yourself and they have to accept you for who you are naturally. Aries and Taurus will help you keep both feet on the ground. You will achieve any goal you set for yourself with Libra and Leo in your corner. A building is only as strong as its foundation. The same is true for a relationship with Virgo and Pisces. Just when you have the pulse of the relationship, Sagittarius will change drastically. Scorpio and Capricorn are not recommended for the faint of heart.

Most Charming Characteristics: Steadfast, exciting, sociable.

Gifts: *For her:* tuition to a class. *For him:* latest gadget.

Sensual Foods: Chocolate soufflé; filet mignon.

Romantic Flowers: The magnolias you send her will let her know you will be around for a while to come. Petunia is to say never despair. Holly will let him know what he is getting into. Pansy will keep you in his thoughts.

Best Date Nights: Wednesday; 9th and 18th of each month.

Colors of Passion: *For her:* pink, lavender. *For him:* white, red.

The Perfect Wedding: Vivacious and sophisticated, lively and diverse—these qualities apply to you and the day you plan. A garden cocktail party or huge banquet hall would work. A five-star hotel with plenty of amenities will ensure your guests have lots to do. Ideal setting: New York.

Wise Words: Miguel de Cervantes: "I have found that a man may do a great deal of good in the world, if only he does not care who gets the credit of it."

Hints of Love: Allow them to know what is in your heart as well as what is in your head.

After the Argument: *For him:* You know he is moody, so you first must find out how mad he is. The best thing for this one is to let him sit and stew for a while. Then when it comes to making up

make sure he thinks it is his idea. There is a need for a lot of game playing with this one. He likes to feel he's the suave one. Let him believe he is. *For her:* This one is a little tricky. You have to have several plans; sometimes flowers will work, other times it will be love letters. Yet another time it may be a night out or even a romantic night in, with a romantic movie. This one can take a ton of work or none at all.

Romantic Places: Places of history bring romance: Scotland; a science museum; Williamsburg, Virginia.

Lucky Love Star: Geminiel—you will never lack commitment.

Beautiful Thought: Expecting from love challenges it; respecting love expands it.

Sharing Secrets: Tomorrow is another day, but why wait? You can do it all today. *For the gals:* Have your date filled from dusk to dawn, and then some. *For the guys:* You may find he needs a nap here and there, but he can last all day and all night if he has a reason.

Judith's Insights

About the Man: You may feel like he cares about nobody, and at times that may be true. Even when he does care for you it will be hard to notice. He does not show his emotions very easily. If you can learn to read the real meaning behind his words, then you will be way ahead of the game. You have to have a lot of stamina to hold on long enough for him to decide whether or not he wants to settle down. He does not mean to trample so many hearts along his path of self-discovery, but it happens nonetheless.

About the Woman: She takes everything to heart. She won't tell you how she feels until she is completely certain about how you feel about her. As a co-worker, she will be the friendliest one in the crowd on her good days. If you catch her on one of her bad days, you had better watch where the pencils fly. Even if there is a strong love between the two of you, you will hear her ask for more and more time to feel safe before entering any commitment. She needs to be completely sure about how you feel and what your intentions are. Don't hesitate to let her know as much as possible.

Soul Mates: Aries and Taurus will give you that sense of balance you are always looking for. Libra and Leo would certainly bring out the best in you. Virgo and Pisces might cause you a little insanity. It would truly take a deep connection for this match to work. When it comes to Sagittarius, it can be a double-edged sword. It can be the best of the best while also being the worst of the worst for you. Scorpio and Capricorn are a roller coaster with many wild turns and twists. Aquarius and Cancer must be able to accept you for who you are for this to work. A fellow Gemini would make a very interesting match. Two people with two sets of personalities is like having multiple partners.

Most Charming Characteristics: Ambitious, sociable, adaptable.

Gifts: *For her:* cell phone. *For him:* dartboard.

Sensual Foods: Steak au poivre; cheesecake.

Romantic Flowers: Iris is your flower if you are the gal sending subtle messages. If you are the man, you will look for clematis. This flower's mental beauty creates emotional stimulation for you.

Best Date Nights: Wednesday; 1st and 19th of each month.

Colors of Passion: *For her:* pink, lavender. *For him:* white, red.

The Perfect Wedding: Vivacious and sophisticated, lively and diverse—these qualities apply to you and the day you plan. A garden cocktail party or huge banquet hall would work. A five-star hotel with plenty of amenities will ensure your guests have lots to do. Ideal setting: New York.

Wise Words: Talford: "Gentleman is a term which does not apply to any station, but to the mind and the feelings in every station."

Hints of Love: Keep both feet on the ground the first time you think you want to jump. This way you won't jump too high too soon.

After the Argument: *For him:* You know he is moody, so you first must find out how mad he is. The best thing for this one is to let him sit and stew for a while. Then when it comes to making up

make sure he thinks it is his idea. There is a need for a lot of game playing with this one. He likes to feel he's the suave one. Let him believe he is. *For her:* This one is a little tricky. You have to have several plans; sometimes flowers will work, other times it will be love letters. Yet another time it may be a night out or even a romantic night in, with a romantic movie. This one can take a ton of work or none at all.

Romantic Places: Places of knowledge bring romance: Spain; a library; San Francisco, California.

Lucky Love Star: Geminiel—you will never lack commitment.

Beautiful Thought: You usually find the right words even when you don't know what to say.

Sharing Secrets: It may need to start with friendship. This isn't the consolation prize; it's the grand prize. *For the gals:* Go slow and allow it to grow one seed at a time. You won't need to push; it will all come in time. *For the guys:* A step here and a step there. Before he knows it, that friendship will be love.

Judith's Insights

About the Man: He does not need to be anyone's hero, but he does need to be everyone's friend. He is a guy who is always lending a helping hand. The challenge about him is that he is abrasive when it comes to love. He only lets on that he feels this way when he has fallen so hard that he can't get back up. He is constantly searching for a place that feels like home. He will go through many relationships and never feel as if he has ever been in love. Pinning this guy down will take a load of patience and time instead of crazy stunts.

About the Woman: She has a voice and knows how to use it. She loves letters and cute little notes. Invite her out in an unusual way. Send a note in a pizza. Or even send her a singing telegram. Do anything to get her attention. Once you do capture her attention in a fabulous way you will keep it very easily. She definitely wants to be part of a relationship. While she craves it, she has a hard time keeping it once she has it. She is constantly looking around for some variety and excitement. This one will intrigue you every step of the way.

Soul Mates: With a fellow Gemini, you will feel as if you are dating many people and never have a reason to stray. Aquarius and Cancer must learn to value you for who you are for anything to work. Push Aries and Taurus off the couch and make sure they have plenty of playtime. Libra and Leo make you see all of the good in yourself. A match with Virgo and Pisces will run you ragged if you let it. Extreme is the name of the game with Sagittarius. Be prepared to go with the flow. If you take a ride with Scorpio and Capricorn, you had better put on your seat belt or you are liable to get thrown around.

Most Charming Characteristics: Domestic, affable, even-tempered.

Gifts: *For her:* surprise destination for a weekend. *For him:* a last-minute cruise.

Sensual Foods: Strawberry shortcake; pineapple; ham.

Romantic Flowers: Any rose of any color for the lady. Roses stand for love regardless of the color. Send them with orchids and you will be saying, "I love you." If you want a gentleman to know you think of him, send pansies, and forget-me-nots for true love.

Best Date Nights: Wednesday; 11th and 20th of each month.

Colors of Passion: *For her:* pink, lavender. *For him:* white, red.

The Perfect Wedding: Vivacious and sophisticated, lively and diverse—these qualities apply to you and the day you plan. A garden cocktail party or huge banquet hall would work. A five-star hotel with plenty of amenities will ensure your guests have lots to do. Ideal setting: New York.

Wise Words: Franklin D. Roosevelt: "Our civilization cannot endure unless we, as individuals, realize our personal responsibility to and dependence on, the rest of the world."

Hints of Love: Laughter alleviates the tension, but so can understanding where another is sitting.

After the Argument: *For him:* You know he is moody, so you first must find out how mad he is. The best thing for this one is to let him sit and stew

for a while. Then when it comes to making up make sure he thinks it is his idea. There is a need for a lot of game playing with this one. He likes to feel he's the suave one. Let him believe he is. *For her:* This one is a little tricky. You have to have several plans; sometimes flowers will work, other times it will be love letters. Yet another time it may be a night out or even a romantic night in, with a romantic movie. This one can take a ton of work or none at all.

Romantic Places: Places of history bring romance: Greece; a shipyard; Philadelphia, Pennsylvania.

Lucky Love Star: Geminiel—you will never lack commitment.

Beautiful Thought: You realize you have a best friend.

Sharing Secrets: This one needs to be the one and only, even if it is only the first date. *For the gals:* Don't talk about your past relationships. Do all you can to make her feel cherished from the first moment. *For the guys:* Play up your innocence. Let him take charge, even in paying the bill. He needs to wear the pants.

Judith's Insights

About the Man: Stay out of this man's way. Whether it is work or play, he does not like anyone to intrude on his business. He sets his boundaries, and these boundaries must be respected. If you allow him this space to breathe, he is more likely to let you in the circle than if you try to smother him. He needs to feel that he can get to that point of his own free will instead of being convinced he is ready. Only he will know that he is ready to do something. It will take a lot of soul-searching for him to come to any kind of commitment.

About the Woman: She would make a great debater, so choose your words wisely. She loves to argue and can do battle with her tongue. All bets are off if her heart is involved. She can be squeamish about change once she has settled with a partner. Give her room to live without feeling closed in. You can always find her in the corner of a party surrounded by people. Everyone is just naturally attracted to her. You have to declare your intentions and then give her plenty of time to check her calendar. She has to be able to explore her options.

Soul Mates: A relationship with another Gemini may give you the variety you crave while keeping you bonded to one person. If Aquarius and Cancer can accept you for who you are, then go for it. Aries and Taurus may baffle you with their settled ways, but they are not a bad thing for you to learn to appreciate. Libra and Leo draw out your greatest qualities and help you shine. Take on Virgo and Pisces only if you are in the mood to work your butt off. When things with Sagittarius are good, they are great, but when they are bad, they are downright ugly! If you like things fast and exciting, then you are going to love Scorpio and Capricorn.

Most Charming Characteristics: Steadfast, confident, domestic.

Gifts: *For her:* dance classes. *For him:* language tapes.

Sensual Foods: Steak fondue; cheese fondue and French bread.

Romantic Flowers: These ladies like everyone to know how faithful they are, so send them violets. To surprise them send tulips. Men like their flowers the same as their relationships, unpretending. Send them camellias with white roses to show your affection.

Best Date Nights: Wednesday; 3rd and 12th of each month.

Colors of Passion: *For her:* pink, lavender. *For him:* white, red.

The Perfect Wedding: Vivacious and sophisticated, lively and diverse—these qualities apply to you and the day you plan. A garden cocktail party or huge banquet hall would work. A five-star hotel with plenty of amenities will ensure your guests have lots to do. Ideal setting: New York.

Wise Words: Charles Dickens: "We all have some bright day—many of us, let us hope, among a crowd of others—to which we revert with particular delight."

Hints of Love: Communication is important here. A script isn't provided for you. You must write it for yourself.

After the Argument: *For him:* You know he is moody, so you first must find out how mad he is. The best thing for this one is to let him sit and stew for a while. Then when it comes to making up make sure he thinks it is his idea. There is a need for a lot of game playing with this one. He likes to feel he's the suave one. Let him believe he is. *For her:* This one is a little tricky. You have to have several plans; sometimes flowers will work, other times it will be love letters. Yet another time it may be a night out or even a romantic night in, with a romantic movie. This one can take a ton of work or none at all.

Romantic Places: Places of knowledge bring romance: Italy; a university; the Smithsonian Institution.

Lucky Love Star: Geminiel—you will never lack commitment.

Beautiful Thought: A compliment from a stranger.

Sharing Secrets: You need to remember never to forget. *For the gals:* Her birthday, holidays, and your anniversary. Even down to each dinner date. *For the guys:* His birthday, his laundry, his mother's birthday, and, of course him, any other day of the year.

Judith's Insights

About the Man: You can find him in the newspaper, or maybe even writing it. He is sure to attend all the events advertised. He loves the spotlight and plenty of attention. If the press will be there, then so will he. I hope you have not only the time but also the patience to get a spot on his calendar. Once you have captured this guy's heart he is very loyal. It takes a lot to get him interested in the first place, however, let alone getting a commitment out of him. Make sure that things do not get routine or boring. If he gets socially deprived there could be a problem.

About the Woman: Trying to get her attention means giving her something of interest. Talk about the local social scene and then invite her to go along with you to an event. She can't stand a boring date or a boring friend. Keep things exhilarating and you will keep her around. Excitement is like an addiction to her, and you may even find her into thrill seeking. Once she commits she is generally loyal but needs to be able to flirt wildly at the same time. Don't take it personally. She knows who she is going home with and won't break that bond.

Soul Mates: When looking for a compatible sign, look no further than your own, Gemini. Make sure you don't change a thing for the benefit of Aquarius and Cancer. They will just have to accept you at face value. Your tendency to play fast and loose with the truth may have Aries and Taurus seeing red. Be careful of what comes out in haste. Libra and Leo will let you revel in your true and best self. If you truly get to know Virgo and Pisces it may work, but it may take a lot of elbow grease. Try to use the bad times with Sagittarius to appreciate the good times. You may come out bruised when you get together with Scorpio and Capricorn.

Most Charming Characteristics: Artistic, congenial, fun-loving.

Gifts: *For her:* tickets to the ballet. *For him:* tickets to a dramatic play.

Sensual Foods: Baked Alaska; seafood.

Romantic Flowers: These ladies like men with taste. Show them you love style by sending fuchsia flowers, or even brightly colored wildflowers will do. To confuse this man, send him lilies along with bright daisies to show your innocence. Keep him guessing.

Best Date Nights: Wednesday; 13th and 22nd of each month.

Colors of Passion: *For her:* pink, lavender. *For him:* white, red.

The Perfect Wedding: Vivacious and sophisticated; lively and diverse—these qualities apply to you and the day you plan. A garden cocktail party or huge banquet hall would work. A five-star hotel with plenty of amenities will ensure your guests have lots to do. Ideal setting: New York.

Wise Words: Henry Wadsworth Longfellow: "Like the swell of some sweet tune, Morning rises into noon, / May glides onward into June."

Hints of Love: Don't dissect every minute of every day. Learn to appreciate each minute as it comes.

After the Argument: *For him:* You know he is moody, so you first must find out how mad he is. The best thing for this one is to let him sit and stew for a while. Then when it comes to making up

make sure he thinks it is his idea. There is a need for a lot of game playing with this one. He likes to feel he's the suave one. Let him believe he is. *For her:* This one is a little tricky. You have to have several plans; sometimes flowers will work, other times it will be love letters. Yet another time it may be a night out or even a romantic night in, with a romantic movie. This one can take a ton of work or none at all.

Romantic Places: Places of knowledge bring romance: Oxford University; a museum; Rome, Italy.

Lucky Love Star: Geminiel—you will never lack commitment.

Beautiful Thought: Friendship is the gift of all gifts.

Sharing Secrets: My house should be your house, especially if you don't have one of your own. *For the gals:* All for one and one for all. Yours and mine must become ours. *For the guys:* If he needs to stand on ceremony, even for the first five minutes, it will be a definite turnoff for this one.

Judith's Insights

About the Man: He is impulsive and very proud of it. This guy finds it impossible to be a stick-in-the-mud. His personality is commanding, but he is never demanding. If you can keep up with his flights of fancy, then more power to you. Be careful how you joke; he might take it the wrong way. He may not seem sensitive but he can be wounded quite easily. He won't let on. He will just fade out of your life and you will never know why. He feels the need to flirt with many people, not as a way to get on to better things but as a way of getting a bit of extra attention.

About the Woman: She is sensitive, and can sometimes take a joke as an insult. I would not make her the butt of too many jokes. Keep your words clear, because she tends to read too much into them. If you are interested in just friendship, you must keep repeating that before it gets through. She can be an exciting person to be around. You have to have a lot of get-up-and-go to keep up with her. She loves to be surrounded by friends and old lovers. Her personality commands attention at all turns. If you can't share her, you can't be happy living life with her.

JUNE

Soul Mates: Aries and Taurus will give you that sense of balance you are always looking for. Libra and Leo would certainly bring out the best in you. Virgo and Pisces might cause you a little insanity. It would truly take a deep connection for this match to work. When it comes to Sagittarius, it can be a double-edged sword. It can be the best of the best while also being the worst of the worst for you. Scorpio and Capricorn are a roller coaster with many wild turns and twists. Aquarius and Cancer must be able to accept you for who you are for this to work. A fellow Gemini would make a very interesting match. Two people with two sets of personalities is like having multiple partners.

Most Charming Characteristics: Steadfast, confident, domestic.

Gifts: *For her:* language tapes. *For him:* magic set.

Sensual Foods: Strawberries and cream; meat loaf.

Romantic Flowers: Iris is your flower if you are the gal sending subtle messages. If you are the man, you will look for clematis. This flower's mental beauty creates emotional stimulation for you.

Best Date Nights: Wednesday; 10th and 19th of each month.

Colors of Passion: *For her:* pink, lavender. *For him:* white, red.

The Perfect Wedding: Vivacious and sophisticated, lively and diverse—these qualities apply to you and the day you plan. A garden cocktail party or huge banquet hall would work. A five-star hotel with plenty of amenities will ensure your guests have lots to do. Ideal setting: New York.

Wise Words: Henry Wadsworth Longfellow: "All the meadows wave with blossoms, / All the woodlands ring with music, / All the trees are dark with foliage."

Hints of Love: They only use the three magic words when they know they mean it, and they already know it is going to be said back to them.

After the Argument: *For him:* You know he is moody, so you first must find out how mad he is. The best thing for this one is to let him sit and stew for a while. Then when it comes to making up

make sure he thinks it is his idea. There is a need for a lot of game playing with this one. He likes to feel he's the suave one. Let him believe he is. *For her:* This one is a little tricky. You have to have several plans; sometimes flowers will work, other times it will be love letters. Yet another time it may be a night out or even a romantic night in, with a romantic movie. This one can take a ton of work or none at all.

Romantic Places: Places of history bring romance: Denmark; an Indian reservation; Fort Worth, Texas.

Lucky Love Star: Geminiel—you will never lack commitment.

Beautiful Thought: The other shoe is finally falling, and someone is there to catch it.

Sharing Secrets: Let them admire something about you first. Show them you have a sense of humor. *For the gals:* Hold their hand and then take them to the next step. *For the guys:* The way to his heart is definitely through his stomach.

Judith's Insights

About the Man: He can wear you out very easily. So, get a good night's sleep before hanging with this guy. He will not be too forthcoming, especially when it comes to his past. He will be secretive and abrasive. Time is the only way you will ever get him to open up. If you give him this, there is no telling what he will give you. He has a loving instinct that will bring people to admire him. He has a strong desire to please those he cares about. Only a chosen few will be invited into his heart. Once you are there he will make sure you never want to leave.

About the Woman: Challenging at best, she seeks constant excitement and is lost at sea. To nail this one down for the first date may be a task in itself. At home it may be all play, but at work she will be all work. Even if you are personally connected to her, business will always be business. There will be no personal feeling mixed in with it. She has a tendency to be erotic when she falls in love. Mix that with her love to please those around her and you will have a very exciting life with her.

Soul Mates: With a fellow Gemini, you will feel as if you are dating many people and never have a reason to stray. Aquarius and Cancer must learn to value you for who you are for anything to work. Push Aries and Taurus off the couch and make sure they have plenty of playtime. Libra and Leo make you see all of the good in yourself. A match with Virgo and Pisces will run you ragged if you let it. Extreme is the name of the game with Sagittarius. Be prepared to go with the flow. If you take a ride with Scorpio and Capricorn, you had better put on your seat belt or you are liable to get thrown around.

Most Charming Characteristics: Artistic, intuitive, domestic.

Gifts: *For her:* spur of the moment getaway. *For him:* night out with the guys.

Sensual Foods: Cherry-apple pie; beef Stroganoff.

Romantic Flowers: Any rose of any color for the lady. Roses stand for love regardless of the color. Send them with orchids and you will be saying, "I love you." If you want a gentleman to know you think of him, send pansies, and forget-me-nots for true love.

Best Date Nights: Wednesday; 11th and 29th of each month.

Colors of Passion: *For her:* pink, lavender. *For him:* white, red.

The Perfect Wedding: Vivacious and sophisticated, lively and diverse—these qualities apply to you and the day you plan. A garden cocktail party or huge banquet hall would work. A five-star hotel with plenty of amenities will ensure your guests have lots to do. Ideal setting: New York.

Wise Words: Henry Wadsworth Longfellow: "For when the heart goes before, like a lamp, and illumines the pathway, / Many things are made clear, that else lie hidden in the darkness."

Hints of Love: Remember to keep the dating fun. Don't act like you are married before your time.

After the Argument: *For him:* You know he is moody, so you first must find out how mad he is. The best thing for this one is to let him sit and stew for a while. Then when it comes to making up make sure he thinks it is his idea. There is a need for a lot of game playing with this one. He likes to feel he's the suave one. Let him believe he is. *For her:* This one is a little tricky. You have to have several plans; sometimes flowers will work, other times it will be love letters. Yet another time it may be a night out or even a romantic night in, with a romantic movie. This one can take a ton of work or none at all.

Romantic Places: Places of knowledge bring romance: Egypt; a poetry-and-quotes reading; Washington, D.C.

Lucky Love Star: Geminiel—you will never lack commitment.

Beautiful Thought: Recognizing you are not alone, just lonely.

Sharing Secrets: Give them the opportunity to notice you first. *For the gals:* They love to be adored; love at first sight. *For the guys:* Remember to always let them believe it was their idea.

Judith's Insights

About the Man: Some may say that he is conceited. He just loves praise and flattery. If you want his attention, all you have to do is give him some of yours. Even if he's your boss, start the conversation with praise and this guy is likely to give you a better raise. When you call attention to his good points it will help him become more sure of himself. He makes a great date and is always up for a good time. Just make sure that the good times end with a bit of rest. If not, both of you will be so burnt out that you won't be going on any more adventures.

About the Woman: Flattery will get you anywhere or everywhere, but it must certainly be genuine. She is practical for the most part. If you want her attention, follow the path of the impractical. Lavish her with anything and everything. She deserves all that you can give and more. It may be hard to get her to commit. She likes her feet in midair and her head in the clouds. Bring her down slowly so she can have time to get used to the change in atmosphere. No matter what the level of commitment you have with her, you have to keep things light so she doesn't run away.

Soul Mates: A relationship with another Gemini may give you the variety you crave while keeping you bonded to one person. If Aquarius and Cancer can accept you for who you are, then go for it. Aries and Taurus may baffle you with their settled ways, but they are not a bad thing for you to learn to appreciate. Libra and Leo draw out your greatest qualities and help you shine. Take on Virgo and Pisces only if you are in the mood to work your butt off. When things with Sagittarius are good, they are great, but when they are bad, they are downright ugly! If you like things fast and exciting, then you are going to love Scorpio and Capricorn.

Most Charming Characteristics: Independent, original, easygoing.

Gifts: *For her:* fine writing paper. *For him:* travel journal.

Sensual Foods: Hot-fudge sundae with all the trimmings; shepherd's pie.

Romantic Flowers: These ladies like everyone to know how faithful they are, so send them violets. To surprise them send tulips. Men like their flowers the same as their relationships, unpretending. Send them camellias with white roses to show your affection.

Best Date Nights: Wednesday; 3rd and 30th of each month.

Colors of Passion: *For her:* pink, lavender. *For him:* white, red.

The Perfect Wedding: Vivacious and sophisticated, lively and diverse—these qualities apply to you and the day you plan. A garden cocktail party or huge banquet hall would work. A five-star hotel with plenty of amenities will ensure your guests have lots to do. Ideal setting: New York.

Wise Words: Henry Wadsworth Longfellow: "Our hearts are lamps for ever burning, / With a steady and unwavering flame, / Pointing upward, for ever the same, / Steadily upward toward the Heaven."

Hints of Love: Make sure you go on more than one date before you jump to conclusions on liking and disliking.

After the Argument: *For him:* You know he is moody, so you first must find out how mad he is.

The best thing for this one is to let him sit and stew for a while. Then when it comes to making up make sure he thinks it is his idea. There is a need for a lot of game playing with this one. He likes to feel he's the suave one. Let him believe he is. *For her:* This one is a little tricky. You have to have several plans; sometimes flowers will work, other times it will be love letters. Yet another time it may be a night out or even a romantic night in, with a romantic movie. This one can take a ton of work or none at all.

Romantic Places: Places of history bring romance: the Taj Mahal; a national monument; Gettysburg, Pennsylvania.

Lucky Love Star: Geminiel—you will never lack commitment.

Beautiful Thought: Someone hands you a blanket when you've just gotten a chill.

Sharing Secrets: This one loves a challenge. *For the gals:* Be consistently inconsistent until you have them hooked. *For the guys:* This one loves to play catch. You may feel like a yo-yo, but as long as he is calling that's all that matters.

Judith's Insights

About the Man: He knows how to change his words, but he does not necessarily do it wisely. He likes to be liked. More important, he needs to be loved. This guy needs to find his own personal satisfaction first before he can be good to anyone else. Making things good for him will make things good for your relationship. As long as you have a tremendous amount of patience, you may just be able to catch him. Keep the word *catch* in mind, because you will always find him in midair on the way to his next adventure.

About the Woman: Talk about living in your own world. The world can be taken over by her, along with her own way to do work. She has her own way to function in a relationship. Unfortunately, she might not always tell you what that way is. You will have to find out what goes and what doesn't by trial and error. If you can keep up with her adventures instead of trying to talk her out of them, you will have a very happy partner. She wants a person to play with and rest with. Any partner of hers has to be hopelessly devoted to make it through.

Soul Mates: When looking for a compatible sign, look no further than your own, Gemini. Make sure you don't change a thing for the benefit of Aquarius and Cancer. They will just have to accept you at face value. Your tendency to play fast and loose with the truth may have Aries and Taurus seeing red. Be careful of what comes out in haste. Libra and Leo will let you revel in your true and best self. If you truly get to know Virgo and Pisces it may work, but it may take a lot of elbow grease. Try to use the bad times with Sagittarius to appreciate the good times. You may come out bruised when you get together with Scorpio and Capricorn.

Most Charming Characteristics: Bright, witty, enthusiastic.

Gifts: *For her:* surprise party. *For him:* night out bowling.

Sensual Foods: Whipped cream, strawberries, brown sugar, and heavy cream.

Romantic Flowers: These ladies like men with taste. Show them you love style by sending fuchsia flowers, or even brightly colored wildflowers will do. To confuse this man, send him lilies along with bright daisies to show your innocence. Keep him guessing.

Best Date Nights: Wednesday; 13th and 22nd of each month.

Colors of Passion: *For her:* pink, lavender. *For him:* white, red.

The Perfect Wedding: Vivacious and sophisticated, lively and diverse—these qualities apply to you and the day you plan. A garden cocktail party or huge banquet hall would work. A five-star hotel with plenty of amenities will ensure your guests have lots to do. Ideal setting: New York.

Wise Words: Henry Wadsworth Longfellow: "Love is sunshine, hate is shadow, / Life is checkered shade and sunshine; rule by love."

Hints of Love: Don't act too needy too soon. It may push this relationship away.

After the Argument: *For him:* You know he is moody, so you first must find out how mad he is.

The best thing for this one is to let him sit and stew for a while. Then when it comes to making up make sure he thinks it is his idea. There is a need for a lot of game playing with this one. He likes to feel he's the suave one. Let him believe he is. *For her:* This one is a little tricky. You have to have several plans; sometimes flowers will work, other times it will be love letters. Yet another time it may be a night out or even a romantic night in, with a romantic movie. This one can take a ton of work or none at all.

Romantic Places: Places of knowledge bring romance: Israel; a planetarium; Baltimore, Maryland.

Lucky Love Star: Geminiel—you will never lack commitment.

Beautiful Thought: Someone tells you how much he or she has always admired your character.

Sharing Secrets: This is a family person at heart; your presence is most important. *For the gals:* Make sure you go to Sunday dinner with her family when you are invited. *For the guys:* If you don't like his mom, you might have a hard time catching this one.

Judith's Insights

About the Man: If you stay out of his way long enough he just may notice you. Even if you work with him, standing back may get you noticed along with your work. Be subtle, especially when asking for a favor. He is much more receptive to change when he is made to feel as if it is his idea in the first place. He has more new and clever ideas than most people have in a lifetime. His mind is always trying to find the next adventure to go on. Give him some ideas of his own to join in on the fun.

About the Woman: This one can go to many extremes. She will vary from too many dates to no dates at all. She wants attention while at the same time she runs from it. Unfortunately, you will have to be the one to determine where she is and then wait for the moment to lavish her with all that she deserves. She is a great seeker of knowledge and is looking for someone who can not only appreciate this but join in as well. You will have a ball hanging with her thanks to her rich imagination.

Soul Mates: The many faces of you and another Gemini will prove to be a fun-filled adventure. Aquarius and Cancer can only change what you let them change. Try to get them to accept who and what you are instead. Aries and Taurus will be the perfect places to turn when you need direction. Libra and Leo bring to light all of the goodness that was there all along, but you couldn't see. When the day with Virgo and Pisces is over you may be too tired to continue. One minute Sagittarius has you in the clouds, the next minute you will feel stuck to the floor. Scorpio and Cancer may leave you a bit bruised and broken when all is said and done.

Most Charming Characteristics: Passionate, enthusiastic, thoughtful.

Gifts: *For her:* tuition to a class. *For him:* latest gadget.

Sensual Foods: Puddings and pastry of all kinds.

Romantic Flowers: You are the lady of distinction, and only carnations will do. Any mix of colors with sprays of mignonette. Sweet peas or red carnations will appeal to this man's heart.

Best Date Nights: Wednesday; 4th and 5th of each month.

Colors of Passion: *For her:* pink, lavender. *For him:* white, red.

The Perfect Wedding: Vivacious and sophisticated, lively and diverse—these qualities apply to you and the day you plan. A garden cocktail party or huge banquet hall would work. A five-star hotel with plenty of amenities will ensure your guests have lots to do. Ideal setting: New York.

Wise Words: Henry Wadsworth Longfellow: "The tidal wave of deeper souls / Into our inmost being rolls, / And lifts us unawares / Out of all meaner cares."

Hints of Love: Keep it fun. Look for new and exciting things to do, especially if you are in a long-term relationship.

After the Argument: *For him:* You know he is moody, so you first must find out how mad he is. The best thing for this one is to let him sit and stew for a while. Then when it comes to making up

make sure he thinks it is his idea. There is a need for a lot of game playing with this one. He likes to feel he's the suave one. Let him believe he is. *For her:* This one is a little tricky. You have to have several plans; sometimes flowers will work, other times it will be love letters. Yet another time it may be a night out or even a romantic night in, with a romantic movie. This one can take a ton of work or none at all.

Romantic Places: Places of history bring romance: Scotland; a science museum; Williamsburg, Virginia.

Lucky Love Star: Geminiel—you will never lack commitment.

Beautiful Thought: Giving someone a second chance may give you one.

Sharing Secrets: Everything in its good time. This one works slowly, but when it is time to pick up speed, watch out. *For the gals:* Don't go by the obvious. Read between the lines. As long as the invitation is being offered go full speed ahead. *For the guys:* Just when you thought you should walk away, he'll say, "I love you." Talk about confusing.

Judith's Insights

About the Man: This guy tends to get himself into compromising situations quite often. Once he learns to know better, this will pass. It can be quite a task to reform him, so don't try. He has an unconventional way about him that can be refreshing if you let it. This guy can be a challenge for even the most flexible person. If you want an adventurous life, step on up to the plate and take a swing. If this is something you can't handle, you should move on. He will never fully see what he might have done to hurt you.

About the Woman: If she only knew what she really wanted, the situation would be much better. She is fickle about everything, from what she is eating for dinner to who her best friend is. Don't try to nail her down. You will only drive yourself crazy. Allow her time to come to the point where she can make a commitment herself. Both of you will be much happier. She could drive you crazy if you are not watching where you are headed. Be the rock in the relationship where she can come back to and rest.

Soul Mates: No one can understand your varied personality quite like a fellow Gemini. If Aquarius and Cancer love you for who you are, you will do the same for them. If love doesn't work out for you and Aries or Taurus, then friendship is a definite possibility. Libra and Leo will help you reach new heights faster than you ever thought possible. A pairing with Virgo and Pisces is not advised for those with weak constitutions. It will take a lot out of you. A relationship with Sagittarius is one of wild extremes. You will get along famously or not at all. Scorpio and Cancer are an accident waiting to happen.

Most Charming Characteristics: Energetic, sympathetic, compelling.

Gifts: *For her:* cell phone. *For him:* dartboard.

Sensual Foods: Champagne with strawberries; fillet of sole.

Romantic Flowers: You love it when you get tulips, declaring love. When you receive a variety, it shows how hopelessly in love your partner is. He will just love a single rose. This shows him you understand his pleasures.

Best Date Nights: Wednesday; 6th and 15th of each month.

Color of Passion: *For her:* pink, lavender. *For him:* white, red.

The Perfect Wedding: Vivacious and sophisticated, lively and diverse—these qualities apply to you and the day you plan. A garden cocktail party or huge banquet hall would work. A five-star hotel with plenty of amenities will ensure your guests have lots to do. Ideal setting: New York.

Wise Words: Henry Wadsworth Longfellow: "For evermore, for evermore, / The reign of violence is o'er!"

Hints of Love: This one is a cautious soul. You may have to find a way to go around to the back door.

After the Argument: *For him:* You know he is moody, so you first must find out how mad he is. The best thing for this one is to let him sit and stew for a while. Then when it comes to making up make sure he thinks it is his idea. There is a need for a lot of game playing with this one. He likes to feel he's the suave one. Let him believe he is. *For her:* This one is a little tricky. You have to have several plans; sometimes flowers will work, other times it will be love letters. Yet another time it may be a night out or even a romantic night in, with a romantic movie. This one can take a ton of work or none at all.

Romantic Places: Places of knowledge bring romance: Spain; a library; San Francisco, California.

Lucky Love Star: Geminiel—you will never lack commitment.

Beautiful Thought: Recognizing a miracle that has happened to you.

Sharing Secrets: This one is a charmer, perhaps even fickle. *For the gals:* If you are patient enough to stick around, this one is worth the wait. *For the guys:* If there is enough time on the clock, stick around past three months. Then maybe he will have noticed you are there.

Judith's Insights

About the Man: This guy is more loyal to others than you might think. He has a flighty type of nature. Not to worry, though, he will be able to settle down when he feels that he is ready. You will usually find him approachable and obtainable. This will come in handy if he is your boss or co-worker. He needs to be stimulated by others around him. His dance card must be full at all times. He might be the guy everyone assumes has plans so no one asks. Be the person to let him know that you are interested in a swing around the dance floor.

About the Woman: She is much more old-fashioned than you might think. She is constantly searching for someone to catch her so that she has a reason to clear her schedule. She wants something real, whether it is a friend or a lover. Where there is true love you will find her. She does not like to stay home unless there is a reason to be there. Cuddling by the fire is a great reason! She wants romance but will never let on how much. It is very important to treat her like she is the one and only, even early in the relationship.

Soul Mates: Another Gemini can be the picture-perfect partner for you. Aquarius and Cancer will only be a good idea if they are willing to love you for you and not try to change you. You might have doubts about Aries and Taurus at first. Just make sure you get to know them before any decisions are made. Everything you wished but never wanted to admit to will suddenly seem possible with Libra and Leo standing by your side. You may find yourself feeling like a limp dish towel after a day with Virgo and Pisces. Like a valley, a pairing with Sagittarius will have its ups and downs. The road with Scorpio and Capricorn is not without its bumps.

Most Charming Characteristics: Impulsive, loyal, sensitive.

Gifts: *For her:* surprise destination for the weekend. *For him:* a last-minute cruise.

Sensual Foods: Chocolates; poached salmon; flambé; filet mignon; potatoes.

Romantic Flowers: Send this girl sunflowers if you want her to know you adore her. You may even add some poppies for a splash of extravagance. His desire for sport and play will be understood when you send him hyacinth and geranium.

Best Date Nights: Wednesday; 15th and 24th of each month.

Colors of Passion: *For her:* pink, lavender. *For him:* white, red.

The Perfect Wedding: Vivacious and sophisticated, lively and diverse—these qualities apply to you and the day you plan. A garden cocktail party or huge banquet hall would work. A five-star hotel with plenty of amenities will ensure your guests have lots to do. Ideal setting: New York.

Wise Words: Ben Jonson: "Ill fortune never crushed that man whom good fortune deceived not. He knows not his own strength that hath not met adversity."

Hints of Love: Passion must be in the picture at all times or you could lose this one's attention quickly.

After the Argument: *For him:* You know he is moody, so you first must find out how mad he is. The best thing for this one is to let him sit and stew for a while. Then when it comes to making up

make sure he thinks it is his idea. There is a need for a lot of game playing with this one. He likes to feel he's the suave one. Let him believe he is. *For her:* This one is a little tricky. You have to have several plans; sometimes flowers will work, other times it will be love letters. Yet another time it may be a night out or even a romantic night in, with a romantic movie. This one can take a ton of work or none at all.

Romantic Places: Places of history bring romance: Greece; a shipyard; Philadelphia, Pennsylvania.

Lucky Love Star: Geminiel—you will never lack commitment.

Beautiful Thought: Taking a moment to have a moment.

Sharing Secrets: If you are looking for love, then you have found the right mate. *For the gals:* This one could be stubborn. It may take forever to get a relationship started, but it is as solid as they come. *For the guys:* Even when he is ready, he might not be willing and able. He will put you through more obstacles than any course. Be patient.

Judith's Insights

About the Man: He can come on way too strong if he is not careful. His lack of ability to be up-front may lead you to believe he is not interested when he is really looking for love. Keep in mind that if he is interested he will usually go about it the wrong way. He wants commitment more than anything and yet he lives as if he is all alone. He is searching for that unconditional love that can only come from his mother or his life partner. Make sure that he is doing the work necessary to make the relationship work.

About the Woman: She can be the best of the best when it comes to being a friend. When it comes to love, she tends to be a little confusing. She will dodge all of your subtle advances and then wonder why you don't ask her out. She is straight out of the book of contradictions. Talk straight and clearly so she will get your point. Misunderstandings are par for the course with her. When this happens, try not to be defensive. Let her know how much she means to you while you allay her fears. Always reinforce your commitment with affection.

JUNE 8

Soul Mates: All signs point to a great partnership with another Gemini. Make Aquarius and Cancer aware of your need to be loved for who you are and things will work out from there. Give Aries and Taurus time. You never know if the planets are in the right place. Libra and Leo will help you recognize how wonderful you have been all along. Daily living with Virgo and Pisces would prove to be difficult. You must decide if it is worth the work. It is either feast or famine with Sagittarius. There is no such thing as middle ground. Scorpio and Capricorn may leave you all shook up.

Most Charming Characteristics: Ambitious, shrewd, friendly.

Gifts: *For her:* dance classes. *For him:* language tapes.

Sensual Foods: Caviar; beef tenderloin; potatoes au gratin.

Romantic Flowers: Rhododendron will let her be on the lookout for trouble. Throw in some chrysanthemum and she'll know it is you she will be looking out for. Cactus will show him warmth. Yellow daffodil is a token of a good time had by all. Chivalry is not dead.

Best Date Nights: Wednesday; 8th and 17th of each month.

Colors of Passion: *For her:* pink, lavender. *For him:* white, red.

The Perfect Wedding: Vivacious and sophisticated, lively and diverse—these qualities apply to you and the day you plan. A garden cocktail party or huge banquet hall would work. A five-star hotel with plenty of amenities will ensure your guests have lots to do. Ideal setting: New York.

Wise Words: William Blake: "The countless gold of a merry heart, / The rubies and pearls of a loving eye, / The indolent never can bring to the mart, / Nor the secret hoard up in his treasury."

Hints of Love: A random act of kindness will go a long way with this one. What can you do for them today?

After the Argument: *For him:* You know he is moody, so you first must find out how mad he is. The best thing for this one is to let him sit and stew for a while. Then when it comes to making up

make sure he thinks it is his idea. There is a need for a lot of game playing with this one. He likes to feel he's the suave one. Let him believe he is. *For her:* This one is a little tricky. You have to have several plans; sometimes flowers will work, other times it will be love letters. Yet another time it may be a night out or even a romantic night in, with a romantic movie. This one can take a ton of work or none at all.

Romantic Places: Places of knowledge bring romance: Italy; a university; the Smithsonian Institution.

Lucky Love Star: Geminiel—you will never lack commitment.

Beautiful Thought: Opening your heart instead of your mouth.

Sharing Secrets: If you can hang around and give constant stimulation, this could be your mate. *For the gals:* She is always looking for the Exit sign. Don't show her where it is or she will be gone. *For the guys:* Fast car, fast food; he likes everything that goes fast. Put on your running shoes. If you can keep up, then he is yours.

Judith's Insights

About the Man: He is a shrewd guy who knows just how to work any room. He throws it on hard when someone just glances his way. You need to give him a healthy dose of stepping back occasionally. If you can do this, he won't be stepping where he shouldn't be. He is quite the observer and may have gotten the hint of your interest already. This, unfortunately, does not mean he will take the initiative. To him, life is an adventure. Part of this adventure is waiting to see what you will do with that interest.

About the Woman: She is willful, determined, and sensitive. This combination can make her seem harsh. It is simply her defense mechanism. There is a fun-loving gal in there somewhere. It will take a lot more than patience to let her come out. Let her know exactly what she means to you, and before you know it, you will have to try to keep up. Don't be offended when you find her immersed in a deep conversation across the room. This is vital to her stimulation. You may feel abandoned, but don't call her on it. She knows who she is going home with.

Soul Mates: With a fellow Gemini, you will have all of the variety you have ever wanted. Aquarius and Cancer must be told that you are not willing to change yourself and they have to accept you for who you are naturally. Aries and Taurus will help you keep both feet on the ground. You will achieve any goal you set for yourself with Libra and Leo in your corner. A building is only as strong as its foundation. The same is true for a relationship with Virgo and Pisces. Just when you have the pulse of the relationship, Sagittarius will change drastically. Scorpio and Capricorn are not recommended for the faint of heart.

Most Charming Characteristics: Charming, gracious, determined.

Gifts: *For her:* tickets to the ballet. *For him:* tickets to a dramatic play.

Sensual Foods: Passion fruit; fillet of sole almondine.

Romantic Flowers: The magnolias you send her will let her know you will be around for a while to come. Petunia is to say never despair. Holly will let him know what he is getting into. Pansy will keep you in his thoughts.

Best Date Nights: Wednesday; 9th and 18th of each month.

Colors of Passion: *For her:* pink, lavender. *For him:* white, red.

The Perfect Wedding: Vivacious and sophisticated, lively and diverse—these qualities apply to you and the day you plan. A garden cocktail party or huge banquet hall would work. A five-star hotel with plenty of amenities will ensure your guests have lots to do. Ideal setting: New York.

Wise Words: Charles Dickens: "Take nothing on its looks; take everything on evidence. There is no better rule."

Hints of Love: Family and friends are important to this one. Don't try to alienate them or it will definitely backfire on you.

After the Argument: *For him:* You know he is moody, so you first must find out how mad he is. The best thing for this one is to let him sit and stew for a while. Then when it comes to making up

make sure he thinks it is his idea. There is a need for a lot of game playing with this one. He likes to feel he's the suave one. Let him believe he is. *For her:* This one is a little tricky. You have to have several plans; sometimes flowers will work, other times it will be love letters. Yet another time it may be a night out or even a romantic night in, with a romantic movie. This one can take a ton of work or none at all.

Romantic Places: Places of knowledge bring romance: Oxford University; a museum; Rome, Italy.

Lucky Love Star: Geminiel—you will never lack commitment.

Beautiful Thought: Appreciating someone else's "thought."

Sharing Secrets: This one may seem like a lot of work. They just need the basics: love, loyalty, and respect. *For the gals:* If you can show her your best side right from the beginning it may work. Be careful of fluff, because she will see right through it. *For the guys:* He loves to be loved. Give him plenty of attention, even if you think you don't stand a chance. Perseverance will win here.

Judith's Insights

About the Man: *Fickle* is not the word here. He finds it hard to make his mind up about anything. If you need an answer right away, it will make the pressure that much worse. Give him time to mull things over in his brain and you will like the answer much more. Once he knows what he wants there is nothing he won't do to get it. He needs many people to talk and hang with. When he wants to hang with his friends don't take it as if he doesn't want to hang with you. Tag along and you will be surprised at how light and fun he can be in a crowd.

About the Woman: Matters of the heart have this gal confused before they are even brought up. She is not sure where her emotions will take her from day to day. You can help her lighten up with a little encouragement and a lot of patience. Once she is loose, then she can be the life of the party. The more people there are for her to talk with, the better mood she will be in. No matter how bad her day was, she will brighten up as soon as she has a crowd to entertain.

Soul Mates: Aries and Taurus will give you that sense of balance you are always looking for. Libra and Leo would certainly bring out the best in you. Virgo and Pisces might cause you a little insanity. It would truly take a deep connection for this match to work. When it comes to Sagittarius, it can be a double-edged sword. It can be the best of the best while also being the worst of the worst for you. Scorpio and Capricorn are a roller coaster with many wild turns and twists. Aquarius and Cancer must be able to accept you for who you are for this to work. A fellow Gemini would make a very interesting match. Two people with two sets of personalities is like having multiple partners.

Most Charming Characteristics: Venturesome, impulsive, love deeply.

Gifts: *For her:* language tapes. *For him:* magic set.

Sensual Foods: Peaches; mousse; shrimp.

Romantic Flowers: Iris is your flower if you are the gal sending subtle messages. If you are the man, you will look for clematis. This flower's mental beauty creates emotional stimulation for you.

Best Date Nights: Wednesday; 1st and 28th of each month.

Colors of Passion: *For her:* pink, lavender. *For him:* white, red.

The Perfect Wedding: Vivacious and sophisticated, lively and diverse—these qualities apply to you and the day you plan. A garden cocktail party or huge banquet hall would work. A five-star hotel with plenty of amenities will ensure your guests have lots to do. Ideal setting: New York.

Wise Words: Charles Dickens: "There are some people who can be merry and can't be wise, and there are some who can be wise (or think they can) and can't be merry."

Hints of Love: Show others how much you adore him or her. They will revel in how others notice.

After the Argument: *For him:* You know he is moody, so you first must find out how mad he is. The best thing for this one is to let him sit and stew for a while. Then when it comes to making up

make sure he thinks it is his idea. There is a need for a lot of game playing with this one. He likes to feel he's the suave one. Let him believe he is. *For her:* This one is a little tricky. You have to have several plans; sometimes flowers will work, other times it will be love letters. Yet another time it may be a night out or even a romantic night in, with a romantic movie. This one can take a ton of work or none at all.

Romantic Places: Places of history bring romance: Denmark; an Indian reservation; Fort Worth, Texas.

Lucky Love Star: Geminiel—you will never lack commitment.

Beautiful Thought: Taking a step toward the fear.

Sharing Secrets: They are looking for love, but that is just their little secret. *For the gals:* Why shouldn't they want to be loved? Of course they do, but they want you to do all of the work. *For the guys:* You must prove yourself repeatedly. Don't expect too much until he knows you are under his thumb.

Judith's Insights

About the Man: As restless as he may seem, he can learn to enjoy the comforts of home. He starts off any relationship dancing around it, including friendship. Sometimes he will feel interested, other times he will seem quite the opposite. If he is sticking around, you know he wants to be there. He won't let the grass grow under his feet unless there is something worth hanging around for. You have to get him interested and keep him interested to make sure his eyes don't wander around the room.

About the Woman: She isn't as needy as she seems to be. She lives in the past because that is where she feels safe. She has a lot of endurance when it comes to love, but you can be certain you will need to sweeten the pot from time to time. Make her feel safe and she will pull back less. If she is finding other things to fill her heart it is time to shake things up and bring something new to the table. Her attention fading is like a fire dying. You need to keep throwing wood on it for it to burn as long as you need to keep warm.

Soul Mates: With a fellow Gemini, you will feel as if you are dating many people and never have a reason to stray. Aquarius and Cancer must learn to value you for who you are for anything to work. Push Aries and Taurus off the couch and make sure they have plenty of playtime. Libra and Leo make you see all of the good in yourself. A match with Virgo and Pisces will run you ragged if you let it. Extreme is the name of the game with Sagittarius. Be prepared to go with the flow. If you take a ride with Scorpio and Capricorn, you had better put on your seat belt or you are liable to get thrown around.

Most Charming Characteristics: Congenial, intellectual, family oriented.

Gifts: *For her:* spur-of-the-moment getaway. *For him:* night out with the guys.

Sensual Foods: Kiwis; cantaloupes; strawberries.

Romantic Flowers: Any rose of any color for the lady. Roses stand for love regardless of the color. Send them with orchids and you will be saying, "I love you." If you want a gentleman to know you think of him, send pansies, and forget-me-nots for true love.

Best Date Nights: Wednesday; 11th and 29th of each month.

Colors of Passion: *For her:* pink, lavender. *For him:* white, red.

The Perfect Wedding: Vivacious and sophisticated, lively and diverse—these qualities apply to you and the day you plan. A garden cocktail party or huge banquet hall would work. A five-star hotel with plenty of amenities will ensure your guests have lots to do. Ideal setting: New York.

Wise Words: Confucius: "From a man's mouth may come forth sharp arrows to wound, and fiery brands to burn. Take good heed, then, that neither issue from your mouth to the injury of others."

Hints of Love: Don't overdo it (dress, attention) too soon or this one will run. Wait until you have them hooked before you become outrageous.

After the Argument: *For him:* You know he is moody, so you first must find out how mad he is.

The best thing for this one is to let him sit and stew for a while. Then when it comes to making up make sure he thinks it is his idea. There is a need for a lot of game playing with this one. He likes to feel he's the suave one. Let him believe he is. *For her:* This one is a little tricky. You have to have several plans; sometimes flowers will work, other times it will be love letters. Yet another time it may be a night out or even a romantic night in, with a romantic movie. This one can take a ton of work or none at all.

Romantic Places: Places of knowledge bring romance: Egypt; a poetry-and-quotes reading; Washington, D.C.

Lucky Love Star: Geminiel—you will never lack commitment.

Beautiful Thought: Humble is knowing your boundaries.

Sharing Secrets: You had better be ready to pull out your romantic side if you want this to work. *For the gals:* Fireplaces, walks on the beach, or even winning a bear at the local carnival. *For the guys:* When you are out shopping bring him something home. Even if it is silly, he will love the thought.

Judith's Insights

About the Man: He will overcomplicate each and every situation he gets into. This is especially true when it comes to matters of the heart. He will always take on too much work, and if it is not there, he will create it himself. At work, you may feel as if he is hogging the boss's attention. Even if you keep the path swept, he will clutter it up with emotional garbage. Getting involved with this guy takes a truly devoted personality. You have to want it to work and put in the time to make that happen.

About the Woman: She can talk herself into it one minute and out of it in the next minute. It is no wonder that you will feel like you are on a seesaw. If you feel like she is pulling away, stand back and wait. In a week or two, she will be charging back for more. She likes things to be complicated more than necessary. She wants to be in love, but when and with whom may take more time and patience that anyone has. Do you have what it takes?

Soul Mates: A relationship with another Gemini may give you the variety you crave while keeping you bonded to one person. If Aquarius and Cancer can accept you for who you are, then go for it. Aries and Taurus may baffle you with their settled ways, but they are not a bad thing for you to learn to appreciate. Libra and Leo draw out your greatest qualities and help you shine. Take on Virgo and Pisces only if you are in the mood to work your butt off. When things with Sagittarius are good, they are great, but when they are bad, they are downright ugly! If you like things fast and exciting, then you are going to love Scorpio and Capricorn.

Most Charming Characteristics: Artistic, affectionate, congenial.

Gifts: *For her:* fine writing paper. *For him:* travel journal.

Sensual Foods: Caramel and chocolate syrup on anything.

Romantic Flowers: These ladies like everyone to know how faithful they are, so send them violets. To surprise them send tulips. Men like their flowers the same as their relationships, unpretending. Send them camellias with white roses to show your affection.

Best Date Nights: Wednesday; 12th and 21st of each month.

Colors of Passion: *For her:* pink, lavender. *For him:* white, red.

The Perfect Wedding: Vivacious and sophisticated, lively and diverse—these qualities apply to you and the day you plan. A garden cocktail party or huge banquet hall would work. A five-star hotel with plenty of amenities will ensure your guests have lots to do. Ideal setting: New York.

Wise Words: Benjamin Franklin: "Do good to thy friend to keep them, to thy enemy to gain him."

Hints of Love: When these folks decide to sit on the fence, don't try to push them off before they are ready. Let them do the jumping themselves.

After the Argument: *For him:* You know he is moody, so you first must find out how mad he is. The best thing for this one is to let him sit and stew

for a while. Then when it comes to making up make sure he thinks it is his idea. There is a need for a lot of game playing with this one. He likes to feel he's the suave one. Let him believe he is. *For her:* This one is a little tricky. You have to have several plans; sometimes flowers will work, other times it will be love letters. Yet another time it may be a night out or even a romantic night in, with a romantic movie. This one can take a ton of work or none at all.

Romantic Places: Places of history bring romance: the Taj Mahal; a national monument; Gettysburg, Pennsylvania.

Lucky Love Star: Geminiel—you will never lack commitment.

Beautiful Thought: Putting two nickels together can create a dime.

Sharing Secrets: It may seem like they are not interested, but ask them out anyway. *For the gals:* Until they absolutely know you are interested, you will never find out that they are. *For the guys:* Ask him out if he doesn't ask you. He may be shy or not. Either way, he may be interested.

Judith's Insights

About the Man: He might get in your way as soon as he gets out of his. When he is ready to dig in, there is no one more dedicated. His lost-at-sea attitude may make it seem as if he would rather be alone. He simply can't find his way to shore yet. Break out the spotlight and guide him if you can. Have no fear, somewhere along the way he will learn to give more than he gets. Until then he may ask for more than his share. The time will come when you are rewarded for all the craziness you have had to put up with in this relationship.

About the Woman: She wants what she wants. When she finally gets to the point at which she figures out what it is, she will want it yesterday. She can be obvious about what makes her happy and what doesn't. It won't take much for you to figure it out. It will be staring you in the face. After she has sowed as many oats as possible and she is ready to settle in, her attitude toward love will be greatly improved. Until then she will resemble an untamed bull. You could get knocked around and bruised while trying to rope her.

Soul Mates: When looking for a compatible sign look no further than your own, Gemini. Make sure you don't change a thing for the benefit of Aquarius and Cancer. They will just have to accept you at face value. Your tendency to play fast and loose with the truth may have Aries and Taurus seeing red. Be careful of what comes out in haste. Libra and Leo will let you revel in your true and best self. If you truly get to know Virgo and Pisces it may work, but it may take a lot of elbow grease. Try to use the bad times with Sagittarius to appreciate the good times. You may come out bruised when you get together with Scorpio and Capricorn.

Most Charming Characteristics: Impulsive, energetic, loyal.

Gifts: *For her:* surprise party. *For him:* night out bowling.

Sensual Foods: Waffles with whipped cream; chocolate soufflé; French wine.

Romantic Flowers: These ladies like men with taste. Show them you love style by sending fuchsia flowers, or even brightly colored wildflowers will do. To confuse this man, send him lilies along with bright daisies to show your innocence. Keep him guessing.

Best Date Nights: Wednesday; 4th and 13th of each month.

Colors of Passion: *For her:* pink, lavender. *For him:* white, red.

The Perfect Wedding: Vivacious and sophisticated, lively and diverse—these qualities apply to you and the day you plan. A garden cocktail party or huge banquet hall would work. A five-star hotel with plenty of amenities will ensure your guests have lots to do. Ideal setting: New York.

Wise Words: Oliver Wendell Holmes: "Memory, imagination, old sentiments and associations are more readily reached through the sense of smell than by almost any other channel."

Hints of Love: Make sure you learn to compromise, but never with your principles.

After the Argument: *For him:* You know he is moody, so you first must find out how mad he is.

The best thing for this one is to let him sit and stew for a while. Then when it comes to making up make sure he thinks it is his idea. There is a need for a lot of game playing with this one. He likes to feel he's the suave one. Let him believe he is. *For her:* This one is a little tricky. You have to have several plans; sometimes flowers will work, other times it will be love letters. Yet another time it may be a night out or even a romantic night in, with a romantic movie. This one can take a ton of work or none at all.

Romantic Places: Places of knowledge bring romance: Israel; a planetarium; Baltimore, Maryland.

Lucky Love Star: Geminiel—you will never lack commitment.

Beautiful Thought: Someone goes out of their way for you and it changes your direction.

Sharing Secrets: Don't be surprised if the first date is with their family. *For the gals:* Make sure you invite her to your family functions. It will be a red flag to her if you don't. *For the guys:* He may seem like a family man, but isn't that what you were looking for?

Judith's Insights

About the Man: He loves to have it all. This is especially true at work. Even if he is an executive, he will be hanging out with everyone in the cafeteria. He can have the best social calendar in his group. Everyone knows his name because he makes sure that they do. He will also be great at remembering everyone else's name. It can be difficult to read between the lines when they are not parallel. He can keep you guessing at every step of the relationship. Life with him can be exciting or frustrating, depending on your point of view.

About the Woman: She is very good at putting her words on paper and into someone else's mouth. This is especially true when her heart is involved. You will have to find out how she feels by how she acts instead of by what she says. Many times, what she does say is the exact opposite of what her actions tell you. Even if she makes it to the altar, her partner may feel as if this fish is about to swim away. Don't pull back to make her stay. Just let her know exactly how you feel in clear and direct language.

Soul Mates: The many faces of you and another Gemini will prove to be a fun-filled adventure. Aquarius and Cancer can only change what you let them change. Try to get them to accept who and what you are instead. Aries and Taurus will be the perfect places to turn when you need direction. Libra and Leo bring to light all of the goodness that was there all along, but you couldn't see. When the day with Virgo and Pisces is over you may be too tired to continue. One minute Sagittarius has you in the clouds, the next minute you will feel stuck to the floor. Scorpio and Cancer may leave you a bit bruised and broken when all is said and done.

Most Charming Characteristics: Generous, considerate, reliable.

Gifts: *For her:* tuition to a class. *For him:* latest gadget.

Sensual Foods: Oysters; mussels; spicy foods.

Romantic Flowers: You are the lady of distinction, and only carnations will do. Any mix of colors with sprays of mignonette. Sweet peas or red carnations will appeal to this man's heart.

Best Date Nights: Wednesday; 4th and 5th of each month.

Colors of Passion: *For her:* pink, lavender. *For him:* white, red.

The Perfect Wedding: Vivacious and sophisticated, lively and diverse—these qualities apply to you and the day you plan. A garden cocktail party or huge banquet hall would work. A five-star hotel with plenty of amenities will ensure your guests have lots to do. Ideal setting: New York.

Wise Words: Charles Dickens: "Who doubts that if we did our duty as faithful as the soldier does his, this world would be a better place?"

Hints of Love: If you try to take a step back, it will be noticed. It could create the domino effect, and everything will start to fall.

After the Argument: *For him:* You know he is moody, so you first must find out how mad he is. The best thing for this one is to let him sit and stew for a while. Then when it comes to making up make sure he thinks it is his idea. There is a need

for a lot of game playing with this one. He likes to feel he's the suave one. Let him believe he is. *For her:* This one is a little tricky. You have to have several plans; sometimes flowers will work, other times it will be love letters. Yet another time it may be a night out or even a romantic night in, with a romantic movie. This one can take a ton of work or none at all.

Romantic Places: Places of history bring romance: Scotland; a science museum; Williamsburg, Virginia.

Lucky Love Star: Geminiel—you will never lack commitment.

Beautiful Thought: Peace is contagious.

Sharing Secrets: Take me as I am could be the anthem for this one. *For the gals:* They will have strong views on just about everything. If you can hang with them, then nothing will be as important as you. *For the guys:* The thing you fall in love with may end up becoming the thing you hate. After a commitment, this one sticks around.

Judith's Insights

About the Man: He can be a real pain in the neck, especially when he does not know what it is he wants. He will be inconsistent, arrogant, and very distracted. He is still capable of being charming underneath all of his indecision. You just have to have patience long enough to find out. He can be more interested in having a great time than having a great love when he is younger. When he starts to grow and mature he will realize that he best times are had when he has his true love by his side. When he finds that love there will be none more devoted than this guy.

About the Woman: She can be known for her candor and honesty. She does not want to feel obligated to anyone. She needs her freedom, so don't try to lasso her in. If you have the diligence to stick around long enough for her to be ready to decide what she wants, you will be pleasantly surprised. You may find that she puts only half a foot forward instead of her best foot forward until she knows for sure that you are interested. Once she is sure that she wants more than friendship, you may be bowled over by the effort she puts into winning you over.

Soul Mates: No one can understand your varied personality quite like a fellow Gemini. If Aquarius and Cancer love you for who you are, you will do the same for them. If love doesn't work out for you and Aries or Taurus, then friendship is a definite possibility. Libra and Leo will help you reach new heights faster than you ever thought possible. A pairing with Virgo and Pisces is not advised for those with weak constitutions. It will take a lot out of you. A relationship with Sagittarius is one of wild extremes. You will get along famously or not at all. Scorpio and Cancer are an accident waiting to happen.

Most Charming Characteristics: Intellectual, diligent, sociable.

Gifts: *For her:* cell phone. *For him:* dartboard.

Sensual Foods: Lobster; watermelon.

Romantic Flowers: You love it when you get tulips, declaring love. When you receive a variety, it shows how hopelessly in love your partner is. He will just love a single rose. This shows him you understand his pleasures.

Best Date Nights: Wednesday; 6th and 15th of each month.

Colors of Passion: *For her:* pink, lavender. *For him:* white, red.

The Perfect Wedding: Vivacious and sophisticated, lively and diverse—these qualities apply to you and the day you plan. A garden cocktail party or huge banquet hall would work. A five-star hotel with plenty of amenities will ensure your guests have lots to do. Ideal setting: New York.

Wise Words: Charles Dickens: "Fashions are like human beings. They come in, nobody knows when, why, or how; and then they go out, nobody knows when, why, or how. Everything is like life, in my opinion, if you look at it in that point of view."

Hints of Love: Consistence and persistence will get this prize every time. They will value the effort.

After the Argument: *For him:* You know he is moody, so you first must find out how mad he is. The best thing for this one is to let him sit and stew for a while. Then when it comes to making up make sure he thinks it is his idea. There is a need

for a lot of game playing with this one. He likes to feel he's the suave one. Let him believe he is. *For her:* This one is a little tricky. You have to have several plans; sometimes flowers will work, other times it will be love letters. Yet another time it may be a night out or even a romantic night in, with a romantic movie. This one can take a ton of work or none at all.

Romantic Places: Places of knowledge bring romance: Spain; a library; San Francisco, California.

Lucky Love Star: Geminiel—you will never lack commitment.

Beautiful Thought: Every thought is the opportunity to learn.

Sharing Secrets: They seem moody until you get to know them. *For the gals:* You may not know whether to say hello or drop dead. As relations progress you will learn not to leave her dangling, and her moods will become more consistent. *For the guys:* To know him is to love him. His bark is much worse than his bite. He just wants someone to love him without criticism.

Judith's Insights

About the Man: He is a guy who wants to have fun, flirt, and live out plenty of fantasies. He can lack patience, but never affection or tolerance. His imagination can make every encounter with him an adventure. Life with him can be fun as long as you take it for what it is. Don't try to make him serious. He will become moody and angry if he is weighed down before he asks to be. He can be the best friend in the world to have as long as he is given the room to fly around as he likes. He is looking for the perfect person to make the promise of a lifetime to.

About the Woman: She has many hidden talents, including juggling her life and her emotions. She can be a great boss or co-worker as long as you don't try to get personal. She sees no need to mix business and pleasure. Her emotions are like a fast train running through an obstacle course. She is not as superficial as she may seem at first glance. As time goes by, you will learn to see her best qualities. These qualities will rise to the top, and you will watch as she becomes unselfish and more affectionate.

Soul Mates: Another Gemini can be the picture-perfect partner for you. Aquarius and Cancer will only be a good idea if they are willing to love you for you and not try to change you. You might have doubts about Aries and Taurus at first. Just make sure you get to know them before any decisions are made. Everything you wished but never wanted to admit to will suddenly seem possible with Libra and Leo standing by your side. You may find yourself feeling like a limp dish towel after a day with Virgo and Pisces. Like a valley, a pairing with Sagittarius will have its ups and downs. The road with Scorpio and Capricorn is not without its bumps.

Most Charming Characteristics: Independent, affectionate, sincere.

Gifts: *For her:* surprise destination for the weekend. *For him:* a last-minute cruise.

Sensual Foods: Strawberries, truffles; shish kebab.

Romantic Flowers: Send this girl sunflowers if you want her to know you adore her. You may even add some poppies for a splash of extravagance. His desire for sport and play will be understood when you send him hyacinth and geranium.

Best Date Nights: Wednesday; 2nd and 6th of each month.

Colors of Passion: *For her:* pink, lavender. *For him:* white, red.

The Perfect Wedding: Vivacious and sophisticated, lively and diverse—these qualities apply to you and the day you plan. A garden cocktail party or huge banquet hall would work. A five-star hotel with plenty of amenities will ensure your guests have lots to do. Ideal setting: New York.

Wise Words: Charles Dickens: "The will to do well . . . is the next thing to having the power."

Hints of Love: Be funny. Laughter will be what keeps this one coming back again and again.

After the Argument: *For him:* You know he is moody, so you first must find out how mad he is. The best thing for this one is to let him sit and stew for a while. Then when it comes to making up

make sure he thinks it is his idea. There is a need for a lot of game playing with this one. He likes to feel he's the suave one. Let him believe he is. *For her:* This one is a little tricky. You have to have several plans; sometimes flowers will work, other times it will be love letters. Yet another time it may be a night out or even a romantic night in, with a romantic movie. This one can take a ton of work or none at all.

Romantic Places: Places of history bring romance: Greece; a shipyard; Philadelphia, Pennsylvania.

Lucky Love Star: Geminiel—you will never lack commitment.

Beautiful Thought: Understanding is the key to communicating.

Sharing Secrets: You had better be able to put your money where your mouth is. *For the gals:* It doesn't need to be lavish, but she does love the loot. The more the better. *For the guys:* He doesn't mind spending his hard-earned cash, but he loves to see you contribute to please him.

Judith's Insights

About the Man: Remember that actions speak much louder than words. For this guy, it may take some time for his actions to even take place. At first, he can seem removed, or even lost. As time passes his disinterest will fade and good actions and a better temperament will emerge. He can only enter a room when he knows where the exits are. He is frightened of getting stuck in a situation that he can't get out of. This is why he is so slow to commit. He knows that once he makes that promise he never wants to break it.

About the Woman: If she stays long enough for you to take her for granted, you may have won yourself a long-lasting relationship. She will keep her distance, but will always show you all the respect that she can. She makes a great boss because she never picks favorites. This gal plays fair and square at all costs. She needs to know that there is a way out of a bad situation just in case. It may take time to nail her down to matrimony. Even after the vows, she will let you know that she could always leave if she needed to.

Soul Mates: All signs point to a great partnership with another Gemini. Make Aquarius and Cancer aware of your need to be loved for who you are and things will work out from there. Give Aries and Taurus time. You never know if the planets are in the right place. Libra and Leo will help you recognize how wonderful you have been all along. Daily living with Virgo and Pisces would prove to be difficult. You must decide if it is worth the work. It is either feast or famine with Sagittarius. There is no such thing as middle ground. Scorpio and Capricorn may leave you all shook up.

Most Charming Characteristics: Artistic, loving, entertaining.

Gifts: *For her:* dance classes. *For him:* language tapes.

Sensual Foods: Grapes; fine cheeses and crackers; taffy.

Romantic Flowers: Rhododendron will let her be on the lookout for trouble. Throw in some chrysanthemum and she'll know it is you she will be looking out for. Cactus will show him warmth. Yellow daffodil is a token of a good time had by all. Chivalry is not dead.

Best Date Nights: Wednesday; 8th and 17th of each month.

Colors of Passion: *For her:* pink, lavender. *For him:* white, red.

The Perfect Wedding: Vivacious and sophisticated, lively and diverse—these qualities apply to you and the day you plan. A garden cocktail party or huge banquet hall would work. A five-star hotel with plenty of amenities will ensure your guests have lots to do. Ideal setting: New York.

Wise Words: Robert Louis Stevenson: "With our chosen friends, and still more between lovers, the truth is easily indicated by the one and aptly comprehended by the other."

Hints of Love: Treat this one like royalty or precious cargo. They will love being valued in this way.

After the Argument: *For him:* You know he is moody, so you first must find out how mad he is. The best thing for this one is to let him sit and stew for a while. Then when it comes to making up make sure he thinks it is his idea. There is a need for a lot of game playing with this one. He likes to feel he's the suave one. Let him believe he is. *For her:* This one is a little tricky. You have to have several plans; sometimes flowers will work, other times it will be love letters. Yet another time it may be a night out or even a romantic night in, with a romantic movie. This one can take a ton of work or none at all.

Romantic Places: Places of knowledge bring romance: Italy; a university; the Smithsonian Institution.

Lucky Love Star: Geminiel—you will never lack commitment.

Beautiful Thought: Open arms are there to let you in, not to block the road.

Sharing Secrets: Nobody likes a weak link, especially not this one. *For the gals:* Make sure you treat her like a lady and act like a man. *For the guys:* Put your best foot forward. Dress your best and keep your manners in check. This man notices.

Judith's Insights

About the Man: He needs to receive all of the attention that he can get. He wants everyone to notice him, even if they are only noticing his tie. He has his own style and sometimes his very own language. He may have to learn how to read minds to keep up with how people view him. His mind changes constantly. He may not be hard to please, but he is certainly hard to catch. He feels that if he keeps moving he can't be caught in a mess he never saw. Even when you have caught him, it takes a lot of energy and imagination to keep him from flying the coop.

About the Woman: She can be a tough boss, but that is only when you are not doing your job. This follows for all of her relationships. You had better be able to step up to the plate or it will be the door she shows you, instead of her inner thoughts. Once the door shuts on you, there is no getting back in. You not only need to be creative, you need to outthink this gal if you want to get her to commit to a relationship. This is easier said than done because she never stops thinking. She may be thinking about how to escape, so stay one step ahead of her.

Soul Mates: With a fellow Gemini, you will have all of the variety you have ever wanted. Aquarius and Cancer must be told that you are not willing to change yourself and they have to accept you for who you are naturally. Aries and Taurus will help you keep both feet on the ground. You will achieve any goal you set for yourself with Libra and Leo in your corner. A building is only as strong as its foundation. The same is true for a relationship with Virgo and Pisces. Just when you have the pulse of the relationship, Sagittarius will change drastically. Scorpio and Capricorn are not recommended for the faint of heart.

Most Charming Characteristics: Modest, charming, sensitive.

Gifts: *For her:* tickets to the ballet. *For him:* tickets to a dramatic play.

Sensual Foods: Champagne; grapes; mangoes; filet mignon.

Romantic Flowers: The magnolias you send her will let her know you will be around for a while to come. Petunia is to say never despair. Holly will let him know what he is getting into. Pansy will keep you in his thoughts.

Best Date Nights: Wednesday; 9th and 18th of each month.

Colors of Passion: *For her:* pink, lavender. *For him:* white, red.

The Perfect Wedding: Vivacious and sophisticated, lively and diverse—these qualities apply to you and the day you plan. A garden cocktail party or huge banquet hall would work. A five-star hotel with plenty of amenities will ensure your guests have lots to do. Ideal setting: New York.

Wise Words: Robert Louis Stevenson: "A man finds a woman admire him where it is only for his acquaintance with geography, he will begin at once to build upon the admiration."

Hints of Love: Affection is important, but only if it comes naturally. Otherwise, the sirens will go off.

After the Argument: *For him:* You know he is moody, so you first must find out how mad he is. The best thing for this one is to let him sit and stew for a while. Then when it comes to making up

make sure he thinks it is his idea. There is a need for a lot of game playing with this one. He likes to feel he's the suave one. Let him believe he is. *For her:* This one is a little tricky. You have to have several plans; sometimes flowers will work, other times it will be love letters. Yet another time it may be a night out or even a romantic night in, with a romantic movie. This one can take a ton of work or none at all.

Romantic Places: Places of knowledge bring romance: Oxford University; a museum; Rome, Italy.

Lucky Love Star: Geminiel—you will never lack commitment.

Beautiful Thought: Laughter is the first sign that happiness could be right behind.

Sharing Secrets: Attention, attention, attention. *For the gals:* Do it any way you can. Presents, phone calls, cards, or flowers. Whatever works for you will work for her. *For the guys:* He would love nostalgic gifts or T-shirts. He also likes phone calls, as long as they don't interrupt his favorite pastimes.

Judith's Insights

About the Man: If you were looking for trouble, then you have found it here. He can drive you crazy with his inconsistent, erratic, and sometimes downright selfish behavior. He does not know how to make up his mind about anything. You will be surprised at what happens when he falls. He will become a horse of a different color. When he has found what he really wants there will be no diverting him from catching it. Make the chase exciting and he will want it even more. Even after he has gotten the prize, excitement must be part of the package for him to hang on to it.

About the Woman: There is never enough time in this gal's life to do all that she needs to get done. At work or at play, she is constantly busy. Wait until the dust has settled around her before you approach her with any serious talk. This includes raises, dates, and any of your needs at all. She loves her home and all of the beautiful things inside. She likes her relationships to be impulsive and exciting. If she gives you an opportunity to show her what you are made of, you have to be up to the challenge. You may have passed the first test but there will be more.

Soul Mates: Aries and Taurus will give you that sense of balance you are always looking for. Libra and Leo would certainly bring out the best in you. Virgo and Pisces might cause you a little insanity. It would truly take a deep connection for this match to work. When it comes to Sagittarius, it can be a double-edged sword. It can be the best of the best while also being the worst of the worst for you. Scorpio and Capricorn are a roller coaster with many wild turns and twists. Aquarius and Cancer must be able to accept you for who you are for this to work. A fellow Gemini would make a very interesting match. Two people with two sets of personalities is like having multiple partners.

Most Charming Characteristics: Retiring, loving, sympathetic.

Gifts: *For her:* language tapes. *For him:* magic set.

Sensual Foods: Châteaubriand; crème brûlée.

Romantic Flowers: Iris is your flower if you are the gal sending subtle messages. If you are the man, you will look for clematis. This flower's mental beauty creates emotional stimulation for you.

Best Date Nights: Wednesday; 1st and 28th of each month.

Colors of Passion: *For her:* pink, lavender. *For him:* green, red.

The Perfect Wedding: Vivacious and sophisticated, lively and diverse—these qualities apply to you and the day you plan. A garden cocktail party or huge banquet hall would work. A five-star hotel with plenty of amenities will ensure your guests have lots to do. Ideal setting: New York.

Wise Words: Robert Louis Stevenson: "There is a fellowship more quiet even than solitude, and which, rightly understood, is solitude made perfect."

Hints of Love: This one likes others to make his or her dreams come true. Be the "fantasy" fulfiller.

After the Argument: *For him:* You know he is moody, so you first must find out how mad he is. The best thing for this one is to let him sit and stew for a while. Then when it comes to making up

make sure he thinks it is his idea. There is a need for a lot of game playing with this one. He likes to feel he's the suave one. Let him believe he is. *For her:* This one is a little tricky. You have to have several plans; sometimes flowers will work, other times it will be love letters. Yet another time it may be a night out or even a romantic night in, with a romantic movie. This one can take a ton of work or none at all.

Romantic Places: Places of history bring romance: Denmark; an Indian reservation; Fort Worth, Texas.

Lucky Love Star: Geminiel—you will never lack commitment.

Beautiful Thought: Excuses work only if they are believable.

Sharing Secrets: Make sure you are not the killjoy. *For the gals:* When she has an idea, try it before you decide you don't like it. She needs to be pleased. *For the guys:* Do the things he loves to do and he will make the things you love ten times more fun.

Judith's Insights

About the Man: This boy just wants to have fun. He is very easy to approach, even by strangers. He is open to anyone and everyone. It won't take much more than a few compliments to get this guy to join you for coffee. Once he is there, however, he will leave it up to you and your ability to keep him interested. Once he comes to terms with the fact that he really wants to be in love it is all downhill from there. Getting to that point is where the work will come in. He won't be caught before his time no matter how hard you try.

About the Woman: She may be your most enjoyable experience in a while. This gal always carries her dancing shoes. It might not seem like it, but this gal is a one-relationship gal. She just loves to have a good time whether she is attached or not. She keeps her calendar full of lucky contenders. To stand out you must keep her attention. Don't forget compliments. Flattery will get you everywhere with her. Just make sure that the compliments are sincere and not just fluff for her ears. She can tell the difference.

Soul Mates: With a fellow Gemini, you will feel as if you are dating many people and never have a reason to stray. Aquarius and Cancer must learn to value you for who you are for anything to work. Push Aries and Taurus off the couch and make sure they have plenty of playtime. Libra and Leo make you see all of the good in yourself. A match with Virgo and Pisces will run you ragged if you let it. Extreme is the name of the game with Sagittarius. Be prepared to go with the flow. If you take a ride with Scorpio and Capricorn, you had better put on your seat belt or you are liable to get thrown around.

Most Charming Characteristics: Original, intense, generous.

Gifts: *For her:* spur-of-the-moment getaway. *For him:* night out with the guys.

Sensual Foods: Shrimp; sinful chocolate cake.

Romantic Flowers: Any rose of any color for the lady. Roses stand for love regardless of the color. Send them with orchids and you will be saying, "I love you." If you want a gentleman to know you think of him, send pansies, and forget-me-nots for true love.

Best Date Nights: Wednesday; 11th and 20th of each month.

Colors of Passion: *For her:* pink, lavender. *For him:* white, red.

The Perfect Wedding: Vivacious and sophisticated, lively and diverse—these qualities apply to you and the day you plan. A garden cocktail party or huge banquet hall would work. A five-star hotel with plenty of amenities will ensure your guests have lots to do. Ideal setting: New York.

Wise Words: Robert Louis Stevenson: "Bugles, and drums, and fifes, are of themselves most excellent things in Nature; and when they carry the mind to marching armies and the picturesque vicissitudes of war, they stir up something proud in heart."

Hints of Love: Stop worrying about next week's date today or there will not be one tomorrow.

After the Argument: *For him:* You know he is moody, so you first must find out how mad he is. The best thing for this one is to let him sit and stew for a while. Then when it comes to making up make sure he thinks it is his idea. There is a need for a lot of game playing with this one. He likes to feel he's the suave one. Let him believe he is. *For her:* This one is a little tricky. You have to have several plans; sometimes flowers will work, other times it will be love letters. Yet another time it may be a night out or even a romantic night in, with a romantic movie. This one can take a ton of work or none at all.

Romantic Places: Places of knowledge bring romance: Egypt; a poetry-and-quotes reading; Washington, D.C.

Lucky Love Star: Geminiel—you will never lack commitment.

Beautiful Thought: If you listen to the music, you learn to create your own words.

Sharing Secrets: You had better be ready to have a relationship. *For the gals:* No lies, no games, and no mistakes. She wants what she wants with as little work possible. *For the guys:* If you have games on your mind, then move on. This one likes fun any way he can get it, but no emotional roller coasters.

Judith's Insights

About the Man: Shower him with love, attention, and gifts, and he will be begging for more. If that does not get this guy's attention, then nothing will. Since there are many people vying for his attention, you must be creative. Try new techniques to keep his eyes on you and your actions. Give him your heart and soul and you will have him eating out of your hand. He will never step on you after you have revealed your feelings to him. If he is not ready to say the same things he will simply pretend he never heard them at all.

About the Woman: Even the finest jewels will not do if you do not give of yourself. She needs to feel your presence in her life. She makes a critical co-worker and a challenging boss. It can be easier than you think to get on her good side. You just need to put in the effort. She will notice and appreciate it when you make time to help her and understand her point of view. Everything you bring to her must be sweet. Sweet food, sweet words, and sweet moments will be the only things that will do. She can be all that you imagine as long as you are all that you can be.

Soul Mates: A relationship with another Gemini may give you the variety you crave while keeping you bonded to one person. If Aquarius and Cancer can accept you for who you are, then go for it. Aries and Taurus may baffle you with their settled ways, but they are not a bad thing for you to learn to appreciate. Libra and Leo draw out your greatest qualities and help you shine. Take on Virgo and Pisces only if you are in the mood to work your butt off. When things with Sagittarius are good, they are great, but when they are bad, they are downright ugly! If you like things fast and exciting, then you are going to love Scorpio and Capricorn.

Most Charming Characteristics: Congenial, even-tempered, witty.

Gifts: *For her:* fine writing paper. *For him:* travel journal.

Sensual Foods: Toasted marshmallows; chocolates.

Romantic Flowers: These ladies like everyone to know how faithful they are, so send them violets. To surprise them send tulips. Men like their flowers the same as their relationships, unpretending. Send them camellias with white roses to show your affection.

Best Date Nights: Wednesday; 3rd and 21st of each month.

Colors of Passion: *For her:* indigo, lavender. *For him:* white, red.

The Perfect Wedding: Vivacious and sophisticated, lively and diverse—these qualities apply to you and the day you plan. A garden cocktail party or huge banquet hall would work. A five-star hotel with plenty of amenities will ensure your guests have lots to do. Ideal setting: New York.

Wise Words: Robert Louis Stevenson: "A good talk is not to be had for the asking. Humors must first be accorded in a kind of overture or prologue."

Hints of Love: Keep the romance in the picture. Don't forget the long walks on the beach and camping out in front of the fireplace.

After the Argument: *For him:* You know he is moody, so you first must find out how mad he is. The best thing for this one is to let him sit and stew for a while. Then when it comes to making up make sure he thinks it is his idea. There is a need for a lot of game playing with this one. He likes to feel he's the suave one. Let him believe he is. *For her:* This one is a little tricky. You have to have several plans; sometimes flowers will work, other times it will be love letters. Yet another time it may be a night out or even a romantic night in, with a romantic movie. This one can take a ton of work or none at all.

Romantic Places: Places of history bring romance: the Taj Mahal; a national monument; Gettysburg, Pennsylvania.

Lucky Love Star: Geminiel—you will never lack commitment.

Beautiful Thought: Watching someone else's dreams come true should encourage you to start yours.

Sharing Secrets: You may have to give this one more than one chance. *For the gals:* Intriguing as she is, expect a handful. She lightens up as time goes on. *For the guys:* His quirks may make you have second thoughts, but that is what separates the men from the boys.

Judith's Insights

About the Man: He wants you to be loyal until it hurts. Expect to prove it on a continuous basis. You must be able to supply proof every time. He can be cynical, especially in the beginning. He comes on much cockier than he could ever be. Don't let that fool you. He is a teddy bear if you can get past that. This guy is the most loyal yet the most flirtatious person there is. Talk about a contradiction. He just needs more stimulation than most people to keep from getting bored. If he is paying attention somewhere else you can always get it back with a compliment or two.

About the Woman: Appeal to her needs at every turn. Approach her by offering her a helping hand wherever she may need it. She wants to know that you went out of your way for her. Expect that you will do all of the driving or all of the work. If you can go the distance, then she will lock on to you instantly. This relationship can be the best of the best and the worst of the worst all rolled up in one. The key is to make the time to treat her with the love she craves and deserves while bracing for the rocky road ahead if she misunderstands your intentions.

Soul Mates: When looking for a compatible sign look no further than your own, Gemini. Make sure you don't change a thing for the benefit of Aquarius and Cancer. They will just have to accept you at face value. Your tendency to play fast and loose with the truth may have Aries and Taurus seeing red. Be careful of what comes out in haste. Libra and Leo will let you revel in your true and best self. If you truly get to know Virgo and Pisces it may work, but it may take a lot of elbow grease. Try to use the bad times with Sagittarius to appreciate the good times. You may come out bruised when you get together with Scorpio and Capricorn.

Most Charming Characteristics: Sensitive, amusing, adventurous.

Gifts: *For her:* antique brooch. *For him:* antique writing desk.

Sensual Foods: Chocolate-covered strawberries; New York steak; scallops.

Romantic Flowers: These ladies like men with taste. Show them you love style by sending fuchsia flowers, or even brightly colored wildflowers will do. To confuse this man, send him lilies along with bright daisies to show your innocence. Keep him guessing.

Best Date Nights: Monday; 4th and 13th of each month.

Colors of Passion: *For her:* lavender, indigo. *For him:* green, white.

The Perfect Wedding: You are inexplicably attracted to the water, so it's no wonder you and yours should spend your special day there. A romantic seashore, a marina, a cruise ship, even an aquarium or seaport should be among the first locations to consider. You demand security and love the domestic life that may lead to a serene bed-and-breakfast wedding overlooking a body of water. Ideal setting: Venice.

Wise Words: Robert Louis Stevenson: "In the closest of all relations—that of love well founded and equally shared—speech is half discarded."

Hints of Love: The mystery is important, but being evasive will create disaster. Make sure you know the difference.

After the Argument: *For him:* Do whatever he wants done around the house or make him a home-cooked meal. Make sure you are really productive. *For her:* Do things you usually hate to do for her. She is sure to notice your socks in the hamper instead of on the floor and appreciate it immensely.

Romantic Places: Places of comfort bring romance: Ireland; a bed-and-breakfast; Key West, Florida.

Lucky Love Star: Cancriel—you will never lack love or domestic comfort.

Beautiful Thought: Detours can change the direction but not the destination.

Sharing Secrets: Talk about high maintenance. *For the gals:* Once she sees that you go out of your way for her, then she will for you. *For the guys:* The bark is definitely much worse than the bite. He comes on stronger and more obstinate than he actually is.

Judith's Insights

About the Man: Once you can get pass the "crabby" side, the rest should be easy. There is no problem approaching this guy, but it will probably be him doing the approaching. Just pay him a compliment or two and see where he takes it. Once you are on his mind he will want you to do the work to keep yourself there. If he is in a relationship he is usually happy. He likes to be in love. He might not want to put in his share of the work to keep the relationship afloat. If you begin to feel as if you are a prize he is bored with, you should pull back so he remembers why he wanted you there in the first place.

About the Woman: She doesn't like being alone. So it may be hard to figure out if she likes you or if you're just filling in the gap until she meets someone more interesting. Well, only time will tell. But once she starts moving the furniture in your house, you know she is comfortable with you. It may take that long to be sure. Once she is comfortable enough to open up to you there is no telling how far she would go to keep you happy and the relationship harmonious. She will greet every challenge with the enthusiasm that is typical of her nature.

Soul Mates: You and another Cancer will be like peanut butter and jelly. You are made for each other. Leo and Libra are wonderful friends for you, but love is not advised. Taurus craves stability. Don't let that pull you to a screeching halt. Just try to get them moving instead. Capricorn and Aries are more than you can handle. Scorpio and Pisces will have emotions overflowing. Things with Virgo and Aquarius are more than you bargained for. You will experience life as never before when you are linked to Sagittarius. You simply have to be open to it. Gemini must be loved for all they are instead of all you want them to be.

Most Charming Characteristics: Enthusiastic, loving, domestic.

Gifts: *For her:* family tree. *For him:* framed picture of his family.

Sensual Foods: Vanilla and strawberry mousse; tiramisù; espresso.

Romantic Flowers: You are the lady of distinction, and only carnations will do. Any mix of colors with sprays of mignonette. Sweet peas or red carnations will appeal to this man's heart.

Best Date Nights: Monday; 5th and 23rd of each month.

Colors of Passion: *For her:* orange, indigo. *For him:* red, russet.

The Perfect Wedding: You are inexplicably attracted to the water, so it's no wonder you and yours should spend your special day there. A romantic seashore, a marina, a cruise ship, even an aquarium or seaport should be among the first locations to consider. You demand security and love the domestic life that may lead to a serene bed-and-breakfast wedding overlooking a body of water. Ideal setting: Venice.

Wise Words: Robert Louis Stevenson: "As, when in the days of summer, through open windows, the fly swift as a breeze and loud as a trump goes by."

Hints of Love: If you learn to back up when things are moving too fast, you won't have to bow out so often.

After the Argument: *For him:* Do whatever he wants done around the house or make him a home-cooked meal. Make sure you are really productive. *For her:* Do things you usually hate to do for her. She is sure to notice your socks in the hamper instead of on the floor and appreciate it immensely.

Romantic Places: Places of leisure bring romance: Bermuda; a spa; Myrtle Beach, South Carolina.

Lucky Love Star: Cancriel—you will never lack love or domestic comfort.

Beautiful Thought: In relationships, friendship is not the consolation prize, it is the prize.

Sharing Secrets: Make sure you have at least five dates before you make up your mind. *For the gals:* They can be cynical, so it could be a few dates before she loosens up. *For the guys:* He still has yesterday on his mind. He needs a reason to forget his past relationship. Make a new history for him.

Judith's Insights

About the Man: You may find your way into his heart quicker than into his head. He won't give you too much information about his past until he believes you'll be in his future. If at first you don't succeed with him, try, and try again. He will be sure to notice the persistence if nothing else. Be consistent and ready to connect and you will do fine here. He likes for things to be uncomplicated, so don't bring up past fights that have been reconciled already. Fighting just for the sake of fighting will make him get right up and leave.

About the Woman: Her love is loyal and her emotions are extremely sensitive. She wants someone who is ready for love. No games are allowed to be played on her turf, unless she is orchestrating them herself. Keep things as simple as they can be and she will appreciate it immensely. She doesn't mind a night at home watching movies as long as you don't forget the popcorn. You may find yourself being the one who does all of the planning for dates and events. She is there to have a good time, not decide when, where, and how things should be.

Soul Mates: Cancer with a Cancer is a perfect match. Leo and Libra are for leaning on instead of loving. Taurus could bore you. Try to teach them to add some excitement to their life. Capricorn and Aries are in love with control. Make sure you are ready to give it up or walk away. Watch out for mood swings with Scorpio and Pisces. The right attitude is essential when you are dealing with Virgo and Aquarius. It can make all the difference. When you are linked with Sagittarius, there is the potential of great things happening if you can go with the flow. Gemini will love you forever if you can love them for all that they are.

Most Charming Characteristics: Decisive, determined, love deeply.

Gifts: *For her:* home-cooked meal. *For him:* antique painting.

Sensual Foods: Raspberries; pound cake; caviar.

Romantic Flowers: You love it when you get tulips, declaring love. When you receive a variety, it shows how hopelessly in love your partner is. He will just love a single rose. This shows him you understand his pleasures.

Best Date Nights: Monday; 6th and 15th of each month.

Colors of Passion: *For her:* orange, indigo. *For him:* green, russet.

The Perfect Wedding: You are inexplicably attracted to the water, so it's no wonder you and yours should spend your special day there. A romantic seashore, a marina, a cruise ship, even an aquarium or seaport should be among the first locations to consider. You demand security and love the domestic life that may lead to a serene bed-and-breakfast wedding overlooking a body of water. Ideal setting: Venice.

Wise Words: Robert Louis Stevenson: "If it be true, as I have heard it said, that drums are covered with asses' skin, what a picturesque irony is there in that?"

Hints of Love: Expecting too much too soon can only build up hopes that will fall down too easily.

After the Argument: *For him:* Do whatever he wants done around the house or make him a home-cooked meal. Make sure you are really productive. *For her:* Do things you usually hate to do for her. She is sure to notice your socks in the hamper instead of on the floor and appreciate it immensely.

Romantic Places: Places of comfort bring romance: Switzerland; a log cabin; Savannah, Georgia.

Lucky Love Star: Cancriel—you will never lack love or domestic comfort.

Beautiful Thought: From where you are sitting, you may not be the best person to take a stand.

Sharing Secrets: Don't be in a hurry, or it will be over before it begins. *For the gals:* Like fine wine and amazing food. Savor a moment until an hour is created. *For the guys:* To do too much too fast will prove risky. Try to give a push and he will just jump ship.

Judith's Insights

About the Man: His voice is known to be mellow. But if he's your boss, and you don't do your job, he will certainly get his point across. He doesn't like friction and is only interested in pure emotions. You must be able to hold up your end of the bargain or you will be dropped like a weak link. You will know where he stands on a number of issues right up front. If you see him dating many people, then he is not ready for commitment and is just having a good time. If he starts spending his nights alone he may be becoming more choosy about who shares his company.

About the Woman: Don't challenge her emotions. There is no one more loyal and centered than this gal. The best way to push her away is to question her ethics. She loves to be loved, and her family is her life; don't try to interfere with the bond between them. Make her aware that you are there to help in any way without trying to take over for her. At times, she jumps into a relationship without thinking it through because she loves to be in love so much. If she is harder to pin down she will make better decisions.

Soul Mates: There is no reason you would not get along famously with a fellow Cancer. Friendship may be your best bet with Leo and Libra. Otherwise, they might get the idea that they are in control. Don't let Taurus's need for stability hinder any excitement coming into your life. Capricorn and Aries are too rigid for your taste. When you get together with Scorpio and Pisces there may be an overload of emotions. When the relationship with Virgo and Aquarius gets you in way over your head, you must be prepared to walk away. With Sagittarius you may feel like running away and staying in the exact same moment. Don't try to change Gemini. Just love them for all that they are.

Most Charming Characteristics: Impulsive, charitable, tolerant.

Gifts: *For her:* pearl necklace. *For him:* leather journal.

Sensual Foods: Flambé; lobster; oysters.

Romantic Flowers: Send this girl sunflowers if you want her to know you adore her. You may even add some poppies for a splash of extravagance. His desire for sport and play will be understood when you send him hyacinth and geranium.

Best Date Nights: Monday; 15th and 24th of each month.

Colors of Passion: *For her:* orange, indigo. *For him:* green, russet.

The Perfect Wedding: You are inexplicably attracted to the water, so it's no wonder you and yours should spend your special day there. A romantic seashore, a marina, a cruise ship, even an aquarium or seaport should be among the first locations to consider. You demand security and love the domestic life that may lead to a serene bed-and-breakfast wedding overlooking a body of water. Ideal setting: Venice.

Wise Words: Charles Dickens: "What is the good of putting things off? Strike while the iron is hot."

Hints of Love: Make sure all the ingredients are present before putting the cake in the oven.

After the Argument: *For him:* Do whatever he wants done around the house or make him a home-cooked meal. Make sure you are really productive. *For her:* Do things you usually hate to do for her. She is sure to notice your socks in the hamper instead of on the floor and appreciate it immensely.

Romantic Places: Places of leisure bring romance: French countryside; a cruise; the Great Lakes.

Lucky Love Star: Cancriel—you will never lack love or domestic comfort.

Beautiful Thought: Even a short walk could lead you in the right direction.

Sharing Secrets: They need to look before they leap, but only in love. *For the gals:* She needs creative and exciting dates to keep her interested. Don't take her for granted too soon. *For the guys:* You may think he gives signs of moving this relationship quickly; make sure you slow it down before he does.

Judith's Insights

About the Man: This is the "man with the moves." That in itself could be a lot of work. If you approach him today and he isn't interested, try tomorrow, or when the moon is full. Until he knows what he wants he will be of no use to you. Try to help him find his niche in life. He is always looking for the next great love of his life. He looks in the right places but his timing can be off. Things have to be introduced slowly into his world if you want him to give them any kind of consideration.

About the Woman: She knows what she wants, she just isn't that manipulating suave lady who knows how to get what she wants. So things usually take her a little longer to get. If you knock, she will certainly let you in. Just don't try to get her to the door faster or she will decide not to answer it at all. Don't even think about opening the door yourself. She has to be the one to let you in or things will not work at all. Move slowly but steer her in the right direction. If you let her think that she is the one in control she will be much easier to lead.

Soul Mates: Cancer with a Cancer is a perfect match. Leo and Libra are for leaning on instead of loving. Taurus could bore you. Try to teach them to add some excitement to their life. Capricorn and Aries are in love with control. Make sure you are ready to give it up or walk away. Watch out for mood swings with Scorpio and Pisces. The right attitude is essential when you are dealing with Virgo and Aquarius. It can make all the difference. When you are in the right frame of mind, things can go very well with Sagittarius. Gemini will love you forever if you can love them for all that they are.

Most Charming Characteristics: Amusing, intellectual, genial.

Gifts: *For her:* cooking tools. *For him:* gardening tools.

Sensual Foods: Crème brûlée; poached salmon.

Romantic Flowers: Rhododendron will let her be on the lookout for trouble. Throw in some chrysanthemum and she'll know it is you she will be looking out for. Cactus will show him warmth. Yellow daffodil is a token of a good time had by all. Chivalry is not dead.

Best Date Nights: Monday; 8th and 26th of each month.

Colors of Passion: *For her:* orange, indigo. *For him:* green, russet.

The Perfect Wedding: You are inexplicably attracted to the water, so it's no wonder you and yours should spend your special day there. A romantic seashore, a marina, a cruise ship, even an aquarium or seaport should be among the first locations to consider. You demand security and love the domestic life that may lead to a serene bed-and-breakfast wedding overlooking a body of water. Ideal setting: Venice.

Wise Words: Charles Dickens: "There are some falsehoods . . . on which men mount, as on bright wings, towards Heaven."

Hints of Love: Simple often turns into complicated with this one. When you overcomplicate the moment, try to step back for a breather.

After the Argument: *For him:* Do whatever he wants done around the house or make him a home-cooked meal. Make sure you are really productive. *For her:* Do things you usually hate to do for her. She is sure to notice your socks in the hamper instead of on the floor and appreciate it immensely.

Romantic Places: Places of comfort bring romance: Turkey; a beach house; wine country, California.

Lucky Love Star: Cancriel—you will never lack love or domestic comfort.

Beautiful Thought: An open mind will improve your vision.

Sharing Secrets: The possibilities are endless, if you can pay the price. *For the gals:* She is hoping chivalry is not dead, and you must be willing to be the man at all costs. *For the guys:* He can be demanding and somewhat controlling. He just needs to be trained.

Judith's Insights

About the Man: Everybody's his friend, even at work, so he is always the most approachable guy. He does better with friends than with intimate relationships. He pushes away when things get too close. He'll run even if it's what he wants, so expect a little yo-yo action here. After a while in a relationship he tends to become bored. You may have to bring a little extra spice to the party to get his attention back on you. He will take everything you give him at face value and not doubt your intentions unless you prove otherwise.

About the Woman: Getting her attention is easier than you may think. She's quiet on the outside, but with plenty to live out. She knows that she wants a relationship and feels like she kissed too many frogs already. She doesn't like doing the work some expect her to do. She is charming and giving but has a tendency to become way too serious. Few people will ever get to know that mind of hers. She will only let you in if you have shown her that you are not there to cause harm. Once bitten, she will not give you another chance to hurt her.

Soul Mates: Cancer's house is your house, so you will get along just fine. When things are always the same, it can get boring. Make sure you and Taurus keep things fresh and new. Leo and Libra can be much too intense for your taste. Mood swings could prevail with Scorpio and Pisces. Capricorn's and Aries's instinct to control all around them will leave you dreaming of greener pastures. If you go in with the right attitude, the problems with Virgo and Aquarius won't seem as big. A relationship with Sagittarius can drive you crazy if you take things too personally. Taking things from moment to moment will make it easier. Enjoy Gemini for the fun-loving spirits they are. If you can do that, then they can love you forever.

Most Charming Characteristics: Loving, ambitious, high ideals.

Gifts: *For her:* day at the beach. *For him:* invite his mom to dinner.

Sensual Foods: Chocolate soufflé; filet mignon.

Romantic Flowers: The magnolias you send her will let her know you will be around for a while to come. Petunia is to say never despair. Holly will let him know what he is getting into. Pansy will keep you in his thoughts.

Best Date Nights: Monday; 9th and 18th of each month.

Colors of Passion: *For her:* orange, indigo. *For him:* green, russet.

The Perfect Wedding: You are inexplicably attracted to the water, so it's no wonder you and yours should spend your special day there. A romantic seashore, a marina, a cruise ship, even an aquarium or seaport should be among the first locations to consider. You demand security and love the domestic life that may lead to a serene bed-and-breakfast wedding overlooking a body of water. Ideal setting: Venice.

Wise Words: Charles Dickens: "The form of religion does not so greatly matter if we try to do good."

Hints of Love: Allow them to know what is in your heart as well as what is in your head.

After the Argument: *For him:* Do whatever he wants done around the house or make him a home-cooked meal. Make sure you are really productive. *For her:* Do things you usually hate to do for her. She is sure to notice your socks in the hamper instead of on the floor and appreciate it immensely.

Romantic Places: Places of leisure bring romance: the Virgin Islands; a five-star hotel; Beverly Hills, California.

Lucky Love Star: Cancriel—you will never lack love or domestic comfort.

Beautiful Thought: If they can make you laugh, they can make you love.

Sharing Secrets: Tomorrow is another day, but why wait? You can do it all today. *For the gals:* Have your date filled from dusk to dawn, and then some. *For the guys:* You may find he needs a nap here and there, but he can last all day and all night if he has a reason.

Judith's Insights

About the Man: As charming as he is, he certainly has a shy side to him. He is quieter than most guys are. When he has something to say it is usually a mouthful. He can be a wanderer with his mind, but seldom with his heart. Once he has set his eyes on his goal there will be no stopping him. He can seem clingy at times but never needy. He can stand alone if he needs to but he prefers to be with a mate. He is easy to hang with because he is always open and ready to like all those he meets.

About the Woman: All she needs is love. She wants and needs it so badly that she will soak it up with a towel if need be. She always puts 100 percent of herself into every relationship she has, including friendship. When you receive her love, you'll never have to worry about disloyalty. Make sure that you are worth the loyalty placed in you. She is a nurturing soul and really loves her domestic side. She might not admit this until later in life while taking care of everyone in her life at the same time. Her kind heart and good advice make her a true partner in any endeavor.

Soul Mates: You and another Cancer are a wonderful match. Leo and Libra can bring out the best or worst in you, depending on the mood in the air. Because push always comes to shove, you and Taurus may have to try some new things together. Aries's and Capricorn's uncompromising nature could put out your fire of passion. When you get together with Scorpio and Pisces you might become overly sensitive to their insecurities. Sometimes Virgo and Aquarius can be worth the risk of being burned. Just be cautious. Sagittarius may grate on your nerves at first, but if you hang in there, it may be worth the effort. Don't try to change Gemini. Accept what you are given.

Most Charming Characteristics: Poetic, ardent, loyal.

Gifts: *For her:* new plant for the garden. *For him:* gourmet cookbook.

Sensual Foods: Steak au poivre; cheesecake.

Romantic Flowers: Iris is your flower if you are the gal sending subtle messages. If you are the man, you will look for clematis. This flower's mental beauty creates emotional stimulation for you.

Best Date Nights: Monday; 1st and 19th of each month.

Colors of Passion: *For her:* orange, indigo. *For him:* green, russet.

The Perfect Wedding: You are inexplicably attracted to the water, so it's no wonder you and yours should spend your special day there. A romantic seashore, a marina, a cruise ship, even an aquarium or seaport should be among the first locations to consider. You demand security and love the domestic life that may lead to a serene bed-and-breakfast wedding overlooking a body of water. Ideal setting: Venice.

Wise Words: Charles Dickens: "A very sublime and great thing is Truth, in its way, though like other sublime and grand things, such as thunderstorms and that, we are not always over and above glad to see it."

Hints of Love: Keep both feet on the ground the first time you think you want to jump. This way you won't jump too high too soon.

After the Argument: *For him:* Do whatever he wants done around the house or make him a home-cooked meal. Make sure you are really productive. *For her:* Do things you usually hate to do for her. She is sure to notice your socks in the hamper instead of on the floor and appreciate it immensely.

Romantic Places: Places of comfort bring romance: London; the beach; Miami, Florida.

Lucky Love Star: Cancriel—you will never lack love or domestic comfort.

Beautiful Thought: Whisper when you really want to be heard.

Sharing Secrets: It may need to start with friendship. This isn't the consolation prize; it's the grand prize. *For the gals:* Go slow and allow it to grow one seed at a time. You won't need to push; it will all come in time. *For the guys:* A step here and a step there. Before he knows it, that friendship will be love.

Judith's Insights

About the Man: He will love to stay home and enjoy a good movie or a game of cards with friends. He is certainly easier to please than many. He doesn't need a barrel of money for a good time. Just no conflict, unless it is his. If you are the one who presents the conflict, he will stop letting you into the party. He has exceptional taste in everything. This is especially true about the people he chooses to spend time with. He is true and loyal, but can tend to be moody when things are not on the right track.

About the Woman: Send her a note and she'll cherish it forever. She doesn't get over crushes too easily and will still linger over her first love all her life. When this gal falls, she falls hard, so you had better be ready to catch her. If you can be as loyal as she is, then you will be a match made in heaven for her. Don't flirt with other people while around her. She will take it as a personal insult, even if it was just for fun. Her sensitivity can make you watch what you do while being one of the reasons why you love her in the first place.

Soul Mates: Cancer's house is your house, so you will get along just fine. When things are always the same, it can get boring. Make sure you and Taurus keep things fresh and new. Leo and Libra can be much too intense for your taste. Mood swings could prevail with Scorpio and Pisces. Capricorn's and Aries's instinct to control all around them will leave you dreaming of greener pastures. If you go in with the right attitude, the problems with Virgo and Aquarius won't seem as big. You will experience life as never before when you are linked to Sagittarius. You simply have to open it. Enjoy Gemini for the fun-loving spirits they are. If you can do that, then they can love you forever.

Most Charming Characteristics: Impulsive, affectionate, determined.

Gifts: *For her:* spectacular candlelit meal at home. *For him:* new recliner.

Sensual Foods: Strawberry shortcake; pineapple; ham.

Romantic Flowers: Any rose of any color for the lady. Roses stand for love regardless of the color. Send them with orchids and you will be saying, "I love you." If you want a gentleman to know you think of him, send pansies, and forget-me-nots for true love.

Best Date Nights: Monday; 2nd and 20th of each month.

Colors of Passion: *For her:* orange, indigo. *For him:* green, russet.

The Perfect Wedding: You are inexplicably attracted to the water, so it's no wonder you and yours should spend your special day there. A romantic seashore, a marina, a cruise ship, even an aquarium or seaport should be among the first locations to consider. You demand security and love the domestic life that may lead to a serene bed-and-breakfast wedding overlooking a body of water. Ideal setting: Venice.

Wise Words: Charles Dickens: "Most men unconsciously judge the world for themselves."

Hints of Love: Laughter alleviates the tension, but so can understanding where another is sitting.

After the Argument: *For him:* Do whatever he wants done around the house or make him a home-cooked meal. Make sure you are really productive. *For her:* Do things you usually hate to do for her. She is sure to notice your socks in the hamper instead of on the floor and appreciate it immensely.

Romantic Places: Places of leisure bring romance: the Caribbean; a mountain resort; Hilton Head, South Carolina.

Lucky Love Star: Cancriel—you will never lack love or domestic comfort.

Beautiful Thought: When you really want to hear the words, close your eyes and listen.

Sharing Secrets: This one needs to be the one and only, even if it is only the first date. *For the gals:* Don't talk about your past relationships. Do all you can to make her feel cherished from the first moment. *For the guys:* Play up your innocence. Let him take charge, even in paying the bill. He needs to wear the pants.

Judith's Insights

About the Man: He lives in a happy world all on his own. If the company is good, he'll take it. If not, he doesn't mind hanging with himself. He enjoys being friends with the people he works with. He needs serenity in every environment. Don't introduce conflict or he will drop you off at the next stop. If you do get him riled up he can have a hot temper. He keeps it under wraps so you won't see this side of him unless you really burn him. Feed his hungry heart with love and affection and the rest will be a piece of cake.

About the Woman: She is looking for that idealistic relationship, and will settle for nothing less. Although she is easy to hang out with, she has a very sensitive nature. Be up-front with her, even if your friendship has been around for ages. They expect the same as what was shown at the beginning. That is why you are still around. Never, ever, question her loyalty to you or anyone else. This will insult her more than you could ever know.

Soul Mates: When you and a fellow Cancer share the what-is-mine-is-yours theory you will be bonded forever. Libra and Leo are too much for you to take. Try to ease away gently. A pairing with Taurus will set off an inner fire that feeds your souls. Capricorn and Aries tend to forget the little joys in life. Try to revel in those same joys. A match with Scorpio and Pisces may result in overly protective or dependent behavior. Don't start a relationship with Virgo and Aquarius if you are not willing to work to keep it going. People can't change simply because you wish it. When you are linked to Sagittarius, there is the potential for great things happening if you can go with the flow. If you can't take Gemini, you should walk away.

Most Charming Characteristics: Reliant, alert-minded, independent.

Gifts: *For her:* family portrait. *For him:* antique furniture.

Sensual Foods: Steak fondue; cheese fondue and French bread.

Romantic Flowers: These ladies like everyone to know how faithful they are, so send them violets. To surprise them send tulips. Men like their flowers the same as their relationships, unpretending. Send them camellias with white roses to show your affection.

Best Date Nights: Monday; 21st and 30th of each month.

Colors of Passion: *For her:* orange, indigo. *For him:* green, russet.

The Perfect Wedding: You are inexplicably attracted to the water, so it's no wonder you and yours should spend your special day there. A romantic seashore, a marina, a cruise ship, even an aquarium or seaport should be among the first locations to consider. You demand security and love the domestic life that may lead to a serene bed-and-breakfast wedding overlooking a body of water. Ideal setting: Venice.

Wise Words: Charles Dickens: "The man who lives from day-to-day by the daily exercise in his sphere of hands and head, and seeks to improve himself . . . acquires for himself that property of soul which has at all times upheld struggling men of every degree."

Hints of Love: Communication is important here. A script isn't provided for you. You must write it for yourself.

After the Argument: *For him:* Do whatever he wants done around the house or make him a home-cooked meal. Make sure you are really productive. *For her:* Do things you usually hate to do for her. She is sure to notice your socks in the hamper instead of on the floor and appreciate it immensely.

Romantic Places: Places of comfort bring romance: Britain; their own living room; Ocean City, Maryland.

Lucky Love Star: Cancriel—you will never lack love or domestic comfort.

Beautiful Thought: Love moves mountains, crosses oceans, and slips through the cracks.

Sharing Secrets: You need to remember never to forget. *For the gals:* Her birthday, holidays, and your anniversary. Even down to each dinner date. *For the guys:* His birthday, his laundry, his mother's birthday, and, of course, him any other day of the year.

Judith's Insights

About the Man: He will rely on no one but himself, unless he gets close enough to rely on you. Then it will be heart-wrenching to him if you disappoint him. He has plenty of self-control when it comes to work, but that's about it. He would not be able to give you another chance if you let him down, so don't. He needs kindness, love, and loyalty to make him happy. He will be disappointed if he does not receive it. He does not recoup from heartache very easily. If you break his heart once you won't get the chance to do it again.

About the Woman: Expect to give her the finer things in life. She knows how to stretch a buck and doesn't mind doing so as long as her mates and friends are not cheap. That will be a big turnoff. She demands and deserves total loyalty. If she is your boss, you had better not be entertaining other offers while still working with her. She can be over-the-top when it comes to the way she treats the people she loves. You have to be able to do the same for her for a relationship with her to work.

JULY

Soul Mates: You and another Cancer are a wonderful match. Leo and Libra can bring out the best or worst in you, depending on the mood in the air. Because push always comes to shove, you and Taurus may have to try some new things together. Aries's and Capricorn's uncompromising nature could put out your fire of passion. When you get together with Scorpio and Pisces you might become overly sensitive to their insecurities. Sometimes Virgo and Aquarius can be worth the risk of being burned. Just be cautious. With Sagittarius, you may feel like running away and staying in the exact same moment. Don't try to change Gemini. Accept what you are given.

Most Charming Characteristics: Gentle, loving, confident.

Gifts: *For her:* antique brooch. *For him:* antique writing desk.

Sensual Foods: Strawberries and cream; meat loaf.

Romantic Flowers: Iris is your flower if you are the gal sending subtle messages. If you are the man, you will look for clematis. This flower's mental beauty creates emotional stimulation for you.

Best Date Nights: Monday; 10th and 28th of each month.

Colors of Passion: *For her:* orange, indigo. *For him:* green, russet.

The Perfect Wedding: You are inexplicably attracted to the water, so it's no wonder you and yours should spend your special day there. A romantic seashore, a marina, a cruise ship, even an aquarium or seaport should be among the first locations to consider. You demand security and love the domestic life that may lead to a serene bed-and-breakfast wedding overlooking a body of water. Ideal setting: Venice.

Wise Words: Thomas à Kempis: "Keep company with the humble, with the devout, and with the virtuous; and confer with them of things that edify."

Hints of Love: They only use the three magic words when they know they mean it, and they already know it is going to be said back to them.

After the Argument: *For him:* Do whatever he wants done around the house or make him a home-cooked meal. Make sure you are really productive. *For her:* Do things you usually hate to do for her. She is sure to notice your socks in the hamper instead of on the floor and appreciate it immensely.

Romantic Places: Places of comfort bring romance: Ireland; a bed and breakfast; Key West, Florida.

Lucky Love Star: Cancriel—you will never lack love or domestic comfort.

Beautiful Thought: A waterfall begins with one single drop of water.

Sharing Secrets: Let them admire something about you first. Show them you have a sense of humor. *For the gals:* Hold their hand and then take them to the next step. *For the guys:* The way to his heart is definitely through his stomach.

Judith's Insights

About the Man: He can be much stronger than anyone gives him credit for. Don't put him against the wall, or it will be you in pain instead of him. He can be very up-front with his emotions when he wants to be. Otherwise, he will hide them very well if he isn't ready to deal with them. Let him get to that point in his own time. He doesn't do single well. The best of him is brought out when he is with a partner. If you are not right for him he will let you know right off the bat. He expects the same in return. He places more importance on giving than receiving.

About the Woman: If you want her attention, you just have to give her yours. She knows what she has and certainly knows how to use it. There will be no games with this gal. This is especially true if you work around her. She may be on the bossy side, but she'll get the job done every time and every way. She is kind, loyal, and true to herself. Once she has established a partnership with someone she will give all that she can give to make things work. She is a great lover of the unknown. Pique her interest with a mystery date or a blind date.

Soul Mates: Cancer's house is your house, so you will get along just fine. When things are always the same, it can get boring. Make sure you and Taurus keep things fresh and new. Leo and Libra can be much too intense for your taste. Mood swings could prevail with Scorpio and Pisces. Capricorn's and Aries's instinct to control all around them will leave you dreaming of greener pastures. If you go in with the right attitude, the problems with Virgo and Aquarius won't seem as big. When you are in the right frame of mind, things can go very well with Sagittarius. Enjoy Gemini for the fun-loving spirits they are. If you can do that, then they can love you forever.

Most Charming Characteristics: Original, forthright; active minded.

Gifts: *For her:* family tree. *For him:* framed picture of his family.

Sensual Foods: Cherry-apple pie; beef Stroganoff.

Romantic Flowers: Any rose of any color for the lady. Roses stand for love regardless of the color. Send them with orchids and you will be saying, "I love you." If you want a gentleman to know you think of him, send pansies, and forget-me-nots for true love.

Best Date Nights: Monday; 11th and 20th of each month.

Colors of Passion: *For her:* orange, indigo. *For him:* green, russet.

The Perfect Wedding: You are inexplicably attracted to the water, so it's no wonder you and yours should spend your special day there. A romantic seashore, a marina, a cruise ship, even an aquarium or seaport should be among the first locations to consider. You demand security and love the domestic life that may lead to a serene bed-and-breakfast wedding overlooking a body of water. Ideal setting: Venice.

Wise Words: George Sand: "Know how to give without hesitation, how to lose without regret, how to acquire without meanness."

Hints of Love: Remember to keep the dating fun. Don't act like you are married before your time.

After the Argument: *For him:* Do whatever he wants done around the house or make him a home-cooked meal. Make sure you are really productive. *For her:* Do things you usually hate to do for her. She is sure to notice your socks in the hamper instead of on the floor and appreciate it immensely.

Romantic Places: Places of leisure bring romance: Bermuda; a spa; Myrtle Beach, South Carolina.

Lucky Love Star: Cancriel—you will never lack love or domestic comfort.

Beautiful Thought: Good things come to those who wait; great things come to those who wait longer.

Sharing Secrets: Give them the opportunity to notice you first. *For the gals:* They love to be adored; love at first sight. *For the guys:* Remember to always let them believe it was their idea.

Judith's Insights

About the Man: Don't try to meddle in this man's business, even if the business is personal. He has a mind of his own and a method to his own madness. Wait for a good day to ask him out or in. If the timing is right, you will be pleasantly surprised by the answer. If you ask at a bad time, the answer will be worse. He is self-reliant, but he certainly loves to choose the right company to keep. It lets him feel as if he is in control. Always let him believe that he is, even when he isn't. He will constantly look to enrich the success of his friends and loved ones.

About the Woman: She doesn't like a busybody, or others intruding in her business. She has her own way of living and won't enjoy criticism too well. If you get close enough to her, you'll learn there are better ways to approach her than between the eyes. She likes a soft approach. If you accommodate her, she will be much easier to take. She will also receive your message more openly. It's all in the presentation. If she feels as if she is in control she won't lash out at you when she feels helpless. Take things nice and easy with no pushing allowed.

Soul Mates: When you and a fellow Cancer share the what-is-mine-is-yours theory you will be bonded forever. Libra and Leo are too much for you to take. Try to ease away gently. A pairing with Taurus will start an inner fire that feeds your souls. Capricorn and Aries tend to forget the little joys in life. Try to revel in those same joys. A match with Scorpio and Pisces may result in overly protective or dependent behavior. Don't start a relationship with Virgo and Aquarius if you are not willing to work to keep it going. People can't change simply because you wish it. A relationship with Sagittarius can drive you crazy if you take things too personally. Taking things from moment to moment will make it easier. If you can't take Gemini, you should walk away.

Most Charming Characteristics: Fun-loving, studious, sympathetic.

Gifts: *For her:* home-cooked meal. *For him:* antique painting.

Sensual Foods: Hot-fudge sundae with all the trimmings; shepherd's pie.

Romantic Flowers: These ladies like everyone to know how faithful they are, so send them violets. To surprise them send tulips. Men like their flowers the same as their relationships, unpretending. Send them camellias with white roses to show your affection.

Best Date Nights: Monday; 3rd and 12th of each month.

Colors of Passion: *For her:* orange, indigo. *For him:* green, russet.

The Perfect Wedding: You are inexplicably attracted to the water, so it's no wonder you and yours should spend your special day there. A romantic seashore, a marina, a cruise ship, even an aquarium or seaport should be among the first locations to consider. You demand security and love the domestic life that may lead to a serene bed-and-breakfast wedding overlooking a body of water. Ideal setting: Venice.

Wise Words: Henri Bergson: "What we do depends on what we are, but we are, to a certain extent, what we do, and we are creating ourselves continually."

Hints of Love: Make sure you go on more than one date before you jump to conclusions on liking and disliking.

After the Argument: *For him:* Do whatever he wants done around the house or make him a home-cooked meal. Make sure you are really productive. *For her:* Do things you usually hate to do for her. She is sure to notice your socks in the hamper instead of on the floor and appreciate it immensely.

Romantic Places: Places of comfort bring romance: Switzerland; a log cabin; Savannah, Georgia.

Lucky Love Star: Cancriel—you will never lack love or domestic comfort.

Beautiful Thought: Obstacles allow us to find alternate routes, which usually include a better destination.

Sharing Secrets: This one loves a challenge. *For the gals:* Be consistently inconsistent until you have them hooked. *For the guys:* This one loves to play catch. You may feel like a yo-yo, but as long as he is calling that's all that matters.

Judith's Insights

About the Man: Do you know what they say about those strong, silent types? They make the best mates. They talk only when they have a purpose. So, you won't be hearing "I love you" until long after he knows for sure that he does. The good news is, you can then count on his words to be true and long-lasting. He never says anything he does not mean. You may have to hold back a little with this one. Don't give him all of your attention all at once. Go slowly and let him yearn for more. Be consistent and persistent but never overwhelming.

About the Woman: She loves everyone, and sometimes it seems there may be too many people in her life. If you want her attention, you have to spike her curiosity. Be a little mysterious, but make sure you are giving her plenty of attention. Words are few and far between with her, but they are always earnest when they come. Don't lay out all of your feelings at her feet and expect her to fall into your arms. Things have to be taken one step at a time with this gal. Call her here and there instead of every day. With this plan, you will be sure to capture her interest.

Soul Mates: There is no reason you would not get along famously with a fellow Cancer. Friendship may be your best bet with Leo and Libra. Otherwise, they might get the idea that they are in control. Don't let Taurus's need for stability hinder any excitement coming into your life. Capricorn and Aries are too rigid for your taste. When you get together with Scorpio and Pisces there may be an overload of emotions. When the relationship with Virgo and Aquarius gets you in way over your head, you must be prepared to walk away. Sagittarius may grate on your nerves at first, but if you hang in there, it may be worth the effort. Don't try to change Gemini. Just love them for all that they are.

Most Charming Characteristics: Passionate, truthful, friendly.

Gifts: *For her:* pearl necklace. *For him:* leather journal.

Sensual Foods: Whipped cream, strawberries, brown sugar, and heavy cream.

Romantic Flowers: These ladies like men with taste. Show them you love style by sending fuchsia flowers, or even brightly colored wildflowers will do. To confuse this man, send him lilies along with bright daisies to show your innocence. Keep him guessing.

Best Date Nights: Monday; 4th and 22nd of each month.

Colors of Passion: *For her:* orange, indigo. *For him:* green, russet.

The Perfect Wedding: You are inexplicably attracted to the water, so it's no wonder you and yours should spend your special day there. A romantic seashore, a marina, a cruise ship, even an aquarium or seaport should be among the first locations to consider. You demand security and love the domestic life that may lead to a serene bed-and-breakfast wedding overlooking a body of water. Ideal setting: Venice.

Wise Words: Pythagoras: "By governing the tongue and being quiet, friendship is produced from strife, the fire of anger being extinguished."

Hints of Love: Don't act too needy too soon. It may push this relationship away.

After the Argument: *For him:* Do whatever he wants done around the house or make him a home-cooked meal. Make sure you are really productive. *For her:* Do things you usually hate to do for her. She is sure to notice your socks in the hamper instead of on the floor and appreciate it immensely.

Romantic Places: Places of leisure bring romance: the French countryside; a cruise; the Great Lakes.

Lucky Love Star: Cancriel—you will never lack love or domestic comfort.

Beautiful Thought: Love is something you cherish.

Sharing Secrets: This is a family person at heart; your presence is most important. *For the gals:* Make sure you go to Sunday dinner with her family when you are invited. *For the guys:* If you don't like his mom, you might have a hard time catching this one.

Judith's Insights

About the Man: Show him something he's never seen before. Enlighten him. That will certainly catch his attention. He doesn't need fireworks, but he'll create them himself if you just give him something to work with. Being mysterious will get him interested as long as you are not playing games. He is independent while wanting the whole world to love him. He doesn't do well when he feels others are not on the same page as he is in social situations. He is exceptionally sensitive and has a warm heart. Keep his heart in mind when doing things he might misunderstand.

About the Woman: She's the one giving everyone advice. It seems as if she is full of information, or even as if she lived a million years. She cherishes note cards and gifts. Her sentimental side is stronger than most. It's easy to get her attention—just put up a flag! She will see it from far away and come to check you out. Don't play games with the emotions that are sure to fly around in this relationship. She will take it personally and close up on you. She can surround herself with loads of people and still seem lonely. Sit with her and hold her hand to let her know you aren't going anywhere.

Soul Mates: You and another Cancer will be like peanut butter and jelly. You are made for each other. Leo and Libra are wonderful friends for you, but love is not advised. Taurus craves stability. Don't let that pull you to a screeching halt. Just try to get them moving instead. Capricorn and Aries are more than you can handle. Scorpio and Pisces will have emotions overflowing. Things with Virgo and Aquarius are more than you bargained for. You will experience life as never before when you are linked to Sagittarius. You simply have to be open to it. Gemini must be loved for all they are instead of all you want them to be.

Most Charming Characteristics: Perseverance, faithful, steadfast.

Gifts: *For her:* cooking tools. *For him:* gardening tools.

Sensual Foods: Puddings and pastry of all kinds.

Romantic Flowers: You are the lady of distinction, and only carnations will do. Any mix of colors with sprays of mignonette. Sweet peas or red carnations will appeal to this man's heart.

Best Date Nights: Monday; 4th and 23rd of each month.

Colors of Passion: *For her:* orange, indigo. *For him:* green, russet.

The Perfect Wedding: You are inexplicably attracted to the water, so it's no wonder you and yours should spend your special day there. A romantic seashore, a marina, a cruise ship, even an aquarium or seaport should be among the first locations to consider. You demand security and love the domestic life that may lead to a serene bed-and-breakfast wedding overlooking a body of water. Ideal setting: Venice.

Wise Words: Robert Louis Stevenson: "Times change, opinions vary to their opposite, and still the world appears a brave gymnasium, full of sea-bathing and horse exercise, and bracing, many virtues."

Hints of Love: Keep it fun. Look for new and exciting things to do, especially if you are in a long-term relationship.

After the Argument: *For him:* Do whatever he wants done around the house or make him a home-cooked meal. Make sure you are really productive. *For her:* Do things you usually hate to do for her. She is sure to notice your socks in the hamper instead of on the floor and appreciate it immensely.

Romantic Places: Places of comfort bring romance: Turkey; a beach house; wine country, California.

Lucky Love Star: Cancriel—you will never lack love or domestic comfort.

Beautiful Thought: Learn to be happy for others and you will learn to be happy with yourself.

Sharing Secrets: Everything in its good time. This one works slowly, but when it is time to pick up speed, watch out. *For the gals:* Don't go by the obvious. Read between the lines. As long as the invitation is being offered go full speed ahead. *For the guys:* Just when you thought you should walk away, he'll say, "I love you." Talk about confusing.

Judith's Insight

About the Man: He knows what he wants eventually in a relationship, but meanwhile he flimflams back and forth and always sends mixed signals. As a co-worker, he has a great work ethic, but his moods may drive you crazy. Learn to just leave him alone when he is having a moment. He thinks that he is consistent and can't understand why everyone thinks that he is moody. Don't attempt to challenge him on this. Just work around him and let him have his space to regain his composure. He will come back to the table fresh and ready for anything.

About the Woman: She is a woman on a mission. The only problem is that you may think her mission has changed because of her mood. *Wrong!* She may just constantly change the way she goes about things. Never take the surface changes for granted. You will end up with egg on your face. A lot of patience goes a long way when dealing with this gal. She will get easier to read in time. One day you may suddenly realize what each mood swing is really all about. Giving her space to work things out in her mind will make all the difference.

Soul Mates: Cancer with a Cancer is a perfect match. Leo and Libra are for leaning on instead of loving. Taurus could bore you. Try to teach them to add some excitement to their life. Capricorn and Aries are in love with control. Make sure you are ready to give it up or walk away. Watch out for mood swings with Scorpio and Pisces. The right attitude is essential when you are dealing with Virgo and Aquarius. It can make all the difference. When you are linked with Sagittarius, there is the potential of great things happening if you can go with the flow. Gemini will love you forever if you can love them for all that they are.

Most Charming Characteristics: Serious, refined, profound thinker.

Gifts: *For her:* day at the beach. *For him:* invite his mom to dinner.

Sensual Foods: Champagne with strawberries; fillet of sole.

Romantic Flowers: You love it when you get tulips, declaring love. When you receive a variety, it shows how hopelessly in love your partner is. He will just love a single rose. This shows him you understand his pleasures.

Best Date Nights: Monday; 6th and 15th of each month.

Colors of Passion: *For her:* orange, indigo. *For him:* green, russet.

The Perfect Wedding: You are inexplicably attracted to the water, so it's no wonder you and yours should spend your special day there. A romantic seashore, a marina, a cruise ship, even an aquarium or seaport should be among the first locations to consider. You demand security and love the domestic life that may lead to a serene bed-and-breakfast wedding overlooking a body of water. Ideal setting: Venice.

Wise Words: Henry Wadsworth Longfellow: "Another lovely day: the lilacs all in bloom and tossing in the wind."

Hints of Love: This one is a cautious soul. You may have to find a way to go around to the back door.

After the Argument: *For him:* Do whatever he wants done around the house or make him a home-cooked meal. Make sure you are really productive. *For her:* Do things you usually hate to do for her. She is sure to notice your socks in the hamper instead of on the floor and appreciate it immensely.

Romantic Places: Places of leisure bring romance: the Virgin Islands; a five-star hotel; Beverly Hills, California.

Lucky Love Star: Cancriel—you will never lack love or domestic comfort.

Beautiful Thought: The more you desire the more you'll accomplish.

Sharing Secrets: This one is a charmer, perhaps even fickle. *For the gals:* If you are patient enough to stick around, this one is worth the wait. *For the guys:* If there is enough time on the clock, stick around past three months. Then maybe he will have noticed you are there.

Judith's Insights

About the Man: He can be rather proper about things, and it may take some time for you to know exactly where he is coming from. He is definitely hard to get a bead on, so don't be discouraged if it takes a while. His moods change like the weather, but never his intentions. Play it straight with this guy and he will appreciate it and even reward you for it. Add water and stir in plenty of love, loyalty, consistency, and patience. He was born to be loved but only wants people in his life who are ready to commit.

About the Woman: It looks easier to make this gal happy than it really is. She can be very set in her ways. Surface happiness will be easy to accomplish. It's tough when it comes to a deep love or longtime relationship. Even when you think it isn't good, it will be. Just hang in there and stay consistent. You may get only one chance with this girl. Two chances if you catch her in a good mood. Make the first one count for everything. She needs to know that you will put the effort into what you want for yourself before she will link her goals with your own.

Soul Mates: Cancer's house is your house, so you will get along just fine. When things are always the same, it can get boring. Make sure you and Taurus keep things fresh and new. Leo and Libra can be much too intense for your taste. Mood swings could prevail with Scorpio and Pisces. Capricorn's and Aries's instinct to control all around them will leave you dreaming of greener pastures. If you go in with the right attitude, the problems with Virgo and Aquarius won't seem as big. With Sagittarius, you may feel like running away and staying in the exact same moment. Enjoy Gemini for the fun-loving spirits they are. If you can do that, then they can love you forever.

Most Charming Characteristics: Generous, energetic, shrewd.

Gifts: *For her:* new plant for the garden. *For him:* gourmet cookbook.

Sensual Foods: Chocolates; poached salmon; flambé; filet mignon; potatoes.

Romantic Flowers: Send this girl sunflowers if you want her to know you adore her. You may even add some poppies for a splash of extravagance. His desire for sport and play will be understood when you send him hyacinth and geranium.

Best Date Nights: Monday; 6th and 24th of each month.

Colors of Passion: *For her:* orange, indigo. *For him:* green, russet.

The Perfect Wedding: You are inexplicably attracted to the water, so it's no wonder you and yours should spend your special day there. A romantic seashore, a marina, a cruise ship, even an aquarium or seaport should be among the first locations to consider. You demand security and love the domestic life that may lead to a serene bed-and-breakfast wedding overlooking a body of water. Ideal setting: Venice.

Wise Words: Robert Louis Stevenson: "What a number of things a river does by simply following Gravity in the innocence of its heart!"

Hints of Love: Passion must be in the picture at all times or you could lose this one's attention quickly.

After the Argument: *For him:* Do whatever he wants done around the house or make him a home-cooked meal. Make sure you are really productive. *For her:* Do things you usually hate to do for her. She is sure to notice your socks in the hamper instead of on the floor and appreciate it immensely.

Romantic Places: Places of comfort bring romance: London; the beach; Miami, Florida.

Lucky Love Star: Cancriel—you will never lack love or domestic comfort.

Beautiful Thought: Being different could make the difference.

Sharing Secrets: If you are looking for love, then you have found the right mate. *For the gals:* This one could be stubborn. It may take forever to get a relationship started, but it is as solid as they come. *For the guys:* Even when he is ready, he might not be willing and able. He will put you through more obstacles than any course. Be patient.

Judith's Insights

About the Man: He likes all the waters of life to be calm. He is not good with worries, and he will seldom create them. This guy is mellow and always up for company, so ask away! You have very little to lose and everything to gain, especially because there is little chance of a no. You won't have to spend money on this guy. The only investment he asks for is your time. He likes for you to give plenty of yourself. He may have fine things in his home, but these objects are not his priority. What he cherishes are prizes of the heart.

About the Woman: She wants to be loved by someone who is more demonstrative than she is. The problem is that she can't show that. She wants you to show it! If you want her attention, appeal to her down-home side by talking about your family. She is very nostalgic. Show your interest when she is reminiscing. Make her the focus of all of your thoughts and she will be in heaven. She wants to be courted with personal notes and handmade gifts instead of expensive jewelry and flowers. If it comes from your heart it will be the best she has ever received.

Soul Mates: Cancer with a Cancer is a perfect match. Leo and Libra are for leaning on instead of loving. Taurus could bore you. Try to teach them to add some excitement to their life. Capricorn and Aries are in love with control. Make sure you are ready to give it up or walk away. Watch out for mood swings with Scorpio and Pisces. The right attitude is essential when you are dealing with Virgo and Aquarius. It can make all the difference. When you are in the right frame of mind, things can go very well with Sagittarius. Gemini will love you forever if you can love them for all that they are.

Most Charming Characteristics: Talented, alert, energetic.

Gifts: *For her:* spectacular candlelit meal at home. *For him:* new recliner.

Sensual Foods: Caviar; beef tenderloin; potatoes au gratin.

Romantic Flowers: Rhododendron will let her be on the lookout for trouble. Throw in some chrysanthemum and she'll know it is you she will be looking out for. Cactus will show him warmth. Yellow daffodil is a token of a good time had by all. Chivalry is not dead.

Best Date Nights: Monday; 8th and 26th of each month.

Colors of Passion: *For her:* orange, indigo. *For him:* green, russet.

The Perfect Wedding: You are inexplicably attracted to the water, so it's no wonder you and yours should spend your special day there. A romantic seashore, a marina, a cruise ship, even an aquarium or seaport should be among the first locations to consider. You demand security and love the domestic life that may lead to a serene bed-and-breakfast wedding overlooking a body of water. Ideal setting: Venice.

Wise Words: Robert Louis Stevenson: "It is the season now to go / About the country high and low, / Among the lilacs hand in hand, / Two by two in fairy land."

Hints of Love: A random act of kindness will go a long way with this one. What can you do for them today?

After the Argument: *For him:* Do whatever he wants done around the house or make him a home-cooked meal. Make sure you are really productive. *For her:* Do things you usually hate to do for her. She is sure to notice your socks in the hamper instead of on the floor and appreciate it immensely.

Romantic Places: Places of leisure bring romance: the Caribbean; a mountain resort; Hilton Head, South Carolina.

Lucky Love Star: Cancriel—you will never lack love or domestic comfort.

Beautiful Thought: Time is the gift of healing; healing is the gift of hope.

Sharing Secrets: If you can hang around and give constant stimulation, this could be your mate. *For the gals:* She is always looking for the Exit sign. Don't show her where it is or she will be gone. *For the guys:* Fast car, fast food; he likes everything that goes fast. Put on your running shoes. If you can keep up, then he is yours.

Judith's Insights

About the Man: He can frustrate the heck out of you. He is always searching for attention. I wouldn't call it flirting, but you might. He will have plenty of people around him, and loads of romantic friendships. Don't get upset as long as he knows whom he is going home with at the end of the day. If you want his attention you can capture it with a song. Music will do it every time. Write him some poetry or even rent a billboard. He wants everyone in the world to know how much he is loved. Do all that you can to show him how much you care.

About the Woman: A relationship with this gal can be as simple or as hard as you want it to be. She expects total attention. She will share everything she owns with you once you have proven yourself to her. To do this you must be able to hang in through thick and thin. Loyalty is a major turn-on for her. Gifts will win her over only if they have come from your soul. You have to demonstrate patience and faith in her to bring her closer to you. She needs to feel that you will be next to her if anything should make her world turn upside down.

Soul Mates: There is no reason you would not get along famously with a fellow Cancer. Frienship may be your best bet with Leo and Libra. Otherwise, they might get the idea that they are in control. Don't let Taurus's need for stability hinder any excitement coming into your life. Capricorn and Aries are too rigid for your taste. When you get together with Scorpio and Pisces there may be an overload of emotions. When the relationship with Virgo and Aquarius gets you in way over your head, you must be prepared to walk away. A relationship with Sagittarius can drive you crazy if you take things too personally. Taking things from moment to moment will make it easier. Don't try to change Gemini. Just love them for all that they are.

Most Charming Characteristics: Ambitious, conscientious, domestic.

Gifts: *For her:* family portrait. *For him:* antique furniture.

Sensual Foods: Passion fruit; fillet of sole almondine.

Romantic Flowers: The magnolias you send her will let her know you will be around for a while to come. Petunia is to say never despair. Holly will let him know what he is getting into. Pansy will keep you in his thoughts.

Best Date Nights: Monday; 9th and 18th of each month.

Colors of Passion: *For her:* orange, indigo. *For him:* green, russet.

The Perfect Wedding: You are inexplicably attracted to the water, so it's no wonder you and yours should spend your special day there. A romantic seashore, a marina, a cruise ship, even an aquarium or seaport should be among the first locations to consider. You demand security and love the domestic life that may lead to a serene bed-and-breakfast wedding overlooking a body of water. Ideal setting: Venice.

Wise Words: Bovee: "The pleasantest things in the world are pleasant thoughts, and the great art in life is to have as many of them as possible."

Hints of Love: Family and friends are important to this one. Don't try to alienate them or it will definitely backfire on you.

After the Argument: *For him:* Do whatever he wants done around the house or make him a home-cooked meal. Make sure you are really productive. *For her:* Do things you usually hate to do for her. She is sure to notice your socks in the hamper instead of the floor and appreciate it immensely.

Romantic Places: Places of comfort bring romance: Britain; their own living room; Ocean City, Maryland.

Lucky Love Star: Cancriel—you will never lack love or domestic comfort.

Beautiful Thought: When our world is falling apart, one hand can make the difference in putting it back together.

Sharing Secrets: This one may seem like a lot of work. They just need the basics: love, loyalty, and respect. *For the gals:* If you can show her your best side right from the beginning it may work. Be careful of fluff, because she will see right through it. *For the guys:* He loves to be loved. Give him plenty of attention, even if you think you don't stand a chance. Perseverance will win here.

Judith's Insights

About the Man: He can bring a lot of anxiety to the table, especially if there is work to be done. No matter how busy he gets, he always finds a way to play. You just have to make sure playing is on terms he agrees with. No mind games here, just pure and simple fun. Let the hair fly in the breeze. If there is such a thing as the marrying kind, you have found it here in this guy. Before he does settle down he needs to have all of his finances and emotional ducks in a row. It may take a little patience on your part to wait for him to get ready, but he will be ready soon.

About the Woman: She needs to take the time to putter around the house. You will find she may keep an unbearable social calendar, but she's the one who takes that Friday night to stay home and wash her hair. This time out of the mix helps her recharge for the next flight of fancy she will go on. She needs time to go to the next step in a relationship. If you push too hard or fast it could create a drowning effect. She will be able to stay around for the long haul as long as she is not ushered to do so before she is ready.

Soul Mates: You and another Cancer are a wonderful match. Leo and Libra can bring out the best or worst in you, depending on the mood in the air. Because push always comes to shove, you and Taurus may have to try some new things together. Aries's and Capricorn's uncompromising nature could put out your fire of passion. When you get together with Scorpio and Pisces you might become overly sensitive to their insecurities. Sometimes Virgo and Aquarius can be worth the risk of being burned. Just be cautious. Sagittarius may grate on your nerves at first, but if you hang in there, it may be worth the effort. Don't try to change Gemini. Accept what you are given.

Most Charming Characteristics: Trustworthy, gentle, love deeply.

Gifts: *For her:* antique brooch. *For him:* antique writing desk.

Sensual Foods: Peaches, mousse; shrimp.

Romantic Flowers: Iris is your flower if you are the gal sending subtle messages. If you are the man, you will look for clematis. This flower's mental beauty creates emotional stimulation for you.

Best Date Nights: Monday; 1st and 28th of each month.

Colors of Passion: *For her:* orange, indigo. *For him:* green, russet.

The Perfect Wedding: You are inexplicably attracted to the water, so it's no wonder you and yours should spend your special day there. A romantic seashore, a marina, a cruise ship, even an aquarium or seaport should be among the first locations to consider. You demand security and love the domestic life that may lead to a serene bed-and-breakfast wedding overlooking a body of water. Ideal setting: Venice.

Wise Words: Johann Wolfgang von Goethe: "Quietly do the next thing that has to be done and allow one thing to follow upon the other."

Hints of Love: Show others how much you adore him or her. They will revel in how others notice.

After the Argument: *For him:* Do whatever he wants done around the house or make him a home-cooked meal. Make sure you are really productive. *For her:* Do things you usually hate to do for her. She is sure to notice your socks in the hamper instead of on the floor and appreciate it immensely.

Romantic Places: Places of comfort bring romance: Ireland; a bed-and-breakfast; Key West, Florida.

Lucky Love Star: Cancriel—you will never lack love or domestic comfort.

Beautiful Thought: A successful person always looks to see what's ahead but never forgets who's behind.

Sharing Secrets: They are looking for love, but that is just their little secret. *For the gals:* Why shouldn't they want to be loved? Of course they do, but they want you to do all of the work. *For the guys:* You must prove yourself repeatedly. Don't expect too much until he knows you are under his thumb.

Judith's Insights

About the Man: He can be here today and gone tomorrow, or at least it will feel like it. This one will be attentive one minute and preoccupied with something else the next. Make sure you are giving him plenty of attention or you'll lose him entirely. Make him feel like an important part of your life. He wants to keep things simple and free of emotional strings. Take one step at a time until he decides that you are the perfect mate for him. That is what he is searching for, after all. If you are the one, you had better be ready to commit.

About the Woman: She wants things to be simple. She does things her own way. She doesn't have a selfish manner, but she will need your undivided attention or the moods will drive you crazy. There will be no beating around the bush with this gal. Be up-front and to the point at all times. If things begin to get stale she will become moody and not want to go out of the house. Bring her back to the land of the living by planning a mystery trip. Her love of the unknown will bring her back to the lively girl you fell for in the first place.

Soul Mates: Cancer's house is your house, so you will get along just fine. When things are always the same, it can get boring. Make sure you and Taurus keep things fresh and new. Leo and Libra can be much too intense for your taste. Mood swings could prevail with Scorpio and Pisces. Capricorn's and Aries's instinct to control all around them will leave you dreaming of greener pastures. If you go in with the right attitude, the problems with Virgo and Aquarius won't seem as big. You will experience life as never before when you are linked to Sagittarius. You simply have to be open to it. Enjoy Gemini for the fun-loving spirits they are. If you can do that, then they can love you forever.

Most Charming Characteristics: Charming, congenial, self-controlled.

Gifts: *For her:* family tree. *For him:* framed picture of his family.

Sensual Foods: Kiwis; cantaloupes; strawberries.

Romantic Flowers: Any rose of any color for the lady. Roses stand for love regardless of the color. Send them with orchids and you will be saying, "I love you." If you want a gentleman to know you think of him, send pansies, and forget-me-nots for true love.

Best Date Nights: Monday; 11th and 20th of each month.

Colors of Passion: *For her:* orange, indigo. *For him:* green, russet.

The Perfect Wedding: You are inexplicably attracted to the water, so it's no wonder you and yours should spend your special day there. A romantic seashore, a marina, a cruise ship, even an aquarium or seaport should be among the first locations to consider. You demand security and love the domestic life that may lead to a serene bed-and-breakfast wedding overlooking a body of water. Ideal setting: Venice.

Wise Words: Edwin Arnold: "Like threads of silver seen through crystal beads, / Let love through good deeds show."

Hints of Love: Don't overdo it (dress, attention)

too soon or this one will run. Wait until you have them hooked before you become outrageous.

After the Argument: *For him:* Do whatever he wants done around the house or make him a home-cooked meal. Make sure you are really productive. *For her:* Do things you usually hate to do for her. She is sure to notice your socks in the hamper instead of on the floor and appreciate it immensely.

Romantic Places: Places of leisure bring romance: Bermuda; a spa; Myrtle Beach, South Carolina.

Lucky Love Star: Cancriel—you will never lack love or domestic comfort.

Beautiful Thought: You really only need one friend.

Sharing Secrets: You had better be ready to pull out your romantic side if you want this to work. *For the gals:* Fireplaces, walks on the beach, or even winning a bear at the local carnival. *For the guys:* When you are out shopping bring him something home. Even if it is silly, he will love the thought.

Judith's Insights

About the Man: Home is where his heart is. That is where you will find it. His heart resides with his family and his long-time friends. If you are loyal to him at work, you will have nothing to worry about and you will have gained a friend for life. Loyalty is the one main requirement of all people in his life. He wants it all, and he will do anything and everything he can to get it. He expects unconditional love from all those around him. If you can give him that level of emotion and commitment, you can be sure that you will receive the same level in return.

About the Woman: Until she has the commitment she is searching for, you will find her moody. She's not the kind of gal who likes to be kept hanging out on a limb. This gal always has her door open. Getting her attention can be as simple as poking your head into the room. If you ask, she will answer. She will never try to mislead you with superficial information. She will get right to the point. Her nurturing nature attracts many people to her side, but only those who give what they receive stay for very long. She will ignore any shortcomings to make any relationship work.

Soul Mates: When you and a fellow Cancer share the what-is-mine-is-yours theory you will be bonded forever. Libra and Leo are too much for you to take. Try to ease away gently. A pairing with Taurus will start an inner fire that feeds your souls. Capricorn and Aries tend to forget the little joys in life. Try to revel in those same joys. A match with Scorpio and Pisces may result in overly protective or dependent behavior. Don't start a relationship with Virgo and Aquarius if you are not willing to work to keep it going. People can't change simply because you wish it. When you are linked with Sagittarius, there is the potential of great things happening if you can go with the flow. If you can't take Gemini, you should walk away.

Most Charming Characteristics: Upright, fastidious, loving.

Gifts: *For her:* home-cooked meal. *For him:* antique painting.

Sensual Foods: Caramel and chocolate syrup on anything.

Romantic Flowers: These ladies like everyone to know how faithful they are, so send them violets. To surprise them send tulips. Men like their flowers the same as their relationships, unpretending. Send them camellias with white roses to show your affection.

Best Date Nights: Monday; 3rd and 21st of each month.

Colors of Passion: *For her:* orange, indigo. *For him:* green, russet.

The Perfect Wedding: You are inexplicably attracted to the water, so it's no wonder you and yours should spend your special day there. A romantic seashore, a marina, a cruise ship, even an aquarium or seaport should be among the first locations to consider. You demand security and love the domestic life that may lead to a serene bed-and-breakfast wedding overlooking a body of water. Ideal setting: Venice.

Wise Words: Henry David Thoreau: "If a man constantly aspires, is he not elevated? Did a man ever try heroism, magnanimity, truth, sincerity, and find that there was no advantage in them, that it was an endeavor?"

Hints of Love: When these folks decide to sit on the fence don't try to push them off before they are ready. Let them do the jumping themselves.

After the Argument: *For him:* Do whatever he wants done around the house or make him a home-cooked meal. Make sure you are really productive. *For her:* Do things you usually hate to do for her. She is sure to notice your socks in the hamper instead of on the floor and appreciate it immensely.

Romantic Places: Places of comfort bring romance: Switzerland; a log cabin; Savannah, Georgia.

Lucky Love Star: Cancriel—you will never lack love or domestic comfort.

Beautiful Thought: There is nothing wrong with a relationship if it is right for you.

Sharing Secrets: It may seem like they are not interested, but ask them out anyway. *For the gals:* Until they absolutely know you are interested, you will never find out that they are. *For the guys:* Ask him out if he doesn't ask you. He may be shy or not. Either way, he may be interested.

Judith's Insights

About the Man: He seems right up-front and almost simple when it comes to love. However, this guy can be your worst nightmare if he isn't ready to commit. Don't challenge him. Just make sure you give him room to breathe. Without it he will drive you crazy with his mood swings that even he can't explain. The best way to get his attention is to give him plenty of yours. The best way to keep him interested in the relationship is to keep it interesting. He loves his home and needs a good reason to leave even for a few hours. Play on his love for the unknown by surprising him.

About the Woman: She lives in her heart and never in her head. She can be the most loyal friend in the world. All that she asks is for the same level of loyalty in return. If she feels threatened, her back will get up, and you may have more than your hands free. Treat her as you would want to be treated. Keep things exciting by giving her unexpected gifts and cards. She will love anything that comes from your heart, so it does not need to be expensive. Give of yourself and she will return the favor and give you her heart.

Soul Mates: There is no reason you would not get along famously with a fellow Cancer. Friendship may be your best bet with Leo and Libra. Otherwise, they might get the idea that they are in control. Don't let Taurus's need for stability hinder any excitement coming into your life. Capricorn and Aries are too rigid for your taste. When you get together with Scorpio and Pisces there may be an overload of emotions. When the relationship with Virgo and Aquarius gets you in way over your head, you must be prepared to walk away. With Sagittarius, you may feel like running away and staying in the exact same moment. Don't try to change Gemini. Just love them for all that they are.

Most Charming Characteristics: Energetic, impulsive, aggressive.

Gifts: *For her:* pearl necklace. *For him:* leather journal.

Sensual Foods: Waffles with whipped cream; chocolate soufflé; French wine.

Romantic Flowers: These ladies like men with taste. Show them you love style by sending fuchsia flowers, or even brightly colored wildflowers will do. To confuse this man, send him lilies along with bright daisies to show your innocence. Keep him guessing.

Best Date Nights: Monday; 13th and 22nd of each month.

Colors of Passion: *For her:* orange, indigo. *For him:* green, russet.

The Perfect Wedding: You are inexplicably attracted to the water, so it's no wonder you and yours should spend your special day there. A romantic seashore, a marina, a cruise ship, even an aquarium or seaport should be among the first locations to consider. You demand security and love the domestic life that may lead to a serene bed-and-breakfast wedding overlooking a body of water. Ideal setting: Venice.

Wise Words: Richard Chenevix Trench: "Every noble life leaves the fibre of itself interwoven for ever in the work of the world."

Hints of Love: Make sure you learn to compromise, but never with your principles.

After the Argument: *For him:* Do whatever he wants done around the house or make him a home-cooked meal. Make sure you are really productive. *For her:* Do things you usually hate to do for her. She is sure to notice your socks in the hamper instead of on the floor and appreciate it immensely.

Romantic Places: Places of leisure bring romance: the French countryside; a cruise; the Great Lakes.

Lucky Love Star: Cancriel—you will never lack love or domestic comfort.

Beautiful Thought: Sometimes you just have to decide to decide.

Sharing Secrets: Don't be surprised if the first date is with their family. *For the gals:* Make sure you invite her to your family functions. It will be a red flag to her if you don't. *For the guys:* He may seem like a family man, but isn't that what you were looking for?

Judith's Insights

About the Man: He definitely has a sensitive side, and sometimes it's both wonderful and scary. Your approach must be clear, and so must your intentions. He doesn't mind playing around, but he hates mind games. Be consistent in your attention to him. If he feels as if it is waning, he will look elsewhere. He is more sensitive than a glance would tell you. As a boss or a co-worker, he has a great heart and does not mind letting you know it. Give him the same respect that he gives you to keep him in your life.

About the Woman: She will make you feel like you have known her forever even if you've just met. She allows everyone in, but that is just the surface. Only a select few actually get really close. If you are lucky enough to have her in your life, you'll never need to question her motives. She would rather be stronger when it comes to her emotions. Her heart can make her do things she is not quite ready for, and she will become moody when she realizes it. Give her time to come to terms with how she is feeling and she will be ready for anything before you know it.

Soul Mates: You and another Cancer will be like peanut butter and jelly. You are made for each other. Leo and Libra are wonderful friends for you, but love is not advised. Taurus craves stability. Don't let that pull you to a screeching halt. Just try to get them moving instead. Capricorn and Aries are more than you can handle. Scorpio and Pisces will have emotions overflowing. Things with Virgo and Aquarius are more than you bargained for. When you are in the right frame of mind, things can go very well with Sagittarius. Gemini must be loved for all they are instead of all you want them to be.

Most Charming Characteristics: Straightforward, generous, idealistic.

Gifts: *For her:* cooking tools. *For him:* gardening tools.

Sensual Foods: Oysters; mussels; spicy foods.

Romantic Flowers: You are the lady of distinction, and only carnations will do. Any mix of colors with sprays of mignonette. Sweet peas or red carnations will appeal to this man's heart.

Best Date Nights: Monday; 4th and 5th of each month.

Colors of Passion: *For her:* orange, indigo. *For him:* green, russet.

The Perfect Wedding: You are inexplicably attracted to the water, so it's no wonder you and yours should spend your special day there. A romantic seashore, a marina, a cruise ship, even an aquarium or seaport should be among the first locations to consider. You demand security and love the domestic life that may lead to a serene bed-and-breakfast wedding overlooking a body of water. Ideal setting: Venice.

Wise Words: Joseph Joubert: "We must put much strength and uprightness into our actions and our judgments, and we must put much kindness and indulgence into our sentiments, in order that the work of life be beautiful."

Hints of Love: If you try to take a step back, it will be noticed. It could create the domino effect, and everything will start to fall.

After the Argument: *For him:* Do whatever he wants done around the house or make him a home-cooked meal. Make sure you are really productive. *For her:* Do things you usually hate to do for her. She is sure to notice your socks in the hamper instead of on the floor and appreciate it immensely.

Romantic Places: Places of comfort bring romance: Turkey; a beach house; wine country, California.

Lucky Love Star: Cancriel—you will never lack love or domestic comfort.

Beautiful Thought: Just look for one minute of fun, and you'll find five.

Sharing Secrets: Take me as I am could be the anthem for this one. *For the gals:* They will have strong views on just about everything. If you can hang with them, then nothing will be as important as you. *For the guys:* The thing you fall in love with may end up becoming the thing you hate. After a commitment, this one sticks around.

Judith's Insights

About the Man: He may seem rather standoffish. He will be the guy standing around listening in, trying to decide whether he wants to enter in on the conversation or not. He can be a loner until he finds the right mate. He will take his time doing so. He wants to make sure that he finds the right one. The one thing he will demand from his partner in life is total loyalty. He can't feel as if he is second banana in any way. If you prove to him your unconditional love and loyalty, he will reward you more handsomely than you could have imagined.

About the Woman: She lives in a world of her own. Home is where she lays her head and where she stores her heart. Feeling comfortable is very important. If her environment is out of whack, her emotions will feel that way, too. If you approach her, expect that she may not jump for joy until after she gets to know you. She needs to feel you out to make sure that her heart is safe in your hands. Once she decides it is safe to move on, she will lavish you with love and warmth. This is when her sunny nature comes through and she shows you what she is really made of.

Soul Mates: Cancer with a Cancer is a perfect match. Leo and Libra are for leaning on instead of loving. Taurus could bore you. Try to teach them to add some excitement to their life. Capricorn and Aries are in love with control. Make sure you are ready to give it up or walk away. Watch out for mood swings with Scorpio and Pisces. The right attitude is essential when you are dealing with Virgo and Aquarius. It can make all the difference. A relationship with Sagittarius can drive you crazy if you take things too personally. Taking things from moment to moment will make it easier. Gemini will love you forever if you can love them for all that they are.

Most Charming Characteristics: Witty, fun-loving, vivid imagination.

Gifts: *For her:* day at the beach. *For him:* invite his mom to dinner.

Sensual Foods: Lobster; watermelon.

Romantic Flowers: You love it when you get tulips, declaring love. When you receive a variety, it shows how hopelessly in love your partner is. He will just love a single rose. This shows him you understand his pleasures.

Best Date Nights: Monday; 15th and 24th of each month.

Colors of Passion: *For her:* orange, indigo. *For him:* green, russet.

The Perfect Wedding: You are inexplicably attracted to the water, so it's no wonder you and yours should spend your special day there. A romantic seashore, a marina, a cruise ship, even an aquarium or seaport should be among the first locations to consider. You demand security and love the domestic life that may lead to a serene bed-and-breakfast wedding overlooking a body of water. Ideal setting: Venice.

Wise Words: Sir Walter Scott: "What an ornament and safeguard is humour, / Far better than wit for a poet and writer, it is a genius itself, and so defends from the insanities."

Hints of Love: Consistence and persistence will get this prize every time. They will value the effort.

After the Argument: *For him:* Do whatever he wants done around the house or make him a home-cooked meal. Make sure you are really productive. *For her:* Do things you usually hate to do for her. She is sure to notice your socks in the hamper instead of on the floor and appreciate it immensely.

Romantic Places: Places of leisure bring romance: the Virgin Islands; a five-star hotel; Beverly Hills, California.

Lucky Love Star: Cancriel—you will never lack love or domestic comfort.

Beautiful Thought: If you think of life as a carnival, you sometimes need not take that ride on the roller coaster.

Sharing Secrets: They seem moody until you get to know them. *For the gals:* You may not know whether to say hello or drop dead. As relations progress you will learn not to leave her dangling, and her moods will become more consistent. *For the guys:* To know him is to love him. His bark is much worse than his bite. He just wants someone to love him without criticism.

Judith's Insights

About the Man: His desire to accomplish a lot will make others think he can be too pushy. That's not this guy at all. He just has his own style of doing things that many don't recognize right away. You will probably not find a nicer guy once you can see inside his soul. Just know that he is on a path and will find his way to the end, detours or not. He likes his environment calm like the waters. He can get overemotional like the waves of the sea. To fully know the depths of his emotions you must be able to prove that your intentions are admirable.

About the Woman: She has a picture in her mind of what she wants her life to be, and she wants that picture to become a reality. This goes for work, school, play, and most certainly love. She will get along with others in business, but also everyone outside of business, too. Those who prove their loyalty will be rewarded. Her home is where she goes to recharge and plan her next step. To be invited to her home is an honor indeed and you should act accordingly. If things in her home are disturbed, her emotions will be also. Tread safely and softly and you will be allowed to stay.

Soul Mates: Cancer's house is your house, so you will get along just fine. When things are always the same, it can get boring. Make sure you and Taurus keep things fresh and new. Leo and Libra can be much too intense for your taste. Mood swings could prevail with Scorpio and Pisces. Capricorn's and Aries's instinct to control all around them will leave you dreaming of greener pastures. If you go in with the right attitude, the problems with Virgo and Aquarius won't seem as big. Sagittarius may grate on your nerves at first, but if you can hang in there, it may be worth the effort. Enjoy Gemini for the fun-loving spirits they are. If you can do that, then they can love you forever.

Most Charming Characteristics: Friendly, intuitive, domestic.

Gifts: *For her:* new plant for the garden. *For him:* gourmet cookbook.

Sensual Foods: Strawberries; truffles; shish kebab.

Romantic Flowers: Send this girl sunflowers if you want her to know you adore her. You may even add some poppies for a splash of extravagance. His desire for sport and play will be understood when you send him hyacinth and geranium.

Best Date Nights: Monday; 6th and 15th of each month.

Colors of Passion: *For her:* orange, indigo. *For him:* green, russet.

The Perfect Wedding: You are inexplicably attracted to the water, so it's no wonder you and yours should spend your special day there. A romantic seashore, a marina, a cruise ship, even an aquarium or seaport should be among the first locations to consider. You demand security and love the domestic life that may lead to a serene bed-and-breakfast wedding overlooking a body of water. Ideal setting: Venice.

Wise Words: Charles Dickens: "Persons don't make their own faces, and it is no more my fault if mine is a good one than it is other people's fault if theirs is a bad one."

Hints of Love: Be funny. Laughter will be what keeps this one coming back again and again.

After the Argument: *For him:* Do whatever he wants done around the house or make him a home-cooked meal. Make sure you are really productive. *For her:* Do things you usually hate to do for her. She is sure to notice your socks in the hamper instead of on the floor and appreciate it immensely.

Romantic Places: Places of comfort bring romance: London; the beach; Miami, Florida.

Lucky Love Star: Cancriel—you will never lack love or domestic comfort.

Beautiful Thought: You make life look so easy; is it?

Sharing Secrets: You had better be able to put your money where your mouth is. *For the gals:* It doesn't need to be lavish, but she does love the loot. The more the better. *For the guys:* He doesn't mind spending his hard-earned cash, but he loves to see you contribute to please him.

Judith's Insights

About the Man: You may find him living in the past because he does that so well in the present. He always thinks yesterday was better than today, and he will strive to top it. Make sure he is completely over his last lover before you get caught up with this guy. If he is not, you may be compared to her at every turn. He wants to be treated as if he is someone with positively no doubts. Honor is important to him. This is true for friendships as well as business relationships. If you are proven worthy you will find no one who is more devoted than this guy.

About the Woman: What a tangled web we weave. That would be her planting webs to catch that dream of love in every corner. She may seem to have a lot of little loves, because she does, but there will only be a few true loves in her life. You can be one of those true loves if you are as loyal as she is. She has to be able to depend on you at all costs. If she feels she can't lean on you when things are bad, she will find someone she can lean on. Consistency is the key to showing this gal what you are made of.

Soul Mates: Cancer with a Cancer is a perfect match. Leo and Libra are for leaning on instead of loving. Taurus could bore you. Try to teach them to add some excitement to their life. Capricorn and Aries are in love with control. Make sure you are ready to give it up or walk away. Watch out for mood swings with Scorpio and Pisces. The right attitude is essential when you are dealing with Virgo and Aquarius. It can make all the difference. You will experience life as never before when you are linked to Sagittarius. You simply have to be open to it. Gemini will love you forever if you can love them for all that they are.

Most Charming Characteristics: Resourceful, entertaining, kind.

Gifts: *For her:* spectacular candlelit meal at home. *For him:* new recliner.

Sensual Foods: Grapes; fine cheeses and crackers; taffy.

Romantic Flowers: Rhododendron will let her be on the lookout for trouble. Throw in some chrysanthemum and she'll know it is you she will be looking out for. Cactus will show him warmth. Yellow daffodil is a token of a good time had by all. Chivalry is not dead.

Best Date Nights: Monday; 8th and 17th of each month.

Colors of Passion: *For her:* orange, indigo. *For him:* green, russet.

The Perfect Wedding: You are inexplicably attracted to the water, so it's no wonder you and yours should spend your special day there. A romantic seashore, a marina, a cruise ship, even an aquarium or seaport should be among the first locations to consider. You demand security and love the domestic life that may lead to a serene bed-and-breakfast wedding overlooking a body of water. Ideal setting: Venice.

Wise Words: Charles Dickens: "The earth had donned her mantle of brightness green, and shed her richest perfumes abroad. It was the prime and the vigor of the year; all things were glad and flourishing."

Hints of Love: Treat this one like royalty or precious cargo. They will love being valued in this way.

After the Argument: *For him:* Do whatever he wants done around the house or make him a home-cooked meal. Make sure you are really productive. *For her:* Do things you usually hate to do for her. She is sure to notice your socks in the hamper instead of on the floor and appreciate it immensely.

Romantic Places: Places of leisure bring romance: the Caribbean; a mountain resort; Hilton Head, South Carolina.

Lucky Love Star: Cancriel—you will never lack love or domestic comfort.

Beautiful Thought: Everyone has his or her own fairy tale; most people just need to recognize the "Happily" in "Ever After."

Sharing Secrets: Nobody likes a weak link, especially not this one. *For the gals:* Make sure you treat her like a lady and act like a man. *For the guys:* Put your best foot forward. Dress your best and keep your manners in check. This man notices.

Judith's Insights

About the Man: He can whine like a girl if he doesn't get his way. Don't worry, his stubborn side will certainly remind you of his manhood. To know this guy is to love him. If you enter a relationship with him without really getting to know him beforehand, it will seem as if it is a constant work in progress. He has so many friends that it may take time to find out if he has any extra interest in you. If he does have the interest, romance will take more time than you think. He needs to get warmed up to you first and learn what makes you tick.

About the Woman: Everybody is always calling her for advice, so expect to be put on hold when you call. She has a busy schedule and likes it that way. Don't be put off by her efforts to change you. It is probably good advice that she is trying to give you. She has no reason to tell you anything but the truth. Getting close to her may take more time than you first thought. Just when you think you know her, you could realize that there is more than what meets the eye in this water. When she is comfortable with your intentions you will find no better mate around.

Soul Mates: There is no reason you would not get along famously with a fellow Cancer. Friendship may be your best bet with Leo and Libra. Otherwise, they might get the idea that they are in control. Don't let Taurus's need for stability hinder any excitement coming into your life. Capricorn and Aries are too rigid for your taste. When you get together with Scorpio and Pisces there may be an overload of emotions. When the relationship with Virgo and Aquarius gets you in way over your head, you must be prepared to walk away. When you are linked to Sagittarius, there is the potential of great things happening if you can go with the flow. Don't try to change Gemini. Just love them for all that they are.

Most Charming Characteristics: Fastidious, original, affectionate.

Gifts: *For her:* family portrait. *For him:* antique furniture.

Sensual Foods: Champagne; grapes; mangoes; filet mignon.

Romantic Flowers: The magnolias you send her will let her know you will be around for a while to come. Petunia is to say never despair. Holly will let him know what he is getting into. Pansy will keep you in his thoughts.

Best Date Nights: Monday; 18th and 27th of each month.

Colors of Passion: *For her:* orange, indigo. *For him:* green, russet.

The Perfect Wedding: You are inexplicably attracted to the water, so it's no wonder you and yours should spend your special day there. A romantic seashore, a marina, a cruise ship, even an aquarium or seaport should be among the first locations to consider. You demand security and love the domestic life that may lead to a serene bed-and-breakfast wedding overlooking a body of water. Ideal setting: Venice.

Wise Words: Charles Dickens: "Only the wisdom that holds the clue to all mysteries can surely know to what extent a man . . . can impose upon himself."

Hints of Love: Affection is important, but only if it comes naturally. Otherwise, the sirens will go off.

After the Argument: *For him:* Do whatever he wants done around the house or make him a home-cooked meal. Make sure you are really productive. *For her:* Do things you usually hate to do for her. She is sure to notice your socks in the hamper instead of on the floor and appreciate it immensely.

Romantic Places: Places of comfort bring romance: Britain; their own living room; Ocean City, Maryland.

Lucky Love Star: Cancriel—you will never lack love or domestic comfort.

Beautiful Thought: Taking responsibility for your own actions can change the outcome.

Sharing Secrets: Attention, attention, attention. *For the gals:* Do it any way you can. Presents, phone calls, cards, or flowers. Whatever works for you will work for her. *For the guys:* He would love nostalgic gifts or T-shirts. He also like phone calls, as long as they don't interrupt his favorite pastimes.

Judith's Insights

About the Man: He wants to be taken care of, and he doesn't care who does that job. He strives to be recognized for his efforts. Charm him and he will love every minute of it. Make sure that you are as honest as he expects. He has no time for people who play games to get what they want. He wants to show his love and for you to show your love in return. Don't interfere with his work or question his loyalty because of his concentration on his work. He will be ready and willing to give you the same amount of attention when he is finished in that area.

About the Woman: She has a heart of gold, but you had better not take that for granted for too long. If you are late once, fine; twice, fine; even three times, you'll get away with it. After that, you may show up and she'll be gone. She only expects what she gives you in return, and that is respect and loyalty. She enters relationships for the long haul but can jump into things she has not thought all the way through. Once she has made a commitment, however, she will work hard to make it work. To make it last, make your love unconditional.

Soul Mates: You and another Cancer are a wonderful match. Leo and Libra can bring out the best or worst in you, depending on the mood in the air. Because push always comes to shove, you and Taurus may have to try some new things together. Aries's and Capricorn's uncompromising nature could put out your fire of passion. When you get together with Scorpio and Pisces you might become overly sensitive to their insecurities. Sometimes Virgo and Aquarius can be worth the risk of being burned. Just be cautious. With Sagittarius you may feel like running away and staying in the exact same moment. Don't try to change Gemini. Accept what you are given.

Most Charming Characteristics: Ambitious, energetic, outdoorsy.

Gifts: *For her:* home-cooked meal. *For him:* antique painting.

Sensual Foods: Châteaubriand; crème brûlée.

Romantic Flowers: Iris is your flower if you are the gal sending subtle messages. If you are the man, you will look for clematis. This flower's mental beauty creates emotional stimulation for you.

Best Date Nights: Monday; 10th and 19th of each month.

Colors of Passion: *For her:* orange, indigo. *For him:* green, russet.

The Perfect Wedding: You are inexplicably attracted to the water, so it's no wonder you and yours should spend your special day there. A romantic seashore, a marina, a cruise ship, even an aquarium or seaport should be among the first locations to consider. You demand security and love the domestic life that may lead to a serene bed-and-breakfast wedding overlooking a body of water. Ideal setting: Venice.

Wise Words: Charles Dickens: "When a frank manner is offensive, it is because it is strained and feigned."

Hints of Love: This one likes others to make his or her dreams come true. Be the "fantasy" fulfiller.

After the Argument: *For him:* Do whatever he wants done around the house or make him a home-cooked meal. Make sure you are really productive. *For her:* Do things you usually hate to do for her. She is sure to notice your socks in the hamper instead of on the floor and appreciate it immensely.

Romantic Places: Places of comfort bring romance: Ireland; a bed-and-breakfast; Key West, Florida.

Lucky Love Star: Cancriel—you will never lack love or domestic comfort.

Beautiful Thought: A gift can sometimes be truly a gift.

Sharing Secrets: Make sure you are not the killjoy. *For the gals:* When she has an idea, try it before you decide you don't like it. She needs to be pleased. *For the guys:* Do the things he loves to do and he will make the things you love ten times more fun.

Judith's Insights

About the Man: As charming as he can be, he can also be as trying to your nerves as you can handle. Offer your help, but don't smother this guy. He enters from the side entrance to take a look around before he gets down to business. He has an unusual way of running his life and his love. Respect the way he does things while trying to encourage different approaches. He doesn't like change, especially when it comes to having a partner. Once the decision is made to commit he will show you his best feature, and that is his loyalty.

About the Woman: The older she gets, the less patient she will become with games and delays. She gives you enough room to hang yourself, so expect to prove yourself time and time again. As time goes on, she will lighten up. Never try to push her to get to that point before she is ready. The never-ending saga of her love life can be amusing when watched from the outside, thanks to her tendency to be overdramatic. While on the inside of that saga, you have to be patient to ride through her many moody periods. As time goes by the challenge becomes a joy.

Soul Mates: Cancer's house is your house, so you will get along just fine. When things are always the same, it can get boring. Make sure you and Taurus keep things fresh and new. Leo and Libra can be much too intense for your taste. Mood swings could prevail with Scorpio and Pisces. Capricorn's and Aries's instinct to control all around them will leave you dreaming of greener pastures. If you go in with the right attitude, the problems with Virgo and Aquarius won't seem as big. When you are in the right frame of mind, things can go very well with Sagittarius. Enjoy Gemini for the fun-loving spirits they are. If you can do that, then they can love you forever.

Most Charming Characteristics: Studious, straightforward, tactful.

Gifts: *For her:* pearl necklace. *For him:* leather journal.

Sensual Foods: Shrimp; sinful chocolate cake.

Romantic Flowers: Any rose of any color for the lady. Roses stand for love regardless of the color. Send them with orchids and you will be saying, "I love you." If you want a gentleman to know you think of him, send pansies, and forget-me-nots for true love.

Best Date Nights: Monday; 20th and 29th of each month.

Colors of Passion: *For her:* orange, indigo. *For him:* red, russet.

The Perfect Wedding: You are inexplicably attracted to the water, so it's no wonder you and yours should spend your special day there. A romantic seashore, a marina, a cruise ship, even an aquarium or seaport should be among the first locations to consider. You demand security and love the domestic life that may lead to a serene bed-and-breakfast wedding overlooking a body of water. Ideal setting: Venice.

Wise Words: Charles Dickens: "Perseverance and strength of character will enable us to bear much."

Hints of Love: Stop worrying about next week's date today or there will not be one tomorrow.

After the Argument: *For him:* Do whatever he wants done around the house or make him a home-cooked meal. Make sure you are really productive. *For her:* Do things you usually hate to do for her. She is sure to notice your socks in the hamper instead of on the floor and appreciate it immensely.

Romantic Places: Places of leisure bring romance: Bermuda; a spa; Myrtle Beach, South Carolina.

Lucky Love Star: Cancriel—you will never lack love or domestic comfort.

Beautiful Thought: You're allowed to enjoy every minute.

Sharing Secrets: You had better be ready to have a relationship. *For the gals:* No lies, no games, and no mistakes. She wants what she wants with as little work possible. *For the guys:* If you have games on your mind, then move on. This one likes fun any way he can get it, but no emotional roller coasters.

Judith's Insights

About the Man: He's a guy who needs a lot of stroking. Start off with noticing his looks, and he will be in your pocket. He certainly has a more stubborn side, so stay away from politics. Debating is one thing, but arguing is quite another, and he does not like to have to fight over his opinions. He loves to be social and makes everyone feel at home when around him. Parties are his specialty, and he will host event after event. Be supportive and let him know you are ready to help. He will ask only if he really needs it, and does not like help before that point.

About the Woman: She will be the floater around the room. She needs to feel busy and important. Her to-do list is far longer than anyone else's. Many times, she will act like the hostess even when she is not. She is really a down-to-earth gal. Don't worry about the show she puts on. If she lets you get close enough, you will see that it is really just an act. She loves to have many goals on the horizon to strive for. She is constantly trying to make today even better than yesterday. If she needs help she will ask, so don't try to butt in before she does.

Soul Mates: When you and a fellow Cancer share the what-is-mine-is-yours theory you will be bonded forever. Libra and Leo are too much for you to take. Try to ease away gently. A pairing with Taurus will start an inner fire that feeds your souls. Capricorn and Aries tend to forget the little joys in life. Try to revel in those same joys. A match with Scorpio and Pisces may result in overly protective or dependent behavior. Don't start a relationship with Virgo and Aquarius if you are not willing to work to keep it going. People can't change simply because you wish it. A relationship with Sagittarius can drive you crazy if you take things too personally. Taking things from moment to moment will make it easier. If you can't take Gemini, you should walk away.

Most Charming Characteristics: Intellectual, adventurous, steadfast.

Gifts: *For her:* cooking tools. *For him:* gardening tools.

Sensual Foods: Toasted marshmallows; chocolates.

Romantic Flowers: These ladies like everyone to know how faithful they are, so send them violets. To surprise them send tulips. Men like their flowers the same as their relationships, unpretending. Send them camellias with white roses to show your affection.

Best Date Nights: Monday; 12th and 30th of each month.

Colors of Passion: *For her:* orange, indigo. *For him:* green, maroon.

The Perfect Wedding: You are inexplicably attracted to the water, so it's no wonder you and yours should spend your special day there. A romantic seashore, a marina, a cruise ship, even an aquarium or seaport should be among the first locations to consider. You demand security and love the domestic life that may lead to a serene bed-and-breakfast wedding overlooking a body of water. Ideal setting: Venice.

Wise Words: Charles Dickens: "It is the highest part of the highest creed to forgive before memory sleeps, and ever to remember how the good overcame the evil."

Hints of Love: Keep the romance in the picture. Don't forget the long walks on the beach and camping out in front of the fireplace.

After the Argument: *For him:* Do whatever he wants done around the house or make him a home-cooked meal. Make sure you are really productive. *For her:* Do things you usually hate to do for her. She is sure to notice your socks in the hamper instead of on the floor and appreciate it immensely.

Romantic Places: Places of comfort bring romance: Switzerland; a log cabin; Savannah, Georgia.

Lucky Love Star: Cancriel—you will never lack love or domestic comfort.

Beautiful Thought: There is always a chance for a new beginning.

Sharing Secrets: You may have to give this one more than one chance. *For the gals:* Intriguing as she is, expect a handful. She lightens up as time goes on. *For the guys:* His quirks may make you have second thoughts, but that is what separates the men from the boys.

Judith's Insights

About the Man: Do not second-guess him, and don't ask too many questions. Let him feel like he is making all the decisions. He may be macho, but he's been known to whine from time to time. Let him get the complaining out of his system before trying to show him how to get things done. His family is the most important thing in his life, so do not underestimate the power they have over his decisions. Keep in mind that if you do become his mate, you will also be a part of his family. Then there will be nothing he won't do for you.

About the Woman: She knows how to dress to the nines, but this gal still has her jeans ready for action. Don't let her fancy look intimidate you. She has enough of a homebody in her to ground her goals in reality. Her phones are always ringing and she likes it that way. Don't allow that to discourage you one bit. The calls may just be from all of her family and friends. These people are very important to her. To impress her, invite her family along on a date. She will be sure to remember it. The key to her heart is to be as close to her family as she is.

Soul Mates: There is no reason you would not get along famously with a fellow Cancer. Friendship may be your best bet with Leo and Libra. Otherwise, they might get the idea that they are in control. Don't let Taurus's need for stability hinder any excitement coming into your life. Capricorn and Aries are too rigid for your taste. When you get together with Scorpio and Pisces there may be an overload of emotions. When the relationship with Virgo and Aquarius gets you in way over your head, you must be prepared to walk away. Sagittarius may grate on your nerves at first, but if you hang in there, it may be worth the effort. Don't try to change Gemini. Just love them for all that they are.

Most Charming Characteristics: Versatile, resourceful, generous.

Gifts: *For her:* day at the beach. *For him:* invite his mom to dinner.

Sensual Foods: Chocolate-covered strawberries; New York steak; scallops.

Romantic Flowers: These ladies like men with taste. Show them you love style by sending fuchsia flowers, or even brightly colored wildflowers will do. To confuse this man, send him lilies along with bright daisies to show your innocence. Keep him guessing.

Best Date Nights: Monday; 22nd and 31st of each month.

Colors of Passion: *For her:* orange, indigo. *For him:* green, russet.

The Perfect Wedding: You are inexplicably attracted to the water, so it's no wonder you and yours should spend your special day there. A romantic seashore, a marina, a cruise ship, even an aquarium or seaport should be among the first locations to consider. You demand security and love the domestic life that may lead to a serene bed-and-breakfast wedding overlooking a body of water. Ideal setting: Venice.

Wise Words: Saint Synesius: "Patience is a tree whose roots are very bitter, but the fruit thereof is very sweet."

Hints of Love: The mystery is important, but being evasive will create disaster. Make sure you know the difference.

After the Argument: *For him:* Do whatever he wants done around the house or make him a home-cooked meal. Make sure you are really productive. *For her:* Do things you usually hate to do for her. She is sure to notice your socks in the hamper instead of on the floor and appreciate it immensely.

Romantic Places: Places of leisure bring romance: the French countryside; a cruise; the Great Lakes.

Lucky Love Star: Cancriel—you will never lack love or domestic comfort.

Beautiful Thought: Being there when you can is good; being there when you can't is a friend.

Sharing Secrets: Talk about high maintenance. *For the gals:* Once she sees that you go out of your way for her, then she will for you. *For the guys:* The bark is definitely much worse than the bite. He comes on stronger and more obstinate than he actually is.

Judith's Insights

About the Man: He is certainly intense to work for, but when you need a day off, he'll be at your side. He can feel sorry for himself and sulk, especially if he gets too lonely. Definitely call this guy. He'll be happy to hear the phone ring even if he doesn't get it. Never let his calendar remain empty. You can always find him at the center of attention at a party. He loves to entertain and accommodate guests, even if he is not the host. Don't forget that home is not only where his heart is but his mind as well. If he seems off-key, maybe something is going on at home.

About the Woman: She certainly has a method to her madness. This gal starts out as everyone's friend. When she feels safe it will then progress to the next stage. She's a classy gal, so appeal to what appeals to her. Make plans to spend time with her family and she will remember that for the rest of her life. She loves to host events at her home to show the world how she lives. She is proud of her home and will be constantly fixing and decorating it. Lend her a hand with the chores and she will come to think of it as your home as well.

Soul Mates: Leos not only love themselves but anyone who is like them. Your good times, as well as the bad times, with Pisces and Virgo will be excessive. Libra and Gemini will bring out the best in you. Scorpio and Taurus will create a strong attraction, but one that is hard to maintain. Aries and Sagittarius will add spice to your life and leave you craving more. A link with Cancer can bring out the best or the worst in you. It all depends on the mood in the air. If you are friends with Aquarius and Capricorn first, it can last forever. Make sure you have that base. You can bring out the best or the worst in each other.

Most Charming Characteristics: Vivacious, energetic, fun-loving.

Gifts: *For her:* tickets to the circus. *For him:* night at a casino.

Sensual Foods: Vanilla and strawberry mousse; tiramisù; espresso.

Romantic Flowers: You are the lady of distinction, and only carnations will do. Any mix of colors with sprays of mignonette. Sweet peas or red carnations will appeal to this man's heart.

Best Date Nights: Sunday; 4th and 23rd of each month.

Colors of Passion: *For her:* yellow, orange. *For him:* green, maroon.

The Perfect Wedding: Anything that promises pleasure to you and your family and friends is right. You love the warmth and the charming, picturesque atmosphere of the theater. Medieval castles, old mansions, or a charming château tucked away in the woods can provide the perfect backdrop for this . . . your special day. Ideal setting: Prague.

Wise Words: Sir H. Wotton: "How happy is he born and taught that serveth not another's will; / Whose armour is his honest thought / And simple truth his utmost skill."

Hints of Love: If you learn to back up when things are moving too fast, you won't have to bow out so often.

After the Argument: *For him:* Saying you're sorry will never be enough unless you overdo it. Overwhelm him. Apologize until he tells you to stop, and then apologize for apologizing so much. *For her:* It had better be roses, and candy, and a night out on the town. And don't forget to stop at a local store and buy her something she would never buy for herself.

Romantic Places: Places of drama bring romance: London; an opera house; Broadway, New York City.

Lucky Love Star: Leonial—you will never lack desire.

Beautiful Thought: Did you know? A guardian angel sits quietly on your shoulders.

Sharing Secrets: Make sure you have at least five dates before you make up your mind. *For the gals:* They can be cynical, so it could be a few dates before she loosens up. *For the guys:* He still has yesterday on his mind. He needs a reason to forget his past relationship. Make a new history for him.

Judith's Insights

About the Man: He can be very temperamental, especially about his toys, and expect him to have plenty of them. So long as you allow this chap his freedom, he will stick around a while. If you try to fence him in where you can keep an eye on him, he will escape and never come back. He will be much more impressed if you give him freedom while giving him the love he so craves. He can be outstandingly generous, not only with his money but with his time and effort as well. Be as generous with yours and he will feel a kinship that may lead to something more.

About the Woman: Don't try to corner this gal, or she'll jump at you. She needs her space, and plenty of breathing room. Remember that flattery will get you everywhere. When in doubt, start with the looks and go from there. Appeal to her love of family to get into her heart for a long time. If she has the opportunity to flirt, and get a little thrill for the attention, she will jump at the chance. The only way to bring things past the flirting stage is to be loyal and consistent. She really does want a long-term commitment in her life.

Soul Mates: If you and a fellow Leo are to be together, you must first establish who will be in charge. Extremes are rampant with Virgo and Pisces. Make sure you balance self-confidence with humility. Everything you forgot people valued in you will shine again when you get together with Gemini and Libra. If you remember that opposites are exciting but difficult, then Scorpio and Taurus will work fine. Aries and Sagittarius have as much energy as you do. Capricorn and Aquarius have many thorns, but all beautiful flowers do. Cancer may bring out your insecurities.

Most Charming Characteristics: Intense, assured, sympathetic.

Gifts: *For her:* acting class. *For him:* sports tickets.

Sensual Foods: Raspberries; pound cake; caviar.

Romantic Flowers: You love it when you get tulips, declaring love. When you receive a variety, it shows how hopelessly in love your partner is. He will just love a single rose. This shows him you understand his pleasures.

Best Date Nights: Sunday; 6th and 24th of each month.

Colors of Passion: *For her:* indigo, orange. *For him:* red, russet.

The Perfect Wedding: Anything that promises pleasure to you and your family and friends is right. You love the warmth and the charming, picturesque atmosphere of the theater. Medieval castles, old mansions, or a charming chateau tucked away in the woods can provide the perfect backdrop for this . . . your special day. Ideal setting: Prague.

Wise Words: William Wordsworth: "Explore the countless springs of silent good; so shall the truth be better understood, / And thy grieved spirit brighten strong in faith."

Hints of Love: Expecting too much too soon can only build up hopes that will fall down too easily.

After the Argument: *For him:* Saying you're sorry will never be enough unless you overdo it. Overwhelm him. Apologize until he tells you to stop, and then apologize for apologizing so much. *For her:* It had better be roses, and candy, and a night out on the town. And don't forget to stop at a local store and buy her something she would never buy for herself.

Romantic Places: Places of wonder bring romance: Rio de Janeiro, a planetarium, Disney World.

Lucky Love Star: Leonial—you will never lack desire.

Beautiful Thought: Knowing that somebody out there really loves you.

Sharing Secrets: Don't be in a hurry, or it will be over before it begins. *For the gals:* Like fine wine and amazing food. Savor a moment until an hour is created. *For the guys:* To do too much too fast will prove risky. Try to give a push and he will just jump ship.

Judith's Insights

About the Man: This guy wants a lot to be going on at all times. He can talk himself in and out of a relationship. This is a guy who just sits on the fence waiting for someone to push him off and into something. To get him started talking all you have to do is ask him about his family. He wants to settle down and be happy more than most people realize. When, how, and with whom he commits still need to be determined. He can be settled one minute and not the next. Stand your ground and wait for the snakes in his head to settle down before asking questions.

About the Woman: She's always open for an invitation. This girl will seldom turn down any kind of fun. She has hundreds of fantasies and is looking to live them all out. She does protect herself by letting others believe she isn't so serious. She is looking for a mate who will let her have fun but be there when she comes home. Her emotions will go haywire if she suspects a lack of loyalty or wandering from her mate. Make sure that you are ready to love her unconditionally. She will reward your patience with warmth and love.

Soul Mates: Leo and a fellow Leo are a good match as long as control is established and agreed upon. Keep your idea of yourself in mind at all times when you try a relationship with Virgo and Pisces. Everything you wished but never seemed possible will be within reach when you have Gemini and Libra in your corner. The rewards in a relationship with Taurus and Scorpio depend on the work you put in. Aries and Sagittarius will have you flying around the world in no time. The rise and fall of a relationship with Aquarius and Capricorn are what make it so much fun. Watch out for Cancer. They will bring out all of your insecurities.

Most Charming Characteristics: Magnetic personality, sincere, love deeply.

Gifts: *For her:* night at a carnival. *For him:* camping out in the woods or the backyard.

Sensual Foods: Flambé; lobster; oysters.

Romantic Flowers: Send this girl sunflowers if you want her to know you adore her. You may even add some poppies for a splash of extravagance. His desire for sport and play will be understood when you send him hyacinth and geranium.

Best Date Nights: Sunday; 15th and 24th of each month.

Colors of Passion: *For her:* yellow, orange. *For him:* red, maroon.

The Perfect Wedding: Anything that promises pleasure to you and your family and friends is right. You love the warmth and the charming, picturesque atmosphere of the theater. Medieval castles, old mansions, or a charming chateau tucked away in the woods can provide the perfect backdrop for this . . . your special day. Ideal setting: Prague.

Wise Words: Edmund Spenser: "The gentle mind by gentle deeds is known, / For a man by nothing is so well betrayed / As by his manners."

Hints of Love: Make sure all the ingredients are present before putting the cake in the oven.

After the Argument: *For him:* Saying you're sorry will never be enough unless you overdo it. Overwhelm him. Apologize until he tells you to stop, and then apologize for apologizing so much. *For her:* It had better be roses, and candy, and a night out on the town. And don't forget to stop at a local store and buy her something she would never buy for herself.

Romantic Places: Places of drama bring romance: Russia; a casino; Toronto, Ontario.

Lucky Love Star: Leonial—you will never lack desire.

Beautiful Thought: When you need a helping hand, there's two.

Sharing Secrets: They need to look before they leap, but only in love. *For the gals:* She needs creative and exciting dates to keep her interested. Don't take her for granted too soon. *For the guys:* You may think he gives signs of moving this relationship quickly; make sure you slow it down before he does.

Judith's Insights

About the Man: Number one, he is complicated but he thinks he's not. Number two, he treats everybody he loves like gold, and enjoys every minute of it. He's charming but seldom disloyal. You really have to push him to make him want to betray you. It is usually only after you have betrayed him. He can interact well with anyone and everyone. Mess with his security and his home and there will be hell to pay. It is very easy to be on his side. Just be nice and sincere. Don't hesitate to make him feel special. He will return the favor tenfold.

About the Woman: She lives a little more in her head than she will care to admit. She wants a mate, but still looks to keep her independence at the same time. Surround her with love and affections straight from your heart. If you keep it romantic you will keep her happy. It doesn't hurt to get her family into the mix to appeal to her sense of home. If you play your cards right you will become part of her family, so it will pay if you become close to them early. Don't play games with this girl's heart. She can give you so much if you are simply the best you can be when you are with her.

Soul Mates: Leo can love Leo when control is established well in advance. Severe swings in the feel of a relationship with Virgo and Pisces are sure to come. Gemini and Libra will let you revel in your true and best self. Taurus and Scorpio pull you in, but you might be overwhelmed once you are there. Say hello to fiery passion and good-bye to the mundane when you hook up with Aries and Sagittarius. Don't let the bumps in the road throw you and Aquarius and Capricorn off course. Cancer will bring out the worst in you if you let them.

Most Charming Characteristics: Dependable, intelligent, capable.

Gifts: *For her:* tickets to a tennis tournament. *For him:* bike tour of local countryside.

Sensual Foods: Crème brûlée; poached salmon.

Romantic Flowers: Rhododendron will let her be on the lookout for trouble. Throw in some chrysanthemum and she'll know it is you she will be looking out for. Cactus will show him warmth. Yellow daffodil is a token of a good time had by all. Chivalry is not dead.

Best Date Nights: Sunday; 17th and 26th of each month.

Colors of Passion: *For her:* yellow, orange. *For him:* red, maroon.

The Perfect Wedding: Anything that promises pleasure to you and your family and friends is right. You love the warmth and the charming, picturesque atmosphere of the theater. Medieval castles, old mansions, or a charming chateau tucked away in the woods can provide the perfect backdrop for this . . . your special day. Ideal setting: Prague.

Wise Words: F. W. Faber: "Have we not always found in our past experience that, on the whole, our kind interpretations were truer than our harsh ones."

Hints of Love: Simple often turns into complicated with this one. When you overcomplicate the moment, try to step back for a breather.

After the Argument: *For him:* Saying you're sorry will never be enough unless you overdo it. Overwhelm him. Apologize until he tells you to stop, and then apologize for apologizing so much. *For her:* It had better be roses, and candy, and a night out on the town. And don't forget to stop at a local store and buy her something she would never buy for herself.

Romantic Places: Places of wonder bring romance: Aztec ruins; a museum; Niagara Falls, New York.

Lucky Love Star: Leonial—you will never lack desire.

Beautiful Thought: Growing up to be rich with knowledge.

Sharing Secrets: The possibilities are endless, if you can pay the price. *For the gals:* She is hoping chivalry is not dead, and you must be willing to be the man at all costs. *For the guys:* He can be demanding and somewhat controlling. He just needs to be trained.

Judith's Insights

About the Man: You know he will need to get in the last word when it comes to a fight. This guy doesn't mind who asks whom out as long as it happens. This guy does not have a shy bone in his body, however. He can be easily found in a crowded party. He is usually the one with a crowd around him. He certainly knows how to have a good time, but he might need to be taught how to go home and get some sleep. He is ageless with his energy. He will have you learning and doing things you had never imagined before.

About the Woman: She just looks to be loved. It sounds simple, but it is not necessarily so simple with this lady. She may have to put you through a few emotional hoops here and there. She can overdo it, but usually that means fun. Let her charm you into her arms and you will never regret it. If she gets depressed it will take plenty of work to get her back to her charming self again. No one will know how to do that better than her family. When in doubt, you can always ask them how to get into her heart.

Soul Mates: Leo and a fellow Leo are a good match as long as control is established and agreed upon. Keep your idea of yourself in mind at all times when you try a relationship with Virgo and Pisces. Everything you wished but never seemed possible will be within reach when you have Gemini and Libra in your corner. The rewards in a relationship with Taurus and Scorpio depend on the work you put in. Aries and Sagittarius will have you flying around the world in no time. The rise and fall of a relationship with Aquarius and Capricorn are what make it so much fun. Watch out for Cancer. They will bring out all of your insecurities.

Most Charming Characteristics: Determined, vivacious, lovable.

Gifts: *For her:* invite her family for a backyard barbecue. *For him:* gold watch.

Sensual Foods: Chocolate soufflé; filet mignon.

Romantic Flowers: The magnolias you send her will let her know you will be around for a while to come. Petunia is to say never despair. Holly will let him know what he is getting into. Pansy will keep you in his thoughts.

Best Date Nights: Sunday; 9th and 27th of each month.

Colors of Passion: *For her:* yellow, orange. *For him:* red, maroon.

The Perfect Wedding: Anything that promises pleasure to you and your family and friends is right. You love the warmth and the charming, picturesque atmosphere of the theater. Medieval castles, old mansions, or a charming chateau tucked away in the woods can provide the perfect backdrop for this . . . your special day. Ideal setting: Prague.

Wise Words: Mary Baker Eddy: "Truth comes from a deep sincerity that must always characterize heroic hearts; it is the better side of man's nature developing itself."

Hints of Love: Allow them to know what is in your heart as well as what is in your head.

After the Argument: *For him:* Saying you're sorry will never be enough unless you overdo it. Overwhelm him. Apologize until he tells you to stop, and then apologize for apologizing so much. *For her:* It had better be roses, and candy, and a night out on the town. And don't forget to stop at a local store and buy her something she would never buy for herself.

Romantic Places: Places of drama bring romance: Greece; a movie set; Los Angeles, California.

Lucky Love Star: Leonial—you will never lack desire.

Beautiful Thought: You are the one who looks on the bright side, even when all the lights are out.

Sharing Secrets: Tomorrow is another day, but why wait? You can do it all today. *For the gals:* Have your date filled from dusk to dawn, and then some. *For the guys:* You may find he needs a nap here and there, but he can last all day and all night if he has a reason.

Judith's Insights

About the Man: Never question this man about his loyalty or his intentions. This man has a heart of pure gold and gives pieces of it away every minute. You won't have any trouble getting his attention or his help. Just ask him! Even if it is above his abilities, he will find a way to get it done for you. He is easy to get along with, especially when he is appreciated by everyone around him. He adores those he keeps company with. Otherwise, they would not be there in the first place. If you are in the inner circle, there are definite possibilities.

About the Woman: Everyone may see her as the life of the party. This is not unusual, because it would be her hosting it nine times out of ten. Your approach can be flirty, but must be fun if you want to keep this gal's attention. Don't question her and she won't question you. Keep her laughing and you will keep her with you forever. She loves her home and enjoys showing it off more than anything else. If you help around the home, making things special, she will make you a part of her life forever.

Soul Mates: Leo will always get along famously with another Leo. Pisces and Virgo bring out the best or worst in you. Sometimes a little bit of both. Libra and Gemini make you see all of the good in yourself. A match with Scorpio and Taurus can work if you both recognize your differences. A pairing with Aries and Sagittarius has sizzle written all over it. Sharpen up your edges. A ride with Aquarius and Capricorn will be exciting indeed. Cancer may be a little too much to handle at times. Hang in there and it will be worth it.

Most Charming Characteristics: Energetic, charming, active mind.

Gifts: *For her:* satin pajamas. *For him:* silk boxer shorts.

Sensual Foods: Steak au poivre; cheesecake.

Romantic Flowers: Iris is your flower if you are the gal sending subtle messages. If you are the man, you will look for clematis. This flower's mental beauty creates emotional stimulation for you.

Best Date Nights: Sunday; 10th and 19th of each month.

Colors of Passion: *For her:* yellow, orange. *For him:* red, maroon.

The Perfect Wedding: Anything that promises pleasure to you and your family and friends is right. You love the warmth and the charming, picturesque atmosphere of the theater. Medieval castles, old mansions, or a charming chateau tucked away in the woods can provide the perfect backdrop for this . . . your special day. Ideal setting: Prague.

Wise Words: Charles Dickens: "What is right is right, and you can neither by tears nor laughter do away with its character."

Hints of Love: Keep both feet on the ground the first time you think you want to jump. This way you won't jump too high too soon.

After the Argument: *For him:* Saying you're sorry will never be enough unless you overdo it. Overwhelm him. Apologize until he tells you to stop, and then apologize for apologizing so much. *For her:* It had better be roses, and candy, and a night out on the town. And don't forget to stop at a local store and buy her something she would never buy for herself.

Romantic Places: Places of wonder bring romance: Jerusalem; the Statue of Liberty; Cape Canaveral, Florida.

Lucky Love Star: Leonial—you will never lack desire.

Beautiful Thought: Someone throws you a life preserver so you don't have to worry about drowning.

Sharing Secrets: It may need to start with friendship. This isn't the consolation prize; it's the grand prize. *For the gals:* Go slow and allow it to grow one seed at a time. You won't need to push; it will all come in time. *For the guys:* A step here and a step there. Before he knows it, that friendship will be love.

Judith's Insights

About the Man: He seems to attract people to him without quite knowing how or why. He can seem young for most of his adult life. He has a tendency to rush into things without thinking them through completely. His quick intuition and remarkable insight may intervene or check his rashness before it is too late. If he does get in over his head, he will still try to make things work as long as possible. His loyalty to himself and those he loves is unmatched. Take time to treat him to the things he denies himself while helping others.

About the Woman: She is a highly emotional lady. Her world and her decisions are ruled by those emotions. She is generous to a fault when these emotions come into play. Never take advantage of what she is willing to give. Make sure that you are ready to give the same level of commitment as she is. Her love is as loyal as it is intense. She is always fighting or ready to fight on behalf of those she loves. She is so sensitive that she can go through life without being understood and appreciated. Let her know just how much she, and everything she does, means to you.

Soul Mates: Leo and a fellow Leo are a good match as long as control is established and agreed upon. Keep your idea of yourself in mind at all times when you try a relationship with Virgo and Pisces. Everything you wished but never seemed possible will be within reach when you have Gemini and Libra in your corner. The rewards in a relationship with Taurus and Scorpio depend on the work you put in. Aries and Sagittarius will have you flying around the world in no time. The rise and fall of a relationship with Aquarius and Capricorn are what make it so much fun. Watch out for Cancer. They will bring out all of your insecurities.

Most Charming Characteristics: Witty, idealistic, affectionate.

Gifts: *For her:* personalized stationery. *For him:* handmade gift.

Sensual Foods: Strawberry shortcake; pineapple; ham.

Romantic Flowers: Any rose of any color for the lady. Roses stand for love regardless of the color. Send them with orchids and you will be saying, "I love you." If you want a gentleman to know you think of him, send pansies, and forget-me-nots for true love.

Best Date Nights: Sunday; 9th and 18th of each month.

Colors of Passion: *For her:* yellow, orange. *For him:* red, maroon.

The Perfect Wedding: Anything that promises pleasure to you and your family and friends is right. You love the warmth and the charming, picturesque atmosphere of the theater. Medieval castles, old mansions, or a charming chateau tucked away in the woods can provide the perfect backdrop for this . . . your special day. Ideal setting: Prague.

Wise Words: Charles Dickens: "Mature affection, homage, devotion, does not easily express itself. Its voice is low. It is modest and retiring, it lies in ambush, waits and waits."

Hints of Love: Laughter alleviates the tension, but so can understanding where another is sitting.

After the Argument: *For him:* Saying you're sorry will never be enough unless you overdo it. Overwhelm him. Apologize until he tells you to stop, and then apologize for apologizing so much. *For her:* It had better be roses, and candy, and a night out on the town. And don't forget to stop at a local store and buy her something she would never buy for herself.

Romantic Places: Places of drama bring romance: India; a theater; Hollywood, California.

Lucky Love Star: Leonial—you will never lack desire.

Beautiful Thought: Remember to touch a snowflake, a drop of rain, or a falling leaf.

Sharing Secrets: This one needs to be the one and only, even if it is only the first date. *For the gals:* Don't talk about your past relationships. Do all you can to make her feel cherished from the first moment. *For the guys:* Play up your innocence. Let him take charge, even in paying the bill. He needs to wear the pants.

Judith's Insights

About the Man: He is a born lover. He can't live without sympathy and affection, just like a plant can't live without water and sunlight. His ever-ready generosity is often the cause of his being imposed upon. It can leave him feeling drained and unappreciated. He will do all he can for you. Just pay him back by doing all you can for him. He will take great care in choosing a mate to keep for life. Once he has chosen that person there will be nothing he would not do to make it work.

About the Woman: She knows things without being taught. As a matter of fact, she will not even know how she knows some things. Her intuition is so strong that it leads her to exactly where she needs to be. She will long remember an act of kindness on your part. The only things she asks from you are loyalty and respect. She has great vitality and will live a long life with the right person by her side. Too many people have taken all they can from her and never given back. Give her all that she gives you and she will love you for it.

Soul Mates: Leo can love Leo when control is established well in advance. Severe swings in the feel of a relationship with Virgo and Pisces are sure to come. Gemini and Libra will let you revel in your true and best self. Taurus and Scorpio pull you in, but you might be overwhelmed once you are there. Say hello to fiery passion and good-bye to the mundane when you hook up with Aries and Sagittarius. Don't let the bumps in the road throw you and Aquarius and Capricorn off course. Cancer will bring out the worst in you if you let them.

Most Charming Characteristics: Perseverance, adaptable, ambitious.

Gifts: *For her:* designer clothes. *For him:* romantic walk.

Sensual Foods: Steak fondue; cheese fondue and French bread.

Romantic Flowers: These ladies like everyone to know how faithful they are, so send them violets. To surprise them send tulips. Men like their flowers the same as their relationships, unpretending. Send them camellias with white roses to show your affection.

Best Date Nights: Sunday; 9th and 27th of each month.

Colors of Passion: *For her:* yellow, orange. *For him:* red, maroon.

The Perfect Wedding: Anything that promises pleasure to you and your family and friends is right. You love the warmth and the charming, picturesque atmosphere of the theater. Medieval castles, old mansions, or a charming chateau tucked away in the woods can provide the perfect backdrop for this . . . your special day. Ideal setting: Prague.

Wise Words: Charles Dickens: "Time is money, and very good money, too, to those who reckon interest by it. Time is money! yes, and time costs money—it is rather an expensive article to some people."

Hints of Love: Communication is important here. A script isn't provided for you. You must write it for yourself.

After the Argument: *For him:* Saying you're sorry will never be enough unless you overdo it. Overwhelm him. Apologize until he tells you to stop, and then apologize for apologizing so much. *For her:* It had better be roses, and candy, and a night out on the town. And don't forget to stop at a local store and buy her something she would never buy for herself.

Romantic Places: Places of wonder bring romance: the Taj Mahal; a cathedral or temple; Niagara Falls, New York.

Lucky Love Star: Leonial—you will never lack desire.

Beautiful Thought: Relationships may seem like work until they really start to work.

Sharing Secrets: You need to remember never to forget. *For the gals:* Her birthday, holidays, and your anniversary. Even down to each dinner date. *For the guys:* His birthday, his laundry, his mother's birthday, and, of course, him any other day of the year.

Judith's Insights

About the Man: He is fiercely independent, and he will resent being commanded to do anything. He can obtain great popularity when he holds a position of power. His charming personality makes people love him instantly. It may take time for him to find the love of his life, but when he does it will be forever. He can be controlled entirely by his feelings. He will live life with passion, especially when surrounded by his loved ones. Generosity and charm radiate from him. He will be sure to notice any good deeds done for him and his family as long as they are from the heart.

About the Woman: This woman is warmhearted and extremely sympathetic. She will feel a friend's pain as keenly as the friend does. If a person has hurt one of her loved ones, she will fight tooth and nail to make that person pay. The way to her heart is through helping others around you. If you do something nice it will stick out in her mind. She will form her opinions of you just by watching how you are with people you come into contact with, not just how you treat her. Pretending to be nice won't work. It must come from your heart and soul for her to believe it.

Soul Mates: Leo and a fellow Leo are a good match as long as control is established and agreed upon. Keep your idea of yourself in mind at all times when you try a relationship with Virgo and Pisces. Everything you wished but never seemed possible will be within reach when you have Gemini and Libra in your corner. The rewards in a relationship with Taurus and Scorpio depend on the work you put in. Aries and Sagittarius will have you flying around the world in no time. The rise and fall of a relationship with Aquarius and Capricorn are what make it so much fun. Watch out for Cancer. They will bring out all of your insecurities.

Most Charming Characteristics: Honest, cautious, keen foresight.

Gifts: *For her:* exotic vacation destination. *For him:* weekend at a spa.

Sensual Foods: Baked Alaska; seafood.

Romantic Flowers: These ladies like men with taste. Show them you love style by sending fuchsia flowers, or even brightly colored wildflowers will do. To confuse this man, send him lilies along with bright daisies to show your innocence. Keep him guessing.

Best Date Nights: Sunday; 4th and 13th of each month.

Colors of Passion: *For her:* yellow, orange. *For him:* red, maroon.

The Perfect Wedding: Anything that promises pleasure to you and your family and friends is right. You love the warmth and the charming, picturesque atmosphere of the theater. Medieval castles, old mansions, or a charming chateau tucked away in the woods can provide the perfect backdrop for this . . . your special day. Ideal setting: Prague.

Wise Words: Charles Dickens: "The affections may not be so easily wounded as the passions, but their hurts are deeper and more lasting."

Hints of Love: Don't dissect every minute of every day. Learn to appreciate each minute as it comes.

After the Argument: *For him:* Saying you're sorry will never be enough unless you overdo it. Overwhelm him. Apologize until he tells you to stop, and then apologize for apologizing so much. *For her:* It had better be roses, and candy, and a night out on the town. And don't forget to stop at a local store and buy her something she would never buy for herself.

Romantic Places: Places of drama bring romance: the French Riviera; a casino; Las Vegas, Nevada.

Lucky Love Star: Leonial—you will never lack desire.

Beautiful Thought: Remember, love starts with like.

Sharing Secrets: My house should be your house, especially if you don't have one of your own. *For the gals:* All for one and one for all. Yours and mine must become ours. *For the guys:* If he needs to stand on ceremony, even for the first five minutes, it will be a definite turnoff for this one.

Judith's Insights

About the Man: These men are great admirers of romantic interludes, although they are not always consistent in their affections. He may confuse you with his contradictory actions. They are only a result of dealing with his strong emotions. Give him time to get used to what he is feeling before asking him for more. He will be the last to forsake a friendship once it is formed. Never get upset at the loads of friends who are asking for his advice. This is probably one of the things that attracted you to him in the first place.

About the Woman: Giving the shirt off her own back to a stranger is just the beginning. If you are close to her, there is nothing she won't do for you. This has gotten her into trouble in the past. Give her the same amount of love that she gives you. If she feels that the relationship is balanced she will stay in it for the long term. Helping her help others will only make your spot in her heart grow each day. Her energy will dwindle if she is not emotionally fed. Make her aware that you, and everyone else, are so happy for what she has done.

AUGUST

Soul Mates: Leo will always get along famously with another Leo. Pisces and Virgo bring out the best or worst in you. Sometimes a little bit of both. Libra and Gemini make you see all of the good in yourself. A match with Scorpio and Taurus can work if you recognize your differences. A pairing with Aries and Sagittarius has sizzle written all over it. Sharpen up your edges. A ride with Aquarius and Capricorn will be exciting indeed. Cancer may be a little too much to handle at times. Hang in there and it will be worth it.

Most Charming Characteristics: Intuitive, bold, outdoorsy.

Gifts: *For her:* acting class. *For him:* sports tickets.

Sensual Foods: Strawberries and cream; meat loaf.

Romantic Flowers: Iris is your flower if you are the gal sending subtle messages. If you are the man, you will look for clematis. This flower's mental beauty creates emotional stimulation for you.

Best Date Nights: Sunday; 1st and 10th of each month.

Colors of Passion: *For her:* yellow, orange. *For him:* red, maroon.

The Perfect Wedding: Anything that promises pleasure to you and your family and friends is right. You love the warmth and the charming, picturesque atmosphere of the theater. Medieval castles, old mansions, or a charming chateau tucked away in the woods can provide the perfect backdrop for this . . . your special day. Ideal setting: Prague.

Wise Words: Charles Dickens: "Love is not passion of earthly moulds, / As a thirst for honour, or fame, or gold; / for when all of these wishes have died away, / The deep strong love of a light brighter day, / Though nourished in secret, consumes the more, / As the slow rust eats to the iron core."

Hints of Love: They only use the three magic words when they know they mean it, and they already know it is going to be said back to them.

After the Argument: *For him:* Saying you're sorry will never be enough unless you overdo it. Overwhelm him. Apologize until he tells you to stop, and then apologize for apologizing so much. *For her:* It had better be roses, and candy, and a night out on the town. And don't forget to stop at a local store and buy her something she would never buy for herself.

Romantic Places: Places of drama bring romance: London; an opera house; Broadway.

Lucky Love Star: Leonial—you will never lack desire.

Beautiful Thought: If you want to see somebody smile, smile first.

Sharing Secrets: Let them admire something about you first. Show them you have a sense of humor. *For the guys:* The way to his heart is definitely through his stomach. *For the gals:* Hold their hand and then take them to the next step.

Judith's Insights

About the Man: You may have to wear a pair of Rollerblades to keep up with him. Expect to keep a flexible schedule. This guy has more energy than most around. You might get tired, but he will always keep any relationship young at heart no matter how long it has been around. You will have much fun with this one. If he is not having fun you will lose his attention fast. This includes simply working with him. If the office is not lively he will get bored. When this guy gets bored his mind will wander to bigger and better things.

About the Woman: You may have to be a mind reader to hang with this gal. She will be saying no but meaning yes, and she will assume that you will know the difference. You have to be persistent to get through the different aspects of her nature. Expect to open your wallet after you open your mouth, and back up your talk with action. You need to put a little passion in the package or she will take to the highway without looking back. Her need for spontaneity and romance has to be understood and participated in, or struggles will arise.

Soul Mates: Leo can love Leo when control is established well in advance. Severe swings in the feel of a relationship with Virgo and Pisces are sure to come. Gemini and Libra will let you revel in your true and best self. Taurus and Scorpio pull you in, but you might be overwhelmed once you are there. Say hello to fiery passion and good-bye to the mundane when you hook up with Aries and Sagittarius. Don't let the bumps in the road throw you and Aquarius and Capricorn off course. Cancer will bring out the worst in you if you let them.

Most Charming Characteristics: Aggressive, buoyant, adaptable.

Gifts: *For her:* night at a carnival. *For him:* camping out in the woods or the backyard.

Sensual Foods: Cherry-apple pie; beef Stroganoff.

Romantic Flowers: Any rose of any color for the lady. Roses stand for love regardless of the color. Send them with orchids and you will be saying, "I love you." If you want a gentleman to know you think of him, send pansies, and forget-me-nots for true love.

Best Date Nights: Sunday; 11th and 20th of each month.

Colors of Passion: *For her:* yellow, orange. *For him:* red, maroon.

The Perfect Wedding: Anything that promises pleasure to you and your family and friends is right. You love the warmth and the charming, picturesque atmosphere of the theater. Medieval castles, old mansions, or a charming chateau tucked away in the woods can provide the perfect backdrop for this . . . your special day. Ideal setting: Prague.

Wise Words: Charles Dickens: "Fortune will not bear chiding—we must not reproach her, or she shuns us."

Hints of Love: Remember to keep the dating fun. Don't act like you are married before your time.

After the Argument: *For him:* Saying you're sorry will never be enough unless you overdo it. Overwhelm him. Apologize until he tells you to stop, and then apologize for apologizing so much. *For her:* It had better be roses, and candy, and a night out on the town. And don't forget to stop at a local store and buy her something she would never buy for herself.

Romantic Places: Places of wonder bring romance: Rio de Janeiro; a planetarium; Disney World.

Lucky Love Star: Leonial—you will never lack desire.

Beautiful Thought: Happiness is a choice you choose.

Sharing Secrets: Give them the opportunity to notice you first. *For the gals:* They love to be adored; love at first sight. *For the guys:* Remember to always let them believe it was their idea.

Judith's Insights

About the Man: This guy likes for life to be a party at all times. You may find him playing cards in a hospital bed. Games are important to him no matter what his situation is at the time. You need to allow this guy to socialize. Give him just enough leeway to feel free but not enough to hang himself. You may feel that his generosity is overwhelming at times. In time you will come to love and count on it. He can be drained by the neediness of his family and friends. Help him take as much time for himself as he does for other people.

About the Woman: She can say exactly what she means right up front. This gal will put it all on the table at the first go-around. She likes to keep the air clear at all times, so make sure you resolve issues right away when they come up. If she feels as if things are hanging overhead she will head for the hills in an instant. She has good intuition and a great memory. She loves excitement and can be the life of the party. Even when there is no party, you will feel as if there is when you are in her company. She hates confrontations of all kinds. Try to stay clear of them.

Soul Mates: Leo and a fellow Leo are a good match as long as control is established and agreed upon. Keep your idea of yourself in mind at all times when you try a relationship with Virgo and Pisces. Everything you wished but never seemed possible will be within reach when you have Gemini and Libra in your corner. The rewards in a relationship with Taurus and Scorpio depend on the work you put in. Aries and Sagittarius will have you flying around the world in no time. The rise and fall of a relationship with Aquarius or Capricorn are what make it so much fun. Watch out for Cancer. They will bring out all of your insecurities.

Most Charming Characteristics: Independent, persistent, demonstrative.

Gifts: *For her:* tickets to a tennis tournament. *For him:* bike tour of local countryside.

Sensual Foods: Hot fudge sundae with all the trimmings; shepherd's pie.

Romantic Flowers: These ladies like everyone to know how faithful they are, so send them violets. To surprise them send tulips. Men like their flowers the same as their relationships, unpretending. Send them camellias with white roses to show your affection.

Best Date Nights: Sunday; 3rd and 30th of each month.

Colors of Passion: *For her:* yellow, orange. *For him:* red, maroon.

The Perfect Wedding: Anything that promises pleasure to you and your family and friends is right. You love the warmth and the charming, picturesque atmosphere of the theater. Medieval castles, old mansions, or a charming chateau tucked away in the woods can provide the perfect backdrop for this . . . your special day. Ideal setting: Prague.

Wise Words: Charles Dickens: "There are few moments in a man's existence when he experiences so much ludicrous distress, or meets with so little charitable commiseration, as when he is in pursuit of his own hat."

Hints of Love: Make sure you go on more than one date before you jump to conclusions on liking and disliking.

After the Argument: *For him:* Saying you're sorry will never be enough unless you overdo it. Overwhelm him. Apologize until he tells you to stop, and then apologize for apologizing so much. *For her:* It had better be roses, and candy, and a night out on the town. And don't forget to stop at a local store and buy her something she would never buy for herself.

Romantic Places: Places of drama bring romance: Russia; a casino; Toronto, Ontario.

Lucky Love Star: Leonial—you will never lack desire.

Beautiful Thought: A compromise is a "co-promise" that two people make, not one.

Sharing Secrets: This one loves a challenge. *For the gals:* Be consistently inconsistent until you have her hooked. *For the guys:* This one loves to play catch. You may feel like a yo-yo, but as long as he is calling that's all that matters.

Judith's Insights

About the Man: He has an ego like you have rarely seen before. It is certainly not hard to capture his attention, although it may be hard to keep it for a long period of time. He loves compliments, so pour them on if you need something from him. There is no such thing as too many as long as they are believable. Paying attention to him is really paying a price. It will cost you big in your time and energy. He is a good and loyal friend, and he knows how to keep a secret. Family plays a large role in his life. To get close to his family is to get close to him.

About the Woman: She likes to be liked. If she is flirting it may not be anything to write home about. She might just be up to her trick of pulling you in. She may or may not be doing something with you once you are in. If she is cooking you dinner, then you are in for sure. If she buys you a gift, then she is interested in a lot more than company. She loves to spend the almighty dollar and loves to have it spent on her. If she shows a sign of being frugal she may just be feeling you out. Her generosity will kick into high gear when she is sure that you are worthy.

Soul Mates: Leos not only love themselves, but anyone like them. Your good times, as well as the bad times, with Pisces and Virgo will be excessive. Libra and Gemini will bring out the best in you. Scorpio and Taurus will create a strong attraction, but one that is hard to maintain. Aries and Sagittarius will add spice to your life and leave you craving more. A link with Cancer can bring out the best or the worst in you. It all depends on the mood in the air. If you are friends with Aquarius and Capricorn first, it can last forever. Make sure you have that base. You can bring out the best or the worst in each other.

Most Charming Characteristics: Domestic, intellectual, sincere.

Gifts: *For her:* invite her family for a backyard barbecue. *For him:* gold watch.

Sensual Foods: Whipped cream, strawberries, brown sugar, and heavy cream.

Romantic Flowers: These ladies like men with taste. Show them you love style by sending fuchsia flowers, or even brightly colored wildflowers will do. To confuse this man, send him lilies along with bright daisies to show your innocence. Keep him guessing.

Best Date Nights: Sunday; 13th and 22nd of each month.

Colors of Passion: *For her:* yellow, orange. *For him:* red, maroon.

The Perfect Wedding: Anything that promises pleasure to you and your family and friends is right. You love the warmth and the charming, picturesque atmosphere of the theater. Medieval castles, old mansions, or a charming chateau tucked away in the woods can provide the perfect backdrop for this . . . your special day. Ideal setting: Prague.

Wise Words: Charles Dickens: "Preserve in a thorough determination to do whatever you have to do as well as you can do it."

Hints of Love: Don't act too needy too soon. It may push this relationship away.

After the Argument: *For him:* Saying you're sorry will never be enough unless you overdo it. Overwhelm him. Apologize until he tells you to stop, and then apologize for apologizing so much. *For her:* It had better be roses, and candy, and a night out on the town. And don't forget to stop at a local store and buy her something she would never buy for herself.

Romantic Places: Places of wonder bring romance: Aztec ruins; a museum; Niagara Falls, New York.

Lucky Love Star: Leonial—you will never lack desire.

Beautiful Thought: When you encourage hope, it makes it easy to cope.

Sharing Secrets: This is a family person at heart; your presence is most important. *For the gals:* Make sure you go to Sunday dinner with her family when you are invited. *For the guys:* If you don't like his mom, you might have a hard time catching this one.

Judith's Insights

About the Man: This guy is the personification of procrastination. Don't wait for him to call. Instead, pick up the phone yourself. You may find that he has been meaning to catch up with you but has been putting it off. Underneath his strong exterior is a guy who is searching for someone to put up with him and all of his toys. He loves to be kept busy at all times. His is one dance card that won't stay empty for long. At work, there is no better boss than one who works with you to get the work done. When it is finished, he is the first to celebrate with you as well.

About the Woman: Send her a singing telegram—or even better, be the singing telegram yourself. Once things get going it will be an adventure that you will not likely forget. Pack an overnight bag and have it ready for fun. Whether she is a friend or a co-worker, she will give your life a new meaning just by being there. You might be looking at things in a whole new light after she gets a hold on you. The more glitz and light in your life the happier she will be. She will give you so much that your head may begin to spin. Give back to her so she does not end up feeling drained.

Soul Mates: Leo will always get along famously with another Leo. Pisces and Virgo bring out the best or worst in you. Sometimes a little bit of both. Libra and Gemini make you see all of the good in yourself. A match with Scorpio and Taurus can work if you recognize your differences. A pairing with Aries and Sagittarius has sizzle written all over it. Sharpen up your edges. A ride with Aquarius and Capricorn will be exciting indeed. Cancer may be a little too much to handle at times. Hang in there and it will be worth it.

Most Charming Characteristics: Witty, alert, fastidious.

Gifts: *For her:* satin pajamas. *For him:* silk boxer shorts.

Sensual Foods: Puddings and pastry of all kinds.

Romantic Flowers: You are the lady of distinction, and only carnations will do. Any mix of colors with sprays of mignonette. Sweet peas or red carnations will appeal to this man's heart.

Best Date Nights: Sunday; 5th and 23rd of each month.

Colors of Passion: *For her:* yellow, orange. *For him:* red, maroon.

The Perfect Wedding: Anything that promises pleasure to you and your family and friends is right. You love the warmth and the charming, picturesque atmosphere of the theater. Medieval castles, old mansions, or a charming chateau tucked away in the woods can provide the perfect backdrop for this . . . your special day. Ideal setting: Prague.

Wise Words: Charles Dickens: "No one is useless in this world who lightens the burdens of it for anyone else."

Hints of Love: Keep it fun. Look for new and exciting things to do, especially if you are in a long-term relationship.

After the Argument: *For him:* Saying you're sorry will never be enough unless you overdo it. Overwhelm him. Apologize until he tells you to stop, and then apologize for apologizing so much. *For her:* It had better be roses, and candy, and a night out on the town. And don't forget to stop at a local store and buy her something she would never buy for herself.

Romantic Places: Places of drama bring romance: Greece; a movie set; Los Angeles, California.

Lucky Love Star: Leonial—you will never lack desire.

Beautiful Thought: Your vision creates destination.

Sharing Secrets: Everything in its good time. This one works slowly, but when it is time to pick up speed, watch out. *For the gals:* Don't go by the obvious. Read between the lines. As long as the invitation is being offered go full speed ahead. *For the guys:* Just when you thought you should walk away, he'll say, "I love you." Talk about confusing.

Judith's Insights

About the Man: He can be so conscientious about things that he can talk himself out of doing anything. No matter how trivial the project might be, he will give it all that he has. This is true of every first date he may have. You will find him going all out to make everything perfect. He may go overboard, but he has fun doing it. He doesn't make it easy to surprise him. He is usually the one who does the spontaneous things. When you try to do the same for him he will catch wind of it fast. You will have to be really sneaky to get away with it, but the look on his face will make it worth it.

About the Woman: She will love it when you do outrageous things for her. The more of a fuss you make over her the better she will feel about herself and the relationship. She can spot a phony from miles away, so make sure that you are genuine. If she feels as if she is being patronized she will turn and walk away. Be a copycat of things she has done for you in the past. This lion won't mind because she will know that your heart is in it. Besides, she always treats people the way she wants to be treated. Follow her lead.

Soul Mates: If you and a fellow Leo are to be together, you must first establish who will be in charge. Extremes are rampant with Virgo and Pisces. Make sure you balance self-confidence with humility. Everything you forgot people valued in you will shine again when you get together with Gemini and Libra. If you remember that opposites are exciting but difficult, then Scorpio and Taurus will work fine. Aries and Sagittarius have as much energy as you do. Capricorn and Aquarius have many thorns, but all beautiful flowers do. Cancer may bring out your insecurities.

Most Charming Characteristics: Ardent, articulate, sociable.

Gifts: *For her:* personalized stationery. *For him:* handmade gift.

Sensual Foods: Champagne with strawberries; fillet of sole.

Romantic Flowers: You love it when you get tulips, declaring love. When you receive a variety, it shows how hopelessly in love your partner is. He will just love a single rose. This shows him you understand his pleasures.

Best Date Nights: Sunday; 15th and 24th of each month.

Colors of Passion: *For her:* yellow, orange. *For him:* red, maroon.

The Perfect Wedding: Anything that promises pleasure to you and your family and friends is right. You love the warmth and the charming, picturesque atmosphere of the theater. Medieval castles, old mansions, or a charming chateau tucked away in the woods can provide the perfect backdrop for this . . . your special day. Ideal setting: Prague.

Wise Words: Mary Baker Eddy: "Goodness and Benevolence never tire. They maintain themselves and others and never stop from exhaustion."

Hints of Love: This one is a cautious soul. You may have to find a way to go around to the back door.

After the Argument: *For him:* Saying you're sorry will never be enough unless you overdo it. Overwhelm him. Apologize until he tells you to stop, and then apologize for apologizing so much. *For her:* It had better be roses, and candy, and a night out on the town. And don't forget to stop at a local store and buy her something she would never buy for herself.

Romantic Places: Places of wonder bring romance: Jerusalem; the Statue of Liberty; Cape Canaveral, Florida.

Lucky Love Star: Leonial—you will never lack desire.

Beautiful Thought: Have the desire to make someone else happy, and love every minute of it.

Sharing Secrets: This one is a charmer, perhaps even fickle. *For the gals:* If you are patient enough to stick around, this one is worth the wait. *For the guys:* If there is enough time on the clock, stick around past three months. Then maybe he will have noticed you are there.

Judith's Insights

About the Man: He is a whole lot complicated. Not only does he expect you to be able to read his mind, he will expect you to mind his heart as well. Keep in mind how things will affect him and his feelings at all times. If you hurt these feelings he will take it personally. Flattery gets you anywhere and everywhere with him. He can certainly entertain the crowd. He will do much better in groups than one-on-one. Expect him to have a lot of guests at his house or he will go out to find some. He needs stimulation to make every day a party in progress.

About the Woman: This is one popular gal, so make your phone calls early in the week to make plans for the weekend. She leaves nothing to chance unless she is at a casino. Make prior arrangements whenever possible and even try to plan ahead in the month. Her laughter will catch you, and her intelligence will keep you interested. Try to do things for her just for the sake of doing them. She will be sure to notice that you are going out of your way for her. This will be a particular treat because she is usually the one going out of her way.

Soul Mates: Leo and a fellow Leo are a good match as long as control is established and agreed upon. Keep your idea of yourself in mind at all times when you try a relationship with Virgo and Pisces. Everything you wished but never seemed possible will be within reach when you have Gemini and Libra in your corner. The rewards in a relationship with Taurus and Scorpio depend on the work you put in. Aries and Sagittarius will have you flying around the world in no time. The rise and fall of a relationship with Aquarius or Capricorn are what make it so much fun. Watch out for Cancer. They will bring out all of your insecurities.

Most Charming Characteristics: Proud, humorous, winning personality.

Gifts: *For her:* designer clothes. *For him:* romantic walk.

Sensual Foods: Chocolates; poached salmon; flambé; filet mignon; potatoes.

Romantic Flowers: Send this girl sunflowers if you want her to know you adore her. You may even add some poppies for a splash of extravagance. His desire for sport and play will be understood when you send him hyacinth and geranium.

Best Date Nights: Sunday; 6th and 15th of each month.

Colors of Passion: *For her:* yellow, orange. *For him:* red, maroon.

The Perfect Wedding: Anything that promises pleasure to you and your family and friends is right. You love the warmth and the charming, picturesque atmosphere of the theater. Medieval castles, old mansions, or a charming chateau tucked away in the woods can provide the perfect backdrop for this . . . your special day. Ideal setting: Prague.

Wise Words: Percy Bysshe Shelley: "Gentleness, Virtue, Wisdom and Endurance, / These are the seals of that most firm assurance / Which bars the pit over Destruction's strength."

Hints of Love: Passion must be in the picture at all times or you could lose this one's attention quickly.

After the Argument: *For him:* Saying you're sorry will never be enough unless you overdo it. Overwhelm him. Apologize until he tells you to stop, and then apologize for apologizing so much. *For her:* It had better be roses, and candy, and a night out on the town. And don't forget to stop at a local store and buy her something she would never buy for herself.

Romantic Places: Places of drama bring romance: India; a theater; Hollywood, California.

Lucky Love Star: Leonial—you will never lack desire.

Beautiful Thought: Being treated like one of the family, when you aren't.

Sharing Secrets: If you are looking for love, then you have found the right mate. *For the gals:* This one could be stubborn. It may take forever to get a relationship started, but it is as solid as they come. *For the guys:* Even when he is ready, he might not be willing and able. He will put you through more obstacles than any course. Be patient.

Judith's Insights

About the Man: He loves his home more than most others. He may love the garage or the basement most of all. Appeal to his desires to get him close to you. Don't ask this guy to a black-tie affair for the first date. Instead, try to find out his favorite restaurant and make reservations before you ask. When he finds out where you are going, there will be only one answer. He keeps old lovers as best friends. He does not like for things to end, so he will just keep everyone around him. Even his bad side is so sincere that it is next to impossible to hate him.

About the Woman: She has a pocketful of jokes and an answer for everything. Her best quality is everything about her. Even if she is not interested in anything further, she will be the best friend you have ever had. She loves to be loved and treated well. Make sure her birthday gift arrives on time and is something very special. She is generous to all those she loves, and that is a lot of people. Try to make her day as special as she makes yours. She can be a handful to live with, but you will make the best memories together when things are going fast and furious.

Soul Mates: Leo can love Leo when control is established well in advance. Severe swings in the feel of a relationship with Virgo and Pisces are sure to come. Gemini and Libra will let you revel in your true and best self. Taurus and Scorpio pull you in, but you might be overwhelmed once you are there. Say hello to fiery passion and good-bye to the mundane when you hook up with Aries and Sagittarius. Don't let the bumps in the road throw you and Aquarius or Capricorn off course. Cancer will bring out the worst in you if you let them.

Most Charming Characteristics: Sensitive, intuitive, affectionate.

Gifts: *For her:* exotic vacation destination. *For him:* weekend at a spa.

Sensual Foods: Caviar; beef tenderloin; potatoes au gratin.

Romantic Flowers: Rhododendron will let her be on the lookout for trouble. Throw in some chrysanthemum and she'll know it is you she will be looking out for. Cactus will show him warmth. Yellow daffodil is a token of a good time had by all. Chivalry is not dead.

Best Date Nights: Sunday; 8th and 17th of each month.

Colors of Passion: *For her:* yellow, orange. *For him:* red, maroon.

The Perfect Wedding: Anything that promises pleasure to you and your family and friends is right. You love the warmth and the charming, picturesque atmosphere of the theater. Medieval castles, old mansions, or a charming chateau tucked away in the woods can provide the perfect backdrop for this . . . your special day. Ideal setting: Prague.

Wise Words: John Clare: "What is there half so sweet and dear, / As sweet discourse from lips we love / In earth's green spots and places where Joys breathe a blessing from above."

Hints of Love: A random act of kindness will go a long way with this one. What can you do for them today?

After the Argument: *For him:* Saying you're sorry will never be enough unless you overdo it. Overwhelm him. Apologize until he tells you to stop, and then apologize for apologizing so much. *For her:* It had better be roses, and candy, and a night out on the town. And don't forget to stop at a local store and buy her something she would never buy for herself.

Romantic Places: Places of wonder bring romance: the Taj Mahal; a cathedral or temple; Niagara Falls, New York.

Lucky Love Star: Leonial—you will never lack desire.

Beautiful Thought: There is nothing like an invitation, especially if it's one you waited for.

Sharing Secrets: If you can hang around and give constant stimulation, this could be your mate. *For the gals:* She is always looking for the Exit sign. Don't show her where it is or she will be gone. *For the guys:* Fast car, fast food; he likes everything that goes fast. Put on your running shoes. If you can keep up, then he is yours.

Judith's Insights

About the Man: He is clever when it comes to just about everything. He always knows just what to say that will get the crowd laughing. When he falls it is hard to peel him off the ground. He can be a workaholic, so find a reason for him to stay at home and relax. Just don't let him know that is why he is home! His energy has the strength of the sun, and his disposition is just as sunny. Give him his own space and time as much as possible. Otherwise, he will run at the first opportunity. If he has his own room he may stay forever.

About the Woman: She can tell you all of the good things about herself. She is not shy in any way and is never ashamed of the bad things about herself. If she is not interested in keeping you company, you will know right away. She will be distracted by anything around. Keep her interested by talking about her. She may spend half of her time trying to make others see things the way she does. Her energy and drive are unmatched. She can be a contradiction at times. One minute she wants to cuddle and the next she will want to dance.

Soul Mates: Leo will always get along famously with another Leo. Pisces and Virgo bring out the best or worst in you. Sometimes a little bit of both. Libra and Gemini make you see all of the good in yourself. A match with Scorpio and Taurus can work if you recognize your differences. A pairing with Aries and Sagittarius has sizzle written all over it. Sharpen up your edges. A ride with Aquarius and Capricorn will be exciting indeed. Cancer may be a little too much to handle at times. Hang in there and it will be worth it.

Most Charming Characteristics: Sincere, honest, just.

Gifts: *For her:* tickets to the circus. *For him:* night at a casino.

Sensual Foods: Passion fruit; fillet of sole almondine.

Romantic Flowers: The magnolias you send her will let her know you will be around for a while to come. Petunia is to say never despair. Holly will let him know what he is getting into. Pansy will keep you in his thoughts.

Best Date Nights: Sunday; 9th and 27th of each month.

Colors of Passion: *For her:* yellow, orange. *For him:* red, maroon.

The Perfect Wedding: Anything that promises pleasure to you and your family and friends is right. You love the warmth and the charming, picturesque atmosphere of the theater. Medieval castles, old mansions, or a charming chateau tucked away in the woods can provide the perfect backdrop for this . . . your special day. Ideal setting: Prague.

Wise Words: Charles Dickens: "Breaking up are capital things in our school days, but in afterlife they are painful enough."

Hints of Love: Family and friends are important to this one. Don't try to alienate them or it will definitely backfire on you.

After the Argument: *For him:* Saying you're sorry will never be enough unless you overdo it. Overwhelm him. Apologize until he tells you to stop, and then apologize for apologizing so much. *For her:* It had better be roses, and candy, and a night out on the town. And don't forget to stop at a local store and buy her something she would never buy for herself.

Romantic Places: Places of drama bring romance: French Riviera; a casino; Las Vegas, Nevada.

Lucky Love Star: Leonial—you will never lack desire.

Beautiful Thought: When all else fails, look for the laughter.

Sharing Secrets: This one may seem like a lot of work. They just need the basics: love, loyalty, and respect. *For the gals:* If you can show her your best side right from the beginning it may work. Be careful of fluff, because she will see right through it. *For the guys:* He loves to be loved. Give him plenty of attention, even if you think you don't stand a chance. Perseverance will win here.

Judith's Insights

About the Man: He needs to have something to talk about. He will always have a handful of answers to any question; whether he is asked in the first place is irrelevant. If you take the time to take a look at this guy he will notice it the first time around. If you are looking for his attention, compliments are your fastest route. He can keep even the most serious relationship simple. He needs to have his own sense of space and he will give you yours. He can let his pride get in the way of progress from time to time, but it never lasts for very long.

About the Woman: She is absolutely brilliant with words. Ask her any question and she will undoubtedly have the answer right away. Even the first time you meet her will not be awkward. She has a talent for making everyone feel at home around her. You will find yourself making excuses to walk past her desk in the office. She loves to do things in a big way. When giving her a gift or throwing her a party, always make sure to go all out to make her happy. She will always be ready to do the same for you. Odds are, she already has.

Soul Mates: Leo will always get along famously with another Leo. Pisces and Virgo bring out the best or worst in you. Sometimes a little bit of both. Libra and Gemini make you see all of the good in yourself. A match with Scorpio and Taurus can work if you recognize your differences. A pairing with Aries and Sagittarius has sizzle written all over it. Sharpen up your edges. A ride with Aquarius and Capricorn will be exciting indeed. Cancer may be a little too much to handle at times. Hang in there and it will be worth it.

Most Charming Characteristics: Generosity, executive ability, good judgment.

Gifts: *For her:* acting class. *For him:* sports tickets.

Sensual Foods: Peaches; mousse; shrimp.

Romantic Flowers: Iris is your flower if you are the gal sending subtle messages. If you are the man, you will look for clematis. This flower's mental beauty creates emotional stimulation for you.

Best Date Nights: Sunday; 19th and 28th of each month.

Colors of Passion: *For her:* yellow, orange. *For him:* red, maroon.

The Perfect Wedding: Anything that promises pleasure to you and your family and friends is right. You love the warmth and the charming, picturesque atmosphere of the theater. Medieval castles, old mansions, or a charming chateau tucked away in the woods can provide the perfect backdrop for this . . . your special day. Ideal setting: Prague.

Wise Words: Charles Dickens: "One person can no more quarrel without an adversity than one can play at chess or fight a duel."

Hints of Love: Show others how much you adore him or her. They will revel in how others notice.

After the Argument: *For him:* Saying you're sorry will never be enough unless you overdo it. Overwhelm him. Apologize until he tells you to stop, and then apologize for apologizing so much. *For her:* It had better be roses, and candy, and a night out on the town. And don't forget to stop at a local store and buy her something she would never buy for herself.

Romantic Places: Places of drama bring romance: London; an opera house; Broadway, New York City.

Lucky Love Star: Leonial—you will never lack desire.

Beautiful Thought: An apology can be a gift for both the person giving it and the person receiving it.

Sharing Secrets: They are looking for love, but that is just their little secret. *For the gals:* Why shouldn't they want to be loved? Of course they do, but they want you to do all of the work. *For the guys:* You must prove yourself repeatedly. Don't expect too much until he knows you are under his thumb.

Judith's Insights

About the Man: He loves to be Mr. Social. Even if his calendar seems full, try to find a way to sneak into his master plan. Learn to take a back seat to him and his needs. Before you know what happened, he will have you in the driver's seat and he will be catering to all of your wants and needs. It is his way of repayment for putting up with him. You may have to be the one to teach him to lie back and relax. Do not expect him to be able to do so overnight. It will take him time to balance his energy and let things flow naturally.

About the Woman: With all of this gal's energy, expect to be jogging to keep up with her. Leave a note on the windshield of her car if you find it hard to keep track of her whereabouts. You may have to come up with a unique way of catching her attention. Once you do, you can be sure that you won't lose it. She needs to know that there is something there that can turn into a long-term relationship. Without that potential, she may feel as if she is wasting her time. Until then, you had better take your vitamins. You will need the extra nutrition to keep up with her active lifestyle.

Soul Mates: Leo can love Leo when control is established well in advance. Severe swings in the feel of a relationship with Virgo and Pisces are sure to come. Gemini and Libra will let you revel in your true and best self. Taurus and Scorpio pull you in, but you might be overwhelmed once you are there. Say hello to fiery passion and good-bye to the mundane when you hook up with Aries and Sagittarius. Don't let the bumps in the road throw you and Aquarius or Capricorn off course. Cancer will bring out the worst in you if you let them.

Most Charming Characteristics: Perseverance, determination, devotion.

Gifts: *For her:* night at a carnival. *For him:* camping out in the woods or the backyard.

Sensual Foods: Kiwis; cantaloupes; strawberries.

Romantic Flowers: Any rose of any color for the lady. Roses stand for love regardless of the color. Send them with orchids and you will be saying, "I love you." If you want a gentleman to know you think of him, send pansies, and forget-me-nots for true love.

Best Date Nights: Sunday; 11th and 20th of each month.

Colors of Passion: *For her:* yellow, orange. *For him:* red, maroon.

The Perfect Wedding: Anything that promises pleasure to you and your family and friends is right. You love the warmth and the charming, picturesque atmosphere of the theater. Medieval castles, old mansions, or a charming chateau tucked away in the woods can provide the perfect backdrop for this . . . your special day. Ideal setting: Prague.

Wise Words: Henry Wadsworth Longfellow: "Sunday is like the stile between the fields of toil, where we can kneel and pray, or sit and meditate."

Hints of Love: Don't overdo it (dress, attention) too soon or this one will run. Wait until you have them hooked before you become outrageous.

After the Argument: *For him:* Saying you're sorry will never be enough unless you overdo it. Overwhelm him. Apologize until he tells you to stop, and then apologize for apologizing so much. *For her:* It had better be roses, and candy, and a night out on the town. And don't forget to stop at a local store and buy her something she would never buy for herself.

Romantic Places: Places of wonder bring romance: Rio de Janeiro; a planetarium; Disney World.

Lucky Love Star: Leonial—you will never lack desire.

Beautiful Thought: Someone loves you and doesn't mind showing it.

Sharing Secrets: You had better be ready to pull out your romantic side if you want this to work. *For the gals:* Fireplaces, walks on the beach, or even winning a bear at the local carnival. *For the guys:* When you are out shopping bring him something home. Even if it is silly, he will love the thought.

Judith's Insights

About the Man: This magnanimous guy will have no trouble attracting dates and projects. He can be picky, however, and you have to be up to snuff for him to choose you over all of the other offers. If you find yourself in his company more than once, then you know he is interested. Be the best you can be to keep him around. He loves to be loved and will never mind when others are demonstrative about their love for him. As long as this guy's partner is able to bring romance and spontaneity to the table there will be no one that is a more loyal mate.

About the Woman: Happiness to her is an ice-cream cone or a night at the carnival. Don't use polished approaches to catch her eye. She likes down-to-earth good stuff. Be genuine and sincere, and that is all she can ever ask for. Keep the splurging and fancy things for later or a special occasion. She can be a slave driver as a boss, but she will always make up for it when the job is done and it is time to celebrate. That is when her generosity kicks into high gear. In love and work, she always rewards a good effort with a more-than-ample bonus.

Soul Mates: Leo and a fellow Leo are a good match as long as control is established and agreed upon. Keep your idea of yourself in mind at all times when you try a relationship with Virgo and Pisces. Everything you wished but never seemed possible will be within reach when you have Gemini and Libra in your corner. The rewards in a relationship with Taurus and Scorpio depend on the work you put in. Aries and Sagittarius will have you flying around the world in no time. The rise and fall of a relationship with Aquarius or Capricorn are what make it so much fun. Watch out for Cancer. They will bring out all of your insecurities.

Most Charming Characteristics: Self-confident, affectionate, loving.

Gifts: *For her:* tickets to a tennis tournament. *For him:* bike tour of local countryside.

Sensual Foods: Caramel and chocolate syrup on anything.

Romantic Flowers: These ladies like everyone to know how faithful they are, so send them violets. To surprise them send tulips. Men like their flowers the same as their relationships, unpretending. Send them camellias with white roses to show your affection.

Best Date Nights: Sunday; 3rd and 12th of each month.

Colors of Passion: *For her:* yellow, orange. *For him:* red, maroon.

The Perfect Wedding: Anything that promises pleasure to you and your family and friends is right. You love the warmth and the charming, picturesque atmosphere of the theater. Medieval castles, old mansions, or a charming chateau tucked away in the woods can provide the perfect backdrop for this . . . your special day. Ideal setting: Prague.

Wise Words: Charles Dickens: "There is no month in the whole year in which nature wears a more beautiful appearance than in the month of August."

Hints of Love: When these folks decide to sit on the fence don't try to push them off before they are ready. Let them do the jumping themselves.

After the Argument: *For him:* Saying you're sorry will never be enough unless you overdo it. Overwhelm him. Apologize until he tells you to stop, and then apologize for apologizing so much. *For her:* It had better be roses, and candy, and a night out on the town. And don't forget to stop at a local store and buy her something she would never buy for herself.

Romantic Places: Places of drama bring romance: Russia; a casino; Toronto, Ontario.

Lucky Love Star: Leonial—you will never lack desire.

Beautiful Thought: There can be many, many firsts; enjoy them all.

Sharing Secrets: It may seem like they are not interested, but ask them out anyway. *For the gals:* Until they absolutely know you are interested, you will never find out that they are. *For the guys:* Ask him out if he doesn't ask you. He may be shy or not. Either way, he may be interested.

Judith's Insights

About the Man: He likes to have people around him whenever possible and has several circles of friends. He will only date those he can see fireworks happening with in the future, or even right now. Passion is his main objective, and life without it is not worth it to him. He is constantly on the search for his Soul Mate. What is good for the goose is not necessarily good for the gander when in a relationship with this guy. He will expect to get away with things that he would never tolerate from you.

About the Woman: She needs to have her date's undivided attention. She is the one and only flirt allowed in her relationship, and don't you forget it. Her flirting is simply a dig for extra stimulation. As a co-worker or a boss, she can be competitive, but that is mainly with herself instead of others. When it comes down to working together, she is ready for anything. Fuss over her as much as you can and you will have her eating out of your hand in no time at all. Family plays a big role in her life. If you can't get along with her family, don't expect her to understand why.

Soul Mates: Leos not only love themselves, but anyone like them. Your good times, as well as the bad times, with Pisces and Virgo will be excessive. Libra and Gemini will bring out the best in you. Scorpio and Taurus will create a strong attraction, but one that is hard to maintain. Aries and Sagittarius will add spice to your life and leave you craving more. A link with Cancer can bring out the best or worst in you. It all depends on the mood in the air. If you are friends with Aquarius and Capricorn first, it can last forever. Make sure you have that base. You can bring out the best or the worst in each other.

Most Charming Characteristics: Ambitious, sentimental, generous.

Gifts: *For her:* invite her family for a backyard barbecue. *For him:* gold watch.

Sensual Foods: Waffles with whipped cream; chocolate soufflé; French wine.

Romantic Flowers: These ladies like men with taste. Show them you love style by sending fuchsia flowers, or even brightly colored wildflowers will do. To confuse this man, send him lilies along with bright daisies to show your innocence. Keep him guessing.

Best Date Nights: Sunday; 13th and 22nd of each month.

Colors of Passion: *For her:* yellow, orange. *For him:* red, maroon.

The Perfect Wedding: Anything that promises pleasure to you and your family and friends is right. You love the warmth and the charming, picturesque atmosphere of the theater. Medieval castles, old mansions, or a charming chateau tucked away in the woods can provide the perfect backdrop for this . . . your special day. Ideal setting: Prague.

Wise Words: Charles Dickens: "Repining is of no use. Of all fruitless errands, sending a tear to look after a day that has gone, is the most fruitless."

Hints of Love: Make sure you learn to compromise, but never with your principles.

After the Argument: *For him:* Saying you're sorry will never be enough unless you overdo it. Overwhelm him. Apologize until he tells you to stop, and then apologize for apologizing so much. *For her:* It had better be roses, and candy, and a night out on the town. And don't forget to stop at a local store and buy her something she would never buy for herself.

Romantic Places: Places of wonder bring romance: Aztec ruins; a museum; Niagara Falls, New York.

Lucky Love Star: Leonial—you will never lack desire.

Beautiful Thought: True love never dies, it just hides for a while.

Sharing Secrets: Don't be surprised if the first date is with their family. *For the gals:* Make sure you invite her to your family functions. It will be a red flag to her if you don't. *For the guys:* He may seem like a family man, but isn't that what you were looking for?

Judith's Insights

About the Man: He gives too much of himself to too many people. You may find him trying to constantly catch up. When you want to capture his attention, and keep it, think about when and where you go. His generosity can get the best of him if he lets it. Don't take advantage of it. Just teach him to hold back a little. He needs to be adored by all those around him. This includes family members, co-workers, and lovers alike. His love is loyal and intense. He may be jealous of any past loves you are friends with, while he may be close with some of his.

About the Woman: She may come across as more of a challenge than she really is. She loves a challenge and may make herself one for you. What she really wants is some good, clean fun. She will only play games that she will have a chance to win. If she feels that there is no chance she will stop playing instantly. Life with her is one big double standard. She will flirt with anyone and everyone while you aren't allowed to even glance away from her. She needs to feel that she has your attention at all times. Treat her like the only lady on the planet.

Soul Mates: Leo can love Leo when control is established well in advance. Severe swings in the feel of a relationship with Virgo and Pisces are sure to come. Gemini and Libra will let you revel in your true and best self. Taurus and Scorpio pull you in, but you might be overwhelmed once you are there. Say hello to fiery passion and good-bye to the mundane when you hook up with Aries and Sagittarius. Don't let the bumps in the road throw you and Aquarius or Capricorn off course. Cancer will bring out the worst in you if you let them.

Most Charming Characteristics: Happy, pleasant disposition, affectionate.

Gifts: *For her:* satin pajamas. *For him:* silk boxer shorts.

Sensual Foods: Oysters; mussels; spicy foods.

Romantic Flowers: You are the lady of distinction, and only carnations will do. Any mix of colors with sprays of mignonette. Sweet peas or red carnations will appeal to this man's heart.

Best Date Nights: Sunday; 4th and 5th of each month.

Colors of Passion: *For her:* yellow, orange. *For him:* red, maroon.

The Perfect Wedding: Anything that promises pleasure to you and your family and friends is right. You love the warmth and the charming, picturesque atmosphere of the theater. Medieval castles, old mansions, or a charming chateau tucked away in the woods can provide the perfect backdrop for this . . . your special day. Ideal setting: Prague.

Wise Words: Charles Dickens: "If the wing of friendship should never moult a feather, the wing of relationship should never be clipped, but be always expanded and serene."

Hints of Love: If you try to take a step back, it will be noticed. It could create the domino effect, and everything will start to fall.

After the Argument: *For him:* Saying you're sorry will never be enough unless you overdo it. Overwhelm him. Apologize until he tells you to stop, and then apologize for apologizing so much. *For her:* It had better be roses, and candy, and a night out on the town. And don't forget to stop at a local store and buy her something she would never buy for herself.

Romantic Places: Places of drama bring romance: Greece; a movie set; Los Angeles, California.

Lucky Love Star: Leonial—you will never lack desire.

Beautiful Thought: Dreams can be inspiration.

Sharing Secrets: Take me as I am could be the anthem for this one. *For the gals:* They will have strong views on just about everything. If you can hang with them, then nothing will be as important as you. *For the guys:* The thing you fall in love with may end up becoming the thing you hate. After a commitment, this one sticks around.

Judith's Insights

About the Man: He can hold a grudge longer than any man around. Get to know this guy very well before you plan to play any jokes on him. Make sure that the joke is something he would find funny instead of insulting. Even as a co-worker, he can be your best playmate or your worst enemy. Don't pour on too much adoration too fast. It may seem as if that is exactly what he wants, but it is not. Straight and steady is what will win the race with all of his other fans. To stand out from the crowd you have to be consistent.

About the Woman: She wants constant attention. Calling today but not tomorrow does not work well for this lady. Call every day! She is a great boss and will give plenty of rewards for a job well done or loyalty of any kind. You will find that the same is true for her in love. She will reward those who are consistent and affectionate. Invite her family over for dinner and she will be connected to you for a lifetime. Argue with any of her family members and you can look for sympathy, and a new mate, somewhere else.

Soul Mates: If you and a fellow Leo are to be together, you must first establish who will be in charge. Extremes are rampant with Virgo and Pisces. Make sure you balance self-confidence with humility. Everything you forgot people valued in you will shine again when you get together with Gemini and Libra. If you remember that opposites are exciting but difficult, then Scorpio and Taurus will work fine. Aries and Sagittarius have as much energy as you do. Capricorn and Aquarius have many thorns, but all beautiful flowers do. Cancer may bring out your insecurities.

Most Charming Characteristics: Versatile, determined, loving.

Gifts: *For her:* personalized stationery. *For him:* handmade gift.

Sensual Foods: Lobster; watermelon.

Romantic Flowers: You love it when you get tulips, declaring love. When you receive a variety, it shows how hopelessly in love your partner is. He will just love a single rose. This shows him you understand his pleasures.

Best Date Nights: Sunday; 6th and 15th of each month.

Colors of Passion: *For her:* yellow, orange. *For him:* red, maroon.

The Perfect Wedding: Anything that promises pleasure to you and your family and friends is right. You love the warmth and the charming, picturesque atmosphere of the theater. Medieval castles, old mansions, or a charming chateau tucked away in the woods can provide the perfect backdrop for this . . . your special day. Ideal setting: Prague.

Wise Words: Charles Dickens: "We all change, but that is with Time: Time does his work honestly. A fig for Time: use him well, and he is a hearty fellow, and scorns to have you at his disadvantage."

Hints of Love: Consistence and persistence will get this prize every time. They will value the effort.

After the Argument: *For him:* Saying you're sorry will never be enough unless you overdo it. Overwhelm him. Apologize until he tells you to stop, and then apologize for apologizing so much. *For her:* It had better be roses, and candy, and a night out on the town. And don't forget to stop at a local store and buy her something she would never buy for herself.

Romantic Places: Places of wonder bring romance: Jerusalem; the Statue of Liberty; Cape Canaveral, Florida.

Lucky Love Star: Leonial—you will never lack desire.

Beautiful Thought: The best kind of charity is giving of your heart.

Sharing Secrets: They seem moody until you get to know them. *For the gals:* You may not know whether to say hello or drop dead. As relations progress you will learn not to leave her dangling, and her moods will become more consistent. *For the guys:* To know him is to love him. His bark is much worse than his bite. He just wants someone to love him without criticism.

Judith's Insights

About the Man: This guy has power over people. You may wonder why until you get close enough to him to understand. Once you are under his emotional spell it is hard to break free. That is, if you even want to. He will cater to all of your wants and needs if you can put up with him long enough for him to do so. He is a big believer in rewarding those who stand by him when he gets a bit crazy. Anything you put into this relationship will be paid back with interest. Investing your time, your energy, and your heart will prove extremely rewarding in the end.

About the Woman: She has a high regard for those who have integrity. If you show her that side of your personality you will capture this lady's attention on the first try. Just make sure that you can keep up this standard. She does not like it when you waver from your first example, nor should she. She is incredibly versatile. She can dress up or down, depending on what the situation calls for. No matter what you have her wear, make sure you take her out and show her a good time. Don't get too serious too soon, and never get moody. Sulking works only for her.

Soul Mates: Leo and a fellow Leo are a good match as long as control is established and agreed upon. Keep your idea of yourself in mind at all times when you try a relationship with Virgo and Pisces. Everything you wished but never seemed possible will be within reach when you have Gemini and Libra in your corner. The rewards in a relationship with Taurus and Scorpio depend on the work you put in. Aries and Sagittarius will have you flying around the world in no time. The rise and fall of a relationship with Aquarius or Capricorn are what make it so much fun. Watch out for Cancer. They will bring out all of your insecurities.

Most Charming Characteristics: Loving, loyal, sympathetic.

Gifts: *For her:* designer clothes. *For him:* romantic walk.

Sensual Foods: Strawberries; truffles; shish kebab.

Romantic Flowers: Send this girl sunflowers if you want her to know you adore her. You may even add some poppies for a splash of extravagance. His desire for sport and play will be understood when you send him hyacinth and geranium.

Best Date Nights: Sunday; 15th and 24th of each month.

Colors of Passion: *For her:* yellow, orange. *For him:* red, maroon.

The Perfect Wedding: Anything that promises pleasure to you and your family and friends is right. You love the warmth and the charming, picturesque atmosphere of the theater. Medieval castles, old mansions, or a charming chateau tucked away in the woods can provide the perfect backdrop for this . . . your special day. Ideal setting: Prague.

Wise Words: Thomas à Kempis: "Lay not thine heart open to every one, but treat of thy affairs with the wise and such as fear God."

Hints of Love: Be funny. Laughter will be what keeps this one coming back again and again.

After the Argument: *For him:* Saying you're sorry will never be enough unless you overdo it. Overwhelm him. Apologize until he tells you to stop, and then apologize for apologizing so much. *For her:* It had better be roses, and candy, and a night out on the town. And don't forget to stop at a local store and buy her something she would never buy for herself.

Romantic Places: Places of drama bring romance: India; a theater; Hollywood, California.

Lucky Love Star: Leonial—you will never lack desire.

Beautiful Thought: Attics are filled with yesterdays; we are filled with tomorrows.

Sharing Secrets: You had better be able to put your money where your mouth is. *For the gals:* It doesn't need to be lavish, but she does love the loot. The more the better. *For the guys:* He doesn't mind spending his hard-earned cash, but he loves to see you contribute to please him.

Judith's Insights

About the Man: He loves to flirt and will do it like crazy until he finds a mate. You can capture his attention by not paying him much attention at all. He will be intrigued, and then the chase is on. He loves the games that are played to win someone over, as long as he can win in the end. He is exceedingly positive. His disposition makes it a pleasure to be around him. The only problem is that you are a mere one out of the many who are enamored of this guy. Stand out by being confident in who you are and what you have to bring into his life.

About the Woman: This gal may seem to be the life of the party. At times it can seem like she has no boundaries at all. That is exactly how she gets noticed. She has a more serious side than those around her could ever imagine. This side comes out when she feels you are worthy to see all of her. Do not ever cross her or make her doubt herself. She is more sensitive than you may think by looking at her. Your approach needs to be from the heart. If you are sincere and consistent she will love you all the more for it.

Soul Mates: Leo will always get along famously with another Leo. Pisces and Virgo bring out the best or worst in you. Sometimes a little bit of both. Libra and Gemini make you see all of the good in yourself. A match with Scorpio and Taurus can work if you recognize your differences. A pairing with Aries and Sagittarius has sizzle written all over it. Sharpen up your edges. A ride with Aquarius and Capricorn will be exciting indeed. Cancer may be a little too much to handle at times. Hang in there and it will be worth it.

Most Charming Characteristics: Affectionate, generous, considerate.

Gifts: *For her:* exotic vacation destination. *For him:* weekend at a spa.

Sensual Foods: Grapes; fine cheeses and crackers; taffy.

Romantic Flowers: Rhododendron will let her be on the lookout for trouble. Throw in some chrysanthemum and she'll know it is you she will be looking out for. Cactus will show him warmth. Yellow daffodil is a token of a good time had by all. Chivalry is not dead.

Best Date Nights: Sunday; 8th and 17th of each month.

Colors of Passion: *For her:* yellow, orange. *For him:* red, maroon.

The Perfect Wedding: Anything that promises pleasure to you and your family and friends is right. You love the warmth and the charming, picturesque atmosphere of the theater. Medieval castles, old mansions, or a charming chateau tucked away in the woods can provide the perfect backdrop for this . . . your special day. Ideal setting: Prague.

Wise Words: Jeremy Taylor: "Friendship is equal to all the world; and itself hath no difference; but it is differenced only by accidents, and by the capacity or incapacity of those that receive it."

Hints of Love: Treat this one like royalty or precious cargo. They will love being valued in this way.

After the Argument: *For him:* Saying you're sorry will never be enough unless you overdo it. Overwhelm him. Apologize until he tells you to stop, and then apologize for apologizing so much. *For her:* It had better be roses, and candy, and a night out on the town. And don't forget to stop at a local store and buy her something she would never buy for herself.

Romantic Places: Places of wonder bring romance: the Taj Mahal; a cathedral or temple; Niagara Falls, New York.

Lucky Love Star: Leonial—you will never lack desire.

Beautiful Thought: Fear can stop everything; encouragement can start anything.

Sharing Secrets: Nobody likes a weak link, especially not this one. *For the gals:* Make sure you treat her like a lady and act like a man. *For the guys:* Put your best foot forward. Dress your best and keep your manners in check. This man notices.

Judith's Insights

About the Man: Don't ever take advantage of his kindness and generosity. As you get to know this guy you will find a soft heart and a strong mind. If you break his trust you will never get it back. If you are loyal and speak from the heart, he will be at your beck and call with pleasure. He loves to have fun but can get the work done, too. There will be no renovations to his nature, so take him as he is. You might be able to get him to buy a new couch, but you can never get him to get rid of his old friends and lovers. Expect to have lots of guests milling around your house.

About the Woman: You had better be as consistent and persistent as she is to catch her attention. Never come between her and her family or her old friends. They won their right to be in her life long before you came along. If she is pushed to choose between you and them, you won't like her choice. Appeal to her impulsiveness and show up unexpectedly. She loves to play games she can win, so let her catch you once in a while. She is better off when she is in control. Let her choose where you eat and dinner will be much more fun.

Soul Mates: Leo and a fellow Leo are a good match as long as control is established and agreed upon. Keep your idea of yourself in mind at all times when you try a relationship with Virgo and Pisces. Everything you wished but never seemed possible will be within reach when you have Gemini and Libra in your corner. The rewards in a relationship with Taurus and Scorpio depend on the work you put in. Aries and Sagittarius will have you flying around the world in no time. The rise and fall of a relationship with Aquarius or Capricorn are what make it so much fun. Watch out for Cancer. They will bring out all of your insecurities.

Most Charming Characteristics: Courageous, positive, resourceful.

Gifts: *For her:* tickets to the circus. *For him:* night at a casino.

Sensual Foods: Champagne; grapes; mangoes; filet mignon.

Romantic Flowers: The magnolias you send her will let her know you will be around for a while to come. Petunia is to say never despair. Holly will let him know what he is getting into. Pansy will keep you in his thoughts.

Best Date Nights: Sunday; 9th and 18th of each month.

Colors of Passion: *For her:* yellow, orange. *For him:* red, maroon.

The Perfect Wedding: Anything that promises pleasure to you and your family and friends is right. You love the warmth and the charming, picturesque atmosphere of the theater. Medieval castles, old mansions, or a charming chateau tucked away in the woods can provide the perfect backdrop for this . . . your special day. Ideal setting: Prague.

Wise Words: Henry Wadsworth Longfellow: "Enjoy the Spring of Love and Youth, / To some good angle leave the rest, / For time will teach thee soon the truth, / There are no birds in last year's nest."

Hints of Love: Affection is important, but only if it comes naturally. Otherwise, the sirens will go off.

After the Argument: *For him:* Saying you're sorry will never be enough unless you overdo it. Overwhelm him. Apologize until he tells you to stop, and then apologize for apologizing so much. *For her:* It had better be roses, and candy, and a night out on the town. And don't forget to stop at a local store and buy her something she would never buy for herself.

Romantic Places: Places of drama bring romance: French Riviera; a casino; Las Vegas, Nevada.

Lucky Love Star: Leonial—you will never lack desire.

Beautiful Thought: A suggestion is always worth receiving.

Sharing Secrets: Attention, attention, attention. *For the gals:* Do it any way you can. Presents, phone calls, cards, or flowers. Whatever works for you will work for her. *For the guys:* He would love nostalgic gifts or T-shirts. He also likes phone calls, as long as they don't interrupt his favorite pastimes.

Judith's Insights

About the Man: You can bring out his best or his worst side. It all depends on how you approach the subject at hand. Flattery will definitely get you an entrance. Once you are there, it is up to you and your ability to hold an interesting conversation with this talker to stay around for any amount of time. Being shy and removed is exactly what it will take to be removed from his little black book in a flash. He will be very impressed if you dig into your own pockets on a date. He might not let you pay, but the thought will be noted and remembered.

About the Woman: She can be sweeter than honey when she wants to be. She can also roar like the lion she is when she wants to. You would do much better with a soft approach than coming on like a steamroller. Once you are in your circle you have to be exciting enough to stay and entertain her. Don't demand too much too fast from her. Take things slow and steady and you will win her over. She likes to have unusual things around her and she will dare to be different at every turn. Take her to an unusual place to get her juices going.

Soul Mates: Leo will always get along famously with another Leo. Pisces and Virgo bring out the best or worst in you. Sometimes a little bit of both. Libra and Gemini make you see all of the good in yourself. A match with Scorpio and Taurus can work if you recognize your differences. A pairing with Aries and Sagittarius has sizzle written all over it. Sharpen up your edges. A ride with Aquarius and Capricorn will be exciting indeed. Cancer may be a little too much to handle at times. Hang in there and it will be worth it.

Most Charming Characteristics: Ambitious, loving, confident.

Gifts: *For her:* acting class. *For him:* sports tickets.

Sensual Foods: Châteaubriand; crème brûlée.

Romantic Flowers: Iris is your flower if you are the gal sending subtle messages. If you are the man, you will look for clematis. This flower's mental beauty creates emotional stimulation for you.

Best Date Nights: Sunday; 1st and 28th of each month.

Colors of Passion: *For her:* yellow, orange. *For him:* red, maroon.

The Perfect Wedding: Anything that promises pleasure to you and your family and friends is right. You love the warmth and the charming, picturesque atmosphere of the theater. Medieval castles, old mansions, or a charming chateau tucked away in the woods can provide the perfect backdrop for this . . . your special day. Ideal setting: Prague.

Wise Words: Johann Herder: "A fool always accuses other people; a partially wise man, himself; a wholly wise man neither himself nor others."

Hints of Love: This one likes others to make his or her dreams come true. Be the "fantasy" fulfiller.

After the Argument: *For him:* Saying you're sorry will never be enough unless you overdo it. Overwhelm him. Apologize until he tells you to stop, and then apologize for apologizing so much. *For her:* It had better be roses, and candy, and a night out on the town. And don't forget to stop at a local store and buy her something she would never buy for herself.

Romantic Places: Places of drama bring romance: London; an opera house; Broadway, New York City.

Lucky Love Star: Leonial—you will never lack desire.

Beautiful Thought: We have character flaws, ceilings, and walls. It is how we use them that counts.

Sharing Secrets: Make sure you are not the killjoy. *For the gals:* When she has an idea, try it before you decide you don't like it. She needs to be pleased. *For the guys:* Do the things he loves to do and he will make the things you love ten times more fun.

Judith's Insights

About the Man: He knows just how to play coy. He will not let you get a hold on his emotions. The walls he builds need to be taken down one brick at a time. It will take a suave mate to start taking any of them down at all. Keep in mind, they didn't go up overnight and they won't come down that quickly, either. Don't be a killjoy around this guy. Remember that every toy he has is important to him. If he is having fun you don't want to be the person who tells him that it is time to go home. He has a tendency to kill the messenger.

About the Woman: She knows how to do it all. Don't expect to be able to teach this lady anything. She longs for a mate who is smart but not a smarty-pants type of person. She will have a good defense for any move toward her emotional core. Make sure you have a good offense, or you won't get far at all. There is absolutely nothing worse than a bad date to this gal. The image will last forever in her mind, and you might not get a second chance. If the first date goes well, however, expect to have to live up to that standard for the rest of the relationship.

Soul Mates: Leo can love Leo when control is established well in advance. Severe swings in the feel of a relationship with Virgo and Pisces are sure to come. Gemini and Libra will let you revel in your true and best self. Taurus and Scorpio pull you in, but you might be overwhelmed once you are there. Say hello to fiery passion and good-bye to the mundane when you hook up with Aries and Sagittarius. Don't let the bumps in the road throw you and Aquarius or Capricorn off course. Cancer will bring out the worst in you if you let them.

Most Charming Characteristics: Jovial, vivacious, friendly.

Gifts: *For her:* night at a carnival. *For him:* camping out in the woods or the backyard.

Sensual Foods: Shrimp; sinful chocolate cake.

Romantic Flowers: Any rose of any color for the lady. Roses stand for love regardless of the color. Send them with orchids and you will be saying, "I love you." If you want a gentleman to know you think of him, send pansies, and forget-me-nots for true love.

Best Date Nights: Sunday; 11th and 20th of each month.

Colors of Passion: *For her:* yellow, violet. *For him:* red, maroon.

The Perfect Wedding: Anything that promises pleasure to you and your family and friends is right. You love the warmth and the charming, picturesque atmosphere of the theater. Medieval castles, old mansions, or a charming chateau tucked away in the woods can provide the perfect backdrop for this . . . your special day. Ideal setting: Prague.

Wise Words: E. Thorneycroft Fowler: "Friendship may pardon our misdeeds; but it is only love that can forgive our mistakes."

Hints of Love: Stop worrying about next week's date today or there will not be one tomorrow.

After the Argument: *For him:* Saying you're sorry will never be enough unless you overdo it. Over-whelm him. Apologize until he tells you to stop, and then apologize for apologizing so much. *For her:* It had better be roses, and candy, and a night out on the town. And don't forget to stop at a local store and buy her something she would never buy for herself.

Romantic Places: Places of wonder bring romance: Rio de Janeiro; a planetarium; Disney World.

Lucky Love Star: Leonial—you will never lack desire.

Beautiful Thought: Generosity is the key; kindness opens all doors to the heart.

Sharing Secrets: You had better be ready to have a relationship. *For the gals:* No lies, no games, and no mistakes. She wants what she wants with as little work possible. *For the guys:* If you have games on your mind, then move on. This one likes fun any way he can get it, but no emotional roller coasters.

Judith's Insights

About the Man: Here is a guy who would not mind receiving a dozen roses or balloons. He likes admiration from anyone, especially his mom. He wants his own life and love to be like those in the movies. He puts up barriers so it is not easy for people to get close and see his dreams. Make sure that you can live up to his first impression of you, because that is exactly what he will expect. A bad first impression with this guy is like the kiss of death. If he feels that you have nothing to bring to his life, you will rarely get a chance to prove him wrong.

About the Woman: This lady spends way too much time making sure she does not get hurt. This causes her to miss out on some great experiences. If you like what you see in her, you have to be a bit pushy in order to get in the door. She likes to be courted and escorted to exciting places. Use your charms to make her feel safe. She does not mind being treated in accordance to her gender. Treat this girl like a lady. Not only will she notice your efforts, but she will enjoy them and want more of the same treatment.

Soul Mates: Leo and a fellow Leo are a good match as long as control is established and agreed upon. Keep your idea of yourself in mind at all times when you try a relationship with Virgo and Pisces. Everything you wished but never seemed possible will be within reach when you have Gemini and Libra in your corner. The rewards in a relationship with Taurus and Scorpio depend on the work you put in. Aries and Sagittarius will have you flying around the world in no time. The rise and fall of a relationship with Aquarius and Capricorn are what make it so much fun. Watch out for Cancer. They will bring out all of your insecurities.

Most Charming Characteristics: Adaptable, accurate, a leader.

Gifts: *For her:* tickets to a tennis tournament. *For him:* bike tour of local countryside.

Sensual Foods: Toasted marshmallows; chocolates.

Romantic Flowers: These ladies like everyone to know how faithful they are, so send them violets. To surprise them send tulips. Men like their flowers the same as their relationships, unpretending. Send them camellias with white roses to show your affection.

Best Date Nights: Sunday; 12th and 21st of each month.

Colors of Passion: *For her:* yellow, orange. *For him:* red, maroon.

The Perfect Wedding: Anything that promises pleasure to you and your family and friends is right. You love the warmth and the charming, picturesque atmosphere of the theater. Medieval castles, old mansions, or a charming chateau tucked away in the woods can provide the perfect backdrop for this . . . your special day. Ideal setting: Prague.

Wise Words: James Russell Lowell: "Love's nobility is shown in this, that it strengthens us to make sacrifices for others, and not for the object of our love alone."

Hints of Love: Keep the romance in the picture. Don't forget the long walks on the beach and camping out in front of the fireplace.

After the Argument: *For him:* Saying you're sorry will never be enough unless you overdo it. Overwhelm him. Apologize until he tells you to stop, and then apologize for apologizing so much. *For her:* It had better be roses, and candy, and a night out on the town. And don't forget to stop at a local store and buy her something she would never buy for herself.

Romantic Places: Places of drama bring romance: Russia; a casino; Toronto, Ontario.

Lucky Love Star: Leonial—you will never lack desire.

Beautiful Thought: Life never stops teaching us what we already know.

Sharing Secrets: You may have to give this one more than one chance. *For the gals:* Intriguing as she is, expect a handful. She lightens up as time goes on. *For the guys:* His quirks may make you have second thoughts, but that is what separates the men from the boys.

Judith's Insights

About the Man: He can handle a tremendous amount of stress at work. When it comes to love, his heart can buckle under so much weight. He is always up for a good time. When it comes time for a serious talk he can have a habit of bailing. Keep even serious matters light and not confrontational to keep him listening to what you have to say. Even though he is a take-charge type of guy, he does not mind being led down a romantic path by the right person. He likes to be the driver, but he won't mind being given directions.

About the Woman: The word *no* is used in her vocabulary way too often. Even if she is interested in dating she will use the word *no* more than the word *yes*. She will only date someone who has potential for more than a fling. She might take the first date too seriously if you let her. She can be very accommodating, and yet she craves to be in control. You can take charge as long as she has the illusion that she is still the one calling the shots. Her family and friends are her world. Make sure that she is not giving them too much and not receiving anything in return.

Soul Mates: Leo will always get along famously with another Leo. Pisces and Virgo bring out the best or worst in you. Sometimes a little bit of both. Libra and Gemini make you see all of the good in yourself. A match with Scorpio and Taurus can work if you recognize your differences. A pairing with Aries and Sagittarius has sizzle written all over it. Sharpen up your edges. A ride with Aquarius and Capricorn will be exciting indeed. Cancer may be a little too much to handle at times. Hang in there and it will be worth it.

Most Charming Characteristics: Winsome, humorous, self-reliant.

Gifts: *For her:* invite her family for a backyard barbecue. *For him:* gold watch.

Sensual Foods: Chocolate-covered strawberries; New York steak; scallops.

Romantic Flowers: These ladies like men with taste. Show them you love style by sending fuchsia flowers, or even brightly colored wildflowers will do. To confuse this man, send him lilies along with bright daisies to show your innocence. Keep him guessing.

Best Date Nights: Sunday; 4th and 22nd of each month.

Colors of Passion: *For her:* cream, orange. *For him:* black, maroon.

The Perfect Wedding: Anything that promises pleasure to you and your family and friends is right. You love the warmth and the charming, picturesque atmosphere of the theater. Medieval castles, old mansions, or a charming chateau tucked away in the woods can provide the perfect backdrop for this . . . your special day. Ideal setting: Prague.

Wise Words: Mary Baker Eddy: "By purifying human thought, the state of mind permeates with increased harmony all the minutes of human affairs."

Hints of Love: The mystery is important, but being evasive will create disaster. Make sure you know the difference.

After the Argument: *For him:* Saying you're sorry will never be enough unless you overdo it. Overwhelm him. Apologize until he tells you to stop, and then apologize for apologizing so much. *For her:* It had better be roses, and candy, and a night out on the town. And don't forget to stop at a local store and buy her something she would never buy for herself.

Romantic Places: Places of wonder bring romance: Aztec ruins; a museum; Niagara Falls, New York.

Lucky Love Star: Leonial—you will never lack desire.

Beautiful Thought: When you think you have it all, it's time to start over again.

Sharing Secrets: Talk about high maintenance. *For the gals:* Once she sees that you go out of your way for her, then she will for you. *For the guys:* The bark is definitely much worse than the bite. He comes on stronger and more obstinate than he actually is.

Judith's Insights

About the Man: This guy lives a little on the edge. He will never mind that last-minute call to see what he has planned for that night. In fact, he would prefer that things are not planned well in advance. That way there is room to change his mind if need be. If you try to catch him in midair he will be much more receptive than if you tie him to a chair. You can intrigue him with any type of date as long as it involves movement. This is no movie-marathon lover. He would much rather be roller skating in the park or walking on the beach.

About the Woman: This gal needs to be understood. She wants to do a lot and have a lot. There will not be any grass growing under this lady's feet if she can help it. Don't stand there and let it grow under yours. If you do wait too long, you will find that she is long gone once you decide to get your feet moving. Even at work you will find that there are not many tasks that she won't undertake and even master. Keep things with her interesting and new without planning ahead of time. Let the day take you where it wants to and see what happens.

Soul Mates: Leo can love Leo when control is established well in advance. Severe swings in the feel of a relationship with Virgo and Pisces are sure to come. Gemini and Libra will let you revel in your true and best self. Taurus and Scorpio pull you in, but you might be overwhelmed once you are there. Say hello to fiery passion and good-bye to the mundane when you hook up with Aries and Sagittarius. Don't let the bumps in the road throw you and Aquarius and Capricorn off course. Cancer will bring out the worst in you if you let them.

Most Charming Characteristics: Energetic, kind, friendly.

Gifts: *For her:* satin pajamas. *For him:* silk boxer shorts.

Sensual Foods: Vanilla and strawberry mousse; tiramisù, espresso.

Romantic Flowers: You are the lady of distinction, and only carnations will do. Any mix of colors with sprays of mignonette. Sweet peas or red carnations will appeal to this man's heart.

Best Date Nights: Sunday; 4th and 23rd of each month.

Colors of Passion: *For her:* yellow, cream. *For him:* red, blue.

The Perfect Wedding: Anything that promises pleasure to you and your family and friends is right. You love the warmth and the charming, picturesque atmosphere of the theater. Medieval castles, old mansions, or a charming chateau tucked away in the woods can provide the perfect backdrop for this . . . your special day. Ideal setting: Prague.

Wise Words: George Herbert: "I would not willingly pass one day of my life without comforting a sad soul or showing mercy."

Hints of Love: If you learn to back up when things are moving too fast, you won't have to bow out so often.

After the Argument: *For him:* Saying you're sorry will never be enough unless you overdo it. Overwhelm him. Apologize until he tells you to stop, and then apologize for apologizing so much. *For her:* It had better be roses, and candy, and a night out on the town. And don't forget to stop at a local store and buy her something she would never buy for herself.

Romantic Places: Places of drama bring romance: Greece; a movie set; Los Angeles, California.

Lucky Love Star: Leonial—you will never lack desire.

Beautiful Thought: Relationships grow if you water and feed them.

Sharing Secrets: Make sure you have at least five dates before you make up your mind. *For the gals:* They can be cynical, so it could be a few dates before they loosen up. *For the guys:* He still has yesterday on his mind. He needs a reason to forget his past relationship. Make a new history for him.

Judith's Insights

About the Man: Entertaining him is your main objective. Make him sing, dance, or even work. Any of it will work as long as he feels like things are happening. He likes people to beg for his company, so leave lots of messages to invite him places. Make him feel wanted and he will want you as his company. You can bring out the best or worst in him just by your approach. Never put this guy on the defensive or you will be the one who ends up being attacked. Make him feel safe and he will love you for it.

About the Woman: She will be in control at all costs. Ask this lady on a date with the expectation that she will have her own opinion of what you should do. Leave it up to her and you will score big points. She will count every dollar you spend, so make each one count. Her generosity will be more than enough to make up for what you invest on making her happy in the beginning. Her reward system is based on loyalty and hard work.

Soul Mates: Only a fellow Virgo can completely understand your need for order in your surroundings and comply with that need as well. Libra will teach you to balance your need of order with a new sense of spontaneity. Aquarius and Cancer will have your head spinning right away. Pisces and Sagittarius will give you all you need to be the very best you can be. Scorpio and Aries will have you wincing from their intimidation. Gemini and Leo take some getting used to, but once you know them, you will love them. Taurus and Capricorn will ground you like never before.

Most Charming Characteristics: Honest, generous, affectionate.

Gifts: *For her:* day of beauty. *For him:* get his car detailed.

Sensual Foods: Raspberries; pound cake; caviar.

Romantic Flowers: You love it when you get tulips, declaring love. When you receive a variety, it shows how hopelessly in love your partner is. He will just love a single rose. This shows him you understand his pleasures.

Best Date Nights: Wednesday; 6th and 15th of each month.

Colors of Passion: *For her:* cream, violet. *For him:* black, blue.

The Perfect Wedding: Practical, but perfect down to the smallest detail, you actually *enjoy* every aspect of planning your wedding day. Your love of romance and need for privacy lend themselves to a lavishly decorated hidden patio or a botanical garden–type location. As with everything you do, your individual personality stamp will be noticed. Ideal setting: Paris.

Wise Words: H. Vandyke: "But often faltering feet come surest to the goal and they who walk in darkness meet the sunrise of the soul."

Hints of Love: Expecting too much too soon can only build up hopes that will fall down too easily.

After the Argument: *For him:* Just tell him how right he was and how wrong you were over and over again. There is no such thing as too much here. *For her:* Grovel, and then grovel some more. They love it. It makes them feel very secure.

Romantic Places: Places of elegance bring romance: Turkey; a cruise; New Orleans, Louisiana.

Lucky Love Star: Virginiel—you will never lack intrigue.

Beautiful Thought: Things must end for new things to begin.

Sharing Secrets: Don't be in a hurry, or it will be over before it begins. *For the gals:* Like fine wine and amazing food. Savor a moment until an hour is created. *For the guys:* To do too much too fast will prove risky. Try to give a push and he will just jump ship.

Judith's Insights

About the Man: If flirting with him does not work, you might have to be the one to ask him out instead of waiting for him to do the asking. He may or may not take the hint. Be blunt if necessary. If he is your neighbor it could be years before he will knock on your door. You will have to take the initiative. He can be one of the best communicators for others, but never for himself. He tends to have selective hearing when it comes to matters of the heart. Make sure your invitation and your intentions are loud and clear.

About the Woman: She wants to jump right in when it comes to love. Then she will get bored very easily and decide to move on. Take things slowly so she can learn new things about you and herself every day. If you have the desire to stay around for a while, make things new and exciting for her to keep her interested. Every once in a while you will have to initiate a conversation to make sure that you are both on the same page. The last thing you want is for this girl to have a different view than yours on how things are going.

Soul Mates: You will find true understanding of your nature when you find a fellow Virgo. Libra will help you see all the good in yourself while improving you at the same time. Aquarius and Cancer will drive you up a wall if you stick around long enough for them to get to you. Pisces and Sagittarius will give you a new purpose and sense of self. You will feel much stronger once under their guidance. Scorpio and Aries will try to bully you. Just stick up for yourself as you are walking to the exit. Gemini and Leo will be a no-no at first glance. If you give them that second look, you might be surprised at what you see. Taurus and Capricorn will give you a solid base for all of your dreams.

Most Charming Characteristics: Affable, sincere, demonstrative.

Gifts: *For her:* closet organizer. *For him:* organizing tool chest.

Sensual Foods: Flambé; lobster; oysters.

Romantic Flowers: Send this girl sunflowers if you want her to know you adore her. You may even add some poppies for a splash of extravagance. His desire for sport and play will be understood when you send him hyacinth and geranium.

Best Date Nights: Wednesday; 6th and 24th of each month.

Colors of Passion: *For her:* cream, violet. *For him:* black, blue.

The Perfect Wedding: Practical, but perfect down to the smallest detail, you actually *enjoy* every aspect of planning your wedding day. Your love of romance and need for privacy lend themselves to a lavishly decorated hidden patio or a botanical garden–type location. As with everything you do, your individual personality stamp will be noticed. Ideal setting: Paris.

Wise Words: Ralph Waldo Emerson: "Power dwells with cheerfulness, hope puts us in a working mood, while despair is no use and untunes the working power."

Hints of Love: Make sure all the ingredients are present before putting the cake in the oven.

After the Argument: *For him:* Just tell him how right he was and how wrong you were over and over again. There is no such thing as too much here. *For her:* Grovel, and then grovel some more. They love it. It makes them feel very secure.

Romantic Places: Places of refinement bring romance: Argentina; New York City.

Lucky Love Star: Virginiel—you will never lack intrigue.

Beautiful Thought: Better to have and hold for a glance than to never get to enjoy the dance.

Sharing Secrets: They need to look before they leap, but only in love. *For the gals:* She needs creative and exciting dates to keep her interested. Don't take her for granted too soon. *For the guys:* You may think he gives signs of moving this relationship quickly; make sure you slow it down before he does.

Judith's Insights

About the Man: He can talk himself into love one minute and right back out of love the next minute. When you think he is being cranky he might be in love and not so sure that he wants to be. Proceed with caution as long as you keep coming. Don't let his indecision ruin a good relationship. He needs for you to communicate to him very clearly. If you don't spell it out for him there is no telling what it is he actually hears. If you waver in your position you will only send all of the wrong signals to an already confused passenger.

About the Woman: She hates being in love because she hates being out of control of her emotions. When she is in love she can decide whether or not she wants to be. She wants what she can't have. When she gets it she gets scared. This gal needs things to go slowly or she will bail when love hits the curves. She will overcomplicate the picture every time. State your intentions clearly right from the start. This will avoid any misunderstandings and make her feel more at ease. When she is at ease she will receive your affection the way it is intended.

Soul Mates: A fellow Virgo will let you know that there is nothing wrong with your nature to begin with. Libra will give you a sense of wholeness when they help you become less rigid. Aquarius and Cancer will leave you numb. This pairing is not recommended for the faint of heart or the easily bruised ego. Pisces and Sagittarius will help you soar to new heights in all you encounter. Scorpio and Aries are too much trouble for you. You will be surprised when you give Gemini and Leo a chance. They just might break your first impression. Taurus and Capricorn will show you all of the wonders that lie in your own life.

Most Charming Characteristics: Artistic, versatile, dependable.

Gifts: *For her:* silk scarf. *For him:* cashmere sweater.

Sensual Foods: Crème brûlée; poached salmon.

Romantic Flowers: Rhododendron will let her be on the lookout for trouble. Throw in some chrysanthemum and she'll know it is you she will be looking out for. Cactus will show him warmth. Yellow daffodil is a token of a good time had by all. Chivalry is not dead.

Best Date Nights: Wednesday; 8th and 17th of each month.

Colors of Passion: *For her:* cream, violet. *For him:* black, blue.

The Perfect Wedding: Practical, but perfect down to the smallest detail, you actually *enjoy* every aspect of planning your wedding day. Your love of romance and need for privacy lend themselves to a lavishly decorated hidden patio or a botanical garden–type location. As with everything you do, your individual personality stamp will be noticed. Ideal setting: Paris.

Wise Words: John Milton: "Through all the winds of doctrine were let loose to play upon the earth, so truth be in the field. We do ingloriously by licensing and prohibiting to misdoubt her strength."

Hints of Love: Simple often turns into complicated with this one. When you overcomplicate the moment, try to step back for a breather.

After the Argument: *For him:* Just tell him how right he was and how wrong you were over and over again. There is no such thing as too much here. *For her:* Grovel, and then grovel some more. They love it. It makes them feel very secure.

Romantic Places: Places of elegance bring romance: Russia; a sculpted garden; Hilton Head, South Carolina.

Lucky Love Star: Virginiel—you will never lack intrigue.

Beautiful Thought: Laughter could cure the anger.

Sharing Secrets: The possibilities are endless, if you can pay the price. *For the gals:* She is hoping chivalry is not dead, and you must be willing to be the man at all costs. *For the guys:* He can be demanding and somewhat controlling. He just needs to be trained.

Judith's Insights

About the Man: His emotions can be very scattered. This is especially true when he starts anything new, but it is almost always true when it comes to love. He does much better when things are getting to the middle or even the end of things. Beginnings are far too stressful for him. Take things slowly to ease him through the tough spots. Some of his friends are old lovers still hanging around. He will keep them around for reassurance. He needs things to continue even if they have changed direction.

About the Woman: She has many clothes, pieces of jewelry, and even many friends. It will take a lot to get this lady to fall in love. Don't mistake her kindness for love. She is just feeling you out to see what you have to offer. You must prove yourself time and time again before this one will risk her heart on you. Although she is a whiz with language, she has a lot of trouble communicating her feelings. She even confuses how people feel about her by overanalyzing their actions. Be clear about how you feel and she will receive what you have to give much more readily.

Soul Mates: Everything will be in its perfect place when you and a fellow Virgo get together. Libra and their scales of balance will teach you how to keep your life level. Aquarius and Cancer will drive you to drink if you stick around too long. Pisces and Sagittarius will help you be all that you can be and more. Scorpio and Aries will try to push you too much to change. Gemini and Leo will surprise you when you least expect it. Taurus and Capricorn will give you something to come home to every time.

Most Charming Characteristics: Kind, loving, studious.

Gifts: *For her:* beauty makeover. *For him:* weekend in the mountains.

Sensual Foods: Chocolate soufflé; filet mignon.

Romantic Flowers: The magnolias you send her will let her know you will be around for a while to come. Petunia is to say never despair. Holly will let him know what he is getting into. Pansy will keep you in his thoughts.

Best Date Nights: Wednesday; 18th and 27th of each month.

Colors of Passion: *For her:* cream, violet. *For him:* black, blue.

The Perfect Wedding: Practical, but perfect down to the smallest detail, you actually *enjoy* every aspect of planning your wedding day. Your love of romance and need for privacy lend themselves to a lavishly decorated hidden patio or a botanical garden–type location. As with everything you do, your individual personality stamp will be noticed. Ideal setting: Paris.

Wise Words: John Locke: "Gentleness is far more successful in all its enterprises than violence. Indeed violence generally frustrates its own purpose while gentleness scarcely ever fails."

Hints of Love: Allow them to know what is in your heart as well as what is in your head.

After the Argument: *For him:* Just tell him how right he was and how wrong you were over and over again. There is no such thing as too much here. *For her:* Grovel, and then grovel some more. They love it. It makes them feel very secure.

Romantic Places: Places of refinement bring romance: the Taj Mahal; an awards ceremony; Boston, Massachusetts.

Lucky Love Star: Virginiel—you will never lack intrigue.

Beautiful Thought: The only thing that replaces love is love.

Sharing Secrets: Tomorrow is another day, but why wait? You can do it all today. *For the gals:* Have your date filled from dusk to dawn, and then some. *For the guys:* You may find he needs a nap here and there, but he can last all day and all night if he has a reason.

Judith's Insights

About the Man: He is never alone if he can help it. Although it may seem as if he is not dating, he will always have someone ready to be picked up in a pinch. He wears a lot of hats and attracts all types of people. This one can be hard to read. He swings between just wanting to hang and being in love. You will never have to look far to find his king-size ego. He can have a chip on his shoulder as well. This is only there for protection. His bruised heart needs to be healed by someone who is sincere and direct with her feelings about him.

About the Woman: She is incredibly cautious. She carries that red flag everywhere she goes, just in case of emotional accidents. She can make even the best of us feel like we are on the string of a yo-yo. She changes her mind more than she would ever be willing to admit. Try to roll with the waves without drowning. She has been thrown around a bit and doesn't like for her emotions to fly uncontrolled. If you have the patience to wait out her insecurities you will be pleasantly surprised by how loving she becomes when she feels safe from harm.

Soul Mates: With a fellow Virgo, all things will be in perfect order. A relationship with Libra is a charmed one. A match of wits happens fast with Cancer and Aquarius. It will be strained just as fast if you don't really get to know each other. Critical is written all over a partnership with Pisces and Sagittarius. Aries and Scorpio will give you a run for your money, then want to go spend it all. Gemini and Leo might cause you a little insanity. You would truly need a deep connection to make this work. Capricorn and Taurus know how to turn on that irresistible charm that you just love.

Most Charming Characteristics: Fair, loving, organized.

Gifts: *For her:* astrological chart. *For him:* box or ringside seats.

Sensual Foods: Steak au poivre; cheesecake.

Romantic Flowers: Iris is your flower if you are the gal sending subtle messages. If you are the man, you will look for clematis. This flower's mental beauty creates emotional stimulation for you.

Best Date Nights: Wednesday; 1st and 10th of each month.

Colors of Passion: *For her:* cream, violet. *For him:* black, blue.

The Perfect Wedding: Practical, but perfect down to the smallest detail, you actually *enjoy* every aspect of planning your wedding day. Your love of romance and need for privacy lend themselves to a lavishly decorated hidden patio or a botanical garden–type location. As with everything you do, your individual personality stamp will be noticed. Ideal setting: Paris.

Wise Words: William Wordsworth: "Give unto me, made lowly wise, / The spirit of self-sacrifice; / the confidence of reason give; / And in the light of truth thy Bondman, / let me live."

Hints of Love: Keep both feet on the ground the first time you think you want to jump. This way you won't jump too high too soon.

After the Argument: *For him:* Just tell him how right he was and how wrong you were over and over again. There is no such thing as too much here. *For her:* Grovel, and then grovel some more. They love it. It makes them feel very secure.

Romantic Places: Places of elegance bring romance: England; a five-star restaurant; Aspen, Colorado.

Lucky Love Star: Virginiel—you will never lack intrigue.

Beautiful Thought: It may be work to love your neighbor, but the reward will be worth it.

Sharing Secrets: It may need to start with friendship. This isn't the consolation prize; it's the grand prize. *For the gals:* Go slow and allow it to grow one seed at a time. You won't need to push; it will all come in time. *For the guys:* A step here and a step there. Before he knows it, that friendship will be love.

Judith's Insights

About the Man: This man changes his mind more often than he changes his shirt. If you think he is just stalling for time, you would be correct. He needs to know exactly where his emotions are going before he makes any kind of big decision. Hang in there and wait for the storm to pass before asking for an answer to your question. Matters of the heart scare him more than you may ever realize. When new things are on the horizon he can shrink back as if he has been hit. Proceed slowly and cautiously to bring him out into the world again.

About the Woman: She comes off as some tough cookie. The walls she shields herself with are there for a reason. She never likes to feel as if she does not have control over her emotions. This can make her seem very cold and distant. She will open up only if she feels that you will be responsible with her heart. Prove yourself worthy. Let her know exactly how you feel. You must be willing to be patient enough to let her emotions emerge. Show your patience just by being near her and not wavering from your position.

Soul Mates: Virgo and Virgo is exactly what you need to feel safe. A partnership with Libra will run like a well-oiled machine. Cancer and Aquarius will make you run away once the temptation has worn off. Loosen up so things with Pisces and Sagittarius can flow as they want to. Just when you think you know Aries and Scorpio, more layers appear out of nowhere. Gemini and Leo will run you ragged if you let them. A solid plan will take you and Capricorn or Taurus to new heights.

Most Charming Characteristics: Amusing, accurate, dependable.

Gifts: *For her:* book about feng shui. *For him:* lottery tickets.

Sensual Foods: Strawberry shortcake; pineapple; ham.

Romantic Flowers: Any rose of any color for the lady. Roses stand for love regardless of the color. Send them with orchids and you will be saying, "I love you." If you want a gentleman to know you think of him, send pansies, and forget-me-nots for true love.

Best Date Nights: Wednesday; 20th and 29th of each month.

Colors of Passion: *For her:* cream, violet. *For him:* black, blue.

The Perfect Wedding: Practical, but perfect down to the smallest detail, you actually *enjoy* every aspect of planning your wedding day. Your love of romance and need for privacy lend themselves to a lavishly decorated hidden patio or a botanical garden–type location. As with everything you do, your individual personality stamp will be noticed. Ideal setting: Paris.

Wise Words: Charles Dickens: "There is not an angel added to the Host of Heaven but does its blessed work on earth in those that loved it here."

Hints of Love: Laughter alleviates the tension, but so can understanding where another is sitting.

After the Argument: *For him:* Just tell him how right he was and how wrong you were over and over again. There is no such thing as too much here. *For her:* Grovel, and then grovel some more. They love it. It makes them feel very secure.

Romantic Places: Places of refinement bring romance: Poland; an opera house; Marina Del Rey, California.

Lucky Love Star: Virginiel—you will never lack intrigue.

Beautiful Thought: If you appreciate, then communicate.

Sharing Secrets: This one needs to be the one and only, even if it is only the first date. *For the gals:* Don't talk about your past relationships. Do all you can to make her feel cherished from the first moment. *For the guys:* Play up your innocence. Let him take charge, even in paying the bill. He needs to wear the pants.

Judith's Insights

About the Man: It may take him some time to warm up to any new idea or person. He is the type who will not be interested the first time around and then will fall in love all of a sudden. It is as if he is truly seeing things for the first time. Let him get to this point slowly, although you can encourage him by hanging around a lot. Attracting a mate is oh so easy for this guy. Choosing a mate is quite a different story. Give him time to weigh his emotions. He wants to know that he has made the best decision for his future.

About the Woman: She has it all on the ball, and others around the workplace can think of her as a show-off. She just has to have it all together or she will feel powerless. She can intimidate those who don't have it all under wraps. If you feel like she does overpower you, you should move on. It takes time for her to warm up to someone enough to feel comfortable. She will demonstrate affection only when others have shown theirs for her. State your feelings clearly and concisely to avoid any misunderstandings in her heart.

Soul Mates: Things will be just as they should when you get together with a fellow Virgo. Remember that where there is smoke there is fire when getting tangled up with Aquarius and Cancer. Libra is the balance you are searching for. Pisces and Sagittarius will give you the wings to fly. Scorpio and Aries will have you twisted in knots trying to keep up with their moods. A pairing with Gemini and Leo is advised only when you want to work your tail off. Capricorn and Taurus will give you the foundation and support you need.

Most Charming Characteristics: Spontaneous, generous, unselfish.

Gifts: *For her:* weekend at a spa. *For him:* astrological chart.

Sensual Foods: Steak fondue; cheese fondue and French bread.

Romantic Flowers: These ladies like everyone to know how faithful they are, so send them violets. To surprise them send tulips. Men like their flowers the same as their relationships, unpretending. Send them camellias with white roses to show your affection.

Best Date Nights: Wednesday; 12th and 21st of each month.

Colors of Passion: *For her:* cream, violet. *For him:* black, blue.

The Perfect Wedding: Practical, but perfect down to the smallest detail, you actually *enjoy* every aspect of planning your wedding day. Your love of romance and need for privacy lend themselves to a lavishly decorated hidden patio or a botanical garden–type location. As with everything you do, your individual personality stamp will be noticed. Ideal setting: Paris.

Wise Words: Charles Dickens: "Father Time is not always a hard parent, and, though he tarries for none of his children, often lays his hand lightly upon those who have used him well."

Hints of Love: Communication is important here. A script isn't provided for you. You must write it for yourself.

After the Argument: *For him:* Just tell him how right he was and how wrong you were over and over again. There is no such thing as too much here. *For her:* Grovel, and then grovel some more. They love it. It makes them feel very secure.

Romantic Places: Places of elegance bring romance: Belgium; a five-star hotel; Savannah, Georgia.

Lucky Love Star: Virginiel—you will never lack intrigue.

Beautiful Thought: You can try to make someone laugh who hardly ever smiles.

Sharing Secrets: You need to remember never to forget. *For the gals:* Her birthday, holidays, and your anniversary. Even down to each dinner date. *For the guys:* His birthday, his laundry, his mother's birthday, and, of course, him any other day of the year.

Judith's Insights

About the Man: He may promise marriage on the first date and then not call you for a month. He can scare himself with his raging emotions. He sits on the fence when it comes to all things before jumping into anything. Please forgive any outbursts that may come prematurely. He will try to make the best decision possible. He is ready, willing, and always waiting for someone to come along and pledge her undying love for him. He wants to feel cherished. He will let you know how he really feels only after you have done so. Tell him how you feel right away.

About the Woman: This gal would much rather walk her dog than hang out with anyone who does not interest her. Find out what her favorite activities and foods are and use them to capture her interest. Learn more about them to keep her around. She wants someone to surprise her with his interest in her. She wants her romance to be like the old movies. She needs for you to do anything to be with her. Make her feel like the center of your universe and she will fall into your arms happily.

Soul Mates: All will be well when you have a Virgo like yourself in your life. Libra will teach you how to balance your personality to find peace within yourself. Aquarius and Cancer will have you running like a madman to keep up. Pisces and Sagittarius understand you more than you could ever imagine. Let them in and you will have a friend for life. Scorpio and Aries will have you doing cartwheels and then ask for more. Be prepared to put your nose to the grindstone with Gemini and Leo. Capricorn and Taurus are the perfect support for your insecure times.

Most Charming Characteristics: Amusing, capable, dependable.

Gifts: *For her:* scented bath products. *For him:* leather wallet.

Sensual Foods: Baked Alaska; seafood.

Romantic Flowers: These ladies like men with taste. Show them you love style by sending fuchsia flowers, or even brightly colored wildflowers will do. To confuse this man, send him lilies along with bright daisies to show your innocence. Keep him guessing.

Best Date Nights: Wednesday; 4th and 31st of each month.

Colors of Passion: *For her:* cream, violet. *For him:* black, blue.

The Perfect Wedding: Practical, but perfect down to the smallest detail, you actually *enjoy* every aspect of planning your wedding day. Your love of romance and need for privacy lend themselves to a lavishly decorated hidden patio or a botanical garden–type location. As with everything you do, your individual personality stamp will be noticed. Ideal setting: Paris.

Wise Words: Charles Dickens: "The greatest felicity that age can know is the contemplation of the happiness of those on whom the warmest affections and tenderest cares of a well-spent life have been unceasingly bestowed."

Hints of Love: Don't dissect every minute of every day. Learn to appreciate each minute as it comes.

After the Argument: *For him:* Just tell him how right he was and how wrong you were over and over again. There is no such thing as too much here. *For her:* Grovel, and then grovel some more. They love it. It makes them feel very secure.

Romantic Places: Places of refinement bring romance: Holland; an art museum; the Russian Tea Room, New York City.

Lucky Love Star: Virginiel—you will never lack intrigue.

Beautiful Thought: Strength is the gift that allows you to move forward.

Sharing Secrets: My house should be your house, especially if you don't have one of your own. *For the gals:* All for one and one for all. Yours and mine must become ours. *For the guys.* If he needs to stand on ceremony, even for the first five minutes, it will be a definite turnoff for this one.

Judith's Insights

About the Man: He is much more shy than anyone would think by looking at him. Even if you see that gleam in his eye you might have to be the one to initiate. Just a little flirt here and a question there will pique his interest. If he still hesitates, it is time to do the asking. It may take forever for him to do it himself. Take things slowly after the first date to prove the stability of your affection. He lives in the dramatic and is always waiting for the next shoe to fall. Be consistent and he will begin to believe that your intentions are admirable.

About the Woman: She will doubt your affection right from the get-go. This is her nature. Your nature must be to go overboard to prove differently. She will love every minute of it if you put your heart into making her see your sincerity. Once she is convinced, she will be yours forever. Her love needs to grow one blade at a time to become beautiful and healthy. Rushing her growth will only result in an uneven partner. You will build the foundation for a lifelong relationship by simply taking your time here.

SEPTEMBER

Soul Mates: With a fellow Virgo, all things will be in perfect order. A relationship with Libra is a charmed one. A match of wits happens fast with Cancer and Aquarius. It will be strained just as fast if you don't really get to know each other. Critical is written all over a partnership with Pisces and Sagittarius. Aries and Scorpio will give you a run for your money, then want to go spend it all. Gemini and Leo might cause you a little insanity. You would truly need a deep connection to make this work. Capricorn and Taurus know how to turn on that irresistible charm that you just love.

Most Charming Characteristics: Generous, sentimental, loyal.

Gifts: *For her:* lottery tickets. *For him:* savings bond.

Sensual Foods: Strawberries and cream; meat loaf.

Romantic Flowers: Iris is your flower if you are the gal sending subtle messages. If you are the man, you will look for clematis. This flower's mental beauty creates emotional stimulation for you.

Best Date Nights: Wednesday; 13th and 22nd of each month.

Colors of Passion: *For her:* cream, violet. *For him:* black, blue.

The Perfect Wedding: Practical, but perfect down to the smallest detail, you actually *enjoy* every aspect of planning your wedding day. Your love of romance and need for privacy lend themselves to a lavishly decorated hidden patio or a botanical garden–type location. As with everything you do, your individual personality stamp will be noticed. Ideal setting: Paris.

Wise Words: Charles Dickens: "Every pleasure is transitory. We can't even eat long."

Hints of Love: They only use the three magic words when they know they mean it, and they already know it is going to be said back to them.

After the Argument: *For him:* Just tell him how right he was and how wrong you were over and over again. There is no such thing as too much here. *For her:* Grovel, and then grovel some more. They love it. It makes them feel very secure.

Romantic Places: Places of elegance bring romance: Spain; a winery; Chicago, Illinois.

Lucky Love Star: Virginiel—you will never lack intrigue.

Beautiful Thought: To know you will be recognized for all your work takes away half the work.

Sharing Secrets: Let them admire something about your first. Show them you have a sense of humor. *For the gals:* Hold their hand and then take them to the next step. *For the guys:* The way to his heart is definitely through his stomach.

Judith's Insights

About the Man: This man may seem complicated because he is. He might want to be the one who does all of the asking. Allow him to believe that he is the one always in control. Subtle will work better with this guy, especially in the work environment. Never make him think that you are demanding things from him or he will shut down all ability to compromise. He can be fickle early on in a partnership until he figures out what it is he really wants out of it. He will change his mind several times before coming to any sort of conclusion.

About the Woman: It can seem as if she has time for everyone but you. That is only true until she decides exactly what it is she wants and doesn't want in a relationship. Until then, she will be sending you mixed signals that will make your head spin. You may have to learn to read between them to get to the core of her character. Asking her a question more than once may work out to your advantage. You might get a different answer each time. So keep asking until you get the answer you are looking for.

Soul Mates: Virgo and Virgo is exactly what you need to feel safe. A partnership with Libra will run like a well-oiled machine. Cancer and Aquarius will make you run away once the temptation has worn off. Loosen up so things with Pisces and Sagittarius can flow as they want to. Just when you think you know Aries and Scorpio, more layers appear out of nowhere. Gemini and Leo will run you ragged if you let them. A solid plan will take you and Capricorn or Taurus to new heights.

Most Charming Characteristics: Witty, adaptable, sincere.

Gifts: *For her:* day of beauty. *For him:* get his car detailed.

Sensual Foods: Cherry-apple pie; beef Stroganoff.

Romantic Flowers: Any rose of any color for the lady. Roses stand for love regardless of the color. Send them with orchids and you will be saying, "I love you." If you want a gentleman to know you think of him, send pansies, and forget-me-nots for true love.

Best Date Nights: Wednesday; 20th and 29th of each month.

Colors of Passion: *For her:* cream, violet. *For him:* black, blue.

The Perfect Wedding: Practical, but perfect down to the smallest detail, you actually *enjoy* every aspect of planning your wedding day. Your love of romance and need for privacy lend themselves to a lavishly decorated hidden patio or a botanical garden–type location. As with everything you do, your individual personality stamp will be noticed. Ideal setting: Paris.

Wise Words: Charles Dickens: "There is a kind of pride, or what may be supposed to be pride, which is mere duty."

Hints of Love: Remember to keep the dating fun. Don't act like you are married before your time.

After the Argument: *For him:* Just tell him how right he was and how wrong you were over and over again. There is no such thing as too much here. *For her:* Grovel, and then grovel some more. They love it. It makes them feel very secure.

Romantic Places: Places of elegance bring romance: Turkey; a cruise; New Orleans, Louisiana.

Lucky Love Star: Virginiel—you will never lack intrigue.

Beautiful Thought: Being silly means the laughter inside of you is alive.

Sharing Secrets: Give them the opportunity to notice you first. *For the gals:* They love to be adored; love at first sight. *For the guys:* Remember to always let them believe it was their idea.

Judith's Insights

About the Man: We can call this guy "Curious George." He is willing to experience anything at any time. So make your first effort your best one. He will make you feel as if you have known each other forever and then not call. If it comes to that, it has to be you who must pick up the phone. Keeping things interesting for him is to keep things changing. Be flexible on the routine elements of your relationship to keep him away from thoughts of changing you. Things around him must be as stimulating as possible. Make him feel special.

About the Woman: This gal will never be afraid to be the one doing the asking. That does not necessarily mean that she will. She likes it better when others do the initiating. This way she can really play the role of being the lady. Treat her as such and she will be hooked. Send her flowers and call her as often as you can. Dazzle her with life and she will love every minute of it. She will give you all of herself if you are the right one to receive it. To become that person you have to give her life the excitement and stimulation it needs.

Soul Mates: Things will be just as they should when you get together with a fellow Virgo. Remember that where there is smoke there is fire when getting tangled up with Aquarius and Cancer. Libra is the balance you are searching for. Pisces and Sagittarius will give you the wings to fly. Scorpio and Aries will have you twisted in knots trying to keep up with their moods. A pairing with Gemini and Leo is only advised when you want to work your tail off. Capricorn and Taurus will give you the foundation and support you need.

Most Charming Characteristics: Versatile, patient, durable.

Gifts: *For her:* closet organizer. *For him:* organizing tool chest.

Sensual Foods: Hot-fudge sundae with all the trimmings; shepherd's pie.

Romantic Flowers: These ladies like everyone to know how faithful they are, so send them violets. To surprise them send tulips. Men like their flowers the same as their relationships, unpretending. Send them camellias with white roses to show your affection.

Best Date Nights: Wednesday; 12th and 21st of each month.

Colors of Passion: *For her:* cream, violet. *For him:* black, blue.

The Perfect Wedding: Practical, but perfect down to the smallest detail, you actually *enjoy* every aspect of planning your wedding day. Your love of romance and need for privacy lend themselves to a lavishly decorated hidden patio or a botanical garden–type location. As with everything you do, your individual personality stamp will be noticed. Ideal setting: Paris.

Wise Words: Charles Dickens: "The good in this state of existence preponderates over the bad, let miscalled philosophers tell us what they will."

Hints of Love: Make sure you go on more than one date before you jump to conclusions on liking and disliking.

After the Argument: *For him:* Just tell him how right he was and how wrong you were over and over again. There is no such thing as too much here. *For her:* Grovel, and then grovel some more. They love it. It makes them feel very secure.

Romantic Places: Places of refinement bring romance: Argentina; high tea; New York City.

Lucky Love Star: Virginiel—you will never lack intrigue.

Beautiful Thought: You don't need all the questions to figure out all the answers.

Sharing Secrets: This one loves a challenge. *For the gals:* Be consistently inconsistent until you have them hooked. *For the guys:* This one loves to play catch. You may feel like a yo-yo, but as long as he is calling that's all that matters.

Judith's Insights

About the Man: Do not think that you don't have his undivided attention just because he is looking elsewhere. He is capable of doing many things at one time. He has attention enough for the whole world. Never whine to this guy. He will bail before you get the chance to truly know him. Keep your self-pity to yourself if you want to keep his attention. He will never admit to his flirtatious side, but expect to hear an earful about yours. While he craves stability in a relationship, he will run away from it if he feels the variety is gone from his life.

About the Woman: She has style and class, and you must appeal to these things when you plan an outing with her. This gal wants someone who will go way out of his way for her. Even if she is your co-worker, she will be in a better mood when she feels that people are working with her instead of against her. As long as her life is stimulating she will not become bored. The reason everyone thinks that she is pushy and impatient is because she is. Let her have her flirtatious ways while she retains the right to come home to you at the end of the night.

Soul Mates: All will be well when you have a Virgo like yourself in your life. Libra will teach you how to balance your personality to find peace within yourself. Aquarius and Cancer will have you running like a madman to keep up. Pisces and Sagittarius understand you more than you could ever imagine. Let them in and you will have a friend for life. Scorpio and Aries will have you doing cartwheels and then ask for more. Be prepared to put your nose to the grindstone with Gemini and Leo. Capricorn and Taurus are the perfect support for your insecure times.

Most Charming Characteristics: Personable, brilliant, loyal.

Gifts: *For her:* silk scarf. *For him:* cashmere sweater.

Sensual Foods: Whipped cream, strawberries, brown sugar, and heavy cream.

Romantic Flowers: These ladies like men with taste. Show them you love style by sending fuchsia flowers, or even brightly colored wildflowers will do. To confuse this man, send him lilies along with bright daisies to show your innocence. Keep him guessing.

Best Date Nights: Wednesday; 13th and 22nd of each month.

Colors of Passion: *For her:* cream, violet. *For him:* black, blue.

The Perfect Wedding: Practical, but perfect down to the smallest detail, you actually *enjoy* every aspect of planning your wedding day. Your love of romance and need for privacy lend themselves to a lavishly decorated, hidden patio or a botanical garden–type location. As with everything you do, your individual personality stamp will be noticed. Ideal setting: Paris.

Wise Words: Charles Dickens: "If you have friends in adversity, stand by them."

Hints of Love: Don't act too needy too soon. It may push this relationship away.

After the Argument: *For him:* Just tell him how right he was and how wrong you were over and over again. There is no such thing as too much here. *For her:* Grovel, and then grovel some more. They love it. It makes them feel very secure.

Romantic Places: Places of elegance bring romance: Russia; a sculpted garden; Hilton Head, South Carolina.

Lucky Love Star: Virginiel—you will never lack intrigue.

Beautiful Thought: Endings only mean new beginnings.

Sharing Secrets: This is a family person at heart; your presence is most important. *For the gals:* Make sure you go to Sunday dinner with her family when you are invited. *For the guys:* If you don't like his mom, you might have a hard time catching this one.

Judith's Insights

About the Man: He may seem like the bossy, macho type with no heart at all. This guy is really all heart and soul. You just have to get close enough to see it. He won't take advantage of you unless you insist. He can break your heart and spirit if he is not ready for love. If he is ready for love, there will be no better partner than him. Even in a crowded room he will stand out like a bright star. He enjoys helping others with their problems, but he is limited when it comes to keeping promises that he makes to others.

About the Woman: Never pick on her about the petty stuff. She hates nitpicking more than anything else in the world, unless she is the one doing it. She is the only one in the crowd allowed to make observations about how people act. If you are around long enough to call it a relationship, then you are already doing well. She will stand on ceremony and protocol, so make sure that every invitation is clear. At times, her actions will be grossly misunderstood. Keep in mind that her intentions are pure. She just has to be taught to find other ways of helping.

Soul Mates: With a fellow Virgo, all will be well in your joined worlds. Libra will give you the peace you are searching for. Aquarius and Cancer are a hard act to keep up with. Pisces and Sagittarius are the best place to start when you are in search of the real you. Scorpio and Aries are too much ruckus for your perfectionist nature. Gemini and Leo are hard work, but well worth the effort. Taurus and Capricorn are the stability you yearn for.

Most Charming Characteristics: Vivacious, winsome, loving.

Gifts: *For her:* a beauty makeover. *For him:* a weekend in the mountains.

Sensual Foods: Puddings and pastry of all kinds.

Romantic Flowers: You are the lady of distinction, and only carnations will do. Any mix of colors with sprays of mignonette. Sweet peas or red carnations will appeal to this man's heart.

Best Date Nights: Wednesday; 4th and 5th of each month.

Colors of Passion: *For her:* cream, violet. *For him:* black, blue.

The Perfect Wedding: Practical, but perfect down to the smallest detail, you actually *enjoy* every aspect of planning your wedding day. Your love of romance and need for privacy lend themselves to a lavishly decorated hidden patio or a botanical garden–type location. As with everything you do, your individual personality stamp will be noticed. Ideal setting: Paris.

Wise Words: Charles Dickens: "There are times of moral danger when the hardest virtuous resolution to form is flight, and when the most heroic bravery is flight."

Hints of Love: Keep it fun. Look for new and exciting things to do, especially if you are in a long-term relationship.

After the Argument: *For him:* Just tell him how right he was and how wrong you were over and over again. There is no such thing as too much here. *For her:* Grovel, and then grovel some more. They love it. It makes them feel very secure.

Romantic Places: Places of refinement bring romance: the Taj Mahal; an awards ceremony; Boston, Massachusetts.

Lucky Love Star: Virginiel—you will never lack intrigue.

Beautiful Thought: Love is something shared, not owned.

Sharing Secrets: Everything in its good time. This one works slowly, but when it is time to pick up speed, watch out. *For the gals:* Don't go by the obvious. Read between the lines. As long as the invitation is being offered go full speed ahead. *For the guys:* Just when you thought you should walk away, he'll say, "I love you." Talk about confusing.

Judith's Insights

About the Man: He is versatile in any aspect except love. He can handle anyone's moody behavior without trouble. The trouble begins when his own emotions come into play. He can't handle not being in control of his emotions, so his behavior may seem erratic suddenly. Let him settle down and he will be the same old rock in no time. He is happiest doing many things at one time. To keep him interested in your relationship, plan a day when you are both constantly on the run. He will be thrilled with your ability to keep up with him.

About the Woman: Do not try to tell this gal what to do. She likes chivalry, but not a bossy mate. She is pretty choosy about who is in her company. If she does the inviting you can be sure that things are going well. If she doesn't invite you out, she may still be thrilled at an invitation from you. She seems so dependable, reliable, and stable that she can seem too good to be true. She is a rock when it comes to all things but love and matters of the heart. The threat of being chained to one thing will scare her, but once she is, there will be an unbreakable bond between you.

Soul Mates: Only a fellow Virgo can completely understand your need for order in your surroundings and comply with that need as well. Libra will teach you to balance your need of order with a new sense of spontaneity. Aquarius and Cancer will have your head spinning right away. Pisces and Sagittarius will give you all you need to be the very best you can be. Scorpio and Aries will have you wincing from their intimidation. Gemini and Leo take some getting used to, but once you know them, you will love them. Taurus and Capricorn will ground you like never before.

Most Charming Characteristics: Faithful, gracious, joyful.

Gifts: *For her:* astrological chart. *For him:* box or ringside seats.

Sensual Foods: Champagne with strawberries; fillet of sole.

Romantic Flowers: You love it when you get tulips, declaring love. When you receive a variety, it shows how hopelessly in love your partner is. He will just love a single rose. This shows him you understand his pleasures.

Best Date Nights: Wednesday; 6th and 15th of each month.

Colors of Passion: *For her:* cream, violet. *For him:* black, blue.

The Perfect Wedding: Practical, but perfect down to the smallest detail, you actually *enjoy* every aspect of planning your wedding day. Your love of romance and need for privacy lend themselves to a lavishly decorated hidden patio or a botanical garden–type location. As with everything you do, your individual personality stamp will be noticed. Ideal setting: Paris.

Wise Words: Charles Dickens: "Oh, there are days in this life, worth life and worth death. Oh, what a bright old song it is, that oh, 'tis love,' tis love, that makes the world go round."

Hints of Love: This one is a cautious soul. You may have to find a way to go around to the back door.

After the Argument: *For him:* Just tell him how right he was and how wrong you were over and over again. There is no such thing as too much here. *For her:* Grovel, and then grovel some more. They love it. It makes them feel very secure.

Romantic Places: Places of elegance bring romance: England; a five-star restaurant; Aspen, Colorado.

Lucky Love Star: Virginiel—you will never lack intrigue.

Beautiful Thought: When opportunity knocks, it helps if you open the door.

Sharing Secrets: This one is a charmer, perhaps even fickle. *For the gals:* If you are patient enough to stick around, this one is worth the wait. *For the guys:* If there is enough time on the clock, stick around past three months. Then maybe he will have noticed you are there.

Judith's Insights

About the Man: He loves romance, but he may feel awkward in making any romantic plans. He just needs to get his romantic muscles warmed up before he dives in. He won't mind coming over to your place for a romantic dinner or a candlelit Jacuzzi. Show him how it is done and he will learn quickly. A relationship with this guy may seem like a roller coaster ride. It will take him time to settle down and allow the possibility of constant companionship to enter his life. He will secretly wish that his partner was more romantic but never admit it.

About the Woman: She may seem like the basic, down-to-earth type. She does like the finer things in life just as much as being a homebody. The best approach for this gal is to invite her to a show, as long as you have great seats! When she does special things she goes all out. Make sure that you do the same for her. Don't introduce too many new ideas into her life all at once. She will shut down almost instantly. Instead, add things one at a time. Make sure she has plenty of time to get used to one idea before going on to the next one.

Soul Mates: You will find true understanding of your nature when you find a fellow Virgo. Libra will help you see all the good in yourself while improving at the same time. Aquarius and Cancer will drive you up a wall if you stick around long enough for them to get to you. Pisces and Sagittarius will give you a new purpose and sense of self. You will feel much stronger once under their guidance. Scorpio and Aries will try to bully you. Just stick up for yourself as you are walking to the exit. Gemini and Leo will be a no-no at first glance. If you give them that second look, you might be surprised at what you see. Taurus and Capricorn will give you a solid base for all of your dreams.

Most Charming Characteristics: Idealistic, self-reliant, likable.

Gifts: *For her:* book about feng shui. *For him:* lottery tickets.

Sensual Foods: Chocolates; poached salmon; flambé; filet mignon; potatoes.

Romantic Flowers: Send this girl sunflowers if you want her to know you adore her. You may even add some poppies for a splash of extravagance. His desire for sport and play will be understood when you send him hyacinth and geranium.

Best Date Nights: Wednesday; 8th and 17th of each month.

Colors of Passion: *For her:* cream, violet. *For him:* black, blue.

The Perfect Wedding: Practical, but perfect down to the smallest detail, you actually *enjoy* every aspect of planning your wedding day. Your love of romance and need for privacy lend themselves to a lavishly decorated hidden patio or a botanical garden–type location. As with everything you do, your individual personality stamp will be noticed. Ideal setting: Paris.

Wise Words: Charles Dickens: "Hunger and recent ill usage are great assistants if you want to cry."

Hints of Love: Passion must be in the picture at all times or you could lose this one's attention quickly.

After the Argument: *For him:* Just tell him how right he was and how wrong you were over and over again. There is no such thing as too much here. *For her:* Grovel, and then grovel some more. They love it. It makes them feel very secure.

Romantic Places: Places of refinement bring romance: Poland; an opera house; Marina Del Rey, California.

Lucky Love Star: Virginiel—you will never lack intrigue.

Beautiful Thought: Putting your best foot forward usually ensures you stable ground.

Sharing Secrets: If you are looking for love, then you have found the right mate. *For the gals:* This one could be stubborn. It may take forever to get a relationship started, but it is as solid as they come. *For the guys:* Even when he is ready, he might not be willing and able. He will put you through more obstacles than any course. Be patient.

Judith's Insights

About the Man: You may find that this guy contradicts himself. He doesn't do it in his words, but in his actions. He finds it very hard to show his affections toward anything and anyone. He almost feels shy about having them in the first place. His emotions scare him when they become strong. Make sure that his environment is in order. He will go ballistic if he can't find something where it was left. The way to his heart is through kindness. He will observe how you interact with the people around you and then form his opinions from there.

About the Woman: Never leave out any details with this gal. If it will be a special night out, let her know it or give her hints. She has a need to dress according to the events taking place. She will be happy only when she is underdressed if she chose to be in the first place. Don't make her feel awkward when you are trying to make her feel special. The only time that she will be comfortable in a romantic situation is when she is in control. The minute she feels her emotions spinning in a direction she didn't mean for them, she will withdraw until she sorts them out.

Soul Mates: A fellow Virgo will let you know that there is nothing wrong with your nature to begin with. Libra will give you a sense of wholeness when they help you become less rigid. Aquarius and Cancer will leave you numb. This pairing is not recommended for the faint of heart or the easily bruised ego. Pisces and Sagittarius will help you soar to new heights in all you encounter. Scorpio and Aries are too much trouble for you. You will be surprised when you give Gemini and Leo a chance. They just might break your first impression. Taurus and Capricorn will show you all of the wonders that lie in your own life.

Most Charming Characteristics: Artistic, musical, loving.

Gifts: *For her:* weekend at a spa. *For him:* astrological chart.

Sensual Foods: Caviar; beef tenderloin; potatoes au gratin.

Romantic Flowers: Rhododendron will let her be on the lookout for trouble. Throw in some chrysanthemum and she'll know it is you she will be looking out for. Cactus will show him warmth. Yellow daffodil is a token of a good time had by all. Chivalry is not dead.

Best Date Nights: Wednesday; 18th and 27th of each month.

Colors of Passion: *For her:* cream, violet. *For him:* black, blue.

The Perfect Wedding: Practical, but perfect down to the smallest detail, you actually *enjoy* every aspect of planning your wedding day. Your love of romance and need for privacy lend themselves to a lavishly decorated hidden patio or a botanical garden–type location. As with everything you do, your individual personality stamp will be noticed. Ideal setting: Paris.

Wise Words: Charles Dickens: "It is a common remark, confirmed by history and experience, that great men rise with the circumstances in which they are placed."

Hints of Love: A random act of kindness will go a long way with this one. What can you do for them today?

After the Argument: *For him:* Just tell him how right he was and how wrong you were over and over again. There is no such thing as too much here. *For her:* Grovel, and then grovel some more. They love it. It makes them feel very secure.

Romantic Places: Places of elegance bring romance: Belgium; a five-star hotel; Savannah, Georgia.

Lucky Love Star: Virginiel—you will never lack intrigue.

Beautiful Thought: Using your ability to give will increase the happiness you live.

Sharing Secrets: If you can hang around and give constant stimulation, this could be your mate. *For the gals:* She is always looking for the Exit sign. Don't show her where it is or she will be gone. *For the guys:* Fast car, fast food; he likes everything that goes fast. Put on your running shoes. If you can keep up, then he is yours.

Judith's Insights

About the Man: He is uncannily observant. If you are checking out someone on the other side of the room he will certainly notice it. He can be easy to catch if you have a slow and easy way about you. If you are a bundle of restless energy the chase will be harder to win. Slow down and let him come to you. He may not be demonstrative with his affections right away. At the same time he may encourage you to be more affectionate from the start. He is afraid that people will discover that he is a real romantic at heart and dreams of a partner who is the same.

About the Woman: This gal can see right through the bull you are planning to tell her even before you start talking. At times she is known to play along and let you get yourself in trouble. That is when she is most amused. She views strength as an intriguing quality. She also guards herself well, so expect defenses to pop up. She will only put words on paper that she really means. Don't expect a card that is signed "Love" until she is sure that she really does. Treat her like a princess even though she pretends she doesn't need to be.

Soul Mates: Everything will be in its perfect place when you and a fellow Virgo get together. Libra and their scales of balance will teach you how to keep your life level. Aquarius and Cancer will drive you to drink if you stick around too long. Pisces and Sagittarius will help you be all that you can be and more. Scorpio and Aries will try to push you too much to change. Gemini and Leo will surprise you when you least expect it. Taurus and Capricorn will give you something to come home to every time.

Most Charming Characteristics: Faithful, considerate, loving.

Gifts: *For her:* scented bath products. *For him:* leather wallet.

Sensual Foods: Passion fruit; fillet of sole almondine.

Romantic Flowers: The magnolias you send her will let her know you will be around for a while to come. Petunia is to say never despair. Holly will let him know what he is getting into. Pansy will keep you in his thoughts.

Best Date Nights: Wednesday; 9th and 27th of each month.

Colors of Passion: *For her:* cream, violet. *For him:* black, blue.

The Perfect Wedding: Practical, but perfect down to the smallest detail, you actually *enjoy* every aspect of planning your wedding day. Your love of romance and need for privacy lend themselves to a lavishly decorated hidden patio or a botanical garden–type location. As with everything you do, your individual personality stamp will be noticed. Ideal setting: Paris.

Wise Words: William Wordsworth: "Serene will be our days and bright, and happy will our nature be, when love is an inuring light, enjoy its own serenity."

Hints of Love: Family and friends are important to this one. Don't try to alienate them or it will definitely backfire on you.

After the Argument: *For him:* Just tell him how right he was and how wrong you were over and over again. There is no such thing as too much here. *For her:* Grovel, and then grovel some more. They love it. It makes them feel very secure.

Romantic Places: Places of refinement bring romance: Holland; art museum; Russian Tea Room, New York City.

Lucky Love Star: Virginiel—you will never lack intrigue.

Beautiful Thought: Giving of yourself is the best gift of all.

Sharing Secrets: This one may seem like a lot of work. They just need the basics: love, loyalty, and respect. *For the gals:* If you can show her your best side right from the beginning it may work. Be careful of fluff, because she will see right through it. *For the guys:* He loves to be loved. Give him plenty of attention, even if you think you don't stand a chance. Perseverance will win here.

Judith's Insights

About the Man: Don't let the strength and power he portrays fool you at all. This guy is as sensitive as they come. Even if he is flirting he may still hold back. He does not trust his emotions when they come on fast and strong. He wants to make sure that they are reliable before he acts on them. Romance will take a lot of energy for him. He can be completely committed to the one he falls in love with. Until then, he will be a shameless flirt. He is great when he is in control, but falling in love is an out-of-control time for him.

About the Woman: Don't expect this girl to be picking up after you anytime soon. Expect that there may be someone picking up after her. This gal is a hard worker and prefers the finer things in life. She will not hesitate to buy those things for herself but would never refuse a gift from you. She secretly dreams of a partner who will come into her life bearing roses and promises of romance. Once a bond has been forged with her it will be nearly impossible to sever it. She will be tempted to run and hide before that bond is formed.

Soul Mates: With a fellow Virgo, all things will be in perfect order. A relationship with Libra is a charmed one. A match of wits happens fast with Cancer and Aquarius. It will be strained just as fast if you don't really get to know each other. Critical is written all over a partnership with Pisces and Sagittarius. Aries and Scorpio will give you a run for your money, then want to go spend it all. Gemini and Leo might cause you a little insanity. You would truly need a deep connection to make this work. Capricorn and Taurus know how to turn on that irresistible charm that you just love.

Most Charming Characteristics: Kind, resourceful, ambitious.

Gifts: *For her:* lottery tickets. *For him:* savings bond.

Sensual Foods: Peaches; mousse; shrimp.

Romantic Flowers: Iris is your flower if you are the gal sending subtle messages. If you are the man, you will look for clematis. This flower's mental beauty creates emotional stimulation for you.

Best Date Nights: Wednesday; 1st and 28th of each month.

Colors of Passion: *For her:* cream, violet. *For him:* black, blue.

The Perfect Wedding: Practical, but perfect down to the smallest detail, you actually *enjoy* every aspect of planning your wedding day. Your love of romance and need for privacy lend themselves to a lavishly decorated hidden patio or a botanical garden–type location. As with everything you do, your individual personality stamp will be noticed. Ideal setting: Paris.

Wise Words: William Makepeace Thackeray: "Compared to the possession of that priceless treasure and happiness unspeakable, a priceless faith, what has life to offer?"

Hints of Love: Show others how much you adore him or her. They will revel in how others notice.

After the Argument: *For him:* Just tell him how right he was and how wrong you were over and over again. There is no such thing as too much here. *For her:* Grovel, and then grovel some more. They love it. It makes them feel very secure.

Romantic Places: Places of elegance bring romance: Spain; a winery; Chicago, Illinois.

Lucky Love Star: Virginiel—you will never lack intrigue.

Beautiful Thought: Looking forward can somehow change the past.

Sharing Secrets: They are looking for love, but that is just their little secret. *For the gals:* Why shouldn't they want to be loved? Of course they do, but they want you to do all of the work. *For the guys:* You must prove yourself repeatedly. Don't expect too much until he knows you are under his thumb.

Judith's Insights

About the Man: This guy won't trust anyone easily. He will put you through test after test. He needs proof that you will be as reliable as he is. He needs more proof than the average judge to make that decision. He can give all of himself in business matters, but not in matters of the heart. To give of himself, he must be completely certain. He is charmed by kindness and impressed by intellect. He doesn't need for life to be fancy, but he never wants to feel as if he has settled for second-best in anything, especially love.

About the Woman: This gal gets tongue-tied with emotional issues, but never at work. It only affects her when she has a personal interest in the outcome. She works on two speeds: slow and fast. There is no in between. She can be shy or completely overwhelming. She will seem removed or be madly in love. Give her the best you have to give at all times. Make her feel special without being lavish and you will have her hooked. Just make sure that you are able to continue the same level of romance you established in the early days of your relationship.

Soul Mates: Virgo and Virgo is exactly what you need to feel safe. A partnership with Libra will run like a well-oiled machine. Cancer and Aquarius will make you run away once the temptation has worn off. Loosen up so things with Pisces and Sagittarius can flow as they want to. Just when you think you know Aries and Scorpio, more layers appear out of nowhere. Gemini and Leo will run you ragged if you let them. A solid plan will take you and Capricorn or Taurus to new heights.

Most Charming Characteristics: Sincere, honest, loving.

Gifts: *For her:* day of beauty. *For him:* get his car detailed.

Sensual Foods: Kiwis; cantaloupes; strawberries.

Romantic Flowers: Any rose of any color for the lady. Roses stand for love regardless of the color. Send them with orchids and you will be saying, "I love you." If you want a gentleman to know you think of him, send pansies, and forget-me-nots for true love.

Best Date Nights: Wednesday; 11th and 20th of each month.

Colors of Passion: *For her:* cream, violet. *For him:* black, blue.

The Perfect Wedding: Practical, but perfect down to the smallest detail, you actually *enjoy* every aspect of planning your wedding day. Your love of romance and need for privacy lend themselves to a lavishly decorated hidden patio or a botanical garden–type location. As with everything you do, your individual personality stamp will be noticed. Ideal setting: Paris.

Wise Words: Ralph Waldo Emerson: "There is no beautifier of complexion or form or behavior like the wish to scatter joy and not pain around us."

Hints of Love: Don't overdo it (dress, attention) too soon or this one will run. Wait until you have them hooked before you become outrageous.

After the Argument: *For him:* Just tell him how right he was and how wrong you were over and over again. There is no such thing as too much here. *For her:* Grovel, and then grovel some more. They love it. It makes them feel very secure.

Romantic Places: Places of elegance bring romance: Turkey; a cruise; New Orleans, Louisiana.

Lucky Love Star: Virginiel—you will never lack intrigue.

Beautiful Thought: Remember to celebrate what you have accomplished.

Sharing Secrets: You had better be ready to pull out your romantic side if you want this to work. *For the gals:* Fireplaces, walks on the beach, or even winning a bear at the local carnival. *For the guys:* When you are out shopping bring him something home. Even if it is silly, he will love the thought.

Judith's Insights

About the Man: His emotions get the best of him right from the start. All that he wants is to be loved unconditionally. His talent for flirting is hidden, but it is there. He won't mind if you make a move, but it would be better to flirt a bit first to lay the groundwork. Once he opens up he will be much easier to understand. When he listens to his intuition he will get along much better. It may take him a few bad relationships to get things done right in his love life. He is a true believer in learning from his mistakes in matters of his heart.

About the Woman: This gal can lack patience. Just when you are about to ask her out she will ask you. If you take too long she might play as if she is too busy to take you up on your offer. She thinks too much, so you may have to think about other things for her to do. Make sure every event is exciting. In early years she may pick a mate because of how nice they look together. The more bad experiences she has with love the more she will know about what works and what doesn't. Keep the thrill in your relationship to keep her from running away.

Soul Mates: Things will be just as they should when you get together with a fellow Virgo. Remember that where there is smoke there is fire when getting tangled up with Aquarius and Cancer. Libra is the balance you are searching for. Pisces and Sagittarius will give you the wings to fly. Scorpio and Aries will have you twisted in knots trying to keep up with their moods. A pairing with Gemini and Leo is only advised when you want to work your tail off. Capricorn and Taurus will give you the foundation and support you need.

Most Charming Characteristics: Faithful, humorous, demonstrative.

Gifts: *For her:* closet organizer. *For him:* organizing tool chest.

Sensual Foods: Caramel and chocolate syrup on anything.

Romantic Flowers: These ladies like everyone to know how faithful they are, so send them violets. To surprise them send tulips. Men like their flowers the same as their relationships, unpretending. Send them camellias with white roses to show your affection.

Best Date Nights: Wednesday; 3rd and 12th of each month.

Colors of Passion: *For her:* cream, violet. *For him:* black, blue.

The Perfect Wedding: Practical, but perfect down to the smallest detail, you actually *enjoy* every aspect of planning your wedding day. Your love of romance and need for privacy lend themselves to a lavishly decorated hidden patio or a botanical garden–type location. As with everything you do, your individual personality stamp will be noticed. Ideal setting: Paris.

Wise Words: Charles Dickens: "The children that we were are not lost to the great knowledge of our Creator. Those innocent creatures will appear with us before Him, and plead for us."

Hints of Love: When these folks decide to sit on the fence don't try to push them off before they are ready. Let them do the jumping themselves.

After the Argument: *For him:* Just tell him how right he was and how wrong you were over and over again. There is no such thing as too much here. *For her:* Grovel, and then grovel some more. They love it. It makes them feel very secure.

Romantic Places: Places of refinement bring romance: Argentina; high tea; New York City.

Lucky Love Star: Virginiel—you will never lack intrigue.

Beautiful Thought: Seasons are like love: stormy, warm, and full of sunshine.

Sharing Secrets: It may seem like they are not interested, but ask them out anyway. *For the gals:* Until they absolutely know you are interested, you will never find out that they are. *For the guys:* Ask him out if he doesn't ask you. He may be shy or not. Either way, he may be interested.

Judith's Insights

About the Man: This guy has no trouble attracting friends. He can keep his distance from an intense love relationship for a long time. Ultimately, this is what he wants, but he will never let on to that fact. This guy is full of contradictions. His actions will confuse you when you compare them with his words. He makes friends easily and will go to the ends of the earth for those he cares about. Be careful about returning his critical judgments of you. He can give more advice than anyone around, but he can seldom take any himself.

About the Woman: She can be very businesslike and may not be close to anyone at work. Once people get to know her they wonder why they didn't notice her kindness before. Go out of your way for her once or twice and she will come around for more. Making her feel worthy of your efforts will put you right on her A-list. You won't find her alone easily. She will constantly surround herself with many friends and family. When she grows out of her critical nature her love life will turn into the fairy tale she has long dreamed about but never admitted to.

Soul Mates: All will be well when you have a Virgo like yourself in your life. Libra will teach you how to balance your personality to find peace within yourself. Aquarius and Cancer will have you running like a madman to keep up. Pisces and Sagittarius understand you more than you could ever imagine. Let them in and you will have a friend for life. Scorpio and Aries will have you doing cartwheels and then ask for more. Be prepared to put your nose to the grindstone with Gemini and Leo. Capricorn and Taurus are the perfect support for your insecure times.

Most Charming Characteristics: Amiable, gracious, loving.

Gifts: *For her:* silk scarf. *For him:* cashmere sweater.

Sensual Foods: Waffles with whipped cream; chocolate soufflé; French wine.

Romantic Flowers: These ladies like men with taste. Show them you love style by sending fuchsia flowers, or even brightly colored wildflowers will do. To confuse this man, send him lilies along with bright daisies to show your innocence. Keep him guessing.

Best Date Nights: Wednesday; 13th and 22nd of each month.

Colors of Passion: *For her:* cream, violet. *For him:* black, blue.

The Perfect Wedding: Practical, but perfect down to the smallest detail, you actually *enjoy* every aspect of planning your wedding day. Your love of romance and need for privacy lend themselves to a lavishly decorated hidden patio or a botanical garden–type location. As with everything you do, your individual personality stamp will be noticed. Ideal setting: Paris.

Wise Words: Charles Dickens: "We are so much in the habit of allowing impressions to be made upon us by external objects, which should be produced by reflection alone, but which, without such visible aids, often escape us."

Hints of Love: Make sure you learn to compromise, but never with your principles.

After the Argument: *For him:* Just tell him how right he was and how wrong you were over and over again. There is no such thing as too much here. *For her:* Grovel, and then grovel some more. They love it. It makes them feel very secure.

Romantic Places: Places of elegance bring romance: Russia; a sculpted garden; Hilton Head, South Carolina.

Lucky Love Star: Virginiel—you will never lack intrigue.

Beautiful Thought: Believing in yourself will help you believe in others.

Sharing Secrets: Don't be surprised if the first date is with their family. *For the gals:* Make sure you invite her to your family functions. It will be a red flag to her if you don't. *For the guys:* He may seem like a family man, but isn't that what you were looking for?

Judith's Insights

About the Man: He is filled with compassion. It is no wonder everyone is looking for his attention. Even if you are dating this guy, people will step over and talk to him at every turn. Don't get your knickers in a knot. He is looking for only one mate. He just wants to make sure that it is the best possible one. For this guy, a promise made is a promise kept. That is why he will be careful about what he says and does. He is looking for his Soul Mate under every rock and in every corner. At times, he can miss what is right in front of him.

About the Woman: Although she might seem to be looking for a challenge, it is simply the way she interacts with others. In business she does much better in communicating. When it comes to matters of emotions, she can freeze up. Her emotions can scare her with their intensity. She can get her dander up on occasion. For the most part, though, her personality is strong and steady. Intrigue her with your talent for listening and your openness to learning. She is hoping for a person who will recognize her insecurities without calling attention to them.

Soul Mates: With a fellow Virgo, all will be well in your joined worlds. Libra will give you the peace you are searching for. Aquarius and Cancer are a hard act to keep up with. Pisces and Sagittarius are the best place to start when you are in search of the real you. Scorpio and Aries are too much ruckus for your perfectionist nature. Gemini and Leo are hard work, but well worth the effort. Taurus and Capricorn are the stability you yearn for.

Most Charming Characteristics: Versatile, humorous, winsome.

Gifts: *For her:* a beauty makeover. *For him:* a weekend in the mountains.

Sensual Foods: Oysters; mussels; spicy foods.

Romantic Flowers: You are the lady of distinction, and only carnations will do. Any mix of colors with sprays of mignonette. Sweet peas or red carnations will appeal to this man's heart.

Best Date Nights: Wednesday; 4th and 5th of each month.

Colors of Passion: *For her:* cream, violet. *For him:* black, blue.

The Perfect Wedding: Practical, but perfect down to the smallest detail, you actually *enjoy* every aspect of planning your wedding day. Your love of romance and need for privacy lend themselves to a lavishly decorated hidden patio or a botanical garden–type location. As with everything you do, your individual personality stamp will be noticed. Ideal setting: Paris.

Wise Words: Charles Dickens: "The cares of the day, old moralists say, are quite enough to perplex one; then drive to-day's sorrow away till tomorrow, / And then put it off until the next one."

Hints of Love: If you try to take a step back, it will be noticed. It could create the domino effect, and everything will start to fall.

After the Argument: *For him:* Just tell him how right he was and how wrong you were over and over again. There is no such thing as too much here. *For her:* Grovel, and then grovel some more. They love it. It makes them feel very secure.

Romantic Places: Places of refinement bring romance: the Taj Mahal; an awards ceremony; Boston, Massachusetts.

Lucky Love Star: Virginiel—you will never lack intrigue.

Beautiful Thought: Stop and think about what you see, then close your eyes and feel what you see.

Sharing Secrets: Take me as I am could be the anthem for this one. *For the gals:* They will have strong views on just about everything. If you can hang with them, then nothing will be as important as you. *For the guys:* The thing you fall in love with may end up becoming the thing you hate. After a commitment, this one sticks around.

Judith's Insights

About the Man: Yes, this guy can get a little hot under the collar. This is especially true if he thinks he is being betrayed. He would not do well if he was ever cheated on in a love affair. He is even worse when he feels he is being talked about behind his back. Always be honest and straightforward to win his trust. Give him plenty of time to feel safe before expecting a lot from him. If he gets into a serious life discussion early on he will freeze up. Take things slowly and steadily with this guy and he will be around much longer.

About the Woman: This gal needs to feel certain that she is number one at all times. This is true in business, too. She must always be on top of the competition. If not, she can feel powerless. She can even be competitive with her family. No matter what her need for being on top, she has the largest heart you will ever see around. There is a caution sign around her neck when it comes to her and relationships. People who get involved with her should proceed slowly into the milestones of the relationship. Talk of the future on the third date will guarantee there is no fourth date.

Soul Mates: Only a fellow Virgo can completely understand your need for order in your surroundings and comply with that need as well. Libra will teach you to balance your need of order with a new sense of spontaneity. Aquarius and Cancer will have your head spinning right away. Pisces and Sagittarius will give you all you need to be the very best you can be. Scorpio and Aries will have you wincing from their intimidation. Gemini and Leo take some getting used to, but once you know them, you will love them. Taurus and Capricorn will ground you like never before.

Most Charming Characteristics: Witty, honest, lovable.

Gifts: *For her:* astrological chart. *For him:* box or ringside seats.

Sensual Foods: Lobster; watermelon.

Romantic Flowers: You love it when you get tulips, declaring love. When you receive a variety, it shows how hopelessly in love your partner is. He will just love a single rose. This shows him you understand his pleasures.

Best Date Nights: Wednesday; 6th and 15th of each month.

Colors of Passion: *For her:* cream, violet. *For him:* black, blue.

The Perfect Wedding: Practical, but perfect down to the smallest detail, you actually *enjoy* every aspect of planning your wedding day. Your love of romance and need for privacy lend themselves to a lavishly decorated hidden patio or a botanical garden–type location. As with everything you do, your individual personality stamp will be noticed. Ideal setting: Paris.

Wise Words: W. H. Davies: "Train up thy mind to feel content, / What matters then how low thy store; / What we enjoy, and not possess, makes rich or poor."

Hints of Love: Consistence and persistence will get this prize every time. They will value the effort.

After the Argument: *For him:* Just tell him how right he was and how wrong you were over and over again. There is no such thing as too much here. *For her:* Grovel, and then grovel some more. They love it. It makes them feel very secure.

Romantic Places: Places of elegance bring romance: England; a five-star restaurant; Aspen, Colorado.

Lucky Love Star: Virginiel—you will never lack intrigue.

Beautiful Thought: Crying is the feathers tickling our emotions.

Sharing Secrets: They seem moody until you get to know them. *For the gals:* You may not know whether to say hello or drop dead. As relations progress you will learn not to leave her dangling, and her moods will become more consistent. *For the guys:* To know him is to love him. His bark is much worse than his bite. He just wants someone to love him without criticism.

Judith's Insights

About the Man: He is drawn to needy people. Just take a look at his former friends and lovers. You won't necessarily think of him as a caretaker. The fact that he is asking is the best sign that he is interested. All other signs are hard to read. Stay away from the green monster syndrome. He will still be trying to save the world. He will panic when he is in love, or even if he likes someone a lot. He will question every move and every word out of his mouth. If you want things to work with him you have to make sure the snakes in his head stay dormant.

About the Woman: This girl walks the planet as if she has it all. For the most part, she may have it all indeed. Don't be fooled by her exterior. She comes across as much more stuck-up than she could ever manage to be. Make her feel needed and she will keep coming around. Don't let her convince herself to back off. She can be lonely and wish with all of her heart to have someone to share her life with. The person she needs is someone who will love her without making her feel drained. Give her what she needs without asking her. She will refuse if given the chance.

Soul Mates: You will find true understanding of your nature when you find a fellow Virgo. Libra will help you see all the good in yourself while improving at the same time. Aquarius and Cancer will drive you up a wall if you stick around long enough for them to get to you. Pisces and Sagittarius will give you a new purpose and sense of self. You will feel much stronger once under their guidance. Scorpio and Aries will try to bully you. Just stick up for yourself as you are walking to the exit. Gemini and Leo will be a no-no at first glance. If you give them that second look, you might be surprised at what you see. Taurus and Capricorn will give you a solid base for all of your dreams.

Most Charming Characteristics: Easygoing, impulsive, domesticated.

Gifts: *For her:* book about feng shui. *For him:* lottery tickets.

Sensual Foods: Strawberries; truffles; shish kebab.

Romantic Flowers: Send this girl sunflowers if you want her to know you adore her. You may even add some poppies for a splash of extravagance. His desire for sport and play will be understood when you send him hyacinth and geranium.

Best Date Nights: Wednesday; 15th and 24th of each month.

Colors of Passion: *For her:* cream, violet. *For him:* black, blue.

The Perfect Wedding: Practical, but perfect down to the smallest detail, you actually *enjoy* every aspect of planning your wedding day. Your love of romance and need for privacy lend themselves to a lavishly decorated hidden patio or a botanical garden–type location. As with everything you do, your individual personality stamp will be noticed. Ideal setting: Paris.

Wise Words: Edwin Arnold: "Bear not false witness, slander not, nor lie; Truth is the speech of inward purity."

Hints of Love: Be funny. Laughter will be what keeps this one coming back again and again.

After the Argument: *For him:* Just tell him how right he was and how wrong you were over and over again. There is no such thing as too much here. *For her:* Grovel, and then grovel some more. They love it. It makes them feel very secure.

Romantic Places: Places of refinement bring romance: Poland; an opera house; Marina Del Rey, California.

Lucky Love Star: Virginiel—you will never lack intrigue.

Beautiful Thought: Timing is everything; everything in its time.

Sharing Secrets: You had better be able to put your money where your mouth is: *For the gals:* It doesn't need to be lavish, but she does love the loot. The more the better. *For the guys:* He doesn't mind spending his hard-earned cash, but he loves to see you contribute to please him.

Judith's Insights

About the Man: Why does he get so much attention? He has that pizzazz and style that make all those around him want to be as close as possible. Don't just feed into his ego like everyone else around him. Be different. He has that player quality inside, but that is not what he is really like at all. When it comes to love, he only expects from his partner what he can give himself. All things must be mutual for him to stay around. He can create harmony out of chaos. The stress he puts himself in the middle of is his worst enemy. Teach him to relax.

About the Woman: Everyone at work loves her. She goes out of her way to help everyone she comes into contact with. She looks down on no one. When it comes to a relationship, she will suddenly become standoffish. Her fear of being hurt or becoming bored loom strongly in her mind at all times. If you treat her like a regular person instead of this higher being that everyone else does, she will notice you much faster. Give her as much affection as she gives you or she will be flying out of the door. She has in mind what she wants and will deviate very little from that.

Soul Mates: A fellow Virgo will let you know that there is nothing wrong with your nature to begin with. Libra will give you a sense of wholeness when they help you become less rigid. Aquarius and Cancer will leave you numb. This pairing is not recommended for the faint of heart or the easily bruised ego. Pisces and Sagittarius will help you soar to new heights in all you encounter. Scorpio and Aries are too much trouble for you. You will be surprised when you give Gemini and Leo a chance. They just might break your first impression. Taurus and Capricorn will show you all of the wonders that lie in your own life.

Most Charming Characteristics: Reliable, content, successful.

Gifts: *For her:* weekend at a spa. *For him:* astrological chart.

Sensual Foods: Grapes; fine cheeses and crackers; taffy.

Romantic Flowers: Rhododendron will let her be on the lookout for trouble. Throw in some chrysanthemum and she'll know it is you she will be looking out for. Cactus will show him warmth. Yellow daffodil is a token of a good time had by all. Chivalry is not dead.

Best Date Nights: Wednesday; 8th and 17th of each month.

Colors of Passion: *For her:* cream, violet. *For him:* black, blue.

The Perfect Wedding: Practical, but perfect down to the smallest detail, you actually *enjoy* every aspect of planning your wedding day. Your love of romance and need for privacy lend themselves to a lavishly decorated hidden patio or a botanical garden–type location. As with everything you do, your individual personality stamp will be noticed. Ideal setting: Paris.

Wise Words: Charles Dickens: "Show me the man who says anything against women, as women, and I boldly declare he is not a man."

Hints of Love: Treat this one like royalty or precious cargo. They will love being valued in this way.

After the Argument: *For him:* Just tell him how right he was and how wrong you were over and over again. There is no such thing as too much here. *For her:* Grovel, and then grovel some more. They love it. It makes them feel very secure.

Romantic Places: Places of elegance bring romance: Belgium; a five-star hotel; Savannah, Georgia.

Lucky Love Star: Virginiel—you will never lack intrigue.

Beautiful Thought: Relationships don't last forever, but that doesn't mean they have less importance.

Sharing Secrets: Nobody likes a weak link, especially not this one. *For the gals:* Make sure you treat her like a lady and act like a man. *For the guys:* Put your best foot forward. Dress your best and keep your manners in check. This man notices.

Judith's Insights

About the Man: This guy can be your greatest dream or your worst nightmare. It all depends on where he is in his life at the time. He starts off intense but becomes selfish. Eventually, though, he will become humble. That is the time to catch him before anyone else snatches him out from under you. Timing is everything here. He will deal with people at work well, but he may deal with emotional pain by running from the mere threat. To live a lifetime with him you must be able to understand all of the contradicting sides to his personality.

About the Woman: This gal stays away from anyone who is flashy. She is looking for a mate she feels will balance her well. She does not mind having her friends all over the place. Her mate, however, must always be right by her side. She needs someone who will stand by her in thick and thin. You have to have a lot of patience to deal with her when she is frightened of her emotions. She likes things to be perfect. Unfortunately, matters of the heart are not so cut-and-dried. This is what drives her crazy most of all.

Soul Mates: Everything will be in its perfect place when you and a fellow Virgo get together. Libra and their scales of balance will teach you how to keep your life level. Aquarius and Cancer will drive you to drink if you stick around too long. Pisces and Sagittarius will help you be all that you can be and more. Scorpio and Aries will try to push you too much to change. Gemini and Leo will surprise you when you least expect it. Taurus and Capricorn will give you something to come home to every time.

Most Charming Characteristics: Kind, tender, understanding.

Gifts: *For her:* scented bath products. *For him:* leather wallet.

Sensual Foods: Champagne; grapes; mangoes; filet mignon.

Romantic Flowers: The magnolias you send her will let her know you will be around for a while to come. Petunia is to say never despair. Holly will let him know what he is getting into. Pansy will keep you in his thoughts.

Best Date Nights: Wednesday; 9th and 18th of each month.

Colors of Passion: *For her:* cream, violet. *For him:* black, blue.

The Perfect Wedding: Practical, but perfect down to the smallest detail, you actually *enjoy* every aspect of planning your wedding day. Your love of romance and need for privacy lend themselves to a lavishly decorated hidden patio or a botanical garden–type location. As with everything you do, your individual personality stamp will be noticed. Ideal setting: Paris.

Wise Words: William Cowper: "Knowledge dwells in heads replete with thoughts of other men; Wisdom in minds attentive to their own."

Hints of Love: Affection is important, but only if it comes naturally. Otherwise, the sirens will go off.

After the Argument: *For him:* Just tell him how right he was and how wrong you were over and over again. There is no such thing as too much here. *For her:* Grovel, and then grovel some more. They love it. It makes them feel very secure.

Romantic Places: Places of refinement bring romance: Holland; art museum; Russian Tea Room, New York City.

Lucky Love Star: Virginiel—you will never lack intrigue.

Beautiful Thought: The twinkling lights in the sky have all the answers; why don't you try?

Sharing Secrets: Attention, attention, attention. *For the gals:* Do it any way you can. Presents, phone calls, cards, or flowers. Whatever works for you will work for her. *For the guys:* He would love nostalgic gifts or T-shirts. He also likes phone calls, as long as they don't interrupt his favorite pastimes.

Judith's Insights

About the Man: This guy is full of passion. The old-fashioned kind. He is constantly searching for a loyal mate he can keep for life. This guy does not like waves. He won't appreciate any games unless they end up in passion. Trying to trick him into things will only make more room between the two of you instead of bringing you closer. He can be the easiest person to get along with if you just play the game his way. He has a certain way of thinking and he will do all that he can to convince you to think the same way.

About the Woman: She wants to be swept off her feet. You will have to do your job well to plan for a clean sweep. She knows just how to get out of you exactly what she needs. There is no beating around the bush with her. You have to lay things out on the table in a clear and concise way. She is playfully affectionate and makes a loyal mate in a committed relationship. The fight will be to get her to that level. She can be afraid of the very thing she craves the most, and that is someone to love her for all that she is.

Soul Mates: With a fellow Virgo, all things will be in perfect order. A relationship with Libra is a charmed one. A match of wits happens fast with Cancer and Aquarius. It will be strained just as fast if you don't really get to know each other. Critical is written all over a partnership with Pisces and Sagittarius. Aries and Scorpio will give you a run for your money, then want to go spend it all. Gemini and Leo might cause you a little insanity. You would truly need a deep connection to make this work. Capricorn and Taurus know how to turn on that irresistible charm that you just love.

Most Charming Characteristics: Ambitious, energetic, conscientious.

Gifts: *For her:* lottery tickets. *For him:* savings bond.

Sensual Foods: Châteaubriand; crème brûlée.

Romantic Flowers: Iris is your flower if you are the gal sending subtle messages. If you are the man, you will look for clematis. This flower's mental beauty creates emotional stimulation for you.

Best Date Nights: Wednesday; 10th and 19th of each month.

Colors of Passion: *For her:* cream, violet. *For him:* black, blue.

The Perfect Wedding: Practical, but perfect down to the smallest detail, you actually *enjoy* every aspect of planning your wedding day. Your love of romance and need for privacy lend themselves to a lavishly decorated hidden patio or a botanical garden–type location. As with everything you do, your individual personality stamp will be noticed. Ideal setting: Paris.

Wise Words: Charles Dickens: "Every failure teaches a man something, if he will learn."

Hints of Love: This one likes others to make his or her dreams come true. Be the "fantasy" fulfiller.

After the Argument: *For him:* Just tell him how right he was and how wrong you were over and over again. There is no such thing as too much here. *For her:* Grovel, and then grovel some more. They love it. It makes them feel very secure.

Romantic Places: Places of elegance bring romance: Spain; a winery; Chicago, Illinois.

Lucky Love Star: Virginiel—you will never lack intrigue.

Beautiful Thought: Boundaries are easy to follow when someone fences them off.

Sharing Secrets: Make sure you are not the killjoy. *For the gals:* When she has an idea, try it before you decide you don't like it. She needs to be pleased. *For the guys:* Do the things he loves to do and he will make the things you love ten times more fun.

Judith's Insights

About the Man: He will evaluate and reevaluate after each and every date. He will pick at the bare bones, making sure he understands every detail. Expect him to compare you to the last person who filled your shoes. If commitment comes along, you could be set. Once he makes that choice he hardly ever turns back. If he is not ready to make that decision, make sure you do not push him. He could clam up—or worse, turn on you. When he can't be sure of which way to go he will feel powerless. Being out of control is his worst fear.

About the Woman: She will become guarded and defensive if your feelings surpass hers. She needs to be the center of your world and more important than anything else. That includes you and your wants and needs. It will scare her, however, if you move too quickly. She is one hard gal to pin down. The more affection she receives the happier she will be. Try not to talk about serious issues in your relationship too early on. Things that belong in the future tend to scare her when they are presented for her to make a decision about now.

Soul Mates: Virgo and Virgo is exactly what you need to feel safe. A partnership with Libra will run like a well-oiled machine. Cancer and Aquarius will make you run away once the temptation has worn off. Loosen up so things with Pisces and Sagittarius can flow as they want to. Just when you think you know Aries and Scorpio, more layers appear out of nowhere. Gemini and Leo will run you ragged if you let them. A solid plan will take you and Capricorn or Taurus to new heights.

Most Charming Characteristics: Unpredictable, easygoing, original.

Gifts: *For her:* day of beauty. *For him:* get his car detailed.

Sensual Foods: Shrimp; sinful chocolate cake.

Romantic Flowers: Any rose of any color for the lady. Roses stand for love regardless of the color. Send them with orchids and you will be saying, "I love you." If you want a gentleman to know you think of him, send pansies, and forget-me-nots for true love.

Best Date Nights: Wednesday; 11th and 29th of each month.

Colors of Passion: *For her:* cream, violet. *For him:* black, blue.

The Perfect Wedding: Practical, but perfect down to the smallest detail, you actually *enjoy* every aspect of planning your wedding day. Your love of romance and need for privacy lend themselves to a lavishly decorated hidden patio or a botanical garden–type location. As with everything you do, your individual personality stamp will be noticed. Ideal setting: Paris.

Wise Words: Charles Dickens: "Friendship's a very good thing in its way . . . no man should have more than two attachments—the first to number one, and the second to the ladies."

Hints of Love: Stop worrying about next week's date today or there will not be one tomorrow.

After the Argument: *For him:* Just tell him how right he was and how wrong you were over and over again. There is no such thing as too much here. *For her:* Grovel, and then grovel some more. They love it. It makes them feel very secure.

Romantic Places: Places of elegance bring romance: Turkey; a cruise; New Orleans, Louisiana.

Lucky Love Star: Virginiel—you will never lack intrigue.

Beautiful Thought: Getting to the bottom of your feelings, not fearing to bring them to the top.

Sharing Secrets: You had better be ready to have a relationship. *For the gals:* No lies, no games, and no mistakes. She wants what she wants with as little work possible. *For the guys:* If you have games on your mind, then move on. This one likes fun any way he can get it, but no emotional roller coasters.

Judith's Insights

About the Man: He wavers on what he actually wants. You will see this in his friendships as well as romantic relationships. You will find yourself feeling close to him one minute and like a stranger in the next. He must get used to the power of his emotions before anything good can come out of a relationship. Stick around and keep plenty of patience in your back pocket. You will need it to put up with his changing mind. Once he feels he can commit, he will stick to it to the end. That is why he doesn't make it there easily.

About the Woman: This lady can put you right into your place in one minute flat. She does this with just a look, and rarely needs any words. There is no reading this girl's thoughts. You must rely on what her actions tell you. If she is inviting you out, then you are definitely on her good side. Getting her into a relationship is harder than you can imagine. Before any kind of commitment can happen, she must dig deep to figure out what she really wants. She will go out of her way to understand others and longs for someone to do the same for her.

Soul Mates: Things will be just as they should be when you get together with a fellow Virgo. Remember that where there is smoke there is fire when getting tangled up with Aquarius and Cancer. Libra is the balance you are searching for. Pisces and Sagittarius will give you the wings to fly. Scorpio and Aries will have you twisted in knots trying to keep up with their moods. A pairing with Gemini and Leo is only advised when you want to work your tail off. Capricorn and Taurus will give you the foundation and support you need.

Most Charming Characteristics: Affectionate, loyal, resourceful.

Gifts: *For her:* closet organizer. *For him:* organizing tool chest.

Sensual Foods: Toasted marshmallows; chocolates.

Romantic Flowers: These ladies like everyone to know how faithful they are, so send them violets. To surprise them send tulips. Men like their flowers the same as their relationships, unpretending. Send them camellias with white roses to show your affection.

Best Date Nights: Wednesday; 12th and 21st of each month.

Colors of Passion: *For her:* cream, violet. *For him:* black, tawny.

The Perfect Wedding: Practical, but perfect down to the smallest detail, you actually *enjoy* every aspect of planning your wedding day. Your love of romance and need for privacy lend themselves to a lavishly decorated hidden patio or a botanical garden–type location. As with everything you do, your individual personality stamp will be noticed. Ideal setting: Paris.

Wise Words: Robert Louis Stevenson: "The rain is raining all around, it rains on field and tree, it rains on umbrellas here, and on the ships at sea."

Hints of Love: Keep the romance in the picture. Don't forget the long walks on the beach and camping out in front of the fireplace.

After the Argument: *For him:* Just tell him how right he was and how wrong you were over and over again. There is no such thing as too much here. *For her:* Grovel, and then grovel some more. They love it. It makes them feel very secure.

Romantic Places: Places of refinement bring romance: Argentina; high tea; New York City.

Lucky Love Star: Virginiel—you will never lack intrigue.

Beautiful Thought: Learning wisdom from the young makes you young yourself.

Sharing Secrets: You may have to give this one more than one chance. *For the gals:* Intriguing as she is, expect a handful. She lightens up as time goes on. *For the guys:* His quirks may make you have second thoughts, but that is what separates the men from the boys.

Judith's Insights

About the Man: Watch how you treat this guy. He hangs around and ends up being everywhere you go. Before you know what happened, he has grown on you. You can find yourself spending your life with him and not be real sure how you got from hating him to loving him. Not that you will be complaining, that is. He has great manners and a sense of how things should be. Everyone is attracted to him, and he can't quite figure out why. He can flirt nonstop while trying to find his true love. That charm will settle down when he does find her.

About the Woman: Even if you have been dating for a while, she might still refer to you as a friend. Don't push her or expect too much too soon. This lady needs space to find out what her feelings are really saying. She must be more than ready to make a commitment with anyone. The devotion you show her will be returned tenfold if you have enough patience to wait out her difficult stages. She can seem egotistical and have low self-esteem at the same time. What she shows the world about herself can be quite different from what she feels inside.

Soul Mates: All will be well when you have a Virgo like yourself in your life. Libra will teach you how to balance your personality to find peace within yourself. Aquarius and Cancer will have you running like a madman to keep up. Pisces and Sagittarius understand you more than you could ever imagine. Let them in and you will have a friend for life. Scorpio and Aries will have you doing cartwheels and then ask for more. Be prepared to put your nose to the grindstone with Gemini and Leo. Capricorn and Taurus are the perfect support for your insecure times.

Most Charming Characteristics: Dreamer, imaginative, well-liked.

Gifts: *For her:* silk scarf. *For him:* cashmere sweater.

Sensual Foods: Chocolate-covered strawberries; New York steak; scallops.

Romantic Flowers: These ladies like men with taste. Show them you love style by sending fuchsia flowers, or even brightly colored wildflowers will do. To confuse this man, send him lilies along with bright daisies to show your innocence. Keep him guessing.

Best Date Nights: Wednesday; 4th and 22nd of each month.

Colors of Passion: *For her:* cream, crimson. *For him:* black, blue.

The Perfect Wedding: Practical, but perfect down to the smallest detail, you actually *enjoy* every aspect of planning your wedding day. Your love of romance and need for privacy lend themselves to a lavishly decorated hidden patio or a botanical garden–type location. As with everything you do, your individual personality stamp will be noticed. Ideal setting: Paris.

Wise Words: Charles Lamb: "The good things of life are not to be had singly, but come to us a mixture, like a schoolboy's holiday, with a task affixed to the tail of it."

Hints of Love: The mystery is important, but being evasive will create disaster. Make sure you know the difference.

After the Argument: *For him:* Just tell him how right he was and how wrong you were over and over again. There is no such thing as too much here. *For her:* Grovel, and then grovel some more. They love it. It makes them feel very secure.

Romantic Places: Places of elegance bring romance: Russia; a sculpted garden; Hilton Head, South Carolina.

Lucky Love Star: Virginiel—you will never lack intrigue.

Beautiful Thought: A thought of caring is easily shown when you are sharing.

Sharing Secrets: Talk about high maintenance. *For the gals:* Once she sees that you go out of your way for her then she will for you. *For the guys:* The bark is definitely much worse than the bite. He comes on stronger and more obstinate than he actually is.

Judith's Insights

About the Man: He will keep his feelings well hidden until he is completely certain that they are returned. He can also be shy when he is not in his own environment. Don't ask for too much right away. Let him give of himself as he feels ready. Before you know it you will have his heart in your hands. He is strong and sensible when it comes to business. His intentions are always honorable, even though his actions seem to say otherwise. He then gets confused if people don't understand what he is trying to do. He is as good at making promises as at keeping them.

About the Woman: This gal stands out in a crowd. If it is not her voice you notice it will be the way she dresses, or even her sensitive presence. Don't be discouraged if it is difficult to get close to her. Many look but can never touch. She will let you in when she is ready to deal with the emotions you will bring. She loves being in love. A big-time premiere, a carnival, and a moonlight walk on the beach are all ways to her heart. Bring in the boardroom and she is all business. If you work with her, try not to bring in personal issues until you are outside the office.

Soul Mates: With a fellow Virgo, all will be well in your joined worlds. Libra will give you the peace you are searching for. Aquarius and Cancer are a hard act to keep up with. Pisces and Sagittarius are the best place to start when you are in search of the real you. Scorpio and Aries are too much ruckus for your perfectionist nature. Gemini and Leo are hard work, but well worth the effort. Taurus and Capricorn are the stability you yearn for.

Most Charming Characteristics: Wise, honest, friendly.

Gifts: *For her:* a beauty makeover. *For him:* a weekend in the mountains.

Sensual Foods: Vanilla and strawberry mousse; tiramisù; espresso.

Romantic Flowers: You are the lady of distinction, and only carnations will do. Any mix of colors with sprays of mignonette. Sweet peas or red carnations will appeal to this man's heart.

Best Date Nights: Wednesday; 4th and 5th of each month.

Colors of Passion: *For her:* cream, violet. *For him:* black, blue.

The Perfect Wedding: Practical, but perfect down to the smallest detail, you actually *enjoy* every aspect of planning your wedding day. Your love of romance and need for privacy lend themselves to a lavishly decorated hidden patio or a botanical garden–type location. As with everything you do, your individual personality stamp will be noticed. Ideal setting: Paris.

Wise Words: Walt Whitman: "To me, every hour of light and dark / Is a miracle, Every inch of space is a miracle, / Every spear of grass."

Hints of Love: If you learn to back up when things are moving too fast, you won't have to bow out so often.

After the Argument: *For him:* Just tell him how right he was and how wrong you were over and over again. There is no such thing as too much here. *For her:* Grovel, and then grovel some more. They love it. It makes them feel very secure.

Romantic Places: Places of refinement bring romance: the Taj Mahal; an awards ceremony; Boston, Massachusetts.

Lucky Love Star: Virginiel—you will never lack intrigue.

Beautiful Thought: Time is so precious and goes too fast; see how long you can make every minute last.

Sharing Secrets: Make sure you have at least five dates before you make up your mind. *For the gals:* She can be cynical, so it could be a few dates before she loosens up. *For the guys:* He still has yesterday on his mind. He needs a reason to forget his past relationship. Make a new history for him.

Judith's Insights

About the Man: He will value every relationship he has, and he will have many. There are only a few that will get into his heart. Many will try to play with his head. He is on the shy side. If he takes the bait by flirting back, ask him out. You might grow old waiting for him to do the asking. There will be no welcoming emotional warfare for this guy. He will step aside before having to get into snake fights or mind games. Be up-front and you will get far with him. Try to hide your real intentions and he will smell it right away.

About the Woman: When you see her at work you will wonder who she goes home with. She keeps her private info private. That is exactly how she likes it. This gal is no cold fish. You just have to get close enough to feel the warmth of her heart. Once you do, you will never want to leave. She has been blessed with fine instincts. She can spot a line of bull before it even reaches her. She puts a lot of energy into what she does, including romance and relationships. Keep in mind that she needs a lot of attention in return.

Soul Mates: Looking at a fellow Libra is like looking in a mirror. Make sure that you can handle what you see. Scorpio and Sagittarius are exactly what the doctor ordered to shake things up a bit. Seeing where things fall will be fun. Capricorn and Aries will bring out the worst in you if you let them feed your insecurities. Aquarius and Gemini will show you more fun than you can handle in a single day. Cancer will have you climbing the walls to get away. Leo and Virgo are more than you can dream of and more. Pisces and Taurus will do all that they can to anchor you to where they feel you should be.

Most Charming Characteristics: Successful, popular, joyful.

Gifts: *For her:* day at a botanical garden. *For him:* cooking class.

Sensual Foods: Raspberries; pound cake; caviar.

Romantic Flowers: You love it when you get tulips, declaring love. When you receive a variety, it shows how hopelessly in love your partner is. He will just love a single rose. This shows him you understand his pleasures.

Best Date Nights: Friday; 6th and 15th of each month.

Colors of Passion: *For her:* lavender, violet. *For him:* blue, tawny.

The Perfect Wedding: You are a lover of art and intrigued by exoticism; you might consider an art gallery or museum as the place you take your vows. A grand hotel-ballroom-turned-paradise or lush green forest can provide the romantic haven you desire. With the emphasis on drama, you'll not only want to woo your beloved but your wedding guests as well. Ideal setting: Egypt; Montreal.

Wise Words: Oliver Goldsmith: "Philosophy is no more than the art of making ourselves happy; that is, of seeking pleasure in regularity, and reconciling what we owe to society with what is due to ourselves."

Hints of Love: Expecting too much too soon can only build up hopes that will fall down too easily.

After the Argument: *For him:* Lavish him with attention. Bring him nice things that are not too overwhelming. Charm him into being that cuddly guy you love. *For her:* A little more stroking than usual. Tickets to a show or even the right evening at home could work.

Romantic Places: Places of movement bring romance: London; the theater; Las Vegas, Nevada.

Lucky Love Star: Libriel—you will never lack serenity.

Beautiful Thought: Tears are us speaking our emotions without words.

Sharing Secrets: Don't be in a hurry, or it will be over before it begins. *For the gals:* Like fine wine and amazing food. Savor a moment until an hour is created. *For the guys:* To do too much too fast will prove risky. Try to give a push and he will just jump ship.

Judith's Insights

About the Man: He may overanalyze so much that he talks himself right out of asking you out to begin with. It may have to be you who must do the dirty work. He will give you the shirt right off his back, but it may take time for him to get that across to you. Let him find the words before pushing too soon. Once you have this guy as a mate it will be smooth sailing. Getting him there is where all of the complications lie. He may be procrastinating, being exclusive until he has a balance in his heart and in his head. Time is all that he is asking for.

About the Woman: She'll do all of the dramatics. Her feelings get hurt often, and you may have to keep your eye on her at all times. She will not commit to anything until she knows that you are both on the same page. It does get easier once she feels that she can trust you with her fragile heart. Let her decide where all of the pieces belong before raising any hard questions. The more stabilized her environment, the more settled you find her emotions. If she seems out of sorts for no reason, find out what is wrong at work or in her family.

Soul Mates: A fellow Libra will understand you more than anyone else ever could. Scorpio and Sagittarius will add spice to your life. You will be surprised at how much you like the new taste of things. Capricorn and Aries are not for the weak-hearted or fragile ego. Aquarius and Gemini will do all that they can think of to show you a good time. Cancer will prey on all the parts of yourself you try to hide. Deal with them before they get a hold on them and they will not be able to hurt you. Leo and Virgo will make the relationship run smoothly by their ability to overlook the bumps in the road. Pisces and Taurus will try to put you on the mantel until they are ready to play with you.

Most Charming Characteristics: Sincere, affectionate, demonstrative.

Gifts: *For her:* friends over for dinner and a movie. *For him:* dinner at a fine restaurant.

Sensual Foods: Flambé, lobster; oysters.

Romantic Flowers: Send this girl sunflowers if you want her to know you adore her. You may even add some poppies for a splash of extravagance. His desire for sport and play will be understood when you send him hyacinth and geranium.

Best Date Nights: Friday; 6th and 24th of each month.

Colors of Passion: *For her:* lavender, crimson. *For him:* black, blue.

The Perfect Wedding: You are a lover of art and intrigued by exoticism; you might consider an art gallery or museum as the place you take your vows. A grand hotel-ballroom-turned-paradise or lush green forest can provide the romantic haven you desire. With the emphasis on drama, you'll not only want to woo your beloved but your wedding guests as well. Ideal setting: Egypt; Montreal.

Wise Words: William Blake: "He who binds to himself a joy, / Doth the winged life destroy; / But he who kisses joy as it flies, / Lives in eternity's sunrise."

Hints of Love: Make sure all the ingredients are present before putting the cake in the oven.

After the Argument: *For him:* Lavish him with attention. Bring him nice things that are not too overwhelming. Charm him into being that cuddly guy you love. *For her:* A little more stroking than usual. Tickets to a show or even the right evening at home could work.

Romantic Places: Places of activity bring romance: Brazil; a carnival; Memphis, Tennessee.

Lucky Love Star: Libriel—you will never lack serenity.

Beautiful Thought: What seems to be the challenge today is an accomplishment of tomorrow.

Sharing Secrets: They need to look before they leap, but only in love. *For the gals:* She needs creative and exciting dates to keep her interested. Don't take her for granted too soon. *For the guys:* You may think he gives signs of moving this relationship quickly; make sure you slow it down before he does.

Judith's Insights

About the Man: This guy may need a lesson or two in dating. He can be pushy and bossy. You must explain to him that although that works in the office, it does not work in matters pertaining to the heart. When this guy does fall in love there is absolutely no one better to be with. He can be the sweetest and most understanding person on the planet. If he smells deceit in any form, there will be no more Mr. Nice Guy. The open-minded person he is naturally will slam shut if he feels he is being lied to. Honesty is the best policy at all times with this guy.

About the Woman: Fussy, picky, and moody; she can be all or none of the above. It all depends on how the waves of the relationship are washing up on the shore. She does not handle the cat-and-mouse game well at all. Play things close to the heart and very straightforward if you ever want to stay around. Relationships in her life may tend to be difficult because she wants predictability at all times, as if she is following a script. She loves compliments on her attire and her home. Treat her like a queen and she will treat you just as royally.

Soul Mates: When in doubt, turn to a fellow Libra. They will give you all of the guidance you will ever need. You will look at the world in a different way when Scorpio and Sagittarius get done with you. Make sure you are at peace with yourself before pairing with Capricorn and Aries. Aquarius and Gemini are all you can ask for in a great relationship. Cancer will prey on any, and all, weakness in your ego. Make sure you are ready to face them. Leo and Virgo will make your life a walk in the park, if you would only let them help. Pisces and Taurus will have you lying on the couch, ready to poke and prod your subconscious.

Most Charming Characteristics: Ambitious, energetic, positive.

Gifts: *For her:* personal shopper. *For him:* tailored suit.

Sensual Foods: Crème brûlée; poached salmon.

Romantic Flowers: Rhododendron will let her be on the lookout for trouble. Throw in some chrysanthemum and she'll know it is you she will be looking out for. Cactus will show him warmth. Yellow daffodil is a token of a good time had by all. Chivalry is not dead.

Best Date Nights: Friday; 8th and 26th of each month.

Colors of Passion: *For her:* lavender, crimson. *For him:* black, tawny.

The Perfect Wedding: You are a lover of art and intrigued by exoticism; you might consider an art gallery or museum as the place you take your vows. A grand hotel-ballroom-turned-paradise or lush green forest can provide the romantic haven you desire. With the emphasis on drama, you'll not only want to woo your beloved but your wedding guests as well. Ideal setting: Egypt; Montreal.

Wise Words: Charles Dickens: "Cheerfulness and content are great beautifiers and are famous preservers of youthful looks."

Hints of Love: Simple often turns into complicated with this one. When you overcomplicate the moment, try to step back for a breather.

After the Argument: *For him:* Lavish him with attention. Bring him nice things that are not too overwhelming. Charm him into being that cuddly guy you love. *For her:* A little more stroking than usual. Tickets to a show or even the right evening at home could work.

Romantic Places: Places of movement bring romance: Paris; an outdoor festival; Times Square, New York City.

Lucky Love Star: Libriel—you will never lack serenity.

Beautiful Thought: If everyone was the same, no one would be different.

Sharing Secrets: The possibilities are endless, if you can pay the price. *For the gals:* She is hoping chivalry is not dead, and you must be willing to be the man at all costs. *For the guys:* He can be demanding and somewhat controlling. He just needs to be trained.

Judith's Insights

About the Man: This guy is full of energy and always on the move. He not only wants to climb that ladder at work, but in life in general. He wants to live each moment with passion. Boring outings will only turn this guy away. When inviting him out, make it something exciting and magical. He is always ready to meet someone new or visit a new place. He craves excitement and change while needing stability. Be his partner in adventure and he will treat you better than anyone else has. Make sure that you are as into hugs and kisses as he is.

About the Woman: She falls in love very seldom, but she has many friends. She looks for that once-in-a-lifetime type of relationship they are always showing in the movies. Instead of going out and searching for it in earnest, she is much like a lady in waiting. She is wishing that it would come and find her. She has dreams of a house with a white picket fence and that dreamboat partner living in it with her. If things are not working out to her expectations after the second date, she will rarely stick around to try harder. She feels her time is better served elsewhere.

Soul Mates: A fellow Libra will give you all you need when you need it without your having to ask. Scorpio and Sagittarius will charm you into anything. Capricorn and Aries will have you tied in knots when they are through. Aquarius and Gemini live to make you happy. Cancer can bring out the worst in you if you let them. Try to be the bigger person. Leo and Virgo will do anything to keep the relationship going without a snag. Pisces and Taurus will have you locked up tight if you let them.

Most Charming Characteristics: Kind, generous, sympathetic.

Gifts: *For her:* day of beauty. *For him:* spa getaway.

Sensual Foods: Chocolate soufflé; filet mignon.

Romantic Flowers: The magnolias you send her will let her know you will be around for a while to come. Petunia is to say never despair. Holly will let him know what he is getting into. Pansy will keep you in his thoughts.

Best Date Nights: Friday; 18th and 27th of each month.

Colors of Passion: *For her:* lavender, crimson. *For him:* black, tawny.

The Perfect Wedding: You are a lover of art and intrigued by exoticism; you might consider an art gallery or museum as the place you take your vows. A grand hotel-ballroom-turned-paradise or lush green forest can provide the romantic haven you desire. With the emphasis on drama, you'll not only want to woo your beloved but your wedding guests as well. Ideal setting: Egypt; Montreal.

Wise Words: Sydney Smith: "People are always happier for having been happy; if you make them happy now, you make them happy twenty years hence by the memory of it."

Hints of Love: Allow them to know what is in your heart as well as what is in your head.

After the Argument: *For him:* Lavish him with attention. Bring him nice things that are not too overwhelming. Charm him into being that cuddly guy you love. *For her:* A little more stroking than usual. Tickets to a show or even the right evening at home could work.

Romantic Places: Places of activity bring romance: Argentina; a nightclub; Miami, Florida.

Lucky Love Star: Libriel—you will never lack serenity.

Beautiful Thought: Everything you learn today creates the outcome of tomorrow.

Sharing Secrets: Tomorrow is another day, but why wait? You can do it all today. *For the gals:* Have your date filled from dusk to dawn, and then some. *For the guys:* You may find he needs a nap here and there, but he can last all day and all night if he has a reason.

Judith's Insights

About the Man: Beauty is in the eye of the beholder. That is how this guy lives his life. You may find that he is critical of his own looks, but he will never be critical of how others look. He has a harmless growl. Don't let that fool you. He is really a teddy bear underneath the grizzly exterior. He needs to know what is going on at all times. If you have been away he will want a blow-by-blow account of the events in your absence. He will also want to know exactly what you are feeling at every turn. Make him secure by being honest.

About the Woman: She has a funny way of showing how she feels. She becomes moody and defensive when she falls in love. Her moods will continue to sway in wide directions until you declare your feelings. She is scared that her feelings are not mutual. If you care for her, you must always tell her at any cost. Her emotions can spiral out of control when she feels that she is in an unbalanced relationship. Don't just tell her how you feel about her. Show her how much you care by holding her hand in public and kissing her cheeks as much as possible.

Soul Mates: Libra and Libra are a match made in heaven. Scorpio and Sagittarius will intrigue you. This could be the best partner no matter what you have in mind. Capricorn and Aries will urge you to reach out and expand. Make sure that they are not bossy, though. Aquarius and Gemini are a perfect example of what can and will go right with a relationship. You will need a great deal of strength to pair with Cancer. Leo and Virgo will work to keep the relationship harmonious and balanced. Pisces and Taurus will be your dream only in a nightmare.

Most Charming Characteristics: Musical, coy, loving.

Gifts: *For her:* big bouquet of flowers. *For him:* day at a botanical garden.

Sensual Foods: Steak au poivre; cheesecake.

Romantic Flowers: Iris is your flower if you are the gal sending subtle messages. If you are the man, you will look for clematis. This flower's mental beauty creates emotional stimulation for you.

Best Date Nights: Friday; 1st and 19th of each month.

Colors of Passion: *For her:* lavender, crimson. *For him:* black, tawny.

The Perfect Wedding: You are a lover of art and intrigued by exoticism; you might consider an art gallery or museum as the place you take your vows. A grand hotel-ballroom-turned-paradise or lush green forest can provide the romantic haven you desire. With the emphasis on drama, you'll not only want to woo your beloved but your wedding guests as well. Ideal setting: Egypt; Montreal.

Wise Words: Robert Louis Stevenson: "By a curious irony of fate, the places to which we are sent when health deserts us are often singularly beautiful."

Hints of Love: Keep both feet on the ground the first time you think you want to jump. This way you won't jump too high too soon.

After the Argument: *For him:* Lavish him with attention. Bring him nice things that are not too overwhelming. Charm him into being that cuddly guy you love. *For her:* A little more stroking than usual. Tickets to a show or even the right evening at home could work.

Romantic Places: Places of movement bring romance: Rome; a ballet; Los Angeles, California.

Lucky Love Star: Libriel—you will never lack serenity.

Beautiful Thought: One sincere gesture is worth a million thoughts.

Sharing Secrets: It may need to start with friendship. This isn't the consolation prize; it's the grand prize. *For the gals:* Go slowly and allow it to grow one seed at a time. You won't need to push; it will all come in time. *For the guys:* A step here and a step there. Before he knows it, that friendship will be love.

Judith's Insights

About the Man: This guy needs a lot of answers, and he has a very long list of questions. Those answers must be truthful and sincere or he will smell a rat. If he finds out that you have indeed been anything but completely honest there will be trouble in paradise. Never hold back what you feel. He needs harmony more than anything, yet he is always expecting to be betrayed. Confrontations will send him heading for the hills. You don't have to go overboard to show him your loyalty and sincerity. You just have to show him your best side at all times.

About the Woman: This lady has a style all her own. You can grab her attention by treating her just like the perfect lady that she is. Even if she is your boss, you must give her the same respect that she gives you. Allow a little tolerance on your part to get any romance started. Her moods may be wild but they are passionate. Her mind is her greatest asset, and she loves being complimented on her intellect. If you want to storm the castle she has built around her heart, you have to be very patient. The guards will be off duty soon.

Soul Mates: A union with a fellow Libra is all you can ever dream of. Scorpio and Sagittarius will ignore any shortcomings you have to keep the relationship running smoothly. Capricorn and Aries will try to change you at almost every turn. Aquarius and Gemini love doing all that they can to make you happy, because that is what makes them happy. Cancer will turn the relationship into a tumultuous one if you are not careful. A joint venture with Leo and Virgo will be balanced in every way. Pisces and Taurus will try to cage you in while you crave your freedom.

Most Charming Characteristics: Courageous, affectionate, venturesome.

Gifts: *For her:* tickets to the opera or symphony. *For him:* tickets to a jazz concert.

Sensual Foods: Strawberry shortcake; pineapple; ham.

Romantic Flowers: Any rose of any color for the lady. Roses stand for love regardless of the color. Send them with orchids and you will be saying, "I love you." If you want a gentleman to know you think of him, send pansies, and forget-me-nots for true love.

Best Date Nights: Friday; 11th and 20th of each month.

Colors of Passion: *For her:* lavender, crimson. *For him:* black, tawny.

The Perfect Wedding: You are a lover of art and intrigued by exoticism; you might consider an art gallery or museum as the place you take your vows. A grand hotel-ballroom-turned-paradise or lush green forest can provide the romantic haven you desire. With the emphasis on drama, you'll not only want to woo your beloved but your wedding guests as well. Ideal setting: Egypt; Montreal.

Wise Words: Charles Dickens: "In the material world . . . nothing can be spared; nor step or atom in the wondrous structure could be lost without a blank being made in the great universe. It is the same with good and evil, happiness and sorrow, in the memories of men."

Hints of Love: Laughter alleviates the tension, but so can understanding where another is sitting.

After the Argument: *For him:* Lavish him with attention. Bring him nice things that are not too overwhelming. Charm him into being that cuddly guy you love. *For her:* A little more stroking than usual. Tickets to a show or even the right evening at home could work.

Romantic Places: Places of activity bring romance: French Rivera; a parade; Detroit, Michigan.

Lucky Love Star: Libriel—you will never lack serenity.

Beautiful Thought: If you learn to expect less, you will feel like you have so much more.

Sharing Secrets: This one needs to be the one and only, even if it is only the first date. *For the gals:* Don't talk about your past relationships. Do all you can to make her feel cherished from the first moment. *For the guys:* Play up your innocence. Let him take charge, even in paying the bill. He needs to wear the pants.

Judith's Insights

About the Man: This guy thinks way too much. Just don't tell him that. He has a subtle flirtation, so you will have to read between the lines. He will always do more than his share of work in the office or at the house. He needs to know just how people feel about him before he can enter into anything new. He likes to take new relationships slowly, so don't push too hard. If you ask him out and get a no right away, it doesn't mean he is not interested. Let him know your intentions and he will feel safer to say yes.

About the Woman: She certainly has a stubborn side, but she would never agree with that. You won't have to do too much convincing to take her out any night. She likes to be treated as the center of attention. She is always willing to try new and exciting things, so make an impression with a great outing for your first date. She can be her own worst enemy. She only seems cold because she is so shy. When you get to know her you will feel like she has been your best friend forever. Once a bond has been forged with her heart she will never abandon it.

Soul Mates: You and a fellow Libra will get along as if you have known each other forever. A partnership with Scorpio and Sagittarius can be a dream made real. Capricorn and Aries tend to move way too fast, and may have you feeling overlooked. Aquarius and Gemini will do all that they can to make the relationship last for a long time. Cancer will bring out a lot of insecurities you forgot were there. Leo and Virgo are on your side all the way and never hesitate to tell you that. Pisces and Taurus can hamper your freedom and make you feel strangled.

Most Charming Characteristics: Considerate, sincere, lovable.

Gifts: *For her:* beauty makeover. *For him:* professional massage.

Sensual Foods: Steak fondue; cheese fondue and French bread.

Romantic Flowers: These ladies like everyone to know how faithful they are, so send them violets. To surprise them send tulips. Men like their flowers the same as their relationships, unpretending. Send them camellias with white roses to show your affection.

Best Date Nights: Friday; 3rd and 21st of each month.

Colors of Passion: *For her:* lavender, crimson. *For him:* black, tawny.

The Perfect Wedding: You are a lover of art and intrigued by exoticism; you might consider an art gallery or museum as the place you take your vows. A grand hotel-ballroom-turned-paradise or lush green forest can provide the romantic haven you desire. With the emphasis on drama, you'll not only want to woo your beloved but your wedding guests as well. Ideal setting: Egypt; Montreal.

Wise Words: Charles Dickens: "When a young lady's as mild as she's game and as game as she's mild, that is all I ask and more than I expect. She then becomes a Queen."

Hints of Love: Communication is important here.

A script isn't provided for you. You must write it for yourself.

After the Argument: *For him:* Lavish him with attention. Bring him nice things that are not too overwhelming. Charm him into being that cuddly guy you love. *For her:* A little more stroking than usual. Tickets to a show or even the right evening at home could work.

Romantic Places: Places of movement bring romance: Rio de Janeiro; a sports event; Hollywood, California.

Lucky Love Star: Libriel—you will never lack serenity.

Beautiful Thought: You can be your own worst enemy, just as long as you are your own best friend.

Sharing Secrets: You need to remember never to forget. *For the gals:* Her birthday, holidays, and your anniversary. Even down to each dinner date. *For the guys:* His birthday, his laundry, his mother's birthday, and, of course, him any other day of the year.

Judith's Insights

About the Man: This guy is a charmer. You can see it in his eyes from across the room. He wants to be romanced, so it is all right with him if you planned a moonlight picnic. Wine and dine him right from the start. He will want to do the same for you. He won't even mind if you pick up the check. He knows exactly how to treat someone when he is in love. Once he charms you into his arms you may never want to leave. If you are honest about your feelings he might let you stay that long or even longer.

About the Woman: She has a unique style of dress and living. You won't likely see many like this lady around. She does not mind acting like a perfect lady at all. In fact, she thrives on it. She also does not mind being independent. She won't date just to avoid being alone. She picks her dates for their potential. Her life's lesson would be to wait with grace and patience for those things and people she wants. Otherwise, she will rush headfirst into something she might not be ready for. Taking things slowly will make them last longer.

OCTOBER

Soul Mates: Libra and Libra are a match made in heaven. Scorpio and Sagittarius will intrigue you. This could be the best partner no matter what you have in mind. Capricorn and Aries will urge you to reach out and expand. Make sure that they are not bossy, though. Aquarius and Gemini are a perfect example of what can and will go right with a relationship. You will need a great deal of strength to pair with Cancer. Leo and Virgo will work to keep the relationship harmonious and balanced. Pisces and Taurus will be your dream only in a nightmare.

Most Charming Characteristics: Sociable, adaptable, sensitive.

Gifts: *For her:* gift certificate to her favorite store. *For him:* enroll him in a book club.

Sensual Foods: Strawberries and cream; meat loaf.

Romantic Flowers: Iris is your flower if you are the gal sending subtle messages. If you are the man, you will look for clematis. This flower's mental beauty creates emotional stimulation for you.

Best Date Nights: Friday; 10th and 19th of each month.

Colors of Passion: *For her:* lavender, crimson. *For him:* black, tawny.

The Perfect Wedding: You are a lover of art and intrigued by exoticism; you might consider an art gallery or museum as the place you take your vows. A grand hotel-ballroom-turned-paradise or lush green forest can provide the romantic haven you desire. With the emphasis on drama, you'll not only want to woo your beloved but your wedding guests as well. Ideal setting: Egypt; Montreal.

Wise Words: Robert Louis Stevenson: "I read, dear friend, in your dear face, Your life's tale told with perfect grace; The river of your life I trace."

Hints of Love: They only use the three magic words when they know they mean it, and they already know it is going to be said back to them.

After the Argument: *For him:* Lavish him with attention. Bring him nice things that are not too overwhelming. Charm him into being that cuddly guy you love. *For her:* A little more stroking than usual. Tickets to a show or even the right evening at home could work.

Romantic Places: Places of activity bring romance: Hong Kong; a street fair; New York City.

Lucky Love Star: Libriel—you will never lack serenity.

Beautiful Thought: Be able to be proud of yourself, and others will follow.

Sharing Secrets: Let them admire something about you first. Show them you have a sense of humor. *For the gals:* hold their hand and then take them to the next step. *For the guys:* The way to his heart is definitely through his stomach.

Judith's Insights

About the Man: He has high hopes when it comes to love, and does not hesitate to make those hopes a reality. He can wear his heart on his sleeve. You can almost always be certain how he is feeling. He has no problem showing his feelings, but hates to have them hurt. Put yourself in his place to see how your words will affect him. He longs for someone to snuggle with. He can have a much softer interior than he would like to admit to. He is the most comfortable in his own space. Snuggling at home is his best evening.

About the Woman: This girl really has a shy side. Even if she is giving you the eye, she is not likely to ask you out on a date. When she is in a business or friendship situation she is much more outgoing. When she feels that her heart or feelings are in danger of getting hurt, she will become quiet. Keep her feelings in mind at all times. She can be sensitive, and a simple misunderstanding can put your relationship back miles in a flash. She loves being in a long-term relationship. She finds comfort in a partnership.

Soul Mates: A union with a fellow Libra is all you can ever dream of. Scorpio and Sagittarius will ignore any shortcomings you have to keep the relationship running smoothly. Capricorn and Aries will try to change you at almost every turn. Aquarius and Gemini love doing all that they can to make you happy, because that is what makes them happy. Cancer will turn the relationship into a tumultuous one if you are not careful. A joint venture with Leo and Virgo will be balanced in every way. Pisces and Taurus will try to cage you in while you crave your freedom.

Most Charming Characteristics: Sweet, musical, kind.

Gifts: *For her:* professional portrait session. *For him:* personal shopper.

Sensual Foods: Cherry-apple pie; beef Stroganoff.

Romantic Flowers: Any rose of any color for the lady. Roses stand for love regardless of the color. Send them with orchids and you will be saying, "I love you." If you want a gentleman to know you think of him, send pansies, and forget-me-nots for true love.

Best Date Nights: Friday; 2nd and 20th of each month.

Colors of Passion: *For her:* lavender, crimson. *For him:* black, tawny.

The Perfect Wedding: You are a lover of art and intrigued by exoticism; you might consider an art gallery or museum as the place you take your vows. A grand hotel-ballroom-turned-paradise or lush green forest can provide the romantic haven you desire. With the emphasis on drama, you'll not only want to woo your beloved but your wedding guests as well. Ideal setting: Egypt; Montreal.

Wise Words: Thomas Carlyle: "All true men are soldiers in the same army, to do battle against the same enemy—the empire of darkness, and wrong."

Hints of Love: Remember to keep the dating fun. Don't act like you are married before your time.

After the Argument: *For him:* Lavish him with attention. Bring him nice things that are not too overwhelming. Charm him into being that cuddly guy you love. *For her:* A little more stroking than usual. Tickets to a show or even the right evening at home could work.

Romantic Places: Places of movement bring romance: Dublin; an amusement park; Seattle, Washington.

Lucky Love Star: Libriel—you will never lack serenity.

Beautiful Thought: I may be talking with my mouth, but it's the words of my heart you are hearing.

Sharing Secrets: Give them the opportunity to notice you first. *For the gals:* They love to be adored; love at first sight. *For the guys:* Remember to always let them believe it was their idea.

Judith's Insights

About the Man: He is not the greatest at making decisions. He needs to have thought everything through. If he is asking you out, he already has a strong interest in you. Don't get upset if he backs off when things get a bit steamy. If you hang in there, he will be back as soon as he has control of his faculties again. Although he wants a strong partnership more than anything, he can have a tendency to overthink every aspect of the relationship. He has great friendships because he knows that relationships take work.

About the Woman: When she finally falls, it is usually hard to abandon the relationship when things get bad. Make sure that her past is really behind her before entering into any emotional bond. If she feels torn between two loves in any way, she will become a half-baked being. Step aside and let her get things straightened out. When the love of her life walks in the door, anything she has ever promised herself will go flying out the window. Tell her how much she means to you and the difference she has made in your life.

Soul Mates: You and a fellow Libra will get along as if you have known each other forever. A partnership with Scorpio and Sagittarius can be a dream made real. Capricorn and Aries tend to move way too fast, and may have you feeling overlooked. Aquarius and Gemini will do all that they can to make the relationship last for a long time. Cancer will bring out a lot of insecurities you forgot were there. Leo and Virgo are on your side all the way and never hesitate to tell you that. Pisces and Taurus can hamper your freedom and make you feel strangled.

Most Charming Characteristics: Faithful, trustworthy, sincere.

Gifts: *For her:* day at a botanical garden. *For him:* cooking class.

Sensual Foods: Hot-fudge sundae with all the trimmings; shepherd's pie.

Romantic Flowers: These ladies like everyone to know how faithful they are, so send them violets. To surprise them send tulips. Men like their flowers the same as their relationships, unpretending. Send them camellias with white roses to show your affection.

Best Date Nights: Friday; 12th and 21st of each month.

Colors of Passion: *For her:* lavender, crimson. *For him:* black, tawny.

The Perfect Wedding: You are a lover of art and intrigued by exoticism; you might consider an art gallery or museum as the place you take your vows. A grand hotel-ballroom-turned-paradise or lush green forest can provide the romantic haven you desire. With the emphasis on drama, you'll not only want to woo your beloved but your wedding guests as well. Ideal setting: Egypt; Montreal.

Wise Words: Henry Wadsworth Longfellow: "Now if my act be good, as I believe, it cannot be recalled. It is already sealed up in Heaven, as a good deed accomplished."

Hints of Love: Make sure you go on more than one date before you jump to conclusions on liking and disliking.

After the Argument: *For him:* Lavish him with attention. Bring him nice things that are not too overwhelming. Charm him into being that cuddly guy you love. *For her:* A little more stroking than usual. Tickets to a show or even the right evening at home could work.

Romantic Places: Places of movement bring romance: London; the theater; Las Vegas, Nevada.

Lucky Love Star: Libriel—you will never lack serenity.

Beautiful Thought: Before you close your eyes at night, forgive the day and take the flight.

Sharing Secrets: This one loves a challenge. *For the gals:* Be consistently inconsistent until you have them hooked. *For the guys:* This one loves to play catch. You may feel like a yo-yo, but as long as he is calling that's all that matters.

Judith's Insights

About the Man: You can get this guy a bouquet of flowers or a pizza with a nice note inside to get his attention. Anything will do if it tells him that you are thinking of him. He appreciates the style with which you can do it. Make sure he knows that you have a mind of your own. It will attract him more than anything. The very thing he is searching for is someone to love him. He needs a team player instead of someone who will challenge him at every turn. He is a willing and devoted friend and partner.

About the Woman: This girl would love it if you showered her with attention. She would give up her family or friends for her love. You must realize, though, that in time she will expect the same from you. Don't ask this girl for something you are unable to give yourself. She will leave right away when she feels no balance in the relationship. She would never ask for something she wouldn't be able to give herself. Repay her kindness and genuine love for you with the same from you. She values what comes back to her.

Soul Mates: There is nothing better than a partnership with someone of your own sign, Libra. Scorpio and Sagittarius can be exactly what you need to spice up your life. Capricorn and Aries will leave your scales in a tangle. Aquarius and Gemini will love to love you and make you happy. Cancer will have you tied in knots in no time. Leo and Virgo will have you doing things you never thought you could until they gave you the support. Pisces and Taurus are rigid. They will try to keep you penned in like a possession.

Most Charming Characteristics: Vigorous, energetic, loving.

Gifts: *For her:* friends over for dinner and a movie. *For him:* dinner at a fine restaurant.

Sensual Foods: Whipped cream, strawberries, brown sugar, and heavy cream.

Romantic Flowers: These ladies like men with taste. Show them you love style by sending fuchsia flowers, or even brightly colored wildflowers will do. To confuse this man, send him lilies along with bright daisies to show your innocence. Keep him guessing.

Best Date Nights: Friday; 4th and 13th of each month.

Colors of Passion: *For her:* lavender, crimson. *For him:* black, tawny.

The Perfect Wedding: You are a lover of art and intrigued by exoticism; you might consider an art gallery or museum as the place you take your vows. A grand hotel-ballroom-turned-paradise or lush green forest can provide the romantic haven you desire. With the emphasis on drama, you'll not only want to woo your beloved but your wedding guests as well. Ideal setting: Egypt; Montreal.

Wise Words: Henry Wadsworth Longfellow: "But the good deed through the ages / Living in historic pages, / Brighter grows and gleams immortal, / Unconsumed by moth or rust."

Hints of Love: Don't act too needy too soon. It may push this relationship away.

After the Argument: *For him:* Lavish him with attention. Bring him nice things that are not too overwhelming. Charm him into being that cuddly guy you love. *For her:* A little more stroking than usual. Tickets to a show or even the right evening at home could work.

Romantic Places: Places of activity bring romance: Brazil; a carnival; Memphis, Tennessee.

Lucky Love Star: Libriel—you will never lack serenity.

Beautiful Thought: Success is when you have become happy with yourself and your accomplishments.

Sharing Secrets: This is a family person at heart; your presence is most important. *For the gals:* Make sure you go to Sunday dinner with her family when you are invited. *For the guys:* If you don't like his mom, you might have a hard time catching this one.

Judith's Insights

About the Man: If you watch this guy's life patterns, you may think that the last thing he is looking for is a lasting love. That is only what he wants you to think. He needs someone who has great intuition and can read what is really behind the words he says. If you can read minds, then this is the man for you. He can be fickle about everything in his life from the food he eats to the people he loves. The only constant is his need to be supported emotionally. He is drawn to unusual surroundings and people.

About the Woman: People think that she is a scatterbrain at times. She puts her business before pleasure at almost every turn. She wants things taken care of before she will go and relax. She won't date just anyone. There has to be a reason and a strong attraction for her to leave her desk in search of love. She is very charming and can flirt in an obvious way. If she is interested, you have to make sure that she doesn't change her mind. Deep down she wants a lot from her mate and needs even more than she wants.

Soul Mates: A fellow Libra will be exactly what you need when you need it. It will be like having a secret connection. Scorpio and Sagittarius will show you things you never dreamed of before. Enjoy the discovery. Capricorn and Aries will have you jumping through hoops to see if you are up to the challenge. Aquarius and Gemini can be the best fun you have had in ages. Cancer will have you ripping your hair out in no time. Leo and Virgo will do all they can to make you feel safe and secure. Pisces and Taurus will have you on a leash and tied to the fence if you don't speak up at the beginning.

Most Charming Characteristics: Impulsive, likable, flexible.

Gifts: *For her:* personal shopper. *For him:* tailored suit.

Sensual Foods: Puddings and pastry of all kinds.

Romantic Flowers: You are the lady of distinction, and only carnations will do. Any mix of colors with sprays of mignonette. Sweet peas or red carnations will appeal to this man's heart.

Best Date Nights: Friday; 4th and 23rd of each month.

Colors of Passion: *For her:* lavender, crimson. *For him:* black, tawny.

The Perfect Wedding: You are a lover of art and intrigued by exoticism; you might consider an art gallery or museum as the place you take your vows. A grand hotel-ballroom-turned-paradise or lush green forest can provide the romantic haven you desire. With the emphasis on drama, you'll not only want to woo your beloved but your wedding guests as well. Ideal setting: Egypt; Montreal.

Wise Words: Aster: "None should dwell too deeply on the past,—full of mistakes, regrets, might-have-beens. By so doing the mind grows limp and discouraged and the soul's energy is dulled."

Hints of Love: Keep it fun. Look for new and exciting things to do, especially if you are in a long-term relationship.

After the Argument: *For him:* Lavish him with attention. Bring him nice things that are not too overwhelming. Charm him into being that cuddly guy you love. *For her:* A little more stroking than usual. Tickets to a show or even the right evening at home could work.

Romantic Places: Places of movement bring romance: Paris; an outdoor festival; Times Square, New York City.

Lucky Love Star: Libriel—you will never lack serenity.

Beautiful Thought: If only you could realize how much today will mean to you tomorrow.

Sharing Secrets: Everything in its good time. This one works slowly, but when it is time to pick up speed, watch out. *For the gals:* Don't go by the obvious. Read between the lines. As long as the invitation is being offered go full speed ahead. *For the guys:* Just when you thought you should walk away, he'll say, "I love you." Talk about confusing.

Judith's Insights

About the Man: You can buy him a cup of coffee or pick up the tab at lunch. Don't go overboard to impress him. He is cautious about what others do for him. You are only allowed to go overboard if you are his mate for life. Otherwise, he will be concerned about what you really want from him. He will go to the ends of the earth for his love, his family, and his friends. He can even sacrifice his own happiness for that of others at times. He is able to adapt to any situation and wishes others in his life were as accommodating as he is.

About the Woman: She may be shy about taking from you— or from anyone, for that matter. Until you have a strong and steady relationship she will be uncomfortable when you try to give her lavish gifts. She sees herself as the one who does for others instead of others doing for her. Once you have been together for a while you had better not forget a birthday or any holiday at all. She is great as long as you don't break her heart. She will do anything to see a smile on your face. Try to return the favor by making her heart sing.

Soul Mates: Looking at a fellow Libra is like looking in a mirror. Make sure that you can handle what you see. Scorpio and Sagittarius are exactly what the doctor ordered to shake things up a bit. Seeing where things fall will be fun. Capricorn and Aries will bring out the worst in you if you let them feed your insecurities. Aquarius and Gemini will show you more fun than you can handle in a single day. Cancer will have you climbing the walls to get away. Leo and Virgo are more than you can dream of and more. Pisces and Taurus will do all that they can to anchor you to where they feel you should be.

Most Charming Characteristics: Able, energetic, wholehearted.

Gifts: *For her:* day of beauty. *For him:* spa getaway.

Sensual Foods: Champagne with strawberries; fillet of sole.

Romantic Flowers: You love it when you get tulips, declaring love. When you receive a variety, it shows how hopelessly in love your partner is. He will just love a single rose. This shows him you understand his pleasures.

Best Date Nights: Friday; 15th and 24th of each month.

Colors of Passion: *For her:* lavender, crimson. *For him:* black, tawny.

The Perfect Wedding: You are a lover of art and intrigued by exoticism; you might consider an art gallery or museum as the place you take your vows. A grand hotel-ballroom-turned-paradise or lush green forest can provide the romantic haven you desire. With the emphasis on drama, you'll not only want to woo your beloved but your wedding guests as well. Ideal setting: Egypt; Montreal.

Wise Words: G. F. Merriman: "Faithfulness is the gold of the heart. To be faithful in darkness, that is the supreme test to which the human spirit is subjected."

Hints of Love: This one is a cautious soul. You may have to find a way to go around to the back door.

After the Argument: *For him:* Lavish him with attention. Bring him nice things that are not too overwhelming. Charm him into being that cuddly guy you love. *For her:* A little more stroking than usual. Tickets to a show or even the right evening at home could work.

Romantic Places: Places of activity bring romance: Argentina; a nightclub; Miami, Florida.

Lucky Love Star: Libriel—you will never lack serenity.

Beautiful Thought: Smiles give strength and power, but only when they are being worn.

Sharing Secrets: This one is a charmer, perhaps even fickle. *For the gals:* If you are patient enough to stick around, this one is worth the wait. *For the guys:* If there is enough time on the clock, stick around past three months. Then maybe he will have noticed you are there.

Judith's Insights

About the Man: Many are attracted to his appearance. You will notice that several people have crushes on him at work. He does have an ego, but it seldom gets out of control. You can let him know that you are interested if you keep it subtle. Going overboard with this guy will only get him to walk away. Once he is yours, don't expect roses and candlelight. He is much more creative than that. He will make romance in the most unusual ways. His friends stay friends for life because of his understanding of what makes a relationship work.

About the Woman: She wears many hats. This gal is great to work for or with. She likes to get everyone to work together instead of against each other. When you meet her for the first time you may feel as if you have known her forever. Allow her time to get to know you before you start asking for things. She enjoys the company of others, so you will seldom find her alone. Her talent for making every occasion special will shine brighter the longer you know her. She will do anything to find a safe and secure life partner.

Soul Mates: A fellow Libra will understand you more than anyone else ever could. Scorpio and Sagittarius will add spice to your life. You will be surprised at how much you like the new taste of things. Capricorn and Aries are not for the weak-hearted or fragile ego. Aquarius and Gemini will do all that they can think of to show you a good time. Cancer will prey on all the parts of yourself you try to hide. Deal with them before they get a hold on them and they will not be able to hurt you. Leo and Virgo will make the relationship run smoothly by their ability to overlook the bumps in the road. Pisces and Taurus will try to put you on the mantel until they are ready to play with you.

Most Charming Characteristics: Honest, faithful, sincere.

Gifts: *For her:* big bouquet of flowers. *For him:* day at a botanical garden.

Sensual Foods: Chocolates; poached salmon; flambé; filet mignon; potatoes.

Romantic Flowers: Send this girl sunflowers if you want her to know you adore her. You may even add some poppies for a splash of extravagance. His desire for sport and play will be understood when you send him hyacinth and geranium.

Best Date Nights: Friday; 6th and 15th of each month.

Colors of Passion: *For her:* lavender, crimson. *For him:* black, tawny.

The Perfect Wedding: You are a lover of art and intrigued by exoticism; you might consider an art gallery or museum as the place you take your vows. A grand hotel-ballroom-turned-paradise or lush green forest can provide the romantic haven you desire. With the emphasis on drama, you'll not only want to woo your beloved but your wedding guests as well. Ideal setting: Egypt; Montreal.

Wise Words: Charles Dickens: "What we have got to do is to keep up our spirits and be neighborly. We shall come all right in the end, never fear."

Hints of Love: Passion must be in the picture at all times or you could lose this one's attention quickly.

After the Argument: *For him:* Lavish him with attention. Bring him nice things that are not too overwhelming. Charm him into being that cuddly guy you love. *For her:* A little more stroking than usual. Tickets to a show or even the right evening at home could work.

Romantic Places: Places of movement bring romance: Rome; a ballet; Los Angeles, California.

Lucky Love Star: Libriel—you will never lack serenity.

Beautiful Thought: Friendship is standing by each other throughout the darkness, patient until we see the light.

Sharing Secrets: If you are looking for love, then you have found the right mate. *For the gals:* This one could be stubborn. It may take forever to get a relationship started, but it is as solid as they come. *For the guys:* Even when he is ready, he might not be willing and able. He will put you through more obstacles than any course. Be patient.

Judith's Insights

About the Man: This guy has a style like no one else around. His approach to life is carefree on the outside, but his mind is always moving on the inside. He has a tendency to procrastinate, even if he is really interested in a project or person. If he does not do the asking, then by all means do so yourself. I wouldn't call him moody, but he can certainly get that way at times. When he feels as if his life is out of sync he may become defensive and emotional. He is ready, willing, and able to help anyone anytime.

About the Woman: She prefers it the old-fashioned way. When you invite her out, expect to be paying the bill. This lady won't mind coughing up her own money as long as she is given time to do so. In her mind, the one who invites is the one who pays. Things have to be at the serious level for her to do the inviting. She needs an honorable mate she can show off to her family and friends. She needs to feel special just by your presence. After tempers flare she is usually the one to patch up the holes and make everything all better.

Soul Mates: When in doubt, turn to a fellow Libra. They will give you all of the guidance you will ever need. You will look at the world in a different way when Scorpio and Sagittarius get done with you. Make sure you are at peace with yourself before pairing with Capricorn and Aries. Aquarius and Gemini are all you can ask for in a great relationship. Cancer will prey on any, and all, weakness in your ego. Make sure you are ready to face them. Leo and Virgo will make your life a walk in the park, if you would only let them help. Pisces and Taurus will have you lying on the couch, ready to poke and prod your subconscious.

Most Charming Characteristics: Sincere, humorous, assured.

Gifts: *For her:* tickets to the opera or symphony. *For him:* tickets to a jazz concert.

Sensual Foods: Caviar; beef tenderloin; potatoes au gratin.

Romantic Flowers: Rhododendron will let her be on the lookout for trouble. Throw in some chrysanthemum and she'll know it is you she will be looking out for. Cactus will show him warmth. Yellow daffodil is a token of a good time had by all. Chivalry is not dead.

Best Date Nights: Friday; 8th and 26th of each month.

Colors of Passion: *For her:* lavender, crimson. *For him:* black, tawny.

The Perfect Wedding: You are a lover of art and intrigued by exoticism; you might consider an art gallery or museum as the place you take your vows. A grand hotel-ballroom-turned-paradise or lush green forest can provide the romantic haven you desire. With the emphasis on drama, you'll not only want to woo your beloved but your wedding guests as well. Ideal setting: Egypt; Montreal.

Wise Words: Marcus Aurelius: "We are all made for co-operation, like feet, like hands, like eye-lids, like the rows of the upper and lower teeth. To act against one another is contrary to nature."

Hints of Love: A random act of kindness will go a long way with this one. What can you do for them today?

After the Argument: *For him:* Lavish him with attention. Bring him nice things that are not too overwhelming. Charm him into being that cuddly guy you love. *For her:* A little more stroking than usual. Tickets to a show or even the right evening at home could work.

Romantic Places: Places of activity bring romance: French Rivera; a parade; Detroit, Michigan.

Lucky Love Star: Libriel—you will never lack serenity.

Beautiful Thought: The chain of love, with no links missing.

Sharing Secrets: If you can hang around and give constant stimulation, this could be your mate. *For the gals:* She is always looking for the Exit sign. Don't show her where it is or she will be gone. *For the guys:* Fast car, fast food; he likes everything that goes fast. Put on your running shoes. If you can keep up then he is yours.

Judith's Insights

About the Man: If this guy is your boss, you may have to take some time to figure him out. He can keep his personal side hidden from view. As a friend, he is the easiest one in the crowd to get along with. As a potential love interest, he can be too serious or not serious enough. There is no middle ground. He does have an understanding heart that is truly a gift. Not everyone is born ready to be in love, but he is. His charm and understanding will win him the attention of the entire room every time.

About the Woman: She likes to be liked and will go out of her way to get people to like her. If you work with this girl you already know that she does not like friction. You have to be a class act to get this lady's attention. Don't just start something with her and let it lie. You have to follow through if you expect her to do the same. She wants a relationship that will last the rest of her life. In business, she will do all that she can to keep the project going and the partnership together. Her need to make everything right after an argument may make her feel drained.

Soul Mates: A fellow Libra will give you all you need when you need it without your having to ask. Scorpio and Sagittarius will charm you into anything. Capricorn and Aries will have you tied in knots when they are through. Aquarius and Gemini live to make you happy. Cancer can bring out the worst in you if you let them. Try to be the bigger person. Leo and Virgo will do anything to keep the relationship going without a snag. Pisces and Taurus will have you locked up tight if you let them.

Most Charming Characteristics: Confident, astute, fun-loving.

Gifts: *For her:* beauty makeover. *For him:* professional massage.

Sensual Foods: Passion fruit; fillet of sole almondine.

Romantic Flowers: The magnolias you send her will let her know you will be around for a while to come. Petunia is to say never despair. Holly will let him know what he is getting into. Pansy will keep you in his thoughts.

Best Date Nights: Friday; 18th and 27th of each month.

Colors of Passion: *For her:* lavender, crimson. *For him:* black, tawny.

The Perfect Wedding: You are a lover of art and intrigued by exoticism; you might consider an art gallery or museum as the place you take your vows. A grand hotel-ballroom-turned-paradise or lush green forest can provide the romantic haven you desire. With the emphasis on drama, you'll not only want to woo your beloved but your wedding guests as well. Ideal setting: Egypt; Montreal.

Wise Words: Charles Dickens: "Power (unless it be the power of intellect or virtue) has ever the greatest attraction for the lowest natures."

Hints of Love: Family and friends are important to this one. Don't try to alienate them or it will definitely backfire on you.

After the Argument: *For him:* Lavish him with attention. Bring him nice things that are not too overwhelming. Charm him into being that cuddly guy you love. *For her:* A little more stroking than usual. Tickets to a show or even the right evening at home could work.

Romantic Places: Places of movement bring romance: Rio de Janeiro; a sports event; Hollywood, California.

Lucky Love Star: Libriel—you will never lack serenity.

Beautiful Thought: If yesterday was better, today wouldn't be such a good tomorrow.

Sharing Secrets: This one may seem like a lot of work. They just need the basics: love, loyalty, and respect. *For the gals:* If you can show her your best side right from the beginning it may work. Be careful of fluff, because she will see right through it. *For the guys:* He loves to be loved. Give him plenty of attention, even if you think you don't stand a chance. Perseverance will win here.

Judith's Insights

About the Man: He has got a style all his own, and it may take you a lifetime to understand it. He has strong convictions when it comes to work. His straight-shooter type of personality may come across all wrong at times. If you like his style, then anything goes. If you don't, you have no chance of changing it. He is in love with all things nostalgic. A relationship with him can be complicated to maintain but well worth the work. There is no middle ground for this guy. He is ready to smile or punch his way out of anything.

About the Woman: Opening the door for her will get you noticed. She wants a mate who stands up for himself and for her. You may have to wine and dine her a bit to get any kind of commitment out of her. She is romantic at heart. To ignore that would clip the relationship before it begins. It is easy to grab her attention, but it takes a high level of romanticism to keep it going. Unless you listen to what she has to say you will get nowhere fast. Honor is very important to her.

Soul Mates: Libra and Libra is a match made in heaven. Scorpio and Sagittarius will intrigue you. This could be the best partner no matter what you have in mind. Capricorn and Aries will urge you to reach out and expand. Make sure that they are not bossy, though. Aquarius and Gemini are a perfect example of what can and will go right with a relationship. You will need a great deal of strength to pair with Cancer. Leo and Virgo will work to keep the relationship harmonious and balanced. Pisces and Taurus will be your dream only in a nightmare.

Most Charming Characteristics: Cheerful, witty, carefree.

Gifts: *For her:* gift certificate to her favorite store. *For him:* enroll him in a book club.

Sensual Foods: Peaches; mousse; shrimp.

Romantic Flowers: Iris is your flower if you are the gal sending subtle messages. If you are the man, you will look for clematis. This flower's mental beauty creates emotional stimulation for you.

Best Date Nights: Friday; 1st and 10th of each month.

Colors of Passion: *For her:* lavender, crimson. *For him:* black, tawny.

The Perfect Wedding: You are a lover of art and intrigued by exoticism; you might consider an art gallery or museum as the place you take your vows. A grand hotel-ballroom-turned-paradise or lush green forest can provide the romantic haven you desire. With the emphasis on drama, you'll not only want to woo your beloved but your wedding guests as well. Ideal setting: Egypt; Montreal.

Wise Words: Charles Dickens: "Though home is a name, a word, it is a strong one; stronger than magician ever spoke, or spirit answered to, in the strongest conjuration."

Hints of Love: Show others how much you adore him or her. They will revel in how others notice.

After the Argument: *For him:* Lavish him with attention. Bring him nice things that are not too overwhelming. Charm him into being that cuddly guy you love. *For her:* A little more stroking than usual. Tickets to a show or even the right evening at home could work.

Romantic Places: Places of activity bring romance: Hong Kong; a street fair; New York City.

Lucky Love Star: Libriel—you will never lack serenity.

Beautiful Thought: Every time you love, you learn something new.

Sharing Secrets: They are looking for love, but that is just their little secret. *For the gals:* Why shouldn't they want to be loved? Of course they do, but they want you to do all of the work. *For the guys:* You must prove yourself repeatedly. Don't expect too much until he knows you are under his thumb.

Judith's Insights

About the Man: He is not perfect and doesn't mind that you aren't, either. He has tremendous compassion and will share of himself at all cost. He will get self-absorbed from time to time. When he does, you have to pull back so you don't feed into his ego. If that ego gets any bigger you might not be able to fit in the room. He never wants to separate from the little child inside of his soul. Appeal to that child and make life a game of excitement. His natural optimism makes it easy for him to cultivate both friends and lovers.

About the Woman: You may never take this gal for being shy. You may look at her intelligence as a strength. She really doesn't want to be anyone's boss. She is looking for someone to get to know her, understand her, and love her in spite of her faults. Never expect her to be perfect and she will return the favor. She must first learn to understand herself before she can ask anyone else to understand where she is coming from. She is happiest at home and rarely feels at peace anywhere else.

Soul Mates: A union with a fellow Libra is all you can ever dream of. Scorpio and Sagittarius will ignore any shortcomings you have to keep the relationship running smoothly. Capricorn and Aries will try to change you at almost every turn. Aquarius and Gemini love doing all that they can to make you happy, because that is what makes them happy. Cancer will turn the relationship into a tumultuous one if you are not careful. A joint venture with Leo and Virgo will be balanced in every way. Pisces and Taurus will try to cage you in while you crave your freedom.

Most Charming Characteristics: Positive, affectionate, understanding, loving.

Gifts: *For her:* professional portrait session. *For him:* personal shopper.

Sensual Foods: Kiwis; cantaloupes; strawberries.

Romantic Flowers: Any rose of any color for the lady. Roses stand for love regardless of the color. Send them with orchids and you will be saying, "I love you." If you want a gentleman to know you think of him send pansies, and forget-me-nots for true love.

Best Date Nights: Friday; 2nd and 20th of each month.

Colors of Passion: *For her:* lavender, crimson. *For him:* black, tawny.

The Perfect Wedding: You are a lover of art and intrigued by exoticism; you might consider an art gallery or museum as the place you take your vows. A grand hotel-ballroom-turned-paradise or lush green forest can provide the romantic haven you desire. With the emphasis on drama, you'll not only want to woo your beloved but your wedding guests as well. Ideal setting: Egypt; Montreal.

Wise Words: Robert Burns: "Hope is the cordial of the human heart, and I endeavor to cherish it as well as I can."

Hints of Love: Don't overdo it (dress, attention) too soon or this one will run. Wait until you have them hooked before you become outrageous.

After the Argument: *For him:* Lavish him with attention. Bring him nice things that are not too overwhelming. Charm him into being that cuddly guy you love. *For her:* A little more stroking than usual. Tickets to a show or even the right evening at home could work.

Romantic Places: Places of movement bring romance: Dublin; an amusement park; Seattle, Washington.

Lucky Love Star: Libriel—you will never lack serenity.

Beautiful Thought: When you let go of today, it will be tomorrow.

Sharing Secrets: You had better be ready to pull out your romantic side if you want this to work. *For the gals:* Fireplaces, walks on the beach, or even winning a bear at the local carnival. *For the guys:* When you are out shopping bring him something home. Even if it is silly, he will love the thought.

Judith's Insights

About the Man: He does not like it when people second-guess his actions in any way. This is especially true when it comes to his work. The best way to this man's heart is to simply read his mind. If you can step in and give him a hand where he needs it, without his having to ask, he will be more than grateful. He just wants to feel as if he is part of the picture instead of pushed off to the side. Include him in as much of your own life as you can. Kindness and sincerity are his greatest attributes.

About the Woman: This lady comes off much more serious than she really is. She is looking for someone to give her a reason to smile. Flirting with her makes the shyness in her soul take over. She just wants to feel the hug of love without arms actually being around her. Let her know your feelings and that you will always be there. Don't just be there physically, but also in spirit when she is away from you. Allow her freedom and encourage her passion at every turn. She fears having to live her life alone.

Soul Mates: You and a fellow Libra will get along as if you have known each other forever. A partnership with Scorpio and Sagittarius can be a dream made real. Capricorn and Aries tend to move way too fast, and may have you feeling overlooked. Aquarius and Gemini will do all that they can to make the relationship last for a long time. Cancer will bring out a lot of insecurities you forgot were there. Leo and Virgo are on your side all the way and never hesitate to tell you that. Pisces and Taurus can hamper your freedom and make you feel strangled.

Most Charming Characteristics: Idealistic, playful, energetic.

Gifts: *For her:* day at a botanical garden. *For him:* cooking class.

Sensual Foods: Caramel and chocolate syrup on anything.

Romantic Flowers: These ladies like everyone to know how faithful they are, so send them violets. To surprise them send tulips. Men like their flowers the same as their relationships, unpretending. Send them camellias with white roses to show your affection.

Best Date Nights: Friday; 3rd and 12th of each month.

Colors of Passion: *For her:* lavender, crimson. *For him:* black, tawny.

The Perfect Wedding: You are a lover of art and intrigued by exoticism; you might consider an art gallery or museum as the place you take your vows. A grand hotel-ballroom-turned-paradise or lush green forest can provide the romantic haven you desire. With the emphasis on drama, you'll not only want to woo your beloved but your wedding guests as well. Ideal setting: Egypt; Montreal.

Wise Words: Charles Dickens: "In very many cases of friendship, or what passes for it, the old axiom is reversed, and like clings to unlike more than like."

Hints of Love: When these folks decide to sit on the fence don't try to push them off before they are ready. Let them do the jumping themselves.

After the Argument: *For him:* Lavish him with attention. Bring him nice things that are not too overwhelming. Charm him into being that cuddly guy you love. *For her:* A little more stroking than usual. Tickets to a show or even the right evening at home could work.

Romantic Places: Places of movement bring romance: London; the theater; Las Vegas, Nevada.

Lucky Love Star: Libriel—you will never lack serenity.

Beautiful Thought: Choices of the paths we are forced to make, perhaps for only a moment it was a heartbreak.

Sharing Secrets: It may seem like they are not interested, but ask them out anyway. *For the gals:* Until they absolutely know you are interested, you will never find out that they are. *For the guys:* Ask him out if he doesn't ask you. He may be shy or not. Either way, he may be interested.

Judith's Insights

About the Man: This man has the patience of a saint. There is nothing he won't tolerate when he is dealing with people. His patience can start to fade when he enters into a relationship that isn't going the way he planned. He has clearly defined views of how things should be. Only someone he loves can change his mind. He can come on too strong at times and not strong enough at others. You have to prove yourself to get close to his heart. Although he is sensitive at heart, he can balance out the mush with a clear mind.

About the Woman: She can be stubborn. That can be the first side of her that you notice. This is especially true in a work environment. She likes things done the way she does them and no other way. She will protect herself at all costs. This is a girl you really have to get to know before you can approach her. If you succeed at winning her over it will be nearly impossible to break the bond between the two of you. She is blessed with charm, wit, and a devoted nature.

Soul Mates: There is nothing better than a partnership with someone of your own sign, Libra. Scorpio and Sagittarius can be exactly what you need to spice up your life. Capricorn and Aries will leave your scales in a tangle. Aquarius and Gemini will love to love you and make you happy. Cancer will have you tied in knots in no time. Leo and Virgo will have you doing things you never thought you could until they gave you the support. Pisces and Taurus are rigid. They will try to keep you penned in like a possession.

Most Charming Characteristics: Quick-witted.

Gifts: *For her:* friends over for dinner and a movie. *For him:* dinner at a fine restaurant.

Sensual Foods: Waffles with whipped cream; chocolate soufflé; French wine.

Romantic Flowers: These ladies like men with taste. Show them you love style by sending fuchsia flowers, or even brightly colored wildflowers will do. To confuse this man, send him lilies along with bright daisies to show your innocence. Keep him guessing.

Best Date Nights: Friday; 4th and 13th of each month.

Colors of Passion: *For her:* lavender, crimson. *For him:* black, tawny.

The Perfect Wedding: You are a lover of art and intrigued by exoticism; you might consider an art gallery or museum as the place you take your vows. A grand hotel-ballroom-turned-paradise or lush green forest can provide the romantic haven you desire. With the emphasis on drama, you'll not only want to woo your beloved but your wedding guests as well. Ideal setting: Egypt; Montreal.

Wise Words: Charles Dickens: "Nature never writes a bad hand. Her writing, as it may be read in the human countenance, is invariably legible, if we come at all trained to the reading of it."

Hints of Love: Make sure you learn to compromise, but never with your principles.

After the Argument: *For him:* Lavish him with attention. Bring him nice things that are not too overwhelming. Charm him into being that cuddly guy you love. *For her:* A little more stroking than usual. Tickets to a show or even the right evening at home could work.

Romantic Places: Places of activity bring romance: Brazil; a carnival; Memphis, Tennessee.

Lucky Love Star: Libriel—you will never lack serenity.

Beautiful Thought: When your wishes do come true, remember the angel that is helping you.

Sharing Secrets: Don't be surprised if the first date is with their family. *For the gals:* Make sure you invite her to your family functions. It will be a red flag to her if you don't. *For the guys:* He may seem like a family man, but isn't that what you were looking for?

Judith's Insights

About the Man: This man is not one of great patience. If he is interested in you it is likely that he will be the pursuer. This way he doesn't have to wait for you to do it. He loves all of the pleasures of life. Tease him with what he loves and he will be hooked to you as long as you want him to be. This quiet soul can be quite the talker when given the chance. He loves to be noticed for his intellect, so compliment him on things he has done at work. He loves fixing broken things whether they are chairs or hearts.

About the Woman: She has a strong desire for entertainment. She never minds having too much to do. Her daily list of goals is usually longer than anyone else's around the office. Invite her out to a night on the town. The way to really impress her is with tickets to the hottest event in town. The more attention she receives the better. She will keep her looks up to par and will get both the first and second glance when she enters the room. Compliments never go unnoticed. She loves to give and receive them.

Soul Mates: A fellow Libra will be exactly what you need when you need it. It will be like having a secret connection. Scorpio and Sagittarius will show you things you never dreamed of before. Enjoy the discovery. Capricorn and Aries will have you jumping through hoops to see if you are up to the challenge. Aquarius and Gemini can be the best fun you have had in ages. Cancer will have you ripping your hair out in no time. Leo and Virgo will do all they can to make you feel safe and secure. Pisces and Taurus will have you on a leash and tied to the fence if you don't speak up at the beginning.

Most Charming Characteristics: Abrupt, impulsive, free-spirited.

Gifts: *For her:* personal shopper. *For him:* tailored suit.

Sensual Foods: Oysters; mussels; spicy foods.

Romantic Flowers: You are the lady of distinction, and only carnations will do. Any mix of colors with sprays of mignonette. Sweet peas or red carnations will appeal to this man's heart.

Best Date Nights: Friday; 4th and 5th of each month.

Colors of Passion: *For her:* lavender, crimson. *For him:* black, tawny.

The Perfect Wedding: You are a lover of art and intrigued by exoticism; you might consider an art gallery or museum as the place you take your vows. A grand hotel-ballroom-turned-paradise or lush green forest can provide the romantic haven you desire. With the emphasis on drama, you'll not only want to woo your beloved but your wedding guests as well. Ideal setting: Egypt; Montreal.

Wise Words: William Penn: "The greatest understandings doubt most, are readiest to learn, and least pleased with themselves. For though they stand on higher ground, and so see farther than their neighbors, they are yet humbled by their prospect."

Hints of Love: If you try to take a step back, it will be noticed. It could create the domino effect, and everything will start to fall.

After the Argument: *For him:* Lavish him with attention. Bring him nice things that are not too overwhelming. Charm him into being that cuddly guy you love. *For her:* A little more stroking than usual. Tickets to a show or even the right evening at home could work.

Romantic Places: Places of movement bring romance: Paris; an outdoor festival; Times Square, New York City.

Lucky Love Star: Libriel—you will never lack serenity.

Beautiful Thought: If I could only take away your pain and bring you the sunshine instead of rain.

Sharing Secrets: Take me as I am could be the anthem for this one. *For the gals:* They will have strong views on just about everything. If you can hang with them, then nothing will be as important as you. *For the guys:* The thing you fall in love with may end up becoming the thing you hate. After a commitment, this one sticks around.

Judith's Insights

About the Man: The more exuberant your personality is, the more likely that this guy will be attracted to you. He likes it if everyone around him likes his mate. There is no such thing as too outgoing for him. You must be able to view life as an adventure to catch his heart. Then he will make it a great adventure for you. He is not cheap in any way, and it is very unlikely that he would ever be with someone who is for very long. Family is very important to him, yet it may cause his greatest stress.

About the Woman: This gal wants no stick-in-the-mud to be around her. She aims for the person who is everyone's heartthrob. She will be very territorial with her mate while relishing how everyone envies her for having him. People can only stand so close before her alarm goes off. To get this lady's heart, you have to have already won the hearts of many. Generosity of spirit is her trademark. To keep a place in her heart you must give to others as well as her. Romance and intimate relationships are extremely important to her.

Soul Mates: Looking at a fellow Libra is like looking in a mirror. Make sure that you can handle what you see. Scorpio and Sagittarius are exactly what the doctor ordered to shake things up a bit. Seeing where things fall will be fun. Capricorn and Aries will bring out the worst in you if you let them feed your insecurities. Aquarius and Gemini will show you more fun than you can handle in a single day. Cancer will have you climbing the walls to get away. Leo and Virgo are more than you can dream of and more. Pisces and Taurus will do all that they can to anchor you to where they feel you should be.

Most Charming Characteristics: Imaginative, enthusiastic, cautious.

Gifts: *For her:* day of beauty. *For him:* spa getaway.

Sensual Foods: Lobster; watermelon.

Romantic Flowers: You love it when you get tulips, declaring love. When you receive a variety, it shows how hopelessly in love your partner is. He will just love a single rose. This shows him you understand his pleasures.

Best Date Nights: Friday; 15th and 24th of each month.

Colors of Passion: *For her:* lavender, crimson. *For him:* black, tawny.

The Perfect Wedding: You are a lover of art and intrigued by exoticism; you might consider an art gallery or museum as the place you take your vows. A grand hotel-ballroom-turned-paradise or lush green forest can provide the romantic haven you desire. With the emphasis on drama, you'll not only want to woo your beloved but your wedding guests as well. Ideal setting: Egypt; Montreal.

Wise Words: Charles Dickens: "It is always the person not in the predicament who knows what ought to have been done in it, and would unquestionably have done it too."

Hints of Love: Consistence and persistence will get this prize every time. They will value the effort.

After the Argument: *For him:* Lavish him with attention. Bring him nice things that are not too overwhelming. Charm him into being that cuddly guy you love. *For her:* A little more stroking than usual. Tickets to a show or even the right evening at home could work.

Romantic Places: Places of activity bring romance: Argentina; a nightclub; Miami, Florida.

Lucky Love Star: Libriel—you will never lack serenity.

Beautiful Thought: As stupid as it is smart.

Sharing Secrets: They seem moody until you get to know them. *For the gals:* You may not know whether to say hello or drop dead. As relations progress you will learn not to leave her dangling, and her moods will become more consistent. *For the guys:* To know him is to love him. His bark is much worse than his bite. He just wants someone to love him without criticism.

Judith's Insights

About the Man: He portrays his individualistic side in a way that makes you think that he never wants a long-term mate. He is just afraid of emotional responsibility, so he will avoid commitment for as long as possible. He will give in eventually, but later rather than sooner. He has to find someone he wants to put up with. He needs to have his life and love be a specific way. He has a tendency to be unrealistic in his expectations of how things should be. Relationships with his friends, lovers, and family mean everything to him.

About the Woman: You may think that once this girl makes a commitment she will stick to it forever. This is only true to a point. You can push her only so far before she pushes back. If you don't live up to her idea of a grown-up she will outgrow you fast. Moving to the next step is important to her. If you can't live up to her expectations it will cause problems in your relationship. She does go with the punches better than you may think, however.

Soul Mates: A fellow Libra will understand you more than anyone else ever could. Scorpio and Sagittarius will add spice to your life. You will be surprised at how much you like the new taste of things. Capricorn and Aries are not for the weak-hearted or fragile ego. Aquarius and Gemini will do all that they can think of to show you a good time. Cancer will prey on all the parts of yourself you try to hide. Deal with them before they get a hold on them and they will not be able to hurt you. Leo and Virgo will make the relationship run smoothly by their ability to overlook the bumps in the road. Pisces and Taurus will try to put you on the mantel until they are ready to play with you.

Most Charming Characteristics: Energetic, forgiving, kind.

Gifts: *For her:* big bouquet of flowers. *For him:* day at a botanical garden.

Sensual Foods: Strawberries; truffles; shish kebab.

Romantic Flowers: Send this girl sunflowers if you want her to know you adore her. You may even add some poppies for a splash of extravagance. His desire for sport and play will be understood when you send him hyacinth and geranium.

Best Date Nights: Friday; 6th and 24th of each month.

Colors of Passion: *For her:* lavender, crimson. *For him:* black, tawny.

The Perfect Wedding: You are a lover of art and intrigued by exoticism; you might consider an art gallery or museum as the place you take your vows. A grand hotel-ballroom-turned-paradise or lush green forest can provide the romantic haven you desire. With the emphasis on drama, you'll not only want to woo your beloved but your wedding guests as well. Ideal setting: Egypt; Montreal.

Wise Words: Thomas Carlyle: "Sincerity, a deep, great, genuine sincerity is the first characteristic of all men in any way heroic."

Hints of Love: Be funny. Laughter will be what keeps this one coming back again and again.

After the Argument: *For him:* Lavish him with attention. Bring him nice things that are not too overwhelming. Charm him into being that cuddly guy you love. *For her:* A little more stroking than usual. Tickets to a show or even the right evening at home could work.

Romantic Places: Places of movement bring romance: Rome; a ballet; Los Angeles, California.

Lucky Love Star: Libriel—you will never lack serenity.

Beautiful Thought: Every ripple in the stream is there to create another dream.

Sharing Secrets: You had better be able to put your money where your mouth is. *For the gals:* It doesn't need to be lavish, but she does love the loot. The more the better. *For the guys:* He doesn't mind spending his hard-earned cash, but he loves to see you contribute to please him.

Judith's Insights

About the Man: He can be a people pleaser at times, so you might not know if he is being nice or flirtatious. He has a nice way about him that makes people want to be close to him. Being coy will get this guy to think twice about you. Don't be overzealous when trying to capture his attention, but be consistent. Think of him as a plant that needs water, food, and attention to grow healthy and strong. Communication is very important here.

About the Woman: Dating others while dating her will not go over well with this lady. She wants to be treated as if she is the most important thing in your life. She wants unconditional love, but wants to have fun while in it. If the romance falls by the wayside, so will the relationship and her attention. Even if you haven't hugged her, she needs to feel as if you have. Showing her how much you love and value her will keep you safe in her heart. She is always eager to assist in anything she can.

Soul Mates: When in doubt, turn to a fellow Libra. They will give you all of the guidance you will ever need. You will look at the world in a different way when Scorpio and Sagittarius get done with you. Make sure you are at peace with yourself before pairing with Capricorn and Aries. Aquarius and Gemini are all you can ask for in a great relationship. Cancer will prey on any, and all, weakness in your ego. Make sure you are ready to face them. Leo and Virgo will make your life a walk in the park, if you would only let them help. Pisces and Taurus will have you lying on the couch, ready to poke and prod your subconscious.

Most Charming Characteristics: Bright, witty, good-natured.

Gifts: *For her:* tickets to the opera or symphony. *For him:* tickets to a jazz concert.

Sensual Foods: Grapes; fine cheeses and crackers; taffy.

Romantic Flowers: Rhododendron will let her be on the lookout for trouble. Throw in some chrysanthemum and she'll know it is you she will be looking out for. Cactus will show him warmth. Yellow daffodil is a token of a good time had by all. Chivalry is not dead.

Best Date Nights: Friday; 8th and 17th of each month.

Colors of Passion: *For her:* lavender, crimson. *For him:* black, tawny.

The Perfect Wedding: You are a lover of art and intrigued by exoticism; you might consider an art gallery or museum as the place you take your vows. A grand hotel-ballroom-turned-paradise or lush green forest can provide the romantic haven you desire. With the emphasis on drama, you'll not only want to woo your beloved but your wedding guests as well. Ideal setting: Egypt; Montreal.

Wise Words: Charles Dickens: "Life must be held sacred among us in more ways than one—Sacred, not merely from the murderous weapon, or the subtle poison, or the cruel blow, but sacred from preventable diseases, distortions and pains."

Hints of Love: Treat this one like royalty or precious cargo. They will love being valued in this way.

After the Argument: *For him:* Lavish him with attention. Bring him nice things that are not too overwhelming. Charm him into being that cuddly guy you love. *For her:* A little more stroking than usual. Tickets to a show or even the right evening at home could work.

Romantic Places: Places of activity bring romance: French Rivera; a parade; Detroit, Michigan.

Lucky Love Star: Libriel—you will never lack serenity.

Beautiful Thought: Simple words can have the most complicated meanings.

Sharing Secrets: Nobody likes a weak link, especially not this one. *For the gals:* Make sure you treat her like a lady and act like a man. *For the guys:* Put your best foot forward. Dress your best and keep your manners in check. This man notices.

Judith's Insights

About the Man: He holds back his emotions because he has a tendency to live in his head. He is afraid of what his heart is telling him. Don't rush to make a move before he is ready to accept it with open arms. Stay close and ready for action. Once he does make up his mind there will be no stopping him. His ideal love is someone who will do the work necessary to keep the relationship healthy. He will also love doing his share. He will hate to have to choose between sides because he thinks that it may rob him of possibilities.

About the Woman: You may have to think up some unusual romantic stunts to capture the attention of this gal. She loves sweetness, charm, and wit. She is much happier when you do the asking, but she won't mind planning the romantic interlude after the date has been set. Get ready for a flood of emotion. She loves the finer things, but she is happy to settle for the basics if they are presented correctly and with love. She gets bored easily, so it may take time to find a person she is willing to stay with for life.

Soul Mates: A fellow Libra will give you all you need when you need it without your having to ask. Scorpio and Sagittarius will charm you into anything. Capricorn and Aries will have you tied in knots when they are through. Aquarius and Gemini live to make you happy. Cancer can bring out the worst in you if you let them. Try to be the bigger person. Leo and Virgo will do anything to keep the relationship going without a snag. Pisces and Taurus will have you locked up tight if you let them.

Most Charming Characteristics: Affectionate, demonstrative, understanding.

Gifts: *For her:* beauty makeover. *For him:* professional massage.

Sensual Foods: Champagne; grapes; mangoes; filet mignon.

Romantic Flowers: The magnolias you send her will let her know you will be around for a while to come. Petunia is to say never despair. Holly will let him know what he is getting into. Pansy will keep you in his thoughts.

Best Date Nights: Friday; 9th and 18th of each month.

Colors of Passion: *For her:* lavender, crimson. *For him:* black, tawny.

The Perfect Wedding: You are a lover of art and intrigued by exoticism; you might consider an art gallery or museum as the place you take your vows. A grand hotel-ballroom-turned-paradise or lush green forest can provide the romantic haven you desire. With the emphasis on drama, you'll not only want to woo your beloved but your wedding guests as well. Ideal setting: Egypt; Montreal.

Wise Words: Charles Dickens: "The truth is the truth, and neither childish absurdities nor unscrupulous contradictions can make it otherwise."

Hints of Love: Affection is important, but only if it comes naturally. Otherwise, the sirens will go off.

After the Argument: *For him:* Lavish him with attention. Bring him nice things that are not too overwhelming. Charm him into being that cuddly guy you love. *For her:* A little more stroking than usual. Tickets to a show or even the right evening at home could work.

Romantic Places: Places of movement bring romance: Rio de Janeiro; a sports event; Hollywood, California.

Lucky Love Star: Libriel—you will never lack serenity.

Beautiful Thought: When reaching out, sometimes you have to get up from the table.

Sharing Secrets: Attention, attention, attention. *For the gals:* Do it any way you can. Presents, phone calls, cards, or flowers. Whatever works for you will work for her. *For the guys:* He would love nostalgic gifts or T-shirts. He also likes phone calls, as long as they don't interrupt his favorite pastimes.

Judith's Insights

About the Man: When he is ready to dive in, there will be no stopping him. He will do all that he can for the love of his life once he finds it. He may not be the most consistent, but he can be the most committed. Never doubt his love and respect once he has declared them. He never says what he doesn't mean. Keep the saying "do unto others as you would have done unto you" close to your heart. He is the personification of this saying.

About the Woman: She can drive you crazy if you work with her. Everything must be done by the book. In love, she is much less uptight. She will take that energy and turn it into passion. The only question is: Can you keep up with her level of emotions? They can be overwhelming if they are not digested well. The better you are to her the better she will be to you. She wants a balanced relationship where both sides put in equal amounts of effort to keep it moving.

Soul Mates: Libra and Libra is a match made in heaven. Scorpio and Sagittarius will intrigue you. This could be the best partner no matter what you have in mind. Capricorn and Aries will urge you to reach out and expand. Make sure that they are not bossy, though. Aquarius and Gemini are a perfect example of what can and will go right with a relationship. You will need a great deal of strength to pair with Cancer. Leo and Virgo will work to keep the relationship harmonious and balanced. Pisces and Taurus will be your dream only in a nightmare.

Most Charming Characteristics: Sensitive, giving, shy.

Gifts: *For her:* gift certificate to her favorite store. *For him:* enroll him in a book club.

Sensual Foods: Châteaubriand; crème brûlée.

Romantic Flowers: Iris is your flower if you are the gal sending subtle messages. If you are the man, you will look for clematis. This flower's mental beauty creates emotional stimulation for you.

Best Date Nights: Friday; 1st and 19th of each month.

Colors of Passion: *For her:* lavender, crimson. *For him:* black, tawny.

The Perfect Wedding: You are a lover of art and intrigued by exoticism; you might consider an art gallery or museum as the place you take your vows. A grand hotel-ballroom-turned-paradise or lush green forest can provide the romantic haven you desire. With the emphasis on drama, you'll not only want to woo your beloved but your wedding guests as well. Ideal setting: Egypt; Montreal.

Wise Words: Charles Dickens: "Under an accumulation of staggerers, no man can be considered a free agent. No man knocks himself down; if his destiny knocks him down, his destiny must pick him up again."

Hints of Love: This one likes others to make his or her dreams come true. Be the "fantasy" fulfiller.

After the Argument: *For him:* Lavish him with attention. Bring him nice things that are not too overwhelming. Charm him into being that cuddly guy you love. *For her.* A little more stroking than usual. Tickets to a show or even the right evening at home could work.

Romantic Places: Places of activity bring romance: Hong Kong; a street fair; New York City.

Lucky Love Star: Libriel—you will never lack serenity.

Beautiful Thought: Understanding means realizing you cannot always be on top.

Sharing Secrets: Make sure you are not the killjoy. *For the gals:* When she has an idea, try it before you decide you don't like it. She needs to be pleased. *For the guys:* Do the things he loves to do and he will make the things you love ten times more fun.

Judith's Insights

About the Man: It will take a lot to get to the bottom of this guy's feelings. You have to do much more than just dig to get there. As time goes on, he will share more and more of his heart. He needs to feel emotional security to do this. Make him feel safe in your arms and there will be nothing he won't tell you. He will only do for you what has been done for him. It is the best way for him to feel that the relationship is balanced. He will suffer in silence before showing any signs of pain of insecurity.

About the Woman: People at work can rub her the wrong way. If this gal is your boss you must show her the respect that she deserves to see any other side of her personality. This is the same with matters of the heart. Treat her well and she will make your life even better. You have to give to receive with her. She looks for others to prove their emotions before she can voice hers. When she feels safe, she will pull down the walls that shelter her emotions. Those who leave her life will usually come back down the road.

Soul Mates: A union with a fellow Libra is all you can ever dream of. Scorpio and Sagittarius will ignore any shortcomings you have to keep the relationship running smoothly. Capricorn and Aries will try to change you at almost every turn. Aquarius and Gemini love doing all that they can to make you happy, because that is what makes them happy. Cancer will turn the relationship into a tumultuous one if you are not careful. A joint venture with Leo and Virgo will be balanced in every way. Pisces and Taurus will try to cage you in while you crave your freedom.

Most Charming Characteristics: Devoted, faithful in duty, reliable.

Gifts: *For her:* professional portrait session. *For him:* personal shopper.

Sensual Foods: Shrimp; sinful chocolate cake.

Romantic Flowers: Any rose of any color for the lady. Roses stand for love regardless of the color. Send them with orchids and you will be saying, "I love you." If you want a gentleman to know you think of him, send pansies, and forget-me-nots for true love.

Best Date Nights: Friday; 2nd and 11th of each month.

Colors of Passion: *For her:* lavender, crimson. *For him:* beige, tawny.

The Perfect Wedding: You are a lover of art and intrigued by exoticism; you might consider an art gallery or museum as the place you take your vows. A grand hotel-ballroom-turned-paradise or lush green forest can provide the romantic haven you desire. With the emphasis on drama, you'll not only want to woo your beloved but your wedding guests as well. Ideal setting: Egypt; Montreal.

Wise Words: Charles Dickens: "Keep yourself cool and equal for anything that may happen, and it will be the better for you."

Hints of Love: Stop worrying about next week's date today or there will not be one tomorrow.

After the Argument: *For him:* Lavish him with attention. Bring him nice things that are not too overwhelming. Charm him into being that cuddly guy you love. *For her:* A little more stroking than usual. Tickets to a show or even the right evening at home could work.

Romantic Places: Places of movement bring romance: Dublin; an amusement park; Seattle, Washington.

Lucky Love Star: Libriel—you will never lack serenity.

Beautiful Thought: I haven't yet concluded what it is we have found in each other, but I know it is definitely good.

Sharing Secrets: You had better be ready to have a relationship. *For the gals:* No lies, no games, and no mistakes. She wants what she wants with as little work possible. *For the guys:* If you have games on your mind, then move on. This one likes fun any way he can get it, but no emotional roller coasters.

Judith's Insights

About the Man: The best way to get to this man's heart is to be consistent. This is true even if he only wants to be friends. Don't take that as a Not Interested sign. He needs for all relationships to grow over time. You have to gain his trust, and he wants to gain yours. If things are not equal, then they won't happen. He needs to be sure that your intentions are real and sincere. It is then that he will give you the best he has inside. He needs a sounding board in order to succeed in other aspects of his life.

About the Woman: This gal will go after what she wants. I know that she may look like the shy and quiet type. She can be that, but also quite the opposite as the situation demands. When it comes to love or business, she won't let obstacles stand in her way of getting exactly what she wants. She will fight hard to make any commitment she has made last a lifetime. As long as you don't take her for granted she will be around for a long time to come. She is a great listener and does not respond unless she feels she has something of substance to say.

Soul Mates: You and a fellow Libra will get along as if you have known each other forever. A partnership with Scorpio and Sagittarius can be a dream made real. Capricorn and Aries tend to move way too fast, and may have you feeling overlooked. Aquarius and Gemini will do all that they can to make the relationship last for a long time. Cancer will bring out a lot of insecurities you forgot were there. Leo and Virgo are on your side all the way and never hesitate to tell you that. Pisces and Taurus can hamper your freedom and make you feel strangled.

Most Charming Characteristics: Charming, gracious, loyal.

Gifts: *For her:* day at a botanical garden. *For him:* cooking class.

Sensual Foods: Toasted marshmallows; chocolates.

Romantic Flowers: These ladies like everyone to know how faithful they are, so send them violets. To surprise them send tulips. Men like their flowers the same as their relationships, unpretending. Send them camellias with white roses to show your affection.

Best Date Nights: Friday; 3rd and 12th of each month.

Colors of Passion: *For her:* scarlet, crimson. *For him:* black, brown.

The Perfect Wedding: You are a lover of art and intrigued by exoticism; you might consider an art gallery or museum as the place you take your vows. A grand hotel-ballroom-turned-paradise or lush green forest can provide the romantic haven you desire. With the emphasis on drama, you'll not only want to woo your beloved but your wedding guests as well. Ideal setting: Egypt; Montreal.

Wise Words: Henry Wadsworth Longfellow: "Filled is Life's goblet to the brim; / And though my eyes with tears are dim, I see its sparkling bubbles swim, / And chant a melancholy hymn / With solemn voice and slow."

Hints of Love: Keep the romance in the picture.

Don't forget the long walks on the beach and camping out in front of the fireplace.

After the Argument: *For him:* Lavish him with attention. Bring him nice things that are not too overwhelming. Charm him into being that cuddly guy you love. *For her:* A little more stroking than usual. Tickets to a show or even the right evening at home could work.

Romantic Places: Places of movement bring romance: London; the theater; Las Vegas, Nevada.

Lucky Love Star: Libriel—you will never lack serenity.

Beautiful Thought: Those who reap for all the rest deserve to have all the best.

Sharing Secrets: You may have to give this one more than one chance. *For the gals:* Intriguing as she is, expect a handful. She lightens up as time goes on. *For the guys:* His quirks may make you have second thoughts, but that is what separates the men from the boys.

Judith's Insights

About the Man: He feels as if he has to be the one to handle everything. Although it may take time for him to allow you to help him, he will eventually. At first, he can be taken aback by a phone call. Once he gets used to it he will expect the calls on a regular basis. If he lets you in it is a sure sign that he won't let you go. He is known for burying his head in the sand when things are going wrong instead of facing them. He can be so loyal that others will go out of their way to become a part of his life.

About the Woman: You may have a hard time reading if this girl is happy or not. She keeps her emotions to herself. She can be a procrastinator. If you are waiting for her to show signs of interest, you might as well just go for it and ask her. Take that step instead of waiting for her to. You might be waiting forever. She is an eternal optimist and holds on to the hope that everything will turn around in time. Try to help her see reality for what it is while not wrecking her optimism. She has many good friends because she works hard at keeping them.

Soul Mates: There is nothing better than a partnership with someone of your own sign, Libra. Scorpio and Sagittarius can be exactly what you need to spice up your life. Capricorn and Aries will leave your scales in a tangle. Aquarius and Gemini will love to love you and make you happy. Cancer will have you tied in knots in no time. Leo and Virgo will have you doing things you never thought you could until they gave you the support. Pisces and Taurus are rigid. They may try to keep you penned up like a possession.

Most Charming Characteristics: Bright, witty, entertaining.

Gifts: *For her:* friends over for dinner and a movie. *For him:* dinner at a fine restaurant.

Sensual Foods: Chocolate-covered strawberries; New York strip steak; scallops.

Romantic Flowers: These ladies like men with taste. Show them you love style by sending fuchsia flowers, or even brightly colored wildflowers will do. To confuse this man, send him lilies along with bright daisies to show your innocence. Keep him guessing.

Best Date Nights: Friday; 4th and 22nd of each month.

Colors of Passion: *For her:* lavender, violet. *For him:* black, tawny.

The Perfect Wedding: You are a lover of art and intrigued by exoticism; you might consider an art gallery or museum as the place you take your vows. A grand hotel-ballroom-turned-paradise or lush green forest can provide the romantic haven you desire. With the emphasis on drama, you'll not only want to woo your beloved but your wedding guests as well. Ideal setting: Egypt; Montreal.

Wise Words: Henry Wadsworth Longfellow: "Strange is the heart of man, with its quick, mysterious instincts."

Hints of Love: The mystery is important, but being evasive will create disaster. Make sure you know the difference.

After the Argument: *For him:* Lavish him with attention. Bring him nice things that are not too overwhelming. Charm him into being that cuddly guy you love. *For her:* A little more stroking than usual. Tickets to a show or even the right evening at home could work.

Romantic Places: Places of activity bring romance: Brazil; a carnival; Memphis, Tennessee.

Lucky Love Star: Libriel—you will never lack serenity.

Beautiful Thought: Everyone is different; the difference is you.

Sharing Secrets: Talk about high maintenance. *For the gals:* Once she sees that you go out of your way for her, then she will for you. *For the guys:* The bark is definitely much worse than the bite. He comes on stronger and more obstinate than he actually is.

Judith's Insights

About the Man: Don't get worried when you realize that a million other people are attracted to him just like you are. It is just because he has such a great personality. In a relationship, you may see a whole other side to him. He can be a bit grumpier than you first suspected. Just remember that it's his heart that you love. He might not come across as sentimental as he really is. One day you might discover that he has kept every card and gift you ever gave him. Friends and family are important to him, although he may push them away early in life.

About the Woman: This gal has plenty of friends and not enough lovers. She is easily misunderstood. She has a naturally sour look, even when she is happy. Make her laugh and you will see an entirely different side to her. Keep her laughing and you will keep her around for as long as you like. She can keep her emotions tucked away inside. It will take time to pull away the layers so she can reveal her true feelings. She will do so when she is ready. She may run away from an unpleasant situation instead of seeking to solve it.

Soul Mates: It is feast or famine with a fellow Scorpio. You will love each other or hate each other, sometimes in the same day. Capricorn and Aries will help you get a hold on all of your wonderful potential. Pisces and Gemini are hard to get used to, but once you do, things will be surpassingly good. Taurus and Cancer may not seem like your type at first, but you would be surprised at how well you end up getting along. If you remember that opposites are exciting but difficult, Aquarius and Leo will work fine. Libra and Sagittarius will do anything for you. All you have to do is ask. Virgo is too rigid for you taste.

Most Charming Characteristics: Kind, affectionate, gracious.

Gifts: *For her:* gift certificate to an on-line trader. *For him:* mutual fund.

Sensual Foods: Vanilla and strawberry mousse; tiramisù; espresso.

Romantic Flowers: You are the lady of distinction, and only carnations will do. Any mix of colors with sprays of mignonette. Sweet peas or red carnations will appeal to this man's heart.

Best Date Nights: Friday; 4th and 23rd of each month.

Colors of Passion: *For her:* violet, lavender. *For him:* brown, black.

The Perfect Wedding: Intensely passionate, you crave a wondrous, exotic environment. Emotional and magnetic, your personality lends itself to a rugged rock garden high on a hill overlooking the ocean. A beachfront wedding may well stir the excitement and emotion you desire. Ideal setting: New Orleans.

Wise Words: Henry Wadsworth Longfellow: "Goodnight! Goodnight, beloved! I come to watch o'er thee!—Alone is peace for me."

Hints of Love: If you learn to back up when things are moving too fast, you won't have to bow out so often.

After the Argument: *For him:* This will take work no matter what is wrong. Making up is always the best with this one. That's why he loves to fight. *For her:* Expect to take money out of the bank for this one. Jewelry or even a trip. It had better be good, or you will need patience.

Romantic Places: Places of suspense bring romance: Stonehenge; dinner theater; New Orleans, Louisiana.

Lucky Love Star: Scorpiel—you will never lack assertiveness and sensuality.

Beautiful Thought: Balance is the key to serenity.

Sharing Secrets: Make sure you have at least five dates before you make up your mind. *For the gals:* She can be cynical, so it could be a few dates before she loosens up. *For the guys:* He still has yesterday on his mind. He needs a reason to forget his past relationship. Make a new history for him.

Judith's Insights

About the Man: You will have to put energy into keeping this guy's attention long enough for him to get to know you. You will find a much more compassionate guy than you would have thought at the beginning. The word *selfish* may be used to describe him, but only by people who don't understand what is behind his behavior. He loves the new and exciting part of the relationship. That is why he has had so many friends and lovers. Relationships may be hard to maintain with a person who doesn't understand his need for thrill-seeking.

About the Woman: She is looking for a thrill. A date with this gal may be hot-air ballooning or scuba diving. She won't expect you to do all of the exciting things that make her happy. She will expect that you do take part in enough to be a part of her life. Otherwise, you will be on the sidelines watching. She needs to have someone who understands her eccentricities and devotion to living life to the fullest. Each moment must be filled with passion for her. Her kindness and patience will draw people to her.

Soul Mates: A fellow Scorpio could be what you need to spice things up. Capricorn and Aries will help you balance your inner self and reach even higher goals than you thought possible. Pisces and Gemini will have you dizzy from their emotional outbursts. Aquarius and Leo could work marvelously when you go in with the right attitude. Taurus and Cancer may have you looking for the Exit sign. Libra and Sagittarius are signs that can make you feel complete. Virgo has caution written all over it.

Most Charming Characteristics: Loyal, determined, tenacious.

Gifts: *For her:* savings bond. *For him:* detective novel.

Sensual Foods: Raspberries; pound cake; caviar.

Romantic Flowers: You love it when you get tulips, declaring love. When you receive a variety, it shows how hopelessly in love your partner is. He will just love a single rose. This shows him you understand his pleasures.

Best Date Nights: Tuesday; 4th and 5th of each month.

Colors of Passion: *For her:* crimson, scarlet. *For him:* tawny, beige.

The Perfect Wedding: Intensely passionate, you crave a wondrous, exotic environment. Emotional and magnetic, your personality lends itself to a rugged rock garden high on a hill overlooking the ocean. A beachfront wedding may well stir the excitement and emotion you desire. Ideal setting: New Orleans.

Wise Words: Oliver Wendell Holmes: "He rests by the storm-swept waves, whose life while tempest roughly tried, whose heart was like streaming caves of ocean throbbing at his side."

Hints of Love: Expecting too much too soon can only build up hopes that will fall down too easily.

After the Argument: *For him:* This will take work no matter what is wrong. Making up is always the best with this one. That's why he loves to fight. *For her:* Expect to take money out of the bank for this one. Jewelry or even a trip. It had better be good, or you will need patience.

Romantic Places: Places of mystery bring romance: the Bermuda Triangle; a train ride; Roswell, New Mexico.

Lucky Love Star: Scorpiel—you will never lack assertiveness and sensuality.

Beautiful Thought: Seven reasons for living every day of the week.

Sharing Secrets: Don't be in a hurry, or it will be over before it begins. *For the gals:* Like fine wine and amazing food. Savor a moment until an hour is created. *For the guys:* To do too much too fast will prove risky. Try to give a push and he will just jump ship.

Judith's Insights

About the Man: He will question your kindness as well as your loyalty. You must prove to him that you are sincere at every turn. Don't take it personally. This guy can be a skeptic through and through. If you want to fight for it, you have to be ready to be consistent in proving him wrong. He is a romantic at heart. You just won't be able to see that side of him until you have taken time to get to know him inside and out.

About the Woman: Just show up at this girl's house in the middle of the winter with a picnic basket for two. That may not only get her attention, but get her to want more as well. She loves spontaneity to be a large part of her life. Make things exciting for her and she will love you for it. You might have already noticed, but she is more unconventional than anyone else. Hanging with her is like being at a carnival every day.

Soul Mates: It is feast or famine with a fellow Scorpio. You will love each other or hate each other, sometimes in the same day. Capricorn and Aries will help you get a hold on all of your wonderful potential. Pisces and Gemini are hard to get used to, but once you do, things will be surpassingly good. Taurus and Cancer may not seem like your type at first, but you would be surprised at how well you end up getting along. Libra and Sagittarius will do anything for you. All you have to do is ask. Virgo is too rigid for you taste.

Most Charming Characteristics: Good sense of humor, proud, determined.

Gifts: *For her:* put her on a treasure hunt. *For him:* tickets to the car races.

Sensual Foods: Flambé; lobster; oysters.

Romantic Flowers: Send this girl sunflowers if you want her to know you adore her. You may even add some poppies for a splash of extravagance. His desire for sport and play will be understood when you send him hyacinth and geranium.

Best Date Nights: Tuesday, 6th and 15th of each month.

Colors of Passion: *For her:* violet, scarlet. *For him:* brown, beige.

The Perfect Wedding: Intensely passionate, you crave a wondrous, exotic environment. Emotional and magnetic, your personality lends itself to a rugged rock garden high on a hill overlooking the ocean. A beachfront wedding may well stir the excitement and emotion you desire. Ideal setting: New Orleans.

Wise Words: Oliver Wendell Holmes: "Marvel to get their message to mankind, in his own verse, the poet still we find. In his own page his memory lies enshrined."

Hints of Love: Make sure all the ingredients are present before putting the cake in the oven.

After the Argument: *For him:* This will take work no matter what is wrong. Making up is always the best with this one. That's why he loves to fight. *For her:* Expect to take money out of the bank for this one. Jewelry or even a trip. It had better be good, or you will need patience.

Romantic Places: Places of suspense bring romance: Ireland; a suspense film; the Alamo, Texas.

Lucky Love Star: Scorpiel—you will never lack assertiveness and sensuality.

Beautiful Thought: When you are feeling down, dress up.

Sharing Secrets: They need to look before they leap, but only in love. *For the gals:* She needs creative and exciting dates to keep her interested. Don't take her for granted too soon. *For the guys:* You may think he gives signs of moving this relationship quickly; make sure you slow it down before he does.

Judith's Insights

About the Man: Most of his words live in his mind and never make it out of his mouth. Even when he falls in love it will take him time to come to terms with it. He loves romance but can't tell you that right away. He will keep his emotions so well hidden that sometimes even he does not know how he feels. After you have proven yourself beyond a shadow of a doubt you may be allowed to enter his inner circle.

About the Woman: If you see her sitting and staring out into space it is not because she is bored. She is really thinking long and hard about someone or something. This gal takes a long time to get over things. She is much too serious. When she has a balanced love in her life she becomes much more balanced herself. Her nature is to block change and to keep the door shut tight. She won't answer the door until you have shown your credentials.

Soul Mates: Only another Scorpio could understand you so well. When you are linked to Capricorn and Aries, you will feel at home and safe. Pisces and Gemini will push your buttons to see what makes you tick. Aquarius and Leo could be the most wonderful people in your life if you let them. Taurus and Cancer are not up your alley at first. Then they will suddenly grow on you and you will be lost without them. Libra and Sagittarius will make life easy with them. Virgo can drive you crazy if you let them. Step back for a breath occasionally.

Most Charming Characteristics: Artistic, well read, personable, likable.

Gifts: *For her:* personal organizer. *For him:* chess set.

Sensual Foods: Crème brûlée; poached salmon.

Romantic Flowers: Rhododendron will let her be on the lookout for trouble. Throw in some chrysanthemum and she'll know it is you she will be looking out for. Cactus will show him warmth. Yellow daffodil is a token of a good time had by all. Chivalry is not dead.

Best Date Nights: Tuesday; 5th and 23rd of each month.

Colors of Passion: *For her:* violet, scarlet. *For him:* brown, beige.

The Perfect Wedding: Intensely passionate, you crave a wondrous, exotic environment. Emotional and magnetic, your personality lends itself to a rugged rock garden high on a hill overlooking the ocean. A beachfront wedding may well stir the excitement and emotion you desire. Ideal setting: New Orleans.

Wise Words: Marie Curie: "We cannot hope to build a better world without improving the individual. Towards this end, each of us must work towards his own highest development, accepting . . . his share of responsibility in the general life of humanity."

Hints of Love: Simple often turns into compli-cated with this one. When you overcomplicate the moment, try to step back for a breather.

After the Argument: *For him:* This will take work no matter what is wrong. Making up is always the best with this one. That's why he loves to fight. *For her:* Expect to take money out of the bank for this one. Jewelry or even a trip. It had better be good, or you will need patience.

Romantic Places: Places of mystery bring romance: Venezuela; an Indian reservation; Devil's Tower, Wyoming.

Lucky Love Star: Scorpiel—you will never lack assertiveness and sensuality.

Beautiful Thought: Sometimes you have to go back out to get back in.

Sharing Secrets: The possibilities are endless, if you can pay the price. *For the gals:* She is hoping chivalry is not dead, and you must be willing to be the man at all costs. *For the guys:* He can be demanding and somewhat controlling. He just needs to be trained.

Judith's Insights

About the Man: To catch this one you need a tremendous amount of patience. Don't try to tell him when he is falling in love. He will run as fast as he can in the opposite direction. He will come back when he is ready to face his emotions. Expect to see the yo-yo syndrome in action with this guy. He is looking for a mate who can understand his need to be constantly entertained. It is in his nature to have as many friends around as possible.

About the Woman: She plays the part of an independent and unromantic woman. She may even pretend that gifts are not necessary. That may work in the beginning. Once you have a real relationship with her you will find that things have changed and you weren't made aware of the changes. There will always be something new that she wants to try or wants to get. In the same breath she will tell you how much she despises change!

Soul Mates: Things with a fellow Scorpio will be smooth as silk or hard as rock. There can be no in-between. Capricorn and Aries will keep you grounded while letting you fly as high as you need to. Pisces and Gemini will be hard to take at times. Let yourself step back when you feel the anger building. Aquarius and Leo will give new meaning to you. Taurus and Cancer take getting used to before you can become wrapped up in their charm. Libra and Sagittarius will make you happy if you would only let them. Virgo is a no-no if you want to keep your sanity.

Most Charming Characteristics: Affectionate, demonstrative, forgiving.

Gifts: *For her:* tuition to an art class. *For him:* pilot lessons.

Sensual Foods: Chocolate soufflé; filet mignon.

Romantic Flowers: The magnolias you send her will let her know you will be around for a while to come. Petunia is to say never despair. Holly will let him know what he is getting into. Pansy will keep you in his thoughts.

Best Date Nights: Tuesday; 9th and 27th of each month.

Colors of Passion: *For her:* violet, scarlet. *For him:* brown, beige.

The Perfect Wedding: Intensely passionate, you crave a wondrous, exotic environment. Emotional and magnetic, your personality lends itself to a rugged rock garden high on a hill overlooking the ocean. A beachfront wedding may well stir the excitement and emotion you desire. Ideal setting: New Orleans.

Wise Words: Oliver Wendell Holmes: "Faith always implies the disbelief of a lesser fact in favor of a greater. A little mind often sees the unbelief, without seeing the belief of a large one."

Hints of Love: Allow them to know what is in your heart as well as what is in your head.

After the Argument: *For him:* This will take work no matter what is wrong. Making up is always the best with this one. That's why he loves to fight. *For her:* Expect to take money out of the bank for this one. Jewelry or even a trip. It had better be good, or you will need patience.

Romantic Places: Places of suspense bring romance: Scotland; a haunted house; Niagara Falls, New York.

Lucky Love Star: Scorpiel—you will never lack assertiveness and sensuality.

Beautiful Thought: Harmony is feeling love in our hearts and joy in our souls.

Sharing Secrets: Tomorrow is another day, but why wait? You can do it all today. *For the gals:* Have your date filled from dusk to dawn, and then some. *For the guys:* You may find he needs a nap here and there, but he can last all day and all night if he has a reason.

Judith's Insights

About the Man: This guy makes a much better date than a husband. On dates he will be constantly looking for something new and exciting to do. When he makes a commitment, he becomes much more of a couch potato. Get him off that couch and back out into the world where he belongs. Remind him of his carefree days by bringing him to his old haunts. He attracts many people around him but has the tendency to let the wind out of the sails too easily.

About the Woman: Her career is important to her, or so she wants to believe. This gal is really a hopeless romantic at heart. She will almost always keep a journal. Don't let her defensive nature keep you away. You may notice that she will become increasingly nervous the closer you get to knowing the real her. Her need for excitement gets her to quit when things slow down. You don't have to keep her flying around, just teach her to enjoy the quiet moments as well.

Soul Mates: A fellow Scorpio could be what you need to spice things up. Capricorn and Aries will help you balance your inner self and reach even higher goals than you thought possible. Pisces and Gemini will have you dizzy from their emotional outbursts. Aquarius and Leo could work marvelously when you go in with the right attitude. Taurus and Cancer may have you looking for the Exit sign. Libra and Sagittarius are signs that can make you feel complete. Virgo has caution written all over it.

Most Charming Characteristics: Generous, light-hearted, sweet-tempered.

Gifts: *For her:* aromatherapy gift set. *For him:* leather journal.

Sensual Foods: Steak au poivre; cheesecake.

Romantic Flowers: Iris is your flower if you are the gal sending subtle messages. If you are the man, you will look for clematis. This flower's mental beauty creates emotional stimulation for you.

Best Date Nights: Tuesday; 4th and 23rd of each month.

Colors of Passion: *For her:* violet, scarlet. *For him:* brown, beige.

The Perfect Wedding: Intensely passionate, you crave a wondrous, exotic environment. Emotional and magnetic, your personality lends itself to a rugged rock garden high on a hill overlooking the ocean. A beachfront wedding may well stir the excitement and emotion you desire. Ideal setting: New Orleans.

Wise Words: Henry Wadsworth Longfellow: "Encamped beside life's rushing stream, in Fancy's misty light, gigantic shapes and shadows gleam portentous through the night."

Hints of Love: Keep both feet on the ground the first time you think you want to jump. This way you won't jump too high too soon.

After the Argument: *For him:* This will take work no matter what is wrong. Making up is always the best with this one. That's why he loves to fight. *For her:* Expect to take money out of the bank for this one. Jewelry or even a trip. It had better be good, or you will need patience.

Romantic Places: Places of mystery bring romance: Aztec ruins; dinner cruise; Salem, Massachusetts.

Lucky Love Star: Scorpiel—you will never lack assertiveness and sensuality.

Beautiful Thought: Paying attention could be your least expensive toll.

Sharing Secrets: It may need to start with friendship. This isn't the consolation prize; it's the grand prize. *For the gals:* Go slowly and allow it to grow one seed at a time. You won't need to push; it will all come in time. *For the guys:* A step here and a step there. Before he knows it, that friendship will be love.

Judith's Insights

About the Man: This guy is a dating master. By the time he settles down he will have many stories to tell about the good old days. Just don't let him revel in old memories for too long. Make new memories by getting him out of the house and on some real adventures. If you let him get serious he will remain so. Get him to laugh like the good old days. He will soon get back in touch with the part of himself that just wants to have fun.

About the Woman: This lady has no problem capturing the hearts of others. It is keeping those hearts that she has problems with. Deciding whether or not she wants to take it to the next stage can be nearly impossible. If you like her, let her know. If you love her, take your time so she has time to get used to the idea. When she has no commitment in her life she will be out doing all that she can to enjoy life. When she has settled down she may become way too serious.

Soul Mates: You and another Scorpio is exactly what the doctor ordered to cure a gray day. With Capricorn and Aries behind you, there is no telling where you will go. Pisces and Gemini are not something you like to deal with. Move on or you will feel anger build up inside. Aquarius and Leo have great potential for fine things to come. Taurus and Cancer will have you wringing your own neck. Libra and Sagittarius will fill the void you don't like to admit is there. Virgo is not advisable if you want to keep your sanity.

Most Charming Characteristics: Accurate, careful, conservative.

Gifts: *For her:* vacation near the water. *For him:* tour of caves.

Sensual Foods: Strawberry shortcake; pineapple; ham.

Romantic Flowers: Any rose of any color for the lady. Roses stand for love regardless of the color. Send them with orchids and you will be saying, "I love you." If you want a gentleman to know you think of him, send pansies, and forget-me-nots for true love.

Best Date Nights: Tuesday; 2nd and 11th of each month.

Colors of Passion: *For her:* violet, scarlet. *For him:* brown, beige.

The Perfect Wedding: Intensely passionate, you crave a wondrous, exotic environment. Emotional and magnetic, your personality lends itself to a rugged rock garden high on a hill overlooking the ocean. A beachfront wedding may well stir the excitement and emotion you desire. Ideal setting: New Orleans.

Wise Words: Henry Wadsworth Longfellow: "All around him was calm, but within him commotion and conflict, / Love contending with friendship, and self with each generous impulse."

Hints of Love: Laughter alleviates the tension, but so can understanding where another is sitting.

After the Argument: *For him:* This will take work no matter what is wrong. Making up is always the best with this one. That's why he loves to fight. *For her:* Expect to take money out of the bank for this one. Jewelry or even a trip. It had better be good, or you will need patience.

Romantic Places: Places of suspense bring romance: Mexico; a magic show; Savannah, Georgia.

Lucky Love Star: Scorpiel—you will never lack assertiveness and sensuality.

Beautiful Thought: Turning the pages gives you more answers.

Sharing Secrets: This one needs to be the one and only, even if it is only the first date. *For the gals:* Don't talk about your past relationships. Do all you can to make her feel cherished from the first moment. *For the guys:* Play up your innocence. Let him take charge, even in paying the bill. He needs to wear the pants.

Judith's Insights

About the Man: This guy is a stud muffin in every way. His conquests will add up until he finds someone to settle down with. This will take time. Don't rush this guy or you will be sorry. He will think that he has his emotions under control when it fact he probably never does. Strong emotions can scare him into being aloof. He enjoys being in a relationship. He just may have too many going all at once. He may overdo in the socializing department.

About the Woman: She is not looking for someone with special style, but for someone up-front she can have a good time with. The only problem is that most people read her wrong and think that she is only out to have fun at any expense. That can be true, but only for the moment. Once she commits, it is all the way. Allow her the room to socialize while still having a relationship that will connect you permanently to her heart.

Soul Mates: Only another Scorpio could understand you so well. When you are linked to Capricorn and Aries, you will feel at home and safe. Pisces and Gemini will push your buttons to see what makes you tick. Aquarius and Leo could be the most wonderful people in your life if you let them. Taurus and Cancer are not up your alley at first. Then they will suddenly grow on you, and you will be lost without them. Libra and Sagittarius will make life easy with them. Virgo can drive you crazy if you let them. Step back for a breath occasionally.

Most Charming Characteristics: Independent, sagacious, self-confident.

Gifts: *For her:* serenity rock garden. *For him:* personal organizer.

Sensual Foods: Steak fondue; cheese fondue and French bread.

Romantic Flowers: These ladies like everyone to know how faithful they are, so send them violets. To surprise them send tulips. Men like their flowers the same as their relationships, unpretending. Send them camellias with white roses to show your affection.

Best Date Nights: Tuesday; 4th and 5th of each month.

Colors of Passion: *For her:* violet, scarlet. *For him:* brown, beige.

The Perfect Wedding: Intensely passionate, you crave a wondrous, exotic environment. Emotional and magnetic, your personality lends itself to a rugged rock garden high on a hill overlooking the ocean. A beachfront wedding may well stir the excitement and emotion you desire. Ideal setting: New Orleans.

Wise Words: Henry Wadsworth Longfellow: "Now be strong, be strong, my heart!"

Hints of Love: Communication is important here. A script isn't provided for you. You must write it for yourself.

After the Argument: *For him:* This will take work no matter what is wrong. Making up is always the best with this one. That's why he loves to fight. *For her:* Expect to take money out of the bank for this one. Jewelry or even a trip. It had better be good, or you will need patience.

Romantic Places: Places of mystery bring romance: Bermuda; the theater; New Orleans, Louisiana.

Lucky Love Star: Scorpiel—you will never lack assertiveness and sensuality.

Beautiful Thought: Because there are differences, and not all can be right, those who do love will also have to fight.

Sharing Secrets: You need to remember never to forget. *For the gals:* Her birthday, holidays, and your anniversary. Even down to each dinner date. *For the guys:* His birthday, his laundry, his mother's birthday, and, of course, him any other day of the year.

Judith's Insights

About the Man: This man has strong principles. You just might not see them put into use in his love life. He can be complex but he has a sensual side that craves someone to be in his life forever. He will, however, fight commitment all the way. His emotions are a battleground for this guy. You may think that it is easy for him to have so much attention. This is not true when he has low self-esteem. It is then that he will misread all of the attention as bad.

About the Woman: She likes to be in love just for the sake of being in love. The only question is, will it last? This girl will have plenty of firsts in her life, but only one last. Having stamina would help to hang with this gal. If you are consistent you will remain on her mind when it comes down to finding her last mate. The more comfortable she becomes with herself the easier the conflicts in her relationships will be to get through.

Soul Mates: There may be power struggles with another Scorpio, but if you work through them, you will be the richer for it. Capricorn and Aries will keep you in line without limiting your potential. Pisces and Gemini will push you to see how far they can go. If you feel yourself losing control, it would be better to step away. Taurus and Cancer will pull you in, although you fight it along the way. Libra and Sagittarius will do anything to make you happy. Don't take advantage of them. You may have to fight to make things work with Aquarius and Leo, but you may be all the richer for the struggle. Virgo will have you pulling your hair out at times. They are just hard to get used to.

Most Charming Characteristics: Compassionate, unshockable, dynamic.

Gifts: *For her:* detective or gossip novel. *For him:* a writing class.

Sensual Foods: Baked Alaska; seafood.

Romantic Flowers: These ladies like men with taste. Show them you love style by sending fuchsia flowers, or even brightly colored wildflowers will do. To confuse this man, send him lilies along with bright daisies to show your innocence. Keep him guessing.

Best Date Nights: Tuesday; 4th and 23rd of each month.

Colors of Passion: *For her:* violet, scarlet. *For him:* brown, beige.

The Perfect Wedding: Intensely passionate, you crave a wondrous, exotic environment. Emotional and magnetic, your personality lends itself to a rugged rock garden high on a hill overlooking the ocean. A beachfront wedding may well stir the excitement and emotion you desire. Ideal setting: New Orleans.

Wise Words: Henry Wadsworth Longfellow: "As unto the bow the cord is, So unto the man is woman: Though she bends him, she obeys him, though she draws him, yet she follows, / Useless each without the other."

Hints of Love: Don't dissect every minute of every day. Learn to appreciate each minute as it comes.

After the Argument: *For him:* This will take work no matter what is wrong. Making up is always the best with this one. That's why he loves to fight. *For her:* Expect to take money out of the bank for this one. Jewelry or even a trip. It had better be good, or you will need patience.

Romantic Places: Places of suspense bring romance: England; a castle tour; Salem, Massachusetts.

Lucky Love Star: Scorpiel—you will never lack assertiveness and sensuality.

Beautiful Thought: Love is wanting the best for someone you love, even when it does not include you.

Sharing Secrets: My house should be your house, especially if you don't have one of your own. *For the gals:* All for one and one for all. Yours and mine must become ours. *For the guys:* If he needs to stand on ceremony, even for the first five minutes, it will be a definite turnoff for this one.

Judith's Insights

About the Man: He wants to be in love. It just takes him a lifetime to find that out. He is easy to please as long as you do what he wants to do. There can be a laundry list of things that he likes, so you will never be bored. As a matter of fact, boredom never enters the picture when you are hanging with this guy. Take trips to new places or eat in restaurants to avoid his seemingly constant search for something to disagree about.

About the Woman: Here is a gal who knows just what she wants. That is, until she changes her mind. Her loyalty usually outweighs her ability to flee her current relationship. If you treat her badly, that will be the reason she is looking to flee and find something new on the horizon. She will try to keep the relationship a bit off balance to keep things interesting and exciting. If she becomes bored she will start looking for things to fight about.

NOVEMBER

Soul Mates: A fellow Scorpio could be what you need to spice things up. Capricorn and Aries will help you balance your inner self and reach even higher goals than you thought possible. Pisces and Gemini will have you dizzy from their emotional outbursts. Aquarius and Leo could work marvelously when you go in with the right attitude. Taurus and Cancer may have you looking for the Exit sign. Libra and Sagittarius are signs that can make you feel complete. Virgo has caution written all over it.

Most Charming Characteristics: Inquisitive, capable, trustworthy.

Gifts: *For her:* gift certificate to on-line trader. *For him:* mutual fund.

Sensual Foods: Strawberries and cream; meat loaf.

Romantic Flowers: Iris is your flower if you are the gal sending subtle messages. If you are the man, you will look for clematis. This flower's mental beauty creates emotional stimulation for you.

Best Date Nights: Tuesday; 4th and 5th of each month.

Colors of Passion: *For her:* violet, scarlet. *For him:* brown, beige.

The Perfect Wedding: Intensely passionate, you crave a wondrous, exotic environment. Emotional and magnetic, your personality lends itself to a rugged rock garden high on a hill overlooking the ocean. A beachfront wedding may well stir the excitement and emotion you desire. Ideal setting: New Orleans.

Wise Words: Henry Wadsworth Longfellow: "With a sober gladness the old year takes up / His bright inheritance of golden fruits."

Hints of Love: They only use the three magic words when they know they mean it, and they already know it is going to be said back to them.

After the Argument: *For him:* This will take work no matter what is wrong. Making up is always the best with this one. That's why he loves to fight. *For her:* Expect to take money out of the bank for this one. Jewelry or even a trip. It had better be good, or you will need patience.

Romantic Places: Places of suspense bring romance: Stonehenge; dinner theater; New Orleans, Louisiana.

Lucky Love Star: Scorpiel—you will never lack assertiveness and sensuality.

Beautiful Thought: Having the patience to allow all your dreams to come true.

Sharing Secrets: Let them admire something about you first. Show them you have a sense of humor. *For the gals:* Hold their hand and then take them to the next step. *For the guys:* The way to his heart is definitely through his stomach.

Judith's Insights

About the Man: This is a date who really knows how to have a good time. Don't ask him too many questions about his past. He plays his hand close to his heart and does not let too many people in. He wants to be paid attention to. The more attention he receives, the better the mood he will be in. Just do not push for too much to be returned too soon. The balancing of the relationship will come without your ever noticing a change.

About the Woman: This gal is temperamental. The good news is, she knows it. The bad news is, she might not care at times. She has a habit of complaining just to complain. You can get used to it after a while. When she gets settled into the relationship, the best of her comes out. This gal does not like to be left hanging, so if you are not interested, move on. If you are interested, then move right in before she moves away.

Soul Mates: You and another Scorpio is exactly what the doctor ordered to cure a gray day. With Capricorn and Aries behind you, there is no telling where you will go. Pisces and Gemini are not something you like to deal with. Move on or you will feel anger build up inside. Aquarius and Leo have great potential for fine things to come. Taurus and Cancer will have you wringing your own neck. Libra and Sagittarius will fill the void you don't like to admit is there. Virgo is not advisable if you want to keep your sanity.

Most Charming Characteristics: Affectionate, charitable, adaptable.

Gifts: *For her:* savings bond. *For him:* detective novel.

Sensual Foods: Cherry-apple pie; beef Stroganoff.

Romantic Flowers: Any rose of any color for the lady. Roses stand for love regardless of the color. Send them with orchids and you will be saying, "I love you." If you want a gentleman to know you think of him, send pansies, and forget-me-nots for true love.

Best Date Nights: Tuesday; 2nd and 20th of each month.

Colors of Passion: *For her:* violet, scarlet. *For him:* brown, beige.

The Perfect Wedding: Intensely passionate, you crave a wondrous, exotic environment. Emotional and magnetic, your personality lends itself to a rugged rock garden high on a hill overlooking the ocean. A beachfront wedding may well stir the excitement and emotion you desire. Ideal setting: New Orleans.

Wise Words: Henry Wadsworth Longfellow: "This goblet, wrought with curious art, / Is filled with waters that upstart, / When the deep fountains of the heart, / By strong convulsions rent apart, / Are running all to waste."

Hints of Love: Remember to keep the dating fun. Don't act like you are married before your time.

After the Argument: *For him:* This will take work no matter what is wrong. Making up is always the best with this one. That's why he loves to fight. *For her:* Expect to take money out of the bank for this one. Jewelry or even a trip. It had better be good, or you will need patience.

Romantic Places: Places of mystery bring romance: the Bermuda Triangle; a train ride; Roswell, New Mexico.

Lucky Love Star: Scorpiel—you will never lack assertiveness and sensuality.

Beautiful Thought: I give to you, so you will have a piece of me.

Sharing Secrets: Give them the opportunity to notice you first. *For the gals:* They love to be adored; love at first sight. *For the guys:* Remember to always let them believe it was their idea.

Judith's Insights

About the Man: He will date you and say that he will be with you forever, and you still may not know whether to call him your boyfriend or not. He certainly has a way of keeping the challenge going. This guy has more experience than most and is known to play a lot of games. Proceed with caution until you know he is giving you the green light. When he is sure that things can go to the next step he will let you know where the traps are and the safe path bends.

About the Woman: This gal has high hopes and certainly intends to fulfill them the best she can. This is true not only in work but also in play. She has a picture in her mind of what it is she wants. She needs to at least attempt to fulfill her wish list. She will want you to respond to her wishes as if you were both in the movies. Sometimes, she will have forgotten to give you the script, but won't hesitate to say you are doing it wrong.

Soul Mates: Only another Scorpio could understand you so well. When you are linked to Capricorn and Aries, you will feel at home and safe. Pisces and Gemini will push your buttons to see what makes you tick. Aquarius and Leo could be the most wonderful people in your life if you let them. Taurus and Cancer are not up your alley at first. Then they will suddenly grow on you and you will be lost without them. Libra and Sagittarius will make life easy with them. Virgo can drive you crazy if you let them. Step back for a breath occasionally.

Most Charming Characteristics: Generous, kind, giving.

Gifts: *For her:* put her on a treasure hunt. *For him:* tickets to the car races.

Sensual Foods: Hot fudge sundae with all the trimmings; shepherd's pie.

Romantic Flowers: These ladies like everyone to know how faithful they are, so send them violets. To surprise them send tulips. Men like their flowers the same as their relationships, unpretending. Send them camellias with white roses to show your affection.

Best Date Nights: Tuesday; 5th and 23rd of each month.

Colors of Passion: *For her:* violet, scarlet. *For him:* brown, beige.

The Perfect Wedding: Intensely passionate, you crave a wondrous, exotic environment. Emotional and magnetic, your personality lends itself to a rugged rock garden high on a hill overlooking the ocean. A beachfront wedding may well stir the excitement and emotion you desire. Ideal setting: New Orleans.

Wise Words: Henry Wadsworth Longfellow: "It has been truly said by some wise man, / That money, grief, and love cannot be hidden."

Hints of Love: Make sure you go on more than one date before you jump to conclusions on liking and disliking.

After the Argument: *For him:* This will take work no matter what is wrong. Making up is always the best with this one. That's why he loves to fight. *For her:* Expect to take money out of the bank for this one. Jewelry or even a trip. It had better be good, or you will need patience.

Romantic Places: Places of suspense bring romance: Ireland; a suspense film; the Alamo, Texas.

Lucky Love Star: Scorpiel—you will never lack assertiveness and sensuality.

Beautiful Thought: A successful person always looks at what is ahead, but never forgets who was behind.

Sharing Secrets: This one loves a challenge. *For the gals:* Be consistently inconsistent until you have them hooked. *For the guys:* This one loves to play catch. You may feel like a yo-yo, but as long as he is calling that's all that matters.

Judith's Insights

About the Man: He can be like a jackrabbit, jumping in and out of your life. You will never know when he will pop up like a groundhog. He will remind you of a rat if you corner him, and a tiger when he is mad, but this guy is really a pussycat with multiple disguises. If he is not ready for love, don't expect to kiss him and have him be your prince. Let him come to the realization that things are fine right where he is and that he doesn't have to chase the dream anymore.

About the Woman: This girl can write romance novels in her head. If you want to get to her heart, start with the depth of her mind. Play games. You start a sentence and have her finish it. This will not only tell you where her head is but if there is room in it for you. Appeal to her weakness, romance, instead of bringing out her strength, defense. She needs to be the one and only on your mind, especially when you are both surrounded by other people.

Soul Mates: There may be power struggles with another Scorpio, but if you work through them, you will be the richer for it. Capricorn and Aries will keep you in line without limiting your potential. Pisces and Gemini will push you to see how far they can go. If you feel yourself losing control, it would be better to step away. Taurus and Cancer will pull you in, although you fight it along the way. Libra and Aquarius will do anything to make you happy. Don't take advantage of them. Sagittarius can make your heart skip a beat. Leo may be more work than you had planned on. Virgo will have you pulling your hair out at times. They are just hard to get used to.

Most Charming Characteristics: Trustworthy, dependable, confident.

Gifts: *For her:* personal organizer. *For him:* chess set.

Sensual Foods: Whipped cream, strawberries, brown sugar, and heavy cream.

Romantic Flowers: These ladies like men with taste. Show them you love style by sending fuchsia flowers, or even brightly colored wildflowers will do. To confuse this man, send him lilies along with bright daisies to show your innocence. Keep him guessing.

Best Date Nights: Tuesday; 4th and 13th of each month.

Colors of Passion: *For her:* violet, scarlet. *For him:* brown, beige.

The Perfect Wedding: Intensely passionate, you crave a wondrous, exotic environment. Emotional and magnetic, your personality lends itself to a rugged rock garden high on a hill overlooking the ocean. A beachfront wedding may well stir the excitement and emotion you desire. Ideal setting: New Orleans.

Wise Words: Henry Wadsworth Longfellow: "Above thy head through rifted clouds there shines a glorious start. Be patient, trust thy star."

Hints of Love: Don't act too needy too soon. It may push this relationship away.

After the Argument: *For him:* This will take work no matter what is wrong. Making up is always the best with this one. That's why he loves to fight. *For her:* Expect to take money out of the bank for this one. Jewelry or even a trip. It had better be good, or you will need patience.

Romantic Places: Places of mystery bring romance: Venezuela; an Indian reservation; Devil's Tower, Wyoming.

Lucky Love Star: Scorpiel—you will never lack assertiveness and sensuality.

Beautiful Thought: Reminiscing brings more smiles than the original moments themselves.

Sharing Secrets: This is a family person at heart; your presence is most important. *For the gals:* Make sure you go to Sunday dinner with her family when you are invited. *For the guys:* If you don't like his mom, you might have a hard time catching this one.

Judith's Insights

About the Man: Here he is, Charming Charlie. He is as lovable as any pet you may ever have. He listens well, even loves to shop. He prefers to do it for himself, but won't mind spending his dollar on you. He will match your generosity if he can, although he can come off like he is cheap, especially in the beginning of a relationship. He is just feeling things out before he makes an investment of money and heart.

About the Woman: The way she handles herself you may think that this gal is out of your league. She carries herself with class, and as if she had a million bucks. You will find she is no follower and would prefer to go about life in her own style. She is looking for a mate who is willing to do the work to have a compatible relationship. She goes deeper than sex appeal. She can possess the things you love to hate, but she will keep your life exciting.

Soul Mates: It is feast or famine with a fellow Scorpio. You will love each other or hate each other, sometimes in the same day. Capricorn and Aries will help you get a hold on all of your wonderful potential. Pisces and Gemini are hard to get used to, but once you do, things will be surpassingly good. Taurus and Cancer may not seem like your type at first, but you would be surprised at how well you end up getting along. Sagittarius can keep up with you like few others. If you are ready to pull up your sleeves and work, you may have a great reward with Leo. Libra and Aquarius will do anything for you. All you have to do is ask. Virgo is too rigid for you taste.

Most Charming Characteristics: Enthusiastic, optimistic, generous.

Gifts: *For her:* tuition to an art class. *For him:* pilot lessons.

Sensual Foods: Puddings and pastry of all kinds.

Romantic Flowers: You are the lady of distinction, and only carnations will do. Any mix of colors with sprays of mignonette. Sweet peas or red carnations will appeal to this man's heart.

Best Date Nights: Tuesday; 4th and 5th of each month.

Colors of Passion: *For her:* violet, scarlet. *For him:* brown, beige.

The Perfect Wedding: Intensely passionate, you crave a wondrous, exotic environment. Emotional and magnetic, your personality lends itself to a rugged rock garden high on a hill overlooking the ocean. A beachfront wedding may well stir the excitement and emotion you desire. Ideal setting: New Orleans.

Wise Words: Henry Wadsworth Longfellow: "In your hearts are the birds and the sunshine, / In your thoughts the brooklet's flow, / But in mine is the wind of Autumn, / And the first fall of the snow."

Hints of Love: Keep it fun. Look for new and exciting things to do, especially if you are in a long-term relationship.

After the Argument: *For him:* This will take work no matter what is wrong. Making up is always the best with this one. That's why he loves to fight. *For her:* Expect to take money out of the bank for this one. Jewelry or even a trip. It had better be good, or you will need patience.

Romantic Places: Places of suspense bring romance: Scotland; a haunted house; Niagara Falls, New York.

Lucky Love Star: Scorpiel—you will never lack assertiveness and sensuality.

Beautiful Thought: There is always room to love one more.

Sharing Secrets: Everything in its good time. This one works slowly, but when it is time to pick up speed, watch out. *For the gals:* Don't go by the obvious. Read between the lines. As long as the invitation is being offered go full speed ahead. *For the guys:* Just when you thought you should walk away, he'll say, "I love you." Talk about confusing.

Judith's Insights

About the Man: If you are going to be intimidated by his flirtatious ways, move on before he lures you into his web. He makes a great mate, but only after he has sowed his wild oats all over the place. Playing with his fire could keep you warm or leave you burned. The difference is how you take him. He needs time to slow down and make a commitment when he is older. The only way to know if he is ready is when he lets you know.

About the Woman: If you are waiting for this girl it could take a while. She is in no hurry to jump on the first bus that rides by. She will need to think long and hard before she enters into any commitment. Give this gal some time. You will probably be standing in the right place at the right time. Keep yourself in this position by being her best friend. She will look at you in a different light when she feels closer to you than anyone else.

Soul Mates: A fellow Scorpio could be what you need to spice things up. Capricorn and Aries will help you balance your inner self and reach even higher goals than you thought possible. Pisces and Gemini will have you dizzy from their emotional outbursts. Aquarius and Leo could work marvelously when you go in with the right attitude. Taurus and Cancer may have you looking for the Exit sign. Libra and Sagittarius are signs that can make you feel complete. Virgo has caution written all over it.

Most Charming Characteristics: Tender, sympathetic, devoted.

Gifts: *For her:* aromatherapy gift set. *For him:* leather journal.

Sensual Foods: Champagne with strawberries; fillet of sole.

Romantic Flowers: You love it when you get tulips, declaring love. When you receive a variety, it shows how hopelessly in love your partner is. He will just love a single rose. This shows him you understand his pleasures.

Best Date Nights: Tuesday; 6th and 14th of each month.

Colors of Passion: *For her:* violet, scarlet. *For him:* brown, beige.

The Perfect Wedding: Intensely passionate, you crave a wondrous, exotic environment. Emotional and magnetic, your personality lends itself to a rugged rock garden high on a hill overlooking the ocean. A beachfront wedding may well stir the excitement and emotion you desire. Ideal setting: New Orleans.

Wise Words: Henry Wadsworth Longfellow: "When the warm sun that brings seed time and harvest has returned again, it is sweet to visit the still wood where springs the first flower of the plane."

Hints of Love: This one is a cautious soul. You may have to find a way to go around to the back door.

After the Argument: *For him:* This will take work no matter what is wrong. Making up is always the best with this one. That's why he loves to fight. *For her:* Expect to take money out of the bank for this one. Jewelry or even a trip. It had better be good, or you will need patience.

Romantic Places: Places of mystery bring romance: Aztec ruins; a dinner cruise; Salem, Massachusetts.

Lucky Love Star: Scorpiel—you will never lack assertiveness and sensuality.

Beautiful Thought: Friendship means having someone who doesn't mind catching you, so you can take the time out to fall.

Sharing Secrets: This one is a charmer, perhaps even fickle. *For the gals:* If you are patient enough to stick around, this one is worth the wait. *For the guys:* If there is enough time on the clock, stick around past three months. Then maybe he will have noticed you are there.

Judith's Insights

About the Man: He can be hopelessly devoted to his mate as long as he has had enough time to grow up. He needs this time to be truly resolved to loving someone else. He can have definite mood swings. Be cautious about the times in which you approach him. You have to wait for the perfect moment. He will keep working until things are perfect when it comes to business. This can be a distraction for his emotions.

About the Woman: She is extremely careful about whom she gives her heart to. Sometimes she is too careful and can lose a good thing before it starts. This lady is more than a challenge at times. Give her plenty of room while stating that you are going to be sticking around for when she is ready. Being a constant in her crazy life will only make you stand out when she really looks around. It will take a while for her to admit how much she wants to be loved.

Soul Mates: It is feast or famine with a fellow Scorpio. You will love each other or hate each other, sometimes in the same day. Capricorn and Aries will help you get a hold on all of your wonderful potential. Pisces and Gemini are hard to get used to, but once you do, things will be surpassingly good. Taurus and Cancer may not seem like your type at first, but you would be surprised at how well you end up getting along. Aquarius and Leo may create a strong attraction, but that is hard to maintain. Libra and Sagittarius will do anything for you. All you have to do is ask. Virgo is too rigid for your taste.

Most Charming Characteristics: Jovial, fun-loving, likable.

Gifts: *For her:* vacation near the water. *For him:* tour of caves.

Sensual Foods: Chocolates; poached salmon; flambé; filet mignon; potatoes.

Romantic Flowers: Send this girl sunflowers if you want her to know you adore her. You may even add some poppies for a splash of extravagance. His desire for sport and play will be understood when you send him hyacinth and geranium.

Best Date Nights: Tuesday; 4th and 23rd of each month.

Colors of Passion: *For her:* violet, scarlet. *For him:* brown, beige.

The Perfect Wedding: Intensely passionate, you crave a wondrous, exotic environment. Emotional and magnetic, your personality lends itself to a rugged rock garden high on a hill overlooking the ocean. A beachfront wedding may well stir the excitement and emotion you desire. Ideal setting: New Orleans.

Wise Words: Henry Wadsworth Longfellow: "My life is cold, and dark, and dreary; / It rains, and the wind is never weary; / My thoughts still cling to the mouldering Past, / But the hopes of youth fall thick in the blast, / And the days are dark and dreary."

Hints of Love: Passion must be in the picture at all times or you could lose this one's attention quickly.

After the Argument: *For him:* This will take work no matter what is wrong. Making up is always the best with this one. That's why he loves to fight. *For her:* Expect to take money out of the bank for this one. Jewelry or even a trip. It had better be good, or you will need patience.

Romantic Places: Places of suspense bring romance: Mexico; a magic show; Savannah, Georgia.

Lucky Love Star: Scorpiel—you will never lack assertiveness and sensuality.

Beautiful Thought: Sweet words, sincere thoughts.

Sharing Secrets: If you are looking for love, then you have found the right mate. *For the gals:* This one could be stubborn. It may take forever to get a relationship started, but it is as solid as they come. *For the guys:* Even when he is ready, he might not be willing and able. He will put you through more obstacles than any course. Be patient.

Judith's Insights

About the Man: His sense of humor is so hidden that it may be hard to find at all. You might not understand what he finds funny. This guy lives in a world all his own. He is very particular about who he lets into that world. Opening the door slowly will intrigue him much more than trying to force it open. He can be quite a challenge to all those he lives and works with. As he grows older and wiser he will become better at showering others with attention.

About the Woman: This gal is a hopeless romantic. This is something you might not realize until you really get to know her. Her strong exterior can confuse all who come into contact with her. Her soft side will allow others to see her in an entirely different light. She just has to be ready to show it. No amount of pulling will make her ready to show things she is not ready to show. Patience is the key to all treasures with her.

Soul Mates: Only another Scorpio could understand you so well. When you are linked to Capricorn and Aries, you will feel at home and safe. Pisces and Gemini will push your buttons to see what makes you tick. Aquarius and Leo could be the most wonderful people in your life if you let them. Taurus and Cancer are not up your alley at first. Then they will suddenly grow on you and you will be lost without them. Libra and Sagittarius will make life easy with them. Virgo can drive you crazy if you let them. Step back for a breath occasionally.

Most Charming Characteristics: Loving, musical, resourceful.

Gifts: *For her:* serenity rock garden. *For him:* personal organizer.

Sensual Foods: Caviar; beef tenderloin; potatoes au gratin.

Romantic Flowers: Rhododendron will let her be on the lookout for trouble. Throw in some chrysanthemum and she'll know it is you she will be looking out for. Cactus will show him warmth. Yellow daffodil is a token of a good time had by all. Chivalry is not dead.

Best Date Nights: Tuesday; 4th and 23rd of each month.

Colors of Passion: *For her:* violet, scarlet. *For him:* brown, beige.

The Perfect Wedding: Intensely passionate, you crave a wondrous, exotic environment. Emotional and magnetic, your personality lends itself to a rugged rock garden high on a hill overlooking the ocean. A beachfront wedding may well stir the excitement and emotion you desire. Ideal setting: New Orleans.

Wise Words: Henry Wadsworth Longfellow: "Happy art thou, as if every day thou hadst picked up a horseshoe."

Hints of Love: A random act of kindness will go a long way with this one. What can you do for them today?

After the Argument: *For him:* This will take work no matter what is wrong. Making up is always the best with this one. That's why he loves to fight. *For her:* Expect to take money out of the bank for this one. Jewelry or even a trip. It had better be good, or you will need patience.

Romantic Places: Places of mystery bring romance: Bermuda; the theater; New Orleans, Louisiana.

Lucky Love Star: Scorpiel—you will never lack assertiveness and sensuality.

Beautiful Thought: Enjoy the moment, for an hour.

Sharing Secrets: If you can hang around and give constant stimulation, this could be your mate. *For the gals:* She is always looking for the Exit sign. Don't show her where it is or she will be gone. *For the guys:* Fast car, fast food; he likes everything that goes fast. Put on your running shoes. If you can keep up, then he is yours.

Judith's Insights

About the Man: This man knows how to hold his tongue because he carries too many of his own secrets in his back pocket. He has a knack with words both in business and in pleasure. He has a style that is all his own, and he loves it. Appeal to his sense of mystery to get in the door. Keep his secrets close to your heart to stay there. He can be easier to work with than be in love with. His first reaction to new emotions is to run away.

About the Woman: She may say one thing and mean another, especially when this gal falls in love. You may see erratic behavior until she feels a steady stream of emotions coming from her mate. Just give her as much time as she needs, along with yourself. The moods will become much smoother with time and patience. She will eventually realize that her feelings will not be going away so she had better deal with them. Then she will just blame her partner.

Soul Mates: Things with a fellow Scorpio will be smooth as silk or hard as rock. There can be no in-between. Capricorn and Aries will keep you grounded while letting you fly as high as you need to. Pisces and Gemini will be hard to take at times. Let yourself step back when you feel the anger building. Aquarius and Leo will give new meaning to you. Taurus and Cancer take getting used to before you can become wrapped up in their charm. Libra and Sagittarius will make you happy if you would only let them. Virgo is a no-no if you want to keep your sanity.

Most Charming Characteristics: Independent, well-liked, content.

Gifts: *For her:* detective or gossip novel. *For him:* a writing class.

Sensual Foods: Passion fruit; fillet of sole almondine.

Romantic Flowers: The magnolias you send her will let her know you will be around for a while to come. Petunia is to say never despair. Holly will let him know what he is getting into. Pansy will keep you in his thoughts.

Best Date Nights: Tuesday; 9th and 18th of each month.

Colors of Passion: *For her:* violet, scarlet. *For him:* brown, beige.

The Perfect Wedding: Intensely passionate, you crave a wondrous, exotic environment. Emotional and magnetic, your personality lends itself to a rugged rock garden high on a hill overlooking the ocean. A beachfront wedding may well stir the excitement and emotion you desire. Ideal setting: New Orleans.

Wise Words: Henry Wadsworth Longfellow: "What I most prize in woman / Is her affections, not her intellect! / The intellect is finite; but the affections / Are infinite, and cannot be exhausted."

Hints of Love: Family and friends are important to this one. Don't try to alienate them or it will definitely backfire on you.

After the Argument: *For him:* This will take work no matter what is wrong. Making up is always the best with this one. That's why he loves to fight. *For her:* Expect to take money out of the bank for this one. Jewelry or even a trip. It had better be good, or you will need patience.

Romantic Places: Places of suspense bring romance: England; a castle tour; Salem, Massachusetts.

Lucky Love Star: Scorpiel—you will never lack assertiveness and sensuality.

Beautiful Thought: Treading lightly gets you to the same places without all the waves.

Sharing Secrets: This one may seem like a lot of work. They just need the basics: love, loyalty, and respect. *For the gals:* If you can show her your best side right from the beginning it may work. Be careful of fluff, because she will see right through it. *For the guys:* He loves to be loved. Give him plenty of attention, even if you think you don't stand a chance. Perseverance will win here.

Judith's Insights

About the Man: As enchanting as he may be, this guy can drive you right up a wall. It will take some time for him to settle down and come to terms with his emotions. He can be looked upon as a swinging bachelor. He may seem whimsical, but he is really much more grounded than he seems. He needs his emotions confirmed, or shall I say validated, constantly. He can be easy to get along with but almost impossible to completely understand.

About the Woman: You may find this gal talking in the cafeteria, but never does the subject of her personal life come up. She likes to have secrets. Every once in a while, when you get close, she may let you in on a few of those secrets. The closer you get the more she will reveal. She will try to make every moment of her life count toward the grand scheme of things. If you help her live her life with passion she will be passionate about you.

Soul Mates: A fellow Scorpio could be what you need to spice things up. Capricorn and Aries will help you balance your inner self and reach even higher goals than you thought possible. Pisces and Gemini will have you dizzy from their emotional outbursts. Aquarius and Leo could work marvelously when you go in with the right attitude. Taurus and Cancer may have you looking for the Exit sign. Libra and Sagittarius are signs that can make you feel complete. Virgo has caution written all over it.

Most Charming Characteristics: Philanthropic, leader, adventuresome.

Gifts: *For her:* aromatherapy gift set. *For him:* leather journal.

Sensual Foods: Peaches; mousse; shrimp.

Romantic Flowers: Iris is your flower if you are the gal sending subtle messages. If you are the man, you will look for clematis. This flower's mental beauty creates emotional stimulation for you.

Best Date Nights: Tuesday; 4th and 5th of each month.

Colors of Passion: *For her:* violet, scarlet. *For him:* brown, beige.

The Perfect Wedding: Intensely passionate, you crave a wondrous, exotic environment. Emotional and magnetic, your personality lends itself to a rugged rock garden high on a hill overlooking the ocean. A beachfront wedding may well stir the excitement and emotion you desire. Ideal setting: New Orleans.

Wise Words: Charles Dickens: "The sea has no appreciation of great men but knocks them about like small fry."

Hints of Love: Show others how much you adore him or her. They will revel in how others notice.

After the Argument: *For him:* This will take work no matter what is wrong. Making up is always the best with this one. That's why he loves to fight. *For her:* Expect to take money out of the bank for this one. Jewelry or even a trip. It had better be good, or you will need patience.

Romantic Places: Places of suspense bring romance: Stonehenge; dinner theater; New Orleans, Louisiana.

Lucky Love Star: Scorpiel—you will never lack assertiveness and sensuality.

Beautiful Thought: When you are feeling low and cold, look for a warm hand to hold yours.

Sharing Secrets: They are looking for love, but that is just their little secret. *For the gals:* Why shouldn't they want to be loved? Of course they do, but they want you to do all of the work. *For the guys:* You must prove yourself repeatedly. Don't expect too much until he knows you are under his thumb.

Judith's Insights

About the Man: With this guy's suspicious nature, if he is interested in you he is probably out finding everything he can about you. He wants to know just what you are all about before he puts his foot into his mouth. If he is not doing the asking, it's all right. He would love it if you would. Earlier in life he can be defensive when it comes to his emotions. Later on, after he has grown, he will be much more spiritual and open-minded.

About the Woman: You may have to wave the white flag of surrender to catch this girl's attention. She likes to know all that she can about people. She is known to have her very own style of doing things and may be restless in business. In love, she is cautious. The course to her heart is slow and littered with others who have tried before. The more up-front you are with her about your feelings and intentions the more likely she will be to let you into her heart.

Soul Mates: You and another Scorpio is exactly what the doctor ordered to cure a gray day. With Capricorn and Aries behind you, there is no telling where you will go. Pisces and Gemini are not something you like to deal with. Move on or you will feel anger build up inside. Aquarius and Leo have great potential for fine things to come. Taurus and Cancer will have you wringing your own neck. Libra and Sagittarius will fill the void you don't like to admit is there. Virgo is not advisable if you want to keep your sanity.

Most Charming Characteristics: Friendly, loving, fair.

Gifts: *For her:* gift certificate to on-line trader. *For him:* mutual fund.

Sensual Foods: Kiwis; cantaloupes; strawberries.

Romantic Flowers: Any rose of any color for the lady. Roses stand for love regardless of the color. Send them with orchids and you will be saying, "I love you." If you want a gentleman to know you think of him, send pansies, and forget-me-nots for true love.

Best Date Nights: Tuesday; 4th and 23rd of each month.

Colors of Passion: *For her:* violet, scarlet. *For him:* brown, beige.

The Perfect Wedding: Intensely passionate, you crave a wondrous, exotic environment. Emotional and magnetic, your personality lends itself to a rugged rock garden high on a hill overlooking the ocean. A beachfront wedding may well stir the excitement and emotion you desire. Ideal setting: New Orleans.

Wise Words: Charles Dickens: "As all partings foreshadow the great final one,—so empty rooms, bereft of a familiar presence, mournfully whisper what your room and what mine must one day be."

Hints of Love: Don't overdo it (dress, attention) too soon or this one will run. Wait until you have them hooked before you become outrageous.

After the Argument: *For him:* This will take work no matter what is wrong. Making up is always the best with this one. That's why he loves to fight. *For her:* Expect to take money out of the bank for this one. Jewelry or even a trip. It had better be good, or you will need patience.

Romantic Places: Places of mystery bring romance: the Bermuda Triangle; a train ride; Roswell, New Mexico.

Lucky Love Star: Scorpiel—you will never lack assertiveness and sensuality.

Beautiful Thought: If you keep both feet on the ground, you are less likely to fly off the handle.

Sharing Secrets: You had better be ready to pull out your romantic side if you want this to work. *For the gals:* Fireplaces, walks on the beach, or even winning a bear at the local carnival. *For the guys:* When you are out shopping bring him something home. Even if it is silly, he will love the thought.

Judith's Insights

About the Man: He is very stubborn, and is known to be selfish. He can also be very demanding of the people around him. He is much more demanding of himself, however. He does have finer qualities and there are special things about him. He will be the first to admit to his downfalls as well as his charms. He will never live his life by a double standard. He will expect higher standards for himself than for anyone else around him.

About the Woman: She only allows people in her life she feels she has a chance of happiness with. She will be uptight during any kind of beginnings, including in work situations. It doesn't take much to change this moody gal's moods. Flowers, candy, and the occasional hug are just the things to do it. She never wants to be caught looking for love in the wrong places. Once things achieve a constant rhythm she will be easier to get along with.

Soul Mates: Only another Scorpio could understand you so well. When you are linked to Capricorn and Aries, you will feel at home and safe. Pisces and Gemini will push your buttons to see what makes you tick. Aquarius and Leo could be the most wonderful people in your life if you let them. Taurus and Cancer are not up your alley at first. Then they will suddenly grow on you and you will be lost without them. Libra and Sagittarius will make life easy with them. Virgo can drive you crazy if you let them. Step back for a breath occasionally.

Most Charming Characteristics: Amiable, magnetic, intuitive, sociable.

Gifts: *For her:* savings bond. *For him:* detective novel.

Sensual Foods: Caramel and chocolate syrup on anything.

Romantic Flowers: These ladies like everyone to know how faithful they are, so send them violets. To surprise them send tulips. Men like their flowers the same as their relationships, unpretending. Send them camellias with white roses to show your affection.

Best Date Nights: Tuesday; 3rd and 12th of each month.

Colors of Passion: *For her:* violet, scarlet. *For him:* brown, beige.

The Perfect Wedding: Intensely passionate, you crave a wondrous, exotic environment. Emotional and magnetic, your personality lends itself to a rugged rock garden high on a hill overlooking the ocean. A beachfront wedding may well stir the excitement and emotion you desire. Ideal setting: New Orleans.

Wise Words: Charles Dickens: "Try to do to others as you would have them do to you, and do not be discouraged if they fail sometimes."

Hints of Love: When these folks decide to sit on the fence don't try to push them off before they are ready. Let them do the jumping themselves.

After the Argument: *For him:* This will take work no matter what is wrong. Making up is always the best with this one. That's why he loves to fight. *For her:* Expect to take money out of the bank for this one. Jewelry or even a trip. It had better be good, or you will need patience.

Romantic Places: Places of suspense bring romance: Ireland; a suspense film; the Alamo, Texas.

Lucky Love Star: Scorpiel—you will never lack assertiveness and sensuality.

Beautiful Thought: Guardian angels protect us from ourselves.

Sharing Secrets: It may seem like they are not interested, but ask them out anyway. *For the gals:* Until they absolutely know you are interested, you will never find out that they are. *For the guys:* Ask him out if he doesn't ask you. He may be shy or not. Either way, he may be interested.

Judith's Insights

About the Man: He is much more likely to fight with himself than with you. He lives inside of his head. He needs to put his two cents in at all times. There is not a shy bone in his body. Sarcasm is a tool, and he will use it as his personal work of art whenever he can. Don't let it get under your skin. He will try to use jealousy to get what he wants until he learns what a terrible mistake that is. After he learns what doesn't work he will find a better way of using his energy.

About the Woman: This brilliant conversationalist will have no problem striking up a conversation with you—or anyone else, for that matter. Don't think that she is a cheater just because she is a chatterer. If you wait too long to make your move, she will be on her way to the next potential candidate. It will take a long time for her to grow out of her temper tantrums. She is famous for going after what she wants in the wrong way.

Soul Mates: There may be power struggles with another Scorpio, but if you work through them, you will be the richer for it. Capricorn and Aries will keep you in line without limiting your potential. Pisces and Gemini will push you to see how far they can go. If you feel yourself losing control, it would be better to step away. Taurus and Cancer will pull you in, although you fight it along the way. Libra and Aquarius will do anything to make you happy. Don't take advantage of them. In Sagittarius you could find the inspiration to go even further than you thought. In Leo you could find more than you bargained for. Virgo will have you pulling your hair out at times. They are just hard to get used to.

Most Charming Characteristics: Honest, content, inquisitive.

Gifts: *For her:* put her on a treasure hunt. *For him:* tickets to the car races.

Sensual Foods: Waffles with whipped cream; chocolate soufflé; French wine.

Romantic Flowers: These ladies like men with taste. Show them you love style by sending fuchsia flowers, or even brightly colored wildflowers will do. To confuse this man, send him lilies along with bright daisies to show your innocence. Keep him guessing.

Best Date Nights: Tuesday; 4th and 22nd of each month.

Colors of Passion: *For her:* violet, scarlet. *For him:* brown, beige.

The Perfect Wedding: Intensely passionate, you crave a wondrous, exotic environment. Emotional and magnetic, your personality lends itself to a rugged rock garden high on a hill overlooking the ocean. A beachfront wedding may well stir the excitement and emotion you desire. Ideal setting: New Orleans.

Wise Words: Hennison: "Self-reverence, self-knowledge, self-control, these three alone lead life to sovereign power."

Hints of Love: Make sure you learn to compromise, but never with your principles.

After the Argument: *For him:* This will take work no matter what is wrong. Making up is always the best with this one. That's why he loves to fight. *For her:* Expect to take money out of the bank for this one. Jewelry or even a trip. It had better be good, or you will need patience.

Romantic Places: Places of mystery bring romance: Venezuela; an Indian reservation; Devil's Tower, Wyoming.

Lucky Love Star: Scorpiel—you will never lack assertiveness and sensuality.

Beautiful Thought: When you close your eyes to sleep, your angel is sitting up to watch over you.

Sharing Secrets: Don't be surprised if the first date is with their family. *For the gals:* Make sure you invite her to your family functions. It will be a red flag to her if you don't. *For the guys:* He may seem like a family man, but isn't that what you were looking for?

Judith's Insights

About the Man: If anyone can drive you crazy, it is this guy. You need more than stamina to keep up with him. You need tremendous patience and a true sense of your own self. This guy is a lot to love. It is a tough job, and many people abandon it. It takes someone special to be able to hang in there through his moody spots. The best thing to do is agree to disagree. From that point all else will fall right into place.

About the Woman: She talks herself in and out of things from one minute to the next. Start putting away a nickel every time she changes her mind. You will be wealthy in no time at all. She is, however, consistent when it comes to work. Some may call her a workaholic. Try to get her out of the office and into the world occasionally. There will be plenty of passion and laughter in your life together. She is well worth the waves to get to the shore.

Soul Mates: It is feast or famine with a fellow Scorpio. You will love each other or hate each other, sometimes in the same day. Capricorn and Aries will help you get a hold on all of your wonderful potential. Pisces and Gemini are hard to get used to, but once you do, things will be surpassingly good. Taurus and Cancer may not seem like your type at first, but you would be surprised at how well you end up getting along. If there is anyone with as much energy as you, it is Sagittarius. A relationship with Leo can grow only with hard work and a lot of love. Libra and Aquarius will do anything for you. All you have to do is ask. Virgo is too rigid for your taste.

Most Charming Characteristics: Leader, forgiving, magnetic.

Gifts: *For her:* personal organizer. *For him:* chess set.

Sensual Foods: Oysters; mussels; spicy foods.

Romantic Flowers: You are the lady of distinction, and only carnations will do. Any mix of colors with sprays of mignonette. Sweet peas or red carnations will appeal to this man's heart.

Best Date Nights: Tuesday; 5th and 23rd of each month.

Colors of Passion: *For her:* violet, scarlet. *For him:* brown, beige.

The Perfect Wedding: Intensely passionate, you crave a wondrous, exotic environment. Emotional and magnetic, your personality lends itself to a rugged rock garden high on a hill overlooking the ocean. A beachfront wedding may well stir the excitement and emotion you desire. Ideal setting: New Orleans.

Wise Words: Henry Wadsworth Longfellow: "Such songs have power to quiet, / The restless pulse of care, / And come like the benediction, / That follows after prayer."

Hints of Love: If you try to take a step back, it will be noticed. It could create the domino effect, and everything will start to fall.

After the Argument: *For him:* This will take work no matter what is wrong. Making up is always the best with this one. That's why he loves to fight. *For her:* Expect to take money out of the bank for this one. Jewelry or even a trip. It had better be good, or you will need patience.

Romantic Places: Places of suspense bring romance: Scotland; a haunted house; Niagara Falls, New York.

Lucky Love Star: Scorpiel—you will never lack assertiveness and sensuality.

Beautiful Thought: Sharing makes everyone feel worthwhile.

Sharing Secrets: Take me as I am could be the anthem for this one. *For the gals:* They will have strong views on just about everything. If you can hang with them, then nothing will be as important as you. *For the guys:* The thing you fall in love with may end up becoming the thing you hate. After a commitment, this one sticks around.

Judith's Insights

About the Man: No matter where he goes, he always gets noticed. He has a great presence that draws people to him. He has a keen way of being a flirt. He won't admit to flirting to a date or a mate, but he does it anyway. It is his personality, and he means nothing against you when he flirts with other people. He loves to challenge others and can be a nudge at times. Although he seems a bit selfish, he is more than capable of being generous.

About the Woman: She has a savvy way about her that makes it very easy to strike up a conversation with her. Just don't go on the offensive with her or she will become the defender of every cause that was ever started. This is no wallflower. Be ready for someone who can battle wits with the best of them. She hates to be taken for granted. Make sure that you give her all that you receive. She loves to be noticed just for being herself.

Soul Mates: A fellow Scorpio could be what you need to spice things up. Capricorn and Aries will help you balance your inner self and reach even higher goals than you thought possible. Pisces and Gemini will have you dizzy from their emotional outbursts. Aquarius and Leo could work marvelously when you go in with the right attitude. Taurus and Cancer may have you looking for the Exit sign. Libra and Sagittarius are signs that can make you feel complete. Virgo has caution written all over it.

Most Charming Characteristics: Persevering, patient, one-of-a-kind.

Gifts: *For her:* tuition to an art class. *For him:* pilot lessons.

Sensual Foods: Lobster; watermelon.

Romantic Flowers: You love it when you get tulips, declaring love. When you receive a variety, it shows how hopelessly in love your partner is. He will just love a single rose. This shows him you understand his pleasures.

Best Date Nights: Tuesday; 6th and 14th of each month.

Colors of Passion: *For her:* violet, scarlet. *For him:* brown, beige.

The Perfect Wedding: Intensely passionate, you crave a wondrous, exotic environment. Emotional and magnetic, your personality lends itself to a rugged rock garden high on a hill overlooking the ocean. A beachfront wedding may well stir the excitement and emotion you desire. Ideal setting: New Orleans.

Wise Words: Henry Wadsworth Longfellow: "There is no flock, however watched and tended, But one dead lamb is there! There is no fireside, howso'er defended, But has one vacant chair."

Hints of Love: Consistence and persistence will get this prize every time. They will value the effort.

After the Argument: *For him:* This will take work no matter what is wrong. Making up is always the best with this one. That's why he loves to fight. *For her:* Expect to take money out of the bank for this one. Jewelry or even a trip. It had better be good, or you will need patience.

Romantic Places: Places of mystery bring romance: Aztec ruins; a dinner cruise; Salem, Massachusetts.

Lucky Love Star: Scorpiel—you will never lack assertiveness and sensuality.

Beautiful Thought: Life is not easy; it's the school of unknown lessons and unlimited degrees.

Sharing Secrets: They seem moody until you get to know them. *For the gals:* You may not know whether to say hello or drop dead. As relations progress you will learn not to leave her dangling, and her moods will become more consistent. *For the guys:* To know him is to love him. His bark is much worse than his bite. He just wants someone to love him without criticism.

Judith's Insights

About the Man: You won't have to have any special style for capturing this guy's heart. All you need is an open mind and the ability to keep up with his conversations. He likes to do anything and everything and is pretty good at doing it all. Invite him out with you to get the creative juices flowing. He loves games as long as everyone is playing fair. He craves constant emotional stimulation but not emotional warfare.

About the Woman: This gal knows exactly what she wants. She is also great at knowing how to get it. You won't be able to snow-job this lady too easily. You can try to charm her, but expect her to know whether you are up to no good. Being on your best behavior with this lady is much advised. You don't want to be caught by her with your hand in the cookie jar. She will make you pay big. She will never expect from you what she doesn't expect from herself.

Soul Mates: It is feast or famine with a fellow Scorpio. You will love each other or hate each other, sometimes in the same day. Capricorn and Aries will help you get a hold on all of your wonderful potential. Pisces and Gemini are hard to get used to, but once you do, things will be surpassingly good. Taurus and Cancer may not seem like your type at first, but you would be surprised at how well you end up getting along. A match with Aquarius and Leo can work only if you recognize your differences and embrace them. Libra and Sagittarius will do anything for you. All you have to do is ask. Virgo is too rigid for your taste.

Most Charming Characteristics: Spiritual, capable, intellectual.

Gifts: *For her:* aromatherapy gift set. *For him:* leather journal.

Sensual Foods: Strawberries; truffles; shish kebab.

Romantic Flowers: Send this girl sunflowers if you want her to know you adore her. You may even add some poppies for a splash of extravagance. His desire for sport and play will be understood when you send him hyacinth and geranium.

Best Date Nights: Tuesday; 4th and 5th of each month.

Colors of Passion: *For her:* violet, scarlet. *For him:* brown, beige.

The Perfect Wedding: Intensely passionate, you crave a wondrous, exotic environment. Emotional and magnetic, your personality lends itself to a rugged rock garden high on a hill overlooking the ocean. A beachfront wedding may well stir the excitement and emotion you desire. Ideal setting: New Orleans.

Wise Words: Henry Wadsworth Longfellow: "If justice rules the universe, / From the good actions of good men / Angels of light should be begotten, / And thus the balance restored again."

Hints of Love: Be funny. Laughter will be what keeps this one coming back again and again.

After the Argument: *For him:* This will take work no matter what is wrong. Making up is always the best with this one. That's why he loves to fight. *For her:* Expect to take money out of the bank for this one. Jewelry or even a trip. It had better be good, or you will need patience.

Romantic Places: Places of suspense bring romance: Mexico; a magic show; Savannah, Georgia.

Lucky Love Star: Scorpiel—you will never lack assertiveness and sensuality.

Beautiful Thought: At the end of the day you should applaud yourself.

Sharing Secrets: You had better be able to put your money where your mouth is. *For the gals:* It doesn't need to be lavish, but she does love the loot. The more the better. *For the guys:* He doesn't mind spending his hard-earned cash, but he loves to see you contribute to please him.

Judith's Insights

About the Man: You can look at his guy as a jigsaw puzzle. Not only are some of his pieces missing, some of them have not even been created yet. He can harbor ill feelings when he doesn't get his way in things. At the same time, he can be loving and honorable if he has the right ingredients. He wants a committed mate as well as the freedom to wander around the planet. He will always give you the same freedom he feels he has.

About the Woman: This girl has all of the right ingredients to be a great politician. Even if she is a housewife, she will always find her way around or through anything. You get more than you expect, but she keeps her wisdom to herself. Allow her to know you are interested for a while and let that simmer in her head. She will always have her invisible guard up. This will be much more apparent as a co-worker than a mate. The guard only comes down for a select few.

Soul Mates: Only another Scorpio could understand you so well. When you are linked to Capricorn and Aries, you will feel at home and safe. Pisces and Gemini will push your buttons to see what makes you tick. Aquarius and Leo could be the most wonderful people in your life if you let them. Taurus and Cancer are not up your alley at first. Then they will suddenly grow on you and you will be lost without them. Libra and Sagittarius will make life easy with them. Virgo can drive you crazy if you let them. Step back for a breath occasionally.

Most Charming Characteristics: Affectionate, tender, dependable.

Gifts: *For her:* vacation near the water. *For him:* tour of caves.

Sensual Foods: Grapes; fine cheeses and crackers; taffy.

Romantic Flowers: Rhododendron will let her be on the lookout for trouble. Throw in some chrysanthemum and she'll know it is you she will be looking out for. Cactus will show him warmth. Yellow daffodil is a token of a good time had by all. Chivalry is not dead.

Best Date Nights: Tuesday; 8th and 26th of each month.

Colors of Passion: *For her:* violet, scarlet. *For him:* brown, beige.

The Perfect Wedding: Intensely passionate, you crave a wondrous, exotic environment. Emotional and magnetic, your personality lends itself to a rugged rock garden high on a hill overlooking the ocean. A beachfront wedding may well stir the excitement and emotion you desire. Ideal setting: New Orleans.

Wise Words: Henry Wadsworth Longfellow: "I have read in the marvelous heart of man, / That strange and mystic scroll, / That an army of phantoms vast and wan / Beleaguer the human soul."

Hints of Love: Treat this one like royalty or precious cargo. They will love being valued in this way.

After the Argument: *For him:* This will take work no matter what is wrong. Making up is always the best with this one. That's why he loves to fight. *For her:* Expect to take money out of the bank for this one. Jewelry or even a trip. It had better be good, or you will need patience.

Romantic Places: Places of mystery bring romance: Bermuda; the theater; New Orleans, Louisiana.

Lucky Love Star: Scorpiel—you will never lack assertiveness and sensuality.

Beautiful Thought: Giving your word is one thing; keeping your word is everything.

Sharing Secrets: Nobody likes a weak link, especially not this one. *For the gals:* Make sure you treat her like a lady and act like a man. *For the guys:* Put your best foot forward. Dress your best and keep your manners in check. This man notices.

Judith's Insights

About the Man: This guy is no cheapskate, but at times he may seem to have short arms and deep pockets. He tests others around him constantly. You need to prove your loyalty and honor before he will keep your company. Once you do prove yourself you will notice that his arms become long enough to get to the bottom of his pockets. If you want to impress him, go out of your way for him. It will certainly score you some brownie points.

About the Woman: All that this girl needs is honest-to-goodness loving. She thinks she is the only one who can play games. The truth is, she doesn't want to play any. Be up front and honest and full of integrity. Even when you prove yourself, she will still give you a run for your money. There is no middle ground with this gal. She will either love you to the ends of the earth or choose to not give you the time of day at all.

Soul Mates: Things with a fellow Scorpio will be smooth as silk or hard as rock. There can be no in-between. Capricorn and Aries will keep you grounded while letting you fly as high as you need to. Pisces and Gemini will be hard to take at times. Let yourself step back when you feel the anger building. Aquarius and Leo will give new meaning to you. Taurus and Cancer take getting used to before you can become wrapped up in their charm. Libra and Sagittarius will make you happy if you would only let them. Virgo is a no-no if you want to keep your sanity.

Most Charming Characteristics: Conscientious, ambitious, accurate.

Gifts: *For her:* serenity rock garden. *For him:* personal organizer.

Sensual Foods: Champagne; grapes; mangoes; filet mignon.

Romantic Flowers: The magnolias you send her will let her know you will be around for a while to come. Petunia is to say never despair. Holly will let him know what he is getting into. Pansy will keep you in his thoughts.

Best Date Nights: Tuesday; 5th and 23rd of each month.

Colors of Passion: *For her:* violet, scarlet. *For him:* brown, beige.

The Perfect Wedding: Intensely passionate, you crave a wondrous, exotic environment. Emotional and magnetic, your personality lends itself to a rugged rock garden high on a hill overlooking the ocean. A beachfront wedding may well stir the excitement and emotion you desire. Ideal setting: New Orleans.

Wise Words: Henry Wadsworth Longfellow: "The day is cold, and dark and dreary; / It rains, and the wind is never weary; / the vine still clings to the mouldering wall, But every gust the dead leaves fall, / And the day is dark and dreary."

Hints of Love: Affection is important, but only if it comes naturally. Otherwise, the sirens will go off.

After the Argument: *For him:* This will take work no matter what is wrong. Making up is always the best with this one. That's why he loves to fight. *For her:* Expect to take money out of the bank for this one. Jewelry or even a trip. It had better be good, or you will need patience.

Romantic Places: Places of suspense bring romance: England; a castle tour; Salem, Massachusetts.

Lucky Love Star: Scorpiel—you will never lack assertiveness and sensuality.

Beautiful Thought: Take your time and do it all; be hasty and you shall fall.

Sharing Secrets: Attention, attention, attention. *For the gals:* Do it any way you can. Presents, phone calls, cards, or flowers. Whatever works for you will work for her. *For the guys:* He would love nostalgic gifts or T-shirts. He also likes phone calls, as long as they don't interrupt his favorite pastimes.

Judith's Insights

About the Man: You can attempt to catch this guy, but there is no guarantee that you will. He can be a tough nut to crack. He can be infantile when it comes to not getting his own way. This is especially true at work. This guy is looking for a whole lot of fun. He only wants special people to share that fun with. He will always be ready to give all that he receives from his business or life partner. His moods will be much happier if work is being done on both sides of the fence.

About the Woman: You may be attracted to her power, but it is really passion that radiates from her. This gal is like an open book. She thinks that she is more complex than she really is. Don't demand too much too fast. As a matter of fact, don't demand anything. If you do, the first date could be your last. She certainly wants to be in love, but it is not how she lives her life. She pretends that commitment doesn't matter when it is all that her soul desires.

Soul Mates: A fellow Scorpio could be what you need to spice things up. Capricorn and Aries will help you balance your inner self and reach even higher goals than you thought possible. Pisces and Gemini will have you dizzy from their emotional outbursts. Aquarius and Leo could work marvelously when you go in with the right attitude. Taurus and Cancer may have you looking for the Exit sign. Libra and Sagittarius are signs that can make you feel complete. Virgo has caution written all over it.

Most Charming Characteristics: Happy, content, honest.

Gifts: *For her:* detective or gossip novel. *For him:* a writing class.

Sensual Foods: Chateaubriand; crème brûleé.

Romantic Flowers: Iris is your flower if you are the gal sending subtle messages. If you are the man, you will look for clematis. This flower's mental beauty creates emotional stimulation for you.

Best Date Nights: Tuesday; 1st and 10th of each month.

Colors of Passion: *For her:* violet, scarlet. *For him:* brown, beige.

The Perfect Wedding: Intensely passionate, you crave a wondrous, exotic environment. Emotional and magnetic, your personality lends itself to a rugged rock garden high on a hill overlooking the ocean. A beachfront wedding may well stir the excitement and emotion you desire. Ideal setting: New Orleans.

Wise Words: Henry Wadsworth Longfellow: "Leafless are the trees; their purple branches, / Spread themselves abroad, like reefs of coral, / Rising silent in the Red Sea of the winter sunset."

Hints of Love: This one likes others to make his or her dreams come true. Be the "fantasy" fulfiller.

After the Argument: *For him:* This will take work no matter what is wrong. Making up is always the best with this one. That's why he loves to fight. *For her:* Expect to take money out of the bank for this one. Jewelry or even a trip. It had better be good, or you will need patience.

Romantic Places: Places of suspense bring romance: Stonehenge; dinner theater; New Orleans, Louisiana.

Lucky Love Star: Scorpiel—you will never lack assertiveness and sensuality.

Beautiful Thought: Compassion is understanding; understanding holds the key.

Sharing Secrets: Make sure you are not the killjoy. *For the gals:* When she has an idea, try it before you decide you don't like it. She needs to be pleased. *For the guys:* Do the things he loves to do and he will make the things you love ten times more fun.

Judith's Insights

About the Man: You can call him crass or sarcastic, but he views it as his way of being humorous. What he thinks of as a sense of humor can be trying to your patience and ego at times. Look at him as a person looking for fun and never take him too seriously. He doesn't mean it that way at all. He may not let you know how he is feeling until you have already let him know your feelings first. His emotions will stay locked inside until he is sure that they are returned.

About the Woman: She is her own biggest conflict. She changes her mind way too quickly and too often. This girl has a temper and can tend to be moody. She is not very up-front with her emotions. She does this to protect herself. She knows what it is like to get her heart broken and doesn't want it to happen again. Your approach needs to be loud and clear so that she knows just where you are coming from. Only when she is sure about the path will she walk on it.

Soul Mates: You and another Scorpio is exactly what the doctor ordered to cure a gray day. With Capricorn and Aries behind you, there is no telling where you will go. Pisces and Gemini are not something you like to deal with. Move on or you will feel anger build up inside. Aquarius and Leo have great potential for fine things to come. Taurus and Cancer will have you wringing your own neck. Libra and Sagittarius will fill the void you don't like to admit is there. Virgo is not advisable if you want to keep your sanity.

Most Charming Characteristics: Trustworthy, reliable.

Gifts: *For her:* gift certificate to on-line trader. *For him:* mutual fund.

Sensual Foods: Shrimp; sinful chocolate cake.

Romantic Flowers: Any rose of any color for the lady. Roses stand for love regardless of the color. Send them with orchids and you will be saying, "I love you." If you want a gentleman to know you think of him, send pansies, and forget-me-nots for true love.

Best Date Nights: Tuesday; 2nd and 11th of each month.

Colors of Passion: *For her:* purple, scarlet. *For him:* royal blue, beige.

The Perfect Wedding: Intensely passionate, you crave a wondrous, exotic environment. Emotional and magnetic, your personality lends itself to a rugged rock garden high on a hill overlooking the ocean. A beachfront wedding may well stir the excitement and emotion you desire. Ideal setting: New Orleans.

Wise Words: Henry Wadsworth Longfellow: "Whene'er a noble deed is wrought, whene'er is spoken a noble thought, our hearts in glad surprise to higher level rise."

Hints of Love: Stop worrying about next week's date today or there will not be one tomorrow.

After the Argument: *For him:* This will take work no matter what is wrong. Making up is always the best with this one. That's why he loves to fight. *For her:* Expect to take money out of the bank for this one. Jewelry or even a trip. It had better be good, or you will need patience.

Romantic Places: Places of mystery bring romance: the Bermuda Triangle; a train ride; Roswell, New Mexico.

Lucky Love Star: Scorpiel—you will never lack assertiveness and sensuality.

Beautiful Thought: When you think you cannot go one more minute, just take one more step.

Sharing Secrets: You had better be ready to have a relationship. *For the gals:* No lies, no games, and no mistakes. She wants what she wants with as little work possible. *For the guys:* If you have games on your mind, then move on. This one likes fun any way he can get it, but no emotional roller coasters.

Judith's Insights

About the Man: He is great at lying to himself. He may have at hand a book of white lies ready for emergency use. You have to keep your eye on this one even if he says that he is unhappy and wants to move on. He may be just trying to get out of responsibility to his feelings. He is likely to complain and not do it right away. He wants others to be more demonstrative than he is. Those around him will be asked to prove themselves over and over.

About the Woman: She needs a lot of stimulation to keep her interested in a single thing or person. Dinner and a movie will do for an appetizer. This girl needs her entertainment to be like a seven-course dinner. Her energy and willpower will astound you. Things with her can seem like a lot of work or an absolute pleasure. It all depends on your depth of feeling for her. She will always do the same amount for you but in her own way, so you might not recognize it for what she intends it to be.

Soul Mates: Only another Scorpio could understand you so well. When you are linked to Capricorn and Aries, you will feel at home and safe. Pisces and Gemini will push your buttons to see what makes you tick. Aquarius and Leo could be the most wonderful people in your life if you let them. Taurus and Cancer are not up your alley at first. Then they will suddenly grow on you and you will be lost without them. Libra and Sagittarius will make life easy with them. Virgo can drive you crazy if you let them. Step back for a breath occasionally.

Most Charming Characteristics: Prompt, dependable, competent.

Gifts: *For her:* savings bond. *For him:* detective novel.

Sensual Foods: Toasted marshmallows; chocolates.

Romantic Flowers: These ladies like everyone to know how faithful they are, so send them violets. To surprise them send tulips. Men like their flowers the same as their relationships, unpretending. Send them camellias with white roses to show your affection.

Best Date Nights: Tuesday; 3rd and 21st of each month.

Colors of Passion: *For her:* violet, olive. *For him:* brown, beige.

The Perfect Wedding: Intensely passionate, you crave a wondrous, exotic environment. Emotional and magnetic, your personality lends itself to a rugged rock garden high on a hill overlooking the ocean. A beachfront wedding may well stir the excitement and emotion you desire. Ideal setting: New Orleans.

Wise Words: Charles Dickens: "Practical jokes are very capital in their way, if you can only get the other party to see the fun in them."

Hints of Love: Keep the romance in the picture. Don't forget the long walks on the beach and camping out in front of the fireplace.

After the Argument: *For him:* This will take work no matter what is wrong. Making up is always the best with this one. That's why he loves to fight. *For her:* Expect to take money out of the bank for this one. Jewelry or even a trip. It had better be good, or you will need patience.

Romantic Places: Places of suspense bring romance: Ireland; a suspense film; the Alamo, Texas.

Lucky Love Star: Scorpiel—you will never lack assertiveness and sensuality.

Beautiful Thought: The truth is the most genuine gift of all.

Sharing Secrets: You may have to give this one more than one chance. *For the gals:* Intriguing as she is, expect a handful. She lightens up as time goes on. *For the guys:* His quirks may make you have second thoughts, but that is what separates the men from the boys.

Judith's Insights

About the Man: His impulsive side might make him ask you out right away. His pensive side might make him think it over until his head hurts. This chap is always out to have some fun. He may just want to hang out without any strings attached. Give him time to decide if he wants to start adding a string at a time. If he is paying attention to you, it might not mean he is in love—but he is definitely interested. He would not waste his time giving his attention to just anyone.

About the Woman: This adventurous woman might be sky-diving one minute and holding board meetings the next minute. She has many hidden talents, and walking while chewing gum is just the beginning. She has style, class, and a whole lot of interest in things around her. You will be doing cartwheels with this girl. Enjoy your time in the rays of her sun. If it lasts an hour it is a good sign. If it lasts the entire day it is the start of something special.

Soul Mates: Things may be exciting or insane with another Sagittarius. It all depends on how you both approach things. Aries and Libra are a dream that becomes a reality. If you keep Scorpio and Capricorn occupied it will prove to be a great experience. Leo and Aquarius are a dream partnership made real. Gemini and Pisces will help you learn more about yourself and what you want. Taurus and Virgo will try to keep you rooted in one spot when you want to dance around. Cancer may grate on your nerves at first, but if you hang in there it may be worth the effort.

Most Charming Characteristics: Serious, studious, careful.

Gifts: *For her:* perfume. *For him:* lottery tickets.

Sensual Foods: Chocolate-covered strawberries; New York steak; scallops.

Romantic Flowers: These ladies like men with taste. Show them you love style by sending fuchsia flowers, or even brightly colored wildflowers will do. To confuse this man, send him lilies along with bright daisies to show your innocence. Keep him guessing.

Best Date Nights: Thursday; 13th and 22nd of each month.

Colors of Passion: *For her:* olive, purple. *For him:* brown, green.

The Perfect Wedding: Your sense of daring in everything you do will, of course, prevail throughout this milestone event. You love the outdoors— it so corresponds with your boundless energy. Something wild and unusual like a casino or a racetrack may tempt your urge to plan a *challenging* experience (yes, adventure triumphs even on your wedding day). Try a resort hotel or, perhaps, try designing your own location . . . all promise to satisfy your need for infinite space. Ideal setting: Australia.

Wise Words: Charles Dickens: "Men who are thoroughly false and hollow, seldom try to hide those vices from themselves; and yet, in the very act of avowing them, they lay claim to the virtues they feign most to despise."

Hints of Love: The mystery is important, but being evasive will create disaster. Make sure you know the difference.

After the Argument: *For him:* Let him just go out hiking, golfing, swimming, or camping. He needs a little adventure and just a little space. *For her:* A trip would be nice. Even a weekend out of town. Something romantic but very adventurous.

Romantic Places: Places of variety bring romance: tropical rain forest; comedy club; Las Vegas, Nevada.

Lucky Love Star: Sagitariel—you will never lack stimulation and spontaneity.

Beautiful Thought: When all else fails, laugh.

Sharing Secrets: Talk about high maintenance. *For the gals:* Once she sees that you go out of your way for her, then she will for you. *For the guys:* The bark is definitely much worse than the bite. He comes on stronger and more obstinate than he actually is.

Judith's Insights

About the Man: This guy has plenty of stamina to go around. You may have to take vitamins to keep up with him and his level of energy. Don't tempt him without being serious. Only play the games that he really wants to play. He is full of laughter, but becoming full of love will take a while. If you are ready to have fun and be plenty busy, then this relationship is one that you will enjoy. Just don't be too pushy on the when, the where, and the what.

About the Woman: She has plenty of friends and gets along with everyone around her. She is a flirt and loves every minute of it. This lady has more desires for where her life should go than most people. Expect to live out a number of fantasies when in her company. She holds nothing back. If you don't like to tag along on her many adventures, you might want to find someone less exuberant. She is not about to slow down for anyone.

Soul Mates: A pairing with a fellow Sagittarius will prove to be loads of fun for both of you. Aries and Libra are all you could dream of and more. Things with Scorpio and Capricorn must be filled with stimulation for them to work. With Leo and Aquarius in your corner, you will reach goals you forgot you set for yourself. Gemini and Pisces will help you open up to the parts in yourself you are not very fond of. If you are ready to do this, you will love it. Taurus and Virgo are like weights on your feet. You have to take them off if you want to run anywhere. Cancer may give you a nervous breakdown if you take things personally. If you don't, then it will roll right off.

Most Charming Characteristics: Determined, venturesome, positive.

Gifts: *For her:* foreign language tapes. *For him:* hire someone to fix the leaky sink.

Sensual Foods: Vanilla and strawberry mousse; tiramisù; espresso.

Romantic Flowers: You are the lady of distinction, and only carnations will do. Any mix of colors with sprays of mignonette. Sweet peas or red carnations will appeal to this man's heart.

Best Date Nights: Thursday; 4th and 23rd of each month.

Colors of Passion: *For her:* scarlet, purple. *For him:* royal blue, green.

The Perfect Wedding: Your sense of daring in everything you do will, of course, prevail throughout this milestone event. You love the outdoors—it so corresponds with your boundless energy. Something wild and unusual like a casino or a racetrack may tempt your urge to plan a *challenging* experience (yes, adventure triumphs even on your wedding day). Try a resort hotel or, perhaps, try designing your own location . . . all promise to satisfy your need for infinite space. Ideal setting: Australia.

Wise Words: Charles Dickens: "In home and all the English virtues which the love of home engenders, lies the only true source of domestic felicity."

Hints of Love: If you learn to back up when things are moving too fast, you won't have to bow out so often.

After the Argument: *For him:* Let him just go out hiking, golfing, swimming, or camping. He needs a little adventure and just a little space. *For her:* A trip would be nice. Even a weekend out of town. Something romantic but very adventurous.

Romantic Places: Places of diversity bring romance: Hong Kong; a casino; Chicago, Illinois.

Lucky Love Star: Sagitariel—you will never lack stimulation and spontaneity.

Beautiful Thought: Laughter is the cure for anger.

Sharing Secrets: Make sure you have at least five dates before you make up your mind. *For the gals:* She can be cynical, so it could be a few dates before she loosens up. *For the guys:* He still has yesterday on his mind. He needs a reason to forget his past relationship. Make a new history for him.

Judith's Insights

About the Man: He can be called a jack-of-all-trades, because he wants to be able to do it all. Not only does he want to do it all, he also wants to be able to do it perfectly the first time. He can get frustrated when it doesn't work out that way. He walks to the beat of a drum of his own design. You have to expect him to travel, and he will likely do it without you. He needs to follow the proverbial yellow brick road.

About the Woman: Don't try to possess this girl. Too much too soon won't work for her at all. She has many aspirations, and one of them may be to settle down, but not yet. She must find a mate who understands her passion for excitement. Until then, she will be out looking for someone to have fun with. She is here to have a good time. She will never mind the work as long as there is more than enough play to along with it.

Soul Mates: You will have laughs beyond imagination with another Sagittarius. Anything you can dream about the perfect partner will be made real in Aries and Libra. Keep open to all things new and exciting and you can fly to new heights with Scorpio and Capricorn. Leo and Aquarius will make the partnership harmonious and balanced. Gemini and Pisces could be a tumultuous paring if you are not careful. Your freedom is nonnegotiable. Make sure that Taurus and Virgo know this. Cancer must be taken at face value instead of personally.

Most Charming Characteristics: Ambitious, idealistic, artistic.

Gifts: *For her:* spa getaway. *For him:* casino trip.

Sensual Foods: Raspberries; pound cake; caviar.

Romantic Flowers: You love it when you get tulips, declaring love. When you receive a variety, it shows how hopelessly in love your partner is. He will just love a single rose. This shows him you understand his pleasures.

Best Date Nights: Thursday; 6th and 24th of each month.

Colors of Passion: *For her:* olive, violet. *For him:* royal blue, green.

The Perfect Wedding: Your sense of daring in everything you do will, of course, prevail throughout this milestone event. You love the outdoors—it so corresponds with your boundless energy. Something wild and unusual like a casino or a racetrack may tempt your urge to plan a *challenging* experience (yes, adventure triumphs even on your wedding day). Try a resort hotel or, perhaps, try designing your own location . . . all promise to satisfy your need for infinite space. Ideal setting: Australia.

Wise Words: Charles Dickens: "There is nothing . . . nothing innocent or good, that dies and is forgotten. Let us hold to that faith or none."

Hints of Love: Expecting too much too soon can only build up hopes that will fall down too easily.

After the Argument: *For him:* Let him just go out hiking, golfing, swimming, or camping. He needs a little adventure and just a little space. *For her:* A trip would be nice. Even a weekend out of town. Something romantic but very adventurous.

Romantic Places: Places of variety bring romance: French Riviera; a carnival; Nashville, Tennessee.

Lucky Love Star: Sagitariel—you will never lack stimulation and spontaneity.

Beautiful Thought: Flowers say so much: I'm here and you've been touched.

Sharing Secrets: Don't be in a hurry or it will be over before it begins. *For the gals:* Like fine wine and amazing food. Savor a moment until an hour is created. *For the guys:* To do too much too fast will prove risky. Try to give a push and he will just jump ship.

Judith's Insights

About the Man: You can ruffle his feathers very easily, especially if you are out in public with him and you are paying attention to someone else. He thinks that he is good at hiding his feelings, but they are usually written all over his face. Let him think that he has you fooled and then work according to what he is really feeling. Whether he likes you or loves you, he will give the relationship his all at all times. The shirt off his back is just the beginning.

About the Woman: This gal has a tendency to put the cart before the horse. She may be planning a wedding in her head without having been on a single date. You will seldom get bored when hanging with her. The furniture and the clothes may change often, as long as she doesn't change mates. Just don't ask too many questions before she is ready to give the answers. If you push too hard all of her charm and grace will go right out of the window.

Soul Mates: A fellow Sagittarius will have you feeling more alive than you have in a long time. Aries and Leo can be the personification of all you dreamed of in a partner. If you are open to new experiences, Scorpio and Capricorn will be your willing guides. Libra and Aquarius will do all that they can to make you happy. Gemini and Pisces will drive you nuts if you let them. Make Taurus and Virgo aware of your need for freedom and they will have to take it or leave it. Cancer may make you feel like running and staying at the same exact moment.

Most Charming Characteristics: Quiet, unassuming, capable.

Gifts: *For her:* skydiving lessons. *For him:* camping trip.

Sensual Foods: Flambé; lobster; oysters.

Romantic Flowers: Send this girl sunflowers if you want her to know you adore her. You may even add some poppies for a splash of extravagance. His desire for sport and play will be understood when you send him hyacinth and geranium.

Best Date Nights: Thursday; 15th and 24th of each month.

Colors of Passion: *For her:* olive, purple. *For him:* royal blue, green.

The Perfect Wedding: Your sense of daring in everything you do will, of course, prevail throughout this milestone event. You love the outdoors—it so corresponds with your boundless energy. Something wild and unusual like a casino or a racetrack may tempt your urge to plan a *challenging* experience (yes, adventure triumphs even on your wedding day). Try a resort hotel or, perhaps, try designing your own location . . . all promise to satisfy your need for infinite space. Ideal setting: Australia.

Wise Words: Charles Dickens: "It is a world we need be careful how we libel, Heaven forgive us, for it is a world of sacred mysteries, and its Creator only knows what lies beneath the surface of His lightest image."

Hints of Love: Make sure all the ingredients are present before putting the cake in the oven.

After the Argument: *For him:* Let him just go out hiking, golfing, swimming, or camping. He needs a little adventure and just a little space. *For her:* A trip would be nice. Even a weekend out of town. Something romantic but very adventurous.

Romantic Places: Places of diversity bring romance: Brazil; a parade; Miami, Florida.

Lucky Love Star: Sagitariel—you will never lack stimulation and spontaneity.

Beautiful Thought: Most people don't understand true kindness.

Sharing Secrets: They need to look before they leap, but only in love. *For the gals:* She needs creative and exciting dates to keep her interested. Don't take her for granted too soon. *For the guys:* You may think he gives signs of moving this relationship quickly; make sure you slow it down before he does.

Judith's Insights

About the Man: With this guy's active mind, he will go around the world and back again in his head. He can be lit up like a Christmas tree with all of his energy. Unfortunately, he can be lazy when it comes to doing the work in a relationship. Find out what he likes and appeal to those preferences. Compromise will take a while to become a part of his vocabulary. He doesn't do well with the moodiness of others. He would rather dish it out than take it.

About the Woman: As enchanting as this girl seems, you will find her moods hard to follow. She either likes you a lot or not at all. There is seldom anything in between. She is much better at pretending interest when it comes to business matters. She can never pretend to be interested when it comes to matters of the heart. She is always up for a good time, however. Capturing her attention will take little more than a carrot. Keeping it is the hard part.

Soul Mates: *Fun* is not the word for when you get together with a fellow Sagittarius. You will feel completely understood by someone cut from the same cloth. Scorpio and Capricorn can take you to places you never imagined if you would open your mind to new possibilities. Libra and Aquarius will do anything to keep the relationship running smoothly. Try not to overstep their flexibility. Gemini and Pisces will try to figure you out. If you share what you can they will be easier to be around. Taurus and Virgo can tend to weigh you down. Try to let them know about your need for freedom. A relationship with Cancer depends on the attitude you go in with. There is no such thing as typical anything when you are linked with Aries and Leo.

Most Charming Characteristics: Kind, generous, upright.

Gifts: *For her:* sapphire necklace. *For him:* beach house for the summer.

Sensual Foods: Crème brûlée; poached salmon.

Romantic Flowers: Rhododendron will let her be on the lookout for trouble. Throw in some chrysanthemum and she'll know it is you she will be looking out for. Cactus will show him warmth. Yellow daffodil is a token of a good time had by all. Chivalry is not dead.

Best Date Nights: Thursday; 17th and 26th of each month.

Colors of Passion: *For her:* olive, purple. *For him:* royal blue, green.

The Perfect Wedding: Your sense of daring in everything you do will, of course, prevail throughout this milestone event. You love the outdoors—it so corresponds with your boundless energy. Something wild and unusual like a casino or a racetrack may tempt your urge to plan a *challenging* experience (yes, adventure triumphs even on your wedding day). Try a resort hotel or, perhaps, try designing your own location . . . all promise to satisfy your need for infinite space. Ideal setting: Australia.

Wise Words: Charles Dickens: "To remember happiness which cannot be restored is pain, but of a softened kind. Our recollections are unfortunately mingled with much that we deplore, and with many actions which we bitterly repent."

Hints of Love: Simple often turns into complicated with this one. When you overcomplicate the moment, try to step back for a breather.

After the Argument: *For him:* Let him just go out hiking, golfing, swimming, or camping. He needs a little adventure and just a little space. *For her:* A trip would be nice. Even a weekend out of town. Something romantic but very adventurous.

Romantic Places: Places of variety bring romance: Greece; a nightclub; Disney World.

Lucky Love Star: Sagitariel—you will never lack stimulation and spontaneity.

Beautiful Thought: Simple can be so simple.

Sharing Secrets: The possibilities are endless, if you can pay the price. *For the gals:* She is hoping chivalry is not dead, and you must be willing to be the man at all costs. *For the guys:* He can be demanding and somewhat controlling. He just needs to be trained.

Judith's Insights

About the Man: It is fight or flight for this guy. He either wants you to stick around and put up with his antics or not. It is easy to get his attention. Just smile and turn on your natural charm. That may never work in business unless you are actually doing your job at the same time you're trying to play nice. At times you might not be sure if he is coming or going. Don't worry. He doesn't know, either. Let him sort out his emotions before asking the tough questions.

About the Woman: You may find more than one person living in her body. The business lady is all work and no play until you get to know the fun-loving, carefree side of her. Then she is a pleasure to know. Don't step on her toes when she is trying to get something done. She has the ability to stomp on yours. She simply wants the perfect partner. She will kiss each and every frog that comes by until she finds that great mate.

Soul Mates: With another Sagittarius, you will be understood like never before. Scorpio and Capricorn will show you new and exciting things when you are ready. Libra and Aquarius try to make you happy at every turn. Let them do it, because it is what makes them happy. Gemini and Pisces will try to push the envelope to see what they can get away with. Aries and Leo will not only bring spice to your life but leave you craving more. Taurus and Virgo need stability in their life and might try to rob you of your freedom to get it. With the right frame of mind, things can go very well with Cancer.

Most Charming Characteristics: Humorous, easygoing, aggressive.

Gifts: *For her:* housekeeper or cleaning service. *For him:* new pet.

Sensual Foods: Chocolate soufflé; filet mignon.

Romantic Flowers: The magnolias you send her will let her know you will be around for a while to come. Petunia is to say never despair. Holly will let him know what he is getting into. Pansy will keep you in his thoughts.

Best Date Nights: Thursday; 9th and 18th of each month.

Colors of Passion: *For her:* olive, purple. *For him:* royal blue, green.

The Perfect Wedding: Your sense of daring in everything you do will, of course, prevail throughout this milestone event. You love the outdoors—it so corresponds with your boundless energy. Something wild and unusual like a casino or a racetrack may tempt your urge to plan a *challenging* experience (yes, adventure triumphs even on your wedding day). Try a resort hotel or, perhaps, try designing your own location . . . all promise to satisfy your need for infinite space. Ideal setting: Australia.

Wise Words: Charles Dickens: "Look upon us, angels of young children, with regards not quite estranged, when the swift river bears us to the ocean."

Hints of Love: Allow them to know what is in your heart as well as what is in your head.

After the Argument: *For him:* Let him just go out hiking, golfing, swimming, or camping. He needs a little adventure and just a little space. *For her:* A trip would be nice. Even a weekend out of town. Something romantic but very adventurous.

Romantic Places: Places of diversity bring romance: Venezuela; a casino; San Francisco, California.

Lucky Love Star: Sagitariel—you will never lack stimulation and spontaneity.

Beautiful Thought: Every relationship counts; add them up.

Sharing Secrets: Tomorrow is another day, but why wait? You can do it all today. *For the gals:* Have your date filled from dusk to dawn, and then some. *For the guys:* You may find he needs a nap here and there, but he can last all day and all night if he has a reason.

Judith's Insights

About the Man: If nothing is appealing to his sweet tooth, then you will have to find the right sweets. He is always protecting himself. He will do that until he meets the love of his life. You may think that he doesn't have a stressed bone in his body, but there are plenty there indeed. He loves to have fun in spite of them. He needs to be noticed by those he loves and admires. If he is not getting the validation he craves at home, he will look elsewhere for it.

About the Woman: She is a good-time Charlene. That is what she would like you to believe, anyway. All at once, her emotions will become erratic. She will ask all of the questions and still need some answers. She can be a walking contradiction in love, but never one in business. She knows just what to do there. She will flirt only to feed her ego, not because she needs many partners. Finding unique ways to make her feel special will put you on her favorite people list.

Soul Mates: Another Sagittarius may drive you around the world, but it may also be the most stimulation you have had in a long time. With so much passion and adventure in Aries and Leo, it would be impossible to bore you. Scorpio and Capricorn need constant stimulation, but that might work well for you. A union with Libra and Aquarius could be picture-perfect. Gemini and Pisces will urge you to reach out and expand. Taurus and Virgo may grate on your nerves. Just let them teach you what they feel they can. Cancer will have you leaping through hoops.

Most Charming Characteristics: Gentle, kind, loving.

Gifts: *For her:* beauty products. *For him:* large backyard barbecue.

Sensual Foods: Steak au poivre; cheesecake.

Romantic Flowers: Iris is your flower if you are the gal sending subtle messages. If you are the man, you will look for clematis. This flower's mental beauty creates emotional stimulation for you.

Best Date Nights: Thursday; 1st and 19th of each month.

Colors of Passion: *For her:* olive, purple. *For him:* royal blue, green.

The Perfect Wedding: Your sense of daring in everything you do will, of course, prevail throughout this milestone event. You love the outdoors—it so corresponds with your boundless energy. Something wild and unusual like a casino or a racetrack may tempt your urge to plan a *challenging* experience (yes, adventure triumphs even on your wedding day). Try a resort hotel or, perhaps, try designing your own location . . . all promise to satisfy your need for infinite space. Ideal setting: Australia.

Wise Words: William Blake: "Joy and woe are woven fine, / A clothing for the soul divine; / Under every grief and pine / Runs a joy with silken twine . . . / And, when this we rightly know, / Safely through the world we go."

Hints of Love: Keep both feet on the ground the first time you think you want to jump. This way you won't jump too high too soon.

After the Argument: *For him:* Let him just go out hiking, golfing, swimming, or camping. He needs a little adventure and just a little space. *For her:* A trip would be nice. Even a weekend out of town. Something romantic but very adventurous.

Romantic Places: Places of variety bring romance: Africa; a cruise; Seattle, Washington.

Lucky Love Star: Sagitariel—you will never lack stimulation and spontaneity.

Beautiful Thought: The soul knows, that's how you knew.

Sharing Secrets: It may need to start with friendship. This isn't the consolation prize; it's the grand prize. *For the gals:* Go slowly and allow it to grow one seed at a time. You won't need to push; it will all come in time. *For the guys:* A step here and a step there. Before he knows it, that friendship will be love.

Judith's Insights

About the Man: He is a bit outspoken at times. The good news is that you will always know where you stand with him. If he puts you next to him, then you are in. Otherwise, expect to be sitting far away. As charming as he can be, you will find him obnoxious at times. Try to remember why you like him in the first place. He is sensitive, but he tries to keep that side of his nature hidden. He will feel safe with a lot of people around him.

About the Woman: Throw her a compliment here and a little gift there. Keep her in the style she dreams about and can become accustomed to. She is fascinated by romance. She wants to live her life as if it is a movie script. Make her dreams a reality and you will have a loving fan. Ultimately, she wants a relationship that will lead to commitment, but not before she is capable of handling that level of responsibility.

Soul Mates: Pairing with a fellow Sagittarius can be the most fun you have had in a long time. Aries and Leo may give you a roller coaster ride, but you will be laughing the entire time. Scorpio and Capricorn need to feel special. If you can give them that, then they will give you the world. Libra and Aquarius will ignore any shortcomings to keep the relationship moving smoothly. Gemini and Pisces will help you expand your horizons. Taurus and Virgo will have you dreaming of greener, and more relaxed, pastures. Cancer will have you trying things you had never imagined before.

Most Charming Characteristics: Quick, impulsive, energetic.

Gifts: *For her:* travel book to plan next trip. *For him:* skydiving lessons.

Sensual Foods: Strawberry shortcake; pineapple; ham.

Romantic Flowers: Any rose of any color for the lady. Roses stand for love regardless of the color. Send them with orchids and you will be saying, "I love you." If you want a gentleman to know you think of him, send pansies, and forget-me-nots for true love.

Best Date Nights: Thursday; 2nd and 11th of each month.

Colors of Passion: *For her:* olive, purple. *For him:* royal blue, green.

The Perfect Wedding: Your sense of daring in everything you do will, of course, prevail throughout this milestone event. You love the outdoors—it so corresponds with your boundless energy. Something wild and unusual like a casino or a racetrack may tempt your urge to plan a *challenging* experience (yes, adventure triumphs even on your wedding day). Try a resort hotel or, perhaps, try designing your own location . . . all promise to satisfy your need for infinite space. Ideal setting: Australia.

Wise Words: Henry Wadsworth Longfellow: "No foe, no dangerous pass, we heed, / Brook no delay—but onward speed / With loosened rein."

Hints of Love: Laughter alleviates the tension, but so can understanding where another is sitting.

After the Argument: *For him:* Let him just go out hiking, golfing, swimming, or camping. He needs a little adventure and just a little space. *For her:* A trip would be nice. Even a weekend out of town. Something romantic but very adventurous.

Romantic Places: Places of diversity bring romance: Jamaica; a street fair; New Orleans, Louisiana.

Lucky Love Star: Sagitariel—you will never lack stimulation and spontaneity.

Beautiful Thought: Feeling the passion of every color of the rainbow.

Sharing Secrets: This one needs to be the one and only, even if it is only the first date. *For the gals:* Don't talk about your past relationships. Do all you can to make her feel cherished from the first moment. *For the guys:* Play up your innocence. Let him take charge, even in paying the bill. He needs to wear the pants.

Judith's Insights

About the Man: He loves to be loved. Send him a love note and invite him out for coffee. More than likely, if you make the first move he will probably make all the ones after that. He may never admit it or even see it for himself, but he is filled with insecurities. Remind him of all the great qualities he has. He can have a way of keeping his defenses up at all times. No one gets inside his walls by mistake. If you find yourself there, be careful of what you touch.

About the Woman: She dabbles in anything and everything. She wants to experience everything she can possibly fit into her life. This is especially true when her love life is not going very well. If you think that she is keeping a busy schedule because she isn't interested in love, you are wrong. You don't have to do much to get an invitation to her inner city. Just ask and odds are she will let you in. Give her time to make sure that you are safe to stay.

Soul Mates: You were made to have fun with someone just like you. That is why Sagittarius would be a great match for you. Aries and Leo will be the perfect image of whatever you dream a partnership should be. Scorpio and Capricorn make your heart skip a beat. Libra and Aquarius love doing all that they can do to make you happy. That is what makes them happy. Change is important, and Gemini and Pisces will not hesitate to initiate it. Taurus and Virgo are like a weight keeping you where they want you to be. You will experience life as never before when you are linked to Cancer.

Most Charming Characteristics: Conscientious, thorough, positive.

Gifts: *For her:* casino trip. *For him:* foreign language tapes.

Sensual Foods: Steak fondue; cheese fondue and French bread.

Romantic Flowers: These ladies like everyone to know how faithful they are, so send them violets. To surprise them send tulips. Men like their flowers the same as their relationships, unpretending. Send them camellias with white roses to show your affection.

Best Date Nights: Thursday; 12th and 21st of each month.

Colors of Passion: *For her:* olive, purple. *For him:* royal blue, green.

The Perfect Wedding: Your sense of daring in everything you do will, of course, prevail throughout this milestone event. You love the outdoors—it so corresponds with your boundless energy. Something wild and unusual like a casino or a racetrack may tempt your urge to plan a *challenging* experience (yes, adventure triumphs even on your wedding day). Try a resort hotel or, perhaps, try designing your own location . . . all promise to satisfy your need for infinite space. Ideal setting: Australia.

Wise Words: Charles Dickens: "Any man may be in good spirits and good temper when he is well dressed. There ain't much credit in that. If I was very ragged and very jolly, then I should begin to feel I had gained a point."

Hints of Love: Communication is important here. A script isn't provided for you. You must write it for yourself.

After the Argument: *For him:* Let him just go out hiking, golfing, swimming, or camping. He needs a little adventure and just a little space. *For her:* A trip would be nice. Even a weekend out of town. Something romantic but very adventurous.

Romantic Places: Places of variety bring romance: Japan; a nightclub; Provincetown, Massachusetts.

Lucky Love Star: Sagitariel—you will never lack stimulation and spontaneity.

Beautiful Thought: An empty nest, leaving room for new visitors.

Sharing Secrets: You need to remember never to forget. *For the gals:* Her birthday, holidays, and your anniversary. Even down to each dinner date. *For the guys:* His birthday, his laundry, his mother's birthday, and, of course, him any other day of the year.

Judith's Insights

About the Man: He has a book full of little white lies that he can use in case of an emergency. These are both to get into and out of relationships. He is the original naughty boy with plenty of toys to play with. Show him yours and I am sure that he can be convinced to play. Be as honest as you would like him to be. He can be the most fun to hang with casually. If you get too serious too fast you may lose him on the way to your destination.

About the Woman: It won't take much to get this gal out of the house if she doesn't already have something to do. It will be making it to dates number two and three that will be the difficult part. If she starts using work as an excuse not to go out, you are on your way off her potential mates list. You are better off letting her say she loves you first. Allow time for that to happen. If you get impatient you can always hold her aside so you don't take things too seriously.

DECEMBER

Soul Mates: Another Sagittarius may drive you around the world, but it may also be the most stimulation you have had in a long time. With so much passion and adventure in Aries and Leo, it would be impossible to bore you. Scorpio and Capricorn need constant stimulation, but that might work well for you. A union with Libra and Aquarius could be picture-perfect. Gemini and Pisces will urge you to reach out and expand. Taurus and Virgo may grate on your nerves. Just let them teach you what they feel they can. Cancer will have you leaping through hoops.

Most Charming Characteristics: Self-confident, reliable, determined.

Gifts: *For her:* perfume: *For him:* lottery tickets.

Sensual Foods: Strawberries and cream; meat loaf.

Romantic Flowers: Iris is your flower if you are the gal sending subtle messages. If you are the man, you will look for clematis. This flower's mental beauty creates emotional stimulation for you.

Best Date Nights: Thursday; 1st and 19th of each month.

Colors of Passion: *For her:* olive, purple. *For him:* royal blue, green.

The Perfect Wedding: Your sense of daring in everything you do will, of course, prevail throughout this milestone event. You love the outdoors—it so corresponds with your boundless energy. Something wild and unusual like a casino or a racetrack may tempt your urge to plan a *challenging* experience (yes, adventure triumphs even on your wedding day). Try a resort hotel or, perhaps, try designing your own location . . . all promise to satisfy your need for infinite space. Ideal setting: Australia.

Wise Words: Charles Dickens: "Nothing is easier for any one of us than to get into a pulpit, or upon a tub, or a stump, or a platform, and blight . . . any class of small people we may choose to select. But it does not follow that because it is easy and safe, it is right."

Hints of Love: They only use the three magic words when they know they mean it, and they already know it is going to be said back to them.

After the Argument: *For him:* Let him just go out hiking, golfing, swimming, or camping. He needs a little adventure and just a little space. *For her:* A trip would be nice. Even a weekend out of town. Something romantic but very adventurous.

Romantic Places: Places of variety bring romance: tropical rain forest; comedy club; Las Vegas, Nevada.

Lucky Love Star: Sagitariel—you will never lack stimulation and spontaneity.

Beautiful Thought: Doing things that will make you feel alive will keep you feeling that way.

Sharing Secrets: Let them admire something about you first. Show them you have a sense of humor. *For the gals:* Hold their hand and then take them to the next step. *For the guys:* The way to his heart is definitely through his stomach.

Judith's Insights

About the Man: Trying to nail down this chap would be a task in itself. He is known for saying one thing and doing another. Loyalty is not his strong point until he decides to settle down. He might already have gone through the never-ending saga of finding himself before you try to get involved with him. If not, you might want to wait until he is ready. If you rub him the wrong way he can cut you off in an instant.

About the Woman: She can be a quiet mouse or a loud tiger. It all depends on the situation. Whatever is at stake, this gal is with you through the good times and the bad times. Just expect for her to make you work for that luxury. You have to be worth her hanging around and helping you through any tough times on the horizon. If you can get past the tollbooth, then you will have a great ride over the bridge. Once you are on the other side it is up to you whether you stay or not.

Soul Mates: Pairing with a fellow Sagittarius can be the most fun you have had in a long time. Aries and Leo may give you a roller coaster ride, but you will be laughing the entire time. Scorpio and Capricorn need to feel special. If you can give them that, then they will give you the world. Libra and Aquarius will ignore any shortcomings to keep the relationship moving smoothly. Gemini and Pisces will help you expand your horizons. Taurus and Virgo will have you dreaming of greener, and more relaxed, pastures. Cancer will have you trying things you had never imagined before.

Most Charming Characteristics: Ambitious, persistent, shrewd.

Gifts: *For her:* foreign language tapes. *For him:* hire someone to fix the leaky sink.

Sensual Foods: Cherry-apple pie; beef Stroganoff.

Romantic Flowers: Any rose of any color for the lady. Roses stand for love regardless of the color. Send them with orchids and you will be saying, "I love you." If you want a gentleman to know you think of him, send pansies, and forget-me-nots for true love.

Best Date Nights: Thursday; 11th and 20th of each month.

Colors of Passion: *For her:* olive, purple. *For him:* royal blue, green.

The Perfect Wedding: Your sense of daring in everything you do will, of course, prevail throughout this milestone event. You love the outdoors—it so corresponds with your boundless energy. Something wild and unusual like a casino or a racetrack may tempt your urge to plan a *challenging* experience (yes, adventure triumphs even on your wedding day). Try a resort hotel or, perhaps, try designing your own location . . . all promise to satisfy your need for infinite space. Ideal setting: Australia.

Wise Words: Henry Wadsworth Longfellow:

"Hands of invisible spirits touch the string of that mysterious instrument, the soul, and pray the prelude of our fate. We hear the voice prophetic and are not alone."

Hints of Love: Remember to keep the dating fun. Don't act like you are married before your time.

After the Argument: *For him:* Let him just go out hiking, golfing, swimming, or camping. He needs a little adventure and just a little space. *For her:* A trip would be nice. Even a weekend out of town. Something romantic but very adventurous.

Romantic Places: Places of diversity bring romance: Hong Kong; a casino; Chicago, Illinois.

Lucky Love Star: Sagitariel—you will never lack stimulation and spontaneity.

Beautiful Thought: You are never alone when you let others in.

Sharing Secrets: Give them the opportunity to notice you first. *For the gals:* They love to be adored; love at first sight. *For the guys:* Remember to always let them believe it was their idea.

Judith's Insights

About the Man: He is one in a million, and he knows it. Even if his self-esteem is running on low, he will still come off as having a big ego. His laughter will get your attention. His ability to have a good time will keep you around. Invite him to an event that involves loads of excitement and good times. He will fall in love with love as long as you don't turn off the romance or the fun. He will become a deflated tire without those two things.

About the Woman: All that this gal needs is love. You won't need a barrel of money, and it's okay if you are ragged and funny. She is a good woman, and make sure you treat her like one. She does not fancy change much, so don't move too fast. A little travel and adventure will certainly put a smile on her face. Plan a weekend getaway without telling her where you are going. She needs to keep wind in her sails to keep moving.

Soul Mates: You were made to have fun with someone just like you. That is why Sagittarius would be a great match for you. Aries and Leo will be the perfect image of whatever you dream a partnership should be. Scorpio and Capricorn make your heart skip a beat. Libra and Aquarius love doing all that they can do to make you happy. That is what makes them happy. Change is important, and Gemini and Pisces will not hesitate to initiate it. Taurus and Virgo are like a weight keeping you where they want you to be. You will experience life as never before when you are linked to Cancer.

Most Charming Characteristics: Idealistic, impatient, judge hastily.

Gifts: *For her:* spa getaway. *For him:* casino trip.

Sensual Foods: Hot-fudge sundae with all the trimmings; shepherd's pie.

Romantic Flowers: These ladies like everyone to know how faithful they are, so send them violets. To surprise them send tulips. Men like their flowers the same as their relationships, unpretending. Send them camellias with white roses to show your affection.

Best Date Nights: Thursday; 3rd and 30th of each month.

Colors of Passion: *For her:* olive, purple. *For him:* royal blue, green.

The Perfect Wedding: Your sense of daring in everything you do will, of course, prevail throughout this milestone event. You love the outdoors—it so corresponds with your boundless energy. Something wild and unusual like a casino or a racetrack may tempt your urge to plan a *challenging* experience (yes, adventure triumphs even on your wedding day). Try a resort hotel or, perhaps, try designing your own location . . . all promise to satisfy your need for infinite space. Ideal setting: Australia.

Wise Words: Charles Dickens: "Those which link the poor man to his humble heart are of the truer metal and bear the stamp of Heaven."

Hints of Love: Make sure you go on more than one date before you jump to conclusions on liking and disliking.

After the Argument: *For him:* Let him just go out hiking, golfing, swimming, or camping. He needs a little adventure and just a little space. *For her:* A trip would be nice. Even a weekend out of town. Something romantic but very adventurous.

Romantic Places: Places of variety bring romance: French Riviera; a carnival; Nashville, Tennessee.

Lucky Love Star: Sagitariel—you will never lack stimulation and spontaneity.

Beautiful Thought: The angel watching over you always understands.

Sharing Secrets: This one loves a challenge. *For the gals:* Be consistently inconsistent until you have them hooked. *For the guys:* This one loves to play catch. You may feel like a yo-yo, but as long as he is calling that's all that matters.

Judith's Insights

About the Man: You might not immediately think of this guy as being moody. If you take away his toys you will see a real mood swing indeed. No matter what, make sure that the first date is full of excitement and fun. If these ingredients are missing, then he will be missing on your second date. This guy won't mind being the responsible mate. Just allow him enough freedom to always let him feel as if he is being fed. This will keep him from looking elsewhere.

About the Woman: Her style is very underplayed, but that can't be said of her voice. When this lady makes a statement she will always get her point across loud and clear. If she is smiling at you, I would advise you to hurry up and ask her out. She can have a here-today-and-gone-tomorrow attitude. Your approach has to be strong and steady. If you wait too long, that smile will be focused on someone else.

Soul Mates: Things may be exciting or insane with another Sagittarius. It all depends on how you both approach things. Aries and Leo are a dream that becomes a reality. If you keep Scorpio and Capricorn occupied, it will prove to be a great experience. Libra and Aquarius are a dream partnership made real. Gemini and Pisces will help you learn more about yourself and what you want. Taurus and Virgo will try to keep you rooted in one spot when you want to dance around. Cancer may grate on your nerves at first, but if you hang in there it may be worth the effort.

Most Charming Characteristics: Shrewd, capable, energetic.

Gifts: *For her:* skydiving lessons. *For him:* camping trip.

Sensual Foods: Whipped cream, strawberries, brown sugar, and heavy cream.

Romantic Flowers: These ladies like men with taste. Show them you love style by sending fuchsia flowers, or even brightly colored wildflowers will do. To confuse this man, send him lilies along with bright daisies to show your innocence. Keep him guessing.

Best Date Nights: Thursday; 13th and 22nd of each month.

Colors of Passion: *For her:* olive, purple. *For him:* royal blue, green.

The Perfect Wedding: Your sense of daring in everything you do will, of course, prevail throughout this milestone event. You love the outdoors—it so corresponds with your boundless energy. Something wild and unusual like a casino or a racetrack may tempt your urge to plan a *challenging* experience (yes, adventure triumphs even on your wedding day). Try a resort hotel or, perhaps, try designing your own location . . . all promise to satisfy your need for infinite space. Ideal setting: Australia.

Wise Words: William Wordsworth: "One impulse from a vernal wood may teach you more of ***, of mortal evil and of good than all the stages can."

Hints of Love: Don't act too needy too soon. It may push this relationship away.

After the Argument: *For him:* Let him just go out hiking, golfing, swimming, or camping. He needs a little adventure and just a little space. *For her:* A trip would be nice. Even a weekend out of town. Something romantic but very adventurous.

Romantic Places: Places of diversity bring romance: Brazil; a parade; Miami, Florida.

Lucky Love Star: Sagitariel—you will never lack stimulation and spontaneity.

Beautiful Thought: The greatest burdens are the ones we put on our own shoulders, and we have the choice if they are there.

Sharing Secrets: This is a family person at heart; your presence is most important. *For the gals:* Make sure you go to Sunday dinner with her family when you are invited. *For the guys:* If you don't like his mom, you might have a hard time catching this one.

Judith's Insights

About the Man: You may have to get your passport ready if you want to hang out with this guy. He has a way about him that keeps his life and his feet in midair. He will come down in his own time. If you try to pull him down before he is ready, he is likely to stay up even longer just for spite. He will usually have many people in his life. If you are a lover of his, you may find it hard to fit into his schedule between his family and friends.

About the Woman: Make sure that you are both looking for the same thing in life. She may have seemed like a free spirit when you first met her. She really knows how to have a good time, but there is no free heart here. With her sensitivity as sharp as it is, her feelings are precious. She does have that quiet side in there that is made for you, and she loves to cuddle. You will get only one chance to hurt her. If you do, she will be gone.

Soul Mates: A pairing with a fellow Sagittarius will prove to be loads of fun for both of you. Aries and Leo are all you could dream of and more. Things with Scorpio and Capricorn must be filled with stimulation for them to work. With Libra and Aquarius in your corner, you will reach goals you forgot you set for yourself. Gemini and Pisces will help you open up to the parts in yourself you are not very fond of. If you are ready to do this, you will love it. Taurus and Virgo are like weights on your feet. You have to take them off if you want to run anywhere. Cancer may give you a nervous breakdown if you take things personally. If you don't, then it will roll right off.

Most Charming Characteristics: Honest, fair-minded, inspiring.

Gifts: *For her:* sapphire necklace. *For him:* beach house for the summer.

Sensual Foods: Puddings and pastry of all kinds.

Romantic Flowers: You are the lady of distinction, and only carnations will do. Any mix of colors with sprays of mignonette. Sweet peas or red carnations will appeal to this man's heart.

Best Date Nights: Thursday; 4th and 5th of each month.

Colors of Passion: *For her:* olive, purple. *For him:* royal blue, green.

The Perfect Wedding: Your sense of daring in everything you do will, of course, prevail throughout this milestone event. You love the outdoors—it so corresponds with your boundless energy. Something wild and unusual like a casino or a racetrack may tempt your urge to plan a *challenging* experience (yes, adventure triumphs even on your wedding day). Try a resort hotel or, perhaps, try designing your own location . . . all promise to satisfy your need for infinite space. Ideal setting: Australia.

Wise Words: William Blake: "For mercy has a human heart, pity a human face, and love the human form Divine and peace the human dress."

Hints of Love: Keep it fun. Look for new and exciting things to do, especially if you are in a long-term relationship.

After the Argument: *For him:* Let him just go out hiking, golfing, swimming, or camping. He needs a little adventure and just a little space. *For her:* A trip would be nice. Even a weekend out of town. Something romantic but very adventurous.

Romantic Places: Places of variety bring romance: Greece; a nightclub; Disney World.

Lucky Love Star: Sagitariel—you will never lack stimulation and spontaneity.

Beautiful Thought: As soon as you use the word *never,* it will happen.

Sharing Secrets: Everything in its good time. This one works slowly, but when it is time to pick up speed, watch out. *For the gals:* Don't go by the obvious. Read between the lines. As long as the invitation is being offered go full speed ahead. *For the guys:* Just when you thought you should walk away, he'll say, "I love you." Talk about confusing.

Judith's Insights

About the Man: You will spot him pretty fast. He is the one with the headache. He is on the run twenty-four hours a day, seven days a week, and he loves it. His charm at work will play like a fiddle, but it won't be quite as easy for him when it comes to love. He will like many but love only a few and trust even less than that. Let him straighten out his emotions before judging his actions. Once you take a good look you might find a person who wants to be romanced.

About the Woman: She has a way of doing things that is all her own, and she will make her path in both work and play. She is like no one else you have ever met. She can have high hopes when it comes to love and can be known for having too many expectations. She wants things to be like they are in the movies. She has a strong sense of family that cannot be underestimated. If the approval from them is not there, then she won't be there, either.

Soul Mates: You will have laughs beyond imagination with another Sagittarius. Anything you can dream about the perfect partner will be made real in Aries and Leo. Keep open to all things new and exciting and you can fly to new heights with Scorpio and Capricorn. Libra and Aquarius will make the partnership harmonious and balanced. Gemini and Pisces could be a tumultuous paring if you are not careful. Your freedom is nonnegotiable. Make sure that Taurus and Virgo know this. Cancer must be taken at face value instead of personally.

Most Charming Characteristics: Original, cautious, accurate.

Gifts: *For her:* housekeeper or cleaning service. *For him:* new pet.

Sensual Foods: Champagne with strawberries; fillet of sole.

Romantic Flowers: You love it when you get tulips, declaring love. When you receive a variety, it shows how hopelessly in love your partner is. He will just love a single rose. This shows him you understand his pleasures.

Best Date Nights: Thursday; 6th and 15th of each month.

Colors of Passion: *For her:* olive, purple. *For him:* royal blue, green.

The Perfect Wedding: Your sense of daring in everything you do will, of course, prevail throughout this milestone event. You love the outdoors— it so corresponds with your boundless energy. Something wild and unusual like a casino or a racetrack may tempt your urge to plan a *challenging* experience (yes, adventure triumphs even on your wedding day). Try a resort hotel or, perhaps, try designing your own location . . . all promise to satisfy your need for infinite space. Ideal setting: Australia.

Wise Words: Johann Wolfgang von Goethe: "To man in his fragile craft a rudder has been given, expressly that he may follow the guidance of his insight and not the caprice of the waves."

Hints of Love: This one is a cautious soul. You may have to find a way to go around to the back door.

After the Argument: *For him:* Let him just go out hiking, golfing, swimming, or camping. He needs a little adventure and just a little space. *For her:* A trip would be nice. Even a weekend out of town. Something romantic but very adventurous.

Romantic Places: Places of diversity bring romance: Venezuela; a casino; San Francisco, California.

Lucky Love Star: Sagitariel—you will never lack stimulation and spontaneity.

Beautiful Thought: The soul knows of tomorrow and helps you through today.

Sharing Secrets: This one is a charmer, perhaps even fickle. *For the gals:* If you are patient enough to stick around, this one is worth the wait. *For the guys:* If there is enough time on the clock, stick around past three months. Then maybe he will have noticed you are there.

Judith's Insights

About the Man: He can justify any wrongdoing like a great defense attorney. He has a great defense even in his love life. This good-time guy may take things a bit more seriously than you might think at first. He must always have a good time. Never attempt to wreck his fun or his moment in the spotlight. Be subtle when asking him anything. Learn to go around to his back door to get inside his head. You will find that once you are knocking at the door he will let you in much easier.

About the Woman: This lady will walk a mile for just one kiss. She is the epitome of the hopeless romantic. She can create romance out of any scenario. Always remember that her heart gets as involved as her head in any relationship she has or thinks she has. When entering into a relationship with her, you have to make sure that you are ready to be responsible for your actions and what they might do to her feelings. Make sure that you are ready.

Soul Mates: A fellow Sagittarius will have you feeling more alive than you have in a long time. Aries and Leo can be the personification of all you dreamed of in a partner. If you are open to new experiences, Scorpio and Capricorn will be your willing guides. Libra and Aquarius will do all that they can to make you happy. Gemini and Pisces will drive you nuts if you let them. Make Taurus and Virgo aware of your need for freedom and they will have to take it or leave it. Cancer may make you feel like running and staying at the same exact moment.

Most Charming Characteristics: Shrewd, intuitive, energetic.

Gifts: *For her:* beauty products. *For him:* large backyard barbecue.

Sensual Foods: Chocolates; poached salmon; flambé; filet mignon; potatoes.

Romantic Flowers: Send this girl sunflowers if you want her to know you adore her. You may even add some poppies for a splash of extravagance. His desire for sport and play will be understood when you send him hyacinth and geranium.

Best Date Nights: Thursday; 6th and 24th of each month.

Colors of Passion: *For her:* olive, purple. *For him:* royal blue, green.

The Perfect Wedding: Your sense of daring in everything you do will, of course, prevail throughout this milestone event. You love the outdoors—it so corresponds with your boundless energy. Something wild and unusual like a casino or a racetrack may tempt your urge to plan a *challenging* experience (yes, adventure triumphs even on your wedding day). Try a resort hotel or, perhaps, try designing your own location . . . all promise to satisfy your need for infinite space. Ideal setting: Australia.

Wise Words: Charles Dickens: "If we try to do our duty by those we employ . . . we know that we do right. Their doing wrong cannot change our doing right, and that should be enough for us."

Hints of Love: Passion must be in the picture at all times or you could lose this one's attention quickly.

After the Argument: *For him:* Let him just go out hiking, golfing, swimming, or camping. He needs a little adventure and just a little space. *For her:* A trip would be nice, even if it's just a weekend out of town. Something romantic but very adventurous.

Romantic Places: Places of variety bring romance: Africa; a cruise; Seattle, Washington.

Lucky Love Star: Sagitariel—you will never lack stimulation and spontaneity.

Beautiful Thought: There is nothing more thoughtful than a kind soul.

Sharing Secrets: If you are looking for love, then you have found the right mate. *For the gals:* This one could be stubborn. It may take forever to get a relationship started, but it is as solid as they come. *For the guys:* Even when he is ready, he might not be willing and able. He will put you through more obstacles than any course. Be patient.

Judith's Insights

About the Man: Where there is smoke there is almost always fire, and this guy has a blazing effect on everything he touches. He comes in and creates warmth. He has a talent for making others feel safe around him, however. He brings out sensitivity and emotions without realizing how or that he is even doing it. Even if he leaves, he always leaves plenty of memories behind to keep you warm.

About the Woman: She can be a bomb or a bombshell. Either way, her presence is known right away and is not easily forgotten once it is gone. She is what dreams are made of. At times these dreams can feel more like nightmares. Even if you date her and lose her, you certainly will have a time to remember. The memory of her will linger in your heart long after she has left for other things.

Soul Mates: *Fun* is not the word for when you get together with a fellow Sagittarius. You will feel completely understood by someone cut from the same cloth. Scorpio and Capricorn can take you to places you never imagined if you would open your mind to new possibilities. Libra and Aquarius will do anything to keep the relationship running smoothly. Try not to overstep their flexibility. The sparks will be flying the instant you hook up with Aries and Leo. Gemini and Pisces will try to figure you out. If you share what you can, they will be easier to be around. Taurus and Virgo can tend to weigh you down. Try to let them know about your need for freedom. A relationship with Cancer depends on the attitude you go in with.

Most Charming Characteristics: Bright, witty, entertaining.

Gifts: *For her:* travel book to plan next trip. *For him:* skydiving lessons.

Sensual Foods: Caviar; beef tenderloin; potatoes au gratin.

Romantic Flowers: Rhododendron will let her be on the lookout for trouble. Throw in some chrysanthemum and she'll know it is you she will be looking out for. Cactus will show him warmth. Yellow daffodil is a token of a good time had by all. Chivalry is not dead.

Best Date Nights: Thursday; 8th and 17th of each month.

Colors of Passion: *For her:* olive, purple. *For him:* royal blue, green.

The Perfect Wedding: Your sense of daring in everything you do will, of course, prevail throughout this milestone event. You love the outdoors—it so corresponds with your boundless energy. Something wild and unusual like a casino or a racetrack may tempt your urge to plan a *challenging* experience (yes, adventure triumphs even on your wedding day). Try a resort hotel or, perhaps, try designing your own location . . . all promise to satisfy your need for infinite space. Ideal setting: Australia.

Wise Words: Charles Dickens: "Pride is one of the seven deadly sins; they cannot be the pride of a mother in her children, for that is a compound of two cardinal virtues—faith and hope."

Hints of Love: A random act of kindness will go a long way with this one. What can you do for them today?

After the Argument: *For him:* Let him just go out hiking, golfing, swimming, or camping. He needs a little adventure and just a little space. *For her:* A trip would be nice. Even a weekend out of town. Something romantic but very adventurous.

Romantic Places: Places of diversity bring romance: Jamaica; a street fair; New Orleans, Louisiana.

Lucky Love Star: Sagitariel—you will never lack stimulation and spontaneity.

Beautiful Thought: Finding the humor in today will get you through tomorrow.

Sharing Secrets: If you can hang around and give constant stimulation, this could be your mate. *For the gals:* She is always looking for the Exit sign. Don't show her where it is or she will be gone. *For the guys:* Fast car, fast food; he likes everything that goes fast. Put on your running shoes. If you can keep up then he is yours.

Judith's Insights

About the Man: You will have to learn to read more than this man's mind to get to the bottom of his feelings. You will have to also read his actions. He will say words that make you feel special and be off in the next second. I wouldn't chase after him unless you are ready to travel the world trying to keep up. He does know how to love, but he needs to be taught how to be committed and to stay around.

About the Woman: She can lose her patience quickly with those who have no stimulation or desire in their lives. You will see this happen in work and with her friends. She is the get-up-and-go girl, and she has no time for those who wait for things to come to them. To get to ride with her you have to make an effort. Don't be a stick-in-the-mud when you are around her. She won't like it one bit. Everyone around will see her as the life of the party.

Soul Mates: With another Sagittarius, you will be understood like never before. Scorpio and Capricorn will show you new and exciting things when you are ready. Libra and Aquarius try to make you happy at every turn. Let them do it, because it is what makes them happy. When Aries and Leo are in your life the journey will be thrilling. Gemini and Pisces will try to push the envelope to see what they can get away with. Taurus and Virgo need stability in their life and to get it might try to rob you of your freedom. With the right frame of mind, things can go very well with Cancer.

Most Charming Characteristics: Kind, versatile, discreet.

Gifts: *For her:* casino trip. *For him:* foreign language tapes.

Sensual Foods: Passion fruit; fillet of sole almondine.

Romantic Flowers: The magnolias you send her will let her know you will be around for a while to come. Petunia is to say never despair. Holly will let him know what he is getting into. Pansy will keep you in his thoughts.

Best Date Nights: Thursday; 9th and 27th of each month.

Colors of Passion: *For her:* olive, purple. *For him:* royal blue, green.

The Perfect Wedding: Your sense of daring in everything you do will, of course, prevail throughout this milestone event. You love the outdoors—it so corresponds with your boundless energy. Something wild and unusual like a casino or a racetrack may tempt your urge to plan a *challenging* experience (yes, adventure triumphs even on your wedding day). Try a resort hotel or, perhaps, try designing your own location . . . all promise to satisfy your need for infinite space. Ideal setting: Australia.

Wise Words: Charles Dickens: "Memory, however sad, is the best and purest link between this world and a better."

Hints of Love: Family and friends are important to this one. Don't try to alienate them or it will definitely backfire on you.

After the Argument: *For him:* Let him just go out hiking, golfing, swimming, or camping. He needs a little adventure and just a little space. *For her:* A trip would be nice. Even a weekend out of town. Something romantic but very adventurous.

Romantic Places: Places of variety bring romance: Japan; a nightclub; Provincetown, Massachusetts.

Lucky Love Star: Sagitariel—you will never lack stimulation and spontaneity.

Beautiful Thought: The best things in life are truly free.

Sharing Secrets: This one may seem like a lot of work. They just need the basics: love, loyalty, and respect. *For the gals:* If you can show her your best side right from the beginning it may work. Be careful of fluff, because she will see right through it. *For the guys:* He loves to be loved. Give him plenty of attention, even if you think you don't stand a chance. Perseverance will win here.

Judith's Insights

About the Man: You may look at him and love the way he is so simple and easygoing. Guess again. He has two distinct sides to his personality. One is adventurous and ready to take a trip around the world. The other is sensitive and wants to be with the one he loves at every waking moment. He wants it all. Try to enjoy the challenge of getting him to settle down. Keep in mind, however, that it could be like walking on eggshells.

About the Woman: This lady has high hopes of living her life in a romantic paradise. It won't sit too well with her when things go off the already planned course. She has a vivid imagination and a heart of gold. Get her imagination in gear by getting her out to a place she has never been to before. She does not know herself as well as she tries to pretend. Asking her will get you nowhere. Finding out yourself will be the fun part.

Soul Mates: Another Sagittarius may drive you around the world, but it may also be the most stimulation you have had in a long time. With so much passion and adventure in Aries and Leo, it would be impossible to bore you. Scorpio and Capricorn need constant stimulation, but that might work well for you. A union with Libra and Aquarius could be picture-perfect. Gemini and Pisces will urge you to reach out and expand. Taurus and Virgo may grate on your nerves. Just let them teach you what they feel they can. Cancer will have you leaping through hoops.

Most Charming Characteristics: Positive, honest, sincere.

Gifts: *For her:* perfume. *For him:* lottery tickets.

Sensual Foods: Peaches; mousse; shrimp.

Romantic Flowers: Iris is your flower if you are the gal sending subtle messages. If you are the man, you will look for clematis. This flower's mental beauty creates emotional stimulation for you.

Best Date Nights: Thursday; 10th and 19th of each month.

Colors of Passion: *For her:* olive, purple. *For him:* royal blue, green.

The Perfect Wedding: Your sense of daring in everything you do will, of course, prevail throughout this milestone event. You love the outdoors—it so corresponds with your boundless energy. Something wild and unusual like a casino or a racetrack may tempt your urge to plan a *challenging* experience (yes, adventure triumphs even on your wedding day). Try a resort hotel or, perhaps, try designing your own location . . . all promise to satisfy your need for infinite space. Ideal setting: Australia.

Wise Words: Charles Dickens: "Nothing is high, because it is in a high place; and nothing is low because it is in a low one. This is the lesson taught us in the great book of nature."

Hints of Love: Show others how much you adore him or her. They will revel in how others notice.

After the Argument: *For him:* Let him just go out hiking, golfing, swimming, or camping. He needs a little adventure and just a little space. *For her:* A trip would be nice. Even a weekend out of town. Something romantic but very adventurous.

Romantic Places: Places of variety bring romance: tropical rain forest; comedy club; Las Vegas, Nevada.

Lucky Love Star: Sagitariel—you will never lack stimulation and spontaneity.

Beautiful Thought: Tomorrows are the stepping-stones of life.

Sharing Secrets: They are looking for love, but that is just their little secret. *For the gals:* Why shouldn't they want to be loved? Of course they do, but they want you to do all of the work. *For the guys:* You must prove yourself repeatedly. Don't expect too much until he knows you are under his thumb.

Judith's Insights

About the Man: This guy may be a bit too blunt when it comes to sharing his emotions or what he may have on his mind. If you can get past this part of his nature, the rest should be much easier to get used to. You may call him evasive, but never call him a liar. He will resent it and you as a result. Because of his cavalier attitude, others may question his loyalties. He needs to be given an amazing amount of energy as well as attention.

About the Woman: Her many talents may lead this lady down many paths, some of them at the same time. That is exactly how she likes it. It makes things more enjoyable for her if she is doing many things at once. You can always get this girl's attention by asking her out in an unusual way. She can love many and trust many as well. Be ready to give all that you have to make her happy. She will love to repay the favor when you least expect it.

Soul Mates: Pairing with a fellow Sagittarius can be the most fun you have had in a long time. Aries and Leo may give you a roller coaster ride, but you will be laughing the entire time. Scorpio and Capricorn need to feel special. If you can give them that, then they will give you the world. Libra and Aquarius will ignore any shortcomings to keep the relationship moving smoothly. Gemini and Pisces will help you expand your horizons. Taurus and Virgo will have you dreaming of greener, and more relaxed, pastures. Cancer will have you trying things you had never imagined before.

Most Charming Characteristics: Bright, witty, vivacious.

Gifts: *For her:* foreign language tapes. *For him:* hire someone to fix the leaky sink.

Sensual Foods: Kiwis; cantaloupes; strawberries.

Romantic Flowers: Any rose of any color for the lady. Roses stand for love regardless of the color. Send them with orchids and you will be saying, "I love you." If you want a gentleman to know you think of him, send pansies, and forget-me-nots for true love.

Best Date Nights: Thursday; 2nd and 20th of each month.

Colors of Passion: *For her:* olive, purple. *For him:* royal blue, green.

The Perfect Wedding: Your sense of daring in everything you do will, of course, prevail throughout this milestone event. You love the outdoors— it so corresponds with your boundless energy. Something wild and unusual like a casino or a racetrack may tempt your urge to plan a *challenging* experience (yes, adventure triumphs even on your wedding day). Try a resort hotel or, perhaps, try designing your own location . . . all promise to satisfy your need for infinite space. Ideal setting: Australia.

Wise Words: Charles Dickens: "I have never believed it possible any natural or improved ability can claim immunity from the companionship of the steady, plain, hard-working qualities, and hope to gain its end."

Hints of Love: Don't overdo it (dress, attention) too soon or this one will run. Wait until you have them hooked before you become outrageous.

After the Argument: *For him:* Let him just go out hiking, golfing, swimming, or camping. He needs a little adventure and just a little space. *For her:* A trip would be nice. Even a weekend out of town. Something romantic but very adventurous.

Romantic Places: Places of diversity bring romance: Hong Kong; a casino; Chicago, Illinois.

Lucky Love Star: Sagitariel—you will never lack stimulation and spontaneity.

Beautiful Thought: The sun shines on you for a rainy day.

Sharing Secrets: You had better be ready to pull out your romantic side if you want this to work. *For the gals:* Fireplaces, walks on the beach, or even winning a bear at the local carnival. *For the guys:* When you are out shopping bring him something home. Even if it is silly, he will love the thought.

Judith's Insights

About the Man: He does much better when he is in love. Otherwise, he will be running around chasing rainbows just to find himself. This guy needs a lot of space, even when he does find his lifelong mate. Find ways of getting answers to your questions without actually asking them. This will make him feel in his own way that he is letting you. Your playing the more cautious role would work better than both of you being carefree.

About the Woman: She needs to have boundaries set for her, but just don't tell her that. She will be walking and talking to a different beat than most anyone around her. This lady has a set of rules for her life that changes on a daily basis. If you try to explain that to her she will simply deny it until the sun comes up. You need to proceed with caution when approaching her, while trying not to let her know that is what you are doing.

Soul Mates: You were made to have fun with someone just like you. That is why Sagittarius would be a great match for you. Aries and Leo will be the perfect image of whatever you dream a partnership should be. Scorpio and Capricorn make your heart skip a beat. Libra and Aquarius love doing all that they can do to make you happy. That is what makes them happy. Change is important, and Gemini and Pisces will not hesitate to initiate it. Taurus and Virgo are like a weight keeping you where they want you to be. You will experience life as never before when you are linked to Cancer.

Most Charming Characteristics: Honest, loving, persevering.

Gifts: *For her:* spa getaway. *For him:* casino trip.

Sensual Foods: Caramel and chocolate syrup on anything.

Romantic Flowers: These ladies like everyone to know how faithful they are, so send them violets. To surprise them send tulips. Men like their flowers the same as their relationships, unpretending. Send them camellias with white roses to show your affection.

Best Date Nights: Thursday; 3rd and 21st of each month.

Colors of Passion: *For her:* olive, purple. *For him:* royal blue, green.

The Perfect Wedding: Your sense of daring in everything you do will, of course, prevail throughout this milestone event. You love the outdoors—it so corresponds with your boundless energy. Something wild and unusual like a casino or a racetrack may tempt your urge to plan a *challenging* experience (yes, adventure triumphs even on your wedding day). Try a resort hotel or, perhaps, try designing your own location . . . all promise to satisfy your need for infinite space. Ideal setting: Australia.

Wise Words: Oliver Wendell Holmes: "With eye undimmed, with strength unwarned, still toiling in your master's field, before you wave the growth unshorn, they will ripen harvest yet to yield."

Hints of Love: When these folks decide to sit on the fence don't try to push them off before they are ready. Let them do the jumping themselves.

After the Argument: *For him:* Let him just go out hiking, golfing, swimming, or camping. He needs a little adventure and just a little space. *For her:* A trip would be nice. Even a weekend out of town. Something romantic but very adventurous.

Romantic Places: Places of variety bring romance: French Riviera; a carnival; Nashville, Tennessee.

Lucky Love Star: Sagitariel—you will never lack stimulation and spontaneity.

Beautiful Thought: Being present is a present.

Sharing Secrets: It may seem like they are not interested, but ask them out anyway. *For the gals:* Until they absolutely know you are interested, you will never find out that they are. *For the guys:* Ask him out if he doesn't ask you. He may be shy or not. Either way, he may be interested.

Judith's Insights

About the Man: He has a style that is classic, and has nostalgia written all over him. You won't have to be a rocket scientist to figure this guy out. He is the typical hunter, and he loves every minute of the game. To him, it is all in good fun and romance. All you have to be is patient while you wait for him to feel safe enough to share things with you. He will show you his hand by himself as soon as he is ready, and you will be pleasantly surprised.

About the Woman: She will get you with either her smile or her laugh. Then there will be her words in any which way. She has great acting skills until her heart takes over her brain. When her emotions are that strong, you will be able to see exactly what she is feeling right on her face. She can be a bit stubborn, even to get the first date with. It all depends on which tactics she uses to lead you in. The funny part is that you will think that you are the one in control the entire time.

Soul Mates: Things may be exciting or insane with another Sagittarius. It all depends on how you both approach things. Aries and Leo are a dream that becomes a reality. If you keep Scorpio and Capricorn occupied it will prove to be a great experience. Libra and Aquarius are a dream partnership made real. Gemini and Pisces will help you learn more about yourself and what you want. Taurus and Virgo will try to keep you rooted in one spot when you want to dance around. Cancer may grate on your nerves at first, but if you hang in there it may be worth the effort.

Most Charming Characteristics: Bold, fearless, venturesome.

Gifts: *For her:* skydiving lessons. *For him:* camping trip.

Sensual Foods: Waffles with whipped cream; chocolate soufflé; French wine.

Romantic Flowers: These ladies like men with taste. Show them you love style by sending fuchsia flowers, or even brightly colored wildflowers will do. To confuse this man, send him lilies along with bright daisies to show your innocence. Keep him guessing.

Best Date Nights: Thursday; 4th and 13th of each month.

Colors of Passion: *For her:* olive, purple. *For him:* royal blue, green.

The Perfect Wedding: Your sense of daring in everything you do will, of course, prevail throughout this milestone event. You love the outdoors—it so corresponds with your boundless energy. Something wild and unusual like a casino or a racetrack may tempt your urge to plan a *challenging* experience (yes, adventure triumphs even on your wedding day). Try a resort hotel or, perhaps, try designing your own location . . . all promise to satisfy your need for infinite space. Ideal setting: Australia.

Wise Words: Oliver Wendell Holmes: "So when

the iron portal shuts behind us, and life forgets us in the noise and world, visions that shun the glaring noon day find us and glimmering starlight shows the gate of pearl."

Hints of Love: Make sure you learn to compromise, but never with your principles.

After the Argument: *For him:* Let him just go out hiking, golfing, swimming, or camping. He needs a little adventure and just a little space. *For her:* A trip would be nice. Even a weekend out of town. Something romantic but very adventurous.

Romantic Places: Places of diversity bring romance: Brazil; a parade; Miami, Florida.

Lucky Love Star: Sagitariel—you will never lack stimulation and spontaneity.

Beautiful Thought: Fantasies and dreams carry us through, for now it is hope that will do.

Sharing Secrets: Don't be surprised if the first date is with their family. *For the gals:* Make sure you invite her to your family functions. It will be a red flag to her if you don't. *For the guys:* He may seem like a family man, but isn't that what you were looking for?

Judith's Insights

About the Man: He likes things very simple. He doesn't think or act like he needs to be in charge, but guess again. His natural instinct is to lead the pack or partnership. He can make a good friend for you until he is completely ready for commitment. Even at work, he may have that Tom Sawyer way about him. This guy can get people to do what he wants, when he wants, without even knowing that he did it at all.

About the Woman: She will always be sending conflicting signals and expecting you to fulfill needs that she has never told you about. You may never know where you stand with this lady until you just sit right down and ask her. It won't take much for her to spill out what she has in her heart. You need to be not only ready for the answers to your questions, but also her expectations of you once she gives you those answers.

Soul Mates: A pairing with a fellow Sagittarius will prove to be loads of fun for both of you. Aries and Leo are all you could dream of and more. Things with Scorpio and Capricorn must be filled with stimulation for them to work. With Libra and Aquarius in your corner, you will reach goals you forgot you set for yourself. Gemini and Pisces will help you open up to the parts in yourself you are not very fond of. If you are ready to do this, you will love it. Taurus and Virgo are like weights on your feet. You have to take them off if you want to run anywhere. Cancer may give you a nervous breakdown if you take things personally. If you don't, then it will roll right off.

Most Charming Characteristics: Positive, aggressive, powerful, enthusiastic.

Gifts: *For her:* sapphire necklace. *For him:* beach house for the summer.

Sensual Foods: Oysters; mussels; spicy foods.

Romantic Flowers: You are the lady of distinction, and only carnations will do. Any mix of colors with sprays of mignonette. Sweet peas or red carnations will appeal to this man's heart.

Best Date Nights: Thursday; 5th and 23rd of each month.

Colors of Passion: *For her:* olive, purple. *For him:* royal blue, green.

The Perfect Wedding: Your sense of daring in everything you do will, of course, prevail throughout this milestone event. You love the outdoors— it so corresponds with your boundless energy. Something wild and unusual like a casino or a racetrack may tempt your urge to plan a *challenging* experience (yes, adventure triumphs even on your wedding day). Try a resort hotel or, perhaps, try designing your own location . . . all promise to satisfy your need for infinite space. Ideal setting: Australia.

Wise Words: Oliver Wendell Holmes: "If a man has a genuine sincere hearty wish to get rid of his liberty, if he is really bent upon becoming a slave, nothing can stop him."

Hints of Love: If you try to take a step back, it will be noticed. It could create the domino effect, and everything will start to fall.

After the Argument: *For him:* Let him just go out hiking, golfing, swimming, or camping. He needs a little adventure and just a little space. *For her:* A trip would be nice. Even a weekend out of town. Something romantic but very adventurous.

Romantic Places: Places of variety bring romance: Greece; a nightclub; Disney World.

Lucky Love Star: Sagitariel—you will never lack stimulation and spontaneity.

Beautiful Thought: Understanding that everything cannot happen today.

Sharing Secrets: Take me as I am could be the anthem for this one. *For the gals:* They will have strong views on just about everything. If you can hang with them, then nothing will be as important as you. *For the guys:* The thing you fall in love with may end up becoming the thing you hate. After a commitment, this one sticks around.

Judith's Insights

About the Man: He has a bit of a wild temper. You may never see it until long after you become involved with him. I wouldn't call him moody, but he can definitely get into a mood. It may not happen often or last for very long. It is his way of trying to tell you that he needs some new stimulation. When he starts really talking about his emotions, you will know that you have him. Never step on his emotions or he will stop sharing them.

About the Woman: You will find that all of her secrets are locked up in a journal. She doesn't like other people to know too much too fast. She is easy to approach, but a little harder to get to know. This gal thrives on attention. Give her a minute of conversation and you will find her chatting away for hours. She will clam up if she feels that her feelings are being invaded. Keep her talking. It will allow you to get to know just how your relationship is growing.

Soul Mates: You will have laughs beyond imagination with another Sagittarius. Anything you can dream about the perfect partner will be made real in Aries and Leo. Keep open to all things new and exciting and you can fly to new heights with Scorpio and Capricorn. Libra and Aquarius will make the partnership harmonious and balanced. Gemini and Pisces could be a tumultuous paring if you are not careful. Your freedom is nonnegotiable. Make sure that Taurus and Virgo know this. Cancer must be taken at face value instead of personally.

Most Charming Characteristics: Bright, witty, entertaining.

Gifts: *For her:* housekeeper or cleaning service. *For him:* new pet.

Sensual Foods: Lobster; watermelon.

Romantic Flowers: You love it when you get tulips, declaring love. When you receive a variety, it shows how hopelessly in love your partner is. He will just love a single rose. This shows him you understand his pleasures.

Best Date Nights: Thursday; 6th and 15th of each month.

Colors of Passion: *For her:* olive, purple. *For him:* royal blue, green.

The Perfect Wedding: Your sense of daring in everything you do will, of course, prevail throughout this milestone event. You love the outdoors—it so corresponds with your boundless energy. Something wild and unusual like a casino or a racetrack may tempt your urge to plan a *challenging* experience (yes, adventure triumphs even on your wedding day). Try a resort hotel or, perhaps, try designing your own location . . . all promise to satisfy your need for infinite space. Ideal setting: Australia.

Wise Words: Charles Dickens: "Who can tell how scenes of peace and quietude sink into the minds of pain-worn dwellers in close and noisy places, and carry their own freshness, deep into their jaded hearts."

Hints of Love: Consistence and persistence will get this prize every time. They will value the effort.

After the Argument: *For him:* Let him just go out hiking, golfing, swimming, or camping. He needs a little adventure and just a little space. *For her:* A trip would be nice. Even a weekend out of town. Something romantic but very adventurous.

Romantic Places: Places of diversity bring romance: Venezuela; a casino; San Francisco, California.

Lucky Love Star: Sagitariel—you will never lack stimulation and spontaneity.

Beautiful Thought: All you need is time; time will show you the way.

Sharing Secrets: They seem moody until you get to know them. *For the gals:* You may not know whether to say hello or drop dead. As relations progress you will learn not to leave her dangling, and her moods will become more consistent. *For the guys:* To know him is to love him. His bark is much worse than his bite. He just wants someone to love him without criticism.

Judith's Insights

About the Man: You may not think that he is capable of being intimidated, but think again. Don't be too demonstrative or overwhelming until you have already laid the emotional groundwork. You can only do that with time and consistency. Don't push what has to come naturally. When he makes a commitment he will stick to it no matter what. He can sometimes still be sticking to it long after it is over.

About the Woman: This lady spends much too much time trying to protect herself. Unfortunately, she can be her own worst enemy. She will challenge many things that don't need to be challenged and question what does not need to be questioned. If a relationship with her is important to you, you have to prove yourself through these challenges. She is an endless romantic, and she seldom gives up. She wants things like they are shown in the movies.

Soul Mates: A fellow Sagittarius will have you feeling more alive than you have in a long time. Aries and Leo can be the personification of all you dreamed of in a partner. If you are open to new experiences, Scorpio and Capricorn will be your willing guides. Libra and Aquarius will do all that they can to make you happy. Gemini and Pisces will drive you nuts if you let them. Make Taurus and Virgo aware of your need for freedom and they will have to take it or leave it. Cancer may make you feel like running and staying at the same exact moment.

Most Charming Characteristics: Spiritual, idealistic, religious.

Gifts: *For her:* beauty products. *For him:* large backyard barbecue.

Sensual Foods: Strawberries; truffles; shish kebab.

Romantic Flowers: Send this girl sunflowers if you want her to know you adore her. You may even add some poppies for a splash of extravagance. His desire for sport and play will be understood when you send him hyacinth and geranium.

Best Date Nights: Thursday; 6th and 24th of each month.

Colors of Passion: *For her:* olive, purple. *For him:* royal blue, green.

The Perfect Wedding: Your sense of daring in everything you do will, of course, prevail throughout this milestone event. You love the outdoors—it so corresponds with your boundless energy. Something wild and unusual like a casino or a racetrack may tempt your urge to plan a *challenging* experience (yes, adventure triumphs even on your wedding day). Try a resort hotel or, perhaps, try designing your own location . . . all promise to satisfy your need for infinite space. Ideal setting: Australia.

Wise Words: Ludwig van Beethoven: "Yes, he who wishes to touch the heart must seek his inspiration from on high. Without this there will be naught but sounds and notes, a soulless body—Is this not true?"

Hints of Love: Be funny. Laughter will be what keeps this one coming back again and again.

After the Argument: *For him:* Let him just go out hiking, golfing, swimming, or camping. He needs a little adventure and just a little space. *For her:* A trip would be nice. Even a weekend out of town. Something romantic but very adventurous.

Romantic Places: Places of variety bring romance: Africa; a cruise; Seattle, Washington.

Lucky Love Star: Sagitariel—you will never lack stimulation and spontaneity.

Beautiful Thought: Sometimes all you need is time to pass, in order for things to happen.

Sharing Secrets: You had better be able to put your money where your mouth is. *For the gals:* It doesn't need to be lavish, but she does love the loot. The more the better. *For the guys:* He doesn't mind spending his hard-earned cash, but he loves to see you contribute to please him.

Judith's Insights

About the Man: He has way too much to accomplish to be weighed down. That is, unless he finds the mate who adds to the goal or can join the path that he has set for himself. His temper can be erratic, as can his love. The only way to his heart is to prove that you can keep up with his pace. Going toward your own goals will certainly grab his attention. Accomplishing your goals will have him eating out of your hand.

About the Woman: You don't need any fancy style with this lady. She will romanticize even a short stroll in the park. If she is in love, she will give you all that she has and more. She will give you her life. She won't ask for much in return. When she does ask, you must make sure that you are capable of being there. She will have a good idea that you are ready to hold up your end if she has asked in the first place.

Soul Mates: *Fun* is not the word for when you get together with a fellow Sagittarius. You will feel completely understood by someone cut from the same cloth. Scorpio and Capricorn can take you to places you never imagined if you would open your mind to new possibilities. Libra and Aquarius will do anything to keep the relationship running smoothly. Try not to overstep their flexibility. Spontaneity is the name of the game when you play with Aries and Leo. Gemini and Pisces will try to figure you out. If you share what you can, they will be easier to be around. Taurus and Virgo can tend to weigh you down. Try to let them know about your need for freedom. A relationship with Cancer depends on the attitude you go in with.

Most Charming Characteristics: Quiet, reserved, imaginative.

Gifts: *For her:* travel book to plan next trip. *For him:* skydiving lessons.

Sensual Foods: Grapes, fine cheeses and crackers; taffy.

Romantic Flowers: Rhododendron will let her be on the lookout for trouble. Throw in some chrysanthemum and she'll know it is you she will be looking out for. Cactus will show him warmth. Yellow daffodil is a token of a good time had by all. Chivalry is not dead.

Best Date Nights: Thursday; 8th and 26th of each month.

Colors of Passion: *For her:* olive, purple. *For him:* royal blue, green.

The Perfect Wedding: Your sense of daring in everything you do will, of course, prevail throughout this milestone event. You love the outdoors—it so corresponds with your boundless energy. Something wild and unusual like a casino or a racetrack may tempt your urge to plan a *challenging* experience (yes, adventure triumphs even on your wedding day). Try a resort hotel or, perhaps, try designing your own location . . . all promise to satisfy your need for infinite space. Ideal setting: Australia.

Wise Words: Charles Dickens: "To surround anything, however monstrous or ridiculous, with an air of mystery, is to invest it with a secret charm, and power of attraction which to the crowd is irresistible."

Hints of Love: Treat this one like royalty or precious cargo. They will love being valued in this way.

After the Argument: *For him:* Let him just go out hiking, golfing, swimming, or camping. He needs a little adventure and just a little space. *For her:* A trip would be nice. Even a weekend out of town. Something romantic but very adventurous.

Romantic Places: Places of diversity bring romance: Jamaica; a street fair; New Orleans, Louisiana.

Lucky Love Star: Sagitariel—you will never lack stimulation and spontaneity.

Beautiful Thought: Such small pebbles make so many ripples in the water.

Sharing Secrets: Nobody likes a weak link, especially not this one. *For the gals:* Make sure you treat her like a lady and act like a man. *For the guys:* Put your best foot forward. Dress your best and keep your manners in check. This man notices.

Judith's Insights

About the Man: He needs more applause than he will ever care to admit to. He has a command-performance attitude when it comes to work. He can be lazy or aggressive when it comes to relationships. It depends on how important that particular relationship and that particular person are to him. The closer you get to his heart, the more complicated this relationship can get. Let him share what is inside in his own time.

About the Woman: You may have to flip a coin to decide if you want to take on this lady. If you have confidence, and you don't mind criticism, then by all means, step up to the plate. To truly know her is to love her. She will keep an invisible wall up to protect her at first. You may not notice this wall because the camouflage of having fun and looking happy disguises it well. The ones who don't take the time to find out who she really is are missing out.

Soul Mates: With another Sagittarius, you will be understood like never before. Scorpio and Capricorn will show you new and exciting things when you are ready. Libra and Aquarius try to make you happy at every turn. Let them do it, because it is what makes them happy. Getting there isn't just half the fun when traveling with Aries and Leo. It can be so much fun that you forget where you were trying to go. Gemini and Pisces will try to push the envelope to see what they can get away with. Taurus and Virgo need stability in their life and might try to rob you of your freedom to get it. With the right frame of mind, things can go very well with Cancer.

Most Charming Characteristics: Strong-willed, aggressive, sympathetic.

Gifts: *For her:* casino trip. *For him:* foreign language tapes.

Sensual Foods: Champagne; grapes; mangoes; filet mignon.

Romantic Flowers: The magnolias you send her will let her know you will be around for a while to come. Petunia is to say never despair. Holly will let him know what he is getting into. Pansy will keep you in his thoughts.

Best Date Nights: Thursday; 18th and 27th of each month.

Colors of Passion: *For her:* olive, purple. *For him:* dark gray, green.

The Perfect Wedding: Your sense of daring in everything you do will, of course, prevail throughout this milestone event. You love the outdoors—it so corresponds with your boundless energy. Something wild and unusual like a casino or a racetrack may tempt your urge to plan a *challenging* experience (yes, adventure triumphs even on your wedding day). Try a resort hotel or, perhaps, try designing your own location . . . all promise to satisfy your need for infinite space. Ideal setting: Australia.

Wise Words: Alfred, Lord Tennyson: "Oh! rest thee sure that I love thee well and cleave to thee."

Hints of Love: Affection is important, but only if it comes naturally. Otherwise, the sirens will go off.

After the Argument: *For him:* Let him just go out hiking, golfing, swimming, or camping. He needs a little adventure and just a little space. *For her:* A trip would be nice. Even a weekend out of town. Something romantic but very adventurous.

Romantic Places: Places of variety bring romance: Japan; a nightclub; Provincetown, Massachusetts.

Lucky Love Star: Sagitariel—you will never lack stimulation and spontaneity.

Beautiful Thought: A fallen leaf starts a new life when someone picks it off the ground.

Sharing Secrets: Attention, attention, attention. *For the gals:* Do it any way you can. Presents, phone calls, cards, or flowers. Whatever works for you will work for her. *For the guys:* He would love nostalgic gifts or T-shirts. He also likes phone calls, as long as they don't interrupt his favorite pastimes.

Judith's Insights

About the Man: Think of him as a tree with a lot of branches. Each of those branches is filled with leaves. They never seem lonely and always look fulfilled. Yet, there they are, standing alone. He may not need a partner, but he really does want one. Don't disturb his branches or his leaves. Just simply stand beside him with your own set of goals and give him the freedom to make up his mind about where to go from there.

About the Woman: She is never sure of what she wants. Life happens to her, and she deals with what comes. She is much more complicated than she would like you to think. Do things the old-fashioned way. Date her and let her get to know you. Don't ask too much from her too soon. She can only show you her true self as she comes to realize it herself. Don't ask for information she might not have yet.

Soul Mates: Another Sagittarius may drive you around the world, but it may also be the most stimulation you have had in a long time. With so much passion and adventure in Aries and Leo, it would be impossible to bore you. Scorpio and Capricorn need constant stimulation, but that might work well for you. A union with Libra and Aquarius could be picture-perfect. Gemini and Pisces will urge you to reach out and expand. Taurus and Virgo may grate on your nerves. Just let them teach you what they feel they can. Cancer will have you leaping through hoops.

Most Charming Characteristics: Ambitious, capable, thrifty.

Gifts: *For her:* perfume. *For him:* lottery tickets.

Sensual Foods: Châteaubriand; crème brûlée.

Romantic Flowers: Iris is your flower if you are the gal sending subtle messages. If you are the man, you will look for clematis. This flower's mental beauty creates emotional stimulation for you.

Best Date Nights: Thursday; 1st and 10th of each month.

Colors of Passion: *For her:* olive, purple. *For him:* royal blue, violet.

The Perfect Wedding: Your sense of daring in everything you do will, of course, prevail throughout this milestone event. You love the outdoors—it so corresponds with your boundless energy. Something wild and unusual like a casino or a racetrack may tempt your urge to plan a *challenging* experience (yes, adventure triumphs even on your wedding day). Try a resort hotel or, perhaps, try designing your own location . . . all promise to satisfy your need for infinite space. Ideal setting: Australia.

Wise Words: Ralph Waldo Emerson: "No truth so sublime but it may be trivial tomorrow in the light of new thoughts. People wish to be settled only as far as they are unsettled; is there any hope for them?"

Hints of Love: This one likes others to make his or her dreams come true. Be the "fantasy" fulfiller.

After the Argument: *For him:* Let him just go out hiking, golfing, swimming, or camping. He needs a little adventure and just a little space. *For her:* A trip would be nice. Even a weekend out of town. Something romantic but very adventurous.

Romantic Places: Places of variety bring romance: tropical rain forest; comedy club; Las Vegas, Nevada.

Lucky Love Star: Sagitariel—you will never lack stimulation and spontaneity.

Beautiful Thought: Anything that matters to you, matters.

Sharing Secrets: Make sure you are not the killjoy. *For the gals:* When she has an idea, try it before you decide you don't like it. She needs to be pleased. *For the guys:* Do the things he loves to do and he will make the things you love ten times more fun.

Judith's Insights

About the Man: He can sometimes expect from others what he can't give himself. He does get disappointed, but he will seldom let you know it. He doesn't stand on ceremony, so he won't mind if you get the ball rolling as long as he gets a turn to decide where it goes and how fast it gets there. As long as you are there to add to his life, things will go smoothly. If you try to smother him he will lose oxygen. Anything that loses oxygen will die.

About the Woman: Watching her, you will notice when she is a blaze of fire or a fire that has been put out. Keep feeding the fire to get her going. You have to get to know who she is to understand her way of life. She is more basic than not, and is looking for a secure pillow to lay her head on. Just don't offer her what you can't actually give. That will be the beginning of the end in her mind. You might not get a chance to make up for it.

Soul Mates: Pairing with a fellow Sagittarius can be the most fun you have had in a long time. Aries and Leo may give you a roller coaster ride, but you will be laughing the entire time. Scorpio and Capricorn need to feel special. If you can give them that, then they will give you the world. Libra and Aquarius will ignore any shortcomings to keep the relationship moving smoothly. Gemini and Pisces will help you expand your horizons. Taurus and Virgo will have you dreaming of greener, and more relaxed, pastures. Cancer will have you trying things you had never imagined before.

Most Charming Characteristics: Honest, trustworthy, affectionate.

Gifts: *For her:* foreign language tapes. *For him:* hire someone to fix the leaky sink.

Sensual Foods: Shrimp; sinful chocolate cake.

Romantic Flowers: Any rose of any color for the lady. Roses stand for love regardless of the color. Send them with orchids and you will be saying, "I love you." If you want a gentleman to know you think of him, send pansies, and forget-me-nots for true love.

Best Date Nights: Thursday; 2nd and 11th of each month.

Colors of Passion: *For her:* violet, purple, brown. *For him:* royal blue, green.

The Perfect Wedding: Your sense of daring in everything you do will, of course, prevail throughout this milestone event. You love the outdoors— it so corresponds with your boundless energy. Something wild and unusual like a casino or a racetrack may tempt your urge to plan a *challenging* experience (yes, adventure triumphs even on your wedding day). Try a resort hotel or, perhaps, try designing your own location . . . all promise to satisfy your need for infinite space. Ideal setting: Australia.

Wise Words: Edwin Arnold: "Like threads of silver seen through crystal beads, let love through good deed show."

Hints of Love: Stop worrying about next week's date today or there will not be one tomorrow.

After the Argument: *For him:* Let him just go out hiking, golfing, swimming, or camping. He needs a little adventure and just a little space. *For her:* A trip would be nice. Even a weekend out of town. Something romantic but very adventurous.

Romantic Places: Places of diversity bring romance: Hong Kong; a casino; Chicago, Illinois.

Lucky Love Star: Sagitariel—you will never lack stimulation and spontaneity.

Beautiful Thought: The road to good intentions will always take you somewhere.

Sharing Secrets: You had better be ready to have a relationship. *For the gals:* No lies, no games, and no mistakes. She wants what she wants with as little work possible. *For the guys:* If you have games on your mind, then move on. This one likes fun any way he can get it, but no emotional roller coasters.

Judith's Insights

About the Man: Send him flowers and he will love it. He will take any kind of attention that he can get his hands on. He doesn't mind being swooned over and gussied up for. As a matter of fact, he prefers it that way. He may make the first move, but once that has happened you can feel free to make any moves you want. He will be open to having a good time, but he needs to have a time and place for everything else. That includes commitment. He can only get to that when the time is right.

About the Woman: She only thinks she knows what she wants. You may have to be the one to teach her how to find out what it really is. She lives for enjoyment. Keep the conversation light until you get the green light to move on to new subjects. She is one live-and-learn type of gal. What may be so good for her today may not work for her tomorrow. She is able to roll through the changes in order for things to go smoothly.

Soul Mates: You were made to have fun with someone just like you. That is why Sagittarius would be a great match for you. Aries and Leo will be the perfect image of whatever you dream a partnership should be. Scorpio and Capricorn make your heart skip a beat. Libra and Aquarius love doing all that they can do to make you happy. That is what makes them happy. Change is important, and Gemini and Pisces will not hesitate to initiate it. Taurus and Virgo are like a weight keeping you where they want you to be. You will experience life as never before when you are linked to Cancer.

Most Charming Characteristics: Optimistic, determined, shrewd.

Gifts: *For her:* spa getaway. *For him:* casino trip.

Sensual Foods: Toasted marshmallows; chocolates.

Romantic Flowers: These ladies like everyone to know how faithful they are, so send them violets. To surprise them send tulips. Men like their flowers the same as their relationships, unpretending. Send them camellias with white roses to show your affection.

Best Date Nights: Thursday; 3rd and 21st of each month.

Colors of Passion: *For her:* olive, purple. *For him:* royal blue, green.

The Perfect Wedding: Your sense of daring in everything you do will, of course, prevail throughout this milestone event. You love the outdoors— it so corresponds with your boundless energy. Something wild and unusual like a casino or a racetrack may tempt your urge to plan a *challenging* experience (yes, adventure triumphs even on your wedding day). Try a resort hotel or, perhaps, try designing your own location . . . all promise to satisfy your need for infinite space. Ideal setting: Australia.

Wise Words: George Eliot: "No soul is desolate as long as there is a human being for whom it can feel trust and reverence."

Hints of Love: Keep the romance in the picture. Don't forget the long walks on the beach and camping out in front of the fireplace.

After the Argument: *For him:* Let him just go out hiking, golfing, swimming, or camping. He needs a little adventure and just a little space. *For her:* A trip would be nice. Even a weekend out of town. Something romantic but very adventurous.

Romantic Places: Places of variety bring romance: French Riviera; a carnival; Nashville, Tennessee.

Lucky Love Star: Sagitariel—you will never lack stimulation and spontaneity.

Beautiful Thought: To be respectful is to be successful.

Sharing Secrets: You may have to give this one more than one chance. *For the gals:* Intriguing as she is, expect a handful. She lightens up as time goes on. *For the guys:* His quirks may make you have second thoughts, but that is what separates the men from the boys.

Judith's Insights

About the Man: He can act macho. They key word here, however, is *act*. He is outgoing yet shy at the same time. You may find him chatting around like no there is tomorrow until emotions come into play. It is not what he really is at all. This guy is definitely a product of his environment. If you change his environment you will see a whole new man. Remember this when he is not acting like his true self.

About the Woman: She comes off with the utmost confidence. This is just a persona that she wants you to see. She needs grounding as much as spontaneity. It may be hard to figure out which one should come first. She can explore her emotions only with someone with whom she feels completely safe. Treat her like the lady she is while you get to know her. When you are inside of her head, you will know just what to do.

Soul Mates: Another Capricorn could be exactly what you are looking for. With Aquarius and Pisces, you will both have a passion for life that you never experienced before. Cancer's and Aries's instinct to control all around them will leave you dreaming of greener pastures. There is not much that can shake the stable foundation you can make with Taurus and Virgo. Scorpio and Gemini will be too much energy focused in every direction for you to take lying down. Libra will fill every minute with a passion for life that can't help but rub off on you. Getting along with the dominating Leo could prove to be a difficult task for you. You and Sagittarius can make a tight partnership.

Most Charming Characteristics: Generous, kind-hearted, affectionate.

Gifts: *For her:* vanilla-scented candles. *For him:* chess set.

Sensual Foods: Chocolate-covered strawberries; New York steak; scallops.

Romantic Flowers: These ladies like men with taste. Show them you love style by sending fuchsia flowers, or even brightly colored wildflowers will do. To confuse this man, send him lilies along with bright daisies to show your innocence. Keep him guessing.

Best Date Nights: Saturday; 4th and 31st of each month.

Colors of Passion: *For her:* green, brown. *For him:* dark gray, brown.

The Perfect Wedding: Earthy goat girls feel most secure on the old terra firma, but climb, climb you must. The top of a mountain in Colorado or the top of a monument in Washington, D.C.; all these locations lend themselves to your powerful persona. Inspired by tradition, you are happiest in a pleasant, conventional location. Ideal setting: Moscow; the Grand Canyon.

Wise Words: J. M. Barrie: "As soon as you can say what you think, and not what some other person has thought for you, you are on your way to being a remarkable man."

Hints of Love: The mystery is important, but being evasive will create disaster. Make sure you know the difference.

After the Argument: *For him:* Pay him extra attention. Send him something at work so everybody notices. Make him feel important. *For her:* Go overboard in a big way. Don't just send flowers at work, but to her home and to her mother's when she is there for Sunday dinner.

Romantic Places: Places of beauty bring romance: the rain forest; a garden; the Grand Canyon.

Lucky Love Star: Capriel—you never like the feeling of loneliness.

Beautiful Thought: Friendship is the entwining of two souls.

Sharing Secrets: Talk about high maintenance. *For the gals:* Once she sees that you go out of your way for her, then she will for you. *For the guys:* The bark is definitely much worse than the bite. He comes on stronger and more obstinate than he actually is.

Judith's Insights

About the Man: There is no better friend than this guy, although he may be a bit of a show-off at times. His theory is that if you have it you have to flaunt it. He has plenty of fantasies about his life. He might not leave any of these fantasies behind until a commitment has been made. You may think of him as a flirt, and he definitely is. That does not necessarily mean that he is not looking for a lifetime commitment.

About the Woman: You will see her as one person before she makes a commitment, but she will be quite another after she does. This lady lightens up and gets more fun to be around. She really won't mind being settled down. It will give her the power to concentrate on so many other things in her life. She longs for love and stability in her life. Without these things, she will walk around aimlessly until someone can give them to her.

Soul Mates: You will be undoubtedly attracted to someone of your own sign, Capricorn. You will make it a good relationship when you accept everything about yourself, for you will see it constantly in them. Virgo and Taurus will be great partners for you because you will each have equal responsibility and reward. Cancer will draw you in but may drive you nuts once you are there. Libra and Aries are brimming with passion. They will give you a new view of the world around you. Leo needs to be in control most of the time. Can you give up as much as they expect? Pisces's charm will prove to be irresistible for you. Keep them occupied and they will do the same for you. Aquarius and Sagittarius can be the perfect combination of yin and yang energy. You will bring out the best in each other at every turn. Gemini and Scorpio are just too much for you to take. Their flirting will leave you boiling.

Most Charming Characteristics: Capable, generous, alert.

Gifts: *For her:* hummingbird feeder. *For him:* day of golf.

Sensual Foods: Vanilla and strawberry mousse; tiramisù; espresso.

Romantic Flowers: You are the lady of distinction, and only carnations will do. Any mix of colors with sprays of mignonette. Sweet peas or red carnations will appeal to this man's heart.

Best Date Nights: Saturday; 4th and 23rd of each month.

Colors of Passion: *For her:* olive, green. *For him:* dark gray, brown.

The Perfect Wedding: Earthy goat girls feel most secure on the old terra firma, but climb, climb you must. The top of a mountain in Colorado or the top of a monument in Washington, D.C.; all these locations lend themselves to your powerful persona. Inspired by tradition, you are happiest in a pleasant, conventional location. Ideal setting: Moscow, the Grand Canyon.

Wise Words: Charles Dickens: "Our affections, however laudable in this transitory world, should never master us, we should guide them."

Hints of Love: If you learn to back up when things are moving too fast, you won't have to bow out so often.

After the Argument: *For him:* Pay him extra attention. Send him something at work so everybody notices. Make him feel important. *For her:* Go overboard in a big way. Don't just send flowers at work, but to her home and to her mother's when she is there for Sunday dinner.

Romantic Places: Places of power bring romance: Russia; a courthouse; Washington, D.C.

Lucky Love Star: Capriel—you never like the feeling of loneliness.

Beautiful Thought: Reflections allow you to inspire yourself.

Sharing Secrets: Make sure you have at least five dates before you make up your mind. *For the gals:* She can be cynical, so it could be a few dates before she loosens up. *For the guys:* He still has yesterday on his mind. He needs a reason to forget his past relationship. Make a new history for him.

Judith's Insights

About the Man: He not only fears commitment, but he will run from it if given the chance. This is only at the first mention of it. Once he gets used to the idea and realizes that it is what his emotions want he will come back to work out the terms. You have to be ready to deal with his indecision. Don't run away when things get sticky with him. Just step back and allow him the time and opportunity to get his emotions settled.

About the Woman: She won't always hit the ball back to you. If that happens, you should take a step back from her game. She is a shy one. She won't let many people know what she is doing or what she wants because it can change from day to day. Patience is the main requirement for a relationship with her. Don't challenge her thoughts or you will still be standing there while she is running away. Once her feelings settle down she will be able to make better decisions.

Soul Mates: A pairing with another Capricorn could be anything but difficult. Achievement of great things is possible when you have Aquarius and Pisces in your corner. Cancer and Aries can wear you a little thin. You don't mind having all of your ducks in a row, but nailed to the floor would drive you crazy. There is wonderful potential for big things when you combine your charm with that of Taurus and Virgo. Scorpio and Gemini will run you ragged with their teasing tendencies. Things with Leo must be up front right away before they decide who is running the show. Libra needs constant stimulation to keep going. You might want to take your vitamins for this one. Sagittarius can be the partner you have always been looking for.

Most Charming Characteristics: Bold, energetic.

Gifts: *For her:* home security system. *For him:* trip to a museum.

Sensual Foods: Raspberries; pound cake; caviar.

Romantic Flowers: You love it when you get tulips, declaring love. When you receive a variety, it shows how hopelessly in love your partner is. He will just love a single rose. This shows him you understand his pleasures.

Best Date Nights: Saturday; 6th and 15th of each month.

Colors of Passion: *For her:* green, brown, violet. *For him:* brown, royal blue.

The Perfect Wedding: Earthy goat girls feel most secure on the old terra firma, but climb, climb you must. The top of a mountain in Colorado or the top of a monument in Washington, D.C.; all these locations lend themselves to your powerful persona. Inspired by tradition, you are happiest in a pleasant, conventional location. Ideal setting: Moscow; the Grand Canyon.

Wise Words: Charles Dickens: "Gold conjures up a mist about a man more destructive of all of his senses and his lulling to his feeling than the fumes of charcoal."

Hints of Love: Expecting too much too soon can only build up hopes that will fall down too easily.

After the Argument: *For him:* Pay him extra attention. Send him something at work so everybody notices. Make him feel important. *For her:* Go overboard in a big way. Don't just send flowers at work, but to her home and to her mother's when she is there for Sunday dinner.

Romantic Places: Places of beauty bring romance: Africa; a hot-air balloon; Yosemite, California.

Lucky Love Star: Capriel—you never like the feeling of loneliness.

Beautiful Thought: Only you and your Guardian Angel know the truth.

Sharing Secrets: Don't be in a hurry, or it will be over before it begins. *For the gals:* Like fine wine and amazing food. Savor a moment until an hour is created. *For the guys:* To do too much too fast will prove risky. Try to give a push and he will just jump ship.

Judith's Insights

About the Man: This man has a big ego, and why not? If he does not like himself, how is he ever going to convince you to? His style may seem overbearing until you get used to it. He has a tendency to overcomplicate things. He has a solid reputation and likes to keep it that way. He will protect his honor along with yours. The way around this guy is to always tell him he is right first. Then go back with a new idea, allowing him to believe it was his all along.

About the Woman: You may think she does not get out much, but you would be sadly mistaken. This is no wallflower, even though she may lead you to believe that she is. She keeps her past behind her, so don't ask too many questions. She will change the flow of the relationship, and the longer she is in it with you the more she will let you in. Everything has its time and its place. If you are flirting at work she may not respond, even if she is interested.

Soul Mates: How can you not get along with someone as much like you as a fellow Capricorn? Pisces and Aquarius will fill your life with never-ending passion and inspiration. Cancer and Aries may try to fence you in. You can't live like that, so make sure they never get the chance. Taurus and Virgo will give you all you need to fulfill even your craziest dreams. Scorpio and Gemini will have you turning green when they turn their flirtatious charm elsewhere. Libras will shine their warm light on you as long as you keep them interested. That feeling is well worth any work that must be done. Leo has to think that they run the show if they are to remain happy anywhere. A partnership with Sagittarius, whether love or not, can be strong and long-lived.

Most Charming Characteristics: Honest, conscientious, methodical.

Gifts: *For her:* tickets to the theater. *For him:* home improvement books.

Sensual Foods: Flambé; lobster; oysters.

Romantic Flowers: Send this girl sunflowers if you want her to know you adore her. You may even add some poppies for a splash of extravagance. His desire for sport and play will be understood when you send him hyacinth and geranium.

Best Date Nights: Saturday; 15th and 24th of each month.

Colors of Passion: *For her:* green, brown, violet. *For him:* dark gray, brown.

The Perfect Wedding: Earthy goat girls feel most secure on the old terra firma, but climb, climb you must. The top of a mountain in Colorado or the top of a monument in Washington, D.C.; all these locations lend themselves to your powerful persona. Inspired by tradition, you are happiest in a pleasant, conventional location. Ideal setting: Moscow; the Grand Canyon.

Wise Words: Charles Dickens: "What is right is right, and you can't either by tears or laughter do away with its character."

Hints of Love: Make sure all the ingredients are present before putting the cake in the oven.

After the Argument: *For him:* Pay him extra attention. Send him something at work so everybody notices. Make him feel important. *For her:* Go overboard in a big way. Don't just send flowers at work, but to her home and to her mother's when she is there for Sunday dinner.

Romantic Places: Places of power bring romance: India; a marina; New York City.

Lucky Love Star: Capriel—you never like the feeling of loneliness.

Beautiful Thought: The world is a circle so it is easier to get around.

Sharing Secrets: They need to look before they leap, but only in love. *For the gals:* She needs creative and exciting dates to keep her interested. Don't take her for granted too soon. *For the guys:* You may think he gives signs of moving this relationship quickly; make sure you slow it down before he does.

Judith's Insights

About the Man: You may think at first that he is emotionless, but that is not this guy at all. As time goes by, you will see a man full of emotions. You may call him cautious, and he may look at himself with a strong opinion of himself. Pride is important to him, and he does things in that manner. I would give him time to make the first move, but if you do it, be subtle. Don't get nervous if he doesn't call right away. He may have his own game plan.

About the Woman: This lady has a lot of class, and you may need to appeal to her classy ways. Invite her to an opera or a concert. It takes her a long time to get over her first love. When she falls in love, every time is like the first time. She can be hard to get to know at first, but as she sees your loyalty she will certainly give you hers. She may not wear status clothes, but she would prefer if you were wearing the hottest designers.

Soul Mates: You cannot help but get along with a Capricorn like yourself. Virgo and Taurus will support you and inspire you in everything you undertake. A relationship with Cancer will start strong but will weaken as time passes. Aries and Libra will open your eyes to dreams and goals you never thought about for yourself. Leo needs someone to lord it over and control. You would be wise to walk away if you don't like giving up control. Pisces will put you under a spell you don't want to wear off. Sagittarius and Aquarius will make you become the perfect you you always dreamed you could be. Gemini and Scorpio are too much for you to handle.

Most Charming Characteristics: Entertaining, fun-loving, intelligent.

Gifts: *For her:* antique furniture. *For him:* gold watch.

Sensual Foods: Crème brûlée; poached salmon.

Romantic Flowers: Rhododendron will let her be on the lookout for trouble. Throw in some chrysanthemum and she'll know it is you she will be looking out for. Cactus will show him warmth. Yellow daffodil is a token of a good time had by all. Chivalry is not dead.

Best Date Nights: Saturday; 10th and 28th of each month.

Colors of Passion: *For her:* green, brown, violet. *For him:* dark gray, brown.

The Perfect Wedding: Earthy goat girls feel most secure on the old terra firma, but climb, climb you must. The top of a mountain in Colorado or the top of a monument in Washington, D.C.; all these locations lend themselves to your powerful persona. Inspired by tradition, you are happiest in a pleasant, conventional location. Ideal setting: Moscow; the Grand Canyon.

Wise Words: Charles Dickens: "Nothing ever happened on this globe for good at which some people did not have their fill of laughter in its outset."

Hints of Love: Simple often turns into complicated with this one. When you overcomplicate the moment, try to step back for a breather.

After the Argument: *For him:* Pay him extra attention. Send him something at work so everybody notices. Make him feel important. *For her:* Go overboard in a big way. Don't just send flowers at work, but to her home and to her mother's when she is there for Sunday dinner.

Romantic Places: Places of beauty bring romance: China; an aquarium; Redwood, California.

Lucky Love Star: Capriel—you never like the feeling of loneliness.

Beautiful Thought: Angels stand with us, so we're never alone.

Sharing Secrets: The possibilities are endless, if you can pay the price. *For the gals:* She is hoping chivalry is not dead, and you must be willing to be the man at all costs. *For the guys:* He can be demanding and somewhat controlling. He just needs to be trained.

Judith's Insights

About the Man: If you start out as friends you will have a much better chance of catching this guy. He will treat you as if he is madly in love with you even if he isn't. It can be very confusing, to say the least. He needs for things to go just so in order for things to progress to making long-term plans. He doesn't do the fly-by-night thing unless it is agreed upon at the beginning. Lay things out right up front to win him over.

About the Woman: She will drive you right up the wall. Every time you may think that you stand no chance she will change her mood and make you think that you do. She does not do this intentionally. She doesn't have a mean bone in her body. She needs to learn what she wants before she can tell you anything about what she is feeling. If you pressure her to do things before she feels that she is ready she will change her mind as soon as you feel things are going well.

Soul Mates: You and a fellow Capricorn are bound to become close and get along for a lifetime. Aquarius and Pisces will have you flying in no time. Things are not so easy for you with Cancer and Aries. Control is the name of the game when it comes to Leo. They love to have it. When you need a solid base to build your dreams, look no further than a Taurus or Virgo. Gemini and Scorpio will leave you cold with their fiery and flirty nature. Libra will have you spinning and laughing at the feeling. You and Sagittarius are natural allies.

Most Charming Characteristics: Calm, collected, considerate.

Gifts: *For her:* jasmine body wash. *For him:* new book.

Sensual Foods: Chocolate soufflé; filet mignon.

Romantic Flowers: The magnolias you send her will let her know you will be around for a while to come. Petunia is to say never despair. Holly will let him know what he is getting into. Pansy will keep you in his thoughts.

Best Date Nights: Saturday; 9th and 18th of each month.

Colors of Passion: *For her:* green, brown, violet. *For him:* dark gray, brown.

The Perfect Wedding: Earthy goat girls feel most secure on the old terra firma, but climb, climb you must. The top of a mountain in Colorado or the top of a monument in Washington, D.C.; all these locations lend themselves to your powerful persona. Inspired by tradition, you are happiest in a pleasant, conventional location. Ideal setting: Moscow; the Grand Canyon.

Wise Words: Robert Browning: "What is a man's age, he must hurry more, that's all. Cram in a day what his youth took a year to hold."

Hints of Love: Allow them to know what is in your heart as well as what is in your head.

After the Argument: *For him:* Pay him extra attention. Send him something at work so everybody notices. Make him feel important. *For her:* Go overboard in a big way. Don't just send flowers at work, but to her home and to her mother's when she is there for Sunday dinner.

Romantic Places: Places of power bring romance: Rome, a yacht; the Lincoln Memorial.

Lucky Love Star: Capriel—you never like the feeling of loneliness.

Beautiful Thought: Everything has a beginning, middle, and end.

Sharing Secrets: Tomorrow is another day, but why wait? You can do it all today. *For the gals:* Have your date filled from dusk to dawn, and then some. *For the guys:* You may find he needs a nap here and there, but he can last all day and all night if he has a reason.

Judith's Insights

About the Man: It is hard to know what he wants because odds are he has not figured that out himself yet. That could take forever. Stay close, but don't expect too much too soon. The longer that you hang in there the better chance you have of being exactly what he has wanted all along. He has to know that you are on his side. If he does, you will never find an easier partner. If he doesn't, you will never find a tougher adversary.

About the Woman: Where you find smoke there is usually fire. You may find her snuffing the fire out instead of feeding it like she is supposed to. She hates to be out of control while longing for it at the same time. Feed the fire slowly, until you know that she is more than ready to take the plunge. Make sure that there is no deceit or lies between the two of you. Playing games with her feelings will get you nowhere. It takes her a long time to be ready. Make sure that you are ready, too.

Soul Mates: You should have no problem having a relationship with your own sign, Capricorn. Two peas in one pod can work well together. Taurus and Virgo would probably be two of the easiest signs for you to get along with, in or out of love. You will be a natural magnet for Cancer, but anticipate complications at times. With Aries and Libra, the passion may draw you in. Even if it is only friendship, it can be a passionate one. Leo would be a hard partner, but it could work if you can stand to be on the bottom once in a while. Pisces, the ingenious wit, will get you together. The great disposition of most Pisces could keep you there. Just make sure they don't get bored. Aquarius and Sagittarius could work well, but be cautious of those flirtatious Gemini and Scorpio. They will drive you crazy. It could test your sense when it comes to loyalty.

Most Charming Characteristics: Energetic, shrewd, diplomatic.

Gifts: *For her:* day of golf. *For him:* membership in exclusive club.

Sensual Foods: Steak au poivre; cheesecake.

Romantic Flowers: Iris is your flower if you are the gal sending subtle messages. If you are the man, you will look for clematis. This flower's mental beauty creates emotional stimulation for you.

Best Date Nights: Saturday; 10th and 19th of each month.

Colors of Passion: *For her:* green, brown, violet. *For him:* dark gray, brown.

The Perfect Wedding: Earthy goat girls feel most secure on the old terra firma, but climb, climb you must. The top of a mountain in Colorado or the top of a monument in Washington, D.C.; all these locations lend themselves to your powerful persona. Inspired by tradition, you are happiest in a pleasant, conventional location. Ideal setting: Moscow; the Grand Canyon.

Wise Words: Robert Browning: "Man's hand first formed to carry a few pounds weight, when taught to marry its strength with an engine lift a mountain."

Hints of Love: Keep both feet on the ground the first time you think you want to jump. This way you won't jump too high too soon.

After the Argument: *For him:* Pay him extra attention. Send him something at work so everybody notices. Make him feel important. *For her:* Go overboard in a big way. Don't just send flowers at work, but to her home and to her mother's when she is there for Sunday dinner.

Romantic Places: Places of beauty bring romance: Africa; a state capital; Miami, Florida.

Lucky Love Star: Capriel—you never like the feeling of loneliness.

Beautiful Thought: Clouds are heavenly pillows.

Sharing Secrets: It may need to start with friendship. This isn't the consolation prize; it's the grand prize. *For the gals:* Go slowly and allow it to grow one seed at a time. You won't need to push; it will all come in time. *For the guys:* A step here and a step there. Before he knows it, that friendship will be love.

Judith's Insights

About the Man: He has a constant poker face if he isn't smiling. He may intrigue you because he is understated. He has hope that someone will find him and love and cherish him for life. You can let him know that you are interested and then take a step back. See if he takes the lead. If not, try again a little less subtly. Then give him time to make up his mind. Once he does know what he wants, there will be nothing that can deter him.

About the Woman: This lassie needs all of the facts before she can make the decision on whether she is interested or not. Then she will want to check your bank accounts. She is thorough in all that she does. This can get a bit over the top at times. Once she gets started there is no stopping her at all. Make sure that you are ready for all that she can give you. She wants to make sure that her heart is not going to get broken.

Soul Mates: Capricorn and Capricorn could work as well as anything out there. You can help Aquarius and Pisces remember the little joys in life so you can find joy in each other for a lifetime. Cancer and Aries could be too rigid for your taste. A solid plan can take a partnership with Taurus and Virgo to new heights. If you like things fast and exciting, you could have loads of fun with Scorpio and Gemini. The passion can be there with Libra as long as someone is feeding the flame. Establish with Leo who the boss is and things can progress from there. You could feel your heart skip a beat with Sagittarius.

Most Charming Characteristics: Resourceful, original, courageous.

Gifts: *For her:* fine bottle of wine. *For him:* royal collectible.

Sensual Foods: Strawberry shortcake; pineapple; ham.

Romantic Flowers: Any rose of any color for the lady. Roses stand for love regardless of the color. Send them with orchids and you will be saying, "I love you." If you want a gentleman to know you think of him, send pansies, and forget-me-nots for true love.

Best Date Nights: Saturday; 2nd and 11th of each month.

Colors of Passion: *For her:* green, brown, violet. *For him:* dark gray, brown.

The Perfect Wedding: Earthy goat girls feel most secure on the old terra firma, but climb, climb you must. The top of a mountain in Colorado or the top of a monument in Washington, D.C.; all these locations lend themselves to your powerful persona. Inspired by tradition, you are happiest in a pleasant, conventional location. Ideal setting: Moscow; the Grand Canyon.

Wise Words: Charles Dickens: "Be as rich as you can honestly be, it is your duty, if not for yourself, for others."

Hints of Love: Laughter alleviates the tension, but so can understanding where another is sitting.

After the Argument: *For him:* Pay him extra attention. Send him something at work so everybody notices. Make him feel important. *For her:* Go overboard in a big way. Don't just send flowers at work, but to her home and to her mother's when she is there for Sunday dinner.

Romantic Places: Places of power bring romance: Athens; a stadium; Los Angeles, California.

Lucky Love Star: Capriel—you never like the feeling of loneliness.

Beautiful Thought: It is easier to look down when you are up.

Sharing Secrets: This one needs to be the one and only, even if it is only the first date. *For the gals:* Don't talk about your past relationships. Do all you can to make her feel cherished from the first moment. *For the guys:* Play up your innocence. Let him take charge, even in paying the bill. He needs to wear the pants.

Judith's Insights

About the Man: This guy does not do well with games unless he is the one initiating them. His sense of humor wavers, but it may be his dry wit that attracted you to him in the first place. Be coy and let him feel as if he is the one in control at all times, even if that is the farthest thing from the truth. Just don't expect too much too soon. Although things may take time to grow with him, it will be well worth the wait once you get there.

About the Woman: This lady enjoys the party. Jokes are okay as long as they are not played on her. Give her attention and show her your more serious side. Expect the relationship to go much like a long, casual walk. You will get to your destination at some point, so it doesn't matter how fast you walk. She can have a speed all her own. At times you may think that her speed is stop. Yes, she can be slow, but she is all about quality instead of quantity.

Soul Mates: You will get along with anyone just like you. That is why you would do well with another Capricorn. If Pisces and Aquarius are on the train, don't let it leave without you. They can give you a true feeling of wellness you never had before. Cancer's and Aries's unyielding nature will have you running in the other direction. Taurus and Virgo know how to turn on that irresistible charm, which you just love. It would be wise to fasten your seat belt. You might be thrown about with Scorpio and Gemini. New and interesting things must be ever present for a relationship with Libra to work. If you can let Leo be in charge, or even think that they are, then you will get along fine. Keep open to all things new and exciting and you can fly to new heights with Sagittarius.

Most Charming Characteristics: Studious, intellectual, cautious.

Gifts: *For her:* gold jewelry. *For him:* antique furniture.

Sensual Foods: Steak fondue; cheese fondue and French bread.

Romantic Flowers: These ladies like everyone to know how faithful they are, so send them violets. To surprise them send tulips. Men like their flowers the same as their relationships, unpretending. Send them camellias with white roses to show your affection.

Best Date Nights: Saturday; 3rd and 21st of each month.

Colors of Passion: *For her:* green, brown, violet. *For him:* dark gray, brown.

The Perfect Wedding: Earthy goat girls feel most secure on the old terra firma, but climb, climb you must. The top of a mountain in Colorado or the top of a monument in Washington, D.C.; all these locations lend themselves to your powerful persona. Inspired by tradition, you are happiest in a pleasant, conventional location. Ideal setting: Moscow; the Grand Canyon.

Wise Words: Charles Dickens: "Disguise it as we may, the reflection will force itself on our minds, that when the next bell announces the arrival of a new year, we may be insensible alike of the timely warning we have so often neglected, and of all of the warm feelings that glow within us now."

Hints of Love: Communication is important here. A script isn't provided for you. You must write it for yourself.

After the Argument: *For him:* Pay him extra attention. Send him something at work so everybody notices. Make him feel important. *For her:* Go overboard in a big way. Don't just send flowers at work, but to her home and to her mother's when she is there for Sunday dinner.

Romantic Places: Places of beauty bring romance: Jamaica; a beach; Key West, Florida.

Lucky Love Star: Capriel—you never like the feeling of loneliness.

Beautiful Thought: Memories are what we are making now.

Sharing Secrets: You need to remember never to forget. *For the gals:* Her birthday, holidays, and your anniversary. Even down to each dinner date. *For the guys:* His birthday, his laundry, his mother's birthday, and, of course, him any other day of the year.

Judith's Insights

About the Man: He is loyal but stubborn. He lets you know his boundaries without using words. You can tell everything by the faces he makes. Generosity does intimidate him. Give to him slowly, not just gifts but your time and love as well. You will know that he is comfortable when he starts giving back. Unfortunately, he can miss a good time because of his fear. He thinks way too much. Make all of your intentions as clear as possible before you start expecting things from him.

About the Woman: She wants you to give her oodles and oodles of attention. At the same time, she makes you feel as if she would frown upon the attention she so craves. She overprotects everything, including herself. Let time take down her barriers instead of trying to rip them down with your hands. The walls she has built around herself for protection did not go up overnight. They have to be dismantled one brick at a time, with each removal being a fight.

Soul Mates: Another Capricorn could be exactly what you are looking for. With Aquarius and Pisces, you will both have a passion for life that you never experienced before. Cancer's and Aries's instinct to control all around them will leave you dreaming of greener pastures. There is not much that can shake the stable foundation you can make with Taurus and Virgo. Scorpio and Gemini will be too much energy focused in every direction for you to take lying down. Libra will fill every minute with a passion for life that can't help but rub off on you. Getting along with the dominating Leo could prove to be a difficult task for you. You and Sagittarius can make a tight partnership.

Most Charming Characteristics: Impulsive, emotional, practical.

Gifts: *For her:* vanilla-scented candles. *For him:* chess set.

Sensual Foods: Baked Alaska; seafood.

Romantic Flowers: These ladies like men with taste. Show them you love style by sending fuchsia flowers, or even brightly colored wildflowers will do. To confuse this man, send him lilies along with bright daisies to show your innocence. Keep him guessing.

Best Date Nights: Saturday; 13th and 31st of each month.

Colors of Passion: *For her:* green, brown, violet. *For him:* dark gray, brown.

The Perfect Wedding: Earthy goat girls feel most secure on the old terra firma, but climb, climb you must. The top of a mountain in Colorado or the top of a monument in Washington, D.C.; all these locations lend themselves to your powerful persona. Inspired by tradition, you are happiest in a pleasant, conventional location. Ideal setting: Moscow; the Grand Canyon.

Wise Words: Charles Dickens: "The year was old, that day, the patient year had lived through the reproaches and misuses of its slanderers, and faithfully performed its work. Spring, summer, autumn, winter; it had laboured through the destined round, and now laid down its weary head to die."

Hints of Love: Don't dissect every minute of every day. Learn to appreciate each minute as it comes.

After the Argument: *For him:* Pay him extra attention. Send him something at work so everybody notices. Make him feel important. *For her:* Go overboard in a big way. Don't just send flowers at work, but to her home and to her mother's when she is there for Sunday dinner.

Romantic Places: Places of power bring romance: Russia; a courthouse; Washington, D.C.

Lucky Love Star: Capriel—you never like the feeling of loneliness.

Beautiful Thought: When you think you are alone, consult the angel on your shoulder.

Sharing Secrets: My house should be your house, especially if you don't have one of your own. *For the gals:* All for one and one for all. Yours and mine must become ours. *For the guys:* If he needs to stand on ceremony, even for the first five minutes, it will be a definite turnoff for this one.

Judith's Insights

About the Man: He loves new beginnings and happy endings. He is much more mushy than one could ever imagine. He finds his own way of creating challenges in love without playing games. You can't find anyone more down-to-earth and loving than this guy right in front of you. He is not hard to figure out at all. Just be there and create an honest and loyal presence in his life. The rest will be a piece of cake.

About the Woman: This gal likes to get it all and do it all. For the most part, she does it alone. She doesn't show her whimsical and spontaneous side very easily. Timing is everything. To see this part of her you have to allow her time. This time will be spent dealing with her fear of being hurt, as she has been in the past. Make her aware that you have been hurt as well and that you understand where she is coming from.

If you would like to share any stories about how the information in this book has touched your life, please send correspondence to the following address:

Judith Turner
1064 River Road
Edgewater, NJ 07020

Or E-mail:
JTPSYCHIC1@aol.com

RESOURCES

The Longfellow Prose Birthday Book, Ticknor and Company, Cambridge, 1886.

The Zodiac and Its Mysteries, Prof. A. F. Seward, Chicago, 1915.

Astrology for All, Alan Leo, London, 1910.

The Pictorial Key to the Tarot, Arthur Edward Waite, William Rider & Son Ltd., London, 1922.

Holmes Birthday Book, Houghton Mifflin & Co., Chicago, 1889.

The Emerson Birthday Book, Houghton Mifflin & Co., New York, 1881.

The Storyteller, Maud Lindsay, M. A. Donahue & Co., Chicago, 1915.

The Sands of Time, Thomas W. Handford, Lothrop Lee & Shepard Co., Boston, 1903.

The World's Famous Orations, William Jennings Bryan, Greece, 1906.

Beautiful Thoughts from Robert Louis Stevenson, James Pott & Co., New York, 1903.

Benjamin Franklin Birthday Book, George W. Jacobs & Co., Philadelphia, 1917.

Longfellow Birthday Book, Barse & Hopkins, New York, 1910.

The Bryant Birthday Book, D. Appleton & Co., New York, 1884.

The Philosophy of Numbers, Mrs. L. Dow Balutti, Atlantic City, 1908.

What Is in Your Name?, Edward J. Clode, 1916.

The Vibration of Numbers, Mrs. L. Dow Balutti, Atlantic City, 1913.

Numerology Up to Date, Karen Adams, Greenberg Publisher Inc., 1925.

Your Destiny in the Zodiac and Its Mysteries, Louise Brightman Brownell, Los Angeles, 1919.

Starlight, C. W. Leadbeater, Theosophical Publishing House, Adyar, Madras, India, 1917.

Our Fate and the Zodiac, Margaret Mayo, Brentano's, New York, 1900.

A Complete Dictionary of Astrology, James Wilson, Samuel Weiser, New York, 1880.

The Influence of the Stars, Rosa Baughan; Kegan Paul, Trench, Truber & Co, London, 1904.

The Key to Astrology, Rapheal, David McKay Publisher, Philadelphia, 1899.

The Magic Seven, Lida A. Churchill, New Tide Publishing, New York, 1901.

An Introduction to Astrology, William Lily, George Bell & Sons, London, 1901.

Heliocentric Astrology, Yarmo Verda, David McKay Publisher, Philadelphia, 1899.

Flower Fables, Louisa May Alcott, Henry Altemus Co., Philadelphia, 1898.

The Birthday Year—Chaucer to Longfellow, Marcus Ward & Co., London, 1879.

Mastery of Fate, Christian D. Larson, L. N. Fowler and Co., Chicago, 1908.

Byron's Shorter Poems, Ralph Hartt Bowels, MacMillan Co., New York, 1922.

Astrology, M. M. MacGregor, Penn Publishing Co., Philadelphia, 1904.

Rapheal's Horay Astrology, Rapheal, W. Foulsham & Co., London, 1897.

Astrosophic Principles, John Hazelrigg, Hermetic Publishing Co., New York, 1917.